TAKAHASHI'S
POCKET
ROMANIZED
ENGLISH-JAPANESE
DICTIONARY

[REVISED EXPANDED EDITION]

by Morio Takahashi
revised by Tomoko Honjo

TAISEIDO

Taiseido shobo Co.
Tokyo and Kobe, Japan
© *Taiseido shobo Co.*

PREFACE

It has been a matter of regret that so few Japanese dictionaries in Roman letters have been available for foreigners. This little dictionary has been compiled for meeting the practical needs of beginners in the study of Japanese.

The vocabularies, phrases and sentences contained in this dictionary are really useful ones, such as, I think, foreign students may learn to use correctly.

This contains 10,000 English words and phrases strictly selected for daily use. English words are classified on the basis of the colloquial language. Each word is explained in Japanese printed both in Roman and Japanese characters. Examples are given side by side with the English equivalents.

The author begs to acknowledge with thanks numerous emendations and valuable suggestions given by Mr. N. Yokochi, Mr. Y. Uzumasa and Mr. M. Saito, without whose kind help the completion of this book would have been impossible. But above all others is he indebted to Mr. W. Dramond, whose assistance throughout has been invaluable.

Any corrections and suggestions that may occur to readers such as likely to improve this little dictionary, will be freely acknowledged.

1937   Morio Takahashi

PREFACE TO REVISED
EXPANDED EDITION

The number of Japanese language learners is increasing dramatically. In the hope of meeting the needs of these Japanese learners, a revision of this dictionary has been made. Words in high frequency of use and words commonly used in business are included, Japanese expressions are given as often as possible with illustrative phrases and sentences, and grammatical information is added to some extent.
The framework of the original dictionary was retained, but now this new edition contains 9149 entries.

Comments and advice by readers and users will be much appreciated.

January, 1993   Tomoko Honjo

HOW TO USE THIS DICTIONARY

1) Abbreviations (and signs) following entries

a.	= adjective – keiyô-shi [形容詞]
abbrev.	= abbreviation – ryakugo [略語]
ad.	= adverb – fukushi [副詞]
aux. v.	= auxiliary verb – jo-dôshi [助動詞]
conj.	= conjunction – setsuzoku-shi [接続詞]
def. art.	= definite article – tei-kanshi [定冠詞]
indef. art.	= indefinite article – futei-kanshi [不定冠詞]
int.	= interjection – kantô-shi [間投詞]
n.	= noun – meishi [名詞]
pl.	= plural – fukusû-kei [複数形]
pref.	= prefix – settô-ji [接頭辞]
prep.	= preposition – zenchi-shi [前置詞]
pron.	= pronoun – dai-meishi [代名詞]
pro-verb	– dai-dôshi [代動詞]
vi.	= intransitive verb – ji-dôshi [自動詞]
vt.	= transitive verb – ta-dôshi [他動詞]

2) List of abbreviations and unabridged words to indicate specialized fields

acc.	= accounting – kaikei[-gaku] [会計(学)]
Air Force	– kûgun [空軍]
American football	– Amerikan futtobôru [アメリカンフットボール]
anat.	= anatomy – kaibô-gaku [解剖学]
arch.	= architecture – kenchiku-gaku [建築学]
astron.	= astronomy – temmon-gaku [天文学]
Aus.	= Australia – Ôsutoraria-de-wa [オーストラリアでは]
aviation	– hikô[-jutsu] [飛行(術)]
baseball	– bêsubôru; yakyû [ベースボール; 野球]
basketball	– basuketto-bôru [バスケットボール]
biol.	= biology – seibutsu-gaku [生物学]
birds	– chôrui [鳥類]

bkpg.	= bookkeeping — boki	[簿記]
bot.	= botany — shokubutsu-gaku	[植物学]
boxing	— bokushingu	[ボクシング]
broadcasting	— hôsô	[放送]
Can.	= Canada — Kanada-de-wa	[カナダでは]
cards	— torampu	[トランプ]
chem.	= chemistry — kagaku	[化学]
colloq.	= colloquial — kôgo-no	[口語の]
com.	= commerce — shôgyô	[商業]
computer	— kompyûta	[コンピュータ]
cooking	— ryôri〔-hô〕	[料理(法)]
dice	— sai〔koro〕	[さいころ]
econ.	= economics — keizai-gaku	[経済学]
educ.	= education — kyôiku〔-gaku〕	[教育(学)]
educ. -psych.	= educational psychology	
	— kyôiku-shinri-gaku	[教育心理学]
elect.	= electricity — denki〔-gaku〕	[電気(学)]
electronics	— denshi-kôgaku	[電子工学]
《(Eng.)》	= England — Eikoku-de-wa	[英国では]
film	— firumu	[フィルム]
fin.	= financial — zaisei-no; kin'yû-no	[財政の; 金融の]
fish	— gyorui	[魚類]
fishing	— tsuri	[釣り]
geog.	= geography — chiri〔-gaku〕	[地理(学)]
geom.	= geometry — kika-gaku	[幾何学]
golf	— gorufu	[ゴルフ]
gram.	= grammar — bumpô	[文法]
horse racing	— keiba	[競馬]
insect	— konchû	[昆虫]
Japan	= Nihon or Nippon	
	— Nihon(Nippon)-de-wa	[日本(日本)では]
L.	= Latin — Raten-go	[ラテン語]
law	— hôritsu	[法律]
log.	= logic — ronri-gaku	[論理学]
marine	— kaiji-no	[海事の]
marine insurance		
	— kaijô-hoken	[海上保険]
math.	= mathematics — sûgaku	[数学]

mech.	= mechanics — kikai-gaku [機械学]
med.	= medical — igaku-no [医学の]
meteorol.	= meteorology — kishô-gaku [気象学]
mil.	= military — guntai-no [軍隊の]
min.	= mining — kôgyô [鉱業]
mountaineering	— tozan [登山]
movie	— eiga [映画]
mus.	= music — ongaku [音楽]
mus. instr.	= musical instrument — gakki [楽器]
Navy	— kaigun [海軍]
newspaper	— shimbun [新聞]
opt.	= optics — kôgaku [光学]
path.	= pathology — byôri-gaku [病理学]
pharmacol.	= pharmacology — yakugaku [薬学]
philos.	= philosophy — tetsugaku [哲学]
phon.	= phonetics — onsei-gaku [音声学]
photo.	= photograph — shashin [写真]
phys.	= physics — butsuri-gaku [物理学]
physiol.	= physiology — seiri-gaku [生理学]
play	— engeki; shibai [演劇; 芝居]
postage stamp	— yûbin-kitte [郵便切手]
printing	— insatsu[-jutsu] [印刷(術)]
prov.	= proverb — kakugen [格言]
psych.	= psychology — shinri-gaku [心理学]
radio	— rajio [ラジオ]
R.R.	= railroad — tetsudô [鉄道]
rugger	— ragubî [ラグビー]
shellfish	— kai-rui [貝類]
slang	— zokugo [俗語]
sports	— supôtsu; undô [スポーツ; 運動]
statistics	— tôkei-gaku [統計学]
stock	— kabushiki [株式]
surg.	= surgery — geka [外科]
swim.	= swimming — suiei [水泳]
teleg.	= telegraph — denshin [電信]
tennis	— tenisu; teikyû [テニス; 庭球]
theater	— gekijô [劇場]
TV	= television — terebijon [テレビジョン]

((US))   = the United States of America
              — Amerika-de-wa [アメリカでは]
zool.   = zoology — dôbutsu-gaku [動物学]

3) Two or more abbreviations in parentheses following entries

A. (*a. & ad.*)

a. Adjective endings *-na*, *-no* are replaceable with adverbial
   endings such as *-de*, *-e*, *-kara*, *-ni*, *-o*, etc.

    cowardly   okubyô-*na*(okubyô-*ni*)
    barefoot   hadashi-*no*(hadashi-*de*); su-ashi-*no*(su-ashi-*de*)
    barehanded   su-de-*no*(-*de*)
    inward   naibu-*no*(-*e*); kokoro-no-naka-*no*(-*e*)
    northeast   hoku-tô-kara-*no*(hoku-tô-*kara*)
    farthest   mottomo-tooku-*no*(mottomo-tooku-*ni*)

b. The principle is the same though the adverb is given first.

    overland   rikuro-*o*(-*no*)

c. Another case of ending replacement

    farther   mottomo-*tooi*(mottomo-*tooku*)

d. Some adjectives do not have corresponding adverbs, though
   others do.

    extra   (*a.*)   yobun-*no*; tokubetsu-*no*; rinji-*no*
            (*ad.*) yobun-*ni*; tokubetsu-*ni*; ———

B. (*a. & n.*)

Adding *-hito*, *-mono*, *-oto*, etc. to adjectives makes noun.

    savage   (*a.*)   zankoku-*na*
            (*n.*)   zankoku-*na-hito*
    spiral   (*a.*)   rasen-jô-*no*
            (*n.*)   rasen-jô-*no-mono*
    humming (*a.*)   bum-bun-*iu*
            (*n.*)   bum-bun-*iu-oto*

C. (*ad. & a.*)

a. Suffixing -*no* to adverbs makes adjectives.

daily   (*ad.*)   hibi; mai-nichi
            (*a.*)   hibi-*no*; mai-nichi-*no*
downward   (*ad.*)   shita-no-hô-e
            (*a.*)   shita-no-hô-e-*no*

b. In the following cases, (Please) See (*a.* & *ad.*).
   headlong   massakasama-*ni*(massakasama-*no*)
   weekly   shû-gime-*de*(-*no*)

D. (*int.* & *n.*) hurray, hurrah (*int.* & *n.*) banzai(-no-koe); furê
                            = (*int.*) banzai; furê
                              (*n.*) banzai-no-koe

E. (*n.* & *a.*)

a. Suffixing -*no*, -*shita*, -*shi-kaketa*, -*no-aru*, -*na*, -*no-yô-na*, -*o-utau*, -*suru*, -*teki-na*, -*sei-no*, -*to-naru*, -*fû-na* to nouns makes adjectives.

adjective	(*n.*)	keiyô-shi
	(*a.*)	keiyô-shi-*no*
adult	(*n.*)	seijin
	(*a.*)	seijin-*shita*
budding	(*n.*)	hatsuga
	(*a.*)	hatsuga-*shi-kaketa*
damp	(*n.*)	shikki
	(*a.*)	shikki-*no-aru*
extreme	(*n.*)	kyokutan
	(*a.*)	kyokutan-*na*
fairy	(*n.*)	yôsei
	(*a.*)	yôsei-*no-yô-na*
humming	(*n.*)	hana-uta
	(*a.*)	hana-uta-*o-utau*
longing	(*n.*)	setsubô
	(*a.*)	setsubô-*suru*
lyric	(*n.*)	jojô-shi
	(*a.*)	jojô-shi-*teki-na*
mineral	(*n.*)	kôbutsu

	(a.)	kôbutsu-*sei-no*
model	(n.)	2)mohan. 3)moderu
	(a.)	2)mohan-*to-naru*. 3)moderu-*to-naru*
narrative	(n.)	monogatari
	(a.)	monogatari-*fû-no*

b. In the following examples, 1) is the nouns 2) the adjectives.

contraband	(n.)	1)mitsuyu-hin; fuhô-torihiki
	(a.)	2)kinsei-*no*
spinning	(n.)	1)bôseki; ito-tsumugi
	(a.)	2)kaiten-*suru*

F. (*n. & a. & ad.*)

downtown	(n.)	hanka-gai
	(a.)	hanka-gai-*no*
	(ad.)	hanka-gai-*e*
inside	(n.)	naibu
	(a.)	naibu-*no*
	(ad.)	naibu-*ni*

G. (*n. & ad.*)

Suffixing -*ni*, -*de* to nouns makes adverbs.

downstairs	(n.)	kaika
	(ad.)	kaika-*ni*
retail	(n.)	ko-uri
	(ad.)	ko-uri-*de*

H. (*n. & vi.*)

a. Adding -*suru*, -*iu*, -*tateru*, -*shaberu*, -*naku*, -*ga-furu*, -*o-tateru*, -*ni-naru*, -*ga-saku*, -*datsu*, -*o-suru*, -*o-hiku*, -*o-harau*, -*to-iu*, -*o-ensô-suru*, -*naru*, -*o-iu*, -*o-tsuku*, -*to-naku*, -*o-toru*, -*o-rôsuru*, -*o-kaburu*, -*de-tsutaeru*, -*o-eru*, -*de-hataraku*, -*o-okasu*, -*de-suberu*, -*ni-noru*, -*o-dasu*, -*o-kaku*, -*fuhei-o-iu*, -*iu*, -*goe-de-iu*, -*de-iku*, -*de-sôshin-suru*, -*de-aruku*, -*de-kakeru*, -*to-tobu* to nouns makes intransitive verbs.

accord	(*n.*)	itchi; chôwa
	(*vi.*)	itchi-*suru*; chôwa-*suru*
buzz	(*n.*)	bum-bun
	(*vi.*)	bum-bun-*iu*
clamor, -our	(*n.*)	sawagi
	(*vi.*)	sawagi-*tateru*
clatter	(*n.*)	pecha-kucha
	(*vi.*)	(hito ga) pecha-kucha-*shaberu*
croak	(*n.*)	kâkâ, gâgâ
	(*vi.*)	(karasu ya kaeru ga) kâkâ, gâgâ-*naku*
drizzle	(*n.*)	kiri-same
	(*vi.*)	kiri-same-*ga-furu*
fizz	(*n.*)	shû-to-iu-oto
	(*vi.*)	shû-to-iu-oto-*o-tateru*
flow	(*n.*)	age-shio
	(*vi.*)	age-shio-*ni-naru*
flower	(*n.*)	hana
	(*vi.*)	hana-*ga-saku*
foam	(*n.*)	awa
	(*vi.*)	awa-*datsu*
golf	(*n.*)	gorufu
	(*vi.*)	gorufu-*o-suru*
harp	(*n.*)	hâpu
	(*vi.*)	hâpu-*o-hiku*
heed	(*n.*)	chûi
	(*vi.*)	chûi-*o-harau*
hiss	(*n.*)	shisshî
	(*vi.*)	shisshî-*to-iu*
jazz	(*n.*)	jazu
	(*vi.*)	jazu-*o-ensô-suru*
jingle	(*n.*)	chirin-chirin
	(*vi.*)	chirin-chirin-*naru*
joke	(*n.*)	jôdan
	(*vi.*)	jôdan-*o-iu*
lie	(*n.*)	uso
	(*vi.*)	uso-*o-tsuku*
low	(*n.*)	mô
	(*vi.*)	mô-*to-naku*

maneuver, -noeuvre (*n.*)   sakusen-kôdô; saku
                      (*vi.*)   sakusen-kôdô-*o-toru*; saku-*o-rôsuru*

mask	(*n.*)	kamen
	(*vi.*)	kamen-*o-kaburu*
megaphone	(*n.*)	megafon
	(*vi.*)	megafon-*de-tsutaeru*
profit	(*n.*)	rieki
	(*vi.*)	rieki-*o-eru*
ranch	(*n.*)	bokujô
	(*vi.*)	bokujô-*de-hataraku*
sin	(*n.*)	tsumi
	(*vi.*)	tsumi-*o-okasu*
ski	(*n.*)	sukî
	(*vi.*)	sukî-*de-suberu*
sleigh	(*n.*)	sori
	(*vi.*)	sori-*ni-noru*
smoke	(*n.*)	kemuri
	(*vi.*)	kemuri-*o-dasu*
snore	(*n.*)	ibiki
	(*vi.*)	ibiki-*o-kaku*
squawk	(*n.*)	bû-bû
	(*vi.*)	bû-bû-*fuhei-o-iu*
squeal	(*n.*)	kî-kî
	(*vi.*)	kî-kî-*iu*; kî-kî-*goe-de-iu*
taxi	(*n.*)	takushî
	(*vi.*)	takushî-*de-iku*
teletype	(*n.*)	teretaipu
	(*vi.*)	teretaipu-*de-sôshin-suru*
tiptoe	(*n.*)	tsuma-saki
	(*vi.*)	tsuma-saki-*de-aruku*
trot	(*n.*)	haya-ashi
	(*vi.*)	haya-ashi-*de-kakeru*
whiz(z)	(*n.*)	hyû
	(*vi.*)	hyû-*to-tobu*

b. Some other endings

    clamor, -our (*n.*)   sake*bi*
                 (*vi.*)   sake*bu*

flow	(*n.*)	nagare
	(*vi.*)	nagare*ru*
giggle	(*n.*)	kusu-kusu-wara*i*
	(*vi.*)	kusu-kusu-wara*u*

I. (*n. & vt.*) dislike (*n. & vt.*) kirai(...o kirau)
        = (*n.*) kirai
        (*vt.*) ...o kirau

J. (*prep. & ad.*) notwithstanding (*prep. & ad.*) ...nimo-kakawarazu
        (sore-nimo-kakawarazu)
        = (*prep.*) ...nimo-kakawarazu
        (*ad.*) sore-nimo-kakawarazu

K. (*prep. & conj.*) until (*prep. & conj.*) 1)...made. 2)yagate;
        tsui-ni
        = (*prep.*) 1)...made
        (*conj.*) 1)...made. 2)yagate, tsui-ni

L. (*pron. & a.*)

(Please) See (*n. & a.*).

    these (*pron.*) kore-ra
        (*a.*) kore-ra-*no*

M. (*pron. & n.*) nothing (*pron. & n.*) 1)nani-mo...nai; mu. 2)
        toru-ni-tarinai-mano
        = (*pron.*) nani-mo-nai
        (*n.*) 1)mu. 2)toru-ni-tarinai-mono

N. (*vi. & n.*)

a. Adding *-koto, -koe, -oto* to intransitive verbs makes nouns.

gape	(*vi.*)	oo-guchi-o-akeru
	(*n.*)	oo-guchi-o-akeru-*koto*
grumble	(*vi.*)	butsu-butsu-iu
	(*n.*)	butsu-butsu-iu-*koe*
purr	(*vi.*)	(neko ga) nodo-o-narasu
	(*n.*)	nodo-o-narasu-*oto*

b. Cases with other forms

     ache   (*vi.*) ita*mu*; uzu*ku*
                  (*n.*) ita*mi*; uzu*ki*

O. (*vi.* & *vt.*)

     argue   (*vi.* & *vt.*) (...o) ronzuru
          = (*vi.*) ronzuru
            (*vt.*) ...o ronzuru
     bay   (*vi.* & *vt.*) (...ni) hoeru
          = (*vi.*) hoeru
            (*vt.*) ...ni hoeru
     flee   (*vi.* & *vt.*) (...kara) nigeru
          = (*vi.*) nigeru
            (*vt.*) ...kara nigeru
     bud   (*vi.* & *vt.*) hatsuga-suru (...o hatsuga-saseru)
          = (*vi.*) hatsuga-suru
            (*vt.*) ...o hatsuga-saseru
     deserve (*vi.* & *vt.*) ukeru-kachi-ga-aru; ...(suru) kachi-ga-aru
          = (*vi.*) ukeru-kachi-ga-aru
            (*vt.*) ...(suru) kachi-ga-aru
     fumble (*vi.* & *vt.*) te-saguri-suru(te-saguri-de...o suru)
          = (*vi.*) te-saguri-suru
            (*vt.*) te-saguri-de...o suru
     shop   (*vi.* & *vt.*) kai-mono-o-suru(...de kai-mono-o-suru)
          = (*vi.*) kai-mono-o-suru
            (*vt.*) ...de kai-mono-o-suru

P. (*vt.* & *n.*)   array (*vt.* & *n.*) ...o yosoou(yosooi)
                   = (*vt.*) ...o yosoou
                    (*n.*) yosooi

Q. (*vt.* & *vi.*) assist (*vt.* & *vi.*) (...o) tetsudau
                   = (*vt.*) ...o tetsudau
                    (*vi.*) tetsudau
             answer (*vt.* & *vi.*) (...ni) kotaeru
                   = (*vt.*) ...ni kotaeru
                    (*vi.*) kotaeru

avenge (*vt. & vi.*) (...no) fukushû-o-suru
    = (*vt.*) ...no fukushû-o-suru
     (*vi.*) fukushû-o-suru

skirt (*vt. & vi.*) (...no) fuchi-ni-sotte-iku
    = (*vt.*) ...no fuchi-ni-sotte-iku
     (*vi.*) fuchi-ni-sotte-iku

box (*vt. & vi.*) (...to) bokushingu-o-suru
    = (*vt.*) ...to bokushingu-o-suru
     (*vi.*) bokushingu-o-suru

determine (*vt. & vi.*) (...to) kesshin-suru
    = (*vt.*) ...to kesshin-suru
     (*vi.*) kesshin-suru

advance (*vt. & vi.*) ...o susumeru(susumu)
    = (*vt.*) ...o susumeru
     (*vi.*) susumu

button (*vt. & vi.*) ...ni-botan-o-kakeru(botan-de-tomaru)
    = (*vt.*) ...ni botan-o-kakeru
     (*vi.*) botan-de-tomaru

dazzle (*vt. & vi.*) ...no me-o-kuramaseru(me-ga-kuramu)
    = (*vt.*) ...no me-o-kuramaseru
     (*vi.*) me-ga-kuramu

1) represents *vt.* and 2) *vi.*

account (*vt. & vi.*) 1)...to omou. 2)setsumei-suru
    = (*vt.*) 1)...to omou
     (*vi.*) 2)setsumei-suru

4) References to the Romanized Letters

a. The Romanized Letters are used according to the system of the attached table.

b. ˆ on the vowel marks 'long vowel'.

c. A geminated consonant is represented by the double consonant letters. However, 「っち」 is represented by *tchi*, not *cchi*.

    aboard   fune-ni-no*tte*
    accord   i*tchi*-suru

REFERENCES TO THE ROMANIZED LETTERS

	a	(あ)(ア)	i	(い)(イ)	u	(う)(ウ)	e	(え)(エ)	o	(お)(オ)
①	ka	(か)(カ)	ki	(き)(キ)	ku	(く)(ク)	ke	(け)(ケ)	ko	(こ)(コ)
②	sa	(さ)(サ)	shi	(し)(シ)	su	(す)(ス)	se	(せ)(セ)	so	(そ)(ソ)
③	ta	(た)(タ)	chi	(ち)(チ)	tsu	(つ)(ツ)	te	(て)(テ)	to	(と)(ト)
	na	(な)(ナ)	ni	(に)(ニ)	nu	(ぬ)(ヌ)	ne	(ね)(ネ)	no	(の)(ノ)
④	ha	(は)(ハ)	hi	(ひ)(ヒ)	fu	(ふ)(フ)	he	(へ)(ヘ)	ho	(ほ)(ホ)
	ma	(ま)(マ)	mi	(み)(ミ)	mu	(む)(ム)	me	(め)(メ)	mo	(も)(モ)
	ya	(や)(ヤ)			yu	(ゆ)(ユ)			yo	(よ)(ヨ)
	ra	(ら)(ラ)	ri	(り)(リ)	ru	(る)(ル)	re	(れ)(レ)	ro	(ろ)(ロ)
	wa	(わ)(ワ)								
	n	(ん)(ン)								

①'	ga	(が)(ガ)	gi	(ぎ)(ギ)	gu	(ぐ)(グ)	ge	(げ)(ゲ)	go	(ご)(ゴ)
②'	za	(ざ)(ザ)	ji	(じ、ぢ)	zu	(ず、づ)	ze	(ぜ)(ゼ)	zo	(ぞ)(ゾ)
				(ジ、ヂ)		(ズ、ヅ)				
③'	da	(だ)(ダ)					de	(で)(デ)	do	(ど)(ド)
④'	ba	(ば)(バ)	bi	(び)(ビ)	bu	(ぶ)(ブ)	be	(べ)(ベ)	bo	(ぼ)(ボ)
④"	pa	(ぱ)(パ)	pi	(ぴ)(ピ)	pu	(ぷ)(プ)	pe	(ぺ)(ペ)	po	(ぽ)(ポ)

kya (きゃ)(キャ)		kyu (きゅ)(キュ)		kyo (きょ)(キョ)
sha (しゃ)(シャ)	shu (しゅ)(シュ)	she (しぇ)(シェ)		sho (しょ)(ショ)
cha (ちゃ)(チャ)	chu (ちゅ)(チュ)	che (ちぇ)(チェ)		cho (ちょ)(チョ)
nya (にゃ)(ニャ)		nyu (にゅ)(ニュ)		nyo (にょ)(ニョ)
hya (ひゃ)(ヒャ)		hyu (ひゅ)(ヒュ)		hyo (ひょ)(ヒョ)
mya (みゃ)(ミャ)		myu (みゅ)(ミュ)		myo (みょ)(ミョ)
rya (りゃ)(リャ)		ryu (りゅ)(リュ)		ryo (りょ)(リョ)
gya (ぎゃ)(ギャ)		gyu (ぎゅ)(ギュ)		gyo (ぎょ)(ギョ)
ja (じゃ)(ジャ)	ju (じゅ)(ジュ)	je (じぇ)(ジェ)		jo (じょ)(ジョ)
bya (びゃ)(ビャ)		byu (びゅ)(ビュ)		byo (びょ)(ビョ)
pya (ぴゃ)(ピャ)		pyu (ぴゅ)(ピュ)		pyo (ぴょ)(ピョ)

	di (ディ)		
fa (ファ)	fi (フィ)	fe (フェ)	fo (フォ)
	ti (ティ)		
	wi (ウィ)	we (ウェ)	wo (ウォ)

d. The syllabic nasal is represented by **m**, which is placed before *b, m, p*.

A-bomb	gem-*b*aku
advisable	kem*m*ei-na
advanced	shim*p*o-shita

e. When a vowel or a sound in the '*ya*' column of the kana syllabary follows a syllabic nasal, ' is placed to make the syllabic boundary clear.

credit	shin'yô
dear	shin'ai-na
prosperity	han'ei
cause	gen'in
disgust	ken'o
dark	in'utsu-na

5) References to parentheses, blackets, etc.

a. The word which may, or need not, be attached to the preceding word is placed in brackets 〔 〕. That is, both *nyûjô* and *nyûjô-ryô* are acceptable. However, in Japanese '-*ryô*' is put in parentheses ( ), instead of 〔 〕.

admission nyûjô〔-ryô〕 [入場(料)]

b. The word in brackets 〔 〕 is either similar with, or contrastive to, the preceding part, and interchangeable with it.
   That is both saigo-no-*sôsha* and saigo-no-*eisha*, and both kimpatsu-no-*dansei* and kimpatsu-no-*josei*, are acceptable.

anchor	saigo-no-sôsha〔-eisha〕 [最後の走者〔泳者〕]
blond(e)	kimpatsu-no-dansei〔-josei〕 [金髪の男性〔女性〕]

6) When the entry word is a compound, its part of speech is not indicated.

7) In principle, Romanized Japanese translation of interjections begins with a capital letter.

A

a (*indef. art.*) 1)hitotsu-no [一つの]; aru [ある]. 2)onaji [同じ].
3)...ni[-tsuki] [...に(付き)].
   (*1*) It is **a** cat. (Sore-wa)*Ippiki-no* neko-de-aru.
   (*2*) girls of **an** age *onaji* nenrei no shôjo
   (*3*) He comes here twice **a** day.
      Kare-wa ichi-nichi-*ni* ni-do koko-e kuru.
abalone (*n.*) awabi [アワビ].
abandon (*vt.*) ...o suteru [...を捨てる]; ...o yameru [...をやめる].
  abandon oneself to ...ni fukeru
abbey (*n.*) dai-shûdô-in [大修道院].
abbreviation (*n.*) shôryaku [省略]; ryakugo [略語]; ryakuji [略字].
abdomen (*n.*)(*anat.*) fuku-bu [腹部].
abhor (*vt.*) ...o hidoku-kirau [...をひどく嫌う].
abide (*vi.*) as '*abide by*' ...o mamoru [...を守る].
    He **abides by** his word. Kare-wa yakusoku-*o mamoru*.
    (*vt.*) taeru [耐える]; ...o gaman-suru [...を我慢する].
    No one can **abide** it. Dare-mo sore-niwa *taerare*-nai.
ability (*n.*) nôryoku [能力]; sainô [才能].
able (*a.*) yûnô-na [有能な].
  be able to (do) (suru)-koto-ga-dekiru
abnormal (*a.*) ijô-na [異常な]; hentai-no [変態の].

aboard (*ad.*) fune-ni-notte [船に乗って].

     All **aboard**! Mina-san *o-nori*-kudasai.

abode (*n.*) jûkyo [住居].

abolish (*vt.*) ...o haishi-suru [...を廃止する].

abolition (*n.*) haishi [廃止].

A-bomb (*n.*) gem-baku [原爆].

abominable (*a.*) 1)iya-na [いやな]. 2)(*colloq.*) hidoi [ひどい].

abound (*vi.*) takusań-aru [沢山ある]; takusan-iru [沢山いる].

about (*prep.*) 1)...ni-tsuite [...に付いて]. 2)...no-mawari-ni [...の回り に]. 3)(masa-ni)...(shi-)yô-to-shite-iru [(まさに)...(し)ようとしている].

  (*1*) Tell me something **about** it.

     Sore-*ni-tsuite* nani-ka o-hanashi-kudasai.

  (*2*) The bees swarm **about** him.

     Mitsu-bachi ga kare-*no-mawari-ni* muragaru.

  (*3*) The sun is **about** to rise. Taiyô ga nobo*rô-to-shite*-iru.

     (*ad.*) 1)...(shi)mawaru [...(し)まわる]. 2)oyoso [およそ]; yaku [約].

  (*1*) A bird is flying **about**. Tori-ga ichi-wa tobi-*mawatte*iru.

  (*2*) I've **about** fifty books.

     Watashi-wa *oyoso* go-jussatsu-no hon-o motte-iru.

above (*ad.*) ue-no-hô-de [上の方で]; zujô-ni [頭上に].

     He was heard **above**. *Ue-no-hô-de* kare-no-koe ga kikoeta.

     (*prep.*) ...yori-ue-ni [...より上に].

     The bridge is **above** the river.

     Hashi ga kawa-*no-ue-ni* kakatte-iru.

     Good health is **above** wealth. Kenkô wa tomi-*ni-masaru*.

  above all toriwake

abridge (*vt.*) ...o tanshuku-suru [...を短縮する]; ...o yôyaku-suru [... を要約する].

abroad (*ad.*) gaikoku-e [外国へ]; kaigai-e [海外へ].

  from abroad kaigai-kara

abrupt (*a.*) 1)totsuzen-no [突然の]. 2)bukkira-bô-na [ぶっきらぼうな].

absent (*a.*) fuzai-de [不在で]; rusu-de [留守で]; kesseki-shite [欠席し て].

     Father is **absent** from home. Chichi wa *rusu*-desu.

     (*vt.*) as '*absent oneself from*' ...o kesseki-suru [...を欠席す る].

     He **absented** himself from the meeting.

Kare-wa sono-kaigô-o *kesseki-shita.*

absent-minded (*a.*) ukkari-shite-iru ［うっかりしている］; uwa-no-sora-no ［上の空の］.

absolute (*a.*) zettai-no ［絶対の］; mu-jôken-no ［無条件の］.

absolutely (*ad.*) 1) zettai-ni ［絶対に］; mattaku ［全く］. 2) masa-ni sono-toori ［まさにそのとおり］.

absorb (*vt.*) 1)...o sui-komu ［…を吸い込む］; ...o kyûshû-suru ［…を吸収する］. 2)(hito)-o muchû-ni-saseru ［(人)を夢中にさせる］.
  (*1*) It does not **absorb** heat. Sore-wa netsu-o *kyûshû-shi*-nai.
  (*2*) He **is absorbed** in playing tennis.
      Kare-wa tenisu-ni-*muchû-da.*

absorbent cotton ((*US*)) dasshi-men ［脱脂綿］.

abstain (*vi.*) tsutsushimu ［慎む］; hikaeru ［控える］.

abstention (*n.*) (tôhyô de-no)kiken ［(投票での)棄権］.

abstract (*a.*) chûshô-teki-na ［抽象的な］.

absurd (*a.*) fu-gôri-na ［不合理な］; baka-geta ［ばかげた］.

abundance (*n.*) hôfu ［豊富］; takusan ［沢山］.

abuse (*vt.*) ...o ran'yô-suru ［…を乱用する］. ...o sokonau ［…をそこなう］.

academy (*n.*) gakkô ［学校］; gakushi-in ［学士院］.

accelerate (*vt.*) ...o kasoku-suru ［…を加速する］.
     (*vi.*) kuruma-no-supîdo-o-masu ［車のスピードを増す］.

accelerator (*n.*) kasoku-suru-mono ［加速するもの］; (*mech.*) akuseru ［アクセル］.

accent (*n.*) 1)akusento ［アクセント］; kyôsei ［強勢］. 2)namari ［なまり］.
     (*vt.*) ...ni akusento-o-oku ［…にアクセントをおく］.

accept (*vt.*) 1)...o uke-toru ［…を受け取る］. 2)...ni ôjiru ［…に応じる］.
  (*1*) He **accepted** the present.
      Kare-wa sono okuri-mono-o *uke-totta.*
  (*2*) I **accepted** his invitation.
      Watashi-wa kare-no shôtai-ni *ôjita.*

acceptance (*n.*) 1)juryô ［受領］. 2)shôdaku ［承諾］.

access (*n.*) 1)sekkin ［接近］. 2)(menkai・de-iri no)kenri ［(面会・出入りの)権利］. 3)(ikari・kanjô no)hossa ［(怒り・感情の)発作］.
  (*2*) Students have **access** to the library.
      Gakusei wa tosho-kan-o-riyô-suru-*kenri*-ga-aru.
      Gakusei wa tosho-kan-o-riyô-*deki*ru.

accessible (*a.*) sekkin-shi-yasui [接近しやすい].

accident (*n.*) 1)jiko [事故]. 2)gûzen-no-deki-goto [偶然の出来事].
  by accident   gûzen-ni

accidental (*a.*) gûzen-no [偶然の]; omoigakenai [思いがけない].

accidentally (*ad.*) gûzen-ni [偶然に]; tama-tama [たまたま]; hakarazu-mo [はからずも]; hyokkori [ひょっこり].

accident insurance   shôgai-hoken [傷害保険].

accommodation (*n.*) 1)tekiô [適応]. 2)yûzû [融通]. 3)wakai [和解].
  4)(*pl.*) (ryokan nado no)shûyô-setsubi [(旅館などの)収容設備].

accompaniment (*n.*) 1)fuzoku-butsu [付属物]; tsuki-mono [付き物].
  2)(*mus.*) bansô [伴奏].

accompany (*vt.*) 1)...ni dôhan-suru [···に同伴する]; ...ni dôkô-suru [···に同行する]. 2)...no bansô-o-suru [···の伴奏をする].

accomplice (*n.*) kyôhan-sha [共犯者].

accomplish (*vt.*) ...o nashi-togeru [···を成し遂げる].

accord (*n. & vi.*) itchi(-suru) [一致(する)]; chôwa(-suru) [調和(する)].

according (*ad.*)
  according to ...ni-yoreba; ...ni-shitagatte

accordingly (*ad.*) sore-yue-ni [それゆえに]; shitagatte [従って].

account (*vt. & vi.*) 1)...to omou [···と思う]. 2)setsumei-suru [説明する].
  (*1*) I **account** him honest.
    Watashi-wa kare-o shôjiki-da-*to omou*.
  (*2*) I cannot **account** for it.
    Watashi-wa sore-ga *setsumei*-deki-nai.
    (*n.*) 1)keisan [計算]; kanjô [勘定]. 2)hanashi [話]. 3)setsumei [説明]. 4)rieki [利益].
  (*1*) I placed it to the cash **account**.
    Watashi-wa sore-o genkin-*kanjô*-ni ireta.
  (*2*) He gave an **account** of his trip.   Kare-wa ryokô-*dan*-o shita.
  (*3*) No satisfactory **account** has been given of it.
    Sore-niwa nan-ra manzoku-na *setsumei*-ga tsuite-i-nai.
  (*4*) Please do so on my **account**.
    Dôzo watashi-no-*tame*-ni sô shite-kudasai.
  on account of ...no-tame-ni; ...to-iu-riyû-de
  on no account ...kesshite...nai

accumulate (*vt.*) ...o tsumi-ageru [···を積み上げる]; ...o chikuseki-suru [···を蓄積する].

　　　　　(*vi.*) tsumoru [積もる]; atsumaru [集まる].

accurate (*a.*) seikaku-na [正確な]; seimitsu-na [精密な].

accursed (*a.*) 1)norowareta [のろわれた]. 2)iya-na [いやな].

accuse (*vt.*) 1)(*law*) ...o kokuso-suru [...を告訴する]. 2)...o hinan-suru [...を非難する].

accustom (*vt.*) ...ni nare-saseru [...に慣れさせる].

　　as '*be accustomed to*' ...ni narete-iru [...に慣れている].

ace (*n.*) 1)(toranpu ya saikoro no)ichi [(トランプやサイコロの)一]. 2)(*sports*) yûshû-senshu [優秀選手].

ache (*vi. & n.*) itamu(itami) [痛む(痛み)]; uzuku(uzuki) [うずく(うずき)].

achieve (*vt.*) ...o nashi-togeru [...を成し遂げる]; (mokuteki)-o tassei-suru [(目的)を達成する].

achievement (*n.*) 1)jôju [成就]; gyôseki [業績]. 2)(*educ.-psych.*) seiseki [成績].

achievement test gakuryoku-kensa [学力検査].

acid (*a.*) 1)suppai [酸っぱい]. 2)(*chem.*) sansei-no [酸性の].
　　(*n.*) 1)suppai-mono [酸っぱいもの]; san [酸].

acknowledge (*vt.*) 1)...o mitomeru [...を認める]. 2)...ni kansha-suru [...に感謝する]. 3)...o uke-totta-koto-o-shiraseru [...を受取ったことを知らせる].

acknowledg(e)ment (*n.*) 1)shônin [承認]. 2)kansha [感謝]. 3)uketori-no-tsûchi [受取の通知].

acorn (*n.*) donguri [どんぐり].

acoustic (*a.*) 1)chôkaku-no [聴覚の]. 2)bôon-yô-no [防音用の].

acquaint (*vt.*) (jijô nado)-o shiraseru [(事情など)を知らせる].
　　be acquainted with ...o yoku-shitte-iru

acquaintance (*n.*) 1)menshiki [面識]. 2)chijin [知人]; shiri-ai [知り合い].

　　(*1*) I have no **acquaintance** with him.
　　　　Watashi-wa kare-ni *menshiki*-ga-nai.
　　(*2*) He is an **acquaintance** of mine.
　　　　Kare-wa watashi no *chijin* da.
　　make one's acquaintance ...to shiri-ai-ni-naru

acquire (*vt.*) ...o eru [...を得る]; ...o kakutoku-suru [...を獲得する].

acre (*n.*) êkâ [エーカー].

across (*prep.*) 1)...o-yoko-gitte [...を横切って]; ...o-watatte [...を渡って]. 2)...no-mukô-ni [...の向こうに].

(1) Go **across** the bridge.   Sono hashi-*o-watari*-nasai.

(2) His house was **across** the river.

    Kare-no ie wa kawa-*mukô-ni* atta.

    (ad.) 1)chokkei-de [直径で]. 2)kôsa-shite [交差して].

(1) The lake is two miles **across**.

    Sono mizuumi wa *chokkei* ni-mairu da.

(2) The knives were laid **across**.   Naifu wa *kôsa-shite* okareta.

act (vt.) ...o enjiru […を演じる].

    He **acted** Lincoln.   Kare-wa Rinkân-*o enjita*.

    (vi.) kôdô-suru [行動する]; furumau [振る舞う].

    He always **acts** patient.

    Kare-wa itsu-mo shimbô-zuyoku-*furumau*.

    (n.) 1)kôi [行為]. 2)(play) ...maku […幕].

(1) It is a kind **act**.   Sore-wa shinsetsu-na *kôi* da.

(2) The third **act** is now going on.

    Ima dai-sam-*maku*-me o yatteiru.

action (n.) 1)kôi [行為]. 2)sayô [作用]. 3)akushon [アクション].
4)(mil.) kôsen [交戦].

active (a.) katsudô-teki-na [活動的な]; kappatsu-na [活発な].

activity (n.) katsudô [活動].

actor (n.) dan'yû [男優].

actress (n.) joyû [女優].

actual (a.) jissai-no [実際の]; genjitsu-no [現実の].

actually (ad.) jissai-ni [実際に]; hontô-ni [本当に].

acute (a.) 1)surudoi [鋭い]. 2)(med.) kyûsei-no [急性の].

ad (n.) (colloq.) kôkoku [広告].

A.D. (abbrev.) Seireki [西暦].

adapt (vt.) 1)...ni tekigô-saseru […に適合させる]. 2)...ni kaisaku-
suru […に改作する].

  adapt oneself to   ...ni junnô-suru

adaptation (n.) tekiô [適応].

add (vt.) ...o kuwaeru […を加える].

    (vi.) (math.) tashi-zan-o-suru [足し算をする].

addition (n.) 1)fuka [付加]. 2)tashi-zan [足し算].

  in addition   sono-ue

additional (a.) fuka-no [付加の]; tsuika-no [追加の].

address (vt.) 1)...ni hanashi-kakeru […に話し掛ける]; ...ni enzetsu-
suru […に演説する]. 2)...ni atesaki-o-kaku […にあて先を書く].

(1) He **addressed** the students. Kare-wa gakusei-ni *enzetsu-shita*.

(2) The letter **was addressed** to me.
     Sono tegami wa watashi-*ate-datta*.
        (n.) 1)enzetsu [演説]. 2)atesaki [あて先].

addressee (n.) jushin-nin [受信人].

addresser, addressor (n.) hasshin-nin [発信人].

adequate (a.) jûbun-na [十分な]; tekishita [適した].

adhere (vi.) 1)nenchaku-suru [粘着する]. 2)koshu-suru [固守する].

adhesive plaster bansô-kô [ばんそうこう].

adieu (int.) Sayô-nara! [さようなら!].

adjacent (a.) (...ni-)rinsetsu-no [(…に)隣接の].

adjective (n. & a.)(gram.) keiyô-shi(-no) [形容詞(の)].

adjust (vt.) 1)...o chôsei-suru [...を調整する]. 2)(mech.)...o chôsetsu-
   suru [...を調節する].
        (vi.) junnô-suru [順応する].

administration (n.) 1)kanri [管理]. 2)gyôsei [行政]. 3)((US))(the A-)
   seifu [政府]; naikaku [内閣].

admirable (a.) appare-na [あっぱれな]; rippa-na [立派な].

admiral (n.) kaigun-taishô [海軍大将].

admire (vt.) ...ni kantan-suru [...に感嘆する].

admission (n.) 1)nyûjô(-ryô) [入場(料)]. 2)shônin [承認].

admit (vt.) 1)...ni nyûgaku-ya-nyûkai-o kyoka-suru [...に入学や入会
   を許可する]. 2)...o mitomeru [...を認める].

(1) I **was admitted** into school.
     Watashi-wa gakkô-ni *nyûgaku-o-kyoka-sareta*.
     Watashi-wa gakkô-ni nyûgaku-shita.

(2) I **admit** that it is so.
     Watashi-wa sore-wa sô-da-*to mitomeru*.

admittance (n.) nyûjô [入場].
     No **admittance**. *Nyûjô*-o-kotowari.

admonition (n.) kunkai [訓戒]; chûkoku [忠告].

adopt (vt.) 1)...o saiyô-suru [...を採用する]. 2)...o yôshi-ni-suru [...
   を養子にする].

(1) The commission **adopted** his plan.
     Iin-kai wa kare-no an-o *saiyô-shita*.

(2) He **adopted** my second son.
     Kare-wa watashi-no jinan-o *yôshi-ni-shita*.

adore (vt.) 1)...o sûhai-suru [...を崇拝する]. 2)(colloq.)...ga dai-suki-de-aru［…が大好きである］.

adorn (*vt.*) …o kazaru［…を飾る］.

adult (*n. & a.*) seijin(-shita)［成人(した)］; otona(-no)［おとな(の)］.

advance (*vt. & vi.*) …o susumeru(susumu)［…を進める(進む)］.

　　　Advance your right foot. Migi-ashi-o *mae-ni-dashi-nasai.*

　　　We **advanced** against them.

　　　　　Ware-ware-wa kare-ra-ni-mukatte *susunda.*

　　　　　(*n.*) 1)zenshin［前進］. 2)shôshin［昇進］. 3)mae-barai［前払
　　　い］.

　　in advance　mae-motte; mae-barai-de

advanced (*a.*) susunda［進んだ］; shimpo-shita［進歩した］.

advantage (*n.*) 1)rieki［利益］. 2)kô-tsugô［好都合］.

　　take advantage of　…o riyô-suru

adventure (*n.*) bôken［冒険］.

adventurer (*n.*) 1)bôken-ka［冒険家］. 2)tôki-ka［投機家］.

adverb (*n.*) (*gram.*) fukushi［副詞］.

adversary (*n.*) teki［敵］; aite［相手］.

adverse (*a.*) gyaku-no［逆の］; hantai-no［反対の］.

adversity (*n.*) gyakkyô［逆境］; fukô［不幸］.

advertise (*vt. & vi.*) (…o) kôkoku-suru［(…を)広告する］.

advice (*n.*) chûkoku［忠告］; jogen［助言］.

　　　He asked for my **advice**.

　　　　　Kare-wa watashi-no *jogen-*o motometa.

advisable (*a.*) tokusaku-no［得策の］; kemmei-na［賢明な］.

advise (*vt.*) …ni-tsuite jogen-suru［…について助言する］;…o susumeru
　　　［…を勧める］.

　　　A doctor **advised** me to go there.

　　　　　Isha wa watashi-ni soko-e iku-yô-*ni* susumeta.

affair (*n.*) 1)jiken［事件］; koto［こと］. 2)(*pl.*) jimu［事務］. 3)
　　　(*colloq.*) mono［もの］.

　　　(*1*) That is my **affair**. Sore-wa watashi-ga-suru *koto* da.

　　　(*2*) He is a man of **affairs**. Kare-wa *jitsumu*-ka da.

affect (*vt.*) 1)…ni eikyô-suru［…に影響する］. 2)(be -ed) okasareru
　　　［冒される］.

　　　(*1*) It does not **affect** my plans.

　　　　　Sore-wa watashi-no keikaku-*ni eikyô-shi*-nai.

　　　(*2*) My throat is **affected** by a cold.

　　　　　Watashi wa kaze-de nodo-o *itamete-iru.*

affect (*vt.*) ...no furi-o-suru [⋯のふりをする].
　　　　He **affected** to be wise.
　　　　Kare-wa fumbetsu-no-aru-*furi-o-shita*.
affectation (*n.*) ki-dori [気取り].
affection (*n.*) aijô [愛情].
affectionate (*a.*) jôai-no-fukai [情愛の深い].
affectionately (*ad.*) yasashiku [優しく].
affirm (*vt.*) ...o...to dangen-suru [⋯を⋯と断言する]; ...o kôtei-suru
　　　[⋯を肯定する].
affirmative (*a.*) kôtei-teki-na [肯定的な]; sansei-no [賛成の].
afflict (*vt.*) (be -ed) kurushimu [苦しむ].
afford (*vt.*) 1)(...suru-)yoyû-ga-aru [(⋯する)余裕がある]. 2)...o
　　　ataeru [⋯を与える].
　　(1) He can **afford** to keep a car.
　　　　Kare-wa kuruma-o motsu-*yoyû-ga-aru*.
　　(2) The place **affords** excellent pasture-land.
　　　　Soko wa subarashii bokusô-chi-*ni-naru*.
afloat (*ad.*) 1)ukande [浮かんで]. 2)(*com.*) ryûtsû-shite [流通して].
afraid (*a.*) 1)kowagatte [怖がって]. 2)zannen-de [残念で].
　　(1) I am much **afraid** of the dog.
　　　　Watashi-wa inu ga totemo *kowai*.
　　(2) I am **afraid** that I cannot go there.
　　　　Zannen-desu-ga watashi-wa soko-e ike-masen.
Africa (*n.*) Afurika [アフリカ].
African (*a.*) Afurika-no [アフリカの]; Afurika-jin-no [アフリカ人の].
　　　(*n.*) Afurika-jin [アフリカ人].
after (*ad.*) ato-ni [あとに].
　　　(*conj.*) (...shi)ta-ato-ni [(⋯し)たあとに].
　　　He came **after** you went out.
　　　　Kimi-ga dekake*ta-ato-ni* kare-ga yatte-kita.
　　　(*prep.*) 1)...no-nochi-ni [⋯の後に]; ...no-ato-ni [⋯のあとに]. 2)
　　　...o-motomete [⋯を求めて]. 3)...ni-naratte [⋯にならって].
　　(1) He died **after** a few days.
　　　　Kare-wa ni-san-nichi-*nochi-ni* shinda.
　　　I'll come **after** you. Watashi-wa *ato-kara* mairi-masu.
　　(2) They are **after** gold. Kare-ra-wa *kin-o-motomete*-iru.
　　(3) He made many toys **after** it.
　　　　Kare-wa sore-*ni-naratte* takusan-no omocha-o tsukutta.

after all kekkyoku; yahari
one after another tsugi-tsugi-to; hiki-tsuzuite
one after the other kawaru-gawaru
the day after (sono-)yokujitsu
　　(*a.*) ato-no [あとの]; nochi-no [後の].
　　He became famous in **after** years.
　　　　Kare-wa *kônen* yûmei-ni-natta.

afternoon (*n.*) gogo [午後].

afterward(s) (*ad.*) nochi-ni [後に]; sono-go [その後].

again (*ad.*) futatabi [再び]; mata [また].
　again and again ikudo-mo; kuri-kaeshite

against (*prep.*) 1)...ni-taishite [⋯に対して]; ...ni-sakaratte [⋯に逆らっ
て]. 2)...ni-motarete [⋯にもたれて]. 3)...ni-sonaete [⋯に備えて].
　　(*1*) It is hard to swim **against** the stream.
　　　　Nagare-*ni-sakaratte* oyogu-no-wa muzukashii.
　　(*2*) Don't lean **against** the wall. Kabe-*ni-motare*ru-na.
　　(*3*) Provide **against** a rainy day. Masaka-no-toki-*ni-sonae*-nasai.

age (*n.*) 1)nenrei [年齢]. 2)hisashii-aida [久しい間]. 3)(the -) jidai
[時代].
　　(*1*) He is thirteen years of **age**. Kare-wa jû-san-*sai* da.
　　(*2*) It's quite an **age** since I saw you last.
　　　　Zuibun o-*hisashi-buri*-desu-ne.
　　(*3*) The 19th century was the **age** of tools.
　　　　Jû-kyû-seiki wa kigu no *jidai* datta.
　come of age seinen-ni-tassuru
　for ages nagai-aida

aged (*a.*) 1)toshi-o-totta [年をとった]. 2)...sai-no [⋯歳の].
　　(*1*) He is now an **aged** man. Kare-wa mô *rôjin* da.
　　(*2*) He has a daughter, **aged** ten.
　　　　Kare-wa ju*ssai-no* musume-ga aru.

agency (*n.*) dairi-ten [代理店].

agent (*n.*) dairi-nin [代理人]; shûsen-nin [周旋人].

aggressive (*a.*) 1)shinryaku-teki-na [侵略的な]. 2)(*colloq.*) sekkyoku-
teki-na [積極的な].

agitate (*vt.*) ...o kaki-mawasu [⋯をかきまわす].
　　(*vi.*) sendô-suru [扇動する].

ago (*ad.*) (ima kara)...mae-ni [(今から)⋯前に].
　a long time ago zuibun-mae-ni

agony (*n.*) kumon ［苦悶］.

agree (*vi.*) 1)shôdaku-suru ［承諾する］. 2)iken-ga-itchi-suru ［意見が一致する］; dôi-suru ［同意する］.

  (*1*) They **agreed** to the proposal.

      Kare-ra-wa sono-teian-o *shôdaku-shita*.

  (*2*) I **agree** with you. Watashi-wa anata-ni *dôi-suru*.

agreeable (*a.*) 1)kanji-no-yoi ［感じのよい］. 2)(...ni-)sansei-suru ［(…に）賛成する］.

agreed (*a.*) 1)dôi-shita ［同意した］. 2)yakusoku-shita ［約束した］; tori-kimerareta ［取決められた］.

  (*1*) We are **agreed**. Ware-ware-wa *dôkan*-desu.

  (*2*) He did not come by the time **agreed** upon.

      Kare-wa *yakusoku-no* jikan-made-ni ko-nakatta.

agreement (*n.*) 1)itchi ［一致］. 2)dôi ［同意］. 3)kyôtei ［協定］.

  come to an agreement kyôtei-ga-matomaru

agricultural products nô-sambutsu ［農産物］.

agriculture (*n.*) nôgyô ［農業］; nôgei ［農芸］.

ah (*int.*) Aa! ［ああ!］; Oo! ［おお!］.

aha (*int.*) Hô! ［ほう!］; Maa! ［まあ!］.

ahead (*ad.*) 1)mae-ni ［前に］; zempô-ni ［前方に］. 2)masatte ［まさって］.

  (*1*) Go **ahead**! *Zen*shin!

      We saw a boat **ahead** of us.

      Ware-ware-no-*zempô-ni* fune-ga isseki mieta.

  (*2*) Tanaka is **ahead** of Suzuki in English.

      Tanaka wa Eigo-de Suzuki-*yori-masatte*-iru.

aid (*vt.*) ...o tasukeru ［…を助ける］.

  I **aided** him with money.

      Watashi-wa kinsen-de kare-o *tasuketa*.

  (*n.*) tasuke ［助け］; enjo ［援助］; kyûjo ［救助］.

  His friends hurried to his **aid**.

      Yûjin-tachi wa kare-no-*kyûjo*-ni isoida.

  first aid ôkyû-teate

ailment (*n.*) (mansei no)byôki ［(慢性の)病気］.

aim (*vt.*) (jû nado)-o mukeru ［(銃など)を向ける］.

  He **aimed** his pistol at me.

      Kare-wa watashi-ni pisutoru-o *tsuki-tsuketa*.

  (*vi.*) nerau ［ねらう］.

He **aimed** at that merchant.
    Kare-wa sono-shônin-o *neratta*.
  (*n.*) 1)nerai [ねらい]. 2)mokuteki [目的].
  (*1*) I took **aim** with my gun. Watashi-wa jû-de *neratta*.
  (*2*) He attained his **aim**. Kare-wa *mokuteki*-o tasshita.

air (*n.*) 1)kûki [空気]. 2)sora [空]. 3)taido [態度].
  (*1*) We must have fresh **air**.
      Ware-ware-wa shinsen-na *kûki*-ga hitsuyô-da.
  (*2*) A bird is flying in the **air**. Tori-ga ichi-wa *sora*-o tondeiru.
  (*3*) You have a lofty **air**. Kimi no *taido* wa gôman da.
  by air hikô-ki-de; muden-de

air force kûgun [空軍].
airmail (*n.*) kôkû-yûbin [航空郵便].
airman (*n.*) hikô-ka [飛行家]; hikô-shi [飛行士].
airplane (*n.*) hikô-ki [飛行機].
airport (*n.*) kûkô [空港].
air pressure kiatsu [気圧].
air raid kûshû [空襲].
airship (*n.*) hikô-sen [飛行船].
airsick (*a.*) hikô-ki-ni-yotta [飛行機に酔った].
airy (*a.*) 1)kûki-no [空気の]. 2)kaze-tooshi-no-yoi [風通しのよい].
aisle (*n.*) tsûro [通路].
alarm (*n.*) 1)keihô [警報]. 2)odoroki [驚き].
  (*1*) An **alarm** was given. *Keihô* ga hasserareta.
  (*2*) "Watch out!" cried he in **alarm**.
      "Ki-o-tsukero!" to kare-wa *odoroite* sakenda.
    (*vt.*) 1)...o hatto-saseru [···をはっとさせる]; ...o fuan-ni-saseru
  [···を不安にさせる]. 2)...ni keihô-o-hassuru [···に警報を発する].
  (*1*) Don't be **alarmed**! *Bikkuri-suru*-na!
alarm clock mezamashi-dokei [目覚まし時計].
alarming (*a.*) odoroku-beki [驚くべき].
alas (*int.*) Aa! [ああ!]; Kanashii-kana! [悲しいかな!].
alert (*a.*) yudan-no-nai [油断のない]; nuke-me-no-nai [抜け目のない].
  (*n.*) keikai-keihô [警戒警報].
algebra (*n.*) daisû[-gaku] [代数(学)].
alien (*a.*) gaikoku[-jin]-no [外国(人)の].
  (*n.*) gaikoku-jin [外国人].
alight (*vi.*) oriru [降りる].

alike (*a.*) onaji-no [同じの]; dôyô-na [同様な].

>They are all **alike** to me.
>>Kare-ra-wa watashi-niwa mina *onaji*-da.

alive (*a.*) ikite [生きて].

all (*a.*) subete-no [すべての]; zembu-no [全部の]; arayuru [あらゆる].

>All the birds were singing. *Subete-no* tori ga saezutteita.

(*pron.*) 1)mina [皆]. 2)subete [すべて]. 3)zembu [全部]; zentai [全体]. 4)banji [万事].

(*1*) **All** are agreed. *Mina* ga dôi-shite-iru.

(*2*) I did **all** I could. Watashi-wa dekiru-koto-wa-*subete* shita.
>>Watashi-wa dekiru-dake-no-koto-o shita.

(*3*) That's **all**. Sore-ga *zembu* da.
>>Sore-dake-da.

(*4*) **All** goes well. *Banji* kô-tsugô-ni iku.

not at all sukoshi-mo...de-nai

>Not at all. Dô-itashi-mashite.

in all zembu-de

(*ad.*) mattaku [全く]; sukkari [すっかり].

>It is all black with the clouds.
>>Sora wa kumo-de *sukkari* kuraku-natte-iru.

all along zutto; shijû

all in (*colloq.*) tsukarete; heto-heto-de

all out zenryoku-o-agete

all over 1)...no-itaru-tokoro-de;....jû 2)sukkari-owatte

1) all over the world sekai-jû

2) The storm is all over. Bôfû-u wa sukkari-yanda.

all right sashi-tsukae-naku

>All right! Yoroshii!; Shôchi-shita!

allege (*vt.*) ...to shuchô-suru […と主張する]; ...to iu [と言う].

allergy (*n.*) (*path.*) arerugî [アレルギー].

alley (*n.*) kôji [小路]; roji [路地].

allied (*a.*) 1)dômei-no [同盟の]; rengô-no [連合の]. 2)dôrui-no [同類の].

alligator (*n.*) wani [ワニ].

allocation (*n.*) wari-ate [割り当て].

allot (*vt.*) ...o wari-ateru […を割り当てる]; ...o bumpai-suru […を分配する].

allow (*vt.*) 1)...o yurusu […を許す]. 2)...ni...sasete-oku […に…させ

ておく].

(1) Father does not **allow** me to go.
    Chichi wa watashi-ga iku-no-o-*yurusa*-nai.

(2) We **allowed** him to do so.
    Ware-ware-wa kare-ni sô *sasete-oita*.

Allow me to... Shitsurei-desu-ga...sasete-kudasai.

allow for (*vi.*) ...o shinshaku-suru [...をしん酌する]; ...o kôryo-ni-ireru [...を考慮に入れる].

    We must **allow** for his youth.
    Kare-no-toshi-no-wakai-ten-o *kôryo-shi*-nakereba-naranai.

allowance (*n.*) 1)teate [手当]. 2)kyoyô [許容]. 3)waribiki [割引].

alloy (*n.*) gôkin [合金].

allusion (*n.*) 1)genkyû [言及]. 2)hiyu [比ゆ].

almanac (*n.*) koyomi [暦]; nenkan [年鑑].

almighty (*a.*) zennô-no [全能の].

almost (*ad.*) hotondo [ほとんど].

aloft (*ad.*) takaku [高く]; ue-ni [上に].

alone (*a.*) hitori-no [一人の]; tandoku-no [単独の].

  leave(let)...alone ...o kamawazu-ni-oku

  let alone ...wa-iu-made-mo-naku

along (*prep.*) ...ni-sotte [...に沿って]; ...zutai-ni [...づたいに].

    A road runs **along** the river.
    Kawa-*ni-sotte* michi-ga ippon aru.

    (*ad.*) 1)sotte [沿って]. 2)mae-e [前へ]; saki-e [先へ]. 3)(mono o)motte [(物を)持って]; (hito to)issho-ni [(人と)一緒に].

(1) A boy walked **along** by the river.
    Hitori-no shônen ga kawa-ni-*sotte* aruite-ita.

(2) Move **along**! *Saki-ni* don-don-aruite!

(3) He took his sister **along**. Kare-wa imôto-o-*tsurete*-itta.

  along with ...to-issho-ni; ...to-kyôryoku-shite; ...ni-kuwaete; ...no-hoka-ni

alongside (*prep.*) ...ni-yoko-zuke-ni [...に横づけに]; ...no-soba-ni [...のそばに].

    We saw several vessels **alongside** the pier.
    Ware-ware-wa sambashi-*ni-yoko-zuke-ni*-natte-iru sû-seki-no fune-o mita.

    (*ad.*) yoko-zuke-ni [横づけに].

    The boat came **alongside**. Bôto ga *yoko-zuke-ni*-natta.

aloud (*ad.*) koe-o-dashite [声を出して]; oo-goe-de [大声で].

alphabet (*n.*) arufabetto [アルファベット]; shoho [初歩].

Alps, the (*n.*) Arupusu-sammyaku [アルプス山脈].

already (*ad.*) sude-ni [すでに]; mô [もう].

also (*ad.*) ...mo-mata […もまた].

　not only...but also ...dake-de-naku...mo-mata

alter (*vt. & vi.*) ...o kaeru (kawaru) […を変える(変わる)].

alteration (*n.*) henkô [変更].

alternative (*n. & a.*) nisha-takuitsu(-no) [二者択一(の)].

although (*conj.*) (...de-aru)keredomo [(…である)けれども].

altitude (*n.*) takasa [高さ]; kôdo [高度].

altogether (*ad.*) 1)zenzen [全然]. 2)zembu-de [全部で].

　(*1*) It's not **altogether** bad.

　　　Sore-wa *zenzen*-warui-wake-de-mo-nai.

　(*2*) It was a day's ride **altogether**.

　　　Zembu-de ichi-nichi-no sôkô-kyori datta.

aluminum, aluminium (*n.*) aruminium [アルミニウム].

always (*ad.*) tsune-ni [常に]; itsu-mo [いつも].

　not always kanarazu-shimo...to-wa-kagira-nai

am (*vi.*) ...de-aru […である].

A.M., a.m. (*abbrev.*) gozen [午前].

amateur (*n.*) shirôto [しろうと]; amachua [アマチュア].

amaze (*vt.*) ...o bikkuri-saseru […をびっくりさせる]; ...o odorokasu […を驚かす].

amazement (*n.*) odoroki [驚き]; bikkuri-suru-koto [びっくりすること].

amazing (*a.*) odoroku-hodo-no [驚くほどの]; mezamashii [目覚ましい].

ambassador (*n.*) taishi [大使].

amber (*n.*) kohaku[-iro] [こはく(色)].

　(*a.*) kohaku-iro-no [こはく色の].

ambition (*n.*) taimô [大望]; yashin [野心];

ambitious (*a.*) taimô-o-idaita [大望をいだいた]; yashin-no-aru [野心のある].

　be ambitious of ...o netsubô-shite-iru

ambulance (*n.*) kyûkyû-sha [救急車]; (*mil.*) yasen-byôin [野戦病院].

amend (*vt.*) ...o shûsei-suru […を修正する]; ...o teisei-suru […を訂正する]; ...o aratameru […を改める].

America (*n.*) Amerika [アメリカ]; Beikoku [米国].

American (*a.*) Amerika-no [アメリカの]; Amerika-jin-no [アメリカ人

の]; Beikoku-no [米国の].

      (n.) Amerika-jin [アメリカ人]; Beikoku-jin [米国人].

amiable (a.) yasashii [優しい]; ki-date-no-yoi [気立てのよい].

amid (prep.) ...no-naka-ni […の中に].

among (prep.) ...no-naka-ni […の中に]; ...no-aida-ni […の間に].

amount (vi.) zembu-de...naru [全部で…なる].

    It **amounted** to 3,000 dollars.

        Zembu-de san-zen-doru-ni *natta*.

      (n.) sôkei [総計]; sôgaku [総額]; ryô [量]; gaku [額].

    The cost reached a large **amount**.

        Genka wa kyo*gaku*-ni nobotta.

ample (a.) hiroi [広い]; jûbun-na [十分な].

amuse (vt.) ...o omoshiro-garaseru […を面白がらせる].

amusement (n.) tanoshimi [楽しみ]; goraku [娯楽].

amusing (a.) omoshiroi [面白い].

an (indef. art.) see. 'a'.

anachronism (n.) jidai-sakugo [時代錯誤].

analysis (n.) bunkai [分解]; bunseki [分析].

anarchist (n.) mu-seifu-shugi-sha [無政府主義者].

anatomy (n.) kaibô[-gaku] [解剖(学)].

ancestor (n.) sosen [祖先].

ancestral (a.) sosen-no [祖先の]; senzo-dai-dai-no [先祖代々の].

anchor (n.) 1)ikari [いかり]. 2)(sports)saigo-no-sôsha[-eisha] [最後
  の走者[泳者]].

  cast anchor　ikari-o-orosu

  lie at anchor　teihaku-shite-iru

  weigh anchor　ikari-o-ageru

      (vt.) ...o ikari-de-tomeru […をいかりで止める].

      (vi.) teihaku-suru [停泊する].

ancient (a.) 1)mukashi-no [昔の]; kodai-no [古代の]. 2)korai-no [古
  来の].

and (conj.) 1)...to […と]; ...oyobi […および]; soshite [そして].
  2)sô-suru-to [そうすると].

    (1) Tom **and** I went there.　Tomu *to* watashi ga soko-e itta.

    (2) Cross the bridge, **and** you'll come to a brick building.

        Sono hashi-o watari-nasai, *sô-suru-to* renga-no tate-mono-
        ni demasu.

  and so on　...nado

and that shikamo; sono-ue

and then sore-kara; soko-de

anecdote (*n.*) itsuwa [逸話].

anew (*ad.*) arata-ni [新たに]; mô-ichi-do [もう一度].

angel (*n.*) 1)tenshi [天使]. 2)yasashii-hito [優しい人].

anger (*n.*) ikari [怒り]; rippuku [立腹].
    (*vt.*) ...o okoraseru […を怒らせる].

angle (*n.*) 1)kaku[do] [角(度)]. 2)kado [かど].

angle (*vi.*) sakana-o-tsuru. [魚を釣る].

angrily (*ad.*) okotte [怒って].

angry (*a.*) okotta [怒った]; hara-o-tateta [腹を立てた].

anguish (*n.*) kutsû [苦痛]; kunô [苦悩].

animal (*n. & a.*) dôbutsu(-no) [動物(の)].

animation (*n.*) 1)kakki [活気]; genki [元気]. 2)(*movie*)manga-eiga [漫画映画]; dôga-seisaku [動画制作].

ankle (*n.*) kurubushi [くるぶし]; ashi-kubi [足首].

annals (*n.*) nenshi [年史]; nempô [年報].

anniversary (*n.*) kinen-bi [記念日]; kinen-sai [記念祭].

announce (*vt.*) ...o shiraseru […を知らせる]; ...o happyô-suru […を発表する].

announcement (*n.*) kokuchi [告知]; happyô [発表].

annoy (*vt.*) ...o nayamasu […を悩ます]; ...o ira-ira-saseru […をいらいらさせる].

annoyance (*n.*) iradachi [いらだち].

annual (*a.*) ichi-nen[-goto]-no [一年(ごと)の]; ichi-nen-ikkai-no [一年一回の].
    (*n.*) nenkan-shi [年刊誌].

another (*a.*) 1)mô-hitotsu-no [もう一つの]. 2)betsu-no [別の].
    (*1*) Have **another** cup. *Mô*-ippai meshi-agare.
    (*2*) He became **another** man. Kare-wa *betsu*jin-ni-natta.
    another time itsu-ka
        (*pron.*) mô-hitotsu-no-mono [もう一つのもの]; betsu-no-mono [別のもの].
        Show me **another**. *Betsu-no-mono*-o misete-kudasai.
    one another tagai-ni

answer (*vt. & vi.*) (...ni) kotaeru [(…に)答える];(...ni) henji-o-suru [(…に)返事をする].
    I must **answer** the letter.

      Sono tegami-*ni henji-o-shi*-nakereba-naranai.

      (*n.*) kotae [答え]; henji [返事].

    I'll send you an **answer** by telephone.

      Denwa-de go-*henji*-itashi-masu.

ant (*n.*) (*insect*) ari [アリ].

Antarctic (*a.*) Nankyoku-no [南極の].

Antarctic Ocean, the Nampyô-yô [南氷洋].

antelope (*n.*) (*zool.*) reiyô [レイヨウ].

antenna (*n.*) 1)(*zool.*) shokkaku [触覚]. 2)antena [アンテナ].

anticipate (*vt.*) 1)...o yosô-suru […を予想する]; ...o yoki-suru […を予期する]. 2)...no sente-o-utsu […の先手を打つ].

antique (*a.*) kottô-no [骨とうの]; kofû-na [古風な].

      (*n.*) kobutsu [古物]; kottô-hin [骨とう品].

antonym (*n.*) han'i-go [反意語].

anxiety (*n.*) 1)shimpai [心配]. 2)setsubô [切望].

anxious (*a.*) 1)shimpai-shite [心配して]. 2)setsubô-shite [切望して].

    (*1*) I am **anxious** about your health.

      Watashi-wa kimi-no-kenkô-ga-*shimpai*-da.

    (*2*) I am **anxious** to avoid mistakes.

      Watashi-wa machigai-o sakeru-koto-o-*setsubô-shite*-iru.

      Watashi-wa ayamachi-o sake-tai.

any (*a.*) 1)ikura-ka [いくらか]. 2)nani-ka [何か]. 3)dono...demo [どの…でも]. 4)nani-mo [何も].

    (*pron.*) ikura-ka [いくらか]; dore-ka [どれか]; dore-mo [どれも].

    (*ad.*) ikura-ka [いくらか]; sukoshi-wa [少しは].

    any longer mohaya(...(shi-)nai)

    any more mohaya

    any one dore-demo; dare-demo

    any time itsu-demo

    if any moshi-are-ba; tatoe-atte-mo

anybody (*pron.*) dare-ka [だれか]; dare-mo [だれも]; dare-demo [だれでも].

anyhow (*ad.*) tomo-kaku [ともかく].

anyone (*pron.*) dare-mo [だれも]; dare-demo [だれでも].

anything (*pron.*) nani-ka [何か]; nani-mo [何も]; nan-demo [何でも].

    as...as anything totemo; hijô-ni

    for anything kesshite(...(shi-)nai)

anyway (*ad.*) tomo-kaku [ともかく]; nan-toka-shite [何とかして].

anywhere (*ad.*) doko-ka-e [どこかへ]; doko-ni-mo [どこにも].

apart (*ad.*) bara-bara-ni [ばらばらに]; hanarete [離れて].
  apart from ...wa-betsu-to-shite
  know(tell)...apart ...o shikibetsu-suru
  take...apart ...o bunkai-suru

apartment (*n.*) heya [部屋]; apâto [アパート].

ape (*n.*) (o-no-nai)saru [(尾のない)さる].

apiece (*ad.*) mei-mei-ni [めいめいに]; ikko-ni-tsuki [一箇に付き];
  hitori-ni-tsuki [一人に付き].

apologize (*vi.*) wabiru [詫びる]; iiwake-o-suru [言い訳をする]; benkai-
  suru [弁解する].

apology (*n.*) shazai [謝罪]; benkai [弁解].

apparatus (*n.*) kikai [機械]; sôchi [装置].

apparent (*a.*) meihaku-na [明白な]; mita-tokoro [見たところ].

apparently (*ad.*) mita-tokoro...rashii [見たところ…らしい]; akiraka-
  ni [明らかに].

appeal (*vi. & n.*) uttaeru(uttae) [訴える(訴え)].

appear (*vi.*) 1)arawareru [現れる]. 2)...to-omowareru […と思われる];
  ...rashii […らしい].
  (*1*) The actress **appeared** on the stage.
      Sono joyû ga butai-ni *arawareta.*
  (*2*) It **appears** that he is ill. Kare-wa byôki-*rashii.*

appearance (*n.*) 1)shutsugen [出現]. 2)gaikan [外観].
  make one's appearance sugata-o-arawasu; shutsugen-suru

appease (*vt.*) 1)...o nadameru […をなだめる]. 2)...o mitasu […を満
  たす].

appendix (*n.*) 1)furoku [付録]. 2)(*anat.*)chûsui [中垂].

appetite (*n.*) shokuyoku [食欲].

applause (*n.*) hakushu-kassai [拍手喝さい]; shôsan [賞賛].

apple (*n.*) ringo [リンゴ].

appliance (*n.*) kigu [器具].

applicant (*n.*) môshi-komi-sha [申込者]; shigan-sha [志願者].

application (*n.*) 1)tekiyô [適用]. 2)môshi-komi[-sho] [申込(書)];
  shinsei [申請].

applied (*a.*) ôyô-no [応用の].
  applied chemistry ôyô-kagaku

apply (*vt.*) 1)...o ôyô-suru […を応用する]. 2)...o ateru […を当てる];
  ...ni mukeru […に向ける].

(1) **Apply** the rule to it. Sono-kisoku-o sore-ni *ôyô-shi-nasai*.

(2) He **applied** his hand to his breast.

    Kare-wa mune-ni te-o *ateta*.

    (*vi.*) 1)ate-hamaru [あてはまる]. 2)môshi-komu [申し込む].

(1) It does not **apply** to this case.

    Sore-wa kono-baai-ni *ate-hamara*-nai.

(2) He **applied** to the seat. Kare-wa sono-seki-o *môshi-konda*.

appoint (*vt.*) 1)...ni nimmei-suru [...に任命する]. 2)...ni shitei-suru [...に指定する].

appointment (*n.*) 1)nimmei [任命]. 2)yakusoku [約束].

(1) He erred by the **appointment** of unsuitable men.

    Kare-wa ayamatte fu-tekinin-na hito-tachi-o *nimmei*-shita.

(2) He kept his **appointment**. Kare-wa *yakusoku*-o mamotta.

   by appointment   yakusoku-ni-yotte

appreciable (*a.*) kanchi-dekiru [感知できる]; kanari-no [かなりの].

appreciate (*vt.*) 1)...no kachi-o-mitomeru [...の価値を認める]. 2)...o kansha-suru [...を感謝する]. 3)...o kanshô-suru [...を鑑賞する].

appreciation (*n.*) tadashii-hyôka [正しい評価]; kanshô [鑑賞]; kansha [感謝].

apprehension (*n.*) ki-zukai [気遣い]; rikai [理解].

approach (*vt. & vi.*) (...ni) chikazuku [(...に)近付く].

    (*n.*) 1)sekkin [接近]. 2)iriguchi [入り口].

approachable (*a.*) chikazuki-yasui [近づきやすい]; (*colloq.*)shitashimi-yasui [親しみやすい].

approbation (*n.*) zenin [是認]; san'i [賛意].

appropriate (*a.*) tekitô-na [適当な].

    (*vt.*) 1)...o chakufuku-suru [...を着服する]. 2)...o jûtô-suru [...を充当する].

approval (*n.*) sansei [賛成]; shônin [承認].

approve (*vt. & vi.*) (...ni) sansei-suru [(...に)賛成する]; (...o) shônin-suru [...を承認する].

approximately (*ad.*) ooyoso [おおよそ]; hobo [ほぼ].

apricot (*n.*) anzu [アンズ].

April (*n.*) Shigatsu [四月].

apron (*n.*) epuron [エプロン]; mae-kake [前掛け].

apt (*a.*) tekisetsu-na [適切な].

    It is an **apt** instance. Sore-wa *tekisetsu-na* rei da.

   be apt at   ...ga jôzu-de-aru

be apt to ...(shi-)gachi-da

Arab (*n.*) Arabu-jin [アラブ人]; Arabia-uma [アラビア馬].

Arabia (*n.*) Arabia [アラビア].

Arabian (*a.*) Arabia-no [アラビアの]; Arabia-jin-no [アラビア人の].
(*n.*) Arabia-jin [アラビア人]; Arabia-uma [アラビア馬].

arbor (*n.*)(*bot.*) jumoku [樹木].

arc (*n.*) 1)yumi-gata [弓形]. 2)(*math.*) enko [円弧]. 3)(*elect.*) âku [アーク].

arcade (*n.*) âkêdo [アーケード]; yane-tsuki-gairo [屋根付き街路].

arch (*n.*)(*arch.*) âchi [アーチ]; serimochi [せりもち].

archbishop (*n.*) dai-shikyô [大司教]; dai-sôjô [大僧正].

architect (*n.*) kenchiku-ka [建築家].

architecture (*n.*) kenchiku-jutsu [建築術]; kenchiku-gaku [建築学]; kenchiku-butsu [建築物].

Arctic (*a.*) Hokkyoku-no [北極の].

Arctic Ocean, the Hoppyô-yô [北氷洋].

ardent (*a.*) nesshin-na [熱心な]; netsuretsu-na [熱烈な].

arduous (*a.*) 1)hone-no-oreru [骨の折れる]. 2)funtô-doryoku-no [奮闘努力の].
   (*1*) It is an **arduous** task. Sore-wa *hone-no-oreru* shigoto da.
   (*2*) He led an **arduous** life.
       Kare-wa *funtô-doryoku-no* jinsei-o okutta.

are (*vi.*) ...de-aru [···である].

area (*n.*) 1)menseki [面積]. 2)chiiki [地域]; chihô [地方]. 3)hiroba [広場]; basho [場所].
   area code ((*US & Can.*)) (denwa-no)shigai-kyokuban

argue (*vi. & vt.*) (...o) ronzuru [(···を)論ずる].

argument (*n.*) giron [議論].

arise (*vi.*) okoru [起こる]; shôzuru [生ずる].

arithmetic (*n.*) sansû [算数].

arm (*n.*) 1)ude [腕]. 2)(*pl.*) buki [武器].
   (*1*) She stood with a child in her **arms**.
       Kano-jo-wa kodomo-o-daite tatte-ita.
   (*2*) They rose in **arms**. Kare-ra-wa *buki*-o-motte tachi-agatta.
   arm in arm ude-o-kumi-atte
       (*vt.*) ...o busô-saseru [···を武装させる].

armament (*n.*) gumbi [軍備].

armchair (*n.*) hiji-kake-isu [ひじかけいす].

armed (*a.*) busô-shita [武装した].

armistice (*n.*) kyûsen [休戦].

armor, -mour (*n.*) yoroi-kabuto [よろいかぶと].

army (*n.*) riku-gun [陸軍]; gun [軍].

around (*ad.*) mawari-ni [回りに]; atari-ni [あたりに].

    It was foggy **around**.

       Atari-ichimen-ni moya-ga-tachi-komete-ita.

   all around shihô-ni; itaru-tokoro-ni

     (*prep.*) ...no-mawari-ni [···の回りに].

    The stars twinkle **around** the moon.

       Hoshi wa tsuki-*no-mawari-ni* kirameku.

arouse (*vt.*) ...no me-o-samasaseru [···の目を覚まさせる].

arrange (*vt.*) 1)...o seiton-suru [···を整とんする]. 2)...o tori-kimeru
   [···を取り決める].

       (*vi.*) jumbi-suru [準備する].

   arrange with one about something aru-koto-ni-tsuite hito-to-
   uchi-awaseru

arrangement (*n.*) 1)seiton [整とん]. 2)(*pl.*) tehai [手配]. 3)tori-kime
   [取り決め].

   flower arrangement ikebana

array (*vt. & n.*) 1)...o yosoou(yosooi) [···を装う(装い)]. 2)...o
   seiretsu-saseru(seiretsu) [···を整列させる(整列)].

arrest (*vt. & n.*) ...o taiho-suru(taiho) [···を逮捕する(逮捕)].

arrive (*vi.*) tôchaku-suru [到着する].

arrogant (*a.*) gôman-na [ごう慢な].

arrow (*n.*) ya [矢].

art (*n.*) 1)geijutsu [芸術]. 2)jinkô [人工]; waza [わざ].

   fine arts bijutsu

artery (*n.*) 1)kansen-dôro [幹線道路]. 2)(*anat.*) dômyaku [動脈].

art gallery garô [画廊].

article (*n.*) 1)kiji [記事]. 2)shinamono [品物]. 3)(*gram.*) kanshi
   [冠詞].

artificial (*a.*) jinkô-no [人工の]; jinzô-no [人造の].

artificially (*ad.*) jinkô-teki-ni [人工的に]; waza-to-rashiku [わざとら
   しく].

artist (*n.*) 1)geijutsu-ka [芸術家]. 2)gaka [画家].

artistic (*a.*) geijutsu-teki-na [芸術的な].

artistically (*ad.*) geijutsu-teki-ni[-mireba] [芸術的に(見れば)].

as (*conj.*) 1)(...no-)yô-ni [（…の）ように]. 2)...(shi-)nagara […（し）ながら]. 3)...(da-)kara […（だ）から]. 4)...toki-ni […ときに]; ...no-aida-ni […の間に]. 5)(...da-)keredomo [（…だ）けれども].

　(1) She did **as** she had been told.
　　　Kano-jo-wa iwareta-*yô-ni* shita.
　(2) She sang **as** she worked.
　　　Kano-jo-wa hataraki-*nagara* uta-o-utatta.
　(3) A fish can swim **as** it has fins.
　　　Hire ga-aru-*kara* sakana wa oyogu-koto-ga-dekiru.
　(4) A sound was heard just **as** I reached the door.
　　　Watashi-ga genkan-ni tsuita-*toki-ni* mono-oto ga kikoeta.
　(5) Young **as** he is, he is very able.
　　　Toshi-koso-wakai-*keredomo*, kare-wa totemo yûnô-da.

　(*prep.*)...to-shite […として].
　　　It can be used **as** a knife, too.
　　　Sore-wa naifu-*to-shite*-mo mochii-rareru.

　as...as possible(...can) dekiru-dake
　as far as ...(surɯ-)kagiri
　as for(to) ...ni-kanshite-wa
　as if(though) ...de-aru-kano-yô-ni
　as it were iwaba
　as yet ima-made-no-tokoro-de-wa　　　　　「上がる].
ascend (*vt. & vi.*) (...ni) noboru [(…に)登る]; (...ni) agaru [(…に)
　(1) We **ascended** the hill. Ware-ware-wa oka-*ni nobotta*.
　(2) The balloon **ascended** to the sky. Kikyû ga sora-ni *agatta*.
ascertain (*vt.*) ...o tashikameru […を確かめる].
ash (*n.*) hai [灰].
　be reduced to ashes shôshitsu-suru; hai-ni-naru
ashamed (*a.*) hajite [恥じて].
　be ashamed of ...o hazukashiku-omou
ashore (*ad.*) kishi-ni [岸に].
　come(go) ashore jôriku-suru
Asia (*n.*) Ajia [アジア].
Asia Minor Shô-Ajia [小アジア].
Asian (*a.*) Ajia-no [アジアの]; Ajia-jin-no [アジア人の].
　　　(*n.*) Ajia-jin [アジア人].
aside (*ad.*) waki-ni [わきに]; hanashite [離して]; betsu-ni-shite [別にして].

aside from ((*US*)) ...wa-sate-oki

joking aside jôdan-wa-sate-oki

put aside 1)...o totte-oku. 2)...o yameru

ask (*vt.*) 1)...o tazuneru [···を尋ねる]; ...o tou [···を問う]. 2)...to tanomu [···と頼む].

　(*1*) He **asked** me a question. Kare-wa boku-ni shitsumon-*shita*.

　(*2*) The man **asked** me to lend him a knife.

　　　　Sono otoko wa watashi-ni naifu-o-kashite-kure-*to tanonda*.

ask one about something aru-koto-ni-tsuite hito-ni kiku

ask one in hito-o toosu

　(*vi.*) 1)tazuneru [尋ねる]. 2)motomeru [求める].

　(*1*) He **asked** after me. Kare-wa watashi-no-ampi-o *tazuneta*.

　(*2*) He **asked** for money. Kare-wa kane-o *motometa*.

asleep (*a. & ad.*) nemutte [眠って].

fall asleep ne-iru

fast asleep gussuri-nemutte

asp (*n.*) Ejiputo-kobura [エジプトコブラ].

aspect (*n.*) 1)yôsu [様子]. 2)kao-tsuki [顔つき]. 3)...muki [···向き].

asphalt (*n.*) (hosô-yô-)asufaruto [(舗装用)アスファルト].

aspire (*vi.*) netsubô-suru [熱望する]; taishi-o-idaku [大志をいだく].

ass (*n.*) 1)(*zool.*) roba [ロバ]. 2)baka [ばか].

assail (*vt.*) ...o osou [···を襲う]; ...o kôgeki-suru [···を攻撃する].

assassin (*n.*) ansatsu-sha [暗殺者].

assassinate (*vt.*) ...o ansatsu-suru [···を暗殺する].

assault (*vt.*) 1)...o kyôshû-suru [···を強襲する]. 2)(*law*) ...ni bôkô-suru [···に暴行する].

　　　(*n.*) kyôshû [強襲]; bôkô [暴行].

assemble (*vt. & vi.*) ...o atsumeru(atsumaru) [···を集める(集まる)].

assembly (*n.*) shûkai [集会].

assembly line nagare-sagyô [流れ作業].

assent (*n. & vi.*) sansei(-suru) [賛成(する)].

assert (*vt.*) 1)...o shuchô-suru [···を主張する]. 2)...o dangen-suru [···を断言する].

assess (*vt.*) 1)...o hyôka-suru [···を評価する]. 2)...o wari-ateru [···を割り当てる].

assessment (*n.*) 1)hyôka [評価]; satei [査定]. 2)zeigaku [税額]. 3) asesumento [アセスメント]; kankyô-eikyô-hyôka [環境影響評価].

asset (*n.*) kichô-na-mono [貴重なもの]; purasu-ni-naru-mono [プラス

になるもの].

assiduous (*a.*) kimben-na [勤勉な].

assign (*vt.*) ...o wari-ateru [···を割り当てる].   「[任務].

assignment (*n.*) wari-ate [割り当て]; kenkyû-kadai [研究課題]; nimmu

assimilate (*vt.*) ...o shôka-suru [···を消化する]; ...o dôka-suru [···を同化する]; ...o yûgô-suru [···を融合する].

       (*vi.*) shôka-sareru [消化される]; dôka-suru [同化する].

assist (*vt. & vi.*) (...o) tetsudau [(···を)手伝う]; (...o) tasukeru [···を助ける].

assistance (*n.*) enjo [援助]; joryoku [助力].

assistant (*n.*) joshu [助手].

associate (*vt.*) 1)...o rengô-saseru [···を連合させる]. 2)...o rensô-suru [···を連想する].

   (2) His name **is associated** with electricity.

       Kare-no na-o-kiku-to denki-*o-rensô-suru.*

       (*vi.*) kôsai-suru [交際する].

     He **associates** with her. Kare-wa kano-jo-to *kôsai-shite-iru.*

association (*n.*) 1)kyôkai [協会]. 2)kôsai [交際].

assorted (*a.*) kakushu-kumi-awase-no [各種組み合わせの].

assume (*vt.*) 1)...o hiki-ukeru [···を引き受ける]. 2)...to katei-suru [···と仮定する]. 3)...o yosoou [···を装う]; ...no furi-o-suru [···のふりをする].

   (1) He **assumed** a responsibility for it.

       Kare-wa sore-ni-taishite sekinin-o *totta.*

   (2) Let us **assume** it to be true.

       Sore-o hontô-da-to *katei-shi-yô.*

   (3) She **assumed** to be surprised.

       Kano-jo-wa bikkuri-shita-*furi-o-shita.*

assumption (*n.*) sôtei [想定].

assurance (*n.*) 1)hoshô [保証]. 2)jishin [自信].

assure (*vt.*) 1)...ni hoshô-suru [···に保証する]. 2)tashika-ni...(to)iu [確かに···(と)言う].

   (1) I **assure** you of his diligence.

       Kare-no-kimben-na-koto-wa watashi-ga *hoshô-suru.*

   (2) I **assured** her that he was present.

       Kare-wa *tashika-ni* i-awaseta *to* watashi-wa kano-jo-ni *itta.*

  I assure you. Tashika-desu-yo.; Daijôbu.

assured (*a.*) tashika-na [確かな].

    Her success is **assured**. Kano-jo-no seikô wa *kakujitsu*-da.

astonish (*vt.*) ...o odorokasu [⋯を驚かす]; ...o bikkuri-saseru [⋯を
びっくりさせる].

    be astonished at ...ni odoroku

astronaut (*n.*) uchû-hikô-shi [宇宙飛行士].

astronomer (*n.*) temmon-gaku-sha [天文学者].

astronomy (*n.*) temmon-gaku [天文学].

at (*prep.*) 1)...ni [⋯に]; ...de [⋯で]. 2)...no-tokoro-ni [⋯のところに].
3)...o-megakete [⋯を目掛けて]. 4)...ni-tsuite [⋯に付いて]. 5)...o-
kiite [⋯を聞いて]. 6)(ikura)-de [(いくら)で].

    (*1*) I met him **at** the station. Watashi-wa kare-ni eki-*de* atta.

         I got up **at** six yesterday. Kinô watashi-wa roku-ji-*ni* okita.

    (*2*) He stood **at** the window.

         Kare-wa mado-*no-tokoro-ni* tatte-ita.

    (*3*) The dog flew **at** me.

         Sono inu wa watashi-*o-megakete* tobi-tsuita.

    (*4*) We sat **at** table. Ware-ware-wa shokutaku-*ni-tsuita.*

    (*5*) They rejoiced **at** the news.

         Kare-ra-wa sono shirase-*o-kiite* yorokonda.

    (*6*) It was sold **at** one pound.

         Sore-wa ichi-pondo(-*ikura*)-*de* ureta.

athlete (*n.*) kyôgi-sha [競技者]; undô-senshu [運動選手].

athlete's foot mizu-mushi [水虫].

athletics (*n.*) undô[-kyôgi] [運動(競技)]; ((*Eng.*)) rikujô-kyôgi [陸上
競技].

Atlantic (Ocean), the Taisei-yô [大西洋].

atlas (*n.*) chizu-sho [地図書].

atmosphere (*n.*) 1)taiki [大気]. 2)fun'iki [雰囲気]; kankyô [環境].

atom (*n.*) genshi [原子].

atom bomb genshi-bakudan [原子爆弾].

atomic energy genshi-ryoku [原子力].

attach (*vt.*) 1)...o tsukeru [⋯を付ける]. 2)...o shitawaseru [⋯をし
たわせる].

attack (*vt.*) 1)...o kôgeki-suru [⋯を攻撃する]. 2)(byôki ga hito)-o
okasu [(病気が人)を冒す].

    (*n.*) 1)kôgeki [攻撃]. 2)hatsubyô [発病].

attain (*vt.*) ...o tassei-suru [⋯を達成する]; ...ni tassuru [⋯に達する].

     (*vi.*) tassuru [達する].

attainment (*n.*) 1)tassei [達成]. 2)gakushiki [学識].

attempt (*vt. & n.*) ...o kuwadateru(kuwadate) [...を企てる(企て)]; ...
o kokoromiru(kokoromi) [...を試みる(試み)].

attend (*vt.*) ...ni shusseki-suru [...に出席する].
     (*vi.*) 1)shusseki-suru [出席する]. 2)tsuki-sou [付き添う]. 3)
chûi-shite-kiku [注意して聞く].
     (2) He **attended** on his sick mother.
          Kare-wa byôki-no-haha-ni *tsuki-sotta*.
     (3) **Attend** to me.   Watashi-no-iu-koto-o *yoku-kike*.

attendance (*n.*) 1)shusseki [出席]; sanretsu [参列]. 2)tsuki-soi [付き
添い].

attention (*n.*) chûi [注意].
   give(pay) attention to ...ni chûi-suru

attentive (*a.*) chûi-bukai [注意深い].

attitude (*n.*) shisei [姿勢]; taido [態度].

attorney (*n.*) 1)((*US*)) bengo-shi [弁護士]. 2)hôtei-dairi-nin [法定代理
人].

attract (*vt.*) ...o hiku [...を引く]; ...o hiki-tsukeru [...を引き付ける].
     It **attracted** my attention
          Sore-wa watashi-no-chûi-o *hiita*.
     A magnet **attracts** steel.   Jishaku wa tetsu-o *hiki-tsukeru*.

attraction (*n.*) 1)hito-o-hiki-tsukeru-mono [人を引きつけるもの]; yobi-
mono [呼び物]. 2)(*phys.*) inryoku [引力].

attractive (*a.*) miryoku-no-aru [魅力のある].

attribute (*vt.*) ...ni kisuru [...に帰する]; ...no sei-ni-suru [...のせいに
する].

auction (*n.*) kyôbai [競売]; ôkushon [オークション].
     (*vt.*) ...o kyôbai-suru [...を競売する].

audience (*n.*) 1)chôshû [聴衆]; (*radio*) chôshu-sha [聴取者]; (*TV*)
shichô-sha [視聴者]. 2)ekken [えっ見].
     (1) The theater was crowded with **audience**.
          Gekijô wa *chôshû*-de ippai-datta.
     (2) The prime minister was received in **audience** by the king.
          Shushô wa ô-ni-*ekken*-shita.

audio-visual (*a.*) shi-chô-kaku-no [視聴覚の].

audio-visual aids shi-chô-kaku-kyôgu [視聴覚教具].

August (*n.*) Hachigatsu [八月].

aunt (*n.*) oba [おば].

auntie, aunty (*n.*) oba-chan [おばちゃん].

Australia (*n.*) Ôsutoraria [オーストラリア].

Australian (*a.*) Ôsutoraria-no [オーストラリアの]; Ôsutoraria-jin-no [オーストラリア人の].
        (*n.*) Ôsutoraria-jin [オーストラリア人].

author (*n.*) chosha [著者]; sakka [作家].

authority (*n.*) 1)ken'i [権威]; kengen [権限]. 2)(*pl.*) tôkyoku [当局].
  the authorities concerned kankei-tôkyoku

authorize (*vt.*) 1)...ni kengen-o-ataeru [...に権限を与える]. 2)...o ninka-suru [...を認可する].

auto (*n.*)(*US colloq.*) jidôsha [自動車].

autobiography (*n.*) jijo-den [自叙伝].

autograph (*n.*) 1)jihitsu [自筆]. 2)jisho [自署].

automatic (*a.*) jidô-no [自動の].

automatically (*ad.*) jidô-teki-ni [自動的に]; kikai-teki-ni [機械的に].

automobile (*n.*) jidôsha [自動車].

autonomy (*n.*) jichi [自治]; jichi-tai [自治体]; jichi-ken [自治権].

autumn (*n.*) aki [秋].

avail (*vi.*) yaku-ni-tatsu [役に立つ].
      (*vt.*) ...ni yaku-datsu [...に役立つ].
  avail oneself of ...o riyô-suru

available (*a.*) riyô-dekiru [利用できる]; te-ni-hairu [手に入る]; yûkô-na [有効な].

avalanche (*n.*) nadare [なだれ].

avarice (*n.*) don'yoku [どん欲].

avenge (*vt. & vi.*) (...no) fukushû-o-suru [(...の)復しゅうをする].

avenue (*n.*) 1)namiki-michi [並木道]. 2)oo-doori [大通り].

average (*n.*) 1)heikin [平均]; nami [並み]. 2)(*marine insurance*) kaison [海損].
  general average (*marine insurance*) kyôdô-kaison
  on an average heikin-shite
  particular average (*marine insurance*) tandoku-kaison
      (*a.*) heikin-no [平均の]; nami-no [並みの].
      (*vt.*) ...o heikin-suru [...を平均する].

avoid (*vt.*) ...o sakeru [...を避ける].

await (*vt.*) ...o matsu [...を待つ].

awake (*vt.*) ...o okosu [...を起こす]; ...kara mezamesaseru [...から目

覚めさせる].

    I'll **awake** him. Watashi-ga kare-*o okoshi*-mashô.

    (*vi.*) me-ga-sameru [目が覚める]; okiru [起きる].

    I **awoke** an hour before his arrival.

        Kare-no tôchaku-ichi-jikan-mae-ni *me-ga-sameta*.

    (*a.*) 1)nemurazu-ni [眠らずに]. 2)ki-zuite [気づいて].

(*1*) He lay **awake**. Kare-wa *nemurazu-ni*-ita.

(*2*) He was **awake** to it. Kare-wa sore-ni *ki-zuite*-ita.

award (*vt.*) ...o juyo-suru [···を授与する].

    (*n.*) shô [賞].

aware (*a.*) shitte [知って]; ki-zuite [気づいて].

away (*ad.*) 1)achira-e [あちらへ]; tooku-e [遠くへ]. 2)rusu-de [留守で]. 3)sesse-to-taezu [せっせと絶えず]; don-don [どんどん]. 4)sukkari...(shite-)shimau [すっかり···(して)しまう].

(*1*) They went **away**. Kare-ra-wa *tachi*-satta.

(*2*) Father is **away** from home. Chichi wa *rusu-de*su.

(*3*) He worked **away**. Kare-wa *sesse-to* hataraita.

(*4*) The snow has melted **away**.

        Yuki wa *sukkari* tokete-*shima*tta.

  far and away haruka-ni

  right away ((*US*)) sugu-sama

awe (*n.*) osore [おそれ].

awful (*a.*) 1)osoroshii [恐ろしい]. 2)(*colloq.*) sugoi [すごい]; hidoi [ひどい].

awfully (*ad.*) totemo [とても]; sugoku [すごく].

awkward (*a.*) 1)bu-kiyô-na [不器用な]. 2)yakkai-na [厄介な].

ax, axe (*n.*) ono [おの].

  get the ax (*colloq.*) kubi-ni-naru

  give one the ax (*colloq.*) hito-o kubi-ni-suru

  have an ax to grind (*colloq.*) mune-ni-ichimotsu-ga-aru

axis (*n.*) jiku [軸].

azalea (*n.*) (*bot.*) tsutsuji [ツツジ].

B

baby (*n.*) akambô [赤ん坊].
bachelor (*n.*) 1)dokushin-no-danshi [独身の男子]. 2)gakushi [学士].
Bachelor of Arts bungaku-shi [文学士].
back (*n.*) 1)se [背]; senaka [背中]. 2)ushiro [後ろ]; ura [裏].
    (*a.*) ushiro-no [後ろの]; ura-no [裏の].
    (*ad.*) ushiro-e [後ろへ]; moto-e [元へ].
backbone (*n.*) 1)se-bone [背骨]. 2)kikotsu [気骨].
background (*n.*) haikei [背景].
backward (*a.*) 1)ushiro-e-no [後ろへの]; gyaku-no [逆の]. 2)okureta
[遅れた]; shimpo-no-osoi [進歩の遅い]. 3)uchiki-na [内気な].
    (*1*) The troops made a **backward** movement.
        Guntai wa *kôtai*-shita.
    (*2*) He is **backward** in his studies.
        Kare-wa benkyô-ga *okurete*-iru.
    (*3*) The girl is very **backward**. Ano shôjo wa totemo *uchiki*-da.
    (*ad.*) ushiro-ni [後ろに]; gyaku-ni [逆に].
bacteria (*n.*) bakuteria [バクテリア]; saikin [細菌].
bad (*a.*) 1)warui [悪い]. 2)hidoi [ひどい]. 3)heta-na [下手な]. 4)
yûgai-na [有害な]. 5)kusatta [腐った]. 6)ki-no-doku-na [気の毒な].
    (*1*) He is a **bad** man. Kare-wa *warui* otoko da.
    (*2*) I have had a **bad** cold. Watashi-wa *hidoi* kaze-o hiiteiru.

　　(3) He is **bad** at drawing.　Kare-wa e-ga-*heta*-da.

　　(4) It is **bad** for your eyes.　Sore-wa kimi-no-me-ni *yoku-nai*.

　　(5) I bought ten eggs, but two of them were **bad**.

　　　　　Watashi-wa tamago-o jukko katta ga, sono-uchi-futatsu
　　　　　wa *kusatte*-ita.

　　(6) That's too **bad**.　Sore-wa o-ki-no-doku-desu.

badge (*n.*) kishô [記章]; bajji [バッジ].

badger (*n.*) ana-guma [アナグマ].

badly (*ad.*) hidoku [ひどく]; totemo [とても].

　　He was **badly** hurt.　Kare-wa *hidoi* kega-o-shita.

　be badly off seikatsu-ga-kurushii

bag (*n.*) 1)fukuro [袋]. 2)kaban [カバン]; te-sage [て さげ].

baggage (*n.*) ((*US*)) te-nimotsu [手荷物].

baggage room ((*US*)) te-nimotsu-ichiji-azukari-sho [手荷物一時預り
　所].

bah (*int.*) Fufun! [ふふん!].

bait (*n.*) esa [えさ].

　　(*vt.*) ...ni esa-o-tsukeru [...にえさを付ける].

bake (*vt.*) (pan nado)-o yaku [(パンなど)を焼く].

baker (*n.*) pan'ya-no-shujin [パン屋の主人].

bakery (*n.*) pan'ya [パン屋].

baking (*n.*) pan-o-yaku-koto [パンを焼くこと].

　　(*a.*) (*Eng. colloq.*) yake-tsuku-yô-na [焼けつくような].

baking powder fukurashi-ko [ふくらし粉].

balance (*n.*) 1)hakari [はかり]. 2)tsuri-ai [釣り合い]; kinkô [均衡].

　　(*vt.*) ...o tsuri-awasu [...を釣り合わす].

balance sheet taishaku-taishô-hyô [貸借対照表].

bald (*a.*) hageta [はげた].

ball (*n.*) tama [たま]; bôru [ボール].

ball (*n.*) butô-kai [舞踏会].

ballad (*n.*) baraddo [バラッド].

ballast (*n.*) (fune no) soko-ni [(船の)底荷]; (dôro nado no)soko-jiki-
　jari [(道路などの)底敷き砂利].

balloon (*n.*) fûsen [風船]; kikyû [気球].

ballot (*n.*) 1)mu-kimei-tôhyô-yôshi [無記名投票用紙]. 2)mu-kimei-
　tôhyô [無記名投票].

balmy (*a.*) kambashii [かんばしい]; sawayaka-na [さわやかな].

balsam (*n.*) 1)barusamu [バルサム]. 2)(*bot.*) hôsenka [ホウセンカ].

bamboo (*n.*) take [竹].

ban (*vt.*) ...o kinjiru [...を禁じる].
　　(*n.*) 1)kinshi [禁止]. 2)hinan [非難].

band (*n.*) 1)obi [帯]; himo [ひも]; bando [バンド]. 2)(*mus.*) gakudan [楽団]. 3)ichi-dan [一団].
　　(*1*) Bring me my **band**. Watashi-no *bando*-o motte-oide.
　　(*2*) The **band** is playing. *Gakudan* ga ensô-shiteiru.
　　(*3*) a **band** of thieves *ichi-dan* no tôzoku

bandage (*n.*) hôtai [包帯].

bang (*vt.*) ...o batan-to-shimeru [...をばたんと閉める].
　　(*n.*) batan [ばたん]; dosun [どすん].
　　(*ad.*) dosun-to [どすんと].

banish (*vt.*) ...o tsuihô-suru [...を追放する].

bank (*n.*) dote [土手]; teibô [堤防]; kawa-gishi [川岸].

bank (*n.*) ginkô [銀行].

banker (*n.*) ginkô-ka [銀行家].

bank note shihei [紙幣]; ginkô-ken [銀行券].

bankruptcy (*n.*) hasan [破産].

banner (*n.*) hata [旗].

banquet (*n.*) enkai [宴会].

baptize (*vt.*) ...ni senrei-o-hodokosu [...に洗礼を施す]; ...ni senrei-mei-o-tsukeru [...に洗礼名を付ける].

bar (*n.*) bô [棒]; yoko-gi [横木]; kannuki [かんぬき].
　　(*vt.*) 1)...ni kannuki-o-suru [...にかんぬきをする]. 2)...o kinshi-suru [...を禁止する].

barbarian (*n.*) yaban-jin [野蛮人].

barbarous (*a.*) zankoku-na [残酷な]; yaban-na [野蛮な].

barber (*n.*) rihatsu-shi [理髪師].

bar code bâ-kôdo [バーコード].

bare (*a.*) 1)hadaka-no [裸の]. 2)...ga-nai [...がない].
　　(*1*) They attacked with **bare** hands.
　　　　Kare-ra-wa *su*-de-de kôgeki-shita.
　　(*2*) The trees are **bare** of leaves. Ki-gi wa ha-*ga*-nai.

barefoot (*a. & ad.*) hadashi-no(hadashi-de) [はだしの(はだしで)]; su-ashi-no (su-ashi-de) [素足の(素足で)].

barehanded (*a. & ad.*) su-de-no(-de) [素手の(で)].

bareheaded (*a. & ad.*) bôshi-o-kabura-nai(-de) [帽子をかぶらない(で)].

barely (*ad.*) yatto-no-koto-de [やっとのことで].

bargain (*n.*) 1)bai-bai-keiyaku [売買契約]. 2)kai-mono [買物].
  (*1*) A **bargain** was made between the two parties.
      Ryô-tôji-sha-no-aida-de *bai-bai-keiyaku* ga seiritsu-shita.
  (*2*) She made a good(bad) **bargain**.
      Kano-jo-wa toku-na(son-na) *kai-mono*-o shita.
bargain sale rembai [れん売].
barge (*n.*) 1)hashike [はしけ]. 2)yûran-sen [遊覧船].
bark (*vi.*) (inu ga) hoeru [(犬が)ほえる].
    (*n.*) hoeru-koe [ほえる声].
bark (*n.*) ki-no-kawa [木の皮].
barley (*n.*) oo-mugi [大麦].
barn (*n.*) 1)naya [納屋]. 2)((*US*)) kachiku-goya [家畜小屋].
barometer (*n.*) 1)sei-u-kei [晴雨計]. 2)shihyô [指標]; baromêtâ [バ
  ロメーター].
baron (*n.*) danshaku [男爵].
barrack (*n.*) (*pl.*) 1)heisha [兵舎]. 2)barakku [バラック].
barrel (*n.*) taru [たる].
barren (*a.*) fumô-no [不毛の].
barricade (*n.*) barikêdo [バリケード].
barrier (*n.*) 1)saku [さく]. 2)shôgai [障害].
barter (*vt. & vi.*) (...o) butsu-butsu-kôkan-suru [(…を)物々交換する].
    (*n.*) butsu-butsu-kôkan [物々交換].
base (*n.*) 1)kiso [基礎] 2)(*mil.*) kichi [基地]. 3)(*baseball*) rui [塁].
base (*a.*) 1)hiretsu-na [卑劣な]. 2)hinshitsu-no-warui [品質の悪い].
baseball (*n.*) yakyû [野球]; bêsubôru [ベースボール].
basement (*n.*) chika-shitsu [地下室]; chikai [地階].
bashful (*a.*) 1)hazukashigari-ya-no [恥ずかしがり屋の]. 2)uchiki-na
  [内気な].
basic (*a.*) kihon-teki-na [基本的な]; kompon-no [根本の].
basic wage kihon-kyû [基本給].
basin (*n.*) 1)tarai [たらい]; suiban [水盤]. 2)bonchi [盆地]; ryûiki
  [流域].
basis (*n.*) kiso [基礎]; konkyo [根拠].
bask (*vi.*) atatamaru [暖まる]; hinata-bokko-o-suru [日なたぼっこを
  する].
basket (*n.*) kago [かご].
bass (*n.*) (*mus.*) teion [低音]; basu [バス].
bat (*n.*) (*zool.*) kômori [コウモリ].

bath (*n.*) 1)nyûyoku [入浴]; mokuyoku [もく浴]. 2)((*Eng.*)) yokusô [浴槽].

bathe (*vt.*) …o mizu-ni-hitasu […を水に浸す].
    (*vi.*) ((*US*)) nyûyoku-suru [入浴する]; ((*Eng.*)) suiei-suru [水泳する].

bathing (*n.*) mizu-abi [水浴び].

bathing suit mizu-gi [水着].

bathroom (*n.*) ((*US*)) yokushitsu [浴室]; toire [トイレ].

batter (*vt.*) …o tataki-kowasu […をたたき壊す].
    (*vi.*) renda-suru [連打する].

batter (*n.*) (*baseball*) dasha [打者].

battery (*n.*) 1)(*elect.*) denchi [電池]. 2)(*baseball*) batterî [バッテリー].

battle (*n.*) sentô [戦闘].

battlefield (*n.*) senjô [戦場].

bay (*n.*) wan [湾]; irie [入り江].

bay (*vi. & vt.*) (…ni) hoeru [(…に)ほえる].

bay window hari-dashi-mado [張出し窓].

bazaar, -zar (*n.*) bazâ [バザー].

B.C. (*abbrev.*) Kigen-zen [紀元前].

be (*vi.*) …de-aru […である].

beach (*n.*) hama [浜]; nagisa [なぎさ].

beacon (*n.*) 1)kagari-bi [かがり火]. 2)kôkû[suiro]-hyôshiki [航空[水路]標識]; ((*US*)) musen-hyôshiki [無線標識].

bead (*n.*) juzu-dama [じゅず玉].

beak (*n.*) kuchibashi [くちばし].

beam (*n.*) 1)(*arch.*) hari [はり]. 2)kôsen [光線].

beaming (*a.*) 1)hikari-kagayaku [光り輝く]. 2)hareyaka-na [晴れやかな].

bean (*n.*) mame [豆].

bear (*n.*) (*zool.*) kuma [クマ].

bear (*vt.*) 1)…o motte-yuku […を持って行く]; …o hakobu […を運ぶ]. 2)…ni taeru […に耐える]; …o gaman-suru […を我慢する]. 3)…o umu […を産む]; (mi)-o musubu [(実)を結ぶ].
    (*1*) I **have borne** the heavy box for two kilometers.
        Watashi-wa sono omoi hako-o ni-kiro *hakonda*.
    (*2*) I cannot **bear** him. Kare wa *gaman*-no-naranu-otoko-da.
    (*3*) He **was born** in London. Kare-wa Rondon-de *umareta*.

　　His efforts **bore** fruit.　Kare-no doryoku wa mi-*o musunda*.
　　(*vi.*) 1)gaman-suru [我慢する]. 2)shinro-o-toru [進路をとる].
　(*1*) I cannot **bear** any more.　Watashi-wa mô *gaman*-deki-nai.
　(*2*) The ship **bore** out to the offing.
　　　Sono fune wa oki-no-hô-e *shinro-o-totta*.
　bear...in mind ...o kokoro-ni-tomeru
beard (*n.*) ago-hige [あごひげ].
bearer (*n.*) 1)umpan-suru-hito [運搬する人]. 2)jisan-nin [持参人].
bearing (*n.*) 1)taido [態度]; furumai [振る舞い]. 2)kankei [関係].
　3)(*pl.*) hôgaku [方角].
　(*1*) He is a youth of noble **bearing**.
　　　Kare-wa *taido*-no-rippa-na-seinen da.
　(*2*) What he says has no **bearing** to this matter.
　　　Kare-no-itte-iru-koto wa kono-ken-to zenzen *kankei* ga-nai.
　(*3*) I can never keep my **bearings** when away from home.
　　　Ittan ie-o-deru-to watashi-wa *hôgaku*-ga wakara-naku-naru.
beast (*n.*) dôbutsu [動物].
beat (*vt.*) 1)...o utsu [...を打つ]. 2)...o makasu [...を負かす].
　(*1*) Children like to **beat** drums.
　　　Kodomo wa taiko-*o-utsu*-no-ga suki-da.
　(*2*) He was **beaten** in the race.　Kare-wa kyôgi-de *maketa*.
　　(*vi.*) utsu [打つ].
　　　His pulse **beats** fast.　Kare-no myaku wa hayaku *utsu*.
　　　　　　Kare-no myaku-haku wa hayai.
　　(*n.*) 1)utsu-koto [打つこと]; utsu-oto [打つ音]. 2)junkai-kuiki
　[巡回区域]. 3)hyôshi [拍子].
　(*1*) We heard the **beat** of a drum.　Taiko-o-*utsu-oto*-ga kikoeta.
　(*2*) The policeman is on his **beat**.　Junsa wa *junkai*-chû-de-aru.
beaten (*a.*) 1)utareta [打たれた]. 2)uchi-makasareta [打ち負かされた].
　3)fumi-narasareta [踏みならされた].
beautiful (*a.*) utsukushii [美しい]; rippa-na [立派な].
beautifully (*ad.*) utsukushiku [美しく].
beauty (*n.*) 1)bi [美]. 2)bijin [美人]. 3)migoto-na-mono [見事なもの].
beauty parlor ((*Eng.*)) biyô-in [美容院].
beaver (*n.*) (*zool.*) bîbâ [ビーバー].
because (*conj.*) 1)...node [...ので]; naze-naraba...dakara [なぜならば...
　だから]. 2)dakara-to-itte...(nai) [だからといって...(ない)].
　(*1*) I smiled **because** it was funny.

Sore-ga okashikatta-*node* watashi-wa waratta.

(2) You must not despise a man **because** he is poor.

Hito ga bimbô-*dakara-to-itte* keibetsu-shite-wa-ike-nai.

because of ...no-tame-ni, ...no-riyû-de

become (*vi.*) ...ni-naru [...になる].

He will **become** famous. Kare-wa yûmei-*ni-naru*-darô.

(*vt.*) ...ni ni-au [...に似合う]; ...ni fusawashii [...にふさわしい].

A white dress **becomes** you.

Kimi-ni-wa shiroi doresu ga *ni-au*.

bed (*n.*) 1)shindai [寝台]. 2)kashô [河床]. 3)nae-doko [苗床].

　go to bed neru

bedclothes (*n.*) shingu [寝具].

bedroom (*n.*) shinshitsu [寝室].

bedside (*n.*) (byônin no) makura-moto [(病人の)まくらもと].

bedtime (*n.*) neru-jikoku [寝る時刻].

bee (*n.*) mitsu-bachi [ミツバチ].

beech (*n.*) (*bot.*) buna-no-ki [ブナの木].

beef (*n.*) gyûniku [牛肉].

beehive (*n.*) mitsu-bachi-no-su[-bako] [ミツバチの巣(箱)].

beer (*n.*) bîru [ビール].

beet (*n.*) (*bot.*) bîto [ビート].

beetle (*n.*) (*insect*) kabuto-mushi [甲虫].

befall (*vt.* & *vi.*) (...ni) okoru [(...に)起こる].

before (*ad.*) mae-ni [前に].

I have heard this **before**.

Watashi-wa *mae-ni* kono-koto-o kiita-koto-ga-aru.

before and behind　*mae* to ushiro *ni*

(*prep.*) ...no-mae-ni [...の前に].

He came **before** six. Kare-wa roku-ji-*mae-ni* kita.

He appeared **before** the judge.

Kare-wa saiban-kan-*no-mae-ni* deta.

before long ma-mo-naku

(*conj.*) ...yori-mae-ni [...より前に].

He arrived **before** I expected.

Kare-wa watashi-ga yoki-shite-ita-*yori-mae-ni* tôchaku-shita.

Kare-wa watashi-ga yoki-shite-ita-*yori-hayaku* tôchaku-shita.

beforehand (*ad.*) mae-motte [前もって]; arakajime [あらかじめ].

beg (*vt.*) ...o tanomu [...を頼む].

beggar (*n.*) kojiki [こじき].

begin (*vt.*) ...o hajimeru [...を始める].

　　　　He **began** writing. Kare-wa kaki-*hajimeta*.

　　　　(*vi.*) hajimaru [始まる].

　　　　School **has begun**. Gakkô ga *hajimatta*.

　to begin with mazu-dai-ichi-ni; somo-somo

beginner (*n.*) shogaku-sha [初学者]; shoshin-sha [初心者].

beginning (*n.*) hajime [始め]; saisho [最初].

　from beginning to end hajime-kara-owari-made

behalf (*n.*)

　on behalf of ...no-kawari-ni; ...no-tame-ni

behave (*vt. & vi.*) furumau [振る舞う].

　behave oneself 1)furumau. 2)gyôgi-yoku-suru

　　1) He **behaved** himself like a gentleman.

　　　　Kare-wa shinshi-rashiku furumatta.

　　2) **Behave** yourself! Gyôgi-yoku-shi-nasai!

behavior, -iour (*n.*) furumai [振る舞い]; taido [態度].

behind (*ad.*) ato-ni [あとに]; okurete [遅れて].

　　　　The clock is five minutes **behind**.

　　　　Sono tokei wa go-fun *okurete*-iru.

　　　　(*prep.*) 1)...no-ato-ni [...のあとに]; ...no-ushiro-ni [...の後ろに].

　　2)...ni-okurete [...に遅れて]. 3)...ni-ototte [に劣って].

　　(*1*) I sat **behind** him. Watashi-wa kare-*no-ushiro-ni* suwatta.

　　(*2*) Robert was a quarter **behind** time.

　　　　Robâto wa jû-go-fun *chikoku*-shita.

　　(*3*) I am **behind** him in English.

　　　　Watashi-wa Eigo-de-wa kare-ni *okure-o-totte*-iru.

being (*n.*) 1)sonzai [存在]. 2)iki-mono [生き物]; ningen [人間].

Belgium (*n.*) Berugî [ベルギー].

belief (*n.*) 1)shinnen [信念]. 2)shin'yô [信用]. 3)shinkô [信仰].

believe (*vt.*) ...o shinjiru [...を信じる]; ...to omou [...と思う].

　　　　I **believe** him. Watashi-wa kare[-no-kotoba]-*o shinjiru*.

　　　　I **believe** him honest. Watashi-wa kare-o shôjiki-da-*to omou*.

　　　　(*vi.*) 1)shinjiru [信じる]. 2)shinkô-suru [信仰する].

　　(*1*) I **believe** in God. Watashi-wa Kami[-no-sonzai]-o *shinjiru*.

(2) I **believe** in Buddhism.

    Watashi-wa Bukkyô-o *shinkô-shite-iru*.

bell (*n.*) kane [鐘]; beru [ベル]; yobi-rin [呼び鈴].

belly (*n.*) (*colloq.*) hara [腹].

belong (*vi.*) ...ni-zokusuru [...に属する]; ...no-shoyû-de-aru [...の所有である].

belongings (*n.*) shoyû-butsu [所有物]; zaisan [財産].

beloved (*a.*) saiai-no [最愛の].

    He is my **beloved** child. Kare-wa watashi-no *saiai-no* ko da.

below (*ad.*) shita[-no-hô]-ni [下(の方)に]; karyû-ni [下流に].

    We saw a village far down **below**.

    Ware-ware-wa zutto *shita-no-hô-ni* mura-ga mieta.

    (*prep.*) 1)...yori-shita-ni [...より下に]. 2)...miman-de [...未満で].

    (2) children **below** the age of sixteen

    jû-roku-sai-*miman-no* kodomo-tachi

belt (*n.*) beruto [ベルト]; obi [帯]; bando [バンド].

belt line ((*US*)) kanjô-sen [環状線].

bench (*n.*) benchi [ベンチ]; naga-isu [長いす].

bend (*vt.*) 1)...o mageru [...を曲げる]. 2)...o mukeru [...を向ける].

    (*1*) **bend** one's elbow hiji-*o mageru*

    (*2*) He **bent** his eyes on it. Kare-wa sore-ni me-*o muketa*.

beneath (*ad.*) shita-ni [下に].

    (*prep.*) ...no-shita-ni [...の下に].

benefactor (*n.*) onjin [恩人].

beneficial (*a.*) tame-ni-naru [ためになる]; yûeki-na [有益な].

benefit (*n.*) rieki [利益]; onkei [恩恵].

benevolent (*a.*) nasake-bukai [情け深い].

bent (*a.*) 1)magatta [曲がった]. 2)kataku-kesshin-shita [固く決心した].

    (*1*) My grandmother is **bent** with age.

    Watashi-no sobo wa toshi-de koshi-ga-*magatte*-iru.

    (*2*) He is **bent** on becoming a musician.

    Kare-wa ongaku-ka-ni-nari-*tagatte*-iru.

    (*n.*) keikô [傾向].

berry (*n.*) berî [ベリー]; mi [実].

beset (*vt.*) 1)...o hôi-suru [...を包囲する]. 2)(be ～) nayamasareru [悩まされる]. 3)...o kazaru [...を飾る]; ...o chiribameru [...をちりばめる].

beside (*prep.*) 1)...no-soba-ni [...のそばに]. 2)...to-kuraberu-to [...と

比べると]. 3)...o-hazurete […を外れて].

(1) He sometimes sits **beside** me.

Kare-wa toki-doki watashi-*no-soba-ni* koshi-kakeru.

(2) He is a mere child **beside** you.

Kare-wa kimi-*to-kuraberu-to* hon-no kodomo da.

(3) His question is **beside** the point.

Kare-no shitsumon wa yôten-*o-hazurete*-iru.

　beside oneself ware-o-wasurete

besides (*ad.*) sono-ue-ni [その上に]; sono-hoka-ni [そのほかに].

I gave him some money **besides**.

Watashi-wa kare-ni *sono-ue-ni* kane-o-sukoshi yatta.

　(*prep.*) ...no-hoka-ni […のほかに].

Besides the moon, we see many stars.

Tsuki-*no-hoka-ni*, takusan-no hoshi-ga mieru.

besiege (*vt.*) ...o hôi-kôgeki-suru […を包囲攻撃する].

best (*a.*) saizen-no [最善の].

This is the **best** book. Kore-wa *ichiban-yoi* hon da.

　(*ad.*) ichiban-yoku [一番よく].

I like honey **best**.

Watashi-wa hachi-mitsu ga *ichiban* suki-da.

　(*n.*) saizen [最善].

　at one's(its) best saizen-no-jôtai-de; massakari-de

　at the best seizei

　do(try) one's best zenryoku-o-tsukusu

　get(have) the best of ...ni katsu; ...o umaku-yaru

　make the best of ...o dekiru-dake-riyô-suru

bestir (*vt.*) as '*bestir oneself*' funki-suru [奮起する].

bestow (*vt.*) ...o ataeru […を与える]; ...o sazukeru […を授ける].

bet (*vt. & vi.*) (...o) kakeru [(…を)賭ける].

　I bet (you) kitto...da

　(*n.*) kake[-kin] [賭け(金)].

betake (*vt.*) as '*betake oneself to*' ...e iku […へ行く].

betray (*vt.*) 1)...o uragiru […を裏切る]. 2)(himitsu)-o morasu [(秘密)をもらす]. 3)...o(-ukkari) sarake-dasu […を(うっかり)さらけ出す].

better (*a.*) yori-yoi [よりよい].

　(*ad.*) yori-yoku [よりよく].

　had better (do) (...suru)-no-ga-yoi; (...suru)-hô-ga-yoi

　know better baka-na-koto-o shi-nai; motto fumbetsu-ga-aru (*n.*) 1)yori-yoi-mono [よりよいもの]. 2)(*pl.*) me-ue-no-hito [目上の人].

better half (*colloq.*) tsuma [妻].

between (*prep.*) ...no-aida-ni [...の間に].
　　　　　(*ad.*) chûkan-ni [中間に].

beverage (*n.*) nomi-mono [飲み物].

beware (*vi. & vt.*) (...ni) ki-o-tsukeru [(...に)気を付ける]; (...ni) yôjin-suru [(...に)用心する].

bewilder (*vt.*) ...o tôwaku-saseru [...を当惑させる]; ...o urotaesaseru [...をうろたえさせる].

beyond (*prep.*) 1)...no-mukô-ni [...の向こうに]; ...o-koete [...を越えて]. 2)...ijô-ni [...以上に]; ...igai-ni [...以外に].
　　(*1*) His house is **beyond** the river.
　　　　　Kare-no ie wa kawa-*mukô-ni*-aru.
　　　　It is **beyond** my power.
　　　　　Sore-wa watashi-no-chikara-*ni-amaru*-koto-da.
　　(*2*) He believes nothing **beyond** his experiences.
　　　　　Kare-wa jibun-no keiken-*igai-wa* nani-mo shinji-nai.
　　　　　(*ad.*) kanata-ni [かなたに]; mukô-ni [向こうに].

bias (*n.*) 1)sennyû-kan [先入観]. 2)baiasu [バイアス].

bib (*n.*) yodare-kake [よだれ掛け].

Bible, the (*n.*) seisho [聖書].

bicycle (*n.*) jitensha [自転車].

bid (*vt.*) 1)(aisatsu)-o noberu [(あいさつ)を述べる]; (wakare)-o tsugeru [(別れ)を告げる]. 2)...o tsukeru [...を付ける].
　　　　　(*vi.*) ne-o-tsukeru [値を付ける].

big (*a.*) 1)ookii [大きい]. 2)(*colloq.*) erai [偉い].

bike (*n.*)(*colloq.*) jitensha [自転車]; ôtobai [オートバイ].

bill (*n.*) kuchibashi [くちばし].

bill (*n.*) 1)kanjô-sho [勘定書]. 2)bira [ビラ]; chirashi [ちらし]. 3) kawase-tegata [為替手形]. 4)(gikai no) hôan [(議会の)法案].

billiards (*n.*) tama-tsuki [玉突き].

billion (*n.*) jû-oku [十億].

bill of lading funa-ni-shôken [船荷証券].

billow (*n.*) oo-nami [大波].

binary (*a.*) futatsu-no [二つの]; (*math.*) nishim-pô-no [二進法の].

bind (*vt.*) 1)...o shibaru [...を縛る]. 2)...o maki-tsukeru [...を巻き付ける]. 3)...o seihon-suru [...を製本する].

binding (*n.*) 1)shibaru-koto [縛ること]. 2)seihon [製本].

binoculars (*n.*) sôgan-kyô [双眼鏡].

biochemistry (*n.*) sei-kagaku [生化学].

biography (*n.*) denki [伝記].

biology (*n.*) seibutsu-gaku [生物学].

birch (*n.*)(*bot.*) kaba-no-ki [カバの木].

bird (*n.*) tori [鳥].

birdie (*n.*) ko-tori [小鳥].

bird's-eye view chôkan-zu [鳥かん図].

birth (*n.*) 1)shussan [出産]; tanjô [誕生]. 2)umare [生まれ].

   give birth to ...o umu

birthday (*n.*) tanjô-bi [誕生日].

birthplace (*n.*) shussei-chi [出生地]; umare-kokyô [生まれ故郷].

biscuit (*n.*) bisuketto [ビスケット].

bishop (*n.*) kantoku [監督]; shikyô [司教]; sôjô [僧正].

bison (*n.*)(*zool.*) baison [バイソン].

bit (*n.*) 1)shôhen [小片]; shôryô [少量]; wazuka [わずか]. 2)(*colloq.*)
   shibaraku-no-aida [しばらくの間].

   a bit chotto; sukoshi

   a bit of sukoshi-no

   bit by bit sukoshi-zutsu; shidai-ni

   not a bit sukoshi-mo...nai

bite (*vt.*) ...o kamu [...をかむ]; ...ni kami-tsuku [...にかみつく].

   (*vi.*) kami-tsuku [かみつく].

   (*n.*) 1)kamu-koto [かむこと]. 2)(esa ni) kui-tsuku-koto [えさに
   食いつくこと].

biting (*a.*) 1)sasu-yô-na [刺すような]. 2)shinratsu-na [辛らつな].

   (*1*) a biting cold hada-o-*sasu-yô-na* tsumetasa

   (*2*) a biting irony *shinratsu-na* hiniku

bitter (*a.*) 1)nigai [苦い]. 2)hidoi [ひどい]; tsurai [つらい].

   (*ad.*) hidoku [ひどく].

bitterly (*ad.*) hidoku [ひどく].

black (*a.*) 1)kuroi [黒い]. 2)makkura-na [真っ暗な]. 3)jaaku-na [邪
   悪な].

   (*n.*) kuro [黒]; kokui [黒衣].

blackberry (*n.*) kuro-ichigo [クロイチゴ].

blackboard (*n.*) kokuban [黒板].

blacken (*vt. & vi.*) ...o kuroku-suru (kuroku-naru) [...を黒くする(黒

くなる)].

blacksmith (*n.*) kajiya [かじ屋].

bladder (*n.*) 1)(*anat.*) bôkô [ぼうこう]. 2)(sakana no) uki-bukuro [魚の)浮き袋].

blade (*n.*) 1)(naifu ya katana no) ha [(ナイフや刀)の刃]. 2)(kusa no) ha [(草の)葉].

  (*1*) The **blade** of the sword glittered in the sun.

      Katana no *ha* wa yôkô-no-naka-de kira-kira-to-hikatta.

blame (*vt.*) ...o hinan-suru […を非難する]; ...o semeru […を責める].

  be to blame seme-o-ou-beki-de-aru

      (*n.*) hinan [非難]; seme [責め]; sekinin [責任].

blameless (*a.*) keppaku-na [潔白な].

blanch (*vt.*) ...o shiroku-suru […を白くする]; ...o hyôhaku-suru […を漂白する].

blank (*a.*) 1)hakushi-no [白紙の]; kûhaku-no [空白の]. 2)pokan-to-shita [ぽかんとした].

  (*1*) Give me a **blank** sheet of paper.

      Hakushi-no kami-o ichi-mai kudasai.

  (*2*) He looked **blank**. Kare-wa *pokan-to-shite*-ita.

      (*n.*) 1)kûhaku [空白]; yohaku [余白]. 2)hakushi [白紙].

  (*1*) Fill the **blank**. *Kûhaku*-o umeyo.

    leave **blanks** *yohaku*-o nokoshite-oku

  (*2*) Give me a telegraph **blank**. Raishin-*shi*-o ichi-mai kudasai.

blanket (*n.*) môfu [毛布].

blast (*n.*) 1)toppû [突風]. 2)bakufû [爆風].

  at a blast ikki-ni

blaze (*n.*) honoo [炎].

  in a blaze moe-agatte

      (*vi.*) moe-tatsu [燃え立つ]; honoo-o-ageru [炎をあげる].

blazing (*a.*) sakan-ni-moete-iru [盛んに燃えている].

bleach (*vt.*) ...o hyôhaku-suru […を漂白する]; ...o sarasu […をさらす].

      (*n.*) hyôhaku[-zai] [漂白(剤)].

bleak (*a.*) areta [荒れた]; fuki-sarashi-no [吹きさらしの].

bleed (*vi.*) shukketsu-suru [出血する].

      (*vt.*) ...kara chi-o-toru […から血を採る].

blend (*vt. & vi.*) ...o mazeru (mazaru) […を混ぜる(混ざる)].

      (*n.*) kongô-butsu [混合物].

bless (*vt.*) ...o shukufuku-suru […を祝福する]; (be -ed) onkei-o-ukeru [恩恵を受ける].

Bless my soul! Saa taihen!; Shimatta!

blessed (*a.*) megumareta [恵まれた].

blessedness (*n.*) megumarete-iru-koto [恵まれていること]; kôfuku [幸福].

blessing (*n.*) shukufuku [祝福]; arigatai-mono [有り難いもの].

blind (*a.*) 1)me-no-mie-nai [目の見えない]. 2)(mono-goto-ga)wakaranai [(物事が)分からない].

(*n.*) hi-yoke [日よけ]; buraindo [ブラインド].

blinding (*a.*) me-o-kuramaseru-yô-na [目をくらませるような].

blindness (*n.*) 1)mômoku [盲目]. 2)mu-fumbetsu [無分別].

blink (*vi.*) mabataki-suru [まばたきする]; (hoshi nado ga)matataku [(星などが)またたく].

(*vt.*) ...o pachikuri-saseru [···をぱちくりさせる].

(*n.*) matataki [またたき]; senkô [せん光].

bliss (*n.*) shijô-no-kôfuku [至上の幸福].

blister (*vt. & vi.*) ...o mizu-bukure-ni-suru (mizu-bukure-ni-naru) [···を水ぶくれにする(水ぶくれになる)].

(*n.*) mizu-bukure [水ぶくれ].

blithe (*a.*) yôki-na [陽気な].

blizzard (*n.*) oo-fubuki [大吹雪].

block (*n.*) 1)(ki ya ishi no) ookina-katamari [(木や石の)大きな塊]. 2)gaiku [街区].

(*1*) The street is paved with **blocks** of stone.

Toori wa *kiri*-ishi-ga shiki-tsumete-aru.

(*2*) The station is three **blocks** away.

Eki wa san-*kukaku*-saki-desu.

(*vt.*) ...o fusagu [···をふさぐ].

blockade (*n.*) fûsa [封鎖].

(*vt.*) ...o fûsa-suru [···を封鎖する].

blond(e) (*a.*) kimpatsu-no [金髪の].

(*n.*) kimpatsu-no-dansei[-josei] [金髪の男性[女性]].

blood (*n.*) chi [血]; ketsueki [血液].

  blood bank ketsueki-ginkô

  blood group ketsueki-gata

  blood pressure ketsuatsu

bloodshed (*n.*) ryûketsu [流血].

bloodshot (*a.*) jûketsu-shita [充血した]; chibashitta [血走った].

bloodstain (*n.*) kekkon [血こん].

bloodstained (*a.*) kekkon-no-tsuita [血こんの付いた]; satsujin-o-okashita [殺人を犯した].

bloody (*a.*) chi-darake-no [血だらけの]; chi-namagusai [血なまぐさい].

bloom (*n.*) hana [花]; kaika [開花].

  in bloom hana-ga-saite

  in full bloom massakari-de

    (*vi.*) (hana-ga-)saku [(花が)咲く]; massakari-de-aru [真っ盛りである].

blooming (*a.*) 1)massakari-no [真っ盛りの]. 2)(*Eng. colloq.*) tohô-mo-nai [途方もない].

blossom (*n.*) hana [花].

  in blossom hana-ga-saite

  in full blossom mankai-de

blot (*n.*) 1)(inki no) shimi [(インキの)しみ]; yogore [汚れ]. 2)oten [汚点].

  (*1*) I have made a **blot** on my paper.

    Kami-ni *shimi-*o koshiraeta.

  (*2*) The scandal brought a **blot** on his character.

    Sono sukyandaru wa kare-no-jinkaku-ni *oten*-o nokoshita.

    (*vt.*) 1)...o yogasu [...を汚す]; ...ni shimi-o-tsukeru [...にしみを付ける]. 2)...o(-suitori-gami-de) sui-toru [...を(吸い取り紙で)吸い取る].

  (*1*) The letter **is blotted** with ink.

    Tegami niwa inki-no-*shimi-ga-aru*.

blouse (*n.*) burausu [ブラウス].

blow (*vi.*) (kaze ga) fuku [(風が)吹く].

    (*vt.*) (hi ya torampetto)-o fuku [(火やトランペット)を吹く].

  blow away ...o fuki-tobasu

  blow in (*colloq.*) hyokkori-arawareru

  blow one's nose hana-o kamu

  blow out ...o fuki-kesu

  blow up 1)...o bakuha-suru. 2)...o fukuramaseru

blow (*n.*) ichigeki [一撃].

  at a blow ichigeki-no-moto-ni; ikkyo-ni

blue (*a.*) 1)ai-iro-no [あい色の]; aoi [青い]. 2)yûutsu-na [憂うつな].

  (*1*) The **blue** dress fits you.

    Sono *ai-iro-no* fuku wa anata-ni ni-au.

  (*2*) The news made him **blue**.

Sono shirase ni kare-wa *yûutsu*-ni-natta.

(*n.*) 1)ai[-iro] [あい(色)]; ao[-iro] [青(色)]. 2)(the –) aozora [青空]; ao-unabara [青海原]. 3)(*pl.*) yûutsu-shô [憂うつ症].

blue book 《*US*》 daigaku-shiken-tôan-yôshi (ao-byôshi-no-sasshi); shiken

blue jeans burû-jînzu; jîpan

be in the blues genki-ga-nai; fusaide-iru

bluff (*a.*) zeppeki-no [絶壁の].

(*n.*) 1)zeppeki [絶壁]. 2)(the B-) yama-no-te [山の手].

bluff (*n.*) kara-ibari [空威張り].

bluish (*a.*) aomi-gakatta [青みがかった].

blunder (*n.*) hema [へま].

(*vi.*) dai-shippai-o-suru [大失敗をする].

blunt (*a.*) 1)nibui [鈍い]. 2)bukkira-bô-na [ぶっきらぼうな].

(*vt. & vi.*) ...o niburaseru (niburu) [...を鈍らせる(鈍る)].

bluntly (*ad.*) bukkira-bô-ni [ぶっきらぼうに].

blur (*n.*) 1)shimi [しみ]. 2)kasumi [かすみ].

(*vt.*) ...o yogosu [...を汚す]; ...o boyakesaseru [...をぼやけさせる].

blush (*vi.*) kao-o-akarameru [顔を赤らめる].

(*n.*) sekimen [赤面].

board (*n.*) 1)ita [板]. 2)shokuji [食事]. 3)iin-kai [委員会].

board and lodging shokuji-tsuki-geshuku

a board of directors riji-kai

go on board a ship jôsen-suru

(*vt.*) 1)...o ita-bari-suru [...を板張りする]. 2)(fune ya kisha)-ni nori-komu [(船や汽車)に乗り込む]. 3)...o makanau [...を賄う].

(*vi.*) kishuku-suru [寄宿する]; geshuku-suru [下宿する].

boardinghouse (*n.*) geshukuya [下宿屋]; kishuku-sha [寄宿舎].

boast (*vi.*) jiman-suru [自慢する].

She **boasted** of her beauty.

Kano-jo-wa jibun-no utsukushi-sa-o *jiman-shita*.

(*vt.*) ...o hokori-ni-suru [...を誇りにする]; ...o motte-iru [...を持っている].

The village **boasts** a good school.

Sono mura niwa rippa-na gakkô-*ga aru*.

(*n.*) jiman [自慢]; hora [ほら].

boastful (*a.*) jiman-suru [自慢する].

boat (*n.*) 1)bôto [ボート]; ko-bune [小舟]. 2)fune [船].

bobbin (*n.*) ito-maki [糸巻き].

bobsled, -sleigh (*n.*) bobusurê [ボブスレー]; ni-ren-zori [二連ぞり].

bodily (*a.*) nikutai-no [肉体の].

body (*n.*) 1)nikutai [肉体]; karada [からだ]. 2)...tai […体]. 3)ichi-dan [一団].
- (*1*) I have a strong **body**.
  - Watashi-wa tsuyoi *karada*-o motte-iru.
- (*2*) The sun and stars are heavenly **bodies**.
  - Taiyô to hoshi wa ten*tai*-de-aru.
- (*3*) They often fly in a **body**.
  - Kare-ra-wa yoku *ichi-dan*-to-natte tobu.

bodyguard (*n.*) goei-tai [護衛隊]; bodîgâdo [ボディーガード].

body language bodî-rangeiji [ボディーランゲイジ]; shintai-gengo [身体言語].

boil (*vt. & vi.*) 1)...o wakasu (waku) […を沸かす(沸く)]. 2)...o niru (nieru) […を煮る(煮える)]. 3)...o futtô-saseru (futtô-suru) […を沸騰させる(沸騰する)].

boiler (*n.*) boirâ [ボイラー]; kikan [汽かん].

boiling point futten [沸点].

boisterous (*a.*) 1)sôzôshii [騒々しい]. 2)oo-are-no [大荒れの].

bold (*a.*) 1)daitan-na [大胆な]. 2)kukkiri-shita [くっきりした]; medatsu [目立つ].
- (*1*) It was a **bold** attempt. Sore-wa *daitan-na* kokoromi datta.
- (*2*) **bold** outlines *kukkiri-shita* rinkaku

boldly (*ad.*) 1)daitan-ni [大胆に]. 2)futoku [太く].

boldness (*n.*) daitan-sa [大胆さ]; zubutosa [図太さ].

bolt (*n.*) boruto [ボルト]; sashi-jô [差し錠].
- (*vt.*) ...o boruto-de-tomeru […をボルトで留める].
- (*vi.*) kake-dasu [駆け出す]; nigeru [逃げる].

bomb (*n.*) bakudan [爆弾].
- (*vt.*) ...o bakugeki-suru […を爆撃する].

bomber (*n.*) bakugeki-ki [爆撃機].

bond (*n.*) 1)(*pl.*) kizuna [きずな]. 2)shômon [証文].
- (*1*) They broke the **bonds** of convention.
  - Kare-ra-wa inshû no *kizuna*-o yabutta.
- (*2*) His word is as good as his **bond**.
  - Kare-no kotoba wa *shômon*-to-onaji-da.

bone (*n.*) hone［骨］.

bonfire (*n.*) oo-kagari-bi［大かがり火］; taki-bi［たき火］.

bonito (*n.*) (*fish*) katsuo［カツオ］.

bonnet (*n.*) bonnetto［ボンネット］.

bonus (*n.*) bônasu［ボーナス］; shôyo［賞与］.

bony (*a.*) hone-batta［骨ばった］.

booby (*n.*) 1)baka-mono［ばか者］. 2)biri［びり］; sai-kai［最下位］.

book (*n.*) hon［本］; shoseki［書籍］.

　know A like a book Ei-ni-seitsû-shite-iru

　　　(*vt.*) 1)...ni kinyû-suru［…に記入する］. 2)...o yoyaku-suru［…
　　　を予約する］.

　　(*1*) This account **is** not **booked.** Kono kanjô wa *kinyû-shite*-nai.

　　　(*vi.*) yoyaku-suru［予約する］.

bookcase (*n.*) hom-bako［本箱］.

booking (*n.*) 1)chôbo-kinyû［帳簿記入］. 2)yoyaku［予約］.

booking clerk ((*Eng.*)) shussatsu-gakari［出札係］.

booking office ((*Eng.*)) shussatsu-sho［出札所］= ticket office.

bookkeeper (*n.*) boki-gakari［簿記係］.

bookkeeping (*n.*) boki［簿記］.

booklet (*n.*) panfuretto［パンフレット］.

bookshelf (*n.*) hon-dana［本棚］.

bookshop = **bookstore** (*n.*) shoten［書店］.

boom (*n.*) bûmu［ブーム］; niwaka-geiki［にわか景気］.

　　　(*vi.*) niwaka-ni-keiki-zuku［にわかに景気づく］.

boon (*n.*) onkei［恩恵］.

boon (*a.*) yukai-na［愉快な］; ki-no-au［気の合う］.

booster (*n.*) 1)kôen-sha［後援者］. 2)(*electronics*) bûsutâ［ブースター］.

bootblack (*n.*) kutsu-migaki［靴みがき］.

booth (*n.*) 1)bûsu［ブース］. 2)kôshû-denwa-bokkusu［公衆電話ボック
　ス］.

boots (*n.*) ((*US*)) naga-gutsu［長靴］; ((*Eng.*)) fuka-gutsu［深靴］.

booty (*n.*) senri-hin［戦利品］; emono［獲物］.

border (*n.*) 1)heri［へり］. 2)kyôkai［境界］; kokkyô［国境］.

　　　(*vt. & vi.*) (...ni) sessuru［(…に)接する］.

　　　The district **borders** the Percian Gulf.

　　　　Sono chiiki wa Perusha-wan-*ni sesshite-iru.*

　　　America **borders** on the two great oceans.

　　　　Amerika wa ryô-taiyô-to *sesshite-iru.*

bore (*vt.*) ...o akeru [···をあける].

bore (*vt.*) ...o unzari-saseru [···をうんざりさせる].

boring (*n.*) ana-o-akeru-koto [穴をあけること].

born (*a.*) umare-nagara-no [生まれながらの]; umareta [生まれた].

borrow (*vt. & vi.*) ...o kariru (kane-o-kariru) [···を借りる（金を借りる）].

bosom (*n.*) mune [胸]; futokoro [ふところ].

boss (*n.*) jôshi [上司]; chô [長].

botanical garden(s) shokubutsu-en [植物園].

botany (*n.*) shokubutsu-gaku [植物学].

both (*a.*) ryôhô-no [両方の]; dochira-no...mo [どちらの···も].

Both (the) brothers are doctors.

Kyôdai wa *dochira-mo* isha da.

(*pron.*) ryôhô [両方].

Both of them are honest. *Ryôhô*-tomo shôjiki-da.

(*ad.*) ...mo...mo [···も···も].

Both he and she are dead. Kare-*mo*-kano-jo-*mo* shinda.

bother (*vt.*) ...o urusa-garaseru [···をうるさがらせる].

Bother it! *Urusai!*

(*vi.*) ku-ni-suru [苦にする].

I never **bother** about it.

Watashi-wa sore-o mattaku-*ku-ni-shi*-nai.

(*n.*) mendô [面倒]; nayami-no-tane [悩みの種].

bottle (*n.*) bin [びん].

bottom (*n.*) 1)soko [底]. 2)shin-soko [心底]. 3)biri [びり].

(*1*) I dived into the **bottom** of the river.

Watashi-wa kawa-no-*soko*-made mogutta.

(*2*) He loves her from the **bottom** of his heart.

Kare-wa *shin-soko*-kara kano-jo-o aishite-iru.

(*3*) He is always at the **bottom** of his class.

Kare-wa itsu-mo kurasu-no-*biri*-ni-iru.

bough (*n.*) oo-eda [大枝].

boulder (*n.*) maru-ishi [丸石].

boulevard (*n.*) hiroi-namiki-michi [広い並木道]; oo-doori [大通り].

bounce (*vt. & vi.*) ...o hazumaseru (hazumu) [···を弾ませる（弾む）].

(*n.*) hazumi [弾み]; hane-kaeri [はね返り].

bound (*vi.*) hane-kaeru [はね返る]; tobi-agaru [跳び上がる]; hazumu [弾む].

(n.) hane-kaeri [はね返り]; baundo [バウンド].

at a bound hito-tobi-de

bound (n.) (pl.) kyôkai [境界]; han'i [範囲]; saigen [際限].

His ambition knows no **bounds**.
Kare-no yashin niwa *saigen*-ga-nai.

(vt.) (be -ed) sakai-o-sessuru [境を接する].

The United States **is bounded** on the north by Canada.
Gasshûkoku wa kita-wa Kanada-ni-*sesshite-iru*.

bound (a.) ...iki-no [···行きの].

boundary (n.) kyôkai-sen [境界線].

boundless (a.) kagiri-no-nai [限りのない].

bow (n.) 1)yumi [弓]. 2)niji [虹]. 3)chô-nekutai [ちょうネクタイ].

bow (vt.) (atama)-o sageru [(頭)を下げる].

Let us **bow** our heads. Atama-*o sage*-mashô.

(vi.) ojigi-o-suru [おじぎをする].

I **bowed** to his father.
Watashi-wa kare-no-o-tô-san-ni *ojigi-o-shita*.

(n.) ojigi [おじぎ].

He made me a **bow**. Kare-wa watashi-ni *ojigi*-o shita.

bow (n.) (marine) senshu [船首].

bowels (n.) chô [腸].

bowl (n.) domburi [どんぶり]; bouru [ボウル].

bowl (vi.) bôringu-o-suru [ボーリングをする].

bowling alley bôringu-jô [ボーリング場].

bowwow (n.) wan-wan [わんわん].

box (n.) 1)hako [箱]. 2) (theater) masu-seki [ます席]; bokkusu [-seki] [ボックス(席)]. 3)tsume-sho [詰め所].

(vt.) ...o hako-ni-ireru [···を箱に入れる]; ...o hako-ni-tsumeru [···を箱に詰める].

box (n.) ichigeki [一撃].

(vt. & vi.) (...to) bokushingu-o-suru [(···と)ボクシングをする].

boxer (n.) kentô-ka [拳闘家]; bokusâ [ボクサー].

boxing (n.) kentô [拳闘]; bokushingu [ボクシング].

boy (n.) shônen [少年].

boycott (n.) boikotto [ボイコット].

(vt.) ...o boikotto-suru [···をボイコットする].

boyhood (n.) shônen-jidai [少年時代].

brace (n.) 1)shime-gane [締め金]. 2) (pl.) chû-kakko [中括弧].

bracelet (*n.*) ude-wa [腕輪].

brag (*vt.* & *vi.*) (...o) jiman-suru [⋯を自慢する].
    (*n.*) jiman [自慢].

braggart (*n.*) hora-fuki [ほら吹き].

braid (*n.*) kumi-himo [組みひも]; uchi-himo [打ちひも].
    (*vt.*) ...o amu [⋯を編む].

brain (*n.*) 1)nô [脳]. 2)(*pl.*) zunô [頭脳].

brake (*n.*) burêki [ブレーキ].
    (*vt.* & *vi.*) (...ni) burêki-o-kakeru [(⋯に)ブレーキをかける].

bramble (*n.*) (*pl.*) ibara [イバラ]; no-bara [野バラ].

branch (*n.*) 1)eda [枝]. 2)shiryû [支流]; shisen [支線]. 3)shiten [支店].
    (*vi.*) bunki-suru [分岐する].

brand (*n.*) hinshitsu [品質]; meigara [銘柄].
    (*vt.*) ...ni yaki-in-o-osu [⋯に焼き印を押す].

brand-new (*a.*) ma-atarashii [真新しい].

brass (*n.*) shinchû [真ちゅう].
  brass band burasu-bando

brave (*a.*) yûkan-na [勇敢な].
    (*vt.*) ...o mono-tomo-shi-nai [⋯をものともしない].

bravely (*ad.*) yûkan-ni [勇敢に].

bravery (*n.*) yûkan [勇敢].

bravo (*int.*) Umai-zo! [うまいぞ!]; Dekashita! [でかした!]; Burabô! [ブラボー!].

breach (*n.*) ihan [違反].

bread (*n.*) pan [パン].
  bread and butter batâ-tsuki-no-pan

breadth (*n.*) haba [幅].

break (*vi.*) 1)kowareru [壊れる]; oreru [折れる]. 2)(kumo nado ga) kireru [(雲などが)切れる]. 3)akeru [明ける].
  (*1*) I struck him with my stick so hard that it **broke** in two.
      Watashi-wa tsue-de kare-o hidoku utta-node tsue ga futatsu-ni *oreta*.
  (*2*) The clouds **broke** and the sun began to shine.
      Kumo ga *kire*-te taiyô ga teri-hajimeta.
  (*3*) Morning **breaks**. Yo ga *akeru*.
    (*vt.*) ...o kowasu [⋯を壊す]; ...o waru [⋯を割る]; ...o oru [⋯を折る].

    She **broke** a teacup.   Kano-jo-wa chawan-*o watta*.

break down 1)koshô-suru. 2)naki-kuzureru

1) The bicycle broke down.   Sono jitensha wa koshô-shita.

2) Mother broke down with grief.

    Haha wa kanashinde naki-kuzureta.

break in 1)oshi-iru. 2)...o kai-narasu

1) They broke in the bank.   Kare-ra-wa ginkô-ni oshi-itta.

2) He is breaking his pony in.

    Kare-wa sono ko-uma-o kai-narashiteiru.

break out okoru; hassei-suru

break up 1)yasumi-ni-naru. 2)kaisan-suru

1) When does your school break up?

    Anata-no gakkô wa itsu yasumi-ni-narimasu-ka?

2) The committee broke up at 3p.m.

    Iin-kai wa gogo-san-ji-ni kaisan-shita.

    (*n.*) 1)ware-me [割れ目]; sake-me [裂け目]. 2)togire [とぎれ].
3)yasumi-jikan [休み時間].

breaker (*n.*) (iwa ni kudakeru) nami [(岩に砕ける)波]; shira-nami [白波].

breakfast (*n.*) chôshoku [朝食].

breast (*n.*) mune [胸].

breaststroke (*n.*) hira-oyogi [平泳ぎ].

breath (*n.*) iki [息].

  out of breath iki-gire-shite

  take one's breath away (hito)-o hatto-saseru

breathe (*vt. & vi.*) (...o) kokyû-suru [(…を)呼吸する].

  breathe freely hotto-suru

  breathe one's last iki-o-hiki-toru

breathing (*n.*) kokyû [呼吸].

breathless (*a.*) iki-o-kirashita [息を切らした].

breed (*vt.*) 1)...ni sodateru […に育てる]. 2)...o umu […を産む]. 3)...
o hiki-okosu […を引き起こす].

    (*vi.*) 1)ko-o-umu [子を産む]. 2)shôjiru [生じる].

    (*n.*) hinshu [品種].

breeding (*n.*) 1)hanshoku [繁殖]; shiiku [飼育]. 2)shitsuke [しつけ].

breeze (*n.*) soyo-kaze [そよ風].

brethren (*n.*) shinkô-nakama [信仰仲間]; dôshi-tachi [同志たち].

brew (*vt. & vi.*) (...o) jôzô-suru [(…を)醸造する].

bribe (*n.*) wairo [賄ろ].
> (*vt. & vi.*) (...ni) wairo-o-okuru [(…に)賄ろを贈る].

bribery (*n.*) zôwai [贈賄]; shûwai [収賄].

brick (*n. & a.*) renga(-no) [れんが(の)].

bridal (*a.*) hana-yome-no [花嫁の]; konrei-no [婚礼の].

bride (*n.*) hana-yome [花嫁].

bridegroom (*n.*) hana-muko [花婿].

bridge (*n.*) hashi [橋].
> (*vt.*) ...ni hashi-o-kakeru […に橋をかける].

bridge (*n.*) (*cards*) burijji [ブリッジ].

bridle (*n.*) baroku [馬ろく].

brief (*a.*) 1)tan-jikan-no [短時間の]; shibaraku-no [しばらくの]. 2) kantan-na [簡単な].
> (*1*) I cannot do it in such a *brief* time.
>   Watashi-wa sonna-*tan-jikan*-de-wa sore-o suru-koto-ga-deki-nai.
> (*2*) This telegram is too **brief** to be clear.
>   Kono dempô wa *kantan*-sugite imi-ga-yoku-wakara-nai.
> **to be brief** temijika-ni-ieba

briefly (*ad.*) kantan-ni [簡単に]; temijika-ni [手短に].

brier, -ar (*n.*) (*bot.*) ibara [イバラ]. buraia-no-ne [ブライアの根].

brigade (*n.*) (*mil.*) ryodan [旅団]; ...tai […隊].

bright (*a.*) 1)hareyaka-na [晴れやかな]; kagayaite-iru [輝いている]. 2)rikô-na [利口な]; yoi [よい]. 3)semmei-na [鮮明な].
> (*1*) He has a **bright** look. Kare-wa *hareyaka-na* kao-o shite-iru.
> a **bright** sunshine *kagayaku* yôkô
> (*2*) He is a **bright** boy Kare-wa *rikô-na* shônen da.
> It is a **bright** idea. Sore-wa *yoi* kangae da.
> (*3*) a **bright** green *semmei-na* midori-iro
>   (*ad.*) = brightly.

brighten (*vt. & vi.*) 1)...o kagayakaseru (kagayaku) […を輝かせる (輝く)]; ...o akaruku-suru (akaruku-naru) […を明るくする(明るくなる)]. 2)...o hareyaka-ni-suru (hareyaka-ni-naru) […を晴れやかにする(晴れやかになる)].

brightly (*ad.*) kagayaite [輝いて].

brilliant (*a.*) 1)hikari-kagayaku [光り輝く]. 2)saiki-no-aru [才気のある]; rippa-na [立派な].

brilliantly (*ad.*) 1)kira-kira-to [きらきらと]. 2)rippa-ni [立派に].

brim (*n.*) (koppu no) fuchi [(コップの)縁]; (bôshi-no) tsuba [(帽子の)つば].

bring (*vt.*) ...o motte-kuru [...を持ってくる]; ...o tsurete-kuru [...を連れてくる].

  bring back ...o kaesu; ...o modosu

  bring down 1)...o taosu. 2)...o sageru

  bring...forth ...o teishutsu-suru

  bring on ...o hiki-okosu

  bring over ...o motte-kuru

    It was brought over from India.

      Sore-wa Indo-kara yunyû-sareta.

  bring up ...o sodateru; ...o shitsukeru

    She was brought up by her aunt.

      Kano-jo-wa oba-ni sodaterareta.

    She was very well brought up.

      Kano-jo-wa yoku shitsukerarete-ita.

brink (*n.*) fuchi [縁]; magiwa [間際].

brisk (*a.*) kappatsu-na [活発な]; kakki-no-aru [活気のある].

briskly (*ad.*) kappatsu-ni [活発に]; genki-yoku [元気よく].

bristle (*n.*) ara-ge [荒毛]; hari-ge [針毛].

  (*vi.*) ke-o-saka-dateru [毛を逆立てる].

British (*a.*) Eikoku-no [英国の]. 「[イギリス英語].

  (*n.*) 1)(the –) Eikoku-jin [英国人]. 2)((US)) Igirisu-Eigo

brittle (*a.*) moroi [もろい]; koware-yasui [壊れやすい].

broad (*a.*) hiroi [広い]; haba-no-hiroi [幅の広い].

broadcast (*vt. & vi.*) (...o) hôsô-suru [(...を)放送する].

  (*n.*) hôsô [放送].

broadcasting station hôsô-kyoku [放送局].

broad jump ((US)) (the –) haba-tobi [幅跳び].

brochure (*n.*) panfuretto [パンフレット].

broil (*vt.*) ...o yaku [...を焼く]; ...o aburu [...をあぶる].

broken (*a.*) 1)kowareta [壊れた]; oreta [折れた]; yabureta [破れた]. 2)hasan-shita [破産した]; suijaku-shita [衰弱した]. 3)togire-togire-no [とぎれとぎれの]. 4)fu-kanzen-na [不完全な]; burôkun-na [ブロークンな].

  (*1*) a **broken** cup *kowareta* koppu

    a **broken** leg *oreta* ashi

    a **broken** promise *yaburareta* yakusoku

   (2) a **broken** bank   *hasan-shita* ginkô

   (3) **broken** words   *togire-togire-no* kotoba

   (4) **broken** English   *detarame-na* Eigo

broker (*n.*) burôkâ [ブローカー].

brokerage (*n.*) naka-gai-tesû-ryô [仲買手数料].

bronchitis (*n.*) (*path.*) kikan-shi-en [気管支炎].

bronchus (*n.*) kikan-shi [気管支].

bronze (*n. & a.*) seidô(-no) [青銅(の)].

brood (*n.*) hito-kaeri-no-hina [一かえりのひな]; hito-hara-no-ko [一腹
   の子].

     (*vi.*) 1)tamago-o-daku [卵を抱く]. 2)kuyo-kuyo-kangae-komu
   [くよくよ考え込む].

   (*1*) The hen **broods** on the eggs for about twenty-one days.

       Men-dori wa oyoso ni-jû-ichi-nichi-kan tamago-o *daku*.

   (*2*) Don't **brood** over past errors.

       Kako-no-ayamachi-o *kuyo-kuyo-kangae-komu*-na.

brook (*n.*) ogawa [小川].

broom (*n.*) hôki [ほうき].

brother (*n.*) 1)kyôdai [兄弟]. 2)nakama [仲間]; shin'yû [親友].

   (*1*) Tom and I are **brothers**. Tomu-to-watashi wa *kyôdai* da.

   (*2*) He is my **brother** in arms. Kare-wa watashi-no sen'*yû* da.

brother-in-law (*n.*) giri-no-kyôdai [義理の兄弟].

brow (*n.*) 1)(*pl.*) mayu [まゆ]. 2)hitai [ひたい].

brown (*n. & a.*) cha iro(no) [茶色(の)].

browse (*vi.*) 1)waka-kusa-o-taberu [若草を食べる]. 2)hiroi-yomi-suru
   [拾い読みする].

     (*vt.*) ...o taberu [...を食べる].

     (*n.*) wakaba [若葉].

bruise (*n.*) daboku-shô [打撲傷]; uchi-mi [打ち身].

     (*vt.*) ...ni kizu-o-tsukeru [...に傷をつける].

     (*vi.*) kizu-tsuku [傷つく].

brush (*n.*) 1)hake [はけ]; burashi [ブラシ]. 2)fude [筆].

     (*vt.*) ...ni burashi-o-kakeru [...にブラシをかける]; ...o migaku
   [...をみがく].

bubble (*n.*) awa [泡].

     (*vi.*) awa-datsu [泡立つ].

bucket (*n.*) baketsu [バケツ].

buckle (*n.*) 1)shime-gane [締め金]; bakkuru [バックル]. 2)magari

［曲がり］.

    (*vt.*) 1)…o bakkuru-de-shimeru ［…をバックルで締める］. 2)…o mageru ［…を曲げる］.

    (*vi.*) magaru ［曲がる］.

bud (*n.*) tsubomi ［つぼみ］.

    (*vi.* & *vt.*) hatsuga-suru (…o hatsuga-saseru) ［発芽する（…を発芽させる）］.

budding (*n.* & *a.*) hatsuga(-shi-kaketa) ［発芽（しかけた）］.

budget (*n.*) yosan[-an] ［予算(案)］.

buffalo (*n.*) (*zool.*) suigyû ［水牛］.

buffet (*n.*) byuffe ［ビュッフェ］.

bug (*n.*) 1)konchû ［昆虫］. 2)nankin-mushi ［ナンキンムシ］.

bugle (*n.*) rappa ［らっぱ］.

build (*vt.*) 1)…o tateru ［…を建てる］; …o kenzô-suru ［…を建造する］. 2)…o setsuritsu-suru ［…を設立する］; …o okosu ［…を興す］. 3)…o tsukuru ［…を作る］. 4)…o okosu ［…をおこす］.

    (*1*) We **build** houses of stone or brick.

        Ware-ware-wa ishi-ka-renga-de ie-*o tateru.*

    (*2*) **build** a business jigyô-*o okosu*

    (*3*) Swallows are **building** their nests.

        Tsubame ga su-*o tsukutteiru.*

    (*4*) Stir the embers and **build** a fire.

        Moe-sashi-*o* kaite hi-*o okose.*

building (*n.*) tate-mono ［建物］; birudingu ［ビルディング］.

bulb (*n.*) 1)(*bot.*) kyûkon ［球根］. 2)(*elect.*) denkyû ［電球］.

bulk (*n.*) ookisa ［大きさ］; kasa ［かさ］.

bulk mail ((*US*)) ryôkin-betsunô-yûbin ［料金別納郵便］.

bulky (*a.*) kasabatta ［かさばった］; ookina ［大きな］.

bull (*n.*) o-ushi ［雄牛］.

bulldozer (*n.*) burudôzâ ［ブルドーザー］.

bullet (*n.*) dangan ［弾丸］.

bulletin (*n.*) 1)kokuji ［告示］. 2)kôhô ［公報］; kaihô ［会報］.

  bulletin board ((*US*)) keiji-ban

bullfighter (*n.*) tôgyû-shi ［闘牛士］.

bullfrog (*n.*) (*zool.*) shokuyô-gaeru ［食用ガエル］.

bump (*vi.* & *vt.*) (…to) butsukaru ［(…と)ぶつかる］.

    (*n.*) shôtotsu ［衝突］; dosun ［どすん］; batan ［ばたん］.

    (*ad.*) dosun-to ［どすんと］; batan-to ［ばたんと］.

bumpy (*a.*) deko-boko-na [でこぼこな]; gata-gata-suru [がたがたする].

bunch (*n.*) 1)fusa [房]; taba [束]. 2)(hito no) atsumari [(人の)集まり].

bundle (*n.*) tsutsumi [包み]; taba [束].
　　　(*vt.*) 1)...o tabaneru [...を束ねる]. 2)...o zonzai-ni-oshi-komu [...をぞんざいに押し込む].

bunk (*n.*) (fune ya kisha no) ne-dana [(船や汽車の)寝棚]; shindai [寝台].

buoy (*n.*) fuhyô [浮標]; bui [ブイ].

buoyant (*a.*) 1)furyoku-no-aru [浮力のある]. 2)genki-na [元気な]; kaikatsu-na [快活な].

burden (*n.*) nimotsu [荷物]; omo-ni [重荷].

bureau (*n.*) 1)((*US*))(kagami-tsuki-no) doressâ [(鏡付きの)ドレッサー]. 2)((*Eng.*))(hiki-dashi-tsuki-no) oo-zukue [引出し付きの)大机]. 3)...kyoku [...局]; ...bu [...部].

bureaucracy (*n.*) kanryô-shugi [官僚主義].

burglar (*n.*) yatô [夜盗]; gôtô [強盗].

burial (*n.*) maisô [埋葬].

burn (*vt. & vi.*) 1)...o yaku (yakeru) [...を焼く(焼ける)]. 2)...o moyasu (moeru) [...を燃やす(燃える)].
　　(*1*) His house **was burnt** down.
　　　　Kare-no ie wa maru-*yake-ni-natta*.
　　(*2*) He **burns** with ambition. Kare-wa yashin-de *moete-iru*.
　burn down shita-bi-ni-naru
　　　The fire has burnt down. Kaji wa shita-bi-ni-natta.
　burn out moe-kiru
　　　The candle has burnt itself out. Rôsoku ga moe-kitta.
　　　(*n.*) yakedo [やけど]; yake-ato [焼け跡].
　　　Does the **burn** smart? *Yakedo* wa hiri-hiri-itami-masu-ka?

burning (*a.*) 1)yakete-iru [焼けている]; atsui [熱い]. 2)hageshii [激しい]. 3)kinkyû-no [緊急の].

burrow (*n.*) (kitsune ya usagi no) ana [(キツネやウサギの)穴].

burst (*vi.*) 1)haretsu-suru [破裂する]; bakuhatsu-suru [爆発する]. 2)patto-hiraku [ぱっと開く].
　　(*1*) He **burst** out with anger.
　　　　Kare-wa kanshaku-dama-o *haretsu-saseta*.
　burst into tears totsuzen-naki-dasu
　burst on ...no-mae-ni-totsuzen-arawareru

burst open patto-hiraku
    (*n.*) haretsu [破裂]; toppatsu [突発].
bury (*vt.*) 1)...o umeru […を埋める]. 2)...o hômuru […を葬る].
bus (*n.*) basu [バス].
bush (*n.*) kamboku [かん木]; kamboku-no-shigemi [かん木の茂み].
busily (*ad.*) isogashiku [忙しく].
business (*n.*) 1)gyômu [業務]; jitsugyô [実業]; shôbai [商売]. 2)yôji
   [用事]; yôken [用件].
  (*1*) What line of **business** is he in?
     Kare-no *shôbai* wa nan-desu-ka?
  (*2*) What is your **business** here? Go-*yô* wa nan-desu-ka?
  on business shôyô-de; yôji-de
  out of business hasan-shite
bust (*n.*) kyôzô [胸像].
bustle (*vi.*) sewashiku-ugoki-mawaru [せわしく動きまわる].
    (*vt.*) ...o seki-tateru […をせきたてる]
    (*n.*) zawameki [ざわめき].
busy (*a.*) isogashii [忙しい]; tabô-na [多忙な].
    The farmer is **busy** making hay.
      Nômin wa hoshi-gusa-zukuri-ni-*isogashii*.
  get busy (*colloq.*) shigoto-ni-kakaru
    (*vt.*) as '*busy oneself*' isogashiku-hataraku [忙しく働く].
    She **busied herself** in the house.
      Kano-jo-wa ie-de *isogashiku-hataraita*.
but (*conj.*) daga [だが]; shikashi [しかし].
    I am old, **but** you are young.
      Watashi-wa toshi-o-totte-iru, *shikashi* kimi-wa wakai.
    (*ad.*) tada [ただ]; honno [ほんの].
    She is **but** a child. Kano-jo-wa *honno* kodomo da.
    (*prep.*) ...o-nozoite […を除いて]; ...igai-ni-wa […以外には].
    No one **but** he could do it.
      Kare-*o-nozoite-wa* sore no dekiru mono wa i-nakatta.
  all but hotondo
    He was all but burnt to death.
      Kare-wa mô-sukoshi-no-tokoro-de yake-shinu-tokoro-datta.
  but for ...ga-nakattara
  cannot but (**do**) (se-)zaru-o-e-nai
butcher (*n.*) nikuya [肉屋].

buttercup (*n.*)(*bot.*) kimpôge [キンポウゲ].

butterfly (*n.*) chô [チョウ].

button (*n.*) botan [ボタン].

    (*vt. & vi.*) ...ni botan-o-kakeru(botan-de-tomaru) [···にボタンを掛ける(ボタンで留まる)].

buttonhole (*n.*) botan-ana [ボタン穴]; botan-hôru [ボタンホール].

buy (*vt.*) ...o kau [···を買う].

buyer (*n.*) kai-te [買い手]; baiyâ [バイヤー].

buyers' market kai-te-ichiba [買い手市場].

buyer's strike shôhi-sha-fubai-dômei [消費者不買同盟].

buzz (*n. & vi.*) bum-bun(-iu) [ぶんぶん(いう)].

by (*ad.*) soba-ni [そばに].

    He was standing **by**. Kare-wa *soba-ni* tatteita.

  by and by yagate; ma-mo-naku

    (*prep.*) 1)...no-soba-ni [···のそばに]; ...no-soba-o [···のそばを]. 2)...made-ni-wa [···までには]. 3)...ni [···に]. 4)...dake [···だけ]. 5)...gime-de [···ぎめで]. 6)...zutsu [···ずつ]. 7)...keiyu-de [···経由で]. 8)...no-aida-wa [···の間は]. 9)...de [···で].

  (*1*) The house is **by** the river. Sono ie wa kawa-*bata-ni*-aru.

  (*2*) **By** the time you come back, I shall have finished this work.

       Anata-ga kae-rareru toki-*made-ni-wa*, watashi-wa kono shigoto-o shi-agete-imasu.

  (*3*) This novel was written **by** him.

       Kono shôsetsu wa kare-*ni-yotte* kakareta.

  (*4*) He is younger than I **by** two years.

       Kare-wa watashi-yori ni-sai-*dake* toshi-shita-da.

  (*5*) We can hire a car **by** the hour.

       Ware-ware-wa jikan-*gime-de* kuruma-ga kari-rareru.

  (*6*) Save money little **by** little.

       Kane-o sukoshi-*zutsu* takuwae-nasai.

  (*7*) He returned home **by** way of Chicago.

       Kare-wa Shikago-*keiyu-de* kikoku-shita.

  (*8*) We work **by** day, and rest **by** night.

       Ware-ware-wa nitchû hataraki, yoru-*no-aida-wa* yasumu.

  (*9*) I go to school **by** bus. Watashi-wa basu-*de* tsûgaku-suru.

bygone (*a.*) sugi-satta [過ぎ去った]; kako-no [過去の].

bypass (*n.*) (jidôsha no) ukai-ro [(自動車の)う回路]; baipasu [バイパス]

(vt.) ...o ukai-suru [⋯をう回する].

bypath (n.) shidô [私道]; kandô [間道].

bystander (n.) kembutsu-nin [見物人]; bôkan-sha [傍観者].

C

cab (n.) takushî [タクシー].

cabbage (n.) kyabetsu [キャベツ].

cabin (n.) 1)koya [小屋]. 2)senshitsu [船室]. 3)kishitsu [機室].

cabinet (n.) 1)yô-dansu [用だんす]; kyabinetto [キャビネット]. 2) naikaku [内閣].

cable (n.) futo-zuna [太綱]; kêburu [ケーブル]; kaitei-densen [海底電線].

cablegram (n.) kaitei-denshin [海底電信]; kaigai-dempô [海外電報].

cactus (n.) (bot.) saboten [サボテン].

cage (n.) tori-kago [鳥かご]; (dôbutsu no) ori [(動物の)おり].

cake (n.) 1)yô-gashi [洋菓子]; kêki [ケーキ]. 2)katamari [固まり].

  (1) Give me a **cake**. *Kêki*-o kudasai.

  (2) There is a **cake** of soap in the box.
      Hako-no-naka-ni sekken-ga *ikko* aru.

calamity (n.) sainan [災難].

calcium (n.) karushium [カルシウム].

calculate (vt. & vi.) (...o) keisan-suru [(⋯を)計算する].

calculating (a.) dasan-teki-na [打算的な].

calculation (*n.*) keisan [計算]; dasan [打算].

calendar (*n.*) koyomi [暦]; karendâ [カレンダー].

calf (*n.*) (*zool.*) ko-ushi [子牛].

calf (*n.*) fukura-hagi [ふくらはぎ].

calico (*n.*) ((*US*)) sarasa [サラサ]; ((*Eng.*)) kyarako [キャラコ].

call (*vt.*) 1)...o yobu […を呼ぶ]. 2)...o shôshû-suru […を招集する].
  3)...ni denwa-o-kakeru […に電話をかける]. 4)...to yobu […と呼ぶ].
  (*1*) Somebody **is calling** you. Dare-ka ga anata-*o yondeiru*.
  (*2*) He **called** the meeting. Kare-wa kaigi-*o shôshû-shita*.
  (*3*) Please **call** me at this number.
      Kono bangô-ni *denwa-kuda*sai.
  (*4*) It is **called** the new moon. Sore-wa shingetsu-*to yobareru*.
    (*vi.*) 1)yobu [呼ぶ]. 2)tachi-yoru [立ち寄る]; hômon-suru [訪問
  する]. 3)denwa-o-kakeru [電話をかける].
  (*1*) They **called** to me from upstairs.
      Kare-ra-wa nikai-kara watashi-o *yonda*(-ni *yobi-kaketa*).
  (*2*) The ship **called** at Kobe. Sono fune wa Kôbe-ni *kikô-shita*.
      I **called** on Uncle John.
      Watashi-wa Jon-oji-san-o *hômon-shita*.
  (*3*) He **called** from Paris.
      Kare-wa Pari-kara *denwa-o-kakete-kita*.

call...after ...no-na-o-totte...to na-zukeru
  He was called Smith after his grandfather.
      Kare-wa sofu-no-na-o-totte Sumisu-to na-zuke-rareta.

call back 1)...ni mata-denwa-o-suru. 2)...o yobi-modosu
  1) I'll call you back. Mata ato-de denwa-shimasu.
  2) Please call her back. Kano-jo-o yobi-modoshite-kudasai.

call for 1)...o hitsuyô-to-suru. 2) ...o sasoi-ni-tachi-yoru
  1) It'll call for a lot of fund.
      Sore-wa ooku-no-shikin-o hitsuyô-to-suru-darô.
  2) I'll call for you at four. Yo-ji-ni sasoi-ni-ikimasu.

call off ...o tori-kesu
  I decided to call the reservation off.
      Watashi-wa yoyaku-o tori-kesu-koto-ni-kimeta.

call on ...o motomeru; ...o tanomu
  They called on me to go with them.
      Kare-ra-wa watashi-ni dôkô-o-motometa.

call up ...ni denwa-o-kakeru; ...o denwa-ni-yobi-dasu

Please call him up on the telephone.

　　Kare-o denwa-ni yobi-dashite-kudasai.

what is called; what you call iwayuru

　(*n.*) 1)yobi-goe [呼び声]; naki-goe [鳴き声]. 2)tsûwa [通話]. 3)
hômon [訪問]. 4)shôshû [召集]; maneki [招き]. 5)yôkyû [要求];
hitsuyô [必要].

(*1*) He is within **call**. Kare-wa *yobeba*-kikoeru-tokoro-ni-iru.

(*2*) a collect **call** ryôkin-jushin-nin-barai-*tsûwa*

(*3*) I have another **call** to make.

　　Mô-ikken *hômon*-suru-tokoro-ga aru.

(*4*) They responded to the **call**. Kare-ra-wa *shôshû*-ni ôjita.

(*5*) You have no **call** to do so.

　　Anata-wa sô-suru-*hitsuyô*-wa nai.

close call (*colloq.*) kiki-ippatsu

calling (*n.*) 1)shôshû [召集]. 2)kami-no-o-meshi [神のお召し]. 3)
tenshoku [天職]; shokugyô [職業].

(*1*) the **calling** of Parliament gikai no *shôshû*

(*2*) **Calling** is the work of God's Spirit.

　　O-meshi wa Kami no Rei no nasu-waza-de-aru.

(*3*) What is your **calling**? Anata-no *shokugyô* wa nan-desu-ka?

calm (*a.*) odayaka-na [穏やか].

　　(*vt. & vi.*) …o shizumeru (shizumaru) […を静める(静まる)].

　　(*n.*) heion [平穏]; nagi [なぎ].

calmly (*ad.*) shizuka-ni [静かに].

camel (*n.*) rakuda [ラクダ].

camellia (*n.*) (*bot.*) tsubaki [ツバキ].

camera (*n.*) shashin-ki [写真機]; kamera [カメラ].

camp (*n.*) yaei [野営]; kyampu [キャンプ].

　　(*vi.*) kyampu-o-suru [キャンプをする].

　camp out yaei-suru; kyampu-seikatsu-o-suru

campaign (*n.*) 1)undô [運動]; kyampên [キャンペーン]. 2)(*mil.*)
gunji-kôdô [軍事行動].

campfire (*n.*) kagari-bi [かがり火]; kyampu-faia [キャンプファイア].

campus (*n.*) (daigaku no) kônai [(大学の)構内]; kyampasu [キャンパ
ス]; gakusha [学舎]; ((*US*)) bunkô [分校].

can (*n.*) (kanzume no) kan [(缶詰の)缶].

　　(*vt.*) …o kanzume-ni-suru […を缶詰にする].

can (*aux. v.*) 1)…dekiru […できる]. 2)…(shite-)mo-yoi […(して)も

よい]. 3)...de-ari-uru […でありうる].

(1) He **can** read the book.
　　　Kare-wa sono hon-o yomu-koto-ga-*dekiru*.
(2) You **can** come with me.
　　　Kimi-wa watashi-to-issho-ni kite-*mo-yoi*.
(3) **Can** it be true?　Sore-wa hontô-*de-ari-uru*-ka?
　　　　　　　　　　　Sore-wa hontô-*ka*-shira?

Canada (n.) Kanada [カナダ].

Canadian (a.) Kanada-no [カナダの]; Kanada-jin-no [カナダ人の].
　　　　(n.) Kanada-jin [カナダ人].

canal (n.) unga [運河].

canary (n.) (*birds*) kanaria [カナリア].

cancel (vt. & vi.) (...o) tori-kesu [(…を)取り消す].

cancer (n.) gan [がん].

candid (a.) sotchoku-na [率直な].

candied (a.) satô-zuke-ni-shita [砂糖づけにした].

candle (n.) rôsoku [ろうそく].

candlestick (n.) shokudai [燭台].

cane (n.) 1)tsue [つえ]; sutekki [ステッキ]. 2)tô [トウ].
(1) He walks with a **cane**.　Kare-wa *tsue*-o-tsuite aruku.
(2) Fetch my **cane** chair.　Watashi-no *tô*-isu-o motte-oide.

canine (n. & a.) inu(-no) [犬(の)].

canine tooth kenshi [犬歯].

canned (a.) kanzume-ni-shita [缶詰にした].

cannon (n.) taihô [大砲].

cannot (aux. v.) 1)...deki-nai […できない]. 2)...hazu-ga-nai […はず
がない].
(1) I **cannot** speak German.
　　　Watashi-wa Doitsu-go-o hanasu-koto-ga-*deki-nai*.
(2) It **cannot** be true.　Sore-wa hontô-no-*hazu-ga-nai*.

canoe (n.) kanû [カヌー]; maruki-bune [丸木舟].

cantaloup(e) (n.) kantarôpu [カンタロープ].

canvas (n.) 1)ho-nuno [帆布]; zukku [ズック]. 2)kambasu [カンバス].

canyon (n.) fukai-kyôkoku [深い峡谷].

cap (n.) 1)(fuchi no nai) bôshi [(縁のない)帽子]. 2)(bin no) futa
[(瓶の)ふた]; kyappu [キャップ].

capable (a.) nôryoku-ga-aru [能力がある]; (...ga-)dekiru [(…が)でき
る].

　　be **capable of** ...ga-dekiru

capacity (*n.*) 1)nôryoku [能力]. 2)shûyô-ryoku [収容力].

cape (*n.*) misaki [岬].

caper (*vi.*) hane-mawaru [はね回る].

　　(*vi.*) waru-fuzake [悪ふざけ].

capital (*a.*) 1)shuyô-na [主要な]; mottomo-jûyô-na [最も重要な]. 2) subarashii [すばらしい].

　　(*1*) The **capital** point is this.　*Jûyô-na* ten wa koko-da.

　　(*2*) We had a **capital** dinner.　*Subarashii* go-chisô deshita.

　　　　(*n.*) 1)shuto [首都]. 2)shihon [資本]. 3)oo-moji [大文字].

　　(*1*) Tokyo is the **capital** of Japan.

　　　　Tôkyô wa Nihon no *shuto*-de-aru.

　　(*2*) He started business with a **capital** of 5,000 dollars.

　　　　Kare-wa go-sen-doru-no-*shihon*-de shôbai-o hajimeta.

　　(*3*) The first word in a sentence begins with a **capital**.

　　　　Bun-no saisho-no go wa *oo-moji*-de hajimaru.

capitalism (*n.*) shihon-shugi [資本主義].

caprice (*n.*) ki-magure [気まぐれ].

captain (*n.*) 1)chô [長]. 2)senchô [船長]; kanchô [艦長]. 3)kyaputen [キャプテン]; shushô [主将].

caption (*n.*) 1)midashi [見出し]. 2)kyapushon [キャプション].

captive (*n.*) horyo [捕虜].

　　　　(*a.*) torawareta [捕らわれた].

capture (*n.*) hokaku [捕獲].

　　　　(*vt.*) ...o horyo-ni-suru [...を捕虜にする]; ...o toraeru [...を捕らえる].

car (*n.*) 1)kuruma [車]; jidôsha [自動車]. 2)sharyô [車両].

　　(*1*) Let's go by **car**.　*Kuruma*(*Jidôsha*)-de ikô.

　　(*2*) That is the second-class **car**.　Are-ga ni-tô-*sha* da.

caravan (*n.*) 1)taishô [隊商]. 2)horo-basha [ほろ馬車]. 3)((*Eng.*)) idô-jûtaku [移動住宅].

carbon (*n.*) 1)(*chem.*) tanso [炭素]. 2)kâbon-shi [カーボン紙]; utsushi [写し] = carbon copy.

carcass, -case (*n.*) (dôbutsu no) shitai [(動物の)死体].

card (*n.*) 1)karuta [カルタ]; torampu-fuda [トランプ札]; (*pl.*) torampu-asobi [トランプ遊び]. 2)meishi [名刺]; kâdo [カード]. 3) hagaki [はがき].

　　(*1*) We played **cards**.　Ware-ware-wa *karuta*-o totta.

                     Ware-ware-wa *torampu-asobi*-o shita.

(2) Please send in this **card**. Kono *meishi*-o o-tori-tsugi-kudasai.

(3) Here is a **card** for you. *Hagaki* ga kimashita-yo.

cardinal numbers kisû [基数].

care (*n.*) 1)shimpai [心配]. 2)sewa [世話]. 3)chûi [注意]. 4)yôjin [用心].

(1) **Care** kills the cat. *Shimpai* wa mi-no-doku-da.

(2) She grew under her uncle's **care**.

    Kano-jo-wa oji-no-*sewa*-no-moto-ni seichô-shita.

(3) The address should be written with **care**.

    Atena wa *chûi*-shite kaka-nakereba-naranai.

(4) Take **care**! *Yôjin*-shi-nasai.

  care of (c/o) ...kata; ...ki-tsuke

  take care of 1)...no sewa-o-suru. 2)...ni ki-o-tsukeru

  take care of oneself karada-o-taisetsu-ni-suru

    (*vi.*) 1)shimpai-suru [心配する]. 2)ki-ni-kakeru [気にかける].

(1) Don't you **care**? Omae-wa *shimpai-shi*-nai-no-ka?

(2) I don't **care** how soon the end may come.

    Owari ga ika-ni-hayaku-tomo watashi-wa *kamawa*-nai.

    (*vt.*) (...shi-)tai-to-omou [(…し)たいと思う].

    Would you **care** to go there? Soko-e iki-*tai*-desu-ka?

  care for 1)...o ki-ni-kakeru; ...o shimpai-suru. 2)...no sewa-o-suru. 3)...o konomu

  2) Mother **cared for** me when I was ill.

    Haha wa watashi-ga byôki-no-toki sewa-o-shite-kureta.

  3) I don't **care for** fruit. Watashi-wa kudamono-o konoma-nai.

career (*n.*) keireki [経歴]; shôgai [生涯].

    (*a.*) semmon-shoku-no [専門職の].

carefree (*a.*) shimpai-no-nai [心配のない]; nonki-na [のんきな].

careful (*a.*) chûi-bukai [注意深い].

careless (*a.*) fu-chûi-na [不注意な]; keisotsu-na [軽率な].

caress (*n.*) aibu [愛ぶ].

    (*vt.*) ...o aibu-suru […を愛ぶする].

cargo (*n.*) funa-ni [船荷]; tsumi-ni [積み荷].

cargo boat kamotsu-sen [貨物船].

caricature (*n.*) manga [漫画]; fûshi-ga [風刺画].

carnival (*n.*) shaniku-sai [謝肉祭].

carol (*n.*) seika [聖歌].

carp (*n.*) (*fish*) koi [コイ].

carpenter (*n.*) daiku [大工].

carpet (*n.*) jûtan [じゅうたん].

carriage (*n.*) 1)kuruma [車]. 2)((*Eng.*)) kyakusha [客車].

carrier pigeon densho-bato [伝書バト].

carrot (*n.*) (*bot.*) ninjin [ニンジン].

carry (*vt.*) 1)...o hakobu […を運ぶ]; .o motte-yuku […を持って行く].
   2)...o sasaeru […を支える]. 3)...o tsutaeru […を伝える].
   (*1*) I never **carry** any money with me.
       Watashi-wa kesshite kane-o *mochi-aruka*-nai.
   (*2*) Four pillars **carry** the roof.
       Shi-hon-no hashira ga yane-o *sasaete-iru*.
   (*3*) The air **carries** sounds. Kûki wa oto-o *tsutaeru*.
   carry on 1)...o tsuzukeru. 2)...o itonamu.
   1) I intend to carry on my father's work.
       Watashi-wa chichi-no-shigoto-o tsuzukeru-tsumori-da.
   2) He carried on the business in Tokyo.
       Kare-wa Tôkyô-de shôbai-o itonanda.
   carry out ...o nashi-togeru
   carry through ...o yari-toosu
       At last he carried through the business.
       Tsui-ni kare-wa sono-shigoto-o yari-tooshita.
   (*vi.*) 1)todoku [届く]. 2)mono-o-hakobu [物を運ぶ].
   (*1*) Her voice **carries** well. Kano-jo-no koe wa yoku *tooru*.

cart (*n.*) ni-basha [荷馬車]; ((*US*)) te-oshi-guruma [手押し車].

cartel (*n.*) (*econ.*) karuteru [カルテル].

cartoon (*n.*) manga [漫画].

carve (*vt. & vi.*) 1)(...o) chôkoku-suru [(…を)彫刻する]. 2)(niku)-o
   kitte-wakeru(niku-o-kitte-wakeru) [(肉)を切って分ける(肉を切って分
   ける)].

cascade (*n.*) chiisai-taki [小さい滝].

case (*n.*) 1)baai [場合]. 2)jitsujô [実情]. 3)kanja [患者]. 4)(*gram.*)
   kaku [格].
   (*1*) in this **case** kono-*baai*-wa
   (*2*) Such being the **case**, I cannot go with you.
       Sô-iu-*jijô*-dakara, watashi-wa kimi-to-issho-ni ike-nai.
   (*3*) Another **case** of cholera broke out.
       Mata-ichi-mei korera-*kanja* ga deta.

(4) the objective **case** mokuteki-*kaku*

  in any case tonikaku; izure-ni-shitemo

  in case of ...no-baai-ni-wa

  in no case kesshite ...nai

case (*n.*) hako [箱]; kêsu [ケース].

casement (*n.*) = casement window hiraki-mado [開き窓].

cash (*n.*) genkin [現金].

    (*vt.*) ...o genkin-to-hiki-kaeru [...を現金と引替える]; ...o genkin-ni-suru [...を現金にする].

cashier (*n.*) reji-gakari [レジ係].

cash on delivery daikin-hiki-kae-barai [代金引替え払い].

cask (*n.*) taru [たる]; oke [おけ].

casket (*n.*) ko-bako [小箱].

cassette (*n.*) kasetto [カセット].

cast (*vt.*) ...o nageru [...を投げる].

    (*n.*) 1)nageru-koto [投げること]; nagerareta-mono [投げられたもの]. 2)(*play*) haiyaku [配役].

caster (*n.*) yakumi-yôki [薬味容器].

castle (*n.*) shiro [城].

casual (*a.*) 1)keishiki-bara-nai [形式ばらない]; kudaketa [くだけた]. 2)gûzen-no [偶然の].

cat (*n.*) neko [ネコ].

catalog, -logue (*n.*) mokuroku [目録]; katarogu [カタログ].

cataract (*n.*) bakufu [ばく布].

catarrh (*n.*) (*med.*) kataru [カタル].

catastrophe (*n.*) (totsuzen-no) dai-hendô [(突然の)大変動].

catch (*vt.*) ...o toraeru [...を捕らえる]. 2)(ame ya arashi ga)-o osou [(雨や嵐が)...を襲う]. 3)...o rikai-suru [...を理解する]; ...o kiki-toru [...を聞き取る]. 4)...ni ma-ni-au [...に間に合う]. 5)...o mitsukeru [...を見付ける].

  (*1*) This cat cannot **catch** a rat.

    Kono neko wa nezumi-*ga tore*-nai.

  (*2*) I **was caught** in the rain. Watashi-wa ame-ni-*atta*.

  (*3*) I didn't **catch** your words.

    Watashi-wa anata-no kotoba-*ga kiki-tore*-masen-deshita.

  (*4*) I got up so early as to **catch** the first train.

    Watashi-wa ichiban-ressha-*ni ma-ni-au*-yô-ni asa-hayaku okita.

(5) I **caught** the boy smoking.

Watashi-wa sono shônen ga tabako-o-sutte-iru-no-o *mitsuketa*.

(*vi.*) tsukamô-to-suru [つかもうとする]; hikkakaru [引っ掛かる].

A drowning man will **catch** at a straw.

Oboreru mono wa wara-o-mo *tsukamu*.

catch on 1)rikai-suru. 2)hitto-suru

1) I can't catch on to the meaning.

Watashi-wa sono-imi-ga rikai-deki-nai.

2) The song caught on. Sono uta wa hitto-shita.

catch up with ...ni oi-tsuku

I could not catch up with him.

Watashi-wa kare-ni oi-tsuku-koto-ga-deki-nakatta.

catcher (*n.*) (*baseball*) kyatchâ [キャッチャー]; hoshu [捕手].

catchphrase (*n.*) utai-monku [うたい文句].

category (*n.*) kategorî [カテゴリー]; hanchû [範ちゅう].

cater (*vi.*) makanau [まかなう].

caterpillar (*n.*) 1)(*insect*) ke-mushi [毛虫]; imomushi [芋虫]. 2) mugen-kidô [無限軌道]; katapira-torakutâ [カタピラトラクター].

cathedral (*n.*) dai-seidô [大聖堂].

Catholic (*a.*) Katorikku-no [カトリックの].

(*n.*) Katorikku-kyô-to [カトリック教徒].

cattle (*n.*) ushi [牛].

cauliflower (*n.*) hana-kyabetsu [花キャベツ]; karifurawâ [カリフラワー].

cause (*n.*) 1)gen'in [原因]. 2)shugi [主義]; risô [理想].

(*1*) The **cause** of his death is unknown.

Kare-no shi*in* wa fumei-da.

(*2*) He stood up for the **cause** of liberty.

Kare-wa jiyû-no-*tame*-ni tachi-agatta.

(*vt.*) 1)...no gen'in-to-naru [···の原因となる]. 2)...ni...saseru [···に···させる].

(*1*) What **has caused** this war?

Dô-iu-*gen'in-de* kono sensô-*ga* okita-no-ka?

(*2*) What **causes** an apple to fall to the ground?

Nani ga ringo-o chijô-*ni* rakka-*saseru*-ka?

caution (*n.*) yôjin [用心].

cautious (*a.*) yôjin-bukai [用心深い].

cave (*n.*) horaana [ほら穴].

cavern (*n.*) dôkutsu [洞くつ].

cavity (*n.*) 1)(*med.*) mushiba [虫歯]. 2)kûdô [空洞].

caw (*n.*) kâkâ [カーカー].

    (*vi.*) (karasu ga) kâkâ-naku [(カラスが)かーかー鳴く].

cease (*vt. & vi.*) …o yameru (yamu) […をやめる(やむ)].

       The soldiers **ceased** fire.

          Heishi-tachi wa shageki-*o yameta*.

       The snow **has ceased**.   Yuki ga *yanda*.

       (*n.*) shûshi [終止].

ceaseless (*a.*) taema-no-nai [絶え間のない].

ceaselessly (*ad.*) taezu [絶えず].

cedar (*n.*) (*bot.*) himaraya-sugi [ヒマラヤスギ].

ceiling (*n.*) tenjô [天井].

  hit the ceiling (*colloq.*) pun-pun-okoru

celebrate (*vt.*) 1)…o iwau […を祝う]. 2)…o ageru […を挙げる]. 3)…
o tataeru […をたたえる].

        (*vi.*) iwau [祝う]; shiki-o-ageru [式を挙げる].

celebrated (*a.*) yûmei-na [有名な].

celebration (*n.*) 1)shukuga[-kai] [祝賀(会)]. 2)(shiki no) kyokô
[(式の)挙行].

celestial (*a.*) ten-no [天の].

celestial body tentai [天体].

cell (*n.*) 1)chiisana-heya [小さな部屋]. 2)(*biol.*) saibô [細胞]. 3)
(*elect.*) denchi [電池].

cellar (*n.*) chika-shitsu [地下室].

cemetery (*n.*) kyôdô-bochi [共同墓地].

censorship (*n.*) ken'etsu [検閲].

censure (*n.*) hinan [非難].

       (*vt.*) …o hinan-suru […を非難する].

census (*n.*) kokusei-chôsa [国勢調査].

center, -tre (*n.*) 1)chûshin [中心]. 2)chûshin-chi [中心地].

  (*1*) It has a black spot in the **center**.

       Sore-wa *chûshin*-ni kuroi ten-ga aru.

  (*2*) Osaka is the **center** of commerce.

       Ôsaka wa shôgyô no *chûshin-chi*-de-aru.

center of gravity jûshin [重心].

centigrade (*a.*) sesshi-no [摂氏の].

centimeter (*n.*) senchi-mêtoru [センチメートル].

central (*a.*) chûshin-no [中心の]; chûô-no [中央の].

centrifugal (*a.*) enshin-sei-no [遠心性の].

centrifugal machine enshin-bunri-ki [遠心分離機].

centripetal (*a.*) kyûshin-sei-no [求心性の].

century (*n.*) seiki [世紀]; hyaku-nen-kan [百年間].

cereals (*n.*) kokumotsu-shoku [穀物食]; shiriaru [シリアル].

cerebral (*a.*) nô-no [脳の].

ceremony (*n.*) gishiki [儀式].

　stand on ceremony gishiki-baru; ki-gane-suru

certain (*a.*) 1)tashika-na [確かな]. 2)aru [ある]; aru-teido-no [ある程度の].

　　(*1*) I am **certain** of his coming.

　　　　Watashi-wa kare wa *tashika*-ni-kuru-to-omou.

　　(*2*) I met a **certain** man yesterday.

　　　　Watashi-wa kinô *aru* hito-ni atta.

　for certain tashika-ni

certainly (*ad.*) 1)tashika-ni [確かに]. 2)yoroshii-tomo [よろしいとも].

　　(*1*) I saw it **certainly**. *Tashika-ni* watashi-wa sore-o mita.

　　(*2*) **Certainly**, sir. Hai, *yoroshii-tomo*.

certificate (*n.*) shômei-sho [証明書]; menkyo-jô [免許状].

　　　a **certificate** of origin gensan-chi-*shômei-sho*

　　　a teacher's **certificate** kyôin-*menkyo-jô*

certify (*vt.*) ...o shômei-suru [⋯を証明する].

cf. (*L.*) confer = *compare* hikaku-seyo [比較せよ].

chaff (*n.*) momi-gara [もみがら].

chain (*n.*) 1)kusari [鎖]. 2)(*pl.*) kôsoku [拘束]. 3)tsuranari [連なり]; ichi-ren [一連]. 4)chên [チェーン].

　　(*1*) The dog is on the **chain**. Inu wa *kusari*-de-tsunaide-iru.

　　(*2*) He is now in **chains**. Kare-wa mokka *kôsoku*-sarete-iru.

　　(*3*) I was involved in a **chain** of events.

　　　　Watashi-wa *ichi-ren* no jiken-ni maki-komareta.

　　(*4*) a hotel **chain** hoteru-*chên*

chain smoker chên-sumôkâ [チェーンスモーカー].

chair (*n.*) isu [いす].

chairperson (*n.*) gichô [議長]; shikai-sha [司会者].

chalk (*n.*) chôku [チョーク]; hakuboku [白墨].

challenge (*n.*) chôsen [挑戦].

　　　　(*vt.*) ...ni chôsen-suru [⋯に挑戦する].
chamber (*n.*) kaikan [会館].
chamber music shitsunai-gaku [室内楽].
chamber of commerce shôgyô-kaigi-sho [商業会議所].
champion (*n.*) 1)yûshô-sha [優勝者]; champion [チャンピオン]. 2)
　　yôgo-sha [擁護者].
chance (*n.*) 1)gûzen [偶然]. 2)kikai [機会]; chansu [チャンス].
　　(*1*) **Chance** governs all.　*Gûzen* ga banji-o shihai-suru.
　　by chance　gûzen-ni; tama-tama
　　leave...to chance　un-makase-ni-suru
　　stand a good chance of...ing　(...suru)mikomi-ga-sôtô-aru
　　　　(*vi.*) gûzen...ga-okoru [偶然⋯が起こる].
change (*n.*) 1)henka [変化]. 2)tsuri-sen [釣り銭]. 3)nori-kae [乗り換
　　え]; ki-gae [着替え].
　　(*1*) There was no **change** in it.
　　　　Sore-ni-wa nan-no *henka* mo nakatta.
　　(*2*) No **change** given.　*Tsuri-sen* o-kotowari.
　　(*3*) He has no **change** of clothes.　Kare-wa *ki-gae*-ga nai.
　　a change of air　tenchi-ryôyô
　　for a change　kibun-o-kaeru-tame-ni
　　small change　ko-zeni
　　　　(*vt.*) ...o kaeru [⋯を替える].
　　　　Now **change** your clothes.　Saa kimono-o *kikae-nasai.*
　　change...into　...o...ni kaeru
　　　　Please change this one hundred note into gold.
　　　　　　Kono hyaku-doru-shihei-o kinka-ni kaete-kudasai.
　　　　(*vi.*) 1)kawaru [変わる]. 2)nori-kaeru [乗り換える].
　　(*1*) A caterpillar **changes** into a butterfly.
　　　　Ke-mushi wa chô-ni *kawaru.*
　　(*2*) **Change** here for Nagoya.　Nagoya-iki *nori-kae.*
changeable (*a.*) kawari-yasui [変わりやすい].
changeful (*a.*) henka-ni-tomu [変化に富む]; fu-antei-na [不安定な].
channel (*n.*) 1)kaikyô [海峡]. 2)(*broadcasting*) channeru [チャンネル].
chap (*n.*) (*colloq.*) yatsu [やつ].
chapel (*n.*) reihai-dô [礼拝堂].
chaps (*n.*) hibi [ひび]; akagire [あかぎれ].
chapter (*n.*) (shomotsu no) shô [《書物の)章].
character (*n.*) 1)jinkaku [人格]; jimbutsu [人物]. 2)moji [文字]. 3)

seikaku [性格].

(1) He is a man of **character**. Kare-wa *jinkaku*-sha-de-aru.

He was a great **character**. Kare-wa idai-na *jimbutsu* datta.

(2) It is very difficult to learn Chinese **characters**.

Kan*ji* o-manabu-no-wa totemo muzukashii.

(3) a **character** actor *seikaku*-haiyû

characteristic (a.) tokuyû-no [特有の].

(n.) tokusei [特性]; tokushoku [特色].

charade (n.) sharêdo [シャレード].

charcoal (n.) mokutan [木炭].

charge (n.) 1)ryôkin [料金]; keihi [経費]. 2)sekinin [責任]; sewa [世話]. 3)hinan [非難]; tsumi [罪]; kokuso [告訴]. 4)(mil.) totsugeki [突撃]. 5)(mil.) sôten [装てん].

(1) He printed it at his own **charge**.

Kare-wa ji*hi*-de sore-o insatsu-shita.

(2) I will take **charge** of the boy.

Watashi-ga sono shônen no *sewa*-o shi-yô.

(3) He was punished on the **charge** of theft.

Kare-wa settô no *tsumi*-de basserareta.

(4) They gave a **charge** upon the enemy.

Kare-ra-wa teki-ni *totsugeki*-shita.

(5) The **charge** was over. *Sôten* wa owatta.

free of charge muryô-de

in charge of ...o-azukatte

(vt.) 1)...o seikyû-suru [...を請求する]. 2)...o takusuru [...を託する]. 3)...no-kado-de semeru [...のかどで責める]; ...o kokuhatsu-suru [...を告発する]. 4)(mil.)...ni sôten-suru [...に装てんする]; ...o mitasu [...を満たす]; ...ni jûden-suru [...に充電する]. 5)(mil.)...ni totsugeki-suru [...に突撃する].

(1) How much will the cabman **charge**?

Takushî-no-unten-shu wa ikura *seikyû-suru*-darô-ka?

(2) I was **charged** with the task.

Watashi-wa sono-shigoto-o *takusareta*.

(3) He was **charged** with murder.

Kare-wa satsujin-zai-de *kokuso-sareta*.

(4) This storage battery must be **charged**.

Kono chikudenchi wa *jûden-suru*-hitsuyô-ga-aru.

(5) They **charged** the enemy. Kare-ra-wa teki-*ni totsugeki-shita*.

　　　　　(*vi.*) 1)shiharai-no-seikyû-o-suru [支払いの請求をする]. 2) totsugeki-suru [突撃する].

charitable (*a.*) nasake-bukai [情け深い]; jizen-no [慈善の].

charity (*n.*) jihi-shin [慈悲心]; jizen [慈善].

charm (*n.*) miryoku [魅力].

　　　　　(*vt. & vi.*) ...o miryô-suru (miryoku-ga-aru) [···を魅了する(魅力がある)].

charming (*a.*) miryoku-teki-na [魅力的な].

chart (*n.*) 1)(*marine*) kaizu [海図]. 2)zuhyô [図表].

charter (*n.*) 1)kenshô [憲章]. 2)taishaku-keiyaku [貸借契約]; châtâ [チャーター].

　　　　　(*vt.*) ...o keiyaku-de-kariru [···を契約で借りる]; ...o châtâ-suru [···をチャーターする].

chase (*vt.*) ...o ou [···を追う]; ...o tsuiseki-suru [···を追跡する].

　　　　　(*n.*) tsuiseki [追跡]; (the -) shuryô [狩猟].

　　give chase to ...o ou

chat (*vi.*) danshô-suru [談笑する].

　　　　　(*n.*) zatsudan [雑談]; seken-banashi [世間話].

　　have a chat with ...to danshô-suru

chatter (*vi.*) 1)pecha-kucha-shaberu [ぺちゃくちゃしゃべる]. 2)(ha ga) gachi-gachi-iu [(歯が)がちがちいう].

chauffeur (*n.*) (jika-yô-sha no) unten-shu [(自家用車の)運転手].

cheap (*a.*) yasui [安い]; yasuppoi [安っぽい].

cheat (*vt.*) ...o damasu [···をだます]; ...o azamuku [···を欺く].

check (*n.*) 1)soshi [阻止]. 2)ai-fuda [合い札]; chikki [チッキ]. 3) ((*US*))ko-gitte [小切手]. 4)kôshi-jima [格子じま].

　　(*1*) We kept the enemy in *check*.
　　　　　Ware-ware-wa teki-o-*soshi*-shita.

　　(*2*) I lost a *check* given for my baggage.
　　　　　Watashi-wa nimotsu-no-*chikki*-o naku-shita.

　　(*3*) I drew a *check* for 500 dollars.
　　　　　Watashi-wa go-hyaku-doru-no-*ko-gitte*-o furi-dashita.

　　　　　(*vt.*) 1)...o soshi-suru [···を阻止する]. 2)...o chikki-de-okuru [···をチッキで送る]. 3)...o chekku-suru [···をチェックする].

　　check in chekkuin-suru; tôjô-te-tsuzuki-o-suru

　　check out chekkuauto-suru

checkbook (*n.*) ((*US*)) ko-gitte-chô [小切手帳].

checked (*a.*) kôshi-jima-no [格子じまの].

checker (*n.*) 1)kôshi-jima [格子じま]. 2)(*pl.*) ((*US*)) chekkâ [チェッカー].

checkmate (*n.*) tsumi [詰み]; iki-zumari [行き詰まり].

checkroom (*n.*) ((*US*)) keitai-hin-azukari-sho [携帯品預り所].

checkup (*n.*) kensa [検査]; tenken [点検]; kenkô-shindan [健康診断].

cheek (*n.*) hoo [ほお].

cheer (*n.*) 1)kassai [喝さい]; kanko [歓呼]. 2)kigen [機嫌].
  (*1*) They gave him three **cheers**.
      Kare-ra-wa kare-no-tame-ni *banzai*-o-san-*shô*-shita.
  (*2*) She is of good **cheer**. Kano-jo-wa jô-*kigen*-da.
    (*vt.*) ...ni kassai-o-okuru […に喝さいを送る]; ...o genki-zukeru
    […を元気づける].
    (*vi.*) genki-zuku [元気づく].
    Cheer up! *Genki-o-dase!*

cheerful (*a.*) kigen-no-yoi [機嫌のよい]; tanoshii [楽しい].

cheerfulness (*n.*) jô-kigen [上機嫌]; yukai [愉快].

cheery (*a.*) kaikatsu-na [快活な]; yôki-na [陽気な]; yukai-na [愉快な].

chef (*n.*) shefu [シェフ].

chemical (*a.*) kagaku-no [化学の].
    (*n.*) (*pl.*) kagaku-seihin [化学製品].

chemist (*n.*) 1)kagaku-sha [化学者]. 2)((*Eng.*)) kusuriya [薬屋];
  yakuzai-shi [薬剤師].

chemistry (*n.*) kagaku [化学].

cheque (*n.*) ((*Eng.*)) ko-gitte [小切手].

cherish (*vt.*) 1)...o kokoro-ni-idaku […を心にいだく]. 2)...o daiji-ni-
  suru […を大事にする].

cherry (*n.*) 1)sakurambo [サクランボ]. 2)sakura-no-ki [桜の木].

cherry blossom sakura-no-hana [桜の花].

chess (*n.*) seiyô-shôgi [西洋将棋]; chesu [チェス].

chest (*n.*) 1)hako [箱]. 2)mune [胸].

chestnut (*n.*) kuri-no-ki [クリの木]; kuri-no-mi [クリの実].

chew (*vt. & vi.*) (...o) yoku-kamu [(…を)よくかむ]; (...o) kami-
  kudaku [(…を)かみ砕く].
  chew the cud 1)(ushi nado ga) hansû-suru. 2)(*colloq.*) yoku-
  kangaeru
    2) Chew the cud for a while. Shibaraku yoku-kangaero.

chick (*n.*) hiyoko [ひよこ]; hina [ひな].

chicken (*n.*) 1)hiyoko [ひよこ]; hina [ひな]. 2)keiniku [鶏肉].

chide (*vt. & vi.*) (...o) shikaru [(…を)しかる]; (...ni) ko-goto-o-iu [… に小言を言う].

chief (*n.*) kashira [かしら]; chô [長].
　(*a.*) omo-na [おもな].

chiefly (*ad.*) omo-ni [おもに]; shu-to-shite [主として].

chilblains (*n.*) shimoyake [しもやけ].

child (*n.*) kodomo [子供]; jidô [児童].

childhood (*n.*) yônen-jidai [幼年時代].

childish (*a.*) kodomo-rashii [子供らしい]; yôchi-na [幼稚な].

chill (*n.*) 1)reiki [冷気]. 2)samu-ke [寒け].
　(*a.*) tsumetai [つめたい]; hiyayaka-na [冷ややかな].
　(*vt.*) ...o hiyasu […を冷やす].

chilly (*a.*) hada-zamui [はだ寒い]; reitan-na [冷淡な].

chime (*n.*) 1)kane [鐘]. 2)chôwa [調和].
　keep chime with ...to chôshi-o-awasete-iku
　　　(*vt. & vi.*) (kane)-o narasu; (kane ga) naru [(鐘)を鳴らす: (鐘が)鳴る].

chimney (*n.*) entotsu [煙突].

chin (*n.*) shita-ago [下あご].

china (*n.*) jiki [磁器]; seto-mono [瀬戸物].

China, the People's Republic of Chûka-jimmin-kyôwa-koku [中華人 民共和国].

Chinese (*a.*) Chûgoku-no [中国の]; Chûgoku-jin-no [中国人の]; Chûgoku-go-no [中国語の].
　(*n.*) Chûgoku-jin [中国人]; Chûgoku-go [中国語].

chip (*n.*) (ki ya ishi no) kire-hashi [(木や石の)切れ端].

chirp (*vi.*) chû-chû-naku [ちゅうちゅう鳴く].
　(*n.*) (ko-tori ya mushi no) naki-goe [(小鳥や虫の)鳴き声].

chisel (*n.*) nomi [のみ].
　(*vt. & vi.*) (...o) nomi-de-horu [(…を)のみで彫る].

choice (*n.*) sentaku [選択].
　at one's own choice zuii-ni
　(*a.*) yori-sugutta [よりすぐった].

choir (*n.*) seika-tai [聖歌隊]; gasshô-dan [合唱団].

choke (*vt.*) 1)...o chissoku-saseru […を窒息させる]. 2)...o fusagu [… をふさぐ].
　(*1*) He **was choked** with smoke.
　　　Kare-wa kemuri-de *iki-gurushi-katta*.

(2) He **choked** up the passage. Kare-wa tsûro-o *fusaida*.
    (n.) chissoku [窒息].

choking (a.) iki-o-tsumaraseru-yô-na [息を詰まらせるような].

cholera (n.) (*med.*) korera [コレラ].

choose (*vt. & vi.*) (...o) erabu [(…を)選ぶ]; (...o) sentaku-suru [(…を)選択する].

chop (*vt.*) (ono ya nata ya hôchô de)...o buchi-giru [(おのやなたやほうちょうで)…をぶち切る].
    (n.) setsudan [切断].

chorus (n.) 1)gasshô [合唱]; kôrasu [コーラス]. 2)gasshô-dan [合唱団].
    a mixed **chorus** konsei-*gasshô*

Christ (n.) Kirisuto [キリスト].
    Jesus Christ Iesu-Kirisuto

christen (*vt.*) 1)...ni senrei-o-hodokosu […に洗礼を施す]. 2)...to meimei-suru […と命名する].

Christian (a.) Kirisuto-no [キリストの]; Kirisuto-kyô-no [キリスト教の].
    Young Men's Christian Association Y.M.C.A. Kirisuto-kyô-seinen-kai
    Young Women's Christian Association Y.W.C.A. Kirisuto-kyô-joshi-seinen-kai
    (n.) Kirisuto-kyô-to [キリスト教徒].

Christianity (n.) Kirisuto-kyô [キリスト教].

Christmas (n.) Kurisumasu [クリスマス].

chronic (a.) (*med.*) mansei-no [慢性の].

chronicle (n.) nendai-ki [年代記].

chrysanthemum (n.) (*bot.*) kiku [キク].

chuckle (*vi. & n.*) kusu-kusu-warau (kusu-kusu-warai) [くすくす笑う(くすくす笑い)].

chum (n.) (*colloq.*) naka-yoshi [仲よし].

church (n.) kyôkai[-dô] [教会(堂)].
    go to church reihai-ni-shusseki-suru

churchyard (n.) (kyôkai-fuzoku no)bochi [(教会付属の)墓地]; kyôkai-no-keidai [教会の境内].

cicada (n.) (*insect*) semi [セミ].

cider (n.) ((*Eng.*)) ringo-shu [リンゴ酒].

cigar (n.) ha-maki [葉巻].

cigarette (*n.*) kami-maki-tabako [紙巻きタバコ].

cinder (*n.*) moe-gara [燃え殻].

cinema (*n.*) (the –) eiga [映画].

circle (*n.*) 1)en [円]; wa [輪]. 2)...kai […界].
  (*vt. & vi.*) (...o) mawaru [(...を)回る]; (...o) senkai-suru [(…を)旋回する].

circuit (*n.*) 1)junkai [巡回]. 2)(*elect.*) kaisen [回線].
  short circuit (*elect.*) shôto

circular (*a.*) marui [丸い]; junkai-no [巡回の]; junkan-no [循環の];
  kairan-no [回覧の].
  (*n.*) kaijô [回状].

circulate (*vt. & vi.*) ...o junkan-saseru (junkan-suru) [...を循環させ
  る(循環する)]; ...o hiromeru (hiromaru) [...を広める(広まる)].

circulation (*n.*) 1)junkan [循環]. 2)(shimbun nado no) hakkô-busû
  [新聞などの)発行部数]. 3)dentatsu [伝達].

circumstance (*n.*) 1)jijô [事情]. 2)deki-goto [出来事]; jiken [事件].
  3)(*pl.*) kyôgû [境遇].
  (*1*) It depends upon **circumstance**. Sore-wa *jijô*-ni yoru.
  (*2*) a victim of **circumstance** *jiken* no gisei-sha
    Ambitions are thwarted by **circumstance**.
    Yashin wa *yoki-senu-jiken*-de zasetsu-suru.
  (*3*) He is in adverse **circumstances**. Kare-wa gyak*kyô*-ni-aru.
  under(in) no circumstances donna-koto-ga-attemo...nai

circus (*n.*) sâkasu [サーカス].

citation (*n.*) in'yô[-bun] [引用(文)].

cite (*vt.*) ...o in'yô-suru [...を引用する].

citizen (*n.*) shimin [市民]; kômin [公民].

citizenship (*n.*) shimin-ken [市民権]; kômin-ken [公民権].

city (*n.*) toshi [都市]; tokai [都会].

city hall shi-yakusho [市役所].

city planning ((*US*)) toshi-keikaku [都市計画].

civil (*a.*) 1)shimin-no [市民の]; (*law*) minji-no [民事の]. 2)reigi-
  tadashii [礼儀正しい]; teinei-na [丁寧な].
  (*1*) The **civil** war broke out in 1850.
    *Nai*ran wa sen-happyaku-go-jû-nen-ni okotta.
  (*2*) He is **civil** to strangers.
    Kare-wa mi-shiranu-hito-ni *teinei*-da.

civil engineering doboku-kôgaku [土木工学].

civilian (*n. & a.*) 1)ippan-shimin(-no) ［一般市民(の)］. 2)bummin (-no) ［文民(の)］.

civilization (*n.*) bummei ［文明］.

civilize (*vt.*) ...o bummei-ka-suru ［…を文明化する］.

civilly (*ad.*) 1)shimin-rashiku ［市民らしく］. 2)reigi-tadashiku ［礼儀正しく］.

civil rights kômin-ken ［公民権］.

claim (*vt.*) 1)...o yôkyû-suru ［…を要求する］; ...o motomeru ［…を求める］. 2)...to shuchô-suru ［…と主張する］.
　　　(*n.*) yôkyû ［要求］; seikyû ［請求］; shuchô ［主張］.

clam (*n.*) (*shellfish*) hamaguri ［ハマグリ］.

clamor, -our (*n. & vi.*) sawagi(-tateru) ［騒ぎ(立てる)］; sakebi (sakebu) ［叫び(叫ぶ)］.

clamp (*n.*) shime-gane ［締め金］.
　　　(*vt.*) ...o shimeru ［…を締める］.

clan (*n.*) ichimon ［一門］; ichizoku ［一族］.

clang (*n.*) garan-to-iu-oto ［ガランという音］.
　　　(*vt. & vi.*) ...o garan-to-narasu (garan-to-naru) ［…をガランと鳴らす(ガランと鳴る)］.

clank (*n.*) gacha-gacha-iu-oto ［ガチャガチャいう音］.
　　　(*vt. & vi.*) ...o gacha-gacha-to-narasu (gacha-gacha-naru) ［…をガチャガチャと鳴らす(ガチャガチャ鳴る)］.

clap (*n.*) 1)hakushu[-no-oto] ［拍手(の音)］. 2)raimei[-no-oto] ［雷鳴(の音)］.
　　　(*vt. & vi.*) (te)-o tataku ［(手)をたたく］; (...ni) hakushu-suru ［(…に)拍手する］.

clarify (*vt. & vi.*) ...o akiraka-ni-suru (akiraka-ni-naru) ［…を明らかにする(明らかになる)］.

clarity (*n.*) meikai ［明快］; meiseki ［明せき］.

clash (*n. & vi.*) shôtotsu(-suru) ［衝突(する)］.

clasp (*vt.*) ...o nigiri-shimeru ［…を握りしめる］; ...o daki-shimeru ［…を抱きしめる］.
　　　(*n.*) 1)shime-gane ［締め金］. 2)hôyô ［抱擁］.

class (*n.*) 1)kurasu ［クラス］; kumi ［組］. 2)tôkyu ［等級］. 3)kaikyû ［階級］.
　　　(*1*) He is at the top of his **class**.
　　　　　Kare-wa *kurasu*-de-toppu-da.
　　　(*2*) She went second-**class**. Kare-wa ni-*tô*-de itta.

(3) Stand by the working **classes**.　Rôdô-sha-*kaikyû*-o-shiji-seyo.

classic (*n.*) (*pl.*) koten [古典].

classical (*a.*) koten-bungaku-no [古典文学の].

classification (*n.*) bunrui [分類].

classify (*vt.*) ...o bunrui-suru [...を分類する].

classmate (*n.*) dôkyû-sei [同級生]; kyûyû [級友].

classroom (*n.*) kyôshitsu [教室].

clatter (*n. & vi.*) (sara ga) gacha-gacha(-iu) [(皿が)がちゃがちゃ(いう)]; (hito ga) pecha-kucha(-shaberu) [(人が)ぺちゃくちゃ(しゃべる)].

clause (*n.*) 1)kajô [箇条]; jôkô [条項]. 2)(*gram.*) setsu [節].

claw (*n.*) (neko ya taka nado no) kagi-tsume [(ネコやタカなどの)かぎつめ].

clay (*n.*) nendo [粘土].

clean (*a.*) seiketsu-na [清潔な].
　　　　(*vt.*) ...o kirei-ni-suru [...をきれいにする]; ...o sôji-suru [...を掃除する].

cleaning (*n.*) sôji [掃除]; sentaku [洗濯].

cleanly (*ad.*) 1)kirei-ni [きれいに]; seiketsu-ni [清潔に]. 2)kiyoraka-ni [清らかに].
　　　　(*a.*) kirei-zuki-na [きれい好きな]; ko-zappari-shita [小ざっぱりした].

cleanse (*vt.*) ...o seiketsu-ni-suru [...を清潔にする]; ...o kiyomeru [...を清める].

clear (*a.*) 1)sumi-kitta [澄みきった]; hareta [晴れた]. 2)meiseki-na [明せきな]; akiraka-na [明らかな]. 3)jama-ga-nai [邪魔がない].

(*1*) The sky is **clear**.　Sora wa *harete*-iru.

(*2*) It seems **clear**.　Sore-wa *akiraka-na*-yô-da.

(*3*) He is **clear** of debt.
　　　　Kare-wa *sukkari* shakkin-o-haratte-*shimatta*.

　　　　(*vt.*) ...o kirei-ni-suru [...をきれいにする]; ...o katazukeru [...を片付ける].

　　Clear the dishes from the table.
　　　　Têburu-no-sara-*o katazuke-nasai*.

　　　　(*vi.*) hareru [晴れる].

　　It began to **clear**.　Sora ga *hare*-hajimeta.

clearance sale zaiko-issô-oo-uri-dashi [在庫一掃大売出し].

clearly (*ad.*) hakkiri-to [はっきりと]; akiraka-ni [明らかに].

clearness (*n.*) meiryô [明りょう]; jama-no-nai-koto [邪魔のないこと].

cleave (*vt. & vi.*) ...o saku (sakeru) ［…を裂く(裂ける)］; ...o waru (wareru) ［…を割る(割れる)］.

cleft (*n.*) sake-me ［裂け目］; ware-me ［割れ目］.

clergyman (*n.*) sei-shoku-sha ［聖職者］.

clerk (*n.*) 1)shoki ［書記］; jimu-in ［事務員］. 2)((*US*)) ten'in ［店員］.

clever (*a.*) 1)rikô-na ［利口な］. 2)kiyô-na ［器用な］; jôzu-na ［上手な］.
   (*1*) He is a **clever** boy. Kare-wa *rikô-na* shônen da.
   (*2*) He is **clever** at drawing. Kare-wa e-ga-*jôzu-da*.

cleverly (*ad.*) rikô-ni ［利口に］; umaku ［うまく］; jôzu-ni ［上手に］.

cleverness (*n.*) rikô ［利口］; kiyô ［器用］.

client (*n.*) 1)(bengo-shi nado no) irai-nin ［(弁護士などの)依頼人］. 2) kokyaku ［顧客］.

cliff (*n.*) gake ［がけ］; zeppeki ［絶壁］.

climate (*n.*) kikô ［気候］; fûdo ［風土］.

climax (*n.*) kuraimakkusu ［クライマックス］.
   (*vt. & vi.*) ...o kuraimakkusu-ni-tôtatsu-saseru (kuraimakkusu-ni-tassuru) ［…をクライマックスに到達させる(クライマックスに達する)］.

climb (*vt. & vi.*) (...ni) noboru ［(…に)登る］; (...ni) yoji-noboru ［(…に)よじ登る］.

clinch (*vt.*) 1)(kugi no saki)-o uchi-mageru ［(くぎの先)を打ち曲げる］. 2)(giron)-no keri-o-tsukeru ［(議論)のけりをつける］.

cling (*vi.*) kuttsuku ［くっつく］; shigami-tsuku ［しがみつく］.

clinic (*n.*) shinryô-sho ［診療所］; (ippan ni) sôdan-sho ［(一般に)相談所］.

clip (*vt.*) ...o hasami-de-kiru ［…をはさみで切る］.
   (*n.*) kiru-koto ［切ること］.

clip (*vt.*) ...o kurippu-de-hasamu ［…をクリップではさむ］.
   (*n.*) kurippu ［クリップ］; kami-basami ［紙ばさみ］.

clipper (*n.*) kiru-hito ［切る人］; (*pl.*) hasami ［はさみ］.

cloakroom (*n.*) (gekijô ya hoteru no) keitai-hin-ichiji-azukari-sho ［(劇場やホテルの)携帯品一時預り所］.

clock (*n.*) kake-dokei ［掛け時計］; oki-dokei ［置き時計］.

clockwise (*a. & ad.*) migi-mawari-no(-ni) ［右回りの(に)］.

close (*a.*) 1)shimeta ［閉めた］; kaze-tooshi-no-warui ［風通しの悪い］. 2)sekkin-shita ［接近した］. 3)shitashii ［親しい］. 4)memmitsu-na ［綿密な］.
   (*1*) I feel ill in a **close** room.
      Watashi-wa *shime-kitta* heya-ni-iru-to kibun-ga-waruku-

       naru.

(2) It was a **close** game. Gêmu wa *sessen* datta.

(3) He is my **close** friend. Kare-wa watashi-no *shin'yû* da.

(4) **close** attention *memmitsu-na* chûi

    (*ad.*) sekkin-shite [接近して]; sugu-chikaku-ni [すぐ近くに].

    He lives **close** to the school.

       Kare-wa gakkô-no-*sugu-chikaku-ni* sunde-iru.

close by sugu-chikaku-ni

    (*n.*) owari [終わり].

    The story soon comes to a **close**.

       Monogatari wa ma-mo-naku *owari*-ni-naru.

    (*vt. & vi.*) 1)...o tojiru [⋯を閉じる]. 2)owaru [終わる].

(1) He **closed** his eyes. Kare-wa me-o *tojita*.

(2) School **closes** at half past two in the afternoon.

       Jugyô wa gogo-ni-ji-han-ni *owaru*.

closely (*ad.*) kitchiri-to [きっちりと]; gemmitsu-ni [厳密に]; missetsu-ni [密接に].

closet (*n.*) oshiire [押入れ].

cloth (*n.*) nuno [布]; orimono [織物].

clothe (*vt.*) ...ni kimono-o-kiseru [⋯に着物を着せる].

clothes (*n.*) ifuku [衣服]; kimono [着物].

clothing (*n.*) iryô-hin [衣料品]; irui [衣類].

cloud (*n.*) kumo [雲].

    There is no **cloud** in the sky. Sora-niwa *kumo* ga-nai.

    (*vt. & vi.*) ...o kumoraseru (kumoru) [⋯を曇らせる(曇る)].

    His face was **clouded**. Kare-no-kao wa *kumotte-ita*.

    It **clouded** up towards evening.

       Yûgata-ni-natte *kumotte-kita*.

cloudless (*a.*) kumo-no-nai [雲のない]; yoku-hareta [よく晴れた].

cloudy (*a.*) kumotta [曇った]; bon'yari-to-shita [ぼんやりとした].

clown (*n.*) dôke-shi [道化師].

club (*n.*) 1)kombô [こん棒]. 2)kurabu [クラブ].

clue (*n.*) itoguchi [糸口]; te-gakari [手がかり].

clumsy (*a.*) bu-kiyô-na [無器用な]; heta-na [下手な]; bu-kakkô-na [ぶかっこうな].

cluster (*n.*) 1)(budô ya sakurambo nado no) fusa [(ブドウやサクランボなどの)房]. 2)shûdan [集団].

    (*vi.*) mure-o-nashite-atsumaru [群れをなして集まる].

Co. = Company kaisha [会社].

c/o, c.o. = care of ...kata […方]; ...ki-tsuke […気付].

coach (*n.*) 1)oo-gata-yon-rin-basha [大型四輪馬車]. 2)((*US*)) (*R.R.*) kyakusha [客車]. 3)((*Eng.*)) chô-kyori-yô-basu [長距離用バス]. 4) (*sports*) kôchi [コーチ].
　　(*vt.*) 1)...o basha-de-hakobu […を馬車で運ぶ]. 2)...no kôchi-o-suru […のコーチをする].

coal (*n.*) sekitan [石炭].

coal mine tankô [炭坑].

coarse (*a.*) 1)somatsu-na [粗末な]. 2)kime-no-arai [きめの荒い]. 3) gehin-na [下品な].

coast (*n.*) kaigan [海岸]; engan [沿岸].
　　(*vi.*) engan-o-kôkô-suru [沿岸を航行する].

coat (*n.*) uwagi [上着]; gaitô [外とう].

coating (*n.*) nuri [塗り]; toryô [塗料].

coax (*vt.*) ...o nadametari-sukashitari-shite...(sa-)seru […をなだめたりすかしたりして…(さ)せる].
　　(*vi.*) nadameru [なだめる]; damasu [だます].

cobweb (*n.*) kumo-no-su [クモの巣].

cock (*n.*) ondori [おんどり].
　　(*vt. & vi.*) ...o pin-to-tateru (pin-to-tatsu) […をぴんと立てる (ぴんと立つ)].

cocktail (*n.*) kakuteru [カクテル].

coco(a)nut (*n.*) kokoyashi-no-mi [ココヤシの実].

cocoon (*n.*) mayu [まゆ].

cod (*n.*) (*fish*) tara [タラ].

code (*n.*) 1)hôten [法典]. 2)kiyaku [規約]. 3)shingô[-taikei] [信号(体系)]; angô [暗号].
　　(*vt.*) ...o angô-bun-ni-suru […を暗号文にする].

code book angô-sho [暗号書].

codliver oil kan'yu [肝油].

coeducation (*n.*) dan-jo-kyôgaku [男女共学].

coffin (*n.*) kan [棺]; hitsugi [ひつぎ].

coherent (*a.*) 1)mitchaku-shita [密着した]. 2)suji-no-tootta [筋の通った].

coil (*vt.*) ...o guru-guru-maku […をぐるぐる巻く].
　　(*n.*) 1)toguro-maki [とぐろ巻き]. 2)(*elect.*) koiru [コイル].

coin (*n.*) kôka [硬貨].

coincide (*vi.*) (...to-)dôji-ni-okoru [(…と)同時に起こる]; itchi-suru
[一致する].

coincidence (*n.*) dôji-hassei [同時発生]; itchi [一致].

cold (*a.*) samui [寒い]; tsumetai [つめたい].
　　　　I don't feel **cold**. Watashi-wa *samuku*-nai.
　　　(*n.*) 1)samu-sa [寒さ]. 2)kaze [かぜ].
　　(*1*) She is shivering with **cold** Kano-jo-wa *samuku*te furueteiru.
　　(*2*) I have caught **cold**. Watashi-wa *kaze*-o hiita.

coldhearted (*a.*) reitan-na [冷淡な].

coldly (*ad.*) reitan-ni [冷淡に].

cold war reisen [冷戦].

collaborate (*vi.*) kyôryoku-suru [協力する]; kyôdô-kenkyû-suru [共同
研究する].

collapse (*n. & vi.*) hôkai(-suru) [崩壊(する)].

collar (*n.*) 1)eri [えり]; karâ [カラー]. 2)(inu no) kubi-wa [(犬の)
首輪].

colleague (*n.*) dôryô [同僚].

collect (*vt. & vi.*) ...o atsumeru (atsumaru) […を集める(集まる)].
　　　　Do you **collect** stamps?
　　　　　　Anata-wa kitte-*o atsumemasu*-ka?
　　　　People **collected** in crowds. Hito-bito ga oozei *atsumatta*.

collection (*n.*) 1)shûshû [収集]. 2)bokin [募金].

collective (*a.*) 1)atsumeta [集めた]. 2)shûdan-teki[-na] [集団的(な)].
　　　　(*n.*) kyôdô-tai [共同体].

collective agreement rôdô-kyôyaku [労働協約].

collective bargaining dantai-kôshô [団体交渉].

college (*n.*) ((*US*)) tanka-daigaku [単科大学]; gakubu [学部]. semmon-
gakkô [専門学校].

collide (*vi.*) shôtotsu-suru [衝突する].

collision (*n.*) shôtotsu [衝突].

colloquial (*a.*) kôgo-no [口語の]; nichijô-kaiwa-no [日常会話の].

colonel (*n.*) taisa [大佐].

colonist (*n.*) nyûshoku-sha [入植者].

colony (*n.*) shokumin-chi [植民地].

color, -our (*n.*) 1)iro [色]. 2)(*pl.*) kokki [国旗]; gunki [軍旗].
　　(*1*) What **color** is that rose? Sono bara wa donna-*iro*-desu-ka?
　　(*2*) the Queen's **colours** Eikoku-*kokki*
　　　　　　(*vt.*) ...ni chakushoku-suru […に着色する].

        (*vi.*) iro-zuku [色づく]; sekimen-suru [赤面する].

colo(u)red (*a.*) chakushoku-no [着色の].

colo(u)rful (*a.*) shikisai-ni-tonda [色彩に富んだ].

colo(u)ring (*n.*) saishiki [彩色].

colossal (*a.*) kyodai-na [巨大な]; (*colloq.*) odoroku-beki [驚くべき].

column (*n.*) 1)(*arch.*) hashira [柱]; enchû [円柱]. 2)(shimbun nado no) ran [(新聞などの)欄]; dan [段]. 3)(*mil.*) jûtai [縦隊].

   (*1*) It sent out a **column** of gray smoke.

      Sore-wa hai-iro-no kemuri-o haita.

   (*2*) Each page has thirteen **columns**.

      Kaku pêji wa jû-san-*dan*-ni-natte-iru.

   (*3*) The company marched on in two **columns**.

      Chûtai wa ni-retsu-*jûtai*-de kôshin-shita.

comb (*n.*) kushi [くし].

      (*vt.*) …o kushi-de-suku […をくしですく].

combat (*n.*) sentô [戦闘].

combination (*n.*) ketsugô [結合].

come (*vi.*) 1)kuru [来る]. 2)(sempô e) iku [(先方へ)行く]. 3)(…ni-) naru [(…に)なる]. 4)Saa! [さあ！]; Oi! [おい！].

   (*1*) He **comes** here once a week.

      Kare-wa shû-ni ichi-do koko-e *kuru*.

   (*2*) I will **come** at once. Sugu *mairi-masu*.

   (*3*) I have **come** to like it. Watashi-wa sore-ga suki-ni-*natta*.

   (*4*) **Come**, stop your play. *Saa*, asobi-o o-yame.

   come about okoru

      How did the event come about?

      Dô-shite sono jiken wa okita-no-ka?

   come across futo…ni de-au

   come along issho-ni-iku

      Come along with us. Ware-ware-to-issho-ni-iki-masen-ka.

   come back kitaku-suru

      He will soon come back.

      Kare-wa ma-mo-naku kitaku-suru-deshô.

   come down orite-kuru

      John, come down to breakfast. Jon, asa-gohan-ni orite-oide.

   come from 1)…kara-kuru. 2)…no-shusshin-de-aru

   1) Where did you come from? Kimi-wa doko-kara-kita-no-da?

   2) He comes from Nagoya. Kare-wa Nagoya-no-shusshin-da.

come home　kitaku-suru

come in　hairu

　　Please come in.　Dôzo o-hairi-kudasai.

come into　...ni haitte-kuru

　　He came into my room without knocking.

　　　　Kare-wa nokku-mo-sezu-ni watashi-no-heya-ni haitte-kita.

come of　1)...kara-kuru. 2)...no-de-de-aru

　1) His illness comes of drinking too much.

　　　Kare-no byôki wa nomi-sugi-kara-kite-iru.

　2) He comes of a good family.　Kare-wa ryôke-no-de-de-aru.

come off　okonawareru

　　The wedding ceremony will come off tomorrow.

　　　　Kekkon-shiki wa asu okonawareru-darô.

Come on!　Saa-ikô!; Saa-koi!; Sô-da!; Sono-chôshi!

come out　1)dete-kuru. 2)(hana-ga) saku. 3)kekka-ga...ni naru

　1) The moon came out.　Tsuki ga dete-kita.

　2) The chrysanthemums will come out soon.

　　　Ma-mo-naku kiku ga saku-deshô.

　3) It came out as we expected.

　　　Kekka wa ware-ware-ga-omotte-ita-toori-ni natta.

come over　1)yatte-kuru. 2)(henka ga)...ni okoru

　1) They came over to our country from America.

　　　Kare-ra-wa haru-baru Amerika-kara waga-kuni-ni yatte-
　　　　kita.

　2) A sudden change has come over him.

　　　Kyûgeki-na henka ga kare-no-kokoro-ni okita.

come round　mawatte-kuru; megutte-kuru

　　Autumn has come round again.

　　　　Aki ga mata megutte-kita.

come up　1)yatte-kuru. 2)me-baeru

　1) My cousin came up to me.　Itoko ga yatte-kita.

　2) Grass comes up in spring.　Kusa wa haru-ni me-baeru.

come up with　...ni oi-tsuku

come upon　1)...ni de-au. 2)...o fui-ni-osou

　1) I came upon her at the station.

　　　Watashi-wa eki-de kano-jo-ni de-atta.

　2) A misfortune came upon his family.

　　　Fukô ga totsuzen kare-no-kazoku-o osotta.

comedian (*n.*) kigeki-haiyû [喜劇俳優]; komedian [コメディアン].

comedy (*n.*) kigeki [喜劇].

comfort (*n.*) 1)nagusame [慰め]. 2)kiraku [気楽].
　(*1*) He is a great **comfort** to his parents.
　　　　Kare-wa ryôshin-ni-totte ookina *nagusame* da.
　(*2*) She lived in **comfort**. Kano-jo-wa *kiraku*-ni kurashita.
　　　　(*vt.*) ...o nagusameru [...を慰める].
　　　He **comforted** his friends.
　　　　Kare-wa tomodachi-o *nagusameta*.

comfortable (*a.*) i-gokochi-no-yoi [居ごこちのよい].

comic (*a.*) kigeki-no [喜劇の]; kokkei-na [こっけいな];
　　　(*n.*) manga-bon[-zasshi] [漫画本[雑誌]].

comical (*a.*) okashina [おかしな]; kokkei-na [こっけいな].

coming (*a.*) kitaru-beki [来たるべき]; tsugi-no [次の].
　　　(*n.*) tôchaku [到着].

comma (*n.*) komma [コンマ].

command (*vt.*) 1)...o meizuru [...を命ずる]; ...o shiki-suru [...を指揮
する]. 2)(keshiki)-o mi-watasu [(景色)を見渡す].
　(*1*) He **commanded** them to go.
　　　　Kare-wa kare-ra-ni ike-*to-meijita*.
　(*2*) The hill **commands** a fine view.
　　　　Sono oka wa *mi-harashi*-ga-yoi.
　　　(*n.*) 1)shiki [指揮]; meirei [命令]. 2)jiyû-ni-tsukau-chikara
[自由に使う力].
　(*1*) They were under the **command** of Captain A.
　　　　Kare-ra-wa Ei-taii-no-*shiki*-no-moto-ni-atta.
　(*2*) He has a good **command** of German.
　　　　Kare-wa Doitsu-go-ga-*jiyû*-ni-tsukaeru.

commander (*n.*) shiki-kan [指揮官]; shirei-kan [司令官].

commanding (*a.*) 1)shiki-suru [指揮する]. 2)dôdô-taru [堂々たる]. 3)
mi-harashi-no-yoi [見晴らしのよい].

commemorate (*vt.*) ...o kinen-suru [...を記念する].

commence (*vt. & vi.*) ...o hajimeru (hajimaru) [...を始める(始まる)].
　　　He **commenced** studying it.
　　　　Kare-wa sore-no-kenkyû-*o-hajimeta*.
　　　The next term **commences** on the 10th of September.
　　　　Tsugi-no gakki wa Kugatsu-tô-ka-ni *hajimaru*.

commencement (*n.*) 1)kaishi [開始]. 2)((US)) sotsugyô-shiki [卒業式].

comment (*n.*) 1)rompyô [論評]. 2)kaisetsu [解説]. 3)iken [意見].
  (*vi.*) rompyô-suru [論評する]; kaisetsu-suru [解説する].
commerce (*n.*) shôgyô [商業]; bôeki [貿易].
commercial (*a.*) 1)shôgyô-no [商業の]. 2)kôkoku-hôsô-no [広告放送の].
  (*n.*) kôkoku-hôsô[-bangumi] [広告放送[番組]]; komâsharu
  [コマーシャル].
commission (*n.*) 1)inin[-jô] [委任(状)]. 2)iin-kai [委員会]. 3)(*com.*)
  tesû-ryô [手数料].
commissioner (*n.*) 1)iin [委員]. 2)bemmu-kan [弁務官]. 3)((*US*))
  komisshonâ [コミッショナー].
commit (*vt.*) 1)(tsumi ya ayamachi)-o okasu [(罪や過ち)を犯す]. 2)
  ...ni yudaneru [···にゆだねる].
  (*1*) He **committed** a crime.　Kare-wa tsumi-o *okashita*.
  (*2*) A warehouse **was committed** to the flames.
   Sôko ga shôshitsu-shita.
committee (*n.*) iin-kai [委員会]; iin [委員].
commodity (*n.*) shôhin [商品]; nichiyô-hin [日用品].
common (*a.*) 1)futsû-no [普通の]; heibon-na [平凡な]. 2)kyôtsû-no
  [共通の].
  (*n.*) kyôyô-chi [共用地].
  Does this village have a **common**?
   Kono mura niwa *kyôyô-chi*-ga arimasu-ka?
 in common　kyôdô-ni
  I have a text in common with him.
   Watashi-wa issatsu-no-kyôka-sho-o kare-to kyôyû-shite-iru.
common law　kanshû-hô [慣習法].
commonly (*ad.*) ippan-ni [一般に].
commonplace (*a.*) heibon-na [平凡な]; ari-fureta [ありふれた].
commonwealth (*n.*) 1)kyôwa-koku [共和国]. 2)rempô [連邦].
communicate (*vt.*) ...o dentatsu-suru [···を伝達する]; ...o shiraseru
  [···を知らせる].
  (*vi.*) tsûshin-suru [通信する].
  I will **communicate** the news to her.
   Watashi-wa sono nyûsu-*o* kano-jo-ni *tsutaema*-shô.
  I **communicate** with a certain Englishman.
   Watashi-wa aru-Eikoku-jin-to *tsûshin-shite-iru*.
communication (*n.*) 1)dentatsu [伝達]; tsûshin [通信]. 2)(*pl.*)
  tsûshin[kôtsû]-kikan [通信[交通]機関].

communist (*n.*) kyôsan-shugi-sha [共産主義者].

community (*n.*) chiiki-shakai [地域社会].

commutation (*n.*) 1)kôkan [交換]; furikae [振替]. 2)((*US*)) teiki-ken-ni-yoru-tsûkin [定期券による通勤]. 3)(*law*) genkei [減刑].

commutation ticket kaisû-ken [回数券]; teiki-ken [定期券].

compact (*a.*) 1)gisshiri-tsumatta [ぎっしり詰まった]. 2)hiki-shimatta [引き締まった]; kanketsu-na [簡潔な].

companion (*n.*) tomodachi [友達]; tsure [連れ]; nakama [仲間].

company (*n.*) 1)kôsai [交際]. 2)tomodachi [友達]. 3)kyaku [客]. 4)ikkô [一行]. 5)kaisha [会社].

　(*1*) She wants his **company**.

　　　Kano-jo-wa kare-to *kôsai*-shi-tagatte-iru.

　(*2*) a boon **company**　yukai-na asobi-*tomodachi*

　(*3*) Mother has **company**.　Haha wa rai-*kyaku*-ga arimasu.

　(*4*) Our **company** consisted of ten men.

　　　Ware-ware-no *ikkô* wa jû-nin-de-atta.

　(*5*) We have established a **company**.

　　　Ware-ware-wa *kaisha*-o setsuritsu-shita.

　in company with　...to-issho-ni; ...to-tsure-datte

comparative (*a.*) hikaku-no [比較の]; kanari-no [かなりの].

comparatively (*ad.*) hikaku-teki-ni [比較的に]; wariai-ni [割合に].

compare (*vt.*) ...to hikaku-suru […と比較する]; ...ni tatoeru […に例える].

　　　　　(*vi.*) hitteki-suru [匹敵する].

　compared with　...to-hikaku-suru-to; ...to-kurabete

comparison (*n.*) hikaku [比較]; taishô [対照].

　in comparison (with)　...(to-)hikaku-shite[-miru-to]

compartment (*n.*) (kyakusha no) koshitsu [(客車の)個室].

compass (*n.*) 1)rashin-ban [羅針盤]. 2)(*pl.*) kompasu [コンパス].

compassion (*n.*) dôjô [同情].

compel (*vt.*) ...o muri-ni...(sa)seru […を無理に…(さ)せる].

　be compelled to (do)　yamu-o-ezu...(suru)

compensation (*n.*) tsugunai [償い]; baisho [賠償].

　in compensation for　...no-tsugunai-to-shite

compete (*vi.*) kyôsô-suru [競争する].

competent (*a.*) 1)nôryoku-no-aru [能力のある]. 2)jûbun-na [十分な].

competition (*n.*) kyôsô [競争]; kyôgi-kai [競技会].

compile (*vt.*) ...o henshû-suru […を編集する].

complain (*vi.*) fuhei-o-iu [不平をいう].

complaint (*n.*) fuhei [不平]; kujô [苦情].

complement (*n.*) hokan-butsu [補完物].
    (*vt.*) ...o hosoku-suru [...を補足する]; ...o kanzen-ni-suru [...を完全にする].

complete (*a.*) kanzen-na [完全な].
    (*vt.*) ...o kansei-saseru [...を完成させる].

complete works zenshû [全集].

completion (*n.*) kansei [完成]; tassei [達成].

complex (*a.*) fukuzatsu-na [複雑な]; fukugô-no [複合の].
    (*n.*) 1)fukugô-tai [複合体]. 2)(*psych.*) kompurekkusu [コンプレックス].

complexion (*n.*) kao-no-iro-tsuya [顔の色つや].

complicate (*vt.*) ...o fukuzatsu-ni-suru [...を複雑にする].

complicated (*a.*) fukuzatsu-na [複雑な]; komi-itta [込み入った].

compliment (*n.*) o-seji [お世辞]; (*pl.*) aisatsu [あいさつ].
    (*vt.*) ...ni o-seji-o-iu [...にお世辞を言う]; ...o homeru [...をほめる].

complimentary (*a.*) o-seji-no-umai [お世辞のうまい]; aisatsu-no [あいさつの].

comply (*vi.*) ôjiru [応じる].

component (*n.*) kôsei-yôso [構成要素].
    (*a.*) kôsei-shite-iru [構成している].

compose (*vt.*) ...o kumi-tateru [...を組み立てる]; ...o tsukuru [...を作る]; ...o sakkyoku-suru [...を作曲する].

composer (*n.*) (*mus.*) sakkyoku-ka [作曲家].

composition (*n.*) 1)sakubun [作文]; (*mus.*) sakkyoku [作曲]. 2) sakuhin [作品].

compound (*vt.*) ...o mazete(...o) tsukuru [...を混ぜて(...を)作る].
    (*a.*) gôsei-no [合成の].

comprehension (*n.*) 1)rikai [理解]. 2)hôkatsu [包括].

comprehensive (*a.*) hôkatsu-teki-na [包括的な].

compress (*vt.*) ...o asshuku-suru [...を圧縮する].

compromise (*n. & vi.*) dakyô(-suru) [妥協(する)].

compulsory (*a.*) kyôsei-teki-na [強制的な]; gimu-teki-na [義務的な].

compulsory education gimu-kyôiku [義務教育].

computer (*n.*) denshi-keisan-ki [電子計算機]; kompyûta [コンピュータ].

comrade (*n.*) nakama [仲間]; tôin [党員].

conceal (*vt.*) ...o kakusu […を隠す].

conceive (*vt.*) ...o omoi-tsuku […を思い付く]; ...to omou […と思う].

concentrate (*vt.*) 1)...ni shûchû-suru […に集中する]. 2)(*chem.*)...o nôshuku-suru […を濃縮する].

      (*vi.*) 1)atsumaru [集まる]. 2)nôshuku-suru [濃縮する].

concept (*n.*) gainen [概念].

conception (*n.*) 1)gainen [概念]. 2)chakusô [着想].

concern (*vt.*) 1)(be -ed) kankei-shite-iru [関係している]. 2)(be -ed) shimpai-suru [心配する].

  (*1*) He is not **concerned** in the affair.

      Kare-wa sono-ken-ni *kankei-shite-i*-nai.

  (*2*) The banker is **concerned** about his debt.

      Ginkô-ka wa fusai-o *shimpai-shite-iru.*

  be concerned with ...ni kankei-ga-aru; ...ni kanshin-o-motsu

  so(as) far as (one) is concerned (dare-sore)-ni-kansuru-kagiri

      (*n.*) 1)kankei [関係]; kanshin [関心]. 2)kaisha [会社].

  have no concern with ...to kankei-ga-nai

concerned (*a.*) kankei-no [関係の]; tôgai-no [当該の].

  the authorities concerned kankei-tôkyoku

  the parties concerned tôji-sha-tachi

concerning (*conj.*) ...ni-tsuite[-no] […について(の)]; ...ni-kanshite […に関して].

concert (*n.*) 1)ongaku-kai [音楽会]. 2)kyôryoku [協力].

concise (*a.*) kanketsu-na [簡潔な].

conclude (*vt.*) 1)...o oeru […を終える]. 2)...to ketsuron-o-kudasu […と結論を下す].

      (*vi.*) 1)owaru [終わる]. 2)kettei-suru [決定する].

  To be concluded. Jikai-kanketsu.

conclusion (*n.*) ketsumatsu [結末]; ketsuron [結論]; kettei [決定].

concrete (*a.*) 1)gutai-teki-na [具体的な]. 2)konkurîto-sei-no [コンクリート製の].

      (*n.*) 1)konkurîto [コンクリート]. 2)gutai-teki-kannen [具体的観念].

condemn (*vt.*) 1)...o yûzai-to-senkoku-suru […を有罪と宣告する]. 2)...o togameru […をとがめる].

condemned (*a.*) yûzai-o-senkoku-sareta [有罪を宣告された].

condense (*vt. & vi.*) (...o) nôshuku-suru [(…を)濃縮する].

condition (*n.*) 1)jôtai [状態]. 2)jôken [条件].

on condition that ...to-iu-jôken-de; moshi ...nara

condole (*vi.*) kuyami-o-iu [悔やみを言う].

conduct (*vt.*) 1)...o annai-suru [...を案内する]. 2)(- oneself) furumau [ふるまう].

　　(*1*) I **conducted** her to the house.

　　　　Watashi-wa kano-jo-o sono-ie-e *annai-shita*.

　　(*2*) He **conducted** himself well.　Kare-wa rippa-ni *furumatta*.

　　　　(*n.*) 1)kôi [行為]. 2)annai [案内].

conductor (*n.*) shashô [車掌]; (*mus.*) shiki-sha [指揮者].

cone (*n.*) ensui[-kei] [円すい(形)].

confectioner (*n.*) kashiya [菓子屋].

confer (*vt.*) ...o sazukeru [...を授ける].

　　The king **conferred** a medal on him.

　　　　Kokuô wa kare-ni kunshô-o *sazuketa*.

　　　　(*vi.*) kyôgi-suru [協議する].

　　The president **conferred** with them.

　　　　Sôsai wa kare-ra-to *kyôgi-shita*.

conference (*n.*) kaigi [会議]; kyôgi-kai [協議会].

confess (*vt.*) ...o hakujô-suru [...を白状する].

confession (*n.*) hakujô [白状]; kokuhaku [告白].

confide (*vt.*) ...o uchi-akeru [...を打ち明ける].

　　　　(*vi.*) 1)himitsu-o-uchi-akeru [秘密を打ち明ける]. 2)shinrai-suru [信頼する].

confidence (*n.*) 1)shinrai [信頼]. 2)jishin [自信]. 3)himitsu [秘密].

　in confidence naisho-de

confident (*a.*) kakushin-shite[-iru] [確信して(いる)]; jishin-no-aru [自信のある].

confidential (*a.*) 1)himitsu-no [秘密の]. 2)uchi-toketa [打ち解けた].

　Confidential Shinten

confine (*vt.*) 1)...o toji-komeru [...を閉じ込める]. 2)...o seigen-suru [...を制限する].

　　(*1*) He **is confined** to bed with a cold.

　　　　Kare-wa kaze-de nete-*iru*.

　　(*2*) It **is confined** to a small limit.

　　　　Sore-wa shô-han'i-ni *kagirarete-iru*.

confirm (*vt.*) 1)...o kakunin-suru [...を確認する]. 2)...o kyôko-ni-suru [...を強固にする].

confiscate (*vt.*) ...o bosshû-suru [...を没収する].

conflict (*n.*) 1) arasoi [争い]. 2) shôtotsu [衝突].
    (*vi.*) mujun-suru [矛盾する].

confound ...o konran-saseru [⋯を混乱させる]; ...o rôbai-saseru
    [⋯をろうばいさせる].

confront (*vt.*) ...ni chokumen-suru [⋯に直面する].

confuse (*vt.*) 1) ...o kondô-suru [⋯を混同する]. 2) ...o mago-tsukaseru
    [⋯をまごつかせる].

  become confused men-kurau

confusion (*n.*) konran [混乱]; rôbai [ろうばい].

congratulate (*vt.*) ...o iwau [⋯を祝う].

congratulation (*n.*) 1) shukuga [祝賀]. 2)(*pl.*) shukuji [祝辞].
    (*int.*) O-medetô!

congress (*n.*) 1) taikai [大会]. 2)((*US*))(C-)kokkai [国会].

conjecture (*vt. & n.*) ...o suisoku-suru(suisoku) [⋯を推測する(推測)].

conjugation (*n.*) (*gram.*) (dôshi no) katsuyô [(動詞の)活用].

conjunction (*n.*) 1)(*gram.*) setsuzoku-shi [接続詞]. 2)ketsugô [結合];
    renketsu [連結].

connect (*vt.*) 1) ...o tsunagu [⋯をつなぐ]. 2) ...to kankei-zukeru [⋯
    と関係づける].

  be connected with ...to kankei-ga-aru

connection (*n.*) 1) setsuzoku [接続]; renraku [連絡]. 2) kankei [関係].
    in connection with ...ni-kanren-shite; ...to-renraku-shite

conquer (*vt.*) ...o seifuku-suru [⋯を征服する]; ...ni uchi-katsu [⋯に
    打ち勝つ].

conqueror (*n.*) seifuku-sha [征服者].

conquest (*n.*) seifuku [征服].

conscience (*n.*) ryôshin [良心].

conscientious (*a.*) ryôshin-teki-na [良心的な]; memmitsu-na [綿密な].

conscious (*a.*) ishiki-shite-iru [意識している]; jikaku-shite-iru [自覚し
    ている].

consciousness (*n.*) 1) ishiki [意識]; kizuku-koto [気づくこと]. 2)
    jikaku [自覚].

consensus (*n.*) konsensasu [コンセンサス]; kankei-sha-no-sôi [関係者
    の総意].

consent (*vi.*) dôi-suru [同意する]; shôdaku-suru [承諾する].
    They **consented** to the demand.
      Kare-ra-wa sono-yôkyû-ni *dôi-shita*.
      (*n.*) dôi [同意]; shôdaku [承諾].

　　　The Diet passed the bill with one **consent**.
　　　Kokkai wa manjô-*itchi*-de sono gian-o kaketsu-shita.

consequence (*n.*) 1)kekka [結果]. 2)jûyô-sei [重要性].
　in consequence of ...no-kekka

consequential (*a.*) hitsuzen-no [必然の]; jûyô-na [重要な].

consequently (*ad.*) sono-kekka [その結果]; shitagatte [従って].

conservative (*a.*) hoshu-teki-na [保守的な].

consider (*vt.*) 1)...o yoku-kangaeru [⋯をよく考える]. 2)...o...to mi-nasu [⋯を⋯と見なす].
　　　　　(*vi.*) yoku-kangaeru [よく考える].

considerable (*a.*) kanari-no [かなりの].

considerate (*a.*) omoi-yari-no-aru [思いやりのある].

consideration (*n.*) kôryo [考慮]; kôsatsu [考察].
　under consideration kôryo-chû

considering (*prep.*) ...o-kangaeru-to [⋯を考えると]; ...nimo-kakawa-razu [⋯にもかかわらず].
　　　　　　(*conj.*) ...de-aru-koto-o-kangaereba [⋯であることを考えれば].

consignment (*n.*) itaku[-hambai] [委託(販売)].

consist (*vi.*) 1)...(kara-)naru [⋯(から)なる]. 2)...(ni-)aru [⋯(に)ある].
　consist in ...ni-aru
　consist of ...kara-naru

consistency (*n.*) 1)ikkan-sei [一貫性]. 2)nôdo [濃度].

consistent (*a.*) ikkan-shita [一貫した]; mujun-shi-nai [矛盾しない].

consolation (*n.*) nagusame [慰め].

consonant (*n.*) (*phon.*) shiin [子音].

conspicuous (*a.*) medatsu [目立つ]; kencho-na [顕著な].

constant (*a.*) kawara-nai [変わらない]; taema-no-nai [絶え間のない].

constantly (*ad.*) taezu [絶えず]; shiba-shiba [しばしば].

constellation (*n.*) (*astron.*) seiza [星座].

constipation (*n.*) bempi [便秘].

constituency (*n.*) senkyo-min [選挙民].

constituent (*n.*) 1)seibun [成分]. 2)yûken-sha [有権者].

constitute (*vt.*) 1)...o kôsei-suru [⋯を構成する]. 2)...ni nimmei-suru [⋯に任命する]. 3)...o seitei-suru [⋯を制定する].

constitution (*n.*) 1)kôsei [構成]. 2)taikaku [体格]. 3)kempô [憲法].

constraint (*n.*) 1)kyôsei [強制]. 2)kyûkutsu [窮屈]; ki-gane [気がね].

construct (*vt.*) ...o kenzô-suru [...を建造する]; ...o kensetsu-suru [...を建設する].

construction (*n.*) kenzô[-butsu] [建造(物)]; (*gram.*) kôzo [構造].
  under construction kenchiku-chû; kôji-chû

consul (*n.*) ryôji [領事].

consul general sô-ryôji [総領事].

consulate (*n.*) ryôji-kan [領事館].

consult (*vt.*) 1)...ni sôdan-suru [...に相談する]. 2)(isha)-ni kakaru [(医者)にかかる]. 3)(jisho)-o hiku [(辞書)を引く].
  (*1*) I must **consult** my parents.
      Watashi-wa ryôshin-*ni sôdan-shi*-nakereba-naranai.
  (*2*) You had better **consult** the doctor.
      Anata-wa isha-*ni mite-moratta*-hô-ga-yoi.
  (*3*) Did you **consult** this dictionary?
      Kono jisho-*o hikimashita*-ka?
      (*vi.*) sôdan-suru [相談する].

consultation (*n.*) sôdan [相談]; shinsatsu [診察].

consulting room shinsatsu-shitsu [診察室].

consume (*vt.*) 1)...o shôhi-suru [...を消費する]. 2)...o yaki-tsukusu [...を焼き尽くす]; ...o tabe-tsukusu [...を食べ尽くす]; ...o nomi-tsukusu [...を飲み尽くす].
  (*2*) The flames **consumed** the whole warehouse.
      Kasai ga sono sôko-*o* sukkari *yaki-tsukushita*.

consumer (*n.*) shôhi-sha [消費者].

consumer resistance kôbai-kyohi [購買拒否].

consumption (*n.*) shôhi [消費].

consumptive (*a.*) shôhi-no [消費の].

contact (*n.*) sesshoku [接触].
  come into contact with ...to sesshoku-suru

contagious (*a.*) densen-sei-no [伝染性の].

contain (*vt.*) 1)...o fukumu [...を含む]; ...ga haitte-iru [...が入っている]. 2)...o osaeru [...を抑える].
  (*1*) The book **contains** lots of pictures.
      Sono hon niwa takusan-no e-*ga haitte-iru*.
  (*2*) I could not **contain** myself for joy.
      Watashi-wa ureshiku-te jibun-*o osaeru*-koto-ga-deki-nakatta.
      Watashi-wa ureshiku-te-tamara-nakatta.

contaminate (*vt.*) ...o osen-suru [...を汚染する].

contemporary (*a.*) 1)gendai-no［現代の］. 2)dô-jidai-no［同時代の］.

contempt (*n.*) keibetsu［軽べつ］.

contemptuous (*a.*) keibetsu-shite［軽べつして］.

contend (*vi.*) arasou［争う］.

content (*n.*) 1)(*pl.*) naka-mi［中身］. 2)(*pl.*) naiyô［内容］. 3)(*pl.*) mokuji［目次］.

content (*n.*) manzoku［満足］.

  to one's heart's content kokoro-yuku-made

      (*vt.*) ...o manzoku-saseru［…を満足させる］.

contest (*n.*) kyôsô［競争］; kyôgi［競技］; kontesuto［コンテスト］.

continent (*n.*) tairiku［大陸］.

continual (*a.*) himpan-na［頻繁な］.

continually (*ad.*) taezu［絶えず］; himpan-ni［頻繁に］.

continue (*vt. & vi.*) ...o tsuzukeru (tsuzuku)［…を続ける(続く)］.

     I **continued** to do so. Watashi-wa sô shi-*tsuzuketa*.

     To be **continued**. Ika-jigô.

     It **continued** an hour. Sore-wa ichi-jikan *tsuzuita*.

continuous (*a.*) taema-no-nai［絶え間のない］.

contraband (*n. & a.*) 1)mitsuyu-hin［密輸品］; fuhô-torihiki［不法取引］. 2)kinsei-no［禁制の］.

contract (*n.*) keiyaku［契約］.

     (*vt. & vi.*) 1)(...o) keiyaku-suru［(…を)契約する］. 2)...o chijimaseru (chijimaru)［…を縮ませる(縮まる)］.

contradiction (*n.*) 1)hambaku［反ばく］. 2)mujun［矛盾］.

  in contradiction to ...to-sei-hantai-ni; ...to-mujun-shite

contradictory (*a.*) mujun-shita［矛盾した］.

contrary (*n. & a.*) hantai(-no)［反対(の)］.

  on the contrary sore-dokoro-ka

contrast (*n.*) taishô［対照］.

     (*vt. & vi.*) ...o taishô-saseru (yoi-taishô-o-nasu)［…を対照させる(よい対照をなす)］.

contribute (*vt. & vi.*) 1)(...ni) kiyo-suru［(…に)寄与する］. 2)(...ni) kikô-suru［(…に)寄稿する］.

contribution (*n.*) 1)kôken［貢献］; kiyo［寄与］. 2)kikô［寄稿］.

contrive (*vt.*) 1)...o kufû-suru［…を工夫する］. 2)dô-nika...(suru)［どうにか…(する)］.

control (*vt.*) ...o tôsei-suru［…を統制する］; ...o yokusei-suru［…を抑制する］.

　　　(n.) tôsei [統制]; yokusei [抑制]; (*baseball*) kontorôru [コントロール].

controversy (*n.*) ronsô [論争]; giron [議論].

contusion (*n.*) daboku-shô [打撲傷].

convenience (*n.*) benri [便利]; kô-tsugô [好都合].

　for convenience' sake　bengi-jô

convenient (*a.*) benri-na [便利な]; tsugô-no-yoi [都合のよい].

convention (*n.*) 1)shûkai [集会]; daihyô-sha-kaigi [代表者会議]. 2) kyôtei [協定]. 3)shikitari [しきたり]; inshû [因習].

conventional (*a.*) inshû-teki-na [因習的な]; kata-ni-hamatta [型にはまった].

conversation (*n.*) kaiwa [会話]; zadan [座談].

conversational (*a.*) kaiwa-no [会話の]; hanashi-zuki-no [話し好きの].

convert (*vt.*) 1)...ni kaeru [...に変える]. 2)...ni kaishû-saseru [...に改宗させる].

　　　(n.) kaishû-sha [改宗者].

convey (*vt.*) 1)...o yusô-suru [...を輸送する]. 2)(shisô ya kanjô)-o tsutaeru [(思想や感情)を伝える].

conveyance (*n.*) yusô[-kikan] [輸送(機関)]; dentatsu [伝達].

conviction (*n.*) 1)kakushin [確信]. 2)(*law*) yûzai-no-hanketsu [有罪の判決].

convince (*vt.*) ...o kakushin-saseru [...を確信させる]; ...o nattoku-saseru [...を納得させる].

convincing (*a.*) settoku-ryoku-no-aru [説得力のある].

convulsions (*n.*) (*med.*) keiren [けいれん]; hikitsuke [ひきつけ].

cook (*vt. & vi.*) (...o) ryôri-suru [(...を)料理する].

　　　(n.) ryôri-nin [料理人]; kokku [コック].

cooking (*n.*) ryôri[-hô] [料理(法)].

cool (*a.*) 1)suzushii [涼しい]. 2)reitan-na [冷淡な]. 3)zûzûshii [ずうずうしい].

　(*1*) It is **cool** here.　Koko-wa *suzushii*.

　(*2*) She is **cool** toward him.　Kano-jo-wa kare-ni *reitan*-da.

　(*3*) He is a **cool** hand.　Kare-wa *zûzûshii*.

　　　(*vt.*) ...o hiyasu [...を冷やす].

coolly (*ad.*) tsumetaku [つめたく]; reitan-ni [冷淡に].

cooperate (*vi.*) kyôdô-suru [協同する].

cooperation (*n.*) kyôdô [協同].

　in cooperation with　...to-kyôdô-shite

cooperative (*a.*) kyôdô-no [協同の]; kyôdô-kumiai-no [協同組合の].
　　　　(*n.*) seikatsu-kyôdô-kumiai [生活協同組合].
cooperative society seikatsu-kyôdô-kumiai [生活協同組合]; shôhi-kumiai [消費組合].
coordinate (*a.*) dôtô-no [同等の]; dôkaku-no [同格の].
　　　　(*vt.*) ...o chôsei-suru [⋯を調整する].
cope (*vi.*) taikô-suru [対抗する].
copper (*n.*) dô [銅]; dôka [銅貨].
copy (*n.*) 1)utsushi [写し]; fukusha [複写]. 2)(shomotsu no)issatsu [(書物の)一冊]. 3)(insatsu-yô no) genkô [(印刷用の)原稿].
　　　　(*vt.*) ...o utsusu [⋯を写す]; ...o fukusha-suru [⋯を複写する].
copyright (*n.*) hanken [版権].
coral (*n. & a.*) sango(-no) [さんご(の)].
coral reef sango-shô [さんご礁].
cord (*n.*) himo [ひも]; (*elect.*) côdo [コード].
　　vocal cords seitai [声帯]
cordially (*ad.*) kokoro-kara [心から].
　　Cordially yours, *Keigu*
corduroy (*n.*) kôruten [コールテン]; (*pl.*) kôruten-no-zubon [コールテンのズボン].
core (*n.*) 1)(kudamono no) shin [(くだものの)芯]. 2)kakushin [核心].
　　to the core tettei-teki-ni
cork (*n.*) koruku[-no-sen] [コルク(の栓)].
corkscrew (*n.*) koruku-sen-nuki [コルク栓抜き].
corn (*n.*) 1)kokumotsu [穀物]. 2)((US)) tômorokoshi [トウモロコシ]; ((Eng.)) ko-mugi [小麦].
corn (*n.*) uo-no-me [うおの目].
corner (*n.*) 1)kado [かど]. 2)sumi [隅].
　　(*1*) The drugstore stands at the **corner** of the street.
　　　　Doraggu-sutoâ wa kono-toori-no-*kado*-ni aru.
　　(*2*) There was a small desk in the **corner** of the room.
　　　　Heya-no-*sumi*-ni chiisai tsukue-ga hitotsu atta.
　　drive...into a corner ...o kyûchi-ni-oi-komu
cornflower (*n.*) (*bot.*) yaguruma-giku [ヤグルマギク].
corolla (*n.*) (*bot.*) kakan [花冠].
corporation (*n.*) hôjin [法人]; ((US)) yûgen-gaisha [有限会社].
corps (*n.*) 1)(*mil.*) gundan [軍団]. 2)dantai [団体].
corpse (*n.*) shitai [死体].

correct (*a.*) seikaku-na [正確な].

(*vt.*) …o teisei-suru […を訂正する].

correspond (*vi.*) 1) fugô-suru [符合する]; taiô-suru [対応する]. 2) buntsû-suru [文通する].

(*1*) Words **correspond** to those ideas which we have.

Go wa ware-ware-no-motte-iru-kannen-ni *taiô-suru*.

(*2*) He **corresponds** with his teacher.

Kare-wa onshi-to *buntsû-shite-iru*.

correspondence (*n.*) 1) buntsû [文通]; tsûshin [通信]; tsûshin-bun [通信文]. 2) fugô [符合]; itchi [一致].

correspondent (*n.*) 1) tsûshin-in [通信員]; buntsû-sha [文通者]. 2) (*com.*) torihiki-saki [取引先].

corresponding (*a.*) 1) fugô-suru [符合する]. 2) tsûshin-suru [通信する].

corridor (*n.*) (*arch.*) rôka [廊下].

corrugated paper dan-bôru-shi [段ボール紙].

corrupt (*a.*) daraku-shita [堕落した]; taihai-shita [退廃した].

cosmic (*a.*) uchû-no [宇宙の].

cosmic rays uchû-sen [宇宙線].

cosmonaut (*n.*) uchû-hikô-shi [宇宙飛行士].

cosmos (*n.*) uchû [宇宙].

cosmos (*n.*) (*bot.*) kosumosu [コスモス].

cost (*vt.*) (hiyô ya rôryoku)-ga kakaru [(費用や労力)が掛かる]; (hito)-ni shuppi-o-kakeru [(人)に出費を掛ける].

(*n.*) 1) hiyô [費用]. 2) genka [原価]. 3) gisei [犠牲].

at any cost donna-gisei-o-haratte-mo

costly (*a.*) kôka-na [高価な].

costume (*n.*) fukusô [服装]; (jidai ya kokumin ya chihô-tokuyû no) ishô [(時代や国民や地方特有の)衣装].

cot (*n.*) kan'i-beddo [簡易ベッド].

cottage (*n.*) 1) shô-jûtaku [小住宅]. 2) ((US)) shô-bessô [小別荘].

cotton (*n.*) 1) (*bot.*) wata [綿]. 2) mempu [綿布].

cough (*n.*) seki [せき]; gohon [ゴホン].

(*vi.*) seki-o-suru [せきをする].

council (*n.*) 1) hyôgi-kai [評議会]. 2) chihô-gikai [地方議会].

counsel (*n.*) 1) sôdan [相談]. 2) jogen [助言].

take counsel (**with**) …(to) sôdan-suru

counsel(l)or (*n.*) jogen-sha [助言者]; komon [顧問]; ((US)) bengo-shi [弁護士].

count (*vt.*) ...o kazoeru […を数える].

    (*vi.*) 1)kazu-o-kazoeru [数を数える]. 2)jûyô-de-aru [重要である].

  count...as ...o ...to mi-nasu

  count in ...o kanjô-ni-ireru

  count on ...o ate-ni-suru

  count out (*colloq.*) ...o jogai-suru

count (*n.*) (Eikoku-igai-no) hakushaku [(英国以外の)伯爵].

countenance (*n.*) kao-tsuki [顔つき]; hyôjô [表情].

counter (*n.*) kanjô-dai [勘定台]; kauntâ [カウンター].

counteract (*vt.*) 1)...ni sakarau […に逆らう]. 2)...o chûwa-suru […を中和する].

counterclockwise (*a. & ad.*) hidari-mawari-no(-ni) [左回りの(に)].

counterfeit (*a.*) mozô-no [模造の]; nise-no [偽の].

    (*n.*) mozô-hin [模造品]; nise-mono [偽物].

    (*vt.*) ...o mozô-suru […を模造する]; ...no nise-mono-o-tsukuru […の偽物を作る].

countless (*a.*) musû-no [無数の].

country (*n.*) 1)kuni [国]. 2)(the -) inaka [田舎]. 3)chihô [地方].

  (*1*) There are so many **countries** in the world.

    Sekai-niwa totemo takusan-no *kuni*-ga-aru.

  (*2*) He has gone to the **country**. Kare-wa *inaka*-e itta.

countryman (*n.*) dôkyô-jin [同郷人].

countryside (*n.*) inaka [田舎]; den'en [田園].

countrywide (*a.*) zenkoku-teki-na [全国的な].

county (*n.*) 1)((*US*)) gun [郡]. 2)((*Eng.*)) shû [州].

couple (*n.*) 1)ittui [一対]; hito-kumi [一組]. 2)fûfu [夫婦].

  (*2*) The new **couple** lived in the city.

    Shin-*fûfu* wa tokai-ni sunda.

  a couple of days ni-san-nichi

coupon (*n.*) kûpon [クーポン].

courage (*n.*) yûki [勇気].

course (*n.*) 1)shinkô [進行]; nari-yuki [成り行き]. 2)katei [課程]. 3)(shokuji no) hito-shina [(食事の)一品].

  (*1*) Be attentive to the **course** of events.

    Jiken-no-*nari-yuki*-ni chûi-shi-nasai.

  (*2*) He completed the junior high school **course**.

    Kare-wa chûgaku-no-*katei*-o oeta.

  (*3*) I took a five-**course** dinner(a dinner of five **courses**).

      Watashi-wa go-*shina*-no-shokuji-o shita.

a matter of course tôzen-no-koto

in the course of ...no-aida-ni

of course mochiron

court (*n.*) 1)saiban-sho [裁判所]; hôtei [法廷]. 2)kyûtei [宮廷]. 3) naka-niwa [中庭]; (*tennis and basketball*) kôto [コート].

  (*1*) He appeared in **court**. Kare-wa shut*tei*-shita.

  (*2*) He went to Court. Kare-wa *kyûchû*-e itta.

  (*3*) The school has a large **court**.

      Gakkô niwa ookina *kôto*-ga aru.

courtesy (*n.*) reigi [礼儀]; teinei [丁寧].

cousin (*n.*) itoko [いとこ].

    a second **cousin** mata-*itoko*

cover (*vt.*) 1)...o oou [...を覆う]; ...o tsutsumu [...を包む]. 2)(aru kyori)-o iku [(ある距離)を行く]. 3)...o tsugunau [...を償う]. 4)...o hôdô-suru [...を報道する].

  (*1*) The top of the mountain **is covered** with snow.

      Sono yama no itadaki wa yuki-de *oowarete-iru*.

  (*2*) An express train **covers** the distance in two hours.

      Kyûkô-ressha wa sono kyori-o ni-jikan-de *hashiru*.

  (*3*) It is enough to **cover** the loss.

      Sore-wa sonshitsu-o *tsugunau*-ni-taru.

  (*4*) He **covered** the accident. Kare-wa sono jiko-o *hôdô-shita*.

    (*n.*) futa [ふた]; ooi [覆い]; (hon no) hyôshi [(本の)表紙]; fûtô [封筒].

    I sent mother a note under a separate **cover**.

      Watashi-wa haha-ni bep*pû*-de tegami-o dashita.

covet (*vt.*) ...o hidoku-hoshigaru [...をひどく欲しがる].

cow (*n.*) me-ushi [雌牛]; nyûgyû [乳牛].

coward (*n.*) okubyô-mono [おく病者]; hikyô-mono [卑きょう者].

cowardice, cowardliness (*n.*) okubyô [おく病]; hikyô [卑きょう].

cowardly (*a. & ad.*) okubyô-na(-ni) [おく病な(に)].

cozy (*a.*) igokochi-no-yoi [居心地のよい].

crab (*n.*) (*zool.*) kani [カニ].

crack (*n.*) 1)pachi! [ぱち!]. 2)hibi [ひび].

    (*vi.*) pachi-tto-iu [ぱちっという]; wareru [割れる].

    (*vt.*) ...o pachi-tto-narasu [...をぱちっと鳴らす]; ...o waru [... を割る].

(*ad.*) pachi-tto [ぱちっと].

cracker (*n.*) 1)kurakkâ [クラッカー]. 2)bakuchiku [爆竹].

cradle (*n.*) yuri-kago [揺りかご].

craft (*n.*) 1)gijutsu [技術]. 2)fune [船].

craftsman (*n.*) shokunin [職人].

craft union shokugyô-betsu-rôdô-kumiai [職業別労働組合].

crafty (*a.*) zurui [ずるい]; waru-gashikoi [悪賢い].

cram (*vt. & vi.*) (*colloq.*)...ni tsume-komi-benkyô-o-saseru (tsume-komi-benkyô-o-suru) [...に詰め込み勉強をさせる(詰め込み勉強をする)].

cramp (*vt.*) 1)(*med.*)...ni keiren-o-okosu [...にけいれんを起こす]. 2)(*arch.*)...o kasugai-de-tomeru [...をかすがいで留める].
  (*n.*) keiren [けいれん]; komura-gaeri [こむら返り].

crane (*n.*) 1)(*birds*) tsuru [ツル]. 2)(*mech.*) kijû-ki [起重機]; kurên [クレーン].

crape (*n.*) kurêpu [クレープ]; chirimen [ちりめん]; kurêpu-no-moshô [クレープの喪章].

crash (*n.*) susamajii-oto [すさまじい音].
  (*vi.*) gara-gara-kudakeru [がらがら砕ける]; tsuiraku-suru [墜落する].
  (*vt.*)...o kowasu [...を壊す].

crater (*n.*) funka-kô [噴火口]; kurêtâ [クレーター].

crave (*vt. & vi.*) (...o) setsubô-suru [(...を)切望する].

crawl (*vi.*) hau [はう]; noro-noro-susumu [のろのろ進む].
  (*n.*) (*swim.*) kurôru [クロール].

crayon (*n.*) kureyon [クレヨン].

crazy (*a.*) 1)kyôki-jimita [狂気じみた]. 2)netchû-shite-iru [熱中している]; muchû-de-aru [夢中である].

creak (*vi. & vt.*) kishimu (...o kishimaseru) [きしむ(...をきしませる)].

cream puff shûkurîmu [シュークリーム].

creamy (*a.*) kurîmu-jô-no [クリーム状の].

create (*vt.*)...o sôzô-suru [...を創造する]; ...o sôsetsu-suru [...を創設する].
  God **created** the heaven and the earth.
    Kami ga ten to chi-o *sôzô-shita*.

creation (*n.*) 1)sôzô [創造]. 2)sôzô-butsu [創造物]; sôsaku-hin [創作品].

creative (*a.*) sôzô-teki-na [創造的な].

creator (*n.*) sôzô-sha [創造者].

creature (*n.*) 1)dôbutsu [動物]; iki-mono [生き物]. 2)hito [人];
   yatsu [やつ].
   (*1*) Living **creatures** are all mortal.   *Iki-mono* wa subete shinu.
   (*2*) Poor **creature**.   Kawaisô-na-*yatsu*.
credible (*a.*) shin'yô-dekiru [信用できる].
credit (*n.*) 1)shin'yô [信用]. 2)meiyo [名誉]; meiyo-to-naru-mono
   [名誉となるもの]. 3)kake-uri [掛け売り]. 4)(*bkpg.*) kashi-kata [貸方].
   (*1*) **Credit** is everything to them.
       Kare-ra-niwa *shin'yô* ga daiichi-da.
   (*2*) Such a student is a **credit** to our school.
       Kono-yô-na seito wa waga-kô-no *meiyo* da.
   (*3*) No **credit** is given in this store.
       Tô-ten-de-wa *kake-uri* wa itashi-ma-sen.
   on credit   kake-de; shin'yô-gashi-de
       (*vt.*) 1)...o shin'yô-suru [...を信用する]. 2)...no kashi-kata-ni-
   kinyû-suru [...の貸方に記入する].
creditor (*n.*) saiken-sha [債権者].
creed (*n.*) shinjô [信条].
creek (*n.*) irie [入り江].
creep (*vi.*) hau [はう]; shinobi-yoru [忍び寄る].
creeper (*n.*) 1)hau-mono [はうもの]. 2)(*bot.*) tsuru-shokubutsu [つ
   る植物].
crescent (*n.*) mika-zuki [三日月].
crest (*n.*) 1)tosaka [とさか]. 2)sanchô [山頂]. 3)nami-gashira [波が
   しら].
crevasse (*n.*) (hyôga no fukai) ware-me [(氷河の深い)割れ目];
   kurebasu [クレバス].
crew (*n.*) jôin [乗員].
cricket (*n.*) (*insect*) koorogi [コオロギ].
crime (*n.*) hanzai [犯罪]; tsumi [罪].
criminal (*a.*) hanzai-no [犯罪の].
   (*n.*) hannin [犯人].
crimson (*n. & a.*) shinkô-shoku(-no) [深紅色(の)].
cripple (*n.*) shintai-shôgai-sha [身体障害者].
   (*vt.*) ...no-te-ashi-o-fu-jiyû-ni-suru [...の手足を不自由にする].
crisis (*n.*) kiki [危機]; jûdai-na-wakare-me [重大な分かれ目].
crisp (*a.*) 1)(shokumotsu ya kami ga) pari-pari-suru [(食物や紙が)
   ぱりぱりする]. 2)(tenki no) suga-suga-shii [(天気の)すがすがしい].

criterion (*n.*) kijun [基準].

critic (*n.*) hihyô-ka [批評家]; hyôron-ka [評論家].

critical (*a.*) 1)hihan-teki-na [批判的な]. 2)kikyû-no [危急の]; kitoku-no [危篤の].

criticize (*vt. & vi.*) (...o) hihyô-suru [···を批評する].

croak (*n. & vi.*) (karasu ya kaeru ga) kâkâ, gâgâ(-naku) [(カラスやカエルが)かーかー, がーがー(鳴く)].

crocodile (*n.*) (*zool.*) wani [ワニ].

crook (*n.*) 1)jizai-kagi [自在かぎ]. 2)wankyoku [湾曲].
　　(*vt.*) ...o mageru [···を曲げる].

crooked (*a.*) 1)magatta [曲がった]. 2)fusei-na [不正な].

crop (*n.*) 1)sakumotsu [作物]. 2)shûkaku-daka [収穫高].
　　(*1*) This weather is not good for the **crop**.
　　　　Kono tenki wa *sakumotsu*-ni-yoku-nai.
　　(*2*) The wheat **crop** was very good this year.
　　　　Kotoshi-wa ko-mugi-no *shûkaku* ga taihen yokatta.

cross (*n.*) jûji-ka [十字架]. 2)(*colloq.*) fu-kigen-na [不機嫌な].
　　(*a.*) 1)kôsa-shita [交差した]. 2)(*colloq.*) fu-kigen-na [不機嫌な].
　　(*vt.*) 1)...o yoko-giru [···を横切る]; ...o-wataru [···を渡る]. 2)
　　(– oneself) mune-no-mae-de-jûji-o-kiru [胸の前で十字を切る].
　　cross over wataru

crossbar (*n.*) yoko-gi [横木].

crossing (*n.*) 1)ôdan [横断]. 2)kôsa-ten [交差点]; ôdan-hodô [横断歩道].

crossroads (*n.*) jûji-ro [十字路]; kôsa-ten [交差点].

crouch (*vi.*) uzukumaru [うずくまる]; kagamu [かがむ].

crow (*n.*) karasu [カラス].

crow (*vi.*) (ondori ga) toki-o-tsugeru [(おんどりが)時を告げる].

crowd (*n.*) gunshû [群衆]; hito-gomi [人込み].
　　(*vi.*) muragaru [群がる]; oshi-kakeru [押しかける].
　　(*vt.*) ...ni muragaru [···に群がる]; ...o gisshiri-tsumeru [···をぎっしり詰める].

crowded (*a.*) komi-atta [込み合った]; man'in-no [満員の].

crown (*n.*) 1)ôkan [王冠]; ôi [王位]. 2)eikan [栄冠]; eiyo [栄誉].
　　(*vt.*) 1)...ni ôkan-o-sazukeru [···に王冠を授ける]; ...o ôi-ni-tsukaseru [···を王位につかせる]. 2)...o eiyo-de-kazaru [···を栄誉で飾る]; ...ni mukuiru [···に報いる].
　　(*1*) She **was crowned** queen. Kano-jo-wa joô-*ni* taterareta.

(2) His labour **was crowned** with success.

      Kare-no doryoku wa seikô-o-motte *mukui-rareta*.

crowning (*a.*) saikô-no [最高の].

crucial (*a.*) kettei-teki-na [決定的な]; inochi-ni-kakawaru [命にかかわる].

crude (*a.*) 1)tennen-no-mama-no [天然のままの]. 2)soya-na [粗野な].

cruel (*a.*) zankoku-na [残酷な].

cruelty (*n.*) 1)zankoku [残酷]. 2)zankoku-na-kôi [残酷な行為].

cruise (*n.*) junkô [巡航].

      (*vi.*) 1)junkô-suru [巡航する]. 2)(takushî nado ga) nagasu [(タクシーなどが)流す].

crumb (*n.*) (*pl.*) pan-kuzu [パンくず].

crumble (*vi.*) boro-boro-ni-kuzureru [ぼろぼろに崩れる].

      (*vt.*) ...o kudaku […を砕く].

crush (*vt.*) ...o oshi-tsubusu […を押しつぶす].

crust (*n.*) 1)pan-no-mimi [パンの耳]. 2)katai-gaihi [堅い外皮].

crutch (*n.*) matsuba-zue [松葉づえ].

cry (*vi.*) 1)sakebu [叫ぶ]. 2)naku [泣く].

    (2) The infant **cried** for milk. Yôji wa chichi-o-motomete *naita*.

      (*vt.*) 1)oogoe-de-sakebu [大声で叫ぶ]. 2)(– oneself) naite...(shite)-shimau [泣いて…(して)しまう].

    (2) He **cried** himself to sleep. Kare-wa *naki*-nagara-nemu*tta*.

      (*n.*) 1)sakebi [叫び]. 2)naki-goe [泣き声].

crybaby (*n.*) naki-mushi [泣き虫].

crystal (*n. & a.*) suishô(-no) [水晶(の)].

crystallize (*vt. & vi.*) ...o kesshô-saseru (kesshô-suru) […を結晶させる(結晶する)]; (...o) gutai-ka-suru [(…を)具体化する].

cube (*n.*) rippô-tai [立方体].

cube sugar kaku-zatô [角砂糖].

cubic (*a.*) rippô-tai-no [立方体の].

cuckoo (*n.*) kakkô [カッコウ].

cucumber (*n.*) (*bot.*) kyûri [キュウリ].

cue (*n.*) kikkake [きっかけ]; aizu [合図].

cuff (*n.*) sode-guchi [そで口]; kafusu [カフス].

cuff links kafusu-botan [カフスボタン].

cuisine (*n.*) ryôri[-ho] [料理(法)].

cultivate (*vt.*) 1)...o tagayasu […を耕す]. 2)(sainô ya shûkan)-o yashinau [(才能や習慣)を養う].

cultivated (*a.*) 1)tagayasareta [耕された]. 2)kyôyô-no-aru [教養のある].

cultivation (*n.*) 1)kôsaku [耕作]. 2)yôsei [養成]. 3)kyôyô [教養].

culture (*n.*) 1)kyôyô [教養]. 2)bunka [文化].

cunning (*a.*) zurui [ずるい]; kôkatsu-na [こうかつな].

cup (*n.*) 1)chawan [茶わん]; chawan-ippai-bun [茶わん一杯分]. 2)
syôhai [賞杯]; kappu [カップ]. 3)(*bot.*) gaku [がく].

  (*1*) Give me a **cup** of tea, please. O-*cha*-o *ippai* kudasai.

  (*2*) He was given a golden **cup**. Kare-wa kim*pai*-o juyo-sareta.

  (*3*) This is a **cup** of the flower.

       Kore-wa sono hana no *gaku* da.

cupboard (*n.*) 1)shokki-dana [食器棚]. 2)((*Eng.*)) to-dana [戸棚].

cure (*n.*) 1)kaifuku [回復]. 2)chiryô[-hô] [治療(法)].

  (*vt.*) ...o chiryô-suru […を治療する].

curiosity (*n.*) sensaku-zuki [せんさく好き]; kôki-shin [好奇心].

  out of curiosity kôki-shin-ni-kararete

curious (*a.*) 1)sensaku-zuki-na [せんさく好きな]. (...shi-)tagaru [(…
し)たがる]. 2)kimyô-na [奇妙な].

  (*1*) He is **curious** to hear such stories.

       Kare-wa sonna hanashi-o kiki-*tagaru*.

  (*2*) That is a **curious** tale. Sore-wa *kimyô-na* hanashi da.

curl (*n.*) maki-ge [巻き毛].

  (*vt.*) ...o maki-ge-ni-suru […を巻き毛にする]; ...o kâru-suru […
をカールする].

  (*vi.*) 1)maki-ge-ni-naru [巻き毛になる]; kâru-suru [カールする].
2)magari-kuneru [曲がりくねる]. 3)rasen-jô-ni-naru [ら旋状になる].

curly (*a.*) maki-ge-no [巻き毛の].

currant (*n.*) (ko-tsubu no tane-nashi) hoshi-budô [(小粒の種なし)干
しブドウ].

currency (*n.*) 1)tsûka [通貨]. 2)ryûtsû [流通].

current (*n.*) 1)nagare [流れ]. 2)(*elect.*) denryû [電流]. 3)fûchô [風
潮].

  (*a.*) 1)genzai-no [現在の]. 2)ryûtsû-shite-iru [流通している].

current account tôza-yokin [当座預金] = checking account.

curriculum (*n.*) kyôka-katei [教科課程]; karikyuramu [カリキュラム].

curry (*n.*) karê-ryôri [カレー料理]; karê-ko [カレー粉].

curse (*n.*) noroi [のろい].

  (*vt. & vi.*) (...o) norou [(…を)のろう].

curve (*n.*) magari [曲がり]; kyokusen [曲線]; (*baseball*) kâbu [カーブ].

    (*vt. & vi.*) ...o mageru (magaru) [...を曲げる(曲がる)].

cushion (*n.*) kusshon [クッション]; shôgeki-o-yawarageru-mono [衝撃を和らげるもの].

custom (*n.*) 1)fûshû [風習]; shûkan [習慣]. 2)tokui-saki [得意先]. 3)(*pl.*) kanzei [関税].

customer (*n.*) tokui-saki [得意先].

customhouse (*n.*) zeikan [税関].

cut (*vt. & vi.*) ...o kiru (kireru) [...を切る(切れる)].

  cut and run (*colloq.*) oo-isogi-de-nige-saru

  cut in   wari-komu

  cut off   ...o kiri-toru

      He cut off a branch of the tree.

        Kare-wa sono ki no eda-o ippon kiri-totta.

  cut out   1)...o kiri-nuku.   2)(*colloq.*)...o yameru

    1)He cut the editorial out of the newspaper.

       Kare-wa shimbun-kara sono shasetsu-o kiri-nuita.

    2)He cut out drinking.   Kare-wa sake-o-yameta.

  cut to pieces   zuta-zuta-ni-kiru

cute (*a.*) 1)((*US*)) kawaii [かわいい]. 2)nuke-me-no-nai [抜け目のない].

cutlery (*n.*) ha-mono-rui [刃物類].

cutlet (*n.*) katsuretsu [カツレツ].

cutter (*n.*) 1)saidan-shi [裁断師]. 2)(*marine*)(gunkan no) kattâ [(軍艦の)カッター].

cutting (*n.*) 1)setsudan [切断]. 2)kiri-nuki [切り抜き].

    (*a.*) mi-o-kiru-yô-na [身を切るような]; shinratsu-na [辛らつな].

cycle (*n.*) 1)shûki [周期]. 2)jitensha [自転車].

cycling (*n.*) saikuringu [サイクリング].

cyclone (*n.*) oo-tatsumaki [大竜巻].

cynical (*a.*) hiniku-na [皮肉な].

D

dad (*n.*) tô-chan [とうちゃん].

daddy (*n.*) = dad.

daffodil (*n.*) (*bot.*) rappa-zuisen [ラッパズイセン].

dahlia (*n.*) (*bot.*) daria [ダリア].

daily (*ad. & a.*) hibi(-no) [日々(の)]; mai-nichi(-no) [毎日(の)].
　　　(*n.*) nikkan-shimbun [日刊新聞].

dainty (*a.*) 1)oishii [おいしい]. 2)yûbi-na [優美な].

dairy (*n.*) rakunô-jô [酪農場]; nyû-seihin-hambai-sho [乳製品販売所].

daisy (*n.*) (*bot.*) hinagiku [ヒナギク]; deijî [デイジー].

dam (*n.*) damu [ダム].
　　　(*vt.*) ...o seki-tomeru [...をせき止める].

damage (*n.*) 1)songai [損害]. 2)(*law; pl.*) songai-baishô [損害賠償].
　　(*1*) Was much **damage** done by the fire?
　　　　　Kaji-de yohodo *higai*-ga arimashita-ka?
　　　　　(*vt.*) ...ni songai-o-ataeru [...に損害を与える].
　　　The Tokaido line **was damaged** at several places by the
　　　flood.
　　　　　Tôkaidô-sen wa kôzui-no-tame-ni sû-kasho-ni *higai-ga-atta*.

damp (*n. & a.*) shikki(-no-aru) [湿気(のある)].
　　　(*vt.*) ...o shimerasu [...を湿らす].

dance (*vt. & vi.*) (...o) odoru [(...を)踊る].

　　　　(n.) dansu [ダンス]; buyô [舞踊].

dancer (n.) dansâ [ダンサー]; buyô-ka [舞踊家].

dandelion (n.) (bot.) tampopo [タンポポ].

dandruff (n.) fuke [ふけ].

dandy (n.) share-otoko [しゃれ男].

Dane (n.) Demmâku-jin [デンマーク人].

danger (n.) kiken [危険].

dangerous (a.) kiken-na [危険な]; abunai [危ない].

Danish (a.) Demmâku-no [デンマークの]; Demmâku-jin-no [デンマーク人の]; Demmâku-go-no [デンマーク語の].

　　　　(n.) Demmâku-go [デンマーク語].

dare (vt.) daitan-ni-mo ...(suru) [大胆にも…(する)]; omoi-kitte ... (suru) [思い切って…(する)].

　　I dare say osoraku; tabun

daring (a.) daitan-na [大胆な]; mukô-mizu-na [向こう見ずな].

dark (a.) 1)kurai [暗い]. 2)koi [濃い]. 3)in'utsu-na [陰うつな].

　　(1) It became **dark**. *Kuraku-natta.*

　　(2) a **dark** green　*koi-midori-iro*

　　(3) They have passed **dark** days.
　　　　　Kare-ra-wa *in'utsu-na* hibi-o sugoshite-kita.

　　　　(n.) (the -) kuragari [暗がり]. yûgure [夕暮れ].

darken (vt. & vi.) 1)...o kuraku-suru (kuraku-naru) [...を暗くする (暗くなる)]. 2)...o inki-ni-suru (inki-ni-naru) [...を陰気にする(陰気になる)].

darkness (n.) ankoku [暗黒]; yami [やみ].

darling (n.) kawaii-hito [かわいい人]; o-ki-ni-iri [お気に入り].

　　My darling! *Anata!; Kimi!*

darn (vt. & vi.) (...o) nui-tsukurou [(…を)縫い繕う].

dart (n.) 1)nage-yari [投げ槍]. 2)tosshin [突進].

　　　　(vt.) (yari nado)-o nageru [(槍など)を投げる].

　　　　(vi.) tosshin-suru [突進する].

dash (vt.) 1)...o nage-tsukeru [...を投げつける]. 2)...o uchi-kudaku [...を打ち砕く].

　　　　(vi.) tosshin-suru [突進する].

　　　　(n.) 1)tosshin [突進]. 2)(the -) tan-kyori-kyôsô [短距離競走]. 3)dasshu [ダッシュ].

　　(1) They made a **dash** at the tower.
　　　　　Kare-ra-wa tô-o-megakete *tosshin-shita.*

   (2) the hundred-meter **dash**   hyaku-mêtoru-*kyôsô*

   (3) A **dash** is a horizontal stroke.

      Dasshu to-wa massugu-ni-hiita sen da.

dashboard (*n.*) keiki-ban [計器板].

data (*n.*) shiryô [資料]; dêta [データ].

date (*n.*) 1)hi-zuke [日付]. 2)jidai [時代]. 3)dêto [デート].

   (*vt.*) …ni hi-zuke-o-kaki-komu […に日付を書き込む]; …to dêto-suru […とデートする].

date line   hi-zuke-henkô-sen [日付変更線].

datum (*n.*) *see.* data.

daughter (*n.*) musume [娘].

dawn (*vi.*) yo-ga-akeru [夜が明ける].

   It **dawns**.   *Yo* ga *akeru.*

   (*n.*) yo-ake [夜明け].

   He rose before **dawn**.   Kare-wa *yo-ake*-mae-ni okita.

day (*n.*) 1)hi [日]; ichi-nichi [一日]. 2)nitchû [日中]; hiru-ma [昼間].

   3)(*pl.*) jidai [時代].

   (1) He goes to school every **day**.

      Kare-wa mai-*nichi* gakkô-e iku.

   (2) It is still **day**.   Mada *nitchû* da.

   (3) golden **days**   zensei-*jidai*

   all day (long); all the day   ichi-nichi-jû

   by day   hiru-ma-wa; nitchû-wa

   call it a day   (*colloq.*) shigoto-o-oeru

   day after day   mainichi-mainichi

   day and night   hiru-mo-yoru-mo; taezu

   in those days   sono-tôji-wa

   one day   aru-hi; katsute; itsu-ka

   some day   sono-uchi; itsu-ka

   the day after tomorrow   myôgo-nichi; asatte

   the day before yesterday   issaku-jitsu; ototoi

   the other day   senjitsu; kono-aida

   these days   chikagoro-wa

   this day week   senshû(*or* raishû)-no-kyô

   to this day   konnichi-made

daybreak (*n.*) yo-ake [夜明け].

daylight (*n.*) 1)nikkô [日光]. 2)hiru-ma [昼間]. 3)yo-ake [夜明け].

daylight saving time   natsu-jikan [夏時間].

daytime (*n.*) hiru-ma [昼間].

dazzle (*vt. & vi.*) ...no me-o-kuramaseru (me-ga-kuramu) [...の目を くらませる(目がくらむ)].

dazzling (*a.*) mabushii [まぶしい].

dead (*a.*) shinda [死んだ]; kareta [枯れた].
>> He **has been dead** four years.
>>> Kare-wa *shinde* yo-nen-ni-naru.
>> (*n.*) (the -) shisha-tachi [死者達].
>>> The **dead** were buried. *Shisha* wa maisô-sareta.

dead end iki-domari [行き止まり].

dead heat hiki-wake [引き分け].

deadly (*a.*) 1)inochi-ni-kakawaru [命にかかわる]. 2)(*colloq.*) kado-no [過度の].
>> (*ad.*) shinin-no-yô-ni [死人のように]; hidoku [ひどく].

deaf (*a.*) 1)mimi-ga-kikoe-nai [耳が聞こえない]. 2)kikô-to-shi-nai [聞こうとしない].
>> (2) He is **deaf** to all my advices.
>>> Kare-wa watashi-no chûkoku-o sukoshi-mo *kikô-to-shi-nai*.

deafen (*vt.*) ...no mimi-o-kikoe-naku-suru [...の耳を聞こえなくする]; ...ni bôon-sôchi-o-suru [...に防音装置をする].

deafening (*a.*) mimi-o-tsunzaku-yô-na [耳をつんざくような].

deal (*vt.*) 1)...o bumpai-suru [...を分配する]; ...o kubaru [...を配る]. 2)(dageki)-o kuwaeru [(打撃)を加える].
>> (1) He is **dealing** cards to each.
>>> Kare-wa torampu-no-fuda-o mei-mei-ni *kubatteiru*.
>> (2) He **dealt** me a heavy blow.
>>> Kare-wa watashi-o hidoku *nagutta*.
>> **deal in** ...o akinau
>> **deal with** ...o tori-atsukau
>> (*n.*) 1)shô-torihiki [商取引]. 2)seisaku [政策].

deal (*n.*) ryô [量]; gaku [額].
>> **a great(good) deal of** kanari-no-ryô-no; takusan-no

dealer (*n.*) 1)hambai-nin [販売人]. 2)(torampu no) kubari-te [(トランプの)配り手].

dean (*n.*) 1)(dai-seidô no) shuseki-shisai [(大聖堂の)主席司祭]. 2)gakubu-chô [学部長]; gakusei-buchô [学生部長].

dear (*a.*) 1)shin'ai-na [親愛な]. 2)taisetsu-na [大切な]. 3)kôka-na [高価な].

   (*n.*) kawaii-hito［かわいい人］.

   My **dear**! *Anata!; Kimi!*

   (*ad.*) kôka-ni［高価に］.

   (*int.*) Oya!［おや!］; Maa!［まあ!］.

dearly (*ad.*) 1)hijô-ni［非常に］. 2)aijô-o-motte［愛情をもって］. 3) ookina-gisei-o-haratte［大きな犠牲を払って］.

   (*2*) She loved the French doll **dearly**.

      Kano-jo-wa sono Furansu-ningyô-o *totemo* kawaigatta.

   (*3*) The battle was bought **dearly**.

      Sono sentô niwa *tadai-no-gisei-ga-haraware*ta.

death (*n.*) shi［死］; shibô［死亡］.

   to death shinu-made

debate (*vt. & vi.*) (...o) tôron-suru［(…を)討論する］.

   (*n.*) tôron［討論］.

debit (*n.*) (*bkpg.*) kari-kata［借方］.

   (*vt.*) ...o kari-kata-ni-kinyû-suru［…を借方に記入する］.

debt (*n.*) 1)shakkin［借金］. 2)ongi［恩義］; giri［義理］.

   (*1*) I am in **debt**. Watashi-wa *shakkin*-o-shite-iru.

   (*2*) I am in her **debt**. Watashi-wa kano-jo-ni-*giri*-ga-aru.

decade (*n.*) jû-nen-kan［十年間］.

dacay (*vi. & vt.*) kuchiru (...o kuchisaseru)［朽ちる(…を朽ちさせる)］; otoroeru (...o otoroesaseru)［衰える(…を衰えさせる)］.

   (*n.*) fuhai［腐敗］; otoroe［衰え］.

decayed (*a.*) kuchita［朽ちた］.

   a **decayed** tooth *mushi*-ba

deceive (*vt.*) ...o damasu［…をだます］; ...o azamuku［…を欺く］.

   (*vi.*) sagi-o-suru［詐欺をする］.

December (*n.*) Jûnigatsu［十二月］.

decent (*a.*) 1)jôhin-na［上品な］. 2)(*colloq.*) kanari-no［かなりの］.

deception (*n.*) sagi［詐欺］; gomakashi［ごまかし］.

decide (*vt. & vi.*) (...o) kettei-suru［(…を)決定する］; ((...shiyô)-to) kesshin-suru［((…しよう)と)決心する］.

decimal (*a.*) jusshim-pô-no［十進法の］.

   (*n.*) shôsû［小数］.

decision (*n.*) kettei［決定］; kesshin［決心］.

decisive (*a.*) 1)kettei-teki-na［決定的な］. 2)danko-to-shita［断固とした］.

deck (*n.*) kampan［甲板］; dekki［デッキ］.

　　　　(*vt.*) ...o kazaru [⋯を飾る].

declaration (*n.*) 1)sengen [宣言]. 2)shinkoku [申告].

declare (*vt.*) 1)...o sengen-suru [⋯を宣言する]; ...to dangen-suru [⋯と断言する]. 2)...o shinkoku-suru [⋯を申告する].

　　　　(*1*) America **declared** war upon Germany.
　　　　　　　Amerika wa Doitsu-ni sensen-*o fukoku-shita.*
　　　　(*2*) Have you anything to **declare**?
　　　　　　　*Shinkoku-su-*beki-mono-ga-nani-ka arimasu-ka?
　　　　　　　(*vi.*) sengen-suru [宣言する]; dangen-suru [断言する].

decline (*vi.*) 1)kotowaru [断る]. 2)katamuku [傾く]. 3)otoroeru [衰える].
　　　　　　　(*vt.*) ...o kotowaru [⋯を断る]; ...o jitai-suru [⋯を辞退する].

decorate (*vt.*) 1)...o kazaru [⋯を飾る]. 2)...ni kunshô-o-sazukeru [⋯に勲章を授ける].

decoration (*n.*) 1)sôshoku [装飾]; kazari-tsuke [飾り付け]. 2)kunshô [勲章].

decorative (*a.*) sôshoku-teki-na [装飾的な].

decoy (*n.*) otori [おとり].

decrease (*vt. & vi.*) ...o genshô-saseru (genshô-suru) [⋯を減少させる (減少する)].
　　　　　　　(*n.*) genshô [減少].

dedicate (*vt.*) 1)...o sasageru [⋯を捧げる]; ...o hônô-suru [⋯を奉納する]. 2)...o kentei-suru [⋯を献呈する].

deduce (*vt.*) 1)...o suiron-suru [⋯を推論する]. 2)...o en'eki-suru [⋯を演えきする].

deduct (*vt.*) ...o sashi-hiku [⋯を差し引く]; ...o kôjo-suru [⋯を控除する].

deed (*n.*) 1)kôi [行為]. 2)(*law*) shôsho [証書].
　　　　(*1*) **Deeds** are better things than words.
　　　　　　　Kôi wa kotoba-ni-masaru.
　　　　(*2*) Give him this **deed**. Kare-ni kono *shôsho-*o watashi-nasai.

deep (*a.*) 1)fukai [深い]; fuka-sa-ga...no [深さが⋯の]. 2)(iro no) koi [(色の)濃い]. 3)(koe nado no) futoi [(声などの)太い].
　　　　(*1*) This lake is **deep**. Kono mizuumi wa *fukai.*
　　　　(*2*) He wears a **deep** brown coat.
　　　　　　　Kare-wa *koi* cha-iro-no uwagi-o kite-iru.
　　　　(*3*) He has a **deep** voice. Kare-wa *futoi* koe-o shite-iru.
　　　　　　　(*ad.*) fukaku [深く].

deep breath   shin-kokyû [深呼吸].

deeply (*ad.*) fukaku [深く].

deer (*n.*) shika [シカ].

defeat (*n.*) haiboku [敗北].
     (*vt.*) ...o makasu [···を負かす].

defect (*n.*) kekkan [欠陥].

defective (*a.*) kekkan-no-aru [欠陥のある].

defend (*vt. & vi.*) 1)(...o) mamoru [(···を)守る]. 2)(...o) bengo-suru [(···を)弁護する].

defense (*n.*) 1)bôgyo [防御]. 2)bengo [弁護].

defenseless (*a.*) bôbi-no-nai [防備のない].

defensive (*a.*) bôgyo-no [防御の].

defer (*vt.*) ...o nobasu [···を延ばす]; ...o enki-suru [···を延期する].

defiance (*n.*) hankô-teki-na-taido [反抗的な態度]; mushi [無視].
  in defiance of   ...o-mushi-shite

deficiency (*n.*) fusoku [不足]; kekkan [欠陥].

deficient (*a.*) fusoku-shite-iru [不足している]; kekkan-no-aru [欠陥のある].

deficit (*n.*) (*acc.*) akaji [赤字]; kesson [欠損].

define (*vt.*) ...o teigi-suru [···を定義する].

definite (*a.*) 1)ittei-no [一定の]. 2)meikaku-na [明確な].

definitely (*ad.*) 1)meikaku-ni [明確に]. 2)(*colloq.*) tashika-ni [確かに].

definition (*n.*) teigi [定義].

deflation (*n.*) (*econ.*) tsûka-shûshuku [通貨収縮]; defure [デフレ].

deform (*vt.*) ...o henkei-saseru [···を変形させる].

defy (*vt.*) 1)...ni idomu [···にいどむ]. 2)...ni hankô-suru [···に反抗する]; ...o mushi-suru [···を無視する].

degree (*n.*) 1)teido [程度]; dankai [段階]. 2)gakui [学位]. 3)(kandan-kei ya ondo-kei no) do [(寒暖計や温度計の)度].
  (*1*) a question of **degree**   *teido* no mondai
  (*2*) He has taken a **degree** recently.
     Kare-wa saikin *gakui*-o totta.
  (*3*) Her temperature is 38 **degrees**.
     Kano-jo-no taion wa san-jû-hachi-*do* da.
  by degrees   shidai-ni; dan-dan
  in some degree   tashô
  to a degree   (*colloq.*) ooi-ni; totemo

deity (*n.*) kami [神].

dejection (*n.*) 1)rakutan [落胆]. 2)(*med.*) bentsû [便通].

delay (*vt. & vi.*) ...o okuraseru (okureru) [···を遅らせる(遅れる)].
　　　(*n.*) chien [遅延].
　without delay　sassoku; tadachi-ni

delegate (*n.*) 1)daihyô [代表]. 2)daigi-in [代議員].
　　　　(*vt.*) ...o daihyô-to-shite-haken-suru [···を代表として派遣する].

delegation (*n.*) daihyô-dan [代表団].

deliberate (*a.*) jukkô-shita [熟考した]; shinchô-na [慎重な].
　　　　　(*vt. & vi.*) (...o) jukuryo-suru [(···を)熟慮する].

delicacy (*n.*) 1)yûbi-sa [優美さ]. 2)bimyô-na-koto [微妙なこと]. 3)
　　sensai-sa [繊細さ]. 4)ka-yowasa [か弱さ]. 5)bimi [美味].

delicate (*a.*) yûbi-na [優美な]; bimyô-na [微妙な]; sensai-na [繊細な];
　　ka-yowai [か弱い].

delicately (*ad.*) yûbi-ni [優美に]; seikô-ni [精巧に]; bimyô-ni [微妙に].

delicious (*a.*) hijô-ni-oishii [非常においしい].

delight (*vt. & vi.*) ...o ooi-ni-yorokobaseru (ooi-ni-yorokobu) [···を
　大いに喜ばせる(大いに喜ぶ)].
　　　(*n.*) oo-yorokobi [大喜び]; tanoshimi [楽しみ].
　take delight in　...o yorokobu; ...o tanoshimu

delightful (*a.*) totemo-yukai-na [とても愉快な].

deliver (*vt.*) 1)...o haitatsu-suru [···を配達する]; ...o todokeru [···を
　届ける]. 2)(enzetsu)-o suru [(演説)をする]. 3)...o sukui-dasu [···を
　救い出す]. 4)(dageki)-o kuwaeru [(打撃)を加える].
　(*1*) The letter **is delivered** twice a day.
　　　Tegami wa hi-ni ni-kai *haitatsu-sareru*.
　(*2*) He **delivered** a speech in French.
　　　Kare-wa Furansu-go-de enzetsu-*o shita*.
　(*3*) He **delivered** me from danger.
　　　Kare-wa watashi-o kiken-kara *sukutte-kureta*.
　(*4*) I **delivered** severe blow on the dog.
　　　Watashi-wa sono inu-o hidoku *nagutta*.

delivery (*n.*) 1)haitatsu [配達]. 2)kyûshutsu [救出]. 3)hanashi-buri
　[話しぶり].

delude (*vt.*) ...o azamuku [···を欺く].

delusion (*n.*) 1)madowasu-koto [惑わすこと]. 2)môsô [妄想].

deluxe (*a.*) gôka-na [豪華な]; derakkusu-na [デラックスな].

demand (*n.*) 1)yôkyû [要求]; seikyû [請求]. 2)juyô [需要].

be in demand juyô-ga-aru

on demand seikyû-shidai

　　　　(vt.) …o yôkyû-suru […を要求する]; …o seikyû-suru […を請求する]; …o yôsuru […を要する].

demerit (n.) ketten [欠点]; tansho [短所]; demeritto [デメリット].

democracy (n.) 1)minshu-shugi [民主主義]. 2)minshu-shugi-koku [民主主義国].

democrat (n.) minshu-shugi-sha [民主主義者].

democratic (a.) minshu-shugi-no [民主主義の]; minshu-teki-na [民主的な].

demon (n.) akuma [悪魔]; oni [鬼].

demonstrate (vt.) …o shômei-suru […を証明する]; …o setsumei-suru […を説明する].

　　　　(vi.) jii-undô-o-suru [示威運動をする].

demonstration (n.) 1)shômei [証明]. 2)jii-undô [示威運動]; demo [デモ].

denial (n.) hitei [否定]; kyozetsu [拒絶].

Denmark (n.) Demmâku [デンマーク].

denominate (vt.) …ni meimei-suru […に命名する]; …o…to yobu […を…と呼ぶ].

denote (vt.) …o shimesu […を示す]; …o imi-suru […を意味する].

denounce (vt.) …o kôzen-to-hinan-suru […を公然と非難する].

dense (a.) misshû-shita [密集した]; koi [濃い].

dental (a.) ha-no [歯の].

dentifrice (n.) neri-ha-migaki [練り歯みがき].

dentist (n.) shika-i [歯科医].

deny (vt.) …o hitei-suru […を否定する]; …o kobamu […を拒む].

deodorant (n.) bôshû-zai [防臭剤].

　　　　(a.) bôshû-no [防臭の].

depart (vi.) shuppatsu-suru [出発する].

department (n.) 1)bumon [部門]; bun'ya [分野]. 2)((US))…shô […省]; ((Eng.))…kyoku […局]; …ka […課]. 3)…gaku-ka […学科].

department store hyakka-ten [百貨店]; depâto [デパート].

departure (n.) shuppatsu [出発].

depend (vi.) 1)tayori-ni-suru [頼りにする]. 2)shinrai-suru [信頼する]. 3)…shidai-de-aru […次第である].

　　(1) Children **depend** upon their parents.

　　　　Kodomo wa oya-ni *tayoru*.

(2) You can **depend** on her. Kano-jo wa *shinrai*-dekiru.

(3) Success **depends** upon your own efforts.

   Seikô wa kimi-jishin-no-doryoku-*shidai*-da.

   depend upon it tashika-ni

   That depends.; It all depends. Sore-wa toki-to-baai-ni-yoru.

dependable (a.) shinrai-dekiru [信頼できる]; ate-ni-naru [当てになる].

dependent (a.) 1)tayotte-iru [頼っている]. 2)(*gram.*) jûzoku-no [従属の].

deplore (vt.) ...o ikan-ni-omou [⋯を遺憾に思う].

deposit (vt.) 1)...o oku [⋯を置く]. 2)...o yokin-suru [⋯を預金する].
   (n.) yokin [預金].

depot (n.) 1)((US)) eki [駅]. 2)sôko [倉庫].

depress (vt.) 1)...o oshi-sageru [⋯を押し下げる]. 2)...o yûutsu-ni-saseru [⋯を憂うつにさせる]. 3)...o fu-keiki-ni-suru [⋯を不景気にする].

depression (n.) 1)teika [低下]. 2)yûutsu [憂うつ]. 3)fu-keiki [不景気].

deprive (vt.) ...o ubau [⋯を奪う].

depth (n.) 1)fuka-sa [深さ]; okuyuki [奥行き]. 2)shinkoku-sa [深刻さ]. 3)okumatta-tokoro [奥まったところ].

(1) The well is 7 meters in **depth**.

   Ido wa *fuka-sa* ga nana-mêtoru aru.

deputy (n.) dairi[-nin] [代理(人)]; daihyô-sha [代表者].

derive (vt.) 1)...o hiki-dasu [⋯を引き出す]. 2)...no yurai-o-tazuneru [⋯の由来を尋ねる].
   (vi.) yurai-suru [由来する].

descend (vi. & vt.) (...o) oriru [(⋯を)降りる]; (...o) kudaru [(⋯を)下る].

descendant (n.) shison [子孫]

descent (n.) 1)kôka [降下]. 2)kudari-zaka [下り坂]. 3)kakei [家系].

describe (vt.) 1)...o kijutsu-suru [⋯を記述する]. 2)...o byôsha-suru [⋯を描写する]. 3)...to iu [⋯と言う].

description (n.) 1)kijutsu [記述]; byôsha [描写]. 2)shurui [種類].
   beyond description kotoba-de-wa-ii-arawase-nai

desert (n.) sabaku [砂漠].

desert (vt.) ...o mi-suteru [⋯を見捨てる].

desert (n.) 1)kôseki [功績]. 2)(pl.) tôzen-no-mukui [当然の報い].

deserted (a.) sabireta [さびれた].

deserter (n.) dassô-hei [脱走兵].

deserve (vi. & vt.) ukeru-kachi-ga-aru [受ける価値がある]; ...(suru)-

kachi-ga-aru [(…する)価値がある].

design (*n.*) 1)zuan [図案]; sekkei-zu [設計図]. 2)keikaku [計画].
　　(*vt.*) …no zuan-o-tsukuru […の図案を作る]; …o keikaku-suru
　　[…を計画する].

designate (*vt.*) …o shiteki-suru […を指摘する]; …o nimmei-suru […
　を任命する].

designer (*n.*) dezainâ [デザイナー]; sekkei-sha [設計者].

desirable (*a.*) nozomashii [望ましい].

desire (*n.*) gambô [願望]; yokubô [欲望].
　　(*vt.*) …o tsuyoku-nozomu […を強く望む]; …o tsuyoku-negau
　　[…を強く願う].

desirous (*a.*) nozonde [望んで]; hoshigatte [欲しがって].

desk (*n.*) tsukue [机].

desolate (*a.*) sabishii [寂しい]; are-hateta [荒れ果てた].

despair (*n. & vi.*) zetsubô(-suru) [絶望(する)].

desperate (*a.*) 1)shinimono-gurui-no [死にもの狂いの]; hisshi-no [必
　死の]. 2)zetsubô-teki-na [絶望的な].

despise (*vt.*) …o keibetsu-suru […を軽べつする].

despite (*prep.*)…nimo-kakawarazu […にもかかわらず].

destination (*n.*) mokuteki-chi [目的地]; shimuke-chi [仕向地].

destiny (*n.*) ummei [運命].

destroy (*vt.*) 1)…o hakai-suru […を破壊する]. 2)…o horobosu […を
　滅ぼす].

destroyer (*n.*) 1)hakai-sha [破壊者]. 2)(*marine*) kuchiku-kan [駆逐艦].

destruction (*n.*) hakai [破壊]; metsubô [滅亡].

destructive (*a.*) hakai-teki-na [破壊的な].

detail (*n.*) 1)(*pl.*) shôjutsu [詳述]. 2)saimoku [細目].
　in detail kuwashiku

detain (*vt.*) 1)…o hiki-tomeru […を引き止める]. 2)…o ryûchi-suru […
　を留置する].

detect (*vt.*) …o mitsukeru […を見付ける]; …o mi-yaburu […を見破る].

detective (*n. & a.*) tantei(-no) [探偵(の)].

determination (*n.*) kettei [決定]; kesshin [決心].

determine (*vt. & vi.*) (…o) kettei-suru [(…を)決定する]; (…to)
　kesshin-suru [(…と)決心する].

determined (*a.*) danko-to-shita [断固とした].

detour (*n.*) mawari-michi [回り道].

deuce (*n.*) 1)(*tennis*) jûse [ジュース]. 2)(*cards*) ni-no-fuda [二の札];

(*dice*) ni-no-me [二の目].

develop (*vt. & vi.*) 1)...o hattatsu-saseru (hattatsu-suru) [...を発達させる(発達する)]. 2)(*photo.*)...o genzô-suru (genzô-sareru) [...を現像する(現像される)].

　　develop ...into hattatsu-shite ...ni naru

development (*n.*) 1)hattatsu [発達]. 2)kaihatsu [開発]. 3)genzô [現像].

device (*n.*) 1)shikake [仕掛け]; kufû [工夫]. 2)ishô [意匠].

devil (*n.*) akuma [悪魔].

devise (*vt.*) ...o kufû-suru [...を工夫する]; ...o anshutsu-suru [...を案出する].

devote (*vt.*) ...o sasageru [...を捧げる].

　　devote oneself to ...ni sennen-suru

devoted (*a.*) chûjitsu-na [忠実な]; kenshin-teki-na [献身的な].

devotion (*n.*) 1)sennen [専念]; kenshin [献身]. 2)(*pl.*) inori [祈り].

devour (*vt.*) ...o musabori-kuu [...をむさぼり食う]; ...o musaboru-yô-ni-yomu [...をむさぼるように読む].

devout (*a.*) shinjin-bukai [信心深い].

dew (*n.*) tsuyu [露].

dewy (*a.*) tsuyu-de-nureta [露でぬれた].

diagnosis (*n.*) (*med.*) shinsatsu [診察]; shindan [診断].

diagram (*n.*) zuhyô [図表].

dial (*n.*) 1)(tokei no) moji-ban [(時計の)文字盤]. 2)daiyaru [ダイヤル].

　　(*vt.*) 1)...ni denwa-o-kakeru [...に電話をかける]. 2)...ni daiyaru-o-awasu [...にダイヤルを合わす].

　　(*vi.*) denwa-o-kakeru [電話をかける].

dialect (*n.*) hôgen [方言].

dialogue (*n.*) taiwa〔-tai〕[対話(体)].

diameter (*n.*) chokkei [直径].

diarrhea, -rhoea (*n.*) (*med.*) geri [下痢].

diary (*n.*) nikki [日記].

dice (*n.*) saikoro〔-asobi〕[さいころ(遊び)].

　　(*vi.*) saikoro-asobi-o-suru [さいころ遊びをする].

　　(*vt.*) ...o sai-no-me-ni-kiru [...をさいの目に切る].

dictate (*vt.*) 1)...o kaki-toraseru [...を書き取らせる]. 2)...o sashizu-suru [...を指図する].

dictation (*n.*) 1)kaki-tori [書き取り]. 2)meirei [命令].

dictionary (*n.*) jisho [辞書].

die (*vi.*) shinu [死ぬ]; kareru [枯れる].

diet (*n.*) 1)jôshoku [常食]. 2)kitei-shoku [規定食].

　(*2*) She is on a **diet**. Kano-jo-wa *shokuji-seigen*-o-shite-iru.

diet (*n.*) (the D-) kokkai [国会].

differ (*vi.*) 1)chigau [違う]; 2)iken-ga-chigau [意見が違う].

　(*1*) They **differ** in custom. Kare-ra-wa fûshû-no-ten-de *chigau*.

　(*2*) I **differ** from you. Watashi-wa anata-to *iken-ga-chigau*.

difference (*n.*) chigai [違い]; sôi-ten [相違点].

　split the difference ayumi-yoru

different (*a.*) chigatta [違った]; iro-iro-na [いろいろな]; betsu-betsu-no [別々の].

difficult (*a.*) konnan-na [困難な]; muzukashii [難しい].

difficulty (*n.*) konnan [困難]; muzukashisa [難しさ].

　with difficulty yatto-no-koto-de

dig (*vt.*) ...o horu [...を掘る].

　dig out ...o hori-dasu

digest (*vt. & vi.*) (...o) shôka-suru [(...を)消化する].

digestion (*n.*) shôka[-ryoku] [消化(力)].

digestive (*n.*) shôka-zai [消化剤].

　(*a.*) shôka-o-tasukeru [消化を助ける].

dignified (*a.*) hin'i-no-aru [品位のある]; igen-no-aru [威厳のある].

dignity (*n.*) hin'i [品位]; igen [威厳].

dike (*n.*) 1)teibô [堤防]. 2)mizo [溝].

dilemma (*n.*) ita-basami [板ばさみ]; jiremma [ジレンマ].

diligent (*a.*) kimben-na [勤勉な].

dim (*a.*) usu-gurai [薄暗い]; bon'yari-to-shita [ぼんやりとした].

dimension (*n.*) 1)sumpô [寸法]. 2)(*pl.*) yôseki [容積]. 3)(*math.*) jigen [次元].

diminish (*vt. & vi.*) ...o herasu (heru) [...を減らす(減る)].

dimly (*ad.*) usu-guraku [薄暗く]; bon'yari[-to] [ぼんやり(と)].

dimple (*n.*) ekubo [えくぼ].

din (*n.*) sôon [騒音]; yakamashii-oto [やかましい音].

dine (*vi. & vt.*) shokuji-suru (...ni shokuji-o-dasu) [食事する(...に食事を出す)].

　dine out soto-de-shokuji-suru ; gaishoku-suru

diner (*n.*) 1)shokuji-suru-hito [食事する人]. 2)shokudô-sha [食堂車].

dingdong (*n.*) gôn-gôn [ごーんごーん]; jan-jan [じゃんじゃん].

dining car　shokudô-sha [食堂車].

dining room　shokudô [食堂].

dining table = dinner table　shokutaku [食卓].

dinner (*n.*)　seisan [正さん].

dinner party　bansan-kai [晩さん会].

dip (*vt. & vi*)　...o chotto-hitasu (chotto-hitaru) [···をちょっと浸す (ちょっと浸る)].

diphtheria (*n.*) (*med.*)　jifuteria [ジフテリア].

diploma (*n.*)　sotsugyô-shôsho [卒業証書]; gakui-ki [学位記].

diplomat (*n.*)　gaikô-kan [外交官].

diplomatic (*a.*)　gaikô-no [外交の]; kake-hiki-no-jôzu-na [駆け引きの上手な].

dipper (*n.*)　hishaku [ひしゃく].

direct (*a.*) 1)chokusetsu-no [直接の]. 2)massugu-na [真っすぐな].
　　　(*ad.*) chokusetsu-ni [直接に]; massugu-ni [真っすぐに].
　　　(*vt.*) 1)(tegami)-ni atena-o-kaku [(手紙)にあて名を書く]. 2)...
　　ni michi-o-oshieru [···に道を教える]. 3)(...suru)-yô-ni sashizu-suru
　　[(···する)ように指図する].
　　　(*1*) The package **was directed** to me.
　　　　　Sono ko-zutsumi wa watashi-*ate-datta*.
　　　(*2*) He **directed** me to the church.
　　　　　Kare-wa sono-kyôkai-e-iku-*michi*-o watashi-*ni oshieta*.
　　　(*3*) I **directed** him to go.
　　　　　Watashi-wa kare-ni iku-*yô-ni sashizu-shita*.

direction (*n.*) 1)hôkô [方向]. 2)sashizu [指図].
　in the direction of　...no-hôkô-ni

directly (*ad.*)　chokusetsu-ni [直接に]; sugu[-ni] [すぐ(に)].

director (*n.*) 1)shidô-sha [指導者]. 2)jûyaku [重役]; riji [理事];
　　shochô [所長]. 3)enshutsu-ka [演出家].

directory (*n.*)　jimmei-bo [人名簿].

dirt (*n.*)　gomi [ごみ]; hokori [ほこり].

dirty (*a.*)　yogoreta [汚れた]; fuketsu-na [不潔な].
　　　(*vt.*)　...o yogosu [···を汚す].

disable (*vt.*)　(be -d) shintai-shôgai-sha-ni-naru [身体障害者になる].

disadvantage (*n.*) 1)furi-na-tachiba [不利な立場]. 2)sonshitsu [損失].

disagree (*vi.*) 1)itchi-shi-nai [一致しない]; iken-ga-awa-nai [意見が合
　　わない]. 2)(kikô ga) awa-nai [(気候が)合わない]; (tabe-mono ga)
　　ataru [(食べ物が)あたる].

　(1) He **disagrees** with other members.

　　　Kare-wa hoka-no-iin-tachi-to *iken-ga-awa-nai*.

　(2) The fish which I ate last night **disagreed** with me.

　　　Sakuya tabeta-sakana ga *atatta*.

disagreeable (*a.*) 1)fu-yukai-na [不愉快な]. 2)ki-muzukashii [気難しい].

disappear (*vi.*) mie-naku-naru [見えなくなる]; kieru [消える].

disappearance (*n.*) 1)mie-naku-naru-koto [見えなくなること]. 2)shissô [失踪].

disappoint (*vt.*) ...o shitsubô-saseru [...を失望させる].

disappointed (*a.*) 1)shitsubô-shita [失望した]. 2)kujikareta [くじかれた].

disappointment (*n.*) shitsubô [失望]; rakutan [落胆].

disapprove (*vt. & vi.*) (...ni) sansei-shi-nai [(...に)賛成しない].

disarmament (*n.*) gumbi-shukushô [軍備縮小].

disaster (*n.*) 1)saigai [災害]. 2)sainan [災難].

disastrous (*a.*) sainan-no [災難の]; hisan-na [悲惨な].

discard (*vt.*) (fuyô-hin, shûkan, shinnen nado)-o suteru [(不用品, 習慣, 信念など)を捨てる]; (*cards*)(ira-nai fuda)-o suteru [(いらない札)を捨てる].

discern (*vt.*) ...o miwakeru [...を見分ける]; ...ni ki-zuku [...に気づく].
　　　(*vi.*) miwakeru [見分ける].

discharge (*vt.*) 1)...o orosu [...を降ろす]. 2)...o utsu [...を撃つ]. 3)...o kaiko-suru [...を解雇する]; ...o kaihô-suru [...を解放する]. 4)...o hatasu [...を果たす]; ...o shiharau [...を支払う]; ...o bensai-suru [...を弁済する].

　(1) They **discharge** a cargo from a ship.

　　　Kare-ra-wa fune-kara ni-*o orosu*.

　(2) He **discharged** his gun.　Kare-wa *happô-shita*.

　(3) I **discharged** one of my clerks.

　　　Watashi-wa jimu-in no hitori-*o kaiko-shita*.

　(4) You must **discharge** your duty.

　　　Kimi-wa shokumu-*o hatasa-nakereba-naranai*.

　　　The surety will **discharge** the debt.

　　　Hoshô-nin ga fusai-*o bensai-suru*-darô.

　　　(*n.*) niage [荷揚げ]; happô [発砲]; kaiko [解雇]; rikô [履行]; bensai [弁済].

discipline (*n.*) 1)kunren [訓練]. 2)kiritsu [規律]. 3)gakumon-no-

　　bun'ya [学問の分野].
　　　　　　(vt.) 1)...o kunren-suru […を訓練する]. 2)...o chôkai-suru
　　[…を懲戒する].
disclose (vt.) 1)...o bakuro-suru […を暴露する]. 2)...o akiraka-ni-
　　suru […を明らかにする]. 3)...o miseru […を見せる].
discontent (n.) fuhei [不平]; fuman [不満].
discord (n.) 1)fuwa [不和]; naka-tagai [仲たがい]. 2)fu-itchi [不一
　　致].
　　　　　　(vi.) itchi-shi-nai [一致しない].
discount (n.) waribiki [割引].
　　　　　　(vt.) ...o waribiki-suru […を割引する].
discourage (vt.) 1)...o rakutan-saseru […を落胆させる]. 2)...ni(-suru-
　　no-o)omoi-todomaraseru […に(するのを)思いとどまらせる].
discouragement (n.) 1)rakutan [落胆]. 2)soshi [阻止].
discourse (n.) 1)kôen [講演]. 2)kaiwa [会話].
discover (vt.) ...o hakken-suru […を発見する].
discovery (n.) hakken[-butsu] [発見(物)].
discredit (n.) fu-shin'yô [不信用]; giwaku [疑惑].
　　　　　　(vt.) ...o shin'yô-shi-nai […を信用しない]; ...no hyôban-o-
　　waruku-suru […の評判を悪くする].
discreet (a.) shinchô-na [慎重な]; hikae-me-na [控え目な].
discrepancy (n.) kui-chigai [食い違い].
discretion (n.) 1)shinchô [慎重]. 2)jiyû-sairyô [自由裁量].
discrimination (n.) kubetsu [区別]; sabetsu-taigû [差別待遇].
discuss (vt.) ...o hanashi-au […を話し合う]; ...o tôgi-suru […を討議
　　する].
discussion (n.) tôron [討論]; tôgi [討議].
disease (n.) byôki [病気].
disengaged (a.) 1)(basho ga) aite-iru [(場所が)空いている]. 2)hima-
　　na [暇な].
disgrace (n.) chijoku [恥辱]; fu-memboku [不面目].
　　in disgrace fukyô-o-katte; memboku-o-ushinatte
　　　　　　(vt.) ...no haji-to-naru […の恥となる].
disguise (vt.) ...o hensô-saseru […を変装させる]; ...o kakusu […を隠
　　す].
　　　　　　(n.) hensô [変装].
　　in disguise hensô-shite
disgust (vt.) ...o iya-ni-naraseru […をいやにならせる].

      (*n.*) ken'o [嫌悪].

dish (*n.*) 1)sara [皿]. 2)(sara ni motta) ryôri [(皿に盛った)料理].

dishearten (*vt.*) ...o gakkari-saseru [...をがっかりさせる].

dishonest (*a.*) fu-shôjiki-na [不正直な]; fu-seijitsu-na [不誠実な].

dishono(u)r (*n.*) fu-meiyo [不名誉]; chijoku [恥辱].
      (*vt.*) ...o hazukashimeru [...を辱める].

disillusion (*n.*) gemmetsu [幻滅].
      (*vt.*) ...ni gemmetsu-o-kanjisaseru [...に幻滅を感じさせる].

disinclination (*n.*) ki-no-susuma-nai-koto [気の進まないこと].

disinfect (*vt.*) ...o shôdoku-suru [...を消毒する].

disinterested (*a.*) 1)shishin-no-nai [私心のない]. 2)mu-kanshin-na [無関心な].

disk (*n.*) emban [円盤]; (*colloq.*) rekôdo [レコード].

dislike (*n. & vt.*) kirai (...o kirau) [嫌い(...を嫌う)].

dismal (*a.*) inki-na [陰気な]; kimi-no-warui [気味の悪い].

dismay (*n.*) rôbai [ろうばい].
      (*vt.*) ...o rôbai-saseru [...をろうばいさせる].

dismiss (*vt.*) 1)...o kaiko-suru [...を解雇する]. 2)...o shirizokeru [...を退ける]; ...o kaisan-saseru [...を解散させる].

disobedient (*a.*) fu-jûjun-na [不従順な].

disobey (*vt.*) ...ni shitagawa-nai [...に従わない].

disorder (*n.*) ranzatsu [乱雑]; mu-chitsujo [無秩序].

dispatch (*vt.*) 1)...o hassô-suru [発送する]. 2)...o hayaku-kata-zukeru [...を早く片付ける].
      (*n.*) 1)tokuha [特派]. 2)shikyû-bin [至急便]. 3)te-bayaku-suru-koto [手早くすること].

dispel (*vt.*) ...o oi-chirasu [...を追い散らす].

dispense (*vt.*) 1)...o bumpai-suru [...を分配する]. 2)(*pharmacol.*) ...o chôzai-suru [...を調剤する].

disperse (*vt.*) 1)...o chirasu [...を散らす]. 2) ...o harasu [...を晴らす]. 3)...o hiromeru [...を広める].
      (*vi.*) chirabaru [散らばる]; hareru [晴れる].

display (*vt.*) 1)...o chinretsu-suru [...を陳列する]; ...o mise-birakasu [...を見せびらかす]. 2)(kanjô)-o arawasu [(感情)を表わす].
      (*n.*) chinretsu [陳列]; mise-birakashi [見せびらかし].
  on display tenji-shite; chinretsu-shite

disposal (*n.*) 1)shobun [処分]. 2)haichi [配置]. 3)shobun-ken [処分権].
  at one's disposal hito-no-jiyû-ni-natte

dispose (*vt.*) 1)...o haichi-suru […を配置する]. 2)...ni...(suru-)ki-ni-naraseru […に…(する)気にならせる].

disposition (*n.*) 1)shobun [処分]. 2)haichi [配置]. 3)kishitsu [気質]; keikô [傾向].

dispute (*n.*) giron [議論].

    (*vt.*) ...o tôron-suru […を討論する]; ...ni hanron-suru […に反論する].

    (*vi.*) tôron-suru [討論する].

disqualify (*vt.*) ...no shikaku-o-ubau […の資格を奪う].

disregard (*vt.*) ...o mushi-suru […を無視する].

disrespect (*n.*) shitsurei [失礼]; keibetsu [軽べつ].

    (*vt.*) ...ni shitsurei-o-suru […に失礼をする]; ...o keibetsu-suru […を軽べつする].

dissatisfy (*vt.*) ...ni fuman-o-idakaseru […に不満をいだかせる].

dissect (*vt.*) ...o kaibô-suru […を解剖する].

dissertation (*n.*) rombun [論文].

dissolve (*vt.*) 1)...o tokasu […を溶かす]. 2)...o kaishô-suru […を解消する].

    (*vi.*) tokeru [溶ける]; shômetsu-suru [消滅する].

distance (*n.*) 1)kyori [距離]. 2)empô [遠方].

  at a distance sukoshi-hanarete

  in the distance empô-ni

distant (*a.*) tooi [遠い].

distil(l) (*vt.*) ...o jôryû-suru […を蒸留する].

distinct (*a.*) 1)hakkiri-shita [はっきりした]. 2)bekko-no [別個の].

distinction (*n.*) 1)kubetsu [区別]. 2)yûshû-sa [優秀さ].

  without distinction mu-sabetsu-ni

distinctive (*a.*) dokutoku-no [独特の]; tokuyû-no [特有の].

distinctly (*ad.*) hakkiri-to [はっきりと].

distinguish (*vt.*) 1)...o...to kubetsu-suru […を…と区別する]. 2)(be-ed/- oneself) medatsu [目立つ]; yûmei-de-aru [有名である].

  (*1*) Can you **distinguish** A from B?

    Kimi-wa Ei-*o*-Bî-*to kubetsu-suru*-koto-ga-dekiru-ka?

  (*2*) She **distinguishes** herself as a scholar.

    Kano-jo-wa gakusha-to-shite *yûmei-da.*

distinguished (*a.*) 1)yûmei-na [有名な]. 2)kencho-na [顕著な].

distort (*vt.*) ...o yugameru […をゆがめる]; ...o ayamari-tsutaeru […を誤り伝える].

distress (*n.*) 1)nayami [悩み]. 2)nangi [難儀].
(*1*) He could not conceal his **distress**.
　　　Kare-wa *nayami*-o kakusu-koto-ga-deki-nakatta.
(*2*) A ship in **distress** was sighted. Sônan-sen ga mieta.

distribute (*vt.*) …o bumpai-suru […を分配する]; …o haifu-suru […
を配布する].

distribution (*n.*) bumpai [分配]; haifu [配布]; bumpu [分布].

district (*n.*) chihô [地方].

distrust (*n.*) fushin-kan [不信感]; giwaku [疑惑].
　　　(*vt.*) …o shinji-nai […を信じない]; …o utagau […を疑う].

disturb (*vt.*) 1)…o kaki-midasu […をかき乱す]. 2)…no jama-o-suru
[…の邪魔をする].

ditch (*n.*) mizo [溝].

dive (*vi.*) (sui-chû e) moguru [(水中へ)潜る]; tobi-komu [飛び込む].
　　　(*n.*) 1)sensui [潜水]. 2)tobi-komi [飛び込み].

diver (*n.*) sensui-fu [潜水夫]; mizu-ni-tobi-komu-hito [水に飛び込む人].

diversity (*n.*) sôi [相違]; tayô-sei [多様性].

divide (*vt.*) 1)…o wakeru […を分ける]. 2)(*math.*)…o waru […を割る].
(*1*) The theory is **divided** into four parts.
　　　Sono gakusetsu wa yottsu-no-bubun-ni *wakareru*.
(*2*) 6 **divided** by 3 is 2. Roku-*waru*-san wa ni.

divine (*a.*) kami-no [神の]; shinsei-na [神聖な].

diving (*n. & a.*) sensui(-no) [潜水(の)]; tobi-komi(-no) [飛び込み(の)].

division (*n.*) 1)bunkatsu [分割]; kubun [区分]. 2)bumon [部門]; ka
[課]. 3)(*math.*) wari-zan [割り算]. 4)(*mil.*) shidan [師団].

divorce (*vt.*) …to rikon-suru […と離婚する].

dizzy (*a.*) me-mai-ga-suru [めまいがする].

do (*vt.*) 1)…o suru […をする]. 2)…o oeru […を終える].
(*1*) **Do** it yourself. Jibun-de sore-*o shi-nasai*.
(*2*) He **has done** crying. Kare-wa naki-*yanda*.
　　　(*vi.*) 1)suru [する]; kôdô-suru [行動する]. 2)oeru [終える]. 3)
kurasu [暮らす]. 4)ma-ni-au [間に合う]; tariru [足りる].
(*1*) **Do** as ordered. Meiji-rareta-yô-ni *shi-nasai*.
(*2*) Have you **done** with this newspaper?
　　　Kono-shimbun-wa o-sumi-ni-narimashita-ka?
(*3*) How do you **do**? *Hajime-mashite*.; *Konnichi-wa*.
(*4*) That will **do**. Sore de *yoroshii*.

do with …ni gaman-suru

　　I can't do with him.
　　　　Watashi-wa kare-ni-wa gaman-deki-nai.
　do without ...nashi-de-sumasu
　have to do with ...to kankei-ga-aru
　　(*aux. v.*)
　(1) Did you see him yesterday?　Kinô kare-ni atta-ka?
　(2) I **do** not speak German.
　　　　Watashi-wa Doitsu-go-wa hanasa-nai.
　(3) **Do** come in.　*Zehi* o-hairi-kudasai.; Dôzo-dôzo.
　　(*pro-verb*)
　(1) You run as fast as I **do**.
　　　　Kimi-wa watashi-*to-onaji-kurai* hayaku hashiru.
　(2) "Do you see him?"　"Yes, I **do**."
　　　　'Kimi-wa kare-ni au-ka?'　'Ee, *ai-masu*.'

docile (*a.*) sunao-na [素直な].
dock (*n.*) dokku [ドック].
dockyard (*n.*) zôsen-jo [造船所].
doctor (*n.*) 1)isha [医者]. 2)hakase [博士].
doctrine (*n.*) kyôgi [教義]; ((*US*)) shugi [主義].
document (*n.*) shorui [書類]; kiroku [記録]; dokyumento [ドキュメント].
documentary (*n.*) kiroku-sakuhin [記録作品].
　　　　　　(*a.*) bunsho-no [文書の]; kiroku-shita [記録した].
dodge (*vi.*) hirari-to[-mi-o]-kawasu [ひらりと(身を)かわす].
　　　　(*vt.*) ...o sakeru […を避ける].
dog (*n.*) inu [犬].
dogma (*n.*) 1)kyôgi [教義]; doguma [ドグマ]. 2)dokudan [独断].
doings (*n.*) (*colloq.*) okonai [行い]; furumai [振る舞い].
doll (*n.*) ningyô [人形].
dollar (*n.*) doru [ドル].
dollar area (*econ.*) doru-chiiki [ドル地域].
dome (*n.*) maru-yane [丸屋根]; maru-tenjô [丸天井].
domestic (*a.*) 1)kokunai-no [国内の]. 2)katei-no [家庭の].
dominant (*a.*) shihai-teki-na [支配的な]; yûryoku-na [有力な].
dominion (*n.*) 1)shuken [主権]. 2)ryôdo [領土].
donkey (*n.*) roba [ロバ].
doom (*n.*) (warui) ummei [(悪い)運命]; hametsu [破滅].
　　　　(*vt.*) ...ni ummei-zukeru […に運命づける].

door (*n.*) 1)to [戸]. 2)de-iriguchi [出入口].
 (*1*) Please open the **door**. Dôka *to*-o akete-kudasai.
 (*2*) Someone is standing at the **door**.
     Dare-ka *iriguchi*-ni tatteiru.
doorbell (*n.*) to-guchi-no-beru [戸口のベル].
doorway (*n.*) to-guchi [戸口].
dope (*n.*) (*slang*) mayaku [麻薬].
dormitory (*n.*) kishuku-sha [寄宿舎].
dose (*n.*) (kusuri no) ippuku [(薬の)一服].
     (*vt.*) ...ni tôyaku-suru [...に投薬する].
dot (*n.*) 1)ten [点]; potsu [ぽつ]. 2)chiisai-mono [小さいもの].
     (*vt. & vi.*) (...ni) ten-o-utsu [(...に)点を打つ].
dotted line tensen [点線].
double (*a.*) ni-bai-no [二倍の]; ni-jû-no [二重の].
doubly (*ad.*) ni-bai-ni [二倍に]; ni-jû-ni [二重に].
doubt (*n.*) utagai [疑い].
  no doubt 1)kitto. 2)tabun
     (*vt. & vi.*) (...o) utagau [(...を)疑う].
doubtful (*a.*) utagawashii [疑わしい].
doubtfully (*ad.*) utagawashiku [疑わしく]; aimai-ni [あいまいに].
doubtless (*ad.*) tashika-ni [確かに]; naruhodo [なるほど].
dove (*n.*) hato [ハト].
down (*ad.*) shita-e [下へ].
     (*prep.*) ...o-kudatte [...を下って]; ...no-shimo-te-ni [...の下手に].
     (*a.*) shita-e-no [下への]; ((*Eng.*)) kudari-no [下りの].
downcast (*a.*) shioreta [しおれた]; utsumuita [うつむいた].
downpour (*n.*) dosha-buri [どしゃ降り].
downstairs (*n. & ad.*) kaika(-ni) [階下(に)].
downtown (*n. & a. & ad.*) hanka-gai(-no)(-e) [繁華街(の)(へ)].
downward (*ad. & a.*) shita-no-hô-e(-no) [下の方へ(の)].
doze (*n. & vi.*) i-nemuri(-suru) [居眠り(する)]; utata-ne(-suru) [う
 たた寝(する)].
dozen (*n.*) dâsu [ダース].
draft (*n.*) 1)suki-ma-kaze [すき間風]. 2)(*com.*) kawase-tegata [為替
 手形]. 3)sôan [草案].
     (*vt.*) 1)...o kisô-suru [...を起草する]; ...no shita-gaki-o-suru [...
 の下書きをする]. 2)((*US*))...o chôhei-ni-toru [...を徴兵にとる].
drag (*vt.*) ...o hiki-zuru [...を引きずる].

　　　They **dragged** themselves along.

　　　　Kare-ra-wa omoi-ashi-o-*hikizutte-aruita*.

　　　(*vi*.) dara-dara-to-sugiru [だらだらと過ぎる].

　　　Time **dragged** by.　Toki ga *dara-dara-to-sugita*.

dragon (*n*.) ryû [竜].

dragonfly (*n*.) (*insect*) tombo [トンボ].

drain (*n*.) haisui-kan [排水管]; gesui-kô [下水溝].

　　　(*vt*.) …no haisui-o-suru […の排水をする]; …o haishutsu-saseru […を排出させる].

　　　(*vi*.) mizu-ga-hakeru [水がはける].

drainpipe (*n*.) gesui-kan [下水管]; haisui-kan [排水管].

drama (*n*.) geki [劇]; gikyoku [戯曲]; dorama [ドラマ].

dramatic (*a*.) geki-no [劇の]; geki-teki-na [劇的な].

draper (*n*.) fukujiya [服地屋].

drastic (*a*.) 1)omoi-kitta [思い切った]. 2)gekiretsu-na [激烈な].

draw (*vt*.) 1)…o hiku […を引く]; …o hipparu […を引っ張る]. 2) (mizu)-o kumu [(水)をくむ]. 3)(zu ya sen)-o hiku [(図や線)を引く]; …o egaku […を描く]. 4)(iki)-o sui-komu [(息)を吸い込む]. 5)(chûi)-o hiku [(注意)を引く]. 6)(*com*.) …o furi-dasu […を振り出す].

　　(*1*) Horses **draw** carts.　Uma wa ni-basha-o *hiku*.

　　(*2*) She went to **draw** water.　Kano-jo-wa mizu-*o kumi*-ni-itta.

　　(*3*) **Draw** a line on the ground.　Jimen-ni sen-*o hiki-nasai*.

　　(*4*) **Draw** breath through your mouth.

　　　　Kuchi-kara iki-*o sui-nasai*.

　　(*5*) The pearl necklace **drew** my attention.

　　　　Sono shinju-no kubi-kazari wa watashi-no chûi-*o hiita*.

　　(*6*) Please **draw** a draft on me.

　　　　Watashi-ate-ni tegata-*o furi-dashite*-kudasai.

　　　(*vi*.) 1)hiku [引く]. 2)e-o-kaku [絵を描く]. 3)chikazuku [近づく].

　　draw near chikazuku

　　draw out 1) (hi ga) nagaku-naru. 2) …o hiki-nobasu

　　1) Days are drawing out.　Hi ga nagaku-natteiru.

drawback (*n*.) ketten [欠点]; furi-na-ten [不利な点].

drawer (*n*.) 1)(*com*.)(tegata no) furi-dashi-nin [(手形の)振出人]. 2) (tsukue no) hiki-dashi [(机の)引き出し]. 3)(*pl*.) zubon-jita [ズボン下]; zurôsu [ズロース].

drawing (*n*.) hiku-koto [引くこと]; senga [線画].

drawing paper gayôshi [画用紙].

drawing room ôsetsu-shitsu [応接室].

drawn game hiki-wake-shiai [引き分け試合]; dorô-gêmu [ドローゲーム].

dread (*vt.*) ...o[-hijô-ni] osoreru [···を(非常に)恐れる].

    (*n.*) kyôfu [恐怖].

dreadful (*a.*) 1)osoroshii [恐ろしい]. 2)(*colloq.*) hidoi [ひどい].

dream (*n.*) yume [夢].

    (*vi.*) yume-o-miru [夢を見る]; sôzô-suru [想像する].

    (*vt.*) ...o yume-miru [···を夢見る]; (...koto)-o yume-ni-miru [(···こと)を夢に見る].

dreamland (*n.*) yume-no-kuni [夢の国].

dreary (*a.*) mono-sabishii [物寂しい]; wabishii [わびしい].

dredge (*vt.*) ...o shunsetsu-suru [···をしゅんせつする].

drench (*vt.*) ...o bisho-nure-ni-suru [···をびしょぬれにする].

dress (*vt.*) 1)...ni fuku-o-kiseru [···に服を着せる]. 2)(kizu)-no teate-o-suru [(傷)の手当をする].

  (*1*) The fields **are dressed** in a fresh robe of green.

    No wa mizumizushii-midori-*no-ishô-o-tsukete-iru*.

  (*2*) My wound **was dressed**. Watashi-no kizu wa *teate-o-uketa*.

    (*vi.*) fuku-o-kiru [服を着る]; mi-jitaku-suru [身支度する].

    (*n.*) 1)fukusô [服装]. 2)(fujin ya kodomo no) doresu [婦人や子供の)ドレス]. 3)reisô [礼装].

dresser (*n.*) ki-tsuke-gakari [着付け係].

dressing (*n.*) 1)shi-age [仕上げ]. 2)doresshingu [ドレッシング].

dressmaking (*n.*) fujin-fuku-shitate [婦人服仕立て]; yôsai [洋裁].

drier (*n.*) kansô-zai [乾燥剤]; kansô-ki [乾燥機]; doraiyâ [ドライヤー].

drift (*n.*) 1)hyôryû [漂流]. 2)(yuki nado no) fuki-yose [(雪などの)吹き寄せ].

    (*vt.*) 1)...o oshi-nagasu [···を押し流す]. 2)...o fuki-yoseru [···を吹き寄せる].

    (*vi.*) tadayou [漂う].

driftwood (*n.*) ryûboku [流木].

drill (*n.*) 1)kunren [訓練]; doriru [ドリル]. 2)kiri [きり].

  (*1*) We had a fire **drill**. Ware-ware-wa shôbô-*kunren*-o shita.

  (*2*) I bored through the board with a **drill**.

    Watashi-wa *kiri*-de ita-ni ana-o-aketa.

    (*vt.*) 1)...o kunren-suru [···を訓練する]. 2)(kiri de)...ni ana-o-akeru [(きりで)···に穴をあける].

    (*vi.*) 1)kyôren-o-ukeru [教練を受ける]. 2)(kiri de) tsuki-toosu

[(きりで)突き通す].

drink (*vt*.) 1)...o nomu [...を飲む]. 2)...o iwatte-kampai-suru [...を祝って乾杯する].

(*vi*.) nomu [飲む]; kampai-suru [乾杯する].

(*n*.) 1)nomi-mono [飲み物]. 2)sake-rui [酒類]. 3)(nomi-mono no) ippai [(飲み物の)一杯].

drip (*vi*.) (mizu ga) shitataru [(水が)滴る].

(*n*.) shizuku [滴].

drive (*vt*.) 1)...o unten-suru [...を運転する]. 2)...o itonamu [...を営む]. 3)muri-ni...(sa-)seru [無理に...(さ)せる]. 4)(kugi ya kui)-o uchi-komu [(くぎやくい)を打ち込む].

(*1*) She cannot **drive** a motorcar.

Kano-jo-wa kuruma-no-*unten*-ga-deki-nai.

(*2*) He **drives** a good trade.

Kare-wa seidai ni shôbai-*o itonande-iru*.

(*3*) This **drove** him into a passion.

Kono-*tame-ni* kare wa okotta.

(*4*) **Drive** the nail aright. Kugi-*o* tadashiku *uchi-kome*.

(*vi*.) 1)kuruma-o-unten-suru [車を運転する]. 2)hagemu [励む].

(*n*.) 1)doraibu [ドライブ]. 2)seiryoku [精力].

drive-in (*n*.) doraibu-in [ドライブイン].

driver (*n*.) (jidôsha no) unten-shu [(自動車の)運転手].

driveway (*n*.) (shitei no) shadô [(私邸の)車道].

driving (*n*.) (kuruma no) unten [(車の)運転].

drizzle (*n*. & *vi*.) kiri-same(-ga-furu) [霧雨(が降る)].

droop (*vi*.) tareru [たれる]; shioreru [しおれる].

(*vt*.) ...o tarasu [...をたらす].

drop (*n*.) shizuku [滴]; itteki [一滴].

Not a single **drop** of rain fell.

Itteki-no-ame mo fura-nakatta.

(*vi*.) shitataru [滴る]; ochiru [落ちる].

An orange **dropped** down from the tree.

Mikan-ga hitotsu ki-kara *ochita*.

(*vt*.) 1)...o shitatarasu [...を滴らす]; ...o otosu [...を落とす]. 2)...o kaki-okuru [...を書き送る].

(*1*) She **dropped** her ink bottle. Kano-jo-wa inku-bin-*o otoshita*.

(*2*) Please **drop** me a line. *O-tegami-o kudasai*.

drop behind rakugo-suru

drop in　chotto-tachi-yoru

drop out　datsuraku-suru; taigaku-suru

drown (*vt.* & *vi.*) ...o dekishi-saseru (dekishi-suru) [...を溺死させる (溺死する)].

　be nearly drowned　oboreru

drowsy (*a.*) nemui [眠い]; nemu-sô-na [眠そうな].

drug (*n.*) kusuri [薬]; mayaku [麻薬].

druggist (*n.*) ((*US*)) yakuzai-shi [薬剤師].

drugstore (*n.*) ((*US*)) doraggu-sutoa [ドラッグストア].

drum (*n.*) taiko [太鼓].

　　(*vi.*) taiko-o-utsu [太鼓を打つ].

　　(*vt.*) ...o taiko-de-ensô-suru [...を太鼓で演奏する].

drunkard (*n.*) oo-zake-nomi [大酒飲み].

drunken (*a.*) yopparatta [酔っ払った].

dry (*a.*) kawaita [乾いた]; kansô-shita [乾燥した]; ame-no-fura-nai [雨の降らない].

　　(*vt.*) ...o kawakasu [...を乾かす]; ...o hosu [...をほす]; ...o fuku [...をふく].

　　　He **dried** them on a towel.

　　　　Kare-wa sore-ra-o taoru-de *fuita*.

　　(*vi.*) kawaku [乾く]; hi-agaru [干上がる].

　　　The well **dried** up.　Ido wa *hi-agatta*.

dry battery　kan-denchi [乾電池].

dry milk　funnyû [粉乳]; kona-miruku [粉ミルク].

duck (*n.*) ahiru [アヒル]; kamo [カモ].

duck (*vt.*) ...o [hyoi-to-mizu-ni-]tsukeru [...を(ひょいと水に)つける].

　　(*vi.*) hyoi-to-mizu-ni-moguru [ひょいと水に潜る].

due (*a.*) 1)tôzen-no [当然の]. 2)tôzen-shiharau-beki [当然支払うべき]; shiharai-kijitsu-no-kita [支払期日のきた]. 3)tôchaku-suru-yotei-no [到着する予定の].

　(*1*) He will advance in life in **due** time.

　　　Sono-uchi-ni kare-wa shusse-suru-darô.

　(*2*) The bill is **due** on the 10th of this month.

　　　Sono tegata wa kongetsu-tô-ka-ga *manki*-desu.

　(*3*) The last train is **due** at 11p.m.

　　　Shû-ressha wa gogo-jû-ichi-ji-ni *tôchaku-suru-hazu*.

be due to　...no-kekka-de-aru; ...no-tame-de-aru

　　His success **is due to** his untiring efforts.

　　　　Kare-no seikô wa kare-no fudan-no doryoku-*no-kekka-de-aru*.

dull (*a.*) 1)nibui ［鈍い］. 2)taikutsu-na ［退屈な］. 3)kusunda ［くすんだ］.

duly (*ad.*) 1)seishiki-ni ［正式に］. 2)jûbun-ni ［十分に］. 3)jikan-doori-ni ［時間どおりに］.

dumb (*a.*) mono-no-ie-nai ［ものの言えない］.

dump (*vt.*) 1)...o suteru ［…を捨てる］; ...o nage-orosu ［…を投げ降ろす］. 2)(*com.*)...o nage-uri-suru ［…を投げ売りする］; ...o dampingu-suru ［…をダンピングする］.
　　　　(*n.*) gomi-sute-ba ［ごみ捨て場］.

dump truck ((*US*)) dampu-kâ ［ダンプカー］.

duplicate (*a.*) ni-jû-no ［二重の］; fuku-no ［副の］; utsushi-no ［写しの］.
　　　　(*n.*) fukusha ［複写］; utsushi ［写し］.
　　　　(*vt.*) 1)...o fukusha-suru ［…を複写する］. 2)...o ni-jû-ni-suru ［…を二重にする］.

durable (*a.*) mochi-ga-yoi ［持ちがよい］.

duration (*n.*) jizoku-kikan ［持続期間］.

during (*prep.*) ...no-aida-ni ［…の間に］; ...no-aida-jû ［…の間じゅう］.

dusk (*n.*) tasogare ［たそがれ］.

dust (*n.*) 1)hokori ［ほこり］. 2)fummatsu ［粉末］.
　(*1*) What a **dust**! Nan-to hidoi *suna-bokori* da!
　(*2*) The coal **dust** found its way everywhere.
　　　　Sekitan-no *kona* ga itaru-tokoro-ni haitte-ita.

dustbin (*n.*) ((*Eng.*)) gomi-ire-kan ［ごみ入れ缶］.

duster (*n.*) hataki ［はたき］; fukin ［ふきん］.

dusty (*a.*) hokori-darake-no ［ほこりだらけの］.

Dutch (*a.*) Oranda-no ［オランダの］; Oranda-jin-no ［オランダ人の］; Oranda-go-no ［オランダ語の］.
　　　　(*n.*) 1)(the D-) Oranda-jin ［オランダ人］. 2)Oranda-go ［オランダ語］.

Dutch treat (*colloq.*) wari-kan-shiki-kaishoku ［割り勘式会食］.

dutiable (*a.*) kanzei-ga-kakaru ［関税がかかる］.

dutiful (*a.*) (shokumu ni) chûjitsu-na ［(職務に)忠実な］.

duty (*n.*) 1)gimu ［義務］; hombun ［本分］; shokumu ［職務］. 2)kanzei ［関税］; zei ［税］.
　(*1*) Every man must do his **duty**.
　　　　Mina *hombun*-o tsukusa-nakereba-naranai.

  He is on(off) **duty**. Kare-wa *tôban(hiban)-da*.

 (2) export **duties** yushutsu-*zei*

duty-free (*a.*) menzei-no [免税の].

dwell (*vi.*) 1)sumu [住む]. 2)(aru jôtai de) kurasu [(ある状態で)暮らす].

 dwell on ...ni-tsuite naga-naga-to-hanasu(-to-kaku); ...o kuyo-kuyo-kangaeru.

  Don't dwell on such a trifle thing.

  Sonna tsumaranai koto-o kuyo-kuyo-kangaeru-na.

dwelling (*n.*) sumai [住居].

dye (*vt. & vi.*) ...o someru (somaru) […を染める(染まる)].

 (*n.*) 1)senryô [染料]. 2)iroai [色合い].

dying (*a.*) shini-kakatte-iru [死にかかっている]; hinshi-no [ひん死の].

dynamic (*a.*) dô-teki-na [動的な]; dainamikku-na [ダイナミックな].

dynamics (*n.*) 1)rikigaku [力学]. 2)dôryoku [動力].

dynamite (*n.*) dainamaito [ダイナマイト].

 (*vt.*) ...o dainamaito-de-bakuha-suru […をダイナマイトで爆破する].

dyspepsia (*n.*) (*med.*) shôka-furyô [消化不良].

E

each (*a.*) ono-ono-no [各々の]; mei-mei-no [めいめいの]; kaku... [各…].

Each student has his own textbooks.

Ono-ono-no seito wa jibun-jishin-no tekisuto-o motte-iru.

(*pron.*) kakuji [各自]; mei-mei [めいめい].

In my home, **each** has his own room.

Watashi-no-ie-de-wa, *mei-mei* ga jibun-no heya-o motte-iru.

(*ad.*) mei-mei[-ni] [めいめい(に)]; hitori[hitotsu]-ni-tsuki [一人[一つ]につき].

I gave them a hundred yen **each**.

Watashi-wa kare-ra-ni *hitori*-hyaku-en-*zutsu* ataeta.

each other tagai-ni

eager (*a.*) 1)nesshin-na [熱心な]. 2)shikiri-ni…(shi-)tagatte [しきりに…(し)たがって].

(*1*) He is very **eager** in his studying.

Kare-wa totemo benkyô-*nesshin*-da.

(*2*) They are **eager** to learn French.

Kare-ra-wa *shikiri-ni* Furansu-go-o manabi-*tagatte*-iru.

eagerly (*ad.*) shikiri-ni [しきりに]; nesshin-ni [熱心に].

eagerness (*n.*) nesshin [熱心].

eagle (*n.*) washi [ワシ].

ear (*n.*) mimi [耳].

ear (*n.*) (*bot.*) (mugi nado no) ho [(麦などの)穂].

earlap (*n.*) mimi-tabu [耳たぶ].

early (*a.*) 1)hayai [早い]. 2)wakai-toki-no [若いときの].

(*1*) in the **early** morning asa-*hayaku*

(*2*) He has been kind at an **early** age.

Kare-wa *wakai-toki*-kara yasashikatta.

(*ad.*) hayaku [早く].

Come **early** in the morning. Asa *hayaku* ki-nasai.

earn (*vt.*) …o kasegu […を稼ぐ]; …o môkeru […をもうける].

earnest (*a.*) majime-na [まじめな]; nesshin-na [熱心な].

earnings (*n.*) shotoku [所得].

earphone (*n.*) 1)(*pl.*) iyafon [イヤフォン]. 2)juwa-ki [受話器].

earth (*n.*) 1)chikyû [地球]. 2)chi [地]; tsuchi [土].

(*1*) The **earth** is round. *Chikyû* wa marui.

(*2*) Oil is found in the **earth**. Sekiyu wa *chi*-chû-ni aru.

Cover it with **earth**. Sore-ni *tsuchi*-o kabuse-nasai.

on earth ittai-zentai

　　　　What on earth is the matter?　Ittai-zentai dô-shita-no-da?

earthen (*a.*) dosei-no [土製の]; tôsei-no [陶製の].

earthenware (*n.*) doki [土器]; tôki [陶器].

earthly (*a.*) kono-yo-no [この世の]; chijô-no [地上の].

earthquake (*n.*) jishin [地震].

earthworm (*n.*) mimizu [ミミズ].

ease (*n.*) 1)kiraku [気楽]; kutsurogi [くつろぎ]. 2)anshin [安心]. 3) yôi [容易].

　(*1*) They drank at their **ease**.
　　　Kare-ra-wa *kutsuroide* sake-o-nonda.

　(*2*) You may set your heart at **ease**.　Go-*anshin* kudasai.

　(*3*) He can do it with **ease**.
　　　Kare-wa sore-o *yôi*-ni suru-koto-ga-dekiru.
　　　Kare-wa sore-o wake-naku suru-koto-ga-dekiru.

　　(*vt.*) ...o raku-ni-suru [...を楽にする]; ...o anshin-saseru [...を安心させる].

easel (*n.*) gaka [画架].

easily (*ad.*) yôi-ni [容易に]; tayasuku [たやすく].

easiness (*n.*) yôi-sa [容易さ]; kiraku [気楽].

east (*n.*) 1)higashi [東]; tôhô [東方]; tôbu [東部]. 2)(the E-)Tôyô [東洋].

　(*1*) The sun rises in the **east**.　Taiyô wa *higashi*-kara noboru.
　　(*a.*) higashi-no [東の]; higashi-kara-no [東からの].
　　　An **east** wind is blowing.　*Higashi*-kaze ga fuiteiru.
　　(*ad.*) higashi-e [東へ]; higashi-ni [東に].

Easter (*n.*) Fukkatsu-sai [復活祭].

eastern (*a.*) higashi-no [東の].

eastward (*a.*) higashi[-e]-no [東(へ)の].

easy (*a.*) 1)yôi-na [容易な]; yasashii [やさしい]. 2)kiraku-na [気楽な]; kutsuroida [くつろいだ].

　(*1*) This work is **easy**.　Kono sagyô wa *yôi*-da.

　(*2*) Make your mind **easy**.　Ki-o o-*raku*-ni.
　　(*ad.*) (*colloq.*) kiraku-ni [気楽に]; nonki-ni [のんきに].
　　　Take it **easy**.　*Aseru-na.*; *Ochitsuke.*; *Shimpai-suru-na.*

easy chair anraku-isu [安楽いす].

easygoing (*a.*) nonki-na [のんきな].

eat (*vt.*) ...o taberu [...を食べる].
　　(*vi.*) shokuji-o-suru [食事をする].

eatable (*a.*) tabe-rareru [食べられる].
　　　　(*n.*) (*pl.*) shokuyô-hin [食用品].
eaves (*n.*) noki [軒].
eavesdrop (*vi.*) tachi-giki-suru [立ち聞きする]; nusumi-giki-suru [盗み聞きする].
ebb (*n.*) hiki-shio [引き潮].
　　　(*vi.*) (shio ga) hiku [(潮が)引く].
E.C. (= European Community) Ôshû-kyôdô-tai [欧州共同体].
eccentric (*a.*) fû-gawari-na [風変わりな].
　　　　　(*n.*) henjin [変人].
echo (*n.*) hankyô [反響]; kodama [こだま].
　　　(*vt. & vi.*) ...o hankyô-saseru (hankyô-suru) [···を反響させる(反響する)]; ...no kodama-o-kaesu (kodama-suru) [···のこだまを返す(こだまする)].
eclipse (*n.*) (*astron.*) (taiyô ya tsuki no) shoku [(太陽や月の)食].
　　　　(*vt.*) ...o ooi-kakusu [···を覆い隠す].
ecliptic (*n.*) (*astron.*) (the -) kôdô [黄道].
ecology (*n.*) seitai-gaku [生態学]; ekorojî [エコロジー].
economic (*a.*) keizai-no [経済の].
economical (*a.*) keizai-teki-na [経済的な]; setsuyaku-suru [節約する].
economically (*ad.*) keizai-teki-ni [経済的に]; setsuyaku-shite [節約して].
economics (*n.*) keizai-gaku [経済学].
economize (*vt. & vi.*) (...o) setsuyaku-suru [(···を)節約する].
economy (*n.*) keizai [経済]; setsuyaku [節約].
ecstasy (*n.*) uchôten [有頂天]; kôkotsu [こうこつ].
edge (*n.*) (ha-mono no) ha [(刃物の)刃]; fuchi [縁]; heri [へり].
edible (*a.*) shokuyô-ni-tekisuru [食用に適する].
　　　(*n.*) (*pl.*) shokuyô-hin [食用品].
edit (*vt.*) ...o henshû-suru [···を編集する].
edition (*n.*) han [版].
editor (*n.*) henshû-sha [編集者]; shuhitsu [主筆].
editorial (*n.*) shasetsu [社説].
　　　　　(*a.*) henshû-no [編集の]; shasetsu-no [社説の].
educate (*vt.*) ...o kyôiku-suru [···を教育する].
education (*n.*) kyôiku [教育].
eel (*n.*) unagi [ウナギ].
effect (*n.*) 1)kekka [結果]; kôka [効果]. 2)(*pl.*) dôsan [動産].

carry...into effect ...o jikkô-suru

come(go) into effect hakkô-suru

effective (*a.*) kiki-me-no-aru [効き目のある]; kôka-teki-na [効果的な].

efficiency (*n.*) nôritsu [能率].

efficient (*a.*) nôritsu-teki-na [能率的な].

effort (*n.*) doryoku [努力].

e.g. = exempli gratia = for example　tatoeba [例えば].

egg (*n.*) tamago [卵].

eggplant (*n.*) (*bot.*) nasu [ナス].

egoistic (*a.*) jiko-hon'i-no [自己本位の].

Egypt (*n.*) Ejiputo [エジプト].

Egyptian (*a.*) Ejiputo-no [エジプトの]; Ejiputo-jin-no [エジプト人の].
　　　　(*n.*) Ejiputo-jin [エジプト人].

eight (*n. & a.*) hachi(-no) [八(の)].

eighteen (*n. & a.*) jû-hachi(-no) [十八(の)].

eighteenth (*n. & a.*) dai-jû-hachi(-no) [第十八(の)].

eighth (*n. & a.*) dai-hachi(-no) [第八(の)].

eightieth (*n. & a.*) dai-hachi-jû(-no) [第八十(の)].

eighty (*n. & a.*) hachi-jû(-no) [八十(の)].

either (*a.*) 1)ryôhô-no [両方の]. 2)dochira-ka-ippô-no [どちらか一方の].
　　(*1*) There are souvenir shops on **either** road.
　　　　Michi-no-*ryôgawa*-ni miyage-mono-ten-ga-arimasu.
　　(*2*) You may take **either** book.
　　　　Dochira-no hon-o totte-mo-yoroshii.
　　　　(*pron.*) dochira-ka [どちらか]; dochira-demo [どちらでも].
　　　　Either will do.　*Dochira-demo* yoroshii.
　　　　(*conj.*) ...ka mata-wa [...かまたは].
　　　　Either he **or** I am at fault.
　　　　Kare-*ka mata-wa* watashi-ga machigatte-iru.
　　　　(*ad.*) ...mo-mata [...もまた].
　　　　John isn't coming **either**.　Jon *mo*[-*mata*] ko-nai.

eject (*vt.*) 1)...o oi-dasu [...を追い出す]. 2)...o haki-dasu [...を吐き出す].

elaborate (*a.*) te-no-konda [手の込んだ]; seikô-na [精巧な].
　　　　(*vt.*) ...o nen-iri-ni-tsukuru [...を念入りに作る].
　　　　(*vi.*) kuwashiku-noberu [詳しく述べる].

elapse (*vi.*) (toki ga) tatsu [(時が)たつ].

elastic (*a.*) danryoku-sei-no-aru [弾力性のある]; yûzû-no-kiku [融通の

　　きく].

　　　　(n.) gomu-himo [ゴムひも].

elbow (n.) hiji [ひじ].

　　(vt.) ...o hiji-de-osu […をひじで押す].

　　He **elbowed** his way through a crowd.

　　　　Kare-wa hito-gomi-no-naka-o *hiji-de-oshi-wakete*-tootta.

elder (a.) toshi-ue-no [年上の].

　　(n.) toshi-ue-no-hito [年上の人].

elderly (a.) shorô-no [初老の].

eldest (a.) ichiban-toshi-ue-no [一番年上の].

elect (vt.) ...o erabu […を選ぶ]; ...o senkyo-suru […を選挙する].

election (n.) 1)senkyo [選挙]. 2)senshutsu [選出].

　　general election sô-senkyo

　　by-election hoketsu-senkyo

election campaign senkyo-undô [選挙運動].

elector (n.) senkyo-nin [選挙人]; yûken-sha [有権者].

electric (a.) denki-no [電気の].

electricity (n.) denki [電気].

electron (n.) (phys. & chem.) denshi [電子]; erekutoron [エレクトロン].

electronics (n.) denshi-kôgaku [電子工学].

electron optics denshi-kôgaku [電子光学].

elegant (a.) yûga-na [優雅な]; jôhin-na [上品な].

element (n.) 1)yôso [要素]; (chem.) genso [元素]. 2)(pl.)(gakumon no) shoho [(学問の)初歩].

elemental (a.) 1)kihon-teki-na [基本的な]. 2)shizen-ryoku-no [自然力の].

elementary (a.) shoho-no [初歩の]; kantan-na [簡単な].

elementary school ((US)) shô-gakkô [小学校].

elephant (n.) zô [ゾウ].

elevate (vt.) ...o ageru […を上げる]; ...o takameru […を高める].

elevator (n.) ((US)) erebêtâ [エレベーター]; shôkô-ki [昇降機].

eleven (n. & a.) jû-ichi(-no) [十一(の)].

eleventh (n. & a.) dai-jû-ichi(-no) [第十一(の)].

　　at the eleventh hour owari-magiwa-ni; kiwadoi-toki-ni

elf (n.) shô-yôsei [小よう精].

eliminate (vt.) ...o sakujo-suru […を削除する].　　　　　　「リート].

elite (n.) (the -) eri-nuki-no-hito-bito [えり抜きの人々]; erîto [エ

ellipsis (*n.*) shôryaku〔-fugô〕[省略(符号)].

elm (*n.*) (*bot.*) nire [ニレ].

eloquent (*a.*) yûben-na [雄弁な]; hyôjô-yutaka-na [表情豊かな].

else (*ad.*) sono-hoka-ni [そのほかに].
> Do you have anything **else** to tell me?
> *Sono-hoka-ni* nani-ka-hanasu-koto-ga arimasu-ka?

elsewhere (*ad.*) doko-ka-hoka-no-tokoro-ni [どこかほかの所に].

elude (*vt.*) ...o〔-umaku〕sakeru […を(うまく)避ける].

emancipate (*vt.*) ...o kaihô-suru […を解放する].

embankment (*n.*) teibô [堤防]; dote [土手].

embark (*vt.*) ...o jôsen-saseru […を乗船させる]; ...o tsumi-komu […を積み込む].
> (*vi.*) jôsen-suru [乗船する].

embarrass (*vt.*) ...o komaraseru […を困らせる].
  be embarrassed kimari-waruku-kanjiru; mago-mago-suru

embarrassment (*n.*) tôwaku [当惑].

embassy (*n.*) taishi-kan [大使館].

emblem (*n.*) shôchô [象徴].

embody (*vt.*) ...o gutai-ka-suru […を具体化する].

embrace (*vt.*) 1)...o daki-shimeru […を抱きしめる]. 2)...o fukumu […を含む].
> (*n.*) hôyô [抱擁].

embroider (*vt. & vi.*) (...o) shishû-suru [(…を)刺しゅうする].

emcee (*n.*) shikai-sha [司会者].
> (*vt. & vi.*) (...o) shikai-suru [(…を)司会する].

emerge (*vi.*) 1)omote-ni-arawareru [表に現れる]. 2)akiraka-ni-naru [明らかになる]. 3)nuke-dasu [抜け出す].

emergency (*n.*) hijô-no-baai [非常の場合]; kinkyû-no-toki [緊急の時].

emigrant (*n.*) (takoku e-no)ijû-min [(他国への)移住民].

emigrate (*vi.*) (takoku e) ijû-suru [(他国へ)移住する].
> (*vt.*) ...o ijû-saseru […を移住させる].

eminence (*n.*) 1)ko-dakai-tokoro [小高い所]. 2)(chii-no-)takai-koto [(地位の)高いこと].

eminent (*a.*) chomei-na [著名な]; takuetsu-shita [卓越した].

emit (*vt.*) 1)(hikari ya netsu)-o hassuru [(光や熱)を発する]. 2)...o kuchi-ni-dasu […を口に出す].

emotion (*n.*) 1)kanjô [感情]. 2)kandô [感動].

emotional (*a.*) 1)kanjô-teki-na [感情的な]. 2)kandô-teki-na [感動的な].

emperor (*n.*) kôtei [皇帝]; tennô [天皇].

emphasis (*n.*) 1)(*phon.*) kyôsei [強勢]. 2)kyôchô [強調].

emphasize (*vt.*) ...o kyôchô-suru [...を強調する].

empire (*n.*) teikoku [帝国].

employ (*vt.*) 1)...o yatou [...を雇う]. 2)...o tsukau [...を使う].

employee (*n.*) jûgyô-in [従業員].

employer (*n.*) yatoi-nushi [雇い主].

employment (*n.*) 1)koyô [雇用]; shiyô [使用]. 2)shokugyô [職業]; shigoto [仕事].

empress (*n.*) jotei [女帝]; kôgô [皇后].

empty (*a.*) kara-no [空の].
   an **empty** bottle   *kara-no* bin
   (*vt.*) ...o kara-ni-suru [...を空にする]; ...o akeru [...をあける].
   She **emptied** the bottle.   Kano-jo-wa bin-*o kara-ni-shita.*
   (*vi.*) 1)kara-ni-naru [空になる]. 2)sosogu [注ぐ].
   (*1*) The classroom **emptied** as soon as the lecture was over.
       Kyôshitsu wa kôgi ga owaru-to-sugu *kara-ni-natta.*
   (*2*) The Shinano **empties** into the Japan Sea.
       Shinano-gawa wa Nihon-kai-ni *sosogu.*

empty-handed (*a.*) te-bura-no [手ぶらの].

enable (*vt.*) ...ni ...(suru-)koto-o-kanô-ni-suru [...に(...する)ことを可能にする].

enamel (*n.*) enameru [エナメル]; hôrô [ほうろう].
   (*vt.*) ...ni enameru-o-nuru [...にエナメルを塗る]; ...ni hôrô-biki-suru [...にほうろう引きする].

enchant (*vt.*) ...o uttori-saseru [...をうっとりさせる].

enchanting (*a.*) uttori-saseru-yô-na [うっとりさせるような].

enclose (*vt.*) 1)...o kakomu [...を囲む]. 2)...o fûnyû-suru [...を封入する].
   (*1*) The garden **is enclosed** with a wall.
       Sono niwa wa kabe-de *kakomarete-iru.*
   (*2*) Please **enclose** a check in your letter.
       Tegami-ni kogitte-*o fûnyû-shite-*kudasai.

enclosure (*n.*) 1)kakoi [囲い]. 2)fûnyû[-butsu] [封入(物)].

encore (*n.*) ankôru [アンコール].

encounter (*vt.*) (hito ya konnan)-ni de-kuwasu. [(人や困難)に出くわす].
   (*n.*) de-au-koto [出会うこと]; sôgû [遭遇].

encourage (*vt.*) ...o yûki-zukeru [...を勇気づける]; ...o shôrei-suru [...

を奨励する].

encouragement (*n.*) gekirei [激励]; shôrei [奨励].

encouraging (*a.*) hagemi-ni-naru [励みになる].

encyclopedia, -paedia (*n.*) hyakka-jiten [百科事典].

end (*n.*) 1)hashi [端]. 2)owari [終わり]; saigo [最後]. 3)mokuteki [目的].

  (*1*) He surveyed the land from **end** to **end**.

    Kare-wa *hashi*-kara-*hashi*-made sono tochi-o sokuryô-shita.

  (*2*) They won victory in the **end**.

    Kare-ra-wa *saigo*-ni-wa shôri-o osameta.

  (*3*) He attained his **end**.　Kare-wa *mokuteki*-o tasshita.

  no end (*colloq.*) ooi-ni

  put an end to …o owaraseru

    (*vt. & vi.*) …o owaraseru (owaru) […を終わらせる(終わる)].

    I shall **end** my life here.

    Watashi-wa koko-de shôgai-o *oeru*-darô.

    His plan **ended** in a failure.

    Kare-no keikaku wa shippai-ni-*owatta*.

endeavor, -our (*n. & vi.*) doryoku(-suru) [努力(する)].

endless (*a.*) kagiri-no-nai [限りのない].

endorse (*vt.*) (*com.*) …ni uragaki-suru […に裏書する].

endow (*vt.*) 1)…ni kikin-o-kifu-suru […に基金を寄付する]. 2)(sainô)-o sazukeru [(才能)を授ける].

endurance (*n.*) nintai[-ryoku] [忍耐(力)]; shimbô [辛抱].

endure (*vt.*) (kutsû ya konnan)-ni taeru [(苦痛や困難)に耐える].

  (*vi.*) mochi-kotaeru [持ちこたえる]; shimbô-suru [辛抱する].

enemy (*n.*) teki [敵].

energetic (*a.*) seiryoku-teki-na [精力的な].

energetically (*ad.*) seiryoku-teki-ni [精力的に].

energetics (*n.*) enerugî-ron [エネルギー論].

energy (*n.*) 1)seiryoku [精力]; enerugî [エネルギー]. 2)(*pl.*) katsudô-ryoku [活動力].

enforce (*vt.*) 1)(*law*)…o shikô-suru […を施行する]. 2)…o kyôyô-suru […を強要する].

engage (*vt*) 1)…o jûji-saseru […を従事させる]. 2)…o yatou […を雇う]. 3)(be -d) kon'yaku-shite-iru [婚約している]. 4)…o yakusoku-suru […を約束する].

  (*1*) Jiro **is engaged** in business.

　　　　Jirô wa shigoto-ni *bottô-shite-iru*.
(2) He **engaged** her as a secretary.
　　　　Kare-wa kano-jo-o hisho-to-shite *yatotta*.
(3) Taro **is engaged** to Hanako.
　　　　Tarô wa Hanako-to *kon'yaku-shite-iru*.
(4) He **engaged** to be here at six.
　　　　Kare-wa roku-ji-ni koko-ni-kuru-*to yakusoku-shita*.
　　　　(*vi.*) jûji-suru [従事する].
　　He **engaged** in trade.　Kare-wa shôbai-o-*shite-ita*.

engaged (*a.*) 1)kon'yaku-chû-no [婚約中の]. 2)shiyô-chû-no [使用中の];
isogashii [忙しい].
(1) an **engaged** couple　*kon'yaku-chu-no* futari
(2) He is now **engaged**.
　　　　Kare-wa ima *isogashi*kute-te-ga-hanase-nai.

engagement (*n.*) 1)kon'yaku [婚約]. 2)yakusoku [約束]. 3)yômu [用
務]. 4)koyô [雇用].

engine (*n.*) enjin [エンジン]; kikan [機関].

engineer (*n.*) gishi [技師].

engineering (*n.*) kôgaku [工学].

England (*n.*) Ingurando [イングランド]; Eikoku [英国].

English (*a.*) 1)Eikoku-no [英国の]; Eikoku-jin-no [英国人の]. 2)Eigo-
no [英語の].
　　　　(*n.*) 1)(the E-) Eikokumin [英国民]. 2)Eigo [英語].

Englishman (*n.*) Eikoku-jin [英国人].

engrave (*vt.*) ...ni chôkoku-suru […に彫刻する]; ...ni hori-komu […
に彫りこむ].

enjoy (*vt.*) 1)...o tanoshimu […を楽しむ]. 2)...o motte-iru […を持っ
ている].
(1) We **enjoyed** the driving.　Doraibu wa *tanoshikatta*.
(2) Are you **enjoying** good health?　O-genki-*desu*-ka?
　　enjoy oneself　yukai-ni-sugosu; tanoshimu

enjoyment (*n.*) tanoshimi [楽しみ]; kyôraku [享楽].

enlarge (*vt. & vi.*) ...o ookiku-suru(ookiku-naru) […を大きくする(大
きくなる)]; (*photo.*) ...o hiki-nobasu(hiki-nobashi-ga-kiku) […を引
き伸ばす(引き伸ばしがきく)].

enlarged edition zôho-ban [増補版].

enlargement (*n.*) kakudai [拡大]; (*photo.*) hiki-nobashi [引き伸ばし].

enlighten (*vt.*) ...o keimô-suru […を啓もうする].

enmity (*n.*) tekii [敵意]; hammoku [反目].

ennoble (*vt.*) ...o kôshô-ni-suru [...を高尚にする].

enormous (*a.*) bakudai-na [ばく大な].

enough (*a.*) jûbun-na [十分な]; ...(suru-ni)-taru [...(するに)足る].

　　　　　(*ad.*) jûbun-ni [十分に]; ...dake [...だけ].

　　　　　(*n.*) jûbun [十分].

　　cannot...enough ikura...(shite-)mo-tari-nai

enrich (*vt.*) ...o yutaka-ni-suru [...を豊かにする].

enrol(l) (*vt.*) ...o meibo-ni-kisai-suru [...を名簿に記載する].

ensure (*vt.*) ...o kakujitsu-ni-suru [...を確実にする]; ...o kakuho-suru [...を確保する].

entangle (*vt.*) ...o motsuresaseru [...をもつれさせる].

　　be entangled in　...ni maki-komareru

enter (*vt.*) ...ni hairu [...に入る]; ...ni kuwawaru [...に加わる].

　　　　　He **entered** the room.　Kare-wa heya-*ni haitta*.

　　　　　He **entered** a contest.　Kare-wa kontesuto-*ni sanka-shita*.

　　　　　(*vi.*) hairu [入る].

enterprise (*n.*) 1)jigyô [事業]. 2)bôken-shin [冒険心].

entertain (*vt.*) 1)...o motenasu [...をもてなす]. 2)...o tanoshimaseru [...を楽しませる].

entertainment (*n.*) 1)motenashi [もてなし]. 2)goraku [娯楽].

enthusiasm (*n.*) nekkyô [熱狂]; netchû [熱中].

enthusiastic (*a.*) nesshin-na [熱心な]; nekkyô-teki-na [熱狂的な].

entire (*a.*) zentai-no [全体の]; mattaku-no [全くの].

entirely (*ad.*) mattaku [全く].

entitle (*vt.*) 1)...ni shikaku-o-ataeru [...に資格を与える]. 2)...to-iu hyôdai-o-tsukeru [...という表題をつける].

　　(*1*) He **is** not **entitled** to a share in the profit.

　　　　　Kare-wa sono rieki no haibun-ni-azukaru-*shikaku-wa*-nai.

　　(*2*) The book **was entitled** "Milton."

　　　　　Sono shomotsu wa "Miruton" *to-iu-hyôdai-datta*.

entrance (*n.*) 1)nyûjô [入場]; nyûgaku [入学]. 2)iriguchi [入り口].

　　(*1*) He took the **entrance** examination.

　　　　　Kare-wa *nyûgaku*-shiken-o uketa.

　　(*2*) At the **entrance** he met with his aunt.

　　　　　Iriguchi-de kare-wa oba-ni atta.

entreat (*vt.*) ...o tangan-suru [...を嘆願する].

entrust (*vt.*) ...o makaseru [...を任せる].

entry (*n.*) 1) hairu-koto [入ること]. 2) sanka-sha [参加者]. 3) kisai-jikô [記載事項].

enumerate (*vt.*) ...o kazoe-ageru [···を数えあげる]; ...o rekkyo-suru [···を列挙する].

envelop (*vt.*) ...o tsutsumu [···を包む].

envelope (*n.*) fûtô [封筒].

envious (*a.*) urayamashi-sô-na [うらやましそうな].

environment (*n.*) shûi [周囲]; kankyô [環境].

envy (*n.*) sembô [せん望].
　　　　(*vt.*) ...o urayamu [···をうらやむ].

epidemic (*a.*) densen-suru [伝染する]; ryûkô-sei-no [流行性の].
　　　　(*n.*) densen-byô [伝染病]; hayari [はやり].

episode (*n.*) sôwa [挿話]; episôdo [エピソード].

epitomize (*vt.*) ...o yôyaku-suru [···を要約する].

epoch (*n.*) (kakki-teki-na)jidai [(画期的な)時代].

epoch-making (*a.*) kakki-teki-na [画期的な].

equal (*a.*) 1) dôtô-no [同等の]; hitoshii [等しい]. 2) (...ni-)taeru [(···に)耐える].
　　(*1*) He is **equal** to his father.
　　　　　Kare-wa chichi-oya-ni-*hitteki-suru*-jimbutsu-da.
　　(*2*) He is not able to be **equal** to the task.
　　　　　Kare-wa sono-shigoto-ni *taeru*-koto-ga-deki-nai.
　　　　(*n.*) 1) dôtô-no-hito [同等の人]. 2) hitteki-suru-mono [匹敵するもの].
　　　　(*vt.*) ...ni hitoshii [···に等しい]; ...ni hitteki-suru [···に匹敵する].

equality (*n.*) dôtô [同等]; byôdô [平等].

equally (*ad.*) hitoshiku [等しく]; dôyô-ni [同様に].

equator (*n.*) (the -) sekidô [赤道].

equip (*vt.*) ...o sôbi-suru [···を装備する]; (- oneself) mi-jitaku-suru [身支度する].

equipment (*n.*) sôbi [装備]; shitaku [支度].

equivalent (*a.*) (...ni-)sôtô-suru [(···に)相当する].

era (*n.*) 1) kigen [紀元]. 2) jidai [時代].

erase (*vt.*) ...o keshi-toru [···を消し取る].

eraser (*n.*) keshi-gomu [消しゴム].

erect (*a.*) chokuritsu-shita [直立した].
　　　　(*vt.*) ...o chokuritsu-saseru [···を直立させる]; ...o tateru [···を建てる].

err (*vi.*) ayamaru [誤る]; machigai-o-suru [間違いをする].

errand (*n.*) yôji [用事]; tsukai [使い].

  go on an errand   tsukai-bashiri-suru

error (*n.*) ayamari [誤り].

erupt (*vi.*) funka-suru [噴火する].

eruption (*n.*) funka [噴火].

escalation (*n.*) dankai-teki-kakudai [段階的拡大]; jôshô [上昇]; esukarêshon [エスカレーション].

escalator (*n.*) ((*US*)) esukarêtâ [エスカレーター].

escape (*vt.*) ...o nogareru […を逃れる]; ...o manukareru […を免れる].

    He narrowly **escaped** being killed.

        Kare-wa yatto korosareru-no-o-*manukareta*.

    (*vi.*) nigeru [逃げる].

    He **escaped** from prison.   Kare-wa *datsugoku-shita*.

    (*n.*) tôbô [逃亡]; nogareru-shudan [逃れる手段].

  have a narrow escape   kyûshi-ni-isshô-o-eru

escort (*n.*) 1)tsuki-soi-no-dansei [付き添いの男性]. 2)goei [護衛].

    (*vt.*) ...ni tsuki-sou […に付き添う]; ...o goei-suru […を護衛する].

especially (*ad.*) toku-ni [特に].

essay (*n.*) zuihitsu [随筆]; essei [エッセイ].

essential (*a.*) honshitsu-teki-na [本質的な]; kaku-koto-no-deki-nai [欠くことのできない].

    (*n.*) honshitsu-teki-yôso [本質的要素].

establish (*vt.*) 1)...o setsuritsu-suru […を設立する]. 2)...o katameru […を固める]. 3)...o risshô-suru […を立証する].

    (*1*) Our school **was established** ten years ago.

        Ware-ware-no gakkô wa jû-nen-mae-ni *setsuritsu-sareta*.

    (*2*) He **established** himself as a writer.

        Kare-wa bumpitsu-ka-to-shite *mi-o-tateta*.

    (*3*) I must **establish** my innocence.

        Watashi-wa mi-no-keppaku-o *risshô-shi*-nakereba-naranai.

establishment (*n.*) 1)setsuritsu [設立]. 2)risshô [立証].

estate (*n.*) 1)jisho [地所]. 2)zaisan [財産].

  real estate   fu-dôsan

esteem (*vt.*) 1)...o sonkei-suru […を尊敬する]. 2)...to kangaeru [… と考える].

    (*1*) You talk gently. We **esteem** you for it.

      Kimi-wa shizuka-ni hanashi-o-suru. Dakara ware-ware-wa
        kimi-o *sonkei-suru*.
       (*n.*) sonkei [尊敬].

estimate (*vt.*) ...to mi-tsumoru […と見積もる]; ...o hyôka-suru […
  を評価する].
       (*vi.*) mitsumori-o-suru [見積もりをする].
       (*n.*) mitsumori [見積もり]; hyôka [評価].

estimation (*n.*) iken [意見]; hyôka [評価]; mitsumori [見積もり].

etc. = et cetera sono-ta [その他]; ...nado […など].

eternal (*a.*) eien-no [永遠の].

eternity (*n.*) eien [永遠]; fumetsu [不滅].

ether (*n.*) (*chem.*) êteru [エーテル].

ethical (*a.*) rinri-no [倫理の]; dôgi-ni-kanatta [道義にかなった].

ethics (*n.*) rinri[-gaku] [倫理(学)].

etiquette (*n.*) sahô [作法]; reigi [礼儀]; echiketto [エチケット].

Europe (*n.*) Yôroppa [ヨーロッパ]; Ôshû [欧州].

European (*a.*) Yôroppa-no [ヨーロッパの]; Yôroppa-jin-no [ヨーロッ
  パ人の].
       (*n.*) Yôroppa-jin [ヨーロッパ人].

evaporation (*n.*) jôhatsu [蒸発].

eve (*n.*) 1)(shukusaijitsu nado no)zen'ya[zenjitsu] [(祝祭日などの)前
  夜[前日]]. 2)(jûyô-jiken nado no)chokuzen [(重要事件などの)直前].
  (*1*) He returned home on Christmas **Eve**.
      Kare-wa Kurisumasu-no-*zen'ya*-ni kaette-kita.
  (*2*) He died on the **eve** of the war.
      Kare-wa sensô-no-*chokuzen*-ni shinda.

even (*a.*) 1)taira-na [平らな]; dôitsu-men-no [同一面の]. 2)taitô-no
  [対等の]; son-toku-no-nai [損得のない]. 3)gûsû-no [偶数の].
  (*1*) an **even** surface *taira-na* hyômen
  (*2*) It was an **even** bargain.
      Sore-wa *son-toku-no-nai* torihiki-datta.
  (*3*) an **even** number *gûsû*

even (*ad.*) ...sae […さえ]; ...sura […すら].
      Even children can get it. Kodomo-de-*sae* wakaru.

evening (*n.*) yûgata [夕方]; ban [晩].

event (*n.*) 1)jiken [事件]; gyôji [行事]. 2)baai [場合]. 3)(*sports*)
  shumoku [種目]; hito-shiai [一試合].
  (*1*) annual **events** nenjû-*gyôji*

(2) in that **event**　sono-*baai*-niwa

(3) track **events**　torakku-*kyôgi*-*shumoku*

　at all events　to-ni-kaku; izure-ni-seyo

eventually (*ad.*) kekkyoku-wa [結局は].

ever (*ad.*) 1)tsune-ni [常に]; itsu-mo [いつも]. 2)katsute [かつて]; ima-made-ni [いままでに]. 3)itsu-ka [いつか]. 4)ittai [いったい].

(1) It is **ever** so.　Sore-wa *itsu-mo* sô-da.

(2) None of us have **ever** seen it.

　　　Ware-ware-no-uchi dare-mo sore-o *ima-made-ni* mita-mono-wa nai.

(3) If you **ever** see him, please tell him that we are all well.

　　　Itsu-ka kare-ni awareta-ra, watashi-tachi-wa mina genki-da-to tsutaete-kudasai.

(4) Why **ever** didn't you say so him?

　　　Ittai naze kare-ni sô iwa-na-katta-no-da?

　as...as ever　ai-kawarazu

　ever since　sore-irai-zutto

　ever so (*colloq.*)　hijô-ni

　for ever　itsu-made-mo

evergreen (*a.*) jôryoku-no [常緑の].

　　　　　(*n.*) jôryoku-ju [常緑樹].

everlasting (*a.*) eikyû-no [永久の].

evermore (*ad.*) tsune-ni [常に]; eikyû-ni [永久に].

every (*a.*) kotogotoku-no [ことごとくの]; ...goto-ni […ごとに].

　every other day　kakujitsu-ni

everybody (*pron.*) dare-demo[-mina] [だれでも(皆)].

everyday (*a.*) mainichi-no [毎日の]; fudan-no [普段の].

everyone (*pron.*) = everybody.

everything (*pron.*) banji [万事].

　　　Everything has its merit.　*Banji* chôsho-o motte-iru.

　　　　　　　　　　　　　　　　　Chôsho-no-nai-mono-wa-nai.

everywhere (*ad.*) doko-ni-mo [どこにも]; itaru-tokoro-de [至る所で].

evidence (*n.*) shôko [証拠].

evident (*a.*) meihaku-na [明白な].

evidently (*ad.*) meihaku-ni [明白に]; akiraka-ni [明らかに].

evil (*a.*) 1)warui [悪い]. 2)yûgai-na [有害な]. 3)fukitsu-na [不吉な].

　　　(*n.*) aku [悪]; saigai [災害].

evil-minded (*a.*) hara-guroi [腹黒い].

evolution (*n.*) 1)hatten [発展]. 2)(*biol.*) shinka [進化].

exact (*a.*) seikaku-na [正確な].

exactly (*ad.*) 1)seikaku-ni [正確に]; chôdo [ちょうど]. 2)mattaku-sono-toori [全くそのとおり].

exaggerate (*vt. & vi.*) (...o) kochô-suru [(…を)誇張する].

exaggerated (*a.*) kochô-shita [誇張した].

exalt (*vt.*) 1)...o takameru […を高める]. 2)...o home-soyasu […をほめそやす].

examination (*n.*) 1)shiken [試験]. 2)shinsatsu [診察]; kensa [検査].
 (*1*) Last week we had an **examination** in physics.
　　　Senshû ware-ware-wa butsuri-no-*shiken*-ga atta.
 (*2*) Did you take a medical **examination**?
　　　Anata-wa kenkô-*shindan*-o ukemashita-ka?

examine (*vt.*) 1)...o shiraberu […を調べる]; ...no shiken-o-suru […の試験をする]. 2)...o shinsatsu-suru […を診察する].
 (*1*) They **are examining** the cause of the car accident.
　　　Kare-ra-wa jidôsha-jiko no gen'in-o *shirabete-imasu*.
　　　Kare-ra-wa jidôsha-jiko no gen'in-o *chôsa-chû-desu*.
 (*2*) The doctor **examined** him. Isha wa kare-o *shinsatsu-shita*.

example (*n.*) 1)rei [例]. 2)tehon [手本]; mohan [模範]. 3)imashime [戒め]; miseshime [みせしめ].
 (*1*) Please give me an **example**. Dôka ichi-*rei*-o agete-kudasai.
 (*2*) He set a good **example** to others.
　　　Kare-wa hoka-no-hito-bito-ni yoi *tehon*-o shimeshita.
 (*3*) The man was made an **example** of them by being hanged.
　　　Ano otoko wa kôshu-kei-ni-sarete *miseshime*-ni-sareta.
 for example tatoeba

exceed (*vt. & vi.*) 1)...o koeru […を超える]. 2)(...ni) masaru [(…に)まさる].

exceeding (*a.*) hijô-na [非常な]; ijô-na [異常な].

exceedingly (*ad.*) hijô-ni [非常に].

excel (*vt. & vi.*) (...ni) masaru [(…に)まさる].

excellence (*n.*) takuetsu [卓越]; yûshû [優秀].

excellency (*n.*) (E-)kakka [閣下].

excellent (*a.*) sugureta [すぐれた]; subarashii [すばらしい].

except (*prep.*)...o-nozoite […を除いて]; ...no-hoka-wa […のほかは].

exception (*n.*) reigai [例外].
 without exception reigai-nashi-ni

exceptional (*a.*) 1)reigai-teki-na ［例外的な］. 2)tokubetsu-sugureta ［特別すぐれた］.

exceptionally (*ad.*) reigai-teki-ni ［例外的に］; hijô-ni ［非常に］.

excess (*n.*) 1)chôka ［超過］. 2)kado ［過度］.

excess of imports yunyû-chôka ［輸入超過］.

excessive (*a.*) kado-no ［過度の］; kyokutan-na ［極端な］.

exchange (*vt.*) 1)...o kôkan-suru ［…を交換する］. 2)(*com.*)...o ryôgae-suru ［…を両替する］.

    (*n.*) 1)kôkan ［交換］. 2)(*com.*) ryôgae ［両替］. 3)(*com.*) torihiki-sho ［取引所］. 4)denwa-kôkan-kyoku ［電話交換局］.

excite (*vt.*) ...o kôfun-saseru ［…を興奮させる］.

excited (*a.*) kôfun-shita ［興奮した］.

excitement (*n.*) kôfun ［興奮］.

exciting (*a.*) 1)kôfun-saseru ［興奮させる］. 2)totemo-omoshiroi ［とても面白い］.

exclaim (*vt. & vi.*) (...to) sakebu ［(…と)叫ぶ］; (...to) iu ［(…と)言う］.

exclamation (*n.*) 1)sakebi ［叫び］; kantan ［感嘆］. 2)(*gram.*) kantan-shi ［感嘆詞］.

exclude (*vt.*) ...o shime-dasu ［…を締め出す］; ...o jogai-suru ［…を除外する］.

exclusive (*a.*) 1)haita-teki-na ［排他的な］. 2)dokusen-teki-na ［独占的な］. 3)kôkyû-na ［高級な］.

  exclusive of ...o-nozoite

exclusively (*ad.*) dokusen-teki-ni ［独占的に］; moppara ［専ら］.

excursion (*n.*) 1)ensoku ［遠足］. 2)shûyû-ryokô ［周遊旅行］.

excuse (*vt.*) 1)...no iiwake-o-suru ［…の言い訳をする］. 2)...o yurusu ［…を許す］.

  (*1*) He **excused** coming late.

    Kare-wa okureta-koto-*no iiwake-o-shita.*

  (*2*) **Excuse** me. *Gomen*-nasai.

    (*n.*) iiwake ［言い訳］; kôjitsu ［口実］.

execute (*vt.*) 1)...o jikkô-suru ［…を実行する］; ...o suikô-suru ［…を遂行する］. 2)...o shokei-suru ［…を処刑する］.

  (*1*) The plan **was** very well **executed**.

    Keikaku wa rippa-ni *jikkô-sareta.*

  (*2*) He **was executed** for murder.

    Kare-wa satsujin-zai-de *shokei-sareta.*

execution (*n.*) 1)jikkô [実行]; suikô [遂行]. 2)shokei [処刑]; shikei-shikkô [死刑執行].

executive (*a.*) 1)shikkô-ryoku-no-aru [執行力のある]. 2)gyôsei-jô-no [行政上の].

    (*n.*) 1)gyôsei-kan [行政官]. 2)kaisha-yakuin [会社役員].

exemplify (*vt.*) ...o reishô-suru [...を例証する]; ...no yoi-rei-to-naru [...のよい例となる].

exempt (*vt.*) ...o menjo-suru [...を免除する].

    (*a.*) menjo-sareta [免除された].

    (*n.*) menjo-sarete-iru-hito [免除されている人].

exemption (*n.*) menjo [免除]; kôjo [控除].

exercise (*n.*) 1)undô [運動]. 2)renshû [練習]; renshû-mondai [練習問題].

    (*1*) Lack of **exercise** is not good for the health.

        Undô-busoku wa kenkô-ni-yoku-nai.

    (*2*) an **exercise** in English grammar   Ei-bumpô-no-*renshû-mondai*

        (*vt.*) 1)(nôryoku ya chikara)-o hatarakaseru [(能力や力)を働かせる]. 2)...o undô-saseru [...を運動させる].

        (*vi.*) undô-suru [運動する]; renshû-suru [練習する].

exert (*vt.*) 1)...o hatarakaseru [...を働かせる]. 2)(– oneself) doryoku-suru [努力する].

exertion (*n.*) 1)doryoku [努力]. 2)kôshi [行使].

exhale (*vt.*) (kûki ya gasu)-o haki-dasu [(空気やガス)を吐き出す].

exhaust (*vt.*) 1)...o tsukare-hatesaseru [...を疲れ果てさせる]. 2)...o tsukai-hatasu [...を使い果たす]. 3)...o kara-ni-suru [...を空にする]. 4)...o kenkyû-shi-tsukusu [...を研究し尽くす].

    (*1*) He **exhausted** himself by hard work.

        Kare-wa isshô-kemmei-hataraite *tsukare-hateta*.

    (*2*) He **exhausted** his money.   Kare-wa kane-o *tsukai-hatashita*.

    (*3*) We **exhausted** the well.

        Ware-ware-wa sono ido-no-mizu-o *kumi-tsukushita*.

        (*vi.*) haishutsu-suru [排出する].

        (*n.*) haiki [排気].

exhibit (*vt.*) 1)...o chinretsu-suru [...を陳列する]; ...o miseru [...を見せる]. 2)...o teishutsu-suru [...を提出する].

        (*vi.*) tenji-kai-o-hiraku [展示会を開く].

        (*n.*) chinretsu-hin [陳列品]; teiji [提示].

exhibition (*n.*) 1)tenran-kai [展覧会]. 2)hakki [発揮].

exhilarate (*vt.*) ...o yôki-ni-saseru [···を陽気にさせる].

exile (*n.*) tsuihô [追放]; bômei [亡命].
(*vt.*) ...o tsuihô-suru [···を追放する].

exist (*vi.*) sonzai-suru [存在する]; ikite-iru [生きている].

existence (*n.*) sonzai [存在]; seizon [生存].

exit (*n.*) 1)deguchi [出口]. 2)(haiyû no) taijô [(俳優の)退場].

exotic (*a.*) ikoku-jôcho-no [異国情緒の].

expand (*vt. & vi.*) ...o hirogeru (hirogaru) [···を広げる(広がる)]; ...o fukuramaseru (fukuramu) [···を膨らませる(膨らむ)].

expansion (*n.*) kakudai [拡大]; bôchô [膨張].

expect (*vt.*) 1)...o kitai-suru [···を期待する]; ...o yoki-suru [···を予期する]. 2)...to omou [···と思う].

expectation (*n.*) kitai [期待]; yoki [予期].
beyond expectation omoi-no-hoka-ni; yosô-ijô-ni

expedition (*n.*) 1)tanken[-tai] [探検(隊)]; ensei[-tai] [遠征(隊)]. 2) jinsoku [迅速].

expel (*vt.*) ...o oi-dasu [···を追い出す].

expenditure (*n.*) 1)shishutsu [支出]; shôhi [消費]. 2)keihi [経費]; hiyô [費用].

expense (*n.*) shuppi [出費]; hiyô [費用].

expensive (*a.*) hiyô-no-kakaru [費用のかかる]; kôka-na [高価な].

experience (*n.*) keiken [経験].
(*vt.*) ...o keiken-suru [···を経験する]; ...o taiken-suru [···を体験する].

experienced (*a.*) keiken-no-aru [経験のある]; rôren-na [老練な].

experiment (*n. & vi.*) jikken(-suru) [実験(する)].

expert (*n.*) kurôto [くろうと]; semmon-ka [専門家].
(*a.*) rôren-na [老練な]; umai [うまい].

expire (*vi.*) shûryô-suru [終了する]; (*com.*) manki-ni-naru [満期になる].

explain (*vt.*) ...o setsumei-suru [···を説明する].

explanation (*n.*) setsumei [説明].

explode (*vt. & vi.*) ...o bakuhatsu-saseru (bakuhatsu-suru) [···を爆発させる(爆発する)]; ...o haretsu-saseru (haretsu-suru) [···を破裂させる(破裂する)].

exploit (*n.*) kôseki [功績]; tegara [手柄].

exploit (*vt.*) ...o kaihatsu-suru [···を開発する].

exploration (*n.*) tanken [探検]; tankyû [探究].

explore (*vt. & vi.*) (...o) tanken-suru [(…を)探検する]; (...o) chôsa-suru [(…を)調査する].

explosion (*n.*) bakuhatsu [爆発]; haretsu [破裂].

explosive (*a.*) bakuhatsu-shi-yasui [爆発しやすい].

      (*n.*) bakuhatsu-butsu [爆発物]; bakuyaku [爆薬].

export (*vt.*) ...o yushutsu-suru […を輸出する].

      (*n.*) 1)yushutsu[-hin] [輸出(品)]. 2)(*pl.*) yushutsu-gaku [輸出額].

  (*1*) The government prohibited the **export** of wheat.

    Seifu wa ko-mugi no *yushutsu*-o kinshi-shita.

  (*2*) **Exports** exceed imports.

    Yushutsu-gaku ga yunyû-gaku-o uwa-mawaru.

    Yushutsu-chôka.

expose (*vt.*) 1)(kiken)-ni(-mi)-o sarasu [(危険)に(身)をさらす]. 2)...o bakuro-suru […を暴露する]. 3)(*photo.*)...o roshutsu-suru […を露出する].

exposition (*n.*) 1)hakuran-kai [博覧会]. 2)setsumei [説明].

exposure (*n.*) 1)mi-o-sarasu-koto [身をさらすこと]. 2)bakuro [暴露]. (*photo.*) roshutsu [露出]; (*film*) hito-koma [一こま].

express (*vt.*) ...o ii-arawasu […を言い表わす]; ...o hyôgen-suru […を表現する].

      (*a.*) 1)meihaku-na [明白な]. 2)tokubetsu-na [特別な]. 3)kyûkô-no [急行の].

      (*n.*) 1)kyûkô-ressha [急行列車]; kyûkô-basu [急行バス]. 2)((*Eng.*)) sokutatsu [速達].

      (*ad.*) 1)((*Eng.*)) sokutatsu-de [速達で]. 2)toku-ni [特に].

express delivery ((*Eng.*)) sokutatsu[-bin] [速達(便)].

expression (*n.*) 1)hyôgen [表現]. 2)hyôjô [表情].

  beyond expression hyôgen-deki-nai-hodo-ni

expressive (*a.*) 1)hyôgen-ni-tomu [表現に富む]. 2)imi-ari-ge-na [意味ありげな].

exquisite (*a.*) 1)totemo-utsukushii [とても美しい]. 2)seikô-na [精巧な]; kotta [凝った].

extend (*vt.*) 1)...o nobasu […を延ばす]; ...o hirogeru […を広げる]; ...o enchô-suru […を延長する]. 2)...o oyobosu […を及ぼす].

      (*vi.*) 1)nobiru [延びる]; hirogaru [広がる]. 2)oyobu [及ぶ].

extension (*n.*) 1)nobasu-koto [延ばすこと]; enchô [延長]; kakuchô [拡張]; hirogeru-koto [広げること]. 2)(denwa no) naisen [(電話の)

内線].

extensive (*a.*) hiroi [広い]; kô-han'i-no [広範囲の].

extensively (*ad.*) hiroku [広く]; dai-kibo-ni [大規模に].

extent (*n.*) 1)hirosa [広さ]; ookisa [大きさ]. 2)han'i [範囲]; teido [程度].

　　to a great extent　hijô-ni

　　to some extent　aru-teido-made

exterior (*a.*) soto-no [外の]; gaikan-jô-no [外観上の].

　　(*n.*) gaibu [外部]; gaikan [外観].

external (*a.*) 1)gaibu-no [外部の]. 2)(*med.*) gaiyô-no [外用の]. 3) hyômen-jô-no [表面上の].

extinct (*a.*) kieta [消えた]; shômetsu-shita [消滅した].

extinct volcano shi-kazan [死火山].

extinguish (*vt.*) …o kesu […を消す]; …o zetsumetsu-saseru […を絶滅させる].

extinguisher (*n.*) shôka-ki [消火器].

extra (*a. & ad.*) yobun-no (yobun-ni) [余分の(余分に)]; tokubetsu-no (tokubetsu-ni) [特別の(特別に)]; rinji-no [臨時の].

　　(*n.*) 1)yobun-na-mono [余分なもの]. 2)gôgai [号外]; rinji-zôkan [臨時増刊]. 3)(*movie*) ekisutora [エキストラ].

extract (*vt.*) 1)…o nuki-toru […を抜き取る]. 2)…o shibori-dasu […を絞り出す]. 3)…o bassui-suru […を抜粋する].

　　(*n.*) 1)bassui [抜粋]. 2)ekisu [エキス].

extraordinary (*a.*) 1)ijô-na [異常な]; hijô-na [非常な]. 2)rinji-no [臨時の].

extravagant (*a.*) 1)kane-zukai-no-arai [金使いの荒い]. 2)tohô-mo-nai [途方もない].

extreme (*n. & a.*) kyokutan(-na) [極端(な)].

extremely (*ad.*) kyokutan-ni [極端に].

exultation (*n.*) oo-yorokobi [大喜び].

eye (*n.*) 1)me [目]. 2)shiryoku [視力].

　　(2) As far as the eye could reach, there extended a large desert.

　　　Me-no-todoku-kagiri, dai-sabaku-ga hirogatte-ita.

　　catch one's eye　hito-no-me-ni-tomaru

　　have(keep) one's eye on　…o mi-haru

　　keep one's eyes open　yudan-naku-chûi-shite-iru

　　naked eye　nikugan

eyeball (*n.*) gankyû [眼球].

eyebrow (*n.*) mayu〔-ge〕［まゆ(毛)］.

eye chart shiryoku-kensa-hyô［視力検査表］.

eyelash (*n.*) matsuge［まつ毛］.

eyelid (*n.*) mabuta［まぶた］.

eyesight (*n.*) shiryoku［視力］; shikai［視界］.

eyesore (*n.*) me-zawari［目障り］.

eyestrain (*n.*) me-no-tsukare［目の疲れ］.

eyewash (*n.*) me-gusuri［目薬］.

eyewitness (*n.*) mokugeki-sha［目撃者］.

      (*vt.*) ...o mokugeki-suru［…を目撃する］.

F

fable (*n.*) gûwa［ぐう話］.

fabric (*n.*) orimono［織物］; ki-ji［生地］.

fabulous (*a.*) 1)densetsu-teki-na［伝説的な］. 2)shinji-gatai［信じ難い］.

face (*n.*) 1)kao［顔］. 2)hyômen［表面］.

  face to face men-to-mukatte

  in (the) face of 1)...ni-chokumen-shite. 2)...nimo-kakawarazu

  look one in the face hito-no-kao-o-matomo-ni-miru

  lose face memboku-o-ushinau

    (*vt.*) 1)...ni mensuru［…に面する］. 2)...ni tachi-mukau［…に立ち向かう］.

  (*1*) The lodge **faces** the sea. Sono koya wa umi-*ni menshite-iru*.

(2) They **faced** the enemy by themselves.
　　　Kare-ra-wa jibun-tachi-dake-de teki-*ni tachi-mukatta*.
　　(*vi.*) muku [向く]; mensuru [面する].

facility (*n.*) 1)bengi [便宜]; (*pl.*) setsubi [設備]. 2)yôi-sa [容易さ].

fact (*n.*) jijitsu [事実]; genjitsu [現実].
　as a matter of fact jijitsu-wa; jissai-wa
　in fact jissai[-no-tokoro]

faction (*n.*) habatsu [派閥].

factor (*n.*) yôso [要素].

factory (*n.*) seizô-sho [製造所]; kôjô [工場].

faculty (*n.*) 1)sainô [才能]; shuwan [手腕]. 2)(*educ.*) (daigaku no) gakubu [(大学の)学部]; ((*US*)) gakubu-kyôju-dan [学部教授団].

fade (*vi.*) 1)(iro ga) aseru [(色が)あせる]. 2)(hikari ga) usureru [(光が)薄れる]. 3)(hana ga) shibomu [(花が)しぼむ].

Fahrenheit (*a.*) kashi-ondo-kei-no [華氏温度計の].

fail (*vi.*) 1)fusoku-suru [不足する]; naku-naru [無くなる]. 2)(kenkô ya shiryoku ga) otoroeru [(健康や視力が)衰える]. 3)shippai-suru [失敗する].
　(1) Our food **failed**. Tabe-mono ga *tsukita*.
　(2) My sight **has failed** lately.
　　　Watashi-no shiryoku wa saikin *otoroeta*.
　(3) He **failed** in the examination.
　　　Kare-wa shiken-ni *shippai-shita*.
　　(*vt.*) 1)...o shitsubô-saseru […を失望させる]; ...no yaku-ni-tata-nai […の役に立たない]. 2)...o okotaru […を怠る]. 3)...ni ochiru […に落ちる].
　(1) Words **failed** me. Kotoba ga *de-nakatta*.
　(2) He **failed** to appear. Kare-wa araware-*nakatta*.
　(3) He **failed** chemistry. Kare-wa kagaku-no-shiken-*ni ochita*.
　never fail to (do) kanarazu...(suru)
　　(*n.*) shippai [失敗].
　without fail machigai-naku; kitto

failure (*n.*) 1)shippai [失敗]. 2)fu-rikô [不履行]. 3)fusoku [不足]. 4)suijaku [衰弱].

faint (*a.*) 1)yowa-yowa-shii [弱々しい]; ki-no-yowai [気の弱い]. 2)bon'yari-shita [ぼんやりした]; kasuka-na [かすかな]. 3)me-mai-
　feel faint me-mai-ga-suru 　　　└ga-shite [目まいがして].

faintly (*ad.*) 1)yowa-yowa-shiku [弱々しく]. 2)kasuka-ni [かすかに].

fair (*n.*) 1)hakuran-kai [博覧会]. 2)himpyô-kai [品評会].
　international trade fair　kokusai-mihon-ichi
fair (*a.*) 1)kôhei-na [公平な]; seitô-na [正当な]. 2)kanari-no [かなり
　の]. 3)(tenki ga) yoi [(天気が)よい]. 4)iro-jiro-no [色白の];
　kimpatsu-no [金髪の]. 5)utsukushii [美しい].
fair-haired (*a.*) kimpatsu-no [金髪の].
fairly (*ad.*) 1)kôhei-ni [公平に]. 2)kanari [かなり]. 3)mattaku [全く];
　mamma-to [まんまと].
　(*1*) The case was treated **fairly**.
　　　Sono jiken wa *kôhei-ni* atsukawareta.
　(*2*) They sing **fairly** well.　Kare-ra-wa *kanari* jôzu-ni utau.
　(*3*) He was **fairly** caught.　Kare-wa *mamma-to* tsukamatta.
fairy (*n. & a.*) yôsei(-no-yô-na) [よう精(のような)].
fairyland (*n.*) otogi-no-kuni [おとぎの国]; senkyô [仙境].
fairy tale　otogi-banashi [おとぎ話]; dôwa [童話].
faith (*n.*) 1)shinrai [信頼]. 2)shinkô [信仰]. 3)shingi [信義].
faithful (*a.*) chûjitsu-na [忠実な]; shinjirareru [信じられる].
faithfully (*ad.*) chûjitsu-ni [忠実に].
　Yours faithfully,; Faithfully yours,　Keigu
fake (*n.*) nise-mono [偽物].
　　(*vt.*) 1)...o gizô-suru [...を偽造する]. 2)(*colloq.*)...no furi-o-suru
　　[...のふりをする].
fall (*vi.*) 1)ochiru [落ちる]; taoreru [倒れる]; (ame ga) furu [(雨が)
　降る]. 2)naru [なる].
　(*1*) They **fell** downstairs.　Kare-ra-wa kaika-ni *ochita*.
　(*2*) The baby **fell** ill.　Akambô wa byôki-ni-*natta*.
　fall on　...ni ataru
　fall to　...shi-hajimeru
　　(*n.*) 1)tsuiraku [墜落]. 2)tentô [転倒]. 3)(*pl.*) taki [滝]. 4)
　　((*US*)) aki [秋].
false (*a.*) 1)ayamatta [誤った]. 2)nise-no [偽の]; jinzô-no [人造の].
　3)fu-seijitsu-na [不誠実な].
　(*1*) It may give him a **false** impression.
　　　Sore-wa kare-ni *ayamatta* inshô-o ataeru-kamo-shirenai.
　(*2*) He made **false** coins.　Kare-wa *nise*-gane-o tsukutta.
　(*3*) I was **false** to myself.　Watashi-wa jibun-ni *fu-seijitsu*-datta.
false eye　gigan [義眼].
falsehood (*n.*) kyogi [虚偽]; uso [うそ].

false teeth gishi [義歯].

fame (*n.*) meisei [名声].

famed (*a.*) nadakai [名高い]; yûmei-na [有名な].

familiar (*a.*) 1)shitashii [親しい]. 2)yoku-shirarete-iru [よく知られている].

family (*n.*) 1)kazoku [家族]. 2)kodomo-tachi [子供たち]. 3)(*biol.*) (seibutsu-bunrui-jô-no) ka [(生物分類上の)科].

famine (*n.*) kikin [飢きん].

famous (*a.*) yûmei-na [有名な].

fan (*n.*) uchiwa [うちわ]; sempû-ki [扇風機].
    (*vt.*) 1)...o aogu […をあおぐ]. 2)...o aoru […をあおる].

fan (*n.*) (*colloq.*)(eiga ya yakyû no) fan [(映画や野球の)ファン].

fanciful (*a.*) ki-magure-na [気まぐれな]; kûsô-teki-na [空想的な].

fancy (*n.*) 1)kûsô [空想]. 2)konomi [好み].
    (*1*) It is a wild **fancy**. Sore-wa toritome-no-nai *kûsô* da.
    (*2*) I have a **fancy** for out-driving.
        Watashi-wa doraibu-ga-*shumi*-da.
    after(to) one's fancy hito-no-ki-ni-itta
        (*vt.*) ...o kûsô-suru […を空想する]; ...to-iu ki-ga-suru […という気がする].
        I **fancy** he is an actor.
        (Watashi-wa) Dômo kare-wa haiyû-*no-yô-na-ki-ga-suru*.
        (*a.*) 1)sôshoku-teki-na [装飾的な]. 2)hôgai-na [法外な]. 3)ki-magure-na [気まぐれな].

fantastic (*a.*) 1)kûsô-teki-na [空想的な]. 2)iyô-na [異様な]. 3)(*colloq.*) subarashii [すばらしい].

far (*ad.*) tooku-ni [遠くに]; haruka-ni [はるかに].
    as far as 1)...made. 2)...(suru)kagiri-wa
    1) as far as Nagoya Nagoya-made
    2) as far as I can watashi-no-dekiru-kagiri
    by far haruka-ni; zutto
    far and near itaru-tokoro-ni
    Far from it! Tonde-mo-nai!
    so far 1)ima-made-wa. 2)soko-made
    so far as (= as far as) ...(suru-)kagiri-wa
    so far from...ing ...(suru-)yori-mushiro; ...no-kawari-ni
    (*a.*) tooi [遠い].
    Far East Kyokutô

faraway (*a.*) tooi [遠い].

fare (*n.*) 1)unchin [運賃]; jôkyaku [乗客]. 2)tabe-mono [食べ物]; ryôri [料理].

  (*1*) What is the **fare** to New York?

      Nyû-Yôku-made *unchin* wa ikura-desu-ka?

  (*2*) simple **fare** shisso-na *ryôri*

    a bill of **fare** menyû

    good(fine) **fare** go-chisô

    (*vi.*) 1)kurasu [暮らす]; yatte-yuku [やって行く]. 2)koto-ga-hakobu [事が運ぶ].

  (*1*) How did you **fare** in your project?

      Keikaku wa umaku-*iki-mashita*-ka?

  (*2*) It **fares** ill with her. Kano-jo-wa *umaku-yatte-i*-nai.

farewell (*n.*) wakare [別れ]; itomagoi [いとまごい].

  bid **farewell** wakare-o-tsugeru; itomagoi-suru

    (*int.*) Go-kigen-yoroshiku! [ご機嫌よろしく!]; Sayô-nara! [さようなら!].

farm (*n.*) nôjô [農場].

    (*vt. & vi.*) (...o) kôsaku-suru [(…を)耕作する].

farmer (*n.*) nôen-nushi [農園主]; nômin [農民].

farming (*n.*) nôjô-keiei [農場経営].

farmyard (*n.*) nôka-no-niwa [農家の庭].

far-sighted (*a.*) 1)((US)) enshi-no [遠視の]. 2)senken-no-mei-no-aru [先見の明のある].

farther (*a. & ad.*) motto-tooi(motto-tooku) [もっと遠い(もっと遠く)].

farthest (*a. & ad.*) mottomo-tooku-no(mottomo-tooku-ni) [最も遠くの(最も遠くに)].

  at (the) **farthest** tooku-temo; osoku-temo

fascinate (*vt.*) ...o uttori-saseru […をうっとりさせる].

fascinating (*a.*) miwaku-teki-na [魅惑的な].

fashion (*n.*) 1)ryûkô [流行]. 2)shikata [仕方]; ryûgi [流儀].

    (*vt.*) ...o katachi-zukuru […を形作る].

fashionable (*a.*) 1)ryûkô-no [流行の]. 2)kôkyû-na [高級な].

fast (*a.*) 1)hayai [速い]. 2)susunde-iru [進んでいる]. 3)shikkari-shita [しっかりした].

  (*1*) He is very **fast** in swimming.

      Kare-wa oyogu-no-ga totemo *hayai*.

  (*2*) My watch is a little **fast**.

Watashi-no tokei wa sukoshi *susunde-iru*.
(3) I laid **fast** hold on him.

Watashi-wa kare-o *shikkari*-tsukanda.

(*ad.*) shikkari-to [しっかりと]; hayaku [速く].

fast (*n. & vi.*) danjiki(-suru) [断食(する)].

fasten (*vt.*) 1)...o kotei-suru [...を固定する]. 2)(chûi nado)-o shûchû-suru [(注意など)を集中する]. 3)...o oshi-tsukeru [...を押しつける].

(*vi.*) 1)shikkari-tomaru [しっかり留まる]; shimaru [締まる]. 2)shigami-tsuku [しがみつく]. 3)me-o-tsukeru [目をつける]. 4)shûchû-suru [集中する].

fastener (*n.*) tome-gu [留め具]; fasunâ [ファスナー]; chakku [チャック].

fastening (*n.*) 1)shimeru-koto [締めること]. 2)(*pl.*) tome-gu [留め具].

fat (*a.*) futotta [太った]; himan-shita [肥満した].

(*n.*) shibô [脂肪]; abura-mi [脂身]; himan [肥満].

fatal (*a.*) 1)chimei-teki-na [致命的な]. 2)ummei-o-kessuru [運命を決する]; kettei-teki-na [決定的な].

fate (*n.*) ummei [運命]; shukumei [宿命].

father (*n.*) chichi [父].

father-in-law (*n.*) gifu [義父]; shûto [しゅうと].

fatigue (*n.*) hirô [疲労].

(*vt.*) ...o tsukaresasu [...を疲れさす].

fatten (*vt. & vi.*) ...o futoraseru (futoru) [...を太らせる(太る)]; ...o koyasu (koeru) [...を肥やす(肥える)].

faucet (*n.*) (suidô no) jaguchi [(水道の)蛇口].

fault (*n.*) 1)kashitsu [過失]. 2)tsumi [罪]; sekinin [責任]. 3)ketten [欠点].

(*1*) He acknowledged his **faults**.

Kare-wa jibun-no *kashitsu*-o mitometa.

(*2*) The **fault** is my own.

Sekinin wa watashi-jishin-ni-aru.

Sore-wa-watashi-no-*sei*-desu.

(*3*) I have many **faults**. Watashi-wa *ketten*-ga-ooi.

find fault with ...no ara-o-sagasu

fault-finding (*n.*) ara-sagashi [あら探し].

(*a.*) kuchi-yakamashii [口やかましい].

faultless (*a.*) môshi-bun-no-nai [申し分のない]; kanzen-na [完全な].

favor, -vour (*n.*) 1)kôi [好意]. 2)jinryoku [尽力]. 3)hen'ai [偏愛].

(1) He won her **favor**. Kare-wa kano-jo-ni-*sukare*ta.

(2) May I ask a **favor** of you?
O-negai-o-*kiite-itadake*-mashô-ka?

(3) She treated him with **favor**.
Kano-jo-wa kare-o *eko-hiiki*-shita.

    (*vt.*) 1)...ni sansei-suru [⋯に賛成する]. 2)...o hiiki-suru [⋯をひいきする]. 3)...ni (...shite-)ageru [⋯に(⋯して)あげる]; ...ni (...shite-)kureru [⋯に(⋯して)くれる].

(1) I **favor** the plan. Watashi-wa sono keikaku-*ni sansei-da*.

(2) I **favor** that wrestler.
Watashi-wa ano resurâ-*ga hiiki-da*.

(3) Will you **favor** us with a song?
Uta-*o kikasete-kudasai-masen*-ka?

favorable (*a.*) 1)kô-tsugô-na [好都合な]. 2)kôi-teki-na [好意的な].

favorite (*n.*) o-ki-ni-iri-no-hito [お気に入りの人]; suki-na-mono [好きなもの].

    (*a.*) o-ki-ni-iri-no [お気に入りの].

fear (*n.*) 1)kyôfu [恐怖]. 2)fuan [不安]; ki-zukai [気遣い].

(1) He was trembling for **fear**.
Kare-wa *kyôfu*-no-tame-ni furueteita.

(2) No **fear**! *Daijôbu-da!*

  for fear that ...no-nai-yô-ni; ...to-ike-nai-kara

    (*vt.*) 1)...o osoreru [⋯を恐れる]. 2)...o shimpai-suru [⋯を心配する].

(1) I **fear** death. Watashi-wa shi-*o osoreru*.

(2) I **fear** that he will be ill.
Watashi wa kare-ga byôki-ni-naru-no-dewa-naika-*to shimpai-shite-iru*.

    (*vi.*) shimpai-suru [心配する]; kenen-suru [懸念する].

    Never **fear**! *Shimpai-suru*-na!

fearful (*a.*) osoroshii [恐ろしい].

fearfully (*ad.*) 1)kowa-gowa [こわごわ]. 2)(*colloq.*) hidoku [ひどく].

fearless (*a.*) osore-nai [恐れない]; daitan-na [大胆な].

feast (*n.*) 1)shukuen [祝宴]; go-chisô [ごちそう]. 2)shukusaijitsu [祝祭日].

    (*vt. & vi.*) 1)...ni go-chisô-suru(go-chisô-ni-naru) [⋯にごちそうする(ごちそうになる)]. 2)...o tanoshimaseru(tanoshimu) [⋯を楽しませる(楽しむ)].

feat (*n.*) 1)hanare-waza [離れ業]. 2)kôseki [功績].

feather (*n.*) hane[-kazari] [羽(飾り)].

    (*vt.*) …ni hane-kazari-o-tsukeru […に羽飾りを付ける].

feathery (*a.*) 1)hane-no-haeta [羽のはえた]. 2)hane-no-yô-na [羽のような].

feature (*n.*) 1)(*pl.*) kao-dachi [顔立ち]; mehanadachi [目鼻立ち]. 2)tokuchô [特徴]; tokushoku [特色]. 3)yobi-mono [呼び物].

  (*1*) She has regular **features**.

    Kano-jo-wa *mehanadachi*-ga totonotte-iru.

  (*2*) the geographical **feature** of a district

    aru chihô no chiri-teki *tokuchô*

  (*3*) the **feature** of tonight's television program

    komban-no terebi-bangumi no *yobi-mono*

    (*vt.*) 1)…o yobi-mono-ni-suru […を呼び物にする]. 2)…no tokushoku-o-nasu […の特色をなす].

February (*n.*) Nigatsu [二月].

federal (*a.*) 1)rempô-no [連邦の]. 2)((*US*))(F-) rempô-seifu-no [連邦政府の].

fee (*n.*) 1)ryôkin [料金]. 2)(*pl.*) jugyô-ryô [授業料]. 3)hôshû [報酬].

feeble (*a.*) yowai [弱い]; yowa-yowa-shii [弱々しい].

feebly (*ad.*) yowa-yowa-shiku [弱々しく].

feed (*vt.*) …o yashinau […を養う]; …ni tabe-mono-o-ataeru […に食べ物を与える].

    (*vi.*) (ushi ya uma ga) mono-o-kuu [(牛や馬が)ものを食う].

  feed on …o jôshoku-to-suru

    (*n.*) magusa [まぐさ]; shiryô [飼料].

feel (*vt.*) …o sawatte-miru […を触ってみる]; …o te-saguri-de-shiru […を手探りで知る]; …o kanjiru […を感じる]; …no kanji-ga-suru […の感じがする].

    Let me **feel** your pulse. Myaku-*o haiken*.

    (*vi.*) kanjiru [感じる].

  feel for …o te-saguri-de-sagasu

  feel like…ing …(shi-)tai-ki-ga-suru

    (*n.*) te-zawari [手触り]; kanji [感じ].

feeler (*n.*) (*zool.*) (*pl.*) shokkaku [触覚].

feeling (*n.*) kanji [感じ]; (*pl.*) kimochi [気持]; kanjô [感情].

feint (*n.*) 1)mise-kake [見せかけ]. 2)(*sports*) feinto [フェイント].

fellow (*n.*) 1)(*pl.*) nakama [仲間]; dôryô [同僚]. 2)yatsu [やつ].

(1) They are **fellows** at school. Kare-ra-wa gakkô-*nakama* da.

(2) Poor **fellow**! Kawaisô-*ni*!

fellowman (*n.*) = fellow creature ningen-dôshi [人間同志]; dôhô [同胞].

felt (*n.*) feruto[-seihin] [フェルト(製品)].

female (*n. & a.*) josei(-no) [女性(の)]; mesu(-no) [雌(の)].

feminine (*a.*) josei-no [女性の]; josei-rashii [女性らしい].

fence (*n.*) kaki [垣]; hei [塀].

fencing (*n.*) fenshingu [フェンシング]; kenjutsu [剣術].

fender (*n.*) (jidôsha no) fendâ [(自動車の)フェンダー].

ferment (*n.*) 1)kôso [酵素]. 2)hakkô [発酵].
    (*vt. & vi.*) ...o hakkô-saseru (hakkô-suru) [···を発酵させる (発酵する)].

fern (*n.*) (*bot.*) shida [シダ].

ferroconcrete (*n.*) tekkin-konkurîto [鉄筋コンクリート].

ferry (*n.*) 1)watashi-bune [渡し船]; ferî[-bôto] [フェリー(ボート)].
    2)watashi-ba [渡し場].
    (*vt. & vi.*) ...o fune-de-watasu (fune-de-wataru) [···を船で渡す (船で渡る)].

fertile (*a.*) (tochi ga) yoku-koeta [(土地が)よく肥えた]; tasan-no [多産の].

fertilizer (*n.*) hiryô [肥料].

fervent (*a.*) atsui [熱い]; netsuretsu-na [熱烈な].

festival (*n.*) matsuri [祭り]; ...sai [···祭]; ...fesutibaru [···フェスティバル].

fetch (*vt.*) (mono)-o itte-totte-kuru [(もの)を行って取って来る].

feudal (*a.*) 1)ryôchi-no [領地の]. 2)hôken-seido-no [封建制度の].

feudalism (*n.*) hôken-seido [封建制度].

fever (*n.*) 1)netsu [熱]. 2)netsubyô [熱病]. 3)nekkyô [熱狂].
  scarlet fever shôkô-netsu

feverish (*a.*) netsu-no-aru [熱のある]; netsuppoi [熱っぽい].

few (*a.*) sukunai [少ない]; shôsû-no [少数の].
    I have **few** friends. Watashi-wa tomodachi-ga *sukunai*.
    He will arrive here in a **few** days.
      Kare-wa *sû*-jitsu-chû-ni koko-e tsuku-darô.
    (*pron.*) shôsû-no-hito [少数の人].
    Few live to the age of ninety.
      Kyû-jussai-made ikiru hito wa *sukunai*.

not a few kanari-ooku-no; zuibun

only a few hon-no-sukoshi-dake-no; goku-wazuka

quite a few (*colloq.*) kanari-no-sû-no

fiancée (*n.*) kon'yaku-sha [婚約者]; fianse [フィアンセ].

fiber, -bre (*n.*) sen'i [繊維].

fiber glass sen'i-garasu [繊維ガラス]; gurasu-faibâ [グラスファイバー].

fiction (*n.*) shôsetsu [小説]; fikushon [フィクション].

fiddle (*n.*) (*colloq.*) baiorin [バイオリン].

fiddlestick (*n.*) baiorin-no-yumi [バイオリンの弓].

fiderity (*n.*) chûjitsu[-do] [忠実(度)]; seikaku-sa [正確さ].

field (*n.*) 1)no-hara [野原]; hatake [畑]. 2)(*sports*) kyôgi-jô [競技場].

    (*vt.*) (bôru)-o toru [(ボール)を取る]; ...o sabaku [...をさばく].

    (*vi.*) (yashu to-shite) shubi-ni-tsuku [(野手として)守備につく].

fielder (*n.*) (*baseball*) yashu [野手].

fiend (*n.*) 1)(*colloq.*)...kyô [...狂]. 2)akuma [悪魔].

fierce (*a.*) dômô-na [どう猛な]; hageshii [激しい].

fiercely (*ad.*) hageshiku [激しく]; môretsu-ni [猛烈に].

fiery (*a.*) hi-no [火の]; hi-no-yô-na [火のような]; netsuretsu-na [熱烈な].

fifteen (*a.*) jû-go-no [十五の].

    (*n.*) jû-go [十五]; (*tennis*) fifutîn [フィフティーン]; (*rugger*) chîmu [チーム].

fifteenth (*n. & a.*) dai-jû-go(-no) [第十五(の)].

fifth (*n. & a.*) dai-go(-no) [第五(の)].

fiftieth (*n. & a.*) dai-go-jû(-no) [第五十(の)].

fifty (*n. & a.*) go-jû(-no) [五十(の)].

fifty-fifty (*a. & ad.*) (*colloq.*) gobu-gobu-no(-ni) [五分五分の(に)]; han-han-no(-ni) [半々の(に)].

go fifty-fifty with ...to yama-wake-suru

fig (*n.*) 1)(*bot.*) ichijiku [イチジク]. 2)goku-wazuka [ごくわずか].

not care a fig(fig's end) for ...o mattaku-mondai-ni-shi-nai

fight (*vi. & vt.*) tatakau (...to tatakau) [戦う(...と戦う)].

    Great Britain **fought** with Germany.

    Eikoku wa Doitsu-to *tatakatta*.

    They **fought** a good battle. Kare-ra-wa yoku *tatakatta*.

    (*n.*) sentô [戦闘]; kenka [けんか].

fighter (*n.*) 1)(*mil.*) = fighter plane sentô-ki [戦闘機]. 2)tôshi [闘

士]

fighting (*n.*) sentô [戦闘].

       (*a.*) kenka-goshi-no [けんか腰の]; sentô-teki-na [戦闘的な].

figure (*n.*) 1)sugata [姿]; katachi [形]. 2)jimbutsu [人物]. 3)moyô [模様]. 4)sûji [数字]. 5)(*pl.*) keisan [計算].

       (*vt.*) 1)...o arawasu [···を表す]. 2)...o(-moyô-de) kazaru [···を(模様で)飾る]. 3)...o sôzô-suru [···を想像する]. 4)...o keisan-suru [···を計算する].

file (*n.*) toji-komi[-chô] [とじ込み(帳)]; fairu [ファイル].

       (*vt.*) ...o toji-komi-ni-suru [···をとじ込みにする].

fill (*vt. & vi.*) ...o ippai-ni-suru (ippai-ni-naru) [···をいっぱいにする(いっぱいになる)].

      The wind **fills** the white sails.

         Kaze ga shiroi ho-o *fukuramaseru*.

      Sails **fill**. Ho ga *kaze-o-haramu*.

  fill in 1)...o kaki-komu. 2)...o umeru

  1) Please fill in the name here.

        Koko-ni namae-o kaki-konde-kudasai.

  2) Fill in the blanks. Kûsho-o ume-nasai.

  fill up ippai-ni-naru

     The hall filled up rapidly.

        Hôru wa tachimachi ippai-ni-natta.

       (*n.*) 1)jûbun [十分]. 2)ippai-no-ryô [一杯の量]; ippuku [一服].

filling (*n.*) tsume-mono [詰め物]; (*med.*) jûten[-butsu] [充てん(物)].

filling station = gas station gasorin-sutando [ガソリンスタンド].

film (*n.*) 1)(*photo.*) firumu [フィルム]. 2) eiga [映画].

filter (*n.*) 1)roka-ki [ろ過器]. 2)(*photo.*) firutâ [フィルター].

filter tip firutâ-zuki-no-tabako [フィルター付きのタバコ].

fin (*n.*) hire [ひれ].

final (*a.*) saigo-no [最後の]; saishû-no [最終の].

       (*n.*) 1)kesshô-sen [決勝戦]. 2)(*pl.*) saishû-shiken [最終試験].

finally (*ad.*) saigo-ni [最後に]; tsui-ni [ついに].

finance (*n.*) 1)zaisei [財政]. 2)(*pl.*) zaigen [財源].

       (*vt.*) ...ni yûshi-suru [···に融資する].

financial (*a.*) zaisei-jô-no [財政上の].

find (*vt.*) 1)...o mitsukeru [···を見付ける]; ...o hakken-suru [···を発見する]. 2)...ga...to wakaru [···が···とわかる].

  (*1*) I will **find** your pen.

　　　　Watashi-ga kimi-no pen-o *mitsukete-ageyô*.
　　(2) I **found** the novel interesting.
　　　　Sono shôsetsu wa omoshiroi-koto-*ga wakatta*.
　find out 1)...o hakken-suru. 2)...o toku
　　1) I found out a mistake.　Watashi-wa ayamari-o hakken-shita.
　　2) Can you find out this riddle?
　　　　Kimi-wa kono-nazo-ga tokeru-ka?
fine (*n.*) bakkin [罰金].
　　　(*vt.*) ...ni bakkin-o-kasuru [⋯に罰金を科する].
fine (*a.*) 1)rippa-na [立派な]. 2)seikô-na [精巧な]. 3)(tsubu nado
　no) komakai [(粒などの)細かい]. 4)(tenki ga) hareta [(天気が)晴れ
　た]. 5)genki-na [元気な].
finely (*ad.*) 1)komakaku [細かく]. 2)rippa-ni [立派に]; umaku [うま
　く].
finger (*n.*) (te no) yubi [(手の)指].
　lay one's finger on (*colloq.*) ...o tekikaku-ni-shiteki-suru; ...no
　　basho-o-tsuki-tomeru
　put the finger on (*US slang*) ...o mikkoku-suru
fingerprint (*n.*) (*pl.*) shimon [指紋].
　　　(*vt.*) ...no shimon-o-toru [⋯の指紋をとる].
finish (*vt.*) ...o sumasu [⋯を済ます]; ...o oeru [⋯を終える].
　　　(*vi.*) owaru [終わる].
　finish off = **finish up**　...o shi-ageru
finished (*a.*) 1)kansei-shita [完成した]. 2)rippa-na [立派な].
fir (*n.*) (*bot.*) momi-no-ki [モミの木].
fire (*n.*) 1)hi [火]. 2)ro-no-hi [炉の火]; taki-bi [たき火]. 3)kaji [火
　事].
　　(*1*) The warehouse caught **fire**.　Sôko ni *hi-ga* tsuita.
　　(*2*) A **fire** is burning on the hearth.　Ro-niwa *hi* ga moeteiru.
　　(*3*) A **fire** broke out last night.　Sakuya *kaji*-ga atta.
　　　(*vt. & vi.*) (...o) hassha-suru [(⋯を)発射する]; ...ni hi-o-tsukeru
　　(hi-ga-tsuku) [⋯に火をつける(火がつく)]; ...o moe-tataseru (moe-
　　agaru) [⋯を燃えたたせる(燃え上がる)].
fire alarm　kasai-keihô [火災警報]; kasai-hôchi-ki [火災報知機].
fire bomb　shôi-dan [焼い弾].
fire brigade ((*US*)) shôbô-kyoku [消防局].
fire escape　kasai-yô-hinan-sôchi [火災用避難装置]; hijô-kaidan [非常
　階段].

fire extinguisher shôka-ki [消火器].

fire fighter = fireman shôbô-shi [消防士].

firefly (*n.*) hotaru [ホタル].

fire insurance kasai-hoken [火災保険].

fireplace (*n.*) danro [暖炉].

fireproof (*a.*) taika-sei-no [耐火性の]; bôka-no [防火の].

firewood (*n.*) takigi [たきぎ].

firework (*n.*) hana-bi [花火].

firm (*a.*) 1)katai [堅い]. 2)kippari-to-shita [きっぱりとした].
    (*ad.*) kataku [堅く]; shikkari-to [しっかりと].
    (*vt. & vi.*) ...o kataku-suru (kataku-naru) [...を堅くする(堅くなる)].

firm (*n.*) shôkai [商会]; kaisha [会社].

firmly (*ad.*) shikkari-to [しっかりと]; kippari-to [きっぱりと].

first (*a. & ad.*) dai-ichi-no (dai-ichi-ni) [第一の(第一に)]; saisho-no
    (saisho-ni) [最初の(最初に)].
  for the first time hajimete
  first of all nani-yori-mo-mazu
    (*n.*) 1)saisho-no-hito [最初の人]; saisho-no-mono [最初のもの].
  2)dai-ichi-nichi [第一日].
  at first saisho-wa; hajime-wa
  from the first hajime-kara

first-rate (*a.*) 1)ichiryû-no [一流の]. 2)(*colloq.*) subarashii [すばら
    しい].

fiscal (*a.*) kokko-no [国庫の]; kaikei-no [会計の].

fiscal stamp shûnyû-inshi [収入印紙].

fiscal year ((*US*)) kaikei-nendo [会計年度].

fish (*n.*) sakana [魚].
    (*vt. & vi.*) ...o tsuru(tsuri-o-suru) [...を釣る(釣りをする)].

fisherman (*n.*) gyofu [漁夫].

fishery (*n.*) gyogyô [漁業]; gyojô [漁場].

fishing (*n.*) sakana-tsuri [魚釣り].

fishing rod tsuri-zao [釣りざお].

fishmonger (*n.*) ((*Eng.*)) sakanaya [魚屋].

fist (*n.*) nigiri-kobushi [握りこぶし]; genkotsu [げんこつ].

fit (*vt.*) 1)...ni au [...に合う]. 2)...o(...ni) tekigô-saseru [...を(...に)
    適合させる].
    (*1*) This hat **fits** me very well.

Kono bôshi wa watashi-ni totemo yoku *au*.

(2) He **fits** living to his circumstances.

Kare-wa seikatsu-o kyôgû-ni *awasete-iru*.

(*vi.*) au [合う]; tekigô-suru [適合する].

This coat **fits** perfectly.　Kono uwagi wa pittari *au*.

(*a.*) 1)tekitô-na [適当な]; fusawashii [ふさわしい].　2)karada-no-chôshi-ga-yoi [体の調子がよい].

feel fit kenkô-de-aru

fit (*n.*) 1)(*med.*) hossa [発作].　2)ichiji-teki-kôfun [一時的興奮]; ki-magure [気まぐれ].

fitting (*n.*) awaseru-koto [合わせること]; kari-nui[no ki-tsuke] [仮縫い(の着付け)].

(*a.*) fusawashii [ふさわしい].

five (*n. & a.*) go(-no) [五(の)].

five-day week shû-itsuka-sei [週五日制].

fix (*vt.*) 1)...o shikkari-kotei-suru [...をしっかり固定する]; ...o sue-tsukeru [...を据え付ける].　2)(me ya chûi)-o jitto-sosogu [(目や注意)をじっと注ぐ].　3)...o sadameru [...を定める]; ...o kimeru [...を決める].　4)...o shûzen-suru [...を修繕する].

(*1*) He **fixed** the post in the ground.

Kare-wa hashira-o jimen-ni *shikkari-to-tateta*.

(*2*) The boy **fixed** his eyes on it.

Sono shônen wa sore-ni *jitto-me-o sosoida*.

(*3*) The date **was fixed** for the next meeting.

Tsugi-no-kaigô-no-hi-ga *tori-kimerareta*.

(*4*) The locksmith **fixed** a broken lock.

Jômaeya wa kowareta jô-o *naoshita*.

(*n.*) 1)(*colloq.*) kurushii-tachiba [苦しい立場].　2)ichi [位置].

be in a fix kurushii-hame-ni-ochiitte-iru

fixed (*a.*) kotei-shita [固定した]; fuhen-no [不変の].

fixed star kôsei [恒星].

fizz (*n. & vi.*) shû-to-iu-oto(-o-tateru) [しゅうという音(を立てる)].

flag (*n.*) hata [旗].

(*vt.*) ...ni hata-o-tateru [...に旗を立てる].　...o hata-de-aizu-suru [...を旗で合図する].

flake (*n.*) (yuki ya hane no) hakuhen [(雪や羽の)薄片].

flaky (*a.*) 1)hakuhen-no [薄片の].　2)hage-ochi-yasui [はげ落ちやすい].

flame (*n.*) 1)honoo [炎].　2)jônetsu [情熱].

burst into flame(s) patto-moe-agaru

in flames moete

　　　(*vi. & vt.*) moe-agaru (…o moyasu) [燃え上がる(…を燃やす)].

flaming (*a.*) moe-agaru [燃え上がる]; moeru-yô-na [燃えるような].

flamingo (*n.*) (*birds*) beni-zuru [ベニヅル]; furamingo [フラミンゴ].

flannel (*n.*) 1)furanneru [フランネル]. 2)(*pl.*) furanneru-seihin [フランネル製品].

flap (*vi.*) pata-pata[bata-bata]-iu [ぱたぱた[ばたばた]いう].

　　　(*n.*) 1)pata-pata [ぱたぱた]; pishari [ぴしゃり]. 2)tarebuta [垂れぶた].

flash (*vi.*) 1)patto-tsuku [ぱっとつく]. 2)patto-ukabu [ぱっと浮かぶ].

　　　(*vt.*) 1)…o patto-tsukeru […をぱっとつける]. 2)…o sokuhô-suru […を速報する].

　　　(*n.*) 1)senkô [閃光]; hirameki [ひらめき]. 2)nyûsu-sokuhô [ニュース速報].

in a flash tachimachi; sokuza-ni

flashlight (*n.*) 1)senkô [閃光]. 2)kaichû-dentô [懐中電灯].

flat (*a.*) 1)taira-na [平らな]. 2)kakki-no-nai [活気のない]. 3)kippari-to-shita [きっぱりとした]; rokotsu-na [露骨な].

　　(*1*) They thought that the earth was **flat**.
　　　　Chikyû wa *taira*-da-to hito-bito-wa omotte-ita.

　　(*2*) The market is **flat**. Shikyô wa *kakki-ga-nai*.

　　(*3*) She gave a **flat** refusal. Kano-jo-wa *kippari*-to kotowatta.

　　　(*n.*) 1)taira-na-bubun [平らな部分]. 2)(*colloq.*) panku-shita-taiya [パンクしたタイヤ].

flat (*n.*) ((*Eng.*)) apâto [アパート].

flatiron (*n.*) airon [アイロン].

flatten (*vt. & vi.*) …o taira-ni-suru (taira-ni-naru) […を平らにする(平らになる)].

flatter (*vt.*) 1)…ni o-seji-o-iu […にお世辞を言う]. 2)…o yorokobasu […を喜ばす]. 3)…o tokui-garaseru […を得意がらせる].

flatterer (*n.*) o-seji-no-umai-hito [お世辞のうまい人].

flattery (*n.*) o-seji [お世辞].

flavor, -vour (*n.*) fûmi [風味]; aji [味].

　　　　　(*vt.*) …ni fûmi-o-soeru […に風味を添える]; …ni aji-o-tsukeru […に味を付ける].

flaw (*n.*) 1)hibi [ひび]. 2)ketten [欠点].

flax (*n.*) (*bot.*) ama [アマ].

flea (*n.*) (*insect*) nomi [ノミ].

flee (*vi. & vt.*) (...kara) nigeru [(…から)逃げる].

fleece (*n.*) yômô [羊毛].

fleecy (*a.*) yômô-no-yô-na [羊毛のような].

fleet (*n.*) kantai [艦隊]; (hikô-ki nado no) ittai [(飛行機などの)一隊].

flesh (*n.*) niku [肉]; (the –) nikutai [肉体].

  in the flesh jitsubutsu-de

flexible (*a.*) 1)mage-yasui [曲げやすい]. 2)yûzû-no-kiku [融通のきく].

flicker (*vi.*) chira-chira-suru [ちらちらする]; yura-yura-suru [ゆらゆらする].

flight (*n.*) 1)hikô [飛行]. 2)...bin […便]. 3)kaidan [階段].
  (*1*) He made the first nonstop **flight** to Paris.
      Kare-wa Pari-made saisho-no mu-chakuriku-*hikô*-o shita.
  (*2*) 353 **Flight** to Chicago.
      Shikago-iki [dai-]sam-byaku-go-jû-sam-*bin*[-hikô]
  (*3*) He ran down a **flight** of steps.
      Kare-wa *kaidan*-o hashiri-orita.

fling (*vt.*) ...o nage-tsukeru […を投げつける].
  (*vi.*) tobi-kakaru [飛びかかる].
  (*n.*) tosshin [突進].

flint (*n.*) 1)hiuchi-ishi [火打石]. 2)(raitâ no) ishi [(ライターの)石].

flinty (*a.*) katai [堅い].

flipper (*n.*) 1)mizu-kaki [水かき]. 2)(sensui-yô) ashi-hire [(潜水用)足ひれ].

flit (*vi.*) sui-sui-tobu [すいすい飛ぶ].

float (*vi. & vt.*) ukabu (...o ukaberu) [浮かぶ(…を浮かべる)].
  (*n.*) uku-mono [浮く物].

floating (*a.*) ukande-iru [浮かんでいる]; ryûdô-teki-na [流動的な].

floating dock uki-dokku [浮きドック].

flock (*n.*) 1)(hitsuji ya yagi ya tori no) mure [(羊ややぎや鳥の)群れ].
  2)(*colloq.*) mure [群れ].
  (*vi.*) muragaru [群がる].

flock (*n.*) hito-fusa-no-yômô [一房の羊毛].

flood (*n.*) 1)kôzui [洪水]. 2)taryô [多量].
  (*vt. & vi.*) ...o hanran-saseru (hanran-suru) […をはん濫させる(はん濫する)].

floor (*n.*) 1)yuka [床]. 2)kai [階].
  (*vt.*) ...ni yuka-ita-o-haru […に床板を張る].

flour (*n.*) ko-mugi-ko [小麦粉]; meriken-ko [メリケン粉].
    (*vt.*) ...o kona-ni-mabusu [...を粉にまぶす]; ...o kona-ni-suru [...
を粉にする].

flourish (*vi.*) sakaeru [栄える]; hanjô-suru [繁盛する].

flour mill seifun-kôjô [製粉工場].

flow (*n. & vi.*) 1)nagare (nagareru) [流れ(流れる)]. 2)age-shio(-ni-
naru) [上げ潮(になる)].

flower (*n. & vi.*) hana(-ga-saku) [花(が咲く)].

flower bed kadan [花壇].

flowerpot (*n.*) ueki-bachi [植木鉢].

flu (*n.*) infuruenza [インフルエンザ]; ryûkan [流感].

fluent (*a.*) ryûchô-na [流ちょうな].

fluid (*n. & a.*) ryûdô-tai(-no) [流動体(の)].

flunk (*vi. & vt.*) (...o) shippai-suru [(...を)失敗する].

fluorescent lamp keikô-tô [蛍光灯].

flush (*vi.*) 1)(mizu ga) hotobashiru [(水が)ほとばしる]. 2)patto-
akaku-naru [ぱっと赤くなる].
    (*vt.*) 1)...o dotto-nagasu [...をどっと流す]. 2)...o akarameru [...
を赤らめる]. 3)(be -ed) kôfun-suru [興奮する].
    (*n.*) 1)sekimen [赤面]. 2)kôfun [興奮]; dai-tokui [大得意].

flute (*n.*) yoko-bue [横笛]; furûto [フルート].

flutter (*vi.*) 1)habataki-suru [羽ばたきする]; (hata ya ho ga)
hatameku [(旗や帆が)はためく]. 2)hira-hira-to-tobu [ひらひらと飛ぶ].
3) sowa-sowa-suru [そわそわする].

fly (*vi.*) tobu [飛ぶ]; hikô-suru [飛行する].
    (*vt.*) ...o tobasu [...を飛ばす]; ...o sôjû-suru [...を操縦する].
    (*n.*) (*baseball*) furai [フライ].

fly (*n.*) (*insect*) hae [ハエ].

flying (*a.*) 1)tonde-iru [飛んでいる]. 2)awatadashii [あわただしい].

foam (*n. & vi.*) awa(-datsu) [泡(立つ)].

focus (*n.*) shôten [焦点].
    (*vt.*) ...no shôten-o-awaseru [...の焦点を合わせる].

foe (*n.*) kataki [かたき]; teki [敵].

fog (*n.*) kiri [霧]; moya [もや].

foggy (*a.*) kiri-no-fukai [霧の深い].

fold (*n.*) ori-me [折り目]; hida [ひだ].
    (*vt.*) 1)...o ori-kasaneru [...を折り重ねる]; ...o ori-tatamu [...を
折り畳む]. 2)(ude)-o kumu [(腕)を組む].

　　(1) I folded the paper in three.
　　　　　Watashi-wa kami-o mittsu-ni *ori-tatanda*.
　　(2) I folded my arms.　Watashi-wa ude-o *kunda*.
　　　　(*vi.*) ori-kasanaru [折り重なる]; ori-tatameru [折り畳める].
foliage (*n.*) ha [葉]; gun'yô [群葉].
folk (*n.*) 1)hito-bito [人々]. 2)(*pl.*)(*colloq.*) kazoku [家族].
follow (*vt.*) 1)...ni tsuzuku [...に続く]; ...ni shitagau [...に従う]. 2)
　...o rikai-suru [...を理解する].
　　　　(*vi.*) tsuite-iku [ついて行く].
　as follows tsugi-no-toori
follower (*n.*) shimpô-sha [信奉者]; monka [門下].
following (*a.*) tsugi-no [次の]; ika-no [以下の].
folly (*n.*) baka-geta-kôi [ばかげた行為]; oroka-sa [愚かさ].
fond (*a.*) kononde [好んで].
　be fond of ...o konomu; ...ga suki-de-aru
food (*n.*) shokumotsu [食物].
foodstuff (*n.*) shokuryô-hin [食料品].
fool (*n.*) baka-mono [ばか者].
　make a fool of ...o baka-ni-suru
　make a fool of oneself baka-na-koto-o-shite-mono-warai-ni-naru
　　　　(*vt.*) ...o baka-ni-suru [...をばかにする]; ...o damasu [...をだます].
　　　　(*vi.*) fuzakeru [ふざける].
　fool about(around) mui-ni-sugosu
foolish (*a.*) baka-na [ばかな]; oroka-na [愚かな].
foolishly (*ad.*) oroka-ni-mo [愚かにも].
foolishness (*n.*) oroka-sa [愚かさ]; baka-geta-koto [ばかげたこと].
foot (*n.*) 1)ashi [足]. 2)(yama no) fumoto [(山の)ふもと]. 3)fîto
　[フィート].
　on foot aruite
football (*n.*) futtobôru [フットボール]; shûkyû [蹴球].
footing (*n.*) 1)ashi-moto [足もと]. 2)ashiba [足場].
footlights (*n.*) (*play*) kyakkô [脚光]; futtoraito [フットライト].
footpath (*n.*) hodô [歩道]; ko-michi [小道].
footprint (*n.*) ashi-ato [足跡].
footstep (*n.*) ashidori [足取り]; ashi-oto [足音]; ashi-ato [足跡].
footwork (*n.*) ashi-sabaki [足さばき].
for (*prep.*) 1)...no-kawari-ni [...の代わりに]. 2)...no(-rieki-no)-tame-
　ni [...の(利益の)ために]. 3)...ni-sansei-shite [...に賛成して]. 4)...o-

uru-tame-ni [⋯を得るために]. 5)...ni-mukatte [⋯に向かって]. 6)...
no-wari-ni-wa [⋯の割には]. 7)...no-aida [⋯の間]. 8)...ni-tekishita
[⋯に適した]. 9)...no-mokuteki-de [⋯の目的で]. 10)...ni-totte [⋯に
とって]. 11)...ni-tsuite-wa [⋯については]. 12)...ni-taishite [⋯に対し
て]. 13)...to-shite [⋯として]. 14)...no-riyû-de [⋯の理由で]. 15)(...
no-kingaku)-de [(⋯の金額)で].

(*1*) I'll start **for** you.
　　Watashi-ga anata-*no-kawari-ni* shuppatsu-shima-shô.
(*2*) They work **for** their society.
　　Kare-ra-wa shakai-*no-tame-ni* hataraku.
(*3*) I am **for** the bill.　Watashi-wa sono-gian-*ni-sansei*-da.
(*4*) They fought **for** liberty.
　　Kare-ra-wa jiyû-*o-uru-tame-ni* tatakatta.
(*5*) He left **for** school.　Kare-wa gakkô-*ni*(-*mukete*) dekaketa.
(*6*) He looks young **for** his age.
　　Kare-wa toshi-*no-wari-ni-wa* wakaku-mieru.
(*7*) We stayed there **for** five days.
　　Ware-ware-wa soko-ni itsuka-*no-aida*(itsuka-*kan*) taizai-
shita.
(*8*) This fish is fit **for** food.
　　Kono sakana wa shoku-*yô-ni*-naru.
(*9*) Mother took me **for** a walk.
　　Haha ga watashi-o sampo-*ni* tsurete-itta.
(*10*) This book is too difficult **for** me.
　　Kono hon wa watashi-*ni-totte*(-*niwa*) muzukashi-sugiru.
(*11*) I'll stop here **for** today.　Kyô-*wa* koko-de yame-masu.
(*12*) Thank you **for** your kind letter.
　　Go-shinsetsu-na o-tegami arigatô.
(*13*) He was elected **for** a chairperson.
　　Kare-wa gichô-*to-shite*(gichô-*ni*) erabareta.
(*14*) This place is famous **for** its beautiful scenery.
　　Koko wa utsukushii-fûkei-*de* yûmei-da.
(*15*) I bought it **for** 500 yen.
　　Watashi-wa sore-o go-hyaku-en-*de* katta.
as for me watashi-to-shite-wa; watashi-ni-kansuru-kagiri-wa
　(*conj.*) naze-nara...dakara [なぜなら⋯だから].
　　He wears spectacles, **for** he is short-sighted.
　　Kare-wa megane-o kakete-iru, kare-wa kinshi-*da-kara*.

forbear (*vt. & vi.*) (...o) sashi-hikaeru [(…を)差し控える]; (...o) gaman-suru [(…を)我慢する].

forbid (*vt.*) ...o kinzuru […を禁ずる]; ...o yuru-sa-nai […を許さない].

force (*n.*) 1)chikara [力]. 2)bôryoku [暴力]. 3)(*pl.*) guntai [軍隊]. 4)shikô [施行].
  by force chikara-zuku-de; muri-ni
  come into force kôryoku-o-hassuru
  in force jisshi-chû-de; yûkô-de
  put...in force ...o jisshi-suru; ...o shikô-suru
    (*vt.*) ...ni kyôsei-suru […に強制する]; ...ni muri-ni...(sa-)seru […に無理に…(さ)せる].

forced (*a.*) kyôsei-sareta [強制された]; muri-jii-no [無理強いの].

forcibly (*ad.*) 1)kyôsei-teki-ni [強制的に]. 2)chikara-zuyoku [力強く].

fore (*a.*) mae-no [前の]; zempô-no [前方の].

forecast (*n.*) yohô [予報]; yosoku [予測].
  (*vt.*) ...o yohô-suru […を予報する]; ...o yogen-suru […を予言する].

forefather (*n.*) (*pl.*) senzo [先祖].

forefinger (*n.*) hitosashi-yubi [人差し指].

foreground (*n.*) zenkei [前景].

forehead (*n.*) hitai [ひたい].

foreign (*a.*) gaikoku-no [外国の].

foreigner (*n.*) gaikoku-jin [外国人].

foremost (*a.*) dai-ichi-i-no [第一位の]; shuyô-na [主要な].
  (*ad.*) massaki-ni [真っ先に].

forenoon (*n.*) gozen [午前].

forerunner (*n.*) 1)senku-sha [先駆者]. 2)mae-bure [前触れ].

foresee (*vt.*) ...o yochi-suru […を予知する].

foresight (*n.*) senken-no-mei [先見の明].

forest (*n.*) shinrin [森林]; sanrin [山林].

foretell (*vt.*) ...o yogen-suru […を予言する]; ...o yokoku-suru […を予告する].

forever (*ad.*) eikyû-ni [永久に].

forfeit (*n.*) 1)bakkin [罰金]. 2)bosshû [没収]. 3)hakudatsu [はく奪].
  (*vt.*) 1)...o bosshû-sareru […を没収される]. 2)...o ushinau […を失う].

forget (*vt. & vi.*) (...o) wasureru [(…を)忘れる].

forgetful (*a.*) wasureppoi [忘れっぽい].

forget-me-not (*n.*) (*bot.*) wasurena-gusa [ワスレナグサ].

forgive (*vt. & vi.*) (...o) yurusu [(…を)許す].

forlorn (*a.*) kodoku-no [孤独の]; wabishii [わびしい].

form (*n.*) 1)katachi [形]; sugata [姿]. 2)shoshiki [書式]; kaki-komi-yôshi [書き込み用紙].

   (*1*) It took the **form** of an angel.

      Sore-wa tenshi no *sugata*-ni natta.

   (*2*) Do you have a telegraph **form**?

      Raishin-*shi*-o o-mochi-desu-ka?

      (*vt.*) ...o katachi-zukuru [⋯を形作る]; ...o tsukuru [⋯を作る]; ...o keisei-suru [⋯を形成する].

formal (*a.*) 1)seishiki-no [正式の]. 2)keishiki-teki-na [形式的な].

formation (*n.*) keisei [形成]; kôzô [構造].

former (*a.*) 1)mae-no [前の]; izen-no [以前の]. 2)(the –) zensha [前者].

  in former times izen-wa; mukashi-wa

formerly (*ad.*) izen-wa [以前は].

formidable (*a.*) 1)osoroshii [恐ろしい]. 2)te-gowai [手ごわい].

formula (*n.*) 1)kimatta-ii-kata [決まった言い方]. 2)(*math.*) (kô)shiki [(公)式].

forsake (*vt.*) ...o mi-suteru [⋯を見捨てる].

fort (*n.*) toride [とりで].

forth (*ad.*) 1)zempô-e [前方へ]. 2)soto-e [外へ].

   (*1*) The lamp swung back and **forth**.

      Rampu wa *zengo*-ni yureta.

   (*2*) He brought a new plan **forth**.

      Kare-wa atarashii keikaku-o *teian*-shita.

  and so forth ...nado

forthcoming (*a.*) yagate-kuru [やがて来る].

forthcoming book kinkan-sho [近刊書].

fortieth (*n. & a.*) dai-yon-jû(-no) [第四十(の)].

fortify (*vt.*) ...ni bôgyo-kôji-o-hodokosu [⋯に防御工事を施す].

  fortify oneself genki-o-tsukeru

fortitude (*n.*) fukutsu-no-seishin [不屈の精神].

fortnight (*n.*) ni-shû-kan [二週間].

fortress (*n.*) yôsai [要さい].

fortunate (*a.*) un-no-yoi [運のよい].

fortunately (*ad.*) un-yoku [運よく].

fortune (*n.*) 1)un [運]. 2)kôun [幸運]. 3)zaisan [財産]. 4)(F-)

　　　ummei-no-me-gami [運命の女神].
forty (*n. & a.*) yon-jû(-no) [四十(の)].
forward (*a.*) 1)zempô-no [前方の]. 2)hayai [早い].
　　　(*ad.*) zempô-e [前方へ]; shôrai-ni-mukatte [将来に向かって].
　　look forward to　…o tanoshimi-ni-shite-matsu
　　　(*n.*) (*sports*) (as *F.W.*) zen'ei [前衛].
　　　(*vt.*) 1)…o tensô-suru […を転送する]. 2)…o sokushin-suru
　　[…を促進する].
fossil (*n. & a.*) kaseki(-no) [化石(の)].
foster (*vt.*) 1)…o sodateru […を育てる]. 2)…o jochô-suru […を助長
　　する]. 3)…o idaku […をいだく].
foul (*a.*) 1)fuketsu-na [不潔な]; kitanai [汚い]. 2)(*colloq.*) iya-na
　　[いやな]. 3)fusei-na [不正な].
　　foul tip　(*baseball*) fauru-chippu
　　　(*n.*) (*sports*) hansoku [反則]; (*baseball*) fauru [ファウル].
found (*vt.*) …o setsuritsu-suru […を設立する]; …o sôritsu-suru […
　　を創立する]; …o(…no-ue-ni)tateru […を(…の上に)建てる].
foundation (*n.*) 1)sôritsu [創立]. 2)kiso [基礎]; konkyo [根拠];
　　yori-dokoro [よりどころ].
foundation stone　soseki [礎石].
founder (*n.*) sôritsu-sha [創立者]; setsuritsu-sha [設立者].
foundry (*n.*) chûzô[-sho] [鋳造(所)].
fountain (*n.*) izumi [泉]; funsui [噴水].
fountain pen　mannen-hitsu [万年筆].
four (*n. & a.*) yon(-no) [四(の)].
fourteen (*n. & a.*) jû-yon(-no) [十四(の)].
fourteenth (*n. & a.*) dai-jû-yon(-no) [第十四(の)].
fourth (*n. & a.*) dai-yon(-no) [第四(の)].
fowl (*n.*) 1)niwatori [にわとり]. 2)ie-de-kau-tori [家で飼う鳥].
fox (*n.*) kitsune [キツネ].
fraction (*n.*) 1)shô-bubun [小部分]. 2)(*math.*) bunsû [分数].
fracture (*n.*) (*med.*) kossetsu [骨折].
　　　(*vi.*) (hone ga)oreru [(骨が)折れる].
fragile (*a.*) koware-yasui [壊れやすい].
fragment (*n.*) hahen [破片]; dampen [断片].
fragrance (*n.*) yoi-kaori [よい香り].
fragrant (*a.*) kaori-no-yoi [香りのよい].
frail (*a.*) moroi [もろい]; yowai [弱い].

frame (*n.*) 1)hone-gumi [骨組み]. 2)taikaku [体格]. 3)gaku-buchi [額縁]; waku [枠].
　　　(*vt.*) ...o kumi-tateru […を組み立てる]; ...o kufû-suru […を工夫する]; ...o waku-ni-hameru […を枠にはめる].

framework (*n.*) 1)kokkaku [骨格]; hone-gumi [骨組み]; waku-gumi [枠組み]. 2)kôsei [構成]; taisei [体制].

franc (*n.*) furan [フラン].

France (*n.*) Furansu [フランス].

frank (*a.*) sotchoku-na [率直な]; kakushi-date-no-nai [隠し立てのない].

frankly (*ad.*) sotchoku-ni [率直に].
　　frankly speaking sotchoku-ni-ieba

frantic (*a.*) kyôran-shita [狂乱した].

fraud (*n.*) sagi [詐欺]; (*colloq.*) peten-shi [ぺてん師].

freckle (*n.*) sobakasu [そばかす].

free (*a.*) 1)jiyû-na [自由な]; hima-na [暇な]. 2)(...ga-)nai [(…が)ない]. 3)muryô-no [無料の]. 4)aite-iru [空いている].
　(*1*) free composition　*jiyû-sakubun*
　　　Are you **free** now?　Ima *o-hima-desu-ka?*
　(*2*) She is quite **free** care.　Kano-jo-wa mattaku kurô-ga-*nai*.
　(*3*) Is it **free** from charge?　Sore-wa *muryô-desu-ka?*
　(*4*) Do you have any rooms **free**?　*Aite-iru* heya-ga arimasu-ka?
　set...free　...o shakuhô-suru; ...o kaihô-suru
　　　(*vt.*) ...o kaihô-suru […を解放する].
　　　(*ad.*) 1)jiyû-ni [自由に]. 2)muryô-de [無料で].

freedom (*n.*) jiyû [自由]; kaihô [解放].

free-lance (*a. & ad.*) jiyû-keiyaku-no(-de) [自由契約の(で)].

free lance jiyû-keiyaku-no-sakka [自由契約の作家]; furî-ransâ [フリーランサー]; jiyû-na-tachiba-no-hito [自由な立場の人].

freely (*ad.*) jiyû-ni [自由に]; ki-garu-ni [気軽に].

freeway (*n.*) ((*US*)) kôsoku-dôro [高速道路].

freeze (*vt. & vi.*) ...o kooraseru(kooru) […を凍らせる(凍る)].
　　　He was **frozen** to death.　Kare-wa *kogoe*-jinda.
　　　Water **freezes** at 32°F.
　　　　Mizu wa kashi-san-jû-ni-do-de *kooru*.
　　　(*n.*) hyôketsu [氷結]; kampa [寒波].

freezer (*n.*) reitô-ko [冷凍庫]; reitô-shitsu [冷凍室].

freight (*vt.*) ...o unsô-suru […を運送する].
　　　(*n.*) 1)kamotsu[-unsô] [貨物(運送)]. 2)unsô-ryô [運送料].

French (*a.*) Furansu-no [フランスの]; Furansu-jin-no [フランス人の]; Furansu-go-no [フランス語の].

    (*n.*) (the –) Furansu-jin [フランス人]. Furansu-go [フランス語].

frequency (*n.*) himpan [頻繁]; hindo [頻度].

frequent (*a.*) tabi-tabi-okoru [たびたび起こる]; tabi-tabi-no [たびたびの].

    (*vt.*) ...ni yoku-de-iri-suru […によく出入りする].

frequently (*ad.*) tabi-tabi [たびたび]; himpan-ni [頻繁に].

fresh (*a.*) 1)shinsen-na [新鮮な]. 2)(...shita-)bakari-no [(…した)ばかりの]. 3)shio-ke-no-nai [塩気のない]. 4)sawayaka-na [さわやかな].

freshen (*vt.*) ...o shinsen-ni-suru […を新鮮にする].

    (*vi.*) shinsen-ni-naru [新鮮になる]; sappari-suru [さっぱりする].

freshman (*n.*) shinnyû-sei [新入生]; ichi-nen-sei [一年生].

freshwater (*n.*) tansui [淡水].

fret (*vt. & vi.*) ...o ira-ira-saseru(iradatsu) […をいらいらさせる(いら立つ)].

friction (*n.*) masatsu [摩擦].

Friday (*n.*) Kin'yô-bi [金曜日].

fried (*a.*) abura-de-ageta [油で揚げた]; furai-no [フライの].

friend (*n.*) yûjin [友人]; mikata [味方].

    He is a **friend** of mine. Kara-wa watashi no *yûjin* desu.

  be friends with ...to-shitashii

friendly (*a.*) shinsetsu-na [親切な]; hito-natsukkoi [人なつっこい].

friendship (*n.*) yûjô [友情].

fright (*n.*) kyôfu [恐怖]; odoroki [驚き].

frighten (*vt.*) ...o gyotto-saseru […をぎょっとさせる].

frightful (*a.*) osoroshii [恐ろしい]; zotto-suru-yô-na [ぞっとするような].

frigid (*a.*) 1)samu-sa-no-kibishii [寒さの厳しい]. 2)reitan-na [冷淡な].

Frigid Zone, the kantai [寒帯].

frill (*n.*) hida-kazari [ひだ飾り].

fringe (*n.*) 1)fusa-kazari [ふさ飾り]. 2)shûhen-bu [周辺部].

    (*vt.*) ...o fuchi-doru […を縁取る].

frivolous (*a.*) 1)keihaku-na [軽薄な]. 2)kudaranai [くだらない].

frizzle (*vi.*) jû-jû-oto-o-tateru [じゅうじゅう音を立てる].

    (*vt.*) ...o jû-jû-itameru […をじゅうじゅういためる].

frog (*n.*) kaeru [カエル].

frolic (*vi.*) fuzakeru [ふざける]; hane-mawaru [はね回る].

(*n.*) fuzake [ふざけ]; ukare-sawagi [浮かれ騒ぎ].

from (*prep.*) 1)...kara […から]. 2)...kara[-no] […から(の)]; ...
shusshin[-no] […出身(の)]. 3)...kara-no […からの]. 4)...ga-gen'in-
de […が原因で]. 5)...kara(-toru) […から(取る)]. 6)...kara(-toru) […
から(とる)]. 7)...to […と].

  (*1*) The station is three miles distant **from** here.
     Eki wa koko-*kara* sam-mairu hanarete-iru.
    I have known him **from** a child.
     Watashi-wa kare-o kodomo-no-toki-*kara* shitte-iru.
  (*2*) He is **from** Oxford. Kare-wa Okkusufôdo-*no-shusshin*-da.
  (*3*) I have just received a letter **from** him.
     Watashi-wa chôdo kare-*kara-no*-tegami-o uketotta-tokoro-
da.
  (*4*) He died **from** overwork.
     Kare-wa karô-*ga-gen'in-de* shinda.
     Kare-wa karô-*ga-moto-de* shinda.
  (*5*) I took his pistol **from** him.
     Watashi-wa kare-*kara* pisutoru-o ubatta.
  (*6*) We make wine **from** grapes.
     Ware-ware-wa budô-*kara* budô-shu-o tsukuru.
  (*7*) Can you distinguish Americans **from** Frenchmen?
     Anata-wa Amerika-jin-*to*-Furansu-jin-no-kubetsu-ga-dekiru-
ka?

front (*n.*) 1)(the ‑) mae [前]; zempô [前方]; shômen [正面]. 2)
(*mil.*) senchi [戦地]; sensen [戦線].

  (*1*) The **front** of my house can be seen from here.
     Watashi-no ie no *shômen* ga koko-kara mieru.
  (*2*) He went to the **front**. Kare-wa *senchi*-e itta.
  come to the front yûmei-ni-naru
    (*a.*) shômen-no [正面の]; omote-no [表の].
    (*vt. & vi.*) (...ni) mensuru [(…に)面する].

frontier (*n.*) 1)kokkyô [国境]. 2)((*US*)) henkyô [辺境].

frost (*n.*) 1)shimo [霜]. 2)shimo-ga-oriru-hodo-no-samu-sa [霜が降
りるほどの寒さ].
  (*vi.*) shimo-ga-oriru [霜が降りる].

frosty (*a.*) 1)shimo-no-oriru [霜の降りる]; kooru-yô-ni-samui [凍るよ
うに寒い]. 2)reitan-na [冷淡な].

frown (*vi.*) kao-o-shikameru [顔をしかめる]; mayu-o-hisomeru [まゆ

をひそめる].

(*n.*) shikamettsura [しかめっ面].

frozen (*a.*) 1)reitô-shita [冷凍した]. 2)hiyayaka-na [冷ややかな].

frugal (*a.*) shisso-na [質素な]; tsumashii [つましい].

frugality (*n.*) shisso [質素]; ken'yaku [倹約].

fruit (*n.*) 1)kudamono [果物]. 2)seika [成果]; mukui [報い].

(*vi.*) mi-o-musubu [実を結ぶ].

fruiterer (*n.*) kudamono-shô [果物商].

fruitful (*a.*) 1)minori-no-ooi [実りの多い]. 2)kôka-no-aru [効果のある].

fruitless (*a.*) minori-no-nai [実りのない]; kôka-no-nai [効果のない].

frustration (*n.*) 1)zasetsu [挫折]. 2)yokkyû-fuman [欲求不満]; furasutorêshon [フラストレーション].

fry (*vt.*) ...o abura-de-ageru […を油で揚げる]; ...o furai-ni-suru […をフライにする].

(*n.*) age-mono [揚げ物]; furai [フライ].

frying pan furai-pan [フライパン].

fuel (*n.*) nenryô [燃料].

fulfil(l) (*vt.*) 1)...o hatasu […を果たす]. 2)...o mitasu […を満たす].

fulfil(l)ment (*n.*) suikô [遂行]; jôju [成就].

full (*a.*) 1)michita [満ちた]. 2)ippai-no [いっぱいの]. 2)kanzen-na [完全な]; jûbun-no [十分の]. 3)ryaku-sa-nai [略さない]. 4)dabu-dabu-no [だぶだぶの].

(*1*) The bus was **full**. Basu wa *man'in*-datta.

(*2*) The **full** moon is to be seen tonight.

　　Komban *man*getsu ga mirareru-hazu-da.

(*3*) Must I write my **full** name?

　　Sei-mei wa *ryaku-sa-nai*-de kaka-nakereba-narimasen-ka?

(*4*) He wears **full** pants.

　　Kare-wa *dabu-dabu-no* zubon-o haite-iru.

(*n.*) (the –) 1)jûbun [十分]. 2)zembu [全部].

(*ad.*) 1)jûbun-ni [十分に]; tappuri [たっぷり]. 2)chôdo [ちょうど].

(*1*) They walked **full** 10 kilometers.

　　Kare-ra-wa *tappuri* jukkiro aruita.

(*2*) **Full** in the middle way there was a lake.

　　Chôdo mannaka-ni mizuumi-ga atta.

fullback (*n.*) (*sports*) furubakku [フルバック]; kôei [後衛].

full-dress (*a.*) 1)seisô-no [正装の]. 2)honkaku-teki-na [本格的な].

full-length (*a.*) tôshin-dai-no [等身大の].

full stop shûshi-fu [終止符]; piriodo [ピリオド].

full-time (*a.*) jôkin-no [常勤の]; sennin-no [専任の].

fully (*ad.*) jûbun-ni [十分に]; maru-maru [まるまる].

fumble (*vi. & vt.*) 1)te-saguri-suru (te-saguri-de...o suru) [手探りする(手探りで…をする)]. 2)(*baseball*) (...o) famburu-suru [(…を)ファンブルする].

fume (*n.*) (*pl.*) kemuri [煙].
　　　(*vi.*) 1)kemuru [煙る]; iburu [いぶる]. 2)pun-pun-okoru [ぷんぷん怒る].

fun (*n.*) 1)tawamure [戯れ]; fuzake [ふざけ]. 2)omoshiro-mi [面白み].

　　make fun of ...o karakau

function (*n.*) 1)kinô [機能]. 2)(*pl.*) shokumu [職務].
　　　(*vi.*) ugoku [動く]; yakume-o-hatasu [役目を果す].

fund (*n.*) shikin [資金]; kikin [基金].

fundamental (*a.*) kihon-teki-na [基本的な].

funeral (*n.*) sôshiki [葬式].

fungus (*n.*) kinrui (kabi ya kinoko nado) [菌類(カビやキノコなど)].

funnel (*n.*) 1)jôgo [じょうご]. 2)entotsu [煙突].

funny (*a.*) okashii [おかしい]; (*colloq.*) kimyô-na [奇妙な].

fur (*n.*) 1)ke-gawa [毛皮]. 2)(*pl.*) ke-gawa-seihin [毛皮製品]; ke-gawa-ifuku [毛皮衣服].

furious (*a.*) ikari-kuruu [怒り狂う]; môretsu-na [猛烈な].

furiously (*ad.*) ikari-kurutte [怒り狂って]; môretsu-ni [猛烈に].

furl (*vt.*) (hata ya ho)-o maite-osameru [(旗や帆)を巻いて収める].

furnace (*n.*) kamado [かまど]; ro [炉].

furnish (*vt.*) 1)...o kyôkyû-suru […を供給する]. 2)...ni kagu-o-sonae-tsukeru […に家具を備え付ける].

　　(*1*) I **furnished** a letter of introduction to him.
　　　　Watashi-wa kare-ni shôkai-jô-*o ataeta*.
　　(*2*) This apartment house is not yet **furnished**.
　　　　Kono apâto wa mada *kagu-ga-haitte-i*-nai.

furnishing (*n.*) 1)kagu-no-sonae-tsuke [家具の備え付け]. 2)(*pl.*) kagu [家具]; bihin [備品].

furniture (*n.*) kagu [家具].

furrow (*n.*) 1)mizo [溝]. 2)(kao no) fukai-shiwa [(顔の)深いしわ].

further (*a. & ad.*) 1)yori-tooi (yori-tooku) [より遠い(より遠く)]. 2)motto-tooi(motto-tooku) [もっと遠い(もっと遠く)]. 3)sore-ijô-no (sore-ijô-ni)［それ以上の（それ以上に）］.

furthermore (*ad.*) omake-ni［おまけに］; sore-dake-de-naku［それだけでなく］.

fury (*n.*) 1)gekido［激怒］. 2)môretsu［猛烈］.
  (*1*) The giant punished him in a **fury**.
　　　Kyojin wa *gekido*-shite kare-o basshita.
  (*2*) The storm blew in all its **fury**.
　　　Arashi wa *môretsu*-ni fuki-areta.

fuse (*n.*) 1)(*elect.*) hyûzu［ヒューズ］. 2)shinkan［信管］.

fusion (*n.*) yôkai［溶解］; yûgô［融合］.

fuss (*n. & vi.*) sawagi(-tateru)［騒ぎ(たてる)］; yaki-moki(-suru)［やきもき(する)］.

futile (*a.*) mueki-na［無益な］; tsumaranai［つまらない］.

future (*n. & a.*) mirai(-no)［未来(の)］; shôrai(-no)［将来(の)］.
  for the future　shôrai-wa
  in the future　mirai-ni; kongo

G

gabble (*vi. & vt.*) haya-kuchi-ni-wake-no-wakara-nai-koto-o-shaberu (...o makushi-tateru)［早口で訳の分からないことをしゃべる（…をまくし立てる）］.

gaiety (*n.*) 1)yôki［陽気］. 2)o-matsuri-sawagi［お祭り騒ぎ］.

gaily (*ad.*) yôki-ni［陽気に］; hade-ni［派手に］.

gain (*vt.*) 1)...o eru [...を得る]. 2)(tokei ga) susumu [(時計が)進む].
3)...o môkeru [...をもうける]. 4)(mokuteki-chi)-ni tassuru [(目的地)
に達する].
　　(*vi.*) 1)môkeru [もうける]; (kenkô ya chikara ga) masu [(健康
や力が)増す]; yoku-naru [よくなる]. 2)(tokei ga) susumu [(時計が)
進む].
　(*1*) I **gained** in weight.　Watashi-wa taijû-ga-*fueta*.
　(*2*) The clock **gains** by 2 minutes a day.
　　　　Sono tokei wa ichi-nichi-ni ni-fun *susumu*.
　　(*n.*) (kenkô ya chishiki no) zôshin [(健康や知識の)増進]; môke
　[もうけ].

gale (*n.*) kyôfû [強風].

gall (*n.*) (*anat.*) tannô [胆のう].

gallant (*a.*) isamashii [勇ましい]; ooshii [雄々しい].

gallery (*n.*) 1)(*theater*) tenjô-sajiki [天井桟敷]. 2)garô [画廊]. 3)
rôka [廊下].

gallop (*n.*) kake-ashi [駆け足]; gyaroppu [ギャロップ].
　　(*vt. & vi.*) ...o gyaroppu-de-kakesaseru (gyaroppu-de-kakeru)
　[...をギャロップで駆けさせる(ギャロップで駆ける)].

gallstone (*n.*) (*med.*) tanseki [胆石].

gamble (*n.*) tobaku [とばく].
　　(*vi.*) tobaku-o-suru [とばくをする]; tôki-o-suru [投機をする].

gambler (*n.*) bakuchi-uchi [ばくち打ち].

game (*n.*) 1)yûgi [遊戯]. 2)kyôgi [競技]; shiai [試合]; gêmu [ゲー
ム]. 3)(ryô no)emono [(猟の)獲物].

gangster (*n.*) gyangu-no-ichi-in [ギャングの一員].

gangway (*n.*) 1)tsûro [通路]. 2)(*marine*) gemmon [舷門].

gap (*n.*) 1)suki-ma [すき間]; ware-me [割れ目]. 2)sôi [相違];
gyappu [ギャップ].

gape (*vi. & n.*) oo-guchi-o-akeru(-koto) [大口をあける(こと)]; pokan-
to-kuchi-o-akete-mitoreru(-koto) [ぽかんと口をあけて見とれる(こと)];
akubi-o-suru(-koto) [あくびをする(こと)].

garage (*n.*) shako [車庫]; garêji [ガレージ]; (jidôsha-)shûri-kôjô
[(自動車)修理工場].

garbage (*n.*) 1)nama-gomi [生ごみ]; kuzu [くず]. 2)garakuta [がら
くた].

garden (*n.*) 1)niwa [庭]. 2)(*pl.*)...en [...園].

gardener (*n.*) uekiya [植木屋]; niwa-shi [庭師].

gardening (*n.*) zôen [造園]; engei [園芸].

gargle (*vt. & vi.*) (...o) ugai-suru [(…を)うがいする].

garland (*n.*) 1)hana-wa [花輪]. 2)eikan [栄冠].
    (*vt.*) ...o hana-wa-de-kazaru […を花輪で飾る].

garment (*n.*) 1)ifuku-no-hito-shina [衣服の一品]. 2)(*pl.*) ifuku [衣服].

gas (*n.*) gasu [ガス]; kitai [気体].

gasoline, -lene (*n.*) gasorin [ガソリン].

gasp (*vi. & n.*) aegu (aegi) [あえぐ(あえぎ)].

gas station ((*US*)) gasorin-sutando [ガソリンスタンド].

gastric (*a.*) i-no [胃の].

gastric ulcer (*med.*) i-kaiyô [胃かいよう].

gastritis (*n.*) (*med.*) i-en [胃炎].

gate (*n.*) mon [門].

gateway (*n.*) irikuchi [入り口]; (...e-no-)michi [(…への)道].

gather (*vt.*) 1)...o atsumeru […を集める]. 2)...rashii […らしい].
  (*1*) They went to **gather** shells.
     Kare-ra-wa kai-gara-*atsume*-ni-itta.
  (*2*) I **gather** from his statement that he has worries.
     Kare-no-itte-iru-koto-kara-sassuru-to kare-wa nayami-goto
     ga aru-*rashii*.
    (*vi.*) atsumaru [集まる].
    (*n.*) 1)yori-atsumari [寄り集まり]. 2)(*pl.*) hida [ひだ]; gyazâ
[ギャザー].

gathering (*n.*) 1)atsumari [集まり]; shûkai [集会]. 2)(*med.*) kanô
[化膿]. 3)hida [ひだ]; gyazâ [ギャザー].

gauge (*n.*) 1)keiki [計器]; gêji [ゲージ]. 2)(*R.R.*) kikan [軌間].
    (*vt.*) ...o hakaru […を計る]; ...o mi-tsumoru […を見積もる].

gay (*a.*) 1)tanoshi-ge-na [楽しげな]; yôki-na [陽気な]; kaikatsu-na
[快活な]. 2)hade-na [派手な].

gaze (*vi.*) jitto-mi-tsumeru [じっと見詰める].
    (*n.*) gyôshi [凝視].

gear (*n.*) 1)ha-guruma [歯車]; gia [ギア]. 2)dôgu [道具]; sôchi [装
置].
    (*vt.*) 1)(be -ed) gia-ga-hairu [ギアが入る]. 2)...o tekigô-saseru
[適合させる].
    (*vi.*) (ha-guruma ga) kami-au [(歯車が)かみ合う].

gee (*int.*) Yaa! [やあ!]; Odoroita-naa! [おどろいたなあ!].

gem (*n.*) hôseki [宝石].

(*vt.*) ...ni hôseki-o-chiribameru [...に宝石をちりばめる].

gender (*n.*) (*gram.*) sei [性].

general (*a.*) ippan-no [一般の]; daitai-no [大体の].

　　　(*n.*) rikugun-taishô [陸軍大将]; shôgun [将軍].

　in general　ippan-ni; gaishite

generalize (*vt.*) ...o ippan-ka-suru [...を一般化する]; ...o fukyû-saseru [...を普及させる].

　　　(*vi.*) gaikatsu-suru [概括する].

generally (*ad.*) ippan-ni [一般に]; gaishite [概して].

　generally speaking　gaishite-ieba

general strike　zenesuto [ゼネスト]

generate (*vt.*) ...o hassei-saseru [...を発生させる].

generation (*n.*) ichi-dai [一代]; ichi-sedai [一世代].

generosity (*n.*) mono-oshimi-shi-nai-koto [物惜しみしないこと]; kandai [寛大].

generous (*a.*) ki-mae-no-yoi [気前のよい]; kandai-na [寛大な].

generously (*ad.*) ki-mae-yoku [気前よく]; kandai-ni [寛大に].

genetic (*a.*) kigen-no [起源の]; iden-gaku-teki-na [遺伝学的な].

genial (*a.*) yasashii [優しい]; shinsetsu-na [親切な]; onwa-na [温和な].

genius (*n.*) tensai [天才].

gentle (*a.*) 1)shinsetsu-na [親切な]; yasashii [優しい]. 2)odayaka-na [穏やかな].

gentleman (*n.*) shinshi [紳士].

gentleness (*n.*) onwa [温和].

gently (*ad.*) odayaka-ni [穏やかに]; shizuka-ni [静かに]; jôhin-ni [上品に].

genuine (*a.*) hommono-no [本物の]; shôshin-shômei-no [正真正銘の].

geographical (*a.*) chiri-gaku-no [地理学の].

geography (*n.*) 1)chiri[-gaku] [地理(学)]. 2)(the –) chisei [地勢].

geology (*n.*) chishitsu-gaku [地質学].

geometry (*n.*) kika-gaku [幾何学].

germ (*n.*) 1)saikin [細菌]; byôgen-kin [病原菌]. 2)me-bae [芽生え]; (*bot.*) hai [はい].

German (*a.*) Doitsu-no [ドイツの]; Doitsu-jin-no [ドイツ人の]; Doitsu-go-no [ドイツ語の].

　　　(*n.*) Doitsu-jin [ドイツ人]; Doitsu-go [ドイツ語].

Germany (*n.*) Doitsu [ドイツ].

gerund (*n.*) (*gram.*) dô-meishi [動名詞].

gesture (*n.*) miburi [身振り]; te-mane [手まね]; jesuchâ [ジェスチ
ャー].

get (*vt.*) 1)...o eru [⋯を得る]; ...o te-ni-ireru [⋯を手に入れる]. 2)...
o tsukamaeru [⋯をつかまえる]. 3)...o kau [⋯を買う]. 4)...o motte-
kuru [⋯を持ってくる]. 5)(byôki)-ni kakaru [(病気)にかかる]. 6)...o
rikai-suru [⋯を理解する]. 7)...o ira-ira-saseru [⋯をいらいらさせる].
8)...o motte-iru [⋯を持っている]. 9)...neba-naranai [⋯ねばならない].
10)...o...(sa-)seru [⋯を⋯(さ)せる]; ...o...(shite-)morau [⋯を⋯(し
て)もらう].

  (*1*) How did you **get** this money?
      Kono kane *o* dôshite *te-ni-ireta-no-ka?*

  (*2*) A detective **got** the thief. Keiji ga dorobô-*o tsukamaeta.*

  (*3*) I'll **get** you a camera. Omae-ni kamera-*o katte-*ageyô.

  (*4*) **Get** my umbrella. Watashi-no kasa-*o motte-oide.*

  (*5*) He **got** the measles. Kare-wa hashika-*ni kakatta.*

  (*6*) I **get** you. *Wakari-mashita.*

  (*7*) The problem **gets** me. Sono mondai de *ira-ira-shite-iru.*

  (*8*) **Has** he **got** a camera? Kare-wa kamera-*o motte-iru-*ka?

  (*9*) I've **got to** go to the dentist's.
      Watashi-wa ha-isha-ni ika-*neba-naranai.*

  (*10*) I **got** my watch repaired.
      Watashi-wa tokei-*o shûzen-shite-moratta.*

    (*vi.*) 1)tsuku [着く]; iku [行く]. 2)...(ni-)naru [⋯(に)なる].

  (*1*) He will **get** here by five o'clock.
      Kare-wa go-ji-made-ni-wa koko-ni *tsuku-*darô.

  (*2*) It will soon **get** dark. Ma-mo-naku kuraku-*naru-*darô.

get along kurasu
  How are you getting along? Ikaga o-kurashi-desu-ka?

get around 1)hiromaru. 2)(*colloq.*)...o-kokufuku-suru
  1) A rumor gets around. Uwasa ga hiromaru.
  2) get around the difficulties konnan-o kokufuku-suru

get away nige-dasu
  He got away from his master successfully.
      Kare-wa shujin-no-tokoro-o umaku nige-dashita.

get away with ...o-umaku-nogareru
  You've got away with it! Umaku-nogareta-na!

get back 1)kaeru. 2)...o-tori-modosu

1) He got back from America yesterday.
　　Kare-wa kinô Amerika-kara kaetta.
2) He would get back his old job.
　　Kare-wa mukashi-no shigoto-o tori-modoshi-takatta.
　　All he wants to do is get his girl friend back.
　　　　Kare-no-shi-tai-koto wa gâru-furendo-o tori-modosu-koto-
　　　　　dake-datta.

get in 1)...ni-noru. 2)tôchaku-suru
1) Did he get in the train?　Kare-wa kisha-ni notta-ka?
2) The train will soon get in.
　　Ressha wa ma-mo-naku tôchaku-shimasu.

get into ...ni-hairu
　　My cousin got into business.
　　　Watashi-no itoko wa jitsugyô-kai-ni haitta.

get off 1)...o oriru. 2)shuppatsu-sru
1) He got off the train at Osaka.
　　Kare-wa Ôsaka-de ressha-o orita.
2) He got off to America.　Kare-wa Amerika-e shuppatsu-shita.

get on 1)...ni-noru. 2) = get along
1) Let's get on the bus.　Basu-ni nori-mashô.

get out deru
　　Get out right away!　Sugu dete-ike!

get over 1)...ni uchi-katsu. 2)...o katazukete-shimau
1) He got over many difficulties.
　　Kare-wa ooku-no konnan-ni uchi-katta.
2) I'll be glad to get it over.　Sore ga katazuku-to ureshii.

get through ...o toori-nukeru
　　The bus got through the tunnel.
　　　Basu wa tonneru-o toori-nuketa.

get through with ...o oeru
　　He got through with the work.
　　　Kare-wa sono shigoto-o oeta.

get to ...ni tôchaku-suru
　　They got to Los Angeles safely.
　　　Kare-ra-wa buji Rosanzerusu-ni tsuita.

get up okiru
　　When did you get up this morning?
　　　Kimi-wa kesa nanji-ni okita-no?

getaway (*n.*) (*colloq.*) tôsô [逃走].

geyser (*n.*) kanketsu-sen [間欠泉].

ghost (*n.*) yûrei [幽霊].

ghostly (*a.*) yûrei-no-yô-na [幽霊のような].

giant (*n.*) kyojin [巨人].

gibberish (*n.*) chimpun-kampun [ちんぷんかんぷん].

giblets (*n.*) zômotsu [臓物]; motsu [もつ].

giddy (*a.*) me-mai-ga-suru[-yô-na] [目まいがする(ような)].

gift (*n.*) 1)okuri-mono [贈り物]. 2)tembu-no-sainô [天賦の才能].

gift certificate keihin-hikikae-ken [景品引換券].

gifted (*a.*) tembu-no-sainô-no-aru [天賦の才能のある].

gigantic (*a.*) kyodai-na [巨大な].

giggle (*n. & vi.*) kusu-kusu-warai(kusu-kusu-warau) [くすくす笑い(くすくす笑う)].

gild (*vt.*) ...ni kim-mekki-suru [···に金めっきする].

gill (*n.*) (*pl.*) era [えら].

ginger (*n.*) (*bot.*) shôga [ショウガ].

ginkgo, gingko (*n.*) (*bot.*) ichô [イチョウ].

giraffe (*n.*) (*zool.*) kirin [キリン].

girdle (*n.*) obi [帯].

girl (*n.*) shôjo [少女]; onna-no-ko [女の子].

girlhood (*n.*) shôjo-jidai [少女時代].

girlish (*a.*) shôjo-rashii [少女らしい].

give (*vt.*) 1)...o ageru [···をあげる]; ...o ataeru [···を与える]; ...o okuru [···を贈る]. 2)...o tsutaeru [···を伝える]. 3)...o moyoosu [···を催す]; ...o hiraku [···を開く].

  (*1*) I'll **give** you a book. Kimi-ni hon-*o* issatsu *age*-yô.

  (*2*) Please **give** my kind regards to your family.

      Go-kazoku-no-minasan-ni yoroshiku *o-tsutae*-kudasai.

  (*3*) I'll **give** you a party in hono(u)r of your graduation.

      Omae-no sotsugyô-o-iwatte pâtî-*o hira*-kô.

    (*vi.*) 1)...ni mono-o-ataeru [···に物を与える]. 2)tawamu [たわむ]. 3)kussuru [屈する].

  give away ...o-yatte-shimau

    He gave his fortune away to his nephew.

    Kare-wa jibun-no zaisan-o oi-ni yatte-shimatta.

  give in kôsan-suru

    The enemy gave in. Teki wa kôsan-shita.

give out …o happyô-suru; …o ooyake-ni-suru

The news was given out on the television.

Sono nyûsu wa terebi-de happyô-sareta.

give up …o yameru

He gave up drinking. Kare-wa sake-o-yameta.

given (*a.*) 1)sadamerareta [定められた]. 2)…ga-ataerareru-to […が与えられると].

glacier (*n.*) hyôga [氷河].

glad (*a.*) 1)yorokobashii [喜ばしい]; ureshii [うれしい]. 2)ureshi-sô-na [うれしそうな].

(*1*) I am very **glad** to see you. Anata-ni o-ai-shite *ureshii.*

Yoku irasshai-mashita.

(*2*) We heard their **glad** songs.

Watashi-tachi-wa kare-ra-no *ureshi-sô-na* uta-o kiita.

gladden (*vt.*) …o yorokobaseru […を喜ばせる].

glade (*n.*) rinkan-no-akichi [林間の空き地].

gladly (*ad.*) yorokonde [喜んで].

gladness (*n.*) ureshisa [うれしさ].

glance (*vi.*) chirari-to-miru [ちらりと見る].

(*n.*) ikken [一見]; hito-me [一目].

at a glance hito-me-de

gland (*n.*) (*anat.*) sen [腺].

glare (*vi.*) 1)gira-gira-hikaru [ぎらぎら光る]. 2)nirami-tsukeru [にらみつける].

(*n.*) 1)mabushii-hikari [まぶしい光]. 2)nirami-tsukeru-koto [にらみつけること].

glaring (*a.*) 1)mabayui [まばゆい]. 2)nirami-tsukeru-yô-na [にらみつけるような].

glass (*n.*) 1)garasu [ガラス]. 2)koppu[-ippai-bun] [コップ(一杯分)]. 3)kagami [鏡]. 4)(*pl.*) megane [めがね].

glassware (*n.*) garasu-seihin [ガラス製品].

gleam (*n. & vi.*) 1)kasuka-na-hikari (kasuka-ni-hikaru) [かすかな光(かすかに光る)]. 2)hirameki (hirameku) [ひらめき(ひらめく)].

glee (*n.*) oo-yorokobi [大喜び]; (*mus.*) gurî-gasshô-kyoku [グリー合唱曲].

glen (*n.*) tani-ma [谷間].

glide (*vi. & vt.*) suberu (…o suberaseru) [すべる(…をすべらせる)]; (*aviation*) kakkû-suru(…o kakkû-saseru) [滑空する(…を滑空させる)].

glimmer (*vi. & n.*) chira-chira-hikaru (chira-chira-suru-hikari) [ち
らちら光る(ちらちらする光)].

glimpse (*n.*) chirari-to-mieru[-miru]-koto [ちらりと見える[見る]こと];
ikken [一見].

　catch(get, have) a glimpse of ...o chirari-to-miru

glitter (*vi.*) pika-pika-hikaru [ぴかぴか光る].

　　　　　(*n.*) kirameki [きらめき].

global (*a.*) 1)kyûkei-no [球形の]. 2)zen-sekai-no [全世界の].

globe (*n.*) 1)kyû [球]. 2)(the -) chikyû [地球]. 3)chikyû-gi [地球儀].
4)kyû-kei-no-mono [球形のもの].

gloom (*n.*) 1)usu-kuragari [薄暗がり]. 2)inki [陰気]; yûutsu [憂うつ].

gloomy (*a.*) 1)usu-gurai [薄暗い]; inki-na [陰気な]. 2)hikan-teki-na
[悲観的な].

glorious (*a.*) 1)kôei-aru [光栄ある]. 2)hikari-kagayaku [光り輝く].
3)(*colloq.*) hijô-ni-yukai-na [非常に愉快な]; suteki-na [すてきな].

glory (*n.*) 1)eikô [栄光]. 2)sôkan [壮観]. 3)han'ei [繁栄].

gloss (*n.*) 1)kôtaku [光沢].

　　　　　(*vt.*) ...ni kôtaku-o-tsukeru […に光沢をつける].

glossary (*n.*) yôgo-kaisetsu [用語解説]; goi-shû [語い集].

glossy (*a.*) kôtaku-no-aru [光沢のある].

glove (*n.*) 1)te-bukuro [手袋]. 2)(*baseball*) gurabu [グラブ].

　fit like a glove pittari-to-au

glow (*vi.*) 1)hakunetsu-shite-kagayaku [白熱して輝く]; shakunetsu-
suru [しゃく熱する]. 2)hoteru [ほてる].

　　　　　(*n.*) 1)hakunetsu [白熱]; moeru-yô-na-iro [燃えるような色]. 2)
hoteri [ほてり].

glowworm (*n.*) (*insect*) tsuchi-botaru [ツチボタル].

glue (*n.*) nikawa [にかわ]; setchaku-zai [接着剤]; nori [のり].

　　　　(*vt.*) ...o setchaku-zai[nikawa]-de-tsukeru […を接着剤[にかわ]で
つける].

gnaw (*vt.*) 1)...o kajiru […をかじる]. 2)...o suri-herasu […をすり減
らす]. 3)...o kurushimeru […を苦しめる]; ...o nayamasu […を悩ます].
　　　　(*vi.*) kajiru [かじる]; kurushimeru [苦しめる]; nayamasu [悩
ます].

go (*vi.*) 1)iku [行く]. 2)kuzureru [崩れる]. 3)naru [鳴る]; (...to)
oto-ga-suru [(…と)音がする]. 4)(...ni) naru [(…に)なる]. 5)(...de-)
iru [(…で)いる]. 6)yaku-ni-tatsu [役に立つ]. 7)ugoku [動く]. 8)
...(shi-)yô-to-suru […(し)ようとする]. 9)tsûyô-suru [通用する];

ryûtsû-suru [流通する].

(1) I **go** to school at eight every day.
　　Watashi-wa mai-nichi hachi-ji-ni gakkô-e *iku*.
(2) The embankment **went**. Teibô ga *kuzureta*.
(3) The whistle **has gone**. Kiteki ga *natta*.
(4) The fish will **go** bad. Sakana ga kusaru-darô.
(5) The dog will have to **go** hungry.
　　Sono inu wa kûfuku-de-*inake*reba-naranai-darô.
(6) The explanation **went** for nothing.
　　Sono setsumei wa nan-no-*yaku-ni*-mo-*tata*-nakatta.
(7) This engine **goes** by steam. Kono enjin wa jôki-de *ugoku*.
(8) It's **going to** snow. Yuki-ga-furi-*sô-da*.
(9) Does a yen bill **go** in this country?
　　En-satsu wa kono kuni-de *tsûyô-shimasu*-ka?

go by sugiru
　　Two months went by. Ni-ka-getsu-ga sugita.
go far seikô-suru
　　He will go far surely. Kare-wa kitto seikô-suru-darô.
go out 1)gaishutsu-suru. 2)kieru
　1) She goes out a great deal at night.
　　　Kano-jo-wa yoru-wa gaishutsu-ga-ooi.
　2) The candle went out in the wind. Rôsoku ga kaze-de kieta.
go over 1)tenkô-suru. 2)...o nen-o-irete-shiraberu
　1) They went over to the enemy.
　　　Kare-ra-wa teki-gawa-ni mawatta.
　2) She is going over the accounts.
　　　Kano-jo-wa keisan-sho-o shirabeteiru.
go through ...o keiken-suru
　　I don't want to go through such trouble again.
　　　Watashi-wa konna monchaku-o ni-do-to keiken-shi-taku-nai.
go through with ...o yari-togeru
go with ...to chôwa-suru
　　Your white dress goes with your face.
　　　Anata-no shiroi doresu wa anata-no kao-ni yoku-utsuru.

goal (*n.*) 1)kesshô-ten [決勝点]; gôru [ゴール]. 2)mokuhyô [目標].
goat (*n.*) yagi [ヤギ].
gobble (*vt. & vi.*) (...o) gatsu-gatsu-taberu [(…を)がつがつ食べる].
god (*n.*) kami [神].

goddess (*n.*) me-gami [女神].

godliness (*n.*) shinjin-bukai-koto [信心深いこと]; keiken [敬けん].

godly (*a.*) shinjin-bukai [信心深い]; keiken-na [敬けんな].

gold (*n.*) kin [金]; kinka [金貨].

golden (*a.*) 1)kin-no [金の]; kin-iro-no [金色の]; kinsei-no [金製の]. 2)kichô-na [貴重な].

    golden opportunity mata-to-nai-kikai

goldfish (*n.*) kingyo [金魚].

goldsmith (*n.*) kin-zaiku-shokunin [金細工職人].

golf (*n. & vi.*) gorufu(-o-suru) [ゴルフ(をする)].

gone (*a.*) 1)satta [去った]. 2)shinda [死んだ].

    (*1*) He **has gone** abroad.   Kare-wa gaikoku-e *itte*-iru.

    (*2*) He **is** dead and **gone**.   Kare-wa *shinde*-shimatta.

gong (*n.*) dora [どら].

good (*a.*) 1)yoi [よい]; zenryô-na [善良な]. 2)shinsetsu-na [親切な]. 3)rippa-na [立派な]. 4)tanoshii [楽しい]. 5)jôzu-na [上手な]. 6)gyôgi-no-yoi [行儀のよい]. 7)kanari-no [かなりの]; jûbun-na [十分な]. 8)yoi [よい].

    (*1*) It is a **good** book.   Sore-wa *yoi* hon da.

    (*2*) It is **good** of you to send me help.

        Watashi-o tasukete-kureru-to-wa go-*shinsetsu-na*-koto.

    (*3*) He has **good** looks.   Kare-wa *rippa-na* kao-dachi-o shite-iru.

    (*4*) We had a very **good** time of it.

        Ware-ware-wa totemo *tanoshii* toki-o sugoshita.

        Ware-ware-wa totemo *tanoshi*-katta.

    (*5*) She is **good** at painting.   Kano-jo-wa e-ga-*jôzu*-da.

    (*6*) She has **good** manners.   Kano-jo-wa *gyôgi-ga-ii*.

    (*7*) It will take a **good** long time to go to the station from here.

        Koko-kara eki-e iku-niwa *kanari* nagai jikan-o yôsuru-darô.

    (*8*) Milk is **good** for everybody.   Gyûnyû wa dare-ni-demo *yoi*.

    as good as ...mo-dôzen

    (as) good as gold (kodomo ga) totemo-otonashii

    feel good (*colloq.*) kibun-ga-yoi; genki-de-aru

    Good for you! Dekashita!; Umai-zo!

    (*n.*) 1)zen [善]; rieki [利益]; kôfuku [幸福]. 2)(*pl.*) dôsan [動産]; shôhin [商品]; ((*Eng.*)) kamotsu [貨物].

(1) Ripe fruits will do him **good**.

    Jukushita kudamono wa kare-no-karada-ni-*ii*-darô.

(2) Almost all stolen **goods** were pawned.

    Tô-*hin*-no-hotondo-subete wa shichi-ni-ire-rareta.

Good afternoon! (*int.*) Konnichi-wa! [今日は!]; Sayô-nara! [さよう なら!].

good-by(e) (*int.*) Sayô-nara! [さようなら!].

    (*n.*) itomagoi [いとまごい].

Good day! (*int.*) Konnichi-wa! [今日は!].

Good evening! (*int.*) Komban-wa [今晩は!]; Sayô-nara! [さような ら!].

good-for-nothing (*a.*) yaku-ni-tata-nai [役にたたない].

good-hearted (*a.*) shinsetsu-na [親切な].

good-humo(u)red (*a.*) aiso-no-yoi [愛想のよい].

good-looking (*a.*) kao-dachi-no-yoi [顔立ちのよい]; utsukushii [美し い].

Good morning! (*int.*) Ohayô! [おはよう!]; Sayô-nara! [さようなら!].

good-natured (*a.*) hito-no-yoi [人のよい]; onkô-na [温厚な].

goodness (*n.*) 1)zenryô-sa [善良さ]; shinsetsu [親切]. 2)chôsho [長所].

    for goodness' sake goshô-da-kara

Good night! (*int.*) Oyasumi! [おやすみ!]; Sayô-nara! [さようなら!].

good-tempered (*a.*) yasashii [優しい]; otonashii [おとなしい].

goodwill (*n.*) kôi [好意]; shinzen [親善].

goody (*int.*) Suteki-da! [すてきだ!].

    (*n.*) (*colloq.*) (*pl.*) 1)tanoshii-mono [楽しいもの]. 2)o-kashi

goose (*n.*) gachô [ガチョウ].   └[お菓子].

gorge (*vt.*) ...o gatsu-gatsu-taberu […をがつがつ食べる].

    (*n.*) 1)kyôkoku [峡谷]. 2)i [胃]; i-no-naka-mi [胃の中味].

gorgeous (*a.*) gôka-na [豪華な]; kirabiyaka-na [きらびやかな].

gorilla (*n.*) (*zool.*) gorira [ゴリラ].

gosh (*int.*) Oya! [おや!].

gospel (*n.*) 1)fukuin [福音]. 2)(G-)fukuin-sho [福音書].

gossip (*n. & vi.*) muda-banashi(-o-suru) [むだ話(をする)]; seken-banashi(o-suru) [世間話(をする)].

Gothic (*a.*) (*arch.*) Goshikku-yôshiki-no [ゴシック様式の].

gourd (*n.*) (*bot.*) hyôtan [ヒョウタン].

gout (*n.*) (*path.*) tsûfû [痛風].

govern (*vt.*) ...o tôchi-suru […を統治する]; ...o shihai-suru […を支配

する].

government (*n.*) seifu [政府]; seiji [政治].

governor (*n.*) 1)《*Eng.*》sôtoku [総督]; 《*US*》chiji [知事]. 2) chôkan [長官].

grab (*vt.*) ...o hittsukamu [⋯をひっつかむ]; ...o hittakuru [⋯をひったくる].
　　　(*vi.*) hittsukamu [ひっつかむ]; hittakuru [ひったくる]; hittakurô-to-suru [ひったくろうとする].
　　　(*n.*) gôdatsu [強奪]; ôryô [横領].

grace (*n.*) 1)yûbi [優美]; shitoyaka-sa [しとやかさ]. 2)shoku-zen [-go]-no-inori [食前[後]の祈り].

graceful (*a.*) shitoyaka-na [しとやかな]; jôhin-na [上品な].

gracefully (*ad.*) shitoyaka-ni [しとやかに].

gracious (*a.*) nasake-bukai [情け深い].

　Good gracious! Saa-taihen!

grade (*n.*) 1)tôkyû [等級]. 2)《*US*》nenkyû [年級]. 3)《*US*》kôbai [こう配].

gradual (*a.*) jojo-no [徐々の]; dan-dan-no [だんだんの].

gradually (*ad.*) dan-dan-to [だんだんと]; shidai-ni [次第に].

graduate (*n.*) sotsugyô-sei [卒業生].
　　　(*vt. & vi.*) ...o sotsugyô-saseru (sotsugyô-suru) [⋯を卒業させる(卒業する)].

graduation (*n.*) sotsugyô [卒業].

grain (*n.*) 1)kokumotsu [穀物]; kokumotsu-no-tsubu [穀物の粒]. 2) honno-sukoshi-no-ryô [ほんの少しの量]. 3)moku-me [木目].

grammar (*n.*) bumpô [文法].

grammatical (*a.*) bumpô[-jô]-no [文法(上)の]; bumpô-ni-kanatta [文法にかなった].

gramophone (*n.*) 《*Eng.*》chikuon-ki [蓄音機].

granary (*n.*) kokusô [穀倉].

grand (*a.*) 1)sôdai-na [壮大な]; yûdai-na [雄大な]; (*colloq.*) subarashii [すばらしい]. 2)shuyô-na [主要な].

grandchild (*n.*) mago [孫].

granddaughter (*n.*) mago-musume [孫娘].

grandeur (*n.*) sôkan [壮観]; igen [威厳]; idai [偉大].

grandfather (*n.*) sofu [祖父].

grandma, grandma(m)ma (*n.*) o-baa-chan [おばあちゃん].

grandmother (*n.*) sobo [祖母].

grandpa, grandpapa (*n.*) o-jii-chan ［おじいちゃん］.

grandson (*n.*) mago-musuko ［孫息子］.

granite (*n.*) mikage-ishi ［みかげ石］.

granny, -nie (*n.*) o-baa-chan ［おばあちゃん］.

grant (*vt.*) ...o kanaeru ［…をかなえる］; ...o ataeru ［…を与える］.
　　take...for granted ...o tôzen-no-koto-to-omou

granulated sugar guranyû-tô ［グラニュー糖］.

grape (*n.*) budô ［ブドウ］.

grapevine (*n.*) budô-no-ki ［ブドウの木］.

graph (*n.*) gurafu ［グラフ］.
　　(*vt.*) ...o gurafu-de-shimesu ［…をグラフで示す］.

grasp (*vt.*) 1)...o tsukamu ［…をつかむ］. 2)...o rikai-suru ［…を理解する］.
　　(*vi.*) tobi-tsuku ［飛びつく］.

grass (*n.*) 1)kusa ［草］. 2)shiba ［芝］. 3)bokusô-chi ［牧草地］.

grasshopper (*n.*) (*insect*) inago ［イナゴ］; batta ［バッタ］.

grassy (*a.*) kusa-no-ooi ［草の多い］; kusa-no-yô-na ［草のような］.

grateful (*a.*) arigataku-omou ［ありがたく思う］; kansha-shite-iru ［感謝している］.

gratefully (*ad.*) arigataku ［ありがたく］; kansha-shite ［感謝して］.

gratify (*vt.*) ...o manzoku-saseru ［…を満足させる］.

gratitude (*n.*) kansha-no-kimochi ［感謝の気持］.

grave (*n.*) haka ［墓］.

grave (*a.*) 1)jûdai-na ［重大な］. 2)igen-no-aru ［威厳のある］; omo-omo-shii ［重々しい］.

gravel (*n.*) jari ［砂利］.

gravely (*ad.*) jûdai-ni ［重大に］; ogosoka-ni ［おごそかに］.

graveyard (*n.*) bochi ［墓地］.

gravity (*n.*) 1)(*phys.*) jûryoku ［重力］; inryoku ［引力］. 2)jûdai-sa ［重大さ］.

gray, grey (*a.*) hai-iro-no ［灰色の］.

gray-headed (*a.*) shira-ga-majiri-no ［白髪まじりの］.

graze (*vi. & vt.*) kusa-o-kuu (...ni kusa-o-kuwaseru) ［草を食う（…に草を食わせる）］.

grease (*n.*) jûshi ［獣脂］; gurîsu ［グリース］.
　　(*vt.*) ...ni gurîsu-o-nuru ［…にグリースを塗る］.

great (*a.*) 1)idai-na ［偉大な］. 2)ookii ［大きい］. 3)hijô-na ［非常な］. 4)(*colloq.*) suteki-na ［すてきな］.

Great Britain　Dai-Buriten-tô［大ブリテン島］.

great-hearted (*a.*) 1)kokoro-no-hiroi［心の広い］. 2)yûki-no-aru［勇気のある］.

greatly (*ad.*) 1)ooi-ni［大いに］; hijô-ni［非常に］. 2)idai-ni［偉大に］.

greatness (*n.*) 1)idai-sa［偉大さ］. 2)tadai［多大］.

Greece (*n.*) Girisha［ギリシャ］.

greedy (*a.*) don'yoku-na［どん欲な］; kui-shimbô-na［食いしんぼうな］.

Greek (*a.*) Girisha-no［ギリシャの］; Girisha-jin-no［ギリシャ人の］; Girisha-go-no［ギリシャ語の］.
　　　(*n.*) Girisha-jin［ギリシャ人］; Girisha-go［ギリシャ語］.

green (*a.*) midori[-iro]-no［緑(色)の］; aoao-to-shita［青々とした］.
　　　(*n.*) 1)midori-iro［緑色］; ryokuchi［緑地］. 2)(*pl.*) aomono［青物］.

greengrocer (*n.*) ((*Eng.*)) aomono-shô［青物商］.

greenhouse (*n.*) onshitsu［温室］.

greenish (*a.*) midori-gakatta［緑がかった］.

greet (*vt.*) 1)...ni aisatsu-suru［…にあいさつする］; ...o mukaeru［…を迎える］. 2)(mimi ya me)-ni hairu［(耳や目)にはいる］; (hana)-o tsuku［(鼻)をつく］.
　　　(*1*) He **greeted** his uncle.　Kare-wa oji-*ni aisatsu-shita*.
　　　(*2*) The odour **greets** my nose.　Sono nioi ga hana-*o tsuku*.

greeting (*n.*) 1)aisatsu［あいさつ］. 2)(*pl.*) aisatsu-no-kotoba［あいさつのことば］.

grid (*n.*) 1)kôshi［格子］. 2)yaki-ami［焼き網］.

gridiron (*n.*) 1)yaki-ami［焼き網］. 2)((*US*)) futtobôru-kyôgi-jô［フットボール競技場］.

grief (*n.*) fukai-kanashimi［深い悲しみ］.
　come to grief　hidoi-me-ni-au; shippai-suru

grieve (*vt. & vi.*) ...o fukaku-kanashimaseru (fukaku-kanashimu)［…を深く悲しませる(深く悲しむ)］.

grim (*a.*) 1)kibishii［厳しい］. 2)danko-taru［断固たる］.

grimly (*ad.*) genkaku-ni［厳格に］; reikoku-ni［冷酷に］; kimi-waruku［気味悪く］.

grimy (*a.*) aka-de-yogoreta［あかで汚れた］.

grin (*vi.*) ha-o-misete-warau［歯を見せて笑う］; niyari-to-warau［にやりと笑う］.
　　　(*n.*) ha-o-mukidasu-koto［歯をむき出すこと］; niya-niya-warai［にやにや笑い］.

grind (*vt.*) 1)...o (usu-de)-hiku […を(うすで)ひく]; ...o chiisaku-
kudaku […を小さく砕く]. 2)...o togu […を研ぐ]. 3)...o kishiraseru
[…をきしらせる].

grip (*vt. & n.*) ...o kataku-nigiru(-koto) […を固く握る(こと)].

grizzly (*a.*) hai-iro-gakatta [灰色がかった].
　　　　　(*n.*) ((*US*)) hai-iro-guma [ハイイログマ].

groan (*vi. & n.*) umeku (umeki-goe) [うめく(うめき声)].

grocer (*n.*) shokuryô-zakka-shônin [食料雑貨商人].

grocery (*n.*) 1)(*pl.*) shokuryô-zakka-rui [食料雑貨類]. 2)shokuryô-
zakka-ten [食料雑貨店].

groom (*n.*) = bridegroom [花婿].

grope (*vi.*) te-saguri-de-sagasu [手探りで探す].

gross (*a.*) 1)zentai-no [全体の]. 2)hidoi [ひどい]. 3)somatsu-na [粗
末な]; gehin-na [下品な].
　　　　(*n.*) gôkei [合計].
　　　　(*vt.*) ...no sô-shûeki-o-ageru […の総収益をあげる].

grossly (*ad.*) gehin-ni [下品に]; hidoku [ひどく].

grotesque (*a.*) kaiki-na [怪奇な]; gurotesuku-na [グロテスクな].
　　　　　　(*n.*) kaiki-na-mono [怪奇なもの].

ground (*n.*) 1)tochi [土地]; jimen [地面]; undô-jô [運動場]. 2)(*pl.*)
niwa [庭]; kônai [構内]. 3)riyû [理由]; gen'in [原因].

ground floor ((*Eng.*)) = first floor ikkai [一階].

groundless (*a.*) konkyo-no-nai [根拠のない]; riyû-no-nai [理由のない].

group (*n.*) mure [群れ]; shûdan [集団]; gurûpu [グループ].

grove (*n.*) ko-dachi [木立ち].

grow (*vi.*) 1)seichô-suru [成長する]; haeru [生える]. 2)...ni naru […
になる].
　　(*1*) Plants would not **grow** without water.
　　　　Mizu-ga-nakereba shokubutsu wa *seichô-shi*-nai-darô-ni.
　　(*2*) The village **grew** into a town.
　　　　Sono mura wa ookiku-natte machi-*ni-natta*.
　　　(*vt.*) 1)...o saibai-suru […を栽培する]. 2)(hige)-o hayasu [(ひ
げ)を生やす].

growl (*vi.*) unaru [うなる]; gami-gami-iu [がみがみ言う].

grown-up (*n. & a.*) seijin(-shita) [成人(した)].

growth (*n.*) 1)seichô [成長]; zôdai [増大]; kakuchô [拡張]. 2)seichô-
shita-mono [成長したもの].

grudge (*n.*) urami [恨み].

　　　　(*vt.*) 1)...o ataeru-no-o-oshimu [⋯を与えるのを惜しむ]. 2)...o
　netamu [⋯をねたむ].
gruel (*n.*) usui-kayu [薄いかゆ].
grumble (*vi. & n.*) butsu-butsu-iu(-koe) [ぶつぶつ言う(声)]; fuhei-o-
　iu(-koto) [不平を言う(こと)].
guarantee (*n.*) hoshô[-nin] [保証(人)].
　　　　　　(*vt.*) ...o hoshô-suru [⋯を保証する]; ...no hoshô-nin-ni-
　naru [⋯の保証人になる].
guaranty (*n.*) hoshô [保証]; tampo[-bukken] [担保(物件)].
guard (*n.*) 1)bannin [番人]; mi-hari [見張り]. 2)((*Eng.*))(ressha no)
　shashô [(列車の)車掌].
　off one's guard yudan-shite
　on one's guard yôjin-shite
　　　　(*vt.*) ...o mamoru [⋯を守る]; ...o mi-haru [⋯を見張る].
　　　　The dog **guards** my house at night.
　　　　　Inu wa yoru watashi-no ie-*no-ban-o-suru*.
　　　　(*vi.*) yôjin-suru [用心する].
　　　　Guard against traffic accidents.　Kôtsû-jiko-ni *yôjin-nasai*.
guardian (*n.*) 1)hogo-sha [保護者]. 2)kanri-sha [管理者]. 3)(*law*)
　kôken-nin [後見人].
guardrail (*n.*) tesuri [手すり]; gâdo-rêru [ガードレール].
guess (*vt.*) ...no kentô-o-tsukeru [⋯の見当をつける]; ...o ii-ateru [⋯
　を言い当てる].
　　　　(*n.*) suiryô [推量]; okusoku [憶測].
　by guess suiryô-de
guest (*n.*) kyaku [客].
guidance (*n.*) annai [案内]; hodô [補導]; gaidansu [ガイダンス].
guide (*n.*) 1)annai-sha [案内者]; gaido [ガイド]. 2)te-biki-sho [手引
　き書].
　　　　(*vt.*) ...o annai-suru [⋯を案内する]; ...o michibiku [⋯を導く].
guidebook (*n.*) ryokô-annai-sho [旅行案内書]; gaido-bukku [ガイドブッ
　ク].
guidepost (*n.*) michi-shirube [道しるべ].
guilt (*n.*) 1)yûzai [有罪]. 2)zaiaku-kan [罪悪感].
guilty (*a.*) yûzai-no [有罪の]; mi-ni-oboe-no-aru [身に覚えのある].
gulf (*n.*) wan [湾].
gull (*n.*) (*birds*) kamome [カモメ].
gum (*n.*) (*pl.*) ha-guki [歯茎].

gum (*n.*) 1)gomu[-no-ki] [ゴム(の木)]. 2)chûin-gamu [チューインガム].

gun (*n.*) jû [銃]; pisutoru [ピストル].

gunpowder (*n.*) kayaku [火薬].

gunshot (*n.*) shageki [射撃]; shatei-kyori [射程距離].

gush (*vi. & n.*) hotobashiru (hotobashiri) [ほとばしる(ほとばしり)].

gust (*n.*) toppû [突風].

gusty (*a.*) toppû-sei-no [突風性の].

gut (*n.*) 1)(*pl.*) chô [腸]; naizô [内臓]. 2)(*pl.*)(*colloq.*) yûki [勇気].

gutter (*n.*) 1)toi [とい]. 2)mizo [溝]. 3)(the –) himmin-gai [貧民街].

guttural (*a.*) nodo-no [のどの].

guy (*n.*) (*colloq.*) otoko [男]; yatsu [やつ].

gymnasium (*n.*) taiiku-kan [体育館].

gymnastics (*n.*) taisô [体操].

gyrocompass (*n.*) kaiten-rashin-gi [回転羅針儀]; jairo-kompasu [ジャイロコンパス].

gyroscope (*n.*) kaiten-gi [回転儀]; jairo-sukôpu [ジャイロスコープ].

H

ha (*int.*) Oya! [おや!]; Haa! [はあ!].

habit (*n.*) shûkan [習慣]; kuse [癖].

habitable (*a.*) sumeru [住める].

habitant (*n.*) jûnin [住人]; kyojû-sha [居住者].

habitation (*n.*) kyojû [居住]; jûsho [住所].

habitual (*a.*) shûkan-teki-na [習慣的な]; itsu-mo-no [いつもの].

haddock (*n.*) (*fish*) tara-no-isshu [タラの一種].

haggard (*a.*) yatsureta [やつれた].

hail (*n. & vi.*) arare(-ga-furu) [あられ(が降る)]; hyô(-ga-furu) [ひょう(が降る)].

hail (*vt.*) 1)...o kanko-shite-mukaeru [...を歓呼して迎える]. 2)...ni yobi-kakeru [...に呼び掛ける].
    (2) **I was hailed** by a friend of mine in the street.
        Watashi-wa toori-de tomodachi-ni *yobi-kakerareta*.
    (*n.*) aisatsu [あいさつ]; yobi-kake [呼び掛け].
    (*int.*) Banzai! [万歳!]; Yôkoso! [ようこそ!].

hair (*n.*) ke [毛]; kami-no-ke [髪の毛].

haircut (*n.*) sampatsu [散髪].

hairdo (*n.*) kami-no-setto [髪のセット].

hairdresser (*n.*) biyô-shi [美容師].

hairstyle (*n.*) kami-gata [髪型]; hea-sutairu [ヘアスタイル].

hale (*a.*) oite-tassha-na [老いて達者な].
    hale and hearty kakushaku-to-shita

half (*n. & a.*) hambun(-no) [半分(の)].
    (*ad.*) hambun-dake [半分だけ]; nakaba [半ば]; hotondo [ほとんど].

halfback (*n.*) (*sports*) hâfu-bakku [ハーフバック].

half-holiday (*n.*) han-don [半ドン].

half-moon (*n.*) hangetsu [半月].

halfway (*a.*) 1)chûkan-no [中間の]. 2)chûto-hampa-na [中途半端な].
    (*ad.*) tochû-de [途中で]; hambun-dake [半分だけ]; fu-jûbun-ni [不十分に].

hall (*n.*) 1)kaikan [会館]. 2)oo-hiroma [大広間]; hôru [ホール]. 3) genkan [玄関].

hallo (*int.*) 1)Moshi-moshi! [もしもし!]. 2)Yaa! [やあ!].

hallow (*vt.*) ...o shinsei-ka-suru [...を神聖化する].

halt (*vt. & vi.*) ...o teishi-saseru (teishi-suru) [...を停止させる(停止する)].
    (*n.*) teishi [停止]; kyûshi [休止].

halve (*vt.*) ...o ni-tôbun-suru [...を二等分する]; ...o hangen-suru [...を半減する].

hammer (*n.*) kana-zuchi [金づち]; hammâ [ハンマー].
    (*vt.*) ...o kana-zuchi-de-tataku [...を金づちでたたく]; ...o

hammâ-de-utsu [⋯をハンマーで打つ].

hand (*n.*) 1)te [手]. 2)(tokei no) hari [(時計の)針]. 3)(*pl.*) shoyû [所有]; shihai [支配]. 4)hisseki [筆跡]. 5)(*pl.*)(hitsuyô-na) hito-de [(必要な)人手]. 6)(...na-)hito [(⋯な)人]. 7)buntan [分担]; sanka [参加]. 8)udemae [腕前].

(*1*) the right **hand** migi-*te*

(*2*) The long **hand** tells the minute. Chô*shin* wa fun-o shimesu.

(*3*) The house fell into my **hands**.
     Sono ie wa watashi-no-*shoyû*-ni natta.

(*4*) He writes a very good **hand**.
     Kare-wa *hisseki* ga totemo rippa-da.

(*5*) My shop is short of **hands**.
     Watashi-no mise wa *hito-de*-ga tari-nai.

(*6*) He is a cool **hand**. Kare-wa zûzûshii.

(*7*) I had a **hand** in this enterprise.
     Watashi-wa kono-jigyô-ni *kuwawatte*-ita.

(*8*) She has a **hand** for pastry.
     Kano-jo-wa kêki-o-tsukuru-no-ga-*jôzu*-da.

  at hand chikaku-ni; chikai-shôrai-ni

  by hand te-de

  come into one's hand ...no te-ni-hairu

  from hand to hand te-kara-te-e

  hand in hand te-ni-te-o-totte

  on all hands itaru-tokoro-de

  on hand 1)temochi-no(-de); ...o-mote-amashite. 2)majika-ni

  on the other hand tahô-de-wa; kore-ni-hanshite
     (*vt.*)...o watasu [⋯を渡す]; ...o te-watasu [⋯を手渡す].

  hand in ...o teishutsu-suru

handbaggage (*n.*) ((*US*)) te-nimotsu [手荷物].

handful (*n.*) hito-nigiri [一握り]; wazuka [わずか].

handicap (*n.*) handikyappu [ハンディキャップ]; fu-rieki [不利益].

handicraft (*n.*) te-zaiku[-hin] [手細工(品)].

handkerchief (*n.*) hankachi [ハンカチ].

handle (*n.*) e [柄]; totte [取っ手]; handoru [ハンドル].
     (*vt.*)...o atsukau [⋯を扱う].

handmade (*a.*) te-sei-no [手製の].

handrail (*n.*) tesuri [手すり].

handsome (*a.*) 1)kao-dachi-no-yoi [顔だちのよい]. 2)sôtô-na [相当な].

handsomely (*ad.*) 1)rippa-ni [立派に]. 2)ki-mae-yoku [気前よく].

handwriting (*n.*) te-gaki [手書き]; hisseki [筆跡].

handy (*a.*) 1)tegoro-na [手ごろな]; benri-na [便利な]. 2)kiyô-na [器用な].

hang (*vt.*) 1)...o kakeru […を掛ける]. 2)...o kôshu-kei-ni-suru […を絞首刑にする].

    (*vi.*) burasagatte-iru [ぶら下がっている].

happen (*vi.*) 1)okoru [起こる]. 2)gûzen...(suru) [偶然…(する)].

  as it happens gûzen; ainiku

happening (*n.*) 1)deki-goto [出来事]; jiken [事件]. 2)hapuningu [ハプニング].

happily (*ad.*) kôfuku-ni [幸福に]; medetaku [めでたく].

happiness (*n.*) kôfuku [幸福].

happy (*a.*) 1)kôfuku-na [幸福な]; medetai [めでたい]. 2)ureshii [うれしい].

  (*1*) You will be **happy** in near future.

    Anata-wa chikai-shôrai *kôfuku*-ni-naru-darô.

  (*2*) I am **happy** to meet you. O-ai-dekite *ureshii*.

harass (*vt.*) ...o nayamasu […を悩ます]; ...o komaraseru […を困らせる].

harbor, -bour (*n.*) minato [港].

hard (*a.*) 1)katai [堅い]. 2)muzukashii [難しい]. 3)nesshin-na [熱心な]. 4)tsurai [つらい]; kibishii [厳しい].

  have a hard time of it hidoi-me-ni-au

  (*ad.*) 1)nesshin-ni [熱心に]. 2)hidoku [ひどく]; hageshiku [激しく].

  (*1*) He works **hard**. Kare-wa *kemmei-ni* hataraku.

  (*2*) It rained very **hard** last night.

    Sakuya ame ga *hageshiku* futta.

hardback (*n.*) = hardcover kata-byôshi-no-hon [堅表紙の本].

hard-boiled (*a.*) kataku-yudeta [固くゆでた].

harden (*vt. & vi.*) ...o kataku-suru(kataku-naru) […を固くする(固くなる)].

hardhearted (*a.*) reikoku-na [冷酷な].

hardly (*ad.*) 1)hotondo...(de-)nai [ほとんど…(で)ない]. 2)yatto [やっと].

  (*1*) There was **hardly** any paper in that time.

    Tôji-wa kami-to-iu-mono wa *hotondo-nakatta*.

(2) He recovered **hardly** what he had lost.

　　Kare-wa sonshitsu-o *yatto* tori-kaeshita.

hardly...when(before) ...(suru-)to-sugu

hardship (*n*.) kunan [苦難]; shinku [辛苦].

hardware (*n*.) 1)kana-mono-rui [金物類]. 2)(*computer*) hâdouea [ハードウェア].

hardworking (*a*.) kimben-na [勤勉な].

hardy (*a*.) ganjô-na [頑丈な]; daitan-na [大胆な].

hare (*n*.) no-usagi [野ウサギ].

harm (*n*.) gai [害]; shôgai [傷害]; songai [損害]; gaiaku [害悪].

　do harm (to) (...ni) kigai-o-kuwaeru

　out of harm's way anzen-na-tokoro-ni

　　　(*vt*.) ...o gai-suru [···を害する]; ...o itameru [···を痛める].

harmful (*a*.) gai-ni-naru [害になる]; yûgai-na [有害な].

harmless (*a*.) mugai-no [無害の]; tsumi-no-nai [罪のない].

harmonious (*a*.) 1)naka-no-yoi [仲のよい]. 2)chôwa-no-toreta [調和のとれた].

harmonize (*vt*.) ...o chôwa-saseru [···を調和させる].

　　　　(*vi*.) chôwa-suru [調和する]; itchi-suru [一致する].

harmony (*n*.) chôwa [調和].

harness (*n*.) bagu [馬具].

harp (*n. & vi*.) hâpu(-o-hiku) [ハープ(をひく)].

harpoon (*n*.) mori [もり].

　　　　(*vt*.) ...ni mori-o-uchi-komu [···にもりを打ち込む].

harsh (*a*.) 1)mimi-zawari-na [耳ざわりな]. 2)kibishii [厳しい].

harshly (*ad*.) ara-ara-shiku [荒々しく]; mimi-zawari-ni [耳ざわりに]; kibishiku [厳しく].

harvest (*n*.) tori-ire [取り入れ]; shûkaku[-ki] [収穫(期)].

haste (*n*.) isogu-koto [急ぐこと]; seikyû [性急].

　make haste isogu

hasten (*vt*.) ...o isogaseru [···を急がせる]; ...o hayameru [···を早める].

　　　　(*vi*.) isogu [急ぐ].

hastily (*ad*.) isoide [急いで]; awatete [あわてて].

hasty (*a*.) isogi-no [急ぎの]; hayamatta [早まった]; keisotsu-na [軽率な].

hat (*n*.) bôshi [帽子].

hatch (*vt. & vi*.) (tamago)-o fuka-suru((tamago ga)kaeru) [(卵)をふ化する((卵が)かえる)].

hatch (*n.*) (*marine*) = hatchway (kampan no) shôkô-guchi [(甲板の) 昇降口]; hatchi [ハッチ].

hate (*vt.*) ...o nikumu […を憎む]; ...o hidoku-kirau […をひどく嫌う].

hateful (*a.*) nikui [憎い].

hatred (*n.*) nikushi-mi [憎しみ]; urami [恨み].

hatter (*n.*) bôshi-seizô-nin [帽子製造人]; bôshiya [帽子屋].

haughty (*a.*) ôhei-na [横柄な].

haul (*vt. & vi.*) (...o) hipparu [(…を)引っ張る].

haunch (*n.*) (*pl.*) dembu [でん部]; shiri [しり].

haunt (*vt.*) ...e tabi-tabi-iku […へたびたび行く]; ...ni shutsubotsu-suru […に出没する].

     (*n.*) yoku-iku-basho [よく行く場所].

have (*vt.*) 1)...o motte-iru […を持っている]; ...o shoyû-suru […を所有する]. 2)...o ukeru […を受ける]. 3)as '*have to*' neba-naranai [ねばならない]. 4)...saseru […させる]. 5)...o suru […をする]. 6)...o taberu […を食べる].

  (*1*) Do you **have** many books?

       Anata-wa takusan hon-*o motte-imasu*-ka?

  (*2*) We **had** no school yesterday.   Kinô jugyô-*ga* na*katta*.

  (*3*) I **have to** write a letter.

       Watashi-wa tegami-o kaka-*neba-naranai*.

  (*4*) I **had** my photo taken.   Watashi-wa shashin-o utsu-*saseta*.

  (*5*) We **had** a game.   Ware-ware-wa shiai-*o shita*.

  (*6*) The patient **had** two eggs.

       Kanja wa tamago-o futatsu *tabeta*.

have on ...o kite-iru; ...o kabutte-iru; ...o haite-iru

have to do with ...to kankei-ga-aru

     (*aux. v.*) 1)...(shite-)shimatta […(して)しまった]. 2)...(shite-)iru […(して)いる]. 3)...(shita-)koto-ga-aru […(した)ことがある].

  (*1*) She **has** gone to England.

       Kano-jo-wa Eikoku-e itte-*shimatta*.

  (*2*) I **have lived** here for ten years.

       Watashi-wa koko-ni jû-nen-kan *sundeiru*.

  (*3*) **Have** you ever **seen** it?

       Anata-wa kore-made-ni sore-o *mita-koto-ga-arimasu*-ka?

havoc (*n.*) oo-are [大荒れ]; dai-hakai [大破壊].

hawk (*n.*) taka [タカ].

hawthorn (*n.*) (*bot.*) sanzashi [サンザシ].

hay (*n.*) hoshi-kusa [干し草]; magusa [まぐさ].

hazard (*n.*) kiken [危険]; bôken [冒険].

    (*vt.*) ...no kiken-o-okasu [···の危険を冒す]; ...o kakeru [···を かける].

haze (*n.*) moya [もや]; kasumi [かすみ].

hazel (*n.*) (*bot.*) hashibami [ハシバミ].

hazy (*a.*) kasunda [かすんだ].

he (*pron.*) kare-wa [彼は]; kare-ga [彼が].

head (*n.*) 1)atama [頭]; zunô [頭脳]. 2)...chô [···長]; kashira [かし ら]. 3)sentô [先頭]. 4)(mono no) sentan [(ものの)先端]; senshu [船首].

    (*1*) He has a good **head**. Kare-wa ii *atama*-o shite-iru.

    (*2*) He is the **head** of the school.

        Kare-wa sono gakkô no *kôchô* da.

    (*3*) She rode away at the **head** of the army.

        Kano-jo-wa gun-no-*sentô*-ni-tatte uma-o-hashirasete-ita.

    (*4*) I went towards the **head** of the cliff.

        Watashi-wa gake-no *sentan*-no-hô-e itta.

    by a head atama-hitotsu-no-sa-de

    go to(turn) one's head ...o-unubore-saseru

      His success has gone to his head.

      Kare-wa seikô-shita-mono-dakara unuborete-iru.

    keep one's head awate-nai

    keep one's head above water shakkin-sezu-ni-iru

    lay(put) heads together hitai-o-atsumete-sôdan-suru

    over one's head rikai-deki-nai

      The matter is over my head. Sono ken wa rikai-deki-nai.

    (*a.*) shuseki-no [首席の].

    (*vt.*) ...no sentô-ni-tatsu [···の先頭に立つ].

    (*vi.*) susumu [進む].

headache (*n.*) zutsû [頭痛].

heading (*n.*) (shimbun nado no) midashi [(新聞などの)見出し].

headline (*n.*) = heading.

headlong (*ad. & a.*) massakasama-ni (massakasama-no) [まっさか さまに(まっさかさまの)]; mukô-mizu-ni (mukô-mizu-no) [向こう見ず に(向こう見ずの)].

head office honten [本店]; honsha [本社].

headquarters (*n.*) hombu [本部]; shirei-bu [司令部].

heal (*vt. & vi.*) ...o naosu (naoru) [···を治す(治る)].

    The doctor **healed** him.   Isha wa kare-no-byôki-o *naoshita*.

    The wound will soon **heal** up.

    Kizu wa ma-mo-naku sukkari *naoru*-darô.

health (*n.*) kenkô [健康].

healthy (*a.*) kenkô-na [健康な].

heap (*n.*) 1)tsumi-kasane [積み重ね]. 2)(*colloq.*) takusan [たくさん]; dossari [どっさり].

    (*1*) The corpses lay in a **heap**.   Shitai ga *yama*-o-nashite-ita.

    (*2*) He has a **heap** of money.

    Kare-wa kane-o *dossari* motte-iru.

    (*vt.*) ...o tsumi-ageru [···を積み上げる].

hear (*vt.*) ...o kiku [···を聞く]; ...ga kikoeru [···が聞こえる].

    (*vi.*) 1)kiku [聞く]. 2)tayori-o-morau [便りをもらう].

    (*1*) Did you **hear** about the accident last night?

    Anata-wa sakuya-no-jiko-o *kikimashita*-ka?

    (*2*) I am waiting to **hear** from him.

    Watashi-wa kare-kara-no-*tayori*-o-matte-imasu.

  hear of ...no-koto-o kiku

  hear out ...o owari-made-kiku

  I hear ...da-sô-da; ...to-iu-hanashi-da

hearing (*n.*) 1)kiku-koto [聞くこと]. 2)chômon-kai [聴問会].

hearing aid hochô-ki [補聴器].

heart (*n.*) 1)shinzô [心臓]. 2)kokoro [心]; aijô [愛情]. 3)yûki [勇気]. 4)chûshin [中心].

    (*1*) He who has a strong **heart** lives long.

        Shinzô ga tsuyoi to naga-iki-suru.

    (*2*) He loves me with all his **heart**.

        Kare-wa *kokoro*-kara watashi-o aishite-iru.

    (*3*) You mustn't lose **heart**.   Kimi-wa *yûki*-o nakushitewa-ikenai.

    (*4*) The hotel stands in the **heart** of the city.

        Sono hoteru wa shi-no-*chûshin*-ni aru.

  at heart kokoro-wa; kokoro-no-soko-de-wa

  break one's heart hito-o-hitan-ni-kure-saseru

  from (the bottom of) one's heart kokoro-no-soko-kara

  learn...by heart ...o anki-suru

heartbeat (*n.*) shinzô-no-kodô [心臓の鼓動].

heartbroken (*a.*) hitan-ni-kureta [悲嘆にくれた].

heartburn (*n.*) mune-yake [胸焼け].

heartfelt (*a.*) kokoro-kara-no [心からの].

hearth (*n.*) rohen [炉辺].

heartily (*ad.*) 1)kokoro-kara [心から]. 2)jûbun-ni [十分に].

heartless (*a.*) hakujô-na [薄情な].

heartstrings (*n.*) fukai-aijô [深い愛情].

hearty (*a.*) 1)kokoro-kara-no [心からの]. 2)takusan-no [沢山の].

　(*1*) The people there gave him a **hearty** welcome.

　　　Soko-no-hito-bito wa kare-o *kokoro-kara* kangei shita.

　(*2*) He took a **hearty** meal.　Kare-wa *takusan* tabeta.

heat (*n.*) 1)netsu [熱]. 2)atsusa [暑さ].

　(*1*) The sun gives us **heat**.

　　　Taiyô wa ware-ware-ni *netsu*-o ataeru.

　(*2*) Don't go out in the **heat** of the day.

　　　Hi-*zakari*-ni gaishutsu-suru-na.

　　(*vt. & vi.*) ...o atsuku-suru (atsuku-naru) […を熱くする（熱くなる）]; ...o kôfun-saseru (kôfun-suru) […を興奮させる（興奮する）].

heater (*n.*) dennetsu-ki [電熱器]; hîtâ [ヒーター].

heathen (*n. & a.*) ikyô-to(-no) [異教徒(の)].

heave (*vt.*) 1)(omoi-mono)-o mochi-ageru [（重い物）を持ち上げる]. 2)(tame-iki)-o-tsuku [（ため息）をつく].

heaven (*n.*) 1)(*pl.*) ten [天]; sora [空]. 2)tengoku [天国]. 3)(H-) kami [神].

　Good heavens! Taihen-da!; Komatta!

heavily (*ad.*) 1)omoku [重く]. 2)hidoku [ひどく]; hageshiku [激しく].

heavy (*a.*) 1)omoi [重い]. 2)hidoi [ひどい]; hageshii [激しい].

　(*1*) Silver is a **heavy** metal.　Gin wa *omoi* kinzoku da.

　(*2*) We had a **heavy** storm last night.

　　　Sakuya *hageshii* arashi-ga atta.

heavy industry jû-kôgyô [重工業].

hedge (*n.*) ikegaki [生け垣].

　　(*vt.*) ...o ikegaki-de-kakomu […を生け垣で囲む].

heed (*n. & vi.*) chûi(-o-harau) [(注意)を払う].

　give(pay) heed to ...ni chûi-o-harau

heedful (*a.*) chûi-bukai [注意深い]; yôjin-bukai [用心深い].

heedless (*a.*) fu-chûi-na [不注意な].

heel (*n.*) kakato [かかと].

　at(on) one's heels ...no-sugu-ato-ni-tsuite

head over heels massakasama-ni

take to one's heels = **show a clean pair of heels** ichimokusan-ni-nigeru

heigh-ho (*int.*) Aa! [ああ!]; Yare-yare! [やれやれ!].

height (*n.*) 1) takasa [高さ]. 2) takai-tokoro [高いところ]. 3) massaichû [真っ最中].

  (*1*) The **height** of that building is 100 meters.

      Ano biru no *takasa* wa hyaku-mêtoru da.

     What is your **height**?

      Kimi-no *se-no-takasa* wa dono-kurai-desu-ka?

  (*2*) I like to ascend a **height**.

      Watashi-wa *takai-tokoro*-ni noboru-no-ga-suki-da.

  (*3*) The party was at its **height**. Pâtî wa *massaichû*-datta.

heighten (*vt. & vi.*) ...o takameru (takamaru) [...を高める(高まる)].

heir (*n.*) sôzoku-nin [相続人]; ato-tori [跡取り].

heiress (*n.*) joshi-sôzoku-nin [女子相続人].

hell (*n.*) jigoku [地獄].

hello (*int.*) Yaa! [やあ!]; Moshi-moshi [もしもし].

helm (*n.*) kaji [かじ]; darin [舵輪].

  (*vt.*) ...no kaji-o-toru [...のかじを取る].

helmet (*n.*) herumetto [ヘルメット].

help (*vt.*) 1)...o tasukeru [...を助ける]; ...o tetsudau [...を手伝う]. 2) (tabe-mono o)...ni totte-yaru [(食べ物を)...にとってやる]; ...o moru [...を盛る]. 3)...o osaeru [...をおさえる]; ...o sakeru [...を避ける].

  (*1*) He **helped** the weak. Kare-wa yowai-hito-bito-o *tasuketa*.

     He **helped** me with my French.

      Kare-wa watashi-no Furansu-go-no-benkyô-o *tetsudatta*.

  (*2*) **Help** her to some sandwiches.

      Kano-jo-ni sandoitchi-o *totte-yari-nasai*.

  (*3*) I cannot **help** it. *Shikata-ga-nai*.

    (*vi.*) tasuke-ni-naru [助けになる]; yaku-datsu [役だつ].

cannot help...ing ...(se-)zu-ni-wa-irare-nai

help oneself to ...o jibun-de-totte-taberu; ...o jibun-de-totte-nomu

    (*n.*) 1)tasuke [助け]; joryoku [助力]; tetsudai [手伝い]. 2) tasuke-ni-naru-hito [助けになる人]; yaku-datsu-mono [役だつもの]. 3)nige-michi [逃げ道].

  (*1*) He cried for **help**.

      Kare-wa *tasuke*-o-motomete oo-goe-o-ageta.

(2) She was a great **help** to her mother.
　　　Kano-jo-no haha wa kano-jo-*no-okage-de* taihen *tasukatta.*
(3) There is no **help** for it. *Shikata-ga-nai.*

helper (*n.*) joshu [助手]; herupâ [ヘルパー].

helpful (*a.*) yaku-ni-tatsu [役に立つ].

helping (*n.*) 1)hito-mori [一盛り]. 2)yaku-ni-tatsu-koto [役に立つこと].
　　a second helping o-kawari
　　　　(*a.*) enjo-no [援助の].

helpless (*a.*) 1)jibun-de-wa-dô-suru-koto-mo-deki-nai [自分ではどうすることもできない]. 2)muryoku-na [無力な]. 3)komatta [困った].

hem (*n.*) fuchi [縁]; heri [へり].
　　　　(*vt.*) …no fuchi-dori-o-suru […の縁取りをする]; …o kakomu […を囲む].

hemisphere (*n.*) hankyû [半球].

hemp (*n.*) (*bot.*) asa [麻].

hen (*n.*) men-dori [めんどり].

her (*pron.*) 1)kano-jo-no [彼女の]. 2)kano-jo-o [彼女を]; kano-jo-ni [彼女に].

herald (*n.*) 1)shisha [使者]. 2)saki-bure [先触れ].
　　　　(*vt.*) …o fukoku-suru […を布告する]; …o saki-bure-suru […を先触れする].

herb (*n.*) kusa [草]; yakusô [薬草].

herd (*n.*) (ushi ya uma nado no) mure [(牛や馬などの)群れ].

here (*ad.*) koko-ni [ここに]; koko-e [ここへ].
　　here and there achi-kochi-ni
　　Here I am. Tada-ima.; Saa, tsuki-mashita.
　　Here's to your health! Go-kenkô-o-shuku-shi-masu!
　　Here you are. Hai, kore.
　　　　(*n.*) koko [ここ]

hereafter (*ad.*) kongo-wa [今後は].

herewith (*ad.*) kore-to-tomo-ni [これと共に]; dôfû-shite [同封して].

heritage (*n.*) sôzoku-zaisan [相続財産].

hermit (*n.*) yo-sute-bito [世捨て人]; inja [隠者].

hero (*n.*) 1)eiyû [英雄]; yûshi [勇士]. 2)(shôsetsu no) shujin-kô [(小説の)主人公].

heroic (*a.*) eiyû-teki-na [英雄的な]; isamashii [勇ましい].

heroine (*n.*) 1)joketsu [女傑]. 2)(shôsetsu no) onna-no-shujin-kô [(小説の)女の主人公].

herring (*n.*) (*fish*) nishin [ニシン].

herringbone (*n.*) sugi-aya [杉あや]; herimbon [ヘリンボン].

hers (*pron.*) kano-jo-no-mono [彼女のもの].

herself (*pron.*) kano-jo-jishin(-o/-ni) [彼女自身(を/に)].

hesitant (*a.*) tamerai-gachi-na [ためらいがちな].

hesitate (*vi.*) tamerau [ためらう].

hew (*vt. & vi.*) (ono nado de)(...o) kiru [(おのなどで)(…を)切る].

hey (*int.*) Chotto! [ちょっと!]; Maa! [まあ!].

hi (*int.*) Yaa! [やあ!]; Konnichi-wa! [今日は!].

hidden (*a.*) kakureta [隠れた]; kakusareta [隠された]; himitsu-no [秘密の].

hide (*vt. & vi.*) ...o kakusu (kakureru) […を隠す(隠れる)].
> He **hid** the ball under the desk.
>> Kare-wa bôru-*o* tsukue-no-shita-ni *kakushita*.
> I will **hide** under the chair.
>> Watashi-wa isu-no-shita-ni *kakure-yô*.

hide-and-seek (*n.*) kakurem-bô [かくれんぼう].

hideous (*a.*) zotto-suru-hodo-osoroshii [ぞっとするほど恐ろしい].

high (*a.*) 1)takai [高い]. 2)kôki-na [高貴な]. 3)kôkyû-na [高級な]; kôka-na [高価な]. 4)(jiki nado ga) takenawa-no [(時期などが)たけなわの].
(*ad.*) takaku [高く].
  high and low subete-no-kaikyû-no

high blood pressure kô-ketsuatsu [高血圧].

highbrow (*n. & a.*) (*colloq.*) chishiki-jin(-no) [知識人(の)].

high fidelity (*n. & a.*) = hi-fi kô-chûjitsu-do(-no) [高忠実度(の)]; haifai(-no) [ハイファイ(の)].

high jump hashiri-taka-tobi [走り高跳び].

highlight (*n.*) yobi-mono [呼び物]; hairaito [ハイライト].
(*vt.*) ...o kyôchô-suru […を強調する].

highly (*ad.*) 1)ooi-ni [大いに]. 2)totemo-homete [とてもほめて].
(*1*) They were **highly** pleased. Kare-ra-wa *ooi-ni* yorokonda.
(*2*) They speak **highly** of him.
  Hito-bito-wa kare-o *totemo-homeru*.

highness (*n.*) 1)takai-koto [高いこと]. 2)(H-)denka [殿下].

high school ((*US*)) kôtô-gakkô [高等学校]; hai-sukûru [ハイスクール].

high-spirited (*a.*) genki-no-ii [元気のいい].

high tide manchô [満潮].

high time shio-doki [潮時].

high-toned (*a.*) kakuchô-no-takai [格調の高い].

highway (*n.*) kansen-dôro [幹線道路]; kaidô [街道].

highwayman (*n.*) oihagi [おいはぎ].

hijack (*vt. & vi.*) ...o gôdatsu-suru [...を強奪する]; (...o) hai-jakku-suru [(...を)ハイジャックする].
   (*n.*) hai-jakku [ハイジャック].

hike (*n. & vi.*) toho-ryokô(-suru) [徒歩旅行(する)]; haikingu(-suru) [ハイキング(する)].

hiker (*n.*) toho-ryokô-sha [徒歩旅行者]; haikâ [ハイカー].

hill (*n.*) oka [丘]; ko-yama [小山].

hillside (*n.*) oka-no-chûfuku [丘の中腹].

him (*pron.*) kare-o [彼を]; kare-ni [彼に].

himself (*pron.*) kare-jishin(-o/-ni) [彼自身(を/に)].

hind (*a.*) ato-no [あとの]; ushiro-no [後ろの].

hinder (*vt. & vi.*) ...no jama-o-suru (jama-ni-naru) [の邪魔をする(邪魔になる)].

hindrance (*n.*) bôgai [妨害]; jama-ni-naru-mono [邪魔になるもの].

hinge (*n.*) 1)chôtsugai [ちょうつがい]. 2)(*postage stamp*) hinji [ヒンジ].
   (*vt. & vi.*) ...ni chôtsugai-o-tsukeru (chôtsugai-de-ugoku) [...にちょうつがいを付ける(ちょうつがいで動く)].

hint (*n.*) anji [暗示]; honomekashi [ほのめかし]; hinto [ヒント].
   (*vt. & vi.*) (...o) anji-suru [(...を)暗示する]; (...o) honomekasu [(...を)ほのめかす].

hip (*n.*) koshi [腰]; shiri [しり].

hippopotamus (*n.*) (*zool.*) kaba [カバ].

hire (*n.*) 1)chin-gashi [賃貸]; chin-gari [賃借り]. 2)kari-chin [借り賃]; shiyô-ryô [使用料].
   (1) He has some boats for **hire**.
       Kare-wa sû-seki-no *kashi*-bôto-o motte-iru.
   (2) I paid five hundred yen for the **hire** of a yacht.
       Watashi-wa yotto-no-*kari-ryô*-ni go-hyaku-en haratta.
   for(on) hire chin-gashi-de
       (*vt.*) 1)...o yatou [...を雇う]. 2)...o chin-gashi-suru [...を賃貸しする]; ...o chin-gari-suru [...を賃借りする].

his (*pron.*) kare-no [彼の]; kare-no-mono [彼のもの].

hiss (*n. & vi.*) shisshî(-to-iu) [しっしー(と言う)].

historian (*n.*) rekishi-ka [歴史家].

historic (*a.*) rekishi-jô-yûmei-na [歴史上有名な]; rekishi-jô-jûyô-na [歴史上重要な].

historical (*a.*) rekishi-teki-na [歴史的な]; shijitsu-ni-motozuku [史実に基づく].

history (*n.*) rekishi [歴史].

hit (*vt.*) 1)...o utsu [⋯を打つ]. 2)...ni meichû-suru [⋯に命中する]; ...ni meichû-saseru [⋯に命中させる].
   (*vi.*) utsu [打つ]; naguru [殴る].
   (*n.*) 1)dageki [打撃]. 2)meichû [命中]. 3)oo-atari [大当り]. 4)(*baseball*) hitto [ヒット].
   make a hit kôhyô-o-hakusuru

hit-and-run (*a.*) 1)(*baseball*) hittendoran-no [ヒッテンドランの]. 2)hiki-nige-no [ひき逃げの]. 3)dengeki-teki-na [電撃的な].

hitch (*n.*) 1)gutto-hiku-koto [ぐっと引くこと]. 2)hikkakari [引っ掛かり].
   without a hitch shubi-yoku
   (*vt.*) 1)...o gutto-hiku [⋯をぐっと引く]. 2)...o tsunagu [⋯をつなぐ]; ...o hikkakeru [⋯を引っ掛ける].
   (*vi.*) 1)gutto-ugoku [ぐっと動く]. 2)hikkakaru [引っ掛かる].

hitchhike (*n. & vi.*) hitchihaiku(-suru) [ヒッチハイク(する)].

hive (*n.*) mitsu-bachi-no-su-bako [ミツバチの巣箱].

hives (*n.*) (*path.*) jimmashin [じんましん].

ho (*int.*) Hô! [ほう!]; Oya! [おや!].

hoard (*n.*) takuwae [蓄え]; chozô-butsu [貯蔵物].
   (*vt. & vi.*) (...o) takuwaeru [(⋯を)蓄える].

hoarse (*a.*) shiwagare-goe-no [しわがれ声の]; hasukî-na [ハスキーな].

hoary (*a.*) shira-ga-no [白髪の]; shiroi [白い]; furui [古い].

hobby (*n.*) dôraku [道楽]; shumi [趣味].

hobbyhorse (*n.*) mokuba [木馬].

hockey (*n.*) hokkê [ホッケー].

hoe (*n.*) kuwa [くわ].
   (*vt.*) ...o kuwa-de-tagayasu [⋯をくわで耕す].
   (*vi.*) kuwa-o-tsukau [くわを使う].

hog (*n.*) ((*Eng.*)) (shokuyô-)buta [(食用)豚].

hoist (*vt.*) ...o ageru [⋯を揚げる]; ...o maki-ageru [⋯を巻き上げる].

hold (*vt.*) 1)...o motsu [⋯を持つ]; ...o nigiru [⋯を握る]. 2)...o sasaeru [⋯を支える]. 3)...o tamotsu [⋯を保つ]. 4)...o hiraku [⋯

を開く]; …o kyokô-suru […を挙行する]. 5)…o ireru-koto-ga-dekiru […を入れることができる]. 6)…to omou […と思う]; …to kangaeru […と考える].

(1) I'll **hold** the baggage for you.   Nimotsu-o *motte*-agemashô.

(2) This shelf won't **hold** the television set.

    Kono tana wa terebi-o *sasae-kire*-nai-darô.

(3) **Hold** your peace.   *Damatte*-ore.

(4) They **held** a party.   Kare-ra-wa pâtî-o *hiraita*.

(5) This bottle **holds** a pint.   Kono bin wa ichi-painto *hairu*.

(6) I **hold** that person to be reliable.

    Watashi-wa sono hito wa tayori-ni-naru-to *kangaete-iru*.

    (*vi.*) 1)tsukamatte-iru [つかまっている]. 2)motsu [もつ]; mochi-kotaeru [持ちこたえる].

(1) She **held** on to the side of the car.

    Kano-jo-wa kuruma-no-kata-gawa-ni *tsukamatte-ita*.

(2) Will this rope **hold**?   Kono rôpu wa *motsu*-darô-ka?

hold on 1)kira-nai-de-oku. 2)tsuzukeru.

1) Hold on, please.   Kira-nai-de-o-machi-kudasai.

2) A fleet of vessels held on in its course.

    Sendan wa sono shinro-o-susumi-tsuzuketa.

hold out 1)…o sashi-dasu. 2)mochi-kotaeru

1) She held out her hand.   Kano-jo-wa te-o sashi-nobeta.

hold up …o tomeru

    The up train was held up by the storm.

    Nobori-ressha wa arashi-de tomatta.

    (*n.*) motsu-koto [持つこと]; hoji [保持].

holder (*n.*) 1)sasaeru-mono [支えるもの]. 2)yôki [容器].

hole (*n.*) ana [穴].

    (*vt.*) …ni ana-o-akeru […に穴をあける].

holiday (*n.*) kyûjitsu [休日]; kyûka [休暇].

    (*a.*) kyûjitsu-no [休日の]; kyûjitsu-ni-fusawashii [休日にふさわしい].

holidaymaker (*n.*) kôraku-kyaku [行楽客]; kyûka-o-totte-iru-hito [休暇を取っている人].

Holland (*n.*) Oranda [オランダ].

hollow (*a.*) kubonda [くぼんだ]; utsuro-na [うつろな].

    (*n.*) kubomi [くぼみ]; utsuro [うつろ].

    (*vt.*) …o utsuro-ni-suru […をうつろにする].

    (*vi.*) utsuro-ni-naru [うつろになる]; kubomu [くぼむ].

holly (*n.*) (*bot.*) seiyô-hiiragi [セイヨウヒイラギ].

holy (*a.*) 1)shinsei-na [神聖な]; shinji-ni-kyôsuru [神事に供する]. 2)
kiyoraka-na [清らかな]; shinjin-bukai [信心深い].

home (*n.*) 1)katei [家庭]; waga-ya [わが家]. 2)hongoku [本国];
kokyô [故郷]; gensan-chi [原産地]. 3)(*baseball*) honrui [本塁];
hômu [ホーム].

  at home 1)zaitaku-shite. 2)kiraku-ni
   1) Were you at home yesterday? Kinô go-zaitaku-deshita-ka?
   2) Make yourself at home. Dôzo o-raku-ni.
    (*a.*) katei-no [家庭の]; kokyô-no [故郷の]; hongoku-no [本国の].
    (*ad.*) waga-ya-e [わが家へ]; hongoku-e [本国へ].

homecoming (*n.*) 1)kikoku [帰国]; kitaku [帰宅]. 2)((*US*)) (daigaku
no) dôsô-kai [(大学の)同窓会].

homeless (*a.*) ie-no-nai [家のない].

homelike (*a.*) waga-ya-no-yô-na [わが家のような]; uchi-toketa [打ち
解けた].

homely (*a.*) 1)utsukushiku-nai [美しくない]. 2)katei-teki-na [家庭的
な]. 3)ari-fure-ta [ありふれた].

homemade (*a.*) 1)jika-sei-no [自家製の]. 2)kokusan-no [国産の].

home run (*baseball*) honrui-da [本塁打]; hômuran [ホームラン].

homesick (*a.*) hômushikku-no [ホームシックの].

homespun (*a.*) te-ori-no [手織りの].
    (*n.*) te-ori-no-rasha [手織りのラシャ]; hômusupan [ホーム
スパン].

homeward(s) (*ad.*) ieji-o-sashite [家路をさして]; hongoku-e-mukatte
[本国へ向かって].
    (*a.*) kito-no [帰途の].

homework (*n.*) 1)shukudai [宿題]; yoshû [予習]. 2)naishoku [内職].

honest (*a.*) shôjiki-na [正直な].

honestly (*ad.*) shôjiki-ni [正直に].
    (*int.*) mattaku [全く]; jissai [実際].

honesty (*n.*) shôjiki [正直].

honey (*n.*) hachi-mitsu [はちみつ].

honeymoon (*n.*) shinkon-ryokô [新婚旅行]; hanemûn [ハネムーン].

honor, -our (*n.*) 1)meiyo [名誉]; meisei [名声]. 2)(*pl.*) yûtô [優等].
3)(H-) kakka [閣下].
   (*1*) He is an **hono(u)r** to our country.

      Kare-wa waga-kuni-no *meiyo* da.

(2) He graduated at Harvard with **hono(u)rs**.

      Kare-wa Hâbâdo-daigaku-o *yûtô*-de sotsugyô-shita.

(3) His **Hono(u)r** is very democratic.

      Kakka wa totemo minshu-teki-na-hito-da.

in honor of ...ni-keii-o-haratte; ...no-kinen-ni

      (vt.) 1)...o sonkei-suru [···を尊敬する]. 2)...ni eiyo-o-ataeru [···に栄誉を与える].

(2) Will you **honor** me with a visit?

      Watashi no ie e go-raihô *itadake*-masen-de-shô-ka?

hono(u)rable *(a.)* meiyo-aru [名誉ある]; sonkei-su-beki [尊敬すべき].

hood *(n.)* 1)zukin [ずきん]; fûdo [フード]. 2)((*US*)) (kuruma no) bonnetto [(車の)ボンネット].

hoof *(n.)* hizume [ひづめ].

hook *(n.)* kagi [かぎ]; hokku [ホック]; tsuri-bari [釣り針].

      (vt.) ...o kagi-de-tomeru [···をかぎで留める]; ...o kagi-jô-ni-mageru [···をかぎ状に曲げる].

      (vi.) kagi-de-tomaru [かぎで留まる].

hoop *(n.)* (kodomo ga mawasu) wa [(子供が回す)輪]; (taru no) taga [(たるの)たが].

hooray *(int.)* Banzai! [万歳!].

hop *(vi.)* pyon-pyon-tobu [ぴょんぴょん跳ぶ].

      (vt.) ...o tobi-kosu [···を跳び越す]; ...ni tobi-noru [···に飛び乗る].

      (n.) hoppu [ホップ]; chôyaku [跳躍].

hop *(n.)* (*bot.*) hoppu [ホップ].

      (vt.) ...ni hoppu-de-niga-mi-o-tsukeru [···にホップで苦味をつける].

hope *(n.)* 1)kibô [希望]; mikomi [見込み]. 2)nozomi-o-kakerarete-iru-mono [望みをかけられているもの].

(1) There is no **hope** of her recovering.

      Kano-jo ga zenkai-suru-*mikomi* wa mattaku-nai.

(2) He is the **hope** of the family.

      Kare-wa ikka-no-naka-de *nozomi-o-kakerarete-iru*.

      (vt. & vi.) (...o) nozomu [(···を)望む]; (...o) kibô-suru [(···を)希望する].

I **hope** you will pass the entrance examination.

      Kimi-ga nyûgaku-shiken-ni gôkaku-suru-koto-*o nozomu*.

hopeful *(a.)* yûbô-na [有望な]; kibô-ni-michita [希望に満ちた].

hopeless *(a.)* kibô-o-ushinatta [希望を失った]; mikomi-no-nai [見込み

のない]; dô-shiyô-mo-nai [どうしようもない].

hopelessly (*ad.*) zetsubô-teki-ni [絶望的に].

hopper (*n.*) jôgo [じょうご].

hop, step(skip), and jump san-dan-tobi [三段跳び].

horizon (*n.*) chihei-sen [地平線]; suihei-sen [水平線].

horizontal (*a.*) chihei[suihei]-sen-no [地平[水平]線の].

horn (*n.*) 1)tsuno [角]. 2)(*mus. instr.*) horun [ホルン]; (jidôsha no) keiteki [(自動車の)警笛].

horrible (*a.*) 1)osoroshii [恐しい]. 2)(*colloq.*) hidoku-iya-na [ひどくいやな].

horribly (*ad.*) osoroshiku [恐ろしく]; (*colloq.*) hidoku [ひどく].

horrid (*a.*) osoroshii [恐しい]; (*colloq.*) hidoi [ひどい].

horrify (*vt.*) ...o zotto-saseru […をぞっとさせる].

horror (*n.*) kyôfu [恐怖]; (*colloq.*) iya-na-mono [いやなもの].

horse (*n.*) 1)uma [馬]. 2)kihei [騎兵].

horseback (*n.*) uma-no-se [馬の背].

horsebreaker (*n.*) chôkyô-shi [調教師].

horse chestnut (*bot.*) seiyô-tochi-no-ki [セイヨウトチノキ].

horselaugh (*n.*) taka-warai [高笑い].

horseman (*n.*) kishu [騎手].

horsemanship (*n.*) bajutsu [馬術].

horsepower (*n.*) bariki [馬力].

horseshoe (*n.*) 1)teitetsu [てい鉄]. 2)Yû-ji-gata-no-mono [U字形のもの].

hose (*n.*) 1)jakan [じゃ管]; hôsu [ホース]. 2)kutsu-shita-rui [靴下類].

hosiery (*n.*) 1)kutsu-shita-rui [靴下類]. 2)kutsu-shita-hambai-gyô [靴下販売業].

hospitable (*a.*) mote-nashi-no-yoi [もてなしのよい]; te-atsui [手厚い].

hospital (*n.*) byôin [病院].

  go to hospital nyûin-suru

hospitality (*n.*) shinsetsu-na-mote-nashi [親切なもてなし]; kôgû [厚遇].

host (*n.*) 1)(kyaku o motenasu) shujin [(客をもてなす)主人]. 2)((*US*))(hoteru no) shihai-nin [(ホテルの)支配人].

host (*n.*) takusan [たくさん]; oozeï [大勢].

hostel (*n.*) hosuteru [ホステル]; kan'i-shukuhaku-sho [簡易宿泊所].

hostess (*n.*) (kyaku o motenasu) onna-shujin [(客をもてなす)女主人].

hostile (*a.*) 1)teki-no [敵の]. 2)tekii-no-aru [敵意のある].

hostility (*n.*) 1)tekii [敵意]. 2)(*pl.*) sentô-kôi [戦闘行為]; kôsen-jôtai [交戦状態].

hot (*a.*) 1)atsui [暑い]; atsui [熱い]. 2)karai [辛い]. 3)hageshii [激しい].

  (*1*) I take some **hot** tea even on **hot** days in August.

      Watashi-wa Hachigatsu-no *atsui*-hi-de-mo *atsui* o-cha-o nomu.

  (*2*) a **hot** curry   *karai* karê

  (*3*) a **hot** contest   *hageshii* kyôsô

hotel (*n.*) ryokan [旅館]; hoteru [ホテル].

hothouse (*n.*) onshitsu [温室].

hot news saishin-no nyûsu [最新のニュース].

hot spring onsen [温泉].

hound (*n.*) ryôken [猟犬].

hour (*n.*) 1)jikan [時間]; jikoku [時刻]. 2)(kimmu-)jikan [(勤務)時間]. 3)(the –) gendai [現代].

  (*1*) He studies 4 **hours** a day.

      Kare-wa ichi-nichi-ni yo-*jikan* benkyô-suru.

  (*2*) The office **hours** are 9 to 4.

      Kimmu-*jikan* wa gozen-ku-ji-kara gogo-yo-ji-made.

  (*3*) He is the man of the **hour**.   Kare-wa *toki* no hito da.

  keep bad(late) hours yo-fukashi[asane]-o-suru

  keep good(early) hours haya-ne[haya-oki]-o-suru

hour hand jishin [時針]; tanshin [短針].

house (*n.*) 1)ie [家]. 2)katei [家庭]; [the H-] ichizoku [一族]. 3)[the H-] giin [議員]. 4)tate-mono [建物]; ...goya [···小屋].

  (*1*) She keeps **house** for her father.

      Kano-jo-wa chichi-no-tame-ni *ie*-no-kiri-mori-o-suru.

  (*2*) The **House** of Tudor is a royal family.

      Tyûdoru-*ke* wa ô-ke-de-aru.

  (*3*) He entered **the House**.   Kare-wa *giin*-ni-natta.

  (*4*) a hen-**house** niwatori-*goya*

  on the house tada-de

  play house mama-goto-o-suru

    (*vt.*) ...o shûyô-suru [···を収容する].

    (*vi.*) sumu [住む].

household (*n.*) kazoku [家族]; kanai-jû [家内じゅう].

housekeeper (*n.*) kasei-fu [家政婦].

housewife (*n.*) shufu [主婦].

housework (*n.*) kaji [家事].

housing (*n.*) jûtaku [住宅]; jûtaku-kyôkyû [住宅供給].

hover (*vi.*) 1)kû-ni-mau [空に舞う]. 2)urotsuku [うろつく].

how (*ad.*) 1)donna-fû-ni [どんなふうに]; ...(suru)shikata [...(する)仕方]. 2)dore-hodo [どれほど]. 3)nanto-maa [なんとまあ]. 4)donna-jôtai-de [どんな状態で].

  (*1*) How is butter made?
     Batâ wa *donna-fû-ni-shite* tsukurareru-ka?

  (*2*) How old is he? Kare-wa *nan*-sai-desu-ka?

  (*3*) How hard he works!
     Nanto-maa kare-wa yoku hataraku-koto!

  (*4*) How are you? Go-kigen *ikaga*-desu-ka?

  and how (*US slang*) totemo; sugoku

  How about...? ...wa dô-desu-ka?

  How goes it? (*colloq.*) Keiki-wa-dô-desu-ka?

  How much? Nedan-wa-ikura-desu-ka?

  (*n.*) (the –) hôhô [方法]; shikata [仕方].

however (*conj.*) keredomo [けれども].

  (*ad.*) donna-ni...de-mo [どんなに...でも].

howl (*vi.*) 1)(inu ya ookami ga) too-boe-suru [(犬やオオカミが)遠ぼえする]. 2)(kaze ga) unaru [(風が)うなる]. 3)umeku [うめく].

  (*n.*) too-boe [遠ぼえ]; wameki-goe [わめき声].

huddle (*vi.*) 1)misshû-suru [密集する]. 2)karada-o-marumeru [体を丸める]. 3)(*colloq.*) dangô-suru [談合する].

  (*vt.*) 1)...o gota-gota-atsumeru [...をごたごた集める]. 2)(–oneself) karada-o-marumeru [体を丸める]. 3)isoide...(o suru) [急いで...(をする)].

  (*n.*) 1)gunshû [群衆]. 2)konran [混乱]. 3)(*American football*) hadoru [ハドル].

hue (*n.*) iro[ai] [色(合い)].

hue (*n.*) sakebi-goe [叫び声].

  hue and cry gô-gô-taru-hinan

hug (*vt.*) 1)...o daki-shimeru [...を抱き締める]. 2)...ni koshitsu-suru [...に固執する].

  (*n.*) hôyô [抱擁].

huge (*a.*) kyodai-na [巨大な].

hullo (*int.*) (= hello) Yaa! [やあ!]; Moshi-moshi! [もしもし!].

hum (*vi.*) 1)(hachi ya sempû-ki ga) bum-bun-iu [(ハチや扇風機が)ぶんぶんいう]. 2)(tameratte) kuchi-gomoru [(ためらって)口ごもる]. 3) hana-uta-o-utau [鼻歌を歌う].

    (*n.*) bum-bun [ぶんぶん]; gaya-gaya [がやがや].

human (*n. & a.*) ningen(-no) [人間(の)].

human being hito [人]; ningen [人間].

humane (*a.*) omoi-yari-no-aru [思いやりのある].

humanism (*n.*) jimpon-shugi [人本主義]; hyûmanizumu [ヒューマニズム].

humanity (*n.*) 1)ningen-rashisa [人間らしさ]; jinrui [人類]. 2)(the *pl.*) jimbun-sho-gakka [人文諸学科].

human race jinrui [人類].

humble (*a.*) 1)kenson-shita [謙そんした]. 2)iyashii [卑しい]. 3) misuborashii [みすぼらしい].

humid (*a.*) shikki-no-ooi [湿気の多い].

humidity (*n.*) shikki [湿気].

humility (*n.*) kenson [謙そん]; hige [卑下].

humming (*n. & a.*) bum-bun-iu-oto (bum-bun-iu) [ぶんぶんいう音(ぶんぶんいう)]; hana-uta(-o-utau) [鼻歌(を歌う)].

humor, -mour (*n.*) 1)kibun [気分]; kigen [機嫌]. 2)kokkei [こっけい]; yûmoa [ユーモア].

    (*1*) He is in a good **humo(u)r**.   Kare-wa jô-*kigen*-da.

    (*2*) He has a sense of **humo(u)r**.   Kare-wa *yûmoa*-o-kaisuru.

    in an ill (a bad) humor fu-kigen-de

humorist (*n.*) share-no-jôzu-na-hito [しゃれの上手な人]; yûmorisuto [ユーモリスト].

humorous (*a.*) kokkei-na [こっけいな]; yûmoa-no-aru [ユーモアのある].

hump (*n.*) 1)(rakuda nado no) kobu [(ラクダなどの)こぶ]. 2)marui-oka [円い丘].

    (*ut.*) ...o maruku-suru […を丸くする].

    (*vi.*) maruku-mori-agaru [丸く盛り上がる].

humpback (*n.*) neko-ze [ねこ背].

hunch (*n.*) yokan [予感]; mushi-no-shirase [虫の知らせ].

hundred (*n. & a.*) hyaku(-no) [百(の)].

    hundreds of nam-byaku-to-iu; takusan-no

hundredfold (*a. & ad.*) hyaku-bai-no(-ni) [百倍の(に)].

hundredth (*n. & a.*) hyaku-ban-me(-no) [百番目(の)].

hunger (*n.*) kûfuku [空腹]; ue [飢え]; katsubô [渇望].

　　　　　(*vi.*) setsubô-suru [切望する].

hunger strike　hansuto [ハンスト].

hungry (*a.*) uete-iru [飢えている]; kûfuku-na [空腹な]; setsubô-shite [切望して].

hunt (*vt.*) …o karu […を狩る].
　　　　　(*vi.*) kari-o-suru [狩りをする].
　　　　　(*n.*) 1)kari [狩り]. 2)shuryô-chi [狩猟地].

hunter (*n.*) 1)ryôshi [猟師]. 2)tankyû-sha [探求者].

hunting (*n.*) kari [狩り].

huntsman (*n.*) shuryô-ka [狩猟家].

hurdle (*n.*) hâdoru [ハードル].
　　　　　(*vt.*) …o tobi-kosu […を飛び越す].

hurdle race　shôgai-butsu-kyôsô [障害物競走]; hâdoru-kyôsô [ハードル競走].

hurl (*vt.*) …o nage-tsukeru […を投げつける].
　　　　　(*n.*) nage-tsukeru-koto [投げつけること].

hurray, hurrah (*int. & n.*) banzai(-no-koe) [万歳(の声)]; furê [フレー].

hurricane (*n.*) dai-bôfû [大暴風]; gufû [ぐ風]; harikên [ハリケーン].

hurried (*a.*) oo-isogi-no [大急ぎの].

hurry (*vt. & vi.*) …o isogaseru (isogu) […を急がせる(急ぐ)].
　hurry up　isogu
　　　　　(*n.*) oo-isogi [大急ぎ].
　in a hurry　isoide

hurt (*vt.*) …o kizu-tsukeru […を傷つける]; …o itameru […を痛める]; …o gaisuru […を害する].
　　　　　(*vi.*) itamu [痛む].
　　　　　(*n.*) kizu [傷]; kega [けが]; sonshô [損傷].

hurtful (*a.*) kanjô-o-gaisuru [感情を害する]; yûgai-na [有害な].

husband (*n.*) otto [夫].

hush (*vt. & vi.*) …o shizuka-ni-saseru (shizuka-ni-naru) […を静かにさせる(静かになる)]; …o damaraseru (damaru) […を黙らせる(黙る)].
　　　　　(*int.*) Shi! [しっ!]; Shizuka-ni! [静かに!].
　　　　　(*n.*) shizukesa [静けさ]; chimmoku [沈黙].

huskily (*ad.*) shagare-goe-de [しゃがれ声で].

husky (*a.*) shagare-goe-no [しゃがれ声の]; hasukî-na [ハスキーな].

hustle (*vi.*) (*colloq.*) sei-o-dasu [精を出す]; hassuru-suru [ハッスルする].

　　　　(n.) (colloq.) hassuru [ハッスル].
hut (n.) koya [小屋].
hyacinth (n.) (bot.) hiyashinsu [ヒヤシンス].
hydrant (n.) kyûsui-sen [給水栓]; shôka-sen [消火栓].
hydroelectric (a.) suiryoku-denki-no [水力電気の].
hydrogen (n.) (chem.) suiso [水素].
hygiene (n.) eisei[-gaku] [衛生(学)].
hymn (n.) sambi-ka [賛美歌].
hyphen (n.) haifun [ハイフン].
　　　　(vt.) ...o haifun-de-renketsu-suru [...をハイフンで連結する].
hypocrite (n.) gizen-sha [偽善者].
hypothesis (n.) kasetsu [仮説].

I

I (pron.) watashi-wa [私は]; watashi-ga [私が].
ice (n.) koori [氷].
　　　　(vt.) ...o koori-de-hiyasu [...を氷で冷やす].
iceberg (n.) hyôzan [氷山].
icebreaker (n.) saihyô-sen [砕氷船].
iced (a.) koori-de-hiyashita [氷で冷やした].
ice field (kyokuchi no) hyôgen [(極地の)氷原].
ice-skate (vi.) aisu-sukêto-o-suru [アイススケートをする].
icicle (n.) tsurara [つらら].

icy (*a.*) koori-no [氷の]; koori-no-hari-tsumeta [氷の張りつめた]; koori-no-yô-ni-tsumetai [氷のようにつめたい].

ID card = identification card mibun-shômei-sho [身分証明書]; ai-dî-kâdo [アイディーカード].

idea (*n.*) 1)kannen [観念]. 2)kangae [考え]. 3)iken [意見].
　(*1*) He has a wrong **idea** of success.
　　　　Kare-wa seikô-ni-taisuru machigatta *kannen*-o motte-iru.
　(*2*) I had no **idea** that she was here, too.
　　　　Kano-jo mo koko-ni iyô-to-wa *kangae*-mo-shi-nakatta.
　(*3*) What's your **idea**? Anata-no go-*iken* wa ikaga-desu-ka?

ideal (*a.*) 1)risô-teki-na [理想的な]. 2)(*philos.*) kannen-teki-na [観念的な].
　(*n.*) risô [理想]; tehon [手本].

idealism (*n.*) risô-shugi [理想主義]; (*philos.*) yuishin-ron [唯心論].

identical (*a.*) dôitsu-no [同一の].

identification (*n.*) dôitsu-da-to-mitomeru-koto [同一だと認めること].

identify (*vt.*) ...o honnin-da-to-kakunin-suru [···を本人だと確認する]; ...o dôitsu-shi-suru [···を同一視する].

identity (*n.*) 1)mi-moto [身元]; shôtai [正体]. 2)honnin-de-aru-koto [本人であること].

ideology (*n.*) (*philos.*) kannen-ron [観念論]. ideorogî [イデオロギー].

idiom (*n.*) kan'yô-go-ku [慣用語句]; idiomu [イディオム].

idiomatic (*a.*) kan'yô-go-hô-teki-na [慣用語法的な].

idiot (*n.*) baka [ばか].

idle (*a.*) 1)taida-na [怠惰な]. 2)muda-na [むだな]. 3)nani-mo-shi-nai [何もしない].
　(*1*) He is an **idle** fellow. Kare-wa *namake*-mono da.
　(*2*) It was an **idle** talk by him.
　　　　Sore-wa kare-no *muda*-banashi datta.
　(*3*) land lying **idle** *asonde*-iru tochi
　　(*vt.*) ...o mui-ni-sugosu [···を無為に過ごす].
　　　He **idled** away his youth.
　　　　Kare-wa seishun-jidai-o *mui-ni-sugoshita*.
　　(*vi.*) namakete-iru [怠けている].
　　　Bees and ants never **idle**.
　　　　Mitsu-bachi ya ari wa kesshite *namake*-nai.

idleness (*n.*) taida [怠惰]; mui [無為].

idly (*ad.*) namakete [怠けて]; muda-ni [むだに].

idol (*n.*) gûzô [偶像]; aidoru [アイドル].

if (*conj.*) 1)moshi...naraba [もし…ならば]. 2)tatoe...demo [たとえ…でも]. 3)...ka-dôka […かどうか].

   (*1*) **If** it rains tomorrow, I shall be at home.

      Asu *moshi*-ame-*nara*, watashi-wa ie-ni ima-shô.

   (*2*) Even **if** it is stormy, I will go.

      Tatoe-arashi-*demo*, watashi-wa iku-tsumori-da.

   (*3*) Ask **if** he is at office.

      Kare-ga jimu-sho-ni iru-*ka-dôka* kiite-kudasai.

ignorance (*n.*) 1)muchi [無知]; mugaku [無学]. 2)shira-nai-koto [知らないこと].

ignorant (*a.*) muchi-no [無知の]; mugaku-no [無学の]; shira-nai [知らない].

ignore (*vt.*) ...o mushi-suru […を無視する].

ill (*a.*) 1)byôki-no [病気の]. 2)warui [悪い]; yûgai-na [有害な].

   (*1*) She has been **ill** a long time.

      Kano-jo-wa nagai-aida *byôki*-da.

   (*2*) **Ill** news runs apace. *Aku*-ji sen-ri.

   be taken (or **fall**) **ill** byôki-ni-kakaru

   (*ad.*) waruku [悪く].

   (*n.*) aku [悪]; fukô [不幸].

illegal (*a.*) hi-gôhô-no [非合法の].

illegible (*a.*) yomi-nikui [読みにくい].

ill-humored (*a.*) fu-kigen-na [不機嫌な]; okorippoi [怒りっぽい].

illness (*n.*) byôki [病気].

ill-tempered (*a.*) ki-muzukashii [気難しい]; okorippoi [怒りっぽい].

illuminate (*vt.*) 1)...o terasu […を照らす]; ...ni shômei-o-hodokosu […に照明を施す]. 2)...o kaimei-suru […を解明する].

illumination (*n.*) shômei [照明]; iruminêshon [イルミネーション].

illusion (*n.*) gen'ei [幻影]; genkaku [幻覚]; kan-chigai [勘違い].

illustrate (*vt.*) ...o reishô-suru […を例証する]; ...o zukai-suru […を図解する].

illustration (*n.*) reishô [例証]; sashie [挿絵]; zukai [図解].

image (*n.*) 1)zô [像]. 2)iki-utsushi [生き写し]. 3)imêji [イメージ].

imaginable (*a.*) sôzô-dekiru [想像できる].

imaginary (*a.*) sôzô-jô-no [想像上の]; jitsuzai-shi-nai [実在しない].

imagination (*n.*) sôzô[-ryoku] [想像(力)].

imagine (*vt. & vi.*) (...o) sôzô-suru [(…を)想像する]; (...to) omou

[(…と)思う].

imbalance (*n.*) fu-kinkô [不均衡]; ambaransu [アンバランス].

imitate (*vt.*) …o maneru […をまねる].

imitation (*n.*) mohô [模倣]; mozô-hin [模造品].

immature (*a.*) mijuku-no [未熟の].

immeasurable (*a.*) hakari-shire-nai [測り知れない].

immediate (*a.*) 1)sokuza-no [即座の]. 2)chokusetsu-no [直接の].

immediately (*ad.*) 1)sugu [すぐ]. 2)chokusetsu-ni [直接に].

immemorial (*a.*) hito-no-kioku-ni-nai [人の記憶にない]; taiko-no [太古の].

immense (*a.*) 1)kôdai-na [広大な]; hakari-shire-nai [測り知れない]. 2)(*colloq.*) subarashii [すばらしい].

immensely (*ad.*) kôdai-ni [広大に]; hakari-shire-nai-hodo [測り知れないほど]; (*colloq.*) sugoku [すごく].

immigrant (*n.*) (takoku-kara-no) ijû-sha [(他国からの)移住者]; imin [移民].

immigrate (*vi.*) (…kara/…e) ijû-suru [(…から/…へ)移住する].

immigration (*n.*) 1)(takoku-kara-no) ijû [(他国からの)移住]. 2)(shutsu-)nyû-koku-kanri [(出)入国管理].

immoral (*a.*) fu-dôtoku-na [不道徳な].

immortal (*a.*) fumetsu-no [不滅の].

immune (*a.*) men'eki-no-aru [免疫のある].
　　　　　(*n.*) men'eki-sha [免疫者].

imp (*n.*) ko-oni [小鬼]; itazurakko [いたずらっ子].

impact (*n.*) shôgeki [衝撃].
　　　　　(*vt.*) 1)…o tsume-komu […を詰め込む]. 2)…ni shôtotsu-suru […に衝突する]; …ni shôgeki-o-ataeru […に衝撃を与える].

impair (*vt.*) …o gaisuru […を害する].

impartial (*a.*) kôhei-na [公平な].

impatience (*n.*) sekkachi [せっかち]; ira-ira [いらいら].

impatient (*a.*) 1)sekkachi-na [せっかちな]. 2)shikiri-ni…(shi-)tagaru [しきりに…(し)たがる].

　(*1*) He grew **impatient** and went out.
　　　Kare-wa *jirettaku*-natte soto-e deta.
　(*2*) She is **impatient** to go shopping.
　　　Kano-jo-wa *shikiri-ni* kaimono-ni-iki-*tagatte-iru*.

impede (*vt.*) …o samatageru […を妨げる].

imperative (*a.*) 1)meirei-teki-na [命令的な]. 2)sakerare-nai [避けられ

ない].

　　　　　(n.) 1)meirei [命令]. 2)kinkyû-kadai [緊急課題].

imperceptible (a.) kanchi-deki-nai [感知できない].

imperfect (a.) fu-kanzen-na [不完全な].

imperial (a.) 1)teikoku-no [帝国の]; kôtei-no [皇帝の]. 2)dôdô-to-shita [堂々とした].

imperialism (n.) teikoku-shugi [帝国主義].

implement (n.) dôgu [道具]; shudan [手段].

implication (n.) fukumi-no-aru-koto [含みのあること].

　by implication an-ni

implore (vt.) ...o aigan-suru […を哀願する].

imply (vt.) ...o sore-to-naku-iu […をそれとなく言う]; ...o honome-kasu […をほのめかす]; ...o an-ni-imi-suru […を暗に意味する].

impolite (a.) bu-sahô-na [無作法な]; shitsurei-na [失礼な].

import (vt.) ...o yunyû-suru […を輸入する].

　　　　　(n.) yunyû[-hin] [輸入(品)].

importance (n.) 1)jûyô-sei [重要性]. 2)kanroku [貫ろく]; yûryoku [有力]. 3)mottai-buri [もったいぶり].

　(1) The matter is of great **importance**.

　　　Sono koto wa totemo *jûyô-da*.

　(2) He lacks **importance**.　Kare-wa *kanroku*-ga tari-nai.

　(3) He walked with an air of **importance**.

　　　Kare-wa *mottai-but*te aruita.

　of no importance jûyô-de-nai

important (a.) 1)jûyô-na [重要な]; taisetsu-na [大切な]. 2)erasô-na [えらそうな]; mottai-butta [もったいぶった].

　(1) I have got a very **important** business.

　　　Watashi-wa totemo *taisetsu-na* shigoto-ga aru.

　(2) He felt very **important**.

　　　Kare-wa hijô-ni *erai-mono-no-yô-ni-omotta*.

importer (n.) yunyû-gyô-sha [輸入業者].

impose (vt.) 1)...o kasu […を課す]. 2)...o oshi-tsukeru […を押しつける].

imposing (a.) dôdô-to-shita [堂々とした].

impossible (a.) fu-kanô-na [不可能な]; ari-e-nai [ありえない].

impotent (a.) mu-kiryoku-na [無気力な].

impractical (a.) jitsuyô-teki-de-nai [実用的でない]; jissai-teki-de-nai [実際的でない].

impress (*vt.*) 1)...no inshô-o-ataeru [⋯の印象を与える]. 2)(be -ed) kandô-suru [感動する].

 (*1*) I **was** unfavorably **impressed** with his arrogance.
  Watashi-wa kare-no sondai-na-taido-kara warui-*inshô-o-uketa.*

 (*2*) I **was** much **impressed** with his adventures.
  Watashi-wa kare-no-kazu-kazu-no-bôken-dan-ni taihen *kandô-shita.*

 (*n.*) 1)ôin [押印]. 2)tokuchô [特徴]. 3)kammei [感銘].

impression (*n.*) inshô [印象]; kandô [感動]; kansô [感想].

impressive (*a.*) inshô-teki-na [印象的な]; kandô-teki-na [感動的な].

imprison (*vt.*) ...o toji-komeru [⋯を閉じ込める]; ...o tôgoku-suru [⋯を投獄する].

improbable (*a.*) ari[okori]-sô-mo-nai [あり[起こり]そうもない]; hontô-rashiku-nai [本当らしくない].

improper (*a.*) tekisetsu-de-nai [適切でない]; tadashiku-nai [正しくない].

improve (*vt.*) ...o kairyô-suru [⋯を改良する]; ...o kaizen-suru [⋯を改善する]; ...o kôjô-saseru [⋯を向上させる].
 (*vi.*) yoku-naru [よくなる]; kaizen-sareru [改善される]; shimpo-suru [進歩する].

improvement (*n.*) 1)kairyô [改良]; kaizen [改善]; kôjô [向上]. 2)kairyô-sareta-ten [改良された点].

imprudent (*a.*) keisotsu-na [軽率な].

impudent (*a.*) atsukamashii [厚かましい]; nama-iki-na [生意気な].

impulse (*n.*) shôdô [衝動]; hazumi [はずみ].

impure (*a.*) fujun-na [不純な].

in (*prep.*) 1)...no-naka-ni [⋯の中に]; ...ni-notte [⋯に乗って]. 2)...ni [⋯に]; ...ni-oite [⋯において]; ...no-aida-ni [⋯の間に]; ...tateba [⋯たてば]. 3)...ni [⋯に]. 4)...o-kite [⋯を着て]. 5)...de [⋯で]. 6)...no-naka-ni [⋯の中に]. 7)...de [⋯で]; ...shite [⋯して]. 8)...wa [⋯は]. 9)(sôkei-)de... [(総計)で⋯]. 10)...o-shite [⋯をして].

 (*1*) It is **in** my hand. Sore-wa watashi-no-te-*no-naka-ni* aru.
  They were **in** a boat. Kare-ra-wa bôto-*ni-notte*-ita.

 (*2*) He was born **in** September. Kare-wa Kugatsu-*ni* umareta.

 (*3*) They went on **in** that direction.
  Kare-ra-wa sono-hôkô-*ni* susumi-tsuzuketa.

 (*4*) She was dressed **in** blue. Kano-jo-wa burû-no-fuku-*o-kite*-ita.

(5) They spoke **in** French. Kare-ra-wa Furansu-go-*de* hanashita.

(6) **In** the works of Pope such an expression is often found.
　　　Pôpu-no-chosaku-*no-naka-ni-wa* konna hyôgen ga yoku dete-kuru.

(7) He is always **in** good health. Kare-wa itsu-mo genki-*de*-iru.

(8) It is five inches **in** width. Sore-wa haba-*ga* go-inchi aru.

(9) They are twenty **in** all. Kare-ra-wa zembu-*de* ni-jû-nin desu.

(10) I spent all day **in** writing letters.
　　　Watashi-wa ichinichi-jû tegami-o-kaite-sugoshita.

　in so far as …(suru-)kagiri-de-wa

　(*ad.*) naka-ni [中に]; zaitaku-shite [在宅して].

　　Is Mr. Smith **in**? Sumisu-san wa go-*zaitaku*-desu-ka?

　(*a.*) uchi-no [内の]; naibu-no [内部の].

inability (*n.*) deki-nai-koto [できないこと].

inaccessible (*a.*) chikazuki-nikui [近づきにくい].

inaccurate (*a.*) fu-seikaku-na [不正確な].

inactive (*a.*) fu-kappatsu-na [不活発な]; taida-na [怠惰な].

inadequate (*a.*) fu-tekitô-na [不適当な]; fu-jûbun-na [不十分な].

inadvertent (*a.*) ukkari-shita [うっかりした].

inadvisable (*a.*) susume-rare-nai [勧められない]; kemmei-de-nai [賢明でない].

inauguration (*n.*) shû-nin[-shiki] [就任(式)].

incapable (*a.*) …ga-deki-nai […ができない].

incendiary (*a.*) 1)hôka-no [放火の]. 2)sendô-teki-na [扇動的な].

incessant (*a.*) taema-no-nai [絶え間のない].

incident (*n.*) deki-goto [出来事]; jiken [事件].

incidental (*a.*) ari-gachi-na [ありがちな]; fuzui-teki-na [付随的な].
　　　(*n.*) 1)fuzui-teki-na-mono [付随的なもの]. 2)(*pl.*) zappi [雑費].

incidentally (*ad.*) tsuide-nagara [ついでながら].

inclination (*n.*) 1)keikô [傾向]. 2)kôbai [こう配]. 3)konomi [好み].

incline (*vt.*) 1)…o katamukeru […を傾ける]. 2)…o…(suru-)ki-ni-saseru […を…(する)気にさせる].

(1) He **inclined** his head. Kare-wa atama-*o kagameta*.

(2) I am **inclined** to think so. Watashi-wa sô omoi-*tai*.
　　　(*vi.*) 1)kokoro-ga-katamuku [心が傾く]. 2)keikô-ga-aru [傾向がある].
　　　(*n.*) keisha [傾斜].

include (*vt.*) ...o fukumu […を含む].

including (*prep.*)...o-fukumete […を含めて].

inclusive (*a.*) sôkatsu-teki-na [総括的な].

　inclusive of ...mo-irete; ...o-fukumete

income (*n.*) shûnyû [収入]; shotoku [所得].

income tax shotoku-zei [所得税].

incompatible (*a.*) ryôritsu-shi-nai [両立しない]; ki-ga-awa-nai [気が合わない].

incomplete (*a.*) fu-kanzen-na [不完全な]; fu-jûbun-na [不十分な].

inconvenience (*n.*) fuben [不便]; fu-jiyû [不自由]; meiwaku [迷惑].
　　　　　　(*vt.*) ...ni fuben-o-kakeru […に不便をかける].

inconvenient (*a.*) fuben-na [不便な].

incorporation (*n.*) 1)ketsugô [結合]; gappei [合併]. 2)(*law*) hôjin-dantai [法人団体].

increase (*vt. & vi.*) ...o fuyasu (fueru) […を増やす(増える)].
　　　　　(*n.*) zôka [増加].

incredible (*a.*) shinji-rare-nai [信じられない]; (*colloq.*) tohô-mo-nai [途方もない].

incur (*vt.*) (kiken nado)-o maneku [(危険など)を招く]; (songai nado)-o ukeru [(損害など)を受ける].

indebted (*a.*) 1)shakkin-ga-aru [借金がある]. 2)on-o-ukete-iru [恩を受けている].

indeed (*ad.*) jitsu-ni [実に]; hontô-ni [本当に]; naruhodo [なるほど].
　Yes, indeed! Ee, sô-desu-tomo!

indefinite (*a.*) 1)aimai-na [あいまいな]. 2)(*gram.*) futei-no [不定の].

indefinitely (*ad.*) 1)itsu-made-mo [いつまでも]. 2)bakuzen-to [漠然と].

independence (*n.*) dokuritsu [独立]; jiritsu [自立].

independent (*a.*) dokuritsu-shita [独立した]; dokuji-no [独自の].
　independent of ...to-wa-betsu-ni; ...to-mu-kankei-ni
　　　　　　　(*n.*) mu-shozoku-giin [無所属議員].

index (*n.*) 1)sakuin [索引]. 2)shisû [指数].
　　　　(*vt.*) ...ni sakuin-o-tsukeru […に索引を付ける].

index finger hitosashi-yubi [人差し指].

index number shisû [指数]; (*econ.*) bukka-shisû [物価指数].

India (*n.*) Indo [インド].

Indian (*a.*) 1)Indo-no [インドの]; Indo-jin-no [インド人の]. 2)Amerika-Indian-no [アメリカインディアンの].
　　　　(*n.*) 1)Indo-jin [インド人]. 2)Amerika-indian [アメリカインディ

アン].

India rubber keshi-gomu [消しゴム].

indicate (*vt.*) ...o sashi-shimesu […を指し示す]; ...o shimesu […を示す].

indicator (*n.*) hyôji-ki [表示器]; shiji-sha [指示者].

indifference (*n.*) 1)mu-kanshin [無関心]. 2)jûyô-de-nai-koto [重要でないこと].

indigestion (*n.*) shôka-furyô [消化不良]; rikai-busoku [理解不足].

indignation meeting kôgi-shûkai [抗議集会].

indigo (*n.*) ai[-iro] [あい(色)].

indirect (*a.*) kansetsu-no [間接の]; massugu-de-nai [真っすぐでない].

indispensable (*a.*) kaku-koto-no-deki-nai [欠くことのできない].

individual (*a.*) ko-ko-no [個々の]; kojin-no [個人の]; dokutoku-no [独特の].
            (*n.*) kojin [個人]; (*colloq.*) hito [人].

individualism (*n.*) kojin-shugi [個人主義]; riko-shugi [利己主義].

individuality (*n.*) kotai [個体]; kosei [個性].

indoor (*a.*) okunai-no [屋内の]; shitsunai-no [室内の].

indoors (*ad.*) okunai-de [屋内で].

induce (*vt.*) ...o toite...(sa-)seru [… を説いて…(さ)せる]; ...o susumete...(sa-)seru [… を勧めて…(さ)せる]; (*log.*)...o kinô-suru [… を帰納する].

indulge (*vt.*) 1)(- oneself) ...ni fukeru [… にふける]. 2)...o amayakasu [… を甘やかす].
         (*vi.*) fukeru [ふける].

industrial (*a.*) sangyô-no [産業の]; kôgyô[-jô]-no [工業(上)の].

industrious (*a.*) kimben-na [勤勉な].

industry (*n.*) 1)sangyô [産業]; kôgyô [工業]. 2)kimben [勤勉].

inefficient (*a.*) nôritsu-no-agara-nai [能率のあがらない]; munô-na [無能な].

inevitable (*a.*) 1)sakerare-nai [避けられない]; hitsuzen-teki-na [必然的な]. 2)(*colloq.*) o-kimari-no [おきまりの].

inexpensive (*a.*) hiyô-no-kakara-nai [費用の掛からない]; yasui [安い].

inexperienced (*a.*) mu-keiken-na [無経験な]; mijuku-na [未熟な].

infamous (*a.*) hazu-beki [恥ずべき]; akumei-no-takai [悪名の高い].

infancy (*n.*) yônen-jidai [幼年時代]; shoki [初期].

infant (*n.*) yôji [幼児].

infantry (*n.*) hohei [歩兵].

infection (*n.*) densen[-byô] [伝染(病)]; kansen [感染].

infectious (*a.*) densen-sei-no [伝染性の].

infer (*vt. & vi.*) (…o) suisoku-suru [(…を)推測する].

inferior (*a.*) kakyû-no [下級の]; ototta [劣った].

  inferior to …yori-otoru

infest (*vt.*) (gaichû ya nezumi ga)…o arasu [(害虫やネズミが)…を荒らす]; …ni habikoru […にはびこる].

infinite (*a.*) mugen-no [無限の]; musû-no [無数の]; bakudai-na [ばく大な].

  (*n.*) (the –) mugen-no-mono [無限のもの].

infinitely (*ad.*) mugen-ni [無限に]; musû-ni [無数に]; hijô-ni [非常に].

infinitive (*n.*) (*gram.*) futei-shi [不定詞].

inflammation (*n.*) nenshô [燃焼]; (*med.*) enshô [炎症].

inflation (*n.*) bôchô [膨張]; (*econ.*) infure [インフレ].

inflection (*n.*) (*gram.*) gokei-henka [語形変化]; katsuyô [活用]; kussetsu [屈折].

inflict (*vt.*) …o kuwaeru […を加える]; (batsu)-o kasu [(罰)を課す].

influence (*n.*) eikyô [影響]; kanka [感化].

  (*vt.*) …ni eikyô-o-oyobosu […に影響を及ぼす]; …o kanka-suru […を感化する].

influential (*a.*) yûryoku-na [有力な]; jûyô-na-yakuwari-o-hatasu [重要な役割を果す].

influenza (*n.*) ryûkô-sei-kambô [流行性感冒]; infuruenza [インフルエンザ].

inform (*vt. & vi.*) (…o) shiraseru [(…を)知らせる].

informal (*a.*) 1)hi-kôshiki-no [非公式の]. 2)kôgo-tai-no [口語体の].

information (*n.*) 1)jôhô [情報]; chishiki [知識]. 2)annai [案内].

ingenious (*a.*) 1)hatsumei-no-sainô-no-aru [発明の才能のある]. 2)kômyô-na [巧妙な].

ingredient (*n.*) seibun [成分].

inhabit (*vt.*) 1)..ni sumu […に住む]. 2)…ni sonzai-suru […に存在する].

inhabitant (*n.*) jûmin [住民].

inhale (*vt. & vi.*) (…o) sui-komu [(…を)吸いこむ].

inherent (*a.*) honrai-sonawatte-iru [本来備わっている].

inherit (*vt. & vi.*) …o sôzoku-suru (zaisan-o-sôzoku-suru) […を相続する(財産を相続する)].

initial (*a.*) saisho-no [最初の]; hajime-no [始めの].

     (*n.*) kashira-moji [頭文字].

(*vt.*) ...ni kashira-moji-o-kaku [···に頭文字を書く].

initiative (*a.*) hajime-no [始めの].
　　　　(*n.*) 1)te-hajime [手始め]. 2)shudô-ken [主導権]; inishiatibu [イニシアティブ]. 3)dokusô-ryoku [独創力].

inject (*vt.*) ...o chûsha-suru [···を注射する]; ...o chûnyû-suru [···を注入する].

injection (*n.*) chûsha[-eki] [注射(液)].

injure (*vt.*) ...ni kega-o-saseru [···にけがをさせる]; ...o gaisuru [···を害する].

injurious (*a.*) yûgai-na [有害な].

injury (*n.*) shôgai [傷害]; kega [けが]; songai [損害].

injustice (*n.*) fu-kôhei [不公平]; fuhô [不法].

ink (*n.*) inku [インク].
　　　　(*vt.*) ...o inku-de-kaku [···をインクで書く].

inland (*n. & a.*) nairiku(-no) [内陸(の)]; oku-chi(-no) [奥地(の)].
　　　　(*ad.*) oku-chi-ni-mukatte [奥地に向かって].

inlay (*vt.*) ...ni zôgan-suru [···に象眼する]; ...o chiribameru [···をちりばめる].
　　　　(*n.*) zôgan-zaiku [象眼細工].

inlet (*n.*) irie [入江].

inn (*n.*) yadoya [宿屋].

inner (*a.*) uchi-no [内の]; naibu-no [内部の].

inning (*n.*) 1)(*baseball*) iningu [イニング]. 2)(*Eng. colloq.*) (*pl.*) kôki [好機].

innocence (*n.*) 1)keppaku [潔白]. 2)mu-jaki [無邪気].

innocent (*a.*) 1)mu-jaki-na [無邪気な]; muzai-no [無罪の]; mugai-no [無害の]. 2)tanjun-na [単純な].

innumerable (*a.*) musû-no [無数の].

input (*n.*) (*computer*) imputto [インプット]; nyûryoku [入力].

inquire (*vt.*) ...o tazuneru [···を尋ねる]; ...o tou [···を問う].
　　　I'll **inquire** his name. Watashi-ga kare-no namae-o *ki-kô*.
　　　　(*vi.*) 1)tazuneru [尋ねる]. 2)chôsa-suru [調査する].
　　(2) May I **inquire** into the matter?
　　　　Watashi-ga sono-ken-o *chôsa-shite*-mo-yoroshii-ka?
　　inquire after ...o mimau

inquiry (*n.*) 1)toi-awase [問い合わせ]. 2)chôsa [調査].
　　(1) I found out by **inquiry** that he was not there at that time.
　　　　Toi-awasete-miru-to kare-wa sono-toki soko-ni inakatta-

koto-ga-wakatta.

(2) I made **inquiries** about the matter.

Watashi-wa sono-ken-ni-tsuite *chôsa*-shita.

inquisitive (*a.*) kiki-tagaru [聞きたがる]; shiri-tagaru [知りたがる].

insane (*a.*) kyôki-no [狂気の].

insanity (*n.*) kyôki [狂気].

inscribe (*vt.*) 1)...o kinyû-suru [···を記入する]; ...o kizamu [···を刻む].
2)...o kenjiru [···を献じる].

inscription (*n.*) mei [銘]; hibun [碑文]; kentei-no-ji [献呈の辞].

insect (*n.*) konchû [昆虫].

insensible (*a.*) 1)jinji-fusei-no [人事不省の]. 2)mu-kankaku-no [無感
覚の]; mu-shinkei-na [無神経な].

inseparable (*a.*) bunri-deki-nai [分離できない].

insert (*vt.*) 1)...o sashi-komu [···を差し込む]; ...o sônyû-suru [···を
挿入する]. 2)...o kaki-komu [···を書き込む].
(*n.*) 1)sônyû-butsu [挿入物]. 2)orikomi-kôkoku [折込み広告].

inside (*n. & a. & ad.*) naibu(-no)(-ni) [内部(の)(に)].
inside out ura-gaeshi-ni
(*prep.*)...no-naibu-ni [···の内部に].

insight (*n.*) dôsatsu[-ryoku] [洞察(力)].

insignificant (*a.*) toru-ni-tari-nai [取るに足りない].

insist (*vi. & vt.*) 1)(...o) shuchô-suru [(···を)主張する]. 2)(...o)
kyôchô-suru [(···を)強調する]. 3)(...o) tsuyoku-yôkyû-suru [(···を)
強く要求する].
(*1*) He **insisted** on his innocence.
Kare-wa jibun-no-muzai-o *shuchô-shita*.
(*2*) I **insisted** on this point.
Watashi-wa kono-ten-o *kyôchô-shita*.
(*3*) They **insisted** on his being present.
Kare-ra-wa *akumade-mo* kare-o shusseki-*sase-yô-to-shita*.

inspect (*vt.*) 1)...o kensa-suru [···を検査する]. 2)...o shisatsu-suru [···
を視察する].

inspection (*n.*) 1)kensa [検査]; ken'etsu [検閲]. 2)shisatsu [視察].

inspector (*n.*) 1)kensa-kan [検査官]. 2)((*Eng.*)) keibu [警部].

inspiration (*n.*) 1)reikan [霊感]; insupirêshon [インスピレーション].
2)kobu [鼓舞]. 3)iki-o-sui-komu-koto [息を吸い込むこと].

inspire (*vt.*) 1)...o fuki-komu [···を吹き込む]. 2)...o kobu-suru [···を
鼓舞する]. 3)...o kangeki-saseru [···を感激させる]. 4)...ni reikan-o-

ataeru [⋯に霊感を与える]. 5)...o sui-komu [⋯を吸い込む].
    (vi.) kobu-suru [鼓舞する]; iki-o-sui-komu [息を吸い込む].

install (vt.) 1)...o nimmei-suru [⋯を任命する]. 2)...o seki-ni-tsukaseru [⋯を席に着かせる]. 3)...o sue-tsukeru [⋯を据え付ける].

installation (n.) 1)shûnin[-shiki] [就任(式)]. 2)setsubi [設備]; (setsubi-sareta) sôchi [(設備された)装置].

instal(l)ment (n.) bunkatsu-harai-komi-kin [分割払い込み金].

instance (n.) rei [例]; jitsurei [実例].
   for instance tatoeba
    (vt.) ...o rei-ni-hiku [⋯を例に引く].

instant (a.) sokuza-no [即座の]; sokuseki-no [即席の].
    (n.) 1)shunkan [瞬間]. 2)(colloq.) insutanto-shokuhin [インスタント食品].
   for an instant chotto-no-aida
   in an instant tachimachi
   the instant (that)... ...(suru-)to-sugu

instantly (ad.) tadachi-ni [直ちに]; sokuza-ni [即座に].

instead (ad.) sono-kawari-ni [その代りに].
   instead of ...no-kawari-ni

instep (n.) ashi-no-kô [足の甲].

instinct (n.) 1)honnô [本能]. 2)soshitsu [素質].

instinctive (a.) honnô-teki-na [本能的な]; chokkan-teki-na [直感的な].

institute (vt.) ...o setsuritsu-suru [⋯を設立する].
    (n.) kyôkai [協会]; gakkai [学会]; ((US)) daigaku [大学].

institution (n.) 1)kôkyô-kikan-no-shisetsu [公共機関の施設]; kôkyô-kikan-no-tate-mono [公共機関の建物]. 2)seido [制度]. 3)setsuritsu [設立].

instruct (vt.) 1)...ni oshieru [⋯に教える]. 2)...ni sashizu-suru [⋯に指図する].
   (1) It will **instruct** you in ideals and habits of service.
    Sore-wa kimi-ni hôshi-no-risô-to-shûkan-o *oshieru*-darô.
   (2) The teacher **instructed** them to sweep the room.
    Sono sensei wa kare-ra-ni sono heya-o sôji-suru-yô-ni-*sashizu-shita*.

instruction (n.) 1)kyôju [教授]. 2)(pl.) sashizu [指図]; meirei [命令].

instructive (a.) tame-ni-naru [ためになる]; yûeki-na [有益な].

instrument (n.) 1)kigu [器具]. 2)gakki [楽器].

instrument board(panel) kêiki-ban [計器板].

insufficient (*a.*) fu-jûbun-na [不十分な].

insulate (*vt.*) 1)...o kakuri-suru [...を隔離する]. 2)...o zetsuen-tai-de-oou [...を絶縁体で覆う].

insult (*n.*) bujoku [侮辱].
　　　(*vt.*) ...o bujoku-suru [...を侮辱する].

insurance (*n.*) hoken[-kin] [保険(金)].

insurance policy hoken-shôken [保険証券].

insure (*vt.*) 1)...ni hoken-o-kakeru [...に保険を掛ける]; ...no hoken-keiyaku-o-suru [...の保険契約をする]. 2)...o hoshô-suru [...を保証する].

integral (*a.*) 1)zettai-hitsuyô-na [絶対必要な]. 2)zentai-no [全体の].

integrate (*vt.*) 1)...o tôgô-suru [...を統合する]. 2)...o yûwa-saseru [...を融和させる].

integrity (*n.*) 1)seijitsu [誠実]. 2)kanzen [完全].

intellect (*n.*) 1)chisei [知性]. 2)(the –) chishiki-jin [知識人].

intellectual (*a.*) chisei-no [知性の].
　　　　　(*n.*) interi [インテリ]; chishiki-jin [知識人].

intelligence (*n.*) 1)chinô [知能]; sômei [そう明]. 2)jôhô [情報].

intelligence quotient chinô-shisû [知能指数].

intelligent (*a.*) sômei-na [そう明な].

intend (*vt.*) ...(suru-)tsumori-de-aru [...(する)つもりである].

intended (*a.*) koi-no [故意の].

intense (*a.*) hageshii [激しい].

intensity (*n.*) kyôretsu-sa [強烈さ]; tsuyo-sa [強さ].

intensive (*a.*) hageshii [激しい]; shûchû-teki-na [集中的な].

intent (*a.*) bottô-shita [没頭した].
　　　(*n.*) (*law*) ito [意図]; mokuteki [目的].

intention (*n.*) ishi [意志]; ikô [意向]; nerai [ねらい].

　with the intention of...ing ...(suru-)tsumori-de

intentional (*a.*) koi-no [故意の].

intently (*ad.*) isshin-ni [一心に]; muchû-de [夢中で].

interchange (*vt.*) ...o kôkan-suru [...を交換する].
　　　　　(*n.*) 1)kôkan [交換]. 2)intâchenji [インターチェンジ].

intercourse (*n.*) 1)kôsai [交際]; kôtsû [交通]. 2)seikô [性交].

interest (*n.*) 1)kyômi [興味]; kanshin [関心]. 2)(*pl.*) rieki [利益]; tame [ため]. 3)rishi [利子].
　(*1*) He takes (an) **interest** in studying history.
　　　Kare-wa rekishi-kenkyû-ni *kyômi*-o motte-iru.
　(*2*) He always looks after only his own **interests**.

　　　　Kare-wa itsu-mo jibun-no-*rieki*-dake-ni ki-o-kubatte-iru.
(3) Its **interest** is 8% a year.　Sono *rishi* wa nen hachi-bu da.
in the interest(s) of ...no-tame-ni
　　　　(*vt.*) ...ni kyômi-o-okosaseru [⋯に興味を起こさせる].
interested (*a.*) 1)kyômi-o-motte-iru [興味を持っている]. 2)rigai-kankei-
no-aru [利害関係のある].
interesting (*a.*) omoshiroi [面白い].
interfere (*vi.*) jama-o-suru [邪魔をする]; kanshô-suru [干渉する].
interference (*n.*) jama [邪魔]; kanshô [干渉].
interior (*a.*) 1)naibu-no [内部の]; uchigawa-no [内側の]. 2)oku-chi-
no [奥地の]. 3)kokunai-no [国内の].
　　interior decoration(design) shitsunai-sôshoku
　　　　(*n.*) 1)naibu [内部]; uchigawa [内側]. 2)oku-chi [奥地];
nairiku [内陸]. 3)shitsunai [室内].
interjection (*n.*) 1)(*gram.*) kantô-shi [間投詞]. 2)kantan [感嘆].
intermediate (*a.*) chûkan-no [中間の].
　　　　(*n.*) chûkan-butsu [中間物].
intermission (*n.*) 1)kyûshi [休止]. 2)(*US theater*) maku-ai [幕間].
internal (*a.*) 1)naibu-no [内部の]; kokunai-no [国内の]. 2)honshitsu-
teki-na [本質的な].
　　　　(*n.*) 1)(*pl.*) naizô [内臓]. 2)naimen-teki-tokushitsu [内面的
特質].
internal-combustion engine nainen-kikan [内燃機関].
international (*a.*) kokusai-teki-na [国際的な].
interpret (*vt.*) 1)...o kaishaku-suru [⋯を解釈する]. 2)...o tsûyaku-
suru [⋯を通訳する].
　　　　(*vi.*) tsûyaku-suru [通訳する].
interpreter (*n.*) tsûyaku[-sha] [通訳(者)]; kaisetsu-sha [解説者].
interrogation (*n.*) shitsumon [質問]; gimon [疑問].
interrupt (*vt. & vi.*) (...no) jama-o-suru [(⋯の)邪魔をする]; (...o)
chûdan-suru [⋯を中断する].
　　　　(*n.*) (*computer*) warikomi [割り込み].
intersection (*n.*) (dôro no) kôsa-ten [(道路の)交差点].
interval (*n.*) 1)kankaku [間隔]. 2)(*theater*) maku-ai [幕間]; kyûkei-
jikan [休憩時間].
　　at intervals toki-doki; tokorodokoro-ni
interview (*n.*) mendan [面談]; intabyû [インタビュー].
　　　　(*vt.*) ...to mendan-suru [⋯と面談する]; ...ni intabyû-suru

[…にインタビューする].

intimate (*a.*) 1)shitashii [親しい]. 2)kuwashii [詳しい].
　　　　(*n.*) shin'yû [親友].

intimate (*vt.*) …o honomekasu […をほのめかす].

intimately (*ad.*) shitashiku [親しく]; kokoro-no-soko-kara [心の底から].

into (*prep.*) 1)…no-naka-e […の中へ]. 2)…ni(-kawaru) […に(変わる)]; …ni(-naru) […に(なる)].
　　　(*1*) I went **into** the room.　Watashi-wa heya-*no-naka-e* haitta.
　　　(*2*) Water turns **into** ice.　Mizu wa koori-*ni*-kawaru.

intolerable (*a.*) taerare-nai [耐えられない].

intonation (*n.*) (*phon.*) (koe no) yokuyô [(声の)抑揚]; intonêshon [イントネーション].

intoxicate (*vt.*) 1)…o yowaseru […を酔わせる]. 2)…o muchû-ni-saseru […を夢中にさせる].

intricate (*a.*) komi-itta [込み入った]; fukuzatsu-na [複雑な].

introduce (*vt.*) 1)…o shôkai-suru […を紹介する]. 2)…o tsutaeru […を伝える]. 3)…o ireru […を入れる]; …o sashi-komu […を差し込む].
　　　(*1*) Allow me to **introduce** my friend Mr. John to you.
　　　　　Watashi-no yûjin Jon-san-*o* go-*shôkai-itashi-masu*.
　　　(*2*) He **introduced** the latest method into his country.
　　　　　Kare-wa sai-shin-no hôhô-*o* kare-no-kuni-ni *tsutaeta*.
　　　(*3*) The doctor **introduced** a tube into the patient's throat.
　　　　　Isha wa kanja-no-nodo-ni kuda-*o* *sashi-konda*.

introduction (*n.*) 1)shôkai [紹介]. 2)dônyû [導入]. 3)joron [序論].

intrude (*vt.*) …ni shiiru […に強いる].
　　　　(*vi.*) oshi-iru [押し入る]; shinnyû-suru [侵入する].

inundate (*vt.*) …o mizu-bitashi-ni-suru […を水浸しにする]; …ni hanran-saseru […にはん濫させる].

invade (*vt.*) …ni shinnyû-suru […に侵入する].

invader (*n.*) shinnyû-sha [侵入者].

invalid (*a.*) byôjaku-na [病弱な].
　　　　(*n.*) byônin [病人].
　　　　(*vt.*) …o byôjaku-ni-suru […を病弱にする].

invalid chair byônin-yô-kuruma-isu [病人用車いす].

invaluable (*a.*) hakari-shire-nai-hodo-kichô-na [計り知れないほど貴重な].

invariably (*ad.*) kanarasu [かならず]; itsu-mo-kawara-nai-de [いつも変わらないで].

invasion (*n.*) shinnyû [侵入].

invent (*vt.*) ...o hatsumei-suru [...を発明する].

invention (*n.*) hatsumei[-hin] [発明(品)].

inventive (*a.*) hatsumei-no-sai-no-aru [発明の才のある]; kiyô-na [器用な].

inventor (*n.*) hatsumei-ka [発明家].

invest (*vt.*) 1)...o tôshi-suru [...を投資する]. 2)...ni sonawatte-iru [...に備わっている].

    (*vi.*) tôshi-suru [投資する].

investigate (*vt. & vi.*) (...o) chôsa-suru [(...を)調査する].

investigation (*n.*) chôsa [調査]; kenkyû [研究]; chôsa-hôkoku [調査報告].

investment (*n.*) 1)tôshi [投資]; shusshi[-kin] [出資(金)]. 2)fuyo [賦与].

invisible (*a.*) me-ni-mie-nai [目に見えない].

invitation (*n.*) shôtai[-jô] [招待(状)]; kan'yû [勧誘].

invite (*vt.*) ...o shôtai-suru [...を招待する]; ...ni susumeru [...に勧める].

    (*n.*) (*colloq.*) shôtai[-jô] [招待(状)].

invoice (*n.*) (*com.*) okuri-jô [送り状].

    (*vt.*) ...ni okuri-jô-o-okuru [...に送り状を送る].

involuntary (*a.*) 1)mu-ishiki-no [無意識の]. 2)fu-hon'i-no [不本意の].

involve (*vt.*) 1)...o fukumu [...を含む]. 2)...ni maki-komu [...に巻きこむ].

inward (*a. & ad.*) naibu-no(-e) [内部の(へ)]; kokoro-no-naka-no(-e) [心の中の(へ)].

    (*n.*) (*pl.*)(*colloq.*) naizô [内臓].

iodine (*n.*) (*colloq.*) yôdochinki [ヨードチンキ].

IOU, I.O.U. shakuyô-shôsho [借用証書].

Iran (*n.*) Iran [イラン].

Iranian (*a.*) Iran-no [イランの]; Iran-jin-no [イラン人の]; Perusha-go-no [ペルシャ語の].

    (*n.*) Iran-jin [イラン人]; Perusha-go [ペルシャ語].

Iraq (*n.*) Iraku [イラク].

Iraqi (*a.*) Iraku-no [イラクの]; Iraku-jin-no [イラク人の]; Iraku-go-no [イラク語の].

    (*n.*) Iraku-jin [イラク人]; Iraku-go [イラク語].

Ireland (*n.*) Airurando [アイルランド].

iris (*n.*) (*bot.*) ayame [アヤメ].

Irish (*a.*) Airurando-no [アイルランドの]; Airurando-jin-no [アイルランド人の]; Airurando-go-no [アイルランド語の].

    (*n.*) Airurando-jin [アイルランド人]; Airurando-go [アイルランド語].

iron (*n.*) 1)tetsu [鉄]. 2)kote [こて]; airon [アイロン].

    (*a.*) tetsu-no [鉄の].

    (*vt.*) ...ni airon-o-kakeru [...にアイロンをかける].

ironic, -ical (*a.*) hiniku-na [皮肉な].

irony (*n.*) hiniku [皮肉]; hango [反語]; hiniku-na-jitai [皮肉な事態].

irrational (*a.*) fu-gôri-na [不合理な]; risei-no-nai [理性のない].

irregular (*a.*) 1)fu-kisoku-na [不規則な]; fu-zoroi-na [不ぞろいな]. 2)fuhô-na [不法な].

    (*n.*) fu-kisoku-na-hito[-mono] [不規則な人[もの]].

irregularity (*n.*) 1)fu-kisoku [不規則]; fu-zoroi [不ぞろい]. 2)hansoku [反則].

irrigation (*n.*) kangai [かんがい].

irritable (*a.*) okorippoi [怒りっぽい]; tanki-na [短気な].

irritate (*vt.*) ...o ira-ira-saseru [...をいらいらさせる]; ...o okoraseru [...を怒らせる].

irritation (*n.*) 1)iradachi [いらだち]; okoraseru-koto [怒らせること]. 2)(*path.*) shigeki [刺激]; enshô [炎症].

is (*vi.*) 1)...de-aru [...である]; aru [ある]; iru [いる]. 2)...(suru-)koto-ni-natte-iru [...(する)ことになっている]; ...(su-)beki-de-aru [...(す)べきである]; ...(suru-)hazu-de-aru [...(する)はずである]. 3)...rareru [...られる]. 4)...(shi-)tsutsu-aru [...(し)つつある].

    (*1*) This is a dog. Kore-wa inu-*de-aru.*

        She is in Nagoya. Kano-jo-wa Nagoya-ni *iru.*

    (*2*) He is to go. Kare-wa iku-*koto-ni-natte-iru.*

        The meeting is to be held today.

            Kai wa kyô hirakareru-*hazu-de-aru.*

    (*3*) Wine is made from grapes.

        Budô-shu wa budô-kara tsuku*rareru.*

    (*4*) The moon is rising. Tsuki ga nobori-*tsutsu-aru.*

island (*n.*) shima [島].

isle (*n.*) ko-jima [小島].

isolate (*vt.*) ...o koritsu-saseru [...を孤立させる]; ...o kakuri-suru [...を隔離する].

Israel (*n.*) Isuraeru[-kyôwa-koku][イスラエル(共和国)].

issue (*n.*) 1)hakkô[発行]. 2)...gô[…号]. 3)ronten[論点].
  (*vt.*) ...o dasu[…を出す]; ...o hakkô-suru[…を発行する].
  (*vi.*) deru[出る].

isthmus (*n.*) chikyô[地峡].

it (*pron.*) 1)sore-wa[それは]; sore-ga[それが]; sore-ni[それに];
  sore-o[それを]. 2)tenkô[天候]; toki[時]; kyori[距離] nado[な
  ど]. 3)...no-wa[…のは]; ...koto-wa[…ことは].
  (*1*) What is **it**? *Sore-wa* nan-desu-ka?
  (*2*) **It** is cold today. Kyô wa samui.
    It is 3 o'clock. Ima san-ji desu.
    It is 3 miles to the station. Eki-made sam-mairu desu.
  (*3*) **It** is certain that we shall succeed.
      Ware-ware-ga seikô-suru-*koto-wa* kakujitsu-da.

Italian (*a.*) Itaria-no[イタリアの]; Itaria-jin-no[イタリア人の]; Itaria-
  go-no[イタリア語の].
    (*n.*) Itaria-jin[イタリア人]; Itaria-go[イタリア語].

Italy (*n.*) Itaria[イタリア]. 「yokubô[欲望].

itch (*n.*) 1)kayumi[かゆみ]; (the –) kaisen[かいせん]. 2)(*colloq.*)
  (*vi.*) kayui[かゆい]; (*colloq.*) muzu-muzu-suru[むずむずする].
  (*vt.*) ...o kayuku-suru[…をかゆくする]; ...o ira-ira-saseru[…を
  いらいらさせる].

item (*n.*) 1)kajô[箇条]; kômoku[項目]. 2)himmoku[品目].

itemize (*vt.*) ...o kajô-gaki-ni-suru[…を箇条書きにする]; ...o
  kômoku-ni-wakeru[…を項目に分ける].

itinerary (*n.*) ryotei[旅程]; ryokô-annai-sho[旅行案内書].
    (*a.*) ryotei-no[旅程の].

its (*pron.*) sore-no[それの].

itself (*pron.*) sore-jishin(-o/-ni)[それ自身(を/に)].

ivory (*n.*) zôge[象げ].

ivy (*n.*) (*bot.*) tsuta[ツタ].

J

jacket (*n.*) jaketto [ジャケット].
jack-in-the-box (*n.*) bikkuri-bako [びっくり箱].
jade (*n.*) hisui [ひすい].
jail (*n.*) keimu-sho [刑務所].
   break jail datsugoku-suru
     (*vt.*) ...o tôgoku-suru [...を投獄する].
jailer, -or (*n.*) kanshu [看守].
jam (*n.*) jamu [ジャム].
jam (*vt.*) ...o fusagu [...をふさぐ]; ...o bôgai-suru [...を妨害する].
   (*vi.*) muragaru [群がる]; oshi-au [押し合う].
   be jammed with ...de ippai-de-aru
     (*n.*) 1)zattô [雑踏]. 2)(*colloq.*) kukyô [苦境].
jam-packed (*a.*) gyû-gyû-zume-no [ぎゅうぎゅう詰めの].
January (*n.*) Ichigatsu [一月].
japan (*n.*) urushi [漆]; shikki [漆器].
     (*vt.*) ...ni urushi-o-nuru [...に漆を塗る].
Japan (*n.*) Nihon [日本]; Nippon [日本].
Japanese (*a.*) Nihon-no [日本の]; Nihon-jin-no [日本人の]; Nihon-go-no [日本語の].
     (*n.*) Nihon-jin [日本人]; Nihon-go [日本語].
jar (*n.*) tsubo [つぼ]; bin [瓶].

jaundice (*n.*) (*med.*) ôdan [黄だん].

javelin (*n.*) (the -) yari-nage [やり投げ]. yari [やり].

jaw (*n.*) ago [あご].

jawbone (*n.*) shita-ago-no-hone [下あごの骨].

jawbreaker (*n.*) (*colloq.*) hatsuon-shi-nikui-kotoba [発音しにくいことば].

jazz (*n. & vi.*) jazu(-o-ensô-suru) [ジャズ(を演奏する)].

jealous (*a.*) 1)shitto-bukai [しっと深い]. 2)netanda [ねたんだ].

jealousy (*n.*) shitto [しっと]; netami [ねたみ].

jeer (*n.*) azakeri [あざけり].
　　(*vi. & vt.*) (...o) azakeru [(…を)あざける].

jellyfish (*n.*) (*zool.*) kurage [クラゲ].

jerk (*vt.*) ...o gui-to-hiku […をぐいと引く]; ...o gui-to-osu […をぐい
と押す]; ...o gui-to-tsuku […をぐいと突く].
　　(*vi.*) kyû-ni-ugoku [急に動く]; gatan-to-ugoku [がたんと動く].
　　(*n.*) kyû-ni-hiku-koto [急に引くこと]; kyû-ni-tsuku-koto [急に突
くこと].

jersey (*n.*) jâjî [ジャージー].

jest (*n.*) 1)jôdan [冗談]. 2)mono-warai-no-tane [物笑いの種].
　in jest jôdan-ni
　　(*vi.*) jôdan-o-iu [冗談を言う].

Jesuit (*n.*) Iezusu-kai-shi [イエズス会士].

Jesus (*n.*) Iesu [イエス].

jet (*n.*) 1)funshutsu [噴出]; funshutsu-guchi [噴出口]. 2) = jet plane
jetto-ki [ジェット機].

jet-propelled (*a.*) jetto-suishin-shiki-no [ジェット推進式の].

Jew (*n.*) Yudaya-jin [ユダヤ人]; Yudaya-kyô-to [ユダヤ教徒].

jewel (*n.*) hôseki [宝石]; sôshin-gu [装身具].

jewel(l)er (*n.*) hôseki-shô [宝石商]; hôseki-shokunin [宝石職人].

jewel(l)ry (*n.*) hôseki-rui [宝石類].

jingle (*n. & vi.*) chirin-chirin(-naru) [ちりんちりん(鳴る)]; rin-rin
(-naru) [りんりん(鳴る)].

job (*n.*) 1)shigoto [仕事]; (*colloq.*) shoku [職]. 2)shigoto-no-seika
[仕事の成果].

jog (*vt.*) ...o chotto-osu […をちょっと押す]; ...o sotto-tsuku […をそっ
と突く].
　　(*vi.*) tobo-tobo-aruku [とぼとぼ歩く]; jogingu-suru [ジョギングす
る].
　　(*n.*) 1)yure [揺れ]. 2)karui-shigeki [軽い刺激].

join (*vt.*) 1)...o musubi-tsuketu [⋯を結び付ける]. 2)...ni sanka-suru [⋯に参加する]; ...ni kuwawaru [⋯に加わる].

　　(*vi.*) 1)musubi-tsuku [結び付く]; tsunagaru [つながる]. 2)sanka-suru [参加する]; kuwawaru [加わる].

　　(*n.*) setsugô-ten [接合点].

joint (*n.*) 1)tsugi-me [継ぎ目]. 2)(*anat.*) kansetsu [関節].

joke (*n. & vi.*) jôdan(-o-iu) [冗談(を言う)].

jolly (*a.*) yôki-na [陽気な]; yukai-na [愉快な]; (*colloq.*) tanoshii [楽しい].

　　(*ad.*) (*Eng. colloq.*) totemo [とても].

jostle (*vt.*) ...o osu [⋯を押す]; ...o tsuku [⋯を突く].

　　(*vi.*) oshi-au [押し合う]; oshi-wakete-susumu [押し分けて進む].

jot (*n.*) sukoshi [少し].

　　(*vt.*) ...o kantan-ni-kaki-tomeru [⋯を簡単に書きとめる].

journal (*n.*) 1)nikkan-shimbun [日刊新聞]; zasshi [雑誌]. 2)nikki [日記].

journalism (*n.*) jânarizumu [ジャーナリズム]; shimbun-zasshi-hôsô-gyô [新聞雑誌放送業].

journalist (*n.*) shimbun-zasshi-kisha [新聞雑誌記者]; shimbun-zasshi-no-kikô-ka [新聞雑誌の寄稿家]; jânarisuto [ジャーナリスト].

journey (*n. & vi.*) tabi(-o-suru) [旅(をする)]; ryokô(-o-suru) [旅行(をする)].

joy (*n.*) yorokobi [喜び]; kanki [歓喜].

joyful (*a.*) (= joyous) yorokobashii [喜ばしい]; ureshii [うれしい].

joyfully (*ad.*) (= joyously) ureshi-sô-ni [うれしそうに].

judge (*n.*) 1)saiban-kan [裁判官]. 2)shimpan[-in] [審判(員)]. 3)kantei-ka [鑑定家].

　　(*vi.*) saiban-o-suru [裁判をする].

　　(*vt.*) ...no hanketsu-o-kudasu [⋯の判決を下す]; ...o handan-suru [⋯を判断する].

　judge one by... hito-o...ni-yotte handan-suru

　judging from ...kara-sassuru-to

judg(e)ment (*n.*) 1)saiban [裁判]; hanketsu [判決]. 2)handan [-ryoku] [判断(力)]. 3)tembatsu [天罰]; batsu [罰]. 4)iken [意見].

judicial (*a.*) 1)shihô-no [司法の]; saiban-no [裁判の]. 2)hihan-teki-na [批判的な].

jug (*n.*) mizu-sashi [水差し]; jagu [ジャグ].

juggler (*n.*) 1)tejina-shi [手品師]. 2)sagi-shi [詐欺師].

juice (*n.*) shiru [汁]; eki [液]; jûsu [ジュース].

juicy (*a.*) 1)shiru-no-ooi [汁の多い]; suibun-no-ooi [水分の多い]. 2) (*colloq.*) kyômi-o-sosoru [興味をそそる].

July (*n.*) Shichigatsu [七月].

jump (*vi.*) tobu [跳ぶ]; tobi-agaru [跳び上がる].

   He **jumped** across a ditch. Kare-wa mizo-o *tobi*-koeta.

   I **jumped** down from it. Watashi-wa sore-kara *tobi*-orita.

   (*vt.*) ...o tobi-koeru […を跳び越える].

   jump about hane-mawaru

   jump at ...ni tobi-tsuku

   jump on(upon) ...ni tobi-kakaru

   jump the queue jumban-o-mata-nai-de-saki-dori-suru; retsu-ni-wari-komu

   (*n.*) 1)chôyaku [跳躍]. 2)kyûtô [急騰].

   at a jump hito-tobi-de

jumper (*n.*) (*sports*) chôyaku-senshu [跳躍選手].

jumper (*n.*) jampâ [ジャンパー].

junction (*n.*) 1)renraku[-eki] [連絡(駅)]. 2)setsugô[-ten] [接合(点)].

June (*n.*) Rokugatsu [六月].

jungle (*n.*) (*nettai-no*) mitsurin [(熱帯の)密林]; janguru [ジャングル].

junior (*a.*) toshi-shita-no [年下の].

   (*n.*) 1)nenshô-sha [年少者]; kôhai [後輩]. 2)((*US*)) daigaku-san-nen-sei [大学三年生].

junior high school chûgakkô [中学校].

junk (*n.*) 1)(*colloq.*) garakuta [がらくた]. 2)(*marine*) janku [ジャンク].

jury (*n.*) baishin[-in-dan] [陪審(員団)].

jury box baishin-in-seki [陪審員席].

just (*a.*) 1)kôsei-na [公正な]. 2)seikaku-na [正確な]; seitô-na [正当な]; tôzen-no [当然の].

   (*1*) He was a wise and **just** man.

      Kare-wa kemmei-de *kôsei-na* hito datta.

   (*2*) It was a **just** comment. Sore-wa *seitô-na* hihyô datta.

   (*ad.*) 1)masa-ni [まさに]; chôdo [ちょうど]. 2)yatto [やっと]; yôyaku [ようやく]. 3)chotto [ちょっと]. 4)ima... hon-no [ほんの]. 4)ima... (shita-) bakari [いま…(した)ばかり]. 5)chotto [ちょっと]. 6) (*colloq.*) mattaku [全く].

   (*1*) It is **just** as you say. Sore-wa *masa-ni*-ossharu-toori-da.

Just then the headlights went off.

Chôdo sono-toki heddoraito ga kieta.

(*2*) We were **just** in time. Ware-ware-wa *yatto* ma-ni-atta.

(*3*) Give me **just** a little more. *Hon-no* mô-sukoshi kudasai.

(*4*) I have **just** finished writing it.

Watashi-wa *ima* sore-o kaki-oeta-*bakari*-da.

(*5*) **Just** show it to me. *Chotto* sore-o misete-kudasai.

(*6*) It is **just** splendid. Sore-wa *mattaku* subarashii.

just now chôdo-ima

just so mattaku-sono-toori-ni

justice (*n.*) 1)seigi [正義]; kôsei [公正]. 2)saiban [裁判].

(*1*) **Justice** ever has been and ever will be pursued.

Seigi wa kore-made tsune-ni motome-rarete-kita, soshite
kongo-mo tsune-ni motome-rareru-darô.

(*2*) They brought robbers to **justice**.

Kare-ra-wa gôtô-tachi-o *saiban*-ni kaketa.

do...justice ...o kôhei-ni-hyôka-suru

justify (*vt.*) ...o seitô-ka-suru [...を正当化する]; ...o bemmei-suru [...
を弁明する].

justly (*ad.*) tadashiku [正しく]; kôsei-ni [公正に].

juvenile (*a.*) shônen-shôjo-muki-no [少年少女向きの].

(*n.*) 1)shônen [少年]; shôjo [少女]. 2)jidô-muki-no-hon [児
童向きの本].

K

kangaroo (*n.*) (*zool.*) kangarû [カンガルー].

keen (*a.*) 1)surudoi [鋭い]; hageshii [激しい]. 2)mi-o-kiru-yô-na [身を切るような]. 3)eiri-na [鋭利な]. 4)nesshin-na [熱心な].

(*1*) The dog has **keen** scent.

     Inu wa *surudoi* kyûkaku-o motte-iru.

    The wound gave me **keen** pangs.

     Sono kizu ga watashi-ni *hageshii* itami-o ataeta.

(*2*) a **keen** wind   *mi-o-kiru-yô-na* kaze

(*3*) This knife has a **keen** edge.

     Kono naifu niwa *eiri-na* ha-ga aru.

(*4*) She is **keen** on tennis.   Kano-jo-wa tenisu-ni *nesshin*-da.

keenly (*ad.*) surudoku [鋭く]; hageshiku [激しく]; nesshin-ni [熱心に].

keep (*vt.*) 1)...o tamotsu [...を保つ]. 2)...o shimatte-oku [...をしまっておく]; ...o hozon-suru [...を保存する]. 3)...o yashinau [...を養う]. 4)...o kau [...を飼う]. 5)...o keiei-suru [...を経営する]. 6)...o mamoru [...を守る]. 7)...o...ni-(shite)oku [...を...に(して)おく]. 8) ...o ryûchi-suru [...を留置する]. 9)...o tsukeru [...をつける]. 10)...o kakusu [...を隠す]. 11)...o mamoru [...を守る]; ...no ban-o-suru [...の番をする].

(*1*) My watch **keeps** very good time.

     Watashi-no tokei wa totemo yoku jikan-*o tamotsu*.

Watashi-no tokei wa totemo yoku au.

(2) You may **keep** it in a dark place.

Sore wa kurai-tokoro-ni *shimatte-oku*-hô-ga-yoi.

(3) He **keeps** four children.

Kare-wa yo-nin-no kodomo-o *yashinatte-iru*.

(4) My daughter **keeps** a dog.

Watashi-no musume wa inu-o ippiki *katte-iru*.

(5) He **keeps** an inn in Takayama.

Kare-wa Takayama-de ryokan-o *keiei-shite-iru*.

(6) I **keep** my promise. Watashi-wa yakusoku-o *mamoru*.

(7) **Keep** the window open. Mado-o akete-*oki-nasai*.

(8) The pickpocket **was kept** in the lockup.

Suri wa ryûchi-jô-ni *irete-okareta*.

(9) I **keep** a diary every day.

Watashi-wa mai-nichi nikki-o *tsukeru*.

(10) Don't **keep** your secrets. Himitsu-o *kakushite-oku*-na.

(11) He **keeps** the goal. Kare-wa gôru-o *mamotte-iru*.

(*vi.*) 1)motsu [もつ]. 2)...(shi-)tsuzukeru [⋯(し)続ける].

(1) This pork will **keep** for a few days.

Kono buta-niku wa ni-san-nichi-wa *motsu*-darô.

(2) We **kept** standing all the time.

Watashi-tachi-wa zutto tachi-*tsuzuketa*.

keep away sakeru

You had better keep away from bad companions.

Warui tomodachi wa saketa-hô-ga-yoi.

keep from ...o sakeru

Keep from danger. Kiken-o sake-nasai.

keep...from ...(sa-)se-nai

You must keep him from smoking.

Kare-ni tabako-o-suwase-nai-yô-ni shi-nakereba-naranai.

keep off ...ni tachi-ira-nai

Keep off the grass. Shiba-fu-ni-tachi-iri-kinshi.

keep out naka-ni-hai-ra-nai

Under construction. Keep out. Kôji-chû. Tachi-iri-kinshi.

keep to ...ni shitagau

We must keep to the rule.

Ware-ware-wa kisoku-ni shitagawa-nakereba-naranai.

keep up with ...ni tsuite-iku

　　　I cannot keep up with you.　Kimi-ni-wa tsuite-ike-nai.

keeper (*n.*) 1)bannin [番人]; mamoru-hito [守る人]. 2)kanri-nin [管理人].

kennel (*n.*) inu-goya [犬小屋].

kernel (*n.*) 1)jin [仁]. 2)(mondai no) kakushin [(問題の)核心].

kerosene (*n.*) tôyu [灯油].

kettle (*n.*) yu-wakashi [湯沸かし]; yakan [やかん].

key (*n.*) 1)kagi [かぎ]. 2)(piano ya taipuraitâ no) ken; kî [(ピアノやタイプライターの)けん；キー]. 3)te-gakari [手がかり]; kaitô[-shû] [解答(集)].
　　　(*vt.*) 1)...ni kagi-o-kakeru [⋯にかぎを掛ける]. 2)...o awaseru [⋯を合わせる].

keyboard (*n.*) kemban [けん盤]; kîbôdo [キーボード].

keyhole (*n.*) kagi-ana [かぎ穴].

key industry kikan-sangyô [基幹産業].

keynote (*n.*) 1)(*mus.*) shuon [主音]. 2)yôshi [要旨]; kihon-hôshin [基本方針].
　　　(*vt.*) ...no kihon-hôshin-o-happyô-suru [⋯の基本方針を発表する]; ...o kyôchô-suru [⋯を強調する].

key punch ((*US*)) kî-panchi [キーパンチ].

keypunch (*vt.*) ...ni kî-panchi-de-ana-o-akeru [⋯にキーパンチで穴をあける].

keystone (*n.*) 1)kaname-ishi [かなめ石]. 2)kompon-genri [根本原理].

kick (*vt. & vi.*) (...o) keru [(⋯を)ける].

kid (*n.*) 1)ko-yagi[-no-kawa] [子やぎ(の皮)]. 2)(*colloq.*) kodomo [子供].

kidnap (*vt.*) ...o yûkai-suru [⋯を誘拐する].

kidney (*n.*) (*anat.*) jinzô [腎臓].

kill (*vt.*) 1)...o korosu [⋯を殺す]; ...o karasu [⋯を枯らす]. 2)(jikan)-o tsubusu [(時間)をつぶす].

　kill oneself jisatsu-suru

kin (*n.*) 1)shinzoku [親族]. 2)ketsuzoku-kankei [血族関係].

kind (*n.*) shurui [種類].
　　　What **kind** of vegetable do you like best?
　　　　Dô-iu-*shurui*-no-yasai-ga ichiban suki-desu-ka?

　a kind of isshu-no

　all kinds of arayuru-shurui-no

　kind of (*colloq.*) chotto; maa

kind (*a.*) shinsetsu-na [親切な].

    Be **kind** to strangers.

        Mi-shiranu-hito-ni-wa *shinsetsu-ni-shi-nasai.*

    Give my kind regards to …ni yoroshiku

kindhearted (*a.*) shinsetsu-na [親切な]; kokoro-no-yasashii [心の優し
い].

kindle (*vt. & vi.*) …ni hi-o-tsukeru (hi-ga-tsuku) […に火をつける（火
がつく）]; …o moyasu (moe-tsuku) […を燃やす（燃えつく）].

kindly (*ad.*) 1)shinsetsu-ni [親切に]. 2)dôzo [どうぞ].

    (*a.*) shinsetsu-na [親切な]; yasashii [優しい].

kindness (*n.*) shinsetsu [親切]; yasashi-sa [優しさ].

kindred (*n.*) shinrui [親類]; ketsuen-kankei [血縁関係].

    (*a.*) 1)dôrui-no [同類の]. 2)ketsuen-no [血縁の].

king (*n.*) [koku-]ô [(国)王].

kingdom (*n.*) 1)ôkoku [王国]. 2)…kai […界].

king-size(d) (*a.*) (*colloq.*) toku-dai-no [特大の]; kingu-saizu-no [キ
ングサイズの].

kiss (*n.*) kisu [キス].

    (*vt. & vi.*) (…ni) kisu-suru [(…に)キスする].

kitchen (*n.*) daidokoro [台所].

kitchen garden katei-saien [家庭菜園].

kite (*n.*) 1)(*birds*) tobi [トビ]. 2)tako [たこ].

kitten (*n.*) ko-neko [子ネコ].

knapsack (*n.*) hainô [背のう]; ryukkusakku [リュックサック].

knee (*n.*) hiza [ひざ].

    fall(go down) on one's knees hizamazuku

kneel (*vi.*) hizamazuku [ひざまずく].

knickerbockers (*n.*) yurui-han-zubon [ゆるい半ズボン]; nikkabokkâ
[ニッカボッカー].

knife (*n.*) naifu [ナイフ]; ko-gatana [小刀].

knight (*n.*) 1)((*Eng.*)) naito-shaku [ナイト爵]. 2)(*chûsei no*) kishi
[(中世の)騎士].

knit (*vt.*) 1)…o amu […を編む]. 2)…o ketsugô-suru […を結合する].
3)(mayu)-o shikameru [(まゆ)をしかめる].

    (*vi.*) ami-mono-o-suru [編み物をする]; musubi-tsuku [結び付く];
(mayu ga) yoru [(まゆが)寄る].

knitting (*n.*) ami-mono [編み物].

knob (*n.*) 1)kobu [こぶ]. 2)(doa no) nigiri [(ドアの)握り]; (rajio ya terebi no) tsumami [(ラジオやテレビの)つまみ].

knock (*vt. & vi.*) (...o) tataku [(…を)たたく]; (...o) nokku-suru [(…を)ノックする].

(*n.*) 1)tataku-koto[-oto] [たたくこと[音]]; nokku [ノック]. 2) (*mech.*)(enjin no) nokkingu [(エンジンの)ノッキング].

knockout (*n.*) (*boxing*) nokkauto [ノックアウト].

knot (*n.*) 1)musubi-me [結び目]. 2)(*marine*) notto [ノット]. 3) kazari-musubi [飾り結び]. 4)nan-mon[dai] [難問(題)].

(*vt.*) ...o musubu […を結ぶ]; ...ni musubi-me-o-tsukuru […に結び目を作る].

(*vi.*) musubareru [結ばれる].

know (*vt.*) 1)...o shitte-iru […を知っている]. 2)...o mi-wakeru […を見分ける].

(*1*) Do you **know** it? Anata-wa sono-koto-o *shitte-imasu*-ka?

(*2*) He could not **know** a sheep from a goat.

Kare-wa hitsuji-*o* yagi-to *mi-wakeru*-koto-ga-deki-nakatta.

(*vi.*) shiru [知る].

He **knows** better.

Kare-wa sonna-koto-gurai *shitte-iru*.

Kare-wa sonna baka-na koto wa shi-nai.

know of ...o shitte-iru

What do you know? (*US colloq.*) Masaka.

you know nee, ...deshô?

knowhow (*n.*) (*colloq.*) (mono-goto-o suru) gijutsu ; kotsu [(物事をする)技術；こつ]; nouhau [ノウハウ].

knowledge (*n.*) chishiki [知識]; ninshiki [認識].

knuckle (*n.*) yubi-no-kansetsu [指の関節].

Korea (*n.*) Chôsen [朝鮮].

Korean (*a.*) Chôsen-no [朝鮮の]; Chôsen-jin-no [朝鮮人の]; Chôsen-go-no [朝鮮語の].

(*n.*) Chôsen-jin [朝鮮人]; Chôsen-go [朝鮮語].

L

label (*n.*) hari-fuda [はり札]; fuda [札]; raberu [ラベル].
    (*vt.*) ...ni hari-fuda-o-haru [···にはり札を貼る]; ...ni raberu-o-haru [···にラベルを貼る].

labor, -bour (*n.*) 1)rôdô [労働]. 2)(hone-no-oreru) shigoto [(骨の折れる)仕事]. 3)rôdô-sha [労働者].
  (*1*) **Labor** is indispensable to production.
    Rôdô wa seisan-niwa kaku-koto-no-deki-nai-mono-da.
  (*2*) You should rest from your **labor**.
    Kimi-wa *shigoto*-o yasumu-beki-da.
       (*vi.*) rôdô-suru [労働する]; hataraku [働く].
       (*vt.*) 1)...o shôsai-ni-ronjiru [···を詳細に論じる]. 2)...ni omo-ni-o-owasu [···に重荷を負わす].

laboratory (*n.*) jikken-shitsu [実験室].

laborer (*n.*) rôdô-sha [労働者].

laborious (*a.*) 1)hone-no-oreru [骨の折れる]. 2)yoku-hataraku [よく働く].

labyrinth (*n.*) meikyû [迷宮]; meiro [迷路].

lace (*n.*) 1)rêsu [レース]. 2)(kutsu nado no) shime-himo [(くつなどの)締めひも].
    (*vt.*) 1)...o himo-de-musubu [···をひもで結ぶ]. 2)(himo nado)-o toosu [(ひもなど)を通す]. 3)...o fuchi-doru [···を縁取る].

    (*vi.*) himo-de-musuberu [ひもで結べる].

lack (*n.*) nai-koto [無いこと]; fusoku [不足]; ketsubô [欠乏].

    He could not go abroad for **lack** of money.

        Kare-wa kane-ga-*nai*-node gaikoku-e ike-nakatta.

    (*vt. & vi.*) ...o kaite-iru (kakete-iru) [...を欠いている(欠けている)]; ...ga fusoku-shite-iru (tari-nai) [...が不足している(足りない)].

    He **lacks** common sense.   Kare-wa jôshiki-*o kaite-iru*.

    Money **is lacking**.   Kane ga *tari-nai*.

lacquer (*n.*) rakkâ [ラッカー].

    (*vt.*) ...ni rakkâ-o-nuru [...にラッカーを塗る].

lad (*n.*) shônen [少年]; waka-mono [若者].

ladder (*n.*) 1)hashigo [はしご]. 2)(shusse no)te-zuru [(出世の)手づる].

lady (*n.*) shukujo [淑女]; go-fujin [ご婦人].

ladybug, ladybird (*n.*) (*insect*) tentô-mushi [テントウムシ].

lag (*vi.*) noro-noro-aruku [のろのろ歩く]; okureru [遅れる].

    (*n.*) okureru-koto [遅れること].

lake (*n.*) mizuumi [湖]; kosui [湖水].

lamb (*n.*) ko-hitsuji[-no-niku] [子羊(の肉)].

lame (*a.*) 1)ashi-no-fu-jiyû-na [足の不自由な]. 2)settoku-ryoku-no-nai [説得力のない]. 3)fu-kanzen-na [不完全な].

    (*vt. & vi.*) ...o-fu-jiyû-ni-suru (fu-jiyû-ni-naru) [...を不自由にする(不自由になる)].

lament (*vt. & vi.*) (...o) nageku [(...を)嘆く]; (...o) kanashimu [(...を)悲しむ].

    (*n.*) hitan [悲嘆]; hika [悲歌].

lamentable (*a.*) nagekawashii [嘆かわしい]; kanashimu-beki [悲しむべき].

lamentation (*n.*) hitan [悲嘆]; aitô [哀悼].

lamp (*n.*) rampu [ランプ]; akari [明かり].

lance (*n.*) yari [やり].

    (*vt.*) ...o tsuku [...を突く].

land (*n.*) riku-chi [陸地]; tochi [土地]; kuni [国].

    At last he discovered **land**.

        Tôtô kare-wa *riku-chi-o* mitsuketa.

    by land rikuro-de

    (*vi.*) 1)jôriku-suru [上陸する]. 2)chakuriku-suru [着陸する].

    (*vt.*) 1)...o riku-age-suru [...を陸揚げする]. 2)...o gesha-saseru [...を下車させる].

(2) He **was landed** at the station.　Kare-wa eki-de *oro-sareta*.

landing (*n.*) 1)jôriku [上陸]; chakuriku [着陸]. 2)riku-age [陸揚げ];
riku-age-ba [陸揚げ場]. 3)(kaidan no) odori-ba [(階段の)踊り場].
　(1) a forced **landing**　fuji-*chaku*[*riku*]
　　　　a soft **landing**　nan-*chakuriku*

landlord (*n.*) ryokan-no-shujin [旅館の主人]; yanushi [家主]; jinushi
[地主].

landscape (*n.*) fûkei[-ga] [風景(画)].

landslide (*n.*) ji-suberi [地すべり]; yama-kuzure [山くずれ].

lane (*n.*) 1)ko-michi [小道]; roji [路地]. 2)shasen [車線].

language (*n.*) gengo [言語]; ...go […語].

languid (*a.*) 1)darui [だるい]; mono-ui [ものうい]. 2)kakki-no-nai
[活気のない].

languish (*vi.*) genki-ga-naku-naru [元気がなくなる]; otoroeru [衰える];
dareru [だれる]; shioreru [しおれる].

lantern (*n.*) chôchin [ちょうちん]; kakutô [角灯].

lap (*n.*) hiza [ひざ].
　　(*vt.*) ...o kasaneru […を重ねる]; ...o tsutsumu […を包む].
　　(*vi.*) ori-kasanaru [折り重なる]; tsutsumareru [包まれる].

lap (*vt.*) ...o nameru […をなめる].
　　(*vi.*) (nami ga) hita-hita-to-uchi-yoseru [(波が)ひたひたと打ち寄
せる].

lapse (*n.*) 1)chotto-shita-machigai [ちょっとした間違い]. 2)keika [経
過].
　(1) a **lapse** of the tongue　ii-*chigai*
　(2) a **lapse** of time　toki no *keika*

lap time rappu-taimu [ラップタイム].

lard (*n.*) râdo [ラード].
　　(*vt.*) ...ni râdo-o-hiku […にラードを引く].

large (*a.*) ookii [大きい].
　at large 1)tsukamara-nai-de. 2)ippan-no; zentai-to-shite-no
　1) The thief is still at large.　Dorobô wa mada tsukamara-nai.
　2) the nation at large　kokumin-ippan

largely (*ad.*) 1)ooi-ni [大いに]. 2)omo-ni [主に].

large-scale (*a.*) dai-kibo-na [大規模な].

lark (*n.*) (*birds*) hibari [ヒバリ].

larva (*n.*) (*insect*) yôchû [幼虫].

lash (*n.*) 1)utsu-koto [打つこと]. 2)(*pl.*) matsuge [まつげ].

    (*vt.*) 1)...o (muchi-)utsu [···を(むち)打つ]. 2)...o hageshiku-ugokasu [···を激しく動かす].

    (*vi.*) hageshiku-ugoku [激しく動く].

lass (*n.*) shôjo [少女].

last (*a.*) 1)saigo-no [最後の]. 2)kono-mae-no [この前の].

  (*1*) the **last** day of the month tsuki no *saigo-no* hi

                            getsumatsu

  (*2*) **last** Sunday *kono-mae-no* Nichiyô-bi

                    senshû-no Nichiyô-bi

    (*ad.*) saigo-ni [最後に]; kono-mae [この前].

  last of all ichiban-owari-ni; saigo-ni

    (*n.*) (the –) 1)saigo-no-hito[-mono/-koto] [最後の人[もの／こと]].

  2)ketsumatsu [結末]; owari [終わり].

  at last tsui-ni; tôtô

  at long last yatto-no-koto-de

last (*vi.*) tsuzuku [続く].

      The festival **lasts** a week. Matsuri wa isshû-kan *tsuzuku*.

    (*vt.*) ...o mochi-kotaesaseru [···を持ちこたえさせる].

      The coat **lasted** me three years.

        Uwagi wa mô san-nen *motta*.

latch (*n.*) kake-gane [掛け金].

    (*vt.*) ...ni kake-gane-o-kakeru [···に掛け金をかける].

late (*a.*) 1)osoi [遅い]; okureta [遅れた]. 2)ko... [故···].

  of late chikagoro; saikin

    (*ad.*) osoku [遅く]; okurete [遅れて].

lately (*ad.*) chikagoro [近ごろ]; saikin [最近].

latent (*a.*) kakureta [隠れた]; senzai-no [潜在の].

later (*ad.*) ato-de [あとで]; nochi-hodo [後ほど].

  later on ato-de

  sooner or later itsu-ka-wa; sôban; osokare-hayakare

latest (*a.*) saikin-no [最近の]; saishin-no [最新の].

  at (the) latest osoku-tomo

Latin (*n.*) Raten-go [ラテン語].

latitude (*n.*) ido [緯度].

latter (*a.*) 1)ato-no [あとの]; kôsha-no [後者の]. 2)(the –) kôsha [後者].

lattice (*n.*) kôshi[-mado] [格子(窓)].

laudable (*a.*) appare-na [あっぱれな]; kanshin-na [感心な].

laugh (*vi.*) warau [笑う].

  laugh at 1)...o mite-warau; ...o kiite-warau. 2)...o azawarau

    (*vt.*) 1)...na-warai-kata-o-suru [···な笑い方をする]. 2)waratte...

  ni suru [笑って···にする].

    (*n.*) 1)warai [笑い]. 2)(*pl.*) ki-barashi [気晴らし].

laughter (*n.*) warai[-goe] [笑い(声)].

launch (*vt.*) ...o shinsui-saseru [···を進水させる]; ...o hassha-suru [···を発射する].

    (*vi.*) hajimeru [始める]; hasshin-suru [発進する].

launch (*n.*) (*marine*) kitei [汽艇]; ranchi [ランチ].

laundry (*n.*) sentakuya [洗濯屋]; sentaku-mono [洗濯もの].

laurel (*n.*) 1)(*bot.*) gekkei-ju [月桂樹]. 2)(*pl.*) eikan [栄冠].

lava (*n.*) yôgan [溶岩].

lavatory (*n.*) 1)semmen-jo [洗面所]. 2)benjo [便所].

lavish (*vt.*) ...o ki-mae-yoku-tsukau [···を気前よく使う]; ...o rôhi-suru [···を浪費する].

    (*a.*) ki-mae-no-yoi [気前のよい]; rôhi-guse-no-aru [浪費癖のある].

law (*n.*) hôritsu [法律]; hôsoku [法則]; ...hô [···法].

lawful (*a.*) gôhô-no [合法の]; hôtei-no [法定の].

lawless (*a.*) muhô-no [無法の].

lawn (*n.*) shiba-fu [芝生].

lawsuit (*n.*) soshô [訴訟].

lawyer (*n.*) hôritsu-ka [法律家]; bengo-shi [弁護士].

lay (*vt.*) 1)...o yokotaeru [···を横たえる]; ...o oku [···を置く]. 2)(tamago)-o umu [(卵)を産む].

  (*1*) The nurse **laid** the patient on the bed.

    Kango-fu wa kanja-o beddo-ni *nekaseta*.

  (*2*) Every other day the hen **laid** an egg.

    Kakujitsu-ni men-dori wa tamago-o *unda*.

  lay aside 1)...o takuwaeru. 2) = give up

  1) She laid aside a large amount of money for her son.

    Kano-jo-wa musuko-no-tame-ni taikin-o takuwaeta.

  lay down ...o suteru

    They laid down their arms. Kare-ra-wa buki-o suteta.

                     Kare-ra-wa kôsan-shita.

  lay on 1)...o kasu. 2)...o nuru. 3) osou

  1) Heavy taxes were laid on. Jûzei ga kaserareta.

  lay out ...no sekkei-o-suru; ...o chinretsu-suru; (*colloq.*) ...o tsukau

　lay up ...o takuwaete-oku; (be laid) ne-komu

layer (*n.*) (kasanatte-iru mono no) sô [(重なっているものの)層].

layoff (*n.*) ichiji-teki-kaiko [一時的解雇]; reiofu [レイオフ].

layout (*n.*) sekkei [設計]; reiauto [レイアウト].

lazily (*ad.*) namakete [怠けて]; norakura-to [のらくらと].

lazy (*a.*) taida-na [怠惰な]; bushô-na [無精な].

lead (*vt.*) 1)...o michibiku [⋯を導く]; ...o annai-suru [⋯を案内する].
　2)...no sentô-ni-tatsu [⋯の先頭に立つ]. 3)...o okuru [⋯を送る].
　(*1*) She will **lead** you into the room.
　　　　Kano-jo-ga sono-heya-ni anata-*o annai-suru*-deshô.
　(*2*) She **led** the way. Kano-jo-ga *sentô-ni-tatte* annai-shita.
　(*3*) I wish to **lead** a quiet life.
　　　　Watashi-wa shizuka-na seikatsu-*o okuri*-tai.
　　(*vi.*) 1)annai-suru [案内する]; sendô-suru [先導する]. 2)tsûjiru
　[通じる]; itaru [至る].
　(*2*) This path **leads** to his house.
　　　　Kono michi wa kare-no-ie-ni *tsûjite-iru.*
　　(*n.*) 1)sendô [先導]; shiki [指揮]. 2)rîdo [リード].
　take the lead sentô-ni-tatsu

lead (*n.*) namari [鉛].

leaden (*a.*) namari-no [鉛の]; namari-iro-no [鉛色の].

leader (*n.*) sendô-sha [先導者]; shiki-sha [指揮者]; ridâ [リーダー].

leadership (*n.*) shidô [指導]; shiki [指揮]; tôsotsu[-ryoku] [統率(力)].

leading (*n.*) sendô [先導]; shidô [指導].
　　(*a.*) shidô-teki-na [指導的な]; shuyô-na [主要な].

leadoff (*a.*) saisho-no [最初の]; sentô-no [先頭の].
　　(*n.*) 1)kaishi [開始]. 2)saisho-ni-yaru-hito [最初にやる人].

leaf (*n.*) 1)ki-no-ha [木の葉]. 2)(shomotsu no) ichi-mai [(書物の)一
　枚]. 3)haku [箔].

leafy (*a.*) ha-no-shigetta [葉の茂った].

league (*n.*) dômei [同盟]; remmei [連盟]; rîgu [リーグ].

leak (*n.*) more[-guchi] [漏れ(口)].
　　(*vt. & vi.*) ...o morasu (moreru) [⋯を漏らす(漏れる)].

lean (*a.*) yaseta [やせた].

lean (*vi.*) 1)yori-kakaru [寄りかかる]; motareru [もたれる]. 2)jôtai-
　o-mageru [上体を曲げる].
　(*1*) The old man **leaned** on his son's arm.

        Sono rôjin wa musuko-no-ude-ni *motareta*.

(2) She **leaned** out at the window.

        Kano-jo-wa mado-kara *jôtai-o-noridashite-ita*.

    (*vt.*) ...o motase-kakeru [···をもたせかける]; ...o tate-kakeru [···を立てかける].

    I **leaned** it against the wall.

        Watashi-wa sore-o kabe-ni *tate-kaketa*.

leaning (*n.*) keikô [傾向].

leap (*vi.*) tobu [跳ぶ].

    He **leaped** for joy.   Kare-wa yorokonde *tobi-agatta*.

    (*vt.*) ...o tobi-koeru [···を跳び越える]; ...ni tobi-koesaseru [···に飛び越えさせる].

    (*n.*) chôyaku [跳躍].

leap year uruu-doshi [うるう年].

learn (*vt. & vi.*) (...o) manabu [(···を)学ぶ]; (...o) oboeru [(···を)覚える]; (...o) shiru [(···を)知る].

learned (*a.*) gakumon-no-aru [学問のある].

learning (*n.*) 1) manabu-koto [学ぶこと]. 2) gakumon [学問]; gakushiki [学識].

lease (*n.*) 1) chin-taishaku-keiyaku [賃貸借契約]; shakuchi-keiyaku [借地契約]; shakuya-keiyaku [借家契約]. 2) shakuyô-kikan [借用期間].

    (*vt.*) ...o chintai-suru [···を賃貸する]; ...o chinshaku-suru [···を賃借する].

least (*a.*) saishô-no [最小の]; mottomo-sukunai [最も少ない].

    There isn't the **least** wind today.

        Kyô-wa kaze ga *sukoshi-mo*-nai.

    (*ad.*) mottomo-sukunaku [最も少なく].

    (*n.*) saishô [最小].

    It is the **least** I can do for her.

        Sore-ga kano-jo-ni-shite-yareru *saishô*-gen-no-koto-da.

  at (the) least sukunaku-tomo

  not in the least chittomo...nai

leather (*n.*) nameshi-gawa [なめし革].

    (*vt.*) ...o nameshi-gawa-ni-suru [···をなめし革にする].

leave (*vt.*) 1)...o saru [···を去る]; ...o shuppatsu-suru [···を出発する]. 2)...o nokosu [···を残す]; ...o oki-wasureru [···を置き忘れる]. 3)...ni makaseru [···に任せる]. 4)...no mama-ni-shite-oku [···のままにしておく].

(1) Yesterday he **left** Tokyo for Nagoya on business.

    Kinô kare-wa shôyô-de Tôkyô-*o shuppatsu-shite* (*o tatte*) Nagoya-e mukatta.

(2) Don't **leave** your textbooks in the classroom.

    Kyôshitsu-ni kyôka-sho-*o oki-wasure*-nai-yô-ni.

(3) I'll **leave** it to you. Anata-ni sore-*o o-makase-shimasu*.

(4) Don't **leave** the window open.

    Mado-o aketa-*mama-ni-shite-oka*-nai-de-kudasai.

    (*vi.*) saru [去る]; shuppatsu-suru [出発する].

leave...alone ...o kamawazu-ni-oku

leave behind ...o ato-ni-nokosu; ...o oki-wasureru

leave off ...o yameru

    He left off crying. Kare-wa naki-yanda.

leave out ...o habuku

    Leave out this paragraph. Kono setsu-o habuki-nasai.

leave (*n.*) 1)kyoka [許可]. 2)wakare [別れ]. 3)kyûka [休暇].

(1) They went out without **leave**.

    Kare-ra-wa *kyoka*-nashi-ni dete-itta.

(2) I must take **leave** of you.

    Watashi-wa anata-to o-*wakare*-shi-nakereba-naranai.

(3) sick **leave** byôki-*kyûka*.

lecture (*n.*) kôen [講演].

    (*vi. & vt.*) (...ni) kôen-suru [(…に)講演する].

lecturer (*n.*) kôen-sha [講演者]; kôshi [講師].

ledge (*n.*) deppari [出っ張り].

ledger (*n.*) (*bkpg.*) moto-chô [元帳].

leech (*n.*) (*zool.*) hiru [ヒル].

leeway (*n.*) 1)(*marine*) fûatsu [風圧]. 2)okure [遅れ]. 3)((US)) yutori [ゆとり].

left (*a.*) hidari-no [左の].

    the **left** hand *hidari*-te

    (*ad.*) hidari-e[-ni] [左へ[に]].

    (*n.*) hidari [左]; hidari-gawa [左側].

left-hand (*a.*) hidari-no [左の]; hidari-gawa-no [左側の].

left-handed (*a.*) hidari-kiki-no [左利きの].

    (*ad.*) hidari-te-de [左手で].

leg (*n.*) 1)ashi [脚]. 2)(*mech.*) ashi [脚].

take to one's legs nige-dasu

legal (*a.*) hôritsu-no [法律の]; gôhô-no [合法の].

legally (*ad.*) hôritsu-teki-ni [法律的に]; gôhô-teki-ni [合法的に].

legend (*n.*) densetsu [伝説].

legion (*n.*) 1)gundan [軍団]. 2)tasû [多数].

legislation (*n.*) 1)rippô [立法]. 2)hôritsu [法律].

legislative (*a.*) rippô-ken-no-aru [立法権のある].
     (*n.*) = legislative body rippô-fu [立法府].

legislator (*n.*) 1)rippô-sha [立法者]. 2)rippô-fu-no-giin [立法府の議員].

legislature (*n.*) 1)rippô-fu [立法府]; rippô-kikan [立法機関]. 2)((*US*))
 shû-gikai [州議会].

leisure (*n.*) hima [暇].
 at leisure hima-de; yukkuri-to
 at one's leisure hima-no-aru-toki-ni

leisurely (*a.*) yukkuri-shita [ゆっくりした]; yuttari-shita [ゆったりし
 た].

lemon (*n.*) remon[-no-ki] [レモン(の木)].

lend (*vt.*) ...o kasu [...を貸す].

length (*n.*) naga-sa [長さ].
 at full length 1)te-ashi-o-naga-naga-to-nobashite. 2)shôsai-ni
 at length 1)tsui-ni. 2)jûbun-ni; shôsai-ni

lengthen (*vt. & vi.*) ...o nagaku-suru (nagaku-naru) [...を長くする
 (長くなる)].

lenient (*a.*) kandai-na [寛大な].

Lent (*n.*) Shijun-setsu [四旬節].

leopard (*n.*) (*zool.*) hyô [ヒョウ].

less (*a.*) yori-sukunai [より少ない].
  He came back in **less** than an hour.
   Kare-wa ichi-jikan-tata-*nai*-uchi-ni kaette-kita.
 (*ad.*) yori-sukunaku [より少なく].
  He is **less** diligent than he was.
   Kare-wa izen-*hodo* kinben-*de-nai*.
 none the less sore-demo-nao
 still(much) less mashite...nai
 no less than ...mo; ...to-dôyô-ni
 (*n.*) yori-sukunai-ryô [より少ない量].

lessen (*vt. & vi.*) ...o sukunaku-suru (sukunaku-naru) [...を少なくす
 る(少なくなる)]; ...o chiisaku-suru (chiisaku-naru) [...を小さくする
 (小さくなる)]; ...o herasu (heru) [...を減らす(減る)].

lesson (*n.*) 1)gakka [学課]; ka [課]. 2)kyôkun [教訓]. 3)(*pl.*)
jugyô [授業]; keiko [けいこ].
  (*1*) Look at **Lesson** 1. Dai-ik*ka*-o go-ran-nasai.
  (*2*) This gave me a good **lesson**.
      Kono-koto-wa watashi-ni yoi *kyôkun*-o ataeta.
      Kono-koto wa watashi-ni yoi *kyôkun*-ni-natta.
  (*3*) He takes **lessons** in music from her.
      Kare-wa kano-jo-ni-tsuite ongaku-no-*keiko*-o shite-iru.
lest (*conj.*)(+should) …(shi-)nai-yô-ni […(し)ないように].
let (*vt.*) 1)…o…(sa-)seru […を…(さ)せる]. 2)…shiyô […しよう]. 3)…
o chintai-suru […を賃貸する]. 4)…o dasu […を出す].
  (*1*) I'll **let** you know it later on.
      Watashi-wa ato-de sore-o anata-ni shira*se*-yô.
      Let him come here by noon.
      Shôgo-made-ni kare-o koko-e ko-*sase-nasai*.
  (*2*) **Let's** take a walk. Sampo-*shiyô*.
  (*3*) He **let** his own house to a tenant, and removed.
      Kare-wa jibun-no mochi-ie-o hito-ni *kashite*, hikkoshita.
      Rooms to **let**. *Kashi*-ma ari.
  (*4*) The wounded man **let** a groan.
      Sono kega-nin wa umeki-goe-o *dashita*.
let down 1)…o shitsubô-saseru. 2)…o orosu.
  1) I shall never **let** you **down**.
      Watashi-wa kimi-o kesshite shitsubô-sase-nai-darô.
let go te-o-hanasu
      He **let go** of the rope and jumped down.
      Kare-wa rôpu-kara-te-o-hanashite tobi-orita.
Let me see. Hate-na.; Ee-to.; Sô-da-ne.
let oneself go shitai-hôdai-ni-yaru
let up yamu
      The rain will **let up** by the evening.
      Ame wa yûgata-made-ni-wa yamu-darô.
letter (*n.*) 1)tegami [手紙]. 2)moji [文字].
  to the letter moji-doori-ni; seikaku-ni
letter box yûbin-uke [郵便受け].
letter of attorney inin-jô [委任状].
letter of credit (*com.*) shin'yô-jô [信用状].
letter paper binsen [便せん].

lettuce (*n.*) (*bot.*) chisha [チシャ]; retasu [レタス].

level (*n.*) 1)suihei [水平]. 2)takasa [高さ]. 3)suijun [水準].
　(*2*) The mountain is 4,000 feet above the sea **level**.
　　　　Sono yama wa kai*batsu*-yon-sen-fîto aru.
　(*a.*) suihei-na [水平な]; onaji-takasa-no [同じ高さの]; onaji-suijun-no [同じ水準の].
　(*vt.*) 1)...o taira-ni-suru […を平らにする]; ...o narasu […をならす]. 2)...no nerai-o-tsukeru […のねらいをつける]; ...o mukeru […を向ける].

lever (*n.*) (*mech.*) teko [てこ].
　(*vt.*) ...o(-teko-de) ugokasu […を(てこで)動かす].
　(*vi.*) teko-o-tsukau [てこを使う].

levy (*n.*) 1)chôshû [徴収]. 2)shôshû [召集].
　(*vt.*) 1)...o chôshû-suru […を徴収する]. 2)...o shôshû-suru […を召集する]. 3)(*law*)...o sashi-osaeru […を差し押さえる].

liable (*a.*) 1)sekinin-ga-aru [責任がある]. 2)...(shi-)gachi-na […(し)がちな]; ...(shi-)yasui […(し)やすい].
　(*1*) He is **liable** to pay debts.
　　　　Kare-wa shakkin-o harau(-beki)-*sekinin-ga-aru*.
　(*2*) Difficulties are **liable** to occur.
　　　　Mendô-na-koto wa *tokaku* okori-*gachi-da*.

liar (*n.*) uso-tsuki [うそつき].

liberal (*a.*) 1)ki-mae-no-yoi [気前のよい]. 2)kandai-na [寛大な]. 3) jiyû-shugi-no [自由主義の].

liberate (*vt.*) ...o jiyû-ni-suru […を自由にする].

liberation (*n.*) kaihô [解放]; kaihô-undô [解放運動]; kenri-kakuchô-undô [権利拡張運動].

liberty (*n.*) 1)jiyû [自由]. 2)shitsurei [失礼]; bu-enryo [無遠慮].
　(*1*) He won his **liberty**. Kare-wa *jiyû*-o kachi-totta.
　(*2*) I take the **liberty** of addressing you.
　　　　Shitsurei-desu-ga o-tegami-o sashi-agemasu.

library (*n.*) 1)tosho-shitsu [図書室]; tosho-kan [図書館]. 2)zôsho [蔵書].

license (*n.*) menkyo[-jô] [免許(状)]; kyoka[-shô] [許可(証)].
　(*vt.*) ...ni menkyo-jô[kyoka]-o ataeru […に免許状[許可]を与える]; ...o ninka-suru […を認可する].

license plate nambâ-purêto [ナンバープレート].

lick (*vt.*) ...o nameru […をなめる]; (honoo ga)...o nameru [(炎が)…

をなめる].

lid (*n.*) 1)futa [ふた]. 2)mabuta = eyelid [まぶた].

lie (*vi.*) 1)yokotawaru [横たわる]; yoko-ni-naru [横になる]. 2)aru [ある]; ichi-suru [位置する].

　(*1*) He **lay** on the grass.　Kare-wa kusa-no-ue-ni *yoko-ni-natta*.

　(*2*) Yokohama **lies** to the west of Tokyo.
　　　　Yokohama wa Tôkyô-no-nishi-ni *ichi-suru(aru)*.

　lie down yoko-ni-natte-yasumu

　(*n.*) (the -) ichi [位置]; ari-kata [あり方].

lie (*n. & vi.*) uso(-o-tsuku) [うそ(をつく)].

life (*n.*) 1)seimei [生命]. 2)jinsei [人生]; seken [世間]. 3)seikatsu [生活]. 4)shôgai [生涯]. 5)denki [伝記]. 6)kakki [活気].

　(*1*) Many **lives** were lost in the accident.
　　　　Sono-jiko-de tasû-no *seimei* ga ushinawareta.

　(*2*) **Life** is compared to a voyage.
　　　　Jinsei wa kôkai-ni tatoerareru.

　(*3*) He leads a happy **life**.
　　　　Kare-wa shiawase-na *seikatsu*-o okutte-iru.

　(*4*) I have never seen such a splendid thing in my **life**.
　　　　Watashi-wa *shôgai*-no-aida-ni konna subarashii mono-o mita-koto-ga-nai.

　(*5*) Have you ever read 'The **Life** of George Washington'?
　　　　Anata-wa 'Jôji Washinton no *denki*'-o yonda-koto-ga-arimasu-ka?

　(*6*) This is the town full of **life**.
　　　　Kore-wa *kakki*-ni-michita-machi da.

　all one's life isshô
　for life isshô

life assurance seimei-hoken [生命保険].

lifeboat (*n.*) kyûmei-tei [救命艇].

life jacket kyûmai-dôi [救命胴衣].

life-size(d) (*a.*) jitsubutsu-dai-no [実物大の]; tôshin-dai-no [等身大の].

lifework (*n.*) isshô-no-shigoto [一生の仕事]; raifuwâku [ライフワーク].

lift (*vt.*) 1)...o mochi-ageru [⋯を持ち上げる]. 2)...o kaijo-suru [⋯を解除する].

　(*vi.*) 1)(kiri nado ga) hareru [(霧などが)晴れる]. 2)mochi-agaru [持ち上がる].

　(*n.*) 1)mochi-ageru-koto [持ち上げること]. 2)((*Eng.*)) erebêtâ [エ

レベーター]. rifuto［リフト].

light (*n.*) 1)hikari［光]. 2)akari［明かり].

  bring...to light ...o akarumi-ni-dasu; ...o bakuro-suru

    (*a.*) 1)akarui［明るい]. 2)(iro ga) usui［(色が)薄い].

    (*vt.*) ...ni akari-o-tsukeru［…に明かりをつける]; ...ni hi-o-tsuketu［…に火をつける]; ...o terasu［…を照らす].

    (*vi.*) hi-ga-tsuku［火がつく]; kagayaku［輝く].

light (*a.*) karui［軽い]; yôi-na［容易な].

  make light of ...o keishi-suru

lighten (*vt.*) 1)...o akaruku-suru［…を明るくする]. 2)...o terasu［…を照らす].

    (*vi.*) 1)akaruku-naru［明るくなる]; kagayaku［輝く]. 2)inabikari-suru［稲光りする].

lighten (*vt. & vi.*) ...o karuku-suru (karuku-naru)［…を軽くする(軽くなる)].

lighter (*n.*) 1)akari-o-tsukeru-hito［明かりをつける人]. 2)raitâ［ライター].

lighter (*n.*) hashike［はしけ].

lighthouse (*n.*) tôdai［灯台].

light industry kei-kôgyô［軽工業].

lightly (*ad.*) 1)karuku［軽く]; keikai-ni［軽快に]. 2)keisotsu-ni［軽率に].

lightning (*n.*) denkô［電光]; inazuma［稲妻].

likable (*a.*) konomashii［好ましい].

like (*vt.*) 1)...o konomu［…を好む]. 2)...(shi-)tai［…(し)たい].

  How do you like it? Sore-wa ikaga-desu-ka?

  if you like yoroshi-kereba

  I should(would) like... ...(shi-)tai-mono-da-ga

    (*n.*) (*pl.*) konomi［好み]; suki-na-mono［好きなもの].

      We have **likes** and dislikes.

        Ware-ware niwa *suki*-kirai-ga-aru.

like (*a.*) nite-iru［似ている].

      The two brothers are very **like**.

        Ano kyôdai wa totemo *nite-iru*.

    (*prep.*)...no-yô-na［…のような]; ...no-yô-ni［…のように].

      What is he **like**? Kare-wa dono-*yô-na*-hito-desu-ka?

      It looks **like** a yellow star.

        Sore-wa kiiro-i hoshi-*no-yô-ni*-mieru.

　　　　Sore-wa kiiro-i hoshi-*no-yô*-da.
　　(*n.*) 1)nita-hito[-mono] [似た人[もの]].
　　　I never saw the **like**.
　　　　Watashi-wa sono-*yô-na-mono*-o mita-koto-ga-nai.
likelihood (*n.*) ari-sô-na-koto [ありそうなこと]; mikomi [見込み].
likely (*a.*) 1)ari-sô-na [ありそうな]; ...rashii […らしい]. 2)yûbô-na
　　[有望な].
　　(*1*) It's a **likely** story.　Sore-wa *ari-sô-na* hanashi da.
　　　It is **likely** to rain.　Ame-ni-nari-sô-*da*.
　　(*2*) He is a **likely** buyer.　Kare-wa *yûbô-na* kai-te da.
　　　　(*ad.*) tabun [たぶん].
　　　Very(Most) **likely** he will try.
　　　　Tabun kare-wa yatte-miru-darô.
liken (*vt.*) ...o tatoeru […をたとえる].
likeness (*n.*) 1)nite-iru-koto [似ていること]. 2)shôzô-ga [肖像画]; ni-
　　gao-e [似顔絵].
liking (*n.*) konomi [好み].
　have a liking for　...ga suki-de-aru
lilac (*n.*) (*bot.*) rairakku [ライラック]; rira [リラ].
　　　(*a.*) usu-murasaki-iro-no [薄紫色の].
lily (*n.*) (*bot.*) yuri [ユリ].
limb (*n.*) te-ashi [手足].
lime (*n.*) sekkai [石灰].
limestone (*n.*) sekkai-gan [石灰岩].
limit (*n.*) 1)genkai [限界]. 2)seigen [制限].
　within limits　tekido-ni
　within the limits of　...no-han'i-nai-de
　without limit　mu-seigen-ni
　　　　(*vt.*) ...o seigen-suru […を制限する]; ...o gentei-suru […を限定
　　する].
limited company ((*Eng.*)) yûgen-sekinin-gaisha [有限責任会社].
limited express tokkyû [特急].
limousine (*n.*) rimujin [リムジン].
limp (*vi.*) fu-jiyû-na-ashi-de-aruku [不自由な足で歩く].
line (*n.*) 1)sen [線]; rain [ライン]. 2)tsuri-ito [釣り糸]. 3)mijikai-
　　tegami [短い手紙]; ippitsu [一筆]. 4)senro [線路]; kôro [航路]. 5)
　　retsu [列]. 6)denwa-sen [電話線]. 7)(*com.*) shurui [種類].
　　(*1*) He drew a dotted **line** on the paper.

　　　　Kare-wa kami-ni ten*sen*-o kaita.
(2) rod and **line** tsuri-zao to *tsuri-ito*
(3) I'll send you a **line**. *Ippitsu* kaki-okuri-masu.
(4) lay a **line** *senro*-o shiku
　　　　This is a ship on the North-American **line**.
　　　　Kore-wa Hokubei-*kôro*-no-fune da.
(5) Stand in two **lines**. Ni-*retsu*-ni narabi-nasai.
(6) Is the **line** busy in rush hours?
　　　　Rasshu-ji-niwa *denwa* wa konde-imasu-ka?
(7) articles in this **line** kono-*te*-no shôhin
　　　(*vt.*) 1)...o ichi-retsu-ni-naraberu [⋯を一列に並べる]; ...ni sotte-naraberu [⋯に沿って並べる]. 2)...ni sen-o-hiku [⋯に線を引く]. 3)...ni shiwa-o-tsukeru [⋯にしわをつける].
(1) Willows **line** the road.
　　　　Yanagi-no-ki ga michi-*ni-sotte-narande-iru*.
(2) **Line** the paper with a pencil.
　　　　Empitsu-de kami-*ni* sen-o-hiki-nasai.
　　　(*vi.*) ichi-retsu-ni-narabu [一列に並ぶ].
line up seiretsu-suru
line (*vt.*) ...ni ura-o-tsukeru [⋯に裏をつける].
　　　　My overcoat **is lined** with silk.
　　　　Watashi-no ôbâ wa kinu-no-*ura-ga-tsuite-iru*.
linear (*a.*) 1)sen-no [線の]; senjô-no [線状の]. 2)naga-sa-no [長さの].
linen (*n.*) rinneru [リンネル].
liner (*n.*) 1)tei-kô-sen [定航船]; teiki-bin [定期便]. 2)(*baseball*) rainâ [ライナー].
linger (*vi.*) guzu-guzu-suru [ぐずぐずする]; bura-bura-suru [ぶらぶらする].
linguistic (*a.*) gengo[-gaku]-no [言語(学)の].
linguistics (*n.*) gengo-gaku [言語学].
lining (*n.*) ura-ji [裏地]; ura [裏].
link (*n.*) 1)wa [輪]. 2)(*pl.*) kafusu-botan [カフスボタン]. 3)kizuna [きずな].
　　　(*vt.*) ...o tsunagu [⋯をつなぐ]; ...o renketsu-suru [⋯を連結する].
links (*n.*) gorufu-jô [ゴルフ場].
linoleum (*n.*) rinoriumu [リノリウム].
lion (*n.*) raion [ライオン]; shishi [シシ].
lip (*n.*) kuchibiru [唇].

lip service kuchi-saki-dake-no-o-seji [口先だけのお世辞].

lipstick (*n.*) kuchi-beni [口紅].

liquid (*a.*) 1)ekitai-no [液体の]; ryûdô-sei-no [流動性の]. 2)sunda [澄んだ].
      (*n.*) ekitai [液体].

liquid capital (*com.*) ryûdô-shihon [流動資本].

liquor (*n.*) 1)arukôru-inryô [アルコール飲料]. 2)shiru [汁].

list (*n.*) hyô [表]; mokuroku [目録]; meibo [名簿].
      a price list kakaku-*hyô*
      a list of graduates sotsugyô-sei-*meibo*
      (*vt.*) …o hyô-ni-noseru [⋯を表に載せる]; …o mokuroku-ni-ireru [⋯を目録に入れる].

listen (*vi.*) kiku [聞く]; keichô-suru [傾聴する].

listener (*n.*) kiku-hito [聞く人]; (rajio no) chôshu-sha [(ラジオの)聴取者].

liter, -tre (*n.*) rittoru [リットル].

literal (*a.*) moji-no [文字の].

literally (*ad.*) moji-doori-ni [文字どおりに].

literary (*a.*) 1)bungaku-no [文学の]; bungei-no [文芸の]. 2)bungaku-ni-tsûjita [文学に通じた]. 3)bungo-no [文語の].

literature (*n.*) 1)bungaku [文学]. 2)bunken [文献].

litter (*n.*) 1)chirakari-mono [散らかりもの]. 2)ranzatsu [乱雑].
      (*vt.*) …o chirakasu [⋯を散らかす].

little (*a.*) 1)chiisai [小さい]. 2)sukoshi-no [少しの]; sukoshi-wa-aru [少しはある]. 3)sukunai [少ない]; hotondo-nai [ほとんどない].
    (*1*) He lives in a little town. Kare-wa *chiisai*-machi-ni sunde-iru.
    (*2*) I have a little money with me.
        Watashi-wa *sukoshi-wa* kane-o motte-iru.
    (*3*) There is little hope for him to recover.
        Kare-ga naoru-mikomi wa *hotondo-nai*.
    (*n.*) 1)shôryô [少量]; sukoshi [少し]. 2)hotondo-nai-mono [ほとんどないもの].
    (*1*) Give me just a little more.
        Watashi-ni mô-honno-*sukoshi*-dake kudasai.
    (*2*) She has seen little of life.
        Kano-jo-wa seken-o *hotondo*-mite-i-*nai*.
        Kano-jo-wa seken-shirazu-da.

little by little sukoshi-zutsu

    (*ad.*) 1)sukoshi-wa [少しは]. 2)mattaku...nai [全く…ない].

  (*1*) I can speak English **a little**.

    Watashi-wa *sukoshi-wa* Eigo-o shabe-re-masu.

  (*2*) These writers are **little** known among us.

    Kore-ra-no   sakka-tachi   wa   ware-ware-no-aida-de-wa

    mattaku-shirarete-i-*nai*.

little more than ...mo-dôzen

not a little sukuna-karazu; zuibun

live (*vi.*) 1)sumu [住む]. 2)ikiru [生きる]; seikatsu-suru [生活する].

  (*1*) He **lives** in Kyushu. Kare-wa Kyûshû-ni *sunde-iru.*

  (*2*) We **live** on rice. Ware-ware-wa kome-o tabete-*ikiru.*

    Ware-ware-wa kome-o jôshoku-to-suru.

  (*vt.*) ...no seikatsu-o-okuru [...の生活を送る].

    He **is living** a peaceful life.

    Kare-wa heiwa-na seikatsu-*o okutteiru.*

live (*a.*) 1)ikite-iru [生きている]. 2)nama-no [生の].

  (*1*) I haven't ever seen a **live** whale.

    Watashi-wa *ikita* kujira-o mita-koto-ga-nai.

  (*2*) **live** programs   *nama*-hôsô

livelihood (*n.*) kurashi [暮らし]; seikei [生計].

lively (*a.*) kappatsu-na [活発な]; genki-no-yoi [元気のよい].

liver (*n.*) 1)(*anat.*) kanzô [肝臓]. 2)rebâ [レバー].

living (*a.*) ikiteiru [生きている]; genson-no [現存の].

    He is the greatest **living** poet.

    Kare-wa *genzai-ikiteiru* saikô-no shijin da.

  (*n.*) kurashi [暮らし]; seikei [生計].

    make a living *seikei*-o-tateru

living room ima [居間].

living wage saitei-seikatsu-chingin [最低生活賃金].

lizard (*n.*) (*zool.*) tokage [トカゲ].

load (*n.*) 1)(tsumi-)ni [(積み)荷]. 2)wari-ate [割り当て]; shigoto-ryô [仕事量]. 3)omo-ni [重荷].

  (*vt.*) 1)...ni ni-o-tsumu [...に荷を積む]; ...o dossari-noseru [...をどっさり載せる]. 2)(*mil.*) ...ni sôten-suru [...に装てんする]. 3)...ni ireru [...に入れる].

  (*1*) The table **is loaded** with fruit.

    Shokutaku niwa kudamono-ga *dossari-nosete-aru.*

  (*2*) I **loaded** the gun. Watashi-wa jû-*ni sôten-shita.*

(3) He **loaded** the camera with film.
    Kare-wa kamera-*ni* firumu-o *ireta*.

loaf (*n.*) pan-ikko [パン一個].

loaf (*vi.*) norakura-shite-kurasu [のらくらして暮らす]; buratsuku [ぶらつく].

loafer (*n.*) norakura-mono [のらくら者]; namake-mono [怠け者].

loan (*n.*) 1)kashi-tsuke [貸し付け]. 2)kôsai [公債].
    (*vt. & vi.*) ...o kasu (kane-o-kasu) [...を貸す(金を貸す)].

lobby (*n.*) robî [ロビー].
    (*vt.*) (giin)-ni hataraki-kakeru [(議員)に働きかける].
    (*vi.*) giin-ni-atsuryoku-o-kakeru [議員に圧力をかける]; gikai-kôsaku-o-suru [議会工作をする].

lobster (*n.*) (*zool.*) ise-ebi [イセエビ].

local (*a.*) 1)jimoto-no [地元の]. 2)kaku-eki-teisha-no [各駅停車の].
    (*n.*) 1)((US)) chihô-kiji [地方記事]. 2)futsû-ressha [普通列車].

locate (*vt.*) 1)...o oku [...を置く]; ...o môkeru [...を設ける]. 2)...no-ichi-o-tsuki-tomeru [...の位置をつきとめる].
  (*1*) The bank **is located** on the ground floor.
        Ginkô wa ikkai-ni *môkerarete-iru*.
  (*2*) We tried to **locate** the cottage.
        Ware-ware-wa sono koya-*no-ichi-o-tsuki-tome*-yô-to-shita.

location (*n.*) 1)ichi [位置]; shozai-chi [所在地]. 2)(*movie*) yagai-satsuei-chi [野外撮影地]; rokêshon [ロケーション].

lock (*n.*) 1)jô [錠]. 2)suimon [水門].
    (*vt.*) 1)...ni kagi-o-kakeru [...にかぎを掛ける]. 2)...o toji-komeru [...を閉じ込める]; ...o daki-shimeru [...を抱き締める]. 3)...o kotei-suru [...を固定する].
  (*1*) He **locked** the door from the outside.
        Kare-wa soto-gawa-kara to-ni *kagi-o-kaketa*.
  (*2*) He **was locked** up in the hut.
        Kare-wa koya-ni *toji-komerareta*.
  (*3*) He **locked** me in a fast embrace.
        Kare-wa watashi-o shikkari *daki-shimeta*.
    (*vi.*) 1)kagi-ga-kakaru [かぎが掛かる]. 2)kumi-au [組み合う].

locker (*n.*) 1)kagi-o-kakeru-hito [かぎを掛ける人]. 2)rokkâ [ロッカー].

locket (*n.*) roketto [ロケット].

lockout (*n.*) kôjô-heisa [工場閉鎖]; rokkuauto [ロックアウト].

locomotive (*n.*) kikan-sha [機関車].

locust (*n.*) (*insect*) inago [イナゴ]; batta [バッタ].

lode (*n.*) kômyaku [鉱脈].

lodge (*vt. & vi.*) ...o tomeru (tomaru) [...を泊める(泊まる)].
> Every house wanted to **lodge** me.
>> Dono ie mo watashi-*o tome*-tagatta.
> I **lodged** with my friend.
>> Watashi-wa tomodachi-no-ie-ni *tomatta*.
> (*n.*) yama-goya [山小屋]; ban-goya [番小屋].

lodging (*n.*) 1)shukuhaku [宿泊]; yado [宿]. 2)(*pl.*) geshuku [下宿]; kashi-ma [貸間].
> (*1*) I asked her for a night's **lodging**.
>> Watashi-wa kano-jo-ni ichi-ya-no *yado*-o tanonda.
> (*2*) I left my bag at my **lodgings**.
>> Watashi-wa *geshuku*-ni kaban-o oki-wasureta.

loft (*n.*) yane-ura [屋根裏].

lofty (*a.*) hijô-ni-takai [非常に高い].

log (*n.*) maruta [丸太].
> **sleep like a log** gussuri-nemuru
> (*vt.*) 1)...o maruta-ni-suru [...を丸太にする]. 2)...o kôkai-nisshi-ni-kinyû-suru [...を航海日誌に記入する].

log cabin maruta-goya [丸太小屋].

logic (*n.*) ronri[-gaku] [論理(学)].

logical (*a.*) ronri-teki-na [論理的な].

loin (*n.*) 1)(*pl.*) koshi [腰]. 2)koshi-niku [腰肉].

loiter (*vi.*) 1)bura-tsuku [ぶらつく]. 2)michikusa-o-kuu [道草を食う].

loneliness (*n.*) sabishi-sa [寂しさ].

lonely (*a.*) sabishii [寂しい]; hitori-botchi-no [独りぼっちの]; hito-zato-hanareta [人里離れた].   「離れた]

lonesome (*a.*) (*colloq.*) sabishii [寂しい]; hito-zato-hanareta [人里

long (*a.*) 1)nagai [長い]. 2)naga-sa-ga...no[de] [長さが...の(で)].
> (*1*) He has been ill for a **long** time.
>> Kare-wa *nagai*-aida byôki-da.
> (*2*) The bar is two feet **long**.
>> Sono bô wa *nagasa-ga*-ni-fîto aru.
> **in the long run** kekkyoku
> (*n.*) nagai-aida [長い間].
> I haven't seen her for **long**.
>> Watashi-wa *nagai-aida* kano-jo-ni atte-i-nai.

before long　chikai-uchi-ni; ma-mo-naku

　　(*ad.*) 1)nagaku [長く]. 2)zutto [ずっと]. 3)...no-aida-jû […の間じゅう].

　　　It was **long** before he got well.

　　　　Kare-wa zenkai-suru-made-ni *nagaku* kakatta.

any longer　mohaya; kore-ijô

as long as　...(suru)kagiri-wa; ...sae-sureba

no longer　mohaya...de-nai

So long!　(*colloq.*) Dewa-sayô-nara.

long (*vi.*) setsubô-suru [切望する]; omoi-kogareru [思いこがれる].

longing (*n. & a.*) setsubô(-suru) [切望(する)]; akogare(-no) [あこがれ(の)].

longitude (*n.*) keido [経度].

long-playing (*a.*) chô-jikan-ensô-no [長時間演奏の].

long-run (*a.*) chôki-kôgyô-no [長期興行の]; rongu-ran-no [ロングランの]; chôki-ni-wataru [長期にわたる].

long-sighted (*a.*) 1)((*Eng.*)) enshi-no [遠視の]. 2)senken-no-mei-no-aru [先見の明のある].

long-winded (*a.*) 1)iki-no-nagaku-tsuzuku [息の長く続く]. 2)naga-tarashii [長たらしい].

look (*vi.*) 1)miru [見る]; nagameru [眺める]. 2)chûmoku-suru [注目する]; ki-o-tsukeru [気を付ける]. 3)...no-yô-da […のようだ]; ...ni-mieru […に見える].

　　(1) She **looked** about her.　Kano-jo-wa atari-o *mi*-mawashita.

　　I **looked** about for my baggage.

　　　Watashi-wa jibun-no-nimotsu-o *sagashita*.

　　Look at this picture.　Kono e-o *goran-nasai*.

　　She **looked** back.　Kano-jo-wa furi-kaette-*mita*.

　　We **looked** down upon the beautiful scenery.

　　　Watashi-tachi-wa utsukushii keshiki-o *mi*-oroshita.

　　I **am looking** for a house on sale.

　　　Watashi-wa uri-ie-o *sagashiteiru*.

　　I'm **looking** forward to seeing you.

　　　Anata-ni *au*-no-ga tanoshimi-da.

　　He **looked** into the water.

　　　Kare-wa mizu-no-naka-o *nozoki*-konda.

　　They **looked** on him as their father.

　　　Kare-ra-wa kare-o chichi-to omotta.

They **looked** up to him as a great musician.

    Kare-ra-wa kare-o idai-na ongaku-ka-to-shite sonkei-shite-ita.

(2) He **looked** after me.

    Kare-wa watashi-no-*mendô-o mite-kureta.*

Look here! *Oi!*

Look out! *Ki-o-tsukero!*

He **looked** over my English composition.

    Kare-wa watashi-no Ei-sakubun-ni me-o-tooshita.

(3) It **looks** like snow. Yuki-ni-nari-*sô-da.*

She **looked** happy. Kano-jo-wa shiawase-*sô-datta.*

    (*vt.*) 1)...no...o jitto-miru [···の···をじっと見る]; ...o shiraberu [···を調べる]. 2)...o me-tsuki-de-shimesu [···を目付きで示す].

(1) He **looked** me in the face. Kare-wa watashi-*no*-kao-o mita.

I **looked** up the word in the dictionary.

    Watashi-wa jisho-de sono-go-o *shirabeta.*

(2) He **looked** his thanks to me.

    Kare-wa *me-tsuki-de* watashi-ni kansha-no-i-o *shimeshita.*

    (*n.*) 1)miru-koto [見ること]; ikken [一見]. 2)me-tsuki [目付き]. 3)yôsu [様子]; gaikan [外観].

(1) He took a **look** at it. Kare-wa sore-o chiratto *mita.*

(2) His scornful **look** irritated me.

    Kare-no keibetsu-shita *me-tsuki* wa watashi-o iradataseta.

(3) Don't judge a man by his **looks**.

    Gaikan-de hito-o handan-suru-na.

looking glass kagami [鏡]; sugata-mi [姿見].

lookout (*n.*) 1)mi-hari [見張り]; yôjin [用心]. 2)zento [前途].

loom (*n.*) hata [機]; shokki [織機].

loom (*vi.*) nutto-arawareru [ぬっと現れる]; bon'yari-mieru [ぼんやり見える].

loop (*n.*) 1)wa [輪]. 2)(*R.R. & teleg. wire*) kanjô-sen [環状線]; rûpu-sen [ループ線].

    (*vt. & vi.*) ...o wa-ni-suru (wa-ni-naru) [···を輪にする(輪になる)].

loose (*a.*) 1)yurunda [緩んだ]. 2)toki-hanatareta [解き放たれた]. 3)geri-o-okoshite-iru [下痢を起こしている].

get loose nigeru

let loose ...o nigasu; ...o jiyû-ni-suru

    (*vt.*) ...o toku [···を解く]; ...o hanatsu [···を放つ]; ...o hodoku

　　[…をほどく].

loosely (*ad.*) yuruku [ゆるく]; shimari-naku [締まりなく]; bara-bara-ni [ばらばらに].

loosen (*vt. & vi.*) …o yurumeru (yurumu) […をゆるめる(ゆるむ)].

lord (*n.*) 1)shuchô [首長]; kunshu [君主]. 2)((*Eng.*))(L-)…kyô […卿]. 3)((*Eng.*)) kizoku [貴族]. 4)(our L-) shu [主].
　　(*vt.*) (…ni) ibari-chiraru [(…に)いばり散らす].

lorry (*n.*) 1)((*Eng.*)) torakku (= truck) [トラック]. 2)torokko [トロッコ].

lose (*vt.*) 1)…o ushinau […を失う]; …o nakusu […をなくす]. 2)…de makeru […で負ける]. 3)…ni nori-okureru […に乗り遅れる]. 4)…ni mayou […に迷う]. 5)…o nogareru […をのがれる]. 6)okureru [遅れる].
　　(*1*) I **lost** my fountain-pen.
　　　　Watashi-wa mannen-hitsu-*o nakushita.*
　　(*2*) We **lost** the race.　Ware-ware-wa rêsu-*ni maketa.*
　　(*3*) Don't **lose** the first train.　Ichi-ban-ressha-*ni nori-okureru*-na.
　　(*4*) He **lost** his way.　Kare-wa michi-*ni mayotta.*
　　(*5*) I have **lost** my stomachache.　I-no-itami ga *naotta.*
　　(*6*) My watch **loses** 2 minutes a day.
　　　　Watashi-no tokei wa ichi-nichi-ni ni-fun *okureru.*
　　(*vi.*) 1)son-o-suru [損をする]. 2)makeru [負ける].
　　(*1*) He **lost** heavily.　Kare-wa *oo-zon-o-shita.*
　　(*2*) He **lost** in the 3rd race.　Kare-wa dai-san-rêsu-de *maketa.*

loss (*n.*) sonshitsu [損失]; funshitsu [紛失].
　　at a loss komatte; tohô-ni-kurete

lost (*a.*) 1)ushinawareta [失われた]. 2)michi-ni-mayotta [道に迷った]. 3)rôhi-sareta [浪費された]. 4)maketa [負けた].

lot (*n.*) 1)ummei [運命]. 2)kuji [くじ]. 3)ichi-kukaku [一区画]. 4)(*colloq.*) takusan [たくさん].
　　(*1*) It falls to my **lot** to do…
　　　　…o suru-no-ga watashi-no *ummei* da.
　　(*2*) The **lot** fell to me.　*Kuji* wa watashi-ni-atatta.
　　(*3*) a parking **lot**　chûsha-*jô*
　　(*4*) What a **lot** of books you have!
　　　　Nan-to *takusan*-no-hon-o motte-iru-koto!

lottery (*n.*) chûsen [抽選].

lotus (*n.*) (*bot.*) hasu [ハス].

loud (*a.*) 1)koe-ga-ookii [声が大きい]; sôzôshii [騒々しい]. 2) kebakebashii [けばけばしい].

    (*ad.*) oo-goe-de [大声で].

loudly (*ad.*) oo-goe-de [大声で].

loudspeaker (*n.*) raudosupîkâ [ラウドスピーカー].

lounge (*n.*) kyûkei-shitsu [休憩室].

    (*vi.*) 1)bura-tsuku [ぶらつく]. 2)yuttari-suwaru [ゆったり座る].

lovable (*a.*) aisu-beki [愛すべき].

love (*n.*) ai [愛].

  give(send) my love to ...ni yoroshiku

    (*vt.*) ...o aisuru […を愛する].

lovely (*a.*) 1)utsukushii [美しい]. 2)(*colloq.*) subarashii [すばらしい].

lover (*n.*) 1)koi-bito [恋人]. 2)(*pl.*) koi-bito-dôshi [恋人同士]. 3) aikô-sha [愛好者].

loving (*a.*) ...o aisuru […を愛する]; aijô-ni-michita [愛情に満ちた].

low (*a.*) 1)hikui [低い]. 2)hette-iru [へっている]. 3)gehin-na [下品な]. 4)genki-no-nai [元気のない].

  (*1*) There was a **low** hill. *Hikui* oka-ga atta.

    He spoke in a **low** voice. Kare-wa *hikui*-koe-de hanashita.

    His room has a **low** ceiling.

        Kare-no heya wa tenjô ga *hikui*.

  (*2*) The well is very **low**. Ido-no-mizu ga totemo *hette-iru*.

  (*3*) a **low** talk *gehin-na* hanashi

  (*4*) He was in **low** spirits. Kare-wa *genki-ga-nakatta*.

    (*ad.*) hikuku [低く].

    (*n.*) 1)soko-ne [底値]. 2)teisoku-gia [低速ギア].

low (*n. & vi.*) mô-(to-naku) [もう(と鳴く)].

lower (*vt.*) ...o hikuku-suru […を低くする]; ...o sageru […を下げる].

    (*vi.*) 1)sagaru [下がる]. 2)hikuku-naru [低くなる].

    (*a.*) (...yori-)hikui [(…より)低い].

    (*n.*) (*US colloq.*) gedan-shindai [下段寝台].

lowly (*a.*) 1)hikui [低い]. 2)kenson-shita [謙そんした].

low tide kanchô [干潮].

loyal (*a.*) chûgi-na [忠義な]; chûjitsu-na [忠実な]; seijitsu-na [誠実な].

loyalty (*n.*) chûjitsu [忠実]; chûsei [忠誠].

lubricate (*vt.*) ...o nameraka-ni-suru […を滑らかにする]; ...ni abura-o-sasu […に油を差す].

luck (*n.*) un [運]; kôun [幸運].
  Good luck (to you)! Kôun-o-inorimasu!
  in luck un-ga-muite
  out of luck un-ga-warui
luckily (*ad.*) un-yoku [運よく]; shiawase-ni-mo [幸せにも].
lucky (*a.*) un-no-yoi [運のよい].
ludicrous (*a.*) kokkei-na [こっけいな].
luggage (*n.*) ((*Eng.*)) te-nimotsu [手荷物].
lukewarm (*a.*) 1)nama-nurui [生ぬるい]. 2)fu-nesshin-na [不熱心な].
lull (*vt.*) 1)…o nadameru […をなだめる]. 2)…o shizumeru […を静める].
  (*vi.*) 1)shizumaru [静まる]. 2)nagu [なぐ].
  (*n.*) nagi [なぎ]; ko-yami [小やみ].
lullaby (*n.*) komori-uta [子もり歌].
lumber (*n.*) mokuzai [木材].
luminous (*a.*) 1)hikari-o-hassuru [光を発する]. 2)akarui [明るい].
luminous paint yakô-toryô [夜光塗料].
lump (*n.*) katamari [かたまり]; (*path.*) kobu [こぶ].
  (*vt.*) …o hito-matome-ni-suru […を一まとめにする].
  (*vi.*) katamari-ni-naru [かたまりになる].
lunar (*a.*) tsuki-no [月の].
lunatic (*a.*) seishin-ijô-no [精神異常の].
lunatic asylum seishin-byôin [精神病院].
lunch (*n.*) chûshoku [昼食]; keishoku [軽食].
luncheon (*n.*) 1) = lunch. 2)chûshoku-kai [昼食会].
lung (*n.*) hai [肺].
lure (*vt.*) 1)…o yûwaku-suru […を誘惑する]. 2)…o obiki-yoseru […をおびき寄せる].
  (*n.*) 1)hiki-tsukeru-mono [引きつけるもの]. 2)(*fishing*) ruâ [ルアー].
lurk (*vi.*) 1)sempuku-suru [潜伏する]. 2)koso-koso-ugoku [こそこそ動く].
lust (*n.*) tsuyoi-yokubô [強い欲望].
  (*vi.*) katsubô-suru [渇望する].
luster, -tre (*n.*) kôtaku [光沢]; tsuya [つや].
luxuriant (*a.*) 1)hammo-shita [繁茂した]; (*tochi no*) koeta [(土地の)肥えた]; (*sôzô-ryoku no*) yutaka-na [(想像力の)豊かな]. 2)karei-na [華麗な].

luxurious (*a.*) zeitaku-na [ぜい沢な].
luxury (*n.*) 1)zeitaku [ぜい沢]. 2)zeitaku-hin [ぜい沢品].
  (*1*) His family all live in **luxury**.
       Kare-no kazoku wa mina *zeitaku*-ni kurashite-iru.
  (*2*) They regard coffee as a **luxury**.
       Kare-ra-wa kôhî-o *zeitaku-hin*-to kangaete-iru.
lymph (*n.*) (*physiol.*) rimpa[-eki] [リンパ(液)].
lynch (*vt.*) ...o rinchi-ni-yotte-korosu [...をリンチによって殺す].
lynx (*n.*) (*zool.*) oo-yamaneko [オオヤマネコ].
lyric (*n. & a.*) jojô-shi(-teki-na) [叙情詩(的な)].

M

ma (*n.*) kaa-chan [かあちゃん].
ma'am (*n.*) ((*US*)) oku-sama [奥さま].
machine (*n.*) 1)kikai [機械]. 2)jidôsha [自動車]; hikô-ki [飛行機].
      (*vt.*) ...o kikai-de-tsukuru [...を機械で作る].
machine gun kikan-jû [機関銃].
machinery (*n.*) 1)kikai-rui [機械類]; kikai-sôchi [機械装置]. 2)kikô
  [機構]; shi-kumi [仕組み].
mackerel (*n.*) (*fish*) saba [サバ].
mackintosh (*n.*) ((*Eng.*)) bôsui-gaitô [防水外とう]; reinkôto [レイン
macro- ookii- [大きい−].   └コート].
mad (*a.*) 1)hakkyô-shita [発狂した]. 2)(*colloq.*) okotta [怒った].

go(run) mad hakkyô-suru

madam (n.) oku-sama [奥さま].

Madame (n.) …fujin […夫人].

made-to-order (a.) atsurae-no [あつらえの].

madly (ad.) kurutta-ka-no-yô-ni [狂ったかのように].

madman (n.) kyôjin [狂人].

madness (n.) kyôki [狂気].

magazine (n.) 1)zasshi [雑誌]. 2)(mil.) kayaku-ko [火薬庫]; dan'yaku-ko [弾薬庫].

magic (n.) mahô [魔法]; kijutsu [奇術].
   (a.) mahô-no [魔法の]; kijutsu-no [奇術の]; fushigi-na [不思議な].

magician (n.) mahô-tsukai [魔法使い]; kijutsu-shi [奇術師].

magistrate (n.) 1)gyôsei-chôkan [行政長官]. 2)chian-hanji [治安判事].

magnet (n.) jishaku [磁石].

magnetic (a.) jishaku-no [磁石の]; miryoku-no-aru [魅力のある].

magnetism (n.) 1)jiki [磁気]. 2)miryoku [魅力].

magnificent (a.) 1)sôdai-na [壮大な]; rippa-na [立派な]. 2)(colloq.) subarashii [すばらしい].

magnify (vt.) 1)…o kakudai-suru […を拡大する]. 2)…o kochô-suru […を誇張する].

magnifying glass kakudai-kyô [拡大鏡]; mushi-megane [虫めがね].

magnitude (n.) 1)ookisa [大きさ]. 2)(jishin no) magunichûdo [(地震の)マグニチュード].

maid (n.) meido [メイド].

maiden (a.) mikon-no [未婚の]; hajimete-no [初めての].
   (n.) shojo [処女]; otome [おとめ].

mail (n.) yûbin[-butsu] [郵便(物)].
   (vt.) ((US)) …o yûsô-suru […を郵送する].

mailbox (n.) ((US)) yûbin-bako [郵便箱].

mailman (n.) ((US)) yûbin-shûhai-nin [郵便集配人].

mail-order (a.) tsûshin-hambai-no [通信販売の].

mail order tsûshin-hambai [通信販売]; mêru-ôdâ [メールオーダー].

maim (vt.) …o sokonau […をそこなう]; …o yaku-ni-tatanaku-suru […を役にたたなくする].

main (a.) omo-na [主な]; shuyô-na [主要な].
   (n.) shuyô-bu[bun] [主要部(分)].

mainland (n.) hondo [本土]; (the M-) Beikoku-hondo [米国本土];

(Nihon no) Honshû [(日本の)本州].

mainly (*ad.*) omo-ni [主に]; dai-bubun-wa [大部分は].

maintain (*vt.*) 1)...o tamotsu […を保つ]; ...o iji-suru […を維持する];
...o hozon-suru […を保存する]. 2)...o shuchô-suru […を主張する].

maintenance (*n.*) 1)iji [維持]; seibi [整備]. 2)shuchô [主張]; shiji
[支持].

maize (*n.*) ((*Eng.*)) tômorokoshi [トウモロコシ].

majesty (*n.*) 1)igen [威厳]. 2)(M-) Heika [陛下].

major (*n.*) 1)(*mil.*) rikugun-shôsa [陸軍少佐]. 2)(*law*) seijin [成人].
3)((*US*)) senkô-kamoku [専攻科目].
　　　(*a.*) 1)ookii-hô-no [大きい方の]; shuyô-na [主要な]. 2)((*Eng.*))
nenchô-no [年長の].
　　　(*vi.*) ((*US*)) senkô-suru [専攻する].

majority (*n.*) 1)dai-tasû [大多数]; ka-hansû [過半数]. 2)seinen [成年].
　　(*1*) The **majority** of people was for him.
　　　　　Dai-tasû-no-hito wa kare-o-shiji-shita.
　　(*2*) He attained his **majority**. Kare-wa *seinen*-ni tasshita.

make (*vt.*) 1)...o tsukuru […を作る]. 2)...o suru […をする]; ...o
okonau […を行なう]. 3)...ni suru […にする]. 4)...ni naru […になる].
5)(zembu de)...ni naru [(全部で)…になる]. 6)...ni tsuku […に着く].
7)...to omou […と思う].
　　(*1*) He **makes** a toy. Kare-wa omocha-*o tsukuru*.
　　(*2*) He will **make** a speech in English.
　　　　　Kare-wa Eigo-de supîchi-*o suru*-darô.
　　(*3*) He **made** them happy. Kare-wa kare-ra-o kôfuku-*ni-shita*.
　　(*4*) Your daughter will **make** a good wife.
　　　　　Kimi-no musume wa ii oku-san-*ni naru*-darô.
　　(*5*) One and one **make(s)** two. Ichi-to-ichi-de ni-*ni naru*.
　　(*6*) I shall **make** Tokyo by six.
　　　　　Watashi-wa roku-ji-made-ni-wa Tôkyô-*ni tsuku*-darô.
　　(*7*) What do you **make** of her? Kano-jo-o dô-*omoi-masu*-ka?
　　　　(*vi.*) iku [行く]; susumu [進む].
　　　　They **made** for the shore.
　　　　　Kare-ra-wa kishi-ni-mukatte *susunda*.

make...from ...de tsukuru
　　Japanese sake is made from rice.
　　　Nihon-shu wa kome-de tsukuru.

make...into ...de...o tsukuru

    We make grape into wine. Budô-de budô-shu-o tsukuru.

make it ((*US*)) umaku-yaru

    You needn't so worry about it, he'll surely make it.

        Ammari-kuyo-kuyo-suru-na, kare-ga kitto umaku-yaru-sa.

make...of ...de...o

    He made a desk of wood. Kare-wa ki-de tsukue-o tsukutta.

make little of ...o keishi-suru

make much of ...o jûshi-shi-sugiru

make out 1)...o sakusei-suru. 2)...o rikai-suru

  1) Please make out a list. Risuto-o tsukutte-kudasai.

  2) Can you make me out ?

      Kimi-wa watashi-no-iu-koto-ga wakaru-ka-ne ?

make up 1)...o tsukuri-ageru. 2)...o oginau; ...o ume-awaseru.
  3)...ni keshô-suru

  1) He made up a baseball team of ten.

      Kare-wa jû-nin-de yakyû-chîmu-o tsukuri-ageta.

  2) He worked hard to make up his losses.

      Kare-wa songai-o ume-awase-yô-to isshô-kemmei hataraita.

  3) Please wait a moment. I'll make up my face.

      Chotto matte-ne. O-keshô-suru-kara.

    (*n.*) 1)...sei […製]. 2)kata [型].

  (*1*) This clock is of German **make**.

      Kono oki-dokei wa Doitsu-*sei*-desu.

make-believe (*n.* & *a.*) itsuwari(-no) [いつわり(の)]; mise-kake(-no)
[見せかけ(の)].

maker (*n.*) seisaku-sha [製作者]; seizô-gyô-sha [製造業者]; mêkâ [メー
カー].

makeup (*n.*) 1)keshô [化粧]. 2)kôzô [構造]; kôsei [構成]. 3)
seishitsu [性質].

making (*n.*) tsukuru-koto [作ること]; keisei [形成].

malaria (*n.*) (*path.*) mararia [マラリア].

Malay (*n.*) Marê-jin [マレー人]; Marê-go [マレー語].

    (*a.*) Marê-jin-no [マレー人の]; Marê-go-no [マレー語の]; Marê-
hantô-no [マレー半島の].

male (*n.* & *a.*) dansei(-no) [男性(の)]; osu(-no) [雄(の)].

malice (*n.*) akui [悪意]; tekii [敵意].

malicious (*a.*) akui-no-aru [悪意のある]; iji-no-warui [意地の悪い].

malt (*n.*) bakuga [麦芽]; moruto [モルト].

mamma (*n.*) kaa-chan [かあちゃん]; mama [ママ].

mammal (*n.*) honyû-dôbutsu [ほ乳動物].

mammoth (*n.*) mammosu [マンモス].

        (*a.*) kyodai-na [巨大な].

mammy (*n.*) kaa-chan [かあちゃん].

man (*n.*) 1)hito [人]; ningen [人間]. 2)otoko [男]; seinen-no-dansei [成年の男性].

    (*1*) Man is mortal. *Ningen wa shinu-mono-da.*

manage (*vt.*) 1)...o umaku-tori-atsukau […をうまく取り扱う]; ...o sôjû-suru […を操縦する]; ...o gyosuru […を御する]. 2)...o shori-suru […を処理する]. 3)...o keiei-suru […を経営する]. 4)...o dô-nika-shite...(suru) […をどうにかして…(する)].

    (*1*) He **manages** a boat well. *Kare-wa bôto-o umaku sôjû-suru.*

    (*2*) Can you **manage** this affair well?

        Kimi-wa kono koto-o umaku shori-suru-koto-ga-dekiru-ka?

    (*3*) He **manages** a hotel. *Kare-wa hoteru-o keiei-shite-iru.*

    (*4*) We **managed** to get there.

        Ware-ware-wa dô-nika-soko-ni tadori-tsuita.

management (*n.*) 1)tori-atsukai [取り扱い]; sôjû [操縦]. 2)shori-nôryoku [処理能力]. 3)keiei [経営].

manager (*n.*) shihai-nin [支配人]; manêjâ [マネージャー]; kanji [幹事].

mane (*n.*) tategami [たてがみ].

maneuver, -noeuvre (*n. & vi.*) 1)(*pl. mil.*) enshû(-suru) [演習(する)]; sakusen-kôdô(-o-toru) [作戦行動(をとる)]. 2)saku(-o-rôsuru) [策(をろうする)].

        (*vt.*) 1)...ni sakusen-kôdô-o-toraseru […に作戦行動をとらせる]. 2)...o(-takumi-ni) ayatsuru […を(巧みに)操る].

manful (*a.*) otoko-rashii [男らしい].

manfully (*ad.*) otoko-rashiku [男らしく]; yûkan-ni [勇敢に].

manhood (*n.*) 1)seijin-de-aru-koto [成人であること]. 2)otoko-rashisa [男らしさ]; yûki [勇気].

-mania ...kyô [⋯狂]; ...mania [⋯マニア].

manifest (*a.*) akiraka-na [明らかな].

        (*vt.*) 1)...o akiraka-ni-suru […を明らかにする]. 2)...o shômei-suru […を証明する].

        (*n.*) tsumi-ni-mokuroku [積荷目録]; okuri-jô [送り状]; jôkyaku-meibo [乗客名簿].

manifold (*a.*) iro-iro-na ［いろいろな］; ta-hômen-no ［多方面の］.
　　　(*vt.*) ...o fukusha-suru ［…を複写する］; ...no kopî-o-toru ［…のコピーをとる］.

mankind (*n.*) jinrui ［人類］.

manly (*a.*) otoko-rashii ［男らしい］.

manner (*n.*) 1)hôhô ［方法］; yari-kata ［やり方］. 2)taido ［態度］; yôsu ［様子］. 3)(*pl.*) gyôgi ［行儀］; sahô ［作法］; manâ ［マナー］. 4)(*pl.*) shûkan ［習慣］.
　　(*1*) He did it in the different **manner**.
　　　　Kare-wa chigatta-*yari-kata*-de sore-o yatta.
　　(*2*) His **manner** was quite natural.
　　　　Kare-no *taido* wa kiwamete shizen-datta.
　　(*3*) He has good **manners**. Kare-wa *gyôgi*-ga-ii.
　　(*4*) Each country has its own customs and **manners**.
　　　　Sore-zore-no kuni niwa tokuyû-no fûzoku-*shûkan*-ga aru.

mansion (*n.*) dai-teitaku ［大邸宅］.

mantelpiece (*n.*) mantorupîsu ［マントルピース］.

mantle (*n.*) manto ［マント］; gaitô ［外とう］.

manual (*a.*) te-no ［手の］; te-de-suru ［手でする］.
　　(*n.*) te-biki ［手引き］.

manufacture (*n.*) seizô ［製造］; (*pl.*) seihin ［製品］.
　　　　(*vt.*) ...o seizô-suru ［…を製造する］.

manufacturer (*n.*) seizô-gyô-sha ［製造業者］.

manufacturing (*n. & a.*) seizô(-no) ［製造(の)］.

manure (*n.*) hiryô ［肥料］.
　　　　(*vt.*) ...ni hiryô-o-yaru ［…に肥料をやる］.

manuscript (*n.*) genkô ［原稿］; shahon ［写本］.
　　　　(*a.*) te-gaki-no ［手書きの］.

many (*n. & a.*) tasû(-no) ［多数(の)］.
　a good many　kanari-ooku-no
　a great many　hijô-ni-ooku-no
　as many as　...mo-no-ooku-no
　how many　ikutsu(-no)

map (*n.*) chizu ［地図］.

maple (*n.*) (*bot.*) kaede ［カエデ］; momiji ［モミジ］.

mar (*vt.*) ...o kizu-tsukeru ［…を傷つける］; ...o dai-nashi-ni-suru ［…を台無しにする］.

marble (*n.*) 1)dairiseki ［大理石］. 2)dairiseki-chôkoku ［大理石彫刻］.

3)(*pl.*) o-hajiki-asobi [おはじき遊び].

    (*a.*) dairiseki-no [大理石の]; katai [硬い]; tsumetai [つめたい].

March (*n.*) Sangatsu [三月].

march (*n.* & *vi.*) kôshin(-suru) [行進(する)].

    (*vt.*) …o kôshin-saseru […を行進させる].

mare (*n.*) mesu-uma [雌馬].

margin (*n.*) 1)fuchi [縁]; yohaku [余白]. 2)yoyû [余裕]. 3)(*com.*) rizaya [利ざや]; mâjin [マージン].

marine (*a.*) 1)umi-no [海の]. 2)sempaku-no [船舶の]; kaiji-no [海事の].

    (*n.*) 1)zen-sempaku [全船舶]. 2)(the Marines) ((*US*)) kaihei-tai [海兵隊].

marine insurance kaijô-hoken [海上保険].

marine products kaisam-butsu [海産物].

mariner (*n.*) sen'in [船員].

marionette (*n.*) ayatsuri-ningyô [操り人形]; marionetto [マリオネット].

maritime (*a.*) 1)umi-no [海の]. 2)engan-chikaku-ni-sumu [沿岸近くに住む].

mark (*n.*) 1)shirushi [しるし]; shimi [しみ]; ato [跡]. 2)kigô [記号]; fugô [符号]. 3)mato [的]; mokuhyô [目標]; hyôteki [標的]. 4)ten [sû] [点(数)].

    (*1*) There is a dirty **mark** on the curtain.

        Kâten-ni kitanai-*shimi*-ga hitotsu aru.

    (*2*) a question **mark**   gimon-*fu*

    (*3*) The shot hit the **mark**.   Tama wa *mato*-ni atatta.

    (*4*) He got full **marks** for English.

        Kare-wa Eigo-de man*ten*-o totta.

    (*vt.*) 1)…ni shirushi-o-tsukeru […にしるしをつける]. 2)…o shimesu […を示す]. 3)…ni chûi-o-harau […に注意を払う].

    (*1*) **Mark** the passages you can't get well.

        Yoku-wakara-nai-bunshô-*ni shirushi-o-tsuke-nasai*.

    (*2*) Wrinkles do not always **mark** age.

        Shiwa wa kanarazu-shimo rônen-o *shimesu*-towa-kagira-nai.

    (*3*) He didn't **mark** his teacher's words.

        Kare-wa sensei-no kotoba-o *chûi-shite-kika*-nakatta.

mark down 1)...o ne-sage-suru. 2)...o kaki-tomeru

1) The $200 overcoat has been marked down 40%.

Ni-hyaku-doru-no-ôbâ ga yon-juppâsento ne-sage-sareta.

2) Mark down carefully what the teacher says.

Sensei-no-iwareru-koto-o chûi-shite kaki-tome-nasai.

market (*n.*) 1)ichiba [市場]; mâketto [マーケット]. 2)sôba [相場].

marking (*n.*) shirushi-ya-tensû-o-tsukeru-koto [しるしや点数をつけること]; shirushi [しるし]; ten [点].

marriage (*n.*) kekkon [結婚].

married (*a.*) kekkon-shita [結婚した]; fûfu-no [夫婦の].

　　get married (to) ...(to) kekkon-suru

marry (*vt.*) ...to kekkon-suru [···と結婚する]; ...o kekkon-saseru [···を結婚させる].

　　　　(*vi.*) kekkon-suru [結婚する].

Mars (*n.*) (*astron.*) Kasei [火星].

marsh (*n.*) numa-chi [沼地].

marshal (*n.*) 1)(*mil.*) rikugun-gensui [陸軍元帥]. 2)((*US*)) rempô-hoan-kan [連邦保安官].

　　　　(*vt.*) 1)...o seiretsu-saseru [···を整列させる]. 2)...o annai-suru [···を案内する].

　　　　(*vi.*) seiretsu-suru [整列する].

marshy (*a.*) numa-chi-no [沼地の].

mart (*n.*) ichiba [市場].

martial (*a.*) 1)sensô-no [戦争の]. 2)yûkan-na [勇敢な]. 3)kôsen-teki-na [好戦的な].

martial law kaigen-rei [戒厳令].

martin (*n.*) (*birds*) iwa-tsubame [イワツバメ].

martyr (*n.*) junkyô-sha [殉教者].

　　　　(*vt.*) ...o junkyô-sha-to-shite-korosu [···を殉教者として殺す]; ...o hakugai-suru [···を迫害する]; ...o kurushimeru [···を苦しめる].

marvel (*n.*) odoroku-beki-koto[-hito] [驚くべきこと[人]].

　　　　(*vt.*) ...ni odoroku [···に驚く]; ...o fushigi-ni-omou [···を不思議に思う].

　　　　(*vi.*) kyôtan-suru [驚嘆する].

marvel(l)ous (*a.*) 1)odoroku-beki [驚くべき]; fushigi-na [不思議な]. 2)(*colloq.*) subarashii [すばらしい].

Marxism (*n.*) Marukusu-shugi [マルクス主義].

masculine (*n. & a.*) dansei(-no) [男性(の)].

mask (*n. & vi.*) kamen(-o-kaburu) [仮面(をかぶる)].

(*vt.*) …o kamen-de-oou […を仮面で覆う].

mason (*n.*) sekkô [石工]; ((*US*)) renga-shokunin [れんが職人].

mass (*n.*) 1)katamari [かたまり]. 2)shûdan [集団]; atsumari [集まり]. 3)tasû [多数]; taryô [多量].

(*vt.*) …o hito-katamari-ni-suru […を一かたまりにする]; …o shûketsu-suru […を集結する].

(*vi.*) hito-katamari-ni-naru [一かたまりになる]; atsumaru [集まる].

mass, Mass (*n.*) misa [ミサ].

massage (*n.*) massâji [マッサージ].

(*vt.*) …o massâji-suru […をマッサージする].

mass communication masukomi [マスコミ].

massive (*a.*) ookikute-omoi [大きくて重い]; dosshiri-to-shita [どっしりとした].

mass media taishû-baitai [大衆媒体]; masu-media [マスメディア].

mass production tairyô-seisan [大量生産]; masupuro [マスプロ].

mast (*n.*) ho-bashira [帆柱]; masuto [マスト].

master (*n.*) 1)shujin [主人]; …chô […長]. 2)((*Eng.*)) sensei [先生]. 3)meijin [名人]; taika [大家]. 4)(M-) shûshi [修士].

(*1*) **master** and man　*shujin* to meshitsukai

(*2*) He is a music **master**.　Kare-wa ongaku-no *sensei* desu.

(*3*) He is a **master** of English literature.
　　Kare-wa Ei-bungaku no *taika* da.

(*4*) **Master** of Arts　bungaku-*shûshi*

(*vt.*) 1)…o seifuku-suru […を征服する]. 2)…ni seitsû-suru […に精通する]; …o masutâ-suru […をマスターする].

(*1*) He could not **master** his fate.
　　Kare-wa jibun-no ummei-o *seifuku-suru-koto-wa-deki-nakatta*.

(*2*) He **has mastered** English.　Kare-wa Eigo-*ni seitsû-shite-iru*.

masterpiece (*n.*) kessaku [傑作]; meisaku [名作].

master plan kihon-keikaku [基本計画]; masutâ-puran [マスタープラン].

mastery (*n.*) 1)shihai [支配]; yûetsu [優越]. 2)jukutatsu [熟達].

mat (*n.*) mushiro [むしろ]; goza [ござ]; tatami [たたみ]; matto [マット]; kutsu-nugui [靴ぬぐい].

(*vt.*) 1)…ni matto-o-shiku […にマットを敷く]. 2)…o

motsuresaseru [⋯をもつれさせる].

   (*vi.*) motsureru [もつれる].

match (*n.*) 1)kô-tekishu [好敵手]. 2)shiai [試合]. 3)engumi [縁組み].

   (*1*) I am no **match** for you in English.

      Watashi-wa Eigo-de-wa kimi-ni-wa *kanawa*-nai.

   (*2*) We had a baseball **match**.

      Ware-ware-wa yakyû-no *shiai*-o yatta.

     (*vt.*) 1)...to kyôsô-saseru [⋯と競争させる]. 2)...ni hitteki-suru [⋯に匹敵する]. 3)...o chôwa-saseru [⋯を調和させる].

     (*vi.*) tsuri-au [釣り合う].

matchless (*a.*) hitteki-suru-mono-ga-nai [匹敵するものがない]; muhi-no [無比の].

mate (*n.*) 1)nakama [仲間]. 2)(*colloq.*) haigû-sha [配偶者]. 3)(*marine*) kôkai-shi [航海士].

     (*vt.*) 1)...o kekkon-saseru [⋯を結婚させる]. 2)...o itchi-saseru [⋯を一致させる].

     (*vi.*) tsugau [つがう]; itchi-suru [一致する].

material (*n.*) 1)zairyô [材料]; genryô [原料]. 2)ki-ji [生地]. 3)(*pl.*) yôgu [用具].

   (*1*) raw **material** gen-*zairyô*

   (*2*) dress **material** fuku*ji*

   (*3*) writing **materials** hikki-*yôgu*

     (*a.*) 1)busshitsu-no [物質の]; busshitsu-teki-na [物質的な]. 2)jûyô-na [重要な].

materialism (*n.*) (*philos.*) yuibutsu-ron [唯物論]; yuibutsu-shugi [唯物主義]. jitsuri-shugi [実利主義].

materialistic (*a.*) yuibutsu-ron-no [唯物論の]; yuibutsu-shugi-teki-na [唯物主義的な]; jitsuri-shugi-no [実利主義の].

materially (*ad.*) 1)busshitsu-teki-ni [物質的に]. 2)jisshitsu-teki-ni [実質的に]. 3)ooi-ni [大いに].

maternal (*a.*) haha-no [母の]; haha-rashii [母らしい].

maternity (*n.*) haha-de-aru-koto [母であること]; bosei [母性].

maternity hospital san'in [産院].

maternity nurse josam-pu [助産婦].

mathematics (*n.*) sûgaku [数学].

matinée, -nee (*n.*) chûkan-kôgyô [昼間興業]; machinê [マチネー].

matrix (*n.*) 1)botai [母体]. 2)igata [鋳型]. 3)(*math.*) gyôretsu [行列]; matorikkusu [マトリックス].

matron (*n.*) 1)(nempai de hin-no-aru) fujin [(年配で品のある)婦人].
2)kasei-fu-chô [家政婦長]; hobo [保母]; ryôbo [寮母]; ((*Eng.*))
kango-fu-chô [看護婦長].

matter (*n.*) 1)busshitsu [物質]. 2)koto-gara [事柄]; jiken [事件]. 3)
(*pl.*) jijô [事情].
(*1*) mind and **matter** seishin to *busshitsu*
(*2*) It's a **matter** of regret. Sore-wa ikan na *koto* da.
    What's the **matter** with you? Dô-shita-no-desu-ka?
(*3*) **Matters** are different in this State.
    Kono-shû-de-wa *jijô* ga chigau.
  no matter how(**what, when, where, who**) tatoe-dô(-nani-ga; -itsu,
   -doko-de, -dare-ga)(...suru-)to-shite-mo
      (*vi.*) jûyô-de-aru [重要である].
    It **matters** little to me.
      Sore-wa watashi-niwa hotondo *jûyô*-ja-nai.
      Sore-wa watashi-niwa dô-demo-ii-koto-da.

mattress (*n.*) (shindai no) shiki-buton [(寝台の)敷布団]; mattoresu
[マットレス].

mature (*a.*) 1)seijuku-shita [成熟した]; enjuku-shita [円熟した]. 2)
(*com.*) shiharai-kigen-no-kita [支払期限の来た].
    (*vt.*) ...o seijuku-saseru [···を成熟させる].
    (*vi.*) 1)seijuku-suru [成熟する]. 2)manki-ni-naru [満期になる].

maturity (*n.*) 1)seijuku [成熟]; enjuku [円熟]. 2)manki [満期].

maxim (*n.*) kakugen [格言]; kingen [金言]; shosei-kun [処世訓].

maximum (*n.*) saidai-gen [最大限]; saidai-sû [最大数]; saidai-ryô
[最大量].
    (*a.*) saidai-no [最大の]; saikô-no [最高の].

May (*n.*) Gogatsu [五月].

may (*aux. v.*) 1)...(shite-)mo-yoi [···(して)もよい]; (...shite-)mo-
sashitsukae-nai [···(して)もさしつかえない]. 2)...kamo-shirenai [···か
もしれない]. 3)...(suru-)yô-ni [···(する)ように]. 4)(tatoe)...de-arô-
tomo [(たとえ)···であろうとも]. 5)negawaku-wa...naran-koto-o [願わ
くは···ならんことを]. 6)dekiru [できる].
(*1*) **May** l go out now? Soto-e itte-*mo-yoroshii*-ka?
(*2*) It **may** rain tomorrow. Asu ame-ga-furu-*kamo-shirenai*.
(*3*) He works hard that he **may** succeed.
    Kare-wa seikô-suru-*yô-ni* isshô-kemmei-ni hataraku.
(*4*) Come what **may**, I'll stay here.

Nani-goto-ga okorô-*tomo*, watashi-wa koko-ni todomaru.

(5) **May** you succeed!

Negawaku-wa anata-ga seikô-*nasaru-koto-o!*

(6) You **may** imagine my rapture.

Kimi-wa boku-no yorokobi-ga sôzô-*deki-yô*.

maybe (*ad.*) tabun [たぶん]; osoraku [おそらく].

May Day Rôdô-sai [労働祭]; Mêdê [メーデー].

mayflower (*n.*) ((*Eng.*)) sanzashi [サンザシ].

mayor (*n.*) shichô [市長].

maze (*n.*) meiro [迷路]; tôwaku [当惑].

me (*pron.*) watashi-o [私を]; watashi-ni [私に].

meadow (*n.*) kusa-chi [草地]; bokusô-chi [牧草地].

meal (*n.*) shokuji [食事]; isshoku-bun [一食分].

meal (*n.*) hikiwari [ひきわり].

mean (*a.*) 1)misuborashii [みすぼらしい]. 2)hiretsu-na [卑劣な]. 3) kechi-na [けちな]. 4)((*US*)) iji-no-warui [意地の悪い].

mean (*vt.*) 1)...(suru-)tsumori-de-aru […(する)つもりである]. 2)...o imi-suru […を意味する].

(1) I **mean** to stay here. Watashi-wa koko-ni iru-*tsumori-da*.

(2) What does this word **mean**? Kono go wa donna-*imi-desu*-ka?

mean (*n. & a.*) heikin(-no) [平均(の)]; chûkan(-no) [中間(の)]; chûi-no [中位の].

meaning (*n.*) 1)imi [意味]; igi [意義]. 2)kôka [効果].

　　　　(*a.*) 1)imi-shinchô-na [意味深長な]. 2)(...suru-)tsumori-no [(…する)つもりの].

means (*n.*) 1)shudan [手段]; hôhô [方法]; hôben [方便]. 2)shiryoku [資力]; shisan [資産].

(1) I told a lie as a **means**. Watashi-wa *hôben*-to-shite uso-o itta.

(2) He is a man of **means**. Kare-wa *shisan*-ka da.

　by all means yoroshii-desu-tomo

　by means of ...ni-yotte; ...de

　by no means kesshite...(shi-)nai

meantime (*n. & ad.*) sô-shite-iru-aida(-ni) [そうしている間(に)].

　in the meantime tokaku-suru-uchi-ni

measles (*n.*) (*med.*) hashika [はしか].

measure (*n.*) 1)sumpô [寸法]; bunryô [分量]. 2)mono-sashi [物差し]; maki-jaku [巻尺]; masu [ます]. 3)shudan [手段]; hôhô [方法];

shochi [処置]. 4)gendo [限度].

above(beyond) measure hôgai-ni

in a great(large) measure yohodo; dai-bubun

in a measure ikura-ka; yaya

　　(*vt.*) 1)...o hakaru [...を測る]; ...no sumpô-o-toru '[...の寸法をとる]. 2)...o hyôka-suru [...を評価する].

　　(*vi.*) (naga-sa ya takasa ya mekata ga)...aru [(長さや高さや目方が)...ある].

measurement (*n.*) 1)hakaru-koto [測ること]. 2)(*pl.*) sumpô [寸法].

meat (*n.*) shokuyô-niku [食用肉].

mechanic (*n.*) kikai-kô [機械工]; shûri-kô [修理工]; jukuren-kô [熟練工].

mechanical (*a.*) kikai[-gaku]-no [機械(学)の]; kikai-teki-na [機械的な].

mechanical engineering kikai-kôgaku [機械工学].

mechanically (*ad.*) kikai-teki-ni [機械的に].

mechanics (*n.*) kikai-gaku [機械学]; rikigaku [力学].

mechanism (*n.*) 1)kikai-sôchi [機械装置]. 2)karakuri [からくり].

medal (*n.*) medaru [メダル]; kishô [記章]; kunshô [勲章].

meddle (*vi.*) kanshô-suru [干渉する]; o-sekkai-suru [おせっかいする].

meddlesome (*a.*) o-sekkai-na [おせっかいな].

medial (*a.*) chûkan-no [中間の]; heikin-no [平均の].

medical (*a.*) 1)igaku-no [医学の]; iryô-no [医療の]. 2)naika-no [内科の].

medicine (*n.*) 1)kusuri [薬]. 2)naika [内科].

medieval (*a.*) chûsei-no [中世の].

meditate (*vt.*) ...o mokuromu [...をもくろむ].

　　(*vi.*) fukaku-kangaeru [深く考える].

meditation (*n.*) 1)jukkô [熟考]; meisô [めい想]. 2)(*pl.*) meisô-roku [めい想録].

Mediterranean, the (*n.*) Chichû-kai [地中海].

medium (*n.*) 1)chûkan [中間]; chûyô [中庸]. 2)baitai [媒体]; baikai [媒介]; shudan [手段].

　　(*a.*) chûkan-no [中間の]; futsû-no [普通の].

medley (*n.*) yose-atsume [寄せ集め].

medley relay medorê-rirê [メドレーリレー].

meek (*a.*) otonashii [おとなしい].

meekly (*ad.*) otonashiku [おとなしく].

meet (*vt.*) 1)...ni de-au [...に出会う]. 2)...o de-mukaeru [...を出迎え

る]. 3)...to shiri-ai-ni-naru […と知り合いになる]. 4)...o mitasu […
を満たす]; ...o kanaeru […をかなえる].
   (*vi.*) 1)de-au [出会う]. 2)tsunagaru [つながる].
  meet with 1)...ni sôgû-suru; ...o keiken-suru. 2)...to yakusoku-
shite-kaidan-suru

meeting (*n.*) shûkai [集会]; kai [会].

megalopolis (*n.*) kyodai-toshi [巨大都市]; megaroporisu [メガロポリ
ス].

megaphone (*n. & vi.*) megafon(-de-tsutaeru) [メガフォン(で伝える)].

melancholy (*n. & a.*) yûutsu(-na) [憂うつ(な)].

mellow (*a.*) juku-shite-amai [熟して甘い]; yutaka-de-utsukushii [豊
かで美しい].

melodious (*a.*) senritsu-no-utsukushii [旋律の美しい].

melodrama (*n.*) merodorama [メロドラマ].

melody (*n.*) senritsu [旋律]; utsukushii-ongaku [美しい音楽]; merodî
[メロディー].

melt (*vi. & vt.*) 1)tokeru(...o tokasu) [溶ける(…を溶かす)]. 2)
yawaragu(...o yawarageru) [和らぐ(…を和らげる)].
  melt away tokete-naku-naru

member (*n.*) 1)kaiin [会員]; seiin [成員]; ichiin [一員]. 2)te-ashi
[手足].

membership (*n.*) 1)kaiin-no-mibun [会員の身分]. 2)kaiin-sû [会員数].

memorandum (*n.*) oboe-gaki [覚え書き]; memo [メモ].

memorial (*a.*) kinen-no [記念の].
          (*n.*) kinen-butsu [記念物]; kinen-hi [記念碑].

memorize (*vt.*) ...o anki-suru […を暗記する]; ...o kioku-suru […を記
憶する].

memory (*n.*) 1)kioku[-ryoku] [記憶(力)]. 2)tsuioku [追憶]; omoi-de
[思い出]. 3)kinen [記念].
  (*1*) He has a bad **memory**. Kare-wa *kioku-ryoku*-ga warui.
  (*2*) World War I became only a **memory**.
      Dai-ichiji-sekai-taisen wa hitotsu-no *tsuioku*-ni suginaku-
natta.
  (*3*) The bronze statue was set up in **memory** of him.
      Kare-o-*kinen*-shite dôzô ga taterareta.

menace (*n.*) kyôi [脅威].
       (*vt.*) ...ni kyôi-o-ataeru […に脅威を与える].
       (*vi.*) kyôhaku-suru [脅迫する].

mend (*vt.*) 1)...o naosu [⋯を直す]; ...o shûzen-suru [⋯を修繕する].
　2)...o aratameru [⋯を改める].
　(*1*) I **had** my watch **mended**. Watashi-wa tokei-o *shûzen-saseta*.
　(*2*) He **mended** his ways. Kare-wa okonai-o *aratameta*.
　　　(*vi.*) kaishin-suru [改心する]; kôten-suru [好転する].
　　　It is never too late to **mend**.
　　　　Aratameru-no-ni oso-sugiru-koto-wa-nai.
　　　(*n.*) shûzen[-kasho] [修繕(箇所)].
meningitis (*n.*) nômaku-en [脳膜炎].
mental (*a.*) 1)kokoro-no [心の]; seishin-no [精神の]. 2)chiteki-na
　[知的な]. 3)(*colloq.*) seishin-byô-no [精神病の].
mention (*vt.*) 1)...to noberu [⋯と述べる]. 2)...no na-o-ageru [⋯の名
　Don't mention it. Dô-itashi-mashite.　　　　　　　　　└をあげる].
　not to mention ...wa iu-made-mo-naku
　　　　(*n.*) genkyû [言及]; chinjutsu [陳述].
menu (*n.*) 1)kon-date-hyô [献立表]; menyû [メニュー]. 2)shokuji [食
　事]; ryôri [料理].
merchandise (*n.*) shôhin [商品].
merchant (*n.*) shônin [商人]; oroshi-uri-shô [卸売商].
merciful (*a.*) jihi-bukai [慈悲深い].
mercury (*n.*) 1)(*chem.*) suigin [水銀]. 2)(*astron.*)(M-) Suisei [水星].
mercy (*n.*) jihi [慈悲]; megumi [恵み].
　at the mercy of ...no nasu-ga-mama-ni-natte
　for mercy's sake goshô-da-kara
mere (*a.*) tan-naru [単なる].
merely (*ad.*) tan-ni [単に]; tada [ただ].
　not merely...but also ...de-aru-bakari-de-wa-naku-te...
merge (*vt.*) ...o-gappei-suru [⋯を合併する]; (be -d) shidai-ni-
　kawatte-iku [次第に変わっていく].
　　　　(*vi.*) toke-konde...ni-naru [溶け込んで⋯になる].
meridian (*n. & a.*) shigo-sen(-no) [子午線(の)].
merit (*n.*) 1)kachi [価値]; torie [取り柄]; chôsho [長所]. 2)(*pl.*)
　kôseki [功績].
　merits and demerits tokushitsu; kôzai
　　　　(*vt.*) ...ni atai-suru [⋯に値する].
merit system 《*US*》jisseki-seido [実績制度]; jitsuryoku-hon'i-sei [実
　力本位制].
mermaid (*n.*) ningyo [人魚].

merrily (*ad.*) tanoshiku [楽しく]; yôki-ni [陽気に].

merry (*a.*) uki-uki-shita [浮き浮きした]; yôki-na [陽気な].

    Merry Christmas! Kurisumasu-o-medetô!

merry-go-round (*n.*) kaiten-mokuba [回転木馬]; merigôrando [メリーゴーランド].

mesh (*n.*) 1) ami-no-me [網の目]. 2) (*pl.*) ami [網]. 3) (*pl.*) wana [わな].

    (*vt. & vi.*) 1)...o ami-de-tsukamaeru (ami-ni-kakaru) […を網でつかまえる(網にかかる)]. 2)...o kami-awaseru (kami-au) […をかみ合わせる(かみ合う)].

mess (*n.*) 1) sanran [散乱]; ranzatsu [乱雑]. 2) kaishoku〔-nakama〕[会食(仲間)]; isshoku-bun-no-shokumotsu [一食分の食物].

    (*1*) The hall was in a **mess**. Hôru wa *konran*-shite-ita.

    (*2*) He failed to appear at **mess**.

        Kare-wa *kaishoku*-ni de-okureta.

    make a mess of ...o-dai-nashi-ni-suru

    (*vt.*) 1)...o chirakasu […を散らかす]. 2) (*colloq.*) ...o dai-nashi-ni-suru […を台無しにする].

    (*vi.*) kaishoku-suru [会食する].

message (*n.*) tsûshin [通信]; dengon [伝言].

    He sent me a **message** on his journey.

        Kare-wa tabi-saki-kara *tayori*-o yokoshita.

messenger (*n.*) shisha [使者]; tsukai-bashiri [使い走り].

metal (*n.*) kinzoku [金属].

metalic (*a.*) kinzoku-no [金属の]; kinzoku-sei-no [金属性の].

meteor (*n.*) ryûsei [流星].

meteoric (*a.*) 1) ryûsei-no-yô-na [流星のような]. 2) taiki-no [大気の].

meter, -tre (*n.*) mêtoru [メートル].

method (*n.*) 1) hôhô [方法]. 2) seizen-to-shita-chitsujo [整然とした秩序].

methodical (*a.*) 1) soshiki-datta [組織立った]. 2) kichô-men-na [き帳面な].

metric (*a.*) mêtoru〔-hô〕-no [メートル(法)の].

metropolis (*n.*) shuto [首都]; shuyô-toshi [主要都市].

metropolitan (*a.*) 1) shuto-no [首都の]; dai-toshi-no [大都市の]. 2) shuto-dai-shikyô-no [首都大司教の].

    (*n.*) 1) dai-toshi-no-jûmin [大都市の住民]. 2) shuto-dai-shikyô [首都大司教].

mew (*n. & vi.*) nyâ(-to-naku) [にゃー(と鳴く)].

Mexican (*a.*) Mekishiko-no [メキシコの]; Mekishiko-jin-no [メキシコ人の].

      (*n.*) Mekishiko-jin [メキシコ人].

Mexico (*n.*) Mekishiko [メキシコ].

micro- chiisai- [小さい−]; wazuka-na- [わずかな−].

microphone (*n.*) maikurofon [マイクロフォン].

microscope (*n.*) kembi-kyô [顕微鏡].

midday (*n.*) shôgo [正午]; ma-hiru [真昼].

middle (*n. & a.*) chûô(-no) [中央(の)]; mannaka(-no) [真ん中(の)]; chûkan(-no) [中間(の)].

middle-aged (*a.*) chûnen-no [中年の].

middle-class (*a.*) chûsan-kaikyû-no [中産階級の].

middle finger naka-yubi [中指].

midnight (*n.*) ma-yonaka [真夜中].

midsummer (*n.*) 1)ma-natsu [真夏]; seika [盛夏]. 2)geshi-no-koro [夏至のころ].

midway (*a. & ad.*) chûto-no(-ni) [中途の(に)].

might (*n.*) chikara [力]; seiryoku [勢力].

  with all one's might; with might and main
      chikara-ippai; zenryoku-o-tsukushite

mightily (*ad.*) tsuyoku [強く]; chikara-o-komete [力をこめて].

mighty (*a.*) 1)kyôryoku-na [強力な]. 2)(*colloq.*) kyodai-na [巨大な]; hijô-na [非常な].

      (*ad.*) (*colloq.*) hijô-ni [非常に]; totemo [とても].

migrate (*vi.*) ijû-suru [移住する]; idô-suru [移動する].

mild (*a.*) yasashii [優しい]; odayaka-na [穏やかな].

mildly (*ad.*) yasashiku [優しく]; odayaka-ni [穏やかに].

milestone (*n.*) 1)ritei-hyô [里程標]. 2)kakki-teki-na-jiken [画期的な事件].

militarism (*n.*) gunkoku-shugi [軍国主義].

military (*a.*) 1)gun-no [軍の]; gunjin-no [軍人の]. 2)rikugun-no [陸軍の].

      (*n.*) (the –) gunjin [軍人]; guntai [軍隊].

milk (*n.*) chichi [乳]; gyûnyû [牛乳]; miruku [ミルク].

    (*vt.*) ...no chichi-o-shiboru […の乳を搾る].

milkmaid (*n.*) chichi-shibori-no-onna [乳搾りの女].

milkman (*n.*) gyûnyûya [牛乳屋]; gyûnyû-haitatsu-nin [牛乳配達人].

milk shake miruku-sêki [ミルクセーキ].

milk-white (*a.*) nyûhaku-shoku-no [乳白色の].

Milky Way, the (*astron.*) Ginga-kei [銀河系]; Ama-no-gawa [天の川].

mill (*n.*) 1)seifun-jo [製粉所]; suisha-ba [水車場]. 2)kôjô [工場]. 3) funsai-ki [粉砕器].

miller (*n.*) seifun-gyô-sha [製粉業者]; konaya [粉屋].

million (*n. & a.*) hyaku-man(-no) [百万(の)].

　millions of nam-byaku-man-mo-no...

millionaire (*n.*) hyaku-man-chôja [百万長者].

millstone (*n.*) 1)ishi-usu [石うす]. 2)omo-ni [重荷].

mimic (*a.*) 1)mohô-no [模倣の]. 2)mozô-no [模造の].

　　　(*n.*) mono-mane-o-suru-hito [物まねをする人]; mohô-sha[-hin] [模倣者[品]].

　　　　(*vt.*) ...no mane-o-suru [...のまねをする].

mince (*vt.*) ...o komakaku-kiri-kizamu [...を細かく切り刻む].

　　　　(*vi.*) ki-dotte-hanasu [気取って話す]; jôhin-butta-furumai-o-suru [上品ぶった振る舞いをする].

　　　　(*n.*) hiki-niku [ひき肉]; minchi-niku [ミンチ肉].

mind (*n.*) 1)kokoro [心]; seishin [精神]. 2)kioku [記憶]. 3)kangae [考え]; iken [意見].

　(1) a scientific **mind** kagaku-teki-na *seishin*

　(2) Out of sight, out of **mind**.

　　　　Mienaku-nareba, *kioku*-kara-too-zakaru.

　　　　Saru-mono hibi-ni utoshi.

　(3) I am of your **mind**. Watashi-wa anata-to-onaji-*iken*-desu.

　bear(keep)...in mind ...o oboete-iru

　change one's mind kangae-ga-kawaru

　come to one's mind hito-no-kokoro-ni-ukabu

　have...on one's mind ...o shimpai-shite-iru

　keep one's mind on ...ni sennen-suru

　make up one's mind ...to kesshin-suru

　out of one's mind ki-ga-kurutte

　to(in) one's mind jibun-no kangae-de-wa

　　　　(*vt.*) 1)...ni chûi-suru [...に注意する]; ...ni ki-o-tsukeru [...に気を付ける]. 2)...o ki-ni-suru [...を気にする]; ...o shimpai-suru [...を心配する]; ...o iyagaru [...をいやがる]. 3)...no sewa-o-suru [...の世話をする]; ...no ban-o-suru [...の番をする].

　(1) **Mind** the step. Ashi-moto-*ni* ki-o-tsuke-nasai.

　　　　　　Ashi-moto-*ni* go-yôjin.

(2) Never **mind** the cost.　Hiyô-nanka *shimpai-suru*-na.

(3) Some of them **were minding** the little children.
　　　　Naka-ni-wa kodomo-*no-sewa-o-shite-iru*-mono-mo-atta.

mind you　ii-kai

Would you mind opening the window?
　　　　Mado-o akete-kudasai-masen-ka?

　　(*vi.*) 1)chûi-suru [注意する]; shimpai-suru [心配する]. 2)iya-garu [いやがる].

(1) Never **mind**!　*Shimpai-suru*-na!

(2) Do you **mind** if I smoke?　Tabako-o-suttemo-*ii-deshô*-ka?

mine (*pron.*) watashi-no-mono [私のもの].

mine (*n.*) 1)kôzan [鉱山]. 2)(*mil.*) jirai [地雷]; kirai [機雷].
　　(*vi. & vt.*) 1)(...o) saikutsu-suru [(…を)採掘する]. 2)(...ni) jirai-o-fusetsu-suru [(…に)地雷を敷設する].

miner (*n.*) kôfu [坑夫].

mineral (*n. & a.*) kôbutsu[-sei-no] [鉱物(性の)].

mingle (*vt. & vi.*) ...o mazeru (mazaru) […を混ぜる(混ざる)].

miniature (*n.*) 1)saimitsu-ga [細密画]. 2)shô-mokei [小模型]; minichua [ミニチュア].
　　(*a.*) ko-gata-no [小型の]; shukushô-shita [縮小した].
　　(*vt.*) ...o saimitsu-ga-ni-kaku […を細密画にかく]; ...o shukusha-suru […を縮写する].

minimum (*n. & a.*) saishô-gen(-no) [最小限(の)].

minister (*n.*) 1)daijin [大臣]. 2)kôshi [公使]. 3)bokushi [牧師].
　　(*vi.*) sewa-o-suru [世話をする].

ministry (*n.*) 1)(M-) shô [省]. 2)(the M-) naikaku [内閣]. 3) bokushi-no-shoku [牧師の職]; seishoku-sha-tachi [聖職者たち].

minor (*a.*) 1)chiisai-hô-no [小さい方の]; shô... [小…]. 2)jûyô-de-nai [重要でない]; ni-ryû-no [二流の]. 3)((*US*)) fuku-senkô-no [副専攻の]. 4)(*law*) mi-seinen-no [未成年の].
　　(*n.*) mi-seinen-sha [未成年者]; ((*US*)) fuku-senkô-kamoku [副専攻科目].

minority (*n.*) 1)shôsû[-ha] [少数(派)]. 2)shôsû-minzoku [少数民族].

mint (*n.*) zôhei-kyoku [造幣局].

mint (*n.*) (*bot.*) hakka [ハッカ].

minus (*prep.*) (*math.*)...o-hiita […を引いた]; (*colloq.*)...no-nai […のない].
　　(*a.*) mainasu-no [マイナスの]; fu-no [負の].

(*n.*) mainasu-fugô [マイナス符号].

minute (*a.*) 1)kiwamete-chiisai [きわめて小さい]. 2)seimitsu-na [精密な].

minute (*n.*) 1)fun [分]. 2)chotto-no-aida [ちょっとの間]; shibaraku [しばらく].

　(*1*) Sixty **minutes** make an hour.

　　　Roku-jup*pun* de ichi-jikan-ni naru.

　(*2*) Wait a **minute**. *Shibaraku* o-machi-kudasai.

　in a minute sugu-ni

minute hand funshin [分針].

minutely (*ad.*) komakaku [細かく]; kuwashiku [詳しく]; seimitsu-ni [精密に].

miracle (*n.*) kiseki [奇跡].

mirror (*n.*) kagami [鏡]; mirâ [ミラー].

　　　(*vt.*) ...o utsusu […を映す]; ...no sugata-o-shimesu […の姿を示す].

mirth (*n.*) yôki-na-sawagi [陽気な騒ぎ].

misanthropy (*n.*) ningen-girai [人間嫌い]; ningen-fushin [人間不信]; ensei [厭世].

misapprehension (*n.*) omoi-chigai [思い違い].

miscarriage (*n.*) 1)shippai [失敗]. 2)gohai [誤配]. 3)ryûzan [流産].

miscellaneous (*a.*) shuju-no [種々の]; zatsu- [雑－].

mischief (*n.*) 1)[ki]gai [(危)害]. 2)itazura [いたずら].

　(*1*) It will do me **mischief**.

　　　Sore-wa watashi-ni *gai*-o oyobosu-darô.

　(*2*) Children get into **mischief**.

　　　Kodomo-tachi wa *itazura*-o hajimeru.

mischievous (*a.*) yûgai-na [有害な]; itazura-zuki-na [いたずら好きな].

misdeed (*n.*) hikô [非行]; akuji [悪事].

miser (*n.*) shusen-do [守銭奴]; kechim-bô [けちん坊].

miserable (*a.*) 1)fukô-na [不幸な]; mijime-na [みじめな]; nasakenai [情けない]. 2)hinjaku-na [貧弱な]; somatsu-na [粗末な]. 3)hazubeki [恥ずべき]; hiretsu-na [卑劣な].

　(*1*) He could not escape **miserable** fate.

　　　Kare-wa *fukô-na* ummei (*hiun*)-o sakeru-koto-ga-deki-nakatta.

　　　I feel **miserable**. Watashi-wa *nasakenai*.

　(*2*) a **miserable** house *misuborashii* ie

(3) It is **miserable** of you to make fun of him.

　　　Kare-o　warai-mono-ni-suru-no-wa　kimi-to-shite-*hazu-beki-koto-da*.

miserably (*ad.*) mijime-ni [みじめに].

misery (*n.*) 1)(*pl.*) fukô [不幸]. 2)hisan-sa [悲惨さ]; kyûjô [窮状].

misfortune (*n.*) 1)fuun [不運]; fukô [不幸]. 2)sainan [災難].

mishap (*n.*) fuun-na-deki-goto [不運な出来事]; sainan [災難].

misjudge (*vt. & vi.*) (...o) ayamatte-handan-suru [(…を)誤って判断する].

mislay (*vt.*) ...o oki-wasureru […を置き忘れる].

misleading (*a.*) hito-o-ayamaraseru [人を誤らせる]; magirawashii [紛らわしい].

misprint (*n.*) goshoku [誤植]; misupurinto [ミスプリント].
　　　(*vt.*) ...o goshoku-suru […を誤植する].

miss (*n.*) 1)(M-)...jô […嬢]; ...san […さん]. 2)musume [娘]. 3)(M-) misu... [ミス…].

miss (*vt.*) 1)...o tori-nigasu […を取り逃がす]; ...ni nori-sokonau […に乗りそこなう]. 2)...o nogasu […を逃がす]. 3)...o mi-otosu […を見落とす]; ...o kiki-otosu […を聞き落す]. 4)...ga (i-)nai-node-sabishiku-omou […が(い)ないのでさびしく思う]; ...ga (i)nai-no-ni-ki-ga-tsuku […が(い)ないのに気が付く].

(1) I **missed** the train.　Watashi-wa kisha-*ni nori-sokonatta*.

(2) I **missed** an opportunity of going abroad.

　　　Watashi-wa kaigai-e iku-kikai-*o nogashita*.

(3) I **missed** the best part of the drama.

　　　Watashi-wa shibai no ichiban-ii tokoro-*o mi-sokonatta*.

(4) I **miss** you very much.

　　　Watashi-wa anata-ga-*i-nai-node* taihen *sabishii*.

　　　I **missed** my purse.

　　　Watashi-wa saifu ga *naku-natte-iru-no-ni-ki-zuita*.

miss fire fuhatsu-ni-owaru
　　　(*vi.*) mato-ni-ate-sokonau [的に当て損なう]; shippai-suru [失敗する].
　　　(*n.*) 1)shippai [失敗]. 2)manukareru-koto [免れること].

missile (*n.*) misairu [ミサイル]; yûdô-dan [誘導弾]; tobi-dôgu [飛び道具].

missing (*a.*) funshitsu-shita [紛失した]; yukue-fumei-no [行方不明の].

mission (*n.*) 1)shimei [使命]; tenshoku [天職]. 2)dendô [伝道]. 3)

shisetsu[-dan] [使節(団)].

missionary (*a.*) dendô-no [伝道の].

 (*n.*) dendô-shi [伝道師]; senkyô-shi [宣教師].

mist (*n.*) kiri [霧]; kasumi [かすみ]; moya [もや].

 (*vt.*) ...o kiri[kasumi/moya]-de-oou [...を霧[かすみ/もや]で覆う].

 (*vi.*) kiri[kasumi/moya]-ga-kakaru [霧[かすみ/もや]がかかる].

mistake (*vt.*) 1)...o machigaeru [...を間違える]. 2)...o gokai-suru [...を誤解する]; ...o omoi-chigai-o-suru [...を思い違いをする].

 (*1*) I **am** often **mistaken** for my sister.

  Watashi-wa yoku ane-to-*machigaerareru*.

 (*2*) She seems to **mistake** me.

  Kano-jo-wa watashi[-no-kotoba]-o *gokai-shite-iru*-rashii.

 (*n.*) machigai [間違い]; gokai [誤解].

 by mistake machigatte

mister (*n.*) (M-)...kun [...君]; ...san [...さん]; ...shi [...氏].

mistress (*n.*) shufu [主婦]; onna-shujin [女主人].

misty (*a.*) kiri-no[-kakatta] [霧の(かかった)]; bon'yari-shita [ぼんやりした].

misunderstand (*vt. & vi.*) (...o) gokai-suru [(...を)誤解する].

misunderstanding (*n.*) gokai [誤解]; iken-no-kui-chigai [意見の食い違い].

misuse (*n.*) goyô [誤用].

 (*vt.*) 1)...o goyô-suru [...を誤用する]. 2)...o gyakutai-suru [...を虐待する].

mitt (*n.*) (*baseball*) mitto [ミット].

mitten (*n.*) miton [ミトン].

mix (*vt.*) ...o mazeru [...を混ぜる]; ...o chôwa-saseru [...を調和させる]; ...o chôgô-suru [...を調合する].

 (*vi.*) mazaru [混ざる].

 (*n.*) kongô[-butsu] [混合(物)].

mixture (*n.*) kongô[-butsu] [混合(物)].

moan (*vi.*) umeku [うめく]; unaru [うなる].

 (*vt.*) (...to) umeku-yô-ni-iu [(...と)うめくように言う].

 (*n.*) umeki-goe [うめき声]; (the -) unari [うなり].

moat (*n.*) hori [堀].

mob (*n.*) 1)gunshû [群衆]. 2)bôto [暴徒].

 (*vt.*) (mure-o-nashite)...o osou [(群をなして)...を襲う].

mobile (*a.*) ryûdô-suru [流動する]; yûzû-sei-no-aru [融通性のある].
    (*n.*) mobîru [モビール].

mock (*vt.*) 1)...o baka-ni-suru [...をばかにする]. 2)...no mane-o-suru [...のまねをする]. 3)...o mushi-suru [...を無視する].
    (*a.*) magai-no [まがいの].

mockery (*n.*) 1)azakeri [あざけり]. 2)warai-mono [笑いもの]. 3) magai-mono [まがいもの].

mode (*n.*) 1)yôshiki [様式]; hôhô [方法]. 2)ryûkô [流行]; môdo [モード].

model (*n. & a.*) 1)mokei(-no) [模型(の)]; hina-gata(-no) [ひな型(の)]. 2)mohan(-to-naru) [模範(となる)]. 3)moderu(-to-naru) [モデル(となる)].
    (*vt.*) ...no mokei-o-tsukuru [...の模型を作る].
    (*vi.*) 1)mokei-o-tsukuru [模型を作る]. 2)moderu-ni-naru [モデルになる].

moderate (*a.*) 1)onken-na [穏健な]. 2)tekido-no [適度の]. 3)koro-ai-no [頃合いの].
    (*1*) He is **moderate** in all things. Kare-wa banji *onken-ni*-yaru.
    (*2*) **Moderate** exercise will do us good.
        Tekido-no undô wa karada-ni-yoi.
    (*3*) The prices are **moderate**. Sore-ra-no kakaku wa *koro-ai*-da.
        (*vt. & vi.*) ...o hikae-me-ni-suru (onken-ni-naru) [...を控え目にする(穏健になる)]; ...o yawarageru (yawaragu) [...を和らげる(和らぐ)].

moderately (*ad.*) hodo-yoku [ほどよく]; tekido-ni [適度に].

modern (*a.*) 1)gendai-no [現代の]; kindai-no [近代の]. 2)gendai-teki-na [現代的な].
    (*n.*) (*pl.*) gendai-jin [現代人].

modest (*a.*) kenson-shita [謙そんした]; tekido-no [適度の].

modestly (*ad.*) kenson-shite [謙そんして]; tekido-ni [適度に].

modesty (*n.*) kenson [謙そん]; tekido [適度].

modify (*vt.*) 1)...o shûsei-suru [...を修正する]; ...o kagen-suru [...を加減する]. 2)(*gram.*) ...o shûshoku-suru [...を修飾する].

moist (*a.*) shimetta [湿った].

moisture (*n.*) shikki [湿気]; suibun [水分].

mold (*n.*) 1)igata [鋳型]. 2)seikaku [性格].
    (*vt.*) ...o kata-ni-irete-tsukuru [...を型に入れて作る].

mole (*n.*) (*zool.*) mogura [モグラ].

mole (*n.*) hokuro [ほくろ]; aza [あざ].

moment (*n.*) 1)shunkan [瞬間]. 2)jiki [時期]. 3)jûyô[-sei] [重要(性)].

　　at any moment itsu-de-mo; itsu-nan-doki

　　for a moment chotto[-no-aida]

　　for the moment sashi-atari

　　in a moment tachimachi; sugu

　　Just(Wait) a moment. Chotto[-matte-kudasai].

　　One moment. Chotto[-matte-kudasai].

　　the(very) moment ...(suru-)ya-ina-ya

momentary (*a.*) 1)shunji-no [瞬時の]. 2)koku-koku-no [刻々の].

monarch (*n.*) kunshu [君主]; ôja [王者].

monarchy (*n.*) kunshu-koku [君主国]; kunshu-sei [君主制].

monastery (*n.*) sôin [僧院]; shûdô-in [修道院].

Monday (*n.*) Getsuyô-bi [月曜日].

monetary (*a.*) kahei-no [貨幣の]; kinsen[-jô]-no [金銭(上)の]; zaisei-jô-no [財政上の].

money (*n.*) kinsen [金銭]; kane [かね]; zaisan [財産].

money order ((*US*)) (yûbin-)kawase [(郵便)かわせ].

Mongol (*n.*) Mongoru-jin [モンゴル人]; Mongoru-go [モンゴル語].

　　(*a.*) Mongoru-no [モンゴルの]; Mongoru-jin-no [モンゴル人の];

　　Mongoru-go-no [モンゴル語の].

mongrel (*n. & a.*) zasshu(-no) [雑種(の)].

monitor (*n.*) 1)gakkyû-iin [学級委員]. 2)monitâ [モニター].

monk (*n.*) shûdô-shi [修道士].

monkey (*n.*) saru [サル].

monochrome (*n.*) tansai-ga [単彩画]; shiro-kuro-shashin [白黒写真].

monopoly (*n.*) dokusen[-ken] [独占(権)]; sembai[-ken] [専売(権)].

monotonous (*a.*) tanchô-na [単調な]; taikutsu-na [退屈な].

monotype (*n.*) monotaipu [モノタイプ].

monsoon (*n.*) kisetsu-fû [季節風]; monsûn [モンスーン].

monster (*n.*) kaibutsu [怪物].

monstrous (*a.*) kaibutsu-no-yô-na [怪物のような]; kyodai-na [巨大な];

　　(*colloq.*) tohô-mo-nai [途方もない].

montage (*n.*) (*photo.*) montâju-shashin [モンタージュ写真].

month (*n.*) tsuki [月].

　　last month sengetsu

　　next month raigetsu

　　this day month raigetsu(*or* sengetsu)-no-kyô

monthly (*a.*) mai-tsuki-no [毎月の]; tsuki-ikkai-no [月一回の].
 (*ad.*) tsuki-ikkai [月一回]; mai-tsuki [毎月].
 (*n.*) gekkan-shi [月刊誌].

monument (*n.*) kinen-hi [記念碑]; kinen-zô [記念像]; kinen-kan [記念館].

moo (*vi. & n.*) mô-to-naku(-koe) [もうと鳴く(声)].

mood (*n.*) kibun [気分]; kimochi [気持].

moody (*a.*) 1)muttsuri-shita [むっつりした]; fu-kigen-na [不機嫌な].
 2)kibun-no-kawari-yasui [気分の変わりやすい].

moon (*n.*) tsuki [月].

moonlight (*n.*) gekkô [月光].
 (*a.*) tsuki-akari-no [月明かりの].

moonlit (*a.*) tsuki-ni-terasareta [月に照らされた].

moor (*n.*) ((*Eng.*)) areno [荒れ野].

moose (*n.*) (*zool.*) hera-jika [ヘラジカ].

mop (*n.*) naga-e-zuki-no-zôkin [長柄付きのぞうきん]; moppu [モップ].
 (*vt.*) ...o(-moppu-de) fuku […を(モップで)ふく]; (ase ya namida)-o nuguu [(汗や涙)をぬぐう].

moral (*a.*) 1)dôtoku[-jô]-no [道徳(上)の]. 2)seishin-teki-na [精神的な].
 (*n.*) 1)kyôkun [教訓]. 2)(*pl.*) hinkô [品行].

morality (*n.*) 1)dôtoku[-gaku] [道徳(学)]; rinri[-gaku] [倫理(学)].
 2)kyôkun [教訓].

more (*a.*) 1)motto-ooku-no [もっと多くの]. 2)sara-ni-ooku-no [さらに多くの]; mô [もう].
 (*1*) I have **more** books than he.
  Watashi-wa kare-yori-mo-*motto-ooku-no*-hon-o motte-iru.
 (*2*) We have one **more** lesson. *Mô* ichi-jikan jugyô-ga aru.
 (*n.*) sarani-tasû[-taryô] [さらに多数[多量]]; sore-ijô-no-mono [それ以上のもの].
 More than one person is needed.
  Hitori-*ijô* ga hitsuyô-da.
  Hitsuyô-na-hito-wa hitori de-wa-nai.
 (*ad.*) motto [もっと]; sono-ue [その上].
 He had to work **more**.
  Kare-wa *motto* hataraka-neba-naranakatta.

all the more nao-sara

more and more shidai-ni; dan-dan

more or less tashô; ikubun-ka; ookare-sukunakare

no more　mohaya...(shi-)nai

no more than　...ni-suginai

no more...than　...to-dôyô..de-nai

not more than　...yori-ooku-nai

still more　nao-sara; mashite

the more...the more　...(sure-)ba(-suru-)hodo...(suru)

moreover (*ad.*) sono-ue-ni [その上に]; sara-ni [さらに].

morning (*n.*) asa [朝]; gozen [午前].

from morning till night　asa-kara-ban-made

morphine (*n.*) moruhine [モルヒネ].

mortal (*a.*) 1)shinu-beki-ummei-no [死ぬべき運命の]. 2)ningen-no [人間の]. 3)chimei-teki-na [致命的な].

(*n.*) ningen [人間].

mortality (*n.*) 1)tasû-no-shi [多数の死]. 2)shibô-sû [死亡数]; shibô-ritsu [死亡率].

mortar (*n.*) morutaru [モルタル].

(*vt.*) ...ni morutaru-o-nuru [...にモルタルを塗る].

mortar (*n.*) suri-bachi [すり鉢]; usu [臼].

mortgage (*n.*) teitô[-ken] [抵当(権)].

(*vt.*) ...o teitô-ni-ireru [...を抵当に入れる].

mosaic (*n.*) mozaiku[-moyô] [モザイク(模様)].

mosquito (*n.*) (*insect*) ka [カ].

moss (*n.*) (*bot.*) koke [コケ].

mossy (*a.*) koke-no-haeta [コケの生えた].

most (*a.*) 1)mottomo-ooku-no [最も多くの]. 2)taitei-no [たいていの]; dai-bubun-no [大部分の].

(*1*) He has **most** apples.

　　Kare-ga *mottomo-takusan* ringo-o motte-iru.

(*2*) **Most** students like baseball.

　　Taitei-no gakusei wa yakyû-ga suki-da.

for the most part　taitei

(*n.*) mottomo-ooku-no-mono [最も多くのもの]; (*US colloq.*) (the –) saikô-no-mono[-hito] [最高のもの[人]].

　　That is the **most** I can do.

　　　Sore-ga watashi-ga dekiru *saikô-no-koto* da.

　　　Sore-ga watashi ni dekiru sei-ippai-no-tokoro da.

(*ad.*) 1)mottomo [最も]. 2)totemo [とても]; hijô-ni [非常に].

(*1*) It is the **most** beautiful scenery.

　　　　　Sore-wa *mottomo* utsukushii keshiki da.

(2) It is a **most** useful animal.

　　　　　Sore-wa *hijô-ni* yaku-ni-tatsu dôbutsu da.

　at the most　seizei

　make the most of　...o saidai-gen-ni-riyô-suru

　most of all　ichiban

mostly (*ad.*) taitei [たいてい]; omo-ni [主に].

moth (*n.*) (*insect*) ga [が].

mother (*n.*) 1)haha[-oya] [母(親)]. 2)(the -) minamoto [源].

mother country　hongoku [本国]; bokoku [母国].

motherhood (*n.*) haha-de-aru-koto [母であること]; bosei[-ai] [母性(愛)]; haha-oya-tachi [母親たち].

mother-in-law (*n.*) gibo [義母]; shûtome [しゅうとめ].

motherly (*a.*) haha-no [母の]; haha-no-yô-na [母のような]; yasashii [優しい].

mother tongue　bokoku-go [母国語].

motif (*n.*) shudai [主題]; mochîfu [モチーフ].

motion (*n.*) 1)undô [運動]; idô [移動]. 2)dôsa [動作]; miburi [身振り]; môshon [モーション]. 3)dôgi [動議].

　in motion　ugoite; unten-chû-no

　　　　　(*vi. & vt.*) (...ni) miburi-de-aizu-suru [(…に)身振りで合図する].

motionless (*a.*) ugoka-nai [動かない]; seishi-shite-iru [静止している].

motive (*n.*) 1)dôki [動機]; mokuteki [目的]. 2)shudai [主題].

　　　　　(*a.*) 1)gen-dôryoku-to-naru [原動力となる]. 2)dôki-to-naru [動機となる].

motor (*n.*) hatsudô-ki [発動機]; môtâ [モーター].

motorbike (*n.*) (*colloq.*) ôtobai [オートバイ]; ((*US*)) môtâbaiku [モーターバイク].

motorcar (*n.*) jidôsha [自動車].

motorization (*n.*) dôryoku-ka [動力化]; jidôsha-ka [自動車化]; môtarizêshon [モータリゼーション].

motto (*n.*) hyôgo [標語]; kingen [金言]; mottô [モットー].

mound (*n.*) 1)tsutsumi [堤]; tsuka [塚]. 2)(*baseball*) maundo [マウンド].

　　　　　(*vt.*) ...o mori-ageru […を盛り上げる].

mount (*vt. & vi.*) 1)(...ni) noboru [(…に)登る]. 2)(...ni) noru [(…に)乗る].

　　　　　(*n.*) 1)agaru-koto [上がること]; noru-koto [乗ること]. 2)

(*photo.*) daishi [台紙].

mount (*n.*) yama [山]; (Mt.) ...yama […山]; ...san […山]; ...zan […山].

mountain (*n.*) 1)yama [山]. 2)(*pl.*) sammyaku [山脈]; renzan [連山]. 3)(a mountain of...) ookina... [大きな…]; taryô-no... [多量の…]; tasû-no... [多数の…].

mountaineering (*n.*) tozan [登山].

mountainous (*a.*) 1)yama-no-ooi [山の多い]; sanchi-no [山地の]. 2)yama-no-yô-na [山のような].

mourn (*vi. & vt.*) 1)(...o) nageku [(…を)嘆く]; (...o) kanashimu [(…を)悲しむ]. 2)(...no) mo-ni-fukusuru [(…の)喪に服する].

mourner (*n.*) kanashimu-hito [悲しむ人]; kaisô-sha [会葬者].

mournful (*a.*) kanashimi-ni-shizunda [悲しみに沈んだ].

mourning (*n.*) 1)kanashimi [悲しみ]. 2)mo [喪]. 3)mofuku [喪服].

mourning band moshô [喪章].

mouse (*n.*) hatsuka-nezumi [ハツカネズミ].

mouth (*n.*) 1)kuchi [口]. 2)kakô [河口]. 3)hito [人].

　　make one's mouth water hito-ni-yodare-o-nagasaseru

mouthful (*n.*) kuchi-ippai [口一杯]; hito-kuchi(-bun) [一口(分)].

move (*vt.*) 1)...o ugokasu […を動かす]. 2)...o kandô-saseru […を感動させる]. 3)(dôgi)-o teishutsu-suru [(動議)を提出する].

　　(*vi.*) 1)ugoku [動く]. 2)tenkyo-suru [転居する].

　　move away tenkyo-suru

　　move in tenkyo-suru

　　move on don-don-susumu

movement (*n.*) 1)ugoki [動き]; dôsa [動作]; undô [運動]. 2)(*pl.*) mono-goshi [物腰]; taido [態度]. 3)(*mus.*) gakushô [楽章].

movie (*n.*) ((*US*)) eiga[-kan] [映画(館)].

moving (*a.*) 1)ugokasu [動かす]. 2)kandô-teki-na [感動的な].

Mr., Mr ...san […さん]; ...shi […氏]; ...sama […さま].

Mrs., Mrs ...san […さん]; ...fujin […夫人]; ...sama […さま].

Ms, Ms. ...san […さん]; ...sama […様].

much (*a.*) takusan-no [たくさんの]; taryô-no [多量の].

　　(*n.*) 1)takusan [たくさん]; taryô [多量]. 2)taishita-mono [たいしたもの]; naka-naka-no-mono [なかなかのもの].

　　(*1*) I learned **much** from him.

　　　　Watashi-wa kare-kara *takusan-no-koto*-o mananda.

　　(*2*) He is very **much** of a scholar.

　　　Kare-wa *naka-naka-no*-gakusha da.

　　(*ad.*) 1)ooi-ni ［大いに］; hijô-ni ［非常に］. 2)zutto ［ずっと］; haruka-ni ［はるかに］.

　　(*1*) Thank you very **much**.　*Dômo arigatô*.

　　(*2*) I'm **much** better.　Watashi-wa *zutto* yoroshii.

　　much more　mashite

　　not so much as　...sae(-shi)-nai: ...hodo...de-nai

　　not so much...as　...yori-mo-mushiro...

　　so much　1)sore-hodo. 2)totemo

mud (*n.*) doro ［泥］.

muddy (*a.*) 1)doro-darake-no ［泥だらけの］; nukarumi-no ［ぬかるみの］. 2)nigotta ［濁った］.

　　(*vt.*) 1)...o doro-darake-ni-suru ［…を泥だらけにする］. 2)...o konran-saseru ［…を混乱させる］.

muffler (*n.*) eri-maki ［えり巻き］; mafurâ ［マフラー］.

mug (*n.*) magu ［マグ］.

muggy (*a.*) (*colloq.*) mushi-atsui ［蒸し暑い］; uttôshii ［うっとうしい］.

mulberry (*n.*) (*bot.*) kuwa[-no-ki] ［クワ(の木)］.

mule (*n.*) 1)(*zool.*) raba ［ラバ］. 2)(*pl.*) myûru ［ミュール］.

multi- ooi- ［多い−］.

multiple (*a.*) tayô-no ［多様の］.

　　(*n.*) (*math.*) baisû ［倍数］.

multiplication (*n.*) 1)(*math.*) kake-zan ［掛け算］. 2)zôka ［増加］; hansyoku ［繁殖］.

multiply (*vt.*) 1)...ni kakeru ［…に掛ける］. 2)...o masu ［…を増す］; ...o fuyasu ［…を増やす］.

　　(*1*) **Multiply** the number by 3.　Sono kazu-*ni* san-o *kake-nasai*.

　　(*2*) The rapid progress of science **multiplies** evils.

　　　　Kagaku no kyûsoku-na shimpo wa gaiaku-*o masu*.

　　(*vi.*) fueru ［増える］; kake-zan-o-suru ［掛け算をする］.

multitude (*n.*) 1)tasû ［多数］. 2)gunshû ［群衆］; (the −)taishû ［大衆］.

　　a multitude of　oozei-no; tasû-no

mummy (*n.*) miira ［ミイラ］.

municipal (*a.*) shi-no ［市の］; chihô-jichi-no ［地方自治の］.

murder (*n.*) satsujin ［殺人］.

　　(*vt.*) 1)...o korosu ［…を殺す］. 2)(*colloq.*) ...o dai-nashi-ni-suru ［…を台無しにする］.

murderer (*n.*) satsujin-han ［殺人犯］.

murmur (*n.*) 1) zawameki ［ざわめき］. 2) sasayaki ［ささやき］; tsubuyaki ［つぶやき］. 3) butsu-butsu-iu-fuhei-no-koe ［ぶつぶつ言う不平の声］.

  (*vi.*) zawameku ［ざわめく］; sasayaku ［ささやく］; tsubuyaku ［つぶやく］; butsu-butsu-iu ［ぶつぶつ言う］.

muscle (*n.*) kinniku ［筋肉］; wanryoku ［腕力］.

muscular (*a.*) kinniku-no[-takumashii] ［筋肉の(たくましい)］.

muse (*vi.*) shizuka-ni-kangaeru ［静かに考える］.

museum (*n.*) hakubutsu-kan ［博物館］; bijutsu-kan ［美術館］.

museum piece chimpin ［珍品］; hakubutsu-kan-mono ［博物館もの］.

mushroom (*n.*) 1) kinoko ［キノコ］; masshurûmu ［マッシュルーム］. 2) kinoko-jô-no-mono ［キノコ状のもの］. 3) seichô-no-hayai-mono ［成長の早いもの］.

  (*vi.*) kinoko-gari-o-suru ［キノコ狩りをする］; kinoko-no-yô-na-katachi-ni-hirogaru ［キノコのような形に広がる］; kyûsoku-ni-seichô-suru ［急速に成長する］.

music (*n.*) 1) ongaku ［音楽］. 2) gakufu ［楽譜］.

music box = **musical box** orugôru ［オルゴール］.

musical (*a.*) ongaku-no ［音楽の］; ongaku-teki-na ［音楽的な］; ongaku-zuki-no ［音楽好きの］.

  (*n.*) myûjikaru ［ミュージカル］.

musical instrument gakki ［楽器］.

musician (*n.*) ongaku-ka ［音楽家］.

muslin (*n.*) 1) mosurin ［モスリン］. 2) ((*US*)) kyarako ［キャラコ］.

must (*aux.v.*) 1) …nakereba-naranai ［…なければならない］. 2) …ni-chigai-nai ［…にちがいない］. 3) (+negative) …(shite-)wa-ikenai ［…(して)はいけない］. 4) …(shi-)nakereba-shôchi-shi-nai ［…(し)なければ承知しない］.

 (*1*) You **must** go. Kimi-ga ika-*nakereba-naranai*.

 (*2*) You **must** have heard of it.

   Anata-wa sono-koto-o kiita-*ni-chigai-nai*.

 (*3*) You **mustn't** go now. Anata-wa ima itte-wa-*ikenai*.

 (*4*) Children **must** play. Kodomo-wa aso ba*zu-niwa-irarenai*.

  (*n.*) zettai-ni-hitsuyô-na-mono ［絶対に必要なもの］; fukaketsu-na-mono ［不可欠なもの］.

mustache, moustache (*n.*) kuchi-hige ［口ひげ］.

mustard (*n.*) karashi ［からし］; masutâdo ［マスタード］.

mute (*a.*) 1) mugon-no ［無言の］. 2) (*phon.*) hatsuon-sare-nai ［発音さ

れない].

    (*n.*) 1)mono-ga-ie-nai-hito [ものが言えない人]. 2)mokuji [黙字];
(*phon.*) mokuon [黙音].

    (*vt.*) ...ni-shôon-ki-o-tsukeru [...に消音器をつける].

mutter (*n. & vi.*) tsubuyaki (tsubuyaku) [つぶやき(つぶやく)]; fuhei
(-o-iu) [不平(を言う)].

mutton (*n.*) hitsuji-no-niku [羊の肉]; maton [マトン].

mutual (*a.*) sôgo-no [相互の]; kyôdô-no [共同の].

my (*pron.*) watashi-no [私の].

  My!; Oh my! Maa!; Oya!

myself (*pron.*) watashi-jishin [私自身]; jibun-o[-ni] [自分を[に]].

mysterious (*a.*) shimpi-teki-na [神秘的な]; fushigi-na [不思議な].

mystery (*n.*) shimpi [神秘]; fushigi-na-koto [不思議なこと]; nazo
[なぞ].

myth (*n.*) 1)shinwa [神話]. 2)tsukuri-banashi [作り話]; kakû-no-
hito [架空の人].

mythology (*n.*) shinwa[-gaku] [神話(学)].

N

nail (*n.*) 1)tsume [つめ]. 2)kugi [くぎ].

  hit the (right) nail on the head ugatta-koto-o-iu; kyûsho-o-
      pitari-to-ii-ateru

    (*vt.*) ...ni kugi-o-utsu [...にくぎを打つ]; ...o kugi-zuke-ni-suru [...

をくぎ付けにする].

naked (*a.*) 1)hadaka-no [裸の]. 2)mukidashi-no [むき出しの]; seki-rara-na [赤裸々な].

naked eye nikugan [肉眼].

name (*n.*) 1)na [名]; seimei [姓名]. 2)meisei [名声]; hyôban [評判].
　　(*1*) I know him by **name**.
　　　　　Watashi-wa kare no *na* dake wa shitte-iru.
　　(*2*) He has a bad **name**. Kare-wa *hyôban*-ga warui.
　　by(of) the name of …to-iu-namae-no
　　call one names hito-no warukuchi-o-iu
　　in name only na-bakari-no
　　　　(*vt.*) 1)…to na-zukeru [⋯と名付ける]. 2)…o shimei-suru [⋯を指名する].
　　(*1*) They **named** him John. Kare-ra-wa kare-o Jon-*to na-zuketa*.
　　(*2*) He **named** Mr. Rogers for the post.
　　　　　Kare-wa Rojâsu-shi-*o* sono chii-ni *nimmei-shita*.

namely (*ad.*) sunawachi [すなわち]; tsumari [つまり].

nap (*n. & vi.*) utata-ne(-suru) [うたた寝(する)]; hiru-ne(-suru) [昼寝(する)].
　　take a nap utata-ne-suru

narcissus (*n.*) (*bot.*) suisen [スイセン].

narcotic (*a.*) masui-no [麻酔の].
　　　　　(*n.*) masui-zai [麻酔剤].

narrate (*vt. & vi.*) (…o) kataru [(⋯を)語る].

narration (*n.*) 1)monogatari [物語]. 2)(*gram.*) wahô [話法].

narrative (*n. & a.*) monogatari(-fû-no) [物語(風の)].

narrow (*a.*) 1)semai [狭い]; hosoi [細い]. 2)yatto-no [やっとの]; karôjite-no [かろうじての]. 3)memmitsu-na [綿密な]. 4)kyôryô-na [狭量な].
　　(*1*) The road is very **narrow**. Sono dôro wa taihen *semai*.
　　(*2*) I had a **narrow** escape. Watashi-wa *yatto* nogareta.
　　(*3*) a **narrow** examination *memmitsu-na* chôsa
　　(*4*) **narrow** views *kyôryô-na* [mono-no-]kangae-kata
　　　　(*vt.*) …o semaku-suru [⋯を狭くする]; …o gentei-suru [⋯を限定する].
　　　　　(*n.*) (*pl.*) seto [瀬戸]; kaikyô [海峡].

narrowly (*ad.*) 1)yatto [やっと]. 2)memmitsu-ni [綿密に]. 3)semaku [狭く].

narrow-minded (*a.*) kokoro-no-semai [心の狭い].

nasty (*a.*) 1)hidoku-kitanai [ひどく汚い]; fuketsu-na [不潔な]. 2)iya-na [いやな]; fukai-na [不快な]. 3)ken'aku-na [険悪な]. 4)iji-no-warui [意地の悪い].

nation (*n.*) 1)kokumin [国民]; minzoku [民族]. 2)kokka [国家].

national (*a.*) kokumin-no [国民の]; kokka-no [国家の].

national anthem kokka [国歌].

nationality (*n.*) 1)kokuseki [国籍]. 2)kokka [国家]; kokumin [国民].

nationalization (*n.*) 1)kokumin-teki-na-mono-ni-suru-koto [国民的なものにすること]. 2)kokuyû-ka [国有化]; kokuei [国営].

national park kokuritsu-kôen [国立公園].

native (*a.*) 1)seikoku-no [生国の]. 2)hae-nuki-no [生え抜きの]; gensan-no [原産の]. 3)umare-tsuki-no [生まれつきの]; seirai-no [生来の].

  (*1*) one's **native** language   *bokoku*-go

  (*2*) the **native** flowers of Japan   Nihon-*gensan-no* hana

  (*3*) His **native** modesty prevents him from doing so.

      Kare-no *seirai-no* tsutsushimi-bukasa ga kare-ni sô sase-nai.

      (*n.*) (…)shusshin-sha [(…)出身者]; gensan-dô-shokubutsu [原産動植物].

natural (*a.*) 1)shizen-no [自然の]; tennen-no [天然の]. 2)umare-tsuki-no [生まれつきの]. 3)tôzen-no [当然の]. 4)shizen-na [自然な]; kazari-ke-no-nai [飾り気のない].

  (*1*) We learned **natural** science.

      Ware-ware-wa *shizen*-kagaku-o naratta.

  (*2*) The deed was done by his **natural** courage.

      Sono kôi wa kare-no *umare-nagara-no* yûki-de nasareta.

  (*3*) It is **natural** that he should say so.

      Kare-ga sô iu-no-wa *tôzen*-da.

  (*4*) He spoke in a **natural** voice.

      Kare-wa *shizen-na*-koe de hanashita.

natural gas tennen-gasu [天然ガス].

naturalist (*n.*) 1)shizen-shugi-sha [自然主義者]. 2)dô-shokubutsu-gakusha [動植物学者].

naturally (*ad.*) 1)shizen-ni [自然に]. 2)umare-tsuki [生まれつき]. 3)mochiron [もちろん].

nature (*n.*) 1)shizen [自然]. 2)seishitsu [性質]; tensei [天性].

  by nature seirai; umare-tsuki

naughty (*a.*) wampaku-na [わんぱくな]; itazura-na [いたずらな].

nautilus (*n.*) (*shellfish*) ômu-gai [オウムガイ].

naval (*a.*) kaigun-no [海軍の].

navel (*n.*) heso [へそ].

navel orange nêburu [ネーブル].

navigate (*vt. & vi.*) 1) (...o) kôkai-suru [(…を)航海する]. 2) (...o) sôjû-suru [(…を)操縦する].

navigation (*n.*) kôkai[-jutsu] [航海(術)]; hikô[-jutsu] [飛行(術)].

navigator (*n.*) kôkai-sha [航海者]; kôkû-shi [航空士].

navy (*n.*) kaigun [海軍].

near (*a.*) 1) chikai [近い]. 2) kinshin-no [近親の]; shitashii [親しい]. 3) yoku-nita [よく似た].
     (*ad.*) 1) chikaku[-ni] [近く(に)]. 2) hotondo [ほとんど].
  near at hand chikaku-ni; chikazuite
  near by chikaku-ni
     (*prep.*) ...no-chikaku-ni […の近くに].
     (*vt. & vi.*) (...ni) chikazuku [(…に)近づく].

nearby (*a.*) chikaku-no [近くの]; fukin-no [付近の].
     (*ad.*) chikaku-ni[-e] [近くに(へ)].

nearly (*ad.*) 1) hotondo [ほとんど]; hobo [ほぼ]. 2) mô-sukoshi-de... (suru-)tokoro [もう少しで…(する)ところ]. 3) missetsu-ni [密接に].

nearsighted (*a.*) 1) kinshi-no [近視の]. 2) kinshi-gan-teki-na [近視眼的な].

neat (*a.*) kichin-to-shita [きちんとした]; ko-girei-na [小ぎれいな]; ko-zappari-shita [小ざっぱりした].

neatly (*ad.*) kichin-to [きちんと]; ko-girei-ni [小ぎれいに]; tegiwa-yoku [手際よく].

nebula (*n.*) 1) (*astron.*) seiun [星雲]. 2) (*med.*) kakumaku-hakudaku [角膜白濁].

necessarily (*ad.*) kanarazu [必ず]; hitsuzen-teki-ni [必然的に].
  not necessarily kanarazu-shimo...de-nai

necessary (*a.*) hitsuyô-na [必要な]; hitsuzen-teki-na [必然的な].
     (*n.*) hitsuju-hin [必需品].

necessity (*n.*) 1) hitsuyô[-hin] [必要(品)]. 2) hitsuju-hin [必需品].

neck (*n.*) kubi [首].

neckerchief (*n.*) eri-maki [襟巻き]; nekkachîfu [ネッカチーフ].

necklace (*n.*) kubi-kazari [首飾り]; nekkuresu [ネックレス].

nectar (*n.*) 1) oishii-nomi-mono [おいしい飲み物]. 2) (*bot.*) (hana-no) mitsu [(花の)みつ].

need (*n.*) nyûyô [入用]; hitsuyô [必要]. 2)konkyû [困窮]; kyûhaku [窮迫]. 3)masaka-no-toki [まさかのとき]. 4)(*pl.*) hitsuyô-na-mono [必要なもの].

  (*1*) There is no **need** for her to come.
      Kano-jo-ga kuru-*hitsuyô*-wa-nai.

  (*2*) He is in great **need**.   Kare-wa taihen *konkyû*-shite-iru.
                    Kare-wa totemo komatte-iru.

  (*3*) A friend in **need** is a friend indeed.
      Masaka-no-toki-no-tomodachi ga hontô-ni tomodachi da.

  (*4*) They supply our **needs**.
      Kare-ra-wa ware-ware-no *hitsuyô-na-mono*-o kyôkyû-suru.

  (*vt.*) 1)...o hitsuyô-to-suru [...を必要とする]; ...ga hitsuyô-de-aru [...が必要である]. 2)...(suru-)hitsuyô-ga-aru [...(する)必要がある].

  (*1*) He **needs** much money.
      Kare-wa tagaku-no kane-*ga hitsuyô-da*.

  (*2*) The operation **needs** to be done with great care.
      Sono shujutsu wa taihen-chûi-bukaku okonau-*hitsuyô-ga-aru*.

  (*aux. v.*) ...(suru-)hitsuyô-ga-aru [...(する)必要がある].

  You **need** not go there at once.
      Sugu soko-e iku-*hitsuyô-wa*-nai.

  Why **need** I do it?
      Naze watashi-ga sore-o suru-*hitsuyô-ga-aru*-no-ka?

needful (*a.*) hitsuyô-na [必要な]; kaku-koto-no-deki-nai [欠くことのできない].

needle (*n.*) hari [針]; nui-bari [縫い針].
  (*vt.*) ...o hari-de-nuu [...を針で縫う].
  (*vi.*) hari-shigoto-o-suru [針仕事をする].

needless (*a.*) fu-hitsuyô-na [不必要な].

needlework (*n.*) hari-shigoto [針仕事]; shishû [刺しゅう].

negative (*a.*) hitei-no [否定の]; shôkyoku-teki-na [消極的な].
  (*n.*) 1)hitei [否定]. 2)(*photo.*) nega [ネガ].
  (*vt.*) ...o hitei-suru [...を否定する]; ...o kyohi-suru [...を拒否する].

negatively (*ad.*) hitei-shite [否定して]; shôkyoku-teki-ni [消極的に].

negative vote hantai-tôhyô [反対投票].

neglect (*vt.*) 1)...o okotaru [...を怠る]. 2)...o orosoka-ni-suru [...を

おろそかにする]; ...o mushi-suru [⋯を無視する].

　　　(n.) 1)taiman [怠慢]. 2)mushi [無視]; keishi [軽視].

negligence (n.) taiman [怠慢]; fu-chûi [不注意]; mu-tonjaku [むとんじゃく].

negotiate (vi.) kyôgi-suru [協議する]; kôshô-suru [交渉する].

　　　(vt.) ...o tori-kimeru [⋯を取決める].

negotiation (n.) kôshô [交渉].

Negro (n. & a.) kokujin(-no) [黒人(の)].

neigh (n. & vi.) inanaki (inanaku) [いななき(いななく)].

neighbor, -bour (n.) tonari-no-hito [隣りの人]; kinjo-no-hito [近所の人].

　　　(vt.) ...ni rinsetsu-suru [⋯に隣接する].

　　　(vi.) chikaku-ni-sumu [近くに住む].

neighbo(u)rhood (n.) 1)kinjo [近所]; fukin [付近]. 2)(the -) kinjo-no-hito-bito [近所の人々].

neighbo(u)ring (a.) kinjo-no [近所の]; rinsetsu-shite-iru [隣接している].

neither (ad.) 1)...demo-naku, mata...demo-nai [⋯でもなく、また⋯でもない]. 2)...mo-mata...de-nai [⋯もまた⋯でない].

(1) He **neither** drinks **nor** smokes.

Kare-wa sake-*mo*-noma-*nai*-*shi mata* tabako-*mo*-suwa-*nai*.

(2) If you don't go, **neither** shall I.

Anata-ga ika-nai-nara, watashi *mo* ika-*nai*.

(a.) dochira-no...mo...de-nai [どちらの⋯も⋯でない].

I like **neither** dictionary.　*Dochira-no* jisho *mo* suki-*de-nai*.

(pron.) dochira-mo...de-nai((shi-)nai) [どちらも⋯でない((し)ない)].

I know **neither** of you.

Watashi-wa kimi-tachi no *dochira-mo* shira-*nai*.

nephew (n.) oi [おい].

Neptune (n.) (astron.) Kaiô-sei [海王星].

nerve (n.) 1)shinkei [神経]. 2)(pl.)(colloq.) shinkei-kabin [神経過敏]. 3)yûki [勇気].

nervous (a.) 1)shinkei-no [神経の]. 2)shinkei-shitsu-na [神経質な]; shinkei-kabin-na [神経過敏な]. 3)kôfun-shi-yasui [興奮しやすい].

nervously (ad.) shinkei-shitsu-ni [神経質に]; ira-ira-shite [いらいらして].

nest (n.) 1)su [巣]. 2)sôkutsu [巣くつ]. 3)kyûsoku-sho [休息所].

　　(*vi.*) su-o-tsukuru [巣を作る].

　　(*vt.*) ...o ireko-ni-suru [···を入れ子にする].

nestle (*vi.*) suri-yoru [すり寄る]; yori-sou [寄りそう]; kokochi-yoku-mi-o-ochitsukeru [心地よく身を落ち着ける].

　　(*vt.*) ...o suri-yoseru [···をすり寄せる]; ...o daki-yoseru [···を抱き寄せる]; ...o su-ni-ireru [···を巣に入れる].

nestling (*n.*) 1)hina-dori [ひな鳥]. 2)akambô [赤ん坊]; yôji [幼児].

net (*n.*) ami [網]; netto [ネット].

　　(*vt.*) ...o ami-de-toraeru [···を網で捕らえる]; ...o ami-de-oou [···を網で覆う].

net (*a.*) shômi-no [正味の].

　　(*vt.*) ...no jun'eki-o-ageru [···の純益をあげる].

network (*n.*) 1)ami-zaiku [網細工]. 2)(*broadcasting*) hôsô-mô [放送網].

neuralgia (*n.*) (*path.*) shinkei-tsû [神経痛].

neurosis (*n.*) (*med.*) shinkei-shô [神経症]; noirôze [ノイローゼ].

neuter (*a.*) chûsei-no [中性の].

　　(*n.*) (*gram.*) chûsei [中性].

neutral (*a.*) 1)chûritsu-no [中立の]. 2)hakkiri-shi-nai [はっきりしない].
　　(*n.*) 1)chûritsu-sha [中立者]. 2)(*mech.*) nyûtoraru [ニュートラル].

never (*ad.*) 1)katsute...(shita-)koto-ga-nai [かつて···(した)ことがない].
　　2)kesshite...(shi-)nai [決して···(し)ない].
　　(*1*) I have **never** seen such a sight.
　　　　　Watashi-wa *katsute* konna kôkei-o mita-*koto-ga-nai.*
　　(*2*) **Never** repeat such a fool.
　　　　　Sonna baka-na-koto-o *kesshite* kuri-kaesu-*na.*

nevertheless (*ad. or conj.*) sore-nimo-kakawarazu [それにもかかわらず];
　　sore-demo [それでも]; yahari [やはり].

new (*a.*) 1)atarashii [新しい]. 2)hajimete-no [初めての]. 3)kondo-no
　　[今度の].
　　A Happy New Year! Shinnen-o-medetô!
　　(*ad.*) saikin [最近]; chikagoro [近ごろ].

newcomer (*n.*) shinrai-sha [新来者].

newly (*ad.*) 1)arata-ni [新たに]. 2)saikin [最近]; chikagoro [近ごろ].

news (*n.*) 1)hôdô [報道]; kiji [記事]; nyûsu [ニュース]. 2)tayori [便
　　り]. 3)nyûsu-ni-naru-hito[-koto] [ニュースになる人[こと]].
　　That's news to me. Sore-wa boku-niwa hatsu-mimi-da.

newscast (*n.*) nyûsu-hôsô [ニュース放送].

newspaper (*n.*) shimbun [新聞].

newspaperman (*n.*) shimbun-kisha [新聞記者]; shimbun-keiei-sha [新聞経営者].

newsreel (*n.*) nyûsu-eiga [ニュース映画].

new year shinnen [新年].

next (*a.*) 1)tsugi-no [次の]. 2)tonari-no [隣りの].

  (*1*) I'll go there **next** Sunday.

    Tsugi-no-Nichiyô-bi-ni watashi-wa soko-e iku.

  (*2*) He lives **next** door to us.

    Kare-wa ware-ware-no-*tonari*-ni sunde-iru.

  in the next place tsugi-ni; dai-ni-ni

  next to (+negative) hotondo

    It is next to impossible. Sore-wa hotondo-fu-kanô-da.

    (*ad.*) tsugi-ni [次に]; tonari-ni [隣りに].

    Next came he. *Tsugi-ni* kare-ga yatte-kita.

    (*prep.*) 1)...no-tsugi-ni[-no] [...の次に(の)]. 2)...no-tonari-ni [-no] [...の隣りに(の)].

  (*1*) Mother loved her niece **next** me.

    Haha wa watashi-*no-tsugi-ni* mei-o kawaigatta.

  (*2*) He sat **next** me. Kare-wa watashi-*no-tonari-ni* suwatta.

next-door (*a.*) tonari-no [隣りの].

nibble (*vt. & vi.*) (...o) sukoshi-zutsu-kajiru [(...を)少しずつかじる].

    (*n.*) hito-kami [ひとかみ]; chotto-kamu-koto [ちょっとかむこと].

nice (*a.*) 1)yoi [よい]. 2)kokochi-yoi [心地よい]. 3)tanoshii [楽しい]. 4)aji-no-yoi [味のよい]. 5)shinsetsu-na [親切な].

  (*1*) This flower smells very **nice**.

    Kono hana wa totemo nioi-ga-*yoi*.

  (*2*) This is a **nice** house to live in.

    Kore-wa sumi-*gokochi-no-yoi* ie da.

  (*3*) We had a **nice** time of it. Ware-ware-wa *tanoshi*-katta.

  (*4*) This orange is very **nice**. Kono mikan wa totemo *aji-ga-yoi*.

  (*5*) It's very **nice** of you to call on me.

    Go-shinsetsu ni yoku tazunete-kuremashita.

  nice and jûbun-ni

nicely (*ad.*) 1)(*colloq.*) yoku [よく]; umaku [うまく]. 2)bimyô-ni [微妙に]; seimitsu-ni [精密に].

nick (*n.*) 1)kizami-me [刻み目]. 2)(*Eng. & Aus. colloq.*) chôshi [調

子]; jôtai [状態].

in the nick of time (*colloq.*) chôdo-yoi-toki-ni; kiwadoi-toki-ni
　　(*vt.*) 1)...ni kizami-me-o-tsukeru […に刻み目をつける]. 2)...ni
ma-ni-au […に間に合う]; ...o umaku-ii-ateru […をうまく言い当てる].
3)(*US colloq.*) ...o damasu […をだます].
　　(*vi.*) 1)chika-mawari-o-suru [近回りをする]. 2)kyû-ni-wari-komu
[急に割り込む].

nickel (*n.*) 1)(*chem.*) nikkeru [ニッケル]. 2)((*US & Can.*)) go-sento-
hakudô-ka [５セント白銅貨].

nickname (*n.*) adana [あだ名]; nikkunêmu [ニックネーム].
　　(*vt.*) ...ni...to adana-o-tsukeru […に…とあだ名をつける].

nicotine (*n.*) (*chem.*) nikochin [ニコチン].

niece (*n.*) mei [めい].

night (*n.*) yoru [夜]; ban [晩].
　　　　The stars appear at **night**. Hoshi wa *yoru* arawareru.
　　　　The moon shines by **night**. Tsuki wa *yoru* kagayaku.
　　　　He stopped there for the **night**.
　　　　　Kare-wa sono-*ban*-wa soko-ni tomatta.
　　　　He was up all **night** long. Kare-wa *yo*-dooshi okite-ita.
　　　　She kept weeping day and **night**.
　　　　　Kano-jo-wa nichi*ya* naki-tsuzuketa.

　have a good night yoku-nemureru
　in the night yakan-ni
　last night sakuban
　late at night yoru-osoku
　night after night mai-ban

nightfall (*n.*) hi-gure [日暮れ].

nightly (*a.*) yoru-no [夜の]; yogoto-no [夜ごとの].
　　(*ad.*) yoru-ni [夜に]; mai-ban [毎晩].

nightmare (*n.*) 1)akumu [悪夢]. 2)osoroshii-keiken [恐ろしい経験].

nihilistic (*a.*) kyomu-shugi-no [虚無主義の]; mu-seifu-shugi-no [無政
府主義の].

nimble (*a.*) 1)subayai [す早い]. 2)rikai-ga-hayai [理解が早い].

nine (*n. & a.*) ku(-no) [九(の)]; kyû(-no) [九(の)].
　nine times out of ten jû-chû-hakku; taitei

nineteen (*n. & a.*) jû-ku(-no) [十九(の)]; jû-kyû(-no) [十九(の)].

nineteenth (*n. & a.*) dai-jû-ku(-no) [第十九(の)]; dai-jû-kyû(-no)
[第十九(の)].

ninetieth (*n. & a.*) dai-kyû-jû(-no) [第九十(の)].

ninety (*n. & a.*) kyû-jû(-no) [九十(の)].

ninth (*n. & a.*) dai-ku(-no) [第九(の)]; dai-kyûmi(-no) [第九(の)].

nip (*vt.*) 1)...o hasamu [...をはさむ]. 2)...o tsumi-toru [...を摘み取る].
  3)(shimo nado ga)...o itameru [(霜などが)...を痛める]; ...o karasu
  [...を枯らす].
  (*1*) I **nipped** my finger in the door.
    Watashi-wa doa-ni yubi-*o hasanda*.
  (*2*) These buds must **be nipped** off.
    Kore-ra-no me wa *tsumi-tora*-neba-naranai.
  (*3*) The buds **were nipped** by the severe frost.
    Me ga hidoi-shimo-de *itanda*.
    (*vi.*) 1)hasamu [はさむ]; tsuneru [つねる]. 2)mi-ni-shimiru [身
  にしみる]. 3)(*Eng. colloq.*) isogu [急ぐ].
    (*n.*) 1)hasamu-koto [はさむこと]; tsuneru-koto [つねること]. 2)
  mi-ni-shimiru-samu-sa [身にしみる寒さ]. 3)tsûretsu-na-kotoba [痛烈
  なことば]. 4)(*Eng. colloq.*) isogu-koto [急ぐこと].

no (*a.*) 1)sukoshi-mo...nai [少しも...ない]. 2)dare-mo...nai [だれも...
  ない]; nani-mo...nai [なにも...ない]. 3)kesshite...nai [決して...ない].
  4)kesshite...(shite-)wa-naranai [決して...(して)はならない].
  (*1*) I have **no** money with me.
    Watashi-wa *sukoshi-mo* kane-o mochi-awasete-*i-nai*.
  (*2*) **No** one knows the fact.   *Dare-mo* sono jijitsu-o shira-*nai*.
  (*3*) He is **no** fool.   Kare-wa *kesshite* baka-dewa-*nai*.
  (*4*) **No** smoking.   Kin'en.
  There is no...ing (*colloq.*) totemo...deki-nai.
    (*ad.*) 1)iie [いいえ]; iya [いや]. 2)hai [はい]; ee [ええ]. 3)
  sukoshi-mo...(de-)nai [少しも...(で)ない].
  (*1*) Do you have a dictionary? — **No**, I don't have.
    Kimi-wa jisho-o motte-iru-ka? — *Iie*, motte-ima-sen.
  (*2*) Isn't he a musician? — **No**, he isn't.
    Kare-wa ongaku-ka dewa-nai-no-desu-ka? — *Ee*, sô-dewa-
    ari-masen.
  (*3*) He is **no** better than yesterday.
    Kare-wa kinô-yori *sukoshi-mo* yoku-natte-*i-nai*.
  no sooner...than ...(suru-)ya-ina-ya

No., no. dai...ban [第...番]; dai...gô [第...号]; ...banchi [...番地].

Nobel laureate(= Nobel prize winner) Nôberu-shô-jushô-sha [ノーベ

ル賞受賞者].

Nobel prize　Nôberu-shô［ノーベル賞］.

nobility (*n.*) 1)kôki-na-umare［高貴な生まれ］. 2)ke-dakasa［気高さ］.

noble (*a.*) 1)ke-dakai［気高い］. 2)kôki-na［高貴な］. 3)sûkô-na［崇高な］. 4)(kinzoku ga) fushoku-shi-nai［(金属が)腐食しない］.

nobody (*pron.*) dare-mo...nai［だれも…ない］.
　　　　　(*n.*) na-mo-nai-hito［名もない人］.

nod (*vi.*) 1)unazuku［うなずく］. 2)i-nemuri-suru［居眠りする］. 3) yureru［揺れる］; nabiku［なびく］.
　　　(*vt.*) 1)...o unazukaseru［…をうなずかせる］. 2)...o yurugasu［…を揺るがす］; ...o nabikasu［…をなびかす］.
　　　(*n.*) unazuki［うなずき］; kokkuri［こっくり］.

noise (*n.*) 1)mono-oto［物音］; sôon［騒音］. 2)noizu［ノイズ］.
　　　(*vt.*) ...o ii-furasu［…を言いふらす］.

noiseless (*a.*) oto-no-shi-nai［音のしない］; shizuka-na［静かな］.

noisy (*a.*) sôzôshii［騒々しい］; yakamashii［やかましい］.

nominal (*a.*) 1)meimoku-dake-no［名目だけの］; môshi-wake[-hodo]-no［申し訳(ほど)の］. 2)na-no［名の］.

nominate (*vt.*) 1)...o shimei-suru［…を指名する］; ...o nimmei-suru［…を任命する］. 2)...o shitei-suru［…を指定する］.

nomination (*n.*) shimei[-ken]［指名(権)］; nimmei[-ken]［任命(権)］.

nominative (*n. & a.*) (*gram.*) shukaku(-no)［主格(の)］.

none (*pron.*) dare-mo...nai［だれも…ない］; sukoshi-mo...nai［少しも…ない］.

nonsense (*n.*) mu-imi［無意味］; baka-geta-koto［ばかげたこと］; nansensu［ナンセンス］.
　　　　(*int.*) Baka-na !［ばかな！］.

nonstop (*a. & ad.*) 1)chokkô-no(-de)［直行の(で)］. 2)mu-chakuriku-no(-de)［無着陸の(で)］; nonsutoppu-no(-de)［ノンストップの(で)］.
　　　　(*n.*) chokkô-bin［直行便］; chokkô-ressha［直行列車］; chokkô-basu［直行バス］.

noodle (*n.*) (*pl.*) nûdoru［ヌードル］.

nook (*n.*) sumi［隅］; hikkonda-tokoro［引っ込んだ所］.

noon (*n.*) 1)shôgo［正午］; ma-hiru［真昼］. 2)(the –) zensei-ki［全盛期］; zetchô［絶頂］.

nor (*conj.*) ...mo-mata...nai［…もまた…ない］.

normal (*a.*) futsû-no［普通の］; seijô-na［正常な］.
　　　　(*n.*) hyôjun［標準］; jôtai［常態］.

north (*n.*) kita [北]; hoppô [北方]; hokubu [北部].
   (*a.*) kita-no [北の]; kita-kara-no [北からの].
   (*ad.*) kita-e [北へ]; kita-ni [北に].

northeast (*n.*) hoku-tô [北東].
   (*a. & ad.*) hoku-tô-no (hoku-tô-e) [北東の(北東へ)]; hoku-tô-kara-no (hoku-tô-kara) [北東からの(北東から)].

northern (*a.*) kita-no [北の].

North Pole, the Hokkyoku [北極].

North Star, the (*astron.*) Hokkyoku-sei [北極星].

northwest (*n.*) hoku-sei [北西].
   (*a. & ad.*) hoku-sei-no (hoku-sei-e) [北西の(北西へ)]; hoku-sei-kara-no (hoku-sei-kara) [北西からの(北西から)].

nose (*n.*) 1)hana [鼻]. 2)kyûkaku [嗅覚]. 3)tosshutsu-bu [突出部].
  count(tell) noses ninzû-o-kazoeru
  follow one's nose massugu-ni-iku   「kanshô-suru
  poke(thrust) one's nose into (*colloq.*) ...ni kuchi-o-dasu; ...ni
  under one's (very) nose hito-no-hana-saki[-menzen]-de
   (*vt.*) 1)...no nioi-o-kagu […のにおいをかぐ]. 2)...ni hana-o-kosuri-tsukeru […に鼻をこすりつける]. 3)(– one's way) yôjin-shi-tsutsu-susumu [用心しつつ進む].
   (*vi.*) 1)nioi-o-kagu [においをかぐ]. 2)o-sekkai-o-yaku [おせっかいをやく]. 3)(yôjin-shi-tsutsu-)susumu [(用心しつつ)進む].

nosegay (*n.*) hana-taba [花束].

nostril (*n.*) bikô [鼻孔].

nosy (*a.*) 1)hana-no-ookii [鼻の大きい]. 2)o-sekkai-na [おせっかいな].

not (*ad.*) ...de-nai […でない]; ...(shi-)nai […(し)ない].
  not...but ...de-wa-nakute...

notable (*a.*) chûmoku-ni-atai-suru [注目に値する]; chomei-na [著名な]; yûmei-na [有名な].
   (*n.*)(*pl.*) chomei-na-hito [著名な人]; meishi [名士].

notarize (*vt.*) ...o ninshô-suru […を認証する]; ...o kôshô-suru […を公証する].

notary (*n.*) kôshô-nin [公証人].

notation (*n.*) 1)hyôki [表記]. 2)kiroku [記録]; memo [メモ].

notch (*n.*) Bui-ji-gata-no-kizami-me [V字型の刻み目].
   (*vt.*) ...ni kizami-me-o-tsukeru […に刻み目を付ける].

note (*n.*) 1)oboe-gaki [覚え書き]; chû [注]. 2)mijikai-tegami [短かい手紙]. 3)chûi [注意]; chûmoku [注目]. 4)(tori no) naki-goe [(鳥の)

鳴き声]. 5)(*mus.*) ompu [音符]. 6)ne-iro [音色]. 7)(*com.*) tegata [手形]. 8)((*Eng.*)) (*com.*) shihei [紙幣].

take note of ...ni chûmoku-suru
   (*vt.*) 1)...ni chûmoku-suru […に注目する]; ...ni chûi-suru […に注意する]; ...ni ki-zuku […に気づく]. 2)...o kaki-tomeru {…を書き留める].
   (*1*) One virtue may **be noted** in him.
      Kare-ni hitotsu *me-ni-tsuku* bitoku ga aru.
   (*2*) I will **note** down every word he said.
      Kare-ga itta-koto-o hito-koto-nokorazu *kaki-tome-yô*.
notebook (*n.*) hikki-chô [筆記帳]; nôto [ノート].
noted (*a.*) yûmei-na [有名な]; chomei-na [著名な].
nothing (*pron. & n.*) 1)nani-mo...nai [なにも…ない]; mu [無]. 2) toru-ni-tarinai-mono [取るに足りないもの].
   (*1*) I have **nothing** to say.
      Watashi-wa *nani-mo* iu-koto-wa-*nai*.
   Nothing will come out of **nothing**.
      Mu-kara nani-mo shôji-nai-darô.
   (*2*) 100,000 yen is **nothing** to his family.
      Kare-no kazoku-niwa jû-man-en wa *toru-ni-tarinai-mono* da.
  for nothing tada-de; muryô-de
  have nothing to do with ...to sukoshi-mo-kankei-ga-nai
  nothing but tada...dake
  There is nothing to it. Sore-wa yôi-na-koto-da.
    (*ad.*) sukoshi-mo...de-nai [少しも…でない].
    These differ **nothing** from those.
      Kore-ra-wa sore-ra-to *sukoshi-mo* chigawa-nai.
notice (*n.*) 1)chûi [注意]; chûmoku [注目]. 2)tsûchi [通知]; yokoku [予告]. 3)tampyô [短評]. 4)hari-fuda [貼り札].
  take notice chûi-suru
  without notice yokoku-nashi-de; mudan-de
    (*vt.*) 1)...ni ki-ga-tsuku […に気が付く]; ...ni chûmoku-suru […に注目する]. 2)...ni tsûchi-suru […に通知する]; ...ni tsûkoku-suru […に通告する]. 3)...o teichô-ni-atsukau […を丁重に扱う]. 4)...ni genkyû-suru […に言及する].
    (*1*) I didn't **notice** it. Watashi-wa sore-*ni ki-ga-tsuka*-nakatta.
    (*2*) He **was noticed** to be dismissed.

　　　　　Kare-wa kaiko-o *tsûkoku-sareta*.

　　　　　(*vi.*) chûi-suru [注意する]; ki-zuku [気づく].

noticeable (*a.*) hito-me-o-hiku [人目を引く]; medatsu [目立つ].

notify (*vt.*) ...ni tsûchi-suru [···に通知する]; ...o keiji-suru [···を掲示する].

notion (*n.*) 1)kannen [観念]; gainen [概念]. 2)kangae [考え]; iken [意見].

notorious (*a.*) akumei-takai [悪名高い].

notwithstanding (*prep. & ad.*) ...nimo-kakawarazu (sore-nimo-kakawarazu) [···にもかかわらず(それにもかかわらず)].

　　　　He started **notwithstanding** the rain.

　　　　　Kare-wa ame-*nimo-kakawarazu* shuppatsu-shita.

　　　　It rained, but he started **notwithstanding**.

　　　　　Ame-ga-futte-ita, shikashi *sore-nimo-kakawarazu* kare-wa
　　　　　　shuppatsu-shita.

nought (*n.*) (*math.*) zero [ゼロ].

noun (*n.*) (*gram.*) meishi [名詞].

nourish (*vt.*) 1)...o yashinau [···を養う]; ...ni eiyô-butsu-o-ataeru [···に栄養物を与える]. 2)(kokoro ni)...o idaku [(心に)···をいだく].

nourishment (*n.*) jiyô-butsu [滋養物]; eiyô-o-ataeru-koto [栄養を与えること]; jochô [助長].

novel (*n.*) shôsetsu [小説].

novel (*a.*) atarashii [新しい]; mezurashii [珍しい]; kibatsu-na [奇抜な].

novelist (*n.*) shôsetsu-ka [小説家].

novelty (*n.*) 1)me-atarashii-koto [目新しいこと]; mezurashisa [珍しさ]. 2)(*pl.*) shin'an-butsu [新案物].

November (*n.*) Jûichigatsu [十一月].

now (*ad.*) 1)ima [今]. 2)sate [さて]; saa [さあ].

　　(*1*) He lives in Osaka **now**.　Kare-wa *ima* Ôsaka-ni sunde-iru.

　　(*2*) **Now**, let's go.　*Saa*, ikô.

　　just now ima-shigata

　　now and then(again) toki-doki

　　　(*n.*) ima [今].

　　　He must have finished writing his English composition by
　　　now.

　　　　　Kare-wa *ima*-goro-wa mô Ei-sakubun-o kaki-oete-iru-ni-
　　　　　chigainai.

from now (**on**) kongo-wa

till now ima-made

  (*conj.*) …(de-aru-)ijô-wa […(である)以上は].

    Now that I am well, I must work.

      Yoku-natta-*ijô-wa*, hataraka-nakucha.

nowadays (*ad.*) konogoro-wa [このごろは]; konnichi-de-wa [今日では].

nowhere (*ad.*) doko-ni-mo…nai [どこにも…ない]; doko-e-mo…(shi-)
nai [どこへも…(し)ない].

  (*n.*) 1)doko-tomo-shire-nai-tokoro [どことも知れないところ].
2)mumei-no-jôtai [無名の状態].

nuclear (*a.*) kaku-no [核の]; genshi-kaku-no [原子核の]; genshi-ryoku-
no [原子力の].

  (*n.*) kaku-heiki [核兵器]; kaku-heiki-hoyû-koku [核兵器保有国].
genshi-ryoku-hatsuden-sho [原子力発電所].

nuclear energy genshi-ryoku [原子力]; kaku-enerugî [核エネルギー].

nucleus (*n.*) kakushin [核心]; chûshin [中心].

nude (*a.*) ratai-no [裸体の].

  (*n.*) ratai [裸体]; ratai-zô [裸体像]; nûdo [ヌード].

nuisance (*n.*) 1)meiwaku-na-kôi [迷惑な行為]. 2)yakkai-na-mono [厄
介なもの]; urusai-hito [うるさい人].

numb (*a.*) kajikanda [かじかんだ]; shibireta [しびれた]; mahi-shita
[麻ひした].

number (*n.*) 1)kazu [数]; sû [数]. 2)bangô [番号]. 3)…ban […番];
…gô […号]; …banchi […番地].

  (*1*) They are superior in **number** to us.

    Kare-ra-wa *kazu*-ni-oite ware-ware-yori masatte-iru.

  an even **number** gûsû

  (*2*) **Number**, please. *Bangô*-o dôzo.

  (*3*) **number** three sam-*ban*

    the May **number** Go-gatsu-*gô*

    a house **number** ie no *banchi*

  a number of takusan-no

  (*vt.*) 1)…o kazoeru […を数える]. 2)…ni bangô-o-tsukeru […
に番号をつける]. 3)…no kazu-ni-tassuru […の数に達する].

  (*vi.*) 1)kazoeru [数える]; keisan-suru [計算する]. 2)sôkei(…
no-)kazu-ni-naru [総計(…の)数になる].

numberless (*a.*) 1)musû-no [無数の]. 2)bangô-no-nai [番号のない].

numeral (*n.*) 1)sûji [数字]; (*gram.*) sûshi [数詞]. 2)(*pl.*)((*US*)) nenjishô [年次章].

　　　(a.) kazu-no [数の].

numerous (a.) tasû-no [多数の]; tasû-kara-naru [多数からなる].

nun (n.) shûdô-jo [修道女]; nisô [尼僧].

nurse (n.) 1)kango-fu [看護婦]. 2)uba [乳母]. 3)hobo [保母].

　　　(vt.) 1)...o kango-suru [⋯を看護する]; ...o kambyô-suru [⋯を看病する]. 2)...ni chichi-o-yaru [⋯に乳をやる]. 3)...o daiji-ni-sodateru [⋯を大事に育てる]. 4)...o chûi-shite-atsukau [⋯を注意して扱う].

　　　(vi.) kango-suru [看護する]; junyû-suru [授乳する].

nursery (n.) 1)kodomo-beya [子供部屋]; ikuji-shitsu [育児室]. 2)nae-doko [苗床]; yôju-en [養樹園].

　　day nursery　takuji-sho; hoiku-sho

nut (n.) 1)ki-no-mi [木の実]; nattsu [ナッツ]. 2)(mech.) tome-neji [留めねじ].

　　　(vi.) ki-no-mi-o-hirou [木の実を拾う].

nutcrackers (n.) kurumi-wari-ki [クルミ割り器]; nattokurakkâ [ナットクラッカー].

nylon (n.) 1)nairon [ナイロン]. 2)(pl.)(colloq.) nairon-no-josei-yô-kutsu-shita [ナイロンの女性用くつ下].

O

O (int.) Oo! [おお!]; Aa! [ああ!]; Maa! [まあ!]; Oya! [おや!]; Ara! [あら!].

oak (*n.*) ôku[-zai] [オーク(材)].

oaken (*a.*) ôku[-sei]-no [オーク(製)の].

oar (*n.*) 1)kai [かい]; ôru [オール]. 2)kogi-te [こぎ手].
　(*vt. & vi.*) (...o)-kogu […を]こぐ].

oasis (*n.*) oashisu [オアシス]; ikoi-no-basho [憩いの場所].

oats (*n.*) karasu-mugi [カラスムギ]; ôto-mugi [オートムギ].

oath (*n.*) 1)chikai [誓い]. 2)(*pl.*) akutai [悪態].

obedience (*n.*) fukujû [服従]; jûjun [従順].

obedient (*a.*) jûjun-na [従順な].

obey (*vt. & vi.*) (...ni) fukujû-suru [(…に)服従する]; (...ni) shitagau
[(…に)従う].

object (*n.*) 1)buttai [物体]; mono [もの]. 2)taishô[-butsu] [対象(物)].
3)mokuteki [目的].
　(*vi.*) hantai-suru [反対する]; igi-o-tonaeru [異義を唱える].
　(*vt.*) ...to hantai-suru […と反対する].

objection (*n.*) 1)hantai [反対]; igi [異義]; fufuku [不服]. 2)hantai-
no-riyû [反対の理由].

objective (*a.*) 1)jitsuzai-no [実在の]. 2)mokuteki-no [目的の]. 3)
(*philos.*) kyakkan-teki-na [客観的な].
　(*n.*) 1)mokuteki [目的]. 2)(*gram.*) mokuteki-kaku [目的格].

objective test kyakkan-tesuto [客観テスト].

obligation (*n.*) 1)gimu [義務]; sekinin [責任]. 2)ongi [恩義]. 3)
saimu [債務]; saiken [債券]. 4)sewa [世話].

oblige (*vt.*) 1)...ni yamu-o-ezu...(sa-)seru […にやむをえず…(さ)せる].
2)...ni shinsetsu-ni-suru […に親切にする]; ...ni onkei-o-hodokosu […
に恩恵を施す].
　(*1*) He **obliged** himself to refrain from smoking.
　　Kare-wa tabako-o tsutsushima-*zaru-o-enakatta*.
　(*2*) I'm much **obliged** to you.　Hontô-ni *arigatô*.
　　(*vi.*) (*colloq.*) kôi-o-shimesu [好意を示す]; hito-no-tame-ni-
tsukusu [人のために尽くす].

obliterate (*vt.*) ...o keshi-saru […を消し去る]; ...o masshô-suru […
を抹消する].

oblivion (*n.*) bôkyaku [忘却].

oblivious (*a.*) wasurete [忘れて]; ki-ga-tsuka-nai [気が付かない].

obscure (*a.*) 1)usu-gurai [薄暗い]; bon'yari-shita [ぼんやりした]. 2)
yo-ni-shirare-nai [世に知られない]. 3)meiryô-de-nai [明りょうでない].
　(*vt.*) 1)...o kuraku-suru […を暗くする]. 2)...o wakari-nikuku-

　　suru［…を分かりにくくする］.

obscurity (*n.*) 1)usu-gura-sa［薄暗さ］. 2)fu-meiryô［不明りょう］; wakari-nikui-ten［分かりにくい点］. 3)mumei［無名］.

observance (*n.*) 1)junshu［順守］. 2)(shukusaijitsu o) iwau-koto［(祝祭日を)祝うこと］. 3)shûkan［習慣］. 4)kansatsu［観察］.

observation (*n.*) 1)kansatsu〔-ryoku〕［観察(力)］; chûi-bukaku-miru-koto［注意深く見ること］. 2)(*pl.*) jôhô［情報］. 3)iken［意見］.

observation car tembô-sha［展望車］.

observe (*vt.*) 1)…o kansatsu-suru［…を観察する］; …ni ki-zuku［…に気づく］. 2)…o mamoru［…を守る］; …o junshu-suru［…を順守する］.
　　　(*vi.*) 1)kansatsu-suru［観察する］. 2)iken-o-noberu［意見を述べる］.

observer (*n.*) 1)kansatsu-sha［観察者］; obuzâbâ［オブザーバー］. 2) junshu-suru-hito［順守する人］.

obstacle (*n.*) shôgai〔-butsu〕［障害(物)］; jama〔-mono〕［邪魔(物)］.

obstacle race shôgai-butsu-kyôsô［障害物競走］.

obstinate (*a.*) ganko-na［頑固な］; gôjô-na［強情な］; shitsuyô-na［執ような］.

obstruct (*vt.*) …o fusagu［…をふさぐ］; …o jama-suru［…を邪魔する］; …o bôgai-suru［…を妨害する］.

obtain (*vt.*) 1)…o eru［…を得る］; …o te-ni-ireru［…を手に入れる］. 2)…o tassei-suru［…を達成する］.

obvious (*a.*) akiraka-na［明らかな］; meiryô-na［明りょうな］.

occasion (*n.*) 1)baai［場合］; ori［折］; toki［時］. 2)kikai［機会］. 3) riyû［理由］; gen'in［原因］.
　　have no occasion to (do) …(suru)-riyû〔hitsuyô〕-ga-nai
　　on occasion toki-doki
　　　　　(*vt.*) 1)…o okosaseru［…を起こさせる］. 2)…ni…(sa-)seru［…に…(さ)せる］.

occasional (*a.*) 1)toki-ori-no［時折の］. 2)tokubetsu-na-baai-no-tame-no［特別な場合のための］; hojo-yô-no［補助用の］.

occasionally (*ad.*) toki-doki［時々］.

occult (*a.*) 1)shimpi-teki-na［神秘的な］; okaruto-teki-na［オカルト的な］; hihô-no［秘法の］. 2)(the -) okaruto［オカルト］; chô-shizen-genshô［超自然現象］.

occupation (*n.*) 1)shokugyô［職業］. 2)sen'yû［占有］.

occupy (*vt.*) 1)…ni sumu［…に住む］; …o shimeru［…を占める］. 2)…o toru［…を取る］; …o fusagu［…をふさぐ］. 3)…ni jûji-saseru［…

に従事させる].

(1) They **have occupied** the same office for the ten years.
   Kare-ra-wa jû-nen-kan onaji ofisu-*ni iru*.
   He **occupies** an important position.
   Kare-wa jûyô-na chii-*o shimete-iru*.
(2) This table **occupies** too much space.
   Kono têburu wa basho-*o tori*-sugiru.
   Troubles **occupy** his mind.
   Yakkai-goto de kare-no atama wa *ippai-da*.
(3) They **are occupied** with opening up wild land.
   Kare-ra-wa are-chi-no-kaitaku-ni *jûji-shite-iru*.

occur (*vi.*) 1)okoru [起こる]. 2)kokoro[atama]-ni-ukabu [心[頭]に浮かぶ]. 3)sonzai-suru [存在する].
(1) A severe earthquake **occurred** last night.
   Sakuya hageshii jishin ga *okita*.
(2) A splendid idea **occurred** to me.
   Subarashii kangae ga *atama-ni-ukanda*.
(3) The word **occurs** twice in the sentence.
   Kono bun-niwa sono go ga ni-do *arawareru*.

ocean (*n.*) taiyô [大洋].
o'clock (*ad.*) ...ji [...時].
octave (*n.*) (*mus.*) okutâbu [オクターブ].
October (*n.*) Jûgatsu [十月].
octopus (*n.*) (*zool.*) tako [タコ].
odd (*a.*) 1)hampa-na [半端な]. 2)hen-na [変な]. 3)kisû-no [奇数の]. 4)rinji-no [臨時の]; toki-tama-no [時たまの].
odds (*n.*) 1)kachi-me [勝ち目]. 2)mikomi [見込み].
(1) The **odds** are in your favo(u)r.
   Kimi-no-hô-ni *kachi-me*-ga-aru.
(2) The **odds** are that he will win.   *Tabun* kare-wa katsu-*darô*.
at odds   arasotte
odor, odour (*n.*) 1)nioi [におい]; kaori [香り]. 2)hyôban [評判].
of (*prep.*) 1)...no [...の]. 2)...no-uchi-de [...のうちで]. 3)...to-iu [...という]. 4)...no-haitte-iru [...の入っている]. 5)...de [...で]. 6)...ni-tsuite [...について]. 7)...kara [...から]. 8)...o [...を]. 9)...ga-gen'in-de [...が原因で].
(1) This is the site **of** a castle.   Koko-wa shiro *no* ato da.
(2) He is the tallest **of** them all.

Mina-*no-uchi-de* kare-ga ichiban-se-ga-takai.

(3) the city **of** Osaka   Ôsaka *to-iu* shi—Ôsaka-shi

(4) a bottle **of** ink   inku *no-haitte-iru* bin

       inku hito-bin; hito-bin-no inku

(5) The bridge is **of** steel.   Sono hashi wa kôtetsu-*de*-dekite-iru.

(6) stories **of** space travel   uchû-ryokô-*ni-tsuite-no* hanashi

(7) He robbed her **of** her money.

     Kare-wa kano-jo-*kara* kane-o nusunda.

     Kare-wa kano-jo-*no* kane-o nusunda.

(8) I am afraid **of** dogs.   Watashi-wa inu-*ga*-kowai.

(9) He died **of** cancer.   Kare-wa gan[-*ga-gen'in*]-*de* shinda.

off (*ad.*) 1)satte [去って]. 2)hanarete [離れて]. 3)dete-shimatte [出てしまって]. 4)kurashi-ga...de [暮らしが…で]. 5)sukkari...(shite-) shimau [すっかり…(して)しまう]. 6)kirete [切れて]; tomatte [止まって]. 7)nuide [脱いで].

(1) He ran **off**. Kare-wa hashiri-*satta*.

(2) The station is four miles **off**.

     Eki wa yom-mairu *hanarete*-iru.

(3) They started **off** on a trip. Kare-ra-wa ryokô-ni *dekaketa*.

     We must be **off** now. Mô o-itoma-shi-nakereba-nari-masen.

(4) He is well **off**. Kare-wa *kurashi-ga*-raku-da.

                 Kare-wa *yûfuku*-da.

(5) I paid **off** my debts.

     Watashi-wa shakkin-o *sukkari*-haratte-*shimatta*.

(6) Turn **off** the television. Terebi-o *kiri*-nasai.

(7) Take your hat **off**. Bôshi-o *tori*-nasai.

off and on toki-doki

  (*prep.*) 1)...kara [⋯から]; ...kara-hanarete [⋯から離れて]. 2)...no-oki-de [⋯の沖で].

(1) He fell **off** a bed. Kare-wa beddo-*kara* ochita.

(2) The ship sank **off** Wakayama.

     Sono fune wa Wakayama-*oki-de* chimbotsu-shita.

  (*a.*) 1)mukô-gawa-no [向こう側の]. 2)hima-na [暇な]; hiban-no [非番の]. 3)kisetsu-hazure-no [季節外れの]. 4)hon-suji-kara-wakareta [本筋から分かれた].

(1) He lives in the **off** side of this river.

     Kare-wa kono-kawa-no-*mukô-gawa*-ni sunde-iru.

(2) an **off** day   *hiban-no* hi

(3) an **off** season   shîzun'*ofu*

(4) an **off** issue   *shiyô-no* mondai

offend (*vt.*) ...o okoraseru [...を怒らせる].

    (*vi.*) 1)tsumi-o-okasu [罪を犯す]. 2)ki-ni-sawaru [気にさわる].

offender (*n.*) ihan-sha [違反者]; fukai-na-mono[-hito] [不快な物[人]].

offense (*n.*) 1)rippuku [立腹]. 2)kôgeki [攻撃]. 3)ihan [違反].

  (*1*) She always takes **offense**.

    Kano-jo-wa itsu-mo *hara-o-tate*te-iru.

  (*2*) The most effective defense is **offence**.

    Saijô-no-bôgyo wa *kôgeki*-de-aru.

  (*3*) It is an **offense** against the law.

    Sore-wa hôritsu-*ihan*-de-aru.

  give offense to ...o okoraseru

offensive (*a.*) 1)iya-na [いやな]. 2)kôgeki-yô-no [攻撃用の].

offer (*vt.*) 1)môshi-deru [申し出る]. 2)...o teikyô-suru [...を提供する].

  (*1*) He **offered** to help them.

    Kare-wa kare-ra-ni enjo-*o môshi-deta*.

  (*2*) I **offered** her the dress material as a gift.

    Watashi-wa kano-jo-ni okuri-mono-to-shite fujin-fukuji-*o teikyô-shita*.

    (*vi.*) 1)...ga arawareru [...が現れる]. 2)môshi-deru [申し出る].

    (*n.*) 1)môshi-ide [申し出]; teikyô [提供]. 2)tsuke-ne [付け値].

offering (*n.*) 1)môshi-ide [申し出]; teikyô [提供]. 2)kenkin [献金]; sonae-mono [供え物].

office (*n.*) 1)jimu-sho [事務所]; shokuba [職場]. 2)shoku [職]; kanshoku [官職]. 3)(*pl.*) sewa [世話]; jinryoku [尽力].

officer (*n.*) 1)shikan [士官]; kôkyû-sen'in [高級船員]. 2)kômu-in [公務員].

official (*a.*) kômu-jô-no [公務上の]; ooyake-no [公の]; kôshiki-no [公式の].

    (*n.*) kômu-in [公務員].

offing (*n.*) oki [沖].

offspring (*n.*) 1)shison [子孫]. 2)kekka [結果].

often (*ad.*) shiba-shiba [しばしば]; tabi-tabi [たびたび].

oh (*int.*) Oo! [おお!]; Maa! [まあ!]; Oya! [おや!].

oho (*int.*) Hohô! [ほほー!].

oil (*n.*) abura [油]; sekiyu [石油].

    (*vt.*) 1)...ni abura-o-nuru [...に油を塗る]; ...ni abura-o-sasu [...

に油を差す]. 2)...o enkatsu-ni-suru […を円滑にする].

oil colo(u)rs abura-enogu [油絵の具].

oil field yuden [油田].

oily (*a.*) 1)abura-no [油の]. 2)o-seji-no-umai [お世辞のうまい].

ointment (*n.*) nankô [軟膏].

O.K., OK (*ad.*) yoroshii [よろしい]; umaku [うまく].

       (*a.*) yoroshii [よろしい]; kekkô-na [結構な].

       (*vt.*) ...o ôkê-suru […をオーケーする]; ...o shônin-suru […を承認する].

を承認する].

       (*n.*) shônin [承認]; kyoka [許可].

old (*a.*) 1)toshi-totta [年とった]. 2)...sai-no […歳の]. 3)furui [古い].

  (*1*) The boy is **old** enough to be able to do it.

      Shônen wa sore-ga-dekiru-*toshi*-da.

  (*2*) He is thirty years **old**. Kare-wa san-jus*sai* da.

  (*3*) I visited an **old** cathedral.

      Watashi-wa *furui* dai-seidô-o otozureta.

  old man (*colloq.*) (the -) oyaji; oya-kata

old-fashioned (*a.*) kyûshiki-na [旧式な]; jidai-okure-no [時代遅れの].

olive (*n.*) (*bot.*) orîbu-no-ki [オリーブの木]; orîbu-no-mi [オリーブの実].

実].

      (*a.*) orîbu[-iro]-no [オリーブ(色)の].

omen (*n.*) zenchô [前兆]; kizashi [きざし].

      (*vt.*) ...no zenchô-to-naru […の前兆となる]; ...o yoji-suru […を予示する].

を予示する].

ominous (*a.*) 1)engi-no-warui [縁起の悪い]. 2)zenchô-no [前兆の].

omission (*n.*) 1)shôryaku [省略]; datsuraku [脱落]. 2)taiman [怠慢]; te-nukari [手抜かり].

te-nukari [手抜かり];

omit (*vt.*) 1)...o shôryaku-suru […を省略する]. 2)...o okotaru […を怠る].

怠る].

omnibus (*n.*) basu [バス].

on (*prep.*) 1)...no-ue-ni(-de) […の上に(で)]. 2)...(shi-)te […(し)て]. 3)...ni-tsuite […について]. 4)...(suru-)to-dôji-ni […(する)と同時に]. 5)(...nichi)-ni [(…日)に]. 6)...no-tame […のため]. 7)...ni-yotte […によって]. 8)...mochi-de […持ちで].

  (*1*) The magazine is **on** the desk.

      Sono zasshi wa tsukue-*no-ue-ni* aru.

  (*2*) I saw a house **on** fire. Ie-ga ikken mo*ete-iru*-no-ga-mieta.

  (*3*) He lectured **on** Japanese history.

Kare-wa Nihon-shi-*ni-tsuite* kôgi-shita.

(4) **On** arriving at the station, I telephoned to him.

Eki-ni tsuku-*to-dôji-ni*, watashi-wa kare-ni denwa-shita.

(5) He was born **on** the 19th of June.

Kare-wa Rokugatsu-jû-ku-nichi-*ni* umareta.

(6) He went to Tokyo **on** official business.

Kare-wa kôyô-*de* Tôkyô-e itta.

(7) We live **on** rice.   Ware-ware-wa kome-*o-tabete* ikite-iru.

(8) The expense is **on** me.

Kono hiyô wa watashi-*ga-harai*-masu.

  (*ad.*) 1)kabutte [かぶって]; kite [着て]. 2)shinkô-shite [進行して];
tsuzukete [続けて].

  (*1*) He had his hat **on**.   Kare-wa bôshi-o *kabutte*-ita.

  (*2*) He went **on**.   Kare-wa *don-don* susunda.

He worked **on**.   Kare-wa hataraki-*tsuzuketa*.

once (*ad.*) 1)ichi-do [一度]. 2)katsute [かつて]; mukashi [昔].

  (*1*) I write a letter to my father **once** a week.

Watashi-wa shû-ni *ichi-do* chichi-ni tegami-o kaku.

  (*2*) **Once** there lived a king here.

Katsute koko-ni ô-sama-ga sunde-ita.

  more than once   nan-do-mo

  once more(again)   mô-ichi-do

    (*conj.*) ittan...(suru-)to [いったん…(する)と].

    Once bit(ten), twice shy.   (*prov.*) *Ichi-do* kamareru-*to*, ni-
do-me-kara-wa kowagaru.

    (*n.*) ichi-do [一度].

  all at once   totsuzen

  at once   tadachi-ni; sugu-ni

  for once   kondo-dake-wa

one (*a.*) 1)hitotsu-no [一つの]. 2)aru [ある].

  (*1*) I have only **one** dictionary.

Watashi-wa jisho-o *issatsu*-dake motte-iru.

  (*2*) **One** day I told it to her.

Aru hi watashi-wa kano-jo-ni sono-koto-o hanashita.

  (*n.*) ichi [一]; ikko [一個]; hitori [一人].

  one by one   hitotsu-zutsu; hitori-zutsu

    (*pron.*) 1)hito [人]; hito-wa-dare-de-mo [人はだれでも]. 2)mono
[もの].

 (*1*) **One** should love one's neighbors.

   Hito wa rinjin-o aisu-beki-da.

 (*2*) Her life was a short **one**.

   Kano-jo-no shôgai wa mijikai *mono* datta.

 every one　dare-de-mo-mina

 no one　dare-mo...nai

 one...the other　...ippô-wa...tahô-wa...

 some one　dare-ka

 the one...the other　...zensha-wa...kôsha-wa...

oneself (*pron.*) jibun-jishin(-o/-ni) [自分自身(を/に)].

 by oneself　hitori-de; dokuryoku-de

 for oneself　jibun-de

 of oneself　hitoride-ni; shizen-ni

one-sided (*a.*) ippô-teki-na [一方的な]; katayotta [片寄った]; kata-gawa-dake-no [片側だけの].

one-way (*a.*) ippô-tsûkô-no [一方通行の]; ichi-hôkô-no [一方向の]; ((*US*)) kata-michi-no [片道の].

onion (*n.*) tamanegi [タマネギ].

only (*a.*) 1)tatta-hitori-no [たった一人の]; tatta-hitotsu-no [たった一つの]. 2)(the –) saiteki-no [最適の]; muhi-no [無比の].

 (*1*) He lost his **only** brother.

   Kare-wa *tatta-hitori-no* kyôdai-o nakushita.

 (*2*) Champagne really is the **only** drink.

   Jitsu-ni shampan wa *saiteki-no* nomi-mono da.

  (*ad.*) tada...dake [ただ…だけ]; honno...bakari [ほんの…ばかり].

  He **only** laughed.　Kare-wa *tada* waratta-*dake*-datta.

  Only you can solve this problem.

   Kimi-*dake*-ga kono mondai-o toku-koto-ga-dekiru.

  He came here from Nagoya **only** a few days ago.

   Kare-wa *honno* ni-san-nichi-mae Nagoya-kara koko-e kita-*bakari*-da.

 have only to (do)　(shi)-sae-sureba-yoi

  You have only to write this passage.

   Kimi-wa kono setsu-o kaki-sae-sureba-yoi.

 if only　...de-sae-areba[-yoi-no-da-ga]

  If only he would come home in safety!

   Kare-ga buji-ni kaeri-sae-sureba-yoi-no-da-ga!

 only just　tatta-ima...(shita-)bakari

only too 1)hijô-ni. 2)zannen-nagara

    1) only too glad hijô-ni-arigatai

    2) only too true zannen-nagara-hontô-de

    (*conj.*) 1)(*colloq.*) tadashi [ただし]; ...daga-shikashi [⋯だがしかし]. 2)...de-sae-nakereba [⋯でさえなければ].

    (*1*) You may go, **only** come back early.

        Itte-mo-yoi, *tadashi* hayaku-kaeri-nasai.

    (*2*) You'd succeed, **only** (that) you're rather lazy.

        Kimi-wa *tada* namake-*sae-shi-nakereba*, seikô-suru-darô.

onward (*ad.*) mae-e [前へ].

    (*a.*) zenshin-suru [前進する]; zempô-e-no [前方への].

open (*vt. & vi.*) 1)(...o) hiraku [(⋯を)開く]. 2)...o hajimeru (hajimaru) [⋯を始める(始まる)].

    (*1*) **Open** the door. To-o akero.

    (*2*) School **opens** at eight. Gakkô wa hachi-ji-ni *hajimaru*.

    (*a.*) 1)aite-iru [開いている]; kôkai-no [公開の]. 2)ooi-no-nai [覆いのない]; sotchoku-na [率直な]. 3)hiro-biro-to-shita [広々とした]. 4)mi-kettei-no [未決定の]; mi-kaiketsu-no [未解決の].

    (*1*) The window is **open**. Ano mado wa *aite-iru*.

    The exhibition is now **open**.

        Hakuran-kai wa mokka *kaisai-chû*-desu.

    (*2*) an **open** car *ôpun*-kâ

    an **open** city *mu-bôbi*-toshi

    an **open** manner *sotchoku-na* taido

    (*3*) an **open** field *hiro-biro-to-shita* no-hara

    (*4*) leave the question **open**

        mondai-o *mi-kaiketsu-no*-mama-ni-shite-oku

opening (*n.*) 1)hiraku-koto [開くこと]; kaikai [開会]; kaishi [開始]; kaitsû [開通]. 2)ana [穴]. 3)akichi [空き地]. 4)ketsuin [欠員].

openly (*ad.*) 1)sotchoku-ni [率直に]. 2)kôzen-to [公然と].

open-minded (*a.*) kokoro-no-hiroi [心の広い].

openwork (*n.*) sukashi-zaiku [透かし細工].

opera (*n.*) kageki [歌劇]; opera [オペラ].

opera house opera-gekijô [オペラ劇場].

operate (*vi.*) 1)hataraku [働く]; sayô-suru [作用する]; kiku [効く]. 2)(*surg.*) shujutsu-suru [手術する].

    (*1*) The medicine **operates** well. Kusuri ga yoku *kiku*.

    (*2*) The surgeon decided to **operate** on him.

　　　　Geka-i wa kare-o *shujutsu-suru*-koto-ni kimeta.
　　　(*vt.*) 1)...o unten-suru [⋯を運転する]; ...o sôjû-suru [⋯を操縦する]. 2)...o keiei-suru [⋯を経営する].

operation (*n.*) 1)hataraki [働き]; sayô [作用]; unten [運転]. 2)shujutsu [手術]. 3)(*mil. pl.*) gunji-kôdô [軍事行動].

operator (*n.*) (kikai no) unten-sha [(機械の)運転者]; musen-tsûshin-shi [無線通信士]; (*teleg.*) kôkan-shu [交換手]; (*surg.*) shujutsu-sha [手術者]; (*stock*) sôba-shi [相場師].

opinion (*n.*) iken [意見]; kenkai [見解].
　　be of (the) opinion that... ...to omou
opinion poll seron-chôsa [世論調査].
opium (*n.*) ahen [あへん].
opponent (*a.*) taikô-suru [対抗する]; hantai-no [反対の].
　　(*n.*) aite [相手]; taikô-sha [対抗者].
opportune (*a.*) tsugô-no-yoi [都合のよい]; jiki-ni-tekishita [時機に適した].
opportunity (*n.*) kikai [機会]; kôki [好機]; chansu [チャンス].
oppose (*vt. & vi.*) (...ni) hantai-suru [(⋯に)反対する]; (...ni) taikô-suru [(⋯に)対抗する].
opposite (*a.*) mukai-gawa-no [向かい側の]; hantai[-gawa]-no [反対(側)の].
　　(*n.*) hantai-no-koto[-mono/-hito] [反対のこと[もの/人]].
　　(*prep.*) ...ni-mukai-atte [⋯に向かい合って].
　　(*ad.*) mukai-gawa-ni [向かい側に]; hantai-no-ichi-ni [反対の位置に].
opposition (*n.*) 1)hantai [反対]; teikô [抵抗]. 2)hantai-tô [反対党]; yatô [野党].
oppress (*vt.*) 1)...o appaku-suru [⋯を圧迫する]; ...o shiitageru [⋯を虐げる]. 2)...o nayamasu [⋯を悩ます].
oppression (*n.*) 1)appaku [圧迫]; assei [圧制]; gyakutai [虐待]. 2)yûutsu [憂うつ]; kunô [苦悩].
optical (*a.*) me-no [目の]; shikaku-no [視覚の]; kôgaku-no [光学の].
optical illusion me-no-sakkaku [目の錯覚].
optimistic (*a.*) rakuten-teki-na [楽天的な]; rakuten-shugi-no [楽天主義の].
option (*n.*) sentaku [選択]; sentaku-dekiru-mono [選択できるもの].
optional (*a.*) zuii-no [随意の].
or (*conj.*) 1)...ka-arui-wa [⋯かあるいは]; ...ka-mata-wa [⋯かまたは].

2)sunawachi [すなわち]. 3)sô-de-nai-to [そうでないと].

(*1*) You **or** I must go.

    Kimi *ka*[-*mata-wa*] watashi ga ika-neba-naranai.

(*2*) The distance is five miles **or** eight kilometers.

    Sono kyori wa go-mairu *sunawachi* hachi-kiro desu.

(*3*) Make haste, **or** you will miss the train.

    Isogi-nasai, *sô-de-nai-to* ressha-ni nori-okuremasu-yo.

or so …ka-sono-kurai

oral (*a.*) kôtô-no [口頭の]; (*anat.*) kuchi-no [口の].

orange (*n. & a.*) orenji(-no) [オレンジ(の)]; orenji-iro(-no) [オレンジ色(の)]; daidai-iro(-no) [だいだい色(の)].

orator (*n.*) enzetsu-sha [演説者]; yûben-ka [雄弁家].

oratorical (*a.*) enzetsu-no [演説の]; yûben-no [雄弁の].

orbit (*n.*) 1)(*astron.*) kidô [軌道]. 2)(chishiki ya katsudô nado no) han'i [(知識や活動などの)範囲].

    (*vi.*) kidô-ni-notte-tobu [軌道に乗って飛ぶ].

    (*vt.*) …o kidô-ni-noseru […を軌道に乗せる]; …no mawari-o-mawaru […の周りを回る].

orchard (*n.*) kaju-en [果樹園].

orchestra (*n.*) kangen-gaku-dan [管弦楽団]; ôkesutora [オーケストラ].

orchid (*n.*) (*bot.*) ran [ラン]; ran-no-hana [ランの花].

ordain (*vt.*) …o(…de-aru-to/…(suru-)yô-ni/…to) sadameru […を(…であると/…(する)ように/…と)定める]; …o seishoku-ni-tsukeru […を聖職につける].

order (*n.*) 1)(*pl.*) meirei [命令]. 2)junjo [順序]. 3)chitsujo [秩序]; kiritsu [規律]. 4)kawase [為替]. 5)(*com.*) chûmon [注文]. 6)tôkyû [等級]; kaikyû [階級]. 7)(the O-) kunshô [勲章]. 8)shûdô-kai [修道会].

(*1*) He gave them **orders** to start.

    Kare-wa kare-ra-ni shuppatsu-no-*meirei*-o kudashita.

(*2*) Arrange them in **order**.

    Sore-ra-o *junjo*-tadashiku narabe-nasai.

(*3*) They keep a social **order**.

    Kare-ra-wa shakai-*chitsujo*-o iji-suru.

(*4*) a postal **order**   yûbin-*kawase*

(*5*) I'll place an **order** with you.

    Watashi-wa anata-ni *chûmon*-shi-yô.

(*6*) all **orders** and degrees of men   ningen no arayuru *kaikyû*

(7) the Order of the Garter   Gâtâ-*kunshô*

(8) the Franciscan **Order** Furanshisuko-*shûdô-kai*

in order that... ...(suru-)tame-ni

in order to (do) ...(suru)-tame-ni

call...to order ...no kaikai-o-sengen-suru

made to order atsurae-no

out of order chôshi-ga-waruku

　　(*vt.*) 1)...ni meijiru [···に命じる]; ...o meirei-suru [···を命令する]. 2)...o chûmon-suru [···を注文する]. 3)...o totonoeru [···を整える]; ...o seiri-suru [···を整理する].

　(*1*) The doctor **ordered** me a complete rest.
　　　Isha wa watashi-ni zettai-ansei-*o meijita.*

　(*2*) I **ordered** a book from New York.
　　　Watashi-wa hon-*o* issatsu Nyû-Yôku-ni *chûmon-shita.*

　(*3*) I want to **order** my thoughts better.
　　　Watashi-wa kangae-*o* yori-yoku *seiri-shi-tai.*

orderly (*a.*) seizen-to-shita [整然とした]; chitsujo-o-mamoru [秩序を守る]; kiritsu-tadashii [規律正しい].

　　(*n.*) (*mil.*) tôban-hei [当番兵]; (byôin no) yômu-in [(病院の)用務員].

ordinal number josû [序数].

ordinary (*a.*) futsû-no [普通の]; heibon-na [平凡な].

ore (*n.*) kôseki [鉱石].

organ (*n.*) 1)(*mus.*) orugan [オルガン]. 2)(*med.*) kikan [器官]. 3) kikan [機関].

　(*2*) **organs** of digestion shôka-*kikan*

　(*3*) **organs** of government seiji-*kikan*

organic (*a.*) 1)(*med.*) kikan-no [器官の]. 2)yûki-tai-no [有機体の]. 3)soshiki-teki-na [組織的な].

organism (*n.*) 1)yûki-tai [有機体]. 2)yûki-teki-soshiki-tai [有機的組織体].

organization (*n.*) 1)soshiki [組織]; kikô [機構]. 2)dantai [団体]; kyôkai [協会].

organize (*vt.*) ...o soshiki-suru [···を組織する]; ...o keitô-dateru [···を系統だてる]; ...o keikaku-suru [···を計画する].

　　(*vi.*) soshiki-teki-ni-danketsu-suru [組織的に団結する]; soshiki[yûki]-ka-suru [組織[有機]化する].

orient (*n.*) 1)(the O-) Tôyô [東洋]; Ajia-shokoku [アジア諸国]. 2)

(shinju no) kôtaku [(真珠の)光沢].
　　(a.) 1)tôhô-no [東方の]. 2)kôtaku-no-aru [光沢のある].
　　(vt.) 1)...o higashi-muki-ni-suru [⋯を東向きにする]. 2)...o tadashii-hôkô-ni-oku [⋯を正しい方向に置く]. 3)...o tekiô-saseru [⋯を適応させる]; ...o hôkô-zukeru [⋯を方向づける]. 4)...no hôgaku-o-shiru [⋯の方角を知る].

oriental (a.) (O-) Tôyô-no [東洋の]; Tôyô-fû-no [東洋風の].

orientation (n.) 1)jumbi-kôshû [準備講習]; orientêshon [オリエンテーション]. 2)hôshin-kettei [方針決定]. 3)higashi-ni-mukeru-koto [東に向けること].

origin (n.) 1)kigen [起源]; gen'in [原因]. 2)umare [生まれ].

original (a.) 1)saisho-no [最初の]; genshi-no [原始の]. 2)dokusô-teki-na [独創的な]. 3)gembun-no [原文の].
　　(n.) gembutsu [原物]; gensho [原書].

originality (n.) dokusô-sei [独創性].

originally (ad.) 1)moto-moto [もともと]; hajime-wa [始めは]. 2)dokusô-teki-ni [独創的に].

originate (vt.) ...o hajimeru [⋯を始める]; ...o okosu [⋯を起こす]; ...o sôsaku-suru [⋯を創作する].
　　(vi.) hajimaru [始まる]; okoru [起こる].

Orion (n.) (astron.) Orion-za [オリオン座].

ornament (n.) kazari [飾り]; sôshin-gu [装身具].
　　(vt.) ...o kazaru [⋯を飾る].

ornamental (a.) kazari-no [飾りの]; sôshoku-yô-no [装飾用の].

orphan (n.) koji [孤児].
　　(vt.) ...o koji-ni-suru [⋯を孤児にする].

orthodox (a.) seitô-ha-no [正統派の]; seisetsu-no [正説の].

ostensibly (ad.) hyômen-jô〔-wa〕[表面上(は)].

ostrich (n.) (birds) dachô [ダチョウ].

other (a.) 1)hoka-no [ほかの]; kotonatta [異なった]. 2)mô-hitotsu-no [もう一つの].
　　(1) She is taller than any **other** girl.
　　　　Hoka-no dono shôjo-yori-mo kano-jo-wa se-ga-takai.
　　(2) Please show me the **other** hand.
　　　　Mô-ippô-no te-o misete-kudasai.
　　every other day kakujitsu-ni
　　the other day senjitsu
　　　　(pron.) hoka-no-hito-tachi [ほかの人たち]; mô-hitotsu-no-hô

[もう一つの方].

Do good to **others**.

Hoka-no-hito-tachi-ni shinsetsu-ni-shi-nasai.

One is light and the **other** is heavy.

Hitotsu wa karuku *mô-hitotsu-no-hô* wa omoi.

some day or other itsu-ka

(*ad.*) (...to-wa-)betsu-no-hôhô-de [(…とは)]別の方法で]; ...igai-ni […以外に].

I can't walk **other** than slowly.

Watashi-wa yukkuri-*de-nakereba* aruke-nai.

otherwise (*ad.*) 1) betsu-no-yari-kata-de [別のやり方で]. 2) sô-de-nakereba [そうでなければ]. 3) sono-ta-no-ten-dewa [その他の点では].

(*1*) I cannot act **otherwise**. Watashi-wa *hoka-ni* yari-yô-ga-nai.

(*2*) He would **otherwise** starve.

Sô-de-nakereba kare-wa gashi-suru-darô.

(*3*) His paper has a few misprints, but **otherwise** it is good.

Kare-no rombun wa ni-san-goshoku-ga aru-ga, *sore-igai-wa* môshi-bun-nai.

(*a.*) betsu-no [別の]; chigatta [違った].

otherworldly (*a.*) chô-sezoku-teki-na [超世俗的な]; raise-no [来世の].

otitis media (*path.*) chûji-en [中耳炎].

otter (*n.*) (*zool.*) kawauso[-no-ke-gawa] [カワウソ(の毛皮)].

ouch (*int.*) Aita! [あいた!]; Itai! [痛い!].

ought (*aux. v.*) 1)...(su-)beki-de-aru […(す)べきである]; ...ga-tôzen-da […が当然だ]. 2)...no-hazu-de-aru […のはずである].

(*1*) We **ought** to obey the social rule.

Ware-ware-wa shakai-kihan-ni shitagau-*beki-da*.

You **ought** not to say such a thing.

Kimi-wa sonna koto-o iu-*beki-de*-nai.

You **ought** to have consulted a doctor.

Kimi-wa isha-ni mite-morau-*beki-datta-noni*.

(*2*) He **ought** to have reached there by this time.

Kare-wa ima-goro soko-e tsuite-iru-*hazu-da*.

ounce (*n.*) onsu [オンス].

our (*pron.*) ware-ware-no [われわれの]; watashi-tachi-no [私たちの].

ours (*pron.*) ware-ware-no-mono [われわれのもの]; watashi-tachi-no-mono [私たちのもの].

ourselves (*pron.*) ware-ware-jishin(-o/-ni) [われわれ自身(を/に)].

out (*ad.*) 1)soto-ni [外に]; soto-e[-dete] [外へ(出て)]. 2)roken-shite [露見して]; saite [咲いて]. 3)owatte [終わって]; sukkari [すっかり]; hakkiri [はっきり]; oo-goe-de [大声で]; kiete [消えて]. 4)(*baseball*) auto-de [アウトで].

(*1*) He is **out**.　Kare-wa *soto-ni-dete*-iru.
　　　　　　　　　Kare-wa rusu-da.
　　The stars are **out**.　Hoshi ga *dete*-iru.

(*2*) The secret has got **out**.
　　　　Himitsu ga *mina-ni-shirete*-shimatta.
　　　　Himitsu ga bareta.
　　The cherryblossoms are **out**.　Sakura-no-hana ga *saita*.

(*3*) The copyright is **out**.　Hanken ga *kireta*.
　　He is tired **out**.　Kare-wa *sukkari* tsukarete-iru.
　　　　　　　　　　Kare-wa tsukare-kitte-iru.
　　Please speak **out**.　*Hakkiri* itte-kudasai.
　　He cried **out**.　Kare-wa *oo-goe-de* naki-sakenda.
　　The fire is **out**.　Hi ga *kiete*-iru.

out of ...kara
　(*a.*) 1)soto-no [外の]. 2)tooku-hanareta [遠く離れた]. 3)nami-hazureta [並はずれた].
　(*prep.*) 1)...kara-soto-e [...から外へ]; ...o-toori-nukete [...を通り抜けて]. 2)...no-soto-gawa-ni [...の外側に].
　(*n.*) (*colloq.*) 1)soto-gawa [外側]. 2)(*pl.*) shoku-o-ushinatta-hito [職を失った人]. 3)iiwake [言い訳]. 4)(*baseball*) auto [アウト].
　(*vt.*) ...o oi-dasu [...を追い出す].

out-and-out (*a.*) mattaku-no [全くの]; tettei-teki-na [徹底的な].

outbreak (*n.*) boppatsu [ぼっ発]; hassei [発生]; bakuhatsu [爆発].

outburst (*n.*) bakuhatsu [爆発]; funshutsu [噴出].

outcome (*n.*) kekka [結果].

outcry (*n.*) 1)sakebi[-goe] [叫び(声)]. 2)kôgi [抗議].

outdoor (*a.*) kogai-no [戸外の].

outdoors (*ad.*) kogai-e [戸外へ]; kogai-de [戸外で].

outer (*a.*) soto-no [外の]; gaibu-no [外部の]; gaimen-no [外面の].

outfit (*n.*) sôbi-isshiki [装備一式]; yôgu-isshiki [用具一式].

outgrow (*vt.*) ...yori ookiku-naru [...より大きくなる]; seichô-shite... ga naku-naru [成長して...がなくなる].

outing (*n.*) ensoku [遠足].

outlaw (*n.*) muhô-mono [無法者].

    (*vt.*) 1)...kara hô-no-hogo-o-ubau [⋯から法の保護を奪う]; ...o hi-gôhô-ka-suru [⋯を非合法化する]. 2)((*US*))...o jikô-ni-suru [⋯を時効にする].

outlet (*n.*) 1)deguchi [出口]. 2)hake-guchi [はけ口]. 3)(*com.*) hanro [販路]. 4)(*elect.*) konsento [コンセント]; sashi-komi-guchi [差し込み口].

outline (*n.*) 1)rinkaku [輪郭]. 2)aramashi [あらまし].
    (*vt.*) ...no rinkaku-o-kaku [⋯の輪郭を描く]; ...no gaiyô-o-noberu [⋯の概要を述べる].

outlook (*n.*) 1)nagame [眺め]; mi-harashi [見晴らし]; mi-tooshi [見通し]. 2)kenkai [見解].

outnumber (*vt.*) ...yori kazu-ga-ooi [⋯より数が多い].

out-of-date (*a.*) kyûshiki-na [旧式な]; jidai-okure-no [時代遅れの].

outpatient (*n.*) gairai-kanja [外来患者].

output (*n.*) 1)seisan-daka [生産高]. 2)(*elect.*) shutsuryoku [出力]. 3)(*computer*) autoputto [アウトプット].

outrage (*n.*) 1)rambô [乱暴]; fuhô-kôi [不法行為]. 2)gekido [激怒].
    (*vt.*) ...o fungai-saseru [⋯を憤慨させる]. 2)...ni bôryoku-o-furuu [⋯に暴力をふるう].

outright (*ad.*) 1)sukkari [すっかり]; mattaku [全く]. 2)sugu-ni [すぐに]. 3)kôzen-to [公然と].
    (*a.*) 1)tettei-teki-na [徹底的な]. 2)akarasama-na [あからさまな].

outset (*n.*) saisho [最初]; hajime [始め].

outside (*n.*) gaibu [外部]; soto-gawa [外側].
    (*a.*) gaibu-no [外部の]; soto-gawa-no [外側の].
    (*ad.*) soto-ni [外に]; soto-e [外へ]; soto-gawa-ni [外側に].
    (*prep.*) ...no-soto-ni[-e] [⋯の外に(へ)].

outsider (*n.*) bugai-sha [部外者]; autosaidâ [アウトサイダー].

outskirts (*n.*) kôgai [郊外].

outspoken (*a.*) enryo-no-nai [遠慮のない]; sotchoku-na [率直な].

outstanding (*a.*) 1)medatsu [目立つ]; kencho-na [顕著な]. 2)(*com.*) mi-harai-no [未払いの]. mi-kaiketsu-no [未解決の].

outward soto-e-mukau [外へ向かう].
    (*ad.*) 1)soto-e [外へ]. 2)soto-no-sekai-e [外の世界へ].

oval (*n. & a.*) tamago-gata(-no) [卵型(の)]; daen-kei(-no) [楕円形(の)].

oven (*n.*) tempi [天火]; ôbun [オーブン].

over (*perp.*) 1)...no-ue-ni [⋯の上に]. 2)...o-koete [⋯を越えて]. 3)...ijô-de [⋯以上で]. 4)...no-ichimen-ni [⋯の一面に]. 5)...ni-tsuite [⋯について]. 6)...(shi-)nagara [⋯(し)ながら].

(*1*) Spread the cloth **over** the table.

　　Têburu-*no-ue-ni* têburu-kake-o hiroge-nasai.

　　Large clouds float **over** our heads.

　　Watashi-tachi-*no-zujô-ni* ookina kumo ga ukande-iru.

(*2*) He jumped **over** the fence.　Kare-wa hei-o tobi-*koeta*.

(*3*) **Over** a thousand applicants were there.

　　Sen-nin-*ijô-no*-shigan-sha ga soko-ni ita.

(*4*) I saw black clouds all **over** the sky.

　　Watashi-wa sora-*ichimen-ni* kuro-kumo-o mita.

(*5*) He frets **over** trifles.　Kare-wa sasai-na-koto-*ni* ira-ira-suru.

(*6*) He talked **over** wine.

　　Kare-wa sake-o-nomi-*nagara* hanashi-o-shita.

　　(*ad.*) 1)mukô-ni [向こうに]; koete [越えて]. 2)sunde [済んで]; owatte [終わって]. 3)hikkuri-kaeshite [ひっくり返して]; taorete [倒れて]. 4)kuri-kaeshite [繰り返して]. 5)ichimen-ni [一面に]. 6)amari [あまり]. 7)zutto [ずっと].

(*1*) The school is **over** there.　Gakkô wa *mukô-ni* aru.

　　He went **over** to America.　Kare-wa Amerika-e *watatta*.

(*2*) School is **over**.　Jugyô ga *owatta*.

(*3*) Turn **over** the page.　Pêji-o *mekuri*-nasai.

(*4*) Read it several times **over**.

　　Nando-demo *kuri-kaeshite* yomi-nasai.

　　Think it **over**.　*Yoku* kangae-nasai.

(*5*) The river is frozen **over**.　Kawa wa *ichimen-ni* kootte-iru.

(*6*) He is not **over** polite.　Kare-wa *amari* teinei-ja-nai.

(*7*) Stay **over** till Sunday.　Nichiyô-made *zutto* i-nasai.

　over again mô-ichi-do; kuri-kaeshite

　over and over kuri-kaeshi-kuri-kaeshi

overcoat (*n.*) gaitô [外とう]; ôbâ [オーバー].

overcome (*vt. & vi.*) (...ni) uchi-katsu [⋯に)打ち勝つ].

overcrowd (*vt.*) ...o ire-sugiru [⋯を入れすぎる]; ...o konzatsu-saseru [⋯を混雑させる].

　　(*vi.*) hidoku-komu [ひどく混む]; konzatsu-suru [混雑する].

overdo (*vt.*) ...o do-o-koshite-suru [⋯を度を越してする].

overdue (*a.*) 1)kigen-ga-sugita [期限が過ぎた]; mi-harai-no [未払いの].

2)enchaku-shita [延着した].

overeat (*vt. & vi.*) (...o) tabe-sugiru [(…を)食べすぎる].

overflow (*vt. & vi.*) (...o) afureru [(…を)あふれる].
    (*n.*) 1)hanran [はん濫]. 2)kajô [過剰].

overhead (*ad. & a.*) zujô-ni(-no) [頭上に(の)].
    (*n.*) ((US)) ippan-sho-keihi [一般諸経費].

overhear (*vt.*) ...o futo-mimi-ni-suru […をふと耳にする].

overheat (*vt. & vi.*) ...o kanetsu-saseru (kanetsu-suru) […を過熱させる(過熱する)]; ...o ôbâhîto-saseru (ôbâhîto-suru) […をオーバーヒートさせる(オーバーヒートする)].
    (*n.*) kanetsu [過熱]; ôbâhîto [オーバーヒート].

overjoyed (*a.*) oo-yorokobi-no [大喜びの].

overland (*ad. & a.*) rikuro-o(-no) [陸路を(の)].

overlook (*vt.*) 1)...o mi-orosu […を見下ろす]. 2)...o oo-me-ni-miru […を大目に見る]. 3)...o mi-otosu […を見落とす]. 4)...o kantoku-suru […を監督する].
    (*1*) The tower **overlooks** the town.
        Tô wa machi-*o mi-oroshite-iru*.
    (*2*) She implored me to **overlook** her blunder.
        Kano-jo-wa jibun-no shissaku-*o oo-me-ni-mite*-kureru-yô-ni watashi-ni tanonda.
    (*3*) I **overlooked** a misspelled word.
        Watashi-wa tsuzuri-no-ayamatta go-*o* ichi-go *mi-otoshita*.
    (*4*) He **overlooks** their works.
        Kare-wa kare-ra-no shigoto-*o kantoku-suru*.

overnight (*ad.*) 1)hito-ban-jû [一晩中]. 2)mae-no-ban-ni [前の晩に]. 3)ichi-ya-no-uchi-ni [一夜のうちに].
    (*a.*) ippaku-no [一泊の]; yo-dooshi-no [夜通しの]; zen'ya-no [前夜の]; ichi-ya-no-uchi-no [一夜のうちの].

overrule (*vt.*) 1)...ni hantai-suru […に反対する]; ...o kutsugaesu […をくつがえす]. 2)...yori masaru […よりまさる].

overrun (*vt.*) 1)(be overrun) habikoru [はびこる]; muragaru [群がる]. 2)...o hashiri-sugiru […を走り過ぎる].

overseas (*a.*) kaigai-no [海外の]; kaigai-muke-no [海外向けの].
    (*ad.*) kaigai-e [海外へ].

oversleep (*vi.*) ne-sugosu [寝過ごす].

overtake (*vt.*) 1)...ni oi-tsuku […に追いつく]. 2)...o totsuzen-osou […を突然襲う].

(1) Poverty cannot **overtake** industry.

    Kasegi-*ni oi-tsuku* bimbô-nashi.

(2) We **were overtaken** by a storm.

    Ware-ware-wa *totsuzen* arashi-ni *osowareta*.

overthrow (*vt.*) 1)...o kutsugaesu [···をくつがえす]; ...o taosu [···を倒す]. 2)(*baseball*) ...o bôtô-suru [···を暴投する].

    (*n.*) 1)tempuku [転覆]. 2)bôtô [暴投].

overtime (*n.*) chôka-kimmu [超過勤務].

    (*a. & ad.*) jikan-gai-no(-ni) [時間外の(に)].

overture (*n.*) 1)(*pl.*) teian [提案]. 2)(*mus.*) jokyoku [序曲].

overturn (*vt. & vi.*) ...o hikkuri-kaesu (hikkuri-kaeru) [···をひっくりかえす(ひっくりかえる)].

overvalue (*vt.*) ...o kai-kaburu [···を買いかぶる].

overweight (*n.*) jûryô-chôka [重量超過]; futori-sugi [太りすぎ].

    (*a.*) jûryô-no-chôka-shita [重量の超過した].

    (*vt.*) 1)...ni tsumi-sugiru [···に積みすぎる]. 2)...o kyôchô-shi-sugiru [···を強調しすぎる].

overwhelming (*a.*) attô-teki-na [圧倒的な].

overwork (*vt. & vi.*) ...o hatarakase-sugiru (hataraki-sugiru) [···を働かせすぎる(働きすぎる)].

    (*n.*) karô [過労].

owe (*vt.*) 1)...ni kari-ga-aru [···に借りがある]; ...ni shakkin-ga-aru [···に借金がある]. 2)...ni otte-iru [···に負っている]; ...ni ongi-ga-aru [···に恩義がある].

(1) Pay what you **owe**. *Karite-iru*-kane-o harai-nasai.

(2) I **owe** my success to my mother.

    Watashi-no seikô wa haha-ni *otte-iru*.

    Watashi-no seikô wa haha-no-*okage-de-aru*.

    (*vi.*) kari-ga-aru [借りがある].

owing (*a.*) kari-to-natte-iru [借りとなっている].

    The **owing** money is too much for me.

    Sono *kari-to-natte-iru* kingaku[Sono *shakkin-no* gaku] wa watashi-niwa ooki-sugiru.

  owing to ...ni-yoru; ...no-tame-ni

    It was put off **owing to** the rain.

    Sore-wa uten-no-tame-ni enki-sareta.

owl (*n.*) fukurô [フクロウ].

own (*a.*) 1)[jibun-]jishin-no [(自分)自身の]. 2)dokutoku-no [独特の].

(1) This is my **own** house. Kore-wa watashi-*jishin-no* ie da.
(2) He has a pitching motion of his **own**.
　　　Kare-wa *dokutoku-no* tôkyû-môshon-o suru.
　on one's own (*colloq.*) dokuryoku-de; hitori-de
　　　(*vt.*) 1)...o shoyû-suru [...を所有する]. 2)...o mitomeru [...を認める].
　　　(*vi.*) mitomeru [認める].
owner (*n.*) mochi-nushi [持ち主]; shoyû-sha [所有者].
ox (*n.*) o-ushi [雄牛].
oxygen (*n.*) (*chem.*) sanso [酸素].
oyster (*n.*) (*shellfish*) kaki [カキ].

P

pa (*n.*) (*colloq.*) tô-chan [とうちゃん].
pace (*n.*) 1)ippo [一歩]. 2)hochô [歩調].
　(1) He advanced fifty **paces**. Kare-wa go-jup*po* susunda.
　(2) He walked at a slow **pace**.
　　　Kare-wa yukkuri-shita-*hochô*-de aruita.
　keep pace with ...ni okure-nai-yô-ni-tsuite-iku; ...to onaji-hayasa-de-iku
　　　(*vt.*) 1)...o yukkuri-aruku [...をゆっくり歩く]. 2)...o hosoku-suru [...を歩測する].
　(2) I **paced** the ground. Boku-wa sono gurando-*o hosoku-shita*.

    (*vi.*) yukkuri-to-aruku [ゆっくりと歩く].

    He **paced** back and forth on the deck.

        Kare-wa kampan-o ittari-kitari *yukkuri-aruita*.

pacific (*a.*) heion-na [平穏な].

Pacific Ocean, the   Taihei-yô [太平洋].

pack (*n.*) 1)tsutsumi [包み]; nimotsu [荷物]. 2)(ryôken no)ichi-gun [(猟犬の)一群]; (akunin no)ichimi [(悪人の)一味]. 3)torampu-no-hito-kumi [トランプの一組]; tabako-no-hito-hako [タバコの一箱].

    (*1*) The peddler carried a heavy **pack** on his back.

        Gyôshô-nin wa omoi *nimotsu*-o se-otte-ita.

    (*2*) a **pack** of greyhounds   *ichi-gun*-no ryôken

        a **pack** of thieves   tôzoku-*ichimi*

    (*3*) a **pack** of cards   *hito-kumi*-no torampu

        a **pack** of cigarettes   tabako *hito-hako*

    (*vt.*) 1)...o ni-zukuri-suru [...を荷造りする]; ...o tsutsumu [...を包む]. 2)...o ippai-ni-tsumeru [...をいっぱいに詰める].

    (*1*) He is busy **packing**.   Kare-wa *ni-zukuri*-ni-isogashii.

    (*2*) The main streets **are packed** with cars.

        Omo-na dôro wa kuruma-de-*ippai-da*.

    (*vi.*) 1)ni-zukuri-suru [荷造りする]. 2)muragaru [群がる]. 3) katamaru [固まる].

package (*n.*) tsutsumi [包み]; ko-zutsumi [小包].

    (*vt.*) ...o ni-zukuri-suru [...を荷造りする]; ((*US*)) ...o hito-matome-ni-suru [...を一まとめにする].

packet (*n.*) tsutsumi [包み]; ko-nimotsu [小荷物].

packing (*n.*) hôsô [包装]; ni-zukuri [荷造り]; pakkingu [パッキング].

pad (*n.*) 1)tsume-mono [詰め物]. 2)(inu ya neko nado no) ashi-ura-no-fukurami [(犬やネコなどの)足裏のふくらみ]. 3)(binsen nado no) hito-tsuzuri [(便せんなどの)一つづり].

    (*vt.*) 1)...ni tsume-mono-o-suru [...に詰め物をする]; ...ni ate-mono-o-suru [...に当て物をする]. 2)...o hiki-nobasu [...を引き延ばす].

paddle (*n.*) padoru [パドル].

    (*vt.*) 1)...o padoru-de-kogu [...をパドルでこぐ]. 2)(*US colloq.*) ...o(hira-te-de-)tataku [...を(平手で)たたく].

paddock (*n.*) 1)shô-hôboku-chi [小放牧地]. 2)(*horse racing*) padokku [パドック].

pagan (*n.*) ikyô-to [異教徒].

    (*a.*) 1)ikyô-to-no [異教徒の]. 2)fu-shinjin-no [不信心の].

page (*n.*) pêji [ページ].

    (*vt.*) …ni pêji-o-tsukeru […にページをつける].

page (*n.*) bôi [ボーイ].

    (*vt.*) …o yobi-dasu […を呼び出す].

pageant (*n.*) yagai-geki [野外劇]; pêjento [ページェント]; gyôretsu [行列]; dashi [だし].

pail (*n.*) te-oke [手おけ].

pain (*n.*) 1)itami [痛み]; kutsû [苦痛]; shintsû [心痛]. 2)(*pl.*) kurô [苦労]; hone-ori [骨折り].

    (*1*) I have a **pain** in the back.　Watashi-wa senaka-ga-*itai*.

    (*2*) I was at great **pains** to explain the passage.

        Watashi-wa sono issetsu-o setsumei-suru-no-ni taihen *kurô*-shita.

   spare no pains rô-o-oshima-nai

    (*vt.*) …ni kutsû-o-ataeru […に苦痛を与える].

    (*vi.*) itamu [痛む].

painful (*a.*) itai [痛い]; kurushii [苦しい]; hone-no-oreru [骨の折れる].

paint (*n.*) enogu [絵の具]; penki [ペンキ].

    (*vt.*) 1)…o egaku […を描く]; …ni saishiki-suru […に彩色する]. 2)…ni penki-o-nuru […にペンキを塗る].

    (*vi.*) 1)e-o-kaku [絵をかく]. 2)keshô-suru [化粧する].

painter (*n.*) gaka [画家]; penkiya [ペンキ屋].

painting (*n.*) e [絵]; e-o-kaku-koto [絵を描くこと]; penki-tosô [ペンキ塗装].

pair (*n.*) ittsui [一対]; issoku [一足]; hito-kumi [一組]; itchô [一丁]; hito-kumi-no-dan-jo [一組の男女].

    a **pair** of shoes　*issoku*-no kutsu

    a **pair** of scissors　hasami-*itchô*

    a **pair** of dancers　*hito-kumi*-no dansâ

    work in **pairs**　*futari-hito-kumi*-ni-natte hataraku

    (*vt.* & *vi.*) …o futari[futatsu]-zutsu-kumi-ni-suru (futari [futatsu]-zutsu-kumi-ni-naru) […を二人[二つ]ずつ組にする(二人[二つ]ずつ組になる)].

pajamas, pyjamas (*n.*) pajama [パジャマ].

Pakistan (*n.*) Pakisutan [パキスタン].

Pakistani (*n.*) Pakisutan-jin [パキスタン人].

    (*a.*) Pakisutan-jin-no [パキスタン人の].

pal (*n.*) nakama [仲間]; aibô [相棒].
    (*vi.*) shitashiku-tsuki-au [親しく付き合う]; naka-yoshi-ni-naru
[仲良しになる].

palace (*n.*) kyûden [宮殿]; dai-teitaku [大邸宅].

palatable (*a.*) aji-no-yoi [味のよい]; kuchi-ni-au [口に合う].

palate (*n.*) 1)(*anat.*) kôgai [口蓋]. 2)mikaku [味覚].

pale (*a.*) 1)aozameta [青ざめた]. 2)(iro ga) usui [(色が)薄い]. 3)
(hikari ga) kasuka-na [(光が)かすかな].
    (*vi.*) aozameru [青ざめる]; usuku-naru [薄くなる].

palm (*n.*) te-no-hira [手の平].
    (*vt.*) ...o te-no-hira-ni-kakusu [...を手の平に隠す].

palm (*n.*) (*bot.*) shuro [シュロ]; yashi [ヤシ].

pamphlet (*n.*) panfuretto [パンフレット]; shô-sasshi [小冊子].

pan (*n.*) hira-nabe [平なべ]; pan [パン].
    (*vt.*) 1)...o hira-nabe-de-chôri-suru [...を平なべで調理する]. 2)...o
nabe-de-sembetsu-suru [...をなべで選別する]. 3)(*colloq.*) ...o
kokuhyô-suru [...を酷評する].

Panama (*n.*) Panama [パナマ]; Panama-shi [パナマ市].

panchromatic (*a.*) (*photo.*) pankuro-no [パンクロの]; zen-seishoku-
no [全整色の].

pancreas (*n.*) (*anat.*) suizô [すい臓].

pane (*n.*) (ichi-mai no) mado-garasu [(一枚の)窓ガラス].

panel (*n.*) 1)kagami-ita [鏡板]. 2)tôron-sha-dan [討論者団]; iin-dan
[委員団].
    (*vt.*) 1)...ni kagami-ita-o-haru [...に鏡板を張る]. 2)...o sentei-
suru [...を選定する].

panel discussion kôkai-tôron-kai [公開討論会]; paneru-disukasshon
[パネルディスカッション].

panic (*n.*) kyôkô [恐慌]; rôbai [ろうばい]; panikku [パニック].
    (*vt.*) ...o urotaesaseru [...をうろたえさせる].

panorama (*n.*) panorama [パノラマ]; zenkei [全景].

panoramic (*a.*) panorama-shiki-no [パノラマ式の]; gaikan-teki-na
[概観的な].

pansy (*n.*) (*bot.*) sanshiki-sumire [サンシキスミレ]; panjî [パンジー].

pant (*vi.*) 1)aegu [あえぐ]; iki-gire-suru [息切れする]. 2)[be -ing]
netsubô-suru [熱望する].
    (*vt.*) ...o aegi-nagara-iu [...をあえぎながら言う].
    (*n.*) aegi [あえぎ]; iki-gire [息切れ].

pantaloon (*n.*) (*pl.*) pantaron [パンタロン].

panther (*n.*) (*zool.*) hyô [ヒョウ].

pantograph (*n.*) 1)shukuzu-ki [縮図器]. 2)(densha no) pantagurafu [(電車の)パンタグラフ].

pantomime (*n.*) mugon-geki [無言劇]; pantomaimu [パントマイム].

pantry (*n.*) shokuryô-hin-shitsu [食料品室]; shokki-shitsu [食器室].

pants (*n.*) ((*Eng.*)) pantsu [パンツ]; ((*US*)) zubon [ズボン].

papa (*n.*) o-tôsan [おとうさん].

paper (*n.*) 1)kami [紙]. 2)shimbun [新聞]. 3)rombun [論文]. 4) (shiken no) tôan [(試験の)答案]. 5)(*pl.*) shorui [書類].
    (*a.*) 1)kami-no [紙の]. 2)meimoku-jô-no [名目上の]. 3)insatsu-sareta [印刷された].
    (*vt.*) 1)...o kami-de-tsutsumu [...を紙で包む]; ...ni kabe-gami-o-haru [...に壁紙を張る]. 2)...ni kami-o-kyôkyû-suru [...に紙を供給する].
    (*vi.*) kabe-gami-o-haru [壁紙を張る].

paperback (*n. & a.*) kami-byôshi-bon(-no) [紙表紙本(の)]; pêpâbakku (-no) [ペーパーバック(の)].

parable (*n.*) tatoe-banashi [たとえ話]; gûwa [ぐう話].

parade (*n.*) 1)gyôretsu [行列]; parêdo [パレード]. 2)(*mil.*) eppei [閲兵].
    (*vt.*) 1)...o neri-aruku [...をねり歩く]. 2)...o mise-birakasu [...を見せびらかす].
    (*vi.*) 1)kôshin-suru [行進する]; parêdo-suru [パレードする]. 2) (*mil.*) eppei-no-tame-ni-seiretsu-suru [閲兵のために整列する].

paradise (*n.*) rakuen [楽園]; paradaisu [パラダイス].

paradox (*n.*) 1)gyakusetsu [逆説]; paradokkusu [パラドックス]. 2) mujun-shita-kotoba [矛盾したことば].

paragraph (*n.*) 1)(bunshô no) danraku [(文章の)段落]; paragurafu [パラグラフ]. 2)(shimbun no) shô-kiji [(新聞の)小記事]; tampyô [短評].
    (*vt.*) ...o danraku-ni-wakeru [...を段落に分ける]; ...ni-tsuite tampen-kiji-o-kaku [...について短篇記事を書く].

parallel (*a.*) 1)heikô-no [平行の]. 2)dôyô-na [同様な].
    (*n.*) 1)heikô-sen [平行線]. 2)ruiji [類似]; hitteki-suru-mono [匹敵するもの].
    (*vt.*) 1)...to heikô-suru [...と平行する]. 2)...ni nite-iru [...に似ている]. 3)...o hikaku-suru [...を比較する].

(*ad.*) heikô-shite [平行して]; dô-hôkô-e [同方向へ].

parallel bars (*sports*) heikô-bô [平行棒].

parallelogram (*n.*) heikô-shihen-kei [平行四辺形].

paralysis (*n.*) (*med.*) mahi [麻ひ]; chûbu [中風].

paralyze, -lyse (*vt.*) ...o mahi-saseru [...を麻ひさせる].

paramount (*a.*) saikô-no [最高の]; mottomo-sugureta [最も優れた].

parapet (*n.*) 1)rankan [欄干]; tesuri [手すり]. 2)(shiro no) kyôheki [(城の)胸壁].

paraphrase (*n.*) iyaku [意訳]; ii-kae [言い換え]; parafurêzu [パラフレーズ].

(*vt. & vi.*) (...o) iyaku-suru [...を意訳する]; (...o) ii-kaeru [...を言い換える]; (...o) parafurêzu-suru [...をパラフレーズする].

parasite (*n.*) (*biol.*) kisei-dôbutsu [寄生動物]; kisei-shokubutsu [寄生植物]; kisei-chû [寄生虫].

parasol (*n.*) parasoru [パラソル]; hi-gasa [日傘].

parcel (*n.*) 1)tsutsumi [包み]; ko-zutsumi [小包]. 2)((US))(tochi no) ichi-kukaku [(土地の)一区画].

  by parcel post   ko-zutsumi-yûbin-de

(*vt.*) 1)...o bumpai-suru [...を分配する]. 2)...o tsutsumi-ni-suru [...を包みにする].

parch (*vt.*) 1)...o hi-agaraseru [...を干上がらせる]. 2)...o iru [...をいる].

pardon (*n.*) yurushi [許し].

  I beg your **pardon**.   1)*Gomen*-kudasai. 2)Mô-ichi-do itte-kudasai.

(*vt.*) ...o yurusu [...を許す].

  Pardon me for being too late.

    Osoku-narimashite *o-yurushi-kudasai*[sumi-masen].

pare (*vt.*) 1)(kudamono)-no kawa-o-muku [(くだもの)の皮をむく]. 2)...o kiru [...を切る]. 3)...o sakugen-suru [...を削減する]; ...o kiri-tsumeru [...を切り詰める].

parent (*n.*) oya [親].

parenthesis (*n.*) 1)(*gram.*) sônyû-go-ku [挿入語句]. 2)(*pl.*) maru-kakko [丸かっこ].

parish (*n.*) kyôku [教区].

park (*n.*) 1)kôen [公園]. 2)chûsha-jô [駐車場].

(*vt.*) 1)...o chûsha-saseru [...を駐車させる]. 2)(*colloq.*) (mono)

　o(...ni) oku [(物)を…に置く].
　　(*vi.*) chûsha-suru [駐車する].
parking (*n.*) chûsha[-basho] [駐車(場所)].
　No parking (**here**). Chûsha-kinshi.
parking lot ((*US*)) chûsha-jô [駐車場].
parliament (*n.*) gikai [議会].
parlor, -lour (*n.*) 1)ima [居間]; ôsetsu-ma [応接間]. 2)(hoteru no)
　kyûkei-shitsu [(ホテルの)休憩室]. 3)((*US*)) eigyô-sho [営業所].
parrot (*n.*) ômu [オウム].
part (*n.*) 1)bubun [部分]; ...no-ichibu […の一部]; hen [編]. 2)
　yakume [役目]; hombun [本分]. 3)gawa [側]; hô [方]. 4)(*pl.*)
　chihô [地方]; ...atari […あたり]. 5)(*pl.*) bubun-hin [部分品].
　(*1*) small **part** shô-*bubun*
　　　　part II dai-ni-*hen*
　(*2*) Each has his **part**. Mei-mei-ga *yakume*-o motte-iru.
　　　　I must do my **part**.
　　　　　Watashi-wa *hombun*-o tsukusa-neba-naranai.
　(*3*) There is no fault on my **part**.
　　　　　Watashi-no-*hô*-ni ochido wa nai.
　(*4*) I have never been in these **parts**.
　　　　　Watashi-wa kono-*hen*-ni kita-koto-wa-ichi-do-mo-nai.
　(*5*) auto **parts** jidôsha-*buhin*
　for my part watashi[-to-shite]-wa
　for the most part taitei
　in part ikubun
　take part in ...ni sanka-suru
　take the part of ...ni mikata-suru
　　(*vi.*) 1)wakareru [分かれる]. 2)wakareru [別れる].
　(*1*) The road **parts** there. Michi wa soko-de *wakareru*.
　(*2*) I **parted** from him at the crossing.
　　　　　Watashi-wa kôsa-ten-de kare-to *wakareta*.
　　(*vt.*) 1)...o wakeru […を分ける]. 2)...o hiki-hanasu […を引き離
　す].
partake (*vi.*) 1)tomo-ni-suru [ともにする]. 2)issho-ni-taberu [一緒に
　食べる]; sanka-suru [参加する]; kuwawaru [加わる].
　partake of ...o tomo-ni-taberu; ikubun...no seishitsu-ga-aru
partial (*a.*) 1)ichi-bubun-no [一部分の]. 2)fu-kôhei-na [不公平な].
partially (*ad.*) bubun-teki-ni [部分的に]; fu-kôhei-ni [不公平に].

participate (*vi.*) 1)sanka-suru [参加する]; tomo-ni-suru [ともにする]. 2)...no-kimi-ga-aru […の気味がある].

particle (*n.*) 1)bi-ryûshi [微粒子]; biryô [微量]. 2)(*gram.*) fu-henka-shi [不変化詞].

particular (*a.*) 1)tokutei-no [特定の]; kakubetsu-no [格別の]. 2) kuwashii [詳しい]. 3)konomi-ga-urusai [好みがうるさい].

  (*1*) I have no **particular** reason to do so.

      Watashi-wa sô-suru-*tokubetsu-na*-riyû-ga aru-wake-dewa-nai.

  (*2*) He gave a **particular** account of his trip.

      Kare-wa *kuwashii* ryokô-dan-o shita.

  (*3*) I am not **particular** about food.

      Watashi-wa tabe-mono-wa-*yakamashiku*-iwa-nai.

    (*n.*) 1)jikô [事項]. 2)(*pl.*) shôsai [詳細].

  in particular toku-ni

particularly (*ad.*) toku-ni [特に]; kuwashiku [詳しく].

parting (*n. & a.*) wakare(-no) [別れ(の)]; bunkatsu(-no) [分割(の)].

partition (*n.*) shikiri [仕切り]; bunkatsu [分割].

    (*vt.*) ...o shikiru […を仕切る]; ...o bunkatsu-suru […を分割する].

partly (*ad.*) bubun-teki-ni [部分的に]; ikubun [いくぶん].

partner (*n.*) 1)kyôdô-shusshi-sha [共同出資者]. 2)nakama [仲間]. 3) (dansu no) pâtonâ [(ダンスの)パートナー].

    (*vt.*) ...to teikei-suru […と提携する].

    (*vi.*) kumu [組む].

partnership (*n.*) 1)kyôdô [協同]. 2)kumiai [組合]; shôkai [商会].

  in partnership with ...to-kyôdô-shite

part-time (*a. & ad.*) pâtotaimu-no(-de) [パートタイムの(で)]; hi-jôkin-no(-de) [非常勤の(で)]; teiji-sei-no(-de) [定時制の(で)].

party (*n.*) 1)ich-dan [一団]; ikkô [一行]. 2)tôha [党派]; seitô [政党]. 3)kai [会]; pâtî [パーティー]. 4)tôji-sha [当事者]; aite[-kata] [相手(方)].

    (*vi.*) pâtî-ni-deru [パーティーに出る].

    (*vt.*) ...o pâtî-de-motenasu […をパーティーでもてなす].

pass (*vi.*) 1)tooru [通る]; toori-sugiru [通り過ぎる]. 2)(toki ga) tatsu [(時が)たつ]. 3)gôkaku-suru [合格する]. 4)tsûka-suru [通過する]. 5)tsûyô-suru [通用する].

  (*1*) They **passed** through the woods.

Kare-ra-wa mori-o *toori*-nuketa.

(2) Ten years **passed**. Jû-nen *tatta*.

(3) He **passed** with much effort. Kare-wa yatto *gôkaku-shita*.

(4) The bill **passed**. Gian wa *tsûka-shita*.

(5) coin that **passes** in Japan Nihon-de *tsûyô-suru*-kôka

   (vt.) 1)...o tooru [⋯を通る]; ...o oi-kosu [⋯を追い越す]. 2)...o [te-]watasu [⋯を(手)渡す]. 3)...ni gôkaku-suru [⋯に合格する]. 4)...o tsûka-suru [⋯を通過する]. 5)(toki)-o sugosu [(時)を過ごす].

pass away shinu

pass for ...to-shite tooru

   (n.) 1)tôge [峠]. 2)muryô-jôsha-ken [無料乗車券]; muryô-nyûjô-ken [無料入場券]; tsûkô-shô [通行証]. 3)gôkaku [合格]. 4)(sports) pasu [パス].

passably (ad.) kanari [かなり].

passage (n.) 1)tsûkô [通行]. 2)(gian no) tsûka [(議案の)通過]. 3) kôkai [航海]; ryokô [旅行]. 4)tsûro [通路]; ((Eng.)) rôka [廊下]. 5)(bunshô no) issetsu [(文章の)一節].

passenger (n.) jôkyaku [乗客]; ryokaku [旅客]; senkyaku [船客].

passer-by (n.) tsûkô-nin [通行人].

passing (a.) 1)toori-gakari-no [通りがかりの]. 2)ichiji-no [一時の]. 3)gôkaku-no [合格の].

   (1) He was saved by a **passing** steamer.

     Kare-wa *toori-gakari-no*-fune-ni kyûjo-sareta.

   (2) This is nothing but a **passing** event.

     Kore-wa *ichiji-no* deki-goto-ni suginai.

   (3) I got a **passing** mark in the examination.

     Watashi-wa shiken-ni *gôkaku*-ten-o totta.

passion (n.) 1)netsujô [熱情]. 2)gekido [激怒].

fly(get) into a passion katto-natte-okoru

passionate (a.) 1)netsuretsu-na [熱烈な]. 2)okorippoi [怒りっぽい].

passionately (ad.) netsuretsu-ni [熱烈に]; katto-natte [かっとなって].

passive (a.) 1)judô-teki-na [受動的な]. 2)mu-teikô-no [無抵抗の]. 3) (gram.) uke-mi-no [受身の].

passport (n.) 1)ryoken [旅券]. 2)shudan [手段].

past (a.) 1)kako-no [過去の]. 2)saikin-no [最近の].

for some time past kore-made-shibaraku-no-aida

   (n.) (the –) kako [過去].

   (prep.) ...o-sugite [⋯を過ぎて]; ...o-koete [⋯を越えて].

It is five **past** four. Yo-ji go-fun *sugi*-desu.

  (*ad.*) toori-koshite [通り越して].

paste (*n.*) 1)nori [のり]. 2)(ryôri yô no) pêsuto [(料理用の)ペースト].
3)neri-mono [練り物].

  (*vt.*) ...o nori-de-tsukeru [⋯をのりでつける]; ...o nori-de-haru
[⋯をのりではる].

pasteboard (*n.*) bôru-gami [ボール紙]; atsugami [厚紙].

pastime (*n.*) 1)ki-barashi [気晴らし]. 2)goraku [娯楽].

pasture (*n.*) bokujô [牧場]; bokusô-chi [牧草地].

  (*vt.*) ...o hôboku-suru [⋯を放牧する].

  (*vi.*) bokusô-o-kuu [牧草を食う].

pat (*vt.*) ...o karuku-tataku [⋯を軽くたたく]; ...o naderu [⋯をなでる].

  (*n.*) karuku-tataku-koto [軽くたたくこと]; naderu-koto [なでるこ
と].

patch (*n.*) 1)(irui nado no) tsugi [(衣類などの)継ぎ]. 2)hanten [はん
点]. 3)shô-jimen [小地面]. 4)(*computer*) patchi [パッチ].

  (*vt.*) ...ni tsugi-o-ateru [⋯に継ぎを当てる]; ...o tsugi-awaseru
[⋯を継ぎ合わせる].

patchwork (*n.*) tsugi-hagi-zaiku [継ぎはぎ細工]; patchiwâku [パッチ
ワーク].

patent (*n. & a.*) tokkyo(-no) [特許(の)].

  (*vt.*) ...no tokkyo[-ken]-o-toru [⋯の特許(権)をとる].

patent right tokkyo-ken [特許権].

path (*n.*) 1)ko-michi [小道]; hodô [歩道]. 2)shinro [進路].

pathetic (*a.*) 1)kanshô-teki-na [感傷的な]; aware-na [哀れな]. 2)
(*colloq.*) toru-ni-tari-nai [取るに足りない].

pathos (*n.*) hiai [悲哀]; pêsosu [ペーソス].

pathway (*n.*) ko-michi [小道]; hodô [歩道].

patience (*n.*) nintai [忍耐]; shimbô [しんぼう].

 have no patience with ...niwa gaman-deki-nai

patient (*a.*) shimbô-zuyoi [しんぼう強い].

  (*n.*) kanja [患者]; byônin [病人].

patiently (*ad.*) shimbô-zuyoku [しんぼう強く].

patriot (*n.*) aikoku-sha [愛国者].

patriotic (*a.*) aikoku-teki-na [愛国的な]; aikoku-shin-no-tsuyoi [愛国
心の強い].

patriotism (*n.*) aikoku-shin [愛国心].

patrol (*n.*) 1)junkai [巡回]; patorôru [パトロール]. 2)teisatsu-tai

［偵察隊］; junshi-sen ［巡視船］.

on patrol junkai-chû; patorôru-chû

　　(*vt. & vi.*) (…o) junkai-suru ［(…を)巡回する］; (…o) patorôru-suru ［(…を)パトロールする］.

patron (*n.*) 1)hogo-sha ［保護者］; kôen-sha ［後援者］; patoron ［パトロン］. 2)hiiki-kyaku ［ひいき客］.

patronage (*n.*) 1)hogo ［保護］; kôen ［後援］; hiiki ［ひいき］. 2)ibatta-taido ［いばった態度］.

under the patronage of …no-kôen-no-moto-ni

patter (*n.*) pera-pera ［ぺらぺら］; para-para ［ぱらぱら］; pata-pata ［ぱたぱた］.

　　(*vi.*) 1)pera-pera-shaberu ［ぺらぺらしゃべる］. 2)para-para-to-oto-ga-suru ［ぱらぱらと音がする］.

　　(2) The rain **pattered** on the window.

　　　　Ame ga mado-ni-atatte *para-para-to-oto-o-tatete-ita.*

pattern (*n.*) 1)mohan ［模範］. 2)kata ［型］. 3)gara ［柄］. 4)mihon ［見本］.

　　(*vt.*) 1)…o…no kata-ni-naratte［…o tehon-ni-shite］-tsukuru ［-okonau］［…を…の型にならって［…を手本にして］作る［行なう］］. 2)…ni moyô-o-tsukeru ［…に模様をつける］.

　　(*vi.*) moyô-o-egaku ［模様を描く］; …no tehon-to-suru ［…の手本とする］.

pause (*n.*) 1)kyûshi ［休止］; togire ［途切れ］. 2)chûcho ［ちゅうちょ］. 3)ku-giri ［句切り］.

make a pause kyûshi-suru; iki-o-tsugu

　　(*vi.*) 1)kyûshi-suru ［休止する］. 2)tamerau ［ためらう］.

pave (*vt.*) …o hosô-suru ［…を舗装する］.

pavement (*n.*) 1)hosô-dôro ［舗装道路］. 2)hodô ［歩道］.

pavilion (*n.*) 1)oo-gata-no-tento ［大型のテント］. 2)tenji-kan ［展示館］; pabirion ［パビリオン］.

paw (*n.*) (inu ya neko nado no)ashi ［(犬やネコなどの)足］.

　　(*vt. & vi.*) 1)(…o) mae-ashi-de-kaku ［(…を)前足でかく］. 2)(…o) te-araku-atsukau ［(…を)手荒く扱う］.

pawn (*vt.*) …o shichi-ni-ireru ［…を質に入れる］.

　　(*n.*) shichi[-ire] ［質(入れ)］.

pawnbroker (*n.*) shichiya ［質屋］.

pay (*vt.*) 1)…o shiharau ［…を支払う］. 2)(chûi)-o harau ［(注意)を払う］. 3)(hômon)-o suru ［(訪問)をする］.

(*vi.*) 1)daikin-o-harau [代金を払う]. 2)hiki-au [引き合う]. 3) tsugunau [償う].

(*1*) I must **pay** for this book.

    Watashi-wa kono-hon-no-*daikin-o-harawa*-neba-naranai.

(*2*) This business **pays**. Kono shôbai wa *hiki-au*.

(*3*) He **paid** dearly for his mistake.

    Kare-wa jibun-no-ayamari〔-no-tame〕-ni takai-*daishô-o-haratta*.

    (*n.*) shiharai [支払い]; kyûryô [給料]; chingin [賃金].

payment (*n.*) shiharai [支払い]; harai-komi [払い込み].

payoff (*n.*) shiharai[-bi] [支払(日)].

pea (*n.*) (*bot.*) endô [エンドウ].

peace (*n.*) 1)heiwa [平和]. 2)anshin [安心]; heisei [平静]. 3) chimmoku [沈黙]. 4)chian [治安].

(*1*) We have hoped for world **peace**.

    Ware-ware-wa sekai-*heiwa*-o nozonde-kita.

(*2*) May he rest in **peace**! Kare-no-rei-yo *yasu*-kare!

(*3*) Hold your **peace**! *Chimmoku*-o tamote!

    Damatte-ore!

(*4*) The policemen keep the **peace**. Keikan wa *chian*-o iji-suru.

peaceable (*a.*) heiwa-o-konomu [平和を好む]; otonashii [おとなしい].

peaceful (*a.*) heiwa-na [平和な]; odayaka-na [穏やかな].

peach (*n.*) momo [桃]; momo-no-ki [桃の木].

peacock (*n.*) (*birds*) osu-no-kujaku [雄のクジャク].

peahen (*n.*) (*birds*) mesu-no-kujaku [雌のクジャク].

peak (*n.*) mine [峰]; sentan [先端]; chôten [頂点].

    (*vt.*) ...o saikô-ni-suru […を最高にする].

    (*vi.*) togaru [とがる]; chôten-ni-tassuru [頂点に達する].

peal (*n.*) (taihô ya kaminari no) todoroki [(大砲やかみなりの)とどろき]; (kane no)hibiki [(鐘の)響き].

    (*vt. & vi.*) ...o todorokaseru (todoroku) […をとどろかせる(とどろく)]; ...o nari-hibikaseru(nari-hibiku) […を鳴り響かせる(鳴り響く)].

peanut (*n.*) nankin-mame [ナンキンマメ]; rakkasei [落花生]; pî-nattsu [ピーナッツ].

pear (*n.*) (*bot.*) seiyô-nashi [セイヨウナシ]; seiyô-nashi-no-ki [セイヨウナシの木].

pearl (*n.*) 1)shinju [真珠]. 2)kichô-na-mono[-hito] [貴重なもの[人]].

    (*a.*) shinju-o-chiribameta [真珠をちりばめた]; shinju-no [真珠の].

    (*vt.*) ...o shinju-de-kazaru […を真珠で飾る].

    (*vi.*) shinju-de-kazaru [真珠で飾る]; shinju-o-toru [真珠を採る].

peasant (*n.*) nômin [農民].

pebble (*n.*) ko-ishi [小石].

peck (*vt. & vi.*) 1)(kuchibashi de)(...o) tsutsuku [(くちばしで)(…を)つつく]. 2)(...o) hon-no-chotto-taberu [(…を)ほんのちょっと食べる]; (...o) iya-iya-taberu [(…を)いやいや食べる].

peculiar (*a.*) 1)dokutoku-no [独特の]; tokuyû-no [特有の]. 2)myô-na [妙な]; hen-na [変な].

    (*1*) This expression is **peculiar** to Japanese.

        Kono hyôgen wa Nihon-go-*tokuyû-no*-mono-da.

    (*2*) He has his own **peculiar** ways.

        Kare niwa *hen-na* kuse-ga aru.

peculiarity (*n.*) 1)tokushoku [特色]. 2)kuse [癖]; kawatta-ten [変わった点].

peculiarly (*ad.*) toku-ni [特に]; kimyô-ni [奇妙に].

pedal (*n.*) pedaru [ペダル].

    (*vt.*) ...no pedaru-o-fumu […のペダルを踏む].

pedantic (*a.*) gakusha-buru [学者ぶる]; pedantikku-na [ペダンティックな].

peddler (*n.*) 1)gyôshô-nin [行商人]. 2)mayaku-no-bainin [麻薬の売人].

pedestal (*n.*) dai [台]; kiso [基礎].

pedestrian (*a.*) 1)hokô-no [歩行の]. 2)sambun-chô-no [散文調の]; heibon-na [平凡な].

        (*n.*) hokô-sha [歩行者].

peel (*vt.*) ...no kawa-o-muku […の皮をむく].

    (*n.*) kawa [皮].

peep (*vi.*) 1)nozoki-mi-suru [のぞき見する]. 2)dan-dan-arawareru [だんだん現れる].

    (*1*) The girl **peeped** into the room.

        Sono shôjo wa heya-no-naka-o *nozoita*.

    (*2*) The moon began to **peep** out. Tsuki ga *mie*-dashita.

    (*n.*) 1)nozoki-mi [のぞき見]. 2)de-hajime [出始め].

    (*1*) I got a **peep** at her room.

        Watashi-wa kano-jo-no-heya-o *nozoki-mi*ta.

    (*2*) Leave here before the **peep** of dawn.

        Yo-ake-mae-ni koko-o tate.

peep (*vi. & n.*) pî-pî-naku(-koe) [ぴーぴー鳴く(声)].

peer (*vi.*) 1)jitto-miru [じっと見る]. 2)shidai-ni-arawareru [次第に現れる].

  (*1*) He **peered** into my face.

    Kare-wa watashi-no kao-o *jitto-mita*.

  (*2*) The moon **peered** through the clouds.

    Tsuki ga kumo-no-ushiro-kara *dete-kita*.

peer (*n.*) 1)dôryô [同僚]. 2)《*Eng.*》jôin-giin [上院議員].

peevish (*a.*) dada-o-koneru [だだをこねる]; sunete-iru [すねている].

peg (*n.*) 1)kugi [くぎ]. 2)kôjitsu [口実]; riyû [理由].

  (*vt.*) 1)...ni kugi-o-utsu […にくぎを打つ]. 2)(kakaku nado)-o kugi-zuke-ni-suru [(価格など)をくぎづけにする].

  peg away at ...o sesse-to-yaru

pelt (*vt. & vi.*) (...o) nage-tsukeru [(…を)投げつける].

pen (*n.*) 1)pen [ペン]. 2)bumpitsu[-katsudô] [文筆(活動)]; buntai [文体].

  (*vt.*) 1)...o kaku […を書く]. 2)(shi ya bun)-o tsukuru [(詩や文)を作る].

pen (*n.*) ori [おり]; kakoi [囲い].

  (*vt.*) ...o kakoi-ni-ireru […を囲いに入れる]; ...o toji-komeru […を閉じ込める].

P.E.N. Kokusai-pen-kurabu [国際ペンクラブ].

penalty (*n.*) batsu [罰]; keibatsu [刑罰]; bakkin [罰金]; penarutî [ペナルティー].

pencil (*n.*) empitsu [鉛筆]; empitsu-gata-no-mono [鉛筆形のもの].

  (*vt.*) ...o empitsu-de-kaku […を鉛筆で書く].

pending (*a.*) mi-kettei-no [未決定の]; pendingu-no [ペンディングの].

  (*prep.*) ...made […まで].

pendulum (*n.*) furi-ko [振り子].

penetrate (*vt.*) 1)...ni shimi-komu […にしみ込む]; ...o kantsû-suru […を貫通する]. 2)...o mi-nuku […を見抜く].

  (*vi.*) hairu [入る]; shimi-komu [しみ込む].

peninsula (*n.*) hantô [半島].

peninsular (*a.*) hantô-no [半島の].

penmanship (*n.*) shûji [習字]; hisseki [筆跡].

pennant (*n.*) 1)《*US*》yûshô-ki [優勝旗]; penanto [ペナント]. 2)(*marine*) sankaku-ki [三角旗].

  win the pennant yûshô-suru

penniless (*a.*) totemo-bimbô-na [とても貧乏な].

pension (*n.*) nenkin [年金]; onkyû [恩給]; fujo-ryô [扶助料].

     an old-age **pension** rôrei-*nenkin*

         (*vt.*) ...ni nenkin-o-ataeru [...に年金を与える].

pensive (*a.*) mono-omoi-ni-shizunda [物思いに沈んだ]; mono-ganashii [物悲しい].

pentagon (*n.*) gokakkei [五角形].

peony (*n.*) (*bot.*) shakuyaku [シャクヤク].

people (*n.*) 1)kokumin [国民]; minzoku [民族]. 2)hito-bito [人々];
seken-no-hito-bito [世間の人々].

     (*1*) The Japanese are an industrious **people**.

         Nihon-jin wa kimben-na *kokumin*-de-aru.

     (*2*) Many **people** were present.

         Ooku-no *hito-bito* ga shusseki-shita.

     People say that... Seken-de-wa ...to itte-iru.

         (*vt.*) ...ni hito-o-sumawaseru [...に人を住まわせる]; ...ni
shokumin-suru [...に植民する].

pep (*n.*) (*colloq.*) genki [元気].

         (*vt.*) (*colloq.*) ...ni kakki-o-ataeru [...に活気を与える]; ...o genki-
zukeru [...を元気づける].

pepper (*n.*) koshô [こしょう]; peppâ [ペパー].

         (*vt.*) ...ni koshô-o-kakeru [...にコショウをかける]; ...ni
chirabaraseru [...に散らばらせる].

peppermint (*n.*) (*bot.*) seiyô-hakka [セイヨウハッカ]; pepaminto [ペ
パミント].

per (*prep.*) ...ni-tsuki [...につき]; ...ni-yotte [...によって].

perceive (*vt.*) ...o chikaku-suru [...を知覚する]; ...ga wakaru [...がわ
かる].

percent, per cent (*n.*) pâsento [パーセント]; hyaku-bun-ritsu [百分率].

         (*ad.*) ...pâsento-dake [...パーセントだけ].

percentage (*n.*) 1)hyaku-bun-ritsu [百分率]. 2)wariai [割合]; bubun
[部分].

perceptible (*a.*) chikaku-dekiru [知覚できる]; kanari-no [かなりの].

perception (*n.*) chikaku [知覚]; ninshiki [認識].

perch (*n.*) tomari-gi [とまり木]; takai-zaseki [高い座席]; (*colloq.*)
takai-chii [高い地位].

         (*vi.*) (tori ga tomari-gi nado ni) tomaru [(鳥がとまり木などに)
とまる]; (takai isu nado ni) koshi-o-kakeru [(高いいすなどに)腰を掛
ける].

   (*vt.*) (tori ya hito nado)-o tomaraseru ［(鳥や人など)をとまらせる］; (tate-mono)-o takai-basho-ni-sueru ［(建物)を高い場所にすえる］.

percolate (*vt. & vi.*) ...o roka-suru (roka-sareru) ［…をろ過する(ろ過される)］.

perfect (*a.*) 1)kanzen-na ［完全な］; môshi-bun-no-nai ［申し分のない］. 2)mattaku-no ［全くの］.
   (*1*) His French is **perfect**. Kare-no Furansu-go wa *kanzen*-da.
   (*2*) He is a **perfect** stranger to me.
      Kare-wa watashi-ga *mattaku* shira-nai-hito da.
     (*vt.*) 1)...o kansei-suru ［…を完成する］; ...o shi-ageru ［…を仕上げる］. 2)(– oneself) jukutatsu-suru ［熟達する］.

perfection (*n.*) kansei ［完成］; shi-age ［仕上げ］; kanzen-na-hito ［完全な人］; kanzen-na-mono ［完全なもの］.
  to perfection kanzen-ni

perfectly (*ad.*) kanzen-ni ［完全に］; mattaku ［全く］.

perform (*vt.*) 1)...o hatasu ［…を果たす］; ...o nashi-togeru ［…を成し遂げる］. 2)...o enjiru ［…を演じる］; ...o jôen-suru ［…を上演する］; ...o ensô-suru ［…を演奏する］.
     (*vi.*) enjiru ［演じる］; jôen-suru ［上演する］; ensô-suru ［演奏する］.

performance (*n.*) 1)suikô ［遂行］; jikkô ［実行］. 2)ensô ［演奏］; engi ［演技］; kôgyô ［興行］.

performer (*n.*) 1)kôi-sha ［行為者］; jikkô-sha ［実行者］. 2)yakusha ［役者］; ensô-sha ［演奏者］.

perfume (*n.*) 1)ii-kaori ［いい香り］. 2)kôsui ［香水］.
     (*vt.*) ...o ii-kaori-de-mitasu ［…をいい香りで満たす］; ...ni kôsui-o-tsukeru ［…に香水をつける］.

perhaps (*ad.*) koto-ni-yoru-to ［ことによると］; hyotto-shita-ra ［ひょっとしたら］.

peril (*n.*) kiken[-butsu] ［危険(物)］.
  at one's peril kiken-o-kakugo-de; jibun-no-sekinin-de

perilous (*a.*) kiken-na ［危険な］.

period (*n.*) 1)kikan ［期間］; jiki ［時期］. 2)jidai ［時代］. 3)(*gram.*) piriodo ［ピリオド］.
     (*a.*) aru-jidai-no ［ある時代の］; aru-jidai-o-arawasu ［ある時代を表す］.

periodical (*a.*) teiki-kankô-no ［定期刊行の］.
     (*n.*) teiki-kankô-butsu ［定期刊行物］; zasshi ［雑誌］.

periscope (*n.*) sembô-kyô [潜望鏡]; perisukôpu [ペリスコープ].

perish (*vi.*) shinu [死ぬ]; horobiru [滅びる].
　　　(*vt.*) ((*Eng.*)) 1)...o kurushimeru […を苦しめる]. 2)...o boro-boro-ni-suru […をぼろぼろにする].

permanent (*a.*) eikyû-teki-na [永久的な]. 2)jôsetsu-no [常設の].
　　　(*n.*) = permanent wave　pâmanento [パーマネント].

permission (*n.*) kyoka [許可]; yurushi [許し].
　without permission　mudan-de

permit (*vt.*) 1)...o yurusu […を許す]; ...o kyoka-suru […を許可する]. 2)...no kikai-o-ataeru […の機会を与える].
　　　(*vi.*) 1)yurusu [許す]. 2)kanô-ni-suru [可能にする].
　weather permitting　tenki-ga-yo-kereba
　　　(*n.*) ninka[-sho] [認可(書)].

perpendicular (*a.*) suichoku-no [垂直の]; chokuritsu-shita [直立した].
　　　(*n.*) suisen [垂線].

perpetual (*a.*) eikyû-no [永久の]; taema-no-nai [絶え間のない].
　　　(*n.*) shiki-zaki-no-shokubutsu [四季咲きの植物].

perpetually (*ad.*) eikyû-ni [永久に]; taema-naku [絶え間なく].

perplex (*vt.*) ...o komaraseru […を困らせる]; ...o nayamasu […を悩ます]; ...o tôwaku-saseru […を当惑させる].

perplexed (*a.*) 1)tôwaku-shita [当惑した]. 2)fukuzatsu-na [複雑な].

perplexity (*n.*) tôwaku [当惑]; nam-mon[dai] [難問(題)].

persecute (*vt.*) ...o hakugai-suru […を迫害する]; ...o kurushimeru […を苦しめる].

persecution (*n.*) hakugai [迫害].

perseverance (*n.*) nintai[-ryoku] [忍耐(力)].

persevere (*vi.*) shimbô-suru [辛抱する]; taeru [耐える].

persimmon (*n.*) kaki [カキ]; kaki-no-ki [カキの木].

persist (*vi.*) 1)shuchô-suru [主張する]. 2)jizoku-suru [持続する]. 3)koshitsu-suru [固執する].

persistent (*a.*) nebari-zuyoi [粘り強い]; jizoku-suru [持続する].

person (*n.*) 1)hito [人]. 2)yôshi [容姿]. 3)hito-gara [人柄].
　in person　honnin-mizukara; jishin-de

personage (*n.*) tôjô-jimbutsu [登場人物]; meishi [名士].

personal (*a.*) 1)kojin-no [個人の]; isshin-jô-no [一身上の]. 2)honnin-mizukara-no [本人自らの]. 3)shintai-no [身体の].

personality (*n.*) 1)kosei [個性]; jinkaku [人格]. 2)meishi [名士]; pâsonaritî [パーソナリティー].

personally (*ad.*) 1)jibun-de ［自分で］; mizukara ［自ら］. 2)kojin-to-shite-wa ［個人としては］; hito-gara[-teki-ni]-wa ［人柄(的に)は］.

personnel (*n.*) sô-shokuin ［総職員］; sô-jin'in ［総人員］.
        (*a.*) jinji-no ［人事の］.

perspective (*n.*) 1)en-kin-gahô ［遠近画法］. 2)chôbô ［眺望］. 3)mikomi ［見込み］; yosô ［予想］.
        (*a.*) en-kin-gahô-ni-yoru ［遠近画法による］.

perspire (*vi.*) ase-o-kaku ［汗をかく］.
        (*vt.*) ...o ase-ni-shite-dasu ［…を汗にして出す］; ...o bumpitsu-suru ［…を分泌する］.

persuade (*vt.*) ...o settoku-suru ［…を説得する］; ...o nattoku-saseru ［…を納得させる］; ...o susumete...(sa-)seru ［…を勧めて…(さ)せる］.

persuasion (*n.*) settoku[-ryoku] ［説得(力)］; kakushin ［確信］.

pertain (*vi.*) 1)fuzoku-suru ［付属する］. 2)fusawashii ［ふさわしい］. 3)kankei-no-aru ［関係のある］.

pertinent (*a.*) tekisetsu-na ［適切な］; chokusetsu-kankei-ga-aru ［直接関係がある］.

pervade (*vt.*) ...ni ichimen-ni-hirogaru ［…に一面に広がる］.

perverse (*a.*) gôjô-na ［強情な］; hinekureta ［ひねくれた］.

pessimistic (*a.*) hikan-teki-na ［悲観的な］; ensei-shugi-no ［えん世主義の］.

pest (*n.*) yakkai-na-mono ［やっかいなもの］; gaichû ［害虫］.

pet (*n.*) 1)petto ［ペット］. 2)o-ki-ni-iri-no-mono ［お気に入りのもの］; o-ki-ni-iri-no-hito ［お気に入りの人］.
        (*a.*) 1)te-gai-no ［手飼いの］. 2)tokui-no ［得意の］. 3)aijô-no-komotta ［愛情のこもった］.
        (*vt.*) ...o kawaigaru ［…をかわいがる］; ...o petto-ni-suru ［…をペットにする］.
        (*vi.*) aibu-suru ［愛撫する］.

petal (*n.*) (*bot.*) hanabira ［花びら］.

petition (*n.*) seigan[-sho] ［請願(書)］; tangan[-sho] ［嘆願(書)］.
        (*vt.*) ...o seikyû-suru ［…を請求する］; ...ni yôsei-suru ［…に要請する］.
        (*vi.*) seigan-suru ［請願する］; seigan-sho-o-teishutsu-suru ［請願書を提出する］.

petrol (*n.*) ((*Eng.*)) gasorin ［ガソリン］.

petroleum (*n.*) sekiyu ［石油］.

petty (*a.*) 1)sasai-na ［さ細な］; toru-ni-tari-nai ［取るに足りない］. 2)

kyôryô-na [狭量な]. 3)kakyû-no [下級の].

phantom (*n.*) yûrei [幽霊]; gen'ei [幻影].

pharmacy (*n.*) yakugaku [薬学]; yakkyoku [薬局]; kusuriya [薬屋].

phase (*n.*) 1)dankai [段階]; men [面]. 2)(*phys.*) isô [位相].

pheasant (*n.*) (*birds*) kiji [キジ].

phenomenal (*a.*) 1)shizen-genshô-no [自然現象の]. 2)odoroku-beki [驚くべき].

phenomenon (*n.*) 1)genshô [現象]. 2)odoroku-beki-koto[-mono/-hito] [驚くべきこと[もの/人]].

philharmonic (*a.*) ongaku-aikô-no [音楽愛好の]; kôkyô-gaku-dan-no [交響楽団の].

           (*n.*) ongaku-kyôkai [音楽協会].

philosopher (*n.*) tetsugakusha [哲学者].

philosophy (*n.*) tetsugaku [哲学].

phone (*n.*) denwa [電話].

           (*vt.*) ...ni denwa-o-kakeru […に電話を掛ける].

phonetic (*a.*) onsei[-gaku]-no [音声(学)の].

phosphoric (*a.*) rin-no [燐の]; rin-o-fukumu [燐を含む].

photo (*n.*) (*colloq.*) shashin [写真].

photograph (*n.*) shashin [写真].

           (*vt. & vi.*) ...no shashin-o-toru (shashin-ni-utsuru) […の写真をとる(写真に写る)].

photographer (*n.*) shashin-ka [写真家]; shashin-o-toru-hito [写真をとる人]; kameraman [カメラマン].

photomontage (*n.*) montâju-shashin [モンタージュ写真].

phrase (*n.*) 1)(*gram.*) ku [句]. 2)kan'yô-ku [慣用句]; furêzu [フレーズ].

physical (*a.*) 1)busshitsu-teki-na [物質的な]. 2)shintai-no [身体の]. 3)butsuri[-gaku]-teki-na [物理(学)的な].

physical examination kenkô-shindan [健康診断].

physically (*ad.*) busshitsu-teki-ni [物質的に]; shintai-jô [身体上]; butsuri-teki-ni [物理的に].

physical science shizen-kagaku [自然科学].

physician (*n.*) naika-i [内科医]; isha [医者].

physicist (*n.*) butsuri-gaku-sha [物理学者].

physics (*n.*) butsuri-gaku [物理学].

piano (*n.*) piano [ピアノ].

pick (*vt.*) 1)...o tsumu […を摘む]. 2)...o tsutsuku […をつつく]. 3)...

o seisen-suru [⋯を精選する]. 4)(mimi ya ha)-o hojikuru [(耳や歯)をほじくる]. 5)...o nuki-toru [⋯を抜き取る].

pick out ...o erabu

pick up 1)...o hiroi-ageru. 2)...o kiki-oboeru. 3)...o nosete-iku. 4)(*colloq.*) kaifuku-suru; kappatsu-ni-naru

1) I picked up a pin on the mat.
  Watashi-wa tatami-no-ue de pin-o ippon hiroi-ageta.

2) He picked up all the necessary English words in a month.
  Kare-wa hitsuyô-na Ei-tango-o subete hito-tsuki-de oboeta.

3) I'll pick up Tom on the way.
  Tochû-de Tomu-o nosete-itte-yarô.

4) Business is gradually picking up.
  Keiki wa jojo-ni kaifuku-shi-tsutsu-aru.

  (*vi.*) 1)tsutsuku [つつく]. 2)seisen-suru [精選する]. 3)hana-o-tsumu [花を摘む].

  (*n.*) 1)sentaku [選択]. 2)shûkaku-butsu [収穫物]. 3)(the –) eri-nuki [えり抜き].

pick (*n.*) 1)(*colloq.*) tsuru-hashi [つるはし]. 2)tsuma-yôji [つまようじ].

pickax(e) (*n.*) tsuru-hashi [つるはし].

picket (*n.*) 1)kui [くい]. 2)pike [ピケ].
  (*vt.*) ...ni kui-o-tateru [⋯にくいを立てる]; ...ni pike-o-haru [⋯にピケをはる].

pickle (*n.*) (*pl.*) tsukemono [つけ物]; pikurusu [ピクルス].
  (*vt.*) ...o pikurusu-ni-suru [⋯をピクルスにする].

pickpocket (*n.*) suri [すり].

picnic (*n.*) ensoku [遠足]; pikunikku [ピクニック].

pictorial (*a.*) e-no[-yô-na] [絵の(ような)]; kaiga-no [絵画の]; e-iri-no [絵入りの].

picture (*n.*) 1)e [絵]. 2)shashin [写真]. 3)((*Eng.*)) eiga [映画].
  (*vt.*) ...o kaku [⋯を描く].

picture book e-hon [絵本].

picturesque (*a.*) 1)e-no-yô-ni-utsukushii [絵のように美しい]; hito-me-o-hiku [人目を引く]. 2)hyôgen-ryoku-ni-tonda [表現力に富んだ].

piece (*n.*) 1)hito-kire [一切れ]; ippen [一片]; ichi-mai [一枚]; ippen [一編]; ikkyoku [一曲]; ikko [一個]. 2)(kôka no) ichi-mai [(硬貨の)一枚]. 3)sakuhin [作品].

in pieces bara-bara-ni-natte

to pieces bara-bara-ni; kona-gona-ni

　　　(*vt.*) ...ni tsugi-o-ateru [...に継ぎを当てる]; ...o tsunagi-awaseru [...をつなぎ合わせる].

pied (*a.*) madara-no [まだらの].

pier (*n.*) sambashi [桟橋]; futô [ふ頭].

pierce (*vt.*) ...o tsuki-sasu [...を突き刺す]; ...o tsuki-toosu [...を突き通す]; ...o tsuranuku [...を貫く].
　　　(*vi.*) kantsû-suru [貫通する].

piety (*n.*) keiken [敬けん]; shinjin [信心].

pig (*n.*) buta [豚].

pigeon (*n.*) hato [ハト].

pigeon breast (*path.*) hato-mune [はと胸].

pile (*n.*) tsumi-kasane [積み重ね]; ...no-yama [...の山].
　　a pile(piles) of takusan-no; yama-no-yô-na
　　　(*vt.*) ...o tsumi-kasaneru [...を積み重ねる].
　　　(*vi.*) tsumoru [積もる].

pilgrim (*n.*) junrei-sha [巡礼者].

pilgrimage (*n.*) junrei[-no-tabi] [巡礼(の旅)].

pill (*n.*) 1)gan'yaku [丸薬]; jôzai [錠剤]. 2)(*colloq.*) (the -) piru ┗[ビル].

pillar (*n.*) hashira [柱].

pillow (*n.*) makura [まくら].
　　　(*vt.*) (atama)-o(...ni)noseru [(頭)を(...に)のせる]; ...no makura-to-naru [...のまくらとなる].
　　　(*vi.*) makura-o-suru [まくらをする].

pilot (*n.*) 1)annai-nin [案内人]. 2)mizusaki-annai-nin [水先案内人]; (*aviation*) pairotto [パイロット].
　　　(*vt.*) ...no mizusaki-annai-o-suru [...の水先案内をする]; ...o sôjû-suru [...を操縦する]; ...o annai-suru [...を案内する].

pimple (*n.*) (*path.*) fukide-mono [吹き出物]; nikibi [にきび].

pin (*n.*) pin [ピン].
　　on pins and needles fuan-ni-kararete
　　　(*vt.*) ...o pin-de-tomeru [...をピンで留める].

pinafore (*n.*) (kodomo nado no) epuron [(子供などの)エプロン].

pincers (*n.*) yattoko [やっとこ]; kugi-nuki [くぎ抜き].

pinch (*vt.*) 1)...o tsuneru [...をつねる]; ...o hasamu [...をはさむ]. 2)...o kurushimeru [...を苦しめる].
　　　(*vi.*) shime-tsukeru [締めつける]; kutsû-de-aru [苦痛である].
　　　(*n.*) 1)tsuneri [つねり]. 2)hito-tsumami [一つまみ]. 3)kitsukute-itai-koto [きつくて痛いこと]; (the -) kiki [危機]; pinchi [ピンチ].

with a pinch of salt   waribiki-shite

pine (*n.*) (*bot.*) matsu [松].

ping-pong (*n.*) pimpon [ピンポン]; takkyû [卓球].

pink (*n.*) 1)(*bot.*) sekichiku [石竹]; nadeshiko [ナデシコ]. 2)momo-iro [桃色]. 3)(*colloq.*) sayoku-gakatta-hito [左翼がかった人].

  in the pink (*colloq.*) genki-de-pichi-pichi-shite

      (*a.*) momo-iro-no [桃色の]; sayoku-gakatta [左翼がかった].

pioneer (*n.*) kaitaku-sha [開拓者]; senku-sha [先駆者].

      (*vt. & vi.*) ...o kaitaku-suru(kaitaku-sha-to-naru) [...を開拓する(開拓者となる)].

pious (*a.*) keiken-na [敬けんな]; shinjin-bukai [信心深い]; shûkyô-jô-no [宗教上の].

pipe (*n.*) 1)kan [管]; paipu [パイプ]. 2)(tabako no)ippuku-bun [(タバコの)一服分]. 3)fue [笛].

      (*vt.*) 1)...o fuku [...を吹く]. 2)...o kan-de-hakobu [...を管で運ぶ]. 3)...ni fuchi-kazari-o-tsukeru [...に縁飾りをつける].

      (*vi.*) fue-o-fuku [笛を吹く]; pî-pî-to-saezuru [ピーピーとさえずる]; kanakiri-goe-o-dasu [金切り声を出す].

pipe organ   paipu-orugan [パイプオルガン].

pique (*n.*) rippuku [立腹].

  out of pique   hara-dachi-magire-ni

      (*vt.*) 1)...no kanjô-o-gaisuru [...の感情を害する]. 2)(kôki-shin)-o sosoru [(好奇心)をそそる].

pirate (*n.*) 1)kaizoku [海賊]. 2)chosaku-ken-shingai-sha [著作権侵害者]; kaizoku-ban-no-shuppan-sha [海賊版の出版者].

      (*vt.*) ...ni kaizoku-kôi-o-hataraku [...に海賊行為を働く]; ...o chosaku-sha-no-kyoka-nashi-ni-shuppan-suru [...を著作者の許可なしに出版する].

pistil (*n.*) (*bot.*) me-shibe [めしべ].

pistol (*n.*) pisutoru [ピストル]; kenjû [拳銃].

      (*vt.*) ...o pisutoru-de-utsu [...をピストルで撃つ].

pit (*n.*) 1)ana [穴]; kubomi [くぼみ]. 2)(*min.*) tate-kô [縦坑].

      (*vt.*) 1)...ni ana-o-akeru [...に穴をあける]. 2)...o tori-kumaseru [...を取り組ませる].

pitch (*n.*) 1)chôten [頂点]. 2)(*mus.*) (oto no) chôshi [(音の)調子]. 3)(fune no) tate-yure [(船の)縦揺れ]. 4)(*baseball*) tôkyû [投球].

    (*1*) She was in the **pitch** of pride.

      Kano-jo-wa tokui-no-*chôten*-ni-atta.

(2) She sings a song at a high **pitch**.

　　Kano-jo-wa takai-*chôshi*-de uta-o-utau.

(3) The ship suddenly gave a **pitch**.

　　Fune wa totsuzen *tate*-ni-hito-*yure*-shita.

　　(*vt*.) 1)...o nageru [···を投げる]. 2)(tento)-o haru [(テント)を張る]. 3)...no chôshi-o-totonoeru [···の調子を整える].

　　(*vi*.) 1)nageru [投げる]; (*baseball*) tôshu-o-tsutomeru [投手を務める]. 2)(fune ga) tate-ni-yureru [(船が)縦に揺れる]. 3) massakasama-ni-ochiru [真っ逆さまに落ちる]; massakasama-ni-taoreru [真っ逆さまに倒れる].

pitch (*n*.) pitchi [ピッチ].

　　(as) black as **pitch** *ma*kkuro-na

　　(as) dark as **pitch** *ma*kkura-na

pitcher (*n*.) (*baseball*) pitchâ [ピッチャー]; tôshu [投手].

pitcher (*n*.) ((*US*)) mizu-sashi [水差し].

pitchfork (*n*.) kuma-de [くま手].

　　(*vt*.) (hoshi-kusa nado)-o kaki-ageru [(干し草など)をかき上げる].

piteous (*a*.) aware-na [哀れな]; itamashii [痛ましい].

pith (*n*.) 1)(kusa ya ki no) zui [(草や木の)髄]. 2)(*anat*.) sekizui [せき髄]. 3)genki [元気]; kiryoku [気力]. 4)(the –) shinzui [真髄].

pitiful (*a*.) aware-na [哀れな]; nasakenai [情けない].

pitiless (*a*.) reikoku-na [冷酷な].

pity (*n*.) 1)awaremi [哀れみ]; dôjô [同情]. 2)oshii-koto [惜しいこと]; zannen-na-koto [残念なこと].

(*1*) He took **pity** on her.

　　Kare-wa kano-jo-o *kawaisô*-da-to-omotta.

(*2*) What a **pity**! Nan-to *oshii-koto*-darô!

　　It is a **pity** that he failed again this year.

　　Kare-ga kotoshi mo shippai-shita-no-wa *zannen-na-koto* da.

　　(*vt. & vi*.) (...o) ki-no-doku-ni-omou [(···を)気の毒に思う].

pivot (*n*.) 1)(*mech*.) sûjiku [枢軸]; pibotto [ピボット]. 2)chûshin-ten [中心点]; yôten [要点].

　　(*vt*.) 1)...o sûjiku-no-ue-ni-oku [···を枢軸の上に置く]. 2)...o kaiten-saseru [···を回転させる].

　　(*vi*.) 1)kaiten-suru [回転する]. 2)izon-suru [依存する]; kimaru [決まる].

placard (*n.*) hari-gami [張り紙]; keiji [掲示]; purakâdo [プラカード].
    (*vt.*) ...ni bira-o-haru [···にビラを貼る]; ...o keiji-shite-shiraseru [···を掲示して知らせる].

place (*n.*) 1)tokoro [所]; basho [場所]. 2)tochi [土地]. 3)seki [席]; yochi [余地]. 4)chii [地位]; mibun [身分].
  give place to ...ni seki-o-yuzuru
  in place of ...no-kawari-ni
  lose one's place chii-o-ushinau
  take one's place chakuseki-suru
  take place okoru; okonawareru
  take the place of ...no kawari-o-suru
    (*vt.*) 1)...o oku [···を置く]. 2)...o nimmei-suru [···を任命する].
3)...o tôshi-suru [···を投資する]. 4)...o chûmon-suru [···を注文する].
5)...ni jun'i-o-tsukeru [···に順位をつける].

placid (*a.*) odayaka-na [穏やかな]; shizuka-na [静かな].

plague (*n.*) 1)ekibyô [疫病]; densen-byô [伝染病]. 2)(the -) pesuto [ペスト].
    (*vt.*) ...o ekibyô-ni-kakaraseru [···を疫病にかからせる]; ...o kurushimeru [···を苦しめる].

plaid (*n.*) kôshi-jima [格子じま].

plain (*a.*) 1)meihaku-na [明白な]. 2)heii-na [平易な]. 3)sotchoku-na [率直な]; kazari-no-nai [飾りのない]; shisso-na [質素な].
    (*ad.*) hakkiri-to [はっきりと]; wakari-yasuku [分かりやすく].
    (*n.*) heigen [平原]; heiya [平野].

plainly (*ad.*) 1)akiraka-ni [明らかに]. 2)sotchoku-ni [率直に]; ari-no-mama-ni [ありのままに]. 3)shisso-ni [質素に].

plait (*n.*) 1)(orimono no) hida [(織物の)ひだ]; purîtsu [プリーツ].
2)o-sage-gami [おさげ髪]; anda-mono [編んだもの].
    (*vt.*) ...o amu [···を編む]; ...ni hida-o-toru [···にひだをとる].

plan (*n.*) 1)keikaku [計画]. 2)heimen-zu [平面図].
  (*1*) The **plan** worked well. Sono *keikaku* wa umaku itta.
  (*2*) This is the **plan** of the building.
    Kore-wa sono biru no *heimen-zu* da.
    (*vt.*) 1)(...suru-)tsumori-de-aru [(···する)つもりである]. 2)...no sekkei-zu-o-kaku [···の設計図を書く].
    (*vi.*) (...suru-)tsumori-de-aru [(···する)つもりである].

plane (*n.*) 1)heimen [平面]; men [面]. 2)(*colloq.*) hikô-ki [飛行機].
3)kanna [かんな].

　　　(*a.*) taira-na [平らな]; heimen-no [平面の].

　　　(*vi.*) kakkû-suru [滑空する]; hikô-ki-de-ryokô-suru [飛行機で旅行する].

planet (*n.*) (*astron.*) wakusei [惑星]; yûsei [遊星].

planetarium (*n.*) (*astron.*) puranetariumu [プラネタリウム]; seiza-tôei-ki [星座投影機].

plank (*n.*) 1)atsu-ita [厚板]. 2)(seitô no) kôryô-no-kômoku [(政党の)綱領の項目].

　　　(*vt.*) ...o ita-bari-suru [...を板張りする].

plant (*n.*) 1)shokubutsu [植物]; sômoku [草木]. 2)kôjô [工場]; puranto [プラント].

　　　(*vt.*) 1)...o ueru [...を植える]. 2)...o nyûshoku-saseru [...を入植させる]. 3)...o ue-tsukeru [...を植え付ける].

plantation (*n.*) 1)dai-nôen [大農園]. 2)ue-komi [植え込み].

planter (*n.*) 1)ue-tsukeru-hito [植えつける人]; (tane o)maku-hito [(種を)まく人]. 2)[dai-]nôen-nushi [(大)農園主]. 3)((*US*)) purantâ [プランター].

plaster (*n.*) 1)shikkui [しっくい]; purasutâ [プラスター]. 2)(*med.*) kôyaku [膏薬].

　　　(*vt.*) ...ni shikkui-o-nuru [...にしっくいを塗る]; ...ni kôyaku-o-haru [...に膏薬をはる].

plastic (*n.*) gôsei-jushi [合成樹脂]; purasuchikku [プラスチック].

　　　(*a.*) 1)purasuchikku-sei-no [プラスチック製の]. 2)zôkei-no [造形の]; sosei-no [そ性の].

plate (*n.*) 1)(asai) sara [(浅い)さら]. 2)(kinzoku ya garasu no) ita [(金属やガラスの)板]. 3)(*baseball*) honrui [本塁]; tôshu-ban [投手板].

　　　(*vt.*) ...o mekki-suru [...をめっきする].

platform (*n.*) 1)dan [壇]; endan [演壇]; kyôdan [教壇]. 2)(eki no) purattofômu [(駅の)プラットフォーム]. 3)(seitô no) kôryô [(政党の)綱領].

　　　(*vt.*) ...o endan-ni-agaraseru [...を演壇に上がらせる].

play (*vi.*) 1)asobu [遊ぶ]. 2)ensô-suru [演奏する]. 3)enjiru [演じる].

　　　(*vt.*) 1)...o shite-asobu [...をして遊ぶ]. 2)...o suru [...をする]. 3)...o ensô-suru [...を演奏する]; ...o hiku [...を弾く]. 4)...o enjiru [...を演じる].

　　　(*1*) The children **play** hide-and-seek.

　　　　　Kodomo-tachi wa kakurem-bô-*o shite-asonde-iru.*

　　　(*2*) We **play** baseball.　Ware-ware-wa yakyû-*o suru.*

(3) Can you **play** the violin? Anata-wa baiorin-*ga hike-masu*-ka?

(4) He **played** the part of King Lear.

Kare-wa Ria-ô no yaku-o *enjita*.

play at …o shite-asobu

play away …o sutte-shimau

play with …o mote-asobu

　　(n.) 1)asobi [遊び]. 2)shôbu-goto [勝負ごと]; kyôgi [競技]. 3) shibai [芝居]; geki [劇].

at play asonde

in play jôdan-ni; fuzakete

player *(n.)* 1)senshu [選手]. 2)haiyû [俳優]; yakusha [役者]. 3)ensô-sha [演奏者]; purêyâ [プレーヤー].

playful *(a.)* fuzaketa [ふざけた]; jôdan-no [冗談の].

playground *(n.)* 1)undô-jô [運動場]; asobi-ba [遊び場]. 2)kôraku-chi [行楽地].

playing card torampu-fuda [トランプ札].

playmate *(n.)* asobi-tomodachi [遊び友だち].

playoff *(n.)* kesshô-shiai [決勝試合]; purêofu [プレーオフ].

plead *(vi.)* 1)bengo-o-suru [弁護をする]. 2)tangan-suru [嘆願する].

　　(1) I'll **plead** for you.

Watashi-wa anata-no-tame-ni *bengo-o-suru*.

　　(2) He **pleaded** for the last chance.

Kare-wa　kore-ga-saigo-da-kara-mô-ichido-yarasete-kure-to *tangan-shita*.

　　(vt.) 1)…o bengo-suru [⋯を弁護する].　2)…o iiwake-to-shite-noberu [⋯を言い訳として述べる].

pleasant *(a.)* yukai-na [愉快な]; tanoshii [楽しい]; kimochi-no-yoi [気持のよい]; aiso-no-yoi [愛想のよい].

have a pleasant time tanoshii-toki-o-sugosu

please *(vt.)* 1)…o yorokobaseru [⋯を喜ばせる]; …no ki-ni-iru [⋯の気に入る]. 2)dôzo [どうぞ].

　　(1) I want to **please** my father.

Watashi-wa chichi-o *yorokobase*te-age-tai.

　　(2) **Please** come in. *Dôzo* o-hairi-kudasai.

　　(vi.) shi-tai-to-omou [したいと思う]; konomu [好む].

Do as you **please**. Anata no *shi-tai-to-omou*-yô-ni shi-nasai.

if you please 1)dôzo; yoroshi-kereba. 2)odoroita-koto-ni

　1) Come in, if you please. Dôzo o-hairi-kudasai.

I will take another cup of coffee, if you please.

Yoroshi-kereba mô-ippai kôhî-o itadake-masu-ka-shira.

2) In his room, if you please, was the missing letter.

Odoroita-koto-ni kare-no-heya-ni nakunatta tegami ga atta-n-desu-yo.

pleasing (*a.*) yukai-na [愉快な]; miryoku-teki-na [魅力的な].

pleasure (*n.*) yukai [愉快]; kairaku [快楽]; konomi [好み].

　at your pleasure go-zui-ni

　for pleasure tanoshimi-ni

　with pleasure yorokonde

pledge (*n.*) 1)seiyaku [誓約]. 2)shichi-ire [質入れ]; teitô[-butsu] [抵当(物)].

　　(*vt.*) ...o chikau [...を誓う]; ...o teitô-ni-ireru [...を抵当に入れる].

Pleiades (*n.*) (*astron.*) Subaru [すばる]; Pureadesu [プレアデス].

plentiful (*a.*) takusan-no [沢山の]; hôfu-na [豊富な].

plenty (*n.*) takusan [沢山]; jûbun [十分]; hôfu-sa [豊富さ].

　plenty of takusan-no

　　(*a.*) takusan-no [沢山の]; hôfu-na [豊富な].

　　(*ad.*) (*colloq.*) tappuri [たっぷり].

pleurisy (*n.*) (*med.*) rokumaku-en [ろく膜炎].

plod (*vi.*) tobo-tobo-aruku [とぼとぼ歩く]; kotsu-kotsu-hataraku [こつこつ働く].

　　(*n.*) tobo-tobo-aruku-koto [とぼとぼ歩くこと].

plot (*n.*) 1)imbô [陰謀]. 2)(shôsetsu ya geki no) suji [(小説や劇の)筋]. 3)shô-jimen [小地面].

　　(*vt.*) ...o takuramu [...をたくらむ]; ...o hakaru [...をはかる].

plow, plough (*n.*) 1)suki [すき]. 2)(the P-)((*Eng.*)) Hokuto-shichisei [北斗七星].

　　　　(*vt.*) ...o suku [...をすく].

　　　　(*vi.*) 1)suki-de-tagayasu [すきで耕す]. 2)hone-otte-susumu [骨折って進む]. 3)kotsu-kotsu-suru [こつこつする].

pluck (*vt.*) 1)(tori no ke)-o mushiri-toru [(鳥の毛)をむしり取る]. 2)...o tsumu [...を摘む]. 3)...o gui-to-hiku [...をぐいと引く].

　　(*vi.*) gui-to-hipparu [ぐいと引っ張る].

　　(*n.*) 1)gui-to-hiku-koto [ぐいと引くこと]. 2)yûki [勇気].

plug (*n.*) 1)sen [栓]. 2)shôka-sen [消火栓]. 3)sashi-komi [差し込み]; puragu [プラグ].

(*vt.*) ...ni sen-o-suru [···に栓をする]; ...o tsumeru [···を詰める].

(*vi.*) 1)(*colloq.*) kotsu-kotsu-tori-kumu [こつこつ取り組む]. 2) tsumaru [詰まる].

plum (*n.*) seiyô-sumomo [セイヨウスモモ]; hoshi-budô [干しブドウ].

plumage (*n.*) (tori no) hane [(鳥の)羽].

plumb (*n.*) ensui [鉛すい].

　　(*a.*) suichoku-na [垂直な].

　　(*ad.*) suichoku-ni [垂直に]; (*Eng. colloq.*) seikaku-ni [正確に].

　　(*vt.*) 1)...no fuka-sa-o-hakaru [···の深さを測る]. 2)...o suichoku-ni-suru [···を垂直にする]. 3)...o saguru [···を探る].

plumbing (*n.*) haikan[-kôji] [配管(工事)].

plume (*n.*) hane [羽]; hane-kazari [羽飾り].

　　(*vt.*) ...o hane-de-kazaru [···を羽で飾る].

plump (*a.*) maru-maru-to-futotta [丸々と太った].

　　(*vt. & vi.*) ...o futoraseru(futoru) [···を太らせる(太る)].

plump (*ad.*) 1)dosun-to [どすんと]. 2)fui-ni [不意に].

　　(*1*) He fell **plump** into the water.

　　　　Kare-wa *dobun-to* sui-chû-ni ochita.

　　(*2*) The enemy came **plump** upon us.

　　　　Teki wa *fui-ni* ware-ware-ni osoi-kakatta.

　　(*vi.*) dosun-to-ochiru [どすんと落ちる].

　　(*vt.*) ...o dosun-to-otosu [···をどすんと落とす].

　　(*n.*) dosun[-to-ochiru-koto] [どすん(と落ちること)].

plunder (*vt.*) ...kara ryakudatsu-suru [···から略奪する].

　　(*n.*) ryakudatsu [略奪].

plunge (*vi.*) tobi-komu [飛び込む]; moguru [潜る]; tosshin-suru [突進する].

　　(*vt.*) 1)...o tsukkomu [···を突っ込む]. 2)...o otoshiireru [···を陥れる].

　　(*n.*) tobi-komi [飛び込み]; totsunyû [突入].

plural (*n. & a.*) (*gram.*) fukusû(-no) [複数(の)].

plus (*prep.*) ...o-kuwaete [···を加えて]; ...no-ue-ni [···の上に].

　　(*a.*) (*math.*) sei-no [正の]; purasu-no [プラスの].

　　(*n.*) 1)(*math.*) seisû [正数]. 2)rieki [利益].

ply (*vt.*) 1)...o sesse-to-tsukau [···をせっせと使う]. 2)...o shitsukoku-suru [···をしつこくする]; ...o shitsukoku-susumeru [···をしつこく勧める].

　　(*vi.*) 1)(fune ya basu ga) teiki-teki-ni-ôfuku-suru [(船やバスが)

　　定期的に往復する]. 2)sei-o-dasu [精を出す].

P.M., p.m. (*abbrev.*) gogo [午後].

pneumonia (*n.*) (*med.*) haien [肺炎].

poach (*vt.*) (tamago)-o yuderu [(たまご)をゆでる].

pocket money　ko-zukai-sen [小遣い銭].

pod (*n.*) saya [さや].

　　(*vt.*) ...no saya-o-muku [...のさやをむく].

　　(*vi.*) saya-ni-naru [さやになる].

poem (*n.*) shi [詩].

poet (*n.*) shijin [詩人].

poetic, poetical (*a.*) shi-no [詩の]; shi-teki-na [詩的な]; shijin-no [詩人の].

poetry (*n.*) shiika [詩歌]; shi [詩]; shijô [詩情].

poignant (*a.*) 1)mi-o-kiru-yô-na [身を切るような]; hageshii [激しい]. 2)shinratsu-na [辛らつな]. 3)kandô-teki-na [感動的な]. 4)hana-o-tsuku [鼻をつく].

point (*n.*) 1)ten [点]. 2)(togatta-)sentan [(とがった)先端]. 3)misaki [岬]. 4)chiten [地点]. 5)yôten [要点]. 6)tokuten [得点]. 7)...do [...度].

　　come to the point　yôten-ni-fureru

　　in point of　...ni-kanshite

　　make a point of (doing)　...(suru)-yô-ni-tsutomeru

　　on the point of　masa-ni...(shi-)yô-to-shite

　　point of view　kenchi; kanten

　　to the point　yôryô-o-ete

　　(*vt.*) 1)...o togaraseru [...をとがらせる]. 2)...o mukeru [...を向ける]. 3)...o sashi-shimesu [...を指し示す]. 4)...o kyôchô-suru [...を強調する].

　　(*vi.*) 1)yubi-sasu [指さす]. 2)...no-hôkô-ni muku [...の方向に向く].

　　point out　shiteki-suru

pointed (*a.*) 1)saki-no-togatta [先のとがった]; surudoi [鋭い]. 2)atetsuketa [当てつけた].

pointer (*n.*) 1)shiji-suru-hito [指示する人]. 2)hinto [ヒント].

poise (*n.*) 1)tsuri-ai [釣り合い]. 2)heisei [平静]. 3)mi-no-konashi [身のこなし]; taido [態度].

　　(*vt.*) 1)...no heikô-o-tamotsu [...の平衡を保つ]. 2)...o chû-ni-ukaseru [...を宙に浮かせる].

   (*vi.*) heikô-o-tamotsu [平衡を保つ].

poison (*n.*) doku [毒].
   (*vt.*) 1)...ni doku-o-ireru [...に毒を入れる]; ...ni doku-o-nuru [...に毒を塗る]. 2)...o dokusatsu-suru [...を毒殺する].

poisonous (*a.*) yûdoku-na [有毒な]; yûgai-na [有害な].

poke (*vt.*) 1)...o tsuku [...を突く]; ...o tsukkomu [...を突っ込む]. 2) ...o kaki-tateru [...をかきたてる].
   (*vi.*) 1)tsuku [突く]; tsuki-deru [突き出る]. 2)sagashi-mawaru [探し回る].
   (*n.*) tsuku-koto [突くこと]; tsutsuku-koto [つつくこと].

polar (*a.*) 1)kyoku[chi]-no [極(地)の]. 2)sei-hantai-no [正反対の].

polar star, the Hokkyoku-sei [北極星].

pole (*n.*) 1)kyoku [極]. 2)sei-hantai [正反対].

pole (*n.*) bô [棒]; sao [さお].
   (*vt.*) ...o sao-de-susumeru [...をさおで進める].

pole jump = pole vault   bô-taka-tobi [棒高飛び].

police (*n.*) 1)keisatsu [警察]. 2)chian [治安].
   (*vt.*) ...no chian-o-tamotsu [...の治安を保つ]; ...o keibi-suru [... を警備する].

policeman (*n.*) kei[satsu]-kan [警(察)官]; junsa [巡査].

police station keisatsu-sho [警察署].

policy (*n.*) 1)seisaku [政策]. 2)chie [知恵].

policy (*n.*) hoken-shôken [保険証券].

polio (*n.*) (*colloq.*) shôni-mahi [小児まひ]; porio [ポリオ].

polish (*vt.*) ...o migaku [...を磨く]; ...o senren-saseru [...を洗練させる].
   (*vi.*) tsuya-ga-deru [つやが出る].
   (*n.*) tsuya-dashi [つや出し]; tsuya [つや]; jôhin-sa [上品さ].

polite (*a.*) teinei-na [丁寧な]; jôhin-na [上品な]; girei-teki-na [儀礼 的な].

political (*a.*) seiji[-jô]-no [政治(上)の]; seiji-gaku-no [政治学の].

political economy seiji-keizai-gaku [政治経済学].

political party seitô [政党].

political science seiji-gaku [政治学].

politician (*n.*) seiji-ka [政治家]; sakushi [策士].

politics (*n.*) seiji [政治]; seiji-gaku [政治学]; seisaku [政策].

polka dots mizu-tama-moyô [水玉模様].

poll (*n.*) 1)tôhyô [投票]; tôhyô-sû [投票数]. 2)(*pl.*) tôhyô-sho [投票 所].

　　(*vt.*) 1)(hyô)-o eru [(票)を得る]. 2)...no seron-chôsa-o-suru […の世論調査をする].

　　(*vi.*) tôhyô-suru [投票する].

pollen (*n.*) (*bot.*) kafun [花粉].

pollute (*vt.*) ...o yogosu […を汚す]; ...o osen-suru […を汚染する]; ...o daraku-saseru […を堕落させる].

pollution (*n.*) osen [汚染]; kôgai [公害]; daraku [堕落].

pond (*n.*) ike [池].

ponder (*vt. & vi.*) (...o) jukkô-suru [(…を)熟考する].

pony (*n.*) ponî [ポニー]; ko-uma [小馬].

pool (*n.*) mizu-tamari [水たまり]; pûru [プール].

pool (*n.*) kyôdô-shikin [共同資金].

　　(*vt.*) ...o kyôdô-shusshi-suru […を共同出資する].

poor (*a.*) 1)bimbô-na [貧乏な]. 2)kawai-sô-na [かわいそうな]; ki-no-doku-na [気の毒な]. 3)yaseta [やせた]. 4)heta-na [下手な].

　be poor at ...ga heta-de-aru

poorly (*a.*) (*Eng. colloq.*) kibun-no-sugure-nai [気分のすぐれない].

　　(*ad.*) mazushiku [貧しく]; misuborashiku [みすぼらしく]; heta-ni [下手に].

pop (*vi.*) 1)pon-to-naru [ぽんと鳴る]. 2)hyoi-to-arawareru [ひょいと現れる]. 3)pon-to-hajikeru [ぽんとはじける].

　(*1*) The cork **popped**.　Koruku ga *pon-to-natta*.

　(*2*) He **popped** right before us.

　　　Kare-wa *hyoi-to* ware-ware-no-mae-ni *arawareta*.

　(*3*) This corn **pops** well.　Kono tômorokoshi wa yoku *hajikeru*.

　　(*vt.*) 1)...ni pon-to-oto-o-dasaseru[-iwaseru] […にポンと音を出させる[言わせる]]. 2)((*US*)) ...o hajikeru-made-iru […をはじけるまでいる]. 3)...o happô-suru […を発砲する].

　　(*n.*) 1)pon-to-iu-oto [ポンという音]. 2)tansan-sui [炭酸水].

　　(*ad.*) pon-to [ポンと]; kyû-ni [急に].

pope (*n.*) Rôma-hôô [ローマ法王].

popgun (*n.*) mame-deppô [豆鉄砲].

poplar (*n.*) (*bot.*) popura [ポプラ].

poppy (*n.*) (*bot.*) keshi [ケシ].

popular (*a.*) 1)ninki-no-aru [人気のある]. 2)tsûzoku-teki-na [通俗的な]. 3)jimmin-no [人民の].

　(*1*) The professor is **popular** with the students.

　　　Ano kyôju wa gakusei-no-aida-de *ninki-ga-aru*.

　　(2) I went to the bookstore to get some **popular** novels.
　　　　　Watashi-wa *tsûzoku*-shôsetsu-o ni-san-satsu kai-ni hon'ya-
　　　　　e itta.
　　(3) **Popular** meetings were often held here.
　　　　　Koko-de-wa *jimmin*-taikai ga tabi-tabi hirakareta.

popularity (*n.*) ninki [人気]; hyôban [評判].
popularly (*ad.*) ippan-ni [一般に]; heii-ni [平易に].
population (*n.*) jinkô [人口]; jûmin [住民].
populous (*a.*) jinkô-no-ooi [人口の多い].
porcelain (*n.*) jiki [磁器].
porch (*n.*) 1)genkan [玄関]; kuruma-yose [車寄せ]; pôchi [ポーチ].
　　2)((*US*)) beranda [ベランダ].
pore (*vi.*) jukudoku-suru [熟読する]; jukkô-suru [熟考する].
pore (*n.*) ke-ana [毛孔]; (*bot.*) kikô [気孔].
pork (*n.*) buta-niku [豚肉].
porridge (*n.*) ((*Eng.*)) kayu [かゆ]; porijji [ポリッジ].
port (*n.*) minato [港].
port (*n.*) (*marine*) sagen [左舷].
　　(*vt.*) ...o sagen-ni-mukeru [...を左舷に向ける].
port (*n.*) pôtowain [ポートワイン].
portable (*a.*) keitai-yô-no [携帯用の].
　　　　　(*n.*) pôtaburu [ポータブル].
porter (*n.*) 1)(eki no) akabô [(駅の)赤帽]; pôtâ [ポーター]. 2)
　　((*US*)) bôi [ボーイ].
porter (*n.*) momban [門番].
porthole (*n.*) (*marine*) gensô [舷窓]. (hikô-ki no) maru-mado [(飛
　　行機の)丸窓].
portion (*n.*) 1)ichibu [一部]. 2)wake-mae [分け前]; (tabe-mono no)
　　ichinin-mae [(食べ物の)一人前].
　　　　　(*vt.*) ...o wakeru [...を分ける].
portrait (*n.*) shôzô-ga [肖像画]; shôzô-shashin [肖像写真]; byôsha
　　[描写].
pose (*n.*) pôzu [ポーズ]; mise-kake [見せかけ].
　　　　　(*vt.*) 1)...ni pôzu-o-toraseru [...にポーズをとらせる]. 2)...o
　　teishutsu-suru [...を提出する].
　　　　　(*vi.*) pôzu-o-toru [ポーズをとる]; mise-kakeru [見せかける].
position (*n.*) 1)ichi [位置]. 2)chii [地位]; shoku [職]. 3)mibun [身
　　分]; kyôgû [境遇]. 4)shisei [姿勢]; taido [態度].

be in a position to (do) ...(suru)-koto-ga-dekiru-tachiba-ni-aru
    (*vt.*) ...o(-tekitô-na-basho-ni) oku […を(適当な場所に)置く].

positive (*a.*) 1)meikaku-na [明確な]. 2)kakushin-no-aru [確信のある].
    3)sekkyoku-teki-na [積極的な]. 4)(*colloq.*) mattaku-no [全くの].
    (*n.*) 1)(*photo.*) yôga [陽画]; poji [ポジ]. 2)(*gram.*)
    genkyû [原級].

positively (*ad.*) kippari-to [きっぱりと]; zettai-ni [絶対に].
    (*int.*) Mochiron! [もちろん!]; Sô-da-tomo! [そうだとも!].

possess (*vt.*) ...o shoyû-suru […を所有する].

possession (*n.*) 1)shoyû [所有]. 2)shoyû-butsu [所有物]; ryôchi [領
    地].

    get(take) possession of ...o te-ni-ireru; ...o sen'yû-suru

possessive (*a.*) shoyû-no [所有の].
    (*n.*) (*gram.*) shoyû-kaku [所有格].

possessor (*n.*) mochi-nushi [持ち主]; shoyû-sha [所有者].

possibility (*n.*) kanô-sei [可能性]; ari-sô-na-koto [ありそうなこと].

possible (*a.*) 1)kanô-na [可能な]; dekiru [できる]. 2)ari-uru [ありう
    る]. 3)dekiru-kagiri-no [できるかぎりの].
    (*1*) Do it yourself if it is **possible**.
       Dekiru-nara jibun-de sore-o shi-nasai.
    (*2*) Is it **possible** that he will succeed?
       Kare-ga seikô-suru-koto-ga hatashite-*ari-uru*-darô-ka?
    (*3*) I'll tell you at the earliest **possible**.
       Dekiru-dake-hayai-kikai-ni hanashi-mashô.

    as...as possible dekiru-dake
    if possible dekiru-koto-nara

possibly (*ad.*) 1)arui-wa [あるいは]; koto-ni-yoru-to [ことによると].
    2)totemo...(nai) [とても…(ない)].
    (*1*) **Possibly** he may recover.
       Arui-wa kare-wa naoru-kamo-shirenai.
    (*2*) He cannot **possibly** do it.
       Kare niwa *totemo* sore wa deki-nai.

post (*n.*) hashira [柱]; kui [くい].
    (*vt.*) (hashira ni bira)-o haru [(柱にビラを)貼る]; ...o keiji-suru
    […を掲示する].

post (*n.*) chii [地位]; busho [部署].
    (*vt.*) ...o busho-ni-tsukaseru […を部署につかせる]; ...o haichi-
    suru […を配置する].

post (*n.*) ((*Eng.*)) yûbin[-butsu] [郵便(物)]; yûbin-posuto [郵便ポスト].
  by post yûbin-de
  by return of post ori-kaeshi
    (*vt.*) ((*Eng.*)) ...o yûsô-suru […郵送する].

postage (*n.*) yûbin-ryôkin [郵便料金].

postage stamp yûbin-kitte [郵便切手].

postal (*a.*) yûbin-no [郵便の].

postal card ((*US*)) kansei-hagaki [官製はがき].

postal order ((*Eng.*)) yûbin-kawase [郵便かわせ].

postbox (*n.*) yûbin-posuto [郵便ポスト].

postcard (*n.*) hagaki [はがき]; e-hagaki [絵はがき].

poster (*n.*) 1)posutâ [ポスター]; kôkoku-bira [広告びら]. 2)bira-o-haru-hito [びらをはる人].
    (*vt.*) ...ni posutâ-o-haru […にポスターをはる].

poste restante kyoku-dome [局留め].

postgraduate (*a.*) daigaku-in-no [大学院の].
    (*n.*) daigaku-in-gakusei [大学院学生]; insei [院生].

postman (*n.*) yûbin-shûhai-nin [郵便集配人].

postmaster (*n.*) yûbin-kyoku-chô [郵便局長].

post office yûbin-kyoku [郵便局].

postpone (*vt.*) ...o enki-suru […を延期する].

postscript (*n.*) tsuishin [追伸]; atogaki [あとがき].

posture (*n.*) 1)shisei [姿勢]; taido [態度]; kokoro-gamae [心構え]. 2)jôsei [情勢].
    (*vi.*) shisei-o-toru [姿勢をとる]; pôzu-o-toru [ポーズをとる].
    (*vt.*) ...ni pôzu-o-toraseru […にポーズをとらせる].

pot (*n.*) tsubo [つぼ]; kame [かめ]; hachi [鉢].
    (*vt.*) ...o yôki-ni-irete-hozon-suru […を容器に入れて保存する]; ...o hachi-ni-ueru […を鉢に植える].

potato (*n.*) jagaimo [ジャガイモ]; poteto [ポテト].

potential (*a.*) hatten-no-kanô-sei-no-aru [発展の可能性のある]; senzai-teki-na [潜在的な].
    (*n.*) 1)kanô-sei [可能性]; senzai[-nô]ryoku [潜在(能)力]. 2) (*elect.*) den'i [電位].

potentiality (*n.*) kanô-sei [可能性]; senzai-ryoku [潜在力]; (*pl.*) kanô-sei-o-yûsuru-mono [可能性を有するもの].

potter (*n.*) tôkô [陶工].

pottery (*n.*) tôki [陶器]; tôki-seizô [陶器製造].

pouch (*n.*) (kangarû nado no) fukuro [(カンガルーなどの)袋]; ko-bukuro [小袋]; pauchi [パウチ]; yûbin-bukuro [郵便袋].
 (*vt.*) ...o fukuro-ni-ireru [⋯を袋に入れる]; ...o fukuro-jô-ni-suru [⋯を袋状にする].
 (*vi.*) fukuro-jô-ni-naru [袋状になる]; fukureru [ふくれる].

poultry (*n.*) kakin [家禽].

pounce (*vi.*) kyû-ni-tobi-kakaru [急に飛びかかる]; kyû-ni-tsukami-kakaru [急につかみかかる].
 (*n.*) kyû-ni-tsukami-kakaru-koto [急につかみかかること].

pound (*n.*) pondo [ポンド].

pound (*vt.*) ...o tsuki-kudaku [⋯をつきくだく]; ...o renda-suru [⋯を連打する].
 (*vi.*) 1)renda-suru [連打する]. 2)dokin-dokin-suru [どきんどきんする]. 3)dosun-dosun-to-aruku [ドスンドスンと歩く].
 (*n.*) renda[-suru-oto] [連打(する音)].

pour (*vt.*) ...o tsugu [⋯をつぐ]; ...o sosogu [⋯を注ぐ]; ...o abiseru [⋯を浴びせる].
 (*vi.*) 1)nagare-deru [流れ出る]. 2)hageshiku-furu [激しく降る]. 3)oshi-yoseru [押し寄せる].

poverty (*n.*) bimbô [貧乏]; hinkon [貧困]; ketsubô [欠乏].

powder (*n.*) 1)kona [粉]; fummatsu [粉末]. 2)kona-oshiroi [粉おしろい]. 3)kayaku [火薬].
 (*vt. & vi.*) 1)...o kona-ni-suru (kona-ni-naru) [⋯を粉にする(粉になる)]. 2)(...ni) kona-oshiroi-o-tsukeru [(⋯に)粉おしろいをつける].

powder magazine kayaku-ko [火薬庫].

power (*n.*) 1)chikara [力]; nôryoku [能力]. 2)kenryoku [権力]; seiken [政権]. 3)dôryoku [動力]; denryoku [電力].
 (*1*) He has the strong mental **power**.
  Kare-wa tsuyoi seishin-*ryoku*-o motte-iru.
 (*2*) The Tokugawas were in **power**.
  Tokugawa-ke ga *seiken*-o-nigitte-ita.
 (*3*) a **power** plant ((US)) *hatsuden*-sho
 in one's **power** ...ni-dekiru-dake-no

powerful (*a.*) kyôryoku-na [強力な]; seiryoku-no-aru [勢力のある].

powerfully (*ad.*) kyôryoku-ni [強力に].

powerless (*a.*) muryoku-na [無力な]; kenryoku-no-nai [権力のない].

practical (*a.*) 1)jissai-teki-na [実際的な]; jitsuyô-teki-na [実用的な].

　　2)jijitsu-jô-no [事実上の].

practically (*ad.*) jissai-ni [実際に]; jijitsu-jô [事実上]; hotondo...modôzen [ほとんど…も同然].

practice (*n.*) 1)renshû [練習]. 2)jitchi [実地]; jissai [実際]. 3)shûkan [習慣]; kanrei [慣例]. 4)gyômu [業務].

　　in practice jijitsu-jô

　　out of practice renshû-busoku-de

　　　　(*vt.*) 1)...o renshû-suru […を練習する]. 2)...ni jûji-suru […に従事する]. 3)...o jikkô-suru […を実行する].

　　　　(*vi.*) 1)renshû-suru [練習する]. 2)kaigyô-suru [開業する].

practiced (*a.*) renshû-o-tsunda [練習をつんだ]; keiken-de-eta [経験で得た].

pragmatism (*n.*) (*philos.*) jitsuyô-shugi [実用主義]; puragumatizumu [プラグマティズム].

prairie (*n.*) dai-sôgen [大草原].

praise (*n.*) shôsan [賞賛]; sambi [賛美].

　　in praise of ...o-home-tataete

　　　　(*vt.*) ...o shôsan-suru […を賞賛する]; ...o sambi-suru […を賛美する].

prank (*n.*) fuzake [ふざけ]; itazura [いたずら].

　　play pranks on ...ni itazura-o-suru; ...o karakau

prawn (*n.*) (*zool.*) kuruma-ebi [クルマエビ].

pray (*vi.*) 1)inoru [祈る]. 2)negau [願う].

　　　　(*vt.*) ...ni inoru […に祈る]; ...o inoru […を祈る].

prayer (*n.*) inori[-no-kotoba] [祈り(の言葉)].

preach (*vi. & vt.*) (...o) sekkyô-suru [(…を)説教する].

preacher (*n.*) sekkyô-sha [説教者]; dendô-sha [伝道者].

precaution (*n.*) yôjin [用心]; keikai [警戒]. 2)yobô-sochi [予防措置].

　　take precautions against ...o yôjin-suru

precede (*vt.*) ...ni saki-datsu […に先だつ]; ...ni senkô-suru […に先行する]; ...ni yûsen-suru […に優先する].

　　　　(*vi.*) senkô-suru [先行する].

precedent (*n.*) senrei [先例]; zenrei [前例]; kanrei [慣例].

preceding (*a.*) mae-no [前の]; zenjutsu-no [前述の].

precept (*n.*) kyôkun [教訓]; kakugen [格言].

precious (*a.*) kôka-na [高価な]; kichô-na [貴重な].

　　　　(*ad.*) (*colloq.*) hijô-ni [非常に]; totemo [とても].

precipice (*n.*) 1)zeppeki [絶壁]. 2)kiki [危機].

precise (*a.*) 1)seikaku-na [正確な]. 2)kichô-men-na [き帳面な].

precisely (*ad.*) 1)seikaku-ni [正確に]. 2)hakkiri-iu-ga [はっきり言うが]. 3)masa-ni-sono-toori [まさにそのとおり].

precision (*n.*) seikaku [正確]; seimitsu [精密].

predecessor (*n.*) zennin-sha [前任者].

predicate (*n.*) (*gram.*) jutsugo [述語]; jutsubu [述部].
    (*vt.*) 1)...o...no-zokusei-de-aru-to-dantei-suru […を…の属性であると断定する]. 2)...no-kiso-o(...ni) oku […の基礎を(…に)置く].

predict (*vt. & vi.*) (...o) yogen-suru [(…を)予言する]; (...o) yohô-suru [(…を)予報する].

predominant (*a.*) medatsu [目立つ]; yûryoku-na [有力な].

preeminent (*a.*) takuetsu-shita [卓越した]; batsugun-no [抜群の].

prefab (*n.*) (*colloq.*) kumi-tate-shiki-tatemono [組立て式建物]; purehabu-jûtaku [プレハブ住宅].

preface (*n.*) jobun [序文]; hashigaki [はしがき].
    (*vt.*) ...ni jobun-o-tsukeru […に序文をつける].

prefecture (*n.*) ken [県]; fu [府].

prefer (*vt.*) mushiro...o erabu [むしろ…を選ぶ]; ...no-hô-o konomu […の方を好む].

preference (*n.*) konomi [好み]; sentaku [選択]; yûsen-ken [優先権].

prefix (*n.*) (*gram.*) settô-ji [接頭辞].
    (*vt.*) ...ni settô-ji-o-tsukeru […に接頭辞をつける].

prejudice (*n.*) henken [偏見]; ke-girai [毛嫌い].
    (*vt.*) 1)...ni henken-o-motaseru […に偏見を持たせる]. 2)...o gaisuru […を害する].

preliminary (*a.*) yobi-no [予備の]; jumbi-no [準備の]; yosen-no [予選の].
    (*n.*) 1)(*pl.*) yobi-kôi [予備行為]; jumbi [準備]. 2)yobi-shiken [予備試験]; yosen [予選].

premature (*a.*) haya-sugiru [早すぎる].

premier (*n.*) sôri-daijin [総理大臣]; shushô [首相].
    (*a.*) shui-no [首位の]; saikô-no [最高の].

premise (*n.*) 1)zentei [前提]. 2)(*pl.*) ie-yashiki [家屋敷].
    (*vt.*) (...da)-to zentei-to-shite-noberu [(…だ)と前提として述べる].

premium (*n.*) 1)wari-mashi-kin [割増し金]; puremiamu [プレミアム]. 2)shôkin [賞金].

preoccupied (*a.*) muchû-ni-natta [夢中になった]; uwa-no-sora-no [上

の空の].

prepaid (*a.*) mae-barai-no [前払いの]; zennô-no [前納の]; puripeido [プリペイド].

preparation (*n.*) jumbi [準備]; yôi [用意]; ((*Eng.*)) yoshû [予習].

prepare (*vt.*) 1)...o jumbi-suru […を準備する]; ...o yôi-suru […を用意する]; ...no shita-shirabe-o-suru […の下調べをする]; ...no shitaku-o-suru […の支度をする]. 2)...ni jumbi-saseru […に準備させる]. 3)...no kakugo-o-saseru […の覚悟をさせる]. 4)...o chôri-suru […を調理する]; ...o chôgô-suru […を調合する].

   (*1*) She is busy **preparing** our supper.
      Kano-jo-wa ware-ware-no yûshoku-*no-shitaku*-ni-isogashii.

   (*2*) He **prepared** himself for the exam.
      Kare-wa shiken-no-*jumbi-o-shita*.

   (*3*) We must always **be prepared** for the worst.
      Ware-ware-wa   tsune-ni   saiaku-no-baai-no-*kakugo-o-shi*-nakereba-naranai.

   (*4*) The doctor **prepared** a medicine.
      Isha wa kusuri-*o chôgô-shita*.

     (*vi.*) 1)jumbi-suru [準備する]; 2)kakugo-o-suru [覚悟をする].

   (*1*) She **is preparing** for her departure to France.
      Kano-jo-wa Furansu-e shuppatsu-suru-*jumbi-o-shiteiru*.

   (*2*) The village **prepared** to do battle.
      Sommin wa tatakau-*kakugo-o-shita*.

prepay (*vt.*) ...o mae-barai-suru […を前払いする]; ...o zennô-suru […を前納する].

preposition (*n.*) (*gram.*) zenchi-shi [前置詞].

prescribe (*vt.*) 1)...o kitei-suru […を規定する]. 2)(*med.*) ...o shohô-suru […を処方する].

     (*vi.*) kitei-suru [規定する]; shohô-o-kaku [処方を書く].

prescription (*n.*) kitei [規定]; (*med.*) shohô[-sen] [処方(せん)].

presence (*n.*) 1)sonzai [存在]. 2)shusseki [出席]. 3)menzen [面前]. 4)fûsai [風さい].

   (*1*) Are you sure of the **presence** of ghosts?
      Kimi-wa yûrei no *sonzai*-o shinjiru-ka?

   (*2*) Your **presence** is requested. Go-*shusseki*-o negaimasu.

   (*3*) Don't scold your sons in the **presence** of others.
      Tanin-no-*menzen*-de musuko-tachi-o shikattewa-ikenai.

   (*4*) He has noble **presence**.

      Kare-wa kihin-no-aru *fûsai*-o shite-iru.

present (*a.*) 1)shusseki-shite-iru [出席している]; i-awasete-iru [居合わせている]. 2)genzai-no [現在の]; ima-no [今の].

  (*1*) I was **present** at the party.

      Watashi-wa sono-pâtî-ni *shusseki-shite-ita*.

  (*2*) the **present** address   *gen*-jûsho

      the **present** student council   *ima-no* seito-kai

      (*n.*) genzai [現在].

  at present ima-no-tokoro

  for the present tôbun

present (*n.*) okuri-mono [贈り物].

    (*vt.*) 1)...o okuru […を贈る]; ...o ataeru […を与える]. 2)...o sashi-dasu […を差し出す]; ...o teishutsu-suru […を提出する]. 3)...o shôkai-suru […を紹介する]. 4)...o arawasu […を表わす]. 5)...o mukeru […を向ける].

  (*1*) I **presented** him with a book.

      Watashi-wa kare-ni hon-o issatsu *okutta*.

  (*2*) He **presented** his card to me.

      Kare-wa jibun-no meishi-*o* watashi-ni *sashi-dashita*.

  (*3*) May I **present** Mr. Sumita to you?

      Sumita-san-*o* go-*shôkai-shimasu*.

  (*4*) This picture **presents** three girls playing in the garden.

      Kono e wa niwa-de asonde-iru san-nin-no shôjo-*o arawashite-iru*.

  (*5*) He **presented** his pistol at me.

      Kare-wa watashi-ni pisutoru-*o muketa*.

presently (*ad.*) 1)yagate [やがて]; ma-mo-naku [間もなく]. 2)mokka [目下]; genzai [現在].

preserve (*vt.*) ...o hozon-suru […を保存する]; ...o hoji-suru […を保持する].

    (*n.*) 1)(*pl.*) satô-zuke [砂糖漬け]. 2)kinryô-ku [禁猟区]. 3)ryôbun [領分].

preside (*vi.*) shikai-suru [司会する]; gichô-o-tsutomeru [議長を務める].

president (*n.*) 1)daitôryô [大統領]. 2)gichô [議長]; kaichô [会長]; ((*US*)) sôchô [総長]; gakuchô [学長]. tôdori [頭取].

press (*vt.*) 1)...o osu […を押す]; ...o assuru […を圧する]. 2)...o kurushimeru […を苦しめる]. 3)...ni puresu-suru […にプレスする]. 4)

...o kyôyô-suru […を強要する]; ...ni segamu […にせがむ].

(1) **Press** the button.　Botan-o *oshi-nasai*.

(2) He **was pressed** by money.　Kare-wa kane-ni *komatte-ita*.

(3) Please **press** my trousers.

Watashi-no zubon-ni *airon-o-kakete*-kudasai.

(4) He **pressed** me for money.

Kare-wa watashi-ni kane-o *seganda*.

(*vi.*) 1)osu [押す]. 2)segamu [せがむ].

(1) People **pressed** against one another.

Hito-bito wa tagai-ni *oshi-atta*.

(2) He **pressed** for my answer.

Kare-wa watashi-no hentô-o *sematta*.

(*n.*) 1)(*colloq.*) airon-o-kakeru-koto [アイロンをかけること]. 2)
appaku [圧迫]. 3)seppaku [切迫]. 4)(the -) shimbun [新聞]. 5)
zattô [雑踏].

press conference kisha-kaiken [記者会見].

pressure (*n.*) 1)atsuryoku [圧力]; appaku [圧迫]; jûatsu [重圧]. 2)
tabô [多忙].

(*vt.*) ...ni atsuryoku-o-kakeru […に圧力をかける].

pressure group atsuryoku-dantai [圧力団体].

prestige (*n.*) ishin [威信].

presume (*vt.*) 1)...to omou […と思う]; ...o suitei-suru […を推定する].
2)aete...(suru) [あえて…(する)].

(*vi.*) deshabaru [出しゃばる].

presumption (*n.*) 1)suitei [推定]; katei [仮定]; okusoku [憶測]. 2)
deshabari [出しゃばり].

pretend (*vt.*) ...no furi-o-suru […のふりをする]; ...o yosoou […を装う].

He **pretended** ignorance.　Kare-wa shira-nai-*furi-o-shita*.

He **pretended** illness.　Kare-wa byôki-o *yosootta*.

Kare-wa *kebyô-o tsukatta*.

(*vi.*) 1)mise-kakeru [見せかける]; furi-o-suru [ふりをする].
2)motsu-to-jishô-suru [持つと自称する].

(*a.*) itsuwari-no [偽りの]; sôzô-jô-no [想像上の].

pretense (*n.*) 1)kôjitsu [口実]. 2)mise-kake [見せかけ]; ki-dori [気取
り].

make a pretense of ...no furi-o-suru

pretty (*a.*) 1)kirei-na [きれいな]; kawairashii [かわいらしい]. 2)
migoto-na [見事な]. 3)(*colloq.*) kanari-no [かなりの].

(*ad.*) (*colloq.*) kanari [かなり]; zuibun [随分].

prevail (*vi.*) 1)fukyû-suru [普及する]. 2)settoku-suru [説得する]. 3) uchi-katsu [打ち勝つ]; masaru [まさる].

prevalent (*a.*) ryûkô-shite-iru [流行している]; fukyû-shite-iru [普及している].

prevent (*vt.*) ...o fusegu […を防ぐ]; ...o samatageru […を妨げる].

prevention (*n.*) bôshi [防止]; yobô [予防].

preview (*n.*) (*movie*) shisha [試写]; yokoku-hen [予告編].

    (*vt.*) ...no shisha-o-miru […の試写を見る]; ...no shisha-o-miseru […の試写を見せる].

previous (*a.*) saki-no [先の]; mae-no [前の].

prey (*n.*) ejiki [え食].

  a beast of prey môjû

  a bird of prey môkin

  fall a prey to 1)...no ejiki-ni-naru. 2)...ni toritsukareru

    (*vi.*) ejiki-ni-suru [え食にする]; kurushimeru [苦しめる].

price (*n.*) 1)kakaku [価格]; nedan [値段]. 2)daishô [代價]. 3)kenshô-kin [懸賞金].

  at any price donna-gisei-o-haratte-mo; dô-atte-mo

    (*vt.*) ...ni nedan-o-tsukeru […に値段をつける].

  price index bukka-shisû [物価指数]

priceless (*a.*) kane-dewa-kae-nai [金では買えない].

prick (*vt.*) 1)...o chikuri-to-sasu […をちくりと刺す]. 2)...o kurushimeru […を苦しめる].

  prick up one's(its) ears (*colloq.*) kiki-mimi-o-tateru

    (*n.*) tsuki-kizu [突き傷]; itami [痛み]; toge [とげ].

pride (*n.*) 1)jiman [自慢]; hokori [誇り]. 2)kôman [高慢]; omoi-agari [思い上がり]. 3)jiman-no-tane [自慢の種].

  (*1*) He takes **pride** in his house.

    Kare-wa jibun-no-ie-o *jiman*-ni-shite-iru.

  (*2*) **Pride** goes before a fall. *Ogori* ga botsuraku-ni-saki-datsu.

                    Ogoreru-mono hisashi-karazu.

  (*3*) He is his father's **pride**.

    Kare-wa chichi-oya-no *jiman-no-tane* da.

    (*vt.*) ...o jiman-suru […を自慢する].

  He **prides** himself on being rich.

    Kare-wa kane-mochi-de-aru-koto-o *jiman-shite-iru*.

priest (*n.*) sôryo [僧侶]; seishoku-sha [聖職者].

primarily (*ad.*) dai-ichi-ni [第一に]; mazu [まず]; honrai [本来].

primary (*a.*) 1)dai-ichi-no [第一の]. 2)kompon-no [根本の]; shoho-no [初歩の].

    (*n.*) ((*US*)) yobi-senkyo [予備選挙].

primary school ((*Eng.*)) shô-gakkô [小学校]; ((*US*)) shôgaku-san(-yo)-nen-made-no-gakkô [小学三(四)年までの学校].

prime (*a.*) dai-ichi-no [第一の]; shuyô-na [主要な].   「盛期].

    (*n.*) (the –) 1)shoki [初期]. 2)seishun [青春]. 3)zensei-ki [全

prime minister sôri-daijin [総理大臣]; shushô [首相].

primer (*n.*) nyûmon-sho [入門書]; te-biki [手引き].

primitive (*a.*) genshi-no [原始の]; genshi-teki-na [原始的な].

    (*n.*) genshi-jin [原始人].

primrose (*n.*) (*bot.*) sakura-sô [サクラソウ].

prince (*n.*) 1)ôji [王子]. 2)(Eikoku-igai-no)kôshaku [(英国以外の)公爵].

princess (*n.*) 1)ôjo [王女]. 2)(Eikoku-igai-no)kôshaku-fujin [(英国以

principal (*a.*) omo-na [主な].   外の)公爵夫人].

    (*n.*) 1)kôchô [校長]; shuyaku [主役]. 2)(*com.*) gankin [元金].

principally (*ad.*) omo-ni [主に].

principle (*n.*) 1)genri [原理]; gensoku [原則]. 2)shugi [主義]. 3)honshitsu [本質].

print (*n.*) 1)insatsu [印刷]. 2)shuppan-butsu [出版物]. 3)purinto-moyô [プリント模様].

  out of print zeppan-ni-natte

    (*vt.*) 1)...o insatsu-suru [...を印刷する]. 2)...o katsuji-tai-de-kaku [...を活字体で書く]. 3)(*photo.*)...o yaki-tsukeru [...を焼き付ける]. 4)...o oshi-tsukeru [...を押しつける].

    (*vi.*) insatsu-suru [印刷する]; insatsu-sareru [印刷される]; katsuji-tai-de-kaku [活字体で書く]; yaki-tsukerareru [焼き付けられる].

printed matter insatsu-butsu [印刷物].

printer (*n.*) 1)insatsu-gyô-sha [印刷業者]; insatsu-kô [印刷工]; insatsu-ki [印刷機]. 2)(*photo.*) yaki-tsuke-ki [焼き付け機].

printing (*n.*) 1)insatsu[-jutsu] [印刷(術)]; (ikkai no) insatsu-busû [(一回の)印刷部数]. 2)(*photo.*) yaki-tsuke [焼き付け].

prior (*a.*) 1)saki-no [先の]; mae-no [前の]. 2)(...yori-)jûyô-na [(...より)重要な]; (...ni-)yûsen-suru [(...に)優先する].

  prior to ...yori-mae-ni[-saki-ni]

prism (*n.*) (*opt.*) purizumu [プリズム]; bunkô-supekutoru [分光スペクトル].

prison (*n.*) keimu-sho [刑務所]; kangoku [監獄].

prisoner (*n.*) shûjin [囚人]; horyo [捕虜].

privacy (*n.*) 1)jiyû-na-shi-seikatsu [自由な私生活]; puraibashî [プライバシー]. 2)intai [隠退]. 2)himitsu [秘密].

private (*a.*) 1)kojin-no [個人の]; shi-teki-na [私的な]. 2)naimitsu-no [内密の]. 3)shiritsu-no [私立の].

    (*1*) This is my **private** affair.

        Kore-wa watashi-*kojin-no* koto da.

    (*2*) a **private** letter   *naimitsu-no* tegami

                        shinten-sho

    (*3*) a **private** school   *shiritsu*-gakkô

privilege (*n.*) tokken [特権]; tokuten [特典].

prize (*n.*) hôbi [ほうび]; shôhin [賞品].

    (*vt.*) ...o omonjiru [⋯を重んじる]; ...o taisetsu-ni-suru [⋯を大切にする].

pro (*n.*) (*colloq.*) puro [プロ]; puro-no-senshu [プロの選手].

probability (*n.*) 1)ari-sô-na-koto [ありそうなこと]. 2)mikomi [見込み]; kôsan [公算].

  in all probability   jû-chû-hakku

probable (*a.*) ari-sô-na [ありそうな].

  It is probable that...   osoraku...darô

probably (*ad.*) tabun [多分]; osoraku [恐らく].

problem (*n.*) 1)mondai [問題]. 2)nayami-no-tane [悩みの種].

procedure (*n.*) tejun [手順]; te-tsuzuki [手続き].

proceed (*vi.*) 1)shinkô-suru [進行する]. 2)tsuzukeru [続ける]. 3) okoru [起こる]; shôjiru [生じる]; hassei-suru [発生する].

    (*1*) The trial **is proceeding.**   Saiban wa mokka *shinkô-chû.*

    (*2*) **Proceed** with your story, please.

        Dôzo o-hanashi-o *o-tsuzuke*-kudasai.

    (*3*) A big sound **proceeded** from the room.

        Ookina oto ga heya-kara *okotta.*

proceeding (*n.*) 1)shinkô [進行]; shochi [処置]. 2)(*pl.*) giji-roku [議事録]. (*law*; *pl.*) soshô-tetsuzuki [訴訟手続き].

  take(institute) proceedings against   ...ni-taishite-soshô-o okosu

proceeds (*n.*) uri-age-daka [売上高]; shûnyû [収入].

process (*n.*) 1)shinkô [進行]; keika [経過]; purosesu [プロセス]. 2) kôtei [工程]; seihô [製法].

  in process of   ...ga-shinkô-chû-de[-no]

　　　　　(*vt.*) 1)...o kakô-suru [⋯を加工する]. 2)...o shori-suru [⋯を処理する].

procession (*n.*) gyôretsu [行列]; kôshin [行進].

proclaim (*vt.*) 1)...o sengen-suru [⋯を宣言する]; ...o fukoku-suru [⋯を布告する]. 2)...o shômei-suru [⋯を証明する].

proclamation (*n.*) sengen[-sho] [宣言(書)]; fukoku [布告].

procurator (*n.*) dairi-nin [代理人].

procure (*vt.*) ...o te-ni-ireru [⋯を手に入れる]; ...o eru [⋯を得る].

prodigal (*a.*) 1)rôhi-suru [浪費する]; hôtô-na [放とうな]. 2)ki-mae-no-yoi [気前のよい].
　　　　　(*n.*) rôhi-sha [浪費者].

prodigious (*a.*) kyodai-na [巨大な]; bakudai-na [ばく大な]; odoroku-beki [驚くべき].

produce (*vt.*) 1)...o seisan-suru [⋯を生産する]; ...o seizô-suru [⋯を製造する]. 2)(*play*) ...o jôen-suru [⋯を上演する]. 3)...o tori-dasu [⋯を取り出す]. 4)...o hiki-okosu [⋯を引き起こす].
　　　　　(*vi.*) seisan-suru [生産する]; seizô-suru [製造する].
　　　　　(*n.*) 1)seisan-daka [生産高]. 2)nô-sambutsu [農産物].

producer (*n.*) 1)seisan-sha [生産者]. 2)((*US*)) seisaku-sha [制作者]; purodyûsâ [プロデューサー].

product (*n.*) 1)[sei]sam-butsu [(生)産物]. 2)kekka [結果]. 3)(*math.*) seki [積].

production (*n.*) 1)seisan [生産]; seizô [製造]. 2)seisan-daka [生産高]. 3)sakuhin [作品]. 4)(*movie*) seisaku [制作]; purodakushon [プロダクション].

productive (*a.*) 1)seisan-teki-na [生産的な]. 2)tasaku-no [多作の]. 3)(...o)-hiki-okosu [(⋯を)引き起こす]. 4)rieki-o-motarasu [利益をもたらす].

profess (*vt.*) 1)...o kôgen-suru [⋯を公言する]. 2)...o yosoou [⋯を装う].

profession (*n.*) 1)shokugyô [職業]. 2)kôgen [公言].

professional (*a.*) shokugyô-no [職業の]; semmon-shoku-no [専門職の]; honshoku-no [本職の].
　　　　　(*n.*) 1)(chiteki-)shokugyô-jin [(知的)職業人]; semmon-ka [専門家]. 2)puro-senshu [プロ選手].

professor (*n.*) (daigaku no) kyôju [(大学の)教授].

proficient (*a.*) jukuren-shita [熟練した]; tannô-na [たん能な].

profile (*n.*) 1)yoko-gao [横顔]; sokumen [側面]; purofîru [プロフィー

ル]. 2)rinkaku [輪郭].

　　　(vt.) ...no rinkaku-o-egaku [···の輪郭を描く].

profit (n. & vi.) rieki(-o-eru) [利益(を得る)].

profitable (a.) môkaru [もうかる]; yûri-na [有利な]; tame-ni-naru [ためになる].

profound (a.) fukai [深い]; shin'en-na [深遠な]; nankai-na [難解な].

program (n.) bangumi [番組]; keikaku [計画]; puroguramu [プログラム].

　　　(vt.) ...no keikaku-o-tateru [···の計画を立てる]; ...no puroguramu-o-tsukuru [···のプログラムを作る].

programmer (n.) (rajio ya terebi no) bangumi-sakusei-sha [(ラジオやテレビの)番組作成者]; (computer) puroguramu-sakusei-sha [プログラム作製者]; puroguramâ [プログラマー].

progress (n. & vi.) shinkô(-suru) [進行(する)]; shimpo(-suru) [進歩(する)]; hattatsu(-suru) [発達(する)].

progressive (a.) shimpo-teki-na [進歩的な]; zenshin-suru [前進する]; zenshin-teki-na [漸進的な].

　　　(n.) shimpo-shugi-sha [進歩主義者].

prohibit (vt.) ...o kinjiru [···を禁じる]; ...ga...o samatageru [···が···を妨げる].

prohibition (n.) kinshi [禁止].

project (n.) keikaku [計画]; kikaku [企画].

　　　(vt.) 1)...o keikaku-suru [···を計画する]; ...o kôan-suru [···を考案する]. 2)...o eisha-suru [···を映写する].

　　　(vi.) tsuki-deru [突き出る].

proletarian (n. & a.) puroretaria(-no) [プロレタリア(の)]; musan-kaikyû-sha(-no) [無産階級者(の)].

prologue, -log (n.) 1)jomaku [序幕]. 2)(jiken no) hottan [(事件の)発端].

prolong (vt.) ...o enchô-suru [···を延長する].

promenade (n.) 1)yûho [遊歩]; sampo [散歩]. 2)((US)) (daigaku nado no) dansupâtî [(大学などの)ダンスパーティー].

　　　(vt.) ...o yûho[sampo]-suru [···を遊歩[散歩]する].

prominent (a.) 1)tsuki-deta [突き出た]. 2)kesshutsu-shita [傑出した].

promise (n.) 1)yakusoku [約束]. 2)mikomi [見込み]; yûbô [有望].

　　(1) He broke his **promise**. Kare-wa *yakusoku*-o yabutta.

　　(2) He is a lad of great **promise**.

　　　　Kare-wa hijô ni *yûbô*-na waka-mono da.

keep one's promise yakusoku-o mamoru
　　(*vt. & vi.*) 1)(...to) yakusoku-suru [(…と)約束する]. 2)(...suru-)mikomi-ga-aru [(…する)見込みがある].

promising (*a.*) mikomi-no-aru [見込みのある]; yûbô-na [有望な].

promote (*vt.*) 1)...o sokushin-suru […を促進する]; ...o shôrei-suru […を奨励する]. 2)...o shôshin-saseru […を昇進させる].

promoter (*n.*) 1)suishin-sha [推進者]; shôrei-sha [奨励者]. 2)kôgyô-sha [興行者].

promotion (*n.*) 1)sokushin [促進]; shôrei [奨励]. 2)shôshin [昇進]; shinkyû [進級]. 3)hokki [発起]; setsuritsu [設立].

prompt (*a.*) sokuza-no [即座の]; binsoku-na [敏速な].
　　(*vt.*) ...ni unagasu […に促す].
　　(*n.*) (*play*) serifu-tsuke [せりふ付け].
　　(*ad.*) chôdo [ちょうど]; kikkari [きっかり].

prompter (*n.*) (*play*) serifu-tsuke-yaku [せりふ付け役]; puromputâ [プロンプター].

pronoun (*n.*) (*gram.*) dai-meishi [代名詞].

pronounce (*vt.*) 1)...o hatsuon-suru […を発音する]. 2)...o senkoku-suru […を宣告する].
　　(*vi.*) 1)hatsuon-suru [発音する]. 2)hanketsu-o-kudasu [判決を下す].

pronounced (*a.*) meihaku-na [明白な]; ichijirushii [著しい]; kippari-shita [きっぱりした].

pronouncement (*n.*) 1)sengen [宣言]. 2)iken [意見].

pronunciation (*n.*) hatsuon [発音].

proof (*n.*) 1)shôko [証拠]; shômei [証明]. 2)taikyû-do [耐久度]. 3)kôsei-zuri [校正刷り].

read(revise) the proof kôsei-o-suru
　　(*a.*) (...ni-)taerareru [(…に)耐えられる].
　　(*vt.*) ...ni bôsui-kakô-o-hodokosu […に防水加工を施す].

propaganda (*n.*) senden [宣伝]; puropaganda [プロパガンダ].

propagate (*vt.*) 1)...o hanshoku-saseru […を繁殖させる]. 2)...o hiromeru […を広める].
　　(*vi.*) hanshoku-suru [繁殖する].

propel (*vt.*) ...o suishin-suru […を推進する]; ...o zenshin-saseru […を前進させる].

propeller (*n.*) puropera [プロペラ]; suishin-ki [推進機]; (fune no) sukuryû [(船の)スクリュー].

proper (*a.*) 1)tekitô-na [適当な]; tadashii [正しい]. 2)koyû-no [固有の].

properly (*ad.*) tekitô-ni [適当に]; tadashiku [正しく]; seitô-ni [正当に].

property (*n.*) 1)zaisan [財産]; shoyû-butsu [所有物]. 2)tokusei [特性]. 3)(*play; pl.*) ko-dôgu [小道具].

prophecy (*n.*) yogen [予言].

prophesy (*vt. & vi.*) (...o) yogen-suru [(…を)予言する].

prophet (*n.*) 1)yogen-sha [予言者]. 2)teishô-sha [提唱者].

proportion (*n.*) 1)wariai [割合]; hiritsu [比率]. 2)kinkô [均衡]. 3)bubun [部分]. 4)(*math.*) hirei [比例].
　in proportion to　...ni-hirei-shite

proposal (*n.*) môshi-komi [申し込み]; teian [提案]; teigi [提議].

propose (*vt.*) 1)...o môshi-komu […を申し込む]; ...o teian-suru […を提案する]. 2)...o kuwadateru […を企てる].
　　　(*vi.*) 1)teian-suru [提案する]. 2)kekkon-o-môshi-komu [結婚を申し込む].

proposition (*n.*) 1)teian [提案]; hatsugi [発議]. 2)(*log.*) meidai [命題].

proprietor (*n.*) shoyû-sha [所有者].

propriety (*n.*) 1)tekitô [適当]; datô [妥当]. 2)reigi-tadashisa [礼儀正しさ].

prose (*n.*) 1)sambun [散文]. 2)tanchô [単調]; heibon [平凡].

prosecute (*vt.*) 1)...o suikô-suru […を遂行する]. 2)...o kiso-suru [(…を)起訴する].

prosecution (*n.*) suikô [遂行]; (*law*) kiso [起訴]; (the -) kensatsu-gawa [検察側].

prosecutor (*n.*) 1)suikô-sha [遂行者]. 2)kensatsu-kan [検察官].

prospect (*n.*) 1)mi-harashi [見晴らし]; nagame [眺め]. 2)mikomi [見込み]; yosô [予想].

prospective (*a.*) mikomi-no-aru [見込みのある]; shôrai-no [将来の].

prosper (*vi.*) han'ei-suru [繁栄する].

prosperity (*n.*) han'ei [繁栄]; kôun [幸運].

prosperous (*a.*) han'ei-shite-iru [繁栄している].

protect (*vt.*) ...o mamoru […を守る]; ...o hogo-suru […を保護する]; ...o fusegu […を防ぐ].

protection (*n.*) hogo [保護]; hogo-suru-mono[-hito] [保護するもの[人]].

protector (*n.*) 1)hogo-sha [保護者]. 2)hogo-sôchi [保護装置]. 3) (*baseball*) purotekutâ [プロテクター].

protein (*n.*) tampaku-shitsu [たん白質].

protest (*vt.*) 1)...o shuchô-suru [···を主張する]. 2)((*US*)) ...ni kôgi-suru [···に抗議する].

　　(*vi.*) kôgi-suru [抗議する]; igi-o-tonaeru [異議を唱える].

　　(*n.*) kôgi [抗議].

Protestant (*n. & a.*) Shinkyô-to(-no) [新教徒(の)].

prototype (*n.*) genkei [原型]; mohan [模範].

proud (*a.*) 1)hokori-o-motte-iru [誇りをもっている]; tokui-na [得意な]. 2)kôman-na [高慢な]. 3)dôdô-to-shita [堂々とした]; migoto-na [見事な].

　be proud of ...o jiman-shite-iru

proudly (*ad.*) hokorashige-ni [誇らしげに]; kôman-ni [高慢に].

prove (*vt.*) 1)...o risshô-suru [···を立証する]; ...o shômei-suru [···を証明する]. 2)...o tamesu [···をためす].

　(*1*) He **proved** himself honest.

　　　Kare-wa jibun ga shôjiki-de-aru-koto-*o risshô-shita.*

　　The fact **proves** her honesty.

　　　Sono jijitsu ga kano-jo-no shôjiki-sa-*o shômei-shite-iru.*

　　(*vi.*) (...de-aru-koto-ga) wakaru [(···であることが)分かる]; hammei-suru [判明する].

　　The book **proved** very interesting.

　　　Sono hon wa totemo omoshiroi-koto-ga *wakatta.*

proverb (*n.*) 1)kotowaza [ことわざ]. 2)hanashi-no-tane [話の種].

provide (*vt.*) 1)...o yôi-suru [···を用意する]. 2)...o kyôkyû-suru [···を供給する].

　(*1*) They **provided** a car for me.

　　　Kare-ra-wa watashi-ni kuruma-*o* ichi-dai *yôi-shita.*

　　(*vi.*) 1)sonaeru [備える]. 2)hitsuyô-na-mono-o-ataeru [必要なものを与える].

　(*1*) You must **provide** against disasters.

　　　Saigai-ni *sonae-*nakereba-naranai.

　(*2*) Parents must **provide** for their children.

　　　Oya wa ko-ni *hitsuyô-na-mono-o-atae-*nakereba-naranai.

providence (*n.*) setsuri [摂理].

providing (*conj.*) moshi...naraba [もし···ならば].

province (*n.*) 1)shû [州]; kuni [国]. 2)(the -s) chihô [地方]. 3)

　ryôiki [領域].

provision (*n.*) 1)yôi [用意]. 2)(*law*) kitei [規定]. 3)(*pl.*) shokuryô [食糧].

　　(*vt.*) ...ni shokuryô-o-kyôkyû-suru [...に食糧を供給する].

provisional (*a.*) kari-no [仮の]; rinji-no [臨時の].

provoke (*vt.*) 1)...o okoraseru [...を怒らせる]. 2)...o hiki-okosu [...を引き起こす]. 3)...o shigeki-shite...(sa-)seru [...を刺激して...(さ)せる].

prow (*n.*) senshu [船首]; hesaki [へさき].

prowl (*vt. & vi.*) (...o) urotsuku [(...を)うろつく].

　　(*n.*) (*colloq.*) urotsuki-mawaru-koto [うろつき回ること].

prudent (*a.*) yôjin-bukai [用心深い]; shinchô-na [慎重な].

pry (*vi.*) nozoki-komu [のぞき込む]; sensaku-suru [せんさくする].

psalm (*n.*) sambi-ka [賛美歌].

pshaw (*int.*) Che! [ちぇっ!]; Baka-na! [ばかな!].

psychology (*n.*) shinri-gaku [心理学]; shinri[-jôtai] [心理(状態)].

public (*a.*) 1)ooyake-no [公の]; kôshû-no [公衆の]. 2)dare-demo-shitte-iru [だれでも知っている].

　　(*n.*) (the -) ippan-no-hito-bito [一般の人々].

publication (*n.*) 1)happyô [発表]. 2)shuppan[-butsu] [出版(物)].

public corporation ((*Eng.*)) kôkyô-kigyô-tai [公共企業体]; kôsha [公社].

publicly (*ad.*) kôzen-to [公然と]; kôteki-ni [公的に]; seron-de [世論で].

public opinion (**poll**) seron(-chôsa) [世論(調査)].

public relations kôhô-katsudô [広報活動]; pîaru [ピーアール] = P.R.

public utility kôeki-jigyô [公益事業].

publish (*vt.*) ...o happyô-suru [...を発表する]; ...o shuppan-suru [...を出版する].

publisher (*n.*) shuppan-gyô-sha [出版業者].

puddle (*n.*) mizu-tamari [水たまり].

　　(*vt.*) 1)(mizu)-o nigosu [(水)を濁す]. 2)...o kone-tsuchi-ni-suru [...をこね土にする].

puff (*vi.*) 1)putto-fuku [ぷっと吹く]; poppotto-dasu [ぽっぽっと出す]. 2)(*colloq.*) putto-fukureru [ぷっとふくれる].

　(*1*) The train **puffed** out of the station.
　　　Kisha wa *poppotto-kemuri-o-haite* eki-o dete-itta.

　(*2*) The blistered skin **puffed**.
　　　Hifu ni mizu-bukure-ga *putto-dekita*.

    (*vt.*) ...o putto-fuku [...をぷっと吹く]; ...o putto-fukuramaseru [...をぷっとふくらませる].

    (*n.*) 1)hito-fuki [一吹き]. 2)putto-fuku-oto [ぷっと吹く音].

pull (*vt. & vi.*) 1)(...o) hiku [(...を)引く]; (...o) hipparu [(...を)引っ張る]. 2)(...o) kogu [(...を)こぐ].

    (*1*) She **pulled** down the blind. Kano-jo-wa buraindo-o *oroshita*.

    He **pulled** at the rope. Kare-wa rôpu-o *hippatta*.

    (*2*) They **pulled** against wind and wave.

        Kare-ra-wa kaze-ya-nami-ni-sakaratte *koida*.

    pull out 1)hassha-suru; (fune ga minato o)deru. 2)te-o-hiku

    1) A ship pulled out of the harbor.

        Fune-ga isseki minato-kara dete-itta.

    pull up 1)...o hiki-nuku. 2)...o tomeru (tomaru)

    1) Pull up all the weeds in the lawn.

        Shiba-fu-no-naka-no-zassô-o nokorazu hiki-nuke.

    2) Pull up the car over there, please.

        Kuruma-o asoko-de tomete-kudasai.

    (*n.*) 1)hiku-koto [引くこと]. 2)doryoku [努力]. 3)(*colloq.*) kone [コネ].

pullover (*n.*) puruôbâ [プルオーバー].

pulp (*n.*) 1)kaniku [果肉]. 2)parupu [パルプ].

    (*vt.*) ...kara kaniku-o-tori-dasu [...から果肉を取り出す]; ...o parupu-jô-ni-suru [...をパルプ状にする].

    (*vi.*) parupu-jô-ni-naru [パルプ状になる].

pulse (*n.*) myakuhaku [脈はく]; hyôshi [拍子].

    (*vi.*) myaku-utsu [脈打つ].

pump (*n.*) pompu [ポンプ].

    (*vt.*) ...o pompu-de-kumi-ageru [...をポンプでくみ上げる].

pumpkin (*n.*) (*bot.*) kabocha [カボチャ].

punch (*n.*) panchi [パンチ].

    (*vt.*) ...ni panchi-o-kurawasu [...にパンチをくらわす]; ...o tataku [...をたたく].

punch (*n.*) ana-ake-ki [穴あけ器]; panchi [パンチ].

    (*vt.*) ...ni ana-o-akeru [...に穴をあける].

puncher (*n.*) panchâ [パンチャー]; kî-panchâ [キーパンチャー].

punctual (*a.*) jikan-o-genshu-suru [時間を厳守する].

punctuation (*n.*) kutô-ten [句読点]; kutô-hô [句読法].

puncture (*n.*) 1)ana-o-akeru-koto [穴をあけること]. 2)(taiya no) panku [(タイヤの)パンク].

    (vt. & vi.) ...o panku-saseru (panku-suru) […をパンクさせる(パンクする)]; ...ni ana-o-akeru (ana-ga-aku) […に穴をあける(穴があく)].

punish (vt.) ...o bassuru […を罰する]; ...o korashimeru […をこらしめる].

punishment (n.) batsu [罰]; shobatsu [処罰].

pupa (n.) (insect) sanagi [さなぎ].

pupil (n.) seito [生徒]; deshi [弟子].

pupil (n.) (anat.) hitomi [ひとみ].

puppet (n.) ayatsuri-ningyô [操り人形]; kairai [かいらい].

    (a.) ayatsuri-ningyô-no [操り人形の]; ayatsurareru [操られる].

puppet government kairai-seifu [かいらい政府].

puppy (n.) ko-inu [小犬].

purchase (vt.) 1)...o kau […を買う]. 2)...o kakutoku-suru […を獲得する].

    (n.) 1)kai-ire [買い入れ]; kônyû [購入]. 2)kônyû-hin [購入品]. 3)te-gakari [手がかり]; sasae [支え].

purchaser (n.) kai-te [買い手]; kôbai-sha [購買者].

purchasing power kôbai-ryoku [購買力].

pure (a.) 1)junsui-na [純粋な]; junketsu-na [純潔な]. 2)(colloq.) mattaku-no [全くの].

purely (ad.) 1)junsui-ni [純粋に]. 2)mattaku [全く]; tan-ni [単に].

purgative (a.) bentsû-o-tsukeru [便通をつける].

    (n.) (med.) gezai [下剤].

purge (vt.) 1)...o kiyomeru […を清める]. 2)...o tsuihô-suru […を追放する]; ...o shukusei-suru […を粛正する].

purify (vt. & vi.) (...o) jôka-suru [(…を)浄化する]; (...o) kiyomeru [(…を)清める].

Puritan (n.) Seikyô-to [清教徒]; Pyûritan [ピューリタン].

purity (n.) junsui [純粋]; junketsu [純潔].

purple (n. & a.) murasaki-iro(-no) [紫色(の)].

purport (n.) shushi [趣旨]; imi [意味].

    (vt.) ...o imi-suru […を意味する]; (...de-aru)-to shôsuru [(…である)と称する].

purpose (n.) 1)mokuteki [目的]. 2)ketsui [決意]. 3)kôka [効果].

  for the purpose of...ing ...(suru)-tame-ni

  on(of) purpose waza-to; kotosara; koi-ni

to no(little) purpose mattaku(hotondo)-yaku-ni-tata-nai

to the purpose yôryô-o-ete; tekisetsu-ni

　　　(*vt.*) ...o kuwadateru [...を企てる].

purposely (*ad.*) koi-ni [故意に]; waza-to [わざと].

purr (*vi. & n.*) (neko ga) nodo-o-narasu(-oto) [(ネコが)のどを鳴らす(音)].

purse (*n.*) 1)saifu [財布]; ((*US*)) handobaggu [ハンドバッグ]. 2)kinsen [金銭]. 3)kenshô-kin [懸賞金].

purser (*n.*) (fune ya hikô-ki no) jimu-chô [(船や飛行機の)事務長]; pâsâ [パーサー].

pursue (*vt.*) 1)...o ou [...を追う]; ...o tsuiseki-suru [...を追跡する]. 2)...ni jûji-suru [...に従事する]. 3)...o tsuzukeru [...を続ける].

　　　(*vi.*) ou [追う]; tsuiseki-suru [追跡する]; tsuzukeru [続ける].

pursuit (*n.*) 1)tsuiseki [追跡]. 2)tsuikyû [追求]. 3)jûji [従事]. 4)kenkyû [研究]; shokugyô [職業].

in pursuit of ...o-motomete; ...o-tsuikyû-shite

push (*vt.*) 1)...o osu [...を押す]. 2)...o oshi-susumeru [...を押し進める]. 3)...o kyôyô-suru [...を強要する].

　(*1*) Don't **push** me so hard.

　　　Sonna-ni hidoku watashi-*o* osa-nai-de-kudasai.

　(*2*) **Push** your plan. Kimi-no keikaku-*o* oshi-susume-nasai.

　(*3*) He **pushed** unwanted goods on me.

　　　Kare-wa watashi-ni fuyô-hin-*o* oshi-tsuketa.

　　　(*vi.*) osu [押す]; oshi-susumu [押し進む].

push away ...o oshi-nokeru

push back ...o oshi-kaesu

　　　(*n.*) 1)osu-koto [押すこと]; oshi [押し]. 2)fumpatsu [奮発]; (*colloq.*) gambari [頑張り].

　(*1*) He gave a **push** at the door. Kare-wa to-o hito-*oshi*-shita.

pussy (*n.*) neko [ネコ].

put (*vt.*) 1)...o oku [...を置く]. 2)...o (sa-)seru [...を(さ)せる]. 3)...suru [...する]. 4)...o ireru [...を入れる]. 5)...o hon'yaku-suru [...を翻訳する]; ...o yakusu [...を訳す].

　(*1*) **Put** a vase on the table. Kabin-*o* têburu-no-ue-ni oki-nasai.

　(*2*) The mother **put** her child to bed.

　　　Sono haha-oya wa kodomo-*o* nekashi-*tsuketa*.

　(*3*) The teacher **put** some questions to him.

　　　Sensei wa kare-ni ni-san-no shitsumon-*o* shita.

(4) She **put** two spoonfuls of sugar in her coffee.
　　Kano-jo-wa kôhî-ni satô-o futa-saji *ireta*.
(5) **Put** it into English.　Sore-o Eigo-ni *yakushi*-nasai.
　　(*vi.*) (fune nado ga) susumu [(船などが)進む].
put away 1)...o katazukeru. 2)...o takuwaeru
　1) Put the books away in the bookcase.
　　　Hon-o hom-bako-ni katazuke-nasai.
　2) You have to put money away for your old age.
　　　Rôgo-ni-sonaete anata-wa kane-o takuwae-neba-naranai.
put back ...o moto-no-tokoro-e-modosu
put down 1)...o shita-ni-oku. 2)...o kaki-tomeru
　1) Put the case down on the floor.　Hako-o yuka-ni oki-nasai.
　2) I put my ideas down in the notebook.
　　　Watashi-wa watashi-no kangae-o nôto-ni kaki-tometa.
put forth (me ya chikara ya hon)-o dasu
put in ...o ireru
put off ...o nobasu (= postpone)
put on ...o kiru
put out 1)...o kesu. 2)...o[-sashi-]dasu
　1) Put out the light.　Hi-o kese.
　2) put out one's hand　te-o sashi-dasu
put together 1)...o kumi-tateru. 2)...o matomeru
　1) The parts of bicycle have come apart, so I put them together
　　　with Tom.
　　　Jitensha no buhin ga bara-bara-ni-natta-node, watashi-wa
　　　　Tomu-to sore-ra-o kumi-tateta.
　2) put together one's thoughts　kangae-o matomeru
put up at ...ni tomaru
put up with ...o gaman-suru
puzzle (*n.*) 1)nammon [難問]; pazuru [パズル]. 2)tôwaku [当惑].
　　(*vt.*) ...o tôwaku-saseru [...を当惑させる]; ...o nayamaseru [...
を悩ませる].
　　(*vi.*) atama-o-nayamasu [頭を悩ます].
puzzling (*a.*) tôwaku-saseru [当惑させる]; wake-no-wakara-nai [訳の
分からない].
pyramid (*n.*) 1)kinji-tô [金字塔]; piramiddo [ピラミッド]. 2)(*geom.*)
kakusui [角すい].

Q

quack (*vi. & n.*) (ahiru ga) gâgâ-naku(-koe) [(アヒルが)がーがー鳴く(声)].

quack (*n.*) nise-isha [にせ医者]; ikasama-shi [いかさま師].

quadrangle (*n.*) 1)shihen-kei [四辺形]. 2)naka-niwa [中庭].

quadruple (*n. & a.*) yom-bai(-no) [四倍(の)].
　　　　(*vt. & vi.*) ...o yom-bai-ni-suru (yom-bai-ni-naru) [...を四倍にする(四倍になる)].

quadruplicate (*a.*) yom-bai-no [四倍の]; yon-jû-no [四重の]; yon-tsû-sakusei-shita [四通作成した].
　　　　(*n.*) yon-tsû-no-hitotsu [四通の一つ].
　　　　(*vt.*) ...o yom-bai-ni-suru [...を四倍にする]; ...o-yon-jû-ni-suru [...を四重にする]; ...o-yon-tsû-sakusei-suru [...を四通作成する].

quail (*n.*) (*birds*) uzura [ウズラ].

quaint (*a.*) iyô-na [異様な]; fû-gawari-de-omoshiroi [風変わりで面白い].

quake (*vi.*) shindô-suru [震動する]; yureru [揺れる].
　　　　(*n.*) (*colloq.*) jishin [地震].

Quaker (*n.*) Kueikâ-kyô-to [クエイカー教徒].

qualification (*n.*) 1)shikaku [資格]. 2)seigen [制限].

qualify (*vt.*) 1)...no shikaku-o-ataeru [...の資格を与える]. 2)...o seigen-suru [...を制限する]. 3)...o mi-nasu [...を見なす]. 4)(*gram.*)

…o shûshoku-suru [⋯を修飾する].

(1) She **is qualified** as a nurse.

　　Kano-jo-wa kango-fu-no-*shikaku-ga-aru*.

(2) The sense of the word **is qualified**.

　　Sono go no imi wa *gentei-sareru*.

(3) I **qualify** her attitude as a rude.

　　Watashi-wa kano-jo-no taido-o burei-da-to *minasu*.

　　(*vi.*) 1)shikaku-o-eru [資格を得る]. 2)(*sports*) yosen-o-tsûka-suru [予選を通過する].

quality (*n.*) 1)hinshitsu [品質]. 2)honshitsu [本質]; tokusei [特性].

quality control hinshitsu-kanri [品質管理].

quantity (*n.*) 1)ryô [量]. 2)taryô [多量].

(1) A large **quantity** of oil is imported.

　　Ta*ryô*-no sekiyu ga yunyû-sareru.

(2) These artificial flowers are made in **quantity**.

　　Kore-ra-no zôka wa *tairyô*-ni tsukurareru.

quarantine (*n.*) kakuri[-sho] [隔離(所)]; ken'eki-sho [検疫所].

　　(*vt.*) …o kakuri-suru [⋯を隔離する]; …o ken'eki-suru [⋯を検疫する].

quarrel (*n. & vi.*) kenka(-suru) [けんか(する)]; kôron(-suru) [口論(する)]; kujô(-o-iu) [苦情(を言う)].

quarrelsome (*a.*) kenka-zuki-na [けんか好きな].

quarry (*n.*) ishikiri-ba [石切り場].

　　(*vt.*) 1)(ishi)-o kiri-dasu [(石)を切り出す]. 2)…o kushin-shite-sagashi-motomeru [⋯を苦心して探し求める].

quarter (*n.*) 1)shibun-no-ichi : yombun-no-ichi [四分の一]. 2)jû-go-fun [十五分]. 3)chiku [地区]. 4)hômen [方面]. 5)(*pl.*) shukusho [宿所].

　　(*vt.*) 1) …o yon-tôbun-suru [⋯を四等分する]. 2) …o shukuhaku-saseru [⋯を宿泊させる].

quarterdeck (*n.*) 1)(*marine*) (the -) kô-kampan [後甲板]. 2)kôkyû-sen'in [高級船員].

quartermaster (*n.*) 1)(*marine*) sôda-shu [操舵手]. 2)(*mil.*) hokyû-gakari-shôkô [補給係将校].

quartet(te) (*n.*) 1)(*mus.*) shijû-sô[-dan] [四重奏(団)]; karutetto [カルテット]. 2)yotsu-zoroi [四つぞろい].

quartz (*n.*) (*min.*) sekiei [石英]; kwôtsu [クォーツ].

quay (*n.*) hato-ba [波止場]; futô [ふ頭].

queen (*n.*) joô [女王]; ôhi [王妃].

queer (*a.*) kimyô-na [奇妙な]; hen-na [変な].
　(*vt.*) 1)...o buchi-kowasu [...をぶち壊す]. 2)...o nayamasu [...を悩ます].

quench (*vt.*) 1)(kawaki)-o iyasu [(かわき)をいやす]. 2)(hi)-o kesu [(火)を消す]. 3)(yokubô)-o osaeru [(欲望)を抑える].

quest (*n.*) tansaku [探索]; tankyû [探求].
　in quest of ...o-sagashi-motomete
　　(*vi.*) sagashi-motomeru [探し求める].

question (*n.*) 1)shitsumon [質問]. 2)utagai [疑い]; gimon [疑問]. 3)mondai [問題].
　beyond question utagai-mo-naku
　in question mondai-no; ronsô-chû-no
　out of the question mattaku-fu-kanô-de
　　(*vt.*) 1)...ni shitsumon-suru [...に質問する]. 2)...o utagau [...を疑う].
　　(*vi.*) shitsumon-suru [質問する].

queue (*vi.*) retsu-o-tsukuru [列を作る]; narande-jumban-o-matsu [並んで順番を待つ].
　　(*n.*) retsu [列].

quick (*a.*) 1)hayai [速い]; binsoku-na [敏速な]. 2)tanki-na [短気な].
　　(*ad.*) hayaku [速く].

quicken (*vt. & vi.*) ...o hayameru (hayaku-naru) [...を速める(速くなる)].

quickly (*ad.*) hayaku [速く]; sugu-ni [すぐに].

quick-witted (*a.*) kiten-no-kiku [機転のきく].

quiet (*a.*) shizuka-na [静かな]; odayaka-na [穏やかな]; ochitsuita [落ち着いた].
　Be(Keep) quiet! Shizuka-ni!
　　(*n.*) shizukesa [静けさ]; heion [平穏].
　　(*vt.*) ...o shizumeru [...を静める]; ...o yawarageru [...を和らげる]; ...o nadameru [...をなだめる].
　　(*vi.*) shizumaru [静まる].

quietly (*ad.*) shizuka-ni [静かに]; odayaka-ni [穏やかに]; jimi-ni [地味に].

quilt (*n.*) kiruto [キルト]; kirutingu-no-shite-aru-kake-buton [キルティングのしてある掛け布団].
　　(*vt.*) ...o kirutingu-ni-suru [...をキルティングにする].

quilting (*n.*) kirutingu［キルティング］; kirutingu-no-zairyô［キルティングの材料］.

quinine (*n.*) kinîne［キニーネ］.

quintet(te) (*n.*) 1)(*mus.*) gojû-sô[-dan]［五重奏(団)］; kuintetto［クインテット］. 2)itsutsu-zoroi［五つぞろい］.

quit (*vt. & vi.*) (...o) yameru［(…を)やめる］.
　　(*a.*) (...o)-manukarete［(…を)免れて］; (...kara)-jiyû-ni-natte［(…から)自由になって］.

quite (*ad.*) 1)mattaku［全く］. 2)kanari［かなり］; (*colloq.*) sono-toori［そのとおり］.

quiver (*vi.*) furueru［震える］; yureru［揺れる］.
　　(*vt.*) ...o furuwaseru［…を震わせる］.
　　(*n.*) furue［震え］.

quiz (*n.*) shitsumon［質問］; kantan-na-tesuto［簡単なテスト］; kuizu［クイズ］.
　　(*vt.*) ...ni shitsumon-suru［…に質問する］; ...ni kantan-na-tesuto-o-suru［…に簡単なテストをする］.

quizmaster (*n.*) kuizu-no-shikai-sha［クイズの司会者］.

quiz show (rajio ya terebi no) kuizu-bangumi［(ラジオやテレビの)クイズ番組］.

quoits (*n.*) wa-nage［輪投げ］.

quotation (*n.*) 1)in'yô［引用］; in'yô-ku［引用句］; in'yô-bun［引用文］. 2)(*com.*) sôba［相場］; mitsumori-gaku［見積もり額］.

quote (*vt.*) 1)...o in'yô-suru［…を引用する］. 2)...o shimesu［…を示す］. 3)(ne)-o tsukeru［(値)をつける］.
　　(*vi.*) in'yô-suru［引用する］.
　　(*n.*) (*colloq.*) in'yô-bun［引用文］.

R

rabbit (*n.*) (kai-)usagi [(飼い)ウサギ].
    (*vi.*) usagi-o-karu [ウサギを狩る].
race (*n.*) 1)kyôsô [競走]. 2)(the *pl.*) keiba [競馬].
    (*vi. & vt.*) (...to) kyôsô-suru [(…と)競走する].
race (*n.*) 1)jinshu [人種]; minzoku [民族]. 2)(*biol.*) rui [類];
    shuzoku [種族].
racial (*a.*) jinshu-no [人種の]; shuzoku-no [種族の].
racing (*n. & a.*) keiba(-no) [競馬(の)]; kyôsô(-no) [競走(の)].
rack (*n.*) 1)tana [棚]. 2)...kake […掛け].
    (*vt.*) 1)...o shibori-toru […をしぼり取る]. 2)...o kurushimeru […
    を苦しめる].
racket (*n.*) 1)oo-sawagi [大騒ぎ]. 2)(*colloq.*) fusei-na-kane-môke
    [不正な金もうけ].
    (*vi.*) asobi-mawaru [遊び回る].
radar (*n.*) dempa-tanchi-ki [電波探知機]; rêdâ [レーダー].
radial (*a.*) 1)kôsen-no [光線の]. 2)hôsha-jô-no [放射状の].
    (*n.*) 1)hôsha-bu [放射部]. 2)rajiaru-taiya [ラジアルタイヤ].
radiant (*a.*) 1)hikari-o-hassuru [光を発する]; kagayaku [輝く];
    mabayui [まばゆい]. 2)hareyaka-na [晴れやかな]. 3)(*phys.*) hôsha-
    no [放射の].
radiant heat hôsha-netsu [放射熱].

radiate (*vi. & vt.*) (...o) hôsha-suru [(…を)放射する].

radiator (*n.*) dambô-ki [暖房器]; rajiêtâ [ラジエーター].

radical (*a.*) 1)kompon-teki-na [根本的な]. 2)kyûshin-teki-na [急進的な].
   (*n.*) 1)kyûshin-ron-sha [急進論者]. 2)(*math.*) kon [根].

radish (*n.*) (*bot.*) hatsuka-daikon [ハツカダイコン]; radisshu [ラディッシュ].

radium (*n.*) rajiumu [ラジウム].

radius (*n.*) hankei [半径]; (katsudô nado no) han'i [(活動などの)範囲].

raffle (*n.*) tomi-kuji[-hambai] [富くじ(販売)].
   (*vt.*) ...o tomi-kuji-hambai-hô-de-uru […を富くじ販売法で売る].

raft (*n.*) ikada [いかだ].
   (*vt.*) ...o ikada-de-hakobu […をいかだで運ぶ].
   (*vi.*) ikada-o-tsukau [いかだを使う].

rag (*n.*) boro[-gire] [ぼろ(ぎれ)]; kire-hashi [切れ端].
   in rags boro-o-kite; boro-boro-de

rage (*n.*) 1)gekido [激怒]; môi [猛威]. 2)netsubô [熱望].
   in a rage hara-o-tatete
   (*vi.*) 1)gekido-suru [激怒する]. 2)abareru [暴れる]; areru [荒れる]; môi-o-furuu [猛威をふるう].

ragged (*a.*) 1)boro-boro-no [ぼろぼろの]; boro-o-kita [ぼろを着た]. 2)giza-giza-no [ぎざぎざの]. 3)teire-o-shite-i-nai [手入れをしていない].

raid (*n.*) 1)shûgeki [襲撃]. 2)teire [手入れ].
   (*vt. & vi.*) (...o) shûgeki-suru [(…を)襲撃する]; (...o) teire-suru [(…を)手入れする].

rail (*n.*) 1)tesuri [手すり]. 2)(*pl.*) rêru [レール]. 3)tetsudô [鉄道].
   by rail tetsudô-de
   (*vt.*) 1)...o saku-de-kakomu […をさくで囲む]. 2)...o tetsudô-de-yusô-suru […を鉄道で輸送する].
   (*vi.*) tetsudô-de-ryokô-suru [鉄道で旅行する].

railroad (*n.*) ((*US*)) tetsudô [鉄道].
   (*vt.*) 1)((*US*)) ...o tetsudô-yusô-suru […を鉄道輸送する]. 2)(hôan nado)-o gôin-ni-tsûka-saseru [(法案など)を強引に通過させる].

railway (*n.*) ((*Eng.*)) tetsudô [鉄道].

rain (*n.*) ame [雨]; ame-furi [雨降り].
   (*vi.*) ame-ga-furu [雨が降る].
   (*vt.*) ...o ame-no-yô-ni-furaseru […を雨のように降らせる].

rainbow (*n.*) niji [にじ].

raindrop (*n.*) ama-dare [雨垂れ].

rainy (*a.*) ame-furi-no [雨降りの]; ame-no-ooi [雨の多い]; ame-moyô-no [雨模様の]; ame-ni-nureta [雨にぬれた].

raise (*vt.*) 1)...o ageru […を上げる]; ...o okosu […を起こす]. 2)...o sodateru […を育てる]; ...o kau […を飼う]; ...o tsukuru […を作る]; ...o yashinau […を養う]. 3)(kane)-o chôtatsu-suru [(かね)を調達する]; ...o kumen-suru […を工面する]. 4)(kakomi)-o toku [(囲み)をとく].

   (*1*) He **raised** his right hand. Kare-wa migi-te-o *ageta*.
      He **raised** himself. Kare-wa mi-o *okoshita*.
   (*2*) He **raises** sheep. Kare-wa hitsuji-o *katte-iru*.
   (*3*) Can you **raise** the necessary fund?
      Kimi-wa hitsuyô-na shikin-o *chôtatsu*-dekiru-ka?
   (*4*) They **raised** the siege. Kare-ra-wa kakomi-o *toita*.
   (*n.*) ((*US*)) shôkyû[-gaku] [昇給(額)].

raisin (*n.*) hoshi-budô [干しブドウ].

rake (*n.*) kuma-de [くま手].
   (*vt.*) 1)...o(-kuma-de-de) kaki-atsumeru […を(くま手で)かき集める]. 2)...o kijû-sôsha-suru […を機銃掃射する]. 3)...o mi-watasu […を見渡す].
   (*vi.*) 1)kuma-de-o-tsukau [くま手を使う]. 2)(...o) kuma-naku-sagasu [(…を)くまなく探す].
  rake in (*colloq.*) ...o oo-môke-suru

rally (*n.*) 1)futatabi-atsumaru-koto [再び集まること]; shûkai [集会]. 2)kaifuku [回復]. 3)(*com.*) hampatsu [反発]. 4)(*sports*) rarî [ラリー].
   (*vt.*) 1)...o futatabi-atsumeru […を再び集める]. 2)...o mori-kaesu […を盛り返す].
   (*vi.*) 1)futatabi-atsumaru [再び集まる]. 2)kaifuku-suru [回復する]. 3)(*com.*) mochi-naosu [持ち直す]. 4)rarî-o-suru [ラリーをする].

ram (*n.*) o-hitsuji [雄羊].
   (*vt.*) 1)...ni shôtotsu-suru […に衝突する]. 2)...o uchi-komu […を打ち込む]. 3)...o tsume-komu […を詰め込む].

ramble (*vi. & n.*) buratsuku (buratsuki) [ぶらつく(ぶらつき)].

ramp (*n.*) keisha-ro [傾斜路]; surôpu [スロープ]; tarappu [タラップ].
   (*vt. & vi.*) ...o keisha-saseru (keisha-suru) […を傾斜させる(傾斜する)].

rampart (*n.*) 1)(*pl.*) jôheki [城壁]. 2)shubi [守備].

ranch (*n. & vi.*) bokujô(-de-hataraku) [牧場(で働く)].

random (*a.*) 1)te-atari-shidai-no [手当たりしだいの]; detarame-no [でたらめの]. 2)(*statistics*) mu-sakui-no [無作為の].
  at random te-atari-shidai-ni

range (*vt.*) 1)...o naraberu [···を並べる]. 2)...o aruki-mawaru [···を歩き回る].
  (*vi.*) 1)narabu [並ぶ]; ichi-retsu-ni-nobiru [一列に伸びる]. 2)(...e) oyonde-iru [(···へ)及んでいる]. 3)bumpu-suru [分布する].
  (*a.*) hôboku-yô-no [放牧用の].
  (*n.*) 1)renzan [連山]; sammyaku [山脈]. 2)han'i [範囲]; kuiki [区域].

ranger (*n.*) ((*US*)) shinrin-keibi-tai [森林警備隊]; kiba-keisatsu-tai-in [騎馬警察隊員]; renjâ [レンジャー].

rank (*n.*) 1)retsu [列]. 2)tôkyû [等級]; kaikyû [階級].
  (*vt.*) 1)...o naraberu [···を並べる]. 2)...o ichi-zukeru [···を位置づける].
  (*vi.*) ichi-suru [位置する].

rank (*a.*) 1)habikotta [はびこった]. 2)mattaku-no [全くの]. 3)akushû-no [悪臭の].

ransom (*n.*) baishô-kin [賠償金]; minoshiro-kin [身の代金].
  (*vt.*) 1)...o mi-uke-suru [···を身請けする]; ...ni minoshiro-kin-o-yôkyû-suru [···に身の代金を要求する]. 2)...no tsumi-o-aganau [···の罪をあがなう].

rap (*vi. & n.*) kotsun-to-tataku(-koto) [こつんとたたく(こと)]; ton-ton-tataku(-oto) [とんとんたたく(音)].

rapid (*a.*) hayai [速い]; kyû-na [急な]; binsoku-na [敏速な].
  (*n.*) 1)(*pl.*) kyûryû [急流]. 2)kôsoku-yusô-shisutemu [高速輸送システム].

rapidly (*ad.*) subayaku [すばやく]; jinsoku-ni [迅速に].

rapture (*n.*) (*pl.*) uchôten [有頂天]; oo-yorokobi [大喜び].
  be in(go into) raptures ...(de) uchôten-ni-naru

rare (*a.*) 1)mare-na [まれな]; mezurashii [珍しい]; usui [薄い]. 2)(*colloq.*) subarashii [すばらしい].

rare (*a.*) ((*US*)) nama-yake-no [なま焼けの]; reâ-no [レアーの].

rarely (*ad.*) mare-ni [まれに]; metta-ni...(shi-)nai [めったに···(し)ない].

rascal (*n.*) akkan [悪漢].

rash (*a.*) mukô-mizu-na [向こう見ずな]; keisotsu-na [軽率な].

rash (*n.*) 1)(*med.*) hosshin [発しん]. 2)tahatsu [多発].

rashly (*ad.*) keisotsu-ni [軽率に]; mu-fumbetsu-ni [無分別に].

rasp (*n.*) 1)ara-yasuri [荒やすり]. 2)iradachi [いらだち].

    (*vt.*) ...ni ara-yasuri-o-kakeru [...に荒やすりをかける]; ...o ira-ira-saseru [...をいらいらさせる].

    (*vi.*) gishi-gishi-oto-o-tateru [ギシギシ音を立てる]; kishiru [きしる].

rat (*n.*) nezumi [ネズミ].

    (*vi.*) 1)nezumi-tori-o-suru [ネズミ取りをする]. 2)(*colloq.*) uragiru [裏切る].

rate (*n.*) 1)wariai [割合]; ritsu [率]. 2)sokudo [速度]. 3)nedan [値段]; ryôkin [料金].

  at any rate tonikaku; sukunaku-tomo

  at the(a) rate of ...no-wariai-de

    (*vt.*) 1)...o hyôka-suru [...を評価する]. 2)...o(...to) kangaeru [...を(...と)考える]. 3)(*US colloq.*) ...ni atai-suru [...に値する].

    (*vi.*) (...to-)mi-nasareru [(...と)見なされる].

rather (*ad.*) 1)mushiro [むしろ]; isso [いっそ]. 2)ikubun [いくぶん]; sukoshi [少し].

  (*1*) It is **rather** good than bad.

      Sore-wa warui-to-iu-yori-wa-*mushiro* ii-to-ieru.

  (*2*) I'm **rather** tired. Watashi-wa *sukoshi* tsukareta.

  I had(would) rather...(than...) (...yori-)mushiro...(suru-)hô-ga-yoi

ratify (*vt.*) ...o hijun-suru [...を批准する]; ...o saika-suru [...を裁可する].

ratio (*n.*) hi [比]; hiritsu [比率]; wariai [割合].

ration (*n.*) 1)(shokuryô no) haikyû-ryô [(食料の)配給量]. 2)(*mil. pl.*) ikkai-bun-no-ryôshoku [一回分の糧食].

    (*vt.*) ...o haikyû-suru [...を配給する].

rational (*a.*) gôri-teki-na [合理的な]; dôri-ni-kanatta [道理にかなった].

rationalize (*vt.*) ((*Eng.*)) ...o gôri-ka-suru [...を合理化する]. ...o ronri-teki-ni-setsumei-suru [...を論理的に説明する]; ...o rikutsu-zukeru [...を理屈づける].

rattle (*vt. & vi.*) ...o gata-gata-iwaseru (gata-gata-iu) [...をがたがたいわせる(がたがたいう)].

    (*n.*) 1)gata-gata [がたがた]; gara-gara [がらがら]. 2)o-shaberi

[おしゃべり].

rattlesnake (*n.*) (*zool.*) garagara-hebi [ガラガラヘビ].

ravage (*n.*) hakai [破壊]; kôhai [荒廃].
　　　　(*vt.*) ...o hakai-suru […を破壊する]; ...o kôhai-saseru […を荒廃させる]; ...o ryakudatsu-suru […を略奪する].

rave (*vi.*) 1)wameki-tateru [わめき立てる]. 2)uwagoto-o-iu [うわ言を言う]. 3)(*colloq.*) gekishô-suru [激賞する]. 4)(umi ga) areru [(海が)荒れる].
　　　　(*vt.*) ...o wameki-tateru […をわめき立てる].
　　　　(*n.*) 1)unari-goe [うなり声]. 2)gekishô [激賞]. 3)(*slang*) muchû [夢中].

raven (*n.*) (*birds*) watari-garasu [ワタリガラス].
　　　　(*a.*) makkuro-na [真黒な].

ravish (*vt.*) 1)...o ubai-saru […を奪い去る]. 2)...o uttori-saseru […をうっとりさせる].

raw (*a.*) 1)nama-no [生の]; ryôri-shite-i-nai [料理していない]. 2)genryô-no-mama-no [原料のままの]; kakô-shite-i-nai [加工していない]. 3)funare-na [不慣れな]; mijuku-na [未熟な].
　　(*1*) They eat fish **raw**. Kare-ra-wa sakana-o *nama-de* taberu.
　　(*2*) We import **raw** materials.
　　　　　Ware-ware-wa *genryô*-o yunyû-suru.
　　(*3*) He is still **raw** to the task.
　　　　　Kare-wa sono-shigoto-ni mada *funare*-da.
　　　　(*n.*) hifu-no-suri-muketa-tokoro [皮膚のすりむけた所]; suri-kizu [すり傷].

ray (*n.*) kôsen [光線]; (*pl.*) hôsha-sen [放射線].
　　　　(*vi.*) (hikari ga) hassuru [(光が)発する].
　　　　(*vt.*) ...o hassuru […を発する].

razor (*n.*) kamisori [かみそり].

reach (*vt.*) 1)(te)-o nobasu [(手)をのばす]. 2)...ni todoku […に届く]; ...ni tassuru […に達する]; ...ni tôchaku-suru […に到着する].
　　(*1*) He **reached** out his hand. Kare-wa te-*o nobashita*.
　　(*2*) He **reached** Nagoya at seven.
　　　　　Kare-wa shichi-ji-ni Nagoya-*ni tsuita*.
　　　　(*vi.*) 1)te-o-nobasu [手をのばす]. 2)tassuru [達する]; todoku [届く].
　　(*1*) He **reached** for the book.
　　　　　Kare-wa *te-o-nobashite* sono hon-o torô-to-shita.

(2) The tendril **reached** down to the ground.

    Tsuru wa jimen-ni *todoita*.

    (*n.*) 1)nobasu-koto ［伸ばすこと］. 2)todoku-kyori ［届く距離］; (chikara-no-oyobu)han'i ［(力の及ぶ)範囲］.

beyond (above, out of) one's reach   hito-no-te-no-todoka-nai-tokoro-ni

within one's reach   hito-no-te-no-todoku-tokoro-ni

react (*vi.*) 1)rendô-suru ［連動する］. 2)hannô-o-shimesu ［反応を示す］.

reaction (*n.*) handô ［反動］; hannô ［反応］; han-sayô ［反作用］; hampatsu ［反発］.

reactor (*n.*) 1)hannô-o-shimesu-hito[-mono] ［反応を示す人［もの］］. 2) (*phys.*) genshi-ro ［原子炉］.

read (*vt.*) 1)...o yonde-rikai-suru ［…を読んで理解する］. 2)..o sasu ［…をさす］.

    (*vi.*) 1)dokusho-suru ［読書する］. 2)(...to) kaite-aru ［(…と)書いてある］.

(1) He always **reads** in bed.

    Kare-wa itsu-mo beddo-no-naka-de *dokusho-suru*.

(2) The letter **reads** as follows.

    Sono tegami niwa tsugi-no-yô-ni *kaite-aru*.

    read through ...o tsûdoku-suru

    (*n.*) dokusho ［読書］; yomi-mono ［読み物］.

reader (*n.*) 1)dokusha ［読者］. 2)tokuhon ［読本］; rîdâ ［リーダー］.

readily (*ad.*) 1)yôi-ni ［容易に］. 2)sugu-ni ［すぐに］; kokoro-yoku ［快く］.

reading (*n.*) 1)dokusho ［読書］; dokusho-ryoku ［読書力］. 2)yomi-mono ［読み物］. 3)kaishaku ［解釈］; gakushiki ［学識］. 4)(me-mori no) dosû ［(目盛の)度数］.

readjust (*vt.*) ...o sai-chôsei-suru ［…を再調整する］.

ready (*a.*) 1)yôi-no-dekita ［用意のできた］; jumbi-no-dekita ［準備のできた］. 2)kakugo-no-dekita ［覚悟のできた］; yorokonde...(suru) ［喜んで…(する)］. 3)(...shi-)gachi-de-aru ［(…し)がちである］. 4)sokuza-no ［即座の］.

(1) Breakfast is **ready**.   Chôshoku-*no-yôi-ga-dekimashita*.

(2) I'm **ready** to go with you.

    Watashi-wa *yorokonde* anata-to-issho-ni mairi*masu*.

(3) John is too **ready** to suspect.   Jon wa *sugu* jasui-*suru*.

(4) He couldn't give a **ready** answer to it.

Kare-wa sore-ni *sokuza-no* hentô-o ataeru-koto-ga-deki-
nakatta.

Kare-wa sore-ni *sokutô-deki-nakatta.

get ready yôi-o-suru; shitaku-o-suru

(*int.*) 《*Eng.*》 Ichi-ni-tsuite! [位置について!].

(*n.*) 1)(*colloq.*) genkin [現金]. 2)jumbi-kanryô-jôtai [準備完了
状態].

(*vt.*) ...o yôi-suru [...を用意する].

ready-made (*a.*) dekiai-no [出来合いの]; redî-mêdo-no [レディーメード
の].

(*n.*) kisei-fuku [既製服].

real (*a.*) 1)shin-no [真の]; hontô-no [本当の]. 2)jissai-no [実際の];
genjitsu-no [現実の].

(*ad.*) (*US colloq.*) hontô-ni [本当に].

(*n.*) (the –) genjitsu [現実]; jitsubutsu [実物].

real estate fu-dôsan [不動産].

realism (*n.*) genjitsu-shugi [現実主義]; shajitsu-shugi [写実主義];
riarizumu [リアリズム].

realistic (*a.*) genjitsu-shugi-no [現実主義の]; genjitsu-teki-na [現実的
な]; shin-ni-sematta [真に迫った].

reality (*n.*) 1)genjitsu [現実]; jitsuzai [実在]; jittai [実体]. 2)shin-
ni-semaru-koto [真に迫ること].

in reality jitsu-wa; jissai-wa

realization (*n.*) 1)ninshiki [認識]. 2)jitsugen [実現]; genjitsu-ka [現
実化]. 3)(the –) genkin-ka [現金化].

realize (*vt.*) 1)...ga wakaru [...が分かる]. 2)...o jitsugen-suru [...を
実現する]. 3)...o kankin-shobun-suru [...を換金処分する].

really (*ad.*) 1)hontô-ni [本当に]; jissai-wa [実際は]. 2)mattaku [全
く].

realm (*n.*) ryôiki [領域].

reap (*vt. & vi.*) 1)(...o) karu [(...を)刈る]; (...o) shûkaku-surí [(...
を)収穫する]. 2)(mukui)-o ukeru [(報い)を受ける].

reaper (*n.*) kari-tori-ki [刈り取り機].

reappear (*vi.*) futatabi-arawareru [ふたたび現われる]; saigen-suru
[再現する].

rear (*n. & a.*) ushiro(-no) [後ろ(の)]; kôbu(-no) [後部(の)].

at(in) the rear of ...no-ushiro-ni

rear (*vt.*) 1)...o sodateru [...を育てる]; ...o shiiku-suru [...を飼育する].

    2)...o tateru [⋯を建てる]. 3)...o okosu [⋯を起こす]; ...o tateru [⋯
を立てる]; ...o ageru [⋯を上げる].

      (*vi.*) ushiro-ashi-de-tatsu [後ろ足で立つ].

rearmament (*n.*) sai-gumbi [再軍備].

reason (*n.*) 1)riyû [理由]. 2)risei [理性].

     (*1*) For this **reason** I did so.

        Kono-*riyû*-no-tame-ni watashi-wa sô-shita.

     (*2*) She has lost her **reason**. Kano-jo-wa *risei*-o ushinatte-ita.

    by(for) reason(s) of ...no-riyû-de

    for some reason or other dô-iu-wake-ka

      (*vi.*) 1)handan-suru [判断する]. 2)dôri-o-toku [道理を説く].

      (*vt.*) ...o ronjiru [⋯を論じる]; ...o suiri-suru [⋯を推理する].

reasonable (*a.*) 1)dôri-ni-kanatta [道理にかなった]; mottomo-na [もっ
ともな]; tegoro-na [手ごろな]. 2)risei-no-aru [理性のある]; fumbetsu-
no-aru [分別のある].

reasonably (*ad.*) dôri-ni-kanatte [道理にかなって]; tekido-ni [適度に];
gôri-teki-ni [合理的に].

rebate (*n.*) harai-modoshi [払い戻し]; waribiki [割引].

      (*vt.*) ...o harai-modosu [⋯を払い戻す]; ...o wari-biku [⋯を割
り引く].

rebel (*n.*) muhon-nin [謀反人].

      (*vi.*) muhon-o-okosu [謀反を起こす]; somuku [背く].

rebellion (*n.*) muhon [謀反]; hanran [反乱]; hankô [反抗].

rebound (*n.*) hane-kaeri [はね返り]; hankyô [反響]; handô [反動].

      (*vi.*) hane-kaeru [はね返る].

rebuild (*vt.*) ...o saiken-suru [⋯を再建する]; ...o tate-naosu [⋯を建
て直す].

rebuke (*vt.*) ...o hinan-suru [⋯を非難する]; ...o shikaru [⋯をしかる].

      (*n.*) hinan [非難].

recall (*vt.*) 1)...o omoi-dasu [⋯を思い出す]. 2)...o shôkan-suru [⋯
を召喚する]. 3)((*US*)) ...o rikôru-suru [⋯をリコールする].

      (*n.*) shôkan [召喚]; rikôru [リコール].

recede (*vi.*) kôtai-suru [後退する].

receipt (*n.*) 1)uketori [受取]; juryô [受領]. 2)ryôshû-sho [領収書];
reshîto [レシート].

   be in receipt of ...o-uke-totta

      (*vt.*) ...ni ryôshû-no-shomei-o-suru [⋯に領収の署名をする].

      (*vi.*) ryôshû-sho-o-kaku [領収書を書く].

receive (*vt.*) 1)...o uke-toru [...を受け取る]. 2)...o mukaeru [...を迎える].

    (*vi.*) 1)uke-toru [受け取る]; (*sports*) reshîbu-suru [レシーブする]. 2)hômon-kyaku-ni-au [訪問客に会う]. 3)jushin-suru [受信する].

receiver (*n.*) uketori-nin [受取人]; juwa-ki [受話器]; reshîbâ [レシーバー].

recent (*a.*) chikagoro-no [近ごろの]; saikin-no [最近の].

recently (*ad.*) chikagoro [近ごろ].

reception (*n.*) 1)settai [接待]; kangei[-kai] [歓迎(会)]. 2)(*broadcasting*) jushin[juzô]-jôtai [受信[受像]状態]. 3)(hoteru no) furonto [(ホテルの)フロント].

recess (*n.*) 1)((*US*)) kyûkei-jikan [休憩時間]. 2)(*pl.*) hikkonda-tokoro [引っ込んだ所]; okumatta-tokoro [奥まった所].

    (*vt.*) 1)...o kubonda-tokoro-ni-oku [...をくぼんだ所に置く]. 2)((*US*)) ...o kyûkei[kyûkai]-ni-suru [...を休憩[休会]にする].

    (*vi.*) kyûkei[kyûkai]-suru [休憩[休会]する].

recipe (*n.*) 1)chôri-hô [調理法]; reshipi [レシピ]. 2)hôhô [方法]; hiketsu [秘訣].

reciprocal (*a.*) sôgo-no [相互の]; gokei-teki-na [互恵的な].

recital (*n.*) 1)(*mus.*) dokusô-kai [独奏会]; dokushô-kai [独唱会]; risaitaru [リサイタル]. 2)anshô [暗唱]; ((*US*)) rôdoku [朗読]. 3)shôsai-na-hanashi [詳細な話]; monogatari [物語].

recitation (*n.*) anshô [暗唱]; rôdoku [ろう読].

recite (*vt.*) 1)...o anshô-suru [...を暗唱する]; ((*US*)) ...o rôdoku-suru [...を朗読する]. 2)(*colloq.*) ...o shôsai-ni-hanasu [...を詳細に話す]. 3)(*colloq.*) ...o rekkyo-suru [...を列挙する].

    (*vi.*) anshô-suru [暗唱する]; rôdoku-suru [朗読する].

reckless (*a.*) mukô-mizu-na [向こう見ずな]; mubô-na [無謀な].

reckon (*vt.*) 1)...o kazoeru [...を数える]. 2)...to mi-nasu [...とみなす]; ...to omou [...と思う].

    (*1*) I **reckon** 40 of them. Sore-ra-wa *kazoeru*-to yon-jû-ni-naru.

    (*2*) I **reckon** him wise. Watashi-wa kare wa kashikoi-*to omou*.

    (*vi.*) keisan-suru [計算する].

  reckon with ...o kôryo-ni-ireru

recline (*vt. & vi.*) ...o yori-kakaraseru (yori-kakaru) [...を寄りかからせる(寄りかかる)]; ...o motase-kakeru (motareru) [...をもたせかける(もたれる)].

recognition (*n.*) mitomeru-koto [認めること]; shônin [承認].

recognize (*vt.*) 1)...o mitomeru [⋯を認める]; ...o shônin-suru [⋯を承認する]. 2)...ni mi[kiki]-oboe-ga-aru [⋯に見[聞き]覚えがある].

recollect (*vt. & vi.*) (...o) omoi-dasu [(⋯を)思い出す]; (...o) kaisô-suru [(⋯を)回想する].

recollection (*n.*) omoi-de [思い出]; kaisô [回想].

recommend (*vt.*) 1)...o suisen-suru [⋯を推薦する]. 2)...o susumeru [⋯を勧める].

    (*1*) Can you **recommend** me a good hotel?
        Ii hoteru-o go-*zonji-ari*-masen-ka?

    (*2*) I **recommended** him to confess.
        Watashi-wa kare-ni jihaku-suru-yô-ni *susumeta*.

recommendation (*n.*) 1)suisen[-jô] [推薦(状)]; susume [勧め]. 2) torie [取り柄].

recompense (*vt.*) ...ni mukuiru [⋯に報いる]; ...o tsugunau [⋯を償う].
    (*n.*) tsugunai [償い].

reconcile (*vt.*) 1)...o wakai-saseru [⋯を和解させる]; ...o chôtei-suru [⋯を調停する]. 2)...o akiramesaseru [⋯をあきらめさせる].

reconstruct (*vt.*) ...o saiken-suru [⋯を再建する]; ...o fukugen-suru [⋯を復元する].

record (*vt.*) 1)...o rokuon-suru [⋯を録音する]; ...o rokuga-suru [⋯を録画する]. 2)...o hyôji-suru [⋯を表示する].
    (*vi.*) rokuon-suru [録音する]; rokuga-suru [録画する].
    (*n.*) 1)kiroku [記録]; rekôdo [レコード]. 2) = (disk) rekôdo [レコード]. 3)keireki [経歴].

recording (*n.*) rokuon [録音]; rokuon-shita-mono [録音したもの].

recover (*vt.*) 1)...o tori-modosu [⋯を取り戻す]. 2)...o kaifuku-suru [⋯を回復する].
    (*vi.*) kaifuku-suru [回復する].

recovery (*n.*) tori-modosu-koto [取り戻すこと]; kaifuku [回復].

recreation (*n.*) ki-barashi [気晴らし]; goraku [娯楽]; kyûyô [休養]; rekuriêshon [レクリエーション].

rectangle (*n.*) chô-hôkei [長方形].

red (*n.*) 1)aka[-iro] [赤(色)]. 2)(the -) akaji [赤字].
    (*a.*) akai [赤い]; aka-iro-no [赤色の].

redcap (*n.*) ((*US*)) akabô [赤帽].

red cross, the (R- C-) seki-jûji-sha [赤十字社].

redden (*vt. & vi.*) ...o akaku-suru (akaku-naru) [赤くする(赤くなる)].

reddish (*a.*) akami-gakatta [赤みがかった].

redeem (*vt.*) 1)...o kai-modosu […を買い戻す]; ...o kaifuku-suru […を回復する]. 2)...o hatasu […を果たす]. 3)...o ume-awaseru […を埋め合わせる].

red-letter day   saijitsu [祭日]; kinen-bi [記念日].

reduce (*vt.*) 1)...o herasu […を減らす]; ...o shukushô-suru […を縮小する]. 2)...o sageru […を下げる]. 3)...o kaeru […を変える]. 4)...ni suru […にする].
     (*vi.*) genshô-suru [減少する]; (*colloq.*) taijû-o-herasu [体重を減らす].

reduction (*n.*) 1)waribiki [割引]. 2)shukushô [縮小]; shukuzu [縮図].

reed (*n.*) (*bot.*) ashi [アシ].

reef (*n.*) anshô [暗礁]; sasu [砂洲].

reel (*n.*) 《*Eng.*》ito-maki [糸巻き]; rîru [リール].
     (*vt.*) (tsuri-ito nado o ito-maki)-ni maki-toru [(釣り糸などを糸巻き)に巻き取る]; ...o rîru-o-maite-taguri-yoseru […をリールを巻いてたぐり寄せる].

refer (*vt.*) 1)...o sashi-mukeru […を差し向ける]. 2)...o sanshô-saseru […を参照させる]. 3)...o itaku-suru […を委託する]; ...o makaseru […をまかせる]. 4)...o(...ni) kisuru […を(…に)帰する].
     (*vi.*) 1)sanshô-suru [参照する]. 2)genkyû-suru [言及する].

referee (*n.*) 1)(futtobôru ya resuringu no) shimban-in [(フットボールやレスリングの)審判員]; referî [レフェリー]; shinsa-in [審査員]. 2)chûsai-nin [仲裁人].
     (*vt. & vi.*) (...no) referî-o-tsutomeru [(…の)レフェリーをつとめる].

reference (*n.*) 1)sankô [参考]; sanshô [参照]. 2)genkyû [言及]. 3)shôkai-saki [照会先].

refine (*vt.*) 1)...o seisei-suru […を精製する]. 2)...o jôhin-ni-suru […を上品にする].

refined (*a.*) 1)seisei-shita [精製した]; seiren-shita [精練した]. 2)jôhin-na [上品な]; senren-sareta [洗練された].

reflect (*vt.*) 1)...o hansha-suru […を反射する]. 2)(kagami nado ga mono)-o utsusu [(鏡などが物)を映す]; ...o han'ei-suru […を反映する]. 3)...o jukkô-suru […を熟考する]. 4)...o motarasu […をもたらす].
     (*vi.*) 1)hansha-suru [反射する]; aku-eikyô-o-oyobosu [悪影響を及ぼす]. 2)jukkô-suru [熟考する].

reflection, reflexion (*n.*) 1)hansha [反射]; han'ei [反映]. 2)jukkô [熟考]. 3)kansô [感想].

reform (*vt.*) ...o kaikaku-suru [⋯を改革する]; ...o kaizen-suru [⋯を改善する]; ...o kaishin-saseru [⋯を改心させる].

  (*vi.*) kaishin-suru [改心する].

  (*n.*) kaizen [改善]; kaikaku [改革].

refrain (*vi.*) yameru [やめる]; tsutsushimu [慎む]; enryo-suru [遠慮する].

 refrain from (smoking) (tabako)-o sashi-hikaeru

refresh (*vt.*) 1)...o sôkai-ni-suru [⋯をそう快にする]; ...o genki-zukeru [⋯を元気づける]; ...no genki-o-kaifuku-saseru [⋯の元気を回復させる]. 2)(– oneself) inshoku-o-shite-kyûkei-suru [飲食をして休憩する].

  (*vi.*) genki-o-kaifuku-suru [元気を回復する]; karui-inshoku-butsu-o-toru [軽い飲食物をとる].

refreshing (*a.*) sawayaka-na [さわやかな]; kimochi-no-yoi [気持のよい].

refreshment (*n.*) 1)genki-kaifuku [元気回復]; kyûyô [休養]. 2)(*pl.*) karui-shokuji [軽い食事].

refrigerate (*vt.*) ...o reizô-suru [⋯を冷蔵する]; ...o reitô-suru [⋯を冷凍する].

refrigerator (*n.*) reizô-ko [冷蔵庫]; reitô-shitsu [冷凍室].

refuge (*n.*) hinan[-jo] [避難(所)].

 take refuge in ...ni hinan-suru

refugee (*n.*) 1)hinan-min [避難民]. 2)bômei-sha [亡命者].

refund (*n.*) harai-modoshi [払い戻し]; hensai [返済].

  (*vt. & vi.*) (...o) harai-modosu [(⋯を)払い戻す]; (...o) hensai-suru [(⋯を)返済する].

refuse (*vt. & vi.*) (...o) kyozetsu-suru [(⋯を)拒絶する]; (...o) kyohi-suru [(⋯を)拒否する].

regain (*vt.*) 1)...o kaifuku-suru [⋯を回復する]; ...o tori-modosu [⋯を取り戻す]. 2)...ni modoru [⋯に戻る].

regard (*vt.*) 1)...o miru [⋯を見る]; ...ni chûi-o-harau [⋯に注意を払う]. 2)...o sonkei-suru [⋯を尊敬する]. 3)...to mi-nasu [⋯と見なす]; ...to kangaeru [⋯と考える]. 4)...ni kankei-suru [⋯に関係する].

 as regards ...ni-tsuite-ieba; ...ni-kanshite-wa

  (*n.*) 1)chûshi [注視]; chûi [注意]. 2)sonkei [尊敬]. 3)kankei [関係]; ten [点]. 4)(*pl.*) yoroshiku-to-no-aisatsu [よろしくとのあいさつ].

 in(with) regard to ...ni-kanshite

regarding (*prep.*)...ni-kanshite[-wa] [⋯に関して(は)].

regardless (*a.*) mu-tonjaku-na [無とん着な].

    (*ad.*) (*colloq.*) sore-nimo-kakawarazu [それにもかかわらず]; sore-demo [それでも]; nani-ga-nan-demo [何が何でも].

regatta (*n.*) bôtorêsu [ボートレース]; regatta [レガッタ].

regiment (*n.*) (*mil.*) rentai [連隊].

    (*vt.*) 1)...o rentai-ni-hensei-suru […を連隊に編成する]. 2)...o kibishiku-kanri-suru […を厳しく管理する].

region (*n.*) chihô [地方]; chiiki [地域]; ryôiki [領域]; sô [層].

register (*vt.*) 1)...o tôroku-suru […を登録する]; ...o tôki-suru […を登記する]; ...o todoke-deru […を届け出る]. 2)...o kakitome-ni-suru […を書留にする].

    (*1*) I **registered** my new car.

        Watashi-wa watashi-no shinsha-*o tôroku-shita*.

    (*2*) I want to **have** this letter **registered**.

        Watashi-wa kono tegami-*o kakitome-ni-shite*-morai-tai.

    (*vi.*) 1)(yado-chô-ni-)kimei-suru [(宿帳に)記名する]; tôroku-suru [登録する]. 2)(*colloq.*) inshô-o-ataeru [印象を与える].

    (*n.*) 1)tôroku-bo [登録簿]; meibo [名簿]. 2)rejisutâ [レジスター]. 3)(dambô no) tsûfû-sôchi [(暖房の)通風装置]. 4)on'iki [音域].

registration (*n.*) tôroku[-shômei-sho] [登録(証明書)]; kakitome [書留].

regret (*vt.*) 1)...o kôkai-suru […を後悔する]. 2)...o zannen-ni-omou […を残念に思う]. 3)...o ki-no-doku-ni-omou […を気の毒に思う].

    (*1*) He **regrets** to have done such a rash act.

        Kare-wa konna keisotsu-na kôi-o shita-koto-*o kôkai-shite-iru*.

    (*2*) I **regret** to say that...   *Zannen-nagara*...de-aru.

    (*3*) I **regret** to hear of his illness.

        Watashi-wa kare ga byôki-de-aru-koto-o-kiite *ki-no-doku-ni-omou*.

    (*n.*) 1)kôkai [後悔]; ikan [遺憾]; zannen [残念]. 2)kanashimi [悲しみ].

    (*1*) I have no **regrets**.   Watashi-wa *kôkai*-shite-i-nai.

    To my great **regret**, I cannot accept your offer.

        Taihen *zannen*-desu-ga, o-môshi-koshi-o o-uke-deki-masen.

regular (*a.*) 1)kisoku-tadashii [規則正しい]. 2)seiki-no [正規の]. 3)teiki-teki-na [定期的な]. 4)tsûjô-no [通常の]. 5)kimatta [決まった].

    (*n.*) 1)(*sports*) regyurâ-no-senshu [レギュラーの選手]. 2)

(*colloq.*) jôkyaku [常客]. 3)seiki-hei [正規兵].

regularly (*ad.*) kisoku-tadashiku [規則正しく]; kichin-to [きちんと].

regulate (*vt.*) 1)...o kisei-suru [...を規制する]; ...o tori-shimaru [...を取り締まる]. 2)...o chôsei-suru [...を調整する].

regulation (*n.*) 1)kisei [規制]; tôsei [統制]; chôsei [調整]. 2)kisoku [規則].

rehabilitation (*n.*) 1)meiyo-kaifuku [名誉回復]. 2)shakai-fukki [社会復帰]; rihabiri[têshon] [リハビリ(テーション)].

rehearsal (*n.*) 1)shita-geiko [下げい古]; rihâsaru [リハーサル]. 2)kuri-kaeshi [繰り返し].

rehearse (*vt.*) 1)...o shita-geiko-suru [...を下げい古する]; ...no yokô-enshû-o-suru [...の予行演習をする]. 2)...o kuri-kaeshite-iu [...を繰り返して言う].

　　　(*vi.*) rihâsaru-o-okonau [リハーサルを行う].

reign (*n.*) 1)tôchi [統治]; shihai [支配]. 2)chisei [治世].

　　　(*vi.*) kunrin-suru [君臨する]; shihai-suru [支配する].

reimburse (*vt.*) ...o hensai-suru [...を返済する]; ...o bensai-suru [...を弁済する]; ...o baishô-suru [...を賠償する].

rein (*n.*) 1)(*pl.*) tazuna [手綱]. 2)(*pl.*) shihai [支配].

　　　(*vt.*) ...o tazuna-de-gyosuru [...を手綱で御する]; ...o seigyo-suru [...を制御する].

reindeer (*n.*) (*zool.*) tonakai [トナカイ].

reinforce (*vt.*) ...o hokyô-suru [...を補強する].

reinforced concrete tekkin-konkurîto [鉄筋コンクリート].

reject (*vt.*) 1)...o kyozetsu-suru [...を拒絶する]; ...o kyakka-suru [...を却下する]. 2)...o haku [...を吐く]; ...o modosu [...をもどす].

　　　(*n.*) fu-gôkaku-hin [不合格品].

rejoice (*vi. & vt.*) ureshigaru(...o ureshigaraseru) [うれしがる(...をうれしがらせる)]; yorokobu(...o yorokobaseru) [喜ぶ(...を喜ばせる)].

　　I am rejoiced to hear it.　Watashi-wa sore-o-kiite *ureshii*.

relate (*vt.*) 1)...o hanasu [...を話す]; ...o monogataru [...を物語る]. 2)...o kankei-saseru [...を関係させる].

　　be related to　...to shinseki-de-aru

　　　(*vi.*) 1)kankei-ga-aru [関係がある]. 2)(...ni)najimu [(...に)なじむ].

relation (*n.*) 1)kankei [関係]. 2)shinrui [親類]. 3)monogatari [物語].

　　in(with) relation to　...ni-kanshite; ...ni-kanren-shite

relative (*a.*) 1)kankei-no-aru [関係のある]. 2)sôtai-teki-na [相対的な].

relative to 1)...ni-kanshite. 2)...ni-kurabete

    (*n.*) 1)shinrui [親類]. 2)(*gram.*) kankei-shi [関係詞].

relatively (*ad.*) 1)hikaku-teki [比較的]; wariai-ni [割合に]. 2)sôtai-teki-ni [相対的に]; (...to-)kanren-shite [(…と)関連して].

relax (*vt. & vi.*) 1)...o yurumeru (yurumu) […をゆるめる(ゆるむ)]. 2)...o kutsurogaseru (kutsurogu) […をくつろがせる(くつろぐ)]; ...o rirakkusu-saseru (rirakkusu-suru) […をリラックスさせる(リラックスする)].

relaxed throat inkô-kataru [いんこうカタル].

relay (*n.*) 1)(*sports*) rirê-kyôsô [リレー競走]; (*broadcasting*) chûkei-hôsô [中継放送]. 2)kôtai[-yôin] [交替(要員)].

    (*vt.*) ...o chûkei-suru […を中継する]; ...to kôtai-suru […と交替する].

release (*vt.*) 1)...o kaihô-suru […を解放する]. 2)...o menjo-suru […を免除する]. 3)...o hanatsu […を放つ]. 4)...o fûgiri-suru […を封切りする]. 5)(*law*)...o jôto-suru […を譲渡する].

    (*n.*) kaihô [解放]; menjo [免除]; fûgiri [封切り]; (*photo.*) rerîzu [レリーズ]; (*law*) jôto[-shôsho] [譲渡(証書)].

relevant (*a.*) kanren-sei-no-aru [関連性のある].

reliable (*a.*) shinrai-dekiru [信頼できる].

relic (*n.*) ihin [遺品]; katami [形見]; kinen-hin [記念品].

relief (*n.*) 1)anshin [安心]. 2)kyûjo [救助]; kyûen [救援]. 3)kôtai [交替]. 4)uki-bori [浮き彫り].

relieve (*vt.*) 1)...o anshin-saseru […を安心させる]. 2)...o kyûjo-suru […を救助する]. 3)...o kôtai-saseru […を交替させる]. 4)...o uki-dataseru […を浮き出たせる].

religion (*n.*) 1)shûkyô [宗教]. 2)shinkô [信仰]. 3)shinjô [信条].

religious (*a.*) 1)shûkyô[-jô]-no [宗教(上)の]. 2)shinjin-bukai [信心深い].

    (*n.*) shûdô-shi [修道士]; shinkô-no-atsui-hito-bito [信仰の厚い人々].

religiously (*ad.*) 1)keiken-ni [敬けんに]; shûkyô-jô [宗教上]. 2)kisoku-tadashiku [規則正しく].

relish (*n.*) 1)aji [味]; kaori [香り]. 2)konomi [好み]. 3)chômi-ryô [調味料].

    (*vt.*) 1)...o ajiwau […を味わう]. 2)...o konomu […を好む].

    (*vi.*) (...no) aji-ga-suru [(…の)味がする]; (...no) kanji-ga-aru [(…の)感じがある].

reluctant (*a.*) ki-no-susuma-nai [気の進まない]; shibu-shibu-no [しぶ
しぶの].

reluctantly (*ad.*) iya-iya [いやいや]; shibu-shibu [しぶしぶ].

rely (*vi.*) shinrai-suru [信頼する]; tayoru [頼る]; ate-ni-suru [当てに
する].

remain (*vi.*) 1)i-nokoru [居残る]; todomaru [とどまる]. 2)...no-
mama-de-iru […のままでいる]; izen...de-aru [いぜん…である].

　(*1*) I can't **remain** here long.

　　　Watashi-wa koko-ni nagaku-wa *ira*-re-nai.

　(*2*) He **remains** my good friend.

　　　Kare-wa *izen-to-shite* watashi-no shin'yû *desu*.

remainder (*n.*) (the -) nokori [残り].

remains (*n.*) 1)nokori [残り]; nokori-mono [残り物]. 2)itai [遺体].
3)ikô [遺稿].

remark (*vt.*) 1)...ni chûi-suru […に注意する]; ...ni ki-zuku […に気づ
く]. 2)...to iu […と言う].

　(*vi.*) shoken-o-noberu [所見を述べる].

　(*n.*) 1)chûmoku [注目]. 2)hatsugen [発言]; iken [意見].

remarkable (*a.*) chûmoku-su-beki [注目すべき]; medatta [目立った];
mezurashii [珍しい].

remarkably (*ad.*) medatte [目立って]; kiwa-datte [際立って].

remedy (*n.*) 1)chiryô(-yaku) [治療(薬)]. 2)kyûsai-shudan [救済手段].

　(*vt.*) ...o chiryô-suru […を治療する]; ...o kyôsei-suru […を矯
正する]; ...o kaizen-suru […を改善する].

remember (*vt.*) 1)...o omoi-dasu […を思い出す]. 2)...o kioku-shite-
iru […を記憶している]; wasurezu-ni...(suru) [忘れずに…(する)]. 3)...
ni yoroshiku-to-iu […によろしくと言う].

　Remember me to... ...ni-yoroshiku.

remembrance (*n.*) 1)kioku [記憶]. 2)kinen [記念]. 3)(*pl.*) yoroshiku-
to-iu-aisatsu [よろしくというあいさつ]. 4)omoi-de [思い出].

remind (*vt.*) ...o omoi-dasaseru […を思い出させる]; ...o omoi-
okosaseru […を思い起こさせる]; ...o ki-zukaseru […を気付かせる].

remit (*vt.*) 1)...o sôkin-suru […を送金する]; ...o okuru […を送る].
2)...o yurusu […を許す]. 3)...o yawarageru […を和らげる]. 4)...o
enki-suru […を延期する].

　(*vi.*) 1)sôkin-suru [送金する]. 2)osamaru [治まる]; yowamaru
[弱まる].

remittance (*n.*) sôkin(-gaku) [送金(額)].

remnant (*n.*) 1)nokori [残り]; nokori-gire [残り切れ]. 2)nagori [名残].

remorse (*n.*) ryôshin-no-kashaku [良心のかしゃく]; kôkai [後悔].

  without remorse yôsha-naku

remote (*a.*) 1)tooku-hanareta [遠く離れた]; hempi-na [辺ぴな]. 2)too-en-no [遠縁の].

removal (*n.*) 1)idô [移動]; iten [移転]. 2)jokyo [除去]. 3)menshoku [免職].

remove (*vt.*) 1)...o utsusu [⋯を移す]; ...o iten-saseru [⋯を移転させる]. 2)...o tori-saru [⋯を取り去る]; ...o nugu [⋯を脱ぐ]. 3)...o kainin-suru [⋯を解任する].

  (*vi.*) iten-suru [移転する]; hikkosu [引っ越す].

  (*n.*) 1)kyori [距離]; hedatari [隔たり]. 2)sôi-no-teido [相違の程度].

renaissance (*n.*) 1)fukkô [復興]; fukkatsu [復活]. 2)(the R-) bungei-fukkô [文芸復興].

render (*vt.*) 1)...o ataeru [⋯を与える]. 2)...o kaesu [⋯を返す]; ...de mukuiru [⋯で報いる]. 3)...o (...ni)-suru [⋯を(に)する].

  (*1*) He **rendered** his services to our country.

    Kare-wa ware-ware-no-kuni-ni enjo-*o ataeta*.

    Kare-wa ware-ware-no-kuni-ni kôken-shita.

  (*2*) **Render** good for evil. Aku-ni-*mukuiru*-ni zen-o-motte-seyo.

  (*3*) **render** his efforts futile kare-no doryoku-*o* muda-ni-*suru*

renew (*vt.*) 1)...o atarashiku-suru [⋯を新しくする]; ...o fukkatsu-suru [⋯を復活する]. 2)...o futatabi-hajimeru [⋯を再び始める]. 3)...o tori-kaeru [⋯を取り替える].

renounce (*vt.*) 1)...o hôki-suru [⋯を放棄する]. 2)...o kyohi-suru [⋯を拒否する]. 3)...to zekkô-suru [⋯と絶交する].

  (*vi.*) hôki-suru [放棄する].

renown (*n.*) meisei [名声]; kômei [高名].

rent (*n.*) 1)sake-me [裂け目]; hokorobi [ほころび]. 2)bunretsu [分裂]; fuwa [不和].

rent (*n.*) 1)yachin [家賃]; heya-dai [部屋代]; chidai [地代]. 2)(kikai nado no) shiyô-ryô [(機械などの)使用料].

  (*vt.*) ...o chinshaku-suru [⋯を賃借する]; ...o chintai-suru [⋯を賃貸する].

  (*vi.*) chintai-sareru [賃貸される].

rent-a-car (*n.*) ((*US*)) renta-kâ [レンタカー].

repair (*vt.*) 1)...o shûri-suru [...を修理する]. 2)...no tsugunai-o-suru [...の償いをする].

  (*n.*) shûzen [修繕]; shûri-sagyô [修理作業]; teire-no-jôtai [手入れの状態].

  under repair shûri-chû [修理中]

repay (*vt.*) 1)...o kaesu [...を返す]; ...o harai-modosu [...を払い戻す]. 2)...ni mukuiru [...に報いる]; ...ni on-gaeshi-o-suru [...に恩返しをする].

  (*1*) I **paid** him the money that I had borrowed.
   Watashi-wa karite-ita-kane-o kare-ni *kaeshita*.

  (*2*) I will **repay** you some day.
   Anata-ni-wa itsu-ka *go-on-gaeshi-o-itashi-masu*.

  (*vi.*) henkin-suru [返金する]; mukuiru [報いる].

repeat (*vt.*) 1)...o kuri-kaesu [...を繰り返す]; ...o kuri-kaeshite-iu [...を繰り返して言う]. 2)...o anshô-suru [...を暗唱する]. 3)...o kôgai-suru [...を口外する].

  (*vi.*) kuri-kaeshite-iu [繰り返して言う].

  (*n.*) hampuku [反復]; (*broadcasting*) saien [再演]; sai-hôsô [再放送]; (*com.*) sai-chûmon [再注文].

repeatedly (*ad.*) kuri-kaeshite [繰り返して]; saisan-saishi [再三再四].

repel (*vt.*) 1)...o oi-harau [...を追い払う]. 2)...o kyozetsu-suru [...を拒絶する]. 3)...o fukai-na-kimochi-ni-suru [...を不快な気持にする].

  (*vi.*) fukai-ni-suru [不快にする].

repent (*vt. & vi.*) (...o) kôkai-suru [(...を)後悔する].

repetition (*n.*) kuri-kaeshi [繰り返し].

replace (*vt.*) 1)...no kôkei-sha-to-naru [...の後継者となる]. 2)...o moto-no-tokoro-ni-oku [...を元のところに置く]. 3)...o tori-kaeru [...を取り替える].

reply (*vi. & vt.*) (...to) kotaeru [(...と)答える].

  (*n.*) 1)kotae [答え]; henji [返事]. 2)ôshû [応酬].

  (*1*) a **reply** to a letter   tegami-ni-taisuru *henji*

  (*2*) I gave him a heavy blow in **reply**.
   Watashi-wa kare-ni-*ôshû*-shite kare-o hidoku nagutta.

report (*vt. & vi.*) (...o) hôkoku-suru [(...を)報告する]; (...o) todoke-deru [(...を)届け出る].

  (*n.*) 1)hôkoku[-sho] [報告(書)]. 2)seiseki-hyô [成績表]. 3)hôdô [報道]. 4)uwasa [うわさ]; hyôban [評判].

reporter (*n.*) hôdô-kisha [報道記者]; repôtâ [レポーター]; hôkokusha [報告者]; shinkoku-sha [申告者].

repose (*vi.*) 1)yasumu [休む]; yoko-ni-naru [横になる]. 2)notte-iru [載っている].

　　　(*n.*) 1)kyûsoku [休息]. 2)heisei [平静].

represent (*vt.*) 1)...o daihyô-suru [...を代表する]; ...o shôchô-suru [...を象徴する]. 2)...o hyôgen-suru [...を表現する]; ...o egaki-dasu [...を描きだす].

representative (*n.*) 1)daihyô-sha [代表者]; daigi-shi [代議士]; ((*US*)) kain-giin [下院議員]. 2)tenkei [典型].

　　the House of Representatives ((*US*)) kain; ((*Japan*)) shûgiin.

　　　(*a.*) 1)hyôgen-suru [表現する]. 2)daihyô-no [代表の]; daihyô-teki-na [代表的な]; tenkei-o-shimesu [典型を示す].

reproach (*n.*) 1)hinan [非難]; shisseki [叱責]. 2)chijoku [恥辱].

　　　(*vt.*) ...o hinan-suru [...を非難する]; ...o shisseki-suru [...を叱責する].

reptile (*n.*) (*zool.*) hachû-rui-no-dôbutsu [は虫類の動物].

republic (*n.*) kyôwa-koku [共和国]; kyôwa-seitai [共和政体].

repulse (*vt.*) ...o gekitai-suru [...を撃退する]; ...o kyozetsu-suru [...を拒絶する].

　　　(*n.*) gekitai [撃退]; kyozetsu [拒絶].

reputation (*n.*) 1)hyôban [評判]. 2)meisei [名声].

　　(*1*) He has a **reputation** for wit.

　　　　Kare-wa kiten-ga-kiku-node *hyôban*-da.

　　(*2*) He has become a man of **reputation**.

　　　　Kare-wa *mei*shi-ni-natta.

request (*n.*) tanomi [頼み]; yôsei [要請].

　　by request motome-ni-ôjite; irai-ni-yotte

　　　(*vt.*) ...o tanomu [...を頼む]; ...o yôsei-suru [...を要請する].

require (*vt.*) 1)...o negau [...を願う]; ...o yôkyû-suru [...を要求する]. 2)...o hitsuyô-to-suru [...を必要とする].

　　(*1*) I **require** all of you to be present.

　　　　Mina-san go-shusseki-*o-negai-masu*.

　　(*2*) Children **require** a plenty of sleep.

　　　　Kodomo wa suimin-*o* jûbun-*toru-hitsuyô-ga-aru*.

requisite (*a.*) hitsuyô-na [必要な].

　　　(*n.*) hitsuyô-butsu [必要物]; yôken [要件].

rescue (*vt.*) ...o sukui-dasu [...を救いだす].

　　　(*n.*) kyûen [救援]; kyûshutsu [救出].

research (*n.*) kenkyû [研究]; chôsa [調査]
 (*vi. & vt.*) (...o) chôsa-suru [(…を)調査する]; (...o) kenkyû-suru [(…を)研究する].

resemblance (*n.*) 1)nite-iru-koto [似ていること]; ruiji [類似]. 2)ni-gao [似顔].

resemble (*vt.*) ...ni nite-iru […に似ている].

resent (*vt.*) ...ni fungai-suru […に憤慨する]; ...o uramu […を恨む].

reservation (*n.*) 1)horyû [保留]. 2)yoyaku [予約]. 3)fuan [不安].

reserve (*vt.*) 1)...o totte-oku […を取っておく]; ...o horyû-suru […を保留する]. 2)...o yoyaku-suru […を予約する].
 (*n.*) 1)(*fin.*) jumbi-kin [準備金]. 2)(*mil. pl.*) yobi-gun [予備軍]. 3)enryo [遠慮]. 4)seigen [制限]. 5)tokubetsu-horyû-chi [特別保留地].
 without reserve enryo-naku

reserved (*a.*) 1)yoyaku-zumi-no [予約済みの]; kashi-kiri-no [貸し切りの]. 2)yobi-no [予備の]. 3)hikae-me-na [控え目な].

reserved seat yoyaku-seki [予約席]; shitei-seki [指定席].

residence (*n.*) teitaku [邸宅]; jûkyo [住居]. 2)kyojû [居住].

resident (*a.*) kyojû-suru [居住する]; sumi-komi-no [住み込みの].
 (*n.*) kyojû-sha [居住者]; zaijû-sha [在住者].

residential (*a.*) kyojû-no [居住の]; jûtaku-no [住宅の].

resign (*vt.*) 1)...o jinin-suru […を辞任する]. 2)...o hôki-suru […を放棄する].
 (*vi.*) jinin-suru [辞任する].
 resign oneself to akiramete...o kanju-suru

resist (*vt. & vi.*) 1)(...ni) teikô-suru [(…に)抵抗する]. 2)(...o) gaman-suru [(…を)我慢する]. 3)(...ni) taeru [(…に)耐える].

resistance (*n.*) teikô[-ryoku] [抵抗(力)].

resistant (*a.*) teikô-suru [抵抗する].
 (*n.*) teikô-sha [抵抗者].

resolute (*a.*) ketsuzen-to-shita [決然とした]; danko-to-shita [断固とした].

resolution (*n.*) 1)ketsui [決意]; kesshin [決心]; ketsudan-ryoku [決断力]. 2)kaiketsu [解決]. 3)(*chem.*) bunkai [分解].

resolve (*vt.*) 1)...to kesshin-suru […と決心する]. 2)...o bunkai-suru […を分解する]. 3)...o kaiketsu-suru […を解決する].
 (*vi.*) 1)kesshin-suru [決心する]. 2)bunkai-shite...to-naru [分解して…となる].

(*n.*) 1)kesshin [決心]; ketsudan[-ryoku] [決断(力)]. 2)ketsugi [決議].

resort (*n.*) 1)hito-de-no-ooi-basho [人出の多い場所]; kôraku-chi [行楽地]. 2)shudan [手段].

　　(*vi.*) 1)shiba-shiba-iku [しばしば行く]. 2)uttaeru [訴える].

resource (*n.*) 1)(*pl.*) shisan [資産]; zaigen [財源]; shigen [資源]. 2)shudan [手段]; hôsaku [方策].

　(*1*) Japan is poor in **resources**.
　　　Nihon wa *shigen*-ni-megumare-nai.

　(*2*) as a last **resource**　saigo-no *shudan*-to-shite
　　　I am at the end of my **resources**.
　　　　Watashi-wa ban*saku*-tsukite-shimatta.

respect (*vt.*) ...o sonkei-suru […を尊敬する].

　as respects　...ni-kanshite

　　(*n.*) 1)sonkei [尊敬]. 2)(*pl.*) yoroshiku-to-no-dengon [よろしくとの伝言]. 3)ten [点].

　(*1*) I have great **respect** for Mr. Shimizu.
　　　Watashi-wa Shimizu-san-o taihen *sonkei*-shite-iru.

　(*2*) Please give your mother my **respects**.
　　　Dôzo o-kâsan-ni *yoroshiku*.

　(*3*) His opinion is true in this **respect**.
　　　Kare-no iken wa kono-*ten*-de-wa tadashii.

　in(with) respect of(to)　...ni-kanshite

respectable (*a.*) 1)chan-to-shita [ちゃんとした]. 2)kanari-no [かなりの]. 3)mi-gurushiku-nai [見苦しくない].

respectful (*a.*) teinei-na [丁寧な]; reigi-tadashii [礼儀正しい].

respectfully (*ad.*) teinei-ni [丁寧に]; uyauyashiku [うやうやしく]; tsutsushinde [慎んで].

respective (*a.*) sore-zore-no [それぞれの]; mei-mei-no [めいめいの]; kakuji-no [各自の].

respond (*vi. & vt.*) (...to) kotaeru [(…と)答える]; (...to) ôtô-suru [(…と)応答する].

responsibility (*n.*) 1)sekinin [責任]. 2)shinrai-do [信頼度].

responsible (*a.*) 1)sekinin-ga-aru [責任がある]; sekinin-o-ou-beki [責任を負うべき]. 2)shinrai-dekiru [信頼できる].

rest (*n.*) kyûsoku [休息].

　at rest　1)kyûsoku-shite. 2)anshin-shite. 3)seishi-shite
　　(*vt.*) 1)...o yasumaseru […を休ませる]. 2)...o oku […を置く].

3)...o motozukaseru [...を基づかせる].

(1) You must **rest** yourself now and then.
　　Kimi-wa toki-doki karada-o *yasume*-nakereba-naranai.

　(*vi.*) 1)yasumu [休む]. 2)motareru [もたれる]. 3)ate-ni-suru [当てにする]. 4)motozuku [基づく].

(1) He **rested** for a while.　Kare-wa shibaraku *yasunda*.

(2) I **rested** against the wall.　Watashi-wa kabe-ni *motarete-ita*.

(3) I **rest** upon his promise.
　　Watashi-wa kare-no yakusoku-o *ate-ni-shite-iru*.

(4) His theory **rests** on many facts.
　　Kare-no riron wa ooku-no jijitsu-ni *motozuite-iru*.

rest (*n.*) (the -) nokori [残り].

　for the rest ato-wa; sono-ta-ni-tsuite-wa
　　(*vi.*) ...no mama-de-aru [...のままである]; izen...de-aru [依然...である].

restaurant (*n.*) resutoran [レストラン]; ryôri-ten [料理店].

restless (*a.*) yasume-nai [休めない]; ochitsuka-nai [落ち着かない].

restoration (*n.*) kaifuku [回復]; fukkô [復興]; fukugen [復元].

restore (*vt.*) 1)...o moto-doori-ni-suru [...を元どおりにする]; ...o kaifuku-suru [...を回復する]. 2)...o henkan-suru [...を返還する].

restrain (*vt.*) 1)...o osaeru [...を抑える]; ...o seigen-suru [...を制限する]. 2)(*law*) ...o kôsoku-suru [...を拘束する].

restraint (*n.*) yokusei [抑制]; seishi [制止]; kôsoku [拘束].

restrict (*vt.*) ...o gentei-suru [...を限定する]; ...o seigen-suru [...を制限する].

restriction (*n.*) seigen[-jôken] [制限(条件)]; gentei [限定].

result (*n.*) kekka [結果].

　as a result of ...no-kekka-to-shite
　in the result kekkyoku
　　(*vi.*) 1)(...no) kekka-to-shite-shôjiru [(...の)結果として生じる]. 2)(..ni) owaru [(...に)終わる].

resume (*vt.*) ...o futatabi-hajimeru [...を再び始める].
　　(*vi.*) futatabi-hajimaru [再び始まる]; tsuzuku [続く].

resurrection (*n.*) fukkatsu [復活]; yomigaeri [よみがえり].

retail (*vt. & vi.*) ...o ko-uri-suru (ko-uri-sareru) [...を小売りする(小売りされる)].
　　(*n. & ad.*) ko-uri(-de) [小売り(で)].

retain (*vt.*) 1)...o hoji-suru [...を保持する]; ...o hoyû-suru [...を保有

する]. 2)...o oboete-iru […を覚えている].

retaliate (*vt. & vi.*) (...ni) hôfuku-suru [(…に)報復する]; (...ni) shi-kaeshi-o-suru [(…に)仕返しをする].

retire (*vi.*) 1)shirizoku [退く]. 2)intai-suru [引退する]. 3)neru [寝る].
  (*1*) After supper he **retired** to his own room.
    Yûshoku-go kare-wa jibun-no-heya-e *shirizoita*.
  (*2*) He **retired** from the world.
    Kare-wa seken-kara *intai-shita*.
    Kare-wa inkyo-shita.
  (*3*) I **retired** earlier than usual.
    Watashi-wa itsumo-yori-hayaku *neta*.
    (*vt.*) ...o taishoku-saseru […を退職させる].
    (*n.*) taikyaku-no-aizu [退却の合図].

retired (*a.*) 1)intai-shita [引退した]; taishoku-shita [退職した]. 2)hito-zato-hanareta [人里離れた]; hempi-na [辺ぴな].
  (*1*) He is a **retired** professor. Kare-wa *taishoku*-kyôju da.
  (*2*) I slept in a **retired** valley.
    Watashi-wa *hito-zato-hanareta*-tani-ma-de nemutta.

retort (*vt. & vi.*) 1)(...to) ii-kaesu [(…と)言い返す]. 2)(...ni) shippe-gaeshi-o-suru [(…に)しっぺ返しをする].
    (*n.*) ii-kaeshi [言い返し]; kuchi-gotae [口答え].

retreat (*n.*) 1)taikyaku [退却]. 2)kakure-ga [隠れ家]; hinan-jo [避難所].
    (*vi.*) taikyaku-suru [退却する]; intai-suru [引退する].

retrieve (*vt.*) 1)...o tori-modosu […を取り戻す]; ...o kaifuku-suru […を回復する]. 2)...o teisei-suru […を訂正する]. 3)...o omoi-dasu […を思い出す].
    (*n.*) tori-kaeshi [取り返し]; kaifuku [回復].

retrospect (*n.*) kaiko [回顧].
    (*vi. & vt.*) (...o) kaiko-suru [(…を)回顧する].

return (*vt.*) ...o kaesu […を返す].
    Please **return** it to me.
      Dôka sore-o watashi-ni *kaeshite*-kudasai.
    (*vi.*) kaeru [帰る]; modoru [戻る].
    Soon he will **return** home.
      Ma-mo-naku kare-wa *kaeru*-deshô.
    (*n.*) 1)kaeri [帰り]. 2)henkyaku [返却]; henrei [返礼]. 3)
    (*pl.*) shûeki [収益]. 4)shinkoku-sho [申告書]; hôkoku-sho [報告書].

(1) Please inform me by **return** of mail.

  Dôka *ori-kaeshi* go-renraku-kudasai.

(2) He sent me many pears in **return**.

  Kare-wa *henrei*-ni nashi-o takusan okutte-kita.

(3) The **returns** were large. *Shûeki* wa ooki-katta.

(4) an income-tax **return** shotoku-zei *shinkoku-sho*

Many happy returns of the day!

  Kono hi o iku-do-mo kasaneraremasu-koto-o!

  (*a.*) hensô-yô-no [返送用の]; kaeri-no [帰りの]; kaesareta [返された]; o-kaeshi-no [お返しの]; moto-ni-modoru [元に戻る].

return match setsujoku-sen [雪辱戦]; ritân-matchi [リターンマッチ].

return ticket 《*Eng.*》 ôfuku-gippu [往復切符].

reveal (*vt.*) 1)...o shimesu […を示す]; ...o akiraka-ni-suru […を明らかにする]. 2)(kami ga)...o keiji-suru [〔神が〕…を啓示する].

revenge (*n.*) fukushû [復しゅう]; shi-kaeshi [仕返し].

  (*vt.*) [- oneself] fukushû-suru [復しゅうする]. ...no shi-kaeshi-o-suru […の仕返しをする].

revenue (*n.*) shûnyû [収入]; sainyû [歳入].

revenue stamp shûnyû-inshi [収入印紙].

reverence (*n.*) sonkei [尊敬]; keii [敬意].

  (*vt.*) ...o sonkei-suru […を尊敬する].

reverend (*a.*) 1)sonkei-su-beki [尊敬すべき]. 2)(the R-) ...shi […師]. 3)seishoku-sha-no [聖職者の].

  (*n.*) seishoku-sha [聖職者]; bokushi [牧師].

reverse (*vt. & vi.*) ...o gyaku-ni-suru (gyaku-ni-naru) […を逆にする（逆になる）].

  (*n. & a.*) gyaku(-no) [逆(の)]; ura(-no) [裏(の)].

review (*n.*) 1)《*US*》 fukushû [復習]. 2)rompyô [論評]. 3)ken'etsu [検閲].

  (*vt.*) ...o fukushû-suru […を復習する]; ...o rompyô-suru […を論評する]; ...o ken'etsu-suru […を検閲する].

  (*vi.*) shohyô-o-kaku [書評を書く].

revise (*vt.*) ...o kaitei-suru […を改訂する]; ...o shûsei-suru […を修正する].

  revised and enlarged kaitei-zôho-no

  (*vi.*) 《*Eng.*》 fukushû-suru [復習する].

  (*n.*) (*printing*) saikô-gera [再校ゲラ].

revival (*n.*) 1)yomigaeri [よみがえり]; fukkatsu [復活]. 2)sai-jôen

[再上演]. 3)tokubetsu-dendô-shûkai [特別伝導集会].

revive (*vt. & vi.*) ...o yomigaeraseru (yomigaeru) [...をよみがえらせる(よみがえる)]; ...o fukkatsu-saseru (fukkatsu-suru) [...を復活させる(復活する)]; ...o kakki-zukeru (kakki-zuku) [...を活気づける(活気づく)].

revolt (*n.*) 1)hankô [反抗]; hanran [反乱]. 2)fukai [不快]; hankan [反感].
　　　(*vi.*) 1)hanran-o-okosu [反乱を起こす]. 2)mune-ga-waruku-naru [胸が悪くなる].
　　　(*vt.*) ...no mune-o-waruku-saseru [...の胸を悪くさせる].

revolution (*n.*) 1)kakumei [革命]. 2)kaiten [回転].

revolutionary (*a.*) kakumei-no [革命の]; kakumei-teki-na [革命的な].
　　　(*n.*) kakumei-ka [革命家].

revolve (*vi.*) kaiten-suru [回転する]; junkan-suru [循環する].
　　　Seasons **revolve**.　Kisetsu wa *junkan-suru*.
　　　(*vt.*) 1)...o kaiten-saseru [...を回転させる]. 2)...o omoi-megurasu [...を思い巡らす].

revolver (*n.*) (kaiten-shiki)rempatsu-pisutoru [(回転式)連発ピストル].

reward (*n.*) hôshû [報酬]; hôbi [ほうび].
　　　(*vt.*) ...ni mukuiru [...に報いる].

rhetoric (*n.*) 1)shûji-gaku [修辞学]; retorikku [レトリック]. 2)oo-gesa-na-kotoba [大げさなことば]. 3)((*US*)) sakubun [作文].

rheumatism (*n.*) (*path.*) ryûmachi [リューマチ].

rhyme (*n.*) in [韻]; dôin-go [同韻語]; (*pl.*) shiika [詩歌].
　　　(*vi.*) 1)shi-o-tsukuru [詩を作る]. 2)in-o-fumu [韻をふむ].
　　　(*vt.*) 1)...o shi-ni-tsukuru [...を詩に作る]. 2)...o(...to) in-o-fumameru [...を(...と)韻をふませる].

rhythm (*n.*) rizumu [リズム]; ritsudô [律動].

rib (*n.*) rokkotsu [ろっ骨].
　　　(*vt.*) ...ni rokkotsu-o-tsukeru [...にろっ骨を付ける].

ribbon (*n.*) ribon [リボン].

rice (*n.*) kome [米]; meshi [めし]; (*bot.*) ine [稲].

rich (*a.*) 1)kane-mochi-no [金持ちの]. 2)hôfu-na [豊富な]. 3)nôkô-na [濃厚な]; (aji no) kotteri-shita [(味の)こってりした]. 4)koeta [肥えた].
　　　(*1*) His uncle is **rich**.　Kare-no oji wa *kane-mochi*-da.
　　　(*2*) China is **rich** in products.
　　　　　Chûgoku wa sambutsu-ga *hôfu*-da.

(3) I always take **rich** food.

     Watashi-wa itsu-mo *kotteri-shita* mono-o taberu.

(4) **rich** soil   *koeta* tochi

riches (*n.*) tomi [富]; zaisan [財産].

richly (*ad.*) hôfu-ni [豊富に]; jûbun-ni [十分に]; nôkô-ni [濃厚に].

rid (*vt.*) ...kara(...o) tori-nozoku [···から(···を)取り除く].

     be rid of ...o manukareru; ...ga naku-naru

     get rid of ...o manukareru; ...o tori-nozoku

riddle (*n.*) nazo [なぞ]; nammon [難問]; fukakai-na-koto [不可解なこと].

     (*vt. & vi.*) ...no nazo-o-toku (nazo-o-kakeru) [···のなぞを解く(なぞをかける)].

ride (*vt.*) 1)(uma ya nori-mono)-ni noru [(馬や乗り物)に乗る]; ...ni notte-iku [···に乗って行く]. 2)...ni ukabu [···に浮かぶ].

     (*vi.*) 1)notte-iku [乗って行く]. 2)(fune ga) ukabu [(船が)浮かぶ]; teihaku-suru [停泊する].

(1) He can **ride** on the horse.   Kare-wa uma-ni *nore*ru.

(2) A ship **is riding** at anchor.   Fune-ga issô *teihaku-shiteiru.*

     (*n.*) noru-koto [乗ること]; nori-mono-ryokô [乗り物旅行].

     It was a four hours' **ride**.   Yo-jikan-no *jôsha* datta.

     I had a very nice **ride**.   *Nori-mono-no-ryokô* ga tanoshikatta.

rider (*n.*) 1)nori-te [乗り手]; kishu [騎手]. 2)tsuika-jôkô [追加条項].

ridge (*n.*) 1)(dôbutsu no) se [(動物の)背]. 2)one [尾根]. 3)une [畝].

     (*vt. & vi.*) ...ni ryûki-o-tsukeru (ryûki-suru) [···に隆起をつける(隆起する)]; ...ni une-o-tsukuru (une-ni-naru) [···に畝を作る(畝になる)].

ridicule (*n.*) chôshô [嘲笑].

     (*vt.*) ...o chôshô-suru [···を嘲笑する].

ridiculous (*a.*) okashii [おかしい]; tohô-mo-nai [途方もない]; baka-geta [ばかげた].

rifle (*n.*) raifuru-jû [ライフル銃]; shijô-jû [施条銃].

right (*a.*) 1)tadashii [正しい]; machigai-no-nai [間違いのない]. 2) tekitô-na [適当な]. 3)tsugô-no-yoi [都合のよい]; môshi-bun-no-nai [申し分のない]. 4)migi-no [右の]. 5)kenkô-na [健康な]. 6)chokkaku-no [直角の].

(1) You are **right**.   Kimi-no-kangae wa *tadashii.*

                  Sono-toori-da.

(2) He is the **right** man in the **right** place.

Kare-koso *teki*zai *teki*sho da.

(3) All's **right** with the world.

Kono-yo-wa banji *môshi-bun-ga-nai*.

(4) The house was on the **right** side.

Sono ie wa *migi*-gawa-ni atta.

(5) Are you **right** now? *Byôki-wa-naorimashita*-ka?

(6) The lines cross at **right** angles.

Kore-ra-no sen wa *chokkaku*-ni majiwaru.

That's right. Sono-toori.

(*ad.*) 1) tadashiku ［正しく］. 2) itchokusen-ni ［一直線に］;
massugu-ni ［真っすぐに］. 3) junchô-ni ［順調に］; umaku ［うまく］. 4)
mattaku ［全く］; chôdo ［ちょうど］.

(1) He is the boy, if I remember **right**.

Watashi no kioku ga *tadashi*-kereba, kare-ga sono
shônen da.

Tashika kare-ga sono shônen da.

(2) He ran **right** down the field.

Kare-wa *massugu-ni* nohara-o kake-orita.

(3) Nothing goes **right** with him.

Kare-wa nani-hitotsu *umaku* ika-nai.

(4) He stood **right** in the middle.

Kare-wa *chôdo* mannaka-ni tatte-ita.

right away(now, off) 《*US*》 sugu-ni

(*n.*) 1) migi ［右］. 2) seigi ［正義］. 3) kenri ［権利］. 4) (*baseball*)
raito ［ライト］.

(1) You'll see the brick building on your **right**.

Migi-gawa-ni renga-zukuri-no tatemono-ga mieru-darô.

(2) might and **right** chikara to *seigi*

(3) You have a **right** to speak.

Kimi-wa hatsugen-suru-*kenri*-ga aru.

do one right hito-o-kôhei-ni-tori-atsukau; seitô-ni-hyôka-suru

(*vt. & vi.*) …o massugu-ni-suru (massugu-ni-naru) ［…を真っ
すぐにする(真っすぐになる)］; …o seijô-ni-suru (seijô-ni-naru) ［…を
正常にする(正常になる)］.

righteous (*a.*) tadashii ［正しい］; kôketsu-na ［高潔な］; kôsei-na ［公
正な］.

rightful (*a.*) tadashii ［正しい］; seitô-na ［正当な］.

rightfully (*ad.*) seitô-ni ［正当に］; gôhô-teki-ni ［合法的に］.

right-handed (*a.*) 1)migi-kiki-no [右利きの]. 2)migi-mawari-no [右回りの].

rightly (*ad.*) 1)tadashiku [正しく]. 2)tôzen [当然].

rigid (*a.*) 1)katai [堅い]. 2)genkaku-na [厳格な].

rim (*n.*) 1)fuchi [縁]; heri [へり]. 2)(sharin no) rimu [(車輪の)リム].
(*vt.*) ...o fuchi-doru [...を縁どる]; ...ni heri-o-tsukeru [...にへりをつける].

ring (*n.*) 1)yubi-wa [指輪]. 2)wa [輪]. 3)(enkei no) kyôgi-jô [(円形の)競技場]; (bokushingu no) ringu [(ボクシングの)リング].
(*vt.*) ...o maruku-tori-kakomu [...を丸く取り囲む]; ...ni wa-o-hameru [...に輪をはめる].

ring (*vi. & vt.*) naru(...o narasu) [鳴る(...を鳴らす)].

  ring off denwa-o-kiru

  ring up 1)...o denwa-guchi-ni-yobi-dasu. 2)(uri-age-kingaku)-o reji-ni-kiroku-suru
(*n.*) 1)narasu-koto [鳴らすこと]; naru-oto [鳴る音]. 2)denwa [-o-kakeru-koto] [電話(を掛けること)].

ring finger hidari-te-no-kusuri-yubi [左手の薬指].

rinse (*vt.*) ...o yusugu [...をゆすぐ].
(*n.*) 1)yusugi [ゆすぎ]. 2)hearinsu [ヘアリンス].

riot (*n.*) sôdô [騒動]; bôdô [暴動].
(*vi.*) 1)bôdô-o-okosu [暴動を起こす]. 2)(...ni) kado-ni-fukeru [(...に)過度にふける]. 3)habikoru [はびこる].

rioter (*n.*) bôto [暴徒].

rip (*vt.*) ...o hiki-saku [...を引き裂く].
(*vi.*) sakeru [裂ける]; yabureru [破れる].
(*n.*) sake-me [裂け目]; hokorobi [ほころび].

ripe (*a.*) jukushita [熟した]; enjuku-shita [円熟した].

ripen (*vi. & vt.*) jukusu(...o jukusaseru) [熟す(...を熟させる)].

ripple (*n.*) saza-nami [さざ波].
(*vi.*) saza-nami-o-tateru [さざ波をたてる]; sara-sara-oto-o-tateru [さらさら音をたてる].

rise (*vi.*) 1)okiru [起きる]; tachi-agaru [立ち上がる]. 2)[mai-]agaru [(舞い)上がる]; noboru [昇る]. 3)seki-o-tatsu [席を立つ]; sankai-suru [散会する]. 4)minamoto-o-hassuru [源を発する]; shôjiru [生じる]. 5)(bukka ga) agaru [(物価が)上がる].
(*1*) He **rises** early. Kare-wa haya-*oki*-da.
(*2*) The sun **rises** in the east. Taiyô wa higashi-kara *noboru*.

　　(*3*) The court **rose** at five. Go-ji-ni *heitei*-shita.

　　(*4*) This river **rises** from the lake.
　　　　　Kono kawa wa ano mizuumi-ni *minamoto-o-hasshite-iru.*

　　(*5*) The prices **are rising.** Bukka wa *agatteiru.*

　　(*n.*) 1)(mono no) okori [(物の)起こり]. 2)agaru-koto [上がること]. 3)shusse [出世].

　give rise to ...o shôjiru; ...o hiki-okosu

risk (*n.*) kiken [危険]; bôken [冒険].

　at one's own risk jibun-no-sekinin-de

　at the risk of ...o-kakugo-de; ...o-kakete

　run(take) risks ichi-ka-bachi-ka-yatte-miru; kiken-o-okasu

　　(*vt.*) ...o kiken-ni-sarasu [...を危険にさらす]; ...o omoi-kitte-yatte-miru [...を思い切ってやってみる].

ritual (*n.*) gishiki [儀式]; gishiki-teki-na-kôi [儀式的な行為].

　　(*a.*) gishiki-no [儀式の]; saishiki-no [祭式の].

rival (*n.*) kyôsô-aite [競走相手]; raibaru [ライバル]; hitteki-suru-mono[-hito] [匹敵するもの[人]].

　　(*a.*) kyôsô-suru [競争する]; kyôsô-aite-no [競争相手の].

　　(*vt.*) ...to kyôsô-suru [...と競争する]; ...ni hitteki-suru [...に匹敵する].

river (*n.*) kawa [川].

river basin ryûiki [流域].

riverside (*n.*) kawa-gishi [川岸]; kahan [河畔].

rivet (*n.*) ribetto [リベット]; byô [びょう].

　　(*vt.*) 1)...o kugi-zuke-ni-suru [...をくぎづけにする]. 2)(chûi nado)-o hiki-tsukeru [(注意など)を引きつける].

road (*n.*) dôro [道路]; michi [道].

road show (*US play*) chihô-jungyô [地方巡業]; rôdoshô [ロードショー].

roadside (*n. & a.*) michibata(-no) [道端(の)].

roadway (*n.*) dôro [道路]; (the –) (toku ni) shadô [(特に)車道].

roam (*vi. & vt.*) (...o) aruki-mawaru [(...を)歩き回る]; (...o) urotsuku [(...を)うろつく].

roar (*vi.*) unaru [うなる]; hoeru [ほえる]; todoroku [とどろく]; (*colloq.*) oo-warai-suru [大笑いする].

　　(*vt.*) ...o oo-goe-de-iu [...を大声で言う].

　　(*n.*) unari-goe [うなり声]; hoeru-koe [ほえる声]; todoroki [とどろき]; ookina-warai-goe [大きな笑い声].

roast (*vt. & vi.*) …o yaku (yakareru) [⋯を焼く(焼かれる)]; …o iru (irareru) [⋯をいる(いられる)].

　　　(*n.*) yaki-niku [焼き肉]; rôsuto [ロースト]; yaku-koto [焼くこと].

rob (*vt.*) …o gôdatsu-suru [⋯を強奪する]; …o ubau [⋯を奪う].

robber (*n.*) gôtô [強盗].

robbery (*n.*) gôdatsu [強奪]; gôtô [強盗]; tônan [盗難].

robe (*n.*) 1)nagaku-yuruyaka-na-fuku [長くゆるやかな服]; rôbu [ローブ]. 2)(*pl.*) reifuku [礼服]; hôi [法衣].

　　　(*vt. & vi.*) …ni rôbu-o-kiseru (rôbu-o-kiru) [⋯にローブを着せる(ローブを着る)].

robin (*n.*) (*birds*) ((*Eng.*)) koma-dori [コマドリ].

robust (*a.*) 1)jôbu-na [丈夫な]; ganken-na [頑健な]. 2)chikara-no-iru [力のいる]. 3)soya-na [粗野な]. 4)koku-no-aru [こくのある].

rock (*n.*) iwa [岩]; kengo-na-sasae [堅固な支え].

rock (*vt.*) …o yuri-ugokasu [⋯を揺り動かす]; …o yurasu [⋯を揺らす].

　　　(*vi.*) 1)hageshiku-yureru [激しく揺れる]. 2)rokkunrôru-o-odoru [ロックンロールを踊る].

　　　(*n.*) yure [揺れ]; dôyô [動揺]; rokkunrôru [ロックンロール].

rockbound (*a.*) iwa-ni-kakomareta [岩に囲まれた]; iwa-darake-no [岩だらけの].

rock-climbing (*n.*) iwa-nobori [岩登り]; rokku-kuraimingu [ロッククライミング].

rocket (*n.*) 1)roketto [ロケット]. 2)noroshi [のろし].

　　　(*vi.*) 1)tosshin-suru [突進する]; roketto-de-tobu [ロケットで飛ぶ]. 2)kyûtô-suru [急騰する].

　　　(*vt.*) …o roketto-dan-de-kôgeki-suru [⋯をロケット弾で攻撃する]; …o roketto-de-uchi-ageru [⋯をロケットで打ち上げる].

rocking chair yuri-isu [揺りいす]; rokkingu-cheâ [ロッキングチェアー].

rock salt gan'en [岩塩].

rocky (*a.*) 1)iwa-no-ooi [岩の多い]; iwa-no-yô-ni-katai [岩のように固い]. 2)ganko-na [頑固な].

rod (*n.*) 1)sao [さお]; tsuri-zao [釣りざお]. 2)muchi [むち].

role (*n.*) yakuwari [役割]; yaku [役].

roll (*vt.*) 1)…o korogasu [⋯を転がす]. 2)…o maku [⋯を巻く]. 3)…o rôrâ-de-narasu [⋯をローラーでならす].

　　　(*vi.*) 1)korogaru [転がる]. 2)(nami ga) uneru [(波が)うねる]. 3)(kaminari nado ga) goro-goro-naru [(かみなりなどが)ごろごろ鳴る].

4)(fune ga) yoko-yure-suru [(船が)横揺れする].

(n.) 1)maki-mono [巻き物]; hito-maki [一巻き]. 2)meibo [名簿]; shusseki-bo [出席簿]. 3)rôru-pan [ロールパン]. 4)(kaminari nado no) todoroki [(雷などの)とどろき]. 5)yoko-yure [横揺れ].

roller (n.) 1)rôrâ [ローラー]. 2)maki-jiku [巻き軸]. 3)oo-nami [大波]. 4)koro [ころ]. 5)heakârâ [ヘアカーラー].

rolling (n.) 1)(fune no) yoko-yure [(船の)横揺れ]. 2)todoroki [とどろき]. 3)(nami nado no) uneri [(波などの)うねり].

(a.) 1)korogaru [転がる]; yoromeku [よろめく]. 2)uneru [うねる]. 3)todoroku [とどろく].

Roman Catholic (a. & n.) Rôma-katorikku-kyôkai-no (Rôma-katorikku-kyô-to) [ローマカトリック教会の(ローマカトリック教徒)].

romance (n.) 1)kûsô-shôsetsu [空想小説]. 2)romansu [ロマンス]; ren'ai [恋愛]. 3)romanchikku-na-fun'iki [ロマンチックな雰囲気].

romantic (a.) kûsô-teki-na [空想的な]; romanchikku-na [ロマンチックな].

(n.) kûsô-ka [空想家]; romanchisuto [ロマンチスト].

rompers (n.) rompâsu [ロンパース].

roof (n.) yane [屋根].

(vt.) ...no yane-o-fuku [...の屋根をふく].

room (n.) 1)heya [部屋]. 2)yochi [余地]. 3)basho [場所].

(1) I swept my **room** myself.
Watashi-wa jibun-de *heya*-o sôji-shita.

(2) There was no **room** for doubt. Utagai-no-*yochi*-wa nakatta.

(3) This table takes up too much **room**.
Kono têburu wa *basho*-o tori-sugiru.

make room for ...no-tame-ni seki-o akeru

(vi.) ((US)) ma-gari-suru [間借りする].

roommate (n.) dôshitsu-sha [同室者]; rûmumeito [ルームメイト].

roost (n.) 1)tomari-gi [止まり木]. 2)negura [ねぐら]; (hito no) kyûsoku-sho [(人の)休息所]; yado [宿].

(vi.) tomari-gi-ni-tomaru [止まり木にとまる]; negura-ni-tsuku [ねぐらにつく]; (hito ga) tomaru [(人が)泊まる].

rooster (n.) ((US)) ondori [おんどり].

root (n.) 1)ne [根]. 2)kiso [基礎]; kongen [根源]; (pl.) rûtsu [ルーツ]. 3)(pl.) konsai-rui [根菜類].

make(take) root ne-o-orosu; teichaku-suru

(vt.) 1)...o ne-zukaseru [...を根付かせる]. 2)...o ne-kosogi-ni-suru [⋯を根こそぎにする].

    (vi.) ne-zuku [根付く]; teichaku-suru [定着する].

root (vi.) (buta nado ga) hana-de-jimen-o-horu [(豚などが)鼻で地面を掘る].

    (vt.) (colloq.) ...o sagashi-dasu [⋯を探し出す].

root (vi.) (US colloq.) ôen-suru [応援する].

rope (n.) tsuna [綱]; nawa [縄].

    (vt.) 1)...o nawa-de-shibaru [⋯を縄で縛る]. 2)...o zairu-de-tsunagu [⋯をザイルでつなぐ]. 3)...o nawa-de-shikiru [⋯を縄で仕切る].

    (vi.) 1)ito-o-hiku [糸をひく]. 2)rôpu-o-tsukatte-nobori-ori-suru [ロープを使って登り降りする]. 3)zairu-de-karada-o-tsunagi-au [ザイルで体をつなぎあう].

ropedancer (n.) tsuna-watari-geinin [綱渡り芸人].

rose (n.) bara [バラ]; bara-iro [バラ色].

rosy (a.) bara-iro-no [バラ色の]; yûbô-na [有望な]; rakkan-teki-na [楽観的な].

rot (vi.) kusaru [腐る]; fuhai-suru [腐敗する]; kuchiru [朽ちる].

    (vt.) ...o kusaraseru [⋯を腐らせる]; ...o kuchisaseru [⋯を朽ちさせる].

    (n.) fuhai [腐敗]; daraku [堕落]; suitai [衰退].

    (int.) Baka-na! [ばかな!]; Kudaranai! [くだらない!].

rotate (vi.) kaiten-suru [回転する]; meguru [巡る]; kôtai-suru [交替する].

    (vt.) ...o kaiten-saseru [⋯を回転させる]; ...o kôtai-saseru [⋯を交替させる].

rotation (n.) kaiten [回転]; (astron.) jiten [自転]. junkan [循環]; kôtai [交替].

rouge (n.) rûju [ルージュ].

    (vt.) ...ni rûju-o-nuru [⋯にルージュをぬる].

rough (a.) 1)deko-boko-no [でこぼこの]; zara-zara-shita [ざらざらした]. 2)arappoi [荒っぽい]; soya-na [粗野な]. 3)kakô-shite-i-nai [加工していない]; migaite-nai [磨いてない]. 4)daitai-no [だいたいの]; gairyaku-no [概略の]. 5)tsurai [つらい].

    (1) a **rough** road   *deko-boko*-michi

    (2) **rough** sports   *arappoi* supôtsu

    (3) a **rough** diamond   *migaite-nai* daiyamondo

                            daiyamondo no genseki

    (4) a **rough** estimate   *gai*san

   (5) She is **rough** on me. Kano-jo-wa watashi-ni *tsuraku*-ataru.
     (*ad.*) arappoku [荒っぽく].
     (*n.*) (*golf*) rafu [ラフ].
     (*vt.*) ...o zara-zara-ni-suru [···をざらざらにする].

roughly (*ad.*) 1)te-ara-ni [手荒に]. 2)zatto [ざっと].

round (*a.*) 1)marui [丸い]. 2)isshû-no [一周の]. 2)kanzen-na [完全な].
   3)daitai-no [大体の]. 4)kanari-no [かなりの]. 5)sotchoku-na [率直
   な]. 6)kappatsu-na [活発な]. 7)rô-rô-to-hibiku [朗々と響く].
     (*n.*) 1)kaiten [回転]; junkai [巡回]. 2)hito-shôbu [一勝負];
   wan-raundo [ワンラウンド]. 3)hito-shikiri [ひとしきり].
     (*prep.*) 1)...no-mawari-ni [···の周りに]; ...o-mawatte [···を回っ
   て]; ...o-kakonde [···を囲んで]. 2)...no-chikaku-ni [···の近くに]. 3)
   yaku [約]; ...goro [···ごろ].
     (*ad.*) 1)megutte [巡って]; mawari-michi-o-shite [回り道をして].
   2)shihô-ni [四方に]. 3)iki-watatte [行き渡って].
   all the year round ichi-nen-jû
     (*vt. & vi.*) ...o maruku-suru (maruku-naru) [···を丸くする(丸
   くなる)]; (...o) mawaru [···を回る].

roundabout (*a.*) too-mawari-no [遠回りの]; too-mawashi-no [遠回し
   の].
       (*n.*) 1)((*Eng.*)) rôtarî [ロータリー]. 2)too-mawashi-no-ii-
   kata [遠回しのいい方]. 3)((*Eng.*)) kaiten-mokuba [回転木馬].

round-shouldered (*a.*) neko-ze-no [猫背の].

round-table conference entaku-kaigi [円卓会議].

round trip ((*Eng.*)) shûyû-ryokô [周遊旅行]; ((*US*)) ôfuku-ryokô [往
   復旅行].

roundup (*n.*) 1)(nyûsu nado no) sôkatsu [(ニュースなどの)総括]. 2)
   kari-atsume [かり集め]. 3)kenkyo [検挙].

rouse (*vt. & vi.*) ...no me-o-samasaseru (me-o-samasu) [···の目を覚
   まさせる(目を覚ます)]; ...o funki-saseru (funki-suru) [···を奮起させ
   る(奮起する)].

route (*n.*) 1)michi-suji [道筋]; rosen [路線]. 2)(...e-no) michi [(···
   への)道]; hôhô [方法]. 3)((*US*)) haitatsu-kuiki [配達区域].
     (*vt.*) 1)...no keiro-o-sadameru [···の経路を定める]. 2)...o hassô-
   suru [···を発送する].

routine (*n.*) kimari-kitta-shigoto [決まり切った仕事]; nikka [日課];
   itsu-mo-no-te-jun [いつもの手順].
     (*a.*) itsu-mo-no [いつもの]; kitei-doori-no [規定どおりの].

row (*n.*) retsu [列]; narabi [並び].
  in a row ichi-retsu-ni-natte

row (*vi.*) bôto-o-kogu [ボートをこぐ]; koide-iku [こいで行く].
  (*vt.*) ...o kogu [...をこぐ].
  (*n.*) kogu-koto [こぐこと].

row (*n.*) (*colloq.*) sawagi [騒ぎ]; kenka [けんか]; kôron [口論].
  (*vi.*) kenka-suru [けんかする]; kôron-suru [口論する].
  (*vt.*) (*colloq.*) ...o togameru [...をとがめる].

royal (*a.*) ô-no [王の]; ôshitsu-no [王室の]; ôja-rashii [王者らしい].

royalty (*n.*) 1)ôi [王位]. 2)ôzoku [王族]. 3)inzei [印税]; roiyarutî [ロイヤルティー].

rub (*vt.*) 1)...o kosuru [...をこする]; ...o kosuri-awaseru [...をこすり合わせる]. 2)...o suri-komu [...をすり込む]. 3)...o suri-muku [...をすりむく].
  (*vi.*) sure-au [すれ合う]; surete-toreru [すれてとれる].

rubber (*n.*) 1)gomu [ゴム]. 2)(*pl.*)((*US*)) ôbâshûzu [オーバーシューズ]. 3)keshi-gomu [消しゴム].

rubbish (*n.*) 1)kuzu [くず]. 2)tsumaranai-kangae [つまらない考え].

ruby (*n.*) rubî[-iro] [ルビー(色)]; kôgyoku [紅玉].
  (*a.*) rubî-iro-no [ルビー色の]; shinku-no [真紅の]; rubî-no [ルビーの].
  (*vt.*) ...o shinku-ni-someru [...を真紅に染める].

rudder (*n.*) kaji [舵]; hôkô-da [方向舵].

rude (*a.*) 1)shitsurei-na [失礼な]; bu-sahô-na [無作法な]. 2)mikai-no [未開の]. 3)sozatsu-na [粗雑な].

rudely (*ad.*) bu-sahô-ni [無作法に]; rambô-ni [乱暴に]; oozappa-ni [大ざっぱに]; dashinuke-ni [出し抜けに].

ruffle (*vt.*) 1)(atama-no-kami ya hane nado)-o kaki-midasu [(頭の髪や羽など)をかき乱す]. 2)...o nami-dataseru [...を波立たせる]. 3)...o iradataseru [...をいらだたせる].
  (*vi.*) shiwa-kucha-ni-naru [しわくちゃになる]; nami-datsu [波立つ]; iradatsu [いらだつ].
  (*n.*) 1)hida-kazari [ひだ飾り]. 2)tori-no-kubi-ge [鳥の首毛]. 3)saza-nami [さざ波]. 4)iradachi [いらだち].

rug (*n.*) shiki-mono [敷き物]; jûtan [じゅうたん].

rugged (*a.*) 1)deko-boko-no [でこぼこの]; gotsu-gotsu-shita [ごつごつした]. 2)kôten-no [荒天の]. 3)soya-na [粗野な].

ruin (*n.*) 1)hametsu [破滅]; metsubô [滅亡]. 2)(*pl.*) haikyo [廃きょ].

 (*vt.*) ...o hametsu-saseru […を破滅させる］; ...o dame-ni-suru [… をだめにする］; ...o hasan-saseru […を破産させる］.

rule (*n.*) 1)kisoku [規則]. 2)jôgi [定規]. 3)shûkan [習慣]. 4)shihai [支配]; tôchi [統治].

 as a rule gaishite; ippan-ni

 make it a rule to (do) ...(suru)-no-o-kimari-ni-suru

 (*vt.*) 1)...o shihai-suru […を支配する］; ...o tôchi-suru […を統治 する］. 2)(sen)-o jôgi-de-hiku [(線)を定規でひく］. 3)...o saiketsu-suru […を裁決する］.

 (*vi.*) 1)shihai-suru [支配する］. 2)saiketsu-suru [裁決する］. 3) ippan-ni...de-aru [一般に…である］.

ruler (*n.*) 1)shihai-sha [支配者]. 2)jôgi [定規].

rum (*n.*) ramu-shu [ラム酒].

rumor, rumour (*n.*) uwasa [うわさ]; hyôban [評判].

 (*vt.*) ...to uwasa-suru […とうわさする］.

run (*vi.*) 1)hashiru [走る］. 2)nagareru [流れる］. 3)kaite-aru [書いて ある］. 4)tsûjite-iru [通じている］. 5)...ni-naru […になる］.

 (*1*) I can **run** very fast.

  Watashi-wa totemo hayaku *hashiru*-koto-ga-dekiru.

 (*2*) The river **runs** through the city.

  Kono kawa wa shi-o kan-*ryû-shite-iru*.

 (*3*) The letter **runs** as follows.

  Sono tegami niwa tsugi-no-yô-ni *kaite-aru*.

 (*4*) A railway **runs** from here to Nagoya.

  Koko-kara Nagoya-made tetsudô-ga *tsûjite-iru*.

 (*5*) The pond **ran** dry. Ike-no-mizu wa hi-agat*ta*.

 (*vt.*) 1)...o hashiraseru […を走らせる］. 2)...o ugokasu […を動か す］. 3)...o keiei-suru […を経営する］. 4)...o okasu […を冒す］.

 (*1*) He **ran** his car to the airport.

  Kare-wa kûkô-made kuruma-*o hashiraseta*.

 (*2*) The machine **is run** by electricity.

  Sono kikai wa denki-de *ugokasareru*.

 (*3*) He **is running** a tearoom near here.

  Kare-wa kono-chikaku-de kissa-ten-*o keiei-shiteiru*.

 (*4*) I don't want you to **run** a risk.

  Watashi-wa kimi-ni kiken-*o okashite*-morai-taku-nai.

 run after ...o ou

 run its course shizen-no-nari-yuki-o-tadoru

run out of ...o tsukai-hatasu

(*n.*) 1)hashiru-koto [走ること]; kyôsô [競走]; sôkô-kyori [走行距離]. 2)(*sports*) tokuten [得点]. 3)(*play*) renzoku-kôen [連続公演].

in the long run nagai-me-de-mireba; kekkyoku

runaway (*n.*) tôbô-sha [逃亡者].

(*a.*) 1)tôsô-shita [逃亡した]. 2)te-ni-oe-nai [手に負えない]. 3)kyûtô-suru [急騰する].

run-down (*a.*) are-hateta [荒れ果てた]; tsukare-hateta [疲れ果てた].

runner (*n.*) 1)hashiru-hito [走る人]. 2)(*baseball*) sôsha [走者]; rannâ [ランナー]. 3)tsukai-bashiri-suru-hito [使い走りする人].

running (*a.*) 1)hashitteiru [走っている]; nagareteiru [流れている]. 2) renzoku-suru [連続する]; tsuzuke-zama-no [続けざまの].

(*ad.*) renzoku-teki-ni [連続的に]; hiki-tsuzuite [引き続いて].

We've won three times **running**.

Ware-ware-wa san-do *tsuzukete* katta.

(*n.*) 1)ranningu [ランニング]; kyôsô [競走]. 2)keiei [経営]. 3)ryûshutsu-butsu[-ryô] [流出物[量]].

rural (*a.*) inaka-no [田舎の]; den'en-no [田園の].

rush (*vi.*) 1)tosshin-suru [突進する]. 2)isogu [急ぐ].

(*1*) We **rushed** on and on.

Ware-ware-wa *tosshin*-ni-tosshin-o tsuzuketa.

(*2*) You mustn't **rush** through your meals.

Isoide shokuji-o *shite*-wa-ikenai.

(*vt.*) 1)...o isoide-okuru […を急いで送る]. 2)...o isoide-suru […を急いでする]. 3)...o seki-tateru […をせきたてる]. 4)...o kyûshû-suru […を急襲する].

(*n.*) 1)tosshin [突進]. 2)sattô [殺到]. 3)awatadashi-sa [あわただしさ]; isogashi-sa [忙しさ]; isogi [急ぎ].

(*1*) He made a **rush** for the door.

Kare-wa toguchi-ni-mukatte *tosshin*-shita.

(*2*) There was a **rush** of orders from every quarter.

Arayuru-hômen-kara chûmon ga *sattô*-shita.

(*3*) I don't like the **rush** of city life.

Watashi-wa tokai-seikatau no *awatadashi-sa*-wa kirai-da.

a **rush** order *dai-shikyû-no* chûmon

Russia (*n.*) Roshia [ロシア].

Russian (*a.*) Roshia-no ［ロシアの］; Roshia-jin-no ［ロシア人の］;
Roshia-go-no ［ロシア語の］.
    (*n.*) Roshia-jin ［ロシア人］; Roshia-go ［ロシア語］.

rust (*n.*) 1)sabi[-iro] ［さび(色)］. 2)donka ［鈍化］.
    (*vi. & vt.*) sabiru(…o sabisaseru) ［さびる(…をさびさせる)］;
niburu(…o niburaseru) ［鈍る(…を鈍らせる)］; sabi-iro-ni-naru(…o
sabi-iro-ni-suru) ［さび色になる(…をさび色にする)］.

rustic (*a.*) 1)inaka-no ［田舎の］; hinabita ［ひなびた］. 2)soya-na ［粗
野な］.
    (*n.*) inaka-mono ［田舎者］.

rustle (*vi. & vt.*) sara-sara-to-oto-ga-suru(…o sara-sara-to-oto-o-
tatesaseru) ［さらさらと音がする(…をさらさらと音をたてさせる)］.
    (*n.*) sara-sara-to-iu-oto ［さらさらという音］.

rusty (*a.*) 1)sabita ［さびた］; sabi-iro-no ［さび色の］. 2)heta-ni-natta
［下手になった］. 3)jidai-okure-no ［時代遅れの］.

rut (*n.*) wadachi ［わだち］.

ruthless (*a.*) mujô-na ［無情な］; reikoku-na ［冷酷な］.

rye (*n.*) (*bot.*) rai-mugi ［ライムギ］.

S

Sabbath (*n.*) Ansoku-bi ［安息日］.

sack (*n.*) oo-bukuro ［大袋］.
    (*vt.*) …o fukuro-ni-ireru ［…を袋に入れる］.

sacred (*a.*) shinsei-na [神聖な]; genshuku-na [厳粛な].

sacrifice (*n.*) 1)ikenie [いけにえ]. 2)gisei [犠牲].
　　　(*vt.*) ...o ikenie-to-shite-sasageru [...をいけにえとして捧げる];
...o gisei-ni-suru [...を犠牲にする].

sad (*a.*) 1)kanashii [悲しい]; aware-na [哀れな]. 2)(*colloq.*) hidoku-
warui [ひどく悪い]. 3)jimi-na [地味な].

saddle (*n.*) kura [くら].
　　　(*vt.*) ...ni kura-o-oku [...にくらを置く].

sadly (*ad.*) 1)kanashi-sô-ni [悲しそうに]. 2)hidoku [ひどく].

sadness (*n.*) kanashimi [悲しみ].

safe (*a.*) 1)anzen-na [安全な]; buji-na [無事な]. 2)(*baseball*) sêfu-
no [セーフの].
　safe and sound buji-ni
　　　(*n.*) kinko [金庫].

safeguard (*n.*) 1)hogo [保護]. 2)anzen-sôchi [安全装置]; yobô-shudan
[予防手段].
　　　(*vt.*) ...o hogo-suru [...を保護する].

safely (*ad.*) anzen-ni [安全に]; buji-ni [無事に]; sashi-tsukae-naku
[差し支えなく].

sagacious (*a.*) sômei-na [そう明な].

sage (*n.*) kenjin [賢人]; tetsujin [哲人].
　　　(*a.*) kashikoi [賢い]; shiryo-bukai [思慮深い].

sail (*n.*) 1)ho [帆]. 2)hansô [帆走]; kôkai [航海].
　(*1*) Put the **sails** up. *Ho*-o ageyo.
　(*2*) Kyushu is one day's **sail** from here.
　　　Kyûshû wa koko-kara ichi-nichi-no *kôkai* desu.
　set sail shuppan-suru; shukkô-suru
　　　(*vi.*) 1)kôkai-suru [航海する]. 2)(tori ya kumo ga)karuku-tobu
[(鳥や雲が)軽く飛ぶ].
　　　(*vt.*) (umi)-o wataru [(海)を渡る]; ...o hansô-saseru [...を帆走
させる].

sailboat (*n.*) ((*US*)) hansen [帆船]; yotto [ヨット].

sailer (*n.*) hansen [帆船].

sailing (*n.*) hansô [帆走]; kôkai-jutsu [航海術]; shuppan [出帆].

sailor (*n.*) sen'in [船員]; kaiin [海員]; suihei [水兵].

saint (*n.*) seijin [聖人]; seija [聖者]; (S-) sei... [聖...].
　　　(*vt.*) ...o seijin-no-retsu-ni-kuwaeru [...を聖人の列に加える]; ...o
seijin-to-mi-nasu [...を聖人と見なす].

sake (*n.*) tame [ため]; riyû [理由]; mokuteki [目的].
　for the sake of ...no-tame-ni
salad (*n.*) sarada [サラダ].
salary (*n.*) kyûryô [給料]; sararî [サラリー].
sale (*n.*) 1)hambai [販売]; ure-yuki [売れ行き]. 2)tokubai [特売].
　for sale uri-mono-no
　on sale hambai-sarete; ((*US*)) tokka-de
salesman (*n.*) danshi-hambai-in [男子販売員]; sêrusuman [セールスマン].
sales slip ((*US*)) uri-age-dempyô [売上伝票]; reshîto [レシート].
saloon (*n.*) 1)(hoteru no) oo-hiroma [(ホテルの)大広間]. 2)(fune no) danwa-shitsu [(船の)談話室]. 3)((*US*)) sakaba [酒場]; bâ [バー].
salt (*n.*) 1)shio [塩]. 2)(*chem.*) en [塩]. 3)kyôshu-o-soeru-mono [興趣を添えるもの]; kichi [機知].
　with a grain of salt (hito no hanashi o)waribiki-shite(-kiku)
　　(*a.*) shio-ke-no-aru [塩気のある]; shio-zuke-no [塩漬けの].
　　(*vt.*) ...ni shio-de-aji-o-tsukeru [···に塩で味をつける]; ...o shio-zuke-ni-suru [···を塩漬けにする].
salutation (*n.*) aisatsu [あいさつ].
salute (*vt. & vi.*) (...ni) aisatsu-suru [(···に)あいさつする]; (...ni) keirei-suru [(···に)敬礼する].
　　(*n.*) aisatsu [あいさつ]; keirei [敬礼]; eshaku [会釈].
salvage (*n.*) kainan-kyûjo [海難救助]; chimbotsu-sen-hiki-age-sagyô [沈没船引揚げ作業]; sarubêji [サルベージ].
　　(*vt.*) ...o sukui-dasu [···を救い出す].
salve (*n.*) 1)nankô [軟膏]. 2)nagusame [慰め].
　　(*vt.*) ...o yawarageru [···を和らげる]; ...o iyasu [···をいやす].
same (*a.*) onaji-no [同じの]; dôyô-na [同様な]; fuhen-no [不変の].
　at the same time dôji-ni
　　(*ad.*) (the -) dôyô-ni [同様に].
　　(*pron.*) onaji-koto[-mono] [同じこと[もの]].
　all the same (*colloq.*) 1)mattaku-onaji. 2)sore-demo-yahari
　The same to you! Go-dôyô-ni!
sample (*n.*) mihon [見本]; sampuru [サンプル]; shikyô-hin [試供品].
　　(*vt.*) 1)...no mihon-o-toru [···の見本を取る]. 2)...o shishoku-suru [···を試食する]; ...o shiin-suru [···を試飲する]; ...o jissai-ni-tamesu [···を実際に試す].

sanatorium (*n.*) sanatoriumu [サナトリウム]; ryôyô-sho [療養所].

sanction (*n.*) 1)ninka [認可]. 2)seisai [制裁].
　　　　(*vt.*) ...o ninka-suru [...を認可する]; ...o shônin-suru [...を承認する].

sanctuary (*n.*) 1)shinsei-na-basho [神聖な場所]. 2)hinan-jo [避難所].

sand (*n.*) 1)suna [砂]. 2)(*pl.*) suna-hara [砂原]; suna-ji [砂地].
　　　(*vt.*) ...ni suna-o-maku [...に砂をまく]; ...o suna-de-migaku [...を砂で磨く].

sandbank (*n.*) sasu [砂州]; asase [浅瀬].

sandglass (*n.*) suna-dokei [砂時計].

sandpaper (*n.*) kami-yasuri [紙やすり]; sandopêpâ [サンドペーパー].

sandwich (*n.*) sandoitchi [サンドイッチ].
　　　　(*vt.*) ...o aida-ni-hasamu [...を間にはさむ].

sandy (*a.*) 1)suna-no [砂の]; suna-darake-no [砂だらけの]. 2)suna-iro-no [砂色の].

sane (*a.*) shôki-no [正気の]; fumbetsu-no-aru [分別のある].

sanitary (*a.*) eisei-no [衛生の]; eisei-teki-na [衛生的な].

sarcasm (*n.*) fûshi [風刺]; hiniku [皮肉]; atekosuri [当てこすり]; iyami [いやみ].

sarcastic (*a.*) hiniku-na [皮肉な].

sardine (*n.*) (*fish*) iwashi [イワシ].

sash (*n.*) mado-waku [窓枠]; sasshi [サッシ].

satelite (*n.*) 1)(*astron.*) eisei [衛星]. 2)jinkô-eisei [人工衛星]. 3)eisei-koku [衛生国]. 4)tori-maki [取り巻き].

satin (*n.*) shusu [しゅす]; saten [サテン].

satisfaction (*n.*) 1)manzoku [満足]; nattoku [納得]. 2)(shakkin no) hensai [(借金の)返済].

satisfactorily (*ad.*) manzoku-dekiru-hodo [満足できるほど]; jûbun-ni [十分に]; môshi-bun-naku [申し分なく].

satisfactory (*a.*) manzoku-na [満足な]; jûbun-na [十分な]..

satisfy (*vt.*) 1)...o manzoku-saseru [...を満足させる]; ...o jûsoku-saseru [...を充足させる]. 2)...o hensai-suru [...を返済する].
　　　(*vi.*) manzoku-o-ataeru [満足を与える].

Saturday (*n.*) Doyô-bi [土曜日].

Saturn (*n.*) (*astron.*) Dosei [土星].

sauce (*n.*) 1)sôsu [ソース]. 2)kyôshu-o-soeru-mono [興趣を添えるもの].
　　　(*vt.*) ...ni sôsu-o-kakeru [...にソースをかける]; ...ni kyômi-o-soeru [...に興味を添える].

saucepan (*n.*) sôsupan [ソースパン].

saucer (*n.*) 1)uke-zara [受け皿]. 2)sora-tobu-emban [空飛ぶ円盤].

saucy (*a.*) 1)nama-iki-na [生意気な]. 2)(*colloq.*) ki-no-kiita [気の利いた].

savage (*a. & n.*) zankoku-na(-hito) [残酷な(人)].

save (*vt.*) 1)...o sukuu [...を救う]; ...o tasukeru [...を助ける]. 2)...o setsuyaku-suru [...を節約する]; ...o chochiku-suru [...を貯蓄する]. 3)...o habuku [...を省く].

   (*1*) He **saved** a child from the fire.

      Kare-wa kodomo-*o* kaji-kara *sukutta*.

   (*2*) I **have saved** little money.

      Watashi-wa *chokin*-ga hotondo nai.

    I **am saving** my strength.

      Watashi-wa chikara-*o takuwaeteiru*.

      Watashi-wa tairyoku-*o muda-zukai-shi-nai-yô-ni-shiteiru*.

   (*3*) A stitch in time **saves** nine.

      Okure-nu-uchi-no hito-hari wa ato-no ku-hari-*o habuku*-koto-ni-naru.

      Kyô-no hito-hari asu-no to-hari.

  save on ...o setsuyaku-suru

  save up chochiku-suru

    (*n.*) (*baseball*) sêbu [セーブ].

save (*prep.*) ...no-hoka-wa [...のほかは]; ...o-nozoite-wa [...を除いては].

    (*conj.*) ...de-aru-koto-o-nozoite [...であることを除いて]; ...wa-betsu-to-shite [...は別として].

saving (*n.*) 1)kyûjo [救助]. 2)setsuyaku [節約]; (*pl.*) chokin [貯金].

savor, -vour (*n.*) 1)aji [味]; fûmi [風味]; mochi-aji [持ち味]. 2)...no-kimi [...の気味].

      (*vi.*) aji-ga-suru [味がする].

      (*vt.*) ...o ajiwau [...を味わう].

saw (*n.*) nokogiri [のこぎり].

      (*vt.*) ...o nokogiri-de-kiru [...をのこぎりで切る].

      (*vi.*) nokogiri-o-tsukau [のこぎりを使う].

say (*vt.*) 1)...o iu [...を言う]; ...to noberu [...と述べる]. 2)...to kaite-aru [...と書いてある]. 3)itte-mireba [言ってみれば].

    (*vi.*) iu [言う]; iken-o-noberu [意見を述べる].

  I say ((*Eng.*)) Oi; Ano-ne; Oya-oya.

I should say... ...de-shô-ne; ...dewa-nai-ka-to-omoimasu.

It goes without saying that... ...wa iu-made-mo-nai.

let us say maa...to-demo-itte-okô; tatoeba

not to say ...to-wa-ie-nai-made-mo

that is to say sunawachi; tsumari

to say nothing of ...wa iu-made-mo-naku

What do you say to...ing? ...wa dô-desu-ka?

You don't say so! (*colloq.*) Masa-ka!; Hontô-desu-ka?

You said it. (*colloq.*) Mattaku-da.

    (*n.*) 1)ii-tai-koto [言いたいこと]. 2)hatsugen-ken [発言権]. 3)kettei-ken [決定権].

saying (*n.*) 1)iu-koto [言うこと]. 2)kotowaza [ことわざ].

    (*1*) I cannot believe his **saying**.

        Watashi-wa kare-no *iu-koto* wa shin'yô-deki-nai.

      sayings and doings *iu-koto* to okonau-koto

    (*2*) This is an old **saying**. Kore-wa furui *kotowaza* da.

say-so (*n.*) 1)(*colloq.*) dokudan [独断]. 2)kyoka [許可]. 3)kettei-ken [決定権].

scaffold (*n.*) 1)ashiba [足場]. 2)yagai-butai [野外舞台]. 3)kôshu-dai [絞首台].

    (*vt.*) ...ni ashiba-o-kakeru […に足場をかける].

scaffolding (*n.*) ashiba [足場].

scald (*vt.*) 1)...o(-nettô ya yuge de) yakedo-saseru […を(熱湯や湯気で)やけどさせる]. 2)...o nettô-shôdoku-suru […を熱湯消毒する]. 3)...o futtô-ten-chikaku-made-nessuru […を沸騰点近くまで熱する].

scale (*n.*) 1)me-mori [目盛り]; shakudo [尺度]; mono-sashi [物差し]. 2)chii [地位]; kaikyû [階級]. 3)kibo [規模]. 4)shukushaku [縮尺]; wariai [割合].

    (*1*) the **scale** of the thermometer ondo-kei no *me-mori*

    (*2*) He is high in the social **scale**.

        Kare-wa shakai-teki *chii*-ga takai.

    (*3*) Everything is on a large **scale** in America.

        Amerika-de-wa banji ga dai-*kibo*-da.

    (*4*) a map with a **scale** of 1cm. to 1km.

        ichi-kiro issenchi-ni-*shukushaku*-shita chizu

    (*vt.*) 1)...o noboru […を登る]. 2)...o shukushaku-de-kaku […を縮尺で書く]; ...o wariai-ni-ôjite-kimeru […を割合に応じてきめる].

scale (*n.*) tembin [天びん]; tembin-no-sara [天びんの皿]; hakari [は

かり].

It turns the **scale**.

Sore-wa *tembin-no-ippô*-o omoku-suru.

Sore-wa kyokumen-o ippen-saseru.

(*vt.*) ...o tembin-de-hakaru […を天びんで量る].

(*vi.*) ...no mekata-ga-aru […の目方がある].

scale (*n.*) 1)(*fish*) uroko [うろこ]. 2)hakuhen [薄片]; kasabuta [かさぶた]. 3)yu-aka [湯あか].

(*vt.*) ...no uroko-o-otosu […のうろこを落とす]; ...o〔hagi-〕toru […を(はぎ)取る]; ...no yu-aka-o-otosu […の湯あかを落とす].

(*vi.*) hage-ochiru [はげ落ちる]; yu-aka-ga-tsuku [湯あかがつく].

scallop (*n.*) hotate-gai [ホタテガイ].

scamper (*vi.*) 1)awatete-nigeru [あわてて逃げる]. 2)hane-mawaru [はね回る].

(*n.*) shissô [疾走].

scan (*vt.*) ...o komakaku-shiraberu […を細かく調べる].

(*n.*) memmitsu-na-chôsa [綿密な調査].

scandal (*n.*) 1)sukyandaru [スキャンダル]; shûbun [醜聞]. 2)hankan [反感]. 3)chûshô [中傷].

scant (*a.*) toboshii [乏しい]; fu-jûbun-na [不十分な].

(*vt.*) ...o kiri-tsumete-ataeru […を切り詰めて与える].

scanty (*a.*) shôryô-no [少量の]; toboshii [乏しい]; fu-jûbun-na [不十分な].

scar (*n.*) kizu-ato [傷跡].

(*vt.*) ...ni kizu-ato-o-tsukeru […に傷跡をつける].

scarce (*a.*) 1)toboshii [乏しい]. 2)mezurashii [珍しい]; mare-na [まれな].

scarcely (*ad.*) 1)hotondo...nai [ほとんど…ない]. 2)yatto [やっと].

(*1*) There was **scarcely** anything to eat in the room.

Sono-heya-niwa tabe-mono wa *hotondo nakatta*.

(*2*) He is **scarcely** twenty.

Kare-wa *yatto* ni-jussai da.

Kare-wa ni-jussai-*ni-naru-ka-nara-nai-ka*-da.

scarcely...when ...(suru-)ka-(shi)nai-uchi-ni

scarcity (*n.*) fusoku [不足]; ketsubô [欠乏]; kikin [飢きん].

scare (*vt.*) ...o obiesaseru […をおびえさせる]; ...o odosu […を脅す].

(*vi.*) obieru [おびえる].

(*n.*) kyôfu [恐怖]; fuan [不安].

scarecrow (*n.*) kakashi [かかし].

scarf (*n.*) sukâfu [スカーフ].

scarlet (*n. & a.*) shinkô-shoku(-no) [深紅色(の)]; hi-iro(-no) [緋色(の)].

scarlet fever   shôkô-netsu [しょう紅熱].

scatter (*vt. & vi.*) ...o maki-chirasu (chirijiri-ni-naru) [...をまき散らす(ちりぢりになる)]; ...o oi-chirasu (chiru) [...を追い散らす(散る)].
    (*n.*) maki-chirasu-koto [まき散らすこと]; shisan [四散].

scene (*n.*) 1)(*play*) ba [場]; butai [舞台]. 2)(jiken no) gemba [(事件の)現場]. 3)fûkei [風景]; keshiki [景色].
    (*1*) Act 1, **Scene** 2   Dai-ichi-maku, dai-ni-*ba*
    (*2*) The policeman arrived on the **scene**.
         Keikan ga *gemba*-ni tôchaku-shita.
    (*3*) I love the country **scene**.
         Watashi-wa inaka-no *fûkei*-ga sukida.

scenery (*n.*) 1)fûkei [風景]; keshiki [景色]. 2)butai-sôchi [舞台装置]; haikei [背景].

scenic (*a.*) 1)keshiki-no [景色の]; keshiki-no-yoi [景色のよい]. 2)butai-no [舞台の].

scent (*vt.*) 1)...o kagi-tsukeru [...をかぎつける]. 2)...o niowaseru [...をにおわせる]; ...ni kôsui-o-tsukeru [...に香水をつける].
    (*1*) They **scent** the lion at a distance.
         Kare-ra-wa tooku-ni raion-*o kagi-tsukeru.*
    (*vi.*) nioi-o-kaide-tsuiseki-suru [においをかいで追跡する].
         The dog **is scenting** about.   Inu ga *kagi-mawatteiru.*
    (*n.*) 1)nioi [におい]. 2)kyûkaku [きゅう覚]. 3)((*Eng.*)) kôsui [香水].

schedule (*n.*) ichiran-hyô [一覧表]; jikan-hyô [時間表]; yotei(-hyô) [予定(表)].
    (*vt.*) ...o yotei-suru [...を予定する]; ...no hyô-o-sakusei-suru [...の表を作成する].

scheme (*n.*) 1)keikaku [計画]; takurami [たくらみ]. 2)soshiki [組織].
    (*vt.*) ...o keikaku-suru [...を計画する]; ...o takuramu [...をたくらむ].

scholar (*n.*) 1)gakusha [学者]. 2)shôgaku-sei [奨学生].

scholarship (*n.*) 1)gakushiki [学識]. 2)shôgaku-kin [奨学金]; sukara-shippu [スカラシップ].

school (*n.*) 1)gakkô [学校]; kôsha [校舎]. 2)jugyô [授業]. 3)zenkô-seito［全校生徒］.

(1) Our **school** stands near the church.

Ware-wara-no *gakkô* wa kyôkai-no-chikaku-ni aru.

(2) We have no **school** today.

Ware-wara-wa kyô-wa *jugyô*-ga nai.

(3) The whole **school** likes him. *Zenkô-seito* ga kare-ga sukida.

after school hôka-go

go to school tsûgaku-suru

leave school taigaku-suru; sotsugyô-suru

schoolboard (*n.*) ((*US*)) kyôiku-iin-kai［教育委員会］.

schoolboy (*n.*) danshi-seito［男子生徒］.

school district gakku［学区］.

schoolfellow (*n.*) gakkô-tomodachi［学校友だち］; gakuyû［学友］ = schoolmate.

schoolgirl (*n.*) joshi-seito［女子生徒］.

schoolhouse (*n.*) kôsha［校舎］.

schooling (*n.*) gakkô-kyôiku［学校教育］.

schoolmaster (*n.*) 1)dansei-kyôshi［男性教師］. 2)kôchô［校長］.

schoolroom (*n.*) kyôshitsu［教室］.

school year gakunen［学年］.

schooner (*n.*) sukûnâ-sen［スクーナー船］.

science (*n.*) 1)kagaku［科学］; ...gaku［…学］. 2)jutsu［術］.

scientific (*a.*) kagaku-no［科学の］; kagaku-teki-na［科学的な］; semmon-teki-gijutsu-o-motsu［専門的技術を持つ］.

scientist (*n.*) kagaku-sha［科学者］.

scissors (*n.*) hasami［ハサミ］.

scold (*vt. & vi.*) ...o shikaru (gami-gami-iu)［…をしかる(がみがみ言う)］.

scoop (*n.*) 1)shô-shaberu［小シャベル］; oo-saji［大さじ］; hishaku［ひしゃく］. 2)sukuu-koto［すくうこと］; hito-sukui［一すくい］. 3)(*newspaper*) toku-dane［特種］.

(*vt.*) 1)...o sukuu［…をすくう］. 2)...o horu［…を掘る］. 3) (*newspaper*) (toku-dane)-o dasu［(特種)を出す］; (tasha)-o dashi-nuku［(他社)を出し抜く］.

scooter (*n.*) ［môtâ-]sukûtâ［(モーター)スクーター］.

(*vi.*) sukûtâ-ni-noru［スクーターに乗る］.

scope (*n.*) 1)han'i［範囲］. 2)kikai［機会］.

scorch (*vt.*) 1)...o kogasu［…を焦がす］. 2)...o shioresaseru［…をしお

れさせる]. 3)...o kokuhyô-suru […を酷評する].

　　　(vi.) kogeru [焦げる]; shioreru [しおれる].

　　　(n.) yake-koge[-no-ato] [焼け焦げ(の跡)].

scorching (a.) yake-tsuku-yô-na [焼けつくような].

score (n.) 1)tokuten [得点]; sukoâ [スコアー]. 2)(mus.) gakufu [楽譜]. 3)kizami-me [刻み目]; (hikkaita-)kizu-ato [(引っかいた)傷跡]. 4)tasû-no [多数の].

　　　(1) What's the **score**? It's three to one.
　　　　　Tokuten wa ikura-desu-ka? San-tai-ichi desu.

　　　(2) a piano **score**　piano-no-*gakufu*

　　　(3) There was a bad **score** on the table.
　　　　　Têburu-ni hidoi *kizu-ato*-ga atta.

　　　(vt.) 1)...o tokuten-suru […を得点する]; ...o saiten-suru […を採点する]. 2)...ni kizami-me-o-tsukeru […に刻み目をつける]; ...ni shirushi-o-tsukeru […にしるしをつける]. 3)(US colloq.) ...o nonoshiru […をののしる].

　　　(vi.) tokuten-suru [得点する]; kizami-me-o-tsukeru [刻み目をつける].

scoreboard (n.) tokuten-keiji-ban [得点掲示板]; sukoabôdo [スコアボード].

scorer (n.) kiroku-gakari [記録係]; sukoarâ [スコアラー].

scorn (n.) keibetsu [軽蔑]; chôshô [嘲笑].

　　　(vt.) 1)...o keibetsu-suru […を軽蔑する]. 2)...o hane-tsukeru […をはねつける].

scornful (a.) keibetsu-shita [軽蔑した].

scornfully (ad.) keibetsu-shite [軽蔑して].

Scorpio (n.) (astron.) Sasori-za [さそり座].

scorpion (n.) (zool.) sasori [サソリ].

Scotch (a.) Sukottorando-no [スコットランドの].

　　　(n.) Sukotchi-uisukî [スコッチウイスキー].

Scotland (n.) Sukottorando [スコットランド].

Scottish (a.) Sukottorando-no [スコットランドの]; Sukottorando-jin-no [スコットランド人の]; Sukottorando-go-no [スコットランド語の].

　　　(the –) Sukottorando-jin [スコットランド人]. Sukottorando-go [スコットランド語].

scour (vt.) 1)...o suri-migaku […をすり磨く]; ...o kosutte-hikaraseru […をこすって光らせる]. 2)...o arai-nagasu […を洗い流す].

　　　(n.) suri-migaku-koto [すり磨くこと]; sabi-otoshi [さび落とし].

scour (*vt. & vi.*) (...o) isoide-sagashi-mawaru [(…を)急いでさがし回る].

scout (*n.*) 1)sekkô [斥候]. 2)shinjin-o-sagasu-hito [新人を探す人]; sukauto [スカウト]. 3)bôi[gâru]-sukauto-no-ichi-in [ボーイ[ガール]スカウトの一員].

    (*1*) He is on the **scout**.　Kare-wa *teisatsu*-shite-iru.

    (*2*) He is a talent **scout**.　Kare-wa tarento-no *sukauto* da.

    (*3*) He entered the boy **scouts**.　Kare-wa bôi-*sukauto*-ni haitta.

    (*vi.*) teisatsu-suru [偵察する]; sagashi-mawaru [探し回る].

scowl (*vi.*) 1)iya-na-kao-o-suru [いやな顔をする]. 2)nirami-tsukeru [にらみつける].

    (*n.*) shikamettsura [しかめっつら].

scramble (*vi.*) 1)yoji-noboru [よじ登る]. 2)ubai-au [奪い合う].

    (*1*) We **scrambled** up a mountain.

        Ware-ware-wa yama-o *yoji-nobotta*.

    (*2*) The boys **scrambled** for seats.

        Kodomo-tachi wa seki-o *ubai-atta*.

        (*vt.*) 1)...o kaki-maze-nagara-iru [… をかきまぜながら炒る]. 2)...o konran-saseru [… を混乱させる].

        (*n.*) 1)yoji-nobori [よじ登り]. 2)ubai-ai [奪い合い]. 3)(*mil.*) sukuramburu [スクランブル].

scrap (*n.*) 1)shôhen [小片]. 2)kuzu-tetsu [くず鉄]; sukurappu [スクラップ]. 3)kiri-nuki [切り抜き].

    (*vt.*) ...o kuzu-ni-suru [… をくずにする]; ...o sukurappu-ni-suru [… をスクラップにする].

scrape (*vt.*) ...o kosuru [… をこする]; ...o suri-muku [… を擦りむく].

    (*vi.*) 1)kosuru [こする]. 2)sureru [擦れる].

    (*n.*) 1)kosuru-koto [こすること]. 2)kasuri-kizu [かすり傷]. 3)(*colloq.*) kukyô [苦境].

scratch (*vt.*) 1)...o hikkaku [… を引っかく]; ...ni kaki-kizu-o-tsukeru [… にかき傷をつける]. 2)...o hashiri-gaki-suru [… を走り書きする]. 3)...o kaki-atsumeru [… をかき集める].

    (*vi.*) hikkaku [引っかく].

    (*n.*) 1)kaku-koto [かくこと]; kaki-kizu [かき傷]. 2)kishiru-oto [きしる音].

scream (*vi.*) kyatto-sakebu [きゃっと叫ぶ]; pî-to-naru [ぴーと鳴る].

    (*vt.*) kanakiri-goe-de...to iu [金切り声で… と言う].

    (*n.*) kanakiri-goe [金切り声]; himei [悲鳴]. pî-to-iu-oto [ぴー

という音].

screech (*vt. & vi.*) (...o) kanakiri-goe-de-sakebu [(…を)金切り声で叫ぶ].

　　　　(*n.*) kan-dakai-sakebi-goe [甲高い叫び声]; kî-to-iu-oto [キーという音].

screen (*n.*) 1)tsuitate [ついたて]; shikiri [仕切り]. 2)(*movie*) eisha-maku [映写幕]; sukurîn [スクリーン]. 3)shahei-butsu [遮へい物].
　　　　(*vt.*) 1)...o shikiru […を仕切る]. 2)...o oou […を覆う]. 3)...o mamoru […を守る]; ...o kabau […をかばう].

screw (*n.*) 1)neji [ねじ]. 2)suishin-ki [推進機]; sukuryû [スクリュー].
　　　　(*vt.*) 1)...o neji-de-shimeru […をねじで締める]; ...o nejiru […をねじる]. 2)...o shikameru […をしかめる].
　　　　(*vi.*) nejireru [ねじれる].

screwdriver (*n.*) neji-mawashi [ねじ回し]; doraibâ [ドライバー].

scripture (*n.*) (the S-) seisho [聖書]; (*pl.*) seiten [聖典].

scrub (*vt.*) 1)...o goshi-goshi-kosuru […をごしごしこする]. 2)...o goshi-goshi-arau […をごしごし洗う].
　　　　(*vi.*) goshi-goshi-kosuru [ごしごしこする]; kosutte-toreru [こすって取れる].
　　　　(*n.*) goshi-goshi-migaku-koto [ごしごし磨くこと].

sculptor (*n.*) chôkoku-ka [彫刻家].

sculpture (*n.*) chôkoku [彫刻].
　　　　(*vt.*) ...o chôkoku-suru […を彫刻する].

sea (*n.*) 1)umi [海]. 2)nami [波].
　　(1) He lives near the **sea**.　Kare-wa *umi*-no-chikaku-ni sunde-iru.
　　(2) a high **sea**　taka-*nami*
　　all at sea　tohô-ni-kurete
　　at sea　kôkai-chû-de; kaijô-de
　　by sea　fune-de
　　go to sea　1)funa-nori-ni-naru. 2)shukkô-suru
　　put to sea　shukkô-suru

sea anemone (*zool.*) isoginchaku [イソギンチャク].

sea bathing kaisui-yoku [海水浴].

sea dog (*zool.*) gomafu-azarashi [ゴマフアザラシ].

sea gull kamome [カモメ].

seal (*n.*) (*zool.*) azarashi [アザラシ].

seal (*n.*) 1)in [印]. 2)fûin [封印].
　　　　(*vt.*) ...ni in-o-osu […に印をおす]; ...ni fû-o-suru […に封をする].

sea level kaimen [海面]; heikin-kaimen [平均海面].

  above sea level kaibatsu

sealing wax fûrô [封ろう].

seam (*n.*) 1)nui-me [縫い目]; tsugi-me [継ぎ目]. 2)shiwa [しわ];
  kizu-ato [傷跡].

      (*vt.*) …o nui-awaseru […を縫い合わせる]; …o tsugi-awaseru […
  を継ぎ合わせる].

seaman (*n.*) sen'in [船員]; kaiin [海員].

seamless (*a.*) nui-me-no-nai [縫い目のない]; tsugi-me-no-nai [継ぎ目
  のない]; shîmuresu-no [シームレスの].

sea otter (*zool.*) rakko [ラッコ].

sear (*vt.*) 1)…o yaku […を焼く]; …no hyômen-o-kogasu […の表面を
  焦がす]. 2)…o shinabisaseru […をしなびさせる]; …o karasu […を
  枯らす]. 3)…o mahi-saseru […を麻ひさせる].

      (*vi.*) yakeru [焼ける]; kogeru [焦げる]; shioreru [しおれる].

search (*vt.*) …o sagasu […を探す]; …o shiraberu […を調べる].

      (*vi.*) sagasu [探す]; motomeru [求める].

      (*n.*) tansaku [探索]; chôsa [調査].

  in search of …o-sagashite; …o-motomete

searchlight (*n.*) tanshô-tô [探照灯]; sâchiraito [サーチライト].

seashore (*n.*) kaigan [海岸]; umi-be [海辺].

seasick (*a.*) fune-ni-yotta [船に酔った].

seasickness (*n.*) funa-yoi [船酔い].

seaside (*n.*) kaigan [海岸]; umi-be [海辺].

season (*n.*) 1)kisetsu [季節]. 2)jiki [時期].

  in season shun-de; jiki-o-ete

  out of season kisetsu-hazure-de; jiki-o-shisshite

  the off-season shîzun-ofu

      (*vt.*) 1)…ni aji-o-tsukeru […に味をつける]. 2)(hito)-o kitaeru
  [(人)を鍛える]. 3)(mokuzai)-o kansô-saseru [(木材)を乾燥させる].

      (*vi.*) 1)nareru [慣れる]. 2)jukusu [熟す].

seasoning (*n.*) chômi[-ryô] [調味(料)].

season ticket 《*Eng.*》 teiki-ken [定期券]. teiki-nyûjô-ken [定期入場券].

seat (*n.*) 1)seki [席]; zaseki [座席]; shîto [シート]. 2)shozai-chi [所
  在地]; chûshin-chi [中心地]. 3)giseki [議席].

  (1) Please take this **seat**. Dôzo kono *seki*-ni o-kake-kudasai.

  (2) Osaka is the **seat** of commerce in Japan.

      Ôsaka wa Nihon-no shôgyô no *chûshin-chi* da.

(3) win a **seat** in an election　senkyo-de *giseki*-o eru

keep one's seat　chakuseki-no-mama-de-iru

　　(*vt.*) 1)…o chakuseki-saseru［…を着席させる］. 2)…o shûyô-suru-zaseki-ga-aru［…を収容する座席がある］. 3)…o giseki-ni-tsukeru［…を議席につける］.

　　(*1*) Please **be seated.**　Dôzo go-*chakuseki*-kudasai.

　　(*2*) The hall **seats** 500 (people).
　　　　Sono shûkai-jo niwa go-hyaku-nin-o *shûyô-suru-zaseki-ga-aru.*

sea urchin (*zool.*) uni［ウニ］.

seaweed (*n.*) kaisô［海草］.

second (*a.*) 1)dai-ni-no［第二の］. 2)mô-hitotsu-no［もう一つの］.

　in the second place　dai-ni-ni; tsugi-ni

　on second thought(s)　kangae-naoshite

　　(*ad.*) dai-ni-ni［第二に］.

　　(*n.*) (the –) dai-ni-bam-me-no-hito[-mono]［第二番目の人［もの］］; dai-ni-nichi［第二日］.

　　(*vt.*) …o shiji-suru［…を支持する］.

second (*n.*) byô［秒］; chotto-no-aida［ちょっとの間］.

　in a second　tachimachi; sugu-ni

secondary (*a.*) dai-ni-i-no［第二位の］; ni-ji-teki-na［二次的な］.

secondhand (*a. & ad.*) chûko-no (chûko-de)［中古の(中古で)］; mata-giki-no (mata-giki-de)［又聞きの(又聞きで)］; kansetsu-no (kansetsu-ni)［間接の(間接に)］.

second hand　byôshin［秒針］.

secondly (*ad.*) dai-ni-ni［第二に］; tsugi-ni［次に］.

secret (*a.*) himitsu-no［秘密の］; kakureta［隠れた］.

　　(*n.*) 1)himitsu［秘密］. 2)hiketsu［秘けつ］.

　keep…a secret from one　…o hito-ni-himitsu-ni-shite-oku

secretary (*n.*) 1)hisho［秘書］; shoki［書記］. 2)((*US*)) chôkan［長官］.

secretly (*ad.*) hisoka-ni［ひそかに］.

sect (*n.*) bumpa［分派］; tôha［党派］; shûha［宗派］.

section (*n.*) 1)bubun［部分］. 2)dammen［断面］. 3)bumon［部門］; …ka［…課］.

secure (*a.*) anzen-na［安全な］; kakujitsu-na［確実な］; anshin-dekiru［安心できる］.

　　(*vt.*) 1)…o anzen-ni-suru［…を安全にする］. 2)…o kakutoku-suru［…を獲得する］; …o te-ni-ireru［…を手に入れる］. 3)…o hoshô-suru [···を保証する].

(1) You must **secure** yourself against loss.

    Kimi-wa jibun-ni-son-*no-nai-yô-ni* shi-nakereba-naranai.

(2) He **secured** a good seat at the theater.

    Kare-wa gekijô-no ii-zaseki-*o te-ni-ireta.*

(3) He **secured** the loan with a pledge.

    Kare-wa tampo-o-tsukete shakkan-no-hensai-*o hoshô-shita.*

security (*n.*) 1)anzen [安全]. 2)hoshô [保証]; tampo [担保].

see (*vt.*) 1)...o miru [···を見る]; ...ga mieru [···が見える]. 2)...ni au [···に会う]; ...o hômon-suru [···を訪問する]. 3)...ga wakaru [···が分かる]; ...o rikai-suru [···を理解する]. 4)...o tashikameru [···を確かめる]; ...o shiraberu [···を調べる]; ...o mite-miru [···を見てみる]. 5)...ni ki-o-tsukeru [···に気をつける].

(1) I **saw** many flowers in the garden.

    Niwa-ni takusan-no hana-*ga mieta.*

(2) I want to **see** him. Watashi-wa kare-*ni ai*-tai.

(3) Now I **see** the use of it. Sore-de sono kôyô-*ga wakatta.*

(4) Go and **see** what the matter is.

    Dô-shita-no-ka *mite*-kinasai.

(5) They **see** that the laws are kept.

    Kare-ra-wa hôritsu ga mamorareru-yô-*ni ki-o-tsukeru.*

  (*vi.*) 1)mieru [見える]. 2)wakaru [分かる]. 3)ki-o-tsukeru [気をつける]; shiraberu [調べる].

(1) Owls can **see** in the dark.

    Fukurô wa kuragari-de me-ga-*mieru.*

(2) You **see**. O-*wakari*-deshô.

(3) I'll **see** to it. Sore-o *shirabete*-miyô.

I see. Wakari-mashita.

see...off ...o mi-okuru

see...through 1)...o mi-nuku. 2)...ga-sumu-made...no mendô-o-miru

see to it that ...(suru)-yô-ni ki-o-tsukeru

seed (*n.*) 1)tane [種]. 2)(*sports*) shîdo〔-sareta〕-senshu [シード(された)選手].

  (*vt.*) (tane)-o maku [(種)をまく]; ...o shîdo-suru [···をシードする].

  (*vi.*) tane-o-maku [種をまく]; tane-ga-dekiru [種ができる].

seek (*vt.*) 1)...o sagasu [···をさがす]; ...o e-yô-to-suru [···を得ようと

する]. 2)(...shi-yô)-to tsutomeru [(…しよう)と努める].

(1) She **is seeking** a job.　Kano-jo-wa shoku-o *sagashiteiru*.

　　He **is** always **seeking** wealth.

　　　　Kare-wa itsu-mo tomi-o *motometeiru*.

(2) He **sought** to become a lawyer.

　　　　Kare-wa bengo-shi-ni-narô-to *doryoku-shita*.

　(*vi.*) motomeru [求める].

seem (*vi.*) ...no-yô-ni-mieru […のように見える]; ...to-omowareru […と思われる].

seeming (*a.*) uwabe-no [うわべの]; mise-kake-no [見せかけの].

seemingly (*ad.*) hyômen-wa [表面は]; mita-tokoro-dewa [見たところでは].

segregation (*n.*) 1)bunri[-jôtai] [分離(状態)]. 2)jinshu-sabetsu [人種差別].

seismometer (*n.*) jishin-kei [地震計].

seize (*vt.*) 1)...o tsukamu […をつかむ]; ...o nigiru […を握る]. 2)...o ubau […を奪う]; (*law*)...o bosshû-suru […を没収する]. 3)(byôki nado)-ga(-hito)-o osou [(病気など)が(人)を襲う].

(1) He **seized** my arm.　Kare-wa watashi-no ude-o *tsukanda*.

(2) They **seized** the fort.　Kare-ra-wa toride-o *dasshu-shita*.

(3) He **was seized** with fear.　Kare-wa kyôfu-ni *osowareta*.

　(*vi.*) tsukamu [つかむ]; toraeru [とらえる]; osou [襲う].

seldom (*ad.*) metta-ni...nai [めったに…ない].

　　He **seldom** goes out.　Kare-wa *metta-ni* gaishutsu-shi-*nai*.

select (*vt. & vi.*) (...o) erabu [(…を)選ぶ].

　　(*a.*) erinuki-no [えり抜きの]; kaiin-o-gentei-shita [会員を限定した].

selection (*n.*) 1)sentaku [選択]; sembatsu [選抜]. 2)eri-nuki-no-mono [えり抜きのもの].

self (*n.*) 1)jibun [自分]; jishin [自身]. 2)honshitsu [本質]; kosei [個性]. 3)shiri [私利].

　　(*a.*) onaji [同じ]; ichiyô-no [一様の].

self-cent(e)red (*a.*) jiko-hon'i-no [自己本位の].

selfish (*a.*) riko-teki-na [利己的な]; jibun-hon'i-no [自分本位の].

sell (*vt. & vi.*) ...o uru (ureru) […を売る(売れる)].

　　The house **was sold** at last.　Sono ie wa yatto *ureta*.

　　These goods will never **sell**.

　　　　Kore-ra-no shinamono wa zettai-ni *ure*-nai-darô.

sell out 1)...o uri-tsukusu. 2)...o uragiru

seller (*n.*) 1)uru-hito [売る人]; uri-te [売り手]. 2)yoku-ureru-mono [よく売れるもの].

sellers' market uri-te-ichiba [売手市場].

sellout (*n.*) (*colloq.*) 1)uri-kire [売り切れ]. 2)oo-iri-man'in-no-kôgyô [大入り満員の興行].

seminar (*n.*) seminâ [セミナー]; zeminâru [ゼミナール].

Senate, the (*n.*) jôin [上院].

senator (*n.*) 1)((*US*)) jôin-giin [上院議員]. 2)(daigaku no) hyôgi-in [(大学の)評議員].

send (*vt.*) 1)...o okuru […を送る]. 2)...o ikaseru […を行かせる]. 3)...o ataete-kudasaru […を与えて下さる].

  (*1*) I **sent** him a book as a gift.
      Watashi-wa kare-ni okuri-mono-to-shite hon-*o* issatsu *okutta.*

  (*2*) He **sent** his eldest son to college.
      Kare-wa chônan-*o* daigaku-ni *ikaseta.*

  (*3*) God **send** you success!
      Kami-ga anata-ni seikô-*o* *atae-raren-*koto-o!
      Go-seikô-o inorimasu!

  (*vi.*) 1)tsukai-o-dasu [使いを出す]. 2)shingô-o-okuru [信号を送る].

  (*1*) The doctor **was sent** for.
      Kakari-tsuke-no-isha-o *yobi-ni-yatta.*

send away ...o oi-harau

send out ...o hassô-suru

send word dengon-suru

senior (*a.*) toshi-ue-no [年上の]; sennin-no [先任の]; jôkyû-no [上級の].

    (*n.*) nenchô-sha [年長者]; sempai [先輩]; ((*Eng.*)) jôkyû-sei [上級生]; ((*US*)) sai-jôkyû-sei [最上級生].

senior high school ((*US*)) kôtô-gakkô [高等学校].

sensation (*n.*) 1)kankaku [感覚]. 2)sensêshon [センセーション]; dai-hyôban [大評判].

sensational (*a.*) seken-o-atto-iwaseru-yô-na [世間をあっと言わせるような]; hito-sawagase-na [人騒がせな]; sensêshonaru-na [センセーショナルな].

sense (*n.*) 1)kankaku [感覚]. 2)kanji [感じ]. 3)(*pl.*) shôki [正気]. 4)shiryo [思慮]; fumbetsu [分別]. 5)imi [意味].

(1) a **sense** of hearing　chôkaku

(2) a **sense** of shame　hazukashii to-iu kanji

(3) They are out of their **senses**.　Kare-ra-wa shôki-de-wa-nai.

(4) He is a man of **sense**.　Kare-wa fumbetsu-no-aru-hito da.

(5) It is true in a **sense**.　Aru-imi-de-wa sore-wa hontô-da.

come to one's senses　shôki[ishiki]-o-tori-modosu

have the sense to (do)　…(suru)-hodo-no-fumbetsu-ga-aru

make sense　dôri-ni-kanau

sensibility (n.) 1)kando [感度]. 2)kanju-sei [感受性].

sensible (a.) 1)kanjirareru [感じられる]; ichijirushii [著しい]. 2)ki-zuite [気づいて]. 3)mono-no-wakatta [もののわかった]; fumbetsu-no-aru [分別のある].

(1) There is no **sensible** difference between them.
　　　Sore-ra-no-aida-niwa ichijirushii sôi wa nai.

(2) He is fully **sensible** of his defects.
　　　Kare-wa jibun-no ketten-niwa jûbun ki-zuite-iru.

(3) He is a **sensible** man.　Kare-wa mono-no-wakatta hito da.

sensitive (a.) 1)binkan-na [敏感な]. 2)kando-no-yoi [感度のよい]. 3)tori-atsukai-ni-shinchô-o-yôsuru [取扱いに慎重を要する]; kimitsu-o-atsukau [機密を扱う].

(1) She is **sensitive** to cold.　Kano-jo-wa samu-sa-ni binkan-da.
　　　　　　　　　　　　　　　　Kano-jo-wa samu-gari-da.

(2) a **sensitive** radio　kando-no-yoi rajio

(3) a **sensitive** position in the government
　　　seifu-no-kimitsu-o-atsukau kanshoku

sensitivity (n.) binkan[-do] [敏感(度)]; kando [感度]; (photo.) (fuirumu no) kando [(フィルムの)感度].

sensual (a.) kannô-teki-na [官能的な].

sentence (n.) 1)(gram.) bun [文]; sentensu [センテンス]. 2)(law) hanketsu [判決].
　　　　(vt.) …ni senkoku-suru […に宣告する]; …ni hanketsu-o-kudasu […に判決を下す].

sentiment (n.) 1)kanjô [感情]; kanshô [感傷]. 2)iken [意見]; kansô [感想].

sentimental (a.) kanjô-teki-na [感情的な]; kanshô-teki-na [感傷的な]; senchimentaru-na [センチメンタルな].

separate (vt. & vi.) …o wakeru (wakareru) […を分ける(分かれる)]; …o hiki-hanasu (hanareru) […を引き離す(離れる)]; …o wakaresaseru (wakareru) [⋯を別れさせる(別れる)].

　　　(a.) hanareta [離れた]; betsu-betsu-no [別々の].

separation (n.) 1)bunri [分離]. 2)bekkyo [別居].

September (n.) Kugatsu [九月].

sequence (n.) 1)renzoku [連続]; junjo [順序]. 2)kekka [結果].

serenade (n.) serenâde [セレナーデ]; sayo-kyoku [小夜曲].

　　　(vi.) serenâde-o-utau [セレナーデを歌う]; serenâde-o-ensô-
suru [セレナーデを演奏する].

serene (a.) 1)hareta [晴れた]. 2)odayaka-na [穏やかな].

sergeant (n.) 1)(mil.) gunsô [軍曹]. 2)junsa-buchô [巡査部長].

serial (a.) renzoku-teki-na [連続的な]; tooshi-no [通しの].

　　　(n.) tsuzuki-mono [続き物].

serial number tooshi-bangô [通し番号].

series (n.) 1)renzoku [連続]; hito-tsuzuki [一続き]. 2)shirîzu-mono
[シリーズもの]; sôsho [双書].

　　　(1) a **series** of events　ichi-ren-no jiken

　　　(2) the Macmillan **series**　Makumiran-sôsho

serious (a.) 1)majime-na [まじめな]; honki-no [本気の]. 2)jûdai-na
[重大な].

　　　(1) Are you **serious**?　Kimi-wa honki-ka?

　　　(2) a **serious** illness　jûbyô

sermon (n.) sekkyô [説教].

serpent (n.) hebi [ヘビ].

servant (n.) 1)meshitsukai [召使い]. 2)hôshi-sha [奉仕者].

serve (vt.) 1)⋯ni tsukaeru [⋯に仕える]. 2)⋯ni yaku-datsu [⋯に役
立つ]; ⋯no tasuke-ni-naru [⋯の助けになる]. 3)⋯o dasu [⋯を出す].
4)⋯o gûsuru [⋯を遇する]; ⋯o atsukau [⋯を扱う]. 5)(sports)⋯o
sâbu-suru [⋯をサーブする].

　　　(1) I cannot **serve** two masters.

　　　　　Watashi-wa nikun-ni tsukaeru-koto-wa-deki-nai.

　　　(2) The fact **serves** to show that he is honest.

　　　　　Sono jijitsu wa kare-ga shôjiki-de-aru-koto-o akiraka-ni-
suru-no-ni-yaku-datsu.

　　　(3) She **was served** with a plate of fish.

　　　　　Kano-jo-wa sakana-ryôri hito-sara-o dasareta.

　　　(4) It **serves** you right.　Tôzen-no mukui-da.

　　　(5) He **served** the ball well.　Kare-wa umaku sâbu-shita.

　　　(vi.) 1)tsukaeru [仕える]; kimmu-suru [勤務する]. 2)yaku-ni-tatsu [役にたつ]. 3)shokuji-no-sewa-o-suru [食事の世話をする]. 4) (*sports*) (aite ni) sâbu-suru [(相手に)サーブする].

(*1*) He **serves** as a clerk in Mr. Suzuki's shop.
　　　Kare-wa Suzuki-san-no-mise-ni jimu-in-to-shite *kimmu-shite-iru.*

(*2*) This **serves** for nothing.
　　　Kore-wa nan-no-*yaku-ni*-mo-*tata*-nai.

(*3*) We **serve** from 5:00p.m. to 10:00p.m.
　　　Tô-ten-no-*eigyô-wa* gogo-go-ji-kara jû-ji-made-*desu.*

(*n.*) (*sports*) sâbu [サーブ].

service (*n.*) 1)tsutome [勤め]; kimmu [勤務]. 2)yaku-ni-tatsu-koto [役にたつこと]. 3)jinryoku [尽力]; sâbisu [サービス]; hone-ori [骨折り]. 4)kôkyô-jigyô [公共事業]; setsubi [設備]; (basu nado no) ben [(バスなどの)便]. 5)reihai [礼拝].

(*1*) sea **service** kaijô-*kimmu*

(*2*) I shall be happy to be of **service** to you.
　　　Watashi-ga o-*yaku-ni-tatsu*-nara saiwai-desu.

(*3*) Will you do me a **service**?
　　　Hitotsu o-*hone-ori*-kudasai-masen-ka?

(*4*) There is a good **service** of buses. Basu no *ben* ga ii.

(*5*) We hold the Sunday **service**.
　　　Ware-ware-wa Nichiyô-*reihai*-o okonau.

　at one's service itsu-demo-hito-no-yaku-ni-tatte
　　　(*vt.*) ...no afutâ-sâbisu-o-suru [...のアフターサービスをする].

serviceable (*a.*) jitsuyô-teki-na [実用的な]; benri-na [便利な].

sesame (*n.*) (*bot.*) goma [ゴマ].

session (*n.*) 1)kaikai [開会]; kaitei [開廷]. 2)kaiki [会期]. 3) (daigaku no) gakunen [(大学の)学年]. 4)atsumari [集まり].

set (*vt.*) 1)...o oku [...を置く]. 2)...o totonoeru [...を整える]; ...o tsugu [...を接ぐ]. 3)...ni awaseru [...に合わせる]. 4)...o ataeru [...を与える]; ...o shimesu [...を示す]. 5)...ni (sa-)seru [...に(さ)せる]. 6)...o kasuru [...を課する].

(*1*) I **set** my hat on the table.
　　　Watashi-wa têburu-no-ue-ni bôshi-o *oita.*

(*2*) The surgeon **set** his broken leg.
　　　Sono geka-i wa kare-no oreta ashi-no-hone-o *tsuida.*

(*3*) He **set** his watch by the TV.
　　　Kare-wa terebi-no-jihô-ni tokei-o *awaseta.*

(4) I **set** him an example.

     Watashi-wa kare-ni tehon-*o shimeshita.*

(5) He **set** the company laughing.

     Kare-wa ichidô-*o* warawa*seta.*

(6) He **set** me to dictation.

     Kare-wa watashi-ni kaki-tori-o *saseta.*

  (vi.) 1)(taiyô nado ga) shizumu [(太陽などが)沈む]. 2)katamaru [固まる]. 3)nagareru [流れる].

(1) The sun **set**. Taiyô ga *shizunda.*

(2) Jelly **sets** as it cools. Zerî wa hieru-to *katamaru.*

(3) The tide **sets** in(out) twice a day.

     Shio wa ichi-nichi-ni ni-do sasu(*hiku*).

set about ...o hajimeru; ...ni tori-kakaru

set back ...o modosu

     Set your watch back one hour.

     Tokei-no-hari-o ichi-jikan modoshi-nasai.

set forth 1) shuppatsu-suru; dekakeru. 2)...o noberu; ...o setsumei-suru

 1) She set forth on a trip. Kano-jo-wa ryokô-ni dekaketa.

 2) He set forth his plans. Kare-wa jibun-no keikaku-o nobeta.

set in hajimaru

     The rainy season will soon set in.

     Ma-mo-naku tsuyu ga hajimaru.

     Ma-mo-naku tsuyu-ni-hairu.

set off 1)shuppatsu-suru(= set forth 1). 2)...o-bakuhatsu-saseru

 2) He set off a dynamite.

     Kare-wa dainamaito-o bakuhatsu-saseta.

set out 1)shuppatsu-suru(= set forth 1). 2)...o-noberu(= set forth 2)

set up 1)...o tateru. 2)...o hajimeru

 1) He set up a hospital. Kare-wa byôin-o tateta.

 2) He has set up a supermarket.

     Kare-wa sûpâ-mâketto-o hajimeta.

  (n.) 1)hito-kumi [一組]; hito-soroi [一そろい]; setto [セット]. 2)*(sports)* setto [セット]. 3)(rajio no) jushin-ki [(ラジオの)受信機]; (terebi no) juzô-ki [(テレビの)受像機]. 4)*(play)* butai-sôchi [舞台装置].

  (a.) 1)danko-to-shita [断固とした]. 2)shotei-no [所定の]; kata-ni-

hamatta［型にはまった］. 3)(...no-)yôi-no-dekita［(…の)用意のできた］.

settle (*vt.*) 1)...o oku［…を置く］; ...o sueru［…を据える］; ...o suwaraseru［…を座らせる］. 2)...ni teijû-saseru［…に定住させる］. 3)...o shizumeru［…を静める］. 4)...o kaiketsu-suru［…を解決する］. 5)...o seisan-suru［…を清算する］; ...o shiharau［…を支払う］.

 (*1*) He **settled** a camera on a tripod.
   Kare-wa kamera-o sankyaku-ni *sueta*.

 (*2*) They have **been settled** in Tokyo these thirty years.
   Kare-ra-wa san-jû-nen-kono-kata Tôkyô-ni *teijû-shiteiru*.

 (*3*) The shower **settled** the dust on the street.
   Sono niwaka-ame de toori-no hokori wa *shizumatta*.

 (*4*) The matter **was** all **settled**.
   Sono ken wa sukkari *kaiketsu-shita*.

 (*5*) **settle** (up) a bill kanjô-o *harau*
  (*vi.*) 1)teijû-suru［定住する］. 2)ochitsuku［落ち着く］. 3)sadamaru［定まる］. 4)shiharau［支払う］.

 settle down ochitsuku

settlement (*n.*) 1)nyûshoku-chi［入植地］. 2)kaiketsu［解決］. 3)seisan［清算］. 4)shakai-fukushi-jigyô-dan［社会福祉事業団］; setsurumento［セツルメント］.

settler (*n.*) 1)kaitaku-sha［開拓者］. 2)ijû-min［移住民］.

seven (*n. & a.*) nana(-no)［七(の)］.

seventeen (*n. & a.*) jû-nana(-no)［十七(の)］.

seventeenth (*n. & a.*) dai-jû-nana(-no)［第十七(の)］.

seventh (*n. & a.*) dai-nana(-no)［第七(の)］.

seventieth (*n. & a.*) dai-nana-jû(-no)［第七十(の)］.

seventy (*n. & a.*) nana-jû(-no)［七十(の)］.

sever (*vt.*) ...o setsudan-suru［…を切断する］; ...o tatsu［…を断つ］.
 (*vi.*) kireru［切れる］; danzetsu-suru［断絶する］.

several (*a.*) 1)ikutsu-ka-no［いくつかの］. 2)mei-mei-no［めいめいの］.

 (*1*) We saw **several** big ships.
   Ware-ware-wa *sû-seki-no* ookii fune-ga mieta.

 (*2*) **Several** men, **several** minds.
   Mei-mei-no hito wa *mei-mei-no* kangae-ga-aru.
   Jû-nin to-iro.

severe (*a.*) 1)kibishii［厳しい］; hidoi［ひどい］. 2)doryoku-o-yôkyû-suru［努力を要求する］. 3)kanso-na［簡素な］.

severely (*ad.*) kibishiku［厳しく］.

sew (*vt. & vi.*) ...o nuu (nui-mono-o-suru) [...を縫う(縫い物をする)].

sewing (*n.*) nui-mono [縫い物]; saihô [裁縫].

sex (*n.*) sei [性]; sekkusu [セックス].

sexual (*a.*) sei-no [性の]; sei-teki-na [性的な].

shabby (*a.*) 1)ki-furushita [着古した]; misuborashii [みすぼらしい]. 2)iyashii [卑しい].

shade (*n.*) 1)kage [陰]; hikage [日陰]. 2)hi-yoke [日よけ]; kasa [かさ]. 3)iroai [色合い]. 4)(a –)sukoshi [少し]. 5)wazuka-na-chigai [わずかな違い]; nyuansu [ニュアンス].

  (*1*) We had lunch under the **shade** of a tree.
      Ware-ware-wa ko-*kage*-de chûshoku-o tabeta.
  (*2*) The silk lamp**shades** matched the curtains.
      Kinu-no sutando-no-*kasa* ga kâten-ni yoku-atte-ita.
  (*3*) different **shades** of green   samazama-na midori no *iroai*
  (*4*) I am a **shade** better today.   Watashi-wa kyô-wa *sukoshi* ii.
  (*5*) This word has some **shades** of meaning.
      Kono go niwa jakkan-no *nyuansu-no-chigau*-imi-ga aru.
      (*vt.*) ...o kage-ni-suru [...を陰にする]; ...ni in'ei-o-tsukeru [...に陰影をつける]; ...o saegiru [...を遮る].
      (*vi.*) jojo-ni-henka-suru [徐々に変化する].

shadow (*n.*) 1)kage [影]; kehai [気配]. 2)koshi-ginchaku [腰ぎんちゃく]. 3)bikô-sha [尾行者]. 4)zenchô [前兆].
      (*vt.*) 1)...o kage-ni-suru [...を陰にする]; ...o kuraku-suru [...を暗くする]. 2)...o honomekasu [...をほのめかす].

shadowy (*a.*) kage-no-ooi [影の多い]; kage-no-yô-na [影のような].

shady (*a.*) kage-no-ooi [陰の多い]; hi-kage-no [日陰の].

shaft (*n.*) 1)yari[-no-e] [やり(の柄)]; e [柄]. 2)(*min.*) tate-kô [縦坑]. 3)(*mech.*) jiku [軸]; shafuto [シャフト].

shaggy (*a.*) ke-bukai [毛深い].

shake (*vt.*) ...o yusaburu [...を揺さぶる]; ...o dôyô-saseru [...を動揺させる].
      (*vi.*) 1)yureru [揺れる]; guratsuku [ぐらつく]. 2)(samu-sa ya osoroshisa de) furueru [(寒さや恐ろしさで)震える].
    shake hands akushu-suru

shall (*aux. v.*) 1)...darô [...だろう]. 2)...shiyô [...しよう]; (...suru-) tsumori-da [(...する)つもりだ]; (...sa-)se-yô [(...させ)よう].
  (*1*) Shall I be well?   Watashi-wa genki-de-iru-*darô*-ka?
      I **shall** be at home at 7.

Watashi-wa shichi-ji-niwa ie-ni iru-*darô*.

Watashi-wa shichi-ji-niwa ie-ni-kaette-iru.

(2) **Shall** I call on him? Kare-o hômon-*shiyô*-ka?

Shall you go to the party on Sunday?

Nichiyô-bi-ni pâtî-ni iku-*tsumori-desu*-ka?

Shall he go there? Kare-o soko-e ika*se-yô*-ka?

You **shall** have an album. Kimi-ni arubamu-o age-*yô*.

He **shall** see it. Kare-ni sore-o mise-*yô*.

shallow (*a.*) asai [浅い]; sempaku-na [浅薄な].

(*n.*) (*pl.*) asase [浅瀬].

(*vi.*) asaku-naru [浅くなる].

sham (*a.*) nise-no [にせの]; gomakashi-no [ごまかしの].

(*n.*) 1)nise-mono [にせもの]; inchiki [いんちき]. 2)peten-shi [ぺてん師].

(*vt.*) ...no furi-o-suru [...のふりをする]; ...o itsuwaru [...を偽る].

(*vi.*) mise-kakeru [見せ掛ける].

shame (*n.*) haji [恥]; fu-meiyo [不名誉].

For shame! **Shame** on you! *Haji*-o-shire! Mittomo-nai!

(*vt.*) ...o hajisaseru [...を恥じさせる]; ...ni fu-meiyo-o-ataeru [...に不名誉を与える]; haji-irasete...(suru-)no-o yamesaseru [恥じ入らせて...(する)のをやめさせる].

shameful (*a.*) hazukashii [恥ずかしい]; fu-memboku-na [不面目な].

shameless (*a.*) haji-shirazu-na [恥知らずな]; zûzûshii [ずうずうしい].

shampoo (*vt.*) (atama-no-kami)-o arau [(頭の髪)を洗う].

(*n.*) sempatsu [洗髪]; shampû [シャンプー].

shape (*n.*) 1)katachi [形]; kakkô [格好]; matomatta-katachi [まとまった形]. 2)jôtai [状態]. 3)shurui [種類]; taipu [タイプ].

(*vt.*) 1)...o katachi-zukuru [...を形作る]. 2)...o kettei-suru [...を決定する]. 3)...o matomeru [...をまとめる]. 4)...o awaseru [...を合わせる].

(*vi.*) katachi-o-nasu [形をなす]; matomaru [まとまる].

shapely (*a.*) kakkô-no-yoi [格好のよい].

share (*n.*) 1)wake-mae [分け前]; yakuwari [役割]. 2)(*com.*) shijô-sen'yû-ritsu [市場占有率]. 3)(*pl.*) ((*Eng.*)) kabu [株]. 「suru

go shares with one in... (*Eng. colloq.*)hito-to...o yama-wake-ni-

(*vt.*) 1)...o wakeru [...を分ける]; ...o wake-au [...を分け合う]; ...o tomo-ni-suru [...を共にする]. 2)...o tsutaeru [...を伝える].

(*vi.*) buntan-suru [分担する]; wake-au [分け合う].

shareholder (*n.*) ((*Eng.*)) kabu-nushi [株主].

shark (*n.*) same [サメ]; fuka [フカ].

sharp (*a.*) 1)surudoi [鋭い]; togatta [とがった]. 2)kyû-na [急な].
3)hakkiri-shita [はっきりした]. 4)rikô-na [利口な]. 5)hageshii [激し
い]. 6)eibin-na [鋭敏な]. 7)(*mus.*) shâpu-no [シャープの].
 (*1*) a **sharp** point *surudoku-togatta* saki
 (*2*) a **sharp** curve *kyû-na* kâbu
 (*3*) the **sharp** outline *hakkiri-shita* rinkaku
 (*4*) a **sharp** boy *rikô-na* shônen
 (*5*) a **sharp** pain *hageshii* itami
 (*6*) a **sharp** nose *eibin-na* hana
  (*ad.*) 1)kakkiri [かっきり]. 2)kyû-ni [急に].
  (*n.*) shâpu [シャープ].

sharpen (*vt.*) 1)...o surudoku-suru […を鋭くする]; (empitsu nado)-o
kezuru [(鉛筆など)を削る]. 2)...o kibishiku-suru […を厳しくする]. 3)
...o hakkiri-saseru […をはっきりさせる].
  (*vi.*) 1)surudoku-naru [鋭くなる]. 2)hageshiku-naru [激しく
なる]. 3)hakkiri-suru [はっきりする]. 4)binkan-ni-naru [敏感になる].

sharply (*ad.*) 1)surudoku [鋭く]. 2)kyû-ni [急に]. 3)hakkiri-to [はっ
きりと]. 4)kibishiku [厳しく]. 5)nuke-me-naku [抜け目なく].

shave (*vt.*) ...o soru […をそる]; ...o usuku-kezuru […を薄く削る].
  (*vi.*) hige-o-soru [ひげをそる].
  (*n.*) hige-o-soru-koto [ひげをそること].

shaving cream hige-sori-yô-kurîmu [ひげそり用クリーム].

shawl (*n.*) kata-kake [肩掛け]; shôru [ショール].
  (*vt.*) ...ni shôru-o-kakeru […にショールを掛ける].

she (*pron.*) kano-jo-wa [彼女は]; kano-jo-ga [彼女が].

shear (*n.*) 1)(*pl.*) oo-basami [大ばさみ]. 2)kari-komi [刈り込み].
  (*vt.*) 1)...o karu […を刈る]. 2)(hitsuji)-no ke-o-karu [(羊)の毛
を刈る].
  (*vi.*) hasami-o-ireru [はさみを入れる]; kireru [切れる].

shed (*n.*) koya [小屋]; shako [車庫].

shed (*vt.*) 1)(namida ya chi nado)-o nagasu [(涙や血など)を流す].
2)...o otosu […を落とす]; ...o nugu […を脱ぐ]. 3)(hikari nado)-o
hassuru [(光など)を発する].

sheep (*n.*) hitsuji [羊].

sheer (*a.*) 1)mattaku-no [全くの]. 2)kiri-tatta [切り立った]. 3)suki-
tootta [透き通った]; goku-usui [ごく薄い].

    (*ad.*) suichoku-ni [垂直に]; massugu-ni [真っすぐに].

sheet (*n.*) 1)shikifu [敷布]; shîtsu [シーツ]. 2)ichi-mai-no-kami [一枚の紙]. 3)usu-ita [薄板]. 4)(koori ya yuki no)usui-hirogari [(氷や雪の)薄い広がり].

    (*vt.*) 1)...ni shikifu-o-tsukeru [···に敷布をつける]. 2)...o usuku-oou [···を薄く覆う].

sheet glass ita-garasu [板ガラス].

sheet iron usu-teppan [薄鉄板].

shelf (*n.*) tana [棚]; iwa-dana [岩だな].

shell (*n.*) 1)kai-gara [貝殻]; (*zool.*) (kame no)kôra [(カメの)甲羅]; (*bot.*) (mame no)kawa [(豆の)皮]. 2)gaikei [外形]. 3)(*mil.*) hôdan [砲弾].

    (*vt.*) 1)...no kara-o-toru [···の殻を取る]; ...no kawa-o-toru [···の皮を取る]. 2)...o hôgeki-suru [···を砲撃する].

    (*vi.*) (kawa nado ga) mukeru [(皮などが)むける]; toreru [とれる].

shelter (*n.*) 1)hinan-jo [避難所]. 2)hogo [保護].

    (*vt.*) ...o hogo-suru [···を保護する]; ...o kakumau [···をかくまう].

    (*vi.*) hinan-suru [避難する].

  shelter oneself mi-o-mamoru; (hito no ken'i nado ni) tayoru

shepherd (*n.*) 1)hitsuji-kai [羊飼い]. 2)bokushi [牧師].

    (*vt.*) ...no sewa-o-suru [···の世話をする]; ...o michibiku [···を導く].

sheriff (*n.*) ((*US*)) gun-hoan-kan [郡保安官]; ((*Eng.*)) shû-chôkan [州長官].

sherry (*n.*) sherî-shu [シェリー酒].

shield (*n.*) 1)tate [盾]. 2)bôgyo-butsu [防御物].

    (*vt.*) 1)...o hogo-suru [···を保護する]. 2)...o kabau [···をかばう]. 3)...o oou [···を覆う]; ...o kakusu [···を隠す].

    (*vi.*) tate-to-naru [盾となる]; hogo-suru [保護する].

shift (*vt.*) 1)...o kaeru [···を変える]; ...o utsusu [···を移す]. 2)...o tori-nozoku [···を取り除く].

    (*vi.*) 1)ichi-o-kaeru [位置を変える]; utsuru [移る]. 2)yarikuri-suru [やりくりする].

  shift for oneself jiriki-de-yarikuri-suru

    (*n.*) 1)henka [変化]. 2)kôtai [交替]. 3)yarikuri [やりくり].

  (2) an eight-hour **shift** hachi-jikan-*kôtai*-sei

shimmer (*vi.*) chira-chira-hikaru［ちらちら光る］; kasuka-ni-hikaru
［かすかに光る］.

　　　(*n.*) kasuka-na-hikari［かすかな光］; chira-chira-suru-hikari
［ちらちらする光］; kirameki［きらめき］.

shine (*vi.*) hikaru［光る］; kagayaku［輝く］; iki-iki-suru［生き生きす
る］.

　　　(*vt.*) 1)...o terasu［…を照らす］; ...o kagayakasu［…を輝かす］.
2)...o migaku［…を磨く］.

　　　(*n.*) hikari［光］; kagayaki［輝き］; tsuya［つや］.

　rain or shine (*colloq.*) sei-u-ni-kakawarazu; don-na-koto-ga-atte-
mo

shiny (*a.*) 1)hikaru［光る］; kagayaku［輝く］; pika-pika-suru［ぴかぴ
かする］. 2)seiten-no［晴天の］.

ship (*n.*) fune［船］.

　　　(*vt.*) ...o fune-ni-tsumu［…を船に積む］; ...o fune-de-okuru［…を
船で送る］; ...o yusô-suru［…を輸送する］.

　　　(*vi.*) fune-ni-noru［船に乗る］; jôsen-suru［乗船する］.

shipment (*n.*) funa-zumi［船積み］; tsumi-ni［積み荷］.

shipper (*n.*) funa-ni-nushi［船荷主］.

shipwreck (*n.*) nampa［難破］; zasetsu［ざ折］.

　　　(*vt.*) ...o nampa-saseru［…を難破させる］; ...o zasetsu-
saseru［…をざ折させる］.

　　　(*vi.*) nampa-suru［難破する］.

shipyard (*n.*) zôsen-jo［造船所］.

shirt (*n.*) 1)waishatsu［ワイシャツ］. 2)((*US*)) shita-gi［下着］.

　　　(*vt.*) ...o shatsu-de-oou［…をシャツで覆う］.

shirting (*n.*) shatsu-ji［シャツ地］; waishatsu-ji［ワイシャツ地］.

shiver (*vi.*) (samu-sa ya kyôfu nado de) buru-buru-furueru［(寒さ
や恐怖などで)ぶるぶる震える］.　　　　　　　　　　　「okan［悪寒］.

　　　(*n.*) mi-burui［身震い］; (*colloq.*) (the *pl.*) samu-ke［寒気］;

shock (*n.*) 1)shôgeki［衝撃］. 2)dageki［打撃］; shokku［ショック］. 3)
(*elect.*) dengeki［電撃］; kanden［感電］.

　(*1*) Several **shocks** of earthquake were felt this month.
　　　Kongetsu-wa *jishin* ga ikudo-ka atta.

　(*2*) The news was a great **shock** to me.
　　　Sono shirase niwa totemo *odoroi*ta.

　(*3*) An electric **shock** may kill people.
　　　Kanden de hito ga shinu-koto-ga-aru.

 (*vt.*) 1)...o gyotto-saseru […をぎょっとさせる]. 2)...o fungai-saseru […を憤慨させる]. 3)...o kanden-saseru […を感電させる].

 (*vi.*) gyotto-suru [ぎょっとする].

shoe (*n.*) 1)(*pl.*) tangutsu [短靴]. 2)teitetsu [てい鉄].

 (*vt.*) ...ni kutsu-o-hakaseru […に靴をはかせる]; ...ni teitetsu-o-utsu […にてい鉄を打つ]; ...ni kana-gu-o-tsukeru […に金具を付ける].

shoeblack (*n.*) ((*Eng.*)) kutsu-migaki [靴磨き].

shoehorn (*n.*) kutsu-bera [靴べら].

shoelace (*n.*) kutsu-himo [靴ひも].

shoemaker (*n.*) kutsuya [靴屋].

shoeshine (*n.*) kutsu-migaki [靴磨き].

shoestring (*n.*) 1)((*US*)) kutsu-himo [靴ひも]. 2)(*colloq.*) wazuka-na-kane [わずかな金].

 (*a.*) 1)hoso-nagai [細長い]. 2)fu-antei-na [不安定な]. 3)shôgaku-no [少額の].

shoot (*vt.*) 1)...o utsu […を撃つ]. 2)(me ya eda)-o dasu [(芽や枝)を出す]. 3)...o abise-kakeru […を浴びせかける]. 4)(*sports*)...o shûto-suru […をシュートする]. 5)(*photo.*)...o satsuei-suru […を撮影する].

 (*1*) They **were** all **shot** to pieces.

  Kare-ra-wa *utare*-te zuta-zuta-ni-natta.

 (*2*) The tree will **shoot** out buds. Sono ki wa me-*o dasu*-darô.

 (*3*) He **shot** questions at me.

  Kare-wa watashi-ni shitsumon-*o abise-kaketa.*

 (*4*) He **shot** the ball into the goal.

  Kare-wa bôru-*o* gôru-ni *shûto-shita.*

 (*5*) He **shot** his first film in Hollywood.

  Kare-wa saisho-no eiga-*o* Hariuddo-de *totta.*

 (*vi.*) 1)utsu [撃つ]. 2)ikioi-yoku-tobi-dasu [勢いよく飛び出す]. 3)me-o-dasu [芽を出す]. 4)shûto-suru [シュートする].

 (*n.*) 1)shageki [射撃]. 2)hatsuga [発芽]; waka-eda [若枝]. 3)shuryô-tai [狩猟隊]; shuryô-chi [狩猟地]. 4)shûto [シュート].

shop (*n.*) 1)mise [店]; ko-uri-ten [小売店]. 2)sagyô-ba [作業場].

 (*vi. & vt.*) kai-mono-o-suru(...de kai-mono-o-suru) [買物をする(…で買物をする)].

shop assistant ((*Eng.*)) ten'in [店員].

shopkeeper (*n.*) tenshu [店主].

shoplifting (*n.*) mambiki [万引き].

shopping (*n.*) kai-mono [買物]; shoppingu [ショッピング].

go shopping kai-mono-ni-iku

shore (*n.*) 1)(umi ya kawa ya mizuumi no) kishi [(海や川や湖の)岸]; riku [陸]. 2)kuni [国].

shoreline (*n.*) kaigan-sen [海岸線]; kogan-sen [湖岸線].

short (*a.*) 1)mijikai [短い]; se-no-hikui [背の低い]. 2)fusoku-shita [不足した]; tari-nai [足りない]. 3)kanketsu-na [簡潔な]; sokke-nai [そっけない].

  (*1*) This is a **short** story. Kore-wa *mijikai* shôsetsu da.
                      Kore-wa *tampen*-shôsetsu da.

  (*2*) We are **short** of money. Ware-ware-wa kane-ga *tarinai*.

  (*3*) To be **short**, she doesn't love me.
      Kantan-ni-ieba, kano-jo-wa watashi-o ai-shite-i-nai-no-da.

  run short fusoku-suru; ketsubô-suru

    (*ad.*) 1)kyû-ni [急に]. 2)fusoku-shite [不足して]. 3)kantan-ni [簡単に].

    (*1*) He stopped **short**. Kare-wa *kyû-ni* tomatta.

    (*n.*) 1)mijikai-mono [短いもの]; kakete-iru-mono [欠けているもの]; (the –) yôten [要点]; (*pl.*) fusoku-bun [不足分]. 2)(*baseball*) shôto [ショート].

  like a shot teppô-dama-no-yô-ni; sugu-ni

shortage (*n.*) fusoku [不足]; ketsubô [欠乏].

shortcoming (*n.*) (*pl.*) ketten [欠点]; tansho [短所].

shortcut (*n.*) chika-michi [近道].

shorten (*vt. & vi.*) ...o mijikaku-suru (mijikaku-naru) [...を短くする (短かくなる)]; ...o chijimeru (chijimu) [...を縮める(縮む)]; ...o tsumeru (tsumaru) [...をつめる(つまる)].

shorthand (*n.*) sokki[-hô] [速記(法)].

short-lived (*a.*) tammei-no [短命の]; hakanai [はかない].

shortly (*ad.*) 1)ma-mo-naku [間もなく]. 2)kantan-ni [簡単に]. 3) sokke-naku [そっけなく].

shortsighted (*a.*) 1)kinshi-no [近視の]. 2)senken-no-mei-no-nai [先見の明のない]; kinshi-gan-teki-na [近視眼的な].

shot (*n.*) 1)dangan [弾丸]. 2)shashu [射手]. 3)shatei [射程]. 4)hito-nage [一投げ]; hito-keri [一けり]; hito-tsuki [一突き]. 5)(*colloq.*) chûsha [注射]. 6)shashin [写真]; sunappu [スナップ].

  like a shot teppô-dama-no-yô-ni; sugu-ni

should (*aux. v.*) 1)...(suru)darô [...(する)だろう] (*see.* would 2). 2) ...(su-)beki-de-aru [...(す)べきである]. 3)...no-wa...da [...のは...だ]; ...to-wa...da [...とは...だ]. 4)man'ichi...nara-ba [万一...ならば].

(2) You **should** study harder.
　　Kimi-wa motto benkyô-su-*beki-da*.
(3) It is strange that he **should** say such a fool.
　　Kare-ga sonna-baka-na-koto-o iu-*to-wa* fushigi-*da*.
(4) If he **should** be free tomorrow, I would call on him.
　　Asu (*man'ichi*) kare-ga hima-*nara*, watashi-wa kare-o-hômon-suru-tsumori-da.

shoulder (*n.*) kata [肩].
　shoulder to shoulder kata-o-narabete
　　(*vt.*) 1)...o katsugu [...をかつぐ]; ...o se-ou [...を背負う]. 2)...o kata-de-osu [...を肩で押す].

shout (*vi.*) sakebu [叫ぶ]; oo-goe-o-dasu [大声を出す].
　　(*vt.*) ...o sakebu [...を叫ぶ].
　　(*n.*) sakebi [叫び]; oo-goe [大声].

shove (*vt.*) ...o osu [...を押す]; ...o tsuku [...を突く]; ...o oshi-nokeru [...を押しのける].
　　(*vi.*) osu [押す]; tsuku [突く].
　　(*n.*) hito-oshi [一押し]; hito-tsuki [一突き].

shovel (*n.*) shaberu [シャベル].
　　(*vt.*) 1)...o shaberu-de-sukuu [...をシャベルですくう]; ...o shaberu-de-tsukuru [...をシャベルで作る]. 2)(tabe-mono nado)-o tairyô-ni[-kuchi-ni]-hôri-komu [(食物など)を大量に(口に)ほうりこむ].
　　(*vi.*) shaberu-o-tsukau [シャベルを使う].

show (*vt.*) 1)...o miseru [...を見せる]; ...o shimesu [...を示す]. 2)...o shômei-suru [...を証明する]. 3)...o annai-suru [...を案内する].
(1) **Show** me another one.　Betsu-no-mono-o *misete*-kudasai.
(2) This **shows** that he is innocent.
　　Kore-wa kare-ga keppaku-de-aru-koto-o *shômei-shite-iru*.
(3) He **showed** me round the campus.
　　Kare-wa watashi-ni sono-gakkô-no-kônai-o achi-kochi *annai-shite-kureta*.
　　(*vi.*) 1)mieru [見える]; arawareru [現れる]. 2)(*colloq.*) tenji-kai-o-hiraku [展示会を開く].
　show up (*colloq.*) arawareru; kao-o-dasu
　　Last night he showed up for the party.
　　Sakuban kare-wa pâtî-ni kao-o-dashita.
　　(*n.*) 1)miseru-koto [見せること]; tenji-kai [展示会]. 2)(*colloq.*) mise-mono [見せもの]; shô [ショー]. 3)gaikan [外観]; mise-kake

［見せ掛け］.

for show mise-birakashi-ni

on show chinretsu-sarete

shower (*n.*) 1)niwaka-ame［にわか雨］. 2)((*US*)) o-iwai-hin-zôtei-pâtî［お祝い品贈呈パーティー］.

    (*vt.*) 1)...o niwaka-ame-de-nurasu［…をにわか雨でぬらす］. 2)...o oshimi-naku-ataeru［…を惜しみなく与える］.

    (*vi.*) 1)niwaka-ame-ga-furu［にわか雨が降る］. 2)ame-no-yô-ni-furi-sosogu［雨のように降りそそぐ］. 3)shawâ-o-abiru［シャワーを浴びる］.

showman (*n.*) (*colloq.*) 1)kôgyô-shi［興行師］. 2)engi-no-saikaku-no-aru-hito［演技の才覚のある人］.

showroom (*n.*) chinretsu-shitsu［陳列室］; shôrûmu［ショールーム］.

show window chinretsu-mado［陳列窓］; shô-uindô［ショーウインドー］.

showy (*a.*) medatsu［目立つ］; kebakebashii［けばけばしい］.

shred (*n.*) 1)dampen［断片］; kire-hashi［切れ端］. 2)wazuka［わずか］.

    cut(tear)...to shreds 1)...o zuta-zuta-ni-saku. 2)...o rompa-suru

    (*vt. & vi.*) ...o zuta-zuta-ni-saku(zuta-zuta-ni-naru)［…をずたずたに裂く（ずたずたになる）］.

shrewd (*a.*) nuke-me-no-nai［抜け目のない］; rikô-na［利口な］.

shriek (*vi.*) kanakiri-goe-o-dasu［金切り声を出す］.

    (*vt.*) ...o kan-dakai-koe-de-iu［…を甲高い声で言う］.

    (*n.*) kanakiri-goe［金切り声］; himei［悲鳴］.

shrill (*a.*) kan-dakai［甲高い］; surudoi［鋭い］.

    (*vt. & vi.*) ...o kan-dakai-koe-de-iu (kan-dakai-koe-o-dasu)［…を甲高い声で言う（甲高い声を出す）］.

shrimp (*n.*) ko-ebi［小エビ］; shurimpu［シュリンプ］.

    (*vi.*) ko-ebi-o-toru［小エビを取る］.

shrine (*n.*) seidô［聖堂］; jinja［神社］.

shrink (*vi.*) 1)chijimu［縮む］. 2)shiri-gomi-suru［しり込みする］. 3)genshô-suru［減少する］.

    (*vt.*) ...o chijimaseru［…を縮ませる］; ...o chiisaku-suru［…を小さくする］; ...o herasu［…を減らす］.

    (*n.*) shûshuku［収縮］.

shrivel (*vi.*) 1)shiwa-ga-yoru［しわがよる］; shibomu［しぼむ］. 2)dame-ni-naru［だめになる］.

    (*vt.*) 1)...ni shiwa-o-yoraseru［…にしわを寄らせる］; ...o

chijimaseru [⋯を縮ませる]. 2)...o dame-ni-suru [⋯をだめにする].

shroud (*vt.*) ...o ooi-kakusu [⋯を覆い隠す]; ...o tsutsumu [⋯を包む].
　　(*n.*) 1)kyô-katabira [経かたびら]. 2)ooi [覆い].

shrub (*n.*) kamboku [かん木].

shrug (*vt.*) (kata)-o sukumeru [(肩)をすくめる].
　　(*vi. & n.*) kata-o-sukumeru(-koto) [肩をすくめる(こと)].

shudder (*n.*) mi-burui [身震い]; furue [震え].
　　(*vi.*) 1)mi-burui-suru [身震いする]; furueru [震える]. 2) yureru [揺れる].

shuffle (*vt.*) 1)(ashi)-o hikizutte-aruku [(足)を引きずって歩く]. 2)...o utsushi-kaeru [⋯を移し替える]. 3)...o gocha-maze-ni-suru [⋯をごちゃ混ぜにする]. 4)...o ii-nukeru [⋯を言い抜ける].
　　(*vi.*) 1)ashi-o-hikizutte-aruku [足を引きずって歩く]; achi-kochi-to-ugoku [あちこちと動く]. 2)(*cards*) kiru [切る]. 3)ii-nukeru [言い抜ける].
　　(*n.*) ashi-o-hikizutte-aruku-koto [足を引きずって歩くこと]; maze-awaseru-koto [混ぜ合わせること]; ii-nogare [言い逃れ].

shun (*vt.*) ...o sakeru [⋯を避ける].

shut (*vt.*) ...o shimeru [⋯を閉める]; ...o tojiru [⋯を閉じる]; ...o toji-komeru [⋯を閉じ込める].
　　(*vi.*) shimaru [閉まる].
　shut off ...o tomeru
　　Shut the gas off. Gasu-o tomete-kure.
　shut out ...o shime-dasu; (*baseball*)...o kampû-suru
　　He shut me out of the house.
　　Kare-wa watashi-o ie-kara shime-dashita.
　shut up (*colloq.*) ...o dama-raseru(damaru)

shutter (*n.*) 1)(*pl.*) yoroi-do [よろい戸]; ama-do [あま戸]. 2)(*photo.*) shattâ [シャッター].

shuttle bus kin-kyori-ôfuku-basu [近距離往復バス].

shy (*a.*) 1)hanikanda [はにかんだ]; uchiki-na [内気な]. 2)(*US colloq.*) fusoku-shite [不足して].

sick (*a.*) 1)byôki-no [病気の]. 2)((*Eng.*)) haki-ke-ga-suru [吐き気がする]. 3)unzari-shite [うんざりして]. 4)koishi-gatte [恋しがって].
　(*1*) He has become **sick** as it was too cold.
　　Amari samukatta-node kare-wa *byôki-ni*-natta.
　(*2*) I always feel **sick** in the bus.
　　Watashi-wa basu-ni-noru-to itsu-mo *haki-sô-ni*-naru.

(3) I'm **sick** of his lecture.
　　　Watashi-wa kare-no kôgi-niwa *unzari-shite*-iru.
(4) She is **sick** for home.　Kano-jo-wa hômu*shikku-ni-kakatte*-iru.

sickle (*n.*) kama [かま].

sickness (*n.*) 1)byôki [病気]. 2)mukatsuki [むかつき]; haki-ke [吐き気].

side (*n.*) 1)gawa [側]; sokumen [側面]. 2)soba [そば]. 3)men [面].
4)mikata [味方].
　(*1*) The sea surrounds it on all **sides**.
　　　Umi ga sono-arayuru-*men*-o tori-kakonde-iru.
　　　Umi ga sono-shi*men*-o tori-kakonde-iru.
　(*2*) A cat is sleeping by my **side**.
　　　Neko-ga ippiki watashi-no-*soba*-de nemutteiru.
　(*3*) The story has two **sides** to it.
　　　Sono-hanashi niwa ryô*men*-ga aru.
　(*4*) Who was on your **side**? Kimi no *mikata* wa dare-datta?
　from side to side sayû-ni; yoko-ni
　side by side narande; tagai-ni-sesshite
　　　(*vi.*) 1)...gawa-ni-tsuku [⋯側につく]. 2)yoko-e-ugoku [横へ動く].
　　　(*vt.*) 1)...ni sokumen-o-tsukeru [⋯に側面をつける]. 2)...to
narabu [⋯と並ぶ]. 3)...no mikata-o-suru [⋯の味方をする].

sideboard (*n.*) shokki-dana [食器棚]; saidobôdo [サイドボード].

sidewalk (*n.*) ((*US*)) hodô [歩道].

siege (*n.*) 1)hôi-kôgeki [包囲攻撃]. 2)(byôki nado no) nagakute-
kurushii-kikan [(病気などの)長くて苦しい期間].

sigh (*n.*) tame-iki [ため息].
　　　(*vi.*) 1)tame-iki-o-tsuku [ため息をつく]. 2)shitau [慕う];
akogareru [あこがれる].
　　　(*vt.*) ...o tame-iki-o-tsuite-iu [⋯をため息をついて言う].

sight (*n.*) 1)miru-koto [見ること]. 2)shiryoku [視力]. 3)kôkei [光景].
4)(the *pl.*) meisho [名所]. 5)mieru-tokoro [見えるところ]; shikai
[視界]. 6)miru-tokoro [見るところ]; kenkai [見解].
　(*1*) He smiled at the **sight** of her.
　　　Kare-wa kano-jo-o-*mite* waratta.
　(*2*) The poor man lost his **sight**.
　　　Kawaisô-ni sono hito wa *shiryoku*-o ushinatta.
　　　Kawaisô-ni sono hito wa shitsumei-shita.
　(*3*) It was a dreadful **sight** to see.

Miru-mo-osoroshii-*kôkei* datta.

(4) Did you do the **sights** of Tokyo?

Tôkyô no *meisho*-kembutsu-o shimashita-ka?

(5) Out of **sight**, out of mind.

Mie-naku-nareba, kokoro-kara-kiete-iku.

Saru-mono hibi-ni-utoshi.

(6) In my **sight** he is honest.

Watashi-no-*miru-tokoro*-de-wa kare-wa shôjiki-da.

at first sight　ikken-shite; hito-me-mite

catch(get) sight of　...o mitsukeru

come in sight　miete-kuru

　　(*vt.*) 1)...o mitsukeru ［…を見付ける］; ...o kansoku-suru ［…を観測する］. 2)...o nerau ［…をねらう］.

sightseeing (*n.*) kankô ［観光］.

sign (*n.*) 1)shirushi ［しるし］; fugô ［符号］. 2)te-mane ［手まね］; mi-buri ［身振り］. 3)kamban ［看板］; hyôshiki ［標識］. 4)keiseki ［形跡］. 5)zenchô ［前兆］; chôkô ［徴候］.

(1) a **sign** of thanks　kansha no *shirushi*

(2) He made me a **sign** to go.

Kare-wa watashi-ni ike-to-*aizu*-shita.

(3) See the neon **sign**board.

Ano neon-sain-no-*kamban*-o goran-nasai.

(4) I saw no **sign** of him.　Kare-no-iru-*keiseki* wa nakatta.

(5) There are **signs** of a storm.　Arashi no *zenchô*-ga-aru.

Are-*moyô*-da.

　　(*vt. & vi.*) 1)(...ni) shomei-suru ［(…に)署名する］. 2)(...ni) aizu-suru ［(…に)合図する］.

signal (*n.*) 1)shingô ［信号］; aizu ［合図］. 2)kikkake ［きっかけ］.

　　(*a.*) 1)shingô-no ［信号の］. 2)ichijirushii ［著しい］.

　　(*vt.*) 1)...ni aizu-suru ［…に合図する］; ...ni shingô-o-okuru ［…に信号を送る］. 2)...no shôko-to-naru ［…の証拠となる］.

　　(*vi.*) aizu-suru ［合図する］; shingô-o-okuru ［信号を送る］.

signature (*n.*) 1)shomei ［署名］; sain ［サイン］. 2)(*mus.*) kigô ［記号］.

signboard (*n.*) kamban ［看板］; keiji-ban ［掲示板］.

significance (*n.*) 1)imi ［意味］. 2)jûyô-sei ［重要性］.

significant (*a.*) imi-no-aru ［意味のある］; jûyô-na ［重要な］.

signify (*vt.*) 1)...o shimesu ［…を示す］; ...o hyômei-suru ［…を表明する］. 2)...o imi-suru ［…を意味する］.

silence (*n.*) 1)shizukesa [静けさ]. 2)chimmoku [沈黙]. 3)mokusatsu [黙殺].

  in silence damatte; shizuka-ni;

      (*vt.*) …o chimmoku-saseru […を沈黙させる].

      (*int.*) Shizuka-ni! [静かに!].

silent (*a.*) 1)damatte-iru [黙っている]. 2)shizuka-na [静かな]. 3) katara-nai [語らない].

  (*1*) Be **silent**, boys! Mina-san, *shizuka-ni!*

  (*2*) Everything is quiet and **silent** all round.

      Atari wa *shizuka*-da.

  (*3*) The newspaper was **silent** about his death.

      Shimbun wa kare-no shi-ni-tsuite *katatte-i-nakatta.*

      Shimbun niwa kare-no shi-ni-tsuite-wa *notte-i-nakatta.*

  (*n.*) (*pl.*) (*colloq.*) musei-eiga [無声映画].

silently (*ad.*) damatte [黙って]; shizuka-ni [静かに].

silk (*n.*) 1)kinu [絹]. 2)(*pl.*) kinu-mono [絹物].

  raw silk kiito

silkworm (*n.*) (*insect*) kaiko [カイコ].

silky (*a.*) 1)kinu-no-yô-na [絹のような]; tsuya-no-aru [つやのある]. 2)mono-yawaraka-na [もの柔らかな].

sill (*n.*) shikii [敷居]; dodai [土台].

silly (*a.*) oroka-na [愚かな]; baka-geta [ばかげた].

  (*n.*) (*colloq.*) O-baka-san [おばかさん].

silver (*n.*) 1)gin [銀]. 2)gin-iro [銀色]. 3)ginka [銀貨]. 4)gin-shokki-rui [銀食器類].

  (*a.*) gin-no [銀の]; gin-iro-no [銀色の]; gin-sei-no [銀製の].

  (*vt.*) …ni gin-o-kabuseru […に銀をかぶせる]; …o gin-iro-ni-suru […を銀色にする].

silvery (*a.*) gin-no-yô-na [銀のような]; gin-hakushoku-no [銀白色の]; gin-o-fukumu [銀を含む].

similar (*a.*) 1)yoku-nita [よく似た]; dôrui-no [同類の]. 2)(*math.*) sôji-no [相似の].

simple (*a.*) 1)tanjun-na [単純な]; kantan-na [簡単な]. 2)o-hitoyoshi-no [お人よしの]. 3)shisso-na [質素な]. 4)ki-dora-nai [気取らない]. 5)junzen-taru [純然たる]. 6)tan'itsu-no [単一の].

simplify (*vt.*) …o kantan-ni-suru […を簡単にする]; …o heii-ni-suru […を平易にする].

simply (*ad.*) 1)kantan-ni [簡単に]. 2)mu-jaki-ni [無邪気に]. 3)tada

[ただ]; mattaku [全く].

simultaneous (*a.*) dôji-ni-okoru [同時に起こる].

simultaneous interpretation dôji-tsûyaku [同時通訳].

sin (*n. & vi.*) tsumi(-o-okasu) [罪(を犯す)].

since (*conj.*) 1)...irai […以来]. 2)...dakara […だから].

 (*1*) It is three years **since** my father died.

   Watashi-no chichi ga shinde-*kara* san-nen-ni-naru.

 (*2*) **Since** you say so, we must admit it.

   Kimi-ga sô iu-no-*dakara*, ware-ware-wa sore-o mitome-
    neba-naranai.

  (*prep.*) ...irai […以来].

  I haven't seen him **since** then.

   Sono-toki-*irai* watashi-wa kare-ni atte-i-nai.

  (*ad.*) 1)sono-go [その後]. 2)...mae-ni […前に].

 (*1*) I have lived here ever **since**.

   Watashi-wa *sono-go*-zutto koko-ni sundeiru.

 (*2*) He died ten years **since**. Kare-wa jû-nen-*mae-ni* shinda.

sincere (*a.*) seijitsu-na [誠実な]; kokoro-kara-no [心からの].

sincerely (*ad.*) seijitsu-ni [誠実に]; kokoro-kara [心から].

 Yours sincerely, or **Sincerely yours**, Keigu

sinew (*n.*) 1)(*anat.*) ken [けん]. 2)(*pl.*) kinniku [筋肉]; tairyoku
[体力]. 3)(*pl.*) chikara [力]; shiryoku [資力].

sing (*vi.*) 1)utau [歌う]. 2)saezuru [さえずる]; naku [鳴く].

  (*vt.*) (uta)-o utau [(歌)を歌う]; ...ni utatte...(sa-)seru […に歌っ
て…(さ)せる]; ...o utatte-sugosu […を歌って過ごす]; ...o tonaeru […
を唱える].

singer (*n.*) kashu [歌手].

single (*a.*) 1)tatta-hitotsu-no [たった一つの]. 2)dokushin-no [独身の].
3)hitori-yô-no [一人用の].

 (*1*) A **single** instance was given.

   Tatta-hitotsu-no rei ga age-rareta.

 (*2*) He remains **single**. Kare-wa mada-*dokushin*-da.

 (*3*) a **single** bed *hitori-yô-no* beddo

  (*n.*) 1)ikko [一個]; hitori [一人]. 2)(*US colloq.*) dokushin-
sha [独身者]. 3)(*colloq.*) hitori-yô-no-heya [一人用の部屋].

  (*vt.*) ...o erabi-dasu […を選び出す].

  (*vi.*) (*baseball*) tanda-o-utsu [単打を打つ].

single-breasted (*a.*) shinguru-no [シングルの]; ichi-retsu-botan-no

［一列ボタンの］.

singular (*a.*) 1)hitotsu-dake-no ［一つだけの］. 2)mare-ni-miru ［まれに見る］. 3)kimyô-na ［奇妙な］. 4)(*gram.*) tansû-no ［単数の］.
　　(*n.*) (*gram.*) tansû ［単数］.

singularly (*ad.*) kiwadatte ［際立って］; toku-ni ［特に］.

sinister (*a.*) 1)fukitsu-na ［不吉な］. 2)akui-no-aru ［悪意のある］.

sink (*vi.*) 1)shizumu ［沈む］. 2)gakkuri-suru ［がっくりする］. 3)ochiiru ［陥る］. 4)yowamaru ［弱まる］.
　　(*1*) She **sank** into the stream.
　　　　Kano-jo-wa nagare-no-naka-ni *shizunda.*
　　(*2*) His heart **sank** at last. Kare-wa tsui-ni *gakkuri-shita.*
　　(*3*) She **sank** into a deep sleep.
　　　　Kano-jo-wa fukai-nemuri-ni *ochita.*
　　(*4*) The wind **sank** down. Kaze ga *shizumatta.*
　　(*vt.*) 1)…o shizumeru ［…を沈める］. 2)…o otosu ［…を落とす］. 3)…o oshi-komeru ［…を押し込める］.
　　(*n.*) 1)(daidokoro no) nagashi ［(台所の)流し］. 2)((*US*)) semmen-dai ［洗面台］. 3)gesui-kô ［下水溝］.

sip (*vt. & vi.*) (…o) chibi-chibi-nomu ［(…を)ちびちび飲む］; (…o) susuru ［(…を)すする］.
　　(*n.*) hito-kuchi ［一口］; chibi-chibi-nomu-koto ［ちびちび飲むこと］.

sir (*n.*) 1)anata-sama ［あなた様］. 2)(S-) Haikei ［拝啓］.
　　(*1*) Good morning, **sir**. Ohayô-gozaimasu.
　　(*2*) Dear **Sirs**, *Haikei*

sister (*n.*) 1)shimai ［姉妹］. 2)shimai-no-yô-ni-shitashii-josei ［姉妹のように親しい女性］.

sister-in-law (*n.*) giri-no-shimai ［義理の姉妹］.

sit (*vi.*) 1)suwaru ［座る］. 2)hirakareru ［開かれる］.
　　(*1*) **Sit** down, please. Dôzo o-*suwari*-kudasai.
　　(*2*) The court will **sit** on Tuesday.
　　　　Hôtei wa Kayô-ni *hirakareru.*
　　sit in on …o sankan-suru; …ni shusseki-suru
　　　　He didn't sit in on the conference.
　　　　Kare-wa kaigi-ni shusseki-shi-nakatta.
　　sit up ne-zu-ni-okiteiru
　　　　He sat up late last night.
　　　　Kare-wa sakuya osoku-made-okite-ita.
　　(*vt.*) 1)…o suwaraseru ［…を座らせる］. 2)(uma)-ni noru ［(馬)に

乗る].

site (*n.*) 1)shikichi [敷地]; yôchi [用地]. 2)iseki [遺跡].
　　(*vt.*) (be -d) ichi-suru [位置する].

sitting room ima [居間].

situated (*a.*) 1)(...ni-)ichi-shite-iru [(…に)位置している]. 2)(*colloq.*)
...no-tachiba-ni-aru […の立場にある].

situation (*n.*) 1)ichi [位置]. 2)keisei [形勢]; jitai [事態]. 3)tsutome-
guchi [勤め口].
　　(*1*) The school stands in a good **situation**.
　　　　Gakkô wa ii-*ichi*-ni aru.
　　(*2*) Can any one save the **situation**?
　　　　Kono *jitai*-o suku-eru-hito-ga-iru-ka?
　　(*3*) John is out of a **situation**. Jon wa shitsu*gyô*-shite-iru.
　　　　Situation wanted. *Shoku*-o-motomu.

six (*n. & a.*) roku(-no) [六(の)].

sixteen (*n. & a.*) jû-roku(-no) [十六(の)].

sixteenth (*n. & a.*) dai-jû-roku(-no) [第十六(の)].

sixth (*n. & a.*) dai-roku(-no) [第六(の)].

sixtieth (*n. & a.*) dai-roku-jû(-no) [第六十(の)].

sixty (*n. & a.*) roku-jû(-no) [六十(の)].

size (*n.*) 1)ookisa [大きさ]. 2)(bôshi ya kutsu nado no)...ban;
saizu [(帽子やくつなどの)…番; サイズ]. 3)kibo [規模]; kiryô [器量].
　　(*1*) They are of the same **size**. Sore-ra-wa onaji-*ookisa*-da.
　　(*2*) What **size** do you wear? Nam-*ban*-o o-tsukai-desu-ka?
　　(*3*) an undertaking of great **size** dai-*kibo* na jigyô
　　　　(*vt.*) ...no ookisa-ni-tsukuru […の大きさに作る]; ...o ookisa-ni-
yotte-wakeru […を大きさによって分ける].

skate (*n.*) (*pl.*) sukêto-gutsu [スケート靴].
　　(*vi.*) sukêto-o-suru [スケートをする].

skeleton (*n.*) 1)gaikotsu [がい骨]. 2)hone-gumi [骨組み]; gairyaku
[概略].

sketch (*n.*) 1)suketchi [スケッチ]. 2)tampen [短編]. 3)taiyô [大要].
　　(*vt.*) ...o suketchi-suru […をスケッチする]; ...no gairyaku-o-
noberu […の概略を述べる].
　　(*vi.*) suketchi-suru [スケッチする].

ski (*n. & vi.*) sukî(-de-suberu) [スキー(で滑る)].

skill (*n.*) jukuren [熟練]; shuwan [手腕]; gijutsu [技術].

skil(l)ful (*a.*) takumi-na [巧みな]; jôzu-na [上手な].

skim (*vt.*) 1)...no-hyômen-ni-uita-mono-o sukui-toru […の表面に浮いたものをすくい取る]. 2)...o sure-sure-ni-tonde-iku […をすれすれに飛んで行く]. 3)...z zatto-yomu […をざっと読む].

 (*vi.*) sure-sure-ni-tonde-iku [すれすれに飛んで行く]; zatto-yomu [ざっと読む].

skin (*n.*) kawa [皮]; hifu [皮膚].

 to the skin hada-made

 (*vt.*) 1)...no kawa-o-muku […の皮をむく]. 2)...o suri-muku […をすりむく].

 (*vi.*) kawa-de-oowareru [皮で覆われる].

skin diver sukin-daibingu-o-suru-hito [スキンダイビングをする人].

skinny (*a.*) yase-koketa [やせこけた]; hone-to-kawa-bakari-no [骨と皮ばかりの].

skip (*vi.*) 1)karuku-tobu [軽く跳ぶ]; sukippu-suru [スキップする]. 2) tobashite-yomu [飛ばして読む]. 3)((*US*)) (*educ.*) tobi-shinkyû-suru [飛び進級する].

 (*vt.*) 1)...o karuku-tobi-kosu […を軽く跳び越す]. 2)...o tobasu […を飛ばす]; ...o habuku […を省く].

 (*n.*) karui-hito-tobi [軽い一跳び]; tobashi-yomi [飛ばし読み]; tobasu-koto [飛ばすこと].

skirt (*n.*) 1)sukâto [スカート]. 2)suso [すそ]. 3)(*pl.*) machi-hazure [町外れ]; (toshi no) shûhen [(都市の)周辺].

 (*vt. & vi.*) 1)(...no) fuchi-ni-sotte-iku [(…の)ふちに沿って行く]. 2)(...o) kaihi-suru [(…を)回避する].

skull (*n.*) zugai-kotsu [頭がい骨].

sky (*n.*) 1)sora [空]; ten [天]. 2)tenkô [天候]. 3)(the -) tengoku [天国].

skylark (*n.*) (*birds*) hibari [ひばり].

skyrocket (*vi. & vt.*) (kakaku ga) hane-agaru [(価格が)はね上がる]; (kakaku)-o hane-agaraseru [(価格)をはね上がらせる].

skyscraper (*n.*) chô-kôsô-biru [超高層ビル].

slab (*n.*) atsu-ita [厚板]; heiban [平板].

slack (*a.*) 1)yurui [ゆるい]; tarunda [たるんだ]. 2)darashi-no-nai [だらしのない]. 3)(*com.*) kakki-no-nai [活気のない]; fu-keiki-na [不景気な].

 (*ad.*) yuruku [ゆるく]; darashi-naku [だらしなく]; fu-kappatsu-ni [不活発に].

 (*n.*) 1)yurunda-bubun [ゆるんだ部分]. 2)chintai [沈滞]; fukyô

[不況].

　　(vt.) 1)...o yurumeru […をゆるめる]; ...o tarumaseru […をたるませる]. 2)...o okotaru […を怠る].

　　(vi.) 1)yurumu [ゆるむ]; tarumu [たるむ]. 2)okotaru [怠る]. 3)chintai-suru [沈滞する].

slacken (vi. & vt.) 1)yurumu(...o yurumeru) [ゆるむ(…をゆるめる)]. 2)sokudo-o-otosu((sokudo)-o otosu) [速度を落とす((速度)を落とす)].

slacks (n.) surakkusu [スラックス].

slam (n.) pishari [ぴしゃり].

　　(vt. & vi.) ...o pishari-to-shimeru (pishari-to-shimaru) […をぴしゃりと閉める(ぴしゃりと閉まる)].

slander (n.) chûshô [中傷]; warukuchi [悪口].

　　(vt.) ...o chûshô-suru […を中傷する].

slang (n.) zokugo [俗語]; surangu [スラング].

slap (n.) 1)hira-te-uchi [平手打ち]. 2)hinan [非難].

　　(vt.) ...o pishari-to-utsu […をぴしゃりと打つ]; ...o patan-to-oku […をぱたんと置く].

　　(vi.) pishari-to-oto-o-tateru [ピシャリと音を立てる].

　　(ad.) (colloq.) massugu-ni [真っすぐに]; matomo-ni [まともに].

slate (n.) surêto [スレート].

　　(vt.) ...o surêto-de-fuku […をスレートでふく].

slaughter (n.) gyakusatsu [虐殺].

　　(vt.) ...o gyakusatsu-suru […を虐殺する].

slave (n.) dorei [奴隷]; akuseku-hataraku-hito [あくせく働く人].

　　(vi.) akuseku-hataraku [あくせく働く].

slavery (n.) 1)dorei-no-kyôgû [奴隷の境遇]. 2)(colloq.) tsurai-shigoto [つらい仕事].

sled (n.) sori [そり].

　　(vi.) sori-ni-noru [そりに乗る]; sori-de-iku [そりで行く].

　　(vt.) ...o sori-de-hakobu […をそりで運ぶ].

sledge (n.) = sled.

sleep (n.) 1)suimin [睡眠]; katsudô-kyûshi [活動休止]. 2)eimin [永眠]. 3)(dôbutsu no) tômin [(動物の)冬眠].

　go to sleep nemuru

　　(vi.) nemuru [眠る]; neru [寝る]; katsudô-shite-i-nai [活動していない]; eimin-shite-iru [永眠している].

　　(vt.) 1)nemuru [眠る]. 2)...o tomerareru […を泊められる].

　sleep...away ...o nete-sugosu

sleeper (*n.*) 1)nemutteiru-hito [眠っている人]. 2)shindai-sha [寝台車]. 3)((*Eng.*)) makura-gi [まくら木]. 4)(*pl.*) ((*US*)) (yôji-yô no) pajama [(幼児用の)パジャマ].

sleeping bag ne-bukuro [寝袋].

sleepy (*a.*) 1)nemui [眠い]; nemu-sô-na [眠そうな]. 2)kakki-no-nai [活気のない]. 3)juku-shi-sugita [熟しすぎた].

sleepyhead (*n.*) nebô [寝坊].

sleeve (*n.*) 1)sode [そで]; surîbu [スリーブ]. 2)((*Eng.*)) rekôdo-no-jaketto [レコードのジャケット].

sleigh (*n. & vi.*) sori(-ni-noru) [そり(に乗る)].
　　　　(*vt.*) ...o sori-de-hakobu […をそりで運ぶ].

slender (*a.*) 1)hossori-to-shita [ほっそりとした]; hoso-nagai [細長い]. 2)wazuka-na [わずかな]. 3)hakujaku-na [薄弱な]; yowai [弱い].

slice (*n.*) (usui-)hito-kire [(薄い)一切れ].
　　　　(*vt.*) ...o usuku-kiru […を薄く切る].
　　　　(*vi.*) (*sports*) suraisu-sasete-utsu [スライスさせて打つ].

slide (*vt. & vi.*) ...o suberaseru (suberu) […を滑らせる(滑る)].
　　　　(*n.*) 1)suberu-koto [滑ること]. 2)suraido [スライド].

slide rule keisan-jaku [計算尺].

slight (*a.*) 1)wazuka-na [わずかな]; sukoshi-no [少しの]; karui [軽い]; toru-ni-tari-nai [取るに足りない]. 2)hossori-shita [ほっそりした].
　　　　(*vt.*) ...o keishi-suru […を軽視する]; ...o naozari-ni-suru […をなおざりにする].
　　　　(*n.*) keishi [軽視]; bujoku [侮辱].

slightly (*ad.*) 1)wazuka-ni [わずかに]; sukoshi [少し]. 2)hossori-to [ほっそりと].

slim (*a.*) 1)hossori-shita [ほっそりした]. 2)wazuka-na [わずかな]. 3)kudaranai [くだらない].
　　　　(*vi.*) yaseru [やせる]; hosoku-naru [細くなる].
　　　　(*vt.*) 1)...o yasesaseru […をやせさせる]. 2)...o sakugen-suru […を削減する].

slime (*n.*) (sakana nado no) nen'eki [(魚などの)粘液]; hedoro [へどろ]; iya-na-mono [いやなもの].

sling (*vt.*) 1)...o nageru […を投げる]. 2)...o tsurusu […をつるす].

slink (*vi.*) kossori-nigeru [こっそり逃げる]; kossori-ugoku [こっそり動く].

slip (*vi.*) 1)suberu [滑る]. 2)shira-nu-ma-ni-sugiru [知らぬ間に過ぎる]. 3)sotto-hairu [そっとはいる]; sotto-deru [そっと出る]. 4)kie-saru

［消え去る］.

(1) His right foot **slipped**.　Kare-no migi-ashi ga *subetta*.

(2) Five years **slipped** away.　Go-nen ga *shira-nu-ma-ni-sugita*.

(3) He **slipped** in without being seen.

Kare-wa hito-ni-mirare-nai-de *sotto*-naka-ni-*haitta*.

(4) The name **slipped** out of my mind.

Watashi wa sono namae ga dô-shite-mo omoi-dase-*nakatta*.

　(*vt.*) 1)...o sururi-to-kiru ［…をするりと着る］; ...o sururi-to-nugu ［…をするりと脱ぐ］. 2)...o toku ［…を解く］.

(1) He **slipped** his coat off.　Kare-wa uwagi-o *sururi-to-nuida*.

(2) The ship **slipped** anchor.　Fune wa ikari-o *toita*.

　(*n.*) 1)suberu-koto ［滑ること］. 2)machigai ［間違い］. 3)surippu ［スリップ］.

　(2) a **slip** of the pen　kaki-*sokonai*

　　　a **slip** of the tongue　*shitsugen*

slip (*n.*) 1)hoso-nagai-ippen ［細長い一片］. 2)sashi-ki ［さし木］.

slippery (*a.*) 1)tsuru-tsuru-suberu ［つるつる滑る］. 2)fu-antei-na ［不安定な］.

slit (*n.*) hoso-nagai-kiri-kuchi ［細長いきり口］; suritto ［スリット］.

　(*vt.*) ...o hoso-nagaku-kiru ［…を細長く切る］; ...o kiri-hiraku ［…を切り開く］.

　(*vi.*) hoso-nagaku-sakeru ［細長く裂ける］.

slogan (*n.*) hyôgo ［標語］; surôgan ［スローガン］; mottô ［モットー］.

slope (*n.*) saka ［坂］; shamen ［斜面］; surôpu ［スロープ］.

　(*vi. & vt.*) keisha-suru(...o keisha-saseru) ［傾斜する（…を傾斜させる）］.

slot machine ((*US*)) surotto-mashîn ［スロットマシーン］; jidô-tobaku-ki ［自動と博機］; ((*Eng.*)) jidô-hambai-ki ［自動販売機］.

slow (*a.*) 1)osoi ［遅い］; noroi ［のろい］. 2)(tokei ga) okurete-iru ［(時計が)遅れている］. 3)taikutsu-na ［退屈な］. 4)nibui ［鈍い］; warui ［悪い］.

(1) He is **slow** but steady.　Kare-wa *osoku*-temo chakujitsu-da.

(2) Your watch is five minutes **slow**.

Kimi-no tokei wa go-fun *okurete-iru*.

(3) a very **slow** book　totemo *taikutsu-na* hon

(4) My son is **slow** to understand.

Watashi-no musuko wa nomi-komi-ga-*warui*.

　　　　(*vi.*) osoku-naru [遅くなる]; yukkuri-suru [ゆっくりする].
　　　　(*vt.*) ...o okuraseru […を遅らせる].
　　　　(*ad.*) osoku [遅く]; yukkuri [ゆっくり].
slowly (*ad.*) osoku [遅く]; yukkuri [ゆっくり].
sluggish (*a.*) 1)bushô-na [無精な]. 2)noroi [のろい]; yuruyaka-na [ゆるやかな]. 3)fu-kappatsu-na [不活発な].
slum (*n.*) suramu-gai [スラム街].
slumber (*n.*) madoromu [まどろむ]; uto-uto-suru [うとうとする].
slump (*n.*) 1)bôraku [暴落]. 2)fushin [不振]; surampu [スランプ].
　　　　(*vi.*) 1)bôraku-suru [暴落する]. 2)ninki-ga-ochiru [人気が落ちる]. 3)dosari-to-ochiru [どさりと落ちる].
sly (*a.*) zurui [ずるい].
smack (*n.*) 1)shita-tsuzumi [舌鼓]. 2)pishari-to-utsu-oto [ピシャリと打つ音].
　　　　(*vt.*) (...ni) shita-tsuzumi-o-utsu [(…に)舌鼓を打つ]; ...o pishari-to-utsu […をピシャリと打つ].
small (*a.*) 1)chiisai [小さい]. 2)tsumaranai [つまらない].
smallpox (*n.*) (*med.*) tennen-tô [天然痘].
smart (*a.*) 1)ki-no-kiita [気のきいた]. 2)shareta [しゃれた]; sumâto-na [スマートな]. 3)rikô-na [利口な]; nuke-me-no-nai [抜け目のない].
　　　　(*vi.*) 1)itamu [痛む]; uzuku [うずく]; hiri-hiri-suru [ひりひりする]. 2)kanjô-o-gaisuru [感情を害する].
　　　　(*ad.*) kibishiku [厳しく].
　　　　(*n.*) itami [痛み]; uzuki [うずき].
smartly (*ad.*) kibishiku [厳しく]; rikô-ni [利口に]; subayaku [す早く]; ko-girei-ni [小ぎれいに].
smash (*vt.*) 1)...o uchi-kowasu […を打ち壊す]. 2)(*sports*) ...o sumasshu-suru […をスマッシュする].
　　　　(*vi.*) 1)kona-gona-ni-naru [粉々になる]. 2)gekitotsu-suru [激突する].
　　　　(*n.*) 1)funsai-suru-oto [粉砕する音]. 2)hageshii-ichigeki [激しい一撃]; dai-shôtotsu [大衝突].
smear (*vt.*) 1)...o nuri-tsukeru […を塗りつける]. 2)...o yogosu […を汚す].
　　　　(*vi.*) yogoreru [汚れる].
　　　　(*n.*) yogore [汚れ]; shimi [しみ].
smell (*vi.*) 1)nioi-o-kagu [においをかぐ]. 2)nioi-ga-suru [においがする].
　　(1) **smell** at a flower　hana-no *nioi-o-kagu*

(2) This flower **smells** bad.   Kono hana wa iya-na-*nioi-ga-suru*.

  (vt.) 1)...no nioi-o-kagu [⋯のにおいをかぐ]. 2)...o kagi-tsukeru [⋯をかぎ付ける].

  (n.) nioi [におい]; kaori [香り].

smile *(vi.)* hohoemu [ほほえむ]; nikkori-warau [にっこり笑う].

  (vt.) hohoende...(sa-)seru [ほほえんで⋯(さ)せる].

  (n.) hohoemi [ほほえみ]; bishô [微笑]; egao [笑顔].

smith *(n.)* kajiya [かじ屋].

smock *(n.)* shigoto-gi [仕事着]; uwappari [上っ張り].

smoke *(n. & vi.)* 1)kemuri(-o-dasu) [煙(を出す)]. 2)kitsuen(-suru) [喫煙(する)].

 have a smoke   ippuku-suru

  (vt.) 1)...o suu [⋯を吸う]. 2)...o kunsei-ni-suru [⋯をくん製にする]. 3)...o ibusu [⋯をいぶす].

smoking *(n.)* kitsuen [喫煙].

  No **smoking**. Kin'*en*.

  Please refrain from **smoking**. *Tabako* go-enryo-kudasai.

  (a.) kemutte-iru [煙っている]; yuge-o-tateru [湯気を立てる].

smooth *(a.)* 1)nameraka-na [滑らかな]. 2)heion-na [平穏な]. 3) yoku-nereta [よく練れた]. 4)ryûchô-na [流ちょうな].

(1) It is as **smooth** as glass.

  Sore-wa garasu-no-yô-ni-*nameraka*-da.

(2) We are now in a **smooth** voyage.

  Ware-ware-wa *heion-na*-kôkai-o-shite-iru.

(3) Please warm the butter to make it **smooth** to spread.

  Nureru-yô-ni batâ-o atatamete-kudasai.

(4) The essay is written in a **smooth** style.

  Sono zuihitsu wa (nameraka-na senren-sareta) *ryûchô-na* buntai-de kakarete-iru.

  (vt.) 1)...o nameraka-ni-suru [⋯を滑らかにする]. 2)...o tairani-suru [⋯を平らにする]. 3)(kami)-o nade-tsukeru [(髪)をなでつける]. 4)...o shizumeru [⋯を静める]. 5)...o senren-suru [⋯を洗練する].

  (vi.) nameraka-ni-naru [滑らかになる]; taira-ni-naru [平らになる]; shizumaru [静まる].

  (n.) taira-ni-suru-koto [平らにすること]; nameraka-na-bubun [滑らかな部分]; heimen [平面].

smoothly *(ad.)* 1)nameraka-ni [滑らかに]. 2)sura-sura-to [すらすらと]; ryûchô-ni [流ちょうに].

smother (*vt.*) 1)...o chissoku-saseru ［…を窒息させる］. 2)...o kami-korosu ［…をかみ殺す］. 3)...o momi-kesu ［…をもみ消す］.

      (*vi.*) chissoku-suru ［窒息する］.

smuggle (*vt.*) ...o mitsuyu-suru ［…を密輸する］; ...o hisoka-ni-mochi-komu ［…をひそかに持ち込む］; ...o hisoka-ni-mochi-dasu ［…をひそかに持ち出す］.

      (*vi.*) mitsuyu-suru ［密輸する］.

snack (*n.*) karui-shokuji ［軽い食事］.

      (*vi.*) ((*US*)) keishoku-o-toru ［軽食をとる］.

snail (*n.*) (*zool.*) katatsumuri ［カタツムリ］.

snake (*n.*) hebi ［ヘビ］.

      (*vt.*) ...o kunerasu ［…をくねらす］; ...o kunette-susumaseru ［…をくねって進ませる］.

      (*vi.*) kunette-susumu ［くねって進む］.

snap (*vt.*) 1)...o pokitto-oru ［…をぽきっと折る］. 2)...o pachin-to-narasu ［…をぱちんと鳴らす］. 3)...ni pakutto-kami-tsuku ［…にぱくっとかみ付く］. 4)...o kami-tsuku-yô-ni-iu ［…をかみつくように言う］. 5)...o subayaku-ugokasu ［…をす早く動かす］. 6)(*colloq.*) ...no sunappu-shashin-o-toru ［…のスナップ写真をとる］.

  (*1*) He **snapped** his cane.   Kare-wa sutekki-*o pokitto-otta*.

  (*2*) I **have snapped** my fingers.

      Watashi-wa yubi-*o pachin-to-narashita*.

  (*3*) The dog **snapped** the piece of meat.

      Sono inu wa niku-hen-*ni pakutto-kami-tsuita*.

  (*4*) Don't **snap** him up so fiercely.

      Sonna-ni hidoku kare-*ni ganari-tsukeru*-na.

  (*5*) He **snapped** the ball at the dog.

      Kare-wa *subayaku* sono inu-ni-mukatte bôru-*o nageta*.

  (*6*) Our photographer **snapped** a nice photograph of us.

      Shashin'ya-san ga ware-ware-no yoi *sunappu-shashin-o-totte-kureta*.

      (*vi.*) pokitto-oreru ［ぽきっと折れる］; pachin-to-iu ［ぱちんという］; kami-tsuku ［かみ付く］; subayaku-ugoku ［す早く動く］.

      (*n.*) 1)pokin ［ぽきん］; pachin ［ぱちん］. 2)(*photo.*) sunappu-shashin ［スナップ写真］. 3)((*US*)) tome-gane ［留め金］; sunappu ［スナップ］. 4)surudoi-kuchô ［鋭い口調］.

      (*ad.*) pokitto ［ぽきっと］; pachin-to ［ぱちんと］.

snapshot (*n.*) sunappu-shashin ［スナップ写真］.

snare (*n.*) wana [わな]; yûwaku [誘惑].

 (*vt.*) ...o wana-ni-kakeru [...をわなにかける]; ...o yûwaku-suru [...を誘惑する].

snarl (*vi. & n.*) 1)unaru(-koto) [うなる(こと)]. 2)gami-gami-iu (-koto) [がみがみ言う(こと)].

snarl (*n.*) motsure [もつれ]; funkyû [紛糾].

 (*vt.*) ...o motsuresaseru [...をもつれさせる]; ...o konran-saseru [...を混乱させる].

 (*vi.*) motsureru [もつれる].

snatch (*vt.*) ...o hittakuru [...をひったくる].

 (*n.*) hittakuri [ひったくり]; gôdatsu [強奪].

sneak (*vi.*) koso-koso-nigeru [こそこそ逃げる]; kossori-hairu [こっそり入る]; kossori-deru [こっそり出る].

 (*vt.*) ...o kossori-mochi-komu [...をこっそり持ち込む]; ...o kossori-mochi-dasu [...をこっそり持ち出す].

 (*n.*) koso-koso-suru-hito [こそこそする人]; hiretsu-na-hito [卑劣な人].

sneer (*n. & vi.*) reishô(-suru) [冷笑(する)].

 (*vt.*) ...o reishô-shite-iu [...を冷笑して言う].

sneeze (*n. & vi.*) kushami(-o-suru) [くしゃみ(をする)].

sniff (*vi.*) 1)hana-o-susuru [鼻をすする]. 2)kun-kun-kagu [くんくんかぐ].

 (*vt.*) ...no nioi-o-kagu [...のにおいをかぐ]; ...ni kan-zuku [...に感付く].

 (*n.*) 1)kun-kun-kagu-koto [くんくんかぐこと]; nioi [におい]. 2)hana-saki-de-ashirau-koto [鼻先であしらうこと].

snip (*vi. & vt.*) (...o) hasami-de-chokin-to-kiru [(...を)はさみでちょきんと切る].

 (*n.*) hito-hasami [一はさみ]; kiri-toru-koto [切り取ること]; ippen [一片]; dampen [断片].

snipe (*n.*) (*birds*) shigi [シギ].

snob (*n.*) sunobbu [スノッブ].

snore (*n. & vi.*) ibiki(-o-kaku) [いびき(をかく)].

snorkel (*n.*) shunôkeru [シュノーケル].

snow (*n. & vi.*) yuki(-ga-furu) [雪(が降る)].

snowball (*n.*) yuki-no-tama [雪の玉].

 (*vt.*) ...ni yuki-no-tama-o-nageru [...に雪の玉を投げる].

 (*vi.*) yuki-gassen-o-suru [雪合戦をする].

snowbound (*a.*) yuki-ni-toji-komerareta [雪に閉じ込められた].

snowcapped (*a.*) yuki-o-itadaita [雪をいただいた].

snowdrift (*n.*) yuki-no-fuki-damari [雪の吹きだまり].

snowfall (*n.*) kôsetsu[-ryô] [降雪(量)].

snowflake (*n.*) seppen [雪片].

snowman (*n.*) yuki-daruma [雪だるま].

snowplow, -plough (*n.*) yuki-kaki [雪かき]; (*R.R.*) josetsu-sha [除雪車].

snowshed (*n.*) nadare-yoke [なだれよけ].

snowslide, -slip (*n.*) nadare [なだれ].

snowstorm (*n.*) fubuki [吹雪].

snow-white (*a.*) masshiro-na [まっ白な]; yuki-no-yô-ni-shiroi [雪のように白い]; jumpaku-no [純白の].

snowy (*a.*) 1)yuki-no-ooi [雪の多い]. 2)yuki-no-furu [雪の降る]. 3) masshiro-na [まっ白な].

  (*1*) Their country is very **snowy**.

      Kare-ra-no kuni wa taihen *yuki-ga-ooi.*

  (*2*) It is **snowy** today. Kyô wa *yuki*-da.

  (*3*) See that **snowy** bird. Ano *masshiro-na* tori-o goran-nasai.

snug (*a.*) 1)igokochi-no-yoi [居心地のよい]. 2)kojimmari-shita [こじんまりした]. 3)pittari-au [ぴったり合う].

  (*ad.*) pittari-to [ぴったりと]; kitchiri-to [きっちりと].

so (*ad.*) 1)sô [そう]; sono-tôri [そのとおり]. 2)sore-hodo [それほど]; sonna-ni [そんなに]. 3)(*colloq.*) hijô-ni [非常に]; totemo [とても]. 4)...mo-sô-de-aru […もそうである].

  (*1*) I think **so**. Watashi-wa *sô* omoimasu.

    Is that **so**? *Sô*-desu-ka?

    Are you a Japanese? **So** I am.

      Anata-wa Nihon-jin desu-ka? *Sô*-desu.

  (*2*) Don't speak **so** fast. *Sonna-ni* hayaku hanasa-nai-de-kure.

  (*3*) I'm **so** hungry. Watashi-wa *totemo* onaka-ga-suite-iru.

  (*4*) You are a Japanese. **So** am I.

    Anata-wa Nihon-jin desu. Watashi *mo sô*-desu.

  or so ...hodo; ...ka-sono-kurai

    We stayed there for a week **or so**.

      Ware-ware-wa soko-ni isshû-kan-*hodo* taizai-shita.

  so as to (do) ...(suru)-tame-ni; ...(suru)-yô-ni

  so...as to(do) ...(suru)-hodo

so that (= therefore) sore-dakara

so...that 1)...(suru-)hodo(-de-aru). 2)amari...na-node

so to speak iwaba

(*conj.*) sore-de [それで].

It was too late, **so** I ran as fast as I could.

Totemo osokatta, *sore-de* watashi-wa dekiru-dake-hayaku-hashitta.

Totemo osokatta-*node*, watashi-wa dekiru-dake-hayaku-hashitta.

(*int.*) 1)sore-de-yoshi! [それでよし!]. 2)hontô-ka [ほんとうか]; masaka [まさか]; yappari [やっぱり].

(1) A little more to the left, **so**!

Mô-sukoshi hidari-no-hô-e, *sore-de-yoshi!*

soak (*vt.*) ...o hitasu [⋯を浸す]; ...o tsukeru [⋯をつける].

(*vi.*) hitaru [浸る]; tsukaru [つかる]; shimi-tooru [染み通る].

so-and-so (*n.*) 1)dare-sore [だれそれ]. 2)kô-kô-iu-koto [こうこういうこと].

soap (*n.*) sekken [石けん].

(*vt.*) ...o sekken-de-arau [⋯を石けんで洗う].

soar (*vi.*) 1)mai-agaru [舞い上がる]. 2)sobie-tatsu [そびえ立つ]. 3)(bukka ga) kyûtô-suru [(物価が)急騰する]. 4)(kibô ga) takamaru [(希望が)高まる].

sob (*vi.*) susuri-naku [すすり泣く].

(*vt.*) susuri-naki-nagara...o iu [すすり泣きながら⋯を言う].

(*n.*) susuri-naki [すすり泣き]; musebi-naki [むせび泣き]; musebi-naku-yô-na-oto [むせび泣くような音].

sober (*a.*) reisei-na [冷静な]; majime-na [まじめな]. 2)yotte-i-nai [酔っていない]. 3)jimi-na [地味な].

(*vt. & vi.*) ...o ochitsukaseru (ochitsuku) [⋯を落ち着かせる(落ち着く)]; ...o majime-ni-suru (majime-ni-naru) [⋯をまじめにする(まじめになる)].

so-called (*a.*) iwayuru [いわゆる].

social (*a.*) 1)shakai-no [社会の]; shakai-teki-na [社会的な]. 2)shakô-jô-no [社交上の]; shakô-kai-no [社交界の].

(*n.*) konshin-kai [懇親会].

socialism (*n.*) shakai-shugi [社会主義].

social science shakai-kagaku [社会科学].

social security shakai-hoshô[-seido] [社会保障(制度)].

society (*n.*) 1)shakai [社会]. 2)...kai […会]; kyôkai [協会]. 3)shakô [社交]; kôsai [交際].

  (*1*) **Society** has one law, and that is custom.

      Shakai niwa hitotsu-no okite-ga aru, sore-wa shûkan-de-aru.

  (*2*) a medical **society**   ishi-*kai*

  (*3*) I enjoyed his **society**.

      Watashi-wa kare-to-no-*kôsai*-o tanoshinda.

sock (*n.*) (*pl.*) mijikai-kutsushita [短かい靴下]; sokkusu [ソックス].

socket (*n.*) uke-guchi [受け口]; soketto [ソケット].

sod (*n.*) shiba-fu [芝生]; shiba-tsuchi [芝土].

soda (*n.*) sôda [ソーダ]; sôda-sui [ソーダ水].

sofa (*n.*) sofâ [ソファー]; naga-isu [長いす].

soft (*a.*) 1)yawarakai [柔らかい]; nameraka-na [滑らかな]. 2)yasashii [優しい]; odayaka-na [穏やかな].

soft drink seiryô-inryô [清涼飲料].

soften (*vt. & vi.*) ...o yawarakaku-suru (yawarakaku-naru) […を柔らかくする(柔らかくなる)]; ...o yawarageru (yawaragu) […を和らげる(和らぐ)].

softly (*ad.*) yawarakaku [柔らかく]; yasashiku [優しく]; shizuka-ni [静かに].

soil (*n.*) tsuchi [土]; tochi [土地].

soil (*vt. & vi.*) ...o yogosu (yogoreru) […を汚す(汚れる)].

  (*n.*) yogore [汚れ]; obutsu [汚物].

sojourn (*n. & vi.*) taizai(-suru) [滞在(する)]; tôryû(-suru) [とう留(する)].

solar (*a.*) taiyô-no [太陽の].

solar system, the (*astron.*) taiyô-kei [太陽系].

soldier (*n.*) gunjin [軍人]; heishi [兵士].

sole (*n.*) ashi-no-ura [足の裏]; kutsu-zoko [靴底].

sole (*a.*) 1)tada-hitotsu-no [ただ一つの]. 2)dokusen-teki-na [独占的な].

sole agent itte-hambai-nin [一手販売人].

solely (*ad.*) 1)tada-hitori-de [ただ一人で]. 2)moppara [もっぱら]; tan-ni [単に].

solemn (*a.*) 1)sôgon-na [荘厳な]. 2)majime-na [まじめな]. 3)shûkyô-jô-no [宗教上の].

solicit (*vt. & vi.*) (...o) kongan-suru [(…を)懇願する].

solid (*a.*) 1)katai [堅い]; kotai-no [固体の]. 2)chûkû-de-nai [中空で

ない]. 3)shikkari-shita [しっかりした].

solitary (*a.*) hitori-botchi-no [独りぼっちの]; hito-zato-hanareta [人里離れた].

　　(*n.*) inton-sha [隠とん者]; yo-sute-bito [世捨て人].

solitude (*n.*) kodoku [孤独]; hito-zato-hanareta-basho [人里離れた場所].

solution (*n.*) 1)kaiketsu [解決]; kaitô [解答]. 2)yôkai [溶解]; yôeki [溶液]. 3)bunkai [分解].

solve (*vt.*) ...o kaiketsu-suru [...を解決する]; ...o toku [...を解く].

somber, -bre (*a.*) 1)usu-gurai [薄暗い]; inki-na [陰気な]. 2)kuro-zunda [黒ずんだ]; jimi-na [地味な].

some (*a.*) 1)ikuraka-no [いくらかの]; ikutsuka-no [いくつかの]. 2)aru [ある]; dare-ka-no [だれかの]; nani-ka-no [何かの]; doko-ka-no [どこかの]. 3)oyoso [およそ]; yaku... [約...]. 4)(*colloq.*) kanari-no [かなりの].

　(*1*) There are **some** notebooks on the desk.

　　　　Tsukue-no-ue-niwa *ikuraka-no* nôto-ga-aru.

　　　Some boys don't like studying.

　　　　Kodomo-*no-naka-ni-wa* benkyô-no-kirai-na-ko-mo-*iru*.

　(*2*) Lend me **some** novel.　*Nani-ka* shôsetsu-o kashite-kudasai.

　(*3*) It is **some** 20 miles off.　*Yaku* ni-jû mairu hanarete-iru.

　(*4*) There was **some** wind last night.

　　　　Sakuya *kanari* kaze ga atta.

　in some way　dô-nika-shite

　some time　1)shibaraku-no-aida. 2)sono-uchi

　　　(*pron.*) 1)aru-hito-tachi [ある人たち]; 2)ikura-ka [いくらか]; ikutsu-ka [いくつか].

　(*1*) **Some** of the boys were late.

　　　　Ano-shônen-tachi-*no-naka-ni-wa* okureta-*mono-mo*-ita.

　(*2*) I have **some** already. Watashi-wa sude-ni *ikura-ka* motte-iru.

　　　(*ad.*) ikubun [いくぶん]; tashô-tomo [多少とも]; sukoshi [少し].

　　　I'm feeling **some** better now.

　　　　Watashi-wa *sukoshi* kibun-ga-yoku-nari-mashita.

somebody (*pron.*) aru-hito [ある人]; dare-ka [だれか].

　　(*n.*) oo-mono [大物]; jûyô-jimbutsu [重要人物].

somehow (*ad.*) 1)dô-nika-shite [どうにかして]. 2)dô-iu-wake-ka [どういう訳か].

　(*1*) I must get it finished **somehow**.

　　　　　Watashi-wa *dô-nika-shite* sore-o shi-age-neba-naranai.

　(2) **Somehow** he never succeeded.

　　　　　Dô-iu-wake-ka kare-wa ichi-do-mo seikô-shi-nakatta.

someone (*pron.*) dare-ka [だれか]; aru-hito [ある人].

somersault, somerset (*n. & vi.*) tombo-gaeri(-o-suru) [とんぼ返り(をする)]; chû-gaeri(-o-suru) [宙返り(をする)].

something (*pron.*) nani-ka-aru-mono[-koto] [何かあるもの[こと]].

　　　　John has **something** in his hand.

　　　　Jon wa *nani-ka* te-ni motte-iru.

　　　　　(*n.*) 1)nani-ka-aru-mono [何かあるもの]. 2)oo-mono [大物].

　(1) I've brought **something** small for you.

　　　　Watashi-wa anata-ni chotto-shita-*mono*-o motte-kimashita-yo.

　(2) He thinks himself **something**.

　　　　Kare-wa jibun-o *oo-mono*-da-to omotte-iru.

　be something of a... chotto-shita...de-aru

　make something of 1)...o katsuyô-suru. 2)...o jûyô-shi-suru

　　　　　(*ad.*) ikubun [いく分]; ikura-ka [いくらか]; yaya [やや].

sometime (*ad.*) itsu-ka [いつか]; aru-toki [ある時].

sometimes (*ad.*) toki-doki [時々]; toki-ni-wa [時には].

somewhat (*ad.*) ikubun [いくぶん]; sukoshi [少し].

somewhere (*ad.*) doko-ka-ni [どこかに]; doko-ka-e [どこかへ].

son (*n.*) musuko [息子].

sonar (*n.*) suichû-ompa-tanchi-ki [水中音波探知機]; sonâ [ソナー].

sonata (*n.*) (*mus.*) sonata [ソナタ]; sômei-kyoku [奏鳴曲].

song (*n.*) uta [歌]; shiika [詩歌].

songster (*n.*) 1)kashu [歌手]. 2)naki-dori [鳴き鳥].

son-in-law (*n.*) musume-muko [娘むこ].

soon (*ad.*) sugu-ni [すぐに]; ma-mo-naku [間もなく]; hayaku [早く].

　as soon as ...(suru-)to-sugu-ni

　as soon as possible dekiru-dake-hayaku

　no sooner...than ...(suru-)to-sugu-ni

　sooner or later osokare-hayakare

soot (*n.*) susu [すす].

　　　　　(*vt.*) ...o susu-darake-ni-suru […をすすだらけにする].

soothe (*vt.*) 1)...o nadameru […をなだめる]. 2)(itami)-o yawarageru [痛み)を和らげる].

sophisticated (*a.*) 1)senren-sareta [洗練された]; kotta [凝った]. 2)

seken-zure-shita [世間ずれした].

sore (*a.*) 1)itai [痛い]; hiri-hiri-suru [ひりひりする]. 2)hitan-ni-kureta [悲嘆に暮れた]. 3)iradatta [いらだった].

sore throat (*path.*) inkô-en [咽喉炎].

sorely (*ad.*) itande [痛んで]; hidoku [ひどく].

sorrow (*n.*) 1)kanashimi [悲しみ]; hitan [悲嘆]. 2)kôkai [後悔].
　　　　　　(*vi.*) kanashimu [悲しむ]; nageku [嘆く].

sorrowful (*a.*) kanashinde-iru [悲しんでいる]; kanashi-sô-na [悲しそうな]; itamashii [痛ましい].

sorry (*a.*) 1)ki-no-doku-ni-omotte [気の毒に思って]. 2)sumanai-to-omotte [すまないと思って]; zannen-de [残念で]; kôkai-shite [後悔して].

　　(*1*) I am **sorry** for you. *O-ki-no-doku*-desu.

　　(*2*) I am **sorry** that I did it. *Sumanai*-koto-o-itashi-mashita.

　　　I am **sorry**. *Môshi-wake-ari-masen.* (Sumimasen.)

　　　I am **sorry** I cannot accept your proposal.
　　　　O-môshi-koshi-o o-uke-deki-zu *zannen*-desu.

　　　You will be **sorry** that you have done it.
　　　　Kimi-wa sore-o shita-koto-o *kôkai-suru*-darô.

sort (*n.*) shurui [種類].

　a sort of isshu-no

　all sorts of arayuru-shurui-no

　out of sorts (*colloq.*) genki-ga-nai

　sort of (*colloq.*) ikubun; tashô

　　(*vt.*) ...o bunrui-suru […を分類する]; ...o shiwake-suru […を仕分けする].

soul (*n.*) 1)tamashii [魂]; seishin [精神]; kihaku [気迫]. 2)(*colloq.*) (+negative) hitori-mo [一人も].

　　(*1*) He has no **soul**. Kare niwa *kihaku*-ga nai.

　　(*2*) Not a **soul** was to be seen. *Hitokko*-hitori i-nakatta.

sound (*n.*) oto [音]; hibiki [響き]; kikoe [聞こえ].

　　(*vi.*) ...no-oto-ga-suru […の音がする]; hibiku [響く]; ...ni-kikoeru […に聞こえる].

　　(*vt.*) ...o narasu […を鳴らす]; ...o shiraseru […を知らせる]; ...o aizu-suru […を合図する].

sound (*a.*) 1)kenzen-na [健全な]; jôbu-na [丈夫な]. 2)kenjitsu-na [堅実な]. 3)jûbun-na [十分な]. 4)yûkô-na [有効な].

　　(*1*) A **sound** mind in a **sound** body.

　　　　Kenzen-na shintai-ni *kenzen-na* seishin(-o).

(2) a **sound** policy　*kenjitsu-na* seisaku

(3) He enjoyed a **sound** sleep.　Kare-wa *jûbun-na* suimin-o totta.

(4) a **sound** title to property　*yûkô-na* zaisan-shoyû-ken

　　　　(*ad.*) jûbun-ni [十分に]; gussuri-to [ぐっすりと].

soundly (*ad.*) 1)kenzen-ni [健全に]; kenjitsu-ni [堅実に]. 2)jûbun-ni [十分に]. 3)hageshiku [激しく]; mattaku [全く].

sour (*a.*) 1)suppai [酸っぱい]. 2)iji-no-warui [意地の悪い]; fu-kigen-na [不機嫌な].

　　　　(*vt.*) 1)...o suppaku-suru […を酸っぱくする]. 2)...o ki-muzuka-shiku-suru […を気難しくする].

　　　　(*vi.*) 1)suppaku-naru [酸っぱくなる]. 2)ki-muzukashiku-naru [気難しくなる]; mazuku-naru [まずくなる].

source (*n.*) 1)suigen[-chi] [水源(地)]; minamoto [源]. 2)gen'in [原因]; shussho [出所].

south (*n.*) minami [南]; nambu [南部]; nampô [南方].

　　　　(*a.*) minami-no [南の]; minami-kara-no [南からの].

　　　　(*ad.*) minami-e [南へ]; minami-ni [南に].

southeast (*n.*) nan-tô [南東].

　　　　(*a. & ad.*) nan-tô-no (nan-tô-e) [南東の(南東へ)]; nan-tô-kara-no (nan-tô-kara) [南東からの(南東から)].

southern (*a.*) minami-no [南の]; minami-ni-aru [南にある]; minami-e-iku [南へ行く]; minami-kara-no [南からの].

Southern Cross, the　Minami-jûji-sei [南十字星].

South Pole, the　Nankyoku[-ten] [南極(点)].

southwest (*n.*) nan-sei [南西].

　　　　(*a. & ad.*) nan-sei-no (nan-sei-e) [南西の(南西へ)]; nan-sei-kara-no (nan-sei-kara) [南西からの(南西から)].

sovereign (*n.*) kunshu [君主]; shuken-sha [主権者].

　　　　(*a.*) 1)kunshu-de-aru [君主である]; shuken-no-aru [主権のある]; ôi-no [王位の]. 2)saikô-no [最高の]; jûyô-na [重要な].

sovereignty (*n.*) shuken [主権]; dokuritsu-koku [独立国].

sow (*vt. & vi.*) ...o maku (tane-o-maku) […をまく(種をまく)].

soybean (*n.*) (*bot.*) daizu [ダイズ].

soy sauce　shôyu [しょう油].

space (*n.*) 1)kûkan [空間]. 2)kankaku [間隔]. 3)basho [場所]. 4)uchû [宇宙].

(1) **Space** is infinite.　*Kûkan* wa mugen-da.

(2) They are separated by a **space** of 10 feet.

    Kare-ra-wa jû-fîto-no-*kankaku*-de hanarete-iru.

(3) It takes too much **space**. Sore-wa *basho*-o tori-sugiru.

(4) a **space** pilot *uchû*-hikô-shi

    (*vt. & vi.*) ...o ittei-no-kankaku-ni-oku (ittei-no-kankaku-o-oku) [···を一定の間隔に置く(一定の間隔を置く)].

spacious (*a.*) hiroi [広い]; hiro-biro-to-shita [広々とした].

spade (*n.*) fumi-guwa [踏みぐわ]; suki [すき].

    (*vt.*) ...o suki-de-horu [···をすきで掘る].

spade (*n.*) (*cards*) supêdo [スペード].

Spain (*n.*) Supein [スペイン].

span (*vt.*) 1)...ni kakatte-iru [···にかかっている]. 2)...ni wataru [···にわたる]; ...ni oyobu [···に及ぶ]. 3)...o yubi-de-hakaru [···を指ではかる].

(1) A long bridge **spans** this river.

    Nagai-hashi ga kono kawa-*ni kakatte-iru*.

(2) His career **spans** half a century.

    Kare-no keireki wa han-seiki-*ni wataru*.

    (*n.*) 1)oya-yubi-to-ko-yubi-o-hirogeta-nagasa [親指と小指を広げた長さ]. 2)zenchô [全長]. 3)(mijikai) kikan [(短い)期間]. 4)(wazuka-na) kyori [(わずかな)距離].

Spaniard (*n.*) Supein-jin [スペイン人].

Spanish (*a.*) Supein-no [スペインの]; Supein-jin-no [スペイン人の]; Supein-go-no [スペイン語の].

    (*n.*) (the –) Supein-jin [スペイン人]. Supein-go [スペイン語].

spare (*a.*) 1)yobi-no [予備の]; yobun-no [余分の]. 2)shisso-na [質素な]. 3)yaseta [やせた].

(1) I have no **spare** time. Watashi-wa *yobun-na* jikan-ga-nai.

(2) a **spare** meal *shisso-na* shokuji

(3) He is a man of **spare** frame. Kare-wa *yaseta* otoko da.

    (*vt.*) 1)...o(-oshinde) tsukawa-nai [···を(惜しんで)使わない]; ...o ken'yaku-suru [···を倹約する]. 2)(inochi)-o tasukeru [(命)を助ける]. 3)...o nashi-de-sumaseru [···をなしで済ませる]; ...o saku [···を割く].

(1) **Spare** the rod, and spoil the child.

    Muchi-o *oshinde-tsukawa-nai*-to, kodomo ga dame-ni-naru.

    Kawaii-ko-ni-wa tabi-o-saseyo.

(2) **Spare** me. Inochi-bakari-wa o-*tasuke*-kudasai.

(3) Lend me any book you can **spare**.

    Anata-ga *nashi-de-sumaseru* hon-nara-nan-demo kashite-kudasai.

    Ira-nai-hon-ga-attara kashite-kudasai.

Can you **spare** me a few minutes?

    Ni-san-pun *saite*-kuremasen-ka?

not spare oneself rô-o-oshima-nai; zenryoku-o-tsukusu

    (*n.*) yobi-hin [予備品].

sparingly (*ad.*) 1) sukoshi [少し]; hikae-me-ni [控え目に]. 2) ken'yaku-shite [倹約して].

spark (*n.*) 1) hi-no-ko [火の粉]. 2) (*elect.*) hi-bana [火花]; supâku [スパーク]. 3) seiki [生気]; kakki [活気]. 4) hirameki [ひらめき].

not a spark sukoshi-mo-nai; mijin-mo-nai

    (*vi.*) hibana-o-dasu [火花を出す]; (*elect.*) supâku-suru [スパークする].

    (*vt.*) ...e-no dôka-sen-to-naru [...への導火線となる]; ...o shigeki-shite...(sa-)seru [...を刺激して...(さ)せる].

sparkle (*n.*) 1) hi-bana [火花]. 2) kagayaki [輝き]; kirameki [きらめき]. 3) kakki [活気]; seiki [生気]. 4) awa-dachi [泡立ち].

    (*vi.*) 1) hi-bana-o-chirasu [火花を散らす]. 2) kagayaku [輝く]; kirameku [きらめく]. 3) hotobashiru [ほとばしる]; isai-o-hanatsu [異彩を放つ].

    (*vt.*) 1) (hi-bana nado)-o hassuru [(火花など)を発する]. 2) ...o kiramekaseru [...をきらめかせる]. 3) (me ga)...o shimesu [(目が)...を示す].

sparrow (*n.*) suzume [スズメ].

Spartan (*a.*) Suparuta-shiki-no [スパルタ式の].

speak (*vi.*) hanashi-o-suru [話しをする].

He always **speaks** loudly.

    Kare-wa itsu-mo oo-goe-de *hanashi-o-suru*.

    (*vt.*) ...o hanasu [...を話す]; ...o iu [...を言う].

Can you **speak** English? Anata-wa Eigo-*ga hanase-masu*-ka?

not to speak of ...wa-iu-made-mo-naku; ...wa-mochiron

speak highly of ...o gekishô-suru

speak ill of ...o waruku-iu

speak of ...no-koto-o iu

speak out enryo-naku-hanasu; oo-goe-de-hanasu

speak to ...ni hanashi-kakeru

speak well of ...o yoku-iu; ...o homeru

speaker (*n.*) 1)hanasu-hito [話す人]. 2) = loudspeaker kakusei-ki [拡声器].

spear (*n.*) yari [やり].
　　　(*vt.*) ...o yari-de-tsuku […をやりで突く].

special (*a.*) tokubetsu-no [特別の]; tokuyû-no [特有の]; semmon-no [専門の]; irei-no [異例の].
　　　(*n.*) 1)tokubetsu-na-hito[-mono] [特別な人[もの]]; tokushi [特使]. 2)(*US colloq.*) tokka-teikyô[-hin] [特価提供(品)].

special delivery ((*US*)) sokutatsu-bin [速達便].

specialist (*n.*) semmon-ka [専門家]; (*med.*) semmon-i [専門医].

speciality (*n.*) 1)semmon [専門]. 2)tokusei-hin [特製品]; meibutsu [名物]. 3)tokushoku [特色]; tokuchô [特徴].
　　make a speciality of ...o semmon-ni-suru

specialize (*vi.*) semmon-ni-suru [専門にする].
　　　(*vt.*) 1)...o tokushu-ka-suru […を特殊化する]. 2)(imi nado)-o gentei-suru [(意味など)を限定する].

specially (*ad.*) tokubetsu-ni [特別に]; waza-waza [わざわざ]; kakubetsu-ni [格別に].

specialty (*n.*) *see.* speciality.

specie (*n.*) shôkin [正金]; seika [正貨].

species (*n.*) 1)(*biol.*) shu [種]. 2)shurui [種類].

specific (*a.*) 1)tokuyû-no [特有の]. 2)meikaku-na [明確な].
　　　(*n.*) tokkô-yaku [特効薬].

specify (*vt.*) ...o meisai-ni-noberu […を明細に述べる]; ...o gutai-teki-ni-ageru […を具体的に挙げる].

specimen (*n.*) mihon [見本]; hyôhon [標本].

speck (*n.*) chiisana-shimi [小さなしみ]; chiri [ちり].
　　　(*vt.*) ...ni shimi-o-tsukeru […にしみをつける].

speckle (*n.*) shô-hanten [小はん点]; potsu-potsu [ぽつぽつ].
　　　(*vt.*) ...ni hanten-o-tsukeru […にはん点をつける].

spectacle (*n.*) 1)kôkei [光景]; mi-mono [見もの]. 2)(*pl.*) megane [めがね].
　　(*1*) It was a splendid **spectacle**.　Sore-wa subarashii *kôkei* datta.
　　(*2*) I bought a pair of **spectacles**.
　　　　Watashi-wa *megane*-o hitotsu katta.

spectator (*n.*) kembutsu-nin [見物人]; mokugeki-sha [目撃者].

spectrum (*n.*) 1)(*opt.*) supekutoru [スペクトル]. 2)(hendô-suru) han'i

[(変動する)範囲].

speculate (*vi.*) 1)tôki-suru [投機する]. 2)suisoku-suru [推測する].
(*vt.*) ...to suisoku-suru […と推測する].

speculation (*n.*) 1)shisaku [思索]; suisoku [推測]. 2)tôki [投機].

speculative (*a.*) shisaku-teki-na [思索的な]; suiron-ni-suginai [推論に
すぎない]; tôki-teki-na [投機的な].

speech (*n.*) 1)gengo(-nôryoku) [言語(能力)]. 2)hanashi-kata [話し方].
3)enzetsu [演説]; supîchi [スピーチ]. 4)(*gram.*) wahô [話法].
(*1*) Man alone expresses his thoughts by **speech**.
　　Ningen-dake-ga kangaete-iru-koto-o *gengo*-de hyôgen-suru.
(*2*) His **speech** is too fast.
　　Kare-no *hanashi-kata* wa haya-sugiru.
(*3*) He made a good **speech**. Kare-wa ii *enzetsu*-o shita.

speechless (*a.*) (shibaraku) kuchi-ga-kikenai [(しばらく)口がきけない];
kotoba-de-arawase-nai-hodo-no [言葉で表わせないほどの].

speed (*n.*) sokuryoku [速力]; sokudo [速度]; supîdo [スピード].
at full(top) speed zen-sokuryoku-de
(*vt.*) ...o hakadoraseru […をはかどらせる]; ...o hayameru […
を早める].
(*vi.*) isogu [急ぐ]; sokudo-o-masu [速度を増す].

speedometer (*n.*) sokudo-kei [速度計].

speedway (*n.*) 1)((*US*)) kôsoku-dôro [高速道路]. 2)jidôsha[ôtobai]-
kyôsô-ro [自動車[オートバイ]競走路].

speedy (*a.*) hayai [速い]; binsoku-na [敏速な].

spell (*vt.*) ...o tsuzuru […をつづる].

spell (*n.*) maryoku [魔力].
　　The magic **spell** was broken.
　　　Majutsu-no-chikara wa yaburareta.

spell (*n.*) 1)hito-tsuzuki(-no-kikan) [一続き(の期間)]; shibaraku-no-
aida [しばらくの間]. 2)hito-shigoto [一仕事].
(*1*) We have a long **spell** of cold weather.
　　Samui tenki ga nagaku-*tsuzuite*-iru.

spelling (*n.*) tsuzuri [つづり]; superu [スペル]; go-no-tsuzuri-kata
[語のつづり方].

spend (*vt.*) 1)(kane)-o tsukau [(金)を使う]; ...o tsuiyasu […を費や
す]. 2)(toki)-o sugosu [(時)を過ごす]. 3)...o dashi-tsukusu […を出
し尽くす]; ...o tsukai-hatasu […を使い果たす].
(*1*) He **has spent** all the money.

Kare-wa kane-o mina *tsukatte*-shimatta.

(2) How did you **spend** your summer vacation?

Natsu-yasumi wa dô *sugoshi-mashita*-ka?

(3) He **spent** his energy on that research.

Kare-wa sono kenkyû-ni seiryoku-o *tsukai-hatashita*.

sphere (*n*.) 1)kyû [球]. 2)tentai [天体]. 3)han'i [範囲].

spice (*n*.) yakumi [薬味]; kôshin-ryô [香辛料]; supaisu [スパイス].

spider (*n*.) kumo [クモ].

spike (*n*.) oo-kugi [大くぎ]; supaiku [スパイク].

(*vt*.) ...ni oo-kugi-o-uchi-tsukeru [···に大くぎを打ちつける]; ...ni supaiku-o-uchi-tsukeru [···にスパイクを打ちつける]; (*sports*)...o supaiku-suru [···をスパイクする].

spill (*vt*.) ...o kobosu [···をこぼす]; ...o maki-chirasu [···をまき散らす]; ...o haki-dasu [···を吐き出す]; (*colloq*.) ...o morasu [···を漏らす].

(*vi*.) koboreru [こぼれる].

(*n*.) 1)koboreru-koto [こぼれること]; koboreta-yogore [こぼれた汚れ]. 2)(*colloq*.) tenraku [転落].

spin (*vt*.) 1)...o tsumuide(...ni)-suru [···を紡いで(···に)する]; (kumo ga su)-o kakeru [(クモが巣)をかける]. 2)(koma)-o mawasu [(こま)を回す]. 3)...o naga-naga-to-hanasu [···を長々と話す]; ...o hiki-nobasu [···を引き延ばす].

(1) They **spin** cotton into thread.

Kare-ra-wa men-o *tsumuide* ito-ni suru.

A spider **is spinning** a web. Kumo ga su-o *kaketeiru*.

(2) Can you **spin** a top? Kimi-wa koma-o *mawaseru*-kai?

(3) He **spun** a yarn about adventures.

Kare-wa *naga-naga-to*-bôken-dan-o-*hanashita*.

(*vi*.) (ito o) tsumugu [(糸を)紡ぐ]; (kumo ga) su-o kakeru [(クモが)巣をかける]; (koma ga) mawaru [(こまが)回る].

(*n*.) kaiten [回転]; (*aviation*) kiri-momi-kôka [きりもみ降下].

spinach (*n*.) hôrensô [ホウレンソウ].

spinal (*a*.) 1)(*anat*.) se-bone-no [背骨の]; sekichû-no [せき柱の]. 2)toge[-jô]-no [とげ(状)の].

spinal cord sekizui [せき髄].

spindle (*n*.) 1)tsumu [つむ]; supindoru [スピンドル]. 2)(*mech*.) shimbô [心棒].

(*vt*.) ...ni tsumu-o-tsukeru [···につむを付ける].

spine (*n*.) 1)(*anat*.) se-bone [背骨]; sekichû [せき柱]. 2)(*bot*.) toge

[とげ]. 3)kikotsu [気骨]; konjô [根性]. 4)(hon no) se [(本の)背].

spinning (*n. & a.*) 1)bôseki [紡績]; ito-tsumugi [糸紡ぎ]. 2)kaiten-suru [回転する].

spinning mill bôseki-kôjô [紡績工場].

spiral (*a. & n.*) rasen-jô-no(-mono) [らせん状の(もの)].

    (*vi.*) 1)rasen-jô-ni-naru [らせん状になる]; rasen-jô-ni-ugoku [らせん状に動く]. 2)(bukka nado ga) kyû-jôshô-suru [(物価などが)急上昇する].

    (*vt.*) ...o rasen-jô-ni-ugokasu [···をらせん状に動かす]; ...o kyû-jôshô-saseru [···を急上昇させる].

spire (*n.*) 1)sentô [尖塔]; senchô [尖頂]. 2)(*bot.*) hosoi-ha [細い葉]; wakai-me [若い芽]. 3)ensui-kei-no-mono [円すい形のもの].

    (*vi.*) tsuki-deru [突き出る]; me-o-dasu [芽を出す].

    (*vt.*) ...ni sentô-o-tsukeru [···に尖塔をつける].

spirit (*n.*) 1)rei [霊]. 2)kokoro [心]; seishin [精神]. 3)yûki [勇気]; (*pl.*) genki [元気]. 4)(*pl.*) arukôru [アルコール].

    (*1*) God is a **spirit**. Kami wa *rei*-de-aru.

    (*2*) We must have public **spirit**.

        Ware-ware-wa kôkyô-(sei)*shin*-o mota-neba-naranai.

    (*3*) Keep up your **spirits**.   *Genki*-o dase.

        Rakutan-suru-na.

  in high(great) spirits genki-yoku; jô-kigen-de

  in low(poor) spirits iki-shôchin-shite

    (*vt.*) 1)...o genki-zukeru [···を元気づける]. 2)...o hisoka-ni-tsure-saru [···をひそかに連れ去る].

spiritual (*a.*) rei-teki-na [霊的な]; seishin-teki-na [精神的な]; sûkô-na [崇高な]; chô-shizen-teki-na [超自然的な].

spit (*vi.*) tsuba-o-haku [つばを吐く].

    (*vt.*) ...o haku [···を吐く].

    (*n.*) tsuba-o-haku-koto [つばを吐くこと]; tsuba [つば].

spite (*n.*) akui [悪意]; urami [恨み].

  in spite of ...nimo-kakawarazu

  in spite of oneself omowazu

splash (*vt.*) 1)(mizu ya doro)-o hane-kakeru [(水や泥)をはねかける]. 2)...o pacha-pacha-sasete-mizu-o-tobi-chirasu [···をぱちゃぱちゃさせて水を飛び散らす]. 3)...ni chirashi-moyô-o-tsukeru [···に散らし模様をつける].

    (*1*) The car **splashed** mud over me.

Jidôsha ga watashi-ni doro-o *hane-kaketa*.

(*vi.*) 1) haneru [はねる]. 2) mizu-o-tobi-chirashi-nagara-susumu [水を飛び散らしながら進む]. 3) zabun-to-tobi-komu [ざぶんと飛び込む].

(*3*) I **splashed** into the water.

Watashi-wa *zabun-to-oto-o-tatete tobi-konda*.

(*n.*) 1) hane [はね]. 2) zabun [ざぶん].

(*1*) It has **splash**boards. Sore niwa *hane-yoke-ga aru*.

(*2*) She jumped into the water with a **splash**.

Kano-jo-wa *zabun-to* sui-chû-ni tobi-konda.

(*ad.*) zabun[bashan]-to-oto-o-tatete [ざぶん[ばしゃん]と音を立てて].

splendid (*a.*) 1) rippa-na [立派な]. 2) (*colloq.*) subarashii [すばらしい].

splendor, -dour (*n.*) 1) kagayaki [輝き]. 2) sôrei [壮麗].

splint (*n.*) (*med.*) soegi [そえ木].

(*vt.*) ...ni soegi-o-ateru [...にそえ木をあてる].

splinter (*n.*) kakera [かけら]; hahen [破片].

(*vt. & vi.*) ...o kona-gona-ni-suru (kona-gona-ni-naru) [...を粉々にする(粉々になる)].

split (*vt.*) 1) ...o waru [...を割る]; ...o saku [...を裂く]. 2) ...o wakeru [...を分ける].

split the difference ayumi-yoru

(*vi.*) wareru [割れる]; sakeru [裂ける].

(*n.*) 1) saku-koto [裂くこと]; sake-me [裂け目]; bunretsu [分裂]. 2) wake-mae [分け前].

(*a.*) saketa [裂けた]; wareta [割れた]; bunretsu-shita [分裂した].

splitting (*a.*) sakeru [裂ける]; wareru[-yô-na] [割れる(ような)]; hageshii [激しい].

spoil (*vt.*) 1) ...o dai-nashi-ni-suru [...を台無しにする]; ...o sogu [...をそぐ]. 2) ...o zôchô-saseru [...を増長させる]; ...o amayakashite-dame-ni-suru [...を甘やかして駄目にする].

(*1*) The rain will **spoil** our picnic.

Ame-ga-furu-to pikunikku wa *dai-nashi-ni-naru*-darô.

That **spoils** our fun. Sore-wa ware-ware-no kyô-o *sogu*.

(*2*) Don't **spoil** the children.

Kodomo-tachi-o *amayakashite-dame-ni-suru*-na.

(*vi.*) 1) dai-nashi-ni-naru [台無しになる]. 2) fuhai-suru [腐敗する].

(*n.*) 1) (*pl.*) ryakudatsu-hin [略奪品]. 2) (*pl.*) ((US)) riken [利

権]. 3)(*pl.*) (doryoku no) seika [(努力の)成果].

spoke (*n.*) 1)(sharin no) ya [(車輪の)や]; supôku [スポーク]. 2) hashigo-no-yoko-san [はしごの横桟].

spoken (*a.*) kôgo-no [口語の].

sponge (*n.*) kaimen [海綿]; suponji [スポンジ].
　　　　(*vt.*) ...o suponji-de-fuku [...をスポンジでふく]; ...o suponji-de-sui-toru [...をスポンジで吸い取る].
　　　　(*vi.*) 1)kaimen-o-toru [海綿を採る]. 2)ekitai-o-kyûshû-suru [液体を吸収する].

sponsor (*n.*) 1)hoshô-nin [保証人]. 2)hokki-nin [発起人]; kôen-sha [後援者]. 3)kôkoku-nushi [広告主]; suponsâ [スポンサー].
　　　　(*vt.*) 1)...no hokki-nin-to-naru [...の発起人となる]. 2)...no suponsâ-ni-naru [...のスポンサーになる]. 3)...no hoshô-nin-to-naru [...の保証人となる].

spontaneous (*a.*) jihatsu-teki-na [自発的な]; shizen-ni-okiru [自然に起きる].

spool (*n.*) ((*US*)) ito-maki [糸巻き].
　　　　(*vt.*) ...o ito-maki-ni-maku [...を糸巻きに巻く].

spoon (*n.*) supûn [スプーン]; saji [さじ].
　　　　(*vt.*) ...o supûn-de-sukuu [...をスプーンですくう].

spoonful (*n.*) supûn-ippai[-bun] [スプーン一杯(分)].

sport (*vi.*) (kodomo ya dôbutsu ga) tawamureru [(子供や動物が)たわむれる].
　　　　(*vt.*) (*colloq.*) ...o mise-birakasu [...を見せびらかす].
　　　　He always **sports** his moustache.
　　　　Kare-wa itsu-mo hige-o *hinette-miseru*.
　　　　(*n.*) 1)tanoshimi [楽しみ]. 2)kyôgi [競技]; supôtsu [スポーツ].
　　　3) (*pl.*) ((*Eng.*)) undô-kai [運動会]. 4)(*colloq.*) supôtsuman [スポーツマン].
　　　(*1*) It may be **sport** to them.
　　　　Sore-wa kare-ra-niwa *tanoshii-koto* kamo-shirenai.
　　　(*2*) He gives himself up to **sport**. Kare-wa *kyôgi*-ni netchû-suru.
　　　(*3*) The **sports** were put off. *Undô-kai* wa enki-sareta.
　　　　(*a.*) 1)supôtsu-no [スポーツの]. 2)keisô-no [軽装の].

sportscast (*n.*) ((*US*)) supôtsu-hôsô [スポーツ放送]; supôtsu-kaisetsu [スポーツ解説].

sportsman (*n.*) supôtsuman [スポーツマン]; undô-ka [運動家].

sportswear (*n.*) supôtsuuea [スポーツウエア].

sporty (*a.*) (*colloq.*) 1)supôtsuman-rashii [スポーツマンらしい];

supôtî-na [スポーティーな]. 2)hade-na [派手な].

spot (n.) 1)madara [まだら]; hanten [はん点]; shimi [しみ]. 2)
(tokutei no) basho [(特定の)場所]; (ittei no) chiten [(一定の)地点].
(1) The bird has many **spots** on her wings.
　　Sono tori wa tsubasa-no ooku-no *hanten*-ga aru.
(2) I know the **spot** where it happened.
　　Sono-koto-ga-okita-*basho*-o watashi-wa shitte-iru.

hit the spot (*colloq.*) môshibun-ga-nai
on the spot sono-ba-de; sokuza-ni
　　(*vt.*) 1)...o yogosu [...を汚す]. 2)...o mitsukeru [...を見付ける].
3)...o oku [...を置く].
　　(*vi.*) shimi-ga-tsuku [しみがつく]; yogoreru [汚れる].
　　(*a.*) 1)sokuza-no [即座の]. 2)genchi-kara-no [現地からの].
　　(*ad.*) (*Eng. colloq.*) chôdo [ちょうど].

spotless (*a.*) 1)shimi-no-nai [しみのない]. 2)ketten-no-nai [欠点のない];
keppaku-na [潔白な].

spouse (n.) haigû-sha [配偶者].

spout (*vt.*) (mizu nado)-o fuki-dasu [(水など)を噴き出す].
　　(*vi.*) hotobashiri-deru [ほとばしり出る].
　　(n.) 1)funsui [噴水]. 2)(kyûsu nado no) kuchi [(きゅうすなど
の)口]; ama-doi [雨どい]; funshutsu-kô [噴出口].

sprain (*vt.*) (te-kubi ya ashi-kubi)-o kujiku [(手首や足首)をくじく]; ...
o nenza-suru [...をねんざする].
　　(n.) nenza [ねんざ].

sprawl (*vi.*) 1)te-ashi-o-nobasu [手足を伸ばす]. 2)(moji ga) notakuru
[(文字が)のたくる]. 3)fu-kisoku-ni-hirogaru [不規則に広がる].
　　(*vt.*) (te-ashi)-o dai-no-ji-ni-hirogeru [(手足)を大の字に広げる].
　　(n.) 1)dai-no-ji-ni-ne-soberu-koto [大の字に寝そべること]. 2)
(machi no) supurôru-genshô [(町の)スプロール現象].

spray (n.) 1)shibuki [しぶき]; mizu-kemuri [水煙]. 2)fummu-ki [噴
霧器].
　　(*vt.*) 1)...ni shibuki-o-kakeru [...にしぶきをかける]. 2)...o fuki-
kakeru [...を吹きかける]; ...ni abiseru [...に浴びせる].
　　(*vi.*) shibuki-ni-naru [しぶきになる]; kiri-o-fuku [霧を吹く].

spread (*vt.*) 1)...o hirogeru [...を広げる]; ...o nobasu [...を伸ばす].
2)...ni usuku-nuru [...に薄く塗る]; ...ni usuku-hirogeru [...に薄く広
げる]. 3)...ni ryôri-o-naraberu [...に料理を並べる]; ...o shokutaku-
ni-naraberu [...を食卓に並べる]. 4)...o sampu-suru [...を散布する]; ...

o maku [⋯をまく]. 5)...no kikan-o-nobasu [⋯の期間を延ばす].

(1) The pheasant **spread** its wings.

Sono kiji wa tsubasa-o *hirogeta*.

(2) She **spread** butter on a piece of toast.

Kano-jo-wa tôsuto-ni batâ-o *nutta*.

(3) The table was **spread** with dishes.

Têburu niwa go-chisô ga *narabete-atta*.

(4) Did you **spread** fertilizer over the soil recently?

Saikin tochi-ni hiryô-o *makimashita*-ka?

(5) You **spread** your payments over 3 years.

Shiharai-kikan-o　san-nen-kan　*hiki-nobashite*-mo-kamai-masen.

　　(vi.) 1)hirogaru [広がる]; hiromaru [広まる]; chirabaru [散らばる]; bumpu-suru [分布する]. 2)wataru [わたる]; nobiru [延びる].

　　(n.) 1)hirogari [広がり]; fukyû [普及]. 2)beddokabâ [ベッドカバー].

sprightly (a.) kappatsu-na [活発な]; genki-na [元気な].

spring (n.) 1)haru [春]. 2)izumi [泉]; gensen [源泉]. 3)zemmai [ぜんまい]; bane [ばね]. 4)tobu-koto [跳ぶこと]; haneru-koto [はねること].

(1) **Spring** has come. *Haru* ga kita.

(2) Japan has many hot **springs**.

Nihon niwa takusan-no on*sen*-ga aru.

(3) The door works by a **spring**.

Kono to wa *bane*-jikake-de ugoku.

(4) The dog was about to make a **spring** upon him.

Sono inu wa kare-ni *tobi-kakar*ô-to-shita.

　　(vi.) 1)tobu [跳ぶ]; haneru [はねる]. 2)shôjiru [生じる]; me-o-dasu [芽を出す]; waki-deru [わき出る].

(1) He **sprang** up from his seat.

Kare-wa seki-kara *patto*-tachi-*agatta*.

(2) Buds began to **spring**. Me ga *de*-hajimeta.

　　(vt.) 1)...o hane-kaeraseru [⋯をはね返らせる]; ...o tobi-agaraseru [⋯を跳び上がらせる]; ...o soraseru [⋯を反らせる]; ...o saku [⋯を裂く]. 3)...o kyû-ni-mochi-dasu [⋯を急に持ち出す].

springtime (n.) haru [春]; haru-no-kisetsu [春の季節].

sprinkle (vt.) ...o furi-kakeru [⋯をふりかける]; ...o maku [⋯をまく].

sprinkler (n.) sansui-ki [散水器]; supurinkurâ [スプリンクラー].

sprout (*vi.*) 1)me-ga-deru [芽が出る]. 2)kyû-ni-nobiru [急にのびる]. 3)umareru [生まれる].

    (*vt.*) 1)...no me-o-dasaseru [···の芽を出させる]. 2)(...no-me)-o toru [(···の芽)を取る]. 3)...o nobasu [···を伸ばす]; ...o hayasu [···をはやす].

    (*n.*) me [芽]; waka-eda [若枝].

spur (*n.*) hakusya [拍車].

    (*vt.*) ...ni-hakusha-o-kakeru [···に拍車をかける].

spurn (*n.*) hane-tsuke [はねつけ].

    (*vt.*) ...o hane-tsukeru [···をはねつける].

sputter (*vi.*) 1)pachi-pachi[butsu-butsu-]oto-o-tateru [ぱちぱち[ぶつぶつ]音を立てる]. 2)haya-kuchi-ni-iu [早口に言う].

    (*vt.*) 1)(tsuba ya tabe-mono nado)-o tobasu [(つばや食べ物など)を飛ばす]. 2)...o haya-kuchi-ni-iu [···を早口に言う].

    (*n.*) pachi-pachi-iu-oto [パチパチいう音]; haya-kuchi-no-kotoba [早口のことば].

spy (*n. & vi.*) supai(-suru) [スパイ(する)].

squadron (*n.*) 1)(*Navy*) sentai [戦隊]. 2)(*US Air Force*) hikô-daitai [飛行大隊].

squander (*vt.*) (toki ya kinsen)-o muda-ni-tsukau [(時や金銭)を無駄に使う].

square (*a.*) 1)sei-hôkei-no [正方形の]; shikaku-no [四角の]. 2)kôhei-na [公平な]. 3)(*math.*) heihô-no [平方の]. 4)(*colloq.*) jûbun-na [十分な].

    (*ad.*) (*colloq.*) 1)shikaku-ni[-naru-yô-ni] [四角に(なるように)]. 2)gasshiri-to [がっしりと]. 3)kôhei-ni [公平に]. 4)matomo-ni [まともに].

    (*n.*) 1)sei-hôkei [正方形]. 2)hiroba [広場]. 3)(*math.*) heihô [平方]; jijô [二乗] = sq.

    (*vt.*) 1)...o sei-hôkei-ni-suru [···を正方形にする]; ...o chokkaku-ni-suru [···を直角にする]. 2)...o jijô-suru [···を二乗する]. 3)(tokuten)-o tai-ni-suru [(得点)をタイにする].

    (*vi.*) 1)chokkaku-ni-naru [直角になる]. 2)(...to-)itchi-suru [(···と)一致する]. 3)kessai-suru [決済する].

square deal (*colloq.*) kôhei-na-torihiki [公平な取引]; kôhei-na-tori-atsukai [公平な取り扱い].

squat (*vi.*) shagamu [しゃがむ]; uzukumaru [うずくまる].

    (*a.*) 1)shaganda [しゃがんだ]. 2)zunguri-shita [ずんぐりした].

squawk (*n. & vi.*) gyâ-gyâ(-naku) [ぎゃーぎゃー(鳴く)]; (*colloq.*) bû-bû(-fuhei-o-iu) [ぶーぶー(不平を言う)].

squeak (*n. & vi.*) chû-chû(-naku) [ちゅーちゅー(鳴く)]; kî-kî(-naru) [きーきー(鳴る)].

squeal (*n. & vi.*) kî-kî(-iu) [きーきー(いう)]; kî-kî-goe(-de-iu) [きーきー声(で言う)].

squeamish (*a.*) 1)mune-no-waruku-naru [胸の悪くなる]. 2)reitan-na [冷淡な]. 3)ki-muzukashii [気難しい].

squeeze (*vt.*) 1)...o shiboru [···を絞る]; ...o assaku-suru [···を圧搾する]. 2)...o hineri-dasu [···をひねり出す].
  (*vi.*) 1)shiboreru [絞れる]. 2)oshi-iru [押し入る].

squid (*n.*) (*zool.*) yari-ika [ヤリイカ].

squire (*n.*) ((*US*)) chian-hanji [治安判事].

squirrel (*n.*) risu [リス].

stab (*vt.*) 1)...o sasu [···を刺す]; ...o tsuki-sasu [···を突き刺す]. 2)...o chûshô-suru [···を中傷する].
  (*n.*) sasu-koto [刺すこと]; tsuki-kizu [突き傷]; chûshô [中傷].

stability (*n.*) antei[-sei] [安定(性)].

stabilize (*vt.*) ...o antei-saseru [···を安定させる].

stable (*a.*) 1)antei-shita [安定した]; ittei-no [一定の]; fuhen-no [不変の]. 2)danko-to-shita [断固とした].

stable (*n.*) umaya [馬屋].
  (*vt.*) ...o umaya-ni-ireru [···を馬屋に入れる].
  (*vi.*) umaya-ni-irete-oku [馬屋に入れておく].

stableman (*n.*) batei [馬丁].

stack (*n.*) 1)hoshi-kusa-no-yama [干し草の山]; taiseki [たい積]. 2)ichi-gun-no-entotsu [一群の煙突]. 3)(*pl.*)(tosho-kan no) shoko [(図書館の)書庫].
  (*vt.*) ...o tsumi-kasaneru [···を積み重ねる]; ...o taba-ni-suru [···を束にする].
  (*vi.*) yama-to-tsumu [山と積む].

stadium (*n.*) sutajiamu [スタジアム]; kyôgi-jô [競技場].

staff (*n.*) 1)buin [部員]; shokuin [職員]. 2)(*mil.*) sambô [参謀].
  (*1*) the editorial **staff** henshû-*buin*
  (*2*) the chief of the general **staff** *sambô*-sôchô
  (*vt.*) (be -ed) haichi-sareru [配置される]; ...no shokuin-to-shite-hataraku [···の職員として働く].

stag (*n.*) (*zool.*) ojika [雄ジカ].

stage (*n.*) 1)butai [舞台]; sutêji [ステージ]. 2)(hattatsu nado no) dankai [(発達などの)段階]; ...ki […期]; jiki [時期]. 3)(roketto no) dan [(ロケットの)段]; (tate-mono no) kai [(建物の)階].

  (*1*) I could only see half the **stage**.

      Butai-no-hambun-shika mie-nakatta.

  (*2*) It is still in experimental **stage**.

      Sore-wa mada jikken-*dankai*-ni-aru.

  (*3*) the second **stage** of a three-**stage**-rocket

      san-*dan*-shiki-roketto no ni-*dan*-me

stagger (*vi. & vt.*) 1)yoromeku(...o yoromekaseru) [よろめく(…をよろめかせる)]. 2)tamerau(...o tamerawaseru) [ためらう(…をためらわせる)].

    (*n.*) 1)yoromeki [よろめき]. 2)furatsuki [ふらつき].

stagnant (*a.*) yodonda [よどんだ]; chintai-shita [沈滞した]; fukappatsu-na [不活発な]; bon'yari-shita [ぼんやりした].

stain (*vt.*) 1)...o yogosu […を汚す]. 2)...o chakushoku-suru […を着色する].

    (*vi.*) yogoreru [汚れる]; shimi-ga-tsuku [しみがつく].

    (*n.*) 1)yogore [汚れ]; shimi [しみ]; kizu [きず]. 2)senryô [染料]; chakushoku-zai [着色剤].

stainless (*a.*) yogore-no-nai [汚れのない]; sabi-nai [さびない].

    (*n.*) sutenresu-sei-no-shokki-rui [ステンレス製の食器類].

stair (*n.*) 1)(kaidan no)ichi-dan [(階段の)一段]. 2)(*pl.*) hashigo-dan [はしご段]; kaidan [階段].

staircase (*n.*) hashigo-dan [はしご段]; kaidan [階段].

stairway (*n.*) kaidan [階段].

stake (*n.*) 1)kui [くい]; bô [棒]. 2)kake-kin [賭け金].

    (*vt.*) 1)...o kui-de-shikiru […をくいで仕切る]; ...o bô-de-sasaeru […を棒で支える]. 2)...o kakeru […を賭ける].

stale (*a.*) 1)shinsen-de-nai [新鮮でない]. 2)chimpu-na [陳腐な]; furukusai [古臭い]. 3)seiki-ga-nai [生気がない]; fuchô-no [不調の].

stalk (*n.*) (*bot.*) kuki [茎]; miki [幹].

stalk (*vi.*) 1)shinobi-yoru [忍び寄る]. 2)oode-o-futte-aruku [大手を振って歩く]. 3)(byôki nado ga) man'en-suru [(病気などが)まん延する].

    (*vt.*) ...ni shinobi-yoru […に忍び寄る]; ...o hisoka-ni-ou […をひそかに追う].

    (*n.*) emono-ni-shinobi-yoru-koto [えものに忍び寄ること]; ibattearuku-koto [威張って歩くこと].

stall (*n.*) 1)umaya-no-hito-shikiri [馬屋の一仕切り]. 2)baiten [売店]; roten [露店]. 3)(*Eng. theater*) ikkai-shômen-no-ittô-seki [一階正面の一等席].

　　(*vt.*) 1)...o umaya[gyûsha]-ni-ireru [...を馬屋[牛舎]に入れる]. 2)...o tachi-ôjô-saseru [...を立ち往生させる]; ...o ensuto-saseru [...をエンストさせる].

　　(*vi.*) umaya[gyûsha]-ni-irete-oku [馬屋[牛舎]に入れておく]; (kuruma ga) tomaru [(車が)止まる].

stamen (*n.*) (*bot.*) o-shibe [雄しべ].

stammer (*vi.*) kuchi-gomoru [口ごもる]; kuchi-gomori-nagara-iu [口ごもりながら言う].

　　He often **stammers**.　Kare-wa *kuchi-gomoru*-koto-ga-ooi.
　　(*vt.*) ...o kuchi-gomori-nagara-iu [...を口ごもりながら言う].
　　He faintly **stammered** out "No."
　　　Kare-wa kasuka-ni "Iie" *to-kuchi-gomori-nagara-itta.*
　　(*n.*) kuchi-gomoru-koto [口ごもること].

stamp (*n.*) 1)han [判]; sutampu [スタンプ]. 2)inshi [印紙]; kitte [切手].

　　(*vt.*) 1)...no han-o-osu [...の判を押す]. 2)...ni kitte-o-haru [...に切手を貼る]. 3)...o fumi-tsukeru [...を踏みつける]. 4)...o inshô-zukeru [...を印象づける]; ...ga...de-aru-koto-o shimesu [...が...であることを示す].

(*1*) He **stamped** his name and address on the book.
　　Kare-wa hon-ni jibun-no jûsho-shimei-*no han-o-oshita.*
(*2*) Please **stamp** your letter.　Tegami-*ni kitte-o-hatte*-kudasai.
(*3*) They **stamped** their feet.　Kare-ra-wa *ashi-bumi-o-shita.*
(*4*) His achievement **stamps** him as one of the masterminds of our era.
　　Kare-no gyôseki *wa* kare-ga ware-ware-no jidai no shidô-sha no hitori-*de-atta-koto-o-shimeshite-iru.*
　　(*vi.*) ashi-o-fumi-narashite-aruku [足を踏みならして歩く].
　　They **stamped** about the room.
　　Kare-ra-wa *ashi-o-fumi-narashite* heya-o-*aruki*-mawatta.

stamp collector kitte-shûshû-ka [切手収集家].

stand (*vi.*) 1)tatsu [立つ]. 2)aru [ある]; ichi-suru [位置する]. 3)(aru jôtai ni) aru [(ある状態に)ある]. 4)takasa-ga...de-aru [高さが...である]; (ondo-kei ga)...(do-o-)shimesu [(温度計が)...(度を)示す].

(*1*) **stand** on tiptoe　tsuma-saki-de *tatsu*

(2) The church **stands** on the hill.　Kyôkai wa oka-no-ue-ni *aru*.

(3) He **stands** in great danger.

　　Kare-wa totemo kiken-na-*jôtai-ni aru*.

(4) The house **stands** 100 feet.

　　Sono ie wa *takasa-ga*-hyaku-fîto-*aru*.

　The thermometer **stands** at 20 degrees.

　　Ondo-kei wa ni-jû-do-o *shimeshite-iru*.

　(vt.) 1)…o tateru […を立てる]. 2)…o gaman-suru […を我慢する]. 3)…ni taeru […に耐える].

(1) I **stood** his umbrella against the wall.

　　Watashi-wa kare-no kasa-*o* kabe-ni *tate-kaketa*.

(2) I cannot **stand** the work any longer.

　　Watashi-wa sono shigoto-*ni tae*rare-nai.

(3) Do you think their music will **stand** the test of time?

　　Anata-wa kare-ra-no ongaku ga toki no shiren-*ni taeru*-to-omoimasu-ka?

stand by　…o tasukeru; …o shiji-suru

　My uncle **stood by** me whenever I was in trouble.

　　Watashi-no oji wa watashi-ga komatte-iru-toki-wa-itsu-mo watashi-o tasukete-kureta.

stand for　…o imi-suru; …o arawasu

　What does this mark **stand for**?

　　Kono mâku wa nani-o arawasu-no-ka?

stand out　medatsu; kukkiri-to-mieru

　The steeple **stood out** against the sky.

　　Sono sentô wa aozora-o-haikei-ni kukkiri-to-sobie-tatte-ita.

　(n.) 1)…kake […掛け]; dai [台]. 2)yatai [屋台]; baiten [売店]. 3)*(pl.)* kanran-seki [観覧席]; sutando [スタンド].

(1) a hat **stand**　bôshi-*kake*

(2) a fruit **stand**　kudamono no *baiten*

(3) the left **stands**　refuto *sutando*

standard *(n.)* 1)hyôjun [標準]; kijun [基準]; kikaku [規格]. 2)hata [旗].

　(a.) 1)hyôjun-no [標準の]; futsû-no [普通の]. 2)ichiryû-no [一流の].

standardize *(vt.)* …o hyôjun-ka-suru […を標準化する]; …o kikaku-ka-suru […を規格化する].

standing *(a.)* 1)tatteiru [立っている]. 2)nagare-nai [流れない]. 3)

jôchi-no [常置の]; sue-tsuke-no [据えつけの].

　　　(n.) 1)tachiba [立場]; mibun [身分]; chii [地位]. 2)meisei [名声]. 3)sonzoku [存続].

standpoint (n.) tachiba [立場]; kenchi [見地]; kanten [観点].

standstill (n.) iki-zumari [行き詰まり]; teishi [停止].

staple (n.) 1)(pl.) shuyô-sambutsu [主要産物]. 2)sen'i [繊維]. 3) genryô [原料].

　　　(a.) shuyô-na [主要な]; jûyô-na [重要な]; chûshin-teki-na [中心的な].

stapler (n.) hotchikisu [ホッチキス].

star (n.) 1)hoshi [星]; hoshi-gata[-no-mono] [星形(のもの)]. 2)sutâ [スター]; hana-gata [花形].

starboard (n.) (marine) ugen [右舷].

starch (n.) dempun [でん粉]; nori [のり].

　　　(vt.) ...ni nori-o-tsukeru [...にのりをつける].

stare (vt. & vi.) (...o) jitto-mi-tsumeru [(...を)じっと見詰める].

　　　(n.) jitto-mi-tsumeru-koto [じっと見詰めること].

starfish (n.) (zool.) hitode [ヒトデ].

starlight (n.) hoshi-akari [星明かり].

starry (a.) hoshi-no-ooi [星の多い]; hoshi-no-yô-ni-kagayaku [星のように輝く]; hoshi-gata-no [星形の]; hoshi-ni-kansuru [星に関する].

start (vi.) 1)shuppatsu-suru [出発する]. 2)hajimaru [始まる]. 3) totsuzen-ugoku [突然動く]; gikutto-suru [ぎくっとする].

　(1) I'll **start** for Europe next month.

　　　Watashi-wa raigetsu Yôroppa-ni-muke *shuppatsu-shimasu*.

　(2) The school year **starts** in April.

　　　Shin-gakunen wa Shigatsu-ni *hajimaru*.

　(3) He **started** in surprise. Kare-wa odoroite *tobi-agatta*.

　　　(vt.) 1)...o hajimeru [...を始める]. 2)...o okosu [...を起こす]; ... o setsuritsu-suru [...を設立する].

　(1) It **started** raining. Ame ga furi-*hajimeta*.

　(2) He **started** business there. Kare-wa soko-de *kaigyô-shita*.

　to start with mazu-dai-ichi-ni; saisho-wa

　　　(n.) 1)shuppatsu [出発]; sutâto [スタート]; kaishi [開始]. 2) saisho-no-bubun [最初の部分]; yûri-na-ichi [有利な位置]. 3)bikkuri-suru-koto [びっくりすること]; totsuzen-ugoki-dasu-koto [突然動き出すこと].

　(1) He got a good **start** in life.

       Kare-wa saisaki-yoku yo-no-naka-ni *sutâto*-shita.

(*2*) The **start** of the play was interesting.

       Sono geki no *saisho-no-bubun* wa omoshirokatta.

       He has a **start** on his classmates.

       Kare-wa kyûyû-yori-*yûri*-da.

(*3*) He began to cry with a **start**.

       Kare-wa *bikkuri*-shite naki-dashita.

at the start hajime-wa; saisho-wa

starter (*n.*) 1)sutâto-aizu-gakari ［スタート合図係］. 2)(enjin no) sutâtâ ［(エンジンの)スターター］. 3)hajimeru-hito[-mono] ［始める人 ［もの］］; kawa-kiri ［皮切り］. 4)shussô-ba ［出走馬］.

starting point shuppatsu-ten ［出発点］.

startle (*vt.*) 1)...o bikkuri-saseru ［…をびっくりさせる］. 2)...o shigeki-shite...(sa-)seru ［…を刺激して…(さ)せる］.

       (*vi.*) odoroku ［驚く］.

       (*n.*) odoroki ［驚き］; hatto-saseru-mono ［はっとさせるもの］.

starvation (*n.*) kiga ［飢餓］; gashi ［餓死］.

starve (*vi.*) ueru ［飢える］; gashi-suru ［餓死する］; (*colloq.*) himojii ［ひもじい］.

       (*vt.*) 1)...o gashi-saseru ［…を餓死させる］. 2)(be -d) setsubô-suru ［切望する］.

state (*n.*) 1)jôtai ［状態］; arisama ［ありさま］. 2)kokka ［国家］; kuni ［国］; ((*US*)) (S-) shû ［州］. 3)igen ［威厳］; igi ［威儀］.

(*1*) Her house is in a bad **state**.

       Kano-jo-no ie wa hidoi-*arisama*-da.

(*2*) an independent **state** dokuritsu-*koku*

(*3*) He always keeps up his **state**.

       Kare-wa itsu-mo *igen*-o-tamotte-iru.

       Kare-wa itsu-mo *mottai-butte*-iru.

in state dôdô-to; mono-mono-shiku

       (*a.*) 1)kokka-no ［国家の］; shû-no ［州の］. 2)girei[-yô]-no ［儀礼 (用)の］; kôshiki-no ［公式の］.

       (*vt.*) ...o noberu ［…を述べる］.

       He **stated** his thoughts. Kare-wa jibun-no kangae-o *nobeta*.

stated (*a.*) sadamerareta ［定められた］; meigen-sareta ［明言された］; hyômei-sareta ［表明された］.

stately (*a.*) igen-no-aru ［威厳のある］; dôdô-to-shita ［堂々とした］.

statement (*n.*) 1)chinjutsu ［陳述］; chinjutsu-no-shikata ［陳述の仕方］;

seimei[-sho] [声明(書)]. 2)(com.) keisan-sho [計算書].

statesman (n.) seiji-ka [政治家].

station (n.) 1)eki [駅]. 2)...sho […署]; ...sho […所]; ...kyoku […局]. 3)basho [場所]; mochi-ba [持ち場].

  (1) I met with him at the **station**.

      Watashi-wa kare-to *eki*-de atta.

  (2) a fire **station**　shôbô-*sho*

    a power **station**　hatsuden-*sho*

    a TV **station**　terebi-*kyoku*

  (3) He was out of **station**.　Kare-wa *mochi-ba*-o hanareta.

     (vt.) ...o busho-ni-tsukaseru […を部署につかせる]; ...o haichi-suru […を配置する].

stationary (a.) seishi-shita [静止した]; henka-no-nai [変化のない]; teijû-no [定住の].

stationer (n.) bumbô-gu-shô [文房具商].

stationery (n.) bumbô-gu [文房具]; binsen [便せん].

stationmaster (n.) ekichô [駅長].

statistic (n.) tôkei-chi[-ryô] [統計値[量]].

statistics (n.) 1)(as singular) tôkei-gaku [統計学]. 2)(as plural) tôkei-hyô [統計表].

statue (n.) zô [像]; chôzô [彫像].

stature (n.) 1)shinchô [身長]. 2)seichô[-do] [成長(度)]; tassei[-no-teido] [達成(の程度)].

status (n.) 1)jôtai [状態]. 2)chii [地位].

statute law (law) hôrei [法令]; kisoku [規則]; teikan [定款].

statute law seibun-hô [成分法].

stay (vi.) 1)todomaru [とどまる]; taizai-suru [滞在する]; (kyaku to-shite) tomaru [(客として)泊まる]. 2)...no-mama-de-aru[-iru] […のままである[いる]]; itsu-made-mo...de-aru [いつまでも…である].

  (1) I'll **stay** here for two more days.

      Watashi-wa koko-ni mô-futsuka-no-aida *taizai-suru*-tsumori-da.

    I **stayed** overnight in Nagoya.

      Watashi-wa Nagoya-de hito-ban *tomatta*.

  (2) She **stays** beautiful.　Kano-jo-wa *itsu-made-mo* utsukushii.

     (vt.) 1)...o tomeru […を止める]. 2)...o mochi-kotaeru […を持ちこたえる]. 3)...o enki-suru […を延期する]; ...o yûyo-suru […を猶予する].

stay away from 1)...o kesseki-suru. 2)...kara hanarete-iru

stay up okite-iru

    (*n.*) taizai [滞在]; (*law*) enki [延期]; yûyo [猶予].

stead (*n.*) kawari [代わり]; tasuke [助け].

in one's stead hito-no-kawari-ni

in stead of ...no-kawari-ni

steadfast (*a.*) shikkari-shita [しっかりした]; fudô-no [不動の].

steadily (*ad.*) chakujitsu-ni [着実に]; tayumazu [たゆまず].

steady (*a.*) 1)antei-shita [安定した]; chakujitsu-na [着実な]; kenjitsu-na [堅実な]. 2)ittei-no [一定の]; mura-no-nai [むらのない].

    (*1*) Slow and **steady** wins the race.

        Yukkuri-to-*chakujitsu-na*-no-ga kekkyoku-wa katsu.

        Isogaba maware.

        He is a **steady** young man. Kare-wa *kenjitsu-na* seinen desu.

    (*2*) The vessel is sailing at a **steady** speed.

        Fune wa *ittei-no*-sokudo-de kôkô-shiteiru.

        (*vt.*) ...o antei-saseru [⋯を安定させる]; ...o ochitsukaseru [⋯を落ち着かせる].

        (*vi.*) ochitsuku [落ち着く].

steak (*n.*) bifuteki [ビフテキ]; sutêki [ステーキ].

steal (*vt.*) ...o nusumu [⋯を盗む].

        (*vi.*) 1)nusumi-o-suru [盗みをする]. 2)kossori-hairu [こっそり入る]; shinobi-yoru [忍び寄る]; kossori-deru [こっそり出る].

    (*2*) Father **stole** into her room.

        Chichi wa *kossori-to* kano-jo-no-heya-ni *haitte*-kita.

        The dusk **is stealing** in. Tasogare ga *shinobi-yotte*-kuru.

        He **stole** away without saying.

        Kare-wa nani-mo-iwa-nai-de *sotto-tachi-satta*.

        (*n.*) (*US colloq.*) nusumi [盗み]; tôhin [盗品]; (*baseball*) tôrui [盗塁].

stealthily (*ad.*) kossori [こっそり]; hisoka-ni [ひそかに].

steam (*n.*) 1)jôki [蒸気]; suchîmu [スチーム]; yuge [湯気]. 2) (*colloq.*) genki [元気]; seiryoku [精力].

        (*vi.*) jôki-de-ugoku [蒸気で動く]; yuge-o-tateru [湯気を立てる].

        (*vt.*) ...ni jôki-o-ateru [⋯に蒸気を当てる]; ...o musu [⋯を蒸す].

steam engine jôki-kikan [蒸気機関].

steamer (*n.*) 1)kisen [汽船]. 2)(*cooking*) seiro [せいろ]; mushi-ki [蒸し器].

steamship (*n.*) kisen [汽船].

steel (*n.*) 1)hagane [はがね]; kôtetsu [鋼鉄]. 2)kata-sa [硬さ]; hijô-sa [非情さ].

    (*vt.*)...o kataku-suru [...を硬くする]. 2)...o hijô-ni-suru [...を非情にする].

steep (*a.*) 1)kyû-na [急な]; kewashii [険しい]. 2)(*colloq.*) hôgai-na [法外な].

steep (*vt.*) 1)...o hitasu [...を浸す]; ...o tsukeru [...をつける]. 2)...ni bottô-saseru [...に没頭させる].

steeple (*n.*) (kyôkai no) sentô [(教会の)尖塔].

steer (*vt.*) ...no kaji-o-toru [...の舵をとる]; ...o sôjû-suru [...を操縦する].

    (*vi.*) kaji-o-toru [舵をとる]; susumu [進む].

    (*n.*) (*US colloq.*) jogen [助言]; sashizu [指図].

steersman (*n.*) sôda-shu [操舵手].

stem (*n.*) 1)(kusa no) kuki [(草の)茎]; (ki no) miki [(木の)幹]. 2)(saji no) e [(さじの)柄]. 3)(*marine*) senshu [船首].

    (*3*) from **stem** to stern　*senshu*-kara-sembi-made

    (*vt.*) ...no kuki-o-tori-saru [...の茎を取り去る].

    (*vi.*) (...kara-)shôjiru [(...から)生じる]; hassei-suru [発生する].

stencil (*n.*) 1)kata-ita [型板]. 2)(tôsha-ban no) genshi [(謄写版の)原紙].

    (*vt.*) ...o sutenshiru-de-suru [...をステンシルで刷る].

stenographer (*n.*) sokki-sha [速記者].

step (*vi.*) aruku [歩く]; susumu [進む]; fumu [踏む].

    (*vt.*) 1)...o fumi-ireru [...を踏み入れる]. 2)...o hosoku-suru [...を歩測する].

    step aside　waki-e-yoru

    (*n.*) 1)ippo [一歩]; ippo-no-kyori [一歩の距離]. 2)ashi-oto [足音]; ashi-ato [足跡]; ashidori [足どり]. 3)fumi-dan [踏み段]; suteppu [ステップ]; (*pl.*) kaidan [階段]. 4)shudan [手段]; shochi [処置].

    (*1*) The child took a **step**. Kodomo wa *ippo*-susunda.

      It is but a **step** to the station.

        Eki-made honno *hito-ashi* da.

    (*2*) I know his **step**. Watashi-wa kare-no *ashi-oto*-ga wakaru.

      He walked with heavy **steps**.

        Kare-wa omoi-*ashidori*-de aruita.

    (*3*) Last night I slipped on the **steps**.

Sakuya watashi-wa *kaidan*-de subette-koronda.
(*4*) You must take **steps** to prevent it.
Kimi-wa sore-o-fusegu-*shudan*-o tora-neba-naranai.
in step hochô-o-soroete
keep step hochô-o-awasete
out of step hochô-o-midashite
step by step chakujitsu-ni; ippo-ippo
stepmother (*n.*) mama-haha [まま母].
stereophonic (*a.*) rittai-onkyô-no [立体音響の]; sutereo-no [ステレオの].
sterling area (the –) (*econ.*) pondo[-tsûyô]-chiiki [ポンド(通用)地域]; sutâringu-chiiki [スターリング地域].
stern (*a.*) 1)genkaku-na [厳格な]; kibishii [厳しい]. 2)ikameshii [いかめしい].
stern (*n.*) (*marine*) sembi [船尾]; tomo [とも].
stew (*vt.*) ...o toro-bi-de-ni-komu [···をとろ火で煮込む].
(*vi.*) toro-toro-nieru [とろとろ煮える].
(*n.*) shichû[-ryôri] [シチュー(料理)].
stick (*n.*) 1)bô-kire [棒切れ]; ki-gire [木切れ]; ko-eda [小枝]. 2)((*Eng.*)) sutekki [ステッキ].
(*1*) We gathered **sticks** to make a fire.
Taki-bi-o suru-tame-ni *ki-gire*-o atsumeta.
(*2*) He has a **stick** in his right hand.
Kare-wa migi-te-ni *sutekki*-o motte-iru.
stick (*vt.*) 1)...o...ni tsuki-sasu [···を···に突き刺す]. 2)...o tsuki-dasu [···を突き出す]. 3)...o hari-tsukeru [···を貼り付ける]; ...o kuttsukeru [···をくっつける].
(*1*) **Stick** a flower in your buttonhole.
Botan-hôru-e hana-*o sashi-nasai*.
(*2*) He always **sticks** out his chest.
Kare-wa itsu-mo mune-*o tsuki-dashite-iru*.
(*3*) I **stuck** a stamp on each of them.
Watashi-wa sore-ra-ni ichi-ichi kitte-*o hatta*.
(*vi.*) 1)kuttsuku [くっつく]. 2)ugoka-naku-naru [動かなくなる]. 3)tsuki-sasaru [突き刺さる].
(*1*) The birdlime **has stuck** to my fingers.
Tori-mochi ga watashi-no-yubi-ni *kuttsuita*.
(*2*) He got through some ten lines and there **stuck**.

　　　Kare-wa　jû-gyô-bakari-wa　umaku-itta　ga,　soko-de
　　　tsukaeta.
　(*3*) A knife **stuck** in his heart.
　　　Naifu ga kare-no shinzô-ni *tsuki-sasatta.*

sticker (*n.*) 1)tsuku-hito［突く人］. 2)bira-o-haru-hito［ビラを貼る人］.
　3)sutekkâ［ステッカー］. 4)nebari-zuyoi-hito［粘り強い人］; gambari-
　ya［がんばり屋］.

sticky (*a.*) 1)neba-neba-shita［ねばねばした］. 2)mushi-atsui［蒸し暑い］.
　3)(*colloq.*) muzukashii［難しい］.

stiff (*a.*) 1)kowabatta［こわ張った］. 2)kata-kurushii［堅苦しい］. 3)
　(kaze ya nagare ga) tsuyoi［(風や流れが)強い］.

stiffen (*vt. & vi.*) 1)...o kataku-suru (kataku-naru)［...を堅くする
　(堅くなる)］; ...o kowabaraseru (kowabaru)［...をこわばらせる(こわ
　ばる)］. 2)...o kata-kurushiku-suru (kata-kurushiku-naru)［...を堅苦
　しくする(堅苦しくなる)］.

stifle (*vt.*) 1)...o chissoku-saseru［...を窒息させる］. 2)(akubi ya
　warai nado)-o osaeru［(あくびや笑いなど)を抑える］. 3)...o kesu［...
　を消す］.
　(*vi.*) chissoku-suru［窒息する］; iki-gurushiku-naru［息苦しくな
　る］.

still (*ad.*) 1)mada［まだ］; ima-demo［今でも］. 2)sara-ni［さらに］;
　motto［もっと］.
　(*1*) It is **still** dark. *Mada* kurai.
　(*2*) It will grow **still** colder. *Motto* samuku-naru-darô.
　　(*a.*) 1)shizuka-na［静かな］; seishi-shita［静止した］. 2)hisoka-na
　［ひそかな］.
　　(*vt.*) ...o shizumeru［...を静める］; ...o nadameru［...をなだめる］.
　　(*n.*) 1) (the -) seijaku［静寂］; shizukesa［静けさ］. 2)suchîru-
　shashin［スチール写真］.

stimulate (*vt.*) ...o shigeki-suru［...を刺激する］; ...o kôfun-saseru［...
　を興奮させる］; ...o genki-zukeru［...を元気づける］.

sting (*n.*) 1)sashi-kizu［刺し傷］; gekitsû［激痛］. 2)(*zool.*) hari［針］;
　dokuga［毒牙］. 3)shinratsu-sa［辛らつさ］.
　　(*vt.*) 1)...o hari-de-sasu［...を針で刺す］; ...o hiri-hiri-saseru［...
　をひりひりさせる］. 2)...o kizu-tsukeru［...を傷つける］. 3)...e-to kari-
　tateru［...へと駆り立てる］.
　　(*vi.*) 1)hiri-hiri-suru［ひりひりする］. 2)kokoro-o-kurushimeru
　［心を苦しめる］.

stingy (*a.*) 1)kechi-na [けちな]; shimittareta [しみったれた]. 2) toboshii [乏しい].

stink (*vi.*) iya-na-nioi-ga-suru [いやなにおいがする].

    (*n.*) akushû [悪臭].

stint (*vt.*) ...o kiri-tsumeru […を切り詰める]; ...o dashi-oshimu [… を出し惜しむ]; ...o seigen-suru […を制限する].

    (*n.*) dashi-oshimi [出し惜しみ]; seigen [制限].

stipulate (*vt.*) ...o kitei-suru […を規定する]. (keiyaku de)...o hoshô-suru [(契約で)…を保証する].

    (*vi.*) yakujô-no-jôken-to-shite-yôkyû-suru [約定の条件として 要求する].

stir (*vt.*) 1)...o ugokasu […を動かす]. 2)...o kaki-mawasu […をかき 回す]. 3)...o funki-saseru […を奮起させる]; ...o kandô-saseru […を 感動させる].

    (*1*) The breeze **stirs** the leaves.

       Soyo-kaze ga ko-no-ha-*o ugokasu*.

    (*2*) Please **stir** the fire. Hi-*o kaki-tatete*-kudasai.

    (*3*) He was deeply **stirred**. Kare-wa fukaku *kandô-shita*.

    (*vi.*) 1)jitto-shite-i-nai [じっとしていない]; ugoku [動く]; soyogu [そよぐ]. 2)(kanjô nado ga) okoru [(感情などが)起こる].

    (*1*) The leaves began to **stir**. Ko-no-ha ga *soyogi*-hajimeta.

stirrup (*n.*) abumi [あぶみ].

stitch (*n.*) hito-hari [一針]; hito-nui [一縫い]; sutetchi [ステッチ].

    (*vt. & vi.*) (...o) nuu [(…を)縫う].

stock (*n.*) 1)kiri-kabu [切り株]. 2)(*US fin.*) kabu [株]; kabushiki [株式]. 3)takuwae [蓄え]. 4)zaiko-hin [在庫品].

    (*1*) I grafted it on a **stock**.

       Watashi-wa sore-*o kiri-kabu*-ni tsuida.

    (*2*) John bought 10% of the company's **stock**.

       Jon wa sono kaisha-no *kabu* no ichi-wari-o kai-shimeta.

    (*3*) She has a great **stock** of knowledge.

       Kano-jo-wa chishiki-no-*takuwae*-ga-hôfu-da.

       Kano-jo-wa totemo chishiki-ga aru.

    (*4*) The shop keeps a large **stock** of socks.

       Ano mise niwa kutsu-shita no *zaiko*-ga ooi.

    out of stock   shina-gire-de; zaiko-ga-kirete

       (*a.*) 1)temochi-no [手持ちの]; zaiko-no [在庫の]. 2)ari-fure-ta [ありふれた]. 3)kabu-no [株の].

(vt.) …ni(…o) shi-ireru［…に(…を)仕入れる］; …o chozô-suru
［…を貯蔵する］.
　　　(vi.) 1)shi-ireru［仕入れる］. 2)shin-me-o-dasu［新芽をだす］.

stockbroker (n.) kabushiki-naka-gai-nin［株式仲買人］.

stock exchange kabushiki-torihiki-sho［株式取引所］; shôken-torihiki-
　　sho［証券取引所］.

stockholder (n.) ((US)) kabu-nushi［株主］.

stocking (n.) (pl.)(nagai) kutsu-shita［(長い)靴下］; sutokkingu［ス
　　トッキング］.

stomach (n.) 1)i［胃］; (colloq.) hara［腹］. 2)shokuyoku［食欲］.
　　　(vt.) 1)…o taberu［…を食べる］. 2)…ni taeru［…に耐える］.

stomachache (n.) itsû［胃痛］; fukutsû［腹痛］.

stone (n.) 1)ishi［石］; ko-ishi［小石］. 2)(kudamono no) tane［(果物
　　の)種］; kaku［核］.
　　(1) A rolling **stone** gathers no moss.
　　　　　Korogaru ishi niwa koke-ga tsuka-nai.
　　　　　Shôbai-gae-wa son-ga-atte-mo toku-wa-nai.
　　　The bridge is built of **stone**.
　　　　　Sono hashi wa ishi-de dekite-iru.
　　(2) Remove the **stones** from the peaches.
　　　　　Momo no tane-o tori-nasai.

　　stonework (n.) ishi-zaiku［石細工］; sekizô-butsu［石造物］; (pl.)
　　　ishikiri-ba［石切り場］.

stony (a.) 1)ishi-no［石の］; ishi-no-ooi［石の多い］. 2)ishi-no-yô-ni-
　　katai［石のように堅い］. 3)reikoku-na［冷酷な］. 4)mu-hyôjô-na［無表
　　情な］.

stool (n.) sutsûru［スツール］.

stoop (vi.) 1)kagamu［かがむ］; mae-kagami-ni-naru［前かがみになる］;
　　koshi-ga-magaru［腰が曲がる］. 2)hin'i-o-otosu［品位を落とす］.
　　　(vt.) …o kagameru［…をかがめる］; …o mageru［…を曲げる］.
　　　(n.) 1)kagamu-koto［かがむこと］; neko-ze［猫背］. 2)hin'i-o-
　　otosu-koto［品位を落とすこと］.

stop (vi.) 1)yamu［やむ］. 2)tomaru［止まる］. 3)tomaru［泊まる］;
　　taizai-suru［滞在する］.
　　(1) The rain **has stopped**. Ame ga yanda.

(2) The train **stopped** at the station.　Kisha ga eki-de *tomatta*.

(3) He **is stopping** at a hotel.　Kare-wa hoteru-ni *tomatteiru*.

　　(vt.) 1)...o yamesru [⋯をやめる]. 2)...o tomeru [⋯を止める].

(1) He **stopped** reading a book.　Kare-wa dokusho-*o yameta*.

(2) He **stopped** a taxicab.　Kare-wa takushî-*o tometa*.

stop off (colloq.) tochû-de-tachi-yoru; tochû-gesha-suru

　　On the way to Tokyo I stopped off at Nagoya.

　　　　Tôkyô-e-iku-tochû watashi-wa Nagoya-de tochû-gesha-shita.

stop over (colloq.) tochû-gesha-suru

　　Can I stop over at Moji?　Moji-de tochû-gesha-dekimasu-ka?

　　(n.) 1)teishi [停止]; teisha [停車]. 2)teiryû-sho [停留所]. 3)tachi-yori [立ち寄り]. 4)sen [栓]. 5)(photo.) shibori [絞り]. 6)shûshi-fu [終止符].

(1) This train goes through from Tokyo to Hakata without any **stop**.

　　　　Kono ressha wa zenzen-*teisha*-sezu-ni Tôkyô-kara Hakata-e chokkô-suru.

(2) Get off the car at the next **stop**.

　　　　Tsugi-no-*teiryû-sho*-de densha-o ori-nasai.

(3) On the way home, I made a **stop** at a bookstore.

　　　　Kito hon'ya-ni *tachi-*yotta.

stopover (n.) tochû-gesha [途中下車].

storage (n.) 1)chozô [貯蔵]. 2)hokan-ryô [保管料]. 3)(computer) kioku-sôchi [記憶装置].

storage battery chikudenchi [蓄電池].

store (n.) 1)takuwae [蓄え]. 2)((US)) mise [店]; (Eng. pl.) hyakka-ten [百貨店].

(1) a **store** of food　shokuryô no *takuwae*

(2) I got this shirt at the **store**.

　　　　Watashi-wa ano-*mise*-de kono shatsu-o katta.

　　My uncle keeps a grocery **store**.

　　　　Watashi-no oji wa shokuryô-hin-*ten*-o keiei-shite-iru.

　　(a.) 1)takuwaerareta [蓄えられた]. 2)mise-de-kaeru [店で買える]; kisei-no [既製の].

　　(vt.) ...o takuwaeru [⋯を蓄える]; ...ni(...o) kyôkyû-suru [⋯に(⋯を)供給する]; ...o sôko-ni-hokan-suru [⋯を倉庫に保管する].

　　Enough food **had been stored** away.

　　　　Shokuryô wa jûbun *takuwaete-atta*.

    (*vi.*) chozô-dekiru [貯蔵できる].

storehouse (*n.*) sôko [倉庫]; hôko [宝庫].

storey (*n.*) = story.

stork (*n.*) (*birds*) kô-no-tori [コウノトリ].

storm (*n.*) 1)arashi [あらし]; bôfû[-u] [暴風(雨)]. 2)kyôshû [強襲].
   3)gekidô [激動].
    (*1*) a heavy **storm** hidoi *arashi*
    (*2*) They took the fort by **storm**.
        Kare-ra-wa *kyôshû*-shite sono toride-o dasshu-shita.
    (*3*) time of social **storm** shakai-teki *gekidô* no jidai
       (*vi.*) areru [荒れる]; arashi-ga-fuku [あらしが吹く].
       (*vt.*)...o kyôshû-suru [...を強襲する]. 2)...ni ganari-tateru
    [...にがなりたてる].

stormy (*a.*) 1)arashi-no [あらしの]. 2)gekiretsu-na [激烈な].

story (*n.*) hanashi [話]; monogatari [物語].

story (*n.*) kai [階].

storybook (*n.*) monogatari-no-hon [物語の本]; dôwa-no-hon [童話の
   本].

stout (*a.*) 1)tsuyoi [強い]; ganjô-na [頑丈な]. 2)futotta [太った];
   himan-tai-no [肥満体の].
    (*1*) a **stout** heart *tsuyoi* kokoro
    (*2*) See that old **stout** gentleman.
        Ano *futotta* rô-shinshi-o goran.
       (*n.*) 1)kuro-bîru [黒ビール]; sutauto [スタウト]. 2)futotta-hito
    [太った人]. 3)(*US pl.*) himan-gata-no-fuku [肥満型の服].

stouthearted (*a.*) yûkan-na [勇敢な]; gôtan-na [豪胆な].

stowaway (*n.*) mikkô-sha [密航者].

straight (*a.*) 1)massugu-na [真っすぐな]. 2)kichin-to-shita [きちんと
   した]; seiton-shita [整とんした]. 3)tadashii [正しい]; sotchoku-na
   [率直な]. 4)renzoku-shita [連続した]; togire-nai [途切れない].
    (*1*) a **straight** road *massugu-na* dôro
    (*2*) Put the things **straight** in the room.
        Shitsu-nai-no-mono-o *seiton*-shi-nasai.
    (*3*) The accounts are **straight**. Keisan wa *tadashii*.
    (*4*) a **straight**-A student *ôru*-Ei-no gakusei
       (*ad.*) 1)massugu-ni [真っすぐに]. 2)sotchoku-ni [率直に]. 3)
   (*colloq.*) kôketsu-ni [高潔に]. shôjiki-ni [正直に]. 4)renzoku-shite
   [連続して]; tsuzuite [続いて].

(1) Go **straight**. *Massugu-ni* iki-nasai.

(2) Tell me **straight**. *Sotchoku-ni* hanashi-nasai.

(3) act **straight**　rippa-ni furumau

(4) sleep **straight** through till 9　ku-ji-made nemuri-*tsuzukeru*

(n.) (the -) massugu [直っすぐ]; chokusen-kôsu [直線コース].

straighten (*vt. & vi.*) …o massugu-ni-suru (massugu-ni-naru) […を真っすぐにする(真っすぐになる)]; …o kichin-to-suru (kichin-to-naru) […をきちんとする(きちんとなる)].

strain (*vt.*) 1)…o 〔-pin-to〕haru […を(ぴんと)張る]. 2)…o (-tsukai-sugite)itameru […を(使いすぎて)痛める]. 3)…o kyokkai-suru […を曲解する].

(1) **Strain** your eyes to see it. Me-o-*mi-hatte* sore-o mi-nasai.

(2) He **has strained** his legs.

　　　Kare-wa *aruki-sugite* ashi-o *itameta*.

(3) He **strained** the meaning of the word.

　　　Kare-wa sono go no imi-o *kyokkai-shita*.

　　(*vi.*) 1)isshô-kemmei-ni-doryoku-suru [一生懸命に努力する]. 2)tsuyoku-hipparu [強く引っ張る]. 3)hizumu [ひずむ].

　　(*n.*) 1)haru-koto [張ること]; kinchô [緊張]. 2)karô [過労].

strait (*n.*) 1)kaikyô [海峡]. 2)(*pl.*) konkyû [困窮].

strand (*n.*) yori-ito [より糸]; ko [こ]; yori [より].

　　(*vt.*) …o nau […をなう].

strange (*a.*) 1)mada-shira-nai [まだ知らない]; hajimete-no [始めての]. 2)hen-na [変な]; kimyô-na [奇妙な].

(1) I saw many **strange** things there.

　　　Watashi-wa soko-de *mezurashii*-mono-o takusan mita.

(2) A **strange** sound was heard.

　　　Hen-na mono-oto ga kikoeta.

　　strange to say　fushigi-ni-mo; myô-na-hanashi-da-ga

stranger (*n.*) 1)mi-shira-nu-hito [見知らぬ人]; yoso-kara-kita-hito [よそから来た人]. 2)fu-annai-na-hito [不案内な人]. 3)keiken-shita-koto-no-nai-hito [経験したことのない人].

(1) A **stranger** called at my house.

　　　Shira-nai-hito ga watashi-no-ie-o tazunete-kita.

(2) I am a **stranger** here. Watashi-wa tôchi-wa *fu-annai* desu.

(3) He is **no stranger** to poverty.

　　　Kare-wa bimbô-no-aji-*o-yoku-shitte*-iru.

strap (*n.*) kawa-himo [革ひも]; tsuri-kawa [つり革].

　　　(*vt.*) ...o kawa-himo-de-shibaru [...を革ひもで縛る]; ...o kawa-himo-de-utsu [...を革ひもで打つ].

　　　(*vi.*) shîto-beruto-o-tsukeru [シートベルトをつける].

stratagem (*n.*) senryaku [戦略]; sakuryaku [策略].

strategic (*a.*) senryaku[-jô]-no [戦略(上)の].

stratosphere (*n.*) (*meteorol.*) seisô-ken [成層圏].

straw (*n.*) 1)wara [わら]; sutorô [ストロー]. 2)kachi-no-nai-mono [価値のないもの].

　　(*1*) A drawing man will catch at a **straw**.
　　　　Oboreru-mono wa *wara*-o-mo tsukamu.

　　(*2*) It's not worth a **straw**.　Sore-wa *nan-no-neuchi-mo-nai*.

　　　(*a.*) mugi-wara-sei-no [麦わら製の]; usu-ki-iro-no [薄黄色の].

strawberry (*n.*) ichigo [イチゴ].

stray (*vi.*) michi-ni-mayou [道に迷う]; samayou [さまよう]; soreru [それる]; dassen-suru [脱線する].

　　　(*a.*) 1)michi-ni-mayotta [道に迷った]. 2)toki-ori-no [時折の].

　　　(*n.*) mayotta-hito[-dôbutsu] [迷った人[動物]]; mai-go [迷い子].

stray child mai-go [まいご].

streak (*n.*) 1)shima [しま]; suji [筋]. 2)...kimi [...気味].

　　　(*vt.*) ...ni shima-o-tsukeru [...にしまをつける].

　　　(*vi.*) 1)shima-ni-naru [しまになる]. 2)shissô-suru [疾走する].

　　3)(*colloq.*) sutorîkingu-suru [ストリーキングする].

stream (*n.*) 1)nagare [流れ]; kawa [川]; ogawa [小川]. 2)nagare [流れ]; dôkô [動向].

　　　(*vi. & vt.*) nagareru(...o nagasu) [流れる(...を流す)].

streamer (*n.*) fuki-nagashi [吹き流し].

streamline (*vt.*) 1)...o ryûsen-kei-ni-suru [...を流線形にする]. 2)...o gôri-ka-suru [...を合理化する]. 3)...o sai-shinshiki-ni-suru [...を最新式にする].

　　　　(*a.*) ryûsen-kei-no [流線形の].

street (*n.*) gairo [街路]; toori [通り]; [S-]....gai [...街].

streetcar (*n.*) ((*US*)) romen-densha [路面電車].

strength (*n.*) 1)chikara [力]; tsuyo-sa [強さ]. 2)chôsho [長所]; tsuyo-mi [強み]. 3)heiryoku [兵力].

strengthen (*vt. & vi.*) ...o tsuyoku-suru(tsuyoku-naru) [...を強くする(強くなる)]; ...o genki-zukeru (genki-zuku) [...を元気づける(元気づく)].

strenuous (*a.*) 1)seiryoku-teki-na [精力的な]. 2)hijô-ni-hone-ga-oreru

[非常に骨が折れる].

stress (*n.*) 1)kyôchô [強調]; jûten [重点]. 2)kinchô [緊張]; sutoresu [ストレス]. 3)(*phon.*) kyôsei [強勢]; akusento [アクセント].
     (*vt.*) 1)...o kyôchô-suru [···を強調する]. 2)...ni kyôsei-o-oku [··· に強勢を置く].

stretch (*vt. & vi.*) 1)...o nobasu (nobiru) [···を伸ばす(伸びる)]. 2)... o hirogeru (hirogaru) [···を広げる(広がる)].
     (*1*) **Stretch** it and make it longer.
         Sore-o *nobashite* motto-nagaku-shi-nasai.
     (*2*) The field **stretches** away for several hundred miles.
         No-hara ga nam-byaku-mairu-mo *hirogatte-iru.*
     (*n.*) 1)nobi [伸び]; hirogari [広がり]. 2)hito-tsuzuki-no-jikan [一続きの時間]. 3)kakudai-kaishaku [拡大解釈].
     (*a.*) nobiru [伸びる]; sutoretchi-no [ストレッチの]; shinshuku-sei-no-aru [伸縮性のある].

strew (*vt.*) ...o maki-chirasu [···をまき散らす].

strict (*a.*) 1)kibishii [厳しい]. 2)seikaku-na [正確な]; gemmitsu-na [厳密な]. 3)zettai-teki-na [絶対的な].

strictly (*ad.*) 1)kibishiku [厳しく]. 2)seikaku-ni [正確に]. 3)mattaku [全く].
     strictly speaking gemmitsu-ni-ieba

stride (*vi.*) 1)oo-mata-ni-aruku [大またに歩く]. 2)matagi-kosu [またぎ越す].
     (*n.*) oo-mata [大また]; hito-matagi [一またぎ].

strife (*n.*) arasoi [争い]; tôsô [闘争].

strike (*vt.*) 1)...o utsu [···を打つ]; ...o naguru [···を殴る]. 2)...ni tsuki-ataru [···に突き当たる]. 3)...ga kokoro-ni-ukabu [···が心に浮かぶ]. 4)(tokei ga toki)-o utsu [(時計が時)を打つ]. 5)(matchi)-o suru [(マッチ)をする]. 6)(ho ya hata)-o orosu [(帆や旗)を降ろす]. 7)((*US*))...ni-taishi sutoraiki-o-suru [···に対しストライキをする].
     (*1*) He **struck** the table with his fist.
         Kare-wa kobushi-de-dosun-to têburu-o *utta.*
     (*2*) A stone **struck** him on the head.
         Ishi ga kare no atama-ni *atatta.*
     (*3*) A bright idea suddenly **struck** me.
         Subarashii kangae ga *kokoro-ni-ukanda.*
     (*4*) The clock **has** just **struck** four.   Tokei ga chôdo yo-ji-o *utta.*
     (*5*) I **struck** a match.   Watashi-wa matchi-o *sutta.*

　　(6) They **struck** the flag.　Kare-ra-wa hata-o oroshita.
　　　　(*vi.*) 1)utsu [打つ]. 2)butsukaru [ぶつかる]. 3)naru [鳴る].
　　4)susumu [進む]. 5)tenka-suru [点火する]. 6)sutoraiki-o-suru [スト
　　ライキをする].
　　　　(*n.*) 1)utsu-koto [打つこと]. 2)(*baseball*) sutoraiku [ストライ
　　ク]. 3)sutoraiki [ストライキ].

strikeout (*n.*) (*baseball*) sanshin [三振].

striking (*a.*) medatsu [目だつ]; ichijirushii [著しい].

string (*n.*) 1)ito [糸]; himo [ひも]. 2)ichi-ren [一連]. 3)(yumi ya
　　gen-gakki no) gen [(弓や弦楽器の)弦]. 4)(the *pl.*) gengakki [弦楽器].
　　　　(*vt.*) 1)...o ito-ni-toosu [...を糸に通す]. 2)...ni gen-o-haru [...
　　に弦を張る]. 3)...no gen-no-chôshi-o-totonoeru [...の弦の調子を整える].
　　3)...o ichi-retsu-ni-tsuraneru [...を一列に連ねる].

strip (*vt.*) 1)...o hagu [...をはぐ]; ...o hadaka-ni-suru [...を裸にする].
　　2)...o ubau [...を奪う]; ...o hagi-toru [...をはぎ取る].
　　　　(1) I **am stripping** the tree of its bark.
　　　　　　Watashi-wa ki-no-kawa-o haideiru.
　　　　(2) He **was stripped** of his clothes.
　　　　　　Kare-wa kimono-o hagi-torareta.
　　　　(*vi.*) ifuku-o-nugu [衣服を脱ぐ].

strip (*n.*) 1)(nuno ya tochi ya ita no) hoso-nagai-kire [-bubun]
　　[(布や土地や板の)細長い切れ[部分]]. 2)kassô-ro [滑走路].

stripe (*n.*) shima [しま]; suji [筋].

striped (*a.*) shima-no-aru [しまのある]; suji-no-aru [筋のある].

strive (*vi.*) doryoku-suru [努力する].

stroke (*n.*) 1)utsu-koto [打つこと]; ichi-geki [一撃]. 2)hito-kogi [一
　　こぎ]. 3)hito-fude [一ふで]. 4)hossa [発作].
　　at a(one) stroke　ichi-geki-de; ikkyo-ni

stroke (*vt.*) ...o naderu [...をなでる]; ...o sasuru [...をさする].
　　　　(*n.*) naderu-koto [なでること]; hito-nade [一なで].

stroll (*vi. & n.*) bura-bura-aruku (bura-bura-aruki) [ぶらぶら歩く(ぶ
　　らぶら歩き)].
　　take a stroll　sampo-suru

strong (*a.*) 1)tsuyoi [強い]. 2)(cha nado ga) koi [(茶などが)濃い].
　　3)yûryoku-na [有力な].
　　one's strong point　hito-no chôsho; hito-no tsuyo-mi

strongly (*ad.*) 1)tsuyoku [強く]. 2)ganjô-ni [頑丈に].

strontium (*n.*) (*chem.*) sutoronchiumu [ストロンチウム].

structure (*n.*) 1)kôzô [構造]. 2)tate-mono [建物]; kenchiku-butsu [建築物]. 3)soshiki-tai [組織体]

(*1*) the **structure** of a house   ie no *kôzô*

(*2*) a marble **structure**   dairi-seki-no *tate-mono*

struggle (*vi.*) 1)mogaku [もがく]. 2)tatakau [闘う].

      (*n.*) mogaki [もがき]; arasoi [争い]; doryoku [努力].

struggle for existence   seizon-kyôsô [生存競争].

stub (*n.*) 1)kiri-kabu [切り株]. 2)((*US*))(ko-gitte nado no) hikae [(小切手などの)控え]. 3)tsukai-nokori [使い残り].

      (*vt.*) 1)...o butsukeru [...をぶつける]. 2)...kara kiri-kabu-o-nozoku [...から切り株を除く]. 3)(tabako)-o oshi-tsubushite-hi-o-kesu [(タバコ)を押しつぶして火を消す].

stubborn (*a.*) ganko-na [頑固な]; gôjô-na [強情な]; atsukai-nikui [扱いにくい].

stuck-up (*a.*) (*colloq.*) unuboreta [うぬぼれた]; kôman-na [高慢な].

stud (*n.*) kazari-byô [飾りびょう]; kazari-botan [飾りボタン].

      (*vt.*) ...ni kazari-botan-o-tsukeru [...に飾りボタンをつける]; (be -ded) (...ga) chiribamerarete-iru [...が)ちりばめられている].

student (*n.*) 1)gakusei [学生]; 2)kenkyû-sha [研究者].

studied (*a.*) 1)koi-no [故意の]. 2)jukuryo-shita-ue-de-no [熟慮した上での].

studio (*n.*) 1)shigoto-ba [仕事場]; atorie [アトリエ]. 2)eiga-satsuei-sho [映画撮影所]; hôsô-shitsu [放送室]; sutajio [スタジオ].

study (*n.*) 1)benkyô [勉強]. 2)kenkyû [研究]; gakumon [学問]. 3)shosai [書斎].

(*1*) The **study** of Latin is hard.

      Raten-go no *benkyô* wa muzukashii.

(*2*) Go on with your **studies**.   Kimi-no *gakumon*-o tsuzuke-nasai.

(*3*) He is always in his **study**.   Kare-wa itsu-mo *shosai*-ni-iru.

      (*vt.*) 1)...o benkyô-suru [...を勉強する]; ...o kenkyû-suru [...を研究する]. 2)...o chôsa-suru [...を調査する]. 3)...o kôryo-suru [...を考慮する].

      (*vi.*) benkyô-suru [勉強する]; kenkyû-suru [研究する]; doryoku-suru [努力する].

stuff (*n.*) 1)mono [もの]; koto [こと]. 2)zairyô [材料]; genryô [原料]. 3)((*Eng.*)) orimono [織物]; ke-orimono [毛織物].

      (*vt.*) ...o tsumeru [...を詰める]; ...ni tsume-mono-o-suru [...に詰め物をする].

　　　　(*vi.*) (*colloq.*) tarafuku-taberu [たらふく食べる].

stuffing (*n.*) tsumeru-koto [詰めること]; tsume-mono [詰め物].

stumble (*vi.*) 1)tsumazuku [つまずく]. 2)tochiru [とちる]. 3)gûzen...
　　(ni) de-kuwasu [偶然…(に)出くわす].
　　　　(*n.*) tsumazuki [つまずき]; shippai [失敗].

stump (*n.*) 1)kiri-kabu [切り株]. 2)kire-hashi [切れ端]. 3)(*colloq.*)
　　(*pl.*) omoi-ashidori [重い足取り].
　　　　(*vt.*) 1)...o kiri-kabu-ni-suru […を切り株にする]. 2)((*US*)) ...o
　　yûzei-shite-mawaru […を遊説して回る]. 3)(*colloq.*) ...o komaraseru
　　[…を困らせる].
　　　　(*vi.*) 1)omoi-ashidori-de-aruku [重い足取りで歩く]. 2)yûzei-
　　suru [遊説する].

stun (*vt.*) 1)...o kizetsu-saseru […を気絶させる]. 2)...o bikkuri-saseru
　　[…をびっくりさせる].

stunning (*a.*) 1)kizetsu-saseru-hodo-no [気絶させるほどの]. 2)(*colloq.*)
　　subarashii [すばらしい].

stupendous (*a.*) tohô-mo-nai [途方もない].

stupid (*a.*) baka-na [ばかな]; tsumara-nai [つまらない].

stupidity (*n.*) 1)oroka-sa [愚かさ]. 2)(*pl.*) oroka-na-okonai [愚かな
　　行い].

sturdy (*a.*) ganjô-na [頑丈な]; jôbu-na [丈夫な]; fukutsu-no [不屈の].

style (*n.*) 1)yôshiki [様式]; kata [型]; sutairu [スタイル]. 2)buntai
　　[文体]. 3)shurui [種類]; taipu [タイプ]. 4)hinkaku [品格].
　　(*1*) the **style** of living　seikatsu-*yôshiki*
　　(*2*) The **style** is better than the matter.
　　　　Buntai(bunshô)-no-hô ga naiyô-yori-mo-yoi.
　　(*3*) This is not my **style** of picture.
　　　　Kore-wa watashi-no suki-na-*taipu*-no-e-dewa-nai.
　　(*4*) She has **style**.　Kano-jo-niwa *hinkaku*-ga-aru.
　　　　He has no **style**.　Kare-wa *hin*-ga nai.
　　　　(*vt.*) 1)...o(...to) yobu […を(…と)呼ぶ]. 2)...o(-ryûkô-ni-
　　awasete) tsukuru […を(流行に合わせて)作る].

subconscious (*n. & a.*) senzai-ishiki(-no) [潜在意識(の)].

subdue (*vt.*) 1)...o seifuku-suru […を征服する]; ...ni uchi-katsu […
　　に打ち勝つ]. 2)...o osaeru […を抑える]; ...o yawarageru […を和ら
　　げる].

subject (*n.*) 1)gakka [学科]. 2)wadai [話題]; daimoku [題目]. 3)
　　kerai [家来]; shimmin [臣民]. 4)(*gram.*) shugo [主語]; shubu [主

部].

　　　(a.) 1)jûzoku-suru [従属する]. 2)(...o-)uke-yasui [(…を)受け
やすい]; (...ni-)kakari-yasui [(…に)かかりやすい]. 3)jôken-to-suru
[条件とする].

　　　(vt.) 1)...o fukujû-saseru […を服従させる]; ...o shihai-suru […
を支配する]. 2)...o(...ni) sarasu […を(…に)さらす].

subjective (a.) (philos.) shukan-teki-na [主観的な]; (gram.) shukaku-
no [主格の].

subjunctive (n. & a.) (gram.) katei-hô(-no) [仮定法(の)].

sublime (a.) 1)yûdai-na [雄大な]; sôgon-na [荘厳な]. 2)takuetsu-
shita [卓越した].

　　　(n.) (the –) 1)sûkô [崇高]. 2)kyokuchi [極地].

　　　(vt. & vi.) ...o kôshô-ni-suru (kôshô-ni-naru) […を高尚にす
る(高尚になる)].

submarine (a.) 1)kaitei-no [海底の]; kaichû-no [海中の]. 2)sensui-
kan-ni-yoru [潜水艦による].

　　　(n.) sensui-kan [潜水艦].

submerge (vt.) ...o suichû-ni-ireru […を水中に入れる]; ...o shizumeru
[…を沈める].

　　　(vi.) 1)sensui-suru [潜水する]. 2)umoreru [埋もれる].

submission (n.) 1)fukujû [服従]. 2)gushin [具申]; teishutsu [提出].

submit (vt.) 1)...o shitagawaseru […を従わせる]; ...o fukujû-saseru
[…を服従させる]. 2)...o gushin-suru […を具申する]; ...o teishutsu-
suru […を提出する].

　　　(vi.) shitagau [従う]; fukujû-suru [服従する]; amanjite(...o)
ukeru [甘んじて(…を)受ける].

subscribe (vt.) 1)...o kifu-suru […を寄付する]. 2)...ni shomei-suru […
に署名する].

　　　(vi.) 1)(shimbun ya zasshi o) yoyaku-suru [(新聞や雑誌を)
予約する]; kôdoku-suru [購読する]. 2)môshi-komu [申し込む]. 3)
kifu-suru [寄付する]. 4)shomei-suru [署名する].

　(1) I **subscribed** for the first volume of a series.

　　　Watashi-wa shirîzu-mono no dai-ikkan-o *yoyaku-chûmon-
shita*.

　(2) He **subscribed** for 2,000 shares.

　　　Kare-wa ni-sen-kabu *môshi-konda*.

　(3) He **subscribed** for $100 to the Red Cross.

　　　Kare-wa Seki-jûji-ni hyaku-doru *kifu-shita*.

(*4*) Will you please **subscribe** to the agreement?
    Gôi-sho-ni *shomei-shite*-kudasai-masen-ka?

subscriber (*n.*) 1)yoyaku-sha [予約者]; kôdoku-sha [購読者]. 2)kifu-sha [寄付者].

subscription (*n.*) 1)〔yoyaku-〕kôdoku [（予約）購読]. 2)kifu [寄付]. 3)shomei [署名].

subsequent (*a.*) sono-go-no [その後の]; ...ni-tsuzuite-okoru [...に続いて起こる].

subside (*vi.*) 1)(kôzui nado ga) hiku [(洪水などが)ひく]; (fûu nado ga) shizumaru [(風雨などが)静まる]. 2)(jimen ga) chinka-suru [(地面が)沈下する]. 3)(*colloq.*) koshi-o-orosu [腰を下ろす].

substance (*n.*) 1)mono [もの]; busshitsu [物質]. 2)(*philos.*) jittai [実体]. honshitsu [本質]. 3)(the -) yôshi [要旨]. 4)shisan [資産]; tomi [富].

substantial (*a.*) 1)genjitsu-no [現実の]; jisshitsu-teki-na [実質的な]. 2)shikkari-shita [しっかりした]; jôbu-na [丈夫な]. 3)sôtô-na [相当な]. 4)yutaka-na [豊かな].

    (*1*) **substantial** progress *jisshitsu-teki-na* shimpo
    (*2*) a **substantial** house *jôbu-na* ie
    (*3*) a **substantial** improvement *sôtô-na* kaizen
    (*4*) a **substantial** farmer *yutaka-na* nômin

substitute (*n.*) dairi-nin [代理人]; daiyô-hin [代用品].
        (*vt. & vi.*) ...o daiyô-suru (daiyô-ni-naru) [...を代用する(代用になる)].

subtle (*a.*) 1)bimyô-na [微妙な]. 2)eibin-na [鋭敏な]. 3)kôkatsu-na [こうかつな].

subtract (*vt.*) ...o hiku [...を引く]; ...o genjiru [...を減じる].
        (*vi.*) hiki-zan-o-suru [引き算をする].

subtraction (*n.*) (*math.*) gempô [減法]; hiki-zan [引き算].

suburb (*n.*) (the *pl.*) kôgai [郊外]. kinkô-chiku [近郊地区].

suburban (*a.*) kôgai-no [郊外の].

subway (*n.*) ((*US*)) chika-tetsu [地下鉄]; ((*Eng.*)) chika-dô [地下道].

succeed (*vi.*) 1)seikô-suru [成功する]. 2)ato-o-tsugu [あとを継ぐ]; keishô-suru [継承する].

    (*1*) He will **succeed** as an engineer.
        Kare-wa gishi-to-shite *seikô-suru*-darô.
    (*2*) He **succeeded** to a hard task.
        Kare-wa konnan-na-shigoto-o *keishô-shita*.
        (*vt.*) ...no ato-o-tsugu [...のあとを継ぐ]; ...ni tsuide-okoru [...

に次いで起こる].

　　Night **succeeds** day.　Yoru wa hiru-*no-ato-ni-kuru*.

success (*n.*) seikô [成功]; seikô-shita-hito[-koto] [成功した人[こと]].

successful (*a.*) seikô-shita [成功した]; umaku-itta [うまくいった].

successfully (*ad.*) shubi-yoku [首尾よく]; migoto-ni [見事に].

succession (*n.*) 1)renzoku [連続]. 2)sôzoku [相続].

　in succession　renzoku-shite; tsuzuite; tsugi-tsugi-ni

successive (*a.*) ai-tsugu [相次ぐ]; renzoku-suru [連続する].

successor (*n.*) kôkei-sha [後継者]; sôzoku-sha [相続者].

succumb (*vi.*) kussuru [屈する]; makeru [負ける].

such (*a.*) 1)sono-yô-na [そのような]; sonna [そんな]. 2)hijô-ni...na [非常に…な]; totemo...na [とても…な].

　(*1*) I don't know **such** a man.

　　　Watashi-wa *sonna* hito-wa shira-nai.

　(*2*) I felt **such** a terrible pain.

　　　Watashi-wa *totemo*-hidoi itami-o kanjita.

　such A as B = **A such as B**　Bî-no-yô-na-Ei

　　(*pron.*) sono-yô-na-mono [そのようなもの]; sono-yô-na-hito [そのような人].

　　　Such is life.　Jinsei-to-wa *sono-yô-na-mono* da.

　and such　...nado

such-and-such (*a.*) kore-kore-no [これこれの]; shika-jika-no [しかじかの].

suck (*vt.*) ...o suu […を吸う]; ...o kyûshû-suru […を吸収する].

　(*vi.*) suu [吸う].

sucker (*n.*) 1)nyûji [乳児]. 2)(*zool.*) kyûban [吸盤].

sudden (*a.*) kyû-na [急な]; totsuzen-no [突然の].

　(all) of a sudden　fui-ni; ikinari

suddenly (*ad.*) kyû-ni [急に]; totsuzen [突然].

sue (*vt.*) 1)...o uttaeru […を訴える]. 2)...o seigan-suru […を請願する].

　(*vi.*) soshô-o-okosu [訴訟を起こす]; (...o-)motomeru [(…を)求める].

suffer (*vt.*) 1)...o ukeru […を受ける]; ...o kômuru […をこうむる]; ...o keiken-suru […を経験する]. 2)...o gaman-suru […を我慢する].

　(*1*) He **suffered** much pain.

　　　Kare-wa taihen-na kutsû-*o keiken-shita*.

　(*2*) I can't **suffer** it.　Watashi-wa sore-niwa *gaman*-deki-nai.

　　(*vi.*) 1)kurushimu [苦しむ]; wazurau [患う]; (byôki ni)

kakaru [(病気に)かかる]. 2)songai-o-ukeru [損害を受ける].

(1) He **has been suffering** from headache.

　　Kare-wa zutsû-ni *nayandeiru*.

(2) The engine **suffered** severely.　Enjin wa dai-*songai-o-uketa*.

sufferer (*n.*) kurushimu-hito [苦しむ人]; kanja [患者]; hisai-sha [被
災者].

suffering (*n.*) 1)kutsû [苦痛]. 2)(*pl.*) kurô [苦労].

sufficient (*a.*) jûbun-na [十分な]; tariru [足りる].

suffocate (*vt. & vi.*) ...o chissoku-saseru (chissoku-suru) […を窒息
させる(窒息する)].

suffrage (*n.*) senkyo-ken [選挙権]; senkyo [選挙]; tôhyô [投票].

sugar (*n.*) satô [砂糖].

　　　(*vt.*) ...ni satô-o-ireru […に砂糖を入れる]; ...ni satô-o-mabusu
[…に砂糖をまぶす].

　　　(*vi.*) amaku-naru [甘くなる].

sugarcane (*n.*) satô-kibi [サトウキビ].

suggest (*vt.*) 1)...o anji-suru […を暗示する]; ...o sore-to-naku-iu […
をそれとなく言う]. 2)...o teian-suru […を提案する]; ...o ii-dasu […を
言い出す]. 3)...o rensô-saseru […を連想させる]; ...o omoi-okosaseru
[…を思い起こさせる].

suggestion (*n.*) 1)anji [暗示]; teian [提案]. 2)...kimi […気味].

suicide (*n.*) jisatsu [自殺].

　　commit suicide　jisatsu-suru

suit (*n.*) 1)itchaku [一着]; sûtsu [スーツ]. 2)(*law*) soshô [訴訟];
kokuso [告訴]. 3)negai [願い]; tangan [嘆願].

(1) a **suit** of clothes　sûtsu-*itchaku*

(2) He has brought a **suit** against me.

　　Kare-wa watashi-o-aite-dotte *soshô*-o okoshita.

(3) He had a **suit** to her.

　　Kare-wa kano-jo-ni *tangan-shi-tai-koto*-ga atta.

　　　(*vt.*) 1)...ni tekisuru […に適する]. 2)...ni ni-au […に似合う]. 3)
...ni tsugô-ga-yoi […に都合がよい]; ...no ki-ni-iru […の気に入る].

　　　(*vi.*) 1)tsugô-ga-yoi [都合がよい]; tekisuru [適する]. 2)((*US*))
kiru [着る].

　　Suit yourself.　Katte-ni-shiro.

suitable (*a.*) tekitô-na [適当な]; fusawashii [ふさわしい]; ni-au [似
合う].

suitcase (*n.*) sûtsukêsu [スーツケース].

suite (*n.*) 1)hito-tsuzuki-no-heya [一続きの部屋]; hito-kumi-no-kagu [一組の家具]. 2)(*mus.*) kumi-kyoku [組曲].

suitor (*n.*) 1)(*law*) genkoku [原告]. 2)seigan-sha [請願者].

sulfur, sulphur (*n.*) iô [硫黄].

sulk (*vi.*) suneru [すねる]; fukureru [ふくれる].
　　(*n.*) (the *pl.*) suneru-koto [すねること]; muttsuri-suru-koto [むっつりすること].

sulky (*a.*) suneta [すねた]; fukureta [ふくれた].

sullen (*a.*) 1)fu-kigen-na [不機嫌な]; muttsuri-shita [むっつりした]. 2)uttôshii [うっとうしい]. 3)(oto ga) nibui [(音が)鈍い].

sultry (*a.*) 1)mushi-atsui [蒸し暑い]; udaru-yô-na [うだるような]. 2)jônetsu-teki-na [情熱的な]; moeru-yô-na [燃えるような].

sum (*n.*) 1)gôkei [合計]. 2)kingaku [金額]. 3)sansû-no-mondai [算数の問題]; (*pl.*) sansû [算数]. 4)taii [大意]; gaiyô [概要].
　　(*1*) The **sum** of one and two is three.
　　　Ichi-to-ni-no-*gôkei* wa san-de-aru.
　　(*2*) He has a large **sum** of money. Kare-wa tai*kin*-o motte-iru.
　　(*3*) You are good at **sums**. Kimi-wa *sansû-ga*-tokui-da.
　　(*4*) in **sum** *yôsuru-ni*
　　(*vt.*) 1)...o gôkei-suru [...を合計する]; ...o yôyaku-suru [...を要約する]. 2)...o mi-nuku [...を見抜く].
　　(*vi.*) yôyaku-suru [要約する]; sôkei...(ni-)naru [総計...(に)なる].
　　to sum up yôyaku-sureba

summary (*n.*) yôyaku [要約]; taiyô [大要].
　　(*a.*) 1)kai-tsumanda [かいつまんだ]; temijika-na [手短な]. 2)(*law*) sokketsu-no [即決の].

summer (*n.*) natsu [夏].

summer solstice, the geshi [夏至].

summit (*n.*) chôjô [頂上]; (the –) shunô[-jin] [首脳(陣)].

summon (*vt.*) 1)...o yobi-dasu [...を呼び出す]; ...o shôkan-suru [...を召喚する]; ...o shôshû-suru [...を召集する]. 2)(yûki ya genki)-o dasu [(勇気や元気)を出す].

summons (*n.*) shôkan[-jô] [召喚(状)]; shôshû [召集].
　　(*vt.*) ...ni shôkan-jô-o-dasu [...に召喚状を出す].

sun (*n.*) 1)taiyô [太陽]. 2)hinata [日なた].
　　(*1*) The **sun** rises in the east. *Taiyô* wa higashi-kara noboru.
　　(*2*) Boys and girls are playing in the **sun**.
　　　Shônen-ya-shôjo-tachi wa *hinata*-de asondeiru.

　　　(*vi.*) hinata-bokko-o-suru [日なたぼっこをする].

　　　(*vt.*) ...o hi-ni-sarasu [...を日にさらす]; ...o hi-ni-hosu [...を日に干す].

sunbeam (*n.*) taiyô-kôsen [太陽光線].

sunburn (*n.*) hi-yake [日焼け].

　　　(*vi. & vt.*) hi-yake-suru(...o-hi-yake-saseru) [日焼けする(...を日焼けさせる)].

sunburned, -burnt (*a.*) 《*Eng.*》hi-yake-shita [日焼けした]; 《*US*》hiri-hiri-suru [ひりひりする]; mizu-bukure-no [水ぶくれの].

Sunday (*n.*) Nichiyô-bi [日曜日].

sundown (*n.*) nichibotsu [日没].

sundry (*a.*) shuju-zatta-no [種々雑多の].

sunflower (*n.*) (*bot.*) himawari [ヒマワリ].

sunglass (*n.*) (*pl.*) sangurasu [サングラス].

sunken (*a.*) 1)shizunda [沈んだ]. 2)kubonda [くぼんだ]; ochi-konda [落ち込んだ].

sunlight (*n.*) nikkô [日光].

sunny (*a.*) hi-atari-no-yoi [日当りのよい]; yôki-na [陽気な].

sunny-side up (*US colloq.*) medama-yaki-no [目玉焼きの].

sunrise (*n.*) hi-no-de[-doki] [日の出(時)].

sunset (*n.*) 1)nichibotsu[-doki] [日没(時)]. 2)yû-yake-zora [夕焼け空].

sunshine (*n.*) 1)nikkô [日光]; hinata [日なた]. 2)kagayaki [輝き]; kaikatsu [快活].

sunstroke (*n.*) nissha-byô [日射病].

suntan (*n.*) hi-yake [日焼け].

super- (*pref.*) chô- [超-].

superb (*a.*) 1)rippa-na [立派な]; tobikiri-jôtô-no [飛び切り上等の]. 2)sôrei-na [壮麗な]; karei-na [華麗な].

superficial (*a.*) 1)hyômen[-jô]-no [表面(上)の]. 2)uwabe-dake-no [うわべだけの]; sempaku-na [浅薄な]; hisô-teki-na [皮相的な].

superfluous (*a.*) yobun-na [余分な]; fu-hitsuyô-na [不必要な].

superintend (*vt.*) ...o shiki-suru [...を指揮する]; ...o kantoku-suru [...を監督する].

superintendent (*n.*) shiki-sha [指揮者]; kantoku-sha [監督者]; kanri-nin [管理人].

　　　(*a.*) kantoku-suru [監督する].

superior (*a.*) 1)sugureta [優れた]; yûshû-na [優秀な]; jôtô-no [上等の]. 2)(...yori-)sugureta [(...より)優れた]; (...ni-)masaru [(...に)ま

さる].

(1) This cloth is very **superior**.　Kono ki-ji wa totemo *jôtô*-da.

(2) It is **superior** in quality to any other machine.

Sore-wa　shitsu-ni-oite　hoka-no-donna-kikai-*yori-sugurete-iru*.

(n.) 1)sugureta-hito [優れた人]. 2)sempai [先輩].

superiority (n.) yûetsu [優越]; takuetsu [卓越]; yûsei [優勢].

superlative (a.) 1)saikô-no [最高の]; saijô-no [最上の]. 2)(*gram.*) saijô-kyû-no [最上級の].

(n.) (*gram.*) 1)saijô-kyû [最上級]. 2)saikô-no-hito [最高の人]; kyokuchi [極致].

supernatural (a.) chô-shizen-no [超自然の]; ningen-banare-shita [人間離れした]; rei-teki-na [霊的な].

(n.) (the –) chô-shizen-genshô [超自然現象].

superstition (n.) meishin [迷信].

supervise (vt.) ...o kantoku-suru […を監督する]; ...o kanri-suru […を管理する]; ...no shiki-o-toru […の指揮をとる].

supper (n.) yûshoku [夕食]; yashoku [夜食].

supplement (n.) hosoku [補足]; hoi [補遺].

(vt.) ...o hosoku-suru […を補足する]; ...o tsuika-suru […を追加する].

supply (vt.) 1)...o kyôkyû-suru […を供給する]. 2)...o oginau […を補う]; ...o hojû-suru […を補充する]; ...o mitasu […を満たす].

(1) Cows **supply** us with milk.

Me-ushi wa ware-ware-ni gyûnyû-o *kyôkyû-suru*.

(2) These articles **supply** the need of the people.

Kore-ra-no shinamono wa kokumin no hitsuyô-o *mitasu*.

(n.) 1)kyôkyû [供給]; hokyû [補給]. 2)(*pl.*) ryôshoku [糧食].

support (vt.) 1)...o sasaeru […を支える]; ...o shiji-suru […を支持する]. 2)...o fuyô-suru […を扶養する]; ...o enjo-suru […を援助する].

(1) Pillars **support** the roof.　Hashira wa yane-o *sasaeru*.

We **are supporting** the plan.

Ware-ware-wa sono keikaku-o *shiji-shiteiru*.

(2) He **supports** a large family.

Kare-wa dai-kazoku-o *fuyô-shite-iru*.

(n.) shiji [支持]; fuyô [扶養]; enjo [援助].

supporter (n.) 1)shiji-sha [支持者]. 2)fuyô-sha [扶養者]. 3)(*sports*) sapôtâ [サポーター].

suppose (*vt.*) 1)...to sôzô-suru [···と想像する]; ...to omou [···と思う].
2)moshi...nara-ba [もし···ならば]. 3)(...shi-)tara-dô-ka [(···し)たら
どうか].

   (*1*) I **suppose** that he will come.

      Watashi-wa kare-wa kuru-*to omou.*

   (*2*) **Suppose** it were so, what would happen?

      Moshi sô-da-to-*suru-to*, dô-naru-darô?

   (*3*) **Suppose** we go. Iku-*to-shiyô-ka.*

suppress (*vt.*) 1)...o chin'atsu-suru [···を鎮圧する]. 2)...o osaeru [···
を抑える]; ...o gaman-suru [···を我慢する]. 3)...o kakusu [···を隠す].

suppurate (*vi.*) umu [うむ]; kanô-suru [化膿する].

supreme (*a.*) saikô-no [最高の]; shijô-no [至上の].

sure (*a.*) 1)tashika-na [確かな]; kakujitsu-na [確実な]; anzen-na [安
全な]. 2)...to-kakushin-shite [···と確信して]; tashika-ni...to-omotte
[確かに···と思って]. 3)kitto...(suru) [きっと···(する)].

   (*1*) a **sure** way to succeed seikô-suru-*kakujitsu-na*-hôhô

   (*2*) I'm **sure** that he is diligent.

      Kare-wa kimben-da-*to* boku-wa *kakushin-shite*-iru.

   (*3*) She is **sure** to come. Kano-jo-wa *kitto*-kuru.

  for sure tashika-ni; kitto

  make sure of ...o tashikameru; ...ni nen-o-ireru

  to be sure tashika-ni

   (*ad.*) 1)tashika-ni [確かに]. 2)ii-desu-tomo [いいですとも];
mochiron [もちろん].

surely (*ad.*) 1)tashika-ni [確かに]; kitto [きっと]. 2)chakujitsu-ni
[着実に].

surf (*n.*) yose-nami [寄せ波].

   (*vi.*) nami-nori-suru [波乗りする]; sâfin-o-suru [サーフィンをする].

surface (*n.*) hyômen [表面]; gaiken [外見]; uwabe [うわべ].

   (*a.*) hyômen-no [表面の]; gaiken-jô-no [外見上の].

   (*vt.*) 1)...no hyômen-o-taira-ni-shi-ageru [···の表面を平らに仕
上げる]. 2)...o uki-agaraseru [···を浮き上がらせる].

   (*vi.*) 1)suimen-ni-fujô-suru [水面に浮上する]. 2)hyômen-ka-
suru [表面化する].

surge (*vi.*) 1)nami-utsu [波うつ]; oo-nami-no-yô-ni-oshi-yoseru [大波
のように押し寄せる]. 2)waki-agaru [沸きあがる].

   (*n.*) 1)oo-nami [大波]; uneri [うねり]. 2)(kanjô no) takamari
[(感情の)高まり].

surgeon (*n.*) geka-i [外科医].

surname (*n.*) sei [姓].

surpass (*vt.*) ...yori masaru […よりまさる]; ...o koeru […を越える].

surplus (*n.*) 1)amari [余り]. 2)(*bkpg.*) jôyo-kin [剰余金].
    (*a.*) amatta [余った]; kajô-no [過剰の].

surprise (*n.*) 1)odoroki [驚き]. 2)odoroku-beki-koto [驚くべきこと];
bikkuri-saseru-mono [びっくりさせるもの]. 3)fui-uchi [不意打ち];
kishû [奇襲].
    (*1*) He jumped up in **surprise**.   Kare-wa *odoroi*te tobi-agatta.
    (*2*) a birthday **surprise**   tanjô-bi no *bikkuri-saseru-okuri-mono*
    (*3*) The fort was taken by **surprise**.
         Kishû-ni-yotte toride wa senryô-sareta.
    to one's surprise   odoroita-koto-ni-wa
        (*vt.*) 1)...o odorokasu […を驚かす]; ...o bikkuri-saseru […
        をびっくりさせる]. 2)...o fui-ni-osou […を不意に襲う].
    (*1*) I am **surprised** to see it.   Sore-o-mite *bikkuri-shita*.

surprising (*a.*) odoroku-beki [驚くべき]; igai-na [意外な].

surrender (*vt.*) ...o hiki-watasu […を引き渡す]; ...o hôki-suru […を
放棄する].
    (*vi.*) kôfuku-suru [降伏する].
    (*n.*) hiki-watashi [引き渡し]; kôfuku [降伏].

surround (*vt.*) ...o kakomu […を囲む]; ...o hôi-suru […を包囲する].
    (*n.*) 1)tori-kakomu-mono [取り囲むもの]. 2)fuchi-kazari
[縁飾り].

surrounding (*a.*) shûi-no [周囲の].

surroundings (*n.*) shûi-no-jôkyô [周囲の状況]; kankyô [環境].

survey (*vt.*) 1)...o mi-watasu […を見渡す]. 2)...o chôsa-suru […を調
査する]; ...o sokuryô-suru […を測量する].
    (*n.*) 1)gaikan [概観]. 2)chôsa [調査]; sokuryô [測量].

survival (*n.*) 1)iki-nokoru-koto [生き残ること]; zanson [残存]. 2)
seizon-sha [生存者]; zanson-butsu [残存物].

survive (*vt.*) ...yori naga-iki-suru […より長生きする]; ...o iki-nokoru
[…を生き残る].
    (*vi.*) iki-nokoru [生き残る].

survivor (*n.*) 1)seizon-sha [生存者]. 2)izoku [遺族]; ibutsu [遺物].

suspect (*vt.*) ...de-nai-ka-to utagau […でないかと疑う]; ...o ayashii-
to-omou […を怪しいと思う].
    (*vi.*) ayashii-to-omou [怪しいと思う]; utagau [疑う].

      (*n.*) yôgi-sha [容疑者].

      (*a.*) ayashii [怪しい]; utagawashii [疑わしい].

suspend (*vt.*) 1)...o tsurusu [···をつるす]; ...o kakeru [···をかける].
2)...o ichiji-teishi-suru [···を一時停止する]. 3)...o horyû-suru [···を
保留する].

    (*1*) She **suspended** a lamp from the ceiling.

         Kano-jo-wa tenjô-kara rampu-o *tsurushita*.

    (*2*) The railway service **was suspended** because of the heavy
         storm.

         Tetsudô wa bôfû-u-no-tame-ni unkô-ga-*ichiji-chûshi-to-
         natta*.

    (*3*) He **suspended** judgment. Kare-wa handan-o *horyû-shita*.

      (*vi.*) 1)shiharai-funô-ni-naru [支払い不能になる]. 2)bura-
sagaru [ぶらさがる].

suspended animation (*physiol.*) jinji-fusei [人事不省]; kashi [仮死].

suspender (*n.*) (*pl.*) ((*Eng.*)) kutsu-shita-dome [靴下留め]; gâtâ [ガー
ター]; ((*US*)) zubon-tsuri [ズボン吊り].

suspense (*n.*) 1)fuan [不安]. 2) ki-gakari [気掛かり]. 2)mi-kettei [未決
定]; chûburarin-no-jôtai [宙ぶらりんの状態].

suspension (*n.*) 1)tsurusu-koto [つるすこと]. 2)mi-kettei [未決定];
horyû [保留]. 3)chûshi [中止]; teishi [停止]; teishoku [停職];
teigaku [停学].

suspension bridge tsuri-bashi [つり橋].

suspicion (*n.*) utagai [疑い]; yôgi [容疑].

suspicious (*a.*) 1)utagawashii [疑わしい]; ayashii [怪しい]. 2)utagai-
bukai [疑い深い].

sustain (*vt.*) 1)...o sasaeru [···を支える]. 2)...o iji-suru [···を維持する].
3)...ni taeru [···に耐える].

swallow (*n.*) (*birds*) tsubame [ツバメ].

swallow (*vt.*) ...o nomi-komu [···を飲み込む]; (*colloq.*) ...o u-nomi-
ni-suru [···をうのみにする].

      (*vi.*) nomi-komu [飲み込む].

      (*n.*) hito-nomi [一飲み].

swamp (*n.*) numa-chi [沼地].

swan (*n.*) hakuchô [ハクチョウ].

swap (*vt.*) ...o kôkan-suru [···を交換する]; ...o suwappingu-suru [···
をスワッピングする].

      (*vi.*) 〔butsu-butsu-〕kôkan-suru [(物々)交換する].

(n.) (colloq.) kôkan[-hin] [交換(品)]; suwappingu [スワッピング].

swarm (n.) mure [群れ]; gunshû [群集].

(vi.) muragaru [群がる]; takaru [たかる].

sway (vi.) 1)yureru [揺れる]. 2)(iken nado ga) guratsuku [(意見な どが)ぐらつく].

(vt.) ...o yuri-ugokasu […を揺り動かす].

(n.) 1)dôyô [動揺]; yure [揺れ]. 2)eikyô[-ryoku] [影響(力)].

swear (vt.) 1)...o chikau […を誓う]. 2)...to dangen-suru […と断言す る]. 3)...ni chikawaseru […に誓わせる].

(vi.) 1)chikau [誓う]. 2)dangen-suru [断言する]. 3)nonoshiru [ののしる].

sweat (n.) ase [汗]; shikki [湿気].

(vi.) ase-o-kaku [汗をかく]; shikki-o-obiru [湿気を帯びる].

(vt.) 1)...ni ase-o-kakaseru […に汗をかかせる]; ...no suibun-o- toru […の水分を取る]. 2)...o yôsetsu-suru […を溶接する].

sweater (n.) sêtâ [セーター].

Sweden (n.) Suwêden [スウェーデン].

Swedish (a.) Suwêden-no [スウェーデンの]; Suwêden-jin-no [スウェー デン人の]; Suwêden-go-no [スウェーデン語の].

(n.) (the –) Suwêden-jin [スウェーデン人]. Suwêden-go [ス ウェーデン語].

sweep (vt.) 1)...o haku […を掃く]; ...o sôji-suru […を掃除する]. 2)... o oshi-nagasu […を押し流す]; ...o issô-suru […を一掃する]. 3)...o sekken-suru […を席けんする].

(1) The children **were sweeping** the floor.
  Kodomo-tachi wa yuka-o haiteita.

(2) Many houses **were swept** away. Ooku-no ie ga nagasareta.

(vi.) 1)sôji-suru [掃除する]. 2)osou [襲う]. 3)sassô-to-aruku [さっそうと歩く]. 4)satto-sugiru [さっと過ぎる].

sweet (a.) 1)amai [甘い]; umai [うまい]. 2)kaori-no-yoi [香りのよい]. 3)koe-no-yoi [声のよい]; oto-no-yoi [音のよい]. 4)(colloq.) airashii [愛らしい]; kawairashii [かわいらしい]. 5)yukai-na [愉快な]; tanoshii [楽しい]. 6)shinsen-na [新鮮な].

(1) The fruit tastes **sweet**. Sono kudamono wa umai.

(2) **Sweet** violet smiles among the grass.
  Kaori-no-yoi sumire ga kusa-no-naka-de egao-o-shite-iru.

(3) She has a **sweet** voice. Kano-jo-wa koe-ga-yoi.

(4) She is a **sweet** girl. Kano-jo-wa kawairashii shôjo da.

(5) a **sweet** home　*tanoshii* katei

(6) **sweet** green vegetables　*shinsen-na* aomono-rui

　　(*ad.*) yasashiku [優しく]; amaku [甘く].

　　(*n.*) 1)amasa [甘さ]; (*pl.*) ((*US*)) kyandî [キャンディー]; amai-
kashi [甘い菓子]. 2)((*Eng.*)) ame [あめ]; kyandî [キャンディー];
amai-dezâto [甘いデザート].

sweeten (*vt. & vi.*) ...o amaku-suru (amaku-naru) […を甘くする(甘
くなる)]; (...no kaori)-o-yoku-suru ((kaori-ga)-yoku-naru) [(…の香
り)をよくする((香りが)よくなる)].

sweetly (*ad.*) 1)amaku [甘く]. 2)yasashiku [優しく]. 3)airashiku
[愛らしく]. 4)chôshi-yoku [調子よく].

sweet potato (*bot.*) satsuma-imo [サツマイモ].

swell (*vi.*) 1)fukureru [ふくれる]; fukuramu [ふくらむ]. 2)zôdai-
suru [増大する]. 3)zôsui-suru [増水する]. 4)mune-ga-ippai-ni-naru
[胸がいっぱいになる].

(1) Her injured ankle **swelled**.

　　Kano-jo-no kega-o-shita ashi-kubi ga *hareta*.

(2) Soon the sea began to **swell** into waves.

　　Ma-mo-naku umi wa nami-ga-tatte *uneri*-hajimeta.

(3) The river **has swelled** with the rain.

　　Kawa wa ame-de *zôsui-shita*.

(4) Her heart **swelled** with happiness.

　　Shiawase-de kano-jo-no mune wa *ippai-ni-natta*.

　　(*vt.*) ...o fukuramaseru […をふくらませる]; ...o zôdai-saseru […
を増大させる].

　　(*n.*) 1)fukurami [ふくらみ]. 2)zôdai [増大]. 3)uneri [うねり].

　　(*a.*) (*US colloq.*) suteki-na [す敵な]; subarashii [すばらしい].

swelter (*vi.*) atsusa-de-kurushimu [暑さで苦しむ]; ase-daku-ni-naru
[汗だくになる].

　　(*n.*) atsu-kurushi-sa [暑苦しさ].

swift (*a.*) 1)hayai [速い]. 2)sokuza-no [即座の]. 3)subayaku...
(suru) [すばやく…(する)].

swim (*vi.*) 1)oyogu [泳ぐ]. 2)me-mai-ga-suru [めまいがする]. 3)
hitaru [ひたる]; afureru [あふれる].

(1) He can **swim** very fast.

　　Kare-wa totemo hayaku *oyogu*-koto-ga-dekiru.

(2) My head **swam**.　Watashi-wa *memai-ga-shita*.

(3) eyes **swimming** with happy tears

　　　　ureshi-namida-de-*afureta* me

　　　(*n.*) oyogi [泳ぎ]; hito-oyogi [一泳ぎ].

swimmer (*n.*) oyogi-te [泳ぎ手].

swimming pool　pûru [プール].

swimsuit (*n.*) mizu-gi [水着].

swing (*vi.*) 1)yureru [揺れる]. 2)genki-yoku-susumu [元気よく進む].
　　3)buranko-ni-noru [ぶらんこに乗る]. 4)(*colloq.*) suingu-chô-de-aru
　　[スイング調である].

　　　(*vt.*) 1)...o furu […を振る]. 2)...o tsurusu […をつるす].

　　　(*n.*) 1)buranko [ぶらんこ]; 2)(yakyû no) suingu [(野球の)スイ
　　ング]. 3)ritsudô-teki-na-ugoki [律動的な動き]; suingu [スイング].

swirl (*vi. & vt.*) uzu-maku(...o uzu-ni-maite-hakobu) [渦巻く(…を渦
　　に巻いて運ぶ)].

　　　(*n.*) uzu-maki [渦巻き].

Swiss (*a.*) Suisu-no [スイスの]; Suisu-jin-no [スイス人の].

　　　(*n.*) Suisu-jin [スイス人].

switch (*n.*) 1)suitchi [スイッチ]. 2)((*US*)) (*R.R.*) tentetsu-ki [転てつ
　　機]. 3)(kyûgeki na) henkô [(急激な)変更]; tenkan [転換].

　　　(*vt.*) (suitchi)-o kiri-kaeru [(スイッチ)を切り換える]; ...o kaeru
　　[…を変える]; ...o tenjiru […を転じる]; ...o kôkan-suru […を交換す
　　る].

　　　(*vi.*) suitchi-o-kiri-kaeru [スイッチを切り換える]; henkô-suru
　　[変更する].

　　switch off　suitchi-o-kiru

　　switch on　suitchi-o-ireru

Switzerland (*n.*) Suisu [スイス].

swoon (*vi.*) 1)kizetsu-suru [気絶する]; sottô-suru [卒倒する]. 2)
　　muga-muchû-ni-naru [無我夢中になる].

　　　(*n.*) kizetsu [気絶]; sottô [卒倒]; kôkotsu [こうこつ].

swoop (*vi.*) (taka nado ga ue kara) tobi-kakaru [(たかなどが上から)
　　飛びかかる]; kyûshû-suru [急襲する].

　　　(*vt.*) ...o hittakuru […をひったくる].

　　　(*n.*) kyûshû [急襲].

sword (*n.*) 1)ken [剣]; katana [刀]. 2)(the -) buryoku [武力];
　　sensô [戦争].

syllable (*n.*) onsetsu [音節]; shiraburu [シラブル].

　　　(*vt.*) ...o onsetsu-goto-ni-hatsuon-suru […を音節ごとに発音す
　　る].

symbol (*n.*) 1)shôchô [象徴]; shimboru [シンボル]. 2)kigô [記号].
  (2) a chemical **symbol** kagaku-*kigô*
    a phonetic **symbol** hatsuon-*kigô*

symbolic (*a.*) 1)shôchô-teki-na [象徴的な]. 2)kigô-ni-yoru [記号による].

symbolize (*vt.*) 1)...o shôchô-suru [...を象徴する]. 2)...o kigô-de-arawasu [...を記号で表す].

symmetrical (*a.*) taishô-teki-na [対称的な]; kinsei-no-toreta [均整のとれた].

sympathetic (*a.*) dôjô-teki-na [同情的な]; omoi-yari-no-aru [思いやりのある]; kyôkan-suru [共感する].

sympathize (*vi.*) dôjô-suru [同情する]; kyômei-suru [共鳴する].

sympathy (*n.*) dôjô [同情]; kyômei [共鳴].

symphony (*n.*) kôkyô-kyoku [交響曲]; shinfonî [シンフォニー].

symptom (*n.*) chôkô [兆候]; (*med.*) shôjô [症状].

synonym (*n.*) dôi-go [同意語]; ruigi-go [類義語]; shinonimu [シノニム].

synthetic (*a.*) 1)(*chem.*) gôsei-no [合成の]. 2)sôgô-no [総合の].
    (*n.*) (*chem.*) gôsei-busshitsu [合成物質].

system (*n.*) 1)soshiki [組織]; seido [制度]. 2)keitô [系統]; taikei [体系]. 3)chitsujo-datta-yarikata [秩序立ったやり方].

systematic (*a.*) soshiki-teki-na [組織的な]; taikei-teki-na [体系的な]; chitsujo-datta [秩序立った].

T

table (*n.*) 1)têburu [テーブル]; shokutaku [食卓]. 2)dai [台]. 3)hyô [表].
　　(*1*) The vase is on the **table**. Kabin wa *têburu*-no-ue-ni aru.
　　(*2*) a billiard **table** tama-tsuki-*dai*
　　(*3*) a time**table** jikoku-*hyô*
　　at table shokuji-chû-de; shokutaku-ni-tsuite
　　wait at(on) table kyûji-suru
table d'hôte teishoku [定食].
table of contents mokuji [目次].
tablet (*n.*) 1)jôzai [錠剤]. 2)meiban [銘板].
tack (*n.*) 1)byô [びょう]. 2)kari-nui [仮縫い]; shitsuke [しつけ]. 3) shinro [針路].
　　(*vt.*) 1)...o byô-de-tomeru […をびょうで留める]. 2)...o tsuke-kuwaeru […を付け加える]. 3)(*marine*) ...no shinro-o-kaeru […の針路を変える].
　　(*vi.*) hôshin-o-kaeru [方針を変える].
tackle (*n.*) (*rugger*) takkuru [タックル].
　　(*vt.*) (*slang*) ...ni kumi-tsuku […に組み付く]. ...ni takkuru-suru […にタックルする].
　　(*vi.*) takkuru-suru [タックルする].
tact (*n.*) kiten [気転]; kotsu [こつ].

tactics (*n.*) 1)senjutsu [戦術]; heihô [兵法]. 2)kake-hiki [駆け引き].

tactile (*a.*) shokkaku-no [触覚の]; shokuchi-dekiru [触知できる].

tadpole (*n.*) (*zool.*) otama-jakushi [オタマジャクシ].

tag (*n.*) 1)(himo-no-saki no)kanagu [(ひもの先の)金具]. 2)ni-fuda [荷札]; sage-fuda [下げ札]; tagu [タグ].

  (*1*) Pull the **tag**, and the fastener will be closed.

     Kanagu o-hike-ba, fasunâ wa shimari-masu.

  (*2*) a name **tag** na-*fuda*

    (*vt.*) 1)...ni kanagu-o-tsukeru [...に金具を付ける]. 2)...ni ni-fuda-o-tsukeru [...に荷札を付ける]. 3)...o(...to) na-zukeru [...を(...と)名付ける]. 4)...ni kôtsû-ihan-kâdo-o-watasu [...に交通違反カードを渡す].

tag (*n.*) oni-gokko [鬼ごっこ].

    (*vt.*) ...o tsukamaeru [...をつかまえる].

tail (*n.*) shippo [しっぽ].

tailor (*n.*) shitateya [仕立て屋]; yôfukuya [洋服屋].

    (*vt.*) ...o shitateru [...を仕立てる]; ...o awaseru [...を合わせる].

    (*vi.*) fuku-o-shitateru [服を仕立てる]; yôfukuya-o-suru [洋服屋をする].

take (*vt.*) 1)...o toru [...を取る]. 2)(shashin)-o toru [(写真)をとる]; (sumpô)-o hakaru [(寸法)を測る]. 3)(byôki)-ni kakaru [(病気)にかかる]. 4)...o ukeru [...を受ける]. 5)...o kariru [...を借りる]. 6)...o kau [...を買う]. 7)...o tsurete-iku [...を連れて行く]. 8)...o taberu [...を食べる]; ...o nomu [...を飲む]. 9)(nori-mono)-ni noru [(乗り物)に乗る]. 10)(jijitsu)-ga kakaru [(時日)がかかる]. 11)...o suru [...をする]. 12)...o rikai-suru [...を理解する].

  (*1*) I **took** a book in my right hand.

     Watashi-wa migi-te-ni hon-*o totta*.

  (*2*) I **took** a nice photo there.

     Watashi-wa soko-de ii shashin-*o totta*.

    Please **take** my measurements.   Sumpô-*o hakatte*-kudasai.

  (*3*) John **has taken** cold.   Jon wa kaze-*o hiiteiru*.

  (*4*) When will you **take** an examination?

     Itsu shiken-*o uke-rare-masu*-ka?

    You had better **take** her advice.

     Kimi-wa kano-jo-no chûkoku-*ni shitagau*-hô-ga-ii.

  (*5*) I **took** the house for the summer.

     Watashi-wa hito-natsu sono ie-*o karita*.

  (*6*) All right, I'll **take** this hat.

Kekkô-desu, kono bôshi-o *moraimasu*.

(7) I'll **take** you to the movie this evening.

Komban eiga-ni *tsurete-itte*-agemasu.

(8) What time did you **take** your breakfast?

Chôshoku wa nan-ji-ni *tabe-mashita*-ka?

Take this medicine every morning.

Mai-asa kono kusuri-o *nomi-nasai*.

(9) Let's **take** a bus. Basu-*ni nori*-mashô.

(10) It **took** me three hours to copy it.

Watashi-wa sore-o utsusu-no-ni san-jikan *kakatta*.

(11) Let's **take** a rest. Hito-yasumi-*shi*-yô.

(12) Do you **take** me? Watashi-no-iu-koto-*ga wakari-masu*-ka?

take after 1)...ni niru. 2)...o tehon-ni-suru

take away ...o mochi-saru; ...o hakobi-saru

take...for ...o...to machigaeru

I took her for her younger sister.

Watashi-wa kano-jo-o kano-jo-no imôto-to machigaeta.

take off 1)...o nugu. 2)...o hanasu. 3)...o kyûka-to-shite-toru.

4)ririku-suru

1) Take your hat off in the room.

Shitsunai-de-wa bôshi-o tori-nasai.

2) Take your hand off the knob.

Doa-no-totte-kara te-o hanashi-nasai.

3) I took one week off in July.

Watashi-wa Shichigatsu-ni isshû-kan kyûka-o-totta.

4) The plane took off at 3:30p.m.

Hikô-ki wa gogo-san-ji-san-juppun-ni ririku-shita.

take on 1)...o hiki-ukeru. 2)...o yatoi-ireru

1) We took on the project.

Ware-ware-wa sono-keikaku-o hiki-uketa.

2) I took on him on a part-time basis.

Watashi-wa kare-o jikan-kyû-de yatoi-ireta.

take over ...o hiki-tsugu

I took over my father's business.

Watashi-wa chichi-no-shigoto-o hiki-tsuida.

take to 1)...ga suki-ni-naru. 2)...ni bottô-suru. 3)...ni uttaeru

1) I took to the poetry soon.

Watashi-wa ma-mo-naku sono-shi-ga suki-ni-natta.

2) He has since taken to drinking.
　　Sore-irai kare-wa inshu-ni fuketteiru.
3) They took to arms.　Kare-ra-wa buki-ni uttaeta.
take up 1)...o tori-ageru. 2)...o shimeru; ...o toru
1) I took up the telephone receiver.
　　Watashi-wa denwa-no-juwa-ki-o tori-ageta.
2) It took up too much space.　Sore-wa basho-o tori-sugita.
　　(*vi.*) 1)ne-zuku [根づく]. 2)ukeru [受ける].
(*1*) The inoculation did not **take**.
　　Sono yobô-sesshu wa *tsuka*-nakatta.
(*2*) The novel **took** well.　Sono shôsetsu wa *hyôban-ga-yokatta*.
takeoff (*n.*) 1)ririku [離陸]. 2)(chôyaku nado no) fumikiri [(跳躍などの)踏切].
tale (*n.*) 1)hanashi [話]; monogatari [物語]. 2)uwasa [うわさ]; (*pl.*) warukuchi [悪口].
talent (*n.*) 1)sainô [才能]. 2)sainô-no-aru-hito-tachi [才能のある人たち]; tarento [タレント].
talk (*vi.*) hanasu [話す]; o-shaberi-o-suru [おしゃべりをする].
　　(*vt.*) ...ni-tsuite hanasu […について話す]; ...o hanasu […を話す].
　talk about ...ni-tsuite hanasu
　talk big hora-o-fuku
　　(*n.*) 1)hanashi [話]; kaiwa [会話]. 2)kôen [講演]. 3)uwasa-no-tane [うわさの種].
talkative (*a.*) hanashi-zuki-no [話し好きの]; o-shaberi-na [おしゃべりな].
talking-to (*n.*) (*colloq.*) kogoto [小言].
tall (*a.*) 1)se-no-takai [背の高い]. 2)se-no-takasa-ga...no [背の高さが…の].
tame (*a.*) 1)nareta [慣れた]. 2)jûjun-na [従順な]. 3)(*colloq.*) tanchô-na [単調な].
　　(*vt.*) 1)...o kai-narasu […を飼いならす]; ...o jûjun-ni-suru […を従順にする]. 2)...o kanri-shite-riyô-suru […を管理して利用する].
　　(*vi.*) nareru [慣れる].
tan (*vt.*) 1)(kawa)-o namesu [(皮)をなめす]. 2)...o hi-yake-saseru […を日焼けさせる].
　　(*vi.*) hi-ni-yakeru [日に焼ける].
　　(*n.*) 1)ko-mugi-iro [小麦色]. 2)tannin [タンニン].
tangle (*vt. & vi.*) ...o motsuresaseru (motsureru) […をもつれさせる

（もつれる）.

　　　(n.) motsure [もつれ]; funkyû [紛糾].

tank (n.) 1)suisô [水槽]; tanku [タンク]. 2)(mil.) sensha [戦車];
tanku [タンク].

tanker (n.) 1)yusô-sen [油そう船]; tankâ [タンカー]. 2)tankurôrî [タンクローリー].

tap (vi. & vt.) (...o) karuku-tataku [(…を)軽くたたく].
　　　(n.) kotsu-kotsu-tataku-oto [こつこつたたく音].

tap (n.) 1)((Eng.)) jaguchi [蛇口]; sen [栓]. 2)tôchô-sôchi [盗聴装置].
　　　(vt.) 1)sen-o-nuite...o dasu [栓を抜いて…を出す]. 2)...o kaihatsu-
suru […を開発する]. 3)...o tôchô-suru […を盗聴する].

tape (n.) 1)têpu [テープ]; maki-jaku [巻き尺] = tapeline. 2)rokuon-
têpu [録音テープ].

　　　breast the **tape** têpu-o kiru

　　　(vt.) 1)...o têpu-de-tsukeru […をテープでつける]; ...o têpu-de-
musubu […をテープで結ぶ]. 2)...o(-têpu-ni) rokuon-suru […を(テープに)録音する].

　　　(vi.) têpu-de-rokuon-suru [テープで録音する].

taper (vi. & vt.) shidai-ni-hosoku-naru(...o shidai-ni-hosoku-suru)
[次第に細くなる(…を次第に細くする)].

tardy (a.) osoi [遅い]; noroi [のろい].

target (n.) mato [的]; mokuhyô [目標].

tariff (n.) 1)kanzei[-hyô] [関税(表)]. 2)(ryokan ya tetsudô no)
ryôkin-hyô [(旅館や鉄道の)料金表].

tart (a.) 1)suppai [酸っぱい]. 2)shinratsu-na [辛らつな].

tart (n.) taruto [タルト].

task (n.) (kaserareta) shigoto [(課せられた)仕事]; kagyô [課業].
　　　(vt.) ...o kokushi-suru […を酷使する]; ...ni omoi-futan-o-kakeru
[…に重い負担を掛ける].

tassel (n.) [kazari-]fusa [(飾り)房].

taste (n.) 1)aji [味]; mikaku [味覚]. 2)shumi [趣味]; konomi [好み].
3)shimbi-gan [審美眼]; sensu [センス].
　　　(vt.) ...o ajiwau […を味わう].
　　　(vi.) (...no)-aji-ga-suru [(…の)味がする].

tasteful (a.) shumi-no-yoi [趣味のよい]; jôhin-na [上品な].

tasteless (a.) 1)aji-no-nai [味のない]. 2)shumi-no-warui [趣味の悪い].

tasty (a.) 1)aji-no-yoi [味のよい]. 2)(colloq.) omoshiroi [面白い].

tattoo (n.) (mil.) kiei-rappa [帰営ラッパ].

　　　　(*vi. & vt.*) (...o) kotsu-kotsu-tataku [(…を)こつこつたたく].

tattoo (*n.*) irezumi [入れ墨].

　　　　(*vt.*) ...ni irezumi-o-suru […に入れ墨をする].

tavern (*n.*) ((*US*)) saka-ba [酒場]; bâ [バー].

tax (*n.*) zei[-kin] [税(金)].

　　　　(*vt.*) 1)...ni kazei-suru […に課税する]; ...ni omoi-futan-o-kakeru […に重い負担を掛ける]. 2)...o satei-suru […を査定する].

taxi (*n. & vi.*) takushî(-de-iku) [タクシー(で行く)].

　　　　(*vt.*) ...o takushî-ni-noseru […をタクシーに乗せる].

tea (*n.*) 1)cha [茶]. 2)((*Eng.*)) gogo-no-o-cha [午後のお茶].

teach (*vt. & vi.*) (...o) oshieru [(…を)教える].

teacher (*n.*) kyôshi [教師]; sensei [先生].

team (*n.*) (*sports*) chîmu [チーム]; kumi [組].

　　　　(*vt.*) ...o chîmu-ni-matomeru […をチームにまとめる].

　　　　(*vi.*) kyôryoku-suru [協力する]; chôwa-suru [調和する].

teamwork (*n.*) kyôdô-sagyô [協同作業]; chîmuwâku [チームワーク].

teapot (*n.*) kyûsu [きゅうす].

tear (*n.*) namida [涙].

　　　　(*vi.*) namida-de-afureru [涙であふれる].

tear (*vt.*) 1)...o hiki-saku […を引き裂く]; ...o yaburu […を破る]. 2) ...o bunretsu-saseru […を分裂させる].

　　　　(*vi.*) sakeru [裂ける]; yabureru [破れる].

　　　　(*n.*) 1)sake-me [裂け目]; hokorobi [ほころび]. 2)tosshin [突進].

tearful (*a.*) namida-gunda [涙ぐんだ]; kanashii [悲しい].

tearoom (*n.*) kissa-ten [喫茶店].

tease (*vt. & vi.*) 1)(...o) ijimeru [(…を)いじめる]; (...o) karakau [(…を)からかう]. 2)(...o) nedaru [(…を)ねだる].

teaspoon (*n.*) cha-saji [茶さじ]; tîsupûn [ティースプーン].

teaspoonful (*n.*) cha-saji-ippai(-bun) [茶さじ一杯(分)].

technical (*a.*) 1)semmon-no [専門の]; gijutsu-teki-na [技術的な]. 2) kôgyô-no [工業の].

technique (*n.*) gijutsu [技術]; gikô [技巧]; tekunikku [テクニック]; kotsu [こつ].

technology (*n.*) kagaku-gijutsu [科学技術]; tekunorojî [テクノロジー].

tedious (*a.*) taikutsu-na [退屈な]; aki-aki-suru [あきあきする].

teenager (*n.*) jû-dai-no-shônen-shôjo [十代の少年少女].

teens (*n.*) jû-dai [十代].

telegram (*n.*) dempô [電報].

telegraph (*n.*) denshin [電信]; dempô [電報].
　　　　(*vt. & vi.*) (...ni) daden-suru [(…に)打電する].
telephone (*n.*) denwa[-ki] [電話(機)].
　　　　(*vt. & vi.*) (...ni) denwa-o-kakeru [(…に)電話をかける].
telephone booth(box) kôshû-denwa-bokkusu [公衆電話ボックス].
telephoto (*a.*) bôen[-renzu]-no [望遠(レンズ)の].
telephoto lens bôen-renzu [望遠レンズ].
telescope (*n.*) bôen-kyô [望遠鏡].
　　　　(*vt.*) ...o ireko-shiki-ni-suru […を入れ子式にする].
　　　　(*vi.*) hamari-komu [はまり込む]; jabara-shiki-ni-shinshuku-suru [蛇腹式に伸縮する].
telescopic (*a.*) bôen-kyô-no [望遠鏡の]; tooku-ga-mieru [遠くが見える]; ireko-shiki-no [入れ子式の].
teletype (*n. & vi.*) Teretaipu(-de-sôshin-suru) [テレタイプ(で送信する)].
televise (*vt.*) ...o terebi-de-hôsô-suru […をテレビで放送する].
television (*n.*) terebi[-hôsô] [テレビ(放送)].
tell (*vt.*) 1)...o hanasu […を話す]; ...o oshieru […を教える]; ...o tsugeru […を告げる]. 2)...to meijiru […と命じる]; ...ni...(shi)nasai-to iu […に…(し)なさいと言う]. 3)...o mi-wakeru […を見分ける].
　(*1*) I'll **tell** you a story.　Hitotsu *o-hanashi* *shima-shô*.
　　　Can you **tell** me the way to the station?
　　　Eki-e-iku-michi-*o oshiete*-kudasai-masen-ka?
　　　I **told** him my name.
　　　Watashi-wa kare-ni watashi-no namae-*o tsugeta*.
　(*2*) I **told** her not to go.　Watashi-wa kano-jo-ni iku-na-*to itta*.
　(*3*) Can you **tell** a goat from a sheep?
　　　Kimi-wa yagi-to-hitsuji-*o mi-wakeru*-koto-ga-dekiru-ka?
　(*vi.*) 1)hanasu [話す]. 2)(karada ni) kotaeru [(からだに)こたえる]; kiki-me-ga-aru [効き目がある]. 3)(*colloq.*) tsuge-guchi-o-suru [告げ口をする]. 4)mi-wakeru [見分ける]; wakaru [わかる].
　(*1*) **tell** of one's experiences　keiken-dan-o *suru*
　(*2*) The strain is beginning to **tell** on him.
　　　Muri ga kare-no-*karada-ni kotae*-hajimeta.
　(*3*) Can you promise not to **tell**?
　　　Tsuge-guchi-o-shi-nai-to yakusoku-shite-kuremasu-ka?
　(*4*) Who can **tell**?　Dare-ni-mo *wakara*-nai.
all told zembu-de
I can tell you. Tashika-ni...desu-yo.

temper (*n.*) 1) kibun [気分]; kigen [機嫌]. 2) ochitsuki [落着き]; heisei [平静]. 3) kishô [気性]; kishitsu [気質]. 4) kanshaku [かんしゃく].

(*1*) He is in a good **temper**. Kare-wa *kigen*-ga-ii.

(*2*) He lost his **temper** at the news.
　　　Kare-wa sono-shirase-o-kiite *heisei-sa*-o ushinatta.

(*3*) She has a sweet **temper**. Kano-jo-wa *kishitsu*-ga-yasashii.

(*4*) She is always in a **temper**.
　　　Kano-jo-wa itsu-mo *kanshaku*-o-okoshite-iru.

　in a bad temper fu-kigen-de

　keep one's temper gaman-suru

　　　(*vt.*) …o chôsetsu-suru […を調節する]; …o tekido-ni-osaeru […を適度に抑える].

　　　(*vi.*) 1) yawaragu [和らぐ]; tekido-ni-naru [適度になる]. 2) kitaerareru [鍛えられる].

temperament (*n.*) kishô [気性]; kishitsu [気質].

temperance (*n.*) sessei [節制]; kinshu [禁酒].

temperate (*a.*) 1) ondan-na [温暖な]. 2) odayaka-na [穏やかな]; setsudo-no-aru [節度のある].

temperature (*n.*) 1) ondo [温度]; taion [体温]. 2) (*colloq.*) kônetsu [高熱].

tempest (*n.*) bôfû-u [暴風雨]; oo-arashi [大あらし].

temple (*n.*) jiin [寺院]; seidô [聖堂].

temple (*n.*) komekami [こめかみ].

temporal (*a.*) 1) toki-no [時の]; gense-no [現世の]; sezoku-no [世俗の]. 2) tsuka-no-ma-no [つかの間の].

temporarily (*ad.*) ichiji-teki-ni [一時的に]; kari-ni [仮に].

temporary (*a.*) ichiji-no [一時の]; kari-no [仮の].

　　　(*n.*) rinji-yatoi-no-hito [臨時雇いの人].

tempt (*vt.*) …o yûwaku-suru […を誘惑する]; …o sosonokashite…(sa-)seru […をそそのかして…(さ)せる]; (…no kanshin)-o-hiku [(…の関心)を惹く].

temptation (*n.*) yûwaku[-butsu] [誘惑(物)].

ten (*n. & a.*) jû(-no) [十(の)].

tenant (*n.*) shakuchi-nin [借地人]; shakuya-nin [借家人]; genjû-sha [現住者].

　　　(*vt.*) …o kariru […を借りる]; …o chinshaku-suru […を賃借する].

tend (*vi.*) 1)...no keikô-ga-aru […の傾向がある]; ...(shi-)gachi-de-aru […(し)がちである]. 2)(...e-)mukau […(…へ)向かう].

tend (*vt.*) ...o sewa-o-suru […を世話をする]; ...no ban-o-suru […の番をする].

　　　(*vi.*) (*US colloq.*) chûi-suru [注意する].

tendency (*n.*) 1)keikô [傾向]; seikô [性向]. 2)tembun [天分].

tender (*a.*) 1)yawarakai [柔らかい]; kizu-tsuki-yasui [傷つきやすい]; yowai [弱い]. 2)yasashii [優しい].

tender (*vt.*) ...o teishutsu-suru […を提出する].

　　　(*vi.*) nyûsatsu-o-suru [入札をする].

　　　(*n.*) teishutsu [提出]; teikyô[-butsu] [提供(物)]; nyûsatsu [入札].

tender (*n.*) sewa-o-suru-hito [世話をする人]; kango-nin [看護人].

tenderly (*ad.*) yasashiku [優しく]; yawarakaku [柔らかく]; sotto [そっと].

tendon (*n.*) (*anat.*) ken [けん].

tendril (*n.*) (*bot.*) tsuru [つる].

tennis (*n.*) tenisu [テニス]; teikyû [庭球].

tenor (*n.*) tenâ[-kashu] [テナー(歌手)].

tense (*a.*) pin-to-hatta [ぴんと張った]; hari-tsumeta [張りつめた].

　　　(*vt. & vi.*) ...o kinchô-saseru (kinchô-suru) […を緊張させる(緊張する)].

tension (*n.*) kinchô [緊張]; shinchô [伸張].

tentative (*a.*) kari-no [仮の]; shiken-teki-na [試験的な].

　　　(*n.*) kokoromi [試み]; shian [試案].

tenth (*n. & a.*) dai-jû(-no) [第十(の)].

term (*n.*) 1)kikan [期間]; gakki [学期]. 2)semmon-yôgo [専門用語]. 3)(*pl.*)(keiyaku ya baibai no) jôken [(契約や売買の)条件]. 4)(*pl.*) aidagara [間柄].

(1) The third **term** has come. San-*gakki* ga hajimatta.

(2) technical **terms** semmon-*yôgo*

(3) I cannot cooperate with you on such **terms**.

　　　Sonna-*jôken*-de-wa kimi-ni kyôryoku-deki-nai.

(4) They are on friendly **terms**.

　　　Kare-ra-wa naka-no-yoi-*aidagara*-da.

　　　Kare-ra-wa naka-yoku-shite-iru.

　　　(*vt.*) ...o...to yobu […を…と呼ぶ]; ...o...to shôsuru […を…と称する].

terminal (*n.*) shûten [終点]; tâminaru [ターミナル].

　　(*a.*) 1)shûten-no [終点の]. 2)saigo-no [最後の]. 3)kimatsu-no [期末の]. 4)(*med.*) makki-no [末期の].

terminate (*vt.*) 1)...o owaraseru [...を終わらせる]. 2)...o kagiru [...を限る].

　　(*vi.*) owaru [終わる].

terrace (*n.*) daichi [台地]; terasu [テラス].

terrible (*a.*) 1)osoroshii [恐ろしい]. 2)(*colloq.*) hidoi [ひどい].

terribly (*ad.*) 1)(*colloq.*) totemo [とても]; hidoku [ひどく]; hijô-ni [非常に]. 2)osoroshiku [恐ろしく].

terrific (*a.*) (*colloq.*) 1)mono-sugoi [ものすごい]. 2)sugoi [すごい]; subarashii [すばらしい].

terrify (*vt.*) ...o kowagaraseru [...を怖がらせる].

territory (*n.*) 1)ryôdo [領土]. 2)(kôdai na) chiiki [(広大な)地域].

terror (*n.*) kyôfu [恐怖]; osoroshii-hito [恐ろしい人]; osoroshii-mono [恐ろしいもの].

test (*n.*) shiken [試験]; kensa [検査]; tesuto [テスト].

　　(*vt.*) ...o shiken-suru [...を試験する]; ...o shiraberu [...を調べる].

testament (*n.*) 1)yuigon [遺言]. 2)(the T-) seisho [聖書].

　　New Testament, the Shin'yaku-seisho

　　Old Testament, the Kyûyaku-seisho

testify (*vi. & vt.*) (...o) shômei-suru [(...を)証明する]; (...o) shôgen-suru [(...を)証言する].

testimony (*n.*) shômei [証明]; shôgen [証言]; shôko [証拠].

text (*n.*) 1)hombun [本文]; gembun [原文]. 2)((*US*)) tekisuto [テキスト].

textbook (*n.*) kyôka-sho [教科書].

textile (*n. & a.*) orimono(-no) [織物(の)].

texture (*n.*) 1)(orimono no) ori-kata [(織物の)織り方]; ki-ji [生地]. 2)soshiki [組織].

than (*conj.*) ...yori-mo [...よりも]; ...yori-hoka-no[-ni] [...よりほかの(に)].

　　(*prep.*) ...yori-mo [...よりも].

thank (*vt.*) ...ni kansha-suru [...に感謝する]; ...ni rei-o-iu [...に礼を言う].

　　Thank God (or Heaven)! *Arigatai.*

　　Thank you. *Arigatô.*

　　No, thank you. Iie, kekkô-desu.

    (*n.*) (*pl.*) kansha [感謝]; shai [謝意].

A thousand(Many) thanks. Makoto-ni arigatô.

 give(return) thanks to ...ni rei-o-noberu

 No, thanks! Arigata-meiwaku-da.

 thanks to ...no-okage-de

thankful (*a.*) kansha-shite-iru [感謝している].

thanksgiving (*n.*) (kami e no) kansha [(神への)感謝].

Thanksgiving Day ((*US*)) Kansha-sai [感謝祭].

that (*a.*) sono [その]; ano [あの].

    (*pron.*) sore [それ]; are [あれ].

   That will do. *Sore* de yoroshii.

That's it. Soko-da.; Sore-da.

That's right! Yoroshii; (*colloq.*) Sansei.

    (*ad.*) sore-hodo [それほど]; sonna-ni [そんなに].

   I can't walk **that** far.

     Watashi-wa *sonna-ni* tooku-wa aruke-nai.

    (*relative pron.*) (...suru)-tokoro-no(-hito) [(…する)ところの(人)];
(...suru)-tokoro-no(-mono) [(…する)ところの(もの)].

   the man **that** lives next door to us

     ware-ware-no-tonari-ni sunde-iru(-*tokoro-no*)-hito

   It is the only dictionary **that** I have.

     Sore-ga watashi no motte-iru(-*tokoro-no*)-yuiitsu-no jisho
desu.

   The day (**that**) he was born was rainy.

     Kare-ga umareta-hi wa ame-datta.

    (*conj.*) 1)...to-iu-koto […ということ]. 2)...(suru-)tame-ni […(する)ために]. 3)hijô-ni...node [非常に…ので]. 4)...no-wa...da […のは…だ].

 (*1*) I know **that** he is honest.

    Watashi-wa kare-ga shôjiki-da-*to-iu-koto*-o shitte-iru.

 (*2*) We eat **that** we may live.

    Ware-ware-wa ikite-iku-*tame-ni* taberu.

 (*3*) I am so tired **that** I cannot go on.

    Watashi-wa *totemo* tsukareta-*node* susumu-koto-ga-deki-
nai.

   He is such a good boy **that** they are proud of him.

    Kare-wa *hijô-ni* ii-ko-na-*node* kare-ra-wa kare-o hokori-ni-
omotte-iru.

(4) It was yesterday **that** she came.

　　Kano-jo-ga kita-*no-wa* kinô *da*tta.

thatch (*n.*) kusa-buki[-no-yane] [草ぶき(の屋根)].

　　(*vt.*) (yane)-o wara-de-fuku [[屋根]をわらでふく].

thaw (*vi.*) 1)tokeru [解ける]. 2)yawaragu [和らぐ]; uchi-tokeru [打ち解ける].

　　(*vt.*) ...o tokasu [...を解かす].

　　(*n.*) yuki-doke [雪解け]; kanwa [緩和].

the (*def. art.*) ano [あの]; sono [その]; kono [この]; rei-no [例の].

(1) Father has bought a watch and a fountain pen. **The** watch is for me and **the** fountain pen is for my sister.

　　Chichi wa tokei to mannen-hitsu-o katta. *Sono* tokei wa watashi-no-de, *sono* mannen-hitsu wa imôto-no-desu.

(2) **the** sun, **the** earth, and **the** moon　taiyô to chikyû to tsuki

(3) **the** Sumida, **the** Japan Sea, **the** Nihon Maru, **the** Japan Alps, **the** Imperial Hotel

　　Sumida-*gawa*, Nihon-kai, Nihon-maru, Nihon-Arupusu, Teikoku-hoteru

(4) **the** Asahi, **the** Sekai　Asahi-*shimbun*, Sekai-*shi*

(5) They are **the** students of our school.

　　Kare-ra-wa honkô no seito-tachi[-no-*zembu*] desu.

(6) **The** horse is a useful animal.

　　Uma wa yaku-ni-tatsu dôbutsu da.

(7) **the** rich and **the** poor　kane-mochi to mazushii *hito-bito*

　　the wounded and **the** missing

　　fushô-*sha* to yukue-fumei-no-*hito-bito*

(8) **the** true, **the** good, and **the** beautiful　shin, zen, bi.

(9) I hired the car by **the** hour.

　　Watashi-wa ichi-jikan-*ikura-to-iu-koto*-de sono kuruma-o karita.

(10) in **the** morning, in **the** afternoon, in **the** evening

　　asa-ni, gogo-ni, yûgata-ni

　　(*ad.*) 1)...ba...hodo-masu-masu [...ば...ほどますます]. 2)sore-dake [それだけ].

(1) **The** more, **the** merrier.　Ninzû-ga-ooi-*hodo* tanoshii.

(2) I like Bill all **the** better for his faults.

　　Watashi-wa Biru-ni ketten-ga-aru-kara-*sore-dake*-issô kare-ga suki-da.

theater, -tre (*n.*) 1)gekijô [劇場]. 2)(the -) engeki [演劇]; gikyoku
theft (*n.*) nusumi [盗み].   ⌐[戯曲].

their (*pron.*) kare-ra-no [彼らの]; kano-jo-ra-no [彼女らの]; sore-ra-
no [それらの].

theirs (*pron.*) kare-ra-no-mono [彼らのもの]; kano-jo-ra-no-mono [彼
女らのもの]; sore-ra-no-mono [それらのもの].

them (*pron.*) kare-ra-o [彼らを]; kare-ra-ni [彼らに]; kano-jo-ra-o
[彼女らを]; kano-jo-ra-ni [彼女らに]; sore-ra-o [それらを]; sore-ra-
ni [それらに].

theme (*n.*) shudai [主題]; têma [テーマ]; dai [題]; wadai [話題].

theme song shudai-ka [主題歌]; têma-songu [テーマソング].

themselves (*pron.*) kare-ra-jishin(-o/-ni) [彼ら自身(を/に)]; kano-jo-ra-
jishin(-o/-ni) [彼女ら自身(を/に)]; sore-ra-jishin(-o/-ni) [それら自身(を/に)].

then (*ad.*) 1)sono-toki [その時]. 2)sore-kara [それから]. 3)sore-de-
wa [それでは].
  (*1*) I was a boy **then**. Watashi-wa *sono-toki* shônen datta.
  (*2*) I went to his house, and **then** to the theater.
      Watashi-wa kare-no-ie-e iki, *sore-kara* gekijô-e itta.
  (*3*) What is that, **then**? *Sore-de-wa* sore-wa nan-desu-ka?
  now and then   toki-doki
    (*n. & a.*) sono-toki(-no) [その時(の)].
  since then   sono-toki-irai

theology (*n.*) shingaku [神学].

theory (*n.*) gakusetsu [学説]; riron [理論]; rikutsu [理屈].

there (*ad.*) 1)soko-ni [そこに]; soko-de [そこで]; soko-e [そこへ]. 2)
...ga-aru [···がある]. 3)sono-ten-de [その点で]. 4)sore [それ].
  (*1*) They lived **there**. Kare-ra-wa *soko-ni* sunde-ita.
    What are you doing **there**?
      Kimi-wa *soko-de* nani-o-shiteiru-no-da?
    When shall you get **there**? Itsu *soko-e* tsuki-masu-ka?
  (*2*) **There** is a desk in the room. Heya-ni tsukue-ga hitotsu *aru*.
    There once lived a young man.
      Katsute seinen-ga hitori sunde-*ita*.
  (*3*) **There** it is, you see. Sâ *sono-ten*-da-yo, kimi.
  (*4*) **There**, it is on the table! *Sore* sono-têbutu-no-ue-ni-aru!
  Are you there? Moshi-moshi.
  There you are! 1)Sore-goran!; Sore-dô-da!. 2)Sore-soko-ni-aru-yo!
    (*n.*) soko [そこ].

therefore (*ad.*) dakara [だから]; shitagatte [従って].

thermometer (*n.*) ondo-kei [温度計]; kandan-kei [寒暖計].

thermostat (*n.*) jidô-ondo-chôsetsu-sôchi [自動温度調節装置]; sâmo-sutatto [サーモスタット].

these (*pron. & a.*) kore-ra(-no) [これら(の)].

thesis (*n.*) 1)shudai [主題]; rondai [論題]. 2)rombun [論文].

they (*pron.*) kare-ra-wa [彼らは]; kare-ra-ga [彼らが]; kano-jo-ra-wa [彼女らは]; kano-jo-ra-ga [彼女らが]; sore-ra-wa [それらは]; sore-ra-ga [それらが]; hito-bito-wa [人々は].

thick (*a.*) 1)atsui [厚い]. 2)shigetta [茂った]. 3)koi [濃い]. 4)futoi [太い]. 5)komi-atta [込み合った].
　(*ad.*) 1)atsuku [厚く]; koku [濃く]. 2)shikiri-ni [しきりに].
　(*n.*) 1)ichiban-atsui[-futoi]-bubun [一番厚い[太い]部分]. 2)(...no-)saichû [(…の)最中].

thicken (*vi. & vt.*) atsuku-naru(...o atsuku-suru) [厚くなる(…を厚くする)]; koku-naru(...o koku-suru) [濃くなる(…を濃くする)].

thicket (*n.*) shigemi [茂み]; yabu [やぶ].

thickly (*ad.*) atsuku [厚く]; futoku [太く]; koku [濃く]; shigette [茂って]; shikiri-ni [しきりに].

thief (*n.*) dorobô [泥棒]; koso-doro [こそ泥].

thieve (*vt. & vi.*) ...o nusumu(mono-o-nusumu) […を盗む(物を盗む)].

thigh (*n.*) 1)futo-momo [太もも]. 2)daitai-kotsu [大たい骨].

thimble (*n.*) yubi-nuki [指ぬき].

thin (*a.*) 1)usui [薄い]. 2)mabara-na [まばらな]. 3)awai [淡い]. 4)hosoi [細い].
　(*ad.*) usuku [薄く]; mabara-ni [まばらに].
　(*vt. & vi.*) ...o usuku-suru (usuku-naru) […を薄くする(薄くなる)]; ...o mabara-ni-suru (mabara-ni-naru) […をまばらにする(まばらになる)].

thing (*n.*) 1)mono [もの]; buttai [物体]. 2)koto [こと]; koto-gara [事柄]. 3)(*pl.*) mochi-mono [持ちもの]; mi-no-mawari-no-shina [身の回りの品]. 4)(*pl.*) jijô [事情]; jitai [事態]. 5)(*pl.*) fûbutsu [風物]. 6)hitsuyô-na-mono[-koto] [必要なもの[こと]]. uttetsuke-no-koto [うってつけのこと]. 7)(*colloq.*) yatsu [やつ].
　(*1*) I found a curious **thing** in the box.
　　　Watashi-wa hako-no-naka-ni mezurashii *mono*-o mitsuketa.
　(*2*) Say the right **thing**. Tadashii *koto*-o ii-nasai.
　(*3*) I have to pack my **things**.

Watashi-wa *mi-no-mawari-no-shina*-no ni-zukuri-o shi-nakereba-naranai.

(4) **Things** are getting better. *Jitai* wa kôten-shi-tsutsu-aru.

(5) **things** Japanese Nihon-no *fûbutsu*

(6) The **thing** is to get there in safety.

Kanjin-na-koto wa soko-e buji-ni tsuku-koto-da.

(7) Poor **thing**! Kawaisô-ni!

think (*vt.*) ...o kangaeru [...を考える]; ...to omou [...と思う]; ...ga wakaru [...がわかる].

    think of 1)...no-koto-o-omou. 2)...o-kangaeru. 3)...o-omoi-dasu. 4)...o-kangae-tsuku. 5)...o...to mi-nasu

    (*n.*) kangaeru-koto [考えること]; shikô [思考].

thinking (*a.*) kangaeru [考える]; fumbetsu-no-aru [分別のある].

    (*n.*) 1)kangaeru-koto [考えること]; shikô [思考]. 2)iken [意見].

thinly (*ad.*) = thin.

third (*a.*) dai-san-no [第三の]; sam-bun-no-ichi-no [三分の一の].

    (*n.*) dai-san-no-hito [第三の人]; sam-bun-no-ichi [三分の一].

    (*ad.*) dai-san-ni [第三に]; sam-ban-me-ni [三番目に].

third-class (*a.*) san-tô-no [三等の]; ((US)) dai-san-shu-no [第三種の].

    (*ad.*) san-tô-de [三等で].

thirdly (*ad.*) dai-san-ni [第三に].

thirst (*n. & vi.*) 1)nodo-no-kawaki (nodo-ga-kawaku) [のどの渇き (のどが渇く)]. 2)katsubô(-suru) [渇望(する)].

thirsty (*a.*) 1)nodo-no-kawaita [のどの渇いた]. 2)katsubô-suru [渇望する]. 3)kansô-shita [乾燥した].

thirteen (*n. & a.*) jû-san(-no) [十三(の)].

thirteenth (*n. & a.*) dai-jû-san(-no) [第十三(の)].

thirtieth (*n. & a.*) dai-san-jû(-no) [第三十(の)].

thirty (*n. & a.*) san-jû(-no) [三十(の)].

this (*a.*) kono [この]; kon... [今...].

    Is **this** book yours? *Kono* hon wa anata-no desu-ka?

    I met her **this** morning. Watashi-wa *kesa* kano-jo-ni atta.

    (*pron.*) kore [これ]; kono-koto [このこと]; kono-hito [この人].

    (*ad.*) (*colloq.*) konna-ni [こんなに]; kore-dake [これだけ]; kore-kurai [これくらい].

    The fish I caught was about **this** big.

    Watashi-ga totta-sakana wa *kore-kurai*-no-ookisa-datta.

thistle (*n.*) (*bot.*) azami [アザミ].

thorn (*n.*) toge [とげ]; ibara [いばら]; toge-no-aru-shokubutsu [とげのある植物].

    (*vt.*) ...o nayamasu […を悩ます].

thorny (*a.*) toge-no-ooi [とげの多い]; toge-no-yô-na [とげのような]; yakkai-na [厄介な].

thorough (*a.*) 1)kanzen-na [完全な]; tettei-teki-na [徹底的な]. 2)kichô-men-na [き帳面な].

thoroughbred (*a.*) 1)junketsu-shu-no [純血種の]. 2)yûshû-na [優秀な].
    (*n.*) 1)junketsu-shu-no-uma [純血種の馬]; sarabureddo [サラブレッド]. 2)sodachi-no-yoi-hito [育ちのよい人]; kyôyô-no-aru-hito [教養のある人].

thoroughfare (*n.*) 1)dôro [道路]; kôdô [公道]. 2)tsûkô [通行].
    No thoroughfare. Tsûkô-dome; Tsûkô-kinshi.

thoroughly (*ad.*) kanzen-ni [完全に]; tettei-teki-ni [徹底的に].

those (*pron. & a.*) sore-ra(-no) [それら(の)].

though (*conj.*) ...nimo-kakawarazu […にもかかわらず]; tatoe...demo [たとえ…でも].
    (*ad.*) (*colloq.*) demo [でも]; yahari [やはり].

thought (*n.*) 1)kangae[-ru-koto] [考え(ること)]; shikô[-ryoku] [思考(力)]. 2)shisô [思想]. 3)(*pl.*) iken [意見]. 4)omoi-yari [思いやり].

thoughtful (*a.*) 1)shiryo-bukai [思慮深い]; chûi-bukai [注意深い]. 2)omoi-yari-no-aru [思いやりのある].

thoughtless (*a.*) shiryo-no-nai [思慮のない]; fu-chûi-na [不注意な]; omoi-yari-no-nai [思いやりのない].

thousand (*n. & a.*) 1)sen(-no) [千(の)]. 2)tasû(-no) [多数(の)]; musû(-no) [無数(の)].
    thousands of nanzen-to-iu

thousandth (*n. & a.*) sem-ban-me(-no) [千番目(の)]; sem-bun-no-ichi(-no) [千分の一(の)].

thrash (*vt.*) ...o(-muchi-de) tataku […を(むちで)たたく].
    (*vi.*) 1)renda-suru [連打する]. 2)mogaku [もがく]. 3)nami-o-kaki-wakete-susumu [波をかき分けて進む].
    (*n.*) 1)hageshiku-utsu-koto [激しく打つこと]. 2)(*swim.*) ashi-no-keri [足のけり]. 3)uchi-makasu-koto [打ち負かすこと].

thread (*n.*) 1)ito [糸]. 2)(hanashi nado no) suji [(話などの)筋].
    (*vt.*) 1)...ni ito-o-toosu […に糸を通す]. 2)...o nuu-yô-ni-toori-nukeru […を縫うように通り抜ける].

     (*vi.*) nuu-yô-ni-tooru [縫うように通る].

threat (*n.*) 1)odoshi [脅し]; kyôhaku [脅迫]. 2)kizashi [兆し].

threaten (*vt.*) 1)...o odosu [⋯を脅す]; ...o kyôhaku-suru [⋯を脅迫する]. 2)...no osore-ga-aru [⋯の恐れがある].

     (*vi.*) 1)kyôhaku-suru [脅迫する]. 2)sematte-iru [迫っている].

three (*n. & a.*) san(-no) [三(の)].

threshold (*n.*) 1)shikii [敷居]; iriguchi [入口]. 2)shuppatsu-ten [出発点].

thrift (*n.*) ken'yaku [倹約]; setsuyaku [節約]; shisso [質素].

thrifty (*a.*) 1)tsumashii [つましい]. 2)((*US*)) hanjô-suru [繁盛する].

thrill (*n.*) 1)zoku-zoku-suru-koto [ぞくぞくすること]; suriru [スリル]. 2)shindô [震動].

     (*vt. & vi.*) ...o zoku-zoku-saseru (zoku-zoku-suru) [⋯をぞくぞくさせる(ぞくぞくする)]; ...o furue-saseru (furueru) [⋯を震えさせる(震える)].

thrilling (*a.*) suriru-manten-no [スリル満点の]; furueru [震える].

thrive (*vi.*) 1)sakaeru [栄える]; hanjô-suru [繁盛する]. 2)oi-shigeru [生い茂る].

throat (*n.*) nodo [のど].

throb (*vi.*) 1)dôki-o-utsu [動きを打つ]. 2)zuki-zuki-itamu [ずきずき痛む]. 3)kôfun-suru [興奮する].

     (*n.*) dôki [動き]; shindô [振動]; zuki-zuki-itamu-koto [ずきずき痛むこと]; kôfun [興奮].

throne (*n.*) ôza [王座]; ôi [王位].

throng (*n.*) gunshû [群衆].

     (*vt. & vi.*) (...ni) muragaru [(⋯に)群がる].

through (*prep.*) 1)...o-tooshite [⋯を通して]. 2)...jû [⋯じゅう]; ...no-aida [⋯の間]. 3)...no-itaru-tokoro-o [⋯の至る所を]. 4)...made [⋯まで]. 5)...o-tsûjite [⋯を通じて]. 6)...no-tame-ni [⋯のために].

  (*1*) The train passed **through** the tunnel.
     Kisha wa tonneru-*o-tootte*-itta.

  (*2*) The rain lasted all **through** the day.
     Ame wa ichi-nichi-*jû* furi-tsuzuita.

  (*3*) He traveled **through** the world.
     Kare-wa sekai-*no-itaru-tokoro-o* ryokô-shita.
     Kare-wa sekai-*jû-o* ryokô-shita.

  (*4*) from Monday **through** Friday
     Getsuyô-bi-kara Kin'yô-bi-*made*

(5) I think I have grown **through** reading.

    Watashi-wa dokusho-o-*tsûjite* seichô-shita-to omou.

(6) I got lost **through** not knowing the way.

    Watashi-wa michi-o-shira-nakatta-*tame-ni* mayotta.

    (ad.) 1)toori-nukete [通り抜けて]. 2)sukkari [すっかり]; mattaku [全く]. 3)owatte [終わって].

(1) May I go **through**? *Toori-nuke-te-*mo yoroshii-ka?

(2) I read the book **through**.

    Watashi-wa sono hon-o *sukkari* yonda.

    Watashi-wa sono hon-o *tsûdoku-shita*.

(3) We are **through** our examination.

    Ware-ware-no shiken wa *owatta*.

be through (with) *(colloq.)* 1)...(o) oeru. 2)...(to) te-o-kiru

 1) Are you through with your home work?

    Anata-wa shukudai-o oemashita-ka?

 2) I'm through with him. Kare-to-wa te-o-kitta.

    I'm through with drinking.

    Watashi-wa o-sake-o yamemashita.

through and through mattaku; tettô-tetsubi

    (a.) tooshi-no [通しの]; chokutsû-no [直通の]; toori-nukerareru [通り抜けられる].

    through ticket *tôshi*-gippu

throughout *(prep.)* ...jû-o [...じゅうを]; ...no-sumi-kara-sumi-made [...のすみからすみまで].

    (ad.) kuma-naku [くまなく]; sukkari [すっかり].

throw *(vt.)* 1)...o nageru [...を投げる]. 2)...o nage-taosu [...を投げ倒す]. 3)...o kyû-ni-ugokasu [...を急に動かす]. 4)...o isoide-kiru [...を急いで着る]. 5)...o...ni otoshiireru [...を...に陥れる].

    (vi.) 1)nageru [投げる]. 2)hôru [ほうる].

    throw away ...o suteru

    throw open ...o patto-akeru; ...o kôkai-suru

    (n.) nageru-koto [投げること]; nagete-todoku-kyori [投げて届く距離].

thrush *(n.)* *(birds)* tsugumi [ツグミ].

thrust *(vt.)* 1)...o gui-to-osu [...をぐいと押す]. 2)...o tsuki-sasu [...を突き刺す]. 3)...o tsuki-dasu [...を突き出す]. 4)...o muri-ni-oshi-tsukeru [...を無理に押し付ける].

    (vi.) 1)gui-to-osu [ぐいと押す]. 2)tsuki-susumu [突き進む]. 3)

don-don-seichô-suru［どんどん生長する］.

   (n.) 1)gui-to-osu-koto［ぐいと押すこと］. 2)shûgeki［襲撃］. 3) suishin［推進］.

thumb (n.) oya-yubi［親指］.

   (vt.) 1)...o oya-yubi-de-mekutte-yogosu［…を親指でめくって汚す］. 2)...o bu-kiyô-ni-yaru［…を不器用にやる］.

   (vi.) (colloq.) hitchihaiku-suru［ヒッチハイクする］.

thump (vi.) 1)tsuyoku-naguru［強くなぐる］. 2)doshin-doshin-to-aruku［どしんどしんと歩く］; (shinzô ga) dokin-dokin-to-utsu［(心臓が)どきんどきんと打つ］.

   (vt.) ...o gotsun-to-tataku［…をごつんとたたく］.

   (n.) gotsun［ごつん］; doshin［どしん］.

thunder (n.) 1)kaminari［雷］; raimei［雷鳴］. 2)ikaku［威嚇］.

   (vi.) 1)kaminari-ga-naru［雷が鳴る］. 2)donaru［どなる］; ookina-oto-o-tateru［大きな音を立てる］.

   (vt.) ...o oo-goe-de-iu［…を大声で言う］; ...o don-don-tataku［…をどんどんたたく］.

thunderbolt (n.) 1)raiden［雷電］; rakurai［落雷］. 2)omoigakenai-koto［思いがけないこと］.

thundering (a.) raimei-no-suru［雷鳴のする］; kaminari-no-yô-ni-todoroku［雷のようにとどろく］; (colloq.) tohô-mo-nai［途方もない］.

thunderstorm (n.) hageshii-raiu［激しい雷雨］.

Thursday (n.) Mokuyô-bi［木曜日］.

thus (ad.) 1)kono-yô-ni［このように］. 2)kore-hodo［これほど］. 3) kô-shite［こうして］; shitagatte［従って］.

thwart (vt.) ...no jama-o-suru［…の邪魔をする］.

tick (n.) 1)chiku-taku［チクタク］; kachi-kachi［カチカチ］. 2)shôgô-no shirushi［照合の印］.

   (vi.) kachi-kachi-to-naru［カチカチとなる］; toki-o-kizamu［時を刻む］.

   (vt.) 1)(toki)-o kizamu［(時)を刻む］. 2)...ni shirushi-o-tsukeru［…にしるしをつける］; ...o shôgô-suru［…を照合する］.

ticker tape kabushiki-sôba-tsûshin-ki-yô-têpu［株式相場通信機用テープ］; (kangei-yô) kami-têpu［(歓迎用)紙テープ］; irogami-hen［色紙片］.

ticket (n.) 1)kippu［切符］; nyûjô-ken［入場券］. 2)kôtsû-ihan-kâdo［交通違反カード］. 3)shô-fuda［正札］.

   (vt.) ...ni shô-fuda-o-tsukeru［…に正札を付ける］; ...ni retteruo-haru [⋯にレッテルを貼る].

ticket office shussatsu-sho [出札所]; kippu-uri-ba [切符売場].

tickle (*vt.*) 1)...o kusuguru [⋯をくすぐる]. 2)...o yorokobaseru [⋯を喜ばせる].

　　　(*vi.*) kusuguttai [くすぐったい]; kosobayui [こそばゆい].

　　　(*n.*) kusuguttai-kanji [くすぐったい感じ]; muzu-gayu-sa [むずがゆさ].

ticktack (*n.*) 1)(tokei no) kachi-kachi [(時計の)かちかち]. 2)(shinzô no) doki-doki [(心臓の)どきどき].

　　　　(*vi.*) chiku-taku-to-oto-o-tateru [チクタクと音を立てる].

tide (*n.*) 1)shio[-no-kamman] [潮(の干満)]. 2)keisei [形勢]; shôchô [消長].

　　(*1*) the rising **tide** age-*shio*

　　(*2*) The **tide** turns. *Keisei* ga ippen-suru.

　　　(*vi.*) shio-no-mani-mani-tadayou [潮のまにまに漂う].

　　　(*vt.*) ...o shio-ni-nosete-hakobu [⋯を潮にのせて運ぶ].

tidily (*ad.*) kichin-to [きちんと]; ko-girei-ni [小ぎれいに].

tidings (*n.*) nyûsu [ニュース]; tayori [便り].

tidy (*a.*) kichin-to-shita [きちんとした]; ko-girei-na [小ぎれいな]; sappari-shita [さっぱりした].

　　　(*vt.*) ...o kichin-to-suru [⋯をきちんとする]; ...o kata-zukeru [⋯を片付ける].

　　　(*n.*) ko-mono-ire [小物入れ].

tie (*vt.*) 1)...o musubu [⋯を結ぶ]. 2)...o shibari-tsukeru [⋯を縛りつける]. 3)(*sports*) ...to dôten-ni-naru [⋯と同点になる].

　　　(*vi.*) musuberu [結べる]; dôten-ni-naru [同点になる].

　tie up 1)...o-shikkari-shibaru. 2)...o-futsû-ni-suru

　　1) He tied up the parcel with the rope.

　　　　Kare-wa rôpu-de ko-zutsumi-o shikkari-shibatta.

　　2) The flood tied up all traffic.

　　　　Kôzui-no-tame-ni kôtsû ga zembu futsû-ni-natta.

　tie up with ...to teikei-suru; ...to tai-appu-suru

　　　(*n.*) 1)musubi[-me] [結び(目)]. 2)nekutai [ネクタイ]. 3)(*pl.*) en [縁]; kizuna [きずな]. 4)(*sports*) dôten [同点]. 5)omo-ni [重荷].

tie-up (*n.*) 1)teikei [提携]; kyôryoku [協力]; tai-appu [タイアップ]. 2)iki-zumari [行き詰まり]; gyômu-no-teitai [業務の停滞].

tiger (*n.*) tora [トラ].

tight (*a.*) 1)(ifuku nado no) kichitto-atta [(衣服などの)きちっと合っ

た]. 2)(nawa nado no) hari-kitta [(なわなどの)張りきった]. 3)
(zubon ya kutsu ga) kitsui [(ズボンやくつが)きつい]. 4)(com.)
kane-zumari-no [金詰まりの]. 5)genkaku-na [厳格な].

   (ad.) kataku [固く]; shikkari-to [しっかりと].

tighten (vt. & vi.) …o shikkari-shimeru (shikkari-shimaru) […をしっ
かり締める(しっかり締まる)]; …o kataku-suru (kataku-naru) […を固
くする(固くなる)].

tile (n.) kawara [かわら]; tairu [タイル].

till (prep.) made [まで].

   (conj.) (…suru toki-)made [(…するとき)まで].

till (vt. & vi.) (…o) tagayasu [(…を)耕す].

tilt (vi. & vt.) katamuku(…o katamukeru) [傾く(…を傾ける)].

   (n.) keisha [傾斜].

timber (n.) 1)zaimoku [材木]; tachi-ki [立木]. 2)(fune no) furêmu
[(船の)フレーム]. 3)jimbutsu [人物].

time (n.) 1)jikoku [時刻]; …ji […時]. 2)toki [時]; jikan [時間];
hima [暇]. 3)jiki [時期]; toki [時]. 4)(pl.) jidai [時代]; keiki
[景気]. 5)…((su-)beki)toki [(…すべき)時]. 6)…do […度]; …kai […
回]; …bai […倍].

   (1) What **time** is it now?　Ima nan-ji-desu-ka?

   (2) **Time** is money.　Toki wa kane nari.

      Shall you have **time** tomorrow?

         Asu o-hima-ga ari-mashô-ka?

   (3) **Time** will show it.　Jiki-ga-tate-ba wakaru-darô.

   (4) He is behind the **times** in his thought.

         Kare-no-kangae-wa jidai-okure-da.

      Times are hard now.　Ima-wa fu-keiki-da.

   (5) It is **time** to go to bed.　Mô neru-toki da.

   (6) Do one thing at a **time**.

         Ichi-do-ni hitotsu-no koto-o shi-nasai.

      three **times** a day　ichi-nichi-ni san-do

      China is twenty-six **times** as large as Japan.

         Chûgoku-no-hirosa wa Nihon-no ni-jû-roku-bai da.

all the time 1)sono-aida-jû-zutto. 2)itsu-mo.

for a time ichiji; shibaraku.

for the time being sashi-atari; tôbun.

from time to time toki-doki.

have a good time (of it) tanoshii-omoi-o-suru.

  in no time toki-o-utsusazu; sugu-ni

  in time ma-ni-atte

  on time jikan-doori-ni

  out of time okurete; kisetsu-hazure-no

  take one's time yukkuri-yaru; jibun-no-pêsu-de-yaru

time bomb jigen-bakudan [時限爆弾].

timely (*a.*) toki-o-eta [時を得た]; taimurî-na [タイムリーな].

timetable (*n.*) (gakkô no) jikan-wari [(学校の)時間割]; (ressha ya basu no) jikoku-hyô [(列車やバスの)時刻表].

timid (*a.*) okubyô-na [おく病な]; ki-no-chiisai [気の小さい].

timidly (*ad.*) okubyô-ni [おく病に]; ozu-ozu-to [おずおずと].

tin (*n.*) 1)suzu [すず]. 2)buriki [ブリキ]. 3)((*Eng.*)) kanzume-no-kan [缶詰の缶].

  (*a.*) suzu[buriki]-sei-no [すず[ブリキ]製の]; yasuppoi [安っぽい].

  (*vt.*) 1)...ni suzu-o-kabuseru [···にすずをかぶせる]. 2)((*Eng.*)) ...o kanzume-ni-suru [···を缶詰にする].

tinge (*n.*) iroai [色合い].

  (*vt.*) ...ni usuku-iro-o-tsukeru [···に薄く色を着ける].

tingle (*vi. & vt.*) hiri-hiri-itamu(...o hiri-hiri-saseru) [ひりひり痛む(···をひりひりさせる)]; zoku-zoku-suru(...o zoku-zoku-saseru) [ぞくぞくする(···をぞくぞくさせる)].

  (*n.*) hiri-hiri-suru-itami [ひりひりする痛み]; zoku-zoku-suru-kôfun [ぞくぞくする興奮].

tinkle (*n.*) chirin-chirin [ちりんちりん].

  (*vi. & vt.*) chirin-chirin-to-naru(...o chirin-chirin-to-narasu) [ちりんちりんと鳴る(···をちりんちりんと鳴らす)].

tinsel (*n.*) pika-pika-hikaru-kinzoku-hen [ぴかぴか光る金属片]; yasu-pika-mono [安ぴか物].

  (*a.*) kim-pika-no [金ぴかの]; mikake-daoshi-no [見かけ倒しの].

  (*vt.*) ...o kim-pika-de-kazaru [···を金ぴかで飾る].

tint (*n.*) 1)iro [色]; iroai [色合い]. 2)tanshoku [淡色]. 3)ke-zome [毛染め].

  (*vt.*) ...ni iroai-o-tsukeru [···に色合いをつける]; ...o someru [···を染める].

tiny (*a.*) chitcha-na [ちっちゃな].

tip (*n.*) saki [先]; sentan [先端].

  (*vt.*) ...no saki-ni(...o)-tsukeru [···の先に(···を)付ける].

tip (*vt. & vi.*) ...o katamukeru (katamuku) [···を傾ける(傾く)]; ...o

hikkuri-kaesu (hikkuri-kaeru) […をひっくり返す（ひっくり返る）].
　(*n.*) keisha [傾斜].

tip (*n.*) 1)chippu [チップ]; kokoro-zuke [心付け]. 2)jogen [助言];
yosô [予想].
　(*vt.*) 1)…ni chippu-o-yaru […にチップをやる]. 2)…ni sotto-
shiraseru […にそっと知らせる].

tip (*n.*) keida [軽打]; (*baseball*) chippu [チップ].
　(*vt.*) …o karuku-utsu […を軽く打つ]; …o chippu-suru […をチッ
プする].
　(*vi.*) tsuma-saki-de-aruku [つま先で歩く].

tiptoe (*n. & vi.*) tsuma-saki(-de-aruku) [つま先（で歩く）].

tire (*n.*) taiya [タイヤ].
　(*vt.*) …ni taiya-o-tsukeru […にタイヤをつける].

tire (*vt. & vi.*) …o tsukare-saseru (tsukareru) […を疲れさせる（疲れ
る）]; …o aki-saseru (akiru) […を飽きさせる（飽きる）].

tired (*a.*) tsukareta [疲れた]; akita [飽きた].
　be tired of …ni akiru; …ga iya-ni-naru
　be tired out tsukarete-heto-heto-ni-naru
　be tired with …de tsukareru

tiresome (*a.*) 1)taikutsu-na [退屈な]; aki-aki-suru [飽き飽きする]. 2)
yakkai-na [厄介な].

tissue (*n.*) 1)(*anat.*) soshiki [組織]. 2)(*usui*) orimono [（薄い）織物].
3)tisshu-pêpâ [ティッシュペーパー].

title (*n.*) 1)hyôdai [表題]; shomei [書名]. 2)shôgô [称号]; kata-
gaki [肩書]. 3)(*sports*) taitoru [タイトル].
　(*vt.*) 1)…ni(…to)-hyôdai-o-tsukeru […に(…と)表題をつける]. 2)
…ni…to-iu-kata-gaki-o-ataeru […に…という肩書を与える].
　(*a.*) 1)hyôdai-no [表題の]; daimei-to-onaji [題名と同じ]. 2)
senshu-ken-no [選手権の].

title page tobira [とびら]; taitoru-pêji [タイトルページ].

to (*prep.*) 1)…e […へ]; …ni […に]; …made […まで]. 2)made-ni
[までに]. 3)…(shita)-koto-ni-wa […(した)ことには]. 4)…(ni-itaru-)
made […(に至る)まで]. 5)…ni-awasete […に合わせて]. 6)…ni-
taishite […に対して]. 7)…(suru-)koto-wa […(する)ことは]. 8)…
(suru-)tame-no […(する)ための]. 9)…(suru-)tame-ni […(する)ため
に]; …(shi-)te […(して)].
　(*1*) Let's go **to** school.　Gakkô-*e* ikô.
　　He sent a letter **to** me.

Kare-wa watashi-*ni* tegami-o yokoshita.

(2) It is five minutes **to** ten.　Jû-ji-*made-ni* go-fun-aru.

Jû-ji-go-fun-mae-da.

(3) **To** my surprise he failed again.

Odoroita-*koto-ni-wa* kare-wa mata shikujitta.

(4) How many hours does it take (for) us from Tokyo **to** Hakata by plane?

Tôkyô-kara Hakata-*made* hikô-ki-de nan-jikan kakari-masu-ka?

(5) They danced **to** the music.

Kare-ra-wa ongaku-*ni-awasete* odotta.

(6) We won the game by 5 to 2.

Ware-ware-wa go-*tai*-ni-de katta.

(7) **To** see is to believe.　Miru-*koto* wa shinjiru-*koto* da.

Hyaku-bun wa ikken-ni-shikazu.

(8) Give me something cold **to** drink.

Nani-ka tsumetai nomi-mono-o kudasai.

(9) We eat **to** live.　Ware-ware-wa ikiru-*tame-ni* taberu.

I'm very glad **to** hear it.　Sore-o-kii*te* taihen ureshii.

(*ad.*) 1)shimatte [閉まって]; tomatte [止まって]; itsu-mo-no-jôtai-ni [いつもの状態に]. 2)katsudô-jôtai-ni [活動状態に].

(*1*) Please put the door **to**.　Doa-o *pittari-shimete*-kudasai.

A ship lies **to**.　Fune-ga issô *tomatte*-iru.

toad (*n.*) (zool.) hiki-gaeru [ヒキガエル]; gama [ガマ].

toadstool (*n.*) kinoko [キノコ]; doku-take [毒タケ].

toast (*n.*) tôsuto [トースト].

(*vt.*) ...o kongari-yaku [...をこんがり焼く]; ...o tôsuto-ni-suru [...をトーストにする].

(*vi.*) kongari-yakeru [こんがり焼ける].

toast (*n.*) kampai [乾杯].

(*vt. & vi.*) (...ni) kampai-suru [(...に)乾杯する].

tobacco (*n.*) kizami-tabako [刻みタバコ].

today, to-day (*n.*) 1)kyô [きょう]. 2)gendai [現代].

(*ad.*) kyô[-wa] [きょう(は)]; konnichi-dewa [今日では]; konogoro-wa [このごろは].

toe (*n.*) 1)ashi-yubi [足指]. 2)tsuma-saki [つま先].

(*vt.*) ...ni tsuma-saki-o-tsukeru [...につま先をつける].

together (*ad.*) 1)tomo-ni [共に]; issho-ni [一緒に]; awasete [合わせ

て]. 2)dôji-ni [同時に].

together with ...to-tomo-ni

toil (*n.*) kurô [苦労]; hone-ori [骨折り].
   (*vi.*) sesse-to-hataraku [せっせと働く].

toilet (*n.*) 1)semmen-jo [洗面所]; benjo [便所]; toire [トイレ]. 2) keshô [化粧].

token (*n.*) 1)shirushi [印]. 2)kinen-hin [記念品].
   as a (*or* **in**) **token of** ...no-shirushi-to-shite

tolerable (*a.*) 1)gaman-no-dekiru [我慢のできる]. 2)kanari-no [かなり
   の]; maa-maa-no [まあまあの].

tolerate (*vt.*) 1)...o gaman-suru [...を我慢する]; ...o oo-me-ni-miru
   [...を大目に見る]. 2)(*med.*) ...ni taisei-ga-aru [...に耐性がある].

toll (*n.*) 1)tsûkô-ryô [通行料]. 2)shi-shô-sha-sû [死傷者数].

toll road yûryô-dôro [有料道路].

tomato (*n.*) tomato [トマト].

tomb (*n.*) haka [墓].

tomorrow (*n.*) ashita [あした]; myônichi [明日]; shôrai [将来].
   (*ad.*) ashita[-wa] [あした(は)]; asu[-wa] [あす(は)].

ton (*n.*) ton [トン].

tone (*n.*) 1)(oto-no-)chôshi [(音の)調子]; ne-iro [音色]. 2)kuchô [口
   調]; gochô [語調]. 3)kifû [気風]. 4)iroai [色合い]. 5)(karada no)
   seijô-na-jôtai [(体の)正常な状態].
   (*vt.*) ...no chôshi-o-tsukeru [...の調子をつける]; ...no chôshi-o-
   totonoeru [...の調子を整える].
   (*vi.*) (aru-)chôshi-o-obiru [(ある)調子を帯びる].

tongs (*n.*) hi-bashi [火ばし]; hasami-dôgu [はさみ道具]; ...basami [...
   ばさみ].

tongue (*n.*) 1)shita [舌]. 2)gengo [言語].
   (*1*) Hold your **tongue**. Damatte-iro.
   (*2*) French is his mother **tongue**.
      Furansu-go wa kare-no bokoku-*go* da.

tonic (*a.*) 1)genki-zukeru [元気づける]. 2)(*mus.*) shuon-no [主音の].
   (*n.*) kyôsô-zai [強壮ざい]; shuon [主音].

tonight (*n.*) kon'ya [今夜]; komban [今晩].
   (*ad.*) kon'ya[-wa] [今夜(は)].

tonnage (*n.*) ton-sû [トン数].

tonsi(l)litis (*n.*) (*med.*) hentôsen-en [へん桃腺炎].

too (*ad.*) 1)sono-ue [その上]; (...mo-)mata [(...も)また]. 2)amari-ni

...sugite [あまりに…すぎて]. 3)(*colloq.*) hijô-ni [非常に]; totemo [とても].

(*1*) I like it, **too**. Watashi-wa sore-*mo-mata* suki-da.

(*2*) This is **too** hot to eat.
      Kore-wa *amari-ni* atsu-*sugite* taberare-nai.
      Kore-wa atsuku-te taberare-nai.

(*3*) I'm **too** happy. Watashi-wa *totemo* shiawase-da.

tool (*n.*) 1)dôgu [道具]; shudan [手段]. 2)te-saki [手先].
    (*vt.*) ...o dôgu-de-tsukuru […を道具で造る]; ...ni kikai-o-sue-tsukeru […に機械を据え付ける].
    (*vi.*) dôgu-o-tsukau [道具を使う]; dôgu-de-saiku-suru [道具で細工する].

tooth (*n.*) ha [歯].

toothache (*n.*) shitsû [歯痛].

toothbrush (*n.*) ha-burashi [歯ブラシ].

toothpaste (*n.*) neri-ha-migaki [練り歯みがき].

toothpick (*n.*) tsuma-yôji [つまようじ].

top (*n.*) koma [こま].

top (*n.*) 1)chôjô [頂上]. 2)(the -) shuseki [首席]. 3)(the -) kyokudo [極度]; zetchô [絶頂].
  at the top of one's voice koe-o-kagiri-ni
  from top to toe sukkari
    (*a.*) ichiban-ue-no [一番上の]; saikô-no [最高の].
    (*vt.*) 1)...no chôjô-o-oou […の頂上を覆う]; ...no chôjô-ni-aru […の頂上にある]; ...no chôjô-ni-tassuru […の頂上に達する]. 2)...yori masaru […よりまさる].

topcoat (*n.*) karui-ôbâ [軽いオーバー]; toppukôto [トップコート].

topic (*n.*) wadai [話題]; topikku [トピック]; rondai [論題].

torch (*n.*) taimatsu [たいまつ]; ((*Eng.*)) kaichû-dentô [懐中電灯].

torment (*n.*) 1)kunô [苦悩]. 2)nayami-no-tane [悩みの種].
    (*vt.*) ...o nayamasu […を悩ます]; ...o hidoku-kurushimeru […をひどく苦しめる].

torpedo (*n.*) 1)gyorai [魚雷]. 2)kanshaku-dama [かんしゃく玉].
    (*vt.*) ...o gyorai-de-kôgeki-suru […を魚雷で攻撃する]; ...o kôgeki-shite-buchi-kowasu […を攻撃してぶち壊す].

torrent (*n.*) 1)kyûryû [急流]. 2)(*pl.*) dosha-buri [どしゃ降り]. 3) rempatsu [連発]; (kanjô no) hotobashiri [(感情の)ほとばしり].

Torrid Zone, the nettai [熱帯].

tortoise (*n.*) kame [カメ].

tortoiseshell (*n.*) bekkô [べっ甲].

torture (*n.*) kutsû[-o-ataeru-koto] [苦痛(を与えること)]; gômon [拷問].

　　　(*vt.*) 1)...o hidoku-kurushimeru [...をひどく苦しめる]; ...o gômon-ni-kakeru [...を拷問にかける]. 2)...o muri-ni-neji-mageru [...を無理にねじ曲げる].

toss (*vt.*) 1)...o poi-to-hôri-ageru [...をぽいとほうり上げる]. 2)...o dôyô-saseru [...を動揺させる]; ...o honrô-suru [...を翻ろうする]. 3) (koin)-o hôri-agete omote-ka-ura-ka-o-mite-jumban-o-kimeru [(コイン)をほうり上げて表か裏かを見て順番を決める].

　　(*1*) He **tossed** the letter on the desk.
　　　　Kare-wa tegami-o tsukue-no-ue-ni *nage-dashita*.
　　(*2*) I saw a ship **tossed** about by the sea.
　　　　Fune ga nami-ni *honrô-sarete-iru*-no-ga mieta.
　　(*3*) The two captains **tossed** a coin.
　　　　Sono futari-no shushô wa koin-o *hôri-agete-jumban-o-kimeta*.

　　(*vi.*) 1)jô-ge-ni-yureru [上下に揺れる]; ne-gaeri-o-utsu [寝返りを打つ]; koroge-mawaru [転げ回る]. 2)koin-nage-de-kimeru [コイン投げで決める].

　　(*n.*) 1)nage-ageru-koto [投げ上げること]; tosu-suru-koto [トスすること]. 2)dôyô [動揺]. 3)(the -) koin-nage [コイン投げ].

total (*a.*) 1)sôkei-no [総計の]. 2)mattaku-no [全くの].

　　(*n.*) sôkei [総計]; gôkei [合計].

　　(*vt.*) gôkei...to-naru [合計...となる]; ...o gôkei-suru [...を合計する].

　　(*vi.*) gôkei...(to-)naru [合計...(と)なる].

totally (*ad.*) mattaku [全く].

totter (*vi.*) yoromeku [よろめく]; guratsuku [ぐらつく].

　　(*n.*) yoromeki [よろめき].

touch (*vt.*) 1)...ni fureru [...に触れる]. 2)...o kandô-saseru [...を感動させる]. 3)...ni genkyû-suru [...に言及する]. 4)...ni kankei-suru [...に関係する].

　　(*vi.*) fureru [触れる].

　　(*n.*) 1)fureru-koto [触れること]; sesshoku [接触]. 2)hitchi [筆致]; tatchi [タッチ]. 3)...kimi [...気味]; shôryô-no... [少量の...].

　　in touch with ...to-sesshoku-shite; ...to-renraku-shite

touching (*a.*) kandô-saseru [感動させる]; mune-o-utsu [胸を打つ].
 (*prep.*) …ni-kanshite […に関して].

tough (*a.*) 1)(niku ya kami nado ga) katai [(肉や紙などが)堅い]. 2)
nebari-no-aru [粘りのある]. 3)ganko-na [頑固な]. 4)hone-no-oreru
[骨の折れる].
 (*n.*) (*colloq.*) rambô-mono [乱暴者]; muhô-mono [無法者].

tour (*n.*) 1)kankô-ryokô [観光旅行]; shûyû-ryokô [周遊旅行]. 2)
kengaku [見学]; jungyô [巡業]. 3)kimmu-kôtai [勤務交替].
 (*vt. & vi.*) (…o) ryokô-suru [(…を)旅行する]; (…o) shûyû-
suru [(…を)周遊する]; (…o) jungyô-suru [(…を)巡業する].

tourist (*n.*) kankô-kyaku [観光客].

tournament (*n.*) kachi-nuki-shiai [勝ち抜き試合]; tônamento [トーナ
メント].

tow (*vt.*) …o tsuna-de-hipparu […を綱で引っ張る]; …o hippatte-
tsurete-iku […を引っ張って連れて行く].
 (*n.*) hiki-zuna [引き綱].

toward (*prep.*) 1)…no-hô-e […の方へ]; …ni-mukatte […に向かって].
2)…goro […ごろ]; …chikaku […近く]. 3)…ni-menshite […に面して].
4)…no-tame-ni […のために].
 (*1*) He hurried **toward** home. Kare-wa ie-*ni-mukatte* isoida.
   Kare-wa ieji-o isoida.
 (*2*) He came back **toward** evening.
   Kare-wa yûgata-*chikaku* kaette-kita.
 (*3*) The house faces **toward** the east.
   Sono ie wa higashi-*ni-menshite*-iru.
 (*4*) I have done all I can **toward** that object.
   Watashi-wa sono-mokuteki-*o-tassuru-tame-ni* zenryoku-o
   tsukushita.

towel (*n.*) taoru [タオル]; tenugui [手ぬぐい].

tower (*n.*) tô [塔].
 (*vi.*) takaku-sobieru [高くそびえる].

town (*n.*) machi [町]; tokai [都会].

town hall shi-yakusho [市役所]; kôkai-dô [公会堂]; machi-yakuba
[町役場].

town planning ((*Eng.*)) toshi-keikaku [都市計画].

toy (*n.*) 1)omocha [おもちゃ]. 2)tsumaranai-mono [つまらないもの].
 make a toy of …o omocha-ni-suru; …o moteasobu
 (*a.*) omocha-no [おもちゃの].

　　　(*vi.*) mote-asobu [もてあそぶ].

trace (*n.*) 1)ashi-ato [足跡]; konseki [こん跡]. 2)hon-no-sukoshi [ほんの少し].

　　　(*vt.*) 1)...o sagashi-dasu [...を捜し出す]. 2)...o torêsu-suru [...をトレースする].

　　　(*vi.*) saka-noboru [さかのぼる]; tsuki-tomeru [突き止める].

trachoma (*n.*) (*med.*) torakôma [トラコーマ].

tracing paper torêshingu-pêpâ [トレーシングペーパー].

track (*n.*) 1)wadachi [わだち]. 2)(*pl.*) ashi-ato [足跡]. 3)ko-michi [小道]. 4)(*sports*) torakku [トラック]. 5)kidô [軌道]; tetsudô-senro [鉄道線路].

　　　(*vt.*) 1)...o tsuiseki-suru [...を追跡する]. 2)((*US*))...ni ashi-ato-o-tsukeru [...に足跡をつける].

tract (*n.*) 1)hiroi-menseki [広い面積]; chiiki [地域]. 2)(*anat.*)...kan [...管]; ...kei [...系].

trade (*n.*) 1)shôbai [商売]; bôeki [貿易]; tsûshô [通商]. 2)shokugyô [職業].

　　　(*vi.*) bôeki-suru [貿易する]; bai-bai-suru [売買する].

　　　(*vt.*) ...o kôkan-suru [...を交換する].

trader (*n.*) bôeki-gyô-sha [貿易業者]; bôeki-sen [貿易船]; shôsen [商船].

trade(s) union ((*Eng.*)) rôdô-kumiai [労働組合].

tradition (*n.*) 1)dentô [伝統]. 2)ii-tsutae [言い伝え].

traditional (*a.*) dentô-teki-na [伝統的な]; densetsu-no [伝説の].

traffic (*n.*) 1)kôtsû[-ryô] [交通(量)]; ôrai [往来]. 2)yusô[-sâbisu] [輸送(サービス)]. 3)bôeki [貿易].

　　　(*vi.*) torihiki-suru [取り引きする]; [fusei-]bai-bai-suru [(不正)売買する].

traffic light kôtsû-shingô-tô [交通信号灯].

tragedy (*n.*) higeki [悲劇]; kanashii-deki-goto [悲しい出来事].

tragic (*a.*) higeki-teki-na [悲劇的な]; hisan-na [悲惨な].

trail (*vt.*) 1)...o hikizuru [...を引きずる]. 2)...no ato-o-tsuite-iku [...のあとをついて行く]. 3)...o hiki-nobasu [...を引き延ばす].

　　　(*vi.*) 1)hiki-zuru [引きずる]. 2)karami-tsuku [からみつく].

　　　(*n.*) 1)ato [跡]. 2)ko-michi [小道].

trailer (*n.*) 1)tsuiseki-sha [追跡者]. 2)torêrâ [トレーラー]; ((*US*)) torêrâhausu [トレーラーハウス].

train (*n.*) 1)ressha [列車]. 2)retsu [列].

    (*vt.*) 1)...o kunren-suru […を訓練する]; ...o kyôiku-suru […を教育する]. 2)...o(-aru-hôkô-ni) nobasu […を(ある方向に)伸ばす].
    (*vi.*) kunren-suru [訓練する].

trainer (*n.*) torênâ [トレーナー]; chôkyô-shi [調教師].

training (*n.*) 1)kunren [訓練]; renshû [練習]; chôkyô [調教]. 2) kyôiku-katei [教育課程].

traitor (*n.*) hangyaku-sha [反逆者]; uragiri-mono [裏切り者].

tram (*n.*) 1)((*Eng.*)) romen-densha [路面電車]. 2)torokko [トロッコ].
    (*vi.*) romen-densha-de-iku [路面電車で行く].
    (*vt.*) ...o torokko-de-hakobu […をトロッコで運ぶ].

tramp (*vi.*) 1)fumi-tsukeru [踏みつける]; dosun-dosun-to-aruku [どすんどすんと歩く].
    (*vt.*) 1)...o teku-teku-aruku […をてくてく歩く]. 2)...o hôrô-suru […を放浪する].
    (*n.*) 1)(the -) dosun-dosun-to-aruku-oto [どすんどすんと歩く音]. 2)toho-ryokô [徒歩旅行]. 3)hôrô-sha [放浪者]. 4)(*marine*) fu-teikô-sen [不定航船] = tramper.

trample (*vi.*) 1)doshin-doshin-to-aruku [どしんどしんと歩く]. 2)fumi-tsukeru [踏みつける].
    (*vt.*) ...o fumi-tsukeru […を踏みつける].
    (*n.*) doshin-doshin-to-aruku-koto[-oto] [どしんどしんと歩くこと[音]]. fumi-tsukeru-koto[-oto] [踏みつけること[音]].

tranquil (*a.*) shizuka-na [静かな]; ochitsuita [落ち着いた]; odayaka-na [穏やかな].

tranquility (*n.*) heisei [平静]; ochitsuki [落ち着き].

transact (*vt.*) 1)(jimu nado)-o shori-suru [(事務など)を処理する]. 2) (torihiki)-o okonau [(取引)を行なう].

transaction (*n.*) (the -) shori [処理]. torihiki [取引].

transfer (*vt.*) 1)...o utsusu […を移す]. 2)...o jôto-suru […を譲渡する]. 3)...o tennin-saseru […を転任させる].
    (*vi.*) 1)tennin-suru [転任する]. 2)nori-kaeru [乗り換える].
    (*n.*) 1)iten [移転]. 2)jôto [譲渡]. 3)norikae[-kippu] [乗り換え(切符)].

transform (*vt.*) 1)...o henkei-saseru […を変形させる]. 2)(*elect.*)...o hen'atsu-suru […を変圧する].
    (*vi.*) (...ni)kawaru [(…に)変わる]; henkei-suru [変形する]; henshitsu-suru [変質する].
    (*n.*) henkei [変形]; henshitsu [変質].

transfusion (*n.*) chûnyû [注入]; yuketsu [輸血].

transit (*n.*) 1)tsûkô [通行]. 2)unsô [運送]; yusô [輸送].

transition (*n.*) utsuri-kawari [移り変わり]; kato-ki [過渡期].

translate (*vt.*) ...o yakusu [...を訳す]; ...o hon'yaku-suru [...を翻訳する].

    (*vi.*) hon'yaku-suru [翻訳する]; hon'yaku-dekiru [翻訳できる].

translation (*n.*) hon'yaku [翻訳]; yakubun [訳文].

transmit (*vt.*) 1)...o okuru [...を送る]. 2)...o tsutaeru [...を伝える]; (*phys.*)...o dendô-suru [...を伝導する]; (*teleg.*)...o sôshin-suru [...を送信する].

transparent (*a.*) 1)tômei-na [透明な]. 2)meihaku-na [明白な]; mie-suita [見え透いた].

transport (*vt.*) ...o yusô-suru [...を輸送する].

    (*n.*) 1)((*Eng.*)) yusô [輸送]; unsô [運送]. 2)yusô-sen [輸送船].

transportation (*n.*) 1)yusô [輸送]; unsô [運送]. 2)((*US*)) yusô-kikan [輸送機関].

trap (*n.*) wana [わな]; keiryaku [計略].

    (*vi. & vt.*) wana-ni-kakeru(...ni wana-o-shi-kakeru) [わなにかける(...にわなを仕掛ける)].

trash (*n.*) 1)((*US*)) kuzu [くず]; garakuta [がらくた]. 2)kudaranai-kangae [くだらない考え]; ((*US*)) kudaranai-hito [くだらない人].

travel (*vi.*) 1)ryokô-suru [旅行する]. 2)tsutawaru [伝わる].

    (*vt.*) ...o ryokô-suru [...を旅行する].

    (*n.*) 1)ryokô [旅行]; (*pl.*) ryokô-ki [旅行記]. 2)idô [移動].

travel(l)er (*n.*) ryokô-sha [旅行者].

traverse (*n.*) 1)ôdan [横断]. 2)(*mountaineering*) torabâsu [トラバース].

    (*vt.*) ...o ôdan-suru [...を横断する].

trawl (*n.*) 1)((*US*)) haenawa [はえなわ]. 2)torôru-ami [トロール網].

    (*vt.*) ...o torôru-ami-de-toru [...をトロール網で捕る].

tray (*n.*) bon [盆]; torei [トレイ]; mori-zara [盛り皿].

tread (*vi. & vt.*) (...o) fumu [(...を)踏む]; (...o) aruku [(...を)歩く].

    (*n.*) ashidori [足取り]; ashi-oto [足音].

treason (*n.*) hangyaku[-zai] [反逆(罪)].

treasure (*n.*) 1)zaihô [財宝]. 2)kichô-hin [貴重品].

    (*vt.*) ...o takuwaeru [...を蓄える]; ...o daiji-ni-suru [...を大

事にする].

treasury (*n.*) 1)hôko [宝庫]. 2)kokko [国庫].

treat (*vt.*) 1)...o atsukau [⋯を扱う]; ...o taigû-suru [⋯を待遇する].
2)...ni-ogoru [⋯におごる]. 3)...o chiryô-suru [⋯を治療する].
　　　(*vi.*) 1)ogoru [おごる]. 2)kôshô-suru [交渉する]. 3)ronzuru [論
ずる].
　　　(*n.*) 1)tanoshimi [楽しみ]. 2)ogori [おごり]; ogoru-ban [おご
る番].

treatment (*n.*) 1)tori-atsukai [取り扱い]; taigû [待遇]. 2)chiryô [治
療].

treaty (*n.*) jôyaku [条約].

tree (*n.*) ki [木]; jumoku [樹木]; moku-sei-no-mono [木製のもの].

tremble (*vi.*) 1)furueru [震える]; mi-burui-suru [身震いする]. 2)(ki
no ha nado ga) soyogu [(木の葉などが)そよぐ].
　　　(*n.*) furue [震え]; mi-burui [身震い]; ononoki [おののき].

tremendous (*a.*) 1)osoroshii [恐ろしい]. 2)(*colloq.*) kyodai-na [巨大
な]. 3)(*colloq.*) subarashii [すばらしい].

trench (*n.*) 1)hori [堀]; mizo [溝]. 2)(*geog.*) kaikô [海溝].
　Japan Trench, the　Nihon-kaikô
　　　(*vt.*) ...ni mizo[hori/gô]-o-horu [⋯に溝[堀／壕]を掘る]; ...o
mizo[hori]-de-kakomu [⋯を溝[堀]で囲む].
　　　(*vi.*) mizo[hori/gô]-o-horu [溝[堀／壕]を掘る].

trend (*n.*) hôkô [方向]; keikô [傾向].
　　　(*vi.*) (...ni-mukau)keikô-ga-aru [(⋯に向かう)傾向がある].

trespass (*vi.*) 1)shinnyû-suru [侵入する]. 2)jama-suru [邪魔する].
　　　(*n.*) fuhô-shinnyû [不法侵入]; jama [邪魔].

trial (*n.*) 1)kokoromi [試み]; shiken [試験]. 2)shiren [試練]. 3)
(*law*) saiban [裁判]; kôhan [公判].
　on trial　1)tameshi-ni. 2)saiban-ni-kakerarete
　　　(*a.*) shiken-teki-na [試験的な].

triangle (*n.*) sankakkei [三角形].

triangular (*a.*) sankakkei-no [三角形の]; san-sha[-kan]-no [三者(間)
の].

tribe (*n.*) 1)shuzoku [種族]; buzoku [部族]. 2)nakama [仲間].

tribute (*n.*) 1)mitsugi-mono [貢ぎ物]. 2)sanji [賛辞].

trick (*n.*) 1)sakuryaku [策略]; torikku [トリック]. 2)itazura [いたず
ら]. 3)tejina [手品]. 4)geitô [芸当]. 5)kotsu [こつ].
　play a trick on a person　hito-ni-itazura-o-suru

    (a.) 1)geitô-no [芸当の]; otoshi-ana-no-aru [落とし穴のある].
    (vt.) 1)...o damasu […をだます]; ...o katsugu […をかつぐ]. 2)
...o kazari-tateru […を飾りたてる].
    (vi.) damasu [だます].

trickle (vi.) 1)shitataru [したたる]. 2)sukoshi-zutsu-kuru [少しずつ来
る]; jojo-ni-tsutawaru [徐々に伝わる].
    (vt.) ...o shitatarasu […をしたたらす].
    (n.) shitatari [したたり]; yukkuri-shita-ugoki [ゆっくりした動
き].

tried (a.) 1)shiken-zumi-no [試験済みの]. 2)shinrai-no-okeru [信頼の
おける].

trifle (n.) 1)sasai-na-koto [ささいなこと]; kudaranai-mono [くだらな
いもの]. 2)shôryô [少量].
    (vi.) 1)moteasobu [もてあそぶ]; ii-kagen-ni-atsukau [いい加減
に扱う]. 2)bura-bura-sugosu [ぶらぶら過ごす]; jikan-o-rôhi-suru [時
間を浪費する].
    (vt.) ...o rôhi-suru […を浪費する].

trifling (a.) 1)wazuka-na [わずかな]; tsumaranai [つまらない]. 2)
fuzaketa [ふざけた].

trim (vt.) 1)...o kari-komu […を刈り込む]; ...no teire-o-suru […の手
入れをする]. 2)...o chôsei-suru […を調整する]; ...no tsuri-ai-o-toru
[…の釣り合いをとる]. 3)...ni kazari-o-tsukeru […に飾りをつける].
    (n.) 1)kari-komi [刈り込み]; chôhatsu [調髪]; seiton [整とん].
2)tsuri-ai [釣り合い]. 3)sôshoku [装飾]. 4)chôshi [調子].
    (a.) kichin-to-shita [きちんとした]; ko-girei-na [小ぎれいな].

trimming (n.) 1)seiton [整とん]; (photo.) torimingu [トリミング].
2)(pl.) kazari [飾り].

trip (n.) ryokô [旅行].
    (vi.) 1)keikai-na-ashidori-de-aruku [軽快な足取りで歩く]. 2)
tsumazuku [つまずく]; ayamachi-o-suru [過ちをする].
    (vt.) ...o tsumazukaseru […をつまずかせる]; ...o shippai-saseru
[…を失敗させる].

triple (a.) sam-bai-no [三倍の]; san-jû-no [三重の].
    (n.) sam-bai [三倍]; (baseball) sanrui-da [三塁打].
    (vi.) sam-bai[san-jû]-ni-naru [三倍[三重]になる]; sanrui-da-o-
utsu [三塁打を打つ].
    (vt.) ...o sam-bai[san-jû]-ni-suru […を三倍[三重]にする].

triplicate (a.) san-jû[sam-bai]-no [三重[三倍]の]; san-tsû-sakuseisareta [三通作成された].

　　　(*n.*) san-kumi-no-hitotsu [三組の一つ]; san-tsû-no-shorui-no-ittsû [三通の書類の一通].

　　　(*vt.*) ...o san-jû-ni-suru […を三重にする]; ...o sam-bai-ni-suru […を三倍にする]; ...o san-tsû-sakusei-suru […を三通作成する].

tripod (*n.*) sankyaku[-dai] [三脚(台)].

triumph (*n.*) 1)shôri [勝利]. 2)dai-seikô [大成功].

　　　(*vi.*) shôri-o-uru [勝利を得る]; kachi-hokoru [勝ち誇る].

triumphal (*a.*) shôri-no [勝利の]; gaisen-no [がい旋の].

triumphant (*a.*) shôri-o-eta [勝利を得た]; tokui-no [得意の].

trivial (*a.*) sasai-na [さ細な]; tsumaranai [つまらない].

trolley, -ly (*n.*) 1)tororî [トロリー]. 2)((*Eng.*)) tororî-basu [トロリーバス]; ((*US*)) romen-densha [路面電車].

troop (*n.*) 1)(dôbutsu no)mure [(動物の)群れ]; ichi-dan-no-hito-bito [一団の人々]; tasû [多数]. 2)(*pl.*) guntai [軍隊]; gunzei [軍勢].

　　　(*vi.*) 1)muragaru [群がる]; (*colloq.*) tai-o-kunde-aruku [隊を組んで歩く].

trophy (*n.*) shôhin [賞品]; torofî [トロフィー]; senri-hin [戦利品]; kinen-hin [記念品].

tropic (*n.*) (*astron. & geog.*) kaiki-sen [回帰線].

　　　(*a.*) nettai-chihô-no [熱帯地方の].

Tropic of Cancer, the Kita-kaiki-sen [北回帰線].

Tropic of Capricorn, the Minami-kaiki-sen [南回帰線].

tropical (*a.*) 1)nettai[-chihô]-no [熱帯(地方)の]. 2)kaiki-sen-no [回帰線の]. 3)netsuretsu-na [熱烈な].

trot (*n. & vi.*) haya-ashi(-de-kakeru) [速足(で駆ける)].

　　　(*vt.*) ...o haya-ashi-de-kakesaseru […を速足で駆けさせる]; (hito)-o isogi-ashi-de-ikaseru [(人)を急ぎ足で行かせる].

trouble (*n.*) 1)shimpai [心配]; kurô [苦労]. 2)byôki [病気]. 3)mendô [面倒]; tesû [手数]; hone-ori [骨折り]. 4)mome-goto [もめ事]; funsô [紛争]; sôgi [争議].

　(*1*) Thank you for your **trouble**.　Go-*kurô*-sama-deshita.

　(*2*) heart **trouble**　shinzô-*byô*

　(*3*) He gave me much **trouble**.

　　　Kare-wa watashi-ni taihen *mendô*-o kaketa.

　　I am sorry for the **trouble** I am giving you.

　　　O-*tesû*-o-kakete môshi-wake-ari-masen.

　(*4*) labor **troubles**　rôdô-*sôgi*

　　in trouble komatte
　　take the trouble to (do) rô-o-oshimazu…(suru); waza-waza…
　　　(suru)
　　　　　(*vt.*) 1)…o komarasu […を困らす]; …o nayamasu […を悩ま
　　す]. 2)…ni tesû-o-kakeru […に手数をかける].
　　　　　(*vi.*) shimpai-suru [心配する]; hone-o-oru [骨を折る].
troublesome (*a.*) yakkai-na [厄介な]; mendô-na [面倒な]; hone-no-
　　oreru [骨の折れる].
trouser (*n.*) (*pl.*) zubon [ズボン].
trout (*n.*) (*fish*) masu [マス]; niji-masu [ニジマス].
truant (*n.*) mudan-kesseki-sha [無断欠席者]; shigoto-o-namakeru-
　　hito [仕事を怠ける人].
　　play truant gakkô-o-zuru-yasumi-suru; shigoto-o-saboru
　　　　　(*a.*) mudan-kesseki-no [無断欠席の]; taida-na [怠惰な].
　　　　　(*vi.*) mudan-kesseki-suru [無断欠席する]; zuru-yasumi-suru
　　[ずる休みする].
truck (*n.*) 1)te-oshi-guruma [手押し車]; torokko [トロッコ]. 2)((*US*))
　　kamotsu-jidôsha [貨物自動車]; torakku [トラック]. 3)((*Eng.*)) mugai-
　　kasha [無がい貨車].
　　　　　(*vt.*) …o torakku-de-hakobu […をトラックで運ぶ].
　　　　　(*vi.*) torakku-o-unten-suru [トラックを運転する].
trudge (*n.*) tobo-tobo-aruku-koto [とぼとぼ歩くこと].
　　　　　(*vi. & vt.*) (…o) tobo-tobo-aruku [(…を)とぼとぼ歩く].
true (*a.*) 1)shin-no [真の]; hontô-no [本当の]. 2)seijitsu-na [誠実な];
　　chûjitsu-na [忠実な]. 3)seikaku-na [正確な]; machigai-no-nai [間違
　　いのない]. 4)seitô-na [正当な]; datô-na [妥当な].
　　(*1*) Is it a **true** story? Sore-wa *hontô-no* hanashi desu-ka?
　　　　　Their wish came **true**. Kare-ra-no negai wa *hontô-ni*-natta.
　　　　　　　　　　　　　　Kare-ra-no negai wa *jitsugen*-shita.
　　(*2*) They were **true** to one another.
　　　　　　Kare-ra-wa tagai-ni *seijitsu*-datta.
　　(*3*) a **true** copy　*seikaku-na* utsushi
　　(*4*) the **true** heir to the throne　*seitô-na* ôi-keishô-sha
truly (*ad.*) shin-ni [真に]; hontô-ni [本当に]; seijitsu-ni [誠実に];
　　chûjitsu-ni [忠実に].
　　Yours truly, ; Truly yours, Keigu
trump (*n.*) (*cards*) kiri-fuda [切り札].
　　play a trump kiri-fuda-o-dasu; oku-no-te-o-dasu

　　　(*vt.*) ...o kiri-fuda-de-kiru [⋯を切り札で切る].

　　　(*vi.*) kiri-fuda-o-dasu [切り札を出す].

trump card　kiri-fuda [切り札]; oku-no-te [奥の手].

trumpet　(*n.*) (*mus.*) torampetto [トランペット]; rappa [らっぱ].

　　　(*vi.*) torampetto-o-fuku [トランペットを吹く].

　　　(*vt.*) 1)...o torampetto-de-shiraseru [⋯をトランペットで知らせる]. 2)...o ii-furasu [⋯を言いふらす].

trunk　(*n.*) 1)(ki no) miki [(木の)幹]. 2)(ningen no) dô [(人間の)胴].
3)kansen [幹線]. 4)(zô no) hana [(象の)鼻]. 5)toranku [トランク].

　　　(*vt.*) ...o toranku-ni-ireru [⋯をトランクに入れる].

trunk road　《*Eng.*》 kansen-dôro [幹線道路].

trust　(*n.*) 1)shin'yô [信用]; shinrai [信頼]. 2)itaku [委託]; hokan
[保管]; (*law*) shintaku [信託]. 3)sekinin [責任]. 4)kakushin [確信].

　　　(*vt.*) 1)...o shin'yô-suru [⋯を信用する]; ...o shinrai-suru [⋯を
信頼する]. 2)...o itaku-suru [⋯を委託する]; ...o azukeru [⋯を預ける].
3)...to kakushin-suru [⋯と確信する].

　　　(*vi.*) 1)shinrai-suru [信頼する]. 2)kakushin-suru [確信する]. 3)
shin'yô-gashi-suru [信用貸しする].

trust company　shintaku-gaisha [信託会社]; shintaku-ginkô [信託銀行].

trustworthy　(*a.*) shinrai-dekiru [信頼できる]; kakujitsu-na [確実な].

truth　(*n.*) 1)shinri [真理]; shinjitsu [真実]. 2)seijitsu [誠実]; shôjiki
[正直].

　　(*1*) I am a lover of **truth**.　Watashi-wa *shinri*-o aisuru-mono da.
　　　　Always speak the **truth**.　Tsune-ni *shinjitsu*-o katare.

　　(*2*) I doubt his **truth**.　Watashi-wa kare-no *seijitsu-sa*-o utagau.

　　to tell the truth (*colloq.*) jitsu-o-ieba

truthful　(*a.*) 1)shôjiki-na [正直な]. 2)hontô-no [本当の].

try　(*vt.*) 1)...o tamesu [⋯を試す]; ...o yatte-miru [⋯をやってみる];
...o kokoromiru [⋯を試みる]; ...to doryoku-suru [⋯と努力する].
2)...o kurushimeru [⋯を苦しめる]; ...o tsukare-saseru [⋯を疲れさ
せる]. 3)(*law*)...o saiban-suru [⋯を裁判する]; ...o shinri-suru [⋯
を審理する].

　　(*1*) Please **try** these shoes on.
　　　　Kono kutsu-o *tameshi*-ni-haite-mite-kudasai.

　　　　I will **try** and get it finished today.
　　　　Naru-beku kyô-jû-ni sore-o *yatte*-shimai-mashô.

　　(*2*) This print **tries** my eyes.

      Kono insatsu wa me-o *tsukare-sasesu.*

  (3) The prisoner **is being tried**.

      Hikoku wa ima-*saiban-o-uketeiru.*

  (*vi.*) yatte-miru [やってみる]; doryoku-suru [努力する].

  (*n.*) 1)kokoromi [試み]; tameshi [試し]. 2)(*rugger*) torai [トライ].

trying (*a.*) 1)kurushii [苦しい]; tsukareru [疲れる]. 2)yakkai-na [厄介な].

tub (*n.*) oke [おけ]; tarai [たらい].

  (*vt.*) 1)...o oke-ni-ireru [...をおけに入れる]. 2)(*Eng. colloq.*) ...o nyûyoku-saseru [...を入浴させる].

  (*vi.*) (*Eng. colloq.*) nyûyoku-suru [入浴する].

tube (*n.*) 1)kuda [管]; tsutsu [筒]; chûbu [チューブ]. 2)((*Eng.*)) chika-tetsu [地下鉄]. 3)((*US*)) shinkû-kan [真空管].

tuberculin (*n.*) tsuberukurin-chûsha-eki [ツベルクリン注射液].

tuberculosis (*n.*) (*path.*) kekkaku [結核].

tuck (*vt.*) 1)...o makuri-ageru [...をまくり上げる]. 2)...ni takku-o-toru [...にタックをとる]. 3)...o oshi-komu [...を押し込む]; ...o kurumu [...をくるむ].

  (*vi.*) takku-o-toru [タックをとる].

  (*n.*) takku [タック].

Tuesday (*n.*) Kayô-bi [火曜日].

tug (*vt.*) ...o gui-to-hipparu [...をぐいと引っ張る]; ...o hiki-bune-de-hiku [...を引き船で引く].

  (*vi.*) tsuyoku-hiku [強く引く].

  (*n.*) 1)tsuyoku-hiku-koto [強く引くこと]. 2)tagubôto [タグボート].

tuition (*n.*) 1)kyôju [教授]. 2)jugyô-ryô [授業料].

tumble (*vi.*) korobu [転ぶ]; taoreru [倒れる].

  (*vt.*) ...o taosu [...を倒す].

tumbler (*n.*) tamburâ [タンブラー].

tuna (*n.*) (*fish*) maguro [マグロ].

tune (*n.*) kyoku [曲]; fushi [節]; senritsu [旋律]; chôwa [調和].

  (*vt. & vi.*) (gakki)-no chôshi-o-awaseru (chôshi-ga-au) [(楽器)の調子を合わせる(調子が合う)].

  tune in (*broadcasting*) daiyaru[channeru]-o-awaseru

  tune up (*mus.*) ...no chôshi-o-awaseru

tunnel (*n.*) tonneru [トンネル]; chika-dô [地下道].

  (*vt. & vi.*) (...ni) tonneru-o-horu [(...に)トンネルを掘る].

turbojet (*n.*) tâbo-jetto-enjin [ターボジェットエンジン]; tâbo-jetto-kôkû-ki [ターボジェット航空機].

turbulent (*a.*) 1)(kaze ya nami nado ga) are-kuruu [(風や波などが) 荒れ狂う]. 2)(kanjô nado ga) kaki-midasareta [(感情などが)かき乱 された]. 3)(bôto nado ga) fuon-na [(暴徒などが)不穏な].

turf (*n.*) shiba-fu [芝生].
     (*vt.*) ...o shiba-de-oou [...を芝で覆う].

Turk (*n.*) Toruko-jin [トルコ人].

Turkey (*n.*) Toruko [トルコ].

turkey (*n.*) (*birds*) shichimen-chô [シチメンチョウ].

Turkish (*a.*) Toruko-no [トルコの]; Toruko-jin-no [トルコ人の]; Toruko-go-no [トルコ語の].
     (*n.*) Toruko-go [トルコ語].

turn (*vt.*) 1)...o kaiten-saseru [...を回転させる]; ...o magaru [...を曲 がる]. 2)...o hikkuri-kaesu [...をひっくり返す]. 3)...o mukeru [...を 向ける]. 4)...o hon'yaku-suru [...を翻訳する]. 5)...o kaeru [...を変え る]. 6)...o oi-harau [...を追い払う].
     (*1*) He **turned** the wheel again.
         Kare-wa futatabi sono sharin-*o kaiten-saseta*.
     He **turned** the corner.   Kare-wa kado-*o magatta*.
     (*2*) He **turned** his coat inside out.
         Kare-wa uwagi-*o ura-gaeshita*.
     (*3*) I **turned** my face that way.
         Watashi-wa kao-*o sochira-e muketa*.
     (*4*) **Turn** this passage into English.
         Kono issetsu-*o Eigo-ni yakushi-nasai*.
     (*5*) The leaves **turn** color.   Kono-ha ga iro-*o kaeru*.
         Kono-ha ga *hen*shoku-suru.
     (*6*) They **turned** the boy out of school.
         Kare-ra-wa sono shônen-*o gakkô-kara oi-dashita*.
     (*vi.*) 1)mawaru [回る]. 2)muku [向く]; magaru [曲がる]. 3) henka-suru [変化する]; ...ni-naru [...になる].
     (*1*) The moon **turns** round the earth.
         Tsuki wa chikyû-no-shûi-o *mawaru*.
     (*2*) **Turn** to the right.   Migi-e *magari-nasai*.
     (*3*) He **turned** pale.   Kare-wa aoku-*natta*.
turn away 1)kao-o-somukeru. 2)...o oi-harau
     1) He turned away and refused to see the sight.

Kare-wa kao-o-somukete sono kôkei-o mi-yô-to-shi-nakatta.

2) Turn him away from the door.

Sono-otoko-o to-guchi-kara oi-dase.

turn off   ...o tomeru; ...o kesu

Turn off the radio.   Rajio-o keshi-nasai.

turn on   ...o tsukeru

Turn on the light, please.   Denki-o tsukete-kudasai.

turn out (*vt.*) 1)...o kesu. 2)...o tsukuru; ...o seisan-suru. 3)...o oi-dasu

1) Turn out the gas.   Gasu-o keshi-nasai.

2) The newly-built factory began to turn out hundreds of TV sets a day.

Atarashiku-dekita-sono-kôjô wa ichi-nichi-ni nam-byaku-dai-to-iu-terebi-o seisan-shi-hajimeta.

3) He was turned out of the village.

Kare-wa sono-mura-kara oi-dasareta.

(*vi.*) kekka-ga...ni-naru.

Everything turned out unfortunate.

Banji fukô-na-kekka-ni-natta.

turn over   ...o mekuru; ...o hikkuri-kaesu

Turn over the page.   Pêji-o mekuri-nasai.

turn round   furi-kaeru

She turned round and smiled at me.

Kano-jo-wa furi-kaette watashi-o-mite-hohoenda.

turn up   1)arawareru; yatte-kuru. 2)...o uwa-mukaseru. 3)...o ori-kaesu

1) He turned up toward evening.

Kare-wa higure-goro yatte-kita.

(*n.*) 1)magari-kado [曲がり角]. 2)kaiten [回転]. 3)henka [変化]. 4)jumban [順番].

(*3*) He has taken a favorable **turn**.

Kare-wa yoi-hô-e *henka*-shita.

Kare-wa kaihô-ni mukatta.

(*4*) I'll wait for my **turn**.   Watashi-wa *jumban*-o ma-tô.

by turns   kawaru-gawaru; kôtai-de

in turn   jumban-ni; tsugi-tsugi-ni

take turns   kôtai-de-suru

turning (*n.*) kaiten [回転]; magari-kado [曲がり角].

turning point　tenkan-ki［転換期］; kawari-me［変わり目］; bunki-ten
　　［分岐点］.

turnip (*n.*) (*bot.*) kabu［カブ］.

turnover (*n.*) 1)tempuku［転覆］. 2)ori-kaeshi［折り返し］.
　　(*a.*) ori-kaeshi-no［折り返しの］.

turnpike (*n.*) yûryô-dôro［有料道路］.

turnstile (*n.*) kaiten-kido［回転木戸］; kaiten-shiki-shussatsu-guchi
　　［回転式出札口］.

turpentine (*n.*) terebin-yu［テレビン油］; matsu-yani［松やに］.

turret (*n.*) (*arch.*) shô-tô［小塔］; taretto［タレット］.

turtle (*n.*) (*zool.*) umi-game［ウミガメ］.

tusk (*n.*) (zô nado no) kiba［(象などの)きば］.
　　(*vt.*) …o kiba-de-tsuku［…をきばで突く］; …o(-kiba-de) hori-
　　kaesu［…を(きばで)掘り返す］.

tutor (*n.*) katei-kyôshi［家庭教師］; ((*Eng.*))(daigaku no)〔kobetsu-〕
　　shidô-kyôkan〔(大学の)(個別)指導教官〕; chûtâ［チューター］.
　　(*vt.*) 1)…ni kojin-kyôju-o-suru［…に個人教授をする］. 2)…o
　　shitsukeru［…をしつける］.
　　(*vi.*) katei-kyôshi-o-suru［家庭教師をする］.

TV terebi［テレビ］.

twelfth (*n. & a.*) dai-jû-ni(-no)［第十二(の)］.

twelve (*n. & a.*) jû-ni(-no)［十二(の)］.

twentieth (*n. & a.*) dai-ni-jû(-no)［第二十(の)］.

twenty (*n. & a.*) ni-jû(-no)［二十(の)］.

twice (*ad.*) 1)ni-do［二度］. 2)ni-bai［-ni］［二倍(に)］.
　　(*1*) I take a walk **twice** a day.
　　　　Watashi-wa ichi-nichi-ni *ni-do* sampo-suru.
　　(*2*) It was **twice** as large as that.
　　　　Sore-wa are-no-*ni-bai*-no-ookisa-ga atta.

twig (*n.*) ko-eda［小枝］; hoso-eda［細枝］.

twilight (*n.*) usu-akari［薄明かり］; tasogare［たそがれ］.

twin (*n.*) 1)futago-no-hitori［双子の一人］. 2)(*pl.*) futago［双子］. 3)
　　ittsui-no-uchi-no-hitori[-hitotsu]［一対のうちの一人[一つ]］.
　　(*a.*) 1)futago-no［双子の］. 2)tsui-no［対の］.
　　(*vi.*) 1)futa-go-o-umu［双子を生む］. 2)tsui-o-nasu［対をなす］.
　　(*vt.*) …o tsui-ni-suru［…を対にする］.

twine (*n.*) yori-ito［より糸］; asa-ito［麻糸］.
　　(*vt.*) 1)…o yoru［…をよる］; …o yori-awasete(…o)-tsukuru［…

をより合わせて(…を)作る]. 2)...o karami-tsukaseru […をからみつかせる]. 3)...o maku […を巻く].
　　　(vi.) maki-tsuku [巻きつく].

twinkle (vi.) pika-pika-hikaru [ぴかぴか光る]; kirameku [きらめく].
　　　(vt.) ...o kira-kira-to-hikaraseru […をきらきらと光らせる].
　　　(n.) 1)kirameki [きらめき]; kagayaki [輝き]. 2)shunkan [瞬間].

twist (vt.) 1)...o yoru […をよる]. 2)...o maku […を巻く]. 3)...o nejiru […をねじる]. 4)...o yugameru […をゆがめる]. 5)...o kojitsukeru […をこじつける].
　　　(vi.) yoreru [よれる]; nejireru [ねじれる].
　　　(n.) 1)yori [より]. 2)nejire [ねじれ]. 3)nejiri-pan [ねじりパン].

twitter (n. & vi.) 1)saezuri (saezuru) [さえずり(さえずる)]. 2)kusu-kusu-warai (kusu-kusu-warau) [くすくす笑い(くすくす笑う)].

two (n. & a.) ni(-no) [二(の)].
　　a day or two   ichi-ryô-jitsu

two-tone (a.) 1)ni-shoku-no [二色の]. 2)tsûton-karâ-no [ツートンカラーの].

tympanic membrane (anat.) komaku [鼓膜].

type (n.) 1)kata [型]; ruikei [類型]; taipu [タイプ]. 2)tehon [手本]; mohan [模範]. 3)katsuji [活字]; jitai [字体].
　　　(vt.) 1)...o taipuraitâ-de-utsu […をタイプライターで打つ]; ...o taipu-suru […をタイプする]. 2)...o(...no)-kata-ni-bunrui-suru […を(…の)型に分類する].
　　　(vi.) taipuraitâ-o-utsu [タイプライターを打つ]; taipu-o-utsu [タイプを打つ].

typhlitis (n.) (med.) môchô-en [盲腸炎].

typhoid fever   chô-chifusu [腸チフス].

typhoon (n.) taifû [台風].

typhus (n.) (med.) hasshin-chifusu [発しんチフス].

typical (a.) 1)tenkei-teki-na [典型的な]; daihyô-teki-na [代表的な]. 2)tokuyû-no [特有の]; tokuchô-o-shimeshite-iru [特徴を示している].

tyranny (n.) sensei-seiji [専制政治]; bôsei [暴政].

tyrant (n.) 1)bôkun [暴君]; sensei-kunshu [専制君主]. 2)wamman [ワンマン].

U

UFO, U.F.O. mi-kakunin-hikô-buttai [未確認飛行物体].

ugly (*a.*) 1)minikui [醜い]; bu-kakkô-na [不かっ好な]. 2)iya-na [いやな]. 3)are-moyô-no [荒れ模様の].

U.K. Rengô-ôkoku [連合王国]; Eikoku [英国].

ulcer (*n.*) (*med.*) kaiyô [かいよう].

ultimate (*a.*) 1)saigo-no [最後の]; saishû-no [最終の]. 2)kompon-teki-na [根本的な].

    (*n.*) 1)(the –) kyûkyoku-ten [究極点]. 2)kihon-teki-jijitsu [基本的事実].

ultimately (*ad.*) kekkyoku [結局]; saishû-teki-ni [最終的に].

umbrella (*n.*) kasa [傘]; ama-gasa [雨傘].

umpire (*n.*) shimban-in [審判員]; ampaia [アンパイア].

    (*vt. & vi.*) (...no) shimban-o-suru [(…の)審判をする]; (...no) chûsai-sha-to-naru [(…の)仲裁者となる].

UN, U.N. Kokusai-rengô [国際連合].

unable (*a.*) ...deki-nai […できない].

unabridged (*a.*) shôryaku-shite-nai [省略してない]; kanzen-na [完全な].

unaccountable (*a.*) 1)setsumei-no-deki-nai [説明のできない]; wake-no-wakara-nai [訳のわからない]. 2)sekinin-ga-nai [責任がない]; bemmei-o-motomerare-nai [弁明を求められない].

unaccustomed (*a.*) narete-i-nai [慣れていない]; futsû-de-nai [普通でな

い].

unanimous (*a.*) manjô-itchi-no [満場一致の].

unavoidable (*a.*) sakerare-nai [避けられない]; yamu-o-e-nai [やむを得ない].

unbearable (*a.*) taerare-nai [耐えられない].

unbind (*vt.*) ...o toku […を解く]; ...o hodoku […をほどく]; ...o kaihô-suru […を解放する].

unbroken (*a.*) 1)kowarete-i-nai [壊れていない]. 2)(kiroku nado ga) yaburarete-i-nai [(記録などが)破られていない]. 3)(kisoku nado ga) mamorarete-iru [(規則などが)守られている]. 4)kujike-nai [くじけない].

unbutton (*vt.*) ...no botan-o-hazusu […のボタンをはずす]; (kokoro no naka)-o uchi-akeru [(心の中)を打ち明ける].
      (*vi.*) botan-o-hazusu [ボタンをはずす].

uncertain (*a.*) kakushin-ga-nai [確信がない]; hakkiri-shi-nai [はっきりしない]; fu-antei-na [不安定な].

unchanged (*a.*) kawara-nai [変わらない]; moto-no-mama-no [元のままの].

uncle (*n.*) oji [おじ].

unclean (*a.*) fuketsu-na [不潔な]; kegareta [汚れた].

uncomfortable (*a.*) kokochi-no-yoku-nai [心地のよくない].

uncommon (*a.*) 1)mare-na [まれな]; mezurashii [珍しい]. 2)ijô-na [異常な]; subarashii [すばらしい].

unconscious (*a.*) 1)ishiki-fumei-no [意識不明の]. 2)ki-zuka-nai [気づかない]. 3)mu-ishiki-no [無意識の].

uncountable (*a.*) musû-no [無数の]; kazoe-kire-nai-hodo-no [数え切れないほどの]; (*gram.*) fu-kasan-no [不可算の].
      (*n.*) (*gram.*) fu-kasan-meishi [不可算名詞].

uncover (*vt.*) 1)...no ooi-o-toru […の覆いを取る]. 2)...o bakuro-suru […を暴露する].
      (*vi.*) ooi[futa]-o-toru [覆い[ふた]を取る].

under (*prep.*) 1)...no-shita-ni […の下に]. 2)...miman-no […未満の]. 3)...no-moto-de […のもとで]. 4)...chû […中].
   (*1*) The vase is **under** the desk.
       Sono kabin wa tsukue-*no-shita-ni* aru.
   (*2*) No one **under** twenty is admitted.
       Ni-jussai-*miman-no*-hito wa nyûjô-o-kotowari.
     a monthly income **under** 500,000 yen
       go-jû-man-en-*miman-no* gesshû

(3) He is studying **under** Dr. Suzuki.

　　Kare-wa Suzuki-hakase-*no-moto-de* kenkyû-shiteiru.

(4) **under** repair　shûri-*chû*

　　(*ad.*) 1)shita-ni [下に]; shita-e [下へ]. 2)osaete [抑えて].

　　(*a.*) 1)shita-no [下の]; yori-sukunai [より少ない]; kai-no [下位の]. 2)shihai-sarete [支配されて].

underclothes (*n.*) shita-gi [下着]; hada-gi [肌着].

underdeveloped (*a.*) 1)hatsuiku-fuzen-no [発育不全の]. 2)kaihatsu-tojô-no [開発途上の].

undergo (*vt.*) ...o keiken-suru […を経験する]; ...o ukeru […を受ける].

undergraduate (*n.*) gakubu-gakusei [学部学生].

underground (*a.*) 1)chika-no [地下の]. 2)himitsu-no [秘密の]; higôhô-teki-na [非合法的な].

　　(*ad.*) 1)chika-ni [地下に]. 2)kakurete [隠れて]; hisonde [潜んで].

　　(*n.*) ((*Eng.*)) chika-tetsu [地下鉄].

undergrown (*a.*) 1)hatsuiku-fu-jûbun-na [発育不十分な]. 2)shita-bae-no-aru [下生えのある].

underline (*vt.*) ...ni kasen-o-hiku […に下線を引く].

　　(*n.*) andârain [アンダーライン]; kasen [下線].

undershirt (*n.*) shatsu [シャツ]; hada-gi [肌着].

understand (*vt.*) 1)...o rikai-suru […を理解する]; ...to ryôkai-suru […と了解する]; ...ga wakaru […がわかる]. 2)...to suisoku-suru […と推測する]; ...to omou […と思う].

(1) I don't **understand** you.

　　Watashi-wa kimi-no-iu-koto-*ga wakara*-nai.

(2) I **understand** him to be satisfied.

　　Watashi-wa kare ga manzoku-shite-iru-koto-*to omou*.

　　(*vi.*) wakaru [わかる]; yoku-shitte-iru [よく知っている]; rikai-o-shimesu [理解を示す].

understanding (*n.*) rikai(-ryoku) [理解(力)]; ryôkai [了解].

come to(arrive at) an understanding with ...to-gôi-ni-tassuru

　　(*a.*) fumbetsu-no-aru [分別のある]; omoi-yari-no-aru [思いやりのある].

undertake (*vt.*) 1)...o hiki-ukeru […を引き受ける]; ...o uke-au […を請け合う]; ...o hoshô-suru […を保証する]. 2)...o kuwadateru […を企てる].

undertaker (*n.*) 1)hiki-uke-nin [引受人]. 2)sôgiya [葬儀屋].

underwear (*n.*) hada-gi[-rui]［肌着(類)］; shita-gi[-rui]［下着(類)］.

underwriter (*n.*) 1)hoken-gyô-sha［保険業者］. 2)(shôken no) hiki-uke-nin［(証券の)引受人］; hoshô-nin［保証人］.

undeveloped (*a.*) mi-hattatsu-no［未発達の］; mi-kaihatsu-no［未開発の］; mijuku-na［未熟な］.

undo (*vt.*) 1)...o moto-doori-ni-suru［…を元どおりにする］. 2)...o hodoku［…をほどく］; ...o hiraku［…を開く］.
　　(*vi.*) hodokeru［ほどける］; hiraku［開く］.

undone (*a.*) mi-kansei-no［未完成の］.

leave...undone ...o hotte-oku; ...o chûto-de-yameru

undoubtedly (*ad.*) utagai-no-yochi-naku［疑いの余地なく］; tashika-ni［確かに］; akiraka-ni［明らかに］.

undress (*vt. & vi.*) ...no fuku-o-nugaseru (fuku-o-nugu)［…の服を脱がせる(服を脱ぐ)］.
　　　(*n.*) 1)heifuku［平服］. 2)hadaka［裸］.

unduly (*ad.*) futô-ni［不当に］.

uneasily (*ad.*) fuan-sô-ni［不安そうに］; kyûkutsu-sô-ni［窮屈そうに］; tôwaku-shite［当惑して］.

uneasy (*a.*) 1)fuan-na［不安な］; ki-ni-kakaru［気にかかる］; kyûkutsu-na［窮屈な］; raku-de-nai［楽でない］. 2)gikochi-nai［ぎこちない］.

unemployed (*a.*) 1)shitsugyô-shita［失業した］. 2)riyô-sarete-i-nai［利用されていない］.

unemployment (*n.*) 1)shitsugyô［失業］. 2)shitsugyô-sha-sû［失業者数］; shitsugyô-ritsu［失業率］.

unequal (*a.*) 1)hitoshiku-nai［等しくない］. 2)fu-kôhei-na［不公平な］. 3)tekisa-nai［適さない］. 4)fu-tsuri-ai-no［不釣り合いな］. 5)ichiyô-de-nai［一様でない］.

uneven (*a.*) 1)heitan-de-nai［平坦でない］; deko-boko-no-aru［でこぼこのある］; mura-no-aru［むらのある］. 2)gokaku-de-nai［互角でない］. 3)kisû-no［奇数の］.

unexpected (*a.*) igai-na［意外な］; omoigakenai［思い掛けない］.

unexpectedly (*ad.*) omoigakenaku［思い掛けなく］; fui-ni［不意に］.

unfavo(u)rable (*a.*) 1)tsugô-no-warui［都合の悪い］; konomashiku-nai［好ましくない］. 2)kôi-teki-de-nai［好意的でない］; hantai-no［反対の］.

unfit (*a.*) fu-tekitô-na［不適当な］; fumuki-na［不向きな］.

unfold (*vt. & vi.*) (...o) hiraku［(…を)開く］; ...o hirogeru (hirogaru)［…を広げる(広がる)］.

unfortunate (*a.*) 1)fukô-na [不幸な]; fuun-na [不運な]. 2)fu-shubi-no [不首尾の]. 3)fu-tekitô-na [不適当な].

        (*n.*) fuun-na-hito [不運な人].

unfortunately (*ad.*) 1)fuun-ni-mo [不運にも]; ainiku [あいにく].

ungrateful (*a.*) 1)on-shirazu-no [恩知らずの]. 2)iya-na [いやな].

unhappily (*ad.*) 1)fukô-ni[-mo] [不幸に(も)]; fuun-ni[-mo] [不運に(も)]. 2)fu-tekisetsu-ni [不適切に]; mazuku [まずく].

unhappy (*a.*) 1)fukô-na [不幸な]. 2)fu-tekisetsu-na [不適切な]; mazui [まずい].

unharmed (*a.*) kizu-o-ukete-i-nai [傷を受けていない]; buji-na [無事な].

unhealthy (*a.*) 1)fu-kenkô-na [不健康な]; fu-kenzen-na [不健全な]. 2) kenkô-ni-warui [健康に悪い].

uniform (*a.*) ichiyô-na [一様な]; soroi-no [そろいの]; ittei-no [一定の]; kawaru-koto-no-nai [変わることのない].

        (*n.*) seifuku [制服]; yunifômu [ユニフォーム].

        (*vt.*) 1)...o ichiyô-ni-suru [...を一様にする]. 2)...ni seifuku-o-kiseru [...に制服を着せる].

unimportant (*a.*) jûyô-de-nai [重要でない]; toru-ni-tari-nai [取るに足りない].

union (*n.*) 1)dômei [同盟]; kumiai [組合]. 2)rengô-shita-mono [連合したもの]. 3)itchi [一致].

unique (*a.*) tada-hitotsu-no [ただ一つの]; dokutoku-no [独特の]; muhi-no [無比の].

unit (*n.*) 1)hitotsu-no-mono [一つのもの]; ikko [一個]. 2)tan'i [単位]; tangen [単元]. 3)(*mil.*) butai [部隊].

unite (*vt. & vi.*) ...o ketsugô-suru (ketsugô-suru) [...を結合する(結合する)]; ...o-gappei-saseru (gappei-suru) [...を合併させる(合併する)].

united (*a.*) rengô-shita [連合した]; danketsu-shita [団結した]; musubareta [結ばれた].

United Kingdom, the Rengô-ôkoku [連合王国]; Eikoku [英国].

United Nations, the Kokusai-rengô [国際連合].

United States of America, the Amerika-gasshû-koku [アメリカ合衆国].

unit price tanka [単価].

unity (*n.*) 1)tôitsu [統一]. 2)itchi [一致]; chôwa [調和]; matomari [まとまり].

universal (*a.*) 1)zen-sekai-no [全世界の]. 2)ippan-teki-na [一般的な]; fuhen-teki-na [普遍的な]; bannô-no [万能の]. 3)uchû-no [宇宙の].

universe (*n.*) 1)(the –) uchû [宇宙]; zen-sekai [全世界]. 2)ryôiki
university (*n.*) sôgô-daigaku [総合大学].   └[領域].
unjust (*a.*) fusei-na [不正な]; fu-kôhei-na [不公平な].
unkempt (*a.*) 1)darashi-no-nai [だらしのない]. 2)kushi-o-irete-i-nai
　[くしを入れていない]. 3)teire-o-shite-i-nai [手入れをしていない].
unkind (*a.*) fu-shinsetsu-na [不親切な].
unknown (*a.*) shirarete-i-nai [知られていない]; michi-no [未知の];
　mumei-no [無名の]; mi-kakunin-no [未確認の].
　　　　(*n.*) shirarete-i-nai-hito[-mono] [知られていない人[もの]].
unlearn (*vt.*) 1)...o jibun-kara-wasureru [⋯を自分から忘れる]. 2)...o
　waza-to-suteru [⋯をわざと捨てる].
unleash (*vt.*) 1)...no kawa-himo-o-toku [⋯の革ひもを解く]. 2)...no
　sokubaku-o-toku [⋯の束縛を解く].
unless (*conj.*) moshi...de-nake-reba [もし⋯でなければ].
　　　　(*prep.*) ...igai-ni [⋯以外に]; ...o-nozoite-wa [⋯を除いては].
unlike (*a.*) chigatta [違った]; nite-i-nai [似ていない].
　　　　(*prep.*) ...to-chigatte [⋯と違って]; ...ni-nite-i-nai-de [⋯に似て
　いないで]; ...rashiku-nai [⋯らしくない].
unlikely (*a.*) ari-sô-mo-nai [ありそうもない]; mikomi-no-nai [見込み
　のない].
unload (*vt.*) 1)(ni)-o orosu [(荷)を降ろす]. 2)...no dangan-o-nuku [⋯
　の弾丸を抜く].
　　　　(*vi.*) ni-oroshi-o-suru [荷降ろしをする]; dangan-o-nuki-toru
　[弾丸を抜き取る].
unlock (*vt. & vi.*) ...no jô-o-akeru (jô-ga-aku) [⋯の錠を開ける(錠が
　開く)].
unlucky (*a.*) 1)un-ga-warui [運が悪い]. 2)fukitsu-na [不吉な]. 3)
　zannen-na [残念な].
unmarried (*a.*) mikon-no [未婚の]; dokushin-no [独身の].
unnatural (*a.*) 1)fu-shizen-na [不自然な]. 2)ninjô-ni-hansuru [人情に
　反する]. 3)jin'i-teki-na [人為的な].
unnecessary (*a.*) fu-hitsuyô-na [不必要な].
unoccupied (*a.*) 1)shigoto-o-shite-i-nai [仕事をしていない]; hima-na
　[暇な]. 2)aite-iru [空いている].
unofficial (*a.*) hi-kôshiki-na [非公式な]; shi-teki-na [私的な].
unorganized (*a.*) mi-soshiki-no [未組織の].
unpack (*vt.*) (tsutsumi)-o toku [(包み)を解く].
　　　　(*vi.*) ni-o-toku [荷を解く]; naka-no-mono-o-tori-dasu [中の物

を取り出す].

unpleasant (*a.*) fu-yukai-na [不愉快な]; iya-na [いやな].

unprecedented (*a.*) senrei-no-nai [先例のない]; kûzen-no [空前の].

unravel (*vt.*) (motsure)-o toku [(もつれ)を解く]; …o hogusu […をほぐす].

　　　(*vi.*) tokeru [解ける]; hogureru [ほぐれる].

unreasonable (*a.*) 1)fu-gôri-na [不合理な]. 2)hôgai-na [法外な]; tohô-mo-nai [途方もない].

unreliable (*a.*) shinrai-deki-nai [信頼できない]; ate-ni-nara-nai [当てにならない].

unreserved (*a.*) 1)enryo-no-nai [遠慮のない]; sotchoku-na [率直な]. 2)seigen-no-nai [制限のない]. 3)(zaseki ga) yoyaku-shite-i-nai [(座席が)予約していない]; jiyû-seki-no [自由席の].

unrest (*n.*) fuan [不安]; fuon [不穏].

unriddle (*vt.*) (nazo)-o toku [(なぞ)を解く].

unroll (*vt.*) (maita-mono)-o toku [(巻いたもの)を解く]; …o hirogeru […を広げる].

unruly (*a.*) 1)shimatsu-ni-oe-nai [始末におえない]. 2)(mono ga) basho-ni-osamari-nikui [(物が)場所に収まりにくい].

unsatisfactory (*a.*) fu-manzoku-na [不満足な]; fu-jûbun-na [不十分な].

unsay (*vt.*) (zengen)-o tori-kesu [(前言)を取り消す].

unseal (*vt.*) 1)…no fû-o-kiru […の封を切る]; …o kaifû-suru […を開封する]. 2)…o jiyû-ni-suru […を自由にする].

unseasonable (*a.*) 1)kisetsu-hazure-no [季節外れの]; fujun-na [不順な]. 2)jiki-o-ayamatta [時機を誤った].

unselfish (*a.*) riko-teki-de-nai [利己的でない]; muyoku-na [無欲な].

unsettled (*a.*) 1)kawari-yasui [変わりやすい]; fu-antei-na [不安定な]. 2)mi-kessai-no [未決済の].

unsparing (*a.*) 1)kibishii [厳しい]. 2)kechi-kechi-shi-nai [けちけちしない].

unspeakable (*a.*) 1)kotoba-ni-arawase-nai [ことばに表せない]. 2)hidoku-warui [ひどく悪い].

unsuccessful (*a.*) fu-seikô-no [不成功の]; shippai-shita [失敗した].

untangle (*vt.*) (motsure)-o toku [(もつれ)を解く]; …o kaiketsu-suru […を解決する].

untidy (*a.*) darashi-no-nai [だらしのない]; ranzatsu-na [乱雑な].

untie (*vt.*) 1)…o toku […を解く]; …o hodoku […をほどく]. 2)…o kaihô-suru […を解放する]. 3)…o kaiketsu-suru […を解決する].

(*vi.*) tokeru [解ける]; hodokeru [ほどける].

until (*prep. & conj.*) 1)...made [...まで]. 2)yagate [やがて]; tsui-ni [ついに].

(*1*) I'll wait for her **until** four.
   Watashi-wa yo-ji-*made* kano-jo-o matô.
   I'll wait **until** he comes back.
   Watashi-wa kare-ga kaette-kuru-*made* matô.

(*2*) They walked and walked, **until** they found a light in the distance.
   Kare-ra-wa don-don-aruite, *tsui-ni* tooku-ni akari-o mitsuketa.

not...until ...made-nai; ...ni-natte-hajimete...(suru)

untrue (*a.*) shinjitsu-de-nai [真実でない]; fu-seijitsu-na [不誠実な]; fu-seikaku-na [不正確な].

untruth (*n.*) uso [うそ].

unusual (*a.*) futsû-de-nai [普通でない]; ijô-na [異常な]; mezurashii [珍しい].

unusually (*ad.*) ijô-ni [異常に]; hijô-ni [非常に]; mezurashiku [珍しく].

unwelcome (*a.*) kangei-sare-nai [歓迎されない]; iya-na [いやな].

unwilling (*a.*) ki-ga-susuma-nai [気が進まない]; iya-iya-nagara-no [いやいやながらの].

unwind (*vt.*) ...o hodoku [...をほどく].
   (*vi.*) 1)hodokeru [ほどける]. 2)(hanashi nado ga) hakkiri-suru [(話などが)はっきりする]. 3)(*colloq.*) kutsurogu [くつろぐ].

unwise (*a.*) mu-fumbetsu-na [無分別な]; ukatsu-na [うかつな].

unwittingly (*ad.*) shirazu-ni [知らずに].

unworthy (*a.*) 1)...ni-atai-shi-nai [...に値しない]; ...ni-fusawashiku-nai [...にふさわしくない]. 2)hazu-beki [恥ずべき].

unzip (*vt. & vi.*) ...no jippâ-o-akeru (jippâ-ga-hiraku) [...のジッパーを開ける(ジッパーが開く)].

up (*ad.*) 1)ue-ni [上に]; ue-e [上へ]. 2)agatte [上がって]. 3)okite [起きて]. 4)sukkari [すっかり]; mattaku [全く]; tsukite [尽きて].

(*1*) What is **up** in the tree? Ki no *ue-ni* nani-ga-arimasu-ka?

(*2*) The sun is **up**. Taiyô wa *nobotte*-iru.

(*3*) I sat **up** late last night.
   Watashi-wa sakuya osoku-made *okite*-ita.

(*4*) He drank it **up**. Kare-wa sore-o nomi-*hoshita*.

    The time is **up**. Jikan ga *kireta*.

up and down jôge-ni; ittari-kitari

up to 1)...made; ...ni-itaru-made. 2)(*colloq.*)...no-sekinin-de

 1) up to the present day konnichi-ni-itaru-made

 2) It's up to you to decide it.

    Sore-o kimeru-no-wa kimi-no-sekinin-da.

    It's up to you. Sore-wa kimi-shidai-da.

               (Kimi-ga-kime-nasai.)

   (*prep.*) 1)...no-ue-e […の上へ]; ...no-ue-ni […の上に]; ...o-nobotte […をのぼって]. 2)...ni-sotte […に沿って].

 (*1*) We rowed **up** the river. Ware-ware-wa kawa-o kogi-*nobotta*.

 (*2*) Go straight **up** this bank.

    Kono-dote-*ni-sotte* massugu iki-nasai.

   (*a.*) 1)((*Eng.*)) nobori-no [上りの]. 2)ue-e-no [上への].

   (*n.*) nobori [上り]; jôshô [上昇]; nobori-ressha[-basu/-erebêtâ] [上り列車[バス/エレベーター]].

   (*vi.*) 1)tachi-agaru [立ち上がる]. 2)fui-ni...(suru) [不意に…(する)].

   (*vt.*) 1)...o mochi-ageru […を持ち上げる]. 2)...o ageru […を上げる]; ...o masu […を増す].

upbraid (*vt.*) ...o hinan-suru […を非難する]; ...o togameru […をとがめる].

uphold (*vt.*) ...o shiji-suru […を支持する].

upholster (*vt.*) (heya)-o kâten-nado-de-kazaru [(部屋)をカーテンなどで飾る].

upon (*prep.*) ...no-ue-ni […の上に]; ...no-ue-e […の上へ].

upper (*a.*) ue-no [上の]; jôbu-no [上部の].

Upper House, the jôin [上院].

upperclassman (*n.*) ((*US*)) jôkyû-sei [上級生].

uppermost (*a.*) saijô-no [最上の]; saikô-no [最高の]; ichiban-ue-no [一番上の].

    (*ad.*) saikô-ni [最高に]; ichiban-ue-ni [一番上に]; ichiban-hajime-ni [一番初めに].

upright (*a.*) 1)massugu-na [真っすぐな]; chokuritsu-shita [直立した]. 2)tadashii [正しい]; shôjiki-na [正直な].

    (*ad.*) massugu-ni [真っすぐに]; chokuritsu-shite [直立して].

    (*n.*) suichoku [垂直].

uproar (*n.*) oo-sawagi [大騒ぎ].

uproot (*vt.*) 1)...o ne-kosogi-ni-suru […を根こそぎにする]. 2)...o oitateru […を追い立てる]. 3)…o konzetsu-suru […を根絶する].

upset (*vt.*) 1)…o hikkuri-kaesu […を引っくり返す]; …o tempuku-saseru […を転覆させる]. 2)…o urotae-saseru […をうろたえさせる]; …no ki-o-tentô-saseru […の気を転倒させる]. 3)…no-chôshi-o kuruwaseru […の調子を狂わせる].

(*1*) He **upset** the vase. Kare-wa kabin-*o hikkuri-kaeshita*.

(*2*) I **was upset** to hear the news of his death.
　　Watashi-wa kare-no shi no shirase-o-kiite *ki-ga-tentô-shita*.

(*3*) A cold drink always **upsets** my stomach.
　　Tsumetai nomi-mono wa itsu-mo watashi-no i-*no-chôshi-o okashiku-suru*.

(*vi.*) hikkuri-kaeru [引っくり返る]; tempuku-suru [転覆する].

(*n.*) 1)tempuku [転覆]. 2)konran [混乱]. 3)(i nado no) fuchô [(胃などの)不調].

(*a.*) tempuku-shita [転覆した]; konran-shita [混乱した]; fuchô-no [不調の].

upside (*n.*) ue-gawa [上側]; jôbu [上部].

upside down sakasama-ni

upstairs (*ad.*) kaijô-e[-de] [階上へ[で]]; ni-kai-e[-de] [二階へ[で]].

(*a.*) kaijô-no [階上の]; ni-kai-no [二階の].

(*n.*) 1)kaijô [階上]; ni-kai [二階]. 2)nobori-kaidan [上り階段].

up-to-date (*a.*) saishin-no [最新の]; gendai-teki-na [現代的な].

uptown (*ad. & a.*) yama-no-te-ni(-no) [山の手に(の)].

(*n.*) yama-no-te [山の手]; jûtaku-chiku [住宅地区].

upward (*a.*) uwa-muki-no [上向きの].

(*ad.*) 1)ue-no-hô-e [上の方へ]. 2)yori-ooku [より多く]. 3) saka-nobotte [さかのぼって].

uranium (*n.*) uraniumu [ウラニウム].

urban (*a.*) toshi-no [都市の]; toshi-tokuyû-no [都市特有の].

urchin (*n.*) wampaku-shônen [わんぱく少年].

urge (*vt.*) 1)…o seki-tateru […をせきたてる]. 2)…o suishin-suru […を推進する]. 3)…ni settoku-suru […に説得する]. 4)…o shuchô-suru […を主張する].

(*vi.*) 1)shigeki-suru [刺激する]. 2)shuchô-suru [主張する].

(*n.*) shôdô [衝動].

urgent (*a.*) 1)kinkyû-no [緊急の]; sashi-sematta [差し迫った]. 2)

saisoku-suru [催促する].

urinate (*vi.*) shôben-o-suru [小便をする].

urticaria (*n.*) (*path.*) jimmashin [じんましん].

us (*pron.*) ware-ware-o [われわれを]; ware-ware-ni [われわれに].

U.S.A. Amerika-gasshû-koku [アメリカ合衆国].

usage (*n.*) 1)shiyô-hô [使用法]; tori-atsukai-kata [取り扱い方]. 2) kanshû [慣習]; kan'yô-hô [慣用法].

use (*n.*) 1)shiyô [使用]. 2)kôyô [効用]; yûyô [有用]; yaku-ni-tatsu-koto [役に立つこと]. 3)yôto [用途]; tsukai-michi [使い道].

  (*1*) things for daily **use**   nichijô-*shiyô-hin*
                                   nichiyô-hin

  (*2*) Oil is of great **use** to us.
       Abura wa ware-ware-ni hijô-ni-*yaku-ni-tatsu*.

  (*3*) I have found a **use** of this money.
       Watashi-wa kono kane no *tsukai-michi*-o mitsuketa.

  make use of ...o shiyô-suru; ...o riyô-suru

  of no use yaku-ni-tata-nai

  of use yaku-ni-tatsu; yûyô-na

  (*vt.*) 1)...o mochiiru [...を用いる]. 2)...o tori-atsukau [...を取り扱う].

  (*1*) Cutting paper, we **use** a paperknife.
       Kami-o-kiru-toki-ni,   ware-ware-wa   kami-kiri-naifu-*o mochiiru*.

  (*2*) He **used** his dog cruelly.   Kare-wa inu-o gyaku*tai-shita*.

  use up ...o tsukai-hatasu

used (*a.*) ...ni-narete [...に慣れて].

  I got **used** to hard work.
       Watashi-wa tsurai-shigoto-*ni nareta*.

  used to yoku...(shita-)mono-da [よく...(した)ものだ]

    He **used to** visit us.
       Kare-wa *yoku* ware-ware-o tazunete-*kita-mono-da*.

used (*a.*) chûko-no [中古の]; sekohan-no [せこはんの]; shiyô-zumi-no [使用済みの].

useful (*a.*) yaku-ni-tatsu [役に立つ]; yûyô-na [有用な].

useless (*a.*) yaku-ni-tata-nai [役に立たない]; mu-eki-na [無益な].

user (*n.*) shiyô-sha [使用者].

usher (*n.*) 1)annai-gakari [案内係]. 2)((*US*)) (kekkon-shiki de no) otoko-no-tsuki-soi-nin [(結婚式での)男の付き添い人].

    (*vt.*) ...o annai-suru [⋯を案内する].

usual (*a.*) futsû-no [普通の]; itsumo-no [いつもの].

  as usual rei-no-toori; ai-kawarazu; itsu-mo-no-yô-ni

    (*n.*) itsu-mo-no-koto [いつものこと]; o-kimari-no-mono [お決まりのもの].

usually (*ad.*) futsû [普通]; itsu-mo-wa [いつもは].

usurp (*vt.*) ...o ubau [⋯を奪う]; ...o gôdatsu-suru [⋯を強奪する].

    (*vi.*) shingai-suru [侵害する].

utensil (*n.*) (katei-)yôhin [(家庭)用品]; kigu [器具]; dôgu [道具].

utility (*n.*) 1)yaku-ni-tatsu-koto [役に立つこと]; kôyô [効用]. 2)

    (*pl.*) jitsuyô-hin [実用品].

utmost (*a.*) saidai-no [最大の]; kyokudo-no [極度の].

    (*n.*) saidai-gen [最大限]; kyokugen [極限].

  do one's utmost saizen-o-tsukusu

utter (*a.*) mattaku-no [全くの]; kanzen-na [完全な].

utter (*vt.*) ...o hassuru [⋯を発する]; ...o noberu [⋯を述べる].

utterly (*ad.*) sukkari [すっかり]; zenzen [全然].

V

vacancy (*n.*) 1)aita-tokoro [空いた所]; kû [空]. 2)ketsuin [欠員]; kûseki [空席].

vacant (*a.*) 1)kara-no [からの]; aite-iru [空いている]. 2)bon'yari-shita [ぼんやりした].

vacate (*vt.*) 1)...o akeru [...を空ける]. 2)...o shirizoku [...を退く].
 (*vi.*) 1)akeru [空ける]. 2)jinin-suru [辞任する].

vacation (*n.*) 1)yasumi [休み]; kyûka [休暇]. 2)(ie nado no) ake-watashi [(家などの)明け渡し]; jishoku [辞職].

vaccinate (*vt.*) ...ni wakuchin-sesshu-o-suru [...にワクチン接種をする]; ...ni shutô-o-suru [...に種痘をする]; ...ni yobô-sesshu-o-suru [...に予防接種をする].
 (*vi.*) shutô-o-suru [種痘をする].

vaccination (*n.*) 1)wakuchin-sesshu [ワクチン接種]; shutô [種痘]; yobô-sesshu [予防接種]. 2)shutô-no-ato [種痘のあと].

vaccine (*n.*) (*med.*) wakuchin [ワクチン]; tôbyô [種苗].

vacuum (*n.*) 1)shinkû [真空]. 2) = vacuum cleaner　denki-sôji-ki [電気掃除機].
 (*vt. & vi.*) (*colloq.*)(...ni) denki-sôji-ki-o-kakeru [(...に)電気掃除機をかける].

vacuum bottle mahô-bin [魔法びん].

vacuum tube shinkû-kan [真空管].

vagabond (*n.*) hôrô-sha [放浪者].
 (*vi.*) hôrô-suru [放浪する]; hôrô-seikatsu-o-suru [放浪生活をする].

vague (*a.*) aimai-na [あいまいな]; bakuzen-to-shita [漠然とした].

vain (*a.*) 1)muda-na [無駄な]. 2)kyoei-shin-no-tsuyoi [虚栄心の強い].
 in vain muda-ni; munashiku

vainly (*ad.*) 1)muda-ni [無駄に]. 2)unuborete [うぬぼれて].

Valentine's day, Saint Sei-Barentain-no-shukujitsu [聖バレンタインの祝日].

valet (*n.*) jûsha [従者]; tsuki-bito [付き人].
 (*vt. & vi.*) (...ni) jûsha-to-shite-tsukaeru [(...に)従者として仕える].

valiant (*a.*) yûkan-na [勇敢な]; ooshii [雄々しい].
 (*n.*) yûkan-na-hito [勇敢な人].

valley (*n.*) 1)tani [谷]; tani-ma [谷間]. 2)ryûiki [流域].

valuable (*a.*) 1)kôka-na [高価な]; kichô-na [貴重な]. 2)hyôka-dekiru [評価できる].
 (*n.*) (*pl.*) kichô-hin [貴重品].

value (*n.*) 1)kachi [価値]. 2)kakaku [価格]. 3)hyôka [評価]. 4)(*math.*) sûchi [数値]. 5)imi [意味]; igi [意義].
 of no value kachi-no-nai

of value kachi-no-aru

   (*vt.*) 1)...o hyôka-suru [⋯を評価する]. 2)...o sonchô-suru [⋯を尊重する].

valve (*n.*) ben [弁]; barubu [バルブ].

van (*n.*) 1)yûgai-torakku [有蓋トラック]; ban [バン]. 2)((*Eng.*)) yûgai-kasha [有蓋貨車].

   (*vt.*) ...o ban-de-umpan-suru [⋯をバンで運搬する].

   (*vi.*) ban-de-iku [バンで行く].

vane (*n.*) kazami [風見]; hane [羽根]; bên [ベーン].

vanish (*vi.*) mie-naku-naru [見えなくなる]; kieru [消える]; usureru [薄れる].

   (*vt.*) ...o kesu [⋯を消す]; ...o mie-naku-suru [⋯を見えなくする].

vanity (*n.*) 1)kûkyo [空虚]; munashisa [むなしさ]. 2)kyoei-shin [虚栄心]; unubore [うぬぼれ]. 3)kyoshoku [虚飾].

vapor, -pour (*n.*) 1)jôki [蒸気]. 2)kyûnyû-yaku [吸入薬].

   (*vi.*) jôki-o-hassuru [蒸気を発する].

   (*vt.*) ...o jôhatsu-saseru [⋯を蒸発させる]; ...o jôki-ni-suru [⋯を蒸気にする].

variable (*a.*) kawari-yasui [変わりやすい]; kahen-no [可変の].

   (*n.*) (*math.*) hensû [変数].

variation (*n.*) 1)henka [変化]; hendô [変動]. 2)sai [差異]. 3)henshu [変種].

varied (*a.*) 1)samazama-na [さまざまな]; henka-ni-tonda [変化に富んだ]. 2)kaerareta [変えられた].

variety (*n.*) 1)henka [変化]; tayô[-sei] [多様(性)]. 2)shurui [種類]. 3)(*biol.*) henshu [変種].

various (*a.*) 1)iro-iro-na [いろいろな]; sûshu-no-kotonatta [数種の異なった]. 2)ikutsu-ka-no [いくつかの].

varnish (*n.*) nisu [ニス].

   (*vt.*) ...ni nisu-o-nuru [⋯にニスを塗る].

vary (*vt.*) 1)...o kaeru [⋯を変える]. 2)...o tayô-ni-suru [⋯を多様にする].

   (*vi.*) 1)kawaru [変わる]; samazama-de-aru [さまざまである]; kotonaru [異なる]. 2)hazureru [外れる].

vase (*n.*) kabin [花びん]; (sôshoku-yô no)tsubo [(装飾用の)つぼ].

Vaseline (*n.*) (*chem.*) waserin [ワセリン].

vast (*a.*) 1)kôdai-na [広大な]; hateshi-no-nai [果てしのない]. 2)

obitadashii [おびただしい].

vault (*n.*) maru-tenjô [丸天井]; âchi-gata-tenjô [アーチ形天井].

veal (*n.*) ko-ushi-no-niku [子牛の肉].

vegetable (*n.*) yasai [野菜]; shokubutsu [植物].
　　　(*a.*) shokubutsu(-sei)-no [植物(性)の].

vegetation (*n.*) shokubutsu [植物]; sômoku [草木].

vehicle (*n.*) 1)kuruma [車]; nori-mono [乗り物]; yusô-kikan [輸送機関]. 2)dentatsu-no-shudan [伝達の手段]; baitai [媒体].

veil (*n.*) bêru [ベール].
　　　(*vt.*) ...ni bêru-o-kakeru […にベールをかける]; ...o kakusu […を隠す].
　　　(*vi.*) bêru-o-kaburu [ベールをかぶる].

vein (*n.*) 1)jômyaku [静脈]; kekkan [血管]. 2)(ichiji-teki na) kibun [(一時的な)気分]. 3)keikô [傾向].
　　　(*vt.*) ...ni myaku[suji]-o-tsukeru […に脈[筋]を付ける].

velocity (*n.*) hayasa [速さ]; (*phys.*) sokudo [速度].

velvet (*n.*) birôdo [ビロード]; berubetto [ベルベット].

vending machine jidô-hambai-ki [自動販売機].

vendor, vender (*n.*) 1)(*law*) uri-te [売り手]. 2) = vending machine jidô-hambai-ki [自動販売機].

venison (*n.*) shika-no-niku [シカの肉].

ventilate (*vt.*) 1)...o kanki-suru […を換気する]. 2)(mondai nado)-o giron-ni-noseru [(問題など)を議論にのせる]; ...o yo-ni-tou […を世に問う].

ventilation (*n.*) 1)tsûfû [通風]; kanki [換気]. 2)kôkai-tôgi [公開討議]; hyômei [表明].

ventilator (*n.*) kanki-mado [換気窓]; kûki-chôsetsu-sôchi [空気調節装置].

venture (*vt.*) 1)...o kiken-ni-sarasu […を危険にさらす]. 2)omoi-kitte... (suru) [思い切って…(する)]; aete...(suru) [あえて…(する)].
　　　(*vi.*) 1)kiken-o-okashite(-suru) [危険を冒して(する)]. 2)omoi-kitte(-suru) [思いきって(する)].
　　　(*n.*) 1)bôken [冒険]; bôken-teki-na-jigyô [冒険的な事業]. 2)tôki [投機].

verb (*n.*) (*gram.*) dôshi [動詞].

verbal (*a.*) 1)kotoba-no [ことばの]; kotoba-no-ue-dake-no [ことばの上だけの]; kôtô-no [口頭の]. 2)(*gram.*) dôshi-no [動詞の].
　　　(*n.*) (*gram.*) jun-dôshi [準動詞].

verdict (*n.*) 1)(*law*) hyôketsu [評決]; tôshin [答申]. 2)(*colloq.*) iken [意見].

verge (*n.*) magiwa [間際]; fuchi [縁]; hashi [端].
  on the verge of ...no-setogiwa-ni; ima-ni-mo...(shi-)yô-to-shite

verify (*vt.*) ...o tashikameru [···を確かめる]; ...ga-jijitsu-de-aru-koto-o kakushô-suru [···が事実であることを確証する].

verse (*n.*) shiika [詩歌]; imbun [韻文]; (shi no) setsu [(詩の)節].

versed (*a.*) seitsû-shita [精通した].

version (*n.*) 1)hon'yaku [翻訳]; yakubun [訳文]; ...han [···版]. 2) setsumei [説明]; kaishaku [解釈].

vertical (*a.*) suichoku-no [垂直の]; chokuritsu-shita [直立した]; tate-no [縦の].
  (*n.*) suichoku-sen [垂直線].

very (*ad.*) 1)hijô-ni [非常に]. 2)hontô-ni [本当に].
  not very amari...de-nai
    (*a.*) 1)mattaku-no [全くの]. 2)...koso-masa-ni-sono [···こそまさにその].
    (*1*) He has shown himself a **very** knave.
      Kare-wa *mattaku-no* akutô de-aru-koto-o mi-o-motte-shimeshita.
    (*2*) This is the **very** thing I want.
      Kore-*koso-masa-ni* watashi-ga nozomu-mono-da.

vessel (*n.*) 1)yôki [容器]; utsuwa [うつわ]. 2)fune [船].

vest (*n.*) ((*US*)) chokki [チョッキ]; besuto [ベスト]; ((*Eng.*)) hada-gi [肌着]; shatsu [シャツ].
  (*vt.*) 1)...ni ifuku-o-kiseru [···に衣服を着せる]. 2)...ni sazukeru [···に授ける].
  (*vi.*) 1)ifuku-o-kiru [衣服を着る]. 2)kizoku-suru [帰属する].

veteran (*n.*) beteran [ベテラン]; kosan-hei [古参兵]; ((*US*)) taieki-gunjin [退役軍人].
  (*a.*) beteran-no [ベテランの]; rôren-na [老練な].

veto (*n.*) kyohi-ken [拒否権].
  (*vt.*) ...ni-taishi kyohi-ken-o-kôshi-suru [···に対し拒否権を行使する].

vex (*vt.*) 1)...o ira-ira-saseru [···をいらいらさせる]; ...o okoraseru [···を怒らせる]. 2)...o ooi-ni-giron-suru [···を大いに議論する].

vexation (*n.*) 1)ira-ira-saseru-koto [いらいらさせること]; haradatashi-sa [腹立たしさ]. 2)iradachi-no-tane [いらだちの種].

via (*prep.*) 1)...keiyu-de [···経由で]. 2)...ni-yotte [···によって]; ...o-tooshite [···を通して].

vibrate (*vi. & vt.*) shindô-suru(...o shindô-saseru) [震動する(···を震動させる)]; yureru(...o yuri-ugokasu) [揺れる(···を揺り動かす)].

vibration (*n.*) 1)shindô [震動]. 2)(*pl.*)(*colloq.*)(hito ya mono nado kara ukeru) kanji [(人や物などから受ける)感じ]; inshô [印象]. 3) (kokoro no) dôyô [(心の)動揺].

vice (*n.*) 1)akutoku [悪徳]; fu-dôtoku [不道徳]. 2)ketten [欠点].

vice- (*pref.*) fuku... [副···]; ...dairi [···代理].

vice-chairperson (*n.*) fuku-gichô [副議長]; fuku-iin-chô [副委員長].

vice-consul (*n.*) fuku-ryôji [副領事].

vice-president (*n.*) fuku-daitôryô [副大統領]; fuku-sôsai [副総裁]; fuku-kaichô [副会長]; fuku-shachô [副社長].

vicinity (*n.*) 1)kinjo [近所]; fukin [付近]. 2)kinsetsu [近接].
   in the vicinity of ...no-chikaku-ni; oyoso...de[...no]

vicious (*a.*) 1)akui-no-aru [悪意のある]. 2)kuse-no-warui [癖の悪い]. 3) (*colloq.*) hidoi [ひどい]. 4)(suiron nado ga) kekkan-no-aru [(推論などが)欠陥のある].

victim (*n.*) gisei[-sha] [犠牲(者)]; hisai-sha [被災者].
   fall a victim to ...no gisei-to-naru

victor (*n.*) shôri-sha [勝利者].

victorious (*a.*) shôri-o-eta [勝利を得た]; shôri-o-shimesu [勝利を示す].

victory (*n.*) 1)shôri [勝利]; senshô [戦勝]. 2)seifuku [征服].

vie (*vi.*) kyôsô-suru [競争する]; hari-au [張り合う].

Vietnam (*n.*) Betonamu [ベトナム].

view (*n.*) 1)miru-koto [見ること]; shikai [視界]. 2)shisatsu [視察]; kembun [検分]. 3)nagame [眺め]; keshiki [景色]; mi-harashi [見晴らし]. 4)iken [意見]; kenkai [見解]. 5)mokuteki [目的]; mokuromi [もくろみ].
   (*1*) Here we have a good **view** of the stage.
      Koko-kara-wa butai ga yoku *mieru*.
   (*2*) They had a **view** of new buildings.
      Kare-ra-wa atarashii tate-mono-o-*mite-mawatta*.
   (*3*) a fine **view** of the lake   mizuumi no utsukushii *keshiki*
      I want a house with a **view** of the sea.
      Umi-no-*mi-harashi*-no-kiku-ie-ga ikken hoshii.
   (*4*) My **views** are quite opposite to yours.
      Watashi-no *iken* wa kimi-no-to-wa sei-hantai-da.

(5) She had a **view** of going to Italy.
　　　Kano-jo-wa Itaria-e-iku-koto-o-*mokuron*-de-ita.
　　(*vt.*) 1)...o miru […を見る]; ...o nagameru […を眺める]. 2)...o kuwashiku-shiraberu […を詳しく調べる]. 3)...to kangaeru […と考える]. 4)...o(...to)-mi-nasu […を(…と)見なす].

viewpoint (*n.*) 1)kenchi [見地]. 2)(aru mono ga)mieru-chiten [(ある物が)見える地点].

vigorous (*a.*) 1)seiryoku-ôsei-na [精力おう盛な]; genki-hatsuratsu-to-shita [元気はつらつとした]. 2)chikara-zuyoi [力強い]. 3)(shokubutsu ga) yoku-sodatsu [(植物が)よく育つ].

vile (*a.*) geretsu-na [下劣な]; (*colloq.*) hidoku-warui [ひどく悪い].

villa (*n.*) bessô [別荘].

village (*n.*) mura [村].

villager (*n.*) sommin [村民].

vine (*n.*) budô-no-ki [ブドウの木]; tsuru-shokubutsu [つる植物].

vinegar (*n.*) 1)su [酢]; binegâ [ビネガー]. 2)fu-kigen [不機嫌].

vineyard (*n.*) budô-en [ブドウ園].

vinyl (*n.*) (*chem.*) biniru-ki [ビニル基].

violate (*vt.*) 1)...ni ihan-suru […に違反する]; ...o yaburu […を破る]. 2)...o kegasu […を汚す]. 3)...o bôgai-suru […を妨害する].

violence (*n.*) 1)hageshisa [激しさ]. 2)rambô [乱暴]; bôkô [暴行]. 3)gai [害].
　　resort to violence wanryoku-ni-uttaeru

violent (*a.*) 1)hageshii [激しい]; rambô-na [乱暴な]. 2)jiko-ni-yoru [事故による].

violet (*n.*) sumire[-iro] [スミレ(色)].

viper (*n.*) (*zool.*) kusari-hebi-no-rui [クサリヘビの類]; doku-hebi [毒ヘビ].

virgin (*n.*) shojo [処女]; otome [おとめ].
　　(*a.*) 1)shojo-no [処女の]; shojo-ni-fusawashii [処女にふさわしい]; kegare-no-nai [汚れのない]. 2)hajimete-no [初めての].

virtually (*ad.*) jisshitsu-teki-ni-wa [実質的には]; jijitsu-jô [事実上].

virtue (*n.*) 1)toku [徳]; bitoku [美徳]. 2)chôsho [長所]. 3)kônô [効能]; kiki-me [ききめ].
　　by(in) virtue of ...no-riyû-de; ...no-o-kage-de

virtuous (*a.*) toku-no-takai [徳の高い]; kôketsu-na [高潔な].

visa (*n.*) biza [ビザ]; sashô [査証]; uragaki [裏書き].
　　(*vt.*) ...o sashô-suru […を査証する]; ...o uragaki-suru […を裏書

きする]; …ni biza-o-ataeru […にビザを与える].

visage (*n.*) kao-tsuki [顔つき].

vise, vice (*n.*) (*mech.*) manriki [万力].
   (*vt.*) …o manriki-de-shimeru […を万力で締める].

visible (*a.*) 1)me-ni-mieru [目に見える]; mite-wakaru [見てわかる]; mi-yasui [見やすい]. 2)menkai-dekiru [面会できる].

vision (*n.*) 1)shiryoku [視力]. 2)risô-zô [理想像]. 3)mi-toosu-chikara [見通す力]. 4)gen'ei [幻影]. 5)kôkei [光景].
   (*vt.*) …o maboroshi-ni-miru […を幻に見る].

visit (*vt.*) 1)…o hômon-suru […を訪問する]. 2)…o mimau […を見舞う]. 3)…o kembutsu-ni-iku […を見物に行く]. 4)(saigai nado ga)…ni furi-kakaru [(災害などが)…に降りかかる].
   (*vi.*) 1)hômon-suru [訪問する]; kembutsu-suru [見物する]. 2)((*US*)) taizai-suru [滞在する]. 3)((*US*)) o-shaberi-o-suru [おしゃべりをする].
   (*n.*) hômon [訪問]; mimai [見舞い]; kembutsu [見物]; taizai [滞在]; shisatsu [視察].
 pay (**one**) **a visit** (hito)-o hômon-suru

visiting card meishi [名刺].

visitor (*n.*) hômon-sha [訪問者]; mimai-kyaku [見舞い客]; kankô-kyaku [観光客]; shukuhaku-kyaku [宿泊客].

visual (*a.*) 1)shikaku-no [視覚の]; me-ni-mieru [目に見える]. 2)shikaku-kyôzai-no [視覚教材の].

vital (*a.*) 1)seimei-no [生命の]. 2)kiwamete-jûyô-na [極めて重要な]. 3)kakki-no-aru [活気のある].

vitality (*n.*) 1)seimei-ryoku [生命力]; katsuryoku [活力]; kakki [活気]. 2)jizoku-ryoku [持続力].

vitamin (*n.*) bitamin [ビタミン].

vivacious (*a.*) kaikatsu-na [快活な]; yôki-na [陽気な].

vivid (*a.*) iki-iki-to-shita [生き生きとした]; semmei-na [鮮明な].

vividly (*ad.*) iki-iki-to [生き生きと]; azayaka-ni [鮮やかに].

vocabulary (*n.*) 1)goi [語い]. 2)tango-shû [単語集].

vocal (*a.*) koe-no [声の]; onsei-no [音声の]; kôtô-no [口頭の]; (*mus.*) seigaku-no [声楽の].
   (*n.*) 1)(*mus.*) bôkaru [ボーカル]. 2)(*phon.*) boin [母音].

vocal cords seitai [声帯].

vocalist (*n.*) seigaku-ka [声楽家]; kashu [歌手].

vocation (*n.*) 1)shokugyô [職業]. 2)tenshoku [天職]. 3)kami-no-o-meshi [神のお召し]. 4)tekisei [適性].

vogue (*n.*) ryûkô [流行]; hayari [はやり]; ninki [人気].
　　in vogue ninki-ga-atte; ryûkô-shite

voice (*n.*) 1)koe [声]. 2)iken [意見]. 3)hatsugen-ken [発言権]. 4)
　　hyômei [表明]. 5)(*gram.*) tai [態].
　　with one voice zen'in-itchi-de
　　　　(*vt.*) 1)...o iu [...を言う]; ...o hyômei-suru [...を表明する]. 2)
　　　　(*phon.*)...o yûsei-on-de-hatsuon-suru [...を有声音で発音する].

void (*a.*) 1)kûkyo-na [空虚な]. 2)(*law*) mukô-no [無効の]. 3)...o-
　　kaite-iru [...を欠いている]. 4)muda-na [無駄な].

volcanic (*a.*) 1)kazan-no [火山の]; kazan-sayô-ni-yoru [火山作用によ
　　る]; kazan-no-ooi [火山の多い]. 2)hijô-ni-hageshii [非常に激しい].

volcano (*n.*) kazan [火山].

volleyball (*n.*) barêbôru [バレーボール].

voltage (*n.*) (*elect.*) den'atsu [電圧]; boruto-sû [ボルト数].

volume (*n.*) 1)hon [本]; ...satsu [...冊]; ...kan [...巻]. 2)yôseki [容
　　積]; ryô [量]. 3)onryô [音量]; boryûmu [ボリューム].

voluntary (*a.*) jihatsu-teki-na [自発的な]; nin'i-no [任意の]; shizen-
　　ni-shôjiru [自然に生じる].

volunteer (*n.*) 1)shigan-sha [志願者]; borantia [ボランティア];
　　tokushi-ka [篤志家]. 2)giyû-hei [義勇兵].
　　　　(*vi.*) susunde-hiki-ukeru [進んで引き受ける]; shigan-suru
　　[志願する].
　　　　(*vt.*) ...o jihatsu-teki-ni-môshi-deru [...を自発的に申し出る].

vomit (*vi.*) 1)haku [吐く]; modosu [もどす]. 2)funshutsu-suru [噴出
　　する].
　　　　(*vt.*) ...o haku [...を吐く]; ...o modosu [...をもどす]; ...o haki-
　　dasu [...を吐き出す].
　　　　(*n.*) ôto[-butsu] [おう吐(物)].

vote (*n.*) tôhyô [投票]; hyôketsu [票決]; tôhyô-ken [投票権].
　　　　(*vi.*) tôhyô-suru [投票する].
　　　　(*vt.*) ...o hyôketsu-suru [...を票決する]; ...o kaketsu-suru [...を
　　可決する].

voting (*n. & a.*) tôhyô(-no) [投票(の)]; senkyo(-no) [選挙(の)].

vow (*n.*) chikai [誓い]; seiyaku [誓約].
　　　　(*vt.*) ...o chikau [...を誓う]; ...o seiyaku-suru [...を誓約する].

vowel (*n.*) boin[-ji] [母音(字)].

voyage (*n.*) kôkai [航海]; funa-tabi [船旅].

(*vi. & vt.*) (...o) kôkai-suru [(…を)航海する].

vulgar (*a.*) 1)gehin-na [下品な]; kyôyô-no-nai [教養のない]. 2)ippan-taishû-no [一般大衆の].

vulture (*n.*) (*birds*) hage-taka [ハゲタカ].

W

waddle (*vi. & n.*) yochi-yochi-aruku(yochi-yochi-aruki) [よちよち歩く(よちよち歩き)].

wade (*vi.*) 1)(kawa nado o) aruite-wataru [(川などを)歩いて渡る]. 2)kurô-shite-susumu [苦労して進む].

wag (*vt. & vi.*) ...o furu(yure-ugoku) […を振る(揺れ動く)].

wage (*n.*) (*pl.*) chingin [賃金]; kyûryô [給料].
　　　(*vt.*) (sensô nado)-o okonau [(戦争など)を行なう].

wage earner chingin-rôdô-sha [賃金労働者].

wager (*n.*) kake-goto [かけ事].
　　　(*vt. & vi.*) 1)(...o) kakeru [(…を)かける]. 2)(...o) uke-au [(…を)請け合う].

wagon, waggon (*n.*) 1)ni-basha [荷馬車]. 2)((*US*)) = station wagon; ((*Eng.*)) mugai-kasha [無蓋貨車]. 3)((*US*)) uba-guruma [乳母車].
　　　(*vt.*) ...o wagon-de-hakobu […をワゴンで運ぶ].
　　　(*vi.*) wagon-de-iku [ワゴンで行く].

wail (*vi.*) 1)naki-sakebu [泣き叫ぶ]; nageki-kanashimu [嘆き悲しむ]. 2)kanashi-ge-na-oto-o-tateru [悲しげな音を立てる].

(*vt.*) ...o nageki-kanashimu ［…を嘆き悲しむ］.

(*n.*) naki-sakebi ［泣き叫び］; kanashi-ge-na-oto ［悲しげな音］.

waist (*n.*) koshi ［腰］; uesuto ［ウエスト］.

waistcoat (*n.*) ((*Eng.*)) chokki ［チョッキ］; besuto ［ベスト］.

wait (*vi.*) 1)matsu ［待つ］. 2)kyûji-suru ［給仕する］.

wait on(upon) ...ni kyûji-suru; (kyaku)-ni ôtai-suru

wait up ne-nai-de-matsu

(*vt.*) ...o matsu ［…を待つ］; ...o machi-ukeru ［…を待ち受ける］.

(*n.*) taiki ［待機］.

waiter (*n.*) weitâ ［ウェイター］.

waiting room machiai-shitsu ［待合室］.

waitress (*n.*) weitoresu ［ウェイトレス］.

wake (*vi.*) 1)me-ga-sameru ［目が覚める］. 2)okite-iru ［起きている］. 3) iki-kaeru ［生き返る］.

(*vt.*) 1)...o(...kara) me-o-samasaseru ［…を(…から)目を覚まさせる］. 2)...o funki-saseru ［…を奮起させる］. 3)...o omoi-dasaseru ［…を思い出させる］.

waken (*vi. & vt.*) = wake.

walk (*vi.*) aruku ［歩く］; sampo-suru ［散歩する］.

(*vt.*) ...o aruku ［…を歩く］; ...o arukaseru ［…を歩かせる］.

(*n.*) 1)hokô ［歩行］; sampo ［散歩］. 2)aruku-kyori ［歩く距離］; aruku-jikan ［歩く時間］. 3)yûho-dô ［遊歩道］. 4)aruki-kata ［歩き方］; aruki-buri ［歩きぶり］. 5)kurashi-buri ［暮らしぶり］; shokugyô ［職業］.

(*1*) I went for a **walk**. Watashi-wa *sampo*-ni dekaketa.

(*2*) It is a ten-minute **walk**. *Aruite* juppun-*no-kyori* desu.

(*3*) An elephant came up the **walk**, carrying some children on his back.

　　　Zô ga senaka-ni sû-nin-no kodomo-o nosete, *yûho-dô*-o yatte-kita.

(*4*) She has a graceful **walk**.

　　　Kano-jo-wa jôhin-na *aruki-kata*-o-suru.

(*5*) people in every **walk** [all **walks**] of life

　　　arayuru *shokugyô*-no hito-bito

take a walk sampo-suru

wall (*n.*) kabe ［壁］; hei ［塀］.

(*vt.*) 1)...o kabe-de-kakou ［…を壁で囲う］; ...ni jôheki-o-megurasu ［…に城壁をめぐらす］. 2)...o(-kabe-de) fusagu ［…を(壁で)ふさぐ］. 3)...o toji-komeru ［…を閉じ込める］.

wallet (*n.*) satsu-ire [札入れ].

walnut (*n.*) kurumi [クルミ].

walrus (*n.*) (*zool.*) seiuchi [セイウチ].

wander (*vi.*) 1)aruki-mawaru [歩き回る]; samayou [さまよう]. 2)
toritome-ga-naku-naru [取り留めがなくなる]. 3)mayou [迷う]; yoko-
michi-ni-soreru [横道にそれる].

　　　(*vt.*) ...o aruki-mawaru […を歩き回る]; ...o samayou […を
さまよう].

　　　(*n.*) (*colloq.*) buratsuku-koto [ぶらつくこと].

wanderer (*n.*) hôrô-sha [放浪者]; samayou-hito [さまよう人]; sasurai-
bito [さすらい人].

wane (*vi.*) 1)(tsuki ga)kakeru [(月が)欠ける]. 2)otoroeru [衰える];
owari-ni-chikazuku [終わりに近づく].

　　　(*n.*) 1)(tsuki no) kake [(月の)欠け]. 2)suibi [衰微].

want (*n.*) 1)ketsubô [欠乏]; fusoku [不足]. 2)hitsuyô [必要].

　　　(*vt.*) 1)...ga kakete-iru […が欠けている]; ...ga tari-nai […が足
りない]. 2)...o hitsuyô-to-suru […を必要とする]; (hito)-ni yô-ga-
aru [(人)に用がある]. 3)...(shi-)tai […(し)たい]; ...o hossuru […を
欲する].

　(*1*) He **wants** judgement.　Kare-wa handan-ryoku-*ni kakete-iru*.

　(*2*) Push this button when you **want** me.
　　　　Go-*yô*-no-toki-wa kono botan-o oshite-kudasai.

　(*3*) I **want** to see you.　Watashi-wa anata-ni ai-*tai*.

　　　(*vi.*) 1)fu-jiyû-suru [不自由する]. 2)totemo...(shi-)tagaru [とて
も…(し)たがる].

　(*1*) Let him **want** for nothing.　Kare-ni *fu-jiyû-saseru*-na.

war (*n.*) sensô [戦争].

　　　(*vi.*) sensô-suru [戦争する]; tekitai-suru [敵対する].

　　　(*a.*) sensô-no [戦争の].

warble (*vi.*) 1)(tori ga)saezuru [(鳥が)さえずる]. 2)koe-o-furuwasete-
utau [声を震わせて歌う]. 3)(ogawa nado ga) seseragi-no-oto-o-
tateru [(小川などが)せせらぎの音を立てる].

　　　(*n.*) saezuri [さえずり]; saezuru-yô-na-uta-goe [さえずるような
歌声].

ward (*n.*) 1)kantoku [監督]; hogo [保護]. 2)...ku […区]. 3)byôshitsu
[病室]; byôtô [病棟].

　　　(*vt.*) ...o kawasu […をかわす].

wardrobe (*n.*) 1)yôfuku-dansu [洋服ダンス]. 2)ishô-beya [衣装部屋].

3)mochi-ishô [持ち衣装].

ware (*n.*) 1)tôki [陶器]. 2)(*pl.*) shôhin [商品].

warehouse (*n.*) sôko [倉庫]; ((*Eng.*)) oroshi-uri-ten [卸売店].
　　　　(*vt.*)...o sôko-ni-ireru [...を倉庫に入れる].

warfare (*n.*) sensô [戦争]; kôsen [交戦]; tôsô [闘争].

warlike (*a.*) 1)kôsen-teki-na [好戦的な]. 2)sensô-no [戦争の]; gunji-no [軍事の].

warm (*a.*) 1)atatakai [暖かい]. 2)kokoro-no-atatakai [心の温かい].
3)nesshin-na [熱心な]; netsuretsu-na [熱烈な].
　　　　(*vt.*) 1)...o atatameru [...を暖める]. 2)...o honobono-to-saseru [...をほのぼのとさせる]. 3)...o netchû-saseru [...を熱中させる].
　　　　(*vi.*) 1)atatamaru [暖まる]. 2)nesshin-ni-naru [熱心になる]. 3)dôjô-o-yoseru [同情を寄せる].

warmly (*ad.*) atatakaku [暖かく]; kokoro-kara [心から]; shinsetsu-ni [親切に].

warmth (*n.*) 1)atataka-sa [暖かさ]. 2)onjô [温情]. 3)nesshin [熱心].

warn (*vt.*) 1)...ni keikoku-suru [...に警告する]. 2)...ni yokoku-suru [...に予告する].
　　　　(*vi.*) keikoku-o-ataeru [警告を与える]; chûi-suru [注意する].

warning (*n.*) keihô [警報]; keikoku [警告]; yokoku [予告].

warrant (*n.*) 1)seitô-na-riyû [正当な理由]. 2)hoshô [保証]. 3)(*law*) reijô [令状]. 4)kyoka-shô [許可証].
　　　　(*vt.*) 1)...o seitô-to-suru [...を正当とする]. 2)...o hoshô-suru [...を保証する]; ...o uke-au [...を請け合う].

warrior (*n.*) bushi [武士]; yûshi [勇士].

warship (*n.*) gunkan [軍艦].

wash (*vt.*) 1)...o arau [...を洗う]; ...o sentaku-suru [...を洗濯する]. 2)(nami ga)...o arau [(波が)...を洗う]; ...ni uchi-yoseru [...に打ち寄せる]. 3)...o oshi-nagasu [...を押し流す].
　　　　(*vi.*) 1)te-o-arau [手を洗う]. 2)sentaku-suru [洗濯する]; sentaku-ga-kiku [洗濯がきく].
　　　　(*n.*) 1)sentaku[-mono] [洗濯(物)]. 2)mizuppoi-tabe-mono [水っぽい食べ物]. 3)shiru-majiri-no-zampan [汁まじりの残飯].
　　　　(*a.*) (*US colloq.*) sentaku-no-kiku [洗濯のきく].

washstand (*n.*) semmen-dai [洗面台].

wasp (*n.*) (*insect*) suzume-bachi [スズメバチ].

waste (*a.*) 1)areta [荒れた]; tagayasarete-i-nai [耕されていない]. 2)haibutsu-no [廃物の]; amari-mono-no [余り物の].

(1) My fields were laid **waste**. Watashi-no hatake wa *arete-ita*.

(2) Put **waste** paper into the box.

　　　Kami-*kuzu* wa kono-hako-ni ire-nasai.

　　　(*vi.*) 1)muda-zukai-suru ［無駄使いする］; muda-ni-naru ［無駄に
なる］. 2)suijaku-suru ［衰弱する］; shômô-suru ［消耗する］. 3)(toki
ga) sugite-iku ［(時が)過ぎていく］.

　　　(*vt.*) 1)…o rôhi-suru ［…を浪費する］. 2)…o otoroe-saseru ［…
を衰えさせる］; …o kôhai-saseru ［…を荒廃させる］.

　　　(*n.*) 1)are-chi ［荒れ地］; are-no ［荒れ野］; sabaku ［砂漠］. 2)
rôhi ［浪費］. 3)haiki-butsu ［廃棄物］; kuzu ［くず］. 4)shômô ［消耗］.

(1) A **waste** of sand was seen. Bôbô-taru-*sabaku* ga mieta.

(2) It's **waste** of time to wait for him any longer.

　　　Kore-ijô kare-o matsu-no-wa jikan no *rôhi* da.

(3) Factory **waste** is polluting rivers and lakes.

　　　Kôjô-no *haieki* ga kawa ya mizuumi-o osen-shiteiru.

(4) **waste** and repair　(karada no) *shômô* to kaifuku

　　run(go) to waste　muda-ni-naru; haibutsu-ni-naru

wasteful (*a.*) 1)rôhi-teki-na ［浪費的な］; muda-na ［無駄な］; fu-keizai-
na ［不経済な］. 2)kôhai-o-motarasu ［荒廃をもたらす］; hakai-teki-na ［
破壊的な］.

wastepaper (*n.*) kami-kuzu ［紙くず］.

watch (*n.*) 1)ude-dokei ［腕時計］. 2)mi-hari ［見張り］. 3)mi-hari[-nin]
［見張り(人)］; gâdoman ［ガードマン］.

　　　(*vi.*) 1)mi-mamoru ［見守る］; mi-haru ［見張る］. 2)kitai-shite-
matsu ［期待して待つ］.

　　　(*vt.*) 1)…o mi-mamoru ［…を見守る］; …o mi-haru ［…を見張る］.
2)…o matsu ［…を待つ］; …o ukagau ［…をうかがう］.

　　watch out　keikai-suru; yôjin-suru

watchdog (*n.*) banken ［番犬］.

watchmaker (*n.*) tokeiya ［時計屋］.

watchman (*n.*) yakei ［夜警］; gâdoman ［ガードマン］.

water (*n.*) 1)mizu ［水］. 2)(*pl.*) umi ［海］; mizuumi ［湖］; kawa ［川］.

　　　(*vt.*) 1)…ni mizu-o-maku ［…に水をまく］; …ni mizu-o-kakeru
［…に水をかける］; …ni mizu-o-nomaseru ［…に水を飲ませる］. 2)…ni
kyûsui-suru ［…に給水する］.

　　　(*vi.*) 1)mizu-o-nomu ［水を飲む］. 2)yodare-o-dasu ［よだれをだす］.
3)namida-o-dasu ［涙を出す］.

water closet suisen-benjo ［水洗便所］; daburu-shî ［ダブルシー］.

watercolo(u)r (*n.*) (*pl.*) suisai-enogu [水彩絵の具]. suisai-ga[-hô] [水彩画(法)].

waterfall (*n.*) taki [滝].

waterfowl (*n.*) mizu-dori [水鳥].

water lily (*bot.*) suiren [スイレン].

watermelon (*n.*) suika [スイカ].

waterpower (*n.*) suiryoku [水力].

waterproof (*a.*) bôsui-sei-no [防水性の]; taisui-sei-no [耐水性の].
　　　　(*n.*) 1)bôsui-nuno [防水布]. 2)((*Eng.*)) reinkôto [レインコート].
　　　　(*vt.*) ...ni bôsui-suru [...に防水する].

watershed (*n.*) 1)bunsui-rei [分水れい]; bunki-ten [分岐点]. 2)((*US*)) (kawa no) ryûiki [(川の)流域].

water ski suijô-sukî [水上スキー].

watery (*a.*) 1)mizuppoi [水っぽい]; shimetta [湿った]. 2)namida-gunda [涙ぐんだ].

wave (*n.*) 1)nami [波]; uneri [うねり]. 2)(tôhatsu nado no) wêbu [(頭髪などの)ウェーブ]. 3)kifuku [起伏]; takamari [高まり].
　　　　(*vi.*) 1)yureru [揺れる]. 2)te[hankachi]-o-furu [手[ハンカチ]を振る]. 3)nami-datsu [波立つ]; unette-iru [うねっている].
　　　　(*vt.*) 1)...o furu [...を振る]. 2)...ni wêbu-o-kakeru [...にウェーブを掛ける]. 3)...o uneraseru [...をうねらせる]; ...o nami-dataseru [...を波立たせる].

waver (*vi.*) yureru [揺れる]; guratsuku [ぐらつく]; dôyô-suru [動揺する]; mayou [迷う].
　　　　(*n.*) yure [揺れ]; tamerai [ためらい]; dôyô [動揺].

wax (*n.*) 1)rô [ろう]. 2)wakkusu [ワックス].
　　　　(*vt.*) ...ni rô-o-nuru [...にろうを塗る].

wax (*vi.*) 1)ookiku-naru [大きくなる]. 2)(tsuki ga) michiru [(月が)満ちる].

waxen (*a.*) rôsei-no [ろう製の]; rô-biki-no [ろう引きの]; rô-no-yô-na [ろうのような]; nameraka-na [滑らかな].

way (*n.*) 1)michi [道]; dôro [道路]. 2)hôhô [方法]; shikata [仕方]. 3)kyori [距離]; michinori [道のり]. 4)hôgaku [方角]; hôkô [方向]. 5)(*colloq.*)...atari [...あたり]. 6)ryûgi [流儀]; kuse [癖]. 7)ten [点].
　　(*1*) Is this the right **way** to the station?
　　　　Eki-e-wa kono *michi*-o-ike-ba ii-desu-ka?
　　(*2*) Where there's a will, there's a **way**.

Ishi no aru tokoro-ni, *hôhô*-ga-aru.

Seishin-ittô nani-goto-ka nara-za-ran.

(3) It's a long **way** from here to the town.

Koko-kara machi-made kanari-no *michinori*-ga-aru.

(4) Come this **way**, please. Kochira-e, dôzo.

(5) He lives somewhere Hiroshima **way**.

Kare-wa doko-ka Hiroshima-*atari*-ni sunde-iru.

(6) This is the **way** of the world.

Kore-ga yo-no-naka no *ryûgi*-to-iu-mono da.

Kore-ga yo no *narawashi* da.

He has tried to mend his **ways**.

Kare-wa jibun-no *kuse*-o nao-sô-to doryoku-shita.

(7) Only in this **way** he is like his brother.

Tada kono-*ten*-de kare-wa kyôdai-ni nite-iru.

all the way 1)haru-baru; (tochû-)zutto. 2)kanzen-ni

by the way tsuide-nagara; tochû-de

by way of 1)...keiyu-de. 2)...no-tsumori-de. 3)...o-shudan-to-shite

give way 1)kowareru. 2)makeru; kussuru. 3)ne-ga-sagaru

 1) The bridge gave way. Hashi ga kowareta.

 2) Don't give way to adversity. Gyakkyô-ni makeru-na.

 3) The stock afterwards gave way.

Kabu wa sono-nochi ne-ga-sagatta.

go one's (own) way jibun-no-omoi-doori-ni-suru

 He always goes his own way.

Kare-wa itsu-mo jibun-no-omoi-doori-ni-suru.

go out of the(one's) way 1)mawari-michi-o-suru. 2)waza-waza
 ...suru. 3)tori-midasu

in the way of 1)...no-ten-de; ...to-shite-wa. 2)...jama-ni-natte

make one's way 1)shusse-suru. 2)susumu

 1) He made his way in the world. Kare-wa shusse-shita.

 2) He made his way to Cambridge.

Kare-wa Kemburijji-e susunde-itta.

make way 1)michi-o-akeru. 2)...ga hakadoru

on the way tochû-de

out of the(one's) way 1)jama-ni-nara-nai-yô-ni. 2)kata-zuite

stand in the way of ...no jama-ni-naru

this way and that achira-kochira[-to]

under way shinkô-chû-de

way (*ad.*) (*US colloq.*) zutto [ずっと]; haruka-ni [はるかに].

waylay (*vt.*) …o machibuse-suru […を待ち伏せする].

wayside (*n. & a.*) michibata(-no) [道端(の)].

wayward (*a.*) 1)waga-mama-na [我がままな]. 2)ki-magure-na [気まぐれな]. 3)yosô-gai-no [予想外の].

we (*pron.*) watashi-tachi-wa [私たちは]; watashi-tachi-ga [私たちが]; ware-ware-wa [われわれは]; ware-ware-ga [われわれが].

weak (*a.*) 1)yowai [弱い]. 2)(cha nado ga) usui [(茶などが)薄い]. 3)ototta [劣った]. 4)fu-jûbun-na [不十分な].

weaken (*vt.*) …o yowameru […を弱める]; …o usumeru […を薄める]. (*vi.*) yowamaru [弱まる].

weakly (*a. & ad.*) yowai (yowaku) [弱い(弱く)]; yowa-yowa-shii (yowa-yowa-shiku) [弱々しい(弱々しく)].

weakness (*n.*) 1)yowasa [弱さ]. 2)jakuten [弱点]. 3)dai-kôbutsu [大好物].

wealth (*n.*) 1)tomi [富]; zaisan [財産]. 2)hôfu [豊富].

wealthy (*a.*) yûfuku-na [裕福な]; hôfu-na [豊富な].

weapon (*n.*) buki [武器]; heiki [兵器]. (*vt.*) …o busô-saseru […を武装させる].

wear (*vt.*) 1)…o kite-iru […を着ている]; …o kakete-iru […をかけている]; (hige)-o hayashite-iru [(ひげ)をはやしている]. 2)…o suri-herasu […をすり減らす].

  (*1*) He always **wears** black.

      Kare-wa itsu-mo kuro-no-fuku-*o kite-iru*.

  Does your sister **wear** glasses?

      Kimi-no nê-san wa megane-*o kakete-iru*-kai?

  He **wears** a mustache. Kare-wa kuchi-hige-*o hayashite-iru*.

  (*2*) His coat **was worn** out. Kare-no uwagi wa *suri-kirete-ita*.

    (*vi.*) 1)shiyô-ni-taeru [使用に耐える]; motsu [もつ]. 2)suri-kireru [すり切れる]; suri-hette…ni-naru [すり減って…になる].

    (*n.*) 1)chakuyô [着用]. 2)ifuku [衣服]. 3)suri-kire [すり切れ]; ki-furushi [着古し]. 4)taikyû-sei [耐久性].

weary (*a.*) 1)tsukarete[-iru] [疲れて(いる)]. 2)aki-aki-shite[-iru] [あきあきして(いる)]. 3)taikutsu-na [退屈な].

  (*1*) I was **weary** with the work.

      Watashi-wa sono-shigoto-de *tsukarete*-ita.

  (*2*) I was **weary** of the work.

      Watashi-wa sono-shigoto-ni *aki-aki-shite*-ita.

　　　　(*vt.*) …o tsukaresaseru […を疲れさせる]; …o taikutsu-saseru […を退屈させる].

　　　　(*vi.*) tsukareru [疲れる]; taikutsu-suru [退屈する].

weasel (*n.*) (*zool.*) itachi [イタチ].

weather (*n.*) tenki [天気]; tenkô [天候].

　　　　(*vt.*) 1)…o fûu-ni-sarasu […を風雨にさらす]. 2)…o kiri-nukeru […を切り抜ける]. 3)(be -ed) fûka-suru [風化する].

　　　　(*vi.*) gaiki-ni-sarasarete-henka-suru [外気にさらされて変化する]; kiri-nukeru [切り抜ける]; fûka-suru [風化する].

weather-beaten (*a.*) 1)fûu-ni-sarasareta [風雨にさらされた]. 2)hi-ni-yaketa [日に焼けた].

weathercock (*n.*) kazami [風見] = weather vane.

weather forecast tenki-yohô [天気予報].

weave (*vt.*) 1)…o oru […を織る]; …o amu […を編む]. 2)…o shi-kumu […を仕組む].

　　　　(*vi.*) orimono-o-oru [織物を織る].

　　　　(*n.*) ori[-kata] [織り(方)]; ami[-kata] [編み(方)]; …ori […織].

web (*n.*) 1)kumo-no-su [クモの巣]. 2)orimono [織物]. 3)(mizu-dori no) mizukaki [(水鳥の)水かき].

　　　　(*vt. & vi.*) (…ni) kumo-no-su-o-haru [(…に)クモの巣を張る].

webbed (*a.*) kumo-no-su-jô-no [クモの巣状の]; mizukaki-no-aru [水かきのある].

wedding (*n.*) 1)kekkon-shiki [結婚式]; konrei [婚礼]. 2)kekkon-kinen-bi [結婚記念日].

wedge (*n.*) kusabi [くさび].

　　　　(*vt.*) 1)…o kusabi-de-tomeru […をくさびで留める]. 2)…o muri-ni-wari-komaseru […を無理に割り込ませる].

Wednesday (*n.*) Suiyô-bi [水曜日].

weed (*n.*) zassô [雑草].

　　　　(*vt.*) …o tori-nozoku […を取り除く].

　　　　(*vi.*) zassô-o-nuku [雑草を抜く].

weedy (*a.*) zassô-no-ooi [雑草の多い]; zassô-no[-yô-na] [雑草の(ような)].

week (*n.*) shû [週]; isshû-kan [一週間]; [W-] …shûkan […週間].

weekday (*n.*) shûjitsu [週日]; heijitsu [平日]; uîkudei [ウイークデイ].

weekend (*n.*) shûmatsu [週末]; uîkuendo [ウイークエンド].

　　　　(*vi.*) shûmatsu-ryokô-o-suru [週末旅行をする]; shûmatsu-o-sugosu [週末を過ごす].

weekly (*ad. & a.*) mai-shû(-no) [毎週(の)]; shû-ikkai(-no) [週一回
(の)]; shû-gime-de(-no) [週ぎめで(の)].
　　　(*n.*) shûkan-shi [週刊誌]; shûhô [週報].

weep (*vi.*) naku [泣く].
　　　(*vt.*) (namida)-o nagasu [(涙)を流す]; ...o naki-kurasu […を泣
き暮らす].

weeping willow (*bot.*) shidare-yanagi [シダレヤナギ].

weigh (*vt.*) 1)...no omosa-o-hakaru […の重さを量る]. 2)...o yoku-
kangaeru […をよく考える]. 3)(be -ed) (...de-)nayamu [(…で)悩む].
4)(*marine*) (ikari)-o ageru [(いかり)を揚げる].
　　　(*vi.*) 1)omo-sa-ga...aru [重さが…ある]. 2)jûyô-shi-sareru [重要
視される]. 3)omo-ni-to-naru [重荷となる]. 4)ikari-o-ageru [いかりを
揚げる].

weight (*n.*) 1)omo-sa [重さ]; jûryô [重量]. 2)omori [おもり]; fundô
[分銅]. 3)jûyô-sei [重要性].
　　gain weight taijû-ga-fueru
　　lose weight taijû-ga-heru
　　　(*vt.*) 1)...o omoku-suru […を重くする]. 2)...ni omo-ni-o-owa-
seru […に重荷を負わせる].

weighty (*a.*) 1)omoi [重い]. 2)yûryoku-na [有力な]. 3)jûdai-na [重
大な].

weir (*n.*) seki [せき]; damu [ダム].

weird (*a.*) 1)bu-kimi-na [不気味な]. 2)(*colloq.*) kimyô-na [奇妙な].

welcome (*int.*) Yô-koso! [ようこそ!].
　　　(*vt.*) 1)...o kangei-suru […を歓迎する]. 2)...o yorokonde-
mukaeru […を喜んで迎える].
　　　(*n.*) kangei [歓迎].
　　give (one) a warm welcome (hito-o-)ooi-ni-kangei-suru
　　　(*a.*) 1)kangei-sareru [歓迎される]. 2)ureshii [うれしい]. 3)
jiyû-ni...(shite-)yoi [自由に…(して)よい].
　　　　You are welcome. Dô-itashi-mashite.

welfare (*n.*) 1)kôfuku [幸福]. 2)han-ei [繁栄]. 3)fukushi-jigyô [福祉
事業].

well (*n.*) ido [井戸]; izumi [泉].
　　　(*vi.*) waki-deru [わき出る]; funshutsu-suru [噴出する]; komi-
ageru [こみ上げる].
　　　(*vt.*) ...o waki-dasaseru […をわき出させる]; ...o fuki-dasu […を

ふき出す].

well (*ad.*) 1)yoku [よく]; jôzu-ni [上手に]. 2)jûbun-ni [十分に];
kanari [かなり]. 3)tsugô-yoku [都合よく]. 4)seitô-ni [正当に].
(*1*) He speaks English **well**. Kare-wa Ei-go-o *jôzu-ni* hanasu.
(*2*) I slept **well** last night.
　　　　Watashi-wa sakuya *jûbun-ni* nemutta.
(*3*) Everything is going **well**. Subete *umaku* itteiru.
(*4*) You may **well** be right. Tabun anata-wa *tadashii*-darô.
as well (*colloq.*) sono-ue; ...mo-mata
as well as ...to-dôyô-ni; ...dake-de-naku
Well done! Dekashita! Umaku-yatta-zo!
　　(*a.*) 1)kenkô-na [健康な]; genki-na [元気な]! 2)manzoku-na [満
足な]; môshi-bun-nai [申し分ない].
(*1*) Are you **well**? O-*genki*-desu-ka?
(*2*) He is **well** enough as a doctor.
　　　　Kare-wa isha-to-shite *môshi-bun-nai*.
It's all very well..., but ...wa kekkô-da-ga, shikashi
　　(*int.*) 1)Maa! [まあ!]; Hê! [へぇー!]. 2)dewa [では]; tokoro-de
[ところで]; sore-de [それで]. 3)ee-to [ええと].
(*1*) **Well**, I never! *Hê*, kore-wa-odoroita!; Masaka!
(*2*) **Well**, let's begin. *Sore-dewa* hajime-yô.
　　(*n.*) yoi-koto [よいこと]; han'ei [繁栄]; kôfuku [幸福].

well-appointed (*a.*) setsubi-no-totonotta [設備の整った].
well-behaved (*a.*) gyôgi-no-yoi [行儀のよい].
well-bred (*a.*) sodachi-no-yoi [育ちのよい].
well-done (*a.*) 1)jûbun-ni-yaketa [十分に焼けた]. 2)rippa-ni-
okonawareta [立派に行われた].
well-established (*a.*) kakuritsu-shita [確立した]; teichaku-shita [定着
した].
well-informed (*a.*) hakushiki-no [博識の]; jijô-ni-tsûjite-iru [事情に通
じている].
well-kept (*a.*) teire-no-iki-todoita [手入れの行き届いた].
well-known (*a.*) 1)yûmei-na [有名な]. 2)najimi-bukai [なじみ深い].
well-mannered (*a.*) gyôgi-no-yoi [行儀のよい].
well-off (*a.*) yûfuku-na [裕福な].
well-to-do (*a.*) (*colloq.*) yûfuku-na [裕福な].
west (*n.*) 1)nishi [西]; seibu [西部]. 2)(the W-) Seiyô [西洋]. 3)
(the W-)《*US*》 Seibu [西部].

    (*a.*) nishi-no [西の]; nishi-kara-no [西からの].

    (*ad.*) nishi-e [西へ]; nishi-ni [西に].

western (*a.*) 1)nishi-no [西の]. 2)(W-)((*US*)) seibu-no [西部の].

westward (*a.*) nishi[-e]-no [西(へ)の].

    (*ad.*) nishi-e[-ni] [西へ[に]]; seihô-e[-ni] [西方へ[に]].

    (*n.*) (the –) nishi [西]; seihô [西方].

wet (*a.*) 1)nureta [ぬれた]. 2)ame[-furi]-no [雨(降り)の].

    (*vt. & vi.*) ...o nurasu(nureru) [...をぬらす(ぬれる)]; ...o shimerasu(shimeru) [...を湿らす(湿る)].

    (*n.*) 1)shimeri [しめり]. 2)(the –) ame [雨].

whack (*vt.*) 1)...o tsuyoku-utsu [...を強く打つ]. 2)((*US*))...o yama-wake-suru [...を山分けする].

    (*vi.*) tsuyoku-utsu [強く打つ].

whale (*n.*) kujira [クジラ].

    (*vi.*) hogei-ni-jûji-suru [捕鯨に従事する].

whale oil geiyu [鯨油].

wharf (*n.*) hatoba [波止場].

what (*a.*) 1)nan-no [何の]; nan-to-iu [何という]; donna [どんな]. 2)nan-to [なんと]; nan-to-iu [なんという].

    (*1*) **What** day of the week is it today?

        Kyô-wa *nan*-yô-bi desu-ka?

    (*2*) **What** a pretty flower it is! *Nan-to* kirei-na hana deshô!

        (*pron.*) 1)nani [何]; nani-o-shite-iru-hito [なにをしている人].

    2)...(suru-)mono [...(する)もの]; ...(suru-)koto [...(する)こと].

    (*1*) **What** do you see over there? Asoko-ni *nani*-ga miemasu-ka?

    What is he? Kare-wa *nani-o-shite-iru-hito* desu-ka?

        Kare no shokugyô wa *nani*-desu-ka?

    (*2*) **What** he said was true. Kare-ga itta-*koto* wa hontô-datta.

    What about...? ...wa-ikaga?

    What ...for? (*colloq.*) nan-no-tame-ni?

    what is called iwayuru

    what is more sono-ue

    (*ad.*) ika-ni [いかに]; dore-hodo [どれほど].

    (*int.*) Nan-datte! [何だって!]; Hee! [へえ!]; Nani! [何!].

whatever (*a.*) 1)donna...demo [どんな...でも]. 2)sukoshi-no...mo [少しの...も].

    (*1*) Take **whatever** book you like.

        Donna-hon-*demo*-yoi-kara kimi-no-suki-na-hon-o tori-nasai.

(2) There is no doubt **whatever**.　*Sukoshi-no*-utagai-*mo* nai.

　　　(*pron.*)　(…suru)-tokoro-no-mono[-koto]-wa-nan-demo　[(…
する)ところのもの[こと]は何でも]；　tatoe-donna-mono[-koto]-ga…
(shiyô)-tomo　[たとえどんなもの[こと]が…(しよう)とも].

　　Do **whatever** you like.

　　　Kimi-no-suki-na-*koto-nara-nan-demo* shi-nasai.

wheat (*n.*) ko-mugi [小麦].

wheel (*n.*) 1)wa [輪]；sharin [車輪]. 2)(*US colloq.*) jitensha [自転
車]. 3)(the -) (jidôsha no) handoru [(自動車の)ハンドル].

　　　(*vt.*) 1)…o ugokasu […を動かす]. 2)…o(…de) hakobu […を(…
で)運ぶ]. 3)…o kaiten-saseru […を回転させる].

　　　(*vi.*) (gururi-to) muki-o-kaeru [(ぐるりと)向きを変える]；senkai-
suru [旋回する].

wheelbarrow (*n.*) te-oshi-guruma [手押し車].

wheeze (*vi. & vt.*) zei-zei-iki-o-suru(…o zei-zei-sase-nagara-hanasu)
[ぜいぜい息をする(…をぜいぜいさせながら話す)].

when (*ad.*) 1)itsu [いつ]. 2)…(suru-)toki […(する)とき].

　　(*1*) **When** is your birthday?　O-tanjô-bi wa *itsu*-desu-ka?

　　(*2*) It was a time **when** I was a boy.

　　　Sore-wa watashi-ga kodomo-no-*toki* deshita.

　　　(*conj.*) (…suru-)toki-ni [(…する)ときに]；(…no-)toki-wa　[(…
の)ときは]；(…suru-)toki-wa-itsu-demo [(…する)ときはいつでも].

　　He was weak **when** he was a boy.

　　　Kare-wa kodomo-no-*toki-wa* karada-ga-yowakatta.

　　　(*pron.*) 1)itsu [いつ]. 2)sono-toki [その時].

　　　(*n.*) (the -) toki [時]；baai [場合].

whence (*ad.*) doko-kara [どこから]；naze [なぜ].

　　　(*pron.*) doko [どこ].

whenever (*conj.*) …(suru)-toki-wa-itsu-demo […(する)ときはいつでも].

where (*ad.*) 1)doko-ni [どこに]；doko-de [どこで]；doko-e [どこへ].
2)…(suru-)tokoro-no(-basho) […(する)ところの(場所)].

　　(*1*) **Where** is the book?　Sono hon wa *doko-ni* arimasu-ka?

　　(*2*) This is the place **where** I was born.

　　　Koko wa watashi-ga umareta-*tokoro* da.

　　　(*conj.*) (…suru-)tokoro-ni [(…する)ところに]；(…suru-)tokoro-
wa-doko[-e]-demo [(…する)ところはどこ(へ)でも]；(…suru-)baai-ni-
wa [(…する)場合には].

　　　(*pron.*) doko [どこ].

(*n.*) (the -) basho [場所].

whereabouts (*ad.*) dono-atari-ni [どのあたりに].

(*n.*) shozai [所在]; arika [ありか]; yukue [行方].

whereas (*conj.*) …de-aru-noni […であるのに]; tokoro-ga (jijitsu wa) [ところが(事実は)].

wherever (*conj.*) (…suru)-tokoro-wa-doko-demo [(…する)ところはどこでも]; doko-e[-ni](…shiyô-)tomo [どこへ[に](…しよう)とも].

whether (*conj.*) 1)…ka-dôka […かどうか]. 2)…de-arô-to-nakarô-to […であろうとなかろうと].

  (*1*) I don't know **whether** it is true or not.

    Hontô-*ka-dôka* watashi-wa shira-nai.

  (*2*) I don't care **whether** it may be true or not.

    Hontô-*de-arô-to-nakarô-to* dottchi-datte-kamawa-nai.

which (*a.*) dono [どの]; dochira-no [どちらの].

    Which book do you want?

    Kimi-wa *dochira-no* hon-ga hoshii-ka?

  (*pron.*) 1)dore [どれ]; dochira [どちら]. 2)…(suru-)tokoro-no […(する)ところの].

  (*1*) **Which** do you like better, spring or autumn?

    Haru-to-aki-to *dochira*-ga suki-desu-ka?

  (*2*) The book **which** he gave me is this.

    Kare-ga watashi-ni kureta(-*tokoro-no*)-hon wa kore-desu.

whichever (*pron. & a.*) dochira-demo [どちらでも]; dochira-ga…de-mo [どちらが…でも].

while (*n.*) aida [間]; jikan [時間]; shibaraku-no-aida [しばらくの間].

    Please wait for a **while**.

    Shibaraku(-no-aida) o-machi-kudasai.

  after a while   shibaraku-shite

  all the while   sono-aida-zutto

  (*conj.*) 1)…(suru-)aida-ni […(する)間に]. 2)…na-noni […なのに]; tokoro-ga-ippô [ところが一方].

  (*1*) He was working **while** the others were playing.

    Kare-wa hito-ga asonde-iru-*aida* hataraiteita.

  (*2*) I am a late riser, **while** my brother is an early one.

    Watashi-wa asa-nebô da-*ga*, otôto wa haya-oki da.

whim (*n.*) ki-magure [気まぐれ].

whine (*vi.*) 1)awareppoku-naku [哀れっぽく泣く]. 2)(inu ga) kun-kun-naku [(犬が)くんくん鳴く].

　　(*vt.*) ...o aware-na-koe-de-iu [···を哀れな声で言う].

　　(*n.*) awareppoi-koe [哀れっぽい声]; naki-goe [泣き声].

whip (*n.*) 1)muchi [むち]. 2)hoippu [ホイップ].

　　(*vt.*) 1)...o muchi-utsu [···をむち打つ]; ...o hageshiku-utsu [···
を激しく打つ]. 2)...o kyû-ni-ugokasu [···を急に動かす]. 3)...o
tsuyoku-kaki-mawashite-awa-dataseru [···を強くかき回して泡立たせる].

　　(*vi.*) 1)kyû-ni-ugoku [急に動く]. 2)(hata nado ga) hatameku
[(旗などが)はためく].

whir, whirr (*vi. & n.*) hyûtto-tobu(hyûtto-iu-oto) [ひゅっと飛ぶ
(ひゅうっという音)]; bûn-to-mawaru(-oto) [ぶうんと回る(音)].

whirl (*vi.*) 1)guru-guru-mawaru [ぐるぐる回る]. 2)kyû-ni-muki-o-
kaeru [急に向きを変える]. 3)shissô-suru [疾走する]. 4)me-mai-ga-
suru [めまいがする].

　　(*vt.*) 1)...o guru-guru-mawasu [···をぐるぐる回す]. 2)...o gui-
to-hipparu [···をぐいと引っ張る]. 3)...o subayaku-hakobu [···をす早
く運ぶ].

　　(*n.*) 1)kaiten [回転]. 2)me-magurushii-renzoku [めまぐるしい連
続]. 3)seishin-no-konran [精神の混乱]. 4)me-mai [めまい].

whirlpool (*n.*) uzu[-maki] [渦(巻)].

whirlwind (*n.*) 1)tsumuji-kaze [つむじ風]; sempû [旋風]. 2)me-
magurushi-sa [目まぐるしさ].

whisk (*vt.*) 1)(gomi nado)-o harau [(ごみなど)をはらう]; ...o hataku
[···をはたく]. 2)((*Eng.*))...o kaki-mawasu [···をかき回す]; ...o awa-
dateru [···を泡立てる].

　　(*vi.*) kyû-ni-saru [急に去る]; kyû-ni-mie-naku-naru [急に見えな
くなる].

　　(*n.*) 1)awa-date-ki [泡立て器]. 2)hito-harai [一はらい].

whisker (*n.*) (*pl.*) hoo-hige [ほおひげ].

whiskey, -ky (*n.*) uisukî [ウイスキー].

whisper (*vi. & n.*) sasayaku(sasayaki) [ささやく(ささやき)]; hiso-
hiso-hanasu(hiso-hiso-banashi) [ひそひそ話す(ひそひそ話)].

whistle (*vi. & vt.*) kuchi-bue-o-fuku(...o kuchi-bue-de-yobu) [口笛を
吹く(···を口笛で呼ぶ)]; keiteki-o-narasu(...ni-keiteki-de-aizu-suru)
[警笛を鳴らす(···に警笛で合図する)].

　　(*n.*) kuchi-bue [口笛]; keiteki [警笛]; hoissuru [ホイッスル].

white (*a.*) shiroi [白い]; hakushoku-no [白色の]; ao-jiroi [青白い].

　　(*n.*) 1)shiro [白]; hakushoku [白色]. 2)(tamago no) shiro-mi
[(玉子の)白身]. 3)shiro-me [白目].

white book hakusho [白書].

white-collar (*a.*) jimu-rôdô-sha-no [事務労働者の]; howaito-karâ-no [ホワイトカラーの]; sararîman-no [サラリーマンの].

white-hot (*a.*) hakunetsu-shita [白熱した]; sai-kôchô-no [最高潮の].

whiten (*vt. & vi.*) ...o shiroku-suru(shiroku-naru) [...を白くする(白くなる)].

whitewash (*n.*) shikkui [漆喰].
      (*vt.*) 1)...ni shikkui-o-nuru [...に漆喰を塗る]. 2)...o tori-tsukurou [...を取り繕う].

whiz(z) (*n. & vi.*) hyû(-to-tobu) [ひゅう(と飛ぶ)].

WHO Sekai-hoken-kikô [世界保健機構].

who (*pron.*) 1)dare [だれ]. 2)...(suru-)tokoro-no(-hito) [...(する)ところの(人)].
    (*1*) **Who** is he? Kare-wa *dare*-desu-ka?
    (*2*) I want a man **who** understands English.
        Watashi-wa Eigo-ga-wakaru(-*tokoro-no*)-hito-ga hoshii.

whoever (*pron.*) 1)(...suru-)hito-wa-dare-demo [(...する)人はだれでも].
  2)dare-ga...(shite-)mo [だれが...(して)も].
    (*1*) We'll welcome **whoever** comes.
        Kuru-*hito-wa-dare-demo* kangei-shimasu.
    (*2*) **Whoever** else objects, I will do.
        Hoka-no *dare-ga* hantai-shiyô-*tomo*, watashi-wa yarimasu.

whole (*a.*) 1)zentai-no [全体の]; subete-no [すべての]; zen... [全...].
  2)maru... [まる...]; man... [満...]. 3)kanzen-na [完全な]; sokkuri-sono-mama-no [そっくりそのままの]; buji-na [無事な].
    (*1*) the **whole** world *zen*-sekai
    (*2*) He stayed there a **whole** year.
        Kare-wa soko-ni *maru*-ichi-nen ita.
    (*3*) I got off with a **whole** skin. Watashi-wa *buji*-ni nigeta.
    (*n.*) zentai [全体]; kanzen-na-mono [完全なもの].
  as a whole zentai-to-shite
  on(upon) the whole zentai-kara-mite

wholesale (*n.*) oroshi-uri [卸売].
    (*a.*) 1)oroshi-uri-no [卸売の]. 2)dai-kibo-na [大規模な].
    (*ad.*) oroshi-uri-de [卸売で]; dai-kibo-ni [大規模に].
    (*vt. & vi.*) (...o) oroshi-uri-suru [(...を)卸売する].

wholesome (*a.*) 1)kenkô-ni-yoi [健康によい]. 2)kenzen-na [健全な]; yûeki-na [有益な].

wholly (*ad.*) mattaku [全く]; sukkari [すっかり]; kanzen-ni [完全に].

whom (*pron.*) 1)dare-o［だれを］; dare-ni［だれに］. 2)…(suru-)tokoro-no(-hito)［…する)ところの(人)］.

whose (*pron.*) 1)dare-no［だれの］. 2)sono(…ga)…(suru-)tokoro-no(-mono)［その(…が)…(する)ところの］. 3)dare-no-mono［だれのもの］.

why (*ad.*) 1)naze［なぜ］; dô-shite［どうして］. 2)…(suru-)tokoro-no(-riyû)［…(する)ところの(理由)］.

    (*1*) **Why** did you go? *Naze* itta-n-da?

    (*2*) That is the reason **why** I cannot agree.

         Sore-ga watashi-ga dôi-deki-nai(-*tokoro-no*)-riyû da.

    Why not? Naze-ike-nai-no-ka?

    (*n.*)(the -) riyû［理由］; wake［わけ］.

    (*int.*) Maa!［まあ!］; Nan-datte!［何だって!］; Mochiron-sa!［もちろんさ!］.

wick (*n.*) (rôsoku ya rampu no) shin［(ろうそくやランプの)芯］.

wicked (*a.*) warui［悪い］; fusei-na［不正な］.

wicket (*n.*) 1)kuguri-do［くぐり戸］. 2)(eki no) kaisatsu-guchi［(駅の)改札口］; mado-guchi［窓口］.

wide (*a.*) 1)haba-no-hiroi［幅の広い］; hiro-biro-to-shita［広々とした］. 2)ookiku-hiraita［大きく開いた］.

    (*ad.*) 1)hiroku［広く］; ookiku-hiraite［大きく開いて］. 2)(…kara-)hazurete［(…から)外れて］; kentô-chigai-ni［見当違いに］.

wide-angle (*a.*) (*opt.*) kôkaku-no［広角の］.

wide-awake (*a.*) 1)sukkari-mezameta［すっかり目覚めた］. 2)yudan-no-nai［油断のない］.

widely (*ad.*) hiroku［広く］; ooi-ni［大いに］.

widen (*vt. & vi.*) …o hiroku-suru(hiroku-naru)［…を広くする(広くなる)］.

wide-open (*a.*) hiroku-hiraita［広く開いた］; (seigen nado ga) mattaku-nai［(制限などが)全くない］.

widespread (*a.*) hiroku-iki-watatta［広く行き渡った］; kô-han'i-ni-wataru［広範囲にわたる］.

widow (*n.*) mibôjin［未亡人］.

    (*vt.*) (be -ed) mibôjin-ni-naru［未亡人になる］.

width (*n.*) haba［幅］; hiro-sa［広さ］.

wield (*vt.*) 1)…o furuu［…を振るう］; …o furi-mawasu［…を振り回す］. 2)…o tsukau［…を使う］; …o mochiiru［…を用いる］.

wife (*n.*) tsuma［妻］.

wig (*n.*) katsura［かつら］.

wild (*a.*) 1)yasei-no [野性の]. 2)mikai-no [未開の]; kôryô-to-shita [荒涼とした]. 3)hageshii [激しい]. 4)kôfun-shita [興奮した]; kyôki-jimita [狂気じみた].

(*1*) **wild** animals *yasei*-dôbutsu

(*2*) **wild** land *mikai-no* tochi

　　wild scenery *kôryô-to-shita* keshiki

(*3*) a **wild** storm *hageshii* arashi

(*4*) with **wild** rage *gekido*-shite

　　He was **wild** with joy. Kare-wa *kyôki*-shita.

　　(*ad.*) rambô-ni [乱暴に]; detarame-ni [出たら目に].

　　(*n.*) (the *pl.*) kôya [荒野]; mikai-chi [未開地].

wildcat (*n.*) 1)(*zool.*) yama-neko [ヤマネコ]. 2)okorippoi-hito [怒りっぽい人]. 3)mubô-na-kikaku [無謀な企画].

　　　　(*a.*) 1)mubô-na [無謀な]. 2)hi-gôhô-na [非合法な].

　　　　(*vt.*) (sekiyu nado)-o bôken-teki-ni-shikutsu-suru [(石油など)を冒険的に試掘する].

wilderness (*n.*) 1) (the –) are-chi [荒れ地]; areno [荒れ野]. 2) hateshi-nai-hirogari [果てしない広がり].

wildly (*ad.*) 1)rambô-ni [乱暴に]; muyami-ni [無やみに]. 2)yasei-teki-ni [野性的に].

will (*aux. v.*) 1)...darô [...だろう]; ...deshô [...でしょう]. 2)...(suru-)tsumori-da [...(する)つもりだ]. 3)yoku...(suru) [よく...(する)]. 4)yahari...da [やはり...だ]. 5)(+ negative) dô-shite-mo...(shi-nai) [どうしても...(しない)]. 6)...(shite-)kure-masen-ka [...(して)くれませんか].

(*1*) You **will** fail. Kimi-wa shippai-suru-*darô*.

　　He **will** succeed. Kare-wa seikô-suru-*darô*.

　　They **will** come to the party. Kare-ra-wa pâtî-ni kuru-*darô*.

(*2*) I **will** start at once.

　　　　Watashi-wa sugu-ni shuppatsu-suru-*tsumori-da*.

(*3*) He **will** sometimes stay up all night.

　　　　Kare-wa toki-doki tetsuya-*suru*.

(*4*) Boys **will** be boys. Kodomo wa *yahari*-kodomo-*da*.

　　　　Itazurakko wa shikata-ga-nai.

(*5*) The door **will** not open. Doa ga *dô-shite-mo* aka-*nai*.

(*6*) **Will** you please post this letter on your way home?

　　　　O-kaeri-gake-ni kono tegami-o posuto-ni-irete-*kure-masen-ka*?

will (*n.*) 1)ishi [意志]; ketsui [決意]. 2)(*law*) yuigon [遺言].
　at will omoi-no-mama-ni
　with a will honki-de
　(*vt.*) 1)...o nozomu [···を望む]. 2)ishi-no-chikara-de...ni...(sa-)
　seru [意志の力で···に···(さ)せる]. 3)...o izô-suru [···を遺贈する].
　(*vi.*) ketsui-suru [決意する].

willful, wilful (*a.*) 1)waga-mama-na [我がままな]. 2)koi-no [故意の].

willing (*a.*) yorokonde...(suru) [喜んで···(する)]; susunde-suru [進ん
　でする].

willingly (*ad.*) yorokonde [喜んで]; kokoroyoku [快く].

willow (*n.*) yanagi [ヤナギ].

win (*vt.*) 1)...ni katsu [···に勝つ]. 2)...o kakutoku-suru [···を獲得す
　る]. 3)...o eru [···を得る]; ...o hakusuru [···を博する]. 4)...o
　settoku-suru [···を説得する]. 5)...ni tassuru [···に達する].
　(*1*) We **won** the game.　Ware-ware-ga sono shiai-ni katta.
　(*2*) She **won** the prize.　Kano-jo-wa shô-o *kakutoku-shita.*
　(*3*) The novel **won** him a reputation.
　　　　Sono shôsetsu de kare-wa kôhyô-o eta.
　(*4*) We must **win** the people to our way of thinking.
　　　　Ware-ware-wa　hito-bito-o　*settoku-shite*　ware-ware-no
　　　　kangae-kata-ni sandô-*sase*-nakereba-naranai.
　(*5*) We finally **won** the top of the mountain.
　　　　Ware-ware-wa tsui-ni yama no chôjô-*ni tasshita.*
　　　(*vi.*) katsu [勝つ]; doryoku-shite...ni-naru [努力して···になる].
　　　(*n.*) kachi [勝ち].
　　　three **wins** five defeats　san-*shô* go-hai

wince (*vi. & n.*) hirumu(hirumi) [ひるむ(ひるみ)].

wind (*n.*) 1)kaze [風]. 2)iki [息]. 3)(*mus.*)(the -) kan-gakki [管楽器].

wind (*vt.*) 1)(neji ya tokei nado)-o-maku [(ねじや時計など)を巻く].
　2)...o maki-tsukeru [···を巻きつける]. 3)(- oneself) takumi-ni-
　tori-iru [巧みに取り入る].
　(*1*) I **wound** (up) the clock.
　　　　Watashi-wa oki-dokei-no-neji-o *maita.*
　(*2*) She **wound** a bandage on my leg.
　　　　Kano-jo-wa watashi-no ashi-ni hôtai-o *maita.*
　(*3*) He **wound** himself into power.
　　　　Kare-wa　*takumi-ni-tori-itte* [*takumi-ni-mi-o-shoshite*]
　　　　kenryoku-o-tsukanda.

　　(*vi.*) 1)uneru [うねる]; magari-kuneru [曲がりくねる]. 2)maki-tsuku [巻きつく].

　(*1*) The river **wound** through the plain.
　　　　Kawa wa heigen-o-*uneri*-nagara nagarete-itta.

　(*2*) The snake **wound** around the branch.
　　　　Hebi wa eda-ni *maki-tsuita*.

wind up (vi.) 1)(*colloq.*) (...to-iu-)hame-ni-naru. 2)(*baseball*) waindappu-suru

　　　　(vt.) 1)...o-maki-ageru. 2)...ni-keri-o-tsukeru; ...o-oeru.
　　　3)...o-seisan-suru

winding (*a.*) magari-kunetta [曲がりくねった].

winding staircase rasen-kaidan [ら旋階段].

windmill (*n.*) fûsha [風車].

window (*n.*) mado [窓].

windowpane (*n.*) mado-garasu [窓ガラス].

window-shop (*vi.*) uindô-shoppingu-o-suru [ウインドーショッピングをする].

window-shopping (*n.*) uindô-shoppingu [ウインドーショッピング].

windpipe (*n.*) kikan [気管]; nodo-bue [のど笛].

windshield (*n.*) ((*US*)) (kuruma no) furonto-garasu [(車の)フロントガラス].

windy (*a.*) kaze-no-fuku [風の吹く]; kaze-no-tsuyoi [風の強い].

wine (*n.*) budô-shu [ブドウ酒]; wain [ワイン].
　　　　(*vt.*) ...o budô-shu-de-motenasu [...をブドウ酒でもてなす].
　　　　(*vi.*) budô-shu-o-nomu [ブドウ酒を飲む].

wing (*n.*) (tori no) tsubasa [(鳥の)翼]; (hikô-ki no) tsubasa [(飛行機の)翼].

on the wing 1)hikô-chû-de. 2)ryokô-chû-de. 3)katsuyaku-chû-de
　　　　(*vt.*) ...o tobasu [...を飛ばす].
　　　　(*vi.*) tonde-iku [飛んで行く].

wink (*vi.*) 1)mabataki-suru [まばたきする]. 2)me-kubase-suru [目くばせする]; uinku-suru [ウインクする]. 3)(hoshi nado ga) kirameku [(星などが)きらめく].
　　　　(*vt.*) 1)...o mabataki-saseru [...をまばたきさせる]. 2)...ni me-kubase-suru [...に目くばせする]; ...o uinku-shite-shiraseru [...をウインクして知らせる]. 3)((*Eng.*))...o temmetsu-saseru [...を点滅させる].
　　　　(*n.*) 1)mabataki [まばたき]. 2)me-kubase [目くばせ]. 3)kirameki [きらめき]. 4)isshun [一瞬]; issui [一睡].

winner (*n.*) shôri-sha [勝利者]; jushô-sha [受賞者].

winning (*a.*) shôri-o-osameta [勝利を収めた]; kesshô-no [決勝の].
    (*n.*) 1)shôri [勝利]. 2)(*pl.*) shôkin [賞金].

winter (*n.*) 1)fuyu [冬]. 2)makki [末期]; bannen [晩年].
    (*vi.*) fuyu-o-sugosu [冬を過ごす].

winter solstice, the tôji [とうじ].

wintry, wintery (*a.*) fuyu-no [冬の]; fuyu-rashii [冬らしい]; wabishii
[わびしい].

wipe (*vt.*) ...o nuguu [···をぬぐう]; ...o fuku [···をふく].
    (*n.*) nuguu-koto [ぬぐうこと]; fuku-koto [ふくこと].

wire (*n.*) 1)harigane [針金]; denwa-sen [電話線]. 2)dempô [電報].
    (*vt.*) ...ni dempô-o-utsu [···に電報を打つ]; ...o harigane-de-
musubu [···を針金で結ぶ].
    (*vi.*) (*colloq.*) dempô-o-utsu [電報を打つ].

wireless (*a.*) musen-no [無線の]; ((*Eng.*)) rajio-no [ラジオの].
    (*n.*) musen-denshin [無線電信]; musen-denwa [無線電話].

wiry (*a.*) 1)kukkyô-na [屈強な]. 2)harigane-jô-no [針金状の].

wisdom (*n.*) chie [知恵]; kemmei [賢明]; hakushiki [博識].

wisdom tooth oya-shirazu [親知らず].

wise (*a.*) kashikoi [賢い]; shiryo-no-aru [思慮のある]; gakushiki-
yutaka-na [学識豊かな].
    (*vi. & vt.*) (...o) shiru [···を知る].

wisely (*ad.*) 1)kemmei-ni [賢明に]. 2)kemmei-ni-mo [賢明にも].

wish (*vt.*) 1)...(shi-)tai-to-omou [···(し)たいと思う]. 2)...de-are-ba-
yoi-to-omou [···であればよいと思う]. 3)...ni...o inoru [···に···を祈る].
    (*1*) I **wish** to go abroad. Watashi-wa gaikoku-e iki-*tai-to-omou*.
    (*2*) I **wish** I were a bird. Watashi-ga tori-*datta-ra-ii-ga-nâ*.
    (*3*) I **wish** you a happy New Year.
        Shinnen o-medetô-gozai-masu.
    (*vi.*) nozomu [望む]; negai-o-kakeru [願いをかける].
    (*n.*) 1)kibô [希望]; nozomi [望み]; negai-goto [願いごと]. 2)
(*pl.*) kôfuku-o-inoru-kimochi [幸福を祈る気持].
    (*1*) He had a great **wish** to go abroad.
        Kare-wa gaikoku-e iki-tai-to-iu-ookina-*nozomi*-ga atta.
    (*2*) With best **wishes** for you. Go-*kôfuku-o-inori*-masu.

wisteria, -taria (*n.*) (*bot.*) fuji [フジ].

wistful (*a.*) 1)mono-hoshi-sô-na [物欲しそうな]; mono-tari-nasa-sô-
na [物足りなさそうな]. 2)mono-omoi-ni-shizunda [物思いに沈んだ].

wit (*n.*) 1)kichi [機知]; kiten [機転]. 2)chiryoku [知力].

witch (*n.*) majo [魔女].

with (*prep.*) 1)...to-tomo-ni [···とともに]; ...to-issho-ni [···と一緒に]. 2)...o-motte [···をもって]; ...de [···で]. 3)...o-motteiru [···を持っている]; ...no-aru [···のある]. 4)...ni-taishite [···に対して]; ...o-aite-ni [···を相手に]. 5)nimo-kakawarazu [···にもかかわらず]. 6)...no-tame-ni [···のために]. 7)...ni-kanshite [···に関して]; ...ni-totte-wa [···にとっては].

(*1*) I have no money **with** me.
    Watashi-wa kane-o mochi-*awasete*-i-nai.

(*2*) The mountain is covered **with** snow.
    Yama wa yuki-*de* oowarete-iru.
    I write **with** a pencil.   Watashi-wa empitsu-*de* kaku.

(*3*) There came an old man **with** gray hair.
    Shiraga-*no*(-*aru*)-rôjin ga kita.

(*4*) We fought **with** an enemy.   Ware-ware-wa teki-*to* tatakatta.

(*5*) **With** all its perils, the life seems to be pleasant.
    Kiken-ga-aru-*nimo-kakawarazu*, sono seikatsu wa tanoshii-yô-ni-omowareru.

(*6*) Her face was pale **with** fear.
    Kano-jo-no kao wa kyôfu-*no-tame-ni* aozamete-ita.

(*7*) It is usual **with** us.   Ware-ware-*ni-totte-wa* sore-ga futsû-da.

    what with A and (what with) B   Ei-yara Bi-yara-de

withdraw (*vt.*) 1)...o hikkomeru [···を引っ込める]. 2)...o tettai-saseru [···を撤退させる]; (yokin)-o hiki-dasu [(預金)を引出す]. 3)...o tori-kesu [···を取り消す].

    (*vi.*) 1)hiki-sagaru [引き下がる]; shirizoku [退く]. 2)tori-kesu [取り消す].

wither (*vi.*) 1)shibomu [しぼむ]; kareru [枯れる]. 2)(iro ga) aseru [(色が)あせる]; (karada ga) otoroeru [(体が)衰える].

    (*vt.*) ...o shibomaseru [···をしぼませる]; ...o karasu [···を枯らす].

withhold (*vt.*) ...o atae-zu-ni-oku [···を与えずにおく]; ...o horyû-suru [···を保留する].

    (*vi.*) hikaeru [控える].

within (*ad.*) 1)naka-ni [中に]; naibu-wa [内部は]; shitsu-nai-ni [室内に]. 2)kokoro-no-naka-de [心の中で].

    (*prep.*) 1)...no-naka-ni [···の中に]. 2)...no-han'i-nai-ni [···の範

　　　囲内に].
　　　　(n.) naibu [内部].

without (ad.) 1)soto-wa [外は]; gaibu-wa [外部は]; ko-gai-ni [戸外に]. 2)gaiken-wa [外見は].
　　　　(prep.) ...nashi-ni [⋯なしに]; ...sezu-ni [⋯せずに].
　　　　(n.) gaibu [外部].

withstand (vt.) ...ni teikô-suru [⋯に抵抗する]; ...ni yoku-taeru [⋯によく耐える].

witness (n.) 1)mokugeki-sha [目撃者]; (law) shônin [証人]. 2)shôko [証拠]; shôgen [証言].
　　　　(vt.) 1)...o mokugeki-suru [⋯を目撃する]. 2)(law) ...ni shomei-suru [⋯に署名する].
　　　　(vi.) (hôtei de) shôgen-suru [(法廷で)証言する].

witty (a.) kichi-ni-tonda [機知に富んだ]; ki-no-kiita [気のきいた].

wizard (n.) mahô-tsukai [魔法使い]; tejina-shi [手品師].

woe (n.) 1)kanashimi [悲しみ]; nayami [悩み]. 2)(pl.) nayami-no-tane [悩みの種]; sainan [災難].

woeful, woful (a.) kanashii [悲しい]; nagekawashii [嘆かわしい].

wolf (n.) ookami [オオカミ].

woman (n.) josei [女性]; fujin [婦人].

womanly (a.) onna-rashii [女らしい]; josei-ni-fusawashii [女性にふさわしい].

wonder (n.) 1)fushigi [不思議]. 2)kyôi [驚異]; odoroki [驚き]. 3)fushigi-na-mono[-koto] [不思議なもの[こと]].
　　(1) It is no **wonder** that he should fail.
　　　　Kare-ga shippai-suru-to-shite-mo *fushigi*-de-wa-nai.
　　(2) They looked at it with **wonder**.
　　　　Kare-ra-wa *kyôi-no-me*-de sore-o mita.
　　(3) the seven **wonders** of the world　sekai no nana-*fushigi*
　　　　(vi.) 1)odoroku [驚く]; fushigi-ni-omou [不思議に思う]. 2)are-kore-kangaeru [あれこれ考える]. 3)utagau [疑う].
　　　　(vt.) 1)...to-wa fushigi-da [⋯とは不思議だ]. 2)...ka-shira-to omou [⋯かしらと思う].
　　(1) I **wonder** that he should have succeeded.
　　　　Kare-ga seikô-shita-*to-wa fushigi-da*.
　　(2) I **wonder** who has come.　Dare-ga kita-*no-ka-shira*.

wonderful (a.) 1)fushigi-na [不思議な]; odoroku-beki [驚くべき]. 2)subarashii [すばらしい].

wont (*n.*) shûkan [習慣]; fûshû [風習].

woo (*vt.*) ...ni kyûkon-suru [···に求婚する]; ...ni kyûai-suru [···に求愛する].

wood (*n.*) 1)mokuzai [木材]. 2)mori [森]; hayashi [林]. 3)maki [まき]; takigi [たきぎ].

wooden (*a.*) 1)ki-no [木の]; moku-sei-no [木製の]. 2)gikochi-nai [ぎこちない]; bu-kiyô-na [不器用な]. 3)mu-hyôjô-na [無表情な].

woodland (*n.*) shinrin[-chitai] [森林(地帯)].

woodpecker (*n.*) (*birds*) kitsutsuki [キツツキ].

woody (*a.*) 1)jumoku-no-ooi [樹木の多い]. 2)mokushitsu-no [木質の].

wool (*n.*) 1)yômô [羊毛]. 2)ke-orimono [毛織物]. 3)ke-ito [毛糸].

wool(l)en (*a.*) 1)yômô[-sei]-no [羊毛(製)の]. 2)ke-orimono-o-atsukau [毛織物を扱う].

　　　　(*n.*) (*pl.*) ke-orimono [毛織物].

wool(l)y (*a.*) 1)(*colloq.*) yômô-no [羊毛の]; yômô-ni-nita [羊毛に似た]. 2)ke-ni-oowareta [毛に覆われた]. 3)konran-shita [混乱した].

　　　　(*n.*) (*pl.*) (*colloq.*) ke-ori-no-ifuku [毛織の衣服].

word (*n.*) 1)kotoba [ことば]; go [語]. 2)shirase [知らせ]; dengon [伝言]. 3)yakusoku [約束]; hoshô [保証]. 4)(the -) meirei [命令]; shiji [指示].

　be as good as one's word yakusoku-o-hatasu

　break one's word yakusoku-o-yaburu

　have a word with ...to chotto-hanashi-o-suru

　have words with ...to kôron-suru

　in a word hito-koto-de-ieba; yôsuru-ni

　in other words ii-kaereba

　keep one's word yakusoku-o-mamoru

　take (one) at one's word (hito-no-)kotoba-doori-ni-toru

work (*n.*) 1)shokugyô [職業]. 2)shigoto [仕事]. 3)sakuhin [作品]; saiku [細工]. 4)(*pl.*) (tokei nado no) shikake [(時計などの)仕掛け]; kikai-bubun [機械部分]. 5)(*pl.*) kôjô [工場].

　at work hataraite

　go to work 1)shigoto-ni-tori-kakaru. 2)shukkin-suru. 3)shoku-ni-tsuku

　out of work shitsugyô-chû-de

　　　　(*vi.*) 1)hataraku [働く]; shigoto-o-suru [仕事をする]; tsutomete-iru [勤めている]; benkyô-suru [勉強する]. 2)ugoku [動く]; kinô-suru [機能する]. 3)umaku-iku [うまくいく].

　(*1*) He **works** for a bank.　Kare-wa ginkô-ni *tsutomete-iru*.

(2) The machine will not **work**.

    Kikai ga dô-shite-mo *ugoka*-nai.

The traffic lights **weren't working** properly.

    Kôtsû-shingô ga kichin-to *kinô-shite-i*-nakat*ta*.

(3) These pills will **work** on you.

    Kono kusuri wa anata-ni *kiku*-deshô.

    (*vt.*) 1)...o hataraku [···を働かせる]. 2)...o tsukau [···を使う]; (kikai nado)-o unten-suru [(機械など)を運転する]. 3)...o motarasu [···をもたらす]. 4)...o keiei-suru [···を経営する]. 5)...o tantô-suru [···を担当する].

(1) He **worked** his employees mercilessly.

    Kare-wa jûgyô-in-tachi-*o* koki-*tsukatta*.

(2) She knows how to **work** a wordprocessor.

    Kano-jo-wa wâpuro-no-*tsukai*-kata-o shitte-iru.

(3) **work** wonders   kiseki-*o motarasu*

(4) **work** a farm   nôjô-*o keiei-suru*

(5) They **worked** the streets round Paddington.

    Kare-ra-wa Padinton-fukin-no-machi-*o tantô-shita*.

work off   ...o-kurô-shite-kata-zukeru

work out (vi.) 1)umaku-iku; yoi-kekka-to-naru. 2)renshû-suru. 3)santei-sareru

    (vt.) 1)...o kushin-shite-tsukuri-ageru; ...o kurô-shite-toku. 2)...o keisan-suru. 3)...o tsukai-tsukusu

work up 1)...o shigeki-suru. 2)...o jumbi-suru. 3)...no nôryoku-o-kôjô-saseru. 4)...o hone-otte-tsukuri-ageru

workaday (*a.*) 1)shigoto-bi-no [仕事日の]; heijitsu-no [平日の]. 2)heibon-na [平凡な].

worker (*n.*) 1)hataraku-hito [働く人]. 2)rôdô-sha [労働者].

workhouse (*n.*) ((*US*)) shônen-in [少年院].

working (*a.*) hataraku [働く]; rôdô-ni-jûji-suru [労働に従事する].

    (*n.*) 1)rôdô [労働]; shigoto [仕事]. 2)sayô [作用]; hataraki [働き]. 3)unten [運転].

working capital   unten-shihon [運転資本].

workingman (*n.*) rôdô-sha [労働者].

workman (*n.*) rôdô-sha [労働者]; shokunin [職人].

workmanship (*n.*) 1)(shokunin no) giryô [(職人の)技量]. 2)(saiku no) deki-bae [(細工の)出来栄え]. 3)saiku-mono [細工もの]; seihin [製品].

workshop (*n.*) 1)sagyô-ba [作業場]. 2)kenkyû-kai [研究会]. 3)kôsaku-shitsu [工作室].

world (*n.*) 1)sekai [世界]. 2)seken [世間]. 3)sekai-no-hito-bito [世界の人々]; seken-no-hito-bito [世間の人々].

  for all the world dô-shite-mo; zettai-ni

  in the world 1)ittai-zentai. 2)kesshite

  out of this world (*colloq.*) suteki-na; tenka-ippin-de

  to the world mattaku; sukkari

worldly (*a.*) 1)kono-yo-no [この世の]. 2)sezoku-teki-na [世俗的な]. 3)meiri-o-ou [名利を追う]; sesai-no-aru [世才のある].

world-wide (*a.*) sekai-teki-na [世界的な].

worm (*n.*) mushi [虫].

    (*vt.*) 1)(– oneself) jojo-ni-tori-iru [徐々に取り入る]; sukoshi-zutsu-susumu [少しずつ進む]. 2)...o jojo-ni-kiki-dasu […を徐々に聞き出す].

worn-out (*a.*) 1)tsukai-furushita [使い古した]. 2)tsukare-hateta [疲れ果てた]. 3)(hyôgen nado ga) furu-kusai [(表現などが)古くさい].

worry (*vt. & vi.*) ...o nayamaseru (nayamu) […を悩ませる(悩む)]; ...o shimpai-saseru (shimpai-suru) […を心配させる(心配する)]; ...o kuyo-kuyo-saseru (kuyo-kuyo-suru) […をくよくよさせる(くよくよする)].

worse (*a. & ad.*) issô-warui (issô-waruku) [いっそう悪い(いっそう悪く)].

    (and) what is worse or **to make matters worse**
      sono-ue-warui-koto-ni-wa

worship (*n.*) 1)reihai [礼拝]. 2)sûhai [崇拝]; sambi [賛美]. 3)《*Eng.*》(Your W-; His W-; Her W-) kakka [閣下].

    (*vt.*) ...o sûhai-suru […を崇拝する]; ...o sambi-suru […を賛美する].

    (*vi.*) reihai-ni-deru [礼拝に出る]; kyôkai-ni-iku [教会に行く].

worship(p)er (*n.*) 1)reihai-sha [礼拝者]; sûhai-sha [崇拝者]. 2)(...no) aikô-sha [(…の)愛好者]; shimpô-sha [信奉者].

worst (*a. & ad.*) mottomo-warui (mottomo-waruku) [最も悪い(最も悪く)].

    (*n.*) saiaku[-no-jitai] [最悪(の事態)].

  at (the) worst saiaku-no-baai-demo; seizei

  get(have) the worst of it makeru

worth (*n.*) 1)kachi [価値]; shinka [真価]. 2)jûyô-sei [重要性]. 3)...sôtô-ryô[-no...] […相当量(の…)].

　　　(a.) …(suru-)dake-no-kachi-no-aru ［…(する)だけの価値のある］;
…(suru-)ni-taru ［…(する)に足る］.
　worth while to or…**ing** …dake-no-kachi-ga-aru

worthless (a.) kachi-no-nai ［価値のない］; tsumaranai ［つまらない］.

worthwhile (a.) shi-gai-no-aru ［しがいのある］; yari-gai-no-aru ［やりがいのある］.

worthy (a.) 1)…no-kachi-ga-aru ［…の価値がある］; …(suru-)ni-taru ［…(する)に足る］; …ni-fusawashii ［…にふさわしい］. 2) sonkei-su-beki ［尊敬すべき］; rippa-na ［立派な］.
　(1) His act is **worthy** of praise.
　　　Kare-no kôi wa shôsan-*ni-atai-suru*.
　(2) a **worthy** man　*rippa-na* jimbutsu

would (aux. v.) 1)…(suru-)tsumori-da ［…(する)つもりだ］. 2)…(suru-)darô ［…(する)だろう］. 3)…(suru-)no-da-ga ［…(する)のだが］. 4) yoku…(shita-)mono-da ［よく…(した)ものだ］. 5) dô-shite-mo…(shi-)takatta ［どうしても…(し)たかった］. 6)…deshô-ka ［…でしょうか］; …(shite-)itadake-masen-ka ［…(して)いただけませんか］.
　(1) He told her that he **would** do his best.
　　　Kare-wa kano-jo-ni zenryoku-o-tsukusu-*tsumori-da*-to itta.
　(2) He said she **would** come soon.
　　　Kano-jo-wa hodo-naku kuru-*darô*-to kare-wa itta.
　(3) If I had money, I **would** get it.
　　　Kane-ga areba, sore-o kau-*no-da-ga*.
　(4) He **would** take a walk early in the morning, when young.
　　　Wakai-toki-ni, kare-wa *yoku* asa-hayaku sampo-shita-*mono-da*.
　(5) He **would** let me go.
　　　Kare-wa *dô-shite-mo* watashi-o ikase-*tagatta*.
　(6) **Would** you please pass me the salt?
　　　Sono shio o totte-*itadake-masen-ka*?

wound (n.) kizu ［傷］.
　　　(vt.) …o kizu-tsukeru ［…を傷つける］.

wow (int.) (colloq.) Waa! ［わあ!］.

wrap (vt.) …o tsutsumu ［…を包む］; …o matou ［…をまとう］. (vi.) 1) kurumaru ［くるまる］. 2) maki-tsuku ［巻きつく］.

wrapping (n.) (pl.) hôsô-zairyô ［包装材料］; hôsô-shi ［包装紙］.

wrath (n.) gekido ［激怒］; ikari ［怒り］.

wreath (n.) 1) hana-wa ［花輪］. 2) (kemuri nado no) wa ［(煙などの)

輪].

wreathe (*vt.*) 1)(hana-wa)-o tsukuru [(花輪)を作る]. 2)...o kazaru [… を飾る]. 3)...o tsutsumu […を包む].

　　(*vi.*) uzu-maku [渦巻く]; karami-tsuku [からみつく].

wreck (*n.*) nampa[-sen] [難破(船)]; zasetsu [ざ折].

　　(*vt. & vi.*) ...o nampa-saseru (nampa-suru) [⋯を難破させる (難破する)]; ...o zasetsu-saseru (zasetsu-suru) [⋯をざ折させる(ざ折 する)].

wren (*n.*) (*birds*) misosazai [ミソサザイ].

wrench (*n.*) 1)(*mech.*)((*US*)) renchi [レンチ]; supana [スパナ]. 2) nenza [ねんざ].

　　(*vt.*) ...o nejiru [⋯をねじる]; ...o nenza-suru [⋯をねんざする].

　　(*vi.*) nejireru [ねじれる]; nejiru [ねじる].

wrestle (*vi.*) 1)resuringu-o-suru [レスリングをする]; kakutô-suru [格 闘する]. 2)tori-kumu [取り組む].

　　(*vt.*) ...to resuringu-suru [⋯とレスリングする].

wrestling (*n.*) resuringu [レスリング].

wretched (*a.*) 1)mijime-na [惨めな]; fukô-na [不幸な]. 2)somatsu-na [粗末な]. 3)hidoi [ひどい].

wriggle (*vi.*) karada-o-kuneraseru [体をくねらせる]; karada-o-kunerasete-susumu [体をくねらせて進む].

　　(*vt.*) ...o kunerasu [⋯をくねらす]; ...o kunerase-nagara-susumu [⋯をくねらせながら進む].

wring (*vt.*) ...o shiboru [⋯を絞る]; ...o nejiru [⋯をねじる].

　　(*vi.*) 1)shiboru [絞る]. 2)mi-o-yojiru [身をよじる].

wrinkle (*n.*) shiwa [しわ].

　　(*vt. & vi.*) ...ni shiwa-o-yoseru (shiwa-ga-yoru) [⋯にしわを 寄せる(しわが寄る)].

wrist (*n.*) te-kubi [手首].

wristwatch (*n.*) ude-dokei [腕時計].

write (*vi.*) 1)ji-o-kaku [字を書く]. 2)tegami-o-kaku [手紙を書く]; tegami-o-dasu [手紙を出す].

　　(*1*) **Write** with a pencil.　Empitsu-de *kaki-nasai*.

　　(*2*) He **writes** to me often.

　　　　Kare-wa yoku watashi-ni *tegami-o-kureru*.

　　(*vt.*) 1)...o kaku [⋯を書く]; ...o shippitsu-suru [⋯を執筆する]. 2)...to tegami-de-shiraseru [⋯と手紙で知らせる].

　　(*1*) He **is writing** a letter.　Kare-wa tegami-*o kaiteiru*.

Who **wrote** this novel?　Dare-ga kono shôsetsu-o *kaita*-no-ka?

(2) He **wrote** that he would leave for Europe.

Kare-wa Yôroppa-ni-iku-*to tegami-de-shirasete-kita.*

write down ...o kaki-tomeru

writer (*n.*) 1)kaku-hito [書く人]. 2)chojutsu-ka [著述家]; sakka [作家]; kisha [記者].

writing (*n.*) 1)kaku-koto [書くこと]; shippitsu [執筆]. 2)hisseki [筆跡]; kakareta-mono [書かれたもの].

written (*a.*) kakareta [書かれた]; bunsho-no [文書の].

wrong (*a.*) 1)warui [悪い]; fusei-na [不正な]. 2)machigatta [間違った]; ayamatta [誤った]. 3)koshô-shita [故障した]. 4)fusawashiku-nai [ふさわしくない]; fu-tekisetsu-na [不適切な].

(*1*) It is **wrong** to waste time.　Jikan-o rôhi-suru-koto-wa *warui.*

(*2*) I think you are **wrong**.

Kimi-no-iu-koto ga *machigatte*-iru-to omou.

(*3*) Something is **wrong** with this machine.

Kono-kikai-wa doko-ka *koshô-shite*-iru.

(*4*) This is the **wrong** time to tell the truth to him.

Kare-ni shinjitsu-o hanasu-no-ni *tekisetsu-na* jiki-de-wa-*nai.*

What's wrong with...? ...wa-dô-ka-shita-no-desu-ka?

(*ad.*) ayamatte [誤って].

He went **wrong**.　Kare-wa *michi-o-machigae*ta.

(*n.*) 1)fusei [不正]; akuji [悪事]. 2)machigai [間違い].

(*vt.*) 1)...ni futô-na-atsukai-o-suru […に不当な扱いをする]. 2)... o gokai-suru […を誤解する]; ...o chûshô-suru […を中傷する].

wrongdoing (*n.*) akuji [悪事]; hanzai [犯罪].

wry (*a.*) 1)shikameta [しかめた]. 2)kojitsuketa [こじつけた].

X

Xmas (*n.*) Kurisumasu [クリスマス].
X ray (*n.*) 1)(*pl.*) Ekkusu-sen [エックス線]; Rentogen-sen [レントゲ
ン線]. 2)Rentogen-shashin [レントゲン写真]. 3)Rentogen-kensa [レ
ントゲン検査].
xylophone (*n.*) mokkin [木琴]; shirohon [シロホン].

Y

yacht (*n. & vi.*) yotto(-ni-noru) [ヨット (に乗る)].

yard (*n.*) yâdo [ヤード]; yâru [ヤール].

yard (*n.*) 1)niwa [庭]; nakaniwa [中庭]. 2)kônai [構内]. 3)sagyô-ba [作業場]; mono-oki-ba [物置き場].
   (*vt.*) ...o kakoi-no-naka-ni-ireru [...を囲いの中に入れる].

yardstick (*n.*) yâdo-jaku [ヤード尺].

yarn (*n.*) 1)(ori-mono yô no) ito [(織物用の)糸]. 2)(*colloq.*) (shin'yô-deki-nai) ryokô-dan [(信用できない)旅行談]; tsukuri-banashi [作り話].
   (*vi.*) hora-banashi-o-suru [ほら話をする].

yawn (*n. & vi.*) akubi(-o-suru) [あくび (をする)].
   (*vt.*) akubi-o-shi-nagara...to iu [あくびをしながら...と言う].

year (*n.*) 1)nen [年]. 2)...sai [...歳]. 3)gakunen [学年]. 4)(*pl.*) jidai [時代].

yearly (*ad. & a.*) nen-ichi-do(-no) [年一度(の)]; mai-toshi(-no) [毎年(の)].
   (*n.*) nen-ichi-do-no-kankô-butsu [年一度の刊行物].

yearn (*vi.*) 1)shitau [慕う]; akogareru [あこがれる]. 2)setsubô-suru [切望する]. 3)dôjô-suru [同情する]; omoi-yaru [思いやる].

yeast (*n.*) 1)kôbo [酵母]; îsuto [イースト]. 2)eikyô-ryoku [影響力].

yell (*vi.*) oo-goe-o-ageru [大声をあげる]; sakebu [叫ぶ]; donaru [ど

なる].

　　(*vt.*) ...o oo-goe-de-iu [...を大声で言う].

　　(*n.*) sakebi-goe [叫び声]; wameki [わめき].

yellow (*n. & a.*) ki-iro(-no) [黄色(の)].

　　(*vt. & vi.*) ...o ki-iro-ni-suru (ki-iro-ni-naru) [...を黄色にする (黄色になる)].

yellowish (*a.*) ki-iroppoi [黄色っぽい].

yellow jacket (*insect*) suzume-bachi [スズメバチ].

yelp (*vi.*) (inu ga) kyan-kyan-naku [(犬が)きゃんきゃん鳴く].

　　(*vt.*) ...o sakende-iu [...を叫んで言う].

　　(*n.*) kyan-kyan-naku-koe [きゃんきゃん鳴く声].

yen (*n.*) en [円].

yes (*ad.*) 1)hai [はい]; sô-desu [そうです]. 2)iie [いいえ]; iya [いや].

yesterday (*n. & ad.*) kinô [きのう]; sakujitsu [昨日].

yet (*ad.*) 1)mada [まだ]. 2)(+ negative) mada(...nai) [まだ(...ない)].
3)sara-ni-issô [さらにいっそう]. 4)sono-uchi-ni [そのうちに]; yagate [やがて]. 5)mô [もう]. 6)sore-nimo-kakawarazu [それにもかかわらず];
demo [でも].

　　(*1*) It is before five **yet**.　*Mada* go-ji-mae-da.

　　(*2*) I haven't had breakfast **yet**.
　　　　Watashi-wa *mada* chôshoku-o tabete-i-*nai*.

　　(*3*) It is **yet** more difficult.　Sore-wa *sara-ni-issô* muzukashii.

　　(*4*) He will get there **yet**.　Kare-wa *yagate* soko-ni tsuku-darô.

　　(*5*) Have you finished writing your composition **yet**?
　　　　Mô sakubun-o kaki-oemashita-ka?

　　(*6*) It sounds strange, and **yet** it is true.
　　　　Hen-ni-kikoeru-keredo, (*sore-nimo-kakawarazu*) sore-wa
　　　　hontô-da.

yew (*n.*) (*bot.*) seiyô-ichii [セイヨウイチイ].

yield (*vt.*) 1)...o shôzuru [...を生ずる]; ...o san-suru [...を産する]. 2)
...o yuzuru [...を譲る]; ...o hôki-suru [...を放棄する].

　　(*vi.*) 1)sakumotsu-o-sanshutsu-suru [作物を産出する]. 2)makeru [負ける]; kussuru [屈する].

　　(*n.*) sanshutsu[-butsu] [産出(物)]; sanshutsu-daka [産出高];
shûeki [収益].

yoke (*n.*) 1)kubiki [くびき]. 2)tembin-bô [天びん棒]. 3)yôku [ヨーク].

　　(*vt.*) 1)...o kubiki-de-tsunagu [...をくびきでつなぐ]. 2)...o
ketsugô-saseru [...を結合させる]; ...o issho-ni-suru [...を一緒にする].

yolk (*n.*) (tamago no) ki-mi [(卵の)黄身].

yonder (*a. & ad.*) asoko-no (asoko-ni) [あそこの(あそこに)]; mukô-no (mukô-ni) [向こうの(向こうに)].

you (*pron.*) 1)anata-wa [あなたは]; anata-ga [あなたが]. 2)anata-gata-wa [あなたがたは]; anata-gata-ga [あなたがたが]. 3)anata-o [あなたを]; anata-ni [あなたに]. 4)anata-gata-o [あなたがたを]; anata-gata-ni [あなたがたに].

young (*a.*) 1)wakai [若い]. 2)nenshô-no [年少の]. 3)(jiki-teki ni) hayai [(時期的に)早い]. 4)shinkô-no [新興の]. 5)mijuku-na [未熟な]; jukushite-i-nai [熟していない].

    (*n.*) (dôbutsu no) ko-tachi [(動物の)子たち].

youngster (*n.*) shônen [少年]; waka-mono [若者].

your (*pron.*) anata-no [あなたの]; anata-gata-no [あなたがたの].

yours (*pron.*) anata-no-mono [あなたのもの]; anata-gata-no-mono [あなたがたのもの].

yourself (*pron.*) anata-jishin(-o/-ni) [あなた自身(を/に)].

yourselves (*pron.*) anata-gata-jishin(-o/-ni) [あなたがた自身(を/に)].

youth (*n.*) 1)seishun[-jidai] [青春(時代)]. 2)waka-sa [若さ]; genki [元気]. 3)wakai-hito-tachi [若い人たち].

youthful (*a.*) 1)waka-waka-shii [若々しい]; genki-na [元気な]; seinen-rashii [青年らしい]. 2)shoki-no [初期の].

Z

zeal (*n.*) nesshin [熱心]; netchû [熱中].

zealous (*a.*) nesshin-na [熱心な]; netchû-shite-iru [熱中している].

zebra (*n.*) (*zool.*) shima-uma [シマウマ].

zenith (*n.*) (*astron.*) (the –) tenchô [天頂]. zetchô [絶頂].

zero (*n.*) zero [ゼロ]; rei [零]; sukoshi-mo-nai-koto [少しもないこと].

zigzag (*n.*) Zeddo-ji-gata [Z字型]; jiguzagu [ジグザグ].

    (*a. & ad.*) jiguzagu-no (jiguzagu-ni) [ジグザグの(ジグザグに)].

    (*vi.*) jiguzagu-ni-susumu [ジグザグに進む].

zinc (*n.*) (*chem.*) aen [亜鉛].

zipper (*n.*) 《*US*》 jippâ [ジッパー]; fasunâ [ファスナー]; chakku [チャック].

    (*vt. & vi.*) (...no) jippâ-o-shimeru [(…の)ジッパーを締める].

zone (*n.*) 1)(*geog.*) ...tai […帯]. 2)chitai [地帯]; kuiki [区域].

    (*vt.*) 1)...o kukaku-suru […を区画する]. 2)...o bunrui-suru […を分類する].

zoo (*n.*) dôbutsu-en [動物園].

zoological (*a.*) dôbutsu-gaku[-jô]-no [動物学(上)の].

zoology (*n.*) dôbutsu-gaku [動物学].

zoom (*vi.*) 1)kyû-jôshô-suru [急上昇する]. 2)supîdo-o-ageru [スピードをあげる]. 3)(*photo.*) zûmu-renzu-de-satsuei-suru [ズームレンズで撮影する].

    (*vt.*) ...o kyû-jôshô-saseru […を急上昇させる]; ...ni zûmu-renzu-o-chôsetsu-suru […にズームレンズを調節する].

Fifth Published in May, 1996

**POCKET
ROMANIZED
ENGLISH-JAPANESE
DICTIONARY**

[Revised Expanded Edition]

(Paperback edition)

by Morio Takahashi
revised by Tomoko Honjo

Publishers Taiseido Shobo Co.
2-4 Kanda Jimbo-cho, Chiyoda-ku,
Tokyo, Japan
4-13 Aotani-cho 4-chome, Nada-ku,
Kobe, Japan

(Printed in Japan)